MACROECONOMICS

erv

In 16

ax 29

EUROPEAN EDITION

MACROECONOMICS

EUROPEAN EDITION

ANDREW B. ABEL

THE WHARTON SCHOOL OF THE
UNIVERSITY OF PENNSYLVANIA

BEN S. BERNANKE

WOODROW WILSON SCHOOL OF
PUBLIC AND INTERNATIONAL AFFAIRS
PRINCETON UNIVERSITY

ROBERT McNABB

CARDIFF BUSINESS SCHOOL
UNIVERSITY OF WALES, CARDIFF

ADDISON-WESLEY

HARLOW, ENGLAND ○ READING, MASSACHUSETTS ○ MENLO PARK, CALIFORNIA ○ NEW YORK
DON MILLS, ONTARIO ○ AMSTERDAM ○ BONN ○ SYDNEY ○ SINGAPORE ○ TOKYO ○ MADRID
SAN JUAN ○ MILAN ○ MEXICO CITY ○ SEOUL ○ TAIPEI

Addison Wesley Longman Limited
Edinburgh Gate
Harlow
Essex CM20 2JE
and Associated Companies throughout the World.

Published in the United States of America by Addison Wesley Longman Inc., New York.

Typeset by 30
Produced by Addison Wesley Longman Singapore Pte Ltd
Printed in Singapore

First published 1998

ISBN 0-201-41996-3

British Library Cataloguing-in-Publication Data
A catalogue record for this book is available from the British Library

Library of Congress Cataloguing-in-Publication Data is available

ABOUT THE AUTHORS

ANDREW B. ABEL

The Wharton School of the
University of Pennsylvania

Robert Morris Professor of Finance at The Wharton School and Professor of Economics at the University of Pennsylvania, Andrew Abel received his A.B. *summa cum laude* from Princeton University and his Ph.D. from the Massachusetts Institute of Technology.

Since his appointment to The Wharton School in 1986, Abel has held the Ronald O. Perelman and the Amoco Foundation Professorships. He began his teaching career at the University of Chicago and Harvard University, and has held visiting appointments at both Tel Aviv University and The Hebrew University of Jerusalem.

A prolific researcher, Abel has published extensively on fiscal policy, capital formation, monetary policy, asset pricing, and social security – as well as serving on the editorial boards of numerous journals. He has been honored as an Alfred P. Sloan Fellow, a National Science Foundation Graduate Fellow, a Fellow of the Econometric Society, and a recipient of the John Kenneth Galbraith Award for teaching excellence. Abel has served as a visiting scholar at the Federal Reserve Bank of Philadelphia and as a member of the Economics Advisory Panel of the National Science Foundation. He is also a Research Associate of the National Bureau of Economic Research and a member of the Advisory Board of the Carnegie-Rochester Conference Series.

BEN S. BERNANKE

Woodrow Wilson School of Public and
International Affairs, Princeton University

Class of 1926 Professor of Economics and Public Affairs at Princeton University, Ben Bernanke received his B.A. in economics from Harvard University, *summa cum laude* – capturing both the Allyn Young Prize for best Harvard undergraduate economics thesis and the John H. Williams prize for outstanding senior in the economics department. Like coauthor Abel, he holds a Ph.D. from the Massachusetts Institute of Technology.

Bernanke began his career at the Stanford Graduate School of Business in 1979, moving to Princeton University in 1985. He has twice been visiting professor at MIT and once at New York University, and has taught in undergraduate, MBA, MPA, and Ph.D. programmes. He has authored more than 50 publications in macroeconomics, macroeconomic history, and finance.

Bernanke has served as a visiting scholar for the Federal Reserve System in Philadelphia, Boston, and New York and is currently an advisor to the Federal Reserve Bank of New York. He is co-editor of *Economic Letters* and associate editor of four other journals. He has been variously honoured as an Alfred P. Sloan Research Fellow, a Hoover Institution National Fellow, a National Science Foundation Graduate Fellow, and a Research Associate of the National Bureau of Economic Research.

ROBERT McNABB

Cardiff Business School
University of Wales, Cardiff

Distinguished Senior Fellow in Economics at Cardiff Business School, University of Wales, Cardiff. Robert McNabb received his B.Sc. in economics from Bristol University and his M.A. in economics from Queen's University in Canada. He holds a Ph.D. from the University of Wales.

McNabb has held visiting appointments at the University of Tasmania, Flinders University, The University of Adelaide, and the University of Bristol. He has taught both undergraduate and postgraduate economics, including MBA programmes and has been commended for excellence in teaching.

McNabb has held visiting and advisory posts with a number of international and public sector organisations, including the Organisation for Economic Co-operation and Development, the United Nations Development Programme, the Office for National Statistics (UK) and the Department for Education and Employment (UK).

He has published on the macroeconomics of developing countries, labour economics, and the application of economics to personal injury law. He is co-author of *Developments in Labour Economics, Inflation in Modern Economics* and *The Market for Training.*

BRIEF CONTENTS

Detailed Contents

Summary Tables

Key Diagrams

PREFACE

Macroeconomics has sold successfully around the World, and has been extremely well received by lecturers and students, who have praised its modern coverage, extensive use of real-world applications, clear writing, and effective learning aids. In writing the European Edition we have built on those strengths while further increasing the book's flexibility to meet the needs of lecturers teaching in a variety of settings. These important strengths include:

- *Real-world applications.* A perennial challenge for lecturers is to help students learn how to actively use the economic ideas developed in the text. The rich variety of applications in this text show by example how economic concepts can be put to work in understanding real-world issues, such as increasing wage inequality, the productivity slowdown, and the problems of making stabilization policy. The European Edition contains many applications from Europe and around the world.

- *Broad coverage.* From its conception, *Macroeconomics* has responded to students' desire to investigate and understand a wider range of macroeconomic issues than permitted by the course's traditional emphasis on short-run fluctuations and stabilization policy. Our text provides a modern treatment of these traditional topics, but also gives in-depth coverage to other important macro issues such as the determinants of long-run economic growth, international trade and capital flows, labour markets, and the political and institutional framework of policy making. This comprehensive coverage also makes our text a useful tool for lecturers with differing views about what they want to cover in their course and the sequence in which they want to present the material.

- *Reliance on a set of core economic ideas.* Although we cover a wide range of topics, we avoid the strategy of developing a new model or theory for each issue and instead emphasize the wide applicability of a set of core economic ideas (such as the production function, the tradeoff between consuming today and saving for tomorrow, and supply-demand analysis). Using these core ideas, we build a theoretical framework that encompasses all of the macroeconomic analyses of our book: long-run and short-run, open-economy and closed-economy, classical and Keynesian.

- *A balanced presentation.* Macroeconomics is full of controversies, many of which arise from the split between classicals and Keynesians (of the old, new, and neo-varieties). Sometimes the controversies overshadow the broad common ground shared between the two schools. Our text emphasizes that common ground: First, we pay greater attention to long-run issues (on which classicals and Keynesians have less disagreement).

Second, we develop the classical and Keynesian analyses of short-run fluctuations within a single overarching framework, in which the two approaches are seen to differ principally in their assumptions about how quickly wages and prices adjust. Where differences in viewpoint remain – for example, in the search versus efficiency-wage interpretations of unemployment – both perspectives are presented and critiqued. This balanced approach gives the student the benefit of hearing all the best ideas in modern macroeconomics. At the same time, a lecturer of either classical or Keynesian inclinations can easily base his or her course on this book.

■ *Innovative pedagogy.* The European edition of *Macroeconomics* provides a wide variety of tools to help students study, understand, and retain the material. These tools, described in more detail later in the Preface, include Summary tables, Key Diagrams, Key Terms, and Key Equations to help students organize their studying; and three types of problems for practice and developing better understanding.

COVERAGE

What is taught in intermediate macroeconomics courses, and how it is taught, has changed substantially in recent years. *Macroeconomics* provides lively and up-to-date coverage of a wide range of macroeconomic issues and ideas, including:

■ *Long-term economic growth.* Because the rate of economic growth plays a central role in determining living standards, we devote much of Part II to growth and related issues. We first discuss factors contributing to growth such as productivity (Chapter 3) and rates of saving and investment (Chapter 4), and then in Chapter 6 we turn to a full-fledged analysis of the growth process, using tools such as growth accounting and the neo-classical growth model. Growth-related topics covered include the post-1973 productivity slowdown, growth 'miracles', the factors that determine long-run living standards, government policies to stimulate growth, and the 'new growth theory'.

■ *International macroeconomic issues.* We address the increasing integration of the world economy in two ways: First, throughout the text we make frequent use of cross-country comparisons and applications that draw on the experiences of countries around the world; for example, Chapter 13 compares sacrifice ratios across countries, Chapter 6 examines the growth experiences of the East Asian tigers, and Chapter 15 discusses strategies for making monetary policy employed around the world. In addition, we devote two chapters specifically to international issues: Chapter 5 shows how the trade balance is related to a nation's rates of saving and investment, then applies this framework to discuss issues such as the debt crisis in less developed countries and the link between the trade deficit and the government budget deficit. Chapter 14 uses a simple supply–demand framework to discuss the determination of exchange rates, and features innovative material on fixed exchange rates and currency unions, including an explanation of why a currency may face a speculative run, and discussions of Bretton Woods, the European Monetary System, and the proposed European Monetary Union.

■ *Business cycles.* Our analysis of business cycles begins with facts rather than theories: Chapter 9 gives a history of European business cycles and then describes the observed cyclical behavior of a variety of important economic variables (the 'business cycle facts'). Alternative classical and Keynesian theories of the cycle, presented in Chapters 10-12, are then evaluated by how well they explain the facts.

■ *Monetary and fiscal policy.* The effects and potential role of macroeconomic policies are discussed in nearly every chapter of the book, in both theory and applications. We present classical (Chapter 11), Keynesian (Chapter 12), and monetarist (Chapter 15) views on the appropriate use of policy. Among the policy-related topics we cover are rational expectations and monetary policy (Chapter 11), the importance of central bank credibility (Chapters 13 and 15), and the intergenerational implications of budget deficits (Chapter 16).

■ *Labour market issues.* We pay close attention to issues relating to employment, unemployment, and real wages. We introduce the basic supply-demand model of the labour market and present a first-pass discussion of unemployment early, in Chapter 3. Unemployment is discussed more extensively in Chapter 13, which covers the inflation-unemployment tradeoff, the costs of unemployment, and government policies for reducing unemployment. Other labour market topics include the dynamics of job creation and job destruction in manufacturing (Chapter 11); efficiency wages (Chapter 12); hysteresis in unemployment (Chapter 13); and the effects of marginal and average tax rate changes on labour supply (Chapter 16).

THE STRUCTURE OF THE EUROPEAN EDITION

We have organized the text in four parts: *Part I* (Chapters 1–2) introduces the field of macroeconomics and discusses issues of economic measurement. *Part II* (Chapters 3–8) focuses on long-run issues, including growth and inflation, and includes an optional chapter (Chapter 8) on the microeconomics of household decision-making. *Part III* (Chapters 9–12) is devoted to the study of short-run economic fluctuations and stabilization policy. Finally, although we discuss macroeconomic policy throughout the book, *Part IV* (Chapters 13–16) looks at issues and institutions of policy-making in greater detail. Appendix A at the end of the book discusses useful algebraic and graphical tools.

Our coverage of short-run fluctuations is intended to aid lecturers who want to concentrate on short-run issues of cyclical fluctuations and macroeconomic stabilization, or who want to take an approach to short-run fluctuations focused more sharply on one or the other of the two major perspectives. *Macroeconomics* introduces the general *IS–LM/AD–AS* framework for macroeconomic analysis *before* the more detailed discussions of the classical and Keynesian models. Specifically, the end of Chapter 9 previews the approach, and Chapter 10 presents the entire model, so that the complete framework for short-run analysis is developed in a logical, unified manner.

We then put these tools to work to study classical theories of cyclical fluctuations in Chapter 11 and the modern Keynesian approach to cycles and stabilization in Chapter 12. Some of the options that this structure opens up for lecturers are discussed in the next section.

FLEXIBILITY

Lecturers of intermediate macroeconomics have different preferences about what to include in their courses, and their choices are often constrained by their students' backgrounds and the length of the term. The structure of our text allows it to accommodate various needs. In planning how to use *Macroeconomics* in your course, you might find it useful to keep the following points in mind:

■ *Core chapters.* We recommend that every course include the following six chapters:

Chapter 1   Introduction to Macroeconomics
Chapter 2   The Measurement and Structure of the National Economy
Chapter 3   Productivity, Output, and Employment
Chapter 4   Consumption, Saving, and Investment
Chapter 7   The Asset Market, Money, and Prices
Chapter 10 The *IS–LM/AD–AS* Model: A General Framework for Macroeconomic Analysis

Chapters 1 and 2 provide an introduction to macroeconomics, including national income accounting. The next four chapters on the list make up the analytical core of the book: Chapter 3 introduces the labour market, Chapters 3 and 4 together develop the goods market, and Chapter 7 discusses the asset market. Chapter 10 combines the three markets into a general equilibrium model usable for short-run analysis (in either a classical or Keynesian mode).

To a syllabus containing the above six chapters, lecturers can add various combinations of the other chapters, depending on the focus of the course. Here are some possible choices:

■ *Short-run focus.* A lecturer who prefers to emphasize short-run issues (business cycle fluctuations and stabilization policy) can omit Chapters 5, 6, and 8 without loss of continuity. It is also possible to go directly from the introductory materials of Chapters 1 and 2 to Chapters 9 and 10, which introduce business cycles and the *IS–LM/AD–AS* framework. Although the presentation in Chapters 9 and 10 is self-contained, it will be helpful in the latter case for the lecturer to provide some background and motivation for the various behavioral relationships and equilibrium conditions.

■ *Classical emphasis.* For lecturers who wish to teach the course with a modern classical emphasis, all the chapters in Part II (including optional Chapter 8 on household decision-making) are recommended. Chapters 9 through 11 provide a self-contained presentation of classical business cycle theory. Other material of interest includes the Friedman-Phelps interpretation of the Phillips curve (Chapter 13), the role of credibility in monetary policy (Chapter 15), and Ricardian equivalence with multiple generations (Chapter 16).

■ *Keynesian emphasis.* Lecturers who prefer a Keynesian emphasis may choose to omit Chapter 8 (household decision-making) and Chapter 11 (classical business cycle analysis). As noted, if a short-run focus is preferred, Chapter 5 (full-employment analysis of the open economy) and Chapter 6 (long-term economic growth) may also be omitted without loss of continuity.

■ *International focus.* Chapter 5 discusses saving, investment, and the trade balance in an open economy with full employment. Chapter 14 discusses exchange rate determination and macroeconomic policy in an open-economy model in which short-run deviations from full employment are possible. (Chapter 5 is a useful but not essential prerequisite for Chapter 14.)

■ *An emphasis on microfoundations.* The basic economics of consumption, saving, and labour supply are discussed in Chapters 3 and 4 as part of the development of our macroeconomic model. However, for lecturers who want to emphasize the microeconomic foundations of macroeconomics, Chapter 8 presents a more formal analysis of household decision-making, using indifference curves and the consumer's budget line to analyze consumption and saving decisions and the concepts of substitution and income effects to discuss the household's labour supply decision. Note that, as Chapter 8 extends material introduced in Chapters 3 and 4, it may be assigned to follow those chapters directly; or it can be assigned as optional background reading for Chapters 3 and 4. Another possibility is to assign only portions of the chapter: Section 8.3 on the life-cycle model of consumption and saving and Section 8.5 on the labour supply decision can be used on a largely stand-alone basis.

APPLYING MACROECONOMICS TO THE REAL WORLD

Economists sometimes get caught up in the elegance of formal models and forget that the ultimate test of a model or theory is its practical relevance. In *Macroeconomics* we dedicate a significant portion of each chapter to showing how the theory can be applied to real events and issues, helping the student learn how to 'think like an economist.'

■ *Applications.* Applications in each chapter show students how they can use theory to understand an important episode or issue, such as the impact of tax reform (Chapter 16) or the causes and effects of the LDC debt crisis (Chapter 5). *Applications* include: discussions of the effects of tax policy on investment (Chapter 4); the recent debate about the sources of East Asian growth (Chapter 6); inflation in the transition economies of Eastern Europe (Chapter 7); European monetary unification (Chapter 14); and inflation targeting (Chapter 15), among others.

■ *Boxes*. Boxes provide interesting additional information or sidelights, often drawn from current research. *Boxes* include (among others) a discussion of the bias in official measures of inflation (Chapter 2); the link between the stock market and investment (Chapter 4); the role of the credit crunch in the 1990–91 recession (Chapter 12); and the credit channel of monetary policy (Chapter 15).

■ *In Touch with the Macroeconomy*. One important component of thinking like an economist is being familiar with macroeconomic data – what's available, its strengths and shortcomings. To help students develop the habit of staying in touch with the macroeconomy, this series of boxes shows where to find important macroeconomic data – such as the index of leading indicators, balance of payments data, and labour market data – and how to interpret them.

■ *The Political Environment*. In talking about economic policy, our students frequently note the discrepancy between the recommendations of economists (assuming they even agree!) and the decisions that politicians or government institutions make. We address this discrepancy in a special series of boxes that highlight *the political environment* of economic issues and policies. These special boxes examine topics such as the link between the state of the economy and presidential elections (Chapter 13) and the relationship between democracy and economic growth (Chapter 6).

LEARNING FEATURES

Our text contains many features aimed at helping students understand, apply, and retain important concepts:

■ *Detailed graphs*. Our book is liberally illustrated with *data graphs*, which emphasize the empirical relevance of the theory, and *analytical graphs*, which guide students through the development of model and theory in a well-paced, step-by-step manner. Both types of graphs include descriptive captions that summarize the details of events shown on the graph.

■ *Key Diagrams*. Key diagrams, a unique study feature found at the end of selected chapters, are self-contained descriptions of the most important analytical graphs in the book (see the Table of Contents for a list). For each key diagram we present the graph (the production function, p. 106, or the *AD–AS* diagram, p. 376, for example) and define and describe its elements in words and equations. We then present an analysis of what the graph reveals and discuss the factors that shift the curves in the graph.

■ *Summary tables*. Summary tables are used throughout the book to bring the main results of an analysis together in one place. Summary tables reduce the time the student must spend writing and memorizing results, allowing a greater concentration on understanding and applying these results.

■ *End-of-chapter review materials*. To facilitate review, at the end of each chapter the student will find a *chapter summary*, covering the chapter's main points; a list of *key terms*, with page references; an annotated list of *key equations*; and *review questions* for self-testing.

- *End-of-chapter problems.* An extensive set of problems for practice and review (more than 160 in all) includes *numerical problems*, which have explicit numerical solutions and are especially useful for checking students' understanding of basic relationships and concepts; and *analytical problems*, which ask the student to use or extend the theory in a qualitative way. Problem answers and additional problems are provided by the Lecturer's Manual.

- *Review of useful analytical tools.* Although we use no mathematics beyond high school algebra, some students will find it handy to have a review of the main analytical tools used in the book. Appendix A (at the end of the text) succinctly discusses functions of one and several variables, graphs, slopes, exponents, and formulas for finding the growth rates of products and ratios.

- *Glossary.* The Glossary at the end of the text includes definitions of all key terms (boldfaced within the chapter and also listed at the end of each chapter) and refers the student to the page on which the term is fully defined and discussed.

SUPPLEMENTARY MATERIALS

For further information regarding supplementary material, please contact Customer Services, Addison Wesley Longman. UK Customers: (01279) 623928; International Customers: +44 1279 623925.

ACKNOWLEDGMENTS

These days a textbook is not the lonely venture of its author or co-authors but is the joint project of dozens of skilled and dedicated people.

We thank the reviewers and colleagues who offered valuable comments on the European Edition.

Reviewers:

Darrin Baines	University of Nottingham
Christopher Tsoukis	University of Hull
Kevin Lawler	University of Sunderland
Anders Paalzow	Stockholm School of Economics

We also give special thanks to:

Ilian Mihov	INSEAD, France
Jon Riley	Cardiff University
Spencer Dale	Bank of England
Anna Brueton	Office for National Statistics
Michele Hainault	OECD
Birgitta Magnusson	Statistics Sweden

Last and most, we thank our families for their patience and support. We dedicate this book to them.

PART I

INTRODUCTION

1

INTRODUCTION TO MACROECONOMICS

1.1   WHAT MACROECONOMICS IS ABOUT

Macroeconomics is the study of the structure and performance of national economies and of the policies that governments use to try to affect economic performance. The issues that macroeconomists address include the following:

■ *What determines a nation's long-run economic growth?* In 1870 income per capita in Norway was smaller than in Argentina. But today, income per capita is more than twice as high in Norway as in Argentina. Why do some nations' economies grow quickly, providing their citizens with rapidly improving living standards, while other nations' economies are relatively stagnant?

■ *What causes a nation's economic activity to fluctuate?* After nearly a decade of prosperity during the 1980s, most European economies began to falter in the early 1990s. For the European Union (EU) as a whole, output in 1993 had fallen by nearly 1% from its 1992 level, though the downturn was much more severe in some countries, such as Sweden, than in others, such as the Netherlands. Why do economies sometimes experience sharp short-run fluctuations, lurching between periods of prosperity and periods of hard times?

■ *What causes unemployment?* During the 1930s nearly one-third of the workforce in the Netherlands was unemployed. A decade later, following World War II, less than 1% of the workforce was unemployed. Why does unemployment sometimes reach very high levels? Why, even during times of relative prosperity, is a significant fraction of the workforce unemployed? Why are unemployment rates now higher in Europe than they are in other countries, such as the United States and Japan?

■ *What causes prices to rise?* The rate of inflation across Europe crept steadily upward during the 1970s, and was in excess of 10% per year in a number of countries in the early 1980s before dropping to less than 4% per year in most European countries in the mid 1980s. Germany's inflation experience has been much more extreme: although Germany has earned a reputation for low inflation in recent decades, following its defeat in World War I Germany experienced an eighteen-month period (July 1922–December 1923) during which prices rose by a factor of several billion! What causes inflation and what can be done about it?

■ *How does being part of a global economic system affect nations' economies?* According to many observers, the recovery from the 1991–92 recession in the UK was hampered by slow economic growth *abroad*, especially by the continued recession in the rest of Europe, which restrained the demand for UK products. During this period tension within the EU heightened as a number of countries were required to persevere with high interest rates in order to maintain the position of their currency within the Exchange Rate Mechanism (ERM) despite the weak state of their domestic economies. How do economic links among nations, such as international trade and borrowing, and through the coordination of policy as among member countries of the EU, affect the performance of individual economies and the world economy as a whole?

■ *Can government policies be used to improve a nation's economic performance?* During the past twenty years, European countries have adopted differing views about the potential role of government in helping to solve a nation's economic problems. The movement towards monetary union and a single currency has highlighted one of the greatest of the perceived problems, the large government budget deficits that exist in most EU countries. How do national economic policies, such as government taxation and spending policies, affect the behaviour of the overall economy? How should economic policy be conducted in order to keep the economy as prosperous and stable as possible?

Macroeconomics seeks to offer answers to such questions, which are of great practical importance and are constantly debated by politicians, the press, and the public. In the rest of this section we consider these key macroeconomic issues in more detail.

Long-Run Economic Growth

If you have ever travelled in a developing country, you could not help but observe the difference in living standards relative to those of Western Europe. The problems of inadequate food, shelter, and health care experienced by the poorest citizens of rich nations often represent the average situation for the people of a developing country. From a macroeconomic perspective, the difference between rich nations and developing nations may be summarized by saying that rich nations have at some point in their history experienced extended periods of rapid economic growth but that the poorer nations either have never experienced sustained growth or have had periods of growth offset by periods of economic decline.

Figure 1.1 summarizes the growth in output of a number of European countries since 1900. The record is an impressive one: Over the past century

**Figure 1.1
Output of selected
European economies
1900–96**

In these graphs the
output of a number of
European countries is
measured by real gross
domestic product (real
GDP) with goods and
services valued at 1990
prices (see Chapter 2)
and expressed in millions
of ECUs. Note the strong
upward trend in output
over time, as well as
sharp fluctuations during
the early 1920s, the
Great Depression
(1929–33), World War II
(1939–45), and the
recessions of 1973–75,
1980–82 and 1990–93.

Sources: 1900–87 from Angus
Maddison, *Dynamic Forces in
Capitalist Development: A
Long-Run Comparative View*,
1991, Oxford University Press,
Oxford, Table A6; 1988–95 from
International Financial Statistics,
Yearbook XLIX, International
Monetary Fund, Washington
D.C., country tables; 1996 from
International Financial Statistics,
Volume L, International
Monetary Fund, Washington
D.C., country tables. All series
have been converted to 1990
ECUs.

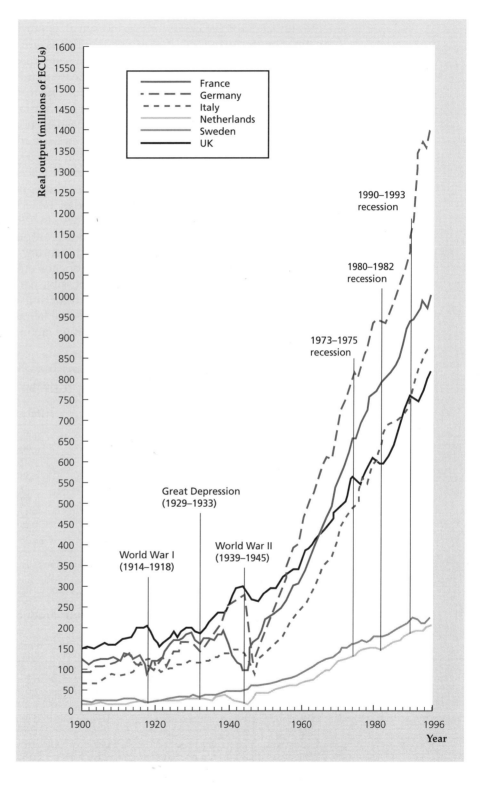

the annual output of goods and services in all countries has increased dramatically. The performance of these economies is not unique, however; other industrial nations have had similar, and in some cases higher, rates of growth over this period of time. This massive increase in the output of industrial economies is one of the central facts of modern history and has had enormous political, military, social, and even cultural implications.

In part, the long-term growth of European economies is the result of rising populations, which have meant a steady increase in the number of available workers. But another significant factor is the increase in the amount of output that can be produced with a given amount of labour. The amount of output produced per unit of labour input – for example, per worker or per hour of work – is called **average labour productivity.** Table 1.1(a) shows how average labour productivity has changed since 1870. In 1987 the average European worker produced more than six times as much output per hour as the average worker at the beginning of the twentieth century. Because today's typical worker is so much more productive, Europeans enjoy a significantly higher standard of living than would have been possible earlier in the century.

Although the long-term record of productivity growth in all European economies is excellent, in recent years average labour productivity in Europe has grown slowly. Table 1.1(b) shows average labour productivity, defined in

Table 1.1(a) Average Labour Productivity (GDP per person hour), 1870–1987

Year	UK	Germany	France	Italy	Netherlands	Sweden
1870	2.15	1.04	1.15	0.85	1.82	0.97
1890	2.86	1.52	1.52	0.99	2.49	1.32
1913	3.63	2.32	2.26	1.72	3.23	2.04
1929	4.58	2.89	3.30	2.38	5.09	2.61
1938	4.97	3.57	4.25	3.12	5.03	3.38
1950	6.49	3.40	4.58	3.52	5.23	5.60
1960	8.15	6.62	7.17	5.52	7.87	7.80
1973	13.36	12.83	14.00	12.82	15.30	15.08
1987	18.46	18.35	21.63	18.25	21.27	18.94

Note: Figures are in US dollars at 1985 prices, adjusted for differences in the purchasing power of the national currencies.
Source: Maddison, *op cit. Figure 1.1,* Table C11

Table 1.1(b) The Growth in Average Labour Productivity (GDP per worker), 1961–96

Year	UK	Germany	France	Italy	Netherlands	Sweden
1961–70	2.6	4.2	4.9	6.2	3.9	3.9
1971–80	1.7	2.6	2.8	2.7	2.7	1.2
1981–90	2.1	1.7	2.1	1.6	1.5	1.3
1991	1.1	2.5	0.7	0.3	0.9	0.4
1992	1.4	0.8	2.1	1.6	1.0	3.2
1993	3.7	−0.3	−0.4	1.8	0.4	3.2
1994	3.8	3.6	2.6	3.7	2.6	3.6
1995	1.8	2.2	1.0	3.4	1.0	1.4
1996	1.5	1.3	1.0	1.6	0.7	0.6

Source: *European Economy 1996: Broad Economic Policy Guidelines*, 1996, European Commission, Brussels, Table 11. GDP at 1990 Market prices per person employed.

this case as output per employed worker, since 1961. As the table shows, with the exception of the UK, the growth rate of output per worker since 1980 compares badly with that recorded in the 1960s. As a result, living standards in many European countries have risen relatively slowly in recent years. Labour productivity growth did rise a little in the mid 1990s, as you can see from Table 1.1(b). However, the possibility that the productivity growth slowdown will continue underlies many of the concerns that have been expressed about the health and long-term future of some European economies.

Because the rates of growth of output and, particularly, of output per worker ultimately determine whether a nation will be rich or poor, understanding what determines growth is one of the most important goals of macroeconomics. Unfortunately, explaining why economies grow is not easy. Why, for example, did resource-poor Japan and Korea experience growth rates that transformed them in a generation or two from war-torn nations to industrial powers, whereas several resource-rich nations of Latin America have had erratic or even negative growth in recent years? Although macroeconomists have nothing close to a complete answer to the question of what determines rates of economic growth, they do have some ideas to offer. For example, as we discuss in some detail in this book, most macroeconomists believe that rates of saving and investment are important for growth. Another key determinant of growth we discuss is the rate at which technological change and other factors help increase the productivity of machines and workers.

Business Cycles

If you look at the history of output of the different countries in Figure 1.1, you will notice that the growth of output is not always smooth but has hills and valleys. Most striking are the periods between 1914 and 1921 and between 1929 and 1945, which contain both World Wars and the Great Depression. Between 1914 and 1918, during World War I, the output of the French and German economies fell by nearly 40%. Over the period 1939–44, output in the UK and Germany, which expanded production of armaments, increased by around 25%. Many other European economies, including both France and the Netherlands, were devastated during World War II and their output fell dramatically. No fluctuations in output in any European economies since 1945 have been as severe as they were during the 1929–45 period. However, during the postwar era there have been periods of unusually rapid economic growth across Europe as a whole, such as during the 1960s, and times during which output in some countries actually declined from one year to the next, as in 1973–75, in the early 1980s, and in the early 1990s.

Macroeconomists use the term *business cycle* to describe short-run, but sometimes sharp, contractions and expansions in economic activity.[1] The downward phase of a business cycle, during which national output may be falling or perhaps growing only very slowly, is called a recession. Even when they are relatively mild, recessions mean hard economic times for many people. Recessions are also a major political concern, because almost every

---

1. A more exact definition is given in Chapter 9. Business cycles do not include fluctuations lasting only a few months, such as the increase in activity that occurs around Christmas.

politician wants to be re-elected and the chances of re-election are better if the nation's economy is expanding rather than declining. Macroeconomists put a lot of effort into trying to figure out what causes business cycles and into deciding what can or should be done about them. In this book we describe a variety of features of business cycles, compare alternative explanations for cyclical fluctuations, and evaluate the policy options that are available for affecting the course of the cycle.

Unemployment

One important aspect of recessions is that they are usually accompanied by an increase in **unemployment,** or the number of people who are available for work and are actively seeking work but cannot find jobs. Along with growth and business cycles, the problem of unemployment is a third major issue in macroeconomics.

The best-known measure of unemployment is the unemployment rate, which is the number of unemployed divided by the total labour force (the number of people either working or seeking work). Figure 1.2 shows the unemployment rate for a number of European countries since 1920. The highest and most prolonged period of unemployment in many countries occurred during the Great Depression of the 1930s. In some countries, such as Germany, the Netherlands and Sweden, the unemployment rate during this period was in excess of 25%, indicating that at least one in every four potential workers was unable to find a job. In contrast, the tremendous increase in economic activity that occurred during the early 1960s significantly reduced unemployment. Many countries saw unemployment drop below 2% and in Germany and the Netherlands it fell to below 1%.

Recessions have led to significant increases in unemployment in recent years. For example, during the 1982–83 recession the unemployment rate in the Netherlands reached 10.8%. Even during periods of economic expansion, however, the unemployment rate can remain well above zero, as you can see from Figure 1.2. In 1990, after a decade of economic growth with no recession, the unemployment rate in France (not shown on graph) remained above 9%. Why the unemployment rate can remain fairly high even when the economy as a whole is doing well is an important question in macroeconomics and is especially important for Europe, where the problem of high unemployment rates has been a major concern in recent years.

Inflation

When the prices of most goods and services are rising over time, the economy is said to be experiencing inflation. Prior to 1950, several European countries including Germany, France and Italy had periods when prices rose very rapidly. This usually occurred during wartime and in the years of rationing that followed. These wartime periods of inflation were often followed by periods of **deflation**, during which the prices of most goods and services fell. In some countries, such as Sweden, the Netherlands and the UK, the result of these offsetting periods of inflation and deflation was that, over the long run, the level of prices was fairly constant. The last significant deflation in Europe

Figure 1.2
Unemployment rates 1920–96
The figure shows the percentage of the civilian labour force (excluding people in the military) that was unemployed in each year. For some countries, data in the early years or during World War II are not available. Unemployment peaked during the Great Depression of the 1930s. It reached its low point in the UK during World War II and in the other countries shown during the 1950s. Since World War II the highest unemployment rates were during the recessions that occurred during 1973–75, 1981–83 and 1993.
Sources: Data for the period 1920–88 from B.R. Mitchell, *International Historical Statistics, Europe 1750–1988*, London Macmillan Publishing, Table B2; Data for the period 1990–96 *European Economy 1996 op cit. Table 1.1(b)*, Table 3.

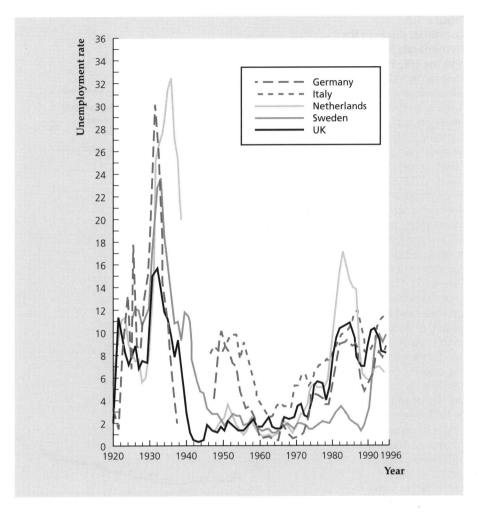

occurred during 1929–33, the initial phase of the Great Depression. Since then inflation without offsetting deflation has become the normal state of affairs. Figure 1.3 shows a measure of the average level of prices[2] faced by consumers in several European countries since 1920. Note the sharp increase in consumer prices across Europe after 1973.

The percentage increase in the average level of prices over a year is called the inflation rate. If the inflation rate in consumer prices is 10%, for example, then on average the prices of items that consumers buy are rising by 10% per year. Rates of inflation may vary dramatically both over time and across countries, from a few per cent per year in low-inflation countries (such as Switzerland) to 1000% per year or more in countries (such as Bolivia or Argentina in recent years) that are experiencing hyperinflations, or extreme

---

2. The measure of the average level of prices is called the consumer or retail price index, which is discussed in Chapter 2. Conceptually, the index is intended to measure the cost of buying a certain fixed set, or 'basket', of consumer goods. However, the construction of a consumer price index over a period as long as two centuries involves many compromises. One is that the basket of goods priced by the index is not literally the same over the entire period shown in Fig. 1.3 but is periodically changed to reflect the different mix of consumer goods available at different times.

Figure 1.3
Consumer prices in the Netherlands, Sweden and the UK, 1920–96
Prior to World War II, the average level of prices faced by consumers remained relatively constant, with periods of inflation (rising prices) offset by periods of deflation (falling prices). Since World War II, however, prices have risen more rapidly. In the figure the average level of prices is measured by the consumer price index (see Chapter 2). The consumer price index measures the cost of a fixed set, or basket, of goods relative to the cost of the same goods in a base period, in this case 1950. Thus a consumer price index for the Netherlands of 115.5 in 1955 means that a basket of consumer goods which cost 100 guilder in 1950 would cost 115.5 guilder in 1955.
Sources: Data for the period 1920–89 from Maddison, *op cit. Figure 1.1*, Tables E3 and E4; data prior to 1990 were converted to a base 1990 = 100; data for the period 1990–96 from *European Economy 1996, op cit. Table 1.1 (b)*, Table 25, data converted to an index with base 1990 = 100.

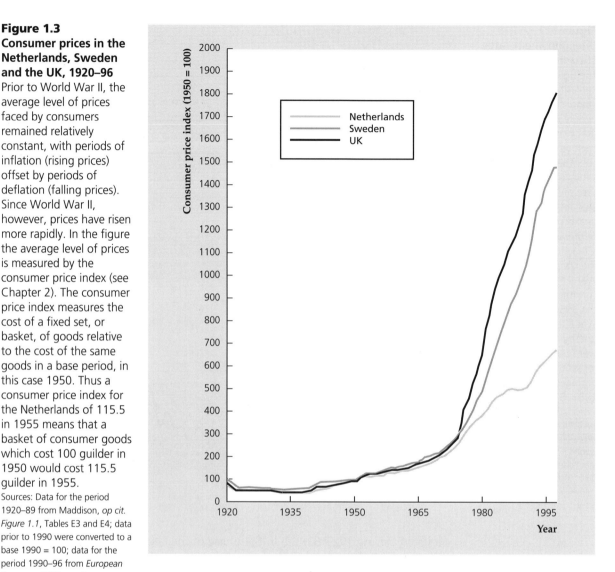

inflations. When the inflation rate reaches an extremely high level, with prices changing daily or hourly, the economy tends to function poorly. High inflation also means that the purchasing power of money erodes quickly, which forces people to scramble to spend their money almost as soon as they receive it.

The International Economy

Today every major economy is an **open economy**, or one that has extensive trading and financial relationships with other national economies. (A **closed economy** does not interact economically with the rest of the world.) Nowhere is this more so than in the European Union. Macroeconomists study patterns of international trade and borrowing to understand better the links between national economies. For example, an important topic in macroeconomics is how international trade and borrowing relationships can help transmit business cycles from country to country. Another significant issue is the move towards monetary union and the introduction of a single currency within Europe.

Another issue for which international considerations are central is trade imbalances. Figure 1.4 shows the historical behaviour of the imports and exports of goods and services by the UK. Imports are goods and services produced abroad and purchased by domestic residents. Exports are goods and services produced in the domestic economy and sold to foreigners. To give you a sense of the relative importance of international trade, Figure 1.4 expresses exports and imports as percentages of total output. Currently, both exports and imports are larger fractions of output than they were during the 1960s, reflecting both the recovery of trade from the disruptions of the Great Depression and World War II and the trend toward greater economic interdependence among nations. However, even a century ago exports and imports were important relative to the size of the overall economy, and this was the case in all European countries.

You can see from Figure 1.4 that exports and imports need not be equal in each year. For example, during the 1930s, UK imports outstripped UK exports because the Great Depression, especially in the USA, reduced the demand for UK goods and services. Similarly, during World War II, the UK economy was

Figure 1.4
UK exports and imports, 1921–95
The figure shows UK exports (dashed line) and UK imports (solid line), each expressed as a percentage of total output. Exports and imports need not be equal in each year: UK imports exceeded exports during much of the twentieth century. During the period 1977–86, however, UK imports were smaller than UK exports.
Source: Data for the period 1921–65 from C.H. Feinstein, *National Income, Expenditure and Output of the United Kingdom 1855–1965*, Cambridge, Cambridge University Press, 1972, Table 2. Data for the period 1966–96 from *International Financial Statistics*, (see notes to Figure 1.1).

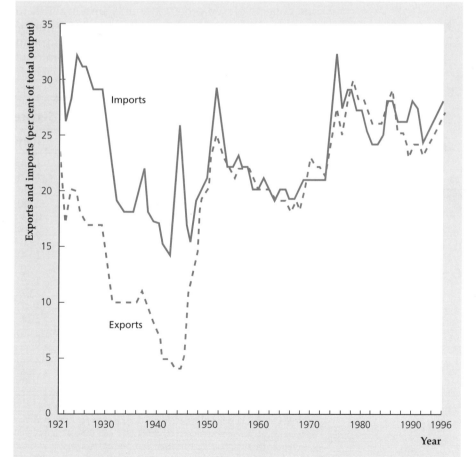

severely constrained and damaged by war and relied on countries such as the USA for many goods. The export of UK goods and services recovered during the 1950s, though in most years since Word War II the UK has imported more goods and services than it has exported. When imports exceed exports, a **trade deficit** exists. In the early 1980s, imports declined sharply relative to exports, as you can see from Figure 1.4. This excess of exports over imports, or **trade surplus**, was, however, short-lived and exports fell sharply in the late 1980s.

Table 1.2 shows the large differences that exist within the EU in terms of the relative size of exports and imports as a proportion of GDP. As you can see, the Netherlands is highly dependent on international trade, importing and exporting the equivalent of half its total output each year, which is between two and three times as large as in France and the UK.

What causes trade imbalances? Are trade deficits bad for countries or their trading partners? These are among the questions that macroeconomists try to answer.

Macroeconomic Policy

A nation's economic performance depends on many factors, including its natural and human resources, its capital stock (buildings and machines), its technology, and the economic choices made by its citizens, both individually and collectively. Another extremely important factor affecting economic performance is the set of macroeconomic policies pursued by the government.

Macroeconomic policies affect the performance of the economy as a whole. The two major types of macroeconomic policy are fiscal policy and

Table 1.2 Export (and Import) of Goods and Services as a percentage of GDP

Year	UK	Germany	France	Italy	Netherlands	Sweden
1961–70	20.5	19.3	13.5	14.6	41.4	21.8
	(20.9)	(17.3)	(13.1)	(14.2)	(41.9)	(22.0)
1971–80	26.5	24.2	19.4	20.8	46.6	27.7
	(26.9)	(22.0)	(19.0)	(21.2)	(45.0)	(27.7)
1981–90	25.9	30.3	22.3	21.4	54.9	32.9
	(26.5)	(26.5)	(22.4)	(21.5)	(50.8)	(31.5)
1991	23.5	25.4	22.7	19.6	54.1	27.9
	(24.7)	(25.5)	(22.3)	(19.4)	(49.3)	(26.4)
1992	23.7	23.7	22.7	20.0	52.2	27.9
	(25.2)	(23.8)	(21.3)	(19.9)	(47.8)	(26.2)
1993	25.3	22.0	22.0	23.3	50.6	32.8
	(26.6)	(21.7)	(19.8)	(19.7)	(45.6)	(29.2)
1994	26.2	22.7	22.8	25.4	51.7	36.7
	(27.1)	(22.1)	(20.6)	(21.3)	(46.3)	(32.5)
1995	27.4	23.0	23.3	28.0	51.8	40.2
	(27.8)	(22.0)	(21.2)	(23.2)	(46.1)	(34.6)
1996	29.2	23.3	23.9	n.a.	53.6	n.a.
	(30.0)	(23.3)	(21.4)		(48.0)	

Note: Figures for Germany pre-1990 show data for West Germany.

Sources: Data for the period 1961–95 from *European Economy 1996, op cit. Table 1.1(b)*, Table 36 'Exports of goods and services at current prices (percentage of GDP)' and Table 42 'Imports of goods and services at current prices (percentage of GDP)'; Data for 1996 from *International Financial Statistics, Volume L, June 1997, op cit. Figure 1.1*, country tables.

monetary policy. **Fiscal policy**, which is determined at the national and local levels, concerns government spending and taxation. **Monetary policy** affects short-term interest rates and the rate of growth of a nation's money supply and is under the control of a government institution known as the central bank. An important issue within the EU is the extent to which central banks should be independent of government, as is the case with both the Bundesbank in Germany and the Bank of England in the UK.

One of the main macroeconomic policy issues of recent years has been in the realm of fiscal policy. This issue concerns the potential effects on the economy of large government budget deficits, the annual excess of government spending over tax collections. The recent deficit is put into a long-term perspective in Figure 1.5, which presents data on government spending and tax revenues for the UK.[3] Again, so that their importance relative to the economy as a whole is indicated, spending, tax collections, and government budget deficits and surpluses are expressed as percentages of total output.

Figure 1.5
Government spending and tax collections, 1920–96

UK government spending (solid line) and UK government tax collections (dashed line) are shown as a percentage of total output. Large deficits occurred during World War II, the Great Depression, and during recessions. The government sector's share of the economy has grown since World War II.
Source: Data for the period 1920–45, from B.R. Mitchell, *International Statistics, Europe 1970–1988*, Macmillan Publishing. Data for the period 1946–96, from *Economic Trends*, Annual Supplement 1996/7.

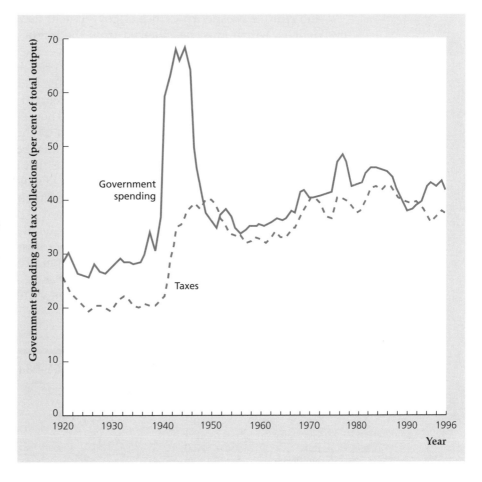

---

3. Government spending includes both government purchases of goods and services, such as purchases of military equipment and the salaries of government officials, and government benefits paid to individuals, such as social welfare payments.

One obvious feature of Figure 1.5 is the peak in government spending and deficit that resulted from World War II. At its high point during World War II, total government spending exceeded 65% of total output. Significant deficits also occurred during the 1920s and the Great Depression of the 1930s because the government increased its spending on social welfare payments and on various programmes designed to help the economy, such as house and road building. Also shown clearly is the increase in the size of the government sector since World War II, an increase reflected in both the major upward shift in government spending and in tax collections relative to national output that occurred in about 1940 and the mild upward trend in both variables that has occurred since then.

Table 1.3 shows what has happened to the government budget deficit in a number of countries since 1961. To highlight their relative significance, the deficits are expressed as percentages of total output. For most EU countries, budget deficits increased significantly in the late 1980s and 1990s. These deficits are historically unusual in that they occurred during a period of peace and relative prosperity. Critics of government fiscal policy argue that these deficits, which must be financed from the public purse, divert funds that might otherwise be put to more productive uses, such as investment in modern equipment, and that they undermine price and exchange rate stability. Some critics also claim a close link between the budget deficits since the mid 1970s and the decline in productivity that occurred in many European countries during the same period (see Table 1.1). The constraints that large budget deficits place on an economy are highlighted by the fact that one of the convergence criteria that must be met by EU member states before they can participate in the European Monetary Union is that their budget deficits must not exceed 3% of GDP (this issue is dealt with in more detail in Chapter 16).

The possible link between the government's budget deficit and productivity growth illustrates an important aspect of macroeconomics: macroeconomic issues and problems are frequently interconnected. For this reason studying one macroeconomic question, such as the effects of the government budget deficit, in isolation is generally not sufficient. Instead, macroeconomists usually study the economy as a complete system, recognizing that changes in one sector or market may affect the behaviour of the entire economy.

Table 1.3 Government Budget Deficits, 1961–96 (as a percentage of GDP)

	1961–73	1974–79	1980–89	1990–96
France	−0.4	0.9	2.3	3.9
Germany	−0.4	2.9	2.0	3.1
Italy	−2.0	8.2	11.2	9.0
Netherlands	0.8	2.7	5.4	3.6
Sweden	n.a.	−3.6	0.8	5.7
UK	0.8	4.0	2.3	5.1

Source: Data for the period 1961–95 from *European Economy 1995, Broad Economic Policy Guidelines*, European Commission, Brussels, Table 120. Data for 1996 from *European Economy 1996, op cit. Table 1.1(b)*, Table 76.

Aggregation

Macroeconomics is one of two broad areas within the field of economics, the other being microeconomics. Macroeconomics and microeconomics have many basic economic ideas and methods in common; the difference between them is the level at which the economy is studied. Microeconomists focus on individual consumers, workers, and firms, each of which is too small to have an impact on the national economy. Macroeconomists ignore the fine distinctions among the many different kinds of goods, firms, and markets that exist in the economy and instead focus on national totals. For example, in their analyses macroeconomists do not care whether consumers are buying VCRs or compact disc players, beef or chicken, Pepsi or Coke. Instead, they add consumer expenditures on all goods and services to get an overall total called aggregate consumption. The process of summing individual economic variables to obtain economy-wide totals is called **aggregation**. The use of aggregation and the emphasis on aggregate quantities such as aggregate consumption, aggregate investment, and aggregate output are the primary factors that distinguish macroeconomics from microeconomics.

1.2   WHAT MACROECONOMISTS DO

How do macroeconomists use their skills, and what do they do with all the data they gather and the theories they develop? Besides teaching economics, macroeconomists engage in a wide variety of activities, including forecasting, macroeconomic analysis, basic research, and data development.

Macroeconomic Forecasting

Many people believe that economists spend most of their time trying to forecast the performance of the economy. In fact, except for a relatively small number of forecasting specialists, forecasting is a minor part of what macroeconomists do. One reason why macroeconomists do not emphasize forecasting is that on the whole they are not terribly good at it! Forecasting is difficult not only because our understanding of how the economy works is imperfect but also because of the impossibility of taking into account *all* the factors – many of them not strictly economic – that might affect future economic trends. Here are some questions that a forecaster, in trying to project the course of the economy, might have to try to answer: How will an ageing population affect future government budget deficits? What oil price will the Organization of Petroleum Exporting Countries (OPEC) decide on at its next meeting? Will there be a severe drought in agricultural regions with adverse effects on food quantities and prices? Will new technologies that are being developed ever come to market? Because answers to such questions are highly uncertain, macroeconomic forecasters rarely offer a single prediction. Instead, they usually combine a 'most likely' forecast with 'optimistic' and 'pessimistic' alternative scenarios.

Does the fact that macroeconomics cannot be used to make highly accurate forecasts of economic activity mean that it is a pointless field of study? Some people may think so, but that is really an unreasonable standard. Meteorology is an example of a field in which forecasting is difficult (will it *definitely* be nice this weekend?) but in which there is also a lot of useful knowledge (meteorologists helped discover the depletion of the earth's ozone layer and pointed out its dangers). Similarly, cardiologists cannot usually predict if or when a patient will have a heart attack – they can only talk about probabilities. Like meteorologists and doctors, economists deal with a system whose complexity makes gaining a thorough understanding difficult and forecasting the system's behaviour even more difficult. Rather than predicting what will happen, most macroeconomists are engaged in analysing and interpreting events as they happen (macroeconomic analysis) or in trying to understand the structure of the economy in general (macroeconomic research).

Macroeconomic Analysis

Macroeconomic analysts monitor the economy and think about the implications of current economic events. Many analysts are employed in the private sector, such as in banks or large corporations. Private-sector analysts try to determine how general economic trends will affect their employers' financial investments, their opportunities for expansion, the demand for their products, and so on. Some private firms specialize in macroeconomic analysis and assist clients on a fee-for-service basis.

The public sector, which includes the EU, national and regional governments and international agencies such as the OECD, the World Bank and the International Monetary Fund, also employs many macroeconomic analysts. The main function of public-sector analysts is to assist in policy making – for example, by writing reports that assess various macroeconomic problems and by identifying and evaluating possible policy options. Among policymakers, the officials who set monetary policy may call on the aid of economists employed within their central banks and the professional staffs of numerous departments and agencies. Economic policymakers also often go outside the government to seek the advice of macroeconomists from business or academia.

If a country has many well-trained macroeconomic analysts, does that mean that its macroeconomic policies will always be intelligent and farsighted? The answer, unfortunately, is 'no'. Because of the complexity of the economy, macroeconomic policy analysis, like macroeconomic forecasting, is often difficult and uncertain. Perhaps even more important, though, *politicians, not economists, usually make economic policy*. Politicians are typically less concerned with the abstract desirability of a policy than with the policy's immediate effects on their constituents. Thus in late 1990 international talks intended to reduce trade barriers failed because European governments found it politically inadvisable to reduce high subsidy payments to their farmers – despite the nearly universal opposition of economists to both trade barriers and farm price support payments. To reflect the importance of politics in economic policy making, at various points in this book we include a feature called 'The Political Environment', in which we discuss political aspects of macroeconomics.

Although the technical advice provided by macroeconomic analysts is not the sole basis on which macroeconomic policy is made, such advice is probably necessary for making good policy decisions, especially if dramatic changes are being considered. In recent years, for example, a number of countries in Eastern Europe, Latin America, and elsewhere have undertaken radical reforms of their economies. In most of these cases the countries' leaders have sought the technical advice of domestic and foreign economists, and this advice has been influential in policy making. In the former Soviet Union, economists have played an important role in the debate over restructuring and reform, both as technical specialists and as political advocates.

Macroeconomic Research

Macroeconomic research takes an amazing variety of forms, from abstract mathematical analysis to psychological experimentation to massive number-crunching projects in which supercomputers are used to process large amounts of economic data. Nevertheless, the goal of all macroeconomic research is to make general statements about how the economy works. The general insights about the economy gained from successful research form the basis for the analyses of specific economic problems, policies, or situations.

To see why research is important, imagine that you are an economist with the International Monetary Fund whose task is to help a small African country control its high rate of inflation. On what basis can you offer advice? Basically, you should know what inflation-fighting policies other countries have used in the past, what the results have been, how the results depended on the characteristics of the country employing the policy, and so on. Particularly if the situation you are analysing is not identical to any of the previous cases, having some theoretical principles would also help identify and understand the main factors contributing to that country's inflation. Analysing the historical cases and working out the theoretical principles by yourself from scratch might involve many years' effort. The value of ongoing research activities is that many of the results and ideas that you would need are already available in books or professional journals or circulated in unpublished form. Because it forms the basis for activities such as economic analysis and forecasting, in a very real sense macroeconomic research is the engine that pulls the whole enterprise of macroeconomics behind it.

Macroeconomic research takes place primarily in colleges and universities, in non-profit institutions (such as the Centre for Economic Policy Research and the National Institute for Economic and Social Research in the UK, and the Business and Social Research Institute in Sweden), and in the public sector (the government and international agencies). Particularly in the public sector, the line between economic analysis and macroeconomic research is much fuzzier than we have drawn it here. The reason is that many economists move back and forth between analysis of specific problems (such as an African country's inflation problem) and more basic macroeconomic research (such as an analysis of inflation in general).

Economic Theory. How is macroeconomic research carried out? As in many other fields, macroeconomic research proceeds primarily through the formulation and testing of theories. An **economic theory** is a set of ideas about the economy that have been organized in a logical framework. Most economic theories are developed in terms of an **economic model,** which is a simplified description of some aspect of the economy, usually expressed in mathematical form. Economists evaluate an economic model or theory by applying four criteria:

1. Are its assumptions reasonable and realistic?

2. Is it understandable and manageable enough to be used in studying real problems?

3. Does it have implications that can be tested by **empirical analysis**? That is, can its implications be evaluated by comparing them with data obtained in the real world?

4. When the implications and the data are compared, are the implications of the theory consistent with the data?

For a theory or model – of any type, not just economic – to be useful, the answer to each of these questions must be 'yes.' Unfortunately, though, economists may not always agree in their evaluation of a particular model, which means that controversies about the best way to model a given economic situation sometimes persist.

We present a summary of the main steps in developing and testing an economic theory or model in Box 1.1.

BOX 1.1

Developing and Testing an Economic Theory

To illustrate the process of developing and testing an economic theory, suppose that we want to develop a theory that explains the routes that people take when they commute from home to work and back. Such a theory would be useful, for example, to a traffic planner who is concerned about how a proposed housing development will affect traffic patterns. Here are the steps we would take:

Step 1. State the research question.

Example: What determines traffic flows in the city during rush hours?

Step 2. Make *provisional* assumptions that describe the economic setting and the behaviour of the economic actors. These assumptions should be simple yet capture the most important aspects of the problem.

Example: The setting is described by the map of the city. The assumption about behaviour is that commuters choose routes that minimize driving time.

Step 3. Work out the implications of the theory.

Example: Use the map of the city to plot a route that minimizes driving time between home and place of work.

Step 4. Conduct an *empirical analysis* to compare the implications of the theory with the data.

Example: Conduct a survey of commuters to identify (1) home locations; (2) work locations; and (3)

routes taken to work. Then see whether the routes predicted by the model are generally the same as those reported in the commuter survey.

Step 5. Evaluate the results of your comparisons.

If the theory fits the data well: Use the theory to predict what would happen if the economic setting or economic policies changed.

Example: Use the minimum-driving time assumption to evaluate the traffic effects of a new housing development by figuring out which routes the residents of the development are likely to take.

If the theory fits the data poorly: Start from scratch with a new model. Repeat steps 2–5.

Example: Change the provisional behavioural assumption to the following: Commuters choose the route that minimizes the *distance* they must drive (not the time they spend driving).

If the theory fits the data moderately well: Either make do with a partially successful theory or modify the model with additional assumptions and then repeat steps 3–5.

Example: A possible modification of the minimum-driving time assumption is that commuters will choose more scenic over less scenic routes, if driving time is not increased by more than a certain number of minutes. To test the model with this modified assumption, you must determine which routes are more scenic (those that pass a lake) and which are less scenic (those that pass a dump).

Data Development

The collection of economic data is a vital part of macroeconomics, and many economists are involved in the data development process. Data on thousands of economic variables are collected and analysed in all major economies. We have already presented some important macroeconomic data series, such as measures of output and the price level, and will look at these and others in more detail in Chapter 2. Macroeconomists use economic data to assess the current state of the economy, make forecasts, analyse policy alternatives, and test macroeconomic theories.

Most economic data are collected and published by individual governments, by public agencies, and by central banks such as the Bank of England and the Bundesbank. To an increasing degree, however, these activities also take place in the private sector. For example, marketing firms and private economic forecasting companies are important collectors, users, and sellers of economic data. In this book, boxes called 'In Touch with the Macroeconomy' describe major macroeconomic data series and tell you how they are collected and where to find them.

Much of the data collection and preparation process is routine. However, because providers of data want their numbers to be as useful as possible while keeping costs down, the organization of major data collection projects is typically the joint effort of many skilled professionals. Providers of data must decide what types of data should be collected based on who is expected to use the data and how. They must take care that measures of economic activity correspond to abstract concepts (such as 'capital' and 'labour') that are suggested by economic theory. In addition, data providers must guarantee the confidentiality of data that may reveal information about individual firms and people in the economy. In a large data-gathering organization, each of these issues is exhaustively analysed by economists and statisticians before data collection begins.[4]

1.3 WHY MACROECONOMISTS DISAGREE

Over the years, the efforts of thousands of analysts, data collectors, and researchers have greatly enhanced the understanding of macroeconomic phenomena. Yet no matter what the macroeconomic issue, the news media can seemingly find an economist to argue either side of it. Why do macroeconomists appear to disagree so much?[5]

---

4. For a readable discussion of issues that face data collectors, see Janet L. Norwood, 'Distinguished Lecture on Economics in Government: Data Quality and Public Policy', *Journal of Economic Perspectives*, Spring 1990, pp. 3–12.
5. Not only do macroeconomists often seem to disagree with each other, but also they are sometimes accused of not being able to agree with themselves. President Harry Truman expressed the frustration of many policymakers when he said he wanted a one-handed economist – one who wouldn't always say, 'On the one hand, . . .; on the other hand. . . .'

To a certain extent, the amount of disagreement among macroeconomists is exaggerated by the tendency of the public and the media to focus on the most difficult and controversial issues. In addition, the very fact that economic policy and performance are of such broad interest and concern contributes to the intensity of debate: more than controversies in many other fields, debates in macroeconomics tend to take place in public, rather than in the seminar room or the laboratory. Although important disagreements among macroeconomists certainly exist, there also are many areas of substantial agreement in macroeconomics.

We can provide an insight into why macroeconomists disagree by drawing the important distinction between positive and normative analyses of economic policy. A **positive analysis** of an economic policy examines the economic consequences of a policy but does not address the question of whether those consequences are desirable. A **normative analysis** of policy tries to determine whether a certain policy *should* be used. For example, if an economist is asked to evaluate the effects on the economy of a 5% rise in the income tax, the response involves a positive analysis. But if asked whether the income tax *should* be raised 5%, the economist's response requires a normative analysis. This normative analysis will involve not only the economist's objective, scientific understanding of how the economy works, but also personal value judgements – for example, about the appropriate size of the government sector or the amount of income redistribution that is desirable.

Economists may agree on the positive analysis of a question yet disagree on the normative part because of differences in values. Value differences are also common in other fields. Physicists may be in perfect agreement on what would happen *if* a nuclear bomb were detonated (a positive analysis). But physicist 'hawks' and physicist 'doves' may disagree strongly about whether nuclear weapons *should* be deployed (a normative question).

Disagreement may occur on positive issues, however, and these differences are important in economics. In macroeconomics there have always been many schools of thought, each with a somewhat different perspective on how the economy works. Examples include monetarism and supply-side economics, both of which we discuss in this book. However, the most important – and enduring – disagreements on positive issues in macroeconomics involve the two schools of thought called the classical approach and the Keynesian approach.

Classicals Versus Keynesians

The classical approach and the Keynesian approach are the two major intellectual traditions in macroeconomics. We discuss the differences between the two approaches briefly here and in much greater detail later in the book.

The Classical Approach. The origins of the classical approach go back more than two centuries, at least to the famous Scottish economist Adam Smith. In 1776 Smith published his classic, *The Wealth of Nations*, in which he proposed the concept of the 'invisible hand'. The idea of the **invisible hand** is that, if there are free markets and individuals conduct their economic affairs in their own best interests, the overall economy will work well. As Smith put it, in a market economy individuals, while pursuing their own self-interest, seem to be led by an invisible hand to maximize the general welfare of everyone in the economy.

However, we must not overstate what Smith claimed. To say that an invisible hand is at work does *not* mean that no one in a market economy will be hungry or dissatisfied; free markets cannot insulate a nation from the effects of drought, war, or political instability. Nor does the invisible hand rule out the existence of great inequalities between the rich and the poor, because in Smith's analysis he took the initial distribution of wealth among people as given. Rather, the invisible-hand idea says that *given* a country's resources (natural, human, and technological) and its initial distribution of wealth, the use of free markets will make people as economically well off as possible.

Validity of the invisible-hand idea depends on a key assumption: the various markets in the economy, including financial markets, labour markets, and markets for goods and services, must function smoothly and without impediments such as minimum wages and interest rate ceilings. In particular, wages and prices must adjust rapidly enough to maintain **equilibrium** – a situation in which the quantities demanded and supplied are equal – in all markets. In markets where quantity demanded exceeds quantity supplied, prices must rise to bring the market into equilibrium. In markets where more of a good is available than people want to buy, prices must fall to bring the market into equilibrium.

Wage and price flexibility is crucial to the invisible-hand idea, because in a free-market system changes in wages and prices are the signals that coordinate the actions of people in the economy. To illustrate, suppose that war abroad disrupts oil imports. This drop in supply will drive up the price of oil. A higher oil price will make it profitable for domestic oil suppliers to pump more oil and to drill more wells. The higher price will also induce domestic consumers to conserve oil and to switch to alternative sources of energy. Increased demand for alternative energy sources will raise their prices and stimulate *their* production, and so on. Thus in the absence of impediments such as government price controls, the adjustment of prices helps the free-market economy respond in a constructive and coordinated way to the initial disruption of supplies.

The classical approach to macroeconomics builds on Smith's basic assumptions that people pursue their own economic self-interest and that prices adjust reasonably quickly to achieve equilibrium in all markets. With these two assumptions as a basis, followers of the classical approach attempt to construct models of the macroeconomy that are consistent with the data and that can be used to answer the questions raised at the beginning of this chapter.

The use of the classical approach carries with it some strong policy implications. Because the classical assumptions imply that the invisible hand works well, classical economists often argue (as a normative proposition) that the government should have, *at most*, a limited role in the economy. As a positive proposition, classical economists also often argue that government policies will be ineffective or counterproductive at achieving their stated goals. Thus, for example, most classicals believe that the government should not try actively to eliminate business cycles.

The Keynesian Approach. Compared with the classical approach, the Keynesian approach is relatively recent. The book that introduced it, *The General Theory of Employment, Interest, and Money,* by British economist John Maynard

Keynes, appeared in 1936 – 160 years after Adam Smith's *The Wealth of Nations*. In 1936 the world was suffering the Great Depression: unprecedentedly high rates of unemployment had afflicted most of the world's economies for years, and the invisible hand of free markets seemed completely ineffective. From the viewpoint of 1936, the classical theory appeared to be seriously inconsistent with the data, creating a need for a new macroeconomic theory. Keynes provided this theory.

In his book Keynes offered an explanation for persistently high unemployment.[6] He based this explanation on an assumption about wage and price adjustment that was fundamentally different from the classical assumption. Instead of assuming that wages and prices adjust rapidly to achieve equilibrium in each market, as in the classical tradition, Keynes assumed that wages and prices adjust slowly. Slow wage and price adjustment meant that markets could be out of equilibrium – with quantities demanded not equal to quantities supplied – for long periods of time. In the Keynesian theory unemployment can persist because wages and prices do not adjust quickly enough to equalize the number of people firms want to employ with the number of people who want to work.

Keynes's proposed solution to high unemployment was to have the government increase its purchases of goods and services, thus raising the demand for output. Keynes argued that this policy would reduce unemployment because, to meet the higher demands for their products, businesses would have to employ more workers. In addition, Keynes suggested, the newly hired workers would have more income to spend, creating another source of demand for output that would raise employment further. More generally, in contrast to classicals, Keynesians tend to be sceptical about the invisible hand and thus are more willing to advocate a role for government in improving macroeconomic performance.

The Evolution of the Classical–Keynesian Debate. Because the Great Depression so strongly shook the faith of many economists in the classical approach, the Keynesian approach dominated macroeconomic theory and policy from World War II until about 1970. At the height of Keynesian influence, economists widely believed that, through the skillful use of macroeconomic policies, the government could promote economic growth while avoiding inflation or recession. The main problems of macroeconomics had apparently been solved, with only some details to be filled in.

However, in the 1970s many European countries as well as the United States suffered from both high unemployment and high inflation – called 'stagflation', or stagnation plus inflation. This experience weakened economists' and policymakers' confidence in the traditional Keynesian approach, much as the Great Depression had undermined the traditional classical approach. In addition, the Keynesian assumption that prices and wages adjust slowly, so that markets may be out of equilibrium, was criticized as being without sound theoretical foundations. While the Keynesian approach

---

6. Actually, Keynes presented a number of explanations of unemployment in his book, and debate continues about 'what Keynes really meant'. Our interpretation of what Keynes meant is the one adopted by his major followers.

was coming under attack, developments in economic theory made classical macroeconomics look more interesting and attractive to many economists. Starting in the early 1970s a modernized classical approach enjoyed a major resurgence among macroeconomic researchers, although classical macroeconomics did not achieve the dominance that Keynesianism enjoyed in the early postwar years.

In the past twenty years advocates of both approaches have reworked them extensively to repair their weaknesses. Economists working in the classical tradition have improved their explanations of business cycles and unemployment. Keynesians have worked on the development of sound theoretical foundations for the slow adjustment of wages and prices, and Keynesian models can now accommodate stagflation. Currently, excellent research is being conducted with both approaches, and substantial communication and cross-fertilization is occurring between them.

A Unified Approach to Macroeconomics

In writing this book, we needed a strategy to deal with the fact that there are two major macroeconomic schools of thought. One strategy would have been to emphasize one of the two schools of thought and to treat the other only briefly. The problem with that strategy is that it would not expose you to the full range of ideas and insights that comprise modern macroeconomics. Alternatively, we might have presented the two approaches separately and then compared and contrasted their conclusions; but you would have missed the opportunity to explore the large common ground shared by the two schools of thought.

Our choice was to take an approach to macroeconomics that is as balanced and unified as possible. In keeping with this unified approach, all our analyses in this book – whether of economic growth, business cycles, inflation, or policy, and whether classical or Keynesian in spirit – are based on a *single economic model,* or on components or extensions of the basic model. This economic model, which draws heavily from both the classical and Keynesian traditions, has the following characteristics.

1. *Individuals, firms, and the government interact in goods markets, asset markets, and labour markets.* We have already discussed the need for aggregation in macroeconomics. In the economic model of this book we follow standard macroeconomic practice and aggregate all the markets in the economy into three major markets: the market for goods and services, the asset market (in which assets such as stocks, bonds, and property are traded), and the labour market. We show how participants in the economy interact in each of these three markets and how these markets relate to each other and the economy as a whole.

2. *The model's macroeconomic analysis is based on the analysis of individual behaviour.* Macroeconomic behaviour reflects the behaviours of many individuals and firms interacting in markets. To understand how individuals and firms behave, we take a 'bottom-up' approach and focus our analysis at the level of individual decision making (as in Box 1.1 where we discussed a model of individual choices about the route to take to work). The insights gained are then used for studying the economy as a whole.

The guiding principle in analysing the behaviour of individuals and firms is the assumption that they *try to maximize their own economic satisfaction, given their needs, desires, and resources.* Although the founder of classical economics, Adam Smith, emphasized this assumption, it is generally accepted by Keynesians and classicals alike; and it is used in virtually all modern macroeconomic research.

3. Although Keynesians reject the classical assumption that wages and prices quickly adjust to achieve equilibrium in the short run, *Keynesians and classicals both agree that in the long run prices and wages fully adjust to achieve equilibrium in the markets for goods, assets, and labour.* Because complete flexibility of wages and prices in the long run is not controversial, we examine the long-term behaviour of the economy (Chapters 3–8) before discussing short-run issues associated with business cycles (Chapters 9–14).

4. *The basic model that we present may be used with either the classical assumption that wages and prices are flexible or the Keynesian assumption that wages and prices are slow to adjust.* This aspect of the model allows us to compare classical and Keynesian conclusions and policy recommendations within a common theoretical framework.

CHAPTER SUMMARY

1. Macroeconomics is the study of the structure and performance of national economies and the policies that governments use to try to affect economic performance. Important topics in macroeconomics include the determinants of long-run economic growth, business cycles, unemployment, inflation, international trade and lending, and macroeconomic policy.

2. Because macroeconomics covers the economy as a whole, macroeconomists ignore the fine distinctions among different kinds of goods, firms, or markets, and focus on national totals such as aggregate consumption. The process of adding individual economic variables to obtain economy wide totals is called aggregation.

3. The activities engaged in by macroeconomists include (in addition to teaching) forecasting, macroeconomic analysis, macroeconomic research, and data development.

4. The goal of macroeconomic research is to be able to make general statements about how the economy works. Macroeconomic research makes

progress toward this goal by developing economic theories and testing them empirically – that is, by seeing whether they are consistent with data obtained from the real world. A useful economic theory is based on reasonable and realistic assumptions, is easy to use, has implications that can be tested in the real world, and is consistent with the data and the observed behaviour of the real-world economy.

5. A positive analysis of an economic policy examines the economic consequences of the policy but does not address the question of whether those consequences are desirable. A normative analysis of a policy tries to determine whether the policy *should* be used. Disagreements among macroeconomists may arise because of differences in normative conclusions, the result of differences in personal values and beliefs, and differences in the positive analysis of a policy proposal.

6. The classical approach to macroeconomics is based on the assumptions that individuals and firms act in their own best interests and that

wages and prices adjust quickly to achieve equilibrium in all markets. Under these assumptions the invisible hand of the free-market economy works well, with only limited scope for government intervention in the economy.

7. The Keynesian approach to macroeconomics assumes that wages and prices do not adjust rapidly and thus the invisible hand may not work well. Keynesians argue that, because of slow wage and price adjustment, unemployment may remain high for a long time. Keynesians are usually more inclined than classicals to believe that government intervention in the economy may help improve economic performance.

Key Terms

aggregation, p. 15
average labour productivity, p. 6
closed economy, p. 10
deflation, p. 8
economic model, p. 17
economic theory, p. 17
empirical analysis, p. 18
equilibrium, p. 21
fiscal policy, p. 13
inflation, p. 8
invisible hand, p. 20
macroeconomics, p. 3
monetary policy, p. 13
normative analysis, p. 20
open economy, p. 10
positive analysis, p. 20
trade deficit, p. 12
trade surplus, p. 12
unemployment, p. 8

Review Questions

1. How have total output and output per worker changed over time in Western Europe? How have these changes affected the lives of typical Europeans?
2. What is a business cycle? How does the unemployment rate behave over the course of a business cycle? Does the unemployment rate ever reach zero?
3. Define *inflation* and *deflation*. Compare the behaviour of consumer prices in Europe in the early 1970s with that in the early 1990s.

4. Define *budget deficit*. Historically, when have governments been most likely to run deficits? What has been the recent experience?
5. What is meant by *aggregation*? Why is aggregation important for macroeconomic analysis?
6. List the principal professional activities of macroeconomists. What role does macroeconomic research play in each of these activities?
7. What steps are involved in developing and testing an economic theory or model? What are the criteria for a useful theory or model?
8. Might two economists agree about the effects of a particular economic policy but disagree about the desirability of implementing the policy? Explain your answer.
9. Compare the classical and Keynesian views on the speed of wage and price adjustment. What are the important consequences of the differences in their views?

Numerical Problems

1. Here are some macroeconomic data for the country of Oz for the years 1996 and 1997.

	1996	1997
Output	12,000 tons of potatoes	14,300 tons of potatoes
Employment	1000 workers	1100 workers
Unemployed	100 workers	50 workers
Total labour force	1100 workers	1150 workers
Prices	2 shekels/ton of potatoes	2.5 shekels/ton of potatoes

As the data suggest, Oz produces only potatoes, and its monetary unit is the shekel. Calculate each of the following macroeconomic variables for Oz, being sure to give units.
   a. Average labour productivity in 1996 and 1997.
   b. The growth rate of average labour productivity between 1996 and 1997.
   c. The unemployment rate in 1996 and 1997.
   d. The inflation rate between 1996 and 1997.
2. In a recent issue of the International Monetary Fund's *International Financial Statistics*, find the data for Denmark. Under the heading 'National Accounts' find data on gross domestic product (a measure of total output), exports and imports. Under the heading 'Government Finance', find data on the government's revenue (taxes) and expenditure.

a. Calculate the ratio of exports to GDP, the ratio of imports to GDP, and the ratio of the trade imbalance to GDP in the latest reported quarter. Compare the answers with the values reported for the previous two complete years.

b. Calculate the ratio of government receipts to GDP, the ratio of government expenditures to GDP, and the ratio of the budget deficit to GDP, for the most recent quarter and for the previous two complete years.

Analytical Problems

1. Can average labour productivity fall even though total output is rising? Can the unemployment rate rise even though total output is rising?
2. Prices were much higher in the United Kingdom in 1996 than in 1890. Does this fact mean that people were economically better off in 1890? Why or why not?
3. State a theory for why people vote conservative or socialist that potentially could satisfy the criteria for a useful theory given in the text. How would you go about testing your theory?

4. Which of the following statements are positive in nature and which are normative?
   a. A tax cut will raise interest rates.
   b. A reduction in income tax would primarily benefit poor and middle-class workers.
   c. Income tax is too high.
   d. A cut in income would improve the government's popularity ratings.
   e. Income tax should not be cut unless capital gains tax is cut too.
5. A heated debate has gone on for a number of years between European and US farmers about the domestic subsidies available to European farmers under the Common Agricultural Policy. US farmers claim that these subsidies enable their European counterparts to sell their products at low prices, thereby undercutting US farm exporters. European farmers argue that any reduction in the support they receive would harm the European economy and European agriculture, and throw European farm workers out of work. How might a classical economist respond to these concerns? Would you expect a Keynesian economist to be more or less sympathetic to these concerns than the classical economist? Why?

CHAPTER 2

THE MEASUREMENT AND STRUCTURE OF THE NATIONAL ECONOMY

Measurement is a crucial part of scientific study. Accurate measurement is essential for making new discoveries, evaluating competing theories, and predicting future events or trends. During the first half of the twentieth century, painstaking research by economists such as Nobel Prize winners Simon Kuznets and Richard Stone (the first people to obtain comprehensive measures of national output) and the team of Arthur Burns and Wesley Mitchell (who performed detailed measurements of the stages of the business cycle) showed that careful economic measurement is not only possible but also necessary for any serious understanding of the economy. Their work, and the efforts of many other researchers, transformed economics from a field in which scholars relied on informal observations and broad generalizations to one in which numbers and statistical analysis play an essential role.

In this chapter we present some of the conceptual and practical issues involved in measuring the macroeconomy. We focus on the national income accounts, a framework for measuring economic activity that is widely used by economic researchers and analysts. Learning about the national income accounts will familiarize you with some useful economic data. In addition, because the national income accounts are set up in a logical way that mirrors the structure of the economy, working through these accounts is an important first step toward understanding how the macroeconomy works. When you finish this chapter, you will have a much clearer understanding of the relationships that exist among key macroeconomic variables and among the different sectors of the economy.

2.1 NATIONAL INCOME ACCOUNTING: THE MEASUREMENT OF PRODUCTION, INCOME, AND EXPENDITURE

The **national income accounts** are an accounting framework used in measuring current economic activity. Almost all countries have some form of official national income accounts. (For background information on national income accounts, see 'In Touch with the Macroeconomy', p. 30.) In this section we discuss the basic idea that underlies national income accounting. We then show how the national income accounts are used in measuring economic activity.

The national income accounts are based on the idea that the amount of economic activity that occurs during a period of time can be measured in terms of

1. the amount of output produced, excluding output used up in intermediate stages of production (the product approach);

2. the incomes received by the producers of output (the income approach); and

3. the amount of spending by the ultimate purchasers of output (the expenditure approach).

Each approach gives a different perspective on the economy. However, the fundamental principle underlying national income accounting is that, except for problems such as incomplete or misreported data, *all three approaches give identical measurements of the amount of current economic activity.*

We can illustrate why these three approaches are equivalent by an example. Imagine an economy with only two businesses, called AppleCo and JuiceCo. AppleCo owns and operates apple orchards. It sells some of its apples directly to the public. It sells the rest of its apples to JuiceCo, which produces and sells apple juice. The following table shows the transactions of each business during a year.

AppleCo Transactions

Wages paid to AppleCo employees	£15,000
Taxes paid to government	5,000
Revenue received from sale of apples	35,000
Apples sold to public	10,000
Apples sold to JuiceCo	25,000

(*Note:* After-tax profit of AppleCo = revenue − costs − taxes = £15,000)

JuiceCo Transactions

Wages paid to JuiceCo employees	£10,000
Taxes paid to government	2,000
Apples purchased from AppleCo	25,000
Revenue received from sale of apple juice	40,000

(*Note:* After-tax profit of JuiceCo = revenue − costs − taxes = £3000)

AppleCo pays £15,000 per year in wages to workers to pick apples, and it sells these apples for £35,000 (£10,000 worth of apples to households and £25,000 worth of apples to JuiceCo). Thus AppleCo's profit before taxes is £35,000 − £15,000 = £20,000. Because AppleCo pays taxes of £5000, its after-tax profit is £15,000.

JuiceCo buys £25,000 of apples from AppleCo and pays wages of £10,000 to workers to process the apples into apple juice. It sells the apple juice for £40,000, so that its profit before taxes is £5000 (£40,000 – £25,000 – £10,000). After paying taxes of £2000, its after-tax profit is £3000.

What is the total value of the economic activity generated by these two businesses? The product approach, income approach, and expenditure approach are three different ways of arriving at the answer to this question; all yield the same answer.

1. The **product approach** measures economic activity by adding the market values of goods and services produced, excluding any goods and services used up in intermediate stages of production. This approach makes use of the value-added concept. The **value added** of any producer is the value of its output minus the value of the inputs it purchases from other producers. The product approach computes economic activity by summing the value added of all producers.

In our example, AppleCo produces output worth £35,000 and JuiceCo produces output worth £40,000. However, measuring overall economic activity by simply adding £35,000 and £40,000 would 'double count' the £25,000 of apples that JuiceCo purchased from AppleCo and processed into juice. To avoid this double counting, we sum value added rather than output: because JuiceCo processed apples worth £25,000 into a product worth £40,000, JuiceCo's value added is £15,000 (£40,000 – £25,000). AppleCo does not use any inputs purchased from other businesses so its value added equals its revenue of £35,000. Thus total value added in the economy is £35,000 + £15,000 = £50,000.

2. The **income approach** measures economic activity by adding all income received, including wages, taxes (the government's income), and after-tax profits (the income of the owners of AppleCo and JuiceCo). The incomes generated in the example are as follows.

Incomes Received

Wage income (£15,000 at AppleCo; £10,000 at JuiceCo)	£25,000
Taxes (£5000 from AppleCo; £2000 from JuiceCo)	7,000
Profits (£15,000 at AppleCo; £3000 at JuiceCo)	18,000
Total income	£50,000

The income approach concludes that the value of economic activity is £50,000, the same amount determined by the product approach.

3. Finally, the **expenditure approach** measures activity by adding the amount spent by all ultimate users of output. In this example, households are ultimate users of apples. JuiceCo is not an ultimate user of apples because it sells the apples (in processed, liquid form) to households. Thus ultimate users purchase £10,000 of apples from AppleCo and £40,000 of apple juice from JuiceCo for a total of £50,000, the same amount computed in both the product and the expenditure approaches.[1]

---

1. In the example, each business also purchases labour services from employees, but as these services are used in production, they are not counted as services purchased by ultimate users.

IN TOUCH *WITH THE MACROECONOMY*

THE NATIONAL INCOME AND PRODUCT ACCOUNTS

In the United Kingdom the national income accounts are officially known as the *United Kingdom National Accounts* and are published in the *Blue Book*. These accounts provide comprehensive measurements of production, income and expenditure for the UK economy. Among the earliest attempts to measure national income were the work of Sir Thomas Petty in England and Pierre Boisguillebert in France in the seventeenth century. Petty produced the first known estimate of national income in England for the early 1680s (£40 million), while Boisguillebert was sent into exile for his attempts to estimate French national income – work which it was felt would undermine the tax system!

For many European countries, estimates of national income started to appear in the early twentieth century, although the foundations for present-day national income accounting were laid in the interwar period by Colin Clark (*The Conditions of Economic Progress*, Macmillan, 1940) and by John Maynard Keynes (*How to Pay for the War*, Macmillan, 1940) in the UK and by the work of Simon Kuznets in the USA and Erik Lindahl in Sweden. The first official UK national income accounts were produced by Richard Stone and James Meade and were published in a 1941 White Paper. They were used primarily as a basis for economic planning during World War II. National income accounts continued to be published in the form of White Papers appended to the UK Budget until the early 1950s when the first *Blue Book* was published.

Currently, national accounts are constructed quarterly by government economists and statisti-cians, such as the Office for National Statistics (ONS) in the UK. In constructing national accounts, the government statisticians rely heavily on data provided by other government departments, such as those dealing with government taxation, industrial production and international trade, and from private sources, such as industry associations.

Initial estimates of quarterly economic activity are typically released three or four weeks after the end of each quarter. Revised estimates, which may differ significantly from the initial estimates, together with fuller breakdowns are then released during each of the next two or three months. More detailed revisions are done annually. Quarterly economic accounts in the UK are published in *UK Economic Accounts: A Quarterly Supplement to Economic Trends*.

Historical national income accounts for the UK may be obtained from several sources, including *Economic Trends: Annual Supplement* and C.H. Feinstein's *National Income, Expenditure and Output of the United Kingdom 1855–1965* (Cambridge University Press, 1972). National income accounts data for all European countries are available in the many national accounts publications produced by government statistical departments, such as Statistics Netherlands. In addition, data are also available in *European Economy*, a publication of the European Commission, the Organization for Economic Co-operation and Development's *National Accounts*, the International Monetary Fund's publication *World Economic Outlook* and the United Nations' *National Accounts Statistics*.

Why the Three Approaches Are Equivalent

That the product, income, and expenditure approaches all give the same answer is no accident. The logic of these three approaches is such that they must *always* give the same answer.

To see why, first observe that the market value of goods and services produced in a given period is *by definition* equal to the amount that buyers must spend to purchase them. JuiceCo's apple juice has a market value of £40,000 only because that is what people are willing to spend to buy it. The market value of a good or service and the spending on that good or service are always the same, so the product approach (which measures market values) and the expenditure approach (which measures spending) must give the same measure of economic activity.[2]

Next, observe that what the seller receives must equal what the buyers spend. The seller's receipts in turn equal the total income generated by the economic activity, including the incomes paid to workers and suppliers, taxes paid to the government, and profits (whatever is left over). Thus total expenditure must equal total income generated, implying that the expenditure and income approaches must also produce the same answer. Finally, as both product value and income equal expenditure, they also must be equal.

Because of the equivalence of the three approaches, over any specified time period

$$\text{total production} = \text{total income} = \text{total expenditure} \qquad (2.1)$$

where production, income, and expenditure all are measured in the same units (for example, in pounds, kronor or lire). Equation (2.1) is called the **fundamental identity of national income accounting** and forms the basis for national income accounting. (An identity is an equation that is true by definition.) In Section 2.2 we show how this fundamental identity is used in measuring current economic activity for the economy as a whole.

2.2 GROSS DOMESTIC PRODUCT

The broadest measure of aggregate economic activity, as well as the best known and most often used, is the gross domestic product, or GDP. As in the example in Section 2.1, a country's GDP may be measured by the product approach, the expenditure approach, or the income approach. Although the three approaches arrive at the same value for GDP, each views GDP differently. Using all three approaches gives a more complete picture of an economy's structure than any single approach could.

The Product Approach to Measuring GDP

The product approach defines a nation's **gross domestic product** (GDP) as the market value of final goods and services newly produced within a nation during a fixed period of time. In working through the various parts of this definition, we discuss some practical issues that arise in measuring GDP.

Market Value. Goods and services are counted in GDP at their market values: that is, at the prices at which they are sold. The advantage of using market values is that it allows adding the production of different goods and services. Imagine, for example, that you want to measure the total output of an economy

---

2. Our explanation implicitly assumes that everything produced is sold. What if a firm produces some goods that it cannot sell? As we demonstrate shortly, the national income accounts treat unsold goods as though they were purchased by the firm from itself: that is, accumulation of unsold goods in inventory is treated as part of expenditure. Thus expenditure and production remain equal even if some goods remain unsold.

that produces 7 cars and 100 pairs of shoes. Adding the number of cars and the number of pairs of shoes to get a total output of 107 would not make much sense because cars and shoes are not of equal economic value. But suppose that each car sells for £10,000 and each pair of shoes sells for £60. Taking these market-determined prices as measures of relative economic values, you can calculate the value of cars produced as £70,000 (7 × £10,000) and the value of shoes produced as £6000 (100 × £60). The total market value of production, or GDP, is £70,000 + £6000 = £76,000. Using market values to measure production makes sense because it takes into account differences in the relative economic importance of different goods and services.

A problem with using market values to measure GDP is that some useful goods and services are not sold in formal markets. Ideally, GDP should be adjusted upward to reflect the existence of these goods and services. However, because of the difficulty of obtaining reliable measures, some non-market goods and services are simply ignored in the calculation of GDP.[3] Home-making and child-rearing services performed within the family without pay, for example, are not included in GDP, although home-making and child care that are provided for pay (for example, by professional housecleaners or by private day-care centres) are included. Similarly, because the benefits of clean air and water are not bought and sold in markets, actions to reduce pollution or otherwise improve environmental quality are not usually reflected in GDP (see Box 2.1).

Some non-market goods and services are partially incorporated in official GDP measures. An example is activities that take place in the so-called underground or informal economy. The **underground economy** includes both legal activities hidden from government record keepers (to avoid payment of taxes or compliance with regulations, for example) and illegal activities such as drug dealing, prostitution, and (in some places) gambling. Some might argue that activities such as drug dealing are 'bads' rather than 'goods' and should not be included in GDP anyway – although a consistent application of this argument might rule out many goods and services currently included in GDP. Clearly, though, the services of a housepainter who is paid in cash in order to avoid taxes should be included in GDP. Government statisticians regularly adjust GDP figures to include estimates of the underground economy's size. Because cash is the favoured means of payment for off-the-books transactions, one clue to the size of the underground economy is the amount of cash in circulation.[4]

A particularly important component of economic activity that does not pass through markets is the services provided by government, such as defence, public education, and the building and maintenance of roads and bridges. The fact that most government services are not sold in markets implies a lack of market values to use when calculating the government's contribution to GDP.

---

3. Periodically, attempts have been made by private economists to devise measures that include non-market economic activity. See, for example, Robert Eisner, 'The Total Incomes System of Accounts', *Survey of Current Business,* January 1985, pp. 24–48, and Luisella Goldschmidt-Clermont and Elisabetta Pagnossin-Aligisakis, '*Measuring Unrecorded Economic Activity in Fourteen Countries*', Human Development Report Office, Occasional Paper no. 20, UNDP, New York, 1992.
4. On the different ways to estimate the size of the underground economy, see J.J. Thomas, *Informal Economic Activity* (Harvester–Wheatsheaf, 1992) and M. Lacko, 'Hungarian Hidden Economy in International Comparisons; Estimation Method Based on Household Electricity Consumption and the Currency Ratio', Institute of Economics, Hungarian Academy of Sciences, 1987.

BOX 2.1

Natural Resources, the Environment, and the National Income Accounts

Much of any country's economic well-being flows from natural, rather than human-made, assets – land, rivers and oceans, natural resources (such as oil and timber), and indeed the air that everyone breathes. Ideally, for the purposes of economic and environmental planning, the use and misuse of natural resources and the environment should be appropriately measured in the national income accounts. Unfortunately, they are not. There are at least two important conceptual problems with the way the national income accounts currently handle the economic use of natural resources and the environment.

1. *Natural resource depletion.* When an oil driller pumps oil from an underground field, the value of the oil produced is counted as part of the nation's GDP; there is no offsetting deduction to account for the fact that non-renewable resources are being depleted. In principle, the draining of the oil field can be thought of as a type of negative inventory investment because in a sense it reduces the inventory of oil. If it were included in the national income accounts, this negative inventory investment would reduce the computed value of GDP.

2. *The costs and benefits of pollution control.* Imagine that a company has the following choices. It can produce £100 million worth of output and in the process pollute the local river by dumping its wastes; alternatively, by using 10% of its workers to dispose properly of its wastes, it can avoid polluting but will get only £90 million of output. Under current national income accounting rules, if the firm chooses to pollute rather than not to pollute, its contribution to GDP will

be larger (£100 million rather than £90 million) because the national income accounts attach no explicit value to a clean river. In an ideal accounting system the economic costs of environmental degradation would be subtracted in the calculation of a firm's contribution to output, and activities that improve the environment – because they provide real economic benefits – would be added to output.

Discussing the national income accounting implications of resource depletion and pollution may seem to trivialize these important problems. Actually, because GDP and related statistics are used continually in policy analyses, abstract questions of measurement may often turn out to have significant real effects. For example, economic development experts have expressed concern that some poor countries, in attempting to raise measured GDP as quickly as possible, have done so in part by overexploiting their natural resources and harming the environment. Conceivably, explicitly incorporating 'hidden' resource and environmental costs into official measures of economic growth might cause these policies to be modified. Similarly, in industrialized countries political debates about the environment have at times emphasized the impact on conventionally measured GDP of proposed pollution control measures, rather than their impact on overall economic welfare. Better accounting for environmental quality might serve to refocus these debates on the more relevant question of whether, for any particular environmental proposal, the benefits (economic and non-economic) exceed the costs.

For these reasons, many countries are currently developing environmental 'satellite' accounts. These will extend the existing national accounts by making allowance for such things as the depletion of natural resources. A new European System of Accounts sets out how this is to be implemented in the EU.[5]

In this case the solution that has been adopted is to value government services at their cost of production. Thus the contribution of national defence to GDP equals the government's cost of providing defence: the salaries of service and civilian personnel, the costs of building and maintaining weapons and bases, and so on. Similarly, the contribution of public education to GDP is measured by the cost of teachers' salaries, new schools and equipment, and so on.

---

5. See, Prasant Vaze, 'Environmental Accounts – Valuing the Depletion of Oil and Gas Reserves', *Economic Trends*, HMSO, April 1996, pp. 36–45 and Steven Keuning, 'Taking the Environment into Account: The NAMEA Approach', *Review of Income and Wealth*, June 1996, pp. 131–48.

Newly Produced Goods and Services. As a measure of current economic activity, GDP includes only goods or services that are newly produced within the current period. GDP excludes purchases or sales of goods that were produced in previous periods. Thus, although the market price paid for a newly constructed house would be included in GDP, the price paid in the sale of a used house is not counted in GDP. (The value of the used house would have been included in GDP for the year it was built.) However, the value of the services of the estate agent involved in the sale of the used house *is* part of GDP, because those services are provided in the current period.

Final Goods and Services. Goods and services produced during a period of time may be classified as either intermediate goods and services or final goods and services. **Intermediate goods and services** are those used up in the production of other goods and services *in the same period that they themselves were produced.* For example, flour that is produced and then used to make bread in the same year is an intermediate good. The transport company that delivers the flour to the bakery provides an intermediate service.

Final goods and services are those goods and services that are not intermediate. Final goods and services are the end products of a process. For example, bread produced by the bakery is a final good, and a shopper's bus ride home from the bakery is a final service. Because the purpose of economic activity is the production of final goods and services, with intermediate goods being but a step along the way, only final goods and services are counted in GDP.

Sometimes the distinction between intermediate goods and final goods is subtle. For example, is a new lathe sold to a furniture manufacturer an intermediate good or a final good? Although the lathe is used to produce other goods, it is not used up during the year. Hence it is not an intermediate good; it is a final good. In particular, the lathe is an example of a type of final good called a capital good. Other more general examples of capital goods include factory equipment, office equipment, and factories and office buildings themselves. A **capital good** is a good that is itself produced (this rules out natural resources such as land) and is used to produce other goods; however, unlike an intermediate good, a capital good is not used up in the same period that it is produced. The preparers of the national income accounts decided to classify capital goods as final goods and thus to include their production in GDP. Their reasoning was that the addition to productive capacity that new capital goods represent is an important purpose of economic activity.

Another subtle distinction between intermediate and final goods arises in the treatment of inventory investment. **Inventories** are stocks of unsold finished goods, goods in process, and raw materials held by firms. Inventory investment is the amount by which inventories increase during the year.[6] For example, suppose that a baker began the year with £1000 worth of flour in her storeroom, and at the end of the year she is holding £1100 worth of flour. The difference between her beginning and ending stocks, or £100 worth of flour, equals the baker's inventory investment during the year. Even though the ultimate purpose of the baker's flour is for making bread, her increase in

---

6. When inventories decline during the year, inventory investment is negative.

inventory represents production of flour that is not used up during the year. As in the case of capital goods, inventory investment is treated as a final good and thus part of GDP because increased inventories on hand imply greater productive capacity in the future.

In the earlier example of AppleCo and JuiceCo, we showed that total economic activity could be measured by summing the value added (value of output minus value of purchased inputs) for each producer. The advantage of the value added technique is that it automatically includes final goods and excludes intermediate goods from the measure of total output. If you go back to that example, you will see that, by summing the value added of the two companies, we obtained a measure of economic activity that included the value of final sales of the two businesses to the public, but that excluded the intermediate goods (unprocessed apples) sold to JuiceCo by AppleCo.

GNP Versus GDP. Until fairly recently many economists focused on a measure of economic activity known as gross national product (GNP) rather than on GDP. The difference between GNP and GDP concerns the treatment of output produced by capital and labour working outside its home (domestic) country. Specifically, **gross national product** is the market value of final goods and services newly produced *by domestic factors of production* during the current period (as opposed to production taking place within a country, which is GDP).

When a country's capital and labour – also called factors of production – are used abroad, they produce output and earn income. This output and income are included in the country's GNP but not in its GDP because they do not represent production taking place within that country. So, for example, the value of roads built by a UK construction company in Saudi Arabia, as measured by the fees that the construction company receives from the Saudi government, is counted in UK GNP but not in UK GDP. Similarly, when foreign capital or labour is used in the UK, the output produced and the income earned are part of UK GDP (because the production occurs within the UK) but not of UK GNP (they are counted in the foreign country's GNP instead). For example, the portion of the value of Japanese cars built in the UK that is attributable to Japanese capital and management counts in Japanese GNP and UK GDP, but not in UK GNP.

We define **net factor payments from abroad** (*NFP*) to be income paid to domestic factors of production by the rest of the world, minus income paid to foreign factors of production by the domestic economy. Using this concept, we express the relationship between GDP and GNP as

$$GDP = GNP - NFP \qquad (2.2)$$

For most European countries, GDP and GNP give slightly different measures of economic activity. For example, in 1994 the UK GDP was £668.87 billion and the UK GNP was £679.39 billion, a difference of about 1.6%. In France, Germany, and the Netherlands, the difference is less than 1%, whilst in Sweden it is about 3%. The distinction between GNP and GDP is important for countries such as Egypt and Turkey that have many citizens working abroad. The reason is that remittances sent home by workers abroad are part of a country's GNP but not its GDP.

The Expenditure Approach to Measuring GDP

A different perspective on the components of GDP is obtained by looking at the expenditure side of the national income accounts. The expenditure approach measures GDP as total spending on final goods and services produced within a nation during a specified period of time. Four major categories of spending are added to get GDP: consumption, investment, government purchases of goods and services, and net exports of goods and services. In symbols,

$$Y = \text{GDP} = \text{total production (or output)}$$
$$= \text{total income}$$
$$= \text{total expenditure};$$
$$C = \text{consumption};$$
$$I = \text{investment};$$
$$G = \text{government purchases of goods and services};$$
$$NX = \text{net exports of goods and services}.$$

With these symbols, we express the expenditure approach to measuring GDP as

$$Y = C + I + G + NX \tag{2.3}$$

Equation (2.3), like equation (2.1), is one of the basic relationships in macro-economics. Equation (2.3) is called the **income–expenditure identity** because it states that income Y equals total expenditure $C + I + G + NX$. Recent UK data for the four categories of spending, along with some major subcategories, are given in Table 2.1. As you read the rest of this section, you should look at Table 2.1 to get some feel for the relative sizes of different components of spending in the UK.

Consumption. **Consumption** is spending by domestic households on final goods and services, including those produced abroad.[7] It is the largest component of expenditure, usually accounting for about two-thirds of GDP. One exception is in Sweden where consumption expenditure accounts for just over half of GDP. Consumption expenditures are grouped into three categories:

1. *consumer durables*, which are long-lived consumer items, such as cars, televisions, furniture, and major appliances (but not houses, which are classified under investment);

2. *non-durable goods*, which are shorter-lived items, such as food, clothing, and fuel; and

3. *services*, such as education, health care, financial services, and transportation.

Investment. **Investment** includes both spending for new capital goods, called *fixed investment*, and increases in firms' inventory holdings, called *inventory investment*. Fixed investment, also known as Gross domestic fixed capital formation, in turn has four major components:

1. *dwellings*, which is residential investment and is spending on the construction of new houses and apartment buildings (houses and apartment buildings are treated as capital because they provide a service (shelter) over a long period of time);

---

7. Later, we subtract imports to get total spending on the goods and services produced in the domestic economy.

Table 2.1 Expenditure Approach to Measuring GDP in the United Kingdom, 1995

	£ billion	% of GDP
Consumers' expenditure	447.25	63.8
Durable goods	40.87	5.8
Non-durable goods	188.77	26.9
Services	217.61	31.0
Gross domestic fixed capital formation	105.39	15.0
Dwellings	21.84	3.1
Other new building and works	28.16	4.0
Plant and machinery	41.08	5.9
Other	14.30	2.0
Value of physical increase in stocks and work in progress	3.85	0.5
General government consumption	149.47	21.3
National government	96.66	13.8
Local government	52.81	7.5
Net exports	−5.49	−0.8
Exports	197.60	28.1
Imports	203.09	28.9
Statistical descrepancy	0.42	0.05
Total (equals GDP)	700.89	100.0

Note: Numbers may not add to totals shown owing to rounding.

Source: *United Kingdom National Accounts 1996, The Blue Book,* London, HMSO, 1996: Table 4.5 'Consumers' expenditure at current market prices'; Table 13.1 'Gross domestic fixed capital formation at market prices'; Table 1.2 'National product; by category of expenditure at current prices'.

2. *other new buildings and works*, which is part of business fixed investment and is spending on structures (e.g. factories, warehouses and office buildings);

3. *plant and machinery*, which is spending on machinery, tools and equipment; and

4. *other investment*, which mainly covers spending on vehicles, ships and aircraft.

Like consumption, investment includes spending on foreign-produced goods. Overall, fixed investment in the United Kingdom is usually about one sixth or one-seventh of GDP, which is similar to that found in Sweden and Italy. It is, however, lower than for Germany and the Netherlands, where fixed investment accounts for about one-quarter or one-fifth of GDP.

As we have mentioned, increases in inventories are included in investment spending, regardless of why inventories rose. In particular, if a firm produces goods that it cannot sell, the resulting rise in inventories counts as investment by the firm. For the purposes of national income accounting, the firm has, in effect, purchased the unsold goods from itself. This accounting rule is useful because it guarantees that production and expenditure will always be equal in the national income accounts. Anything that is produced must by definition either be bought by a customer or 'purchased' by the firm itself. In the UK national accounts, inventory investment is called 'the value of physical increase in stocks and work in progress'.

Government Purchases of Goods and Services. **Government purchases** of goods and services, which include any expenditure by the government for a currently produced good or service, foreign or domestic, is the third major component of spending. Government purchases include those made by local and municipal authorities and governments. Government purchases in the United Kingdom have recently been about one-fifth of GDP. In Europe, government purchases are highest in Scandanavia (in Sweden, for example, they represent just under 30% of GDP) where welfare spending is also high. Government purchases are lowest in the Benelux countries: in the Netherlands they have recently been about 14% of GDP.

Not all the cheques written by the government are for purchases of goods and services. **Transfers,** a category that includes government payments for state pensions, unemployment benefits, welfare payments, and so on, are payments (primarily to individuals) by the government that are not made in exchange for current goods or services. As a result, they are excluded from the government purchases category and are not counted in GDP as calculated by the expenditure approach. Similarly, interest payments on the national debt are not counted as part of government purchases.

Net Exports. **Net exports** are exports minus imports. As discussed in Chapter 1, exports are the goods and services produced within a country that are purchased by foreigners; imports are the goods and services produced abroad that are purchased by a country's residents. Net exports are positive if exports are greater than imports and negative if imports exceed exports.

Exports are added to total spending because they represent spending (by foreigners) on final goods and services produced in a country. Imports are subtracted from total spending because consumption, investment, and government purchases are defined to include imported goods and services. Subtracting imports ensures that total spending, $C + I + G + NX$, reflects spending only on output produced in the country. For example, an increase in Italian imports may mean that Italians are buying German cars instead of Italian cars. For fixed total spending by domestic residents, therefore, an increase in imports lowers spending on domestic production.

The Income Approach to Measuring GDP

The third and final way to measure GDP is the income approach. It calculates GDP by adding the incomes received by producers, including profits, and taxes paid to the government. (see Table 2.2 for recent UK data). Five types of income are identified.

1. *Income from employment*, the income of workers (excluding the self-employed) and includes wages, salaries, employee benefits (including contributions by employers to pension plans), and employer national insurance and social security contributions. As you can see from Table 2.2, income

Table 2.2   Income Approach to Measuring GDP in the United Kingdom, 1995

	£ billion	% of GDP
Income from employment	377.70	53.9
Income from self-employment	67.27	9.6
Gross trading profits of companies	86.58	12.4
Gross trading surplus of public corporations and general government enterprises	5.24	0.7
Rent	62.76	8.9
Imputed charge for consumption of non-trading capital	4.73	0.7
Total domestic income	**604.26**	**86.2**
Plus Statistical discrepancy	0.49	0.06
Plus Indirect taxes	96.63	13.8
Equals **GDP**	**700.89**	**100**
Plus Net property income from abroad	9.57	1.4
Equals **GNP**	**710.46**	**101.4**
Less Capital consumption	−72.88	10.4
Equals **Net national product** (NNP)	**637.58**	**91.0**
Less Indirect taxes	−96.63	13.8
Equals **National income**	**540.95**	**77.2**

Source: *Economic Trends, Annual Supplement*, 1996, Table 14.1.

from employment is the largest component of national income, comprising 53.9% of GDP in 1995.[8]

2. *Income from self-employment* is the income of the non-incorporated self-employed. As many self-employed people own some capital (examples are a farmer's tractor or a dentist's X-ray machine), so income from self-employment includes both labour income and capital income. Income from self-employment was 9.6% of UK GDP in 1995.

3. *Gross trading profits of companies* are the profits earned by corporations and represent the remainder of corporate revenue after wages, rents, and other costs have been paid. Corporate profits are used to pay taxes levied on corporations and interest payments, and to pay dividends to shareholders. The rest of corporate profits after taxes, interest payments and dividends, called retained earnings, is kept within the corporation. Gross trading profits are generally about 12% of GDP, but the amount of profits earned by corporations may change dramatically from year to year or even from quarter to quarter.

---

8. Income from employment overstates the take-home income of workers. As in each of the other measures of income on this list, part of the income received by employees must be paid to the government as taxes.

4. *Gross trading surplus of public corporations and general government enterprises* are the profits earned by all nationalized industries and other businesses owned by the government and local authorities.

5. *Rent* is the income earned by individuals who own land or structures that they rent to others. Some miscellaneous types of income, such as royalty income paid to authors, recording artists and others, also are included in this category. Rent was 8.9% of GDP in 1995.

6. *Imputed charge for consumption of non-trading capital* is the national rental income which the government receives from government departments for the use of government-owned property. In 1995 this repesented 0.7% of GDP.

In addition to the six income components just described, one other item needs to be accounted for to obtain GDP. *Indirect taxes*, such as VAT and excise taxes, are paid by businesses to the government. Indirect taxes do not appear in any of the five categories of income discussed, but because they are income to the government, they must be added in order to measure all of a country's income.[9]

A key part of the income approach is a concept known as national income. **National income** is simply the total income of a country's residents. In order to calculate national income two further items have to be accounted for. The first is net factor payments from abroad (called net property income from abroad in the UK national accounts). As we discussed earlier, when we add net factor payments, *NFP*, to GDP this gives GNP.

Second, we need to allow for depreciation. **Depreciation** (also known as capital consumption) is the value of the capital that wears out during the period over which economic activity is being measured.[10] Gross national product and gross domestic product are called *gross* because they measure the nation's total production or output of goods and services without subtracting depreciation. In the calculation of national income, depreciation must be subtracted from total, or gross, income. Gross national product less depreciation equals **net national product.** Because national income is the total income of all residents, excluding the government, it is also necessary to subtract indirect taxes from net national product to obtain national income, as indicated in Table 2.2.

Private Sector and Government Sector Income. In this section we have measured economic activity as the sum of all the incomes received in an economy. Sometimes, however, economists need to know how much of total income was received by the private sector (households and businesses) and how much accrues to the government sector. For example, in trying to predict the demand for consumer goods, focusing on the income available to the private sector might be more useful than focusing on the income of the economy as a whole.

The income of the private sector, known as **private disposable income**, measures the amount of income the private sector has available to spend. In

9. A few small additional items are included such as net subsidies to government enterprises. We do not discuss these items here.
10. Depreciation includes both capital that physically wears out and capital that is scrapped because it is no longer economically useful. For instance, still-functioning computers that are scrapped because they have been made obsolete by later models would be included in depreciation.

general, as for an individual family, the disposable income of the private sector as a whole equals income received from private-sector activities, plus payments received by the private sector from the government, minus taxes paid to the government. The precise definition is

$$\text{private disposable income} = Y + NFP + TR + INT - T \qquad (2.4)$$

where

$$Y = \text{gross domestic product (GDP)};$$
$$NFP = \text{net factor payments from abroad};$$
$$TR = \text{transfers received from the government};$$
$$INT = \text{interest payments on the government's debt};$$
$$T = \text{taxes}.$$

As you can see from equation (2.4), private disposable income equals private sector income earned at home (GDP) and abroad (net factor payments from abroad, NFP);[11] plus payments to the private sector from the government sector (transfers, TR, and interest on the government debt, INT); minus taxes paid to the government, T.

The part of GDP that is not at the disposal of the private sector is the net income of the government sector. The government's net income equals taxes paid by the private sector, T, minus payments from the government to the private sector (transfers, TR, and interest payments on the government debt, INT):

$$\text{net government income} = T - TR - INT \qquad (2.5)$$

Adding equations (2.4) and (2.5) yields the sum of private disposable income and net government income, $Y + NFP$, which is gross national product.

2.3 SAVING AND WEALTH

If you wanted to assess the economic situation of a household, the current income of the household would be an important piece of information. However, someone with a high current income is not necessarily better off economically than someone with a low current income. For example, a retired tycoon who has no current earnings but owns property worth £10 million is probably economically better off than a newly graduated doctor with a high salary but heavy debts left over from medical school. To determine how well off a household is, in addition to knowing current income, you also need to know what the household owns (its assets) and owes (its liabilities). The difference between assets and liabilities is called **wealth.**

As for a household, the economic well-being of a country depends not only on its income but also on its wealth. The wealth of an entire nation is called **national wealth.**

An important determinant of wealth is the rate of saving. A family that puts aside a quarter of its income each month will accumulate wealth much more quickly than a family that spends nearly all its income. Similarly, the rate at which national wealth increases depends on the rate at which individuals,

---

11. Note that the sum of incomes earned at home and abroad, GDP + NFP, equals GNP.

businesses, and governments in the economy save. Thus rates of saving and wealth accumulation are closely related.

In this section we present some concepts of aggregate saving and wealth and examine the relationships among them. Our main interest here is measurement. Questions such as what determines the rate of saving in a country are covered in later chapters.

Measures of Aggregate Saving

In general, the **saving** of any economic unit is the unit's current income minus its spending on current needs. The saving *rate* of an economic unit is its saving divided by its income. From a macroeconomic perspective, three important measures of saving are private saving, government saving, and national saving. Summary table 1 outlines the definitions of each measure.

Private Saving. The saving of the private sector, known as **private saving**, equals private disposable income minus consumption. Using the definition of private disposable income from equation (2.4), we have

$$S_{pvt} = \text{private disposable income} - \text{consumption}$$
$$= (Y + NFP - T + TR + INT) - C \qquad (2.6)$$

where S_{pvt} is private saving. Consumption is subtracted from private disposable income to obtain private saving because consumption represents the private sector's spending to meet current needs. Investment, although part of private-sector spending, is not subtracted from private disposable income because capital goods are purchased to enhance future productive capacity rather than to satisfy current needs. The private saving *rate* is private saving divided by private disposable income.[12]

Government Saving. **Government saving** equals net government income minus government purchases of goods and services, G. With the definition of net government income from equation (2.5), government saving, S_{govt}, is

$$S_{govt} = \text{net government income} - \text{government purchases} \qquad (2.7)$$
$$= (T - TR - INT) - G$$

If you think of government purchases as the government's spending to meet current needs, this definition of government saving fits the general definition of saving. In reality, though, some goods that the government purchases – roads, military aircraft, and government buildings, for example – are not used up during the year and thus are available to satisfy future needs. An ideal measure of government saving would exclude these longer-lived items from

---

12. A measure of aggregate saving that you may hear reported and discussed is *personal saving*, which is the saving of the household portion of the private sector. Personal saving differs from private saving by excluding saving done within businesses. The personal saving rate in the UK and in Scandanavia has been notoriously low, as it has been in the USA. However, because businesses are owned and controlled by households, it makes little economic sense to distinguish between the portion of private saving done within households and the portion done within businesses. Thus we focus on private rather than personal saving.

SUMMARY 1	Saving Measure	Definition and Formula
Measures of Aggregate Saving	**Private saving**	Private disposable income less consumption $$S_{pvt} = (Y + NFP - T + TR + INT) - C$$
	Government saving	Government receipts less government outlays $$S_{govt} = T - (G + TR + INT)$$
	National saving	Private saving plus government saving; also GNP ($Y+NFP$) less consumption and government purchases $$S = S_{pvt} + S_{govt}$$ $$= Y + NFP - C - G$$

current government purchases. However, although the national accounts of most European countries do distinguish these longer-lived government purchases from spending to meet current needs, for simplicity we define government saving to be net government income less *all* government purchases, even though this definition tends to underestimate the true amount of saving that the government does.[13]

Another, probably more familiar, name for government saving is the government **budget surplus**, which equals government receipts minus government outlays. **Government receipts** equal tax revenue, T. **Government outlays** are the sum of government purchases of goods and services, G, transfers, TR, and interest payments on government debt, INT. Thus the government budget surplus equals $T - (G + TR + INT)$, which, as you can see from equation (2.7), is the same as government saving.

When government receipts are less than government outlays, the difference between outlays and receipts is known as the government **budget deficit.** Thus, when the government runs a budget deficit, with its outlays greater than its receipts, government saving is negative.

National Saving. **National saving,** or the saving of the economy as a whole, equals private saving plus government saving. Using the definitions of private and government saving, equations (2.6) and (2.7), we obtain national saving, S:

$$S = S_{pvt} + S_{govt}$$
$$= (Y + NFP - T + TR + INT - C) + (T - TR - INT - G) \qquad (2.8)$$
$$= Y + NFP - C - G$$

Equation (2.8) shows that national saving equals the total income of the economy, $Y + NFP$ (which equals GNP), minus spending to satisfy current needs (consumption, C, and government purchases, G).

---

13. A similar argument suggests that expenditures on cars and other long-lived consumer durables should not be subtracted from disposable income in the calculation of private saving, although in practice they are subtracted.

The Uses of Private Saving

How is private saving in an economy put to use? Here we show that private saving is used to fund new capital investment, provide the resources the government needs to finance its budget deficits, and acquire assets from or lend to foreigners.

To derive an important identity that illustrates the uses of private saving, we first use the income–expenditure identity (equation 2.3) and substitute $C + I + G + NX$ for Y in the expression for national saving (equation 2.8):

$$S = (C + I + G + NX) + NFP - C - G$$

Simplifying the above expression, we obtain

$$S = I + (NX + NFP) \tag{2.9}$$

The expression for national saving in equation (2.9) contains the term $NX + NFP$, which is the sum of net exports and net factor payments, and is called the current account balance, CA.[14] The **current account balance** equals payments received from abroad in exchange for currently produced goods and services (including factor services), minus the analogous payments made to foreigners by the domestic economy. Substituting CA for $NX + NFP$ in equation (2.9), we obtain

$$S = I + CA \tag{2.10}$$

We now have an expression for national saving, S; our goal is an expression for private saving, S_{pvt}. Equation (2.8) shows that private saving, S_{pvt}, equals national saving, S, minus government saving, S_{govt}. Then, subtracting S_{govt} from both sides of equation (2.10), we get

$$S_{pvt} = I + (-S_{govt}) + CA \tag{2.11}$$

where $-S_{govt}$ is the government budget deficit.

Equation (2.11) is another important macroeconomic identity, called the **uses-of-saving identity**. It states that an economy's private saving is used in three ways:

1. *Investment* (I). Firms borrow from private savers to finance the construction and purchase of new capital (including residential capital) and inventory investment.

2. *The government budget deficit* ($-S_{govt}$). When the government runs a budget deficit (so that S_{govt} is negative and $-S_{govt}$ is positive), it must borrow from private savers to cover the difference between outlays and receipts.

3. *The current account balance* (CA). When the Italian current account balance is positive, foreigners' receipts of payments from Italy are not sufficient to cover the payments they make to Italy. To make up the difference, foreigners must either borrow from Italian private savers or sell to Italian savers some of their assets, such as land, factories, stocks, and bonds. Thus financing the current account balance is a use of a country's private saving.

---

14. Actually, the current account balance also includes a term called net unilateral transfers, which measures transfers between countries such as private gifts or official foreign aid (see Chapter 5). In our analysis we generally ignore this term.

In contrast, when the Italian current account balance is negative, as during most of the 1980s and early 1990s, Italian receipts of payments from foreigners are not sufficient to cover Italian payments to foreigners. To offset this excess of payments over receipts, Italy must borrow from foreigners or sell to foreigners some Italian assets. In this case foreigners use their saving to lend to the Italy or to acquire Italian assets.[15]

APPLICATION
The Uses of Saving and the Government Budget Deficit in the 1980s and 1990s

Understanding the uses-of-saving identity is a helpful first step for analysing some complicated macroeconomic issues. For example, the effects of government budget deficits on the economy are argued endlessly. Equation (2.11) shows that if the government budget deficit increases, at least one of the following three things, or a combination of them, must happen: (1) private saving must rise, (2) investment must fall, and/or (3) the current account balance must fall.

Figure 2.1 shows the behaviour of private saving and its three uses in Germany, Italy, Sweden, and the UK since 1980. During the 1980s, government budget deficits tended to fall, with the decline in Sweden being especially striking. In both Sweden and the UK, this decline was accompanied by a widening gap between national investment and private saving, whereas in Germany it was offset by a corresponding fall in the current account surplus. Since the late 1980s, the surge in the government budget deficit has been associated with a deterioration in national investment relative to saving in both Sweden and the UK and by a sharp fall in the current account surplus. The data for Italy show that during the fifteen-year period the behaviour of private saving and its three uses have remained fairly constant and that the large budget deficit has been accompanied by a wide gap between national saving and investment.

Relating Saving and Wealth

Saving is a key economic variable because it is closely related to the rate of wealth accumulation. In the rest of this section we discuss the relationship of saving and wealth. To do so, however, we must first introduce the concept of stocks versus flows.

Stocks and Flows. The economic variables we have discussed so far in this chapter – such as GDP and the various types of expenditure, income, and saving – are measured per unit of time (for example, per quarter or per year). For instance, annual GDP figures measure the economy's production per year. Variables that are measured per unit of time are called **flow variables**.

In contrast, some economic variables, called **stock variables**, are defined at a point in time. Examples of stock variables are the amount of money in your bank account on 15 September of this year and the total value of all houses in Sweden on 1 January 1997.

In many applications a flow variable is the rate of change in a stock variable. A classic example is a bath with water flowing in from a tap. The amount of water in the bath at any moment is a stock variable. The units of a stock

---

15. The current account and its relationship to international borrowing and lending are discussed in greater detail in Chapter 5.

Figure 2.1
The uses-of-saving identity in Germany, Italy, Sweden and the UK, 1980–96
The figure illustrates the uses-of-saving identity – which states that private saving equals the sum of investment, the government budget deficit, and the current account balance – for Germany, Italy, Sweden, and the UK over the period 1980–96. All variables are measured as a percentage of GDP.

Source: *European Economy*, *1996, op cit. Table 1.1(b)*, Table 48 'Gross saving: private sector'; Table 49 'Gross saving; general government'; Table 46 'Balance of current transactions with the rest of the world; Table 19 'Gross fixed capital formation. All are expressed as a percentage of GDP at current market prices.

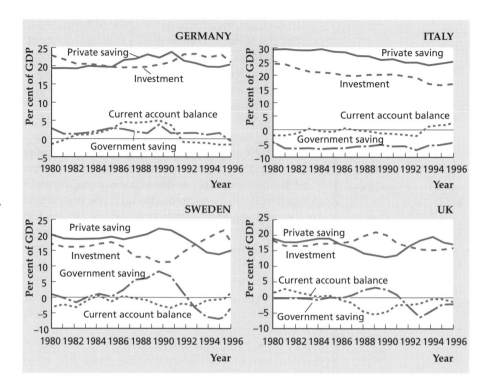

variable (litres, in this case) do not have a time dimension. The rate at which water enters the bath is a flow variable; its units (litres per minute) have a time dimension. In this case the flow is equal to the rate of change of the stock.

Wealth and Saving as Stock and Flow. Saving and wealth are related to each other in much the same way that the flow and stock of water in a bath are related. The wealth of any economic unit, also called net worth, is its assets (the things that it owns, including IOUs from other economic units) minus its liabilities (what it owes to other units). Wealth is measured in a currency at a point in time and is a stock variable. Saving is measured in a currency per unit time and is a flow variable. Because saving takes the form of an accumulation of assets or a reduction in liabilities (for example, if saving is used to pay off debts), it adds to wealth just as water flowing into a bath adds to the stock of water.

National Wealth. National wealth is the total wealth of the residents of a country. National wealth consists of two parts: (1) the country's domestic physical assets, such as its stock of capital goods and land;[16] and (2) its net foreign assets. The **net foreign assets** of a country equal the country's foreign assets (foreign stocks, bonds, and factories owned by domestic residents) minus its foreign liabilities (domestic physical and financial assets owned by foreigners). Net foreign assets are part of national wealth because they represent claims on foreigners that are not offset by foreigners' claims on the domestic economy.

---

16. In principle, national wealth should also include the value of the skills and training of the country's residents – what economists call human capital. In practice, because of measurement problems, human capital is not usually included in measures of national wealth.

Domestic financial assets held by domestic residents are not part of national wealth because the value of any domestic financial asset is offset by a domestic financial liability. For example, a cheque account held by an Italian in an Italian bank is an asset for the depositor but a liability for the bank; it thus does not represent wealth for the economy as a whole. In contrast, an Italian's bank account in a Swiss bank has no corresponding domestic liability (it is a liability of a foreigner) and so is part of Italy's national wealth.

National wealth can change in two ways over time. First, the value of the existing assets or liabilities that make up national wealth may change. Thus an increase in the value of Italian farmland raises Italian national wealth, as does an increase in the value of foreign stocks held by Italians. The wearing out or depreciation of physical assets, which corresponds to a fall in the value of those assets, reduces national wealth.

The second way that national wealth can change is through national saving. Over any particular period of time, with the value of existing assets and liabilities held constant, each extra amount of national saving adds that amount to national wealth. That is,

$$S = I + CA$$

which you will recognize as equation (2.10). This equation shows that national saving has two uses: (1) to increase the stock of domestic physical capital through investment, I, and (2) to increase the nation's stock of net foreign assets by lending to foreigners or acquiring foreign assets in an amount equal to the current account balance, CA. But each amount by which domestic physical assets or net foreign assets increase is an amount by which national wealth increases. Thus, as we claimed, increases in national saving increase national wealth to the same extent. As in the example of water flowing into a bath, the more rapid the flow of national saving, the more quickly the stock of national wealth will rise.

APPLICATION

An International Comparison of National Saving and Investment Rates

How do national saving and investment in Europe compare with saving and investment in other developed countries? Figure 2.2 shows saving and investment for 1963–91 for some member countries of the Organization for Economic Cooperation and Development (OECD), a group of 25 industrialized countries. National saving as a percentage of GDP, investment as a percentage of GDP, and current account balances are shown for each of the seven largest OECD countries and for all OECD countries combined. From the relationship $S = I + CA$ (equation 2.10), we know that the excess of national saving over investment, $S - I$, for each country equals the country's current account balance, CA. In the diagram, green shading indicates a positive current account balance (national saving greater than investment), while grey indicates a negative current account balance (investment greater than national saving).

Figure 2.2 shows that the United Kingdom and the United States are both low-saving countries, with national saving rates well below that of all OECD countries taken together. As a percentage of GDP, investment in the United States is also fairly low. Japan stands out as the country with the highest saving rate.

Two other conclusions may be drawn from Figure 2.2. First, national saving rates of many countries have fallen substantially since 1970. Second, within individual OECD countries national saving and investment generally have tended to move in tandem. This point implies that the current account balances of individual OECD countries, which equal the difference between each country's national saving and investment, typically have been small as a percentage of GDP. The exception is the period since the early 1980s, during which the United States, the United Kingdom, and Canada generally have had sharply negative current account balances (investment greater than saving), whereas Japan and Germany have had positive current account balances (saving greater than investment).

Figure 2.2
Trends in national saving and investment rates, 1963–91

National saving and investment as a percentage of GDP are shown for 1963–91 for seven OECD countries separately and for all 25 OECD countries taken together. The shaded areas indicate the current account balance, or the excess of national saving over investment. Green shading indicates a positive current account balance (national saving greater than investment); grey shading indicates a negative current account balance (investment greater than national saving).

Source: *National Accounts*, 1970–91, OECD. (This publication contains data prior to 1970 for national saving and investment.)

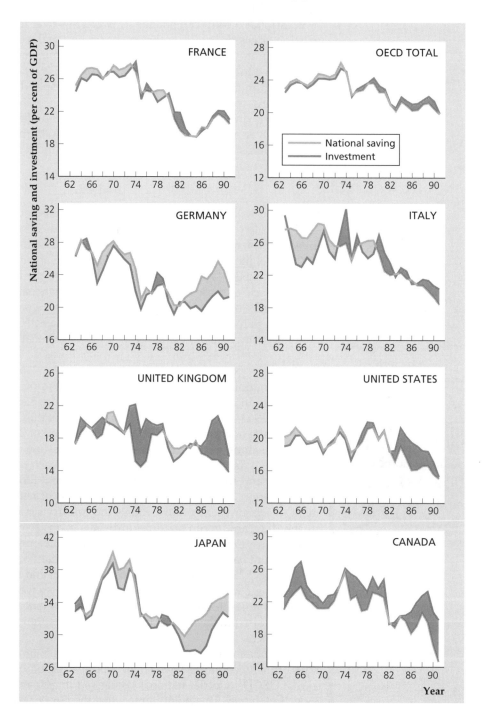

2.4 PRICE INDEXES, INFLATION, AND INTEREST RATES

All the key macroeconomic variables that we have discussed so far in this chapter – GDP, the components of expenditure and income, national wealth, and saving – are measured in terms of current market values. Such variables are called **nominal variables.** The advantage of using market values to measure economic activity is that it allows summing of different types of goods and services.

However, a problem with measuring economic activity in nominal terms arises if you want to compare the values of an economic variable – GDP, for example – at two different points in time. If the current market value of the goods and services included in GDP changes over time, you cannot tell whether this change reflects changes in the quantities of goods and services produced, changes in the prices of goods and services, or a combination of these factors. For example, a large increase in the current market value of GDP might mean that a country has greatly expanded its production of goods and services, or it might mean that the country has experienced inflation, which raised the prices of goods and services.

Economists have devised methods for breaking down changes in nominal variables into the part owing to changes in physical quantities and the part owing to changes in prices. Consider the numerical example in Table 2.3, which gives production and price data for the Outasite Golf Ball Company. Five years ago the nominal value of Outasite's production was £200,000 (60,000 golf balls worth £3.00 each and 40,000 tees worth £0.50 each). This year the nominal value of Outasite's production is £480,000 (80,000 balls at £5.00 plus 80,000 tees at £1.00). Although the nominal value of Outasite's production has increased by 140% over the past five years, this increase does not reflect either a 140% increase in output or a 140% increase in prices. Instead, as you can see from Table 2.3, both quantities and prices rose.

Table 2.3   Production and Price Data for Outasite Golf Ball Company

	Five Years Ago (Base Year)	This Year (Current Year)	Change from Five Years Ago
Product			
Balls	60,000	80,000	+20,000
Tees	40,000	80,000	+40,000
Price			
Balls	£3.00/ball	£5.00/ball	+£2.00/ball
Tees	£0.50/tee	£1.00/tee	+£0.50/tee
Value			
Balls	£180,000	£400,000	+£220,000
Tees	£20,000	£80,000	+£60,000
Total	**£200,000**	**£480,000**	**+£280,000**

Suppose that you were interested primarily in the growth of Outasite's output, perhaps because you wanted to study how the company's workforce productivity has changed over time. How much of the increase in the nominal value of Outasite's production reflects changes in the quantity of balls and tees produced, not changes in price? A standard way to eliminate the influence of price changes is to measure the value of production in each period by using prices from some base year. For this example, let's choose five years ago as the base year. For Outasite's current production of 80,000 balls at £3.00 per ball (the price of balls five years ago) and its current production of 80,000 tees at £0.50 per tee (the price of tees five years ago), the value of Outasite's production this year is £280,000. This calculation is summarized in Table 2.4, step 1.

In general, an economic variable that is measured by the prices of a base year is called a **real variable**. Thus £280,000 is the real value of Outasite's current production. Real economic variables measure the physical volume of economic activity.

What was Outasite's real production five years ago? To find it, multiply Outasite's production of balls and tees from five years ago by the prices of balls and tees in the base year, or five years ago. This calculation gives (60,000 balls × £3.00 per ball) + (40,000 tees × £0.50 per tee) = £200,000. This value is the same as that for Outasite's nominal production five years ago. This result is a general one: Because current and base-year prices are the same in the base year, real and nominal quantities are also the same in the base year.

Comparing Outasite's current real production of £280,000 with its real production of £200,000 five years ago shows that the company's real production rose by 40% over the five years. Note that the estimated increase in real production of 40% lies between the 33% increase in ball production and the 100% increase in tee production. The overall increase in production is actually closer to 33% than 100% because the value of ball production is much greater than the value of tee production. Hence the increase in ball production receives greater weight in the overall growth rate.

Real Versus Nominal GDP

Just as an individual firm's production can be expressed in either nominal or real terms, the output of an entire economy also can be expressed in both nominal and real terms. **Nominal GDP**, also called GDP at current prices, is the market value of an economy's final output at current market prices. **Real GDP**, also called GDP at constant prices, measures the market value of an economy's final output at prices that prevailed during a specified base year or period. Use real rather than nominal GDP when looking at how an economy's physical production has evolved over time. (Figure 1.1, p. 5, shows the long-run behaviour of real output in a number of European countries.)

Currently, the base year used to calculate real GDP is 1990. Thus to calculate real GDP for, say, 1996 multiply the quantities of goods and services produced in 1996 by the 1990 prices for those goods and services. In contrast, to calculate nominal GDP for 1996 multiply the quantities of goods and services produced in 1996 by their 1996 prices. Nominal GDP in the Netherlands in 1996 of 661.8 billion guilders exceeded real GDP in 1996 of 587.6 billion guilders because prices generally rose between 1990 and 1996. In contrast, real and nominal GDP were equal at 516.3 billion guilders in 1990 because current and base-year prices were the same in that year.

Table 2.4   Calculation of Real Output and Price Level for Outasite Golf Ball Company

1. Calculation of the real value of current output

Real value of current output =

	current quantities	x	base-year prices		
Balls	80,000		£3.00	=	£240,000
Tees	80,000		£0.50	=	£40,000
				Total	£280,000

2. Calculation of the price level (variable-weight index)

$$\text{Price level} = \frac{\text{value of current output at current prices}}{\text{value of current output at base-year prices}}$$

Value of current output at current prices =

	current quantities	x	current prices		
Balls	80,000		£5.00	=	£400,000
Tees	80,000		£1.00	=	£80,000
				Total	£480,000

Value of current output at base-year prices =

	current quantities	x	base-year prices		
Balls	80,000		£3.00	=	£240,000
Tees	80,000		£0.50	=	£40,000
				Total	£280,000

$$\text{Price level (variable-weight)} = \frac{£480,000}{£280,000} = 1.71$$

3. Calculation of the price level (fixed-weight index)

$$\text{Price level} = \frac{\text{value of base-year output at current prices}}{\text{value of base-year output at base-year prices}}$$

Value of base-year output at current prices =

	base-year quantities	x	current prices		
Balls	60,000		£5.00	=	£300,000
Tees	40,000		£1.00	=	£40,000
				Total	£340,000

Value of base-year output at base-year prices =

	base-year quantities	x	base-year prices		
Balls	60,000		£3.00	=	£180,000
Tees	40,000		£0.50	=	£20,000
				Total	£200,000

$$\text{Price level (fixed-weight)} = \frac{£340,000}{£200,000} = 1.70$$

All macroeconomic variables discussed in this chapter – consumption, investment, saving, wealth, and so on – may be expressed in real terms. Because they measure physical quantities, real variables are better indicators than nominal variables of how a country's living standards and productive capacity are changing over time. In most of this book we focus on the real determinants of economic well-being. Therefore from now on, unless otherwise stated, when we refer to output, Y, consumption, C, investment, I, and so on, we are referring to these variables measured in real rather than nominal terms.

Price Indexes and Inflation

Measuring GDP in real terms eliminates the effects of price changes from the measure of national output. Sometimes, however, as when studying the determinants of inflation, you may want to determine how much prices have changed over a period of time. A measure of the average level of prices for some specified set of goods and services, relative to the prices in a specified base year, is called a **price index.**

The simplest type of price index is an index for one good, say, pizzas. Suppose that pizzas cost £3.00 each in the base year, say, 1990, and cost £4.50 each today. The price index for pizzas, which measures the price of pizzas today relative to 1990, is £4.50/£3.00 = 1.50, indicating that pizza prices have risen 50% since 1990.

Usually, however, economists want to know how prices have changed not just for one good but for a larger set of goods and services, perhaps even all the goods and services produced in the economy. So they must somehow combine the prices of many goods into a single index. Two basic types of price index, called variable-weight indexes and fixed-weight indexes, are used to measure average price change for a set of goods and services.

A **variable-weight price index** starts with the set of goods and services produced in the current period and compares today's cost of those goods and services with what they would have cost in the base year. More precisely:

$$\text{variable-weight price index} = \frac{\text{value of current output at current prices}}{\text{value of current output at base-year prices}}$$

If the goods and services produced today are much more costly than in the base year, the variable-weight price index will be high. Table 2.4, step 2, shows how to calculate a variable-weight price index for Outasite. Its current output is worth £480,000 at today's prices and £280,000 at the prices of five years ago. Thus the price index for Outasite for the current year is £480,000/£280,000 = 1.71. Thus, on average, Outasite's prices now are 71% higher than five years earlier.

An often-used variable-weight price index, which is constructed as part of the national income accounts, is the GDP deflator. For any period, the **GDP deflator** is the ratio of current nominal GDP to current real GDP:

$$\text{GDP deflator} = \frac{\text{nominal GDP}}{\text{real GDP}}$$

The GDP deflator is the variable-weight price index that covers all final goods and services in the economy. The value of current output in current prices is the same as nominal GDP, and the value of current output in base-year prices equals real GDP. Thus the definition of the GDP deflator fits the general form of a variable-weight price index. Published values of the GDP deflator and other price indexes often are multiplied by 100 to get rid of the decimal point. In that case you will see a notation such as 1990 = 100, which means that the index equals 100 (rather than 1.00) in the base year, 1990.

The second type of price index is a fixed-weight index. A **fixed-weight price index** measures how much a fixed basket of goods costs relative to a base period:

$$\text{fixed-weight price index} = \frac{\text{value of fixed basket at current prices}}{\text{value of fixed basket at base-year prices}}$$

The fixed-weight price index for Outasite is calculated in Table 2.4, step 3, for a fixed basket that equals Outasite's base-year production. The value of Outasite's base-year output in current prices is £340,000, and the value of its base-year output in base-year prices is £200,000. Thus the fixed-weight price index is £340,000/£200,000 = 1.70, or not much different from the value of 1.71 obtained for the variable-weight index.

The most-used fixed-weight price index is the **consumer price index**, or CPI.[17] (See Figure 1.3 for historical values of the CPI.) Government statisticians construct CPIs by sending people out each month to find the current prices of a fixed list, or basket, of consumer items, including many specific items of food, clothing, housing, and fuel. The CPI for that month is then calculated as the current cost of the basket of consumer items divided by the cost of the basket of items in the base year.[18]

Variable-weight and fixed-weight indexes of the price level have different advantages. The advantage of variable-weight indexes over fixed-weight indexes is that they reflect the prices of the basket of goods that people actually purchased in the current year, rather than the basket they purchased in the base year. The relative disadvantage of variable-weight indexes is that the current basket may contain many goods that did not exist or were of different quality in the base year (see Box 2.2, p. 55). For such goods, statisticians must estimate what a new or improved good would have cost had it existed in the base year, which introduces a source of error.[19]

An important variable that is measured with price indexes is the rate of inflation. The rate of inflation equals the percentage rate of increase in the price index per period. Thus if the CPI rises from 100 in one year to 105 the next, the rate of inflation between the two years is (105 − 100)/100 = 5/100 = 0.05 = 5% per year. If in the third year the CPI is 112, the rate of inflation between the second and third years is (112 − 105)/105 = 7/105 = 0.0667 = 6.67% per year. More generally, if P_t is the price level in period t and P_{t+1} is the price level in period $t + 1$, the rate of inflation between t and $t + 1$, or π_{t+1}, is

$$\pi_{t+1} = \frac{(P_{t+1} - P_t)}{P_t} = \frac{\Delta P_{t+1}}{P_t}$$

17. In the UK the consumer price index is called the retail price index, or RPI.

18. Like the GDP deflator, the CPI often is multiplied by 100, so base-year prices equal 100 rather than 1.00.

19. Base years also are periodically changed, so as not to be too far in the past. Updating the base year reduces the problem of having current goods that are very different from the goods that existed in the base year.

where ΔP_{t+1}, or $P_{t+1} - P_t$, represents the change in P_t.

Figure 2.3 shows the inflation rate for Italy, Germany, Sweden and the UK for the period 1961–96, based on the GDP deflator as the measure of the price level. Inflation rose sharply during the 1970s and fell sharply in the early 1980s, especially in the UK and Italy.

Interest Rates

Interest rates are another important – and familiar – type of economic variable. An **interest rate** is a rate of return promised by a borrower to a lender. If, for example, the interest rate on a £100, one-year loan is 8%, the borrower has promised to repay the lender £108 one year from now, or £8 interest plus repayment of the £100 borrowed.

As we discuss in more detail in Chapter 4, there are many different interest rates in the economy. Interest rates vary according to who is doing the borrowing, how long the funds are borrowed for, and other factors. There are also many assets in the economy, such as shares of corporate stock, that do not pay a specified interest rate but do pay their holders a return; for shares of stock the return comes in the form of dividends and capital gains (increases in the stock's market price). The existence of so many different assets, each with

Figure 2.3
The inflation rate in Germany, Italy, Sweden and the UK, 1961–96
Here, inflation is measured as the annual percentage change in the GDP deflator. Inflation rose during the 1970s and fell sharply in the early 1980s.

Source: *European Economy 1996, op cit. Table 1.1(b)*, Table 25.

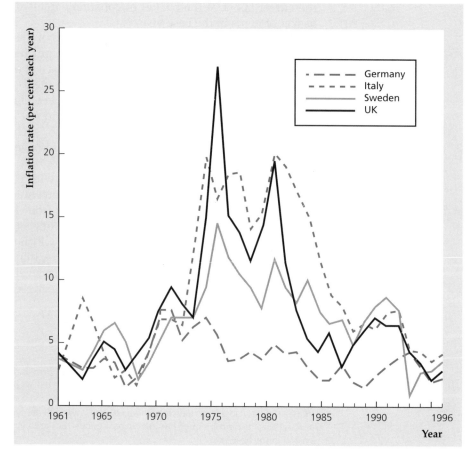

BOX 2.2

Does CPI Inflation Overstate Increases in the Cost of Living?

Official inflation rates play a crucial role in macro-economic analysis and policy making. The Bundes-bank and the Bank of England are two European central banks which target inflation rates in Germany and the UK respectively when setting interest rates, and in many European countries state pensions and social security benefits are linked to the CPI. It is therefore important that the price indexes which measure the rate of inflation do so accurately. In 1996 a US government commission (headed by Michael Boskin of Stanford University, former chief economic advisor to President Bush) presented a report on the accuracy of official inflation measures in the USA, raising issues that are equally relevant to other countries. The Boskin report concluded that inflation as measured by the CPI may overstate true increases in the cost of living by as much as one to two percentage points per year. In other words, if the official inflation rate is 3% per year, the 'true' inflation rate may well be 2% per year or less.

Why might it be the case that increases in the CPI overstate the actual rate at which the cost of living rises? One problem is that it is hard for government statisticians to measure changes in the quality of goods. If the design of an air conditioner is improved, for example, so that it can put out 10% more cold air without increased use of electricity, then a 10% increase in the price of the air conditioner should not be considered inflation; although the consumer is paying 10% more, he or she is also receiving 10% more cooling capacity. However, if the government statisticians fail to take account of the improved quality of the air conditioner and simply note its 10% increase in price, they will erroneously ascribe the price change to inflation. Although measuring the output of an air conditioner is not difficult, for some products, and especially services, quality change is hard to measure. By what percentage does the availability of 24-hour cash machines improve the quality of banking services, for example? To the extent that the CPI fails to account for quality improvements in the goods and services people use, inflation will be overstated. This overstatement is called the *quality adjustment bias*.

Another problem with CPI inflation as a measure of increases in the cost of living can be illustrated by the following example. Suppose that consumers like chicken and turkey about equally well, and in the base year they consume equal amounts of each. But then for some reason the price of chicken rises sharply, leading consumers to switch to eating turkey almost exclusively. Since consumers are about equally satisfied with chicken and turkey, this switch does not make them significantly worse off; their true cost of living has not been much affected by the rise in the price of chicken. However, the official CPI, which measures the cost of buying the base-year basket of goods, will register a significant increase when the price of chicken skyrockets. Thus the rise in the CPI exaggerates the true increase in the cost of living. The problem is that the CPI assumes that consumers purchase a basket of goods and services that is fixed over time, ignoring the option that consumers have of substituting cheaper goods or services for more expensive ones. This source of overstatement of the true increase in the cost of living is called the *substitution bias*. The seriousness of the problem clearly depends upon how regularly the basket of goods used to construct the CPI is updated: in the UK it is updated every twelve months, though in many other countries the updating is less frequent – it is every ten years in the USA.

If official inflation measures do in fact overstate true inflation, there are important implications. First, if rises in the cost of living are overstated, then rises in important quantities like real family income and firm productivity are correspondingly understated. Thus the bias in the CPI may lead to a too-gloomy view of how well an economy has done in the past few decades. Second, many government payments and taxes are tied, or *indexed*, to the CPI. Social security benefits, for example, often automatically increase each year by the same percentage as the CPI. If CPI inflation overstates true inflation, then social security recipients have been receiving greater benefit increases than necessary to compensate them for increases in the cost of living. It has been estimated for the USA that if social security and other transfer payments were set to increase at the rate of 'true' inflation, rather than at the CPI inflation rate, much of the Federal government budget deficit would be eliminated.

Note: For a detailed discussion of biases in the CPI in the USA, see Matthew Shapiro and David Wilcox, 'Mismeasurement in the Consumer Price Index: An Evaluation', in Ben Bernanke and Julio Rotemberg (eds.), *NBER Macroeconomics Annual*, 1996.

its own rate of return, has the potential to complicate greatly the study of macroeconomics. Fortunately, however, most interest rates and other rates of return tend to move up and down together. For purposes of macroeconomic analysis we usually speak of 'the' interest rate, as if there were only one. If we say that a certain policy causes 'the' interest rate to rise, for example, we mean that interest rates and rates of return in general are likely to rise.

Real Versus Nominal Interest Rates. Interest rates and other rates of return share a measurement problem with nominal GDP: an interest rate indicates how quickly the nominal value of an interest-bearing asset increases over time, but it does not reveal how quickly the value of the asset changes in real, or purchasing-power, terms. Consider, for example, a savings account with an interest rate of 4% per year that has £300 in it at the beginning of the year. At the end of the year the savings account is worth £312, which is a relatively good deal for the depositor if inflation is zero; with no inflation the price level is unchanged over the year, and £312 buys 4% more goods and services in real terms than the initial £300 did a year earlier. If inflation is 4%, however, what cost £300 a year earlier now costs £312, and in real terms the savings account is worth no more today than it was a year ago.

To distinguish changes in the real value of assets from changes in nominal value, economists frequently use the concept of the real interest rate. The **real interest rate** (or real rate of return) on an asset is the rate at which the real value or purchasing power of the asset increases over time. To distinguish them from real interest rates, we refer to conventionally measured interest rates, such as those reported in the newspaper, as nominal interest rates. The **nominal interest rate** (or nominal rate of return) tells us the rate at which the nominal value of an asset increases over time. The symbol for the nominal interest rate is i.

The real interest rate is related to the nominal interest rate and the inflation rate:

$$\text{real interest rate} = \text{nominal interest rate} - \text{inflation rate}$$
$$= i - \pi \tag{2.12}$$

We derive and discuss equation (2.12) further at the end of the book in Appendix A, Section A.7.[20] For now, consider again the savings account paying 4% interest. If the inflation rate is zero, the real interest rate on that savings account is the 4% nominal interest rate minus the 0% inflation rate, or 4%. A 4% real interest rate on the account means that the depositor will be able to buy 4% more goods and services at the end of the year than at the beginning. But, if inflation is 4%, the real interest rate on the savings account is the 4% nominal interest rate minus the 4% inflation rate, or 0%. In this case the purchasing power of the account is no greater at the end of the year than at the beginning.

Nominal and real interest rates for 1965–96 are shown in Figure 2.4. The real interest rate was unusually low in the mid 1970s; indeed, it was negative in many European countries, which means that the real values of interest-bearing assets were actually declining over time. Nominal interest rates rose to

---

20. Equation (2.12) is an approximation, rather than an exact relationship. This approximation holds most closely when interest rates and inflation rates are not too high.

Figure 2.4(a)
Nominal interests in Germany, Italy, Sweden and the UK, 1965–96
The nominal interest rate for Germany is measured by the interest rate on mortgage bonds, for Italy the interest rate on medium term government bonds, for Sweden the interest rate on government bonds, and for the UK the interest rate on the short-term government bonds. The nominal rate of interest was very high during the early 1980s but fell sharply in the mid 1980s.
Source: Data for the period 1966–95 from *International Financial Statistics Yearbook XLIX*, International Monetary Fund, Washington D.C., country tables. Data for 1996 from *International Financial Statistics, Volume L*, June 1997 *op cit. Figure 1.1*, country tables.

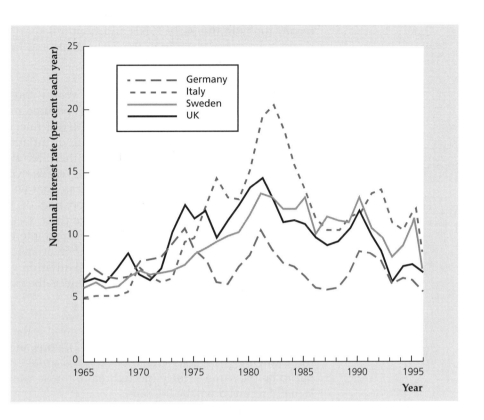

Figure 2.4(b)
Real interest rates in Germany, Italy, Sweden and the UK, 1965–96
The real rate of interest is measured as the nominal rate of interest minus the average inflation rate (using the GDP deflator) over the current and subsequent two years. The real rate of interest was unusually low (actually negative) in the mid 1970s in Italy, Sweden and the UK. In the early 1980s real interest rates rose sharply as they did again in the early 1990s in Italy and Sweden.
Source: Data for the period 1966–95 from *International Financial Statistics Yearbook XLIX*, International Monetary Fund, Washington D.C., country tables. Data for 1996 from *International Financial Statistics, Volume L*, June 1997 *op cit. Figure 1.1*, country tables.

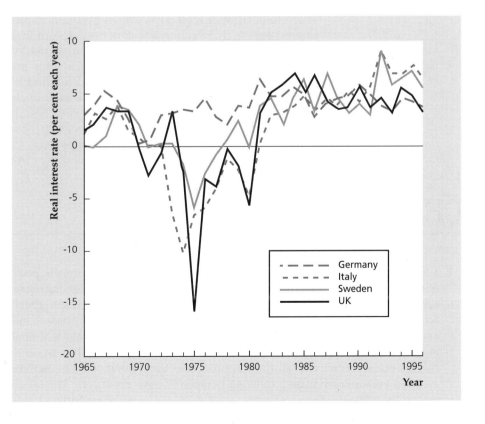

record highs in the early 1980s and then fell sharply in the late 1980s. Real interest rates rose sharply in the early 1980s and have continued to increase slightly since then.

The Expected Real Interest Rate. When you borrow, lend, or make a bank deposit, the nominal interest rate is specified in advance. But what about the real interest rate? For any nominal interest rate, equation (2.12) states that the real interest rate depends on the rate of inflation over the period of the loan or deposit – say, a year. However, the rate of inflation during the year generally cannot be determined until the year is over. Thus at the time that a loan or deposit is made, the real interest rate that will be received is uncertain.

Because borrowers, lenders, and depositors do not know what the actual real interest rate will be, they must make their decisions about how much to borrow, lend, or deposit on the basis of the real interest rate they expect to prevail. They know the nominal interest rate in advance, so the real interest rate they expect depends on what they think inflation will be. The **expected real interest rate** is the nominal interest rate minus the expected rate of inflation, or

$$r = i - \pi^e \tag{2.13}$$

where r is the expected real interest rate and π^e is the expected rate of inflation.

Comparing equations (2.13) and (2.12), you can see that if people are correct in their expectations – so that expected inflation and actual inflation turn out to be the same – the expected real interest rate and the real interest rate actually received will be the same.

The expected real interest rate is the correct interest rate to use for studying most types of economic decision, such as people's decisions about how much to borrow or lend. However, a problem in measuring the expected real interest rate is that economists generally do not know exactly what the public's expected rate of inflation is. Economists use various means to measure expected inflation. One approach is to survey the public and simply ask what rate of inflation people expect. A second method is to assume that the public's expectations of inflation are the same as publicly announced government or private forecasts. A third possibility is to assume that people's inflation expectations are an extrapolation of recently observed rates of inflation. Unfortunately, none of these methods is perfect, so the measurement of the expected real interest rate always contains some error.

CHAPTER SUMMARY

1. The national income accounts are an accounting framework used in measuring current economic activity. The national income accounts measure activity in three ways: the product approach, the expenditure approach, and the income approach. Although each gives the same value for current economic activity, all three approaches are used because each gives a different perspective on the economy.

2. Gross domestic product (GDP) is the broadest measure of aggregate economic activity occurring during a specified period of time. The product approach measures GDP by adding the market values of final goods and services newly produced in an economy; this approach is implemented by summing the value added by all producers. The expenditure approach measures GDP by adding the four categories of spending:

consumption, investment, government purchases, and net exports. The income approach measures GDP by adding all the incomes, including taxes and profits, generated by economic activity.

3. The income of the private sector (domestic households and businesses) is called private disposable income. Private disposable income equals income received from private-sector activities (GDP plus net factor payments from abroad, or GNP) plus payments received from the government (transfers and interest on government debt) minus taxes paid to the government. The net income of the government sector equals taxes collected minus transfer payments and interest paid on government debt. Private disposable income and net government income sum to GNP, which is the income of all domestic factors of production.

4. Saving is the portion of an economic unit's current income that it does not spend to meet current needs. Saving by the private sector, called private saving, equals private disposable income minus consumption. Government saving, which is the same as the government budget surplus, equals the government's net income minus its purchases of goods and services; equivalently, government saving equals government receipts minus government outlays. National saving is the sum of private saving and government saving; it equals GDP plus net factor payments from abroad minus consumption and government purchases.

5. The uses-of-saving identity states that private saving equals the sum of investment, the government budget deficit, and the current account balance. Equivalently, national saving equals the sum of investment and the current account balance.

6. The national wealth of a country equals its physical assets, such as capital, plus its net foreign assets. National wealth increases in two ways: through changes in the value of existing assets and through national saving. National saving adds to national wealth because national saving is used either for investment, thus adding to physical capital, or for lending to foreigners an amount that equals the current account balance, which increases the country's net foreign assets.

7. Nominal GDP is the value of an economy's final output measured at current market prices. Real GDP measures the market value of the economy's final output at prices that prevailed in some base year or period. Because prices are held constant in the calculation of real GDP, changes in real GDP over time capture changes in production volume. More generally, nominal variables measure current market values; real variables are intended to measure physical quantities.

8. A price index is a measure of the current price level relative to a base year. A variable-weight price index, such as the GDP deflator, compares the cost of a set of goods and services produced in the current period with what that set of goods and services would have cost in the base year. A fixed-weight price index, such as the consumer price index, measures how much a fixed basket of goods and services costs in each period, relative to what they cost in the base year. Inflation is the percentage rate of change of the price level, as measured by a price index such as the GDP deflator or the CPI.

9. An interest rate is a rate of return promised by a borrower to a lender. The nominal interest rate is the rate at which the nominal value of an interest-bearing asset increases over time. The real interest rate, or the nominal interest rate minus the rate of inflation, is the rate at which the value of an asset grows in real, or purchasing-power, terms. Borrowing and lending decisions are based on the expected real interest rate, which is the nominal interest rate less the expected rate of inflation.

Key Terms

Key Equations

$$\text{total production} = \text{total income} = \text{total expenditure} \tag{2.1}$$

The fundamental identity of national income accounting states that the same measure of total economic activity is obtained whether activity is measured by the production of final goods and services, the amount of income generated by the economic activity, or the expenditure on final goods and services.

$$Y = C + I + G + NX \tag{2.3}$$

According to the income–expenditure identity, total income or product or output, Y, equals the sum of the four types of expenditure: consumption, C, investment, I, government purchases, G, and net exports, NX.

$$S_{pvt} = (Y + NFP - T + TR + INT) - C \tag{2.6}$$

Private saving equals private disposable income less consumption, C. Private disposable income equals gross domestic product, Y, plus net factor payments from abroad, NFP, plus transfers, TR, and interest, INT, received from the government, less taxes paid, T.

$$S_{govt} = (T - TR - INT) - G \tag{2.7}$$

Government saving equals government receipts from taxes, T, less outlays for transfers, TR, interest on the national debt, INT, and government purchases, G. Government saving is the same as the government budget surplus and is the negative of the government budget deficit.

$$S = S_{pvt} + S_{govt} = Y + NFP - C - G \tag{2.8}$$

National saving, S, is the sum of private saving and government saving. Equivalently, national saving equals gross domestic product, Y, plus net factor payments from abroad, NFP, less consumption, C, and government purchases, G.

$$S = I + CA \tag{2.10}$$

National saving, S, has two uses: to finance investment, I, and to lend to foreigners (or to acquire foreign assets) an amount that equals the current account balance, CA. The current account balance equals the increase in net foreign assets.

$$S_{pvt} = I + (-S_{govt}) + CA \tag{2.11}$$

According to the uses-of-saving identity, private saving is used to finance investment spending, I, to provide the government with the funds it needs to cover its budget deficit, $-S_{govt}$, and to lend to foreigners (or to acquire foreign assets) an amount that equals the current account balance, CA.

$$r = i - \pi^e \tag{2.13}$$

The expected real interest rate, r, equals the nominal interest rate, i, minus expected inflation π^e.

Review Questions

1. What are the three approaches to measuring economic activity? Why do they give the same answer?

2. Why are goods and services counted in GDP at market value? Are there any disadvantages or problems in using market values to measure production?

3. What is the difference between intermediate and final goods and services? In which of these categories do capital goods, such as factories and machines, fall? Why is the distinction between intermediate and final goods important for measuring GDP?

4. List the four components of total spending. Why are imports subtracted when GDP is calculated in the expenditure approach?

5. Define private saving. How is private saving used in the economy? What is the relationship between private saving and national saving?

6. What is national wealth, and why is it important? How is national wealth linked to national saving?

7. For the purposes of assessing an economy's growth performance, which is the more important statistic: real GDP or nominal GDP? Why?

8. Describe how the GDP deflator and the CPI are calculated. What are the basic differences between these two price indexes?

9. Explain the differences among the nominal interest rate, the real interest rate, and the expected real interest rate. Which interest rate concept is the most important for the decisions made by borrowers and lenders? Why?

Numerical Problems

1. After a boat rescues everyone else from Gilligan's Island, the Professor and Gilligan remain behind, afraid of getting shipwrecked again with the same bunch of people. The Professor grows coconuts and catches fish. Last year he harvested 1,000 coconuts and caught 500 fish. He values one fish as worth two coconuts. The Professor gave 200 coconuts to Gilligan in exchange for help in the harvest, and he gave Gilligan 100 fish in exchange for collecting worms for use in fishing. The Professor stored 100 of his coconuts in his hut for consumption at some future time. He also used 100 fish as fertilizer for the coconut trees, as he must every year to keep the trees producing. Gilligan consumed all his coconuts and fish.

   In terms of fish, what is the GDP of Gilligan's Island? What are consumption and investment? What are the incomes of the Professor and Gilligan?

2. ABC Computer Company has a £20,000,000 factory in Silicon Valley. During the current year ABC builds £2,000,000 worth of computer components. ABC's costs are labour, £1,000,000; interest on debt, £100,000; and taxes, £200,000.

   ABC sells all its output to XYZ Supercomputer. Using ABC's components, XYZ builds four super-computers at a cost of £800,000 each (£500,000 worth of components, £200,000 in labour costs, and £100,000 in taxes per computer). XYZ has a £30,000,000 factory.

   XYZ sells three of the supercomputers for £1,000,000 each; but at year's end, it had not sold the fourth. The unsold computer is carried on XYZ's books as an £800,000 increase in inventory.

   a. Calculate the contributions to GDP of these transactions, showing that all three approaches give the same answer.

   b. Repeat part (a), but now assume that in addition to its other costs, ABC also paid £500,000 for imported computer chips.

3. For each of the following transactions, determine the contribution to the current year's GDP. Explain the effects on the product, income, and expenditure accounts.

   a. On 1 January you purchase 100 litres of petrol at £0.70 per litre. The petrol station purchased the petrol the previous week at a wholesale price (transportation included) of £0.65 per litre.

   b. Colonel Hogwash purchases a Victorian mansion for £500,000. The broker's fee is 6%.

   c. A homemaker enters the workforce, taking a job that will pay £10,000 over the year. The homemaker must pay £5000 over the year for professional child care services.

   d. The Japanese build a car plant in Wales for £100,000,000, using only local labour and materials. (*Hint:* The car plant is a capital good produced in the UK and purchased by the Japanese.)

   e. You are informed that you have won £3,000,000 on the National Lottery, to be paid to you, in total, immediately.

   f. The promoters pay you an additional £5000 fee to appear in a TV commercial publicizing the National Lottery.

g. Hertz Rent-a-Car replaces its rental fleet by buying £100,000,000 worth of new cars from Ford . It sells its old fleet to a consortium of used-car dealers for £40,000,000. The consortium resells the used cars to the public for a total of £60,000,000.

4. You are given the following data on an economy.

Gross national product	1000
Government purchases of goods and services	200
Government deficit	50
National saving	200
Investment	150
Net factor payments from abroad	25

Find the following:
a. Consumption
b. Private saving
c. Disposable income
d. Gross domestic product
e. Net exports

5. Consider an economy that produces only three types of fruit: apples, oranges, and bananas. In the base year (a few years ago), the production and price data were as follows.

Fruit	Quantity	Price
Apples	3000 bags	£2 per bag
Bananas	6000 bunches	£3 per bunch
Oranges	8000 bags	£4 per bag

In the current year the production and price data are as follows.

Fruit	Quantity	Price
Apples	4000 bags	£3 per bag
Bananas	14,000 bunches	£2 per bunch
Oranges	32,000 bags	£5 per bag

a. What are the values of nominal and real GDP in the base year and the current year?
b. How much did nominal GDP grow between the base year and the current year?
c. How much did real GDP grow between the base year and the current year?
d. What was the percentage change in the price level between the base year and the current year, as measured by the GDP deflator? As measured by a fixed-weight price index that takes actual production in the base year as the fixed basket of goods?

6. For the consumer price index values shown, calculate the rate of inflation in each year from 1930 to 1933. What is unusual about this period, relative to recent experience?

Year	1929	1930	1931	1932	1933
CPI	51.3	50.0	45.6	40.9	38.8

7. Hy Marks buys a one-year government bond on 1 January, 1996, for £500. He receives principal plus interest totaling £545 on 1 January, 1997. Suppose that the CPI is 200 on 1 January, 1996 and 214 on 1 January, 1997. This increase in prices is more than Hy had anticipated; his guess was that the CPI would be at 210 by the beginning of 1997.

Find the nominal interest rate, the inflation rate, the real interest rate, Hy's expected inflation rate, and Hy's expected real interest rate.

8. The GDP deflator in Econoland is 200 on 1 January, 1993. The deflator rises to 242 by 1 January, 1995, and to 266.2 by 1 January, 1996.

a. What is the annual rate of inflation over the two-year period between 1 January, 1993, and 1 January, 1995? In other words, what constant yearly rate of inflation would lead to the price rise observed over those two years?
b. What is the annual rate of inflation over the three-year period from 1 January, 1993, to 1 January, 1996?
c. In general, if P_0 is the price level at the beginning of an n-year period, and P_n is the price level at the end of that period, show that the annual rate of inflation π over that period satisfies the equation $(1 + \pi)^n = (P_n/P_0)$.

Analytical Problems

1. A reputable study shows that a particular new workplace safety regulation will reduce the growth of real GDP. Is this an argument against implementing the regulation? Explain.

2. Economists have tried to measure the GDPs of virtually all the world's nations. This problem asks you to think about some practical issues that arise in that effort.

a. Before the fall of communism, the economies of the Soviet Union and Eastern Europe were centrally planned. One aspect of central planning is that most prices are set by the government. A government-set price may be too low, in that people want to buy more of the good at the fixed price than there are supplies available; or the price may be too high, so that large stocks of the good sit unsold on store shelves. In recent years central planning has been largely eliminated in Eastern Europe and the former Soviet Union, but government price setting has not been completely abandoned. For example, Russia still keeps energy prices well below market-clearing levels.

What problem does government control of prices create for economists attempting to measure a country's GDP? Suggest a strategy for dealing with this problem.

b. In very poor, agricultural countries, many people grow their own food, make their own clothes, and provide services for each other within a family or village group. Official GDP estimates for these countries are often extremely low, perhaps just a few hundred pounds per person.

Some economists have argued that the official GDP figures underestimate these nations' actual GDPs. Why might this be so? Again, can you suggest a strategy for dealing with this measurement problem?

3. In the EU publication *European Economy*, find Tables 21, 46, 50 and 111 ('Gross fixed capital formation', 'Balance of current transactions with the rest of the world', 'Gross private savings' and 'Gross savings: general government', respectively). Using the tables, find private saving and national saving for Finland. Show that private saving equals the sum of its three uses in each year.

THE MACROECONOMICS OF FULL EMPLOYMENT

3

PRODUCTIVITY, OUTPUT, AND EMPLOYMENT

In Chapter 2 we discussed the measurement of several economic variables used to gauge the economy's health. The measurement of economic performance is a prelude to the main objective of macroeconomics: *to understand how the economy works.* Understanding how the economy works requires a shift from economic *measurement* to economic *analysis.*

In Part II of this book, which begins with this chapter, we have two main goals. The first is to analyse the factors that affect the longer-term performance of the economy, including the rate of economic growth, productivity and living standards, the long-run levels of employment and unemployment, saving and capital formation, and the rate of inflation, among others.

The second goal is to develop a theoretical model of the macroeconomy that you can use to analyse the economic issues covered in this book and others that you may encounter in the future. As outlined in Chapter 1, our model is based on the assumption that individuals, firms, and the government interact in three composite markets: the labour market (covered in this chapter), the goods market (Chapter 4), and the asset market (Chapter 7). In developing and using this model in Part II, we generally assume that the economy is at full employment, with quantities supplied and demanded equal in each of the three major markets. As we are focusing on the long-term behaviour of the economy, this assumption is a reasonable one. In Part III, in which we explore business cycles, we allow for the possibility that quantities supplied and demanded may not be equal in the short run.

This chapter begins the discussion of how the economy works with what is perhaps the most fundamental determinant of economic well-being in a society: the economy's productive capacity. Everything else being equal, the greater the quantity of goods and services an economy can produce, the more people will be able to consume in the present and the more they will be able to save and invest for the future.

The first section of the chapter shows that the amount of output an economy produces depends on two factors: (1) the quantities of inputs (such as labour, capital, and raw materials) utilized in the production process; and (2) the **productivity** of the inputs – that is, the effectiveness with which they are used. As discussed in Chapter 1, an economy's productivity is basic to determining living standards. In this chapter we show how productivity affects people's incomes by helping to determine how many workers are employed and how much they receive in wages.

Of the various inputs to production, the most important (as measured by share of total cost) is labour. For this reason, we spend most of the chapter analysing the labour market, using the tools of supply and demand. We first consider the factors that affect how much labour employers demand and workers supply and then look at the forces that tend to bring the labour market into equilibrium. Equilibrium in the labour market determines wages and employment; in turn, the level of employment, together with the quantities of other inputs (such as capital) and the level of productivity, determines how much output an economy produces.

Our basic model of the labour market rests on the assumption that the quantities of labour supplied and demanded are equal so that all labour resources are fully utilized. In reality, however, some fraction of workers is always unemployed. The latter part of the chapter introduces unemployment and looks at the relationship between the unemployment rate and the amount of output produced in the economy.

3.1   HOW MUCH DOES THE ECONOMY PRODUCE? THE PRODUCTION FUNCTION

Every day the business news reports many economic variables that influence the economy's performance – the rate of consumer spending, the value of the domestic currency, the gyrations of the stock market, the growth rate of the money supply, and so on. All of these variables are important. However, no determinant of economic performance and living standards is more basic than the economy's physical capacity to produce goods and services. If an economy's factories, farms, and other businesses all shut down for some reason, other economic factors would not mean much.

What determines the quantity of goods and services that an economy can produce? A key factor is the quantity of inputs – such as capital goods, labour, raw materials, land, and energy – that producers in the economy use. Economists refer to inputs to the production process as **factors of production**. All else being equal, the greater the quantities of factors of production used, the more goods and services are produced.

Of the various factors of production, the two most important are capital (factories and machines, for example) and labour (workers). Hence we focus on these two factors in discussing an economy's capacity to produce goods and services. In modern economies, however, output often responds strongly to changes in the supply of other factors, such as energy or raw materials. Later in this chapter the Application 'Output, Employment, and the Real Wage During Oil Price Shocks', p. 90, discusses the effects of a disruption in oil supplies on the economy.

The quantity of capital and labour (and other inputs) used in production does not completely determine the amount of output produced. Equally important is how effectively these factors are used. For the same stocks of capital and labour, an economy with superior technologies and management practices, for example, will produce more output than an economy without those strengths.

The effectiveness with which capital and labour are used may be summarized by a relationship called the production function. The **production function** is a mathematical expression relating the amount of output produced to quantities of capital and labour utilized. A convenient way to write the production function is

$$Y = AF(K, N) \tag{3.1}$$

where

Y = real output produced in a given period of time;
A = a number measuring overall productivity;
K = the capital stock, or quantity of capital used in the period;
N = the number of workers employed in the period;
F = a function relating output Y to capital K and labour N.

The production function in equation (3.1) applies both to an economy as a whole (where Y, K, and N refer to the economy's output, capital stock, and number of workers) and to an individual firm, in which case Y, K, and N refer to the firm's output, capital, and number of workers.

According to equation (3.1), the amount of output Y that an economy (or firm) can produce during any period of time depends on the size of the capital stock K and the number of workers N. The symbol A in equation (3.1), which multiplies the function $F(K, N)$, is a measure of the overall effectiveness with which capital and labour are used. We refer to A as total factor productivity, or simply productivity. Note that, for any values of capital and labour, an increase in productivity A of, say, 10% implies a 10% increase in the amount of output that can be produced. Thus increases in productivity A correspond to improvements in production technology or to any other change in the economy that allows capital and labour to be utilized more effectively.

APPLICATION

The Production Function of an Economy and Productivity Growth

Empirical studies show that the relationship between output and inputs in many European economies is described reasonably well by the following production function:[1]

$$Y = AK^{0.3}N^{0.7} \tag{3.2}$$

The production function in equation (3.2) is a specific example of the general production function in equation (3.1), in which we set the general function $F(K, N)$ equal to $K^{0.3}N^{0.7}$. (Note that this production function contains exponents; if you need to review the properties of exponents, see Appendix A, Section A.6.)

Equation (3.2) shows how output Y relates to the use of factors of production, capital K and labour N, and to productivity A. Table 3.1 presents

---

1. This type of production function is called a Cobb–Douglas production function. Cobb–Douglas production functions take the form $Y = AK^aN^{1-a}$, where $0 < a < 1$. Under certain conditions, the parameter a in the Cobb–Douglas production function corresponds to the share of income received by owners of capital, whereas labour receives a share of income equal to $1 - a$. Thus observing the actual shares of income received by capital and labour provides a way of estimating the parameter a.

data on these variables for the UK economy since 1980. Columns (1), (2), and (3) show output (real GDP), capital stock, and labour for each year. Real GDP and the capital stock are measured in billions of 1990 pounds, and labour is measured in millions of employed workers. Column (4) shows the UK economy's productivity for each year.

Output, capital, and labour in Table 3.1 are measured directly, but there is no way to measure productivity directly. Instead, the productivity index A shown in column (4) is measured indirectly by assigning to A the value necessary to satisfy equation (3.2). Specifically, for each year A is determined by the formula $A = Y/(K^{0.3}N^{0.7})$, which is just another way of writing equation (3.2). In 1994, for example, Table 3.1 reports that $Y = 570.72$, $K = 973.46$, and $N = 21.660$; therefore the value of A for 1994 is $570.72/[(973.46)^{0.3}(21.660)^{0.7}]$, or $A = 8.41$. Calculating productivity in this way ensures that the production function relationship, equation (3.2), is satisfied exactly for each year.

The levels of the productivity index A reported in Table 3.1 depend on the units in which output, capital, and labour are measured – for example, the values of A would change if we measured workers in thousands rather than millions – and thus are hard to interpret. In contrast, the year-to-year growth rates of the productivity measure shown in column (5) are units-free and are therefore easier to work with. A close look at the productivity growth rates shown in Table 3.1 emphasizes two points.

Table 3.1   The Production Function of the United Kingdom, 1980–95

Year	(1) Real GDP, Y (billions of 1990 pounds)	(2) Capital, K (billions of 1990 pounds)	(3) Labour, N (millions of workers)	(4) Total Factor Productivity, A[a]	(5) Growth in Total Factor Productivity (% Change in A)
1980	423.49	1095.0	22.991	5.77	
1981	418.03	1044.1	21.892	5.99	3.8
1982	425.25	990.2	21.414	6.29	5.0
1983	440.89	968.7	21.067	6.64	5.6
1984	451.13	967.3	21.238	6.76	1.8
1985	468.07	968.7	21.423	6.96	3.0
1986	488.12	996.3	21.387	7.21	3.6
1987	511.62	1020.2	21.584	7.46	3.5
1988	537.22	1069.6	22.258	7.55	1.2
1989	548.94	1123.9	22.661	7.51	–0.5
1990	551.12	1157.0	22.918	7.42	–1.2
1991	540.31	989.76	22.262	7.77	4.7
1992	537.45	937.80	21.938	7.94	2.2
1993	549.59	930.14	21.629	8.22	3.5
1994	570.72	973.46	21.660	8.41	2.3
1995	584.34	1018.65	21.984	8.41	0.0

[a] Total factor productivity is calculated by the formula $A = Y/(K^{0.3}N^{0.7})$.

Sources: Y is in billions of 1990 pounds from *Economic Trends: Annual Supplement 1997*, Table 1.3; K is in constant-cost net stock of fixed private non-residential capital in billions of 1990 pounds from *UK National Accounts, The Blue Book* (various years) Table 14.7; N is the number of employees in employment from *Economic Trends, Annual Supplement 1997*, Table 3.2..

3.1 How Much Does the Economy Produce?
The Production Function

7 1

First, productivity growth can vary sharply from year to year. Most strikingly, productivity growth in the United Kingdom was low in 1984 and was negative in 1989 and 1990. In many countries, productivity normally falls in recessions and rises in recoveries, although this relationship is relatively weak in the UK. Explanations for the behaviour of productivity over the business cycle are controversial and we return to this issue in Part III of this book, which is devoted to business cycles.

Second, since 1980, productivity growth in the UK has been relatively strong, averaging more than 2%. This result is better than the performance of the 1970s, when productivity growth was about 0.5% per year, and as good as the 1960s. This trend is exceptional in Europe with most European countries having experienced a general slowdown in productivity growth since the 1960s. Chapter 6 discusses in greater detail these trends and the consequences they have for living standards.

The Shape of the Production Function

The production function in equation (3.1) can be shown graphically. The easiest way to graph it is to hold one of the two factors of production, either capital or labour, constant and then graph the relationship between output and the other factor.[2] Suppose that we use the UK production function for the year 1991 and hold labour N at its actual 1991 value of 22.262 million workers (see Table 3.1). We also use the actual 1991 value of 7.77 for A. The production function (equation 3.2) becomes

$$Y = AK^{0.3}N^{0.7} = (7.77)(K^{0.3})(22.262^{0.7}) = 68.19K^{0.3}$$

This relationship is graphed in Figure 3.1, with capital stock K on the horizontal axis and output Y on the vertical axis. With labour and productivity held at their 1991 values, the graph shows the amount of output that could have been produced in that year for any value of the capital stock. Point A on the graph shows the situation that actually occurred in 1991: the value of the capital stock (£989.76 billion) appears on the horizontal axis, and the value of real GDP (£540.31 billion) appears on the vertical axis.

The production function graphed in Figure 3.1 shares two properties with most production functions:

1. *The production function slopes upward from left to right.* The slope of the production function tells us that, as the capital stock increases, more output can be produced.

2. *The slope of the production function becomes flatter from left to right.* This property implies that, although more capital always leads to more output, it does so at a decreasing rate.

Before discussing the economics behind the second property of the production function, we can illustrate it numerically using Figure 3.1. Suppose that we are initially at point B, where the capital stock is £500 billion. Adding £100 billion in capital moves us to point C, where the capital stock is £600

---

2. To show the relationship among output and both factors of production simultaneously would require a three-dimensional graph.

Figure 3.1
The production function relating output and capital
This production function shows how much output the UK economy could produce for each level of UK capital stock, holding UK labour and productivity at 1991 levels. Point *A* corresponds to the actual 1991 output and capital stock. The production function has diminishing marginal productivity of capital: Raising the capital stock by £100 billion in order to move from point *B* to point *C* raises output by £24.73 billion, but adding another £100 billion in capital to go from point *C* to point *D* increases output by only £21.99 billion.

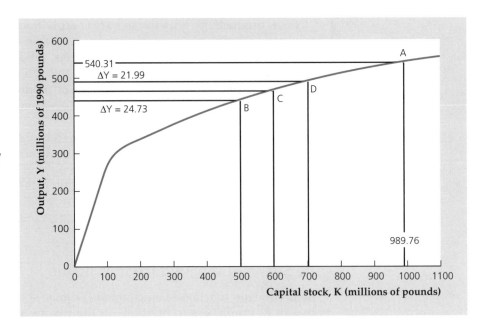

billion. How much extra output has this expansion in capital provided? The difference in output between points *B* and *C* is £24.73 billion (£464.69 billion output at point *C* minus £439.96 million output at point *B*). This extra £24.73 billion in output is the benefit from raising the capital stock from £500 billion to £600 billion, with productivity and employment held constant.

Now suppose that, starting at *C*, we add another £100 billion of capital. This new addition of capital takes us to *D*, where the capital stock is £700 billion. The difference in output between *C* and *D* is only £21.99 billion (£486.68 billion output at point *D* minus £464.69 million output at point *C*), which is less than the £24.73 billion increase in output between *B* and *C*. Thus, although the second £100 billion of extra capital raises total output, it does so by less than did the first £100 billion of extra capital. This result illustrates that the production function rises less steeply between points *C* and *D* than between points *B* and *C*.

The Marginal Product of Capital. The two properties of the production function are closely related to a concept known as the marginal product of capital. To understand this concept, let's suppose that we start from some given capital stock *K* and increase the capital stock by some amount ΔK (other factors held constant). This increase in capital would cause output *Y* to increase by some amount ΔY. The **marginal product of capital**, or **MPK**, is the increase in output produced resulting from a one-unit increase in the capital stock. Because ΔK additional units of capital permit the production of ΔY additional units of output, the amount of additional output produced per additional unit of capital is $\Delta Y/\Delta K$. Thus the marginal product of capital is $\Delta Y/\Delta K$.

The marginal product of capital $\Delta Y/\Delta K$ is the change in the variable on the vertical axis of the production function graph (ΔY) divided by the change in the variable on the horizontal axis (ΔK), which you might recognize as a slope.[3] For small increases in the capital stock, the *MPK* can be measured by the slope of a line drawn at a tangent to the production function. Figure 3.2 illustrates this way of measuring the *MPK*. When the capital stock is 500, for example, the *MPK* equals the slope of the line tangent to the production function at point *B*.[4] We can use the concept of the marginal product of capital to restate the two properties of production functions listed earlier.

1. *The marginal product of capital is positive.* Whenever the capital stock is increased, more output can be produced. Because the marginal product of capital is positive, the production function slopes upward from left to right.

2. *The marginal product of capital declines as the capital stock is increased.* Because the marginal product of capital is the slope of the production function, the slope of the production function decreases as the capital stock is increased. As Figure 3.2 shows, the slope of the production function at point *D*, where the capital stock is 700, is smaller than the slope at point *B*, where the capital stock is 500. Thus the production function becomes flatter from left to right.

The tendency for the marginal product of capital to decline as the amount of capital in use increases is called the **diminishing marginal productivity** of capital. The economic reason for diminishing marginal productivity of capital is as follows: when the capital stock is low, there are many workers for each machine, and the benefits of increasing capital further are great; but when the capital stock is high, workers already have plenty of capital to work with, and

---

3. For definitions and a discussion of slopes of lines and curves, see Appendix A, Section A.2.
4. We often refer to the slope of the line tangent to the production function at a given point as simply the slope of the production function at that point, for short.

Figure 3.2
The production function and the marginal product of capital
The marginal product of capital (*MPK*) at any point can be measured as the slope of the line tangent to the production function at that point. Because the slope of the line tangent to the production function at point *B* is greater than the slope of the line tangent to the production function at point *D*, we know that the *MPK* is greater at *B* than at *D*. At higher levels of capital stock, the *MPK* is lower, reflecting diminishing marginal productivity of capital.

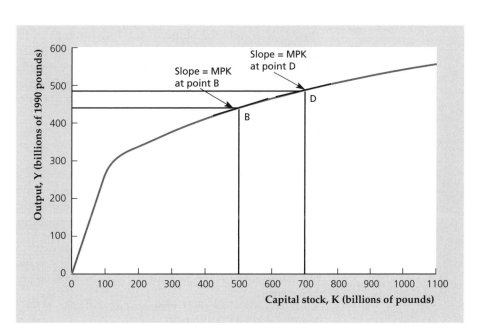

little benefit is to be gained from expanding capital further. For example, in a secretarial pool in which there are many more secretaries than word processors, each word processor is constantly being utilized and secretaries must waste time waiting for a free machine. In this situation, the benefits in terms of increased output of adding extra word processors are high. However, if there are already as many word processors as secretaries, so that word processors are often idle and there is no waiting for a machine to become available, little additional output can be obtained by adding yet another word processor.

The Marginal Product of Labour. In Figures 3.1 and 3.2 we graphed the relationship between output and capital implied by the 1991 UK production function, holding constant the amount of labour. Similarly, we can look at the relationship between output and labour, holding constant the quantity of capital. Suppose that we fix capital K at its actual 1991 value of £989.76 billion and hold productivity A at its actual 1991 value of 7.77 (see Table 3.1). The production function (equation 3.2) becomes

$$Y = AK^{0.3}N^{0.7} = (7.77)(989.76^{0.3})(N^{0.7}) = 61.53N^{0.7}$$

This relationship is shown graphically in Figure 3.3. Point A, where $N = 22.262$ million workers and $Y = $ £540.31 billion, corresponds to the actual 1991 values.

The production function relating output and labour looks generally the same as the production function relating output and capital.[5] As in the case of capital, increases in the number of workers raise output but do so at a diminishing rate. Thus the principle of diminishing marginal productivity also applies to labour, and for similar reasons: the greater the number of workers already using a fixed amount of capital and other inputs, the smaller the benefit (in terms of increased output) of adding even more workers.

The **marginal product of labour**, or **MPN**, is the additional output produced by each additional unit of labour, $\Delta Y / \Delta N$. As with the marginal product of capital, for small increases in employment the MPN can be measured by the slope of the line tangent to a production function that relates output and labour. In Figure 3.3, when employment equals 5 million workers, the MPN equals the slope of the line tangent to the production function at point B; and when employment is 15 million workers, the MPN is the slope of the line that touches the production function at point C. Because of the diminishing marginal productivity of labour, the slope of the production function relating output to labour is greater at B than at C, and the production function flattens from left to right.

Supply Shocks

The production function of an economy does not usually remain fixed over time. Economists use the term **supply shock** – or, sometimes, productivity shock – to refer to a change in an economy's production function.[6] A positive, or beneficial, supply shock raises the amount of output that can be produced

---

5. Because N is raised to the power of 0.7 but K is raised to the power of 0.3, the production function relating output and labour is not as sharply bowed as the production function relating output and capital.

6. The term 'shock' is a slight misnomer. Not all changes in the production function are sharp or unpredictable, although many are.

3.1 How Much Does the Economy Produce?
The Production Function

75

Figure 3.3
The production function and the marginal product of labour
This production function shows how much output the UK economy could produce at each level of employment (labour input), holding productivity and the capital stock constant at 1991 levels. Point *A* corresponds to actual 1991 output and employment. The marginal product of labour (*MPN*) at any point is measured as the slope of the line tangent to the production function at that point. The *MPN* is lower at higher levels of employment, reflecting diminishing marginal productivity of labour.

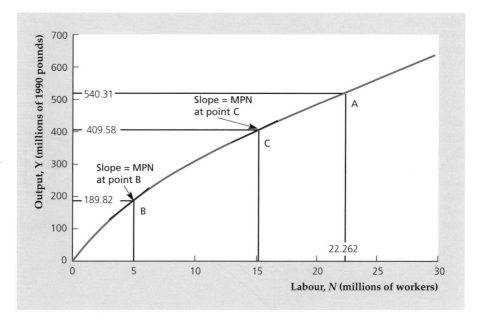

for given quantities of capital and labour. A negative, or adverse, supply shock lowers the amount of output that can be produced for each capital–labour combination.

Real-world examples of supply shocks include changes in the weather, such as a drought or an unusually cold winter; inventions or innovations in management techniques that improve efficiency, such as minicomputers or statistical analysis in quality control; and changes in government regulations, such as anti-pollution laws, that affect the technologies or production methods used. Also included in the category of supply shocks are changes in the supplies of factors of production *other than capital and labour* that affect the amount that can be produced.

Figure 3.4 shows the effects of an adverse supply shock on the production function relating output and labour. The negative supply shock shifts the production function downward so that less output can be produced for specific quantities of labour and capital. In addition, the supply shock shown reduces the slope of the production function so that the output gains from adding a worker (the marginal product of labour) are lower at every level of employment.[7] Similarly, a beneficial supply shock makes possible the production of more output with given quantities of capital and labour and thus shifts the production function upward.[8]

---

7. Logically, an adverse supply shock need not always reduce the marginal products of labour and capital: for example, the production function could make a parallel downward shift. However, thinking of an adverse supply shock reducing marginal products as being the normal case seems reasonable. A shift of the production function like that shown in Figure 3.4 would occur if there were a decline in total factor productivity *A*, for example.
8. The effects of supply shocks on the production function relating output and capital would be similar.

Figure 3.4
An adverse supply shock that lowers the *MPN*
An adverse supply shock is a downward shift of the production function. For any level of labour, the amount of output that can be produced is now less than before. The adverse shock reduces the slope of the production function at every level of employment.

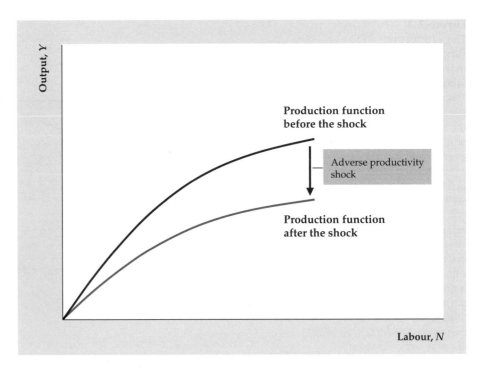

3.2   THE DEMAND FOR LABOUR

We have shown that the amount of output produced by a country, or by a firm, depends both on productivity and the quantities of inputs used in the production process. In Section 3.1 our focus was on productivity – its measurement and factors such as supply shocks that cause it to change. In this section we examine what determines the quantities of inputs that producers use. Recall that the two most important inputs are capital and labour. The capital stock in an economy changes over time as a result of investment by firms and the scrapping of worn-out or obsolete capital. However, because the capital stock is long-lived and has been built up over many years, new investment and the scrapping of old capital only slowly have a significant effect on the overall quantity of capital available. Thus, for analyses spanning only a few quarters or years, economists often treat the economy's capital stock as fixed. For now we follow this practice and assume a fixed capital stock. In taking up long-term economic growth in Chapter 6, we drop this assumption and examine how the capital stock evolves over time.

In contrast to the amount of capital, the amount of labour employed in the economy can change fairly quickly. For example, firms may lay off workers or ask them to work overtime without much notice. Workers may quit or decide to enter the work force quickly. Thus year-to-year changes in production can often be traced to changes in employment. To explain why employment changes, for the remainder of this chapter we focus on how the labour market works, using a supply and demand approach. In this section we look at labour demand, and in Section 3.3 we discuss factors affecting labour supply.

As a step toward understanding the overall demand for labour in the economy we consider how an individual firm decides how many workers to employ. To keep things simple for the time being, we make the following assumptions:

1. *Workers are all alike.* We ignore differences in workers' aptitudes, skills, ambition, and so on.

2. *Firms view the wage of the workers they hire as being determined in a competitive labour market and not set by the firms themselves.* For example, a competitive firm in Liverpool that wants to hire machinists knows that it must pay the going local wage for machinists if it wants to attract qualified workers. The firm then decides how many machinists to employ.

3. *In making the decision about how many workers to employ, a firm's goal is to earn the highest possible level of profit* (the value of its output minus its costs of production, including taxes). The firm will demand the amount of labour that maximizes its profit.

To work out the profit-maximizing amount of labour, the firm must compare the costs and benefits of hiring each additional worker. The cost of an extra worker is the worker's wage, and the benefit of an extra worker is the value of the additional goods or services the worker produces. As long as the benefits of additional labour exceed the costs, hiring more labour will increase the firm's profits. The firm will continue to hire additional labour until the benefit of an extra worker (the value of extra goods or services produced) equals the cost (the wage).

The Marginal Product of Labour and Labour Demand: An Example

Let's make the discussion of labour demand more concrete by looking at Dandy Dogs, a small business that grooms dogs. Dandy Dogs uses both capital, such as clippers, baths, and brushes, and labour to produce its output of groomed dogs.

The production function that applies to Dandy Dogs appears in Table 3.2. For given levels of productivity and the capital stock, it shows how Dandy Dogs' daily output of groomed dogs, column (2), depends on the number of workers employed, column (1). The more workers Dandy Dogs has, the greater its daily output is.

The *MPN* of each worker at Dandy Dogs is shown in column (3). Employing the first worker raises Dandy Dogs' output from 0 to 11, so the *MPN* of the first worker is 11. Employing the second worker raises Dandy Dogs' output from 11 to 20, an increase of 9, so the *MPN* of the second worker is 9; and so on. Column (3) also shows that, as the number of workers at Dandy Dogs increases, the *MPN* falls so that labour at Dandy Dogs has diminishing marginal productivity. The more workers there are on the job, the more they must share the fixed amount of capital (baths, clippers, brushes), and the less benefit there is to adding yet another worker.

The marginal product of labour measures the benefit of employing an additional worker in terms of the extra *output* produced. A related concept, the **marginal revenue product of labour**, or *MRPN*, measures the benefit of

Table 3.2 Dandy Dogs' Production Function

(1) Number of Workers, N	(2) Number of Dogs Groomed, Y	(3) Marginal Product of Labour, MPN	(4) Marginal Revenue Product of Labour, $MRPN = MPN \times P$ (when $P = £10$ per grooming)
0	0		
		11	£110
1	11		
		9	£90
2	20		
		7	£70
3	27		
		5	£50
4	32		
		3	£30
5	35		
		1	£10
6	36		

employing an additional worker in terms of the extra *revenue* produced. To calculate the *MRPN*, we need to know the price of the firm's output. If Dandy Dogs receives £10 for each dog it grooms, the *MRPN* of the first worker is £110 per day (11 additional dogs groomed per day at £10 per grooming). More generally, the marginal revenue product of an additional worker equals the price of the firm's output, P, times the extra output gained by adding the worker, *MPN*:

$$MRPN = P \times MPN \qquad (3.3)$$

At Dandy Dogs the price of output P is £10 per grooming, so the *MRPN* of each worker, column (4), equals the *MPN* of the worker, column (3), multiplied by £10.

Now suppose that the wage W that Dandy Dogs must pay to attract qualified workers is £80 per day. (We refer to the wage W, when measured in the conventional way in terms of today's pounds, as the *nominal* wage.) How many workers should Dandy Dogs employ in order to maximize its profits? To answer this question, Dandy Dogs compares the benefits and costs of employing each additional worker. The benefit of employing an additional worker, in pounds per day, is the worker's marginal revenue product *MRPN*. The cost of an additional worker, in pounds per day, is the nominal daily wage W.

Table 3.2 shows that the *MRPN* of the first worker is £110 per day, which exceeds the daily wage of £80, so employing the first worker is profitable for Dandy Dogs. Adding a second worker increases Dandy Dogs' profit as well because the *MRPN* of the second worker (£90 per day) also exceeds the daily wage. However, employing a third worker reduces Dandy Dogs' profit because the third worker's *MRPN* of £70 per day is less than the £80 daily wage. Therefore Dandy Dogs' profit-maximizing level of employment at

£80/day – equivalently, the quantity of labour demanded by Dandy Dogs – is two workers.

In finding the quantity of labour demanded by Dandy Dogs, we measured the benefits and costs of an extra worker in nominal, or pounds, terms. If we measured the benefits and costs of an extra worker in real terms, the results would be the same. In real terms the benefit to Dandy Dogs of an extra worker is the number of extra groomings that the extra worker provides, which is the marginal product of labour, MPN. The real cost of adding another worker is the **real wage**, which is the wage measured in terms of units of output. Algebraically, the real wage, w, equals the nominal wage, W, divided by the price of output, P.

In this example the nominal wage W is £80 per day and the price of output P is £10 per grooming, so the real wage w equals (£80 per day)/(£10 per grooming), or 8 groomings per day. To find the profit-maximizing level of employment, Dandy Dogs compares this real cost of an additional worker with the real benefit of an additional worker, the MPN. The MPN of the first worker is 11 groomings per day, which exceeds the real wage of 8 groomings per day, so employing this worker is profitable. The second worker also should be hired, as the second worker's MPN of 9 groomings per day also exceeds the real wage of 8 groomings per day. However, a third worker should not be hired, as the third worker's MPN of 7 groomings per day is less than the real wage. The quantity of labour demanded by Dandy Dogs is therefore two workers, which is the same result we got when we compared costs and benefits in nominal terms.

This example shows that when the benefit of an additional worker exceeds the cost of an additional worker, the firm should increase employment in order to maximize profits. Similarly, if at the firm's current employment level the benefit of the last worker employed is less than the cost of the worker, the firm should reduce employment. Summary table 2 compares benefits and costs of additional labour in both real and nominal terms. In the choice of the profit-maximizing level of employment, comparison of benefits and costs in real or nominal terms is equally valid.

SUMMARY 2	To maximize profits, the firm should:	Increase employment if	Decrease employment if
Comparing the Benefits and Costs of Changing the Amount of Labour	Real terms	$MPN > w$ $(MPN > W/P)$	$MPN < w$ $(MPN < W/P)$
	Nominal terms	$P \times MPN > W$ $(MRPN > W)$	$P \times MPN < W$ $(MRPN < W)$

MPN = marginal product of labour
P = price of output
$MRPN$ = marginal revenue product of labour = $P \times MPN$
W = nominal wage
w = real wage = W/P

A Change in the Wage

Dandy Dogs' decision to employ two workers was based on a nominal wage of £80 per day. Now suppose that for some reason the nominal wage needed to attract qualified workers drops to £60 per day. How will the reduction in the nominal wage affect the number of workers that Dandy Dogs wants to employ?

To find the answer, we can compare costs and benefits in either nominal or real terms. Let's make the comparison in real terms. If the nominal wage drops to £60 per day while the price of groomings remains at £10, the real wage falls to (£60 per day)/(£10 per grooming), or 6 groomings per day. Column (3) of Table 3.2 shows that the *MPN* of the third worker is 7 groomings per day, which is now greater than the real wage. Thus, at the lower wage, expanding the quantity of labour demanded from two to three workers is profitable for Dandy Dogs. However, the firm will not hire a fourth worker because the *MPN* of the fourth worker (5 groomings per day) is less than the new real wage (6 groomings per day).

This example illustrates a general point about the effect of the real wage on labour demand: All else being equal, *a decrease in the real wage raises the amount of labour demanded.* Similarly, *an increase in the real wage decreases the amount of labour demanded.*

The Marginal Product of Labour and the Labour Demand Curve

Using Dandy Dogs as an example, we showed the negative relationship between the real wage and the quantity of labour that a firm demands. Figure 3.5 shows in more general terms how the link between the real wage and the quantity of labour demanded is determined. The amount of labour N is on the horizontal axis. The *MPN* and the real wage, both of which are measured in goods per unit of labour, are on the vertical axis. The downward-sloping curve is the *MPN* curve; it relates the marginal product of labour, *MPN*, to the amount of labour employed by the firm, N. The *MPN* curve slopes downward because of the diminishing marginal productivity of labour. The horizontal line represents the real wage faced by firms in the labour market, which the firms take as given. Here, the real wage is w^*.

For any real wage w^*, the amount of labour that yields the highest profit (and therefore the amount of labour demanded) is determined at point A, the intersection of the real-wage line and the *MPN* curve. At A the quantity of labour demanded is N^*. Why is N^* a firm's profit-maximizing level of labour input? At employment levels of less than N^*, the marginal product of labour exceeds the real wage (the *MPN* curve lies above the real-wage line); thus, if the firm's employment is initially less than N^*, it can increase its profit by expanding the amount of labour it uses. Similarly, if the firm's employment is initially greater than N^*, the marginal product of labour is less than the real wage ($MPN < w^*$) and the firm can raise profits by reducing employment. Only when employment equals N^* will the firm be satisfied with the number of workers it has. More generally, for any real wage, the profit-maximizing amount of labour input – labour demanded – corresponds to the point at which the *MPN* curve and the real-wage line intersect.

Figure 3.5
The determination of labour demand
The amount of labour demanded is determined by locating the point on the *MPN* curve at which the *MPN* equals the real wage rate; the amount of labour corresponding to that point is the amount of labour demanded. For example, when the real wage is *w**, the *MPN* equals the real wage at point *A* and the quantity of labour demanded is *N**. The labour demand curve, *ND*, shows the amount of labour demanded at each level of the real wage. The labour demand curve is identical to the *MPN* curve.

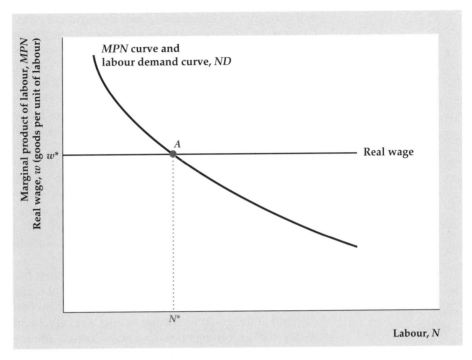

The graph of the relationship between the amount of labour demanded by a firm and the real wage that the firm faces is called the *labour demand curve*. Because the *MPN* curve also shows the amount of labour demanded at any real wage, *the labour demand curve is the same as the MPN curve*, except that the vertical axis measures the real wage for the labour demand curve and measures the marginal product of labour for the *MPN* curve.[9] Like the *MPN* curve, the labour demand curve slopes downward, indicating that the quantity of labour demanded falls as the real wage rises.

This labour demand curve is more general than that in the example of Dandy Dogs in a couple of ways that are worth mentioning. First, we referred to the demand for labour and not specifically to the demand for workers, as in Dandy Dogs example. In general, labour *N* can be measured in various ways – for example, as total hours worked, total weeks worked, or the number of employees – depending on the application. Second, although we assumed in the example that Dandy Dogs had to hire a whole number of workers, the labour demand curve shown in Figure 3.5 allows labour *N* to have any positive value, whole or fractional. Allowing *N* to take any value is sensible because people may work fractions of an hour.

Factors that Shift the Labour Demand Curve

Because the labour demand curve shows the relation between the real wage and the amount of labour that firms want to employ, changes in the real wage are represented as movements *along* the labour demand curve. Changes in the

---

9. Recall that the real wage and the *MPN* are measured in the same units, goods per unit of labour.

real wage do not cause the labour demand curve to shift. The labour demand curve shifts in response to factors that change the amount of labour that firms want to employ *at any given level of the real wage*. For example, we showed earlier in this chapter that beneficial or positive supply shocks are likely to increase the *MPN* at all levels of labour input, and adverse or negative supply shocks are likely to reduce the *MPN* at all levels of labour input. Thus a beneficial supply shock shifts the *MPN* curve upward and to the right and raises the quantity of labour demanded at any given real wage; an adverse supply shock does the reverse.

The effect of a supply shock on Dandy Dogs' demand for labour can be illustrated by imagining that the proprietor of Dandy Dogs discovers that playing jazz music soothes the dogs. It makes them more cooperative and doubles the number of groomings per day that the same number of workers can produce. This technological improvement gives Dandy Dogs a new production function, as described in Table 3.3. Note that doubling total output doubles the *MPN* at each employment level.

Dandy Dogs demanded two workers when faced with the original production function (Table 3.2) and a real wage of 8 groomings per day. Table 3.3 shows that the productivity improvement increases Dandy Dogs' labour demand at the given real wage to four workers, because the *MPN* of the fourth worker (10 groomings per day) now exceeds the real wage. Dandy Dogs will not hire a fifth worker, however, because this worker's *MPN* (6 groomings per day) is less than the real wage.

The effect of a beneficial supply shock on a labour demand curve is shown in Figure 3.6. The shock causes the *MPN* to increase at any level of labour

Table 3.3   Dandy Dogs' Production Function After a Beneficial Productivity Shock

(1) Number of Workers, *N*	(2) Number of Dogs Groomed, *Y*	(3) Marginal Product of Labour, *MPN*	(4) Marginal Revenue Product of Labour, *MRPN* = *MPN* × *P* (when *P* = £10 per grooming)
0	0		
		22	£220
1	22		
		18	£180
2	40		
		14	£140
3	54		
		10	£100
4	64		
		6	$60
5	70		
		2	$20
6	72		

input, so the *MPN* curve shifts upward and to the right. Because the *MPN* and labour demand curves are identical, the labour demand curve also shifts upward and to the right, from ND^1 to ND^2 in Fig. 3.6. When the labour demand curve is ND^2, the firm hires more workers at any real wage level than when the labour demand curve is ND^1. Thus worker productivity and the amount of labour demanded are closely linked.

Another factor that may affect labour demand is the size of the capital stock. Generally, an increase in the capital stock K – by giving each worker more machines or equipment to work with – raises workers' productivity and increases the *MPN* at any level of labour. Hence an increase in the capital stock will cause the labour demand curve to shift upward and to the right, raising the amount of labour that a firm demands at any particular real wage.[10]

Aggregate Labour Demand

So far we have focused on the demand for labour by an individual firm, such as Dandy Dogs. For macroeconomic analysis, however, we usually work with the concept of the **aggregate demand for labour**, or the sum of the labour demands of all the firms in an economy.

Because the aggregate demand for labour is the sum of firms' labour demands, the factors that determine the aggregate demand for labour are the same as for an individual firm. Thus the aggregate labour demand curve looks the same as the labour demand curve for an individual firm (Figure 3.5). Like the firm's labour demand curve, the aggregate labour demand curve slopes

---

10. An increase in the capital stock may reduce the demand for labour if the new capital substitutes for the use of labour. For example, the installation of automatic elevators reduced the marginal product of elevator operators and thus the demand for these workers.

Figure 3.6
The effect of a beneficial supply shock on labour demand
A beneficial supply shock that raises the *MPN* at every level of labour shifts the *MPN* curve upward and to the right. Because the labour demand curve is identical to the *MPN* curve, the labour demand curve shifts upward and to the right from ND^1 to ND^2. For any real wage, firms demand more labour after a beneficial supply shock.

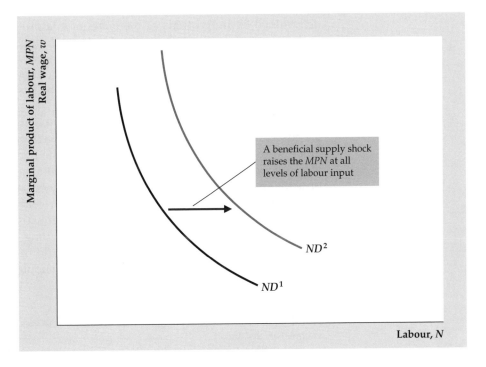

SUMMARY 3	An increase in	Causes the labour demand curve to shift	Reason
Factors that Shift the Aggregate Labour Demand Curve	Productivity	Right	Beneficial supply shock increases *MPN* and shifts *MPN* curve up and to the right.
	Capital stock	Right	Higher capital stock increases *MPN* and shifts *MPN* curve up and to the right.

downward, showing that an increase in the economy-wide real wage reduces the total amount of labour that firms want to use. Similarly, a beneficial supply shock or an increase in the aggregate capital stock shifts the aggregate labour demand curve upward and to the right; an adverse supply shock or a drop in the aggregate capital stock shifts it downward and to the left. The factors affecting aggregate labour demand are listed for convenience in Summary table 3.

3.3 THE SUPPLY OF LABOUR

The demand for labour is determined by firms, but the supply of labour is determined by individuals or members of a family making a joint decision. Each person of working age must decide how much (if at all) to work in the wage-paying sector of the economy versus non-wage-paying alternatives, such as taking care of the home and children, going to school, or being retired. The **aggregate supply of labour** is the sum of the labour supplied by everyone in the economy.

Recall that, in determining how much labour to demand, firms compare the costs and benefits of hiring additional workers. Similarly, in deciding how much to work, an individual should weigh the benefits against the costs of working. Beyond any psychological satisfaction gained from having a job, the principal benefit of working is the income earned, which can be used to buy necessities and luxuries. The principal cost of working is that it involves time and effort that are no longer available for other activities. Economists use the term **leisure**[11] for all off-the-job activities, including eating, sleeping, working around the house, spending time with family and friends, and so on. To make themselves as well off as possible, individuals should choose to supply labour

---

11. The term 'leisure' does not imply that all off-the-job activities (housework or schoolwork, for example) are 'leisurely'!

up to the point at which the income obtained from working an extra hour just makes up for the extra hour of leisure they have to forgo.

We discuss the details of the labour supply decision in Chapter 8. Here we present a general discussion that begins with the relationship between the real wage and labour supply.

The Labour Supply Curve

The economic benefit that people derive from working is the real value of the income that they receive for each unit of time spent at work, which is the same as the real wage. Recall that the real wage w equals the nominal wage W divided by the price level P. Thus, if the nominal wage is £12/hour and the price level is £3/good, the real wage is 4 goods/hour. In this case, the worker earns wages with purchasing power equal to 4 goods by working an additional hour.

In discussing labour supply, we distinguish between the *current* real wage (which the worker can earn by working today) and the *expected future* real wage (which the worker expects to earn at some future date). Labour supply reacts differently to changes in the current real wage and the expected future real wage. We consider first the effect of the current real wage.

When the current real wage rises, working (instead of enjoying leisure) becomes more attractive. For example, if shelf stacking pays very little in real terms, a student may prefer going to the seaside to taking a summer job at the supermarket. But if the supermarket pays a high real wage – high enough, say, to allow the student to buy a used car by the beginning of the autumn term – the student may choose to work. Thus increases in the current real wage should raise the quantity of labour supplied.

The *labour supply curve* of an individual worker relates the amount of labour supplied to the current real wage, with other factors (including the expected future real wage) held constant. Figure 3.7 is a graph of a typical labour supply curve. The current real wage is measured on the vertical axis, and the amount of labour supplied is measured on the horizontal axis. The labour supply curve slopes upward because an increase in the current real wage leads to an increase in the amount of labour supplied.

Factors that Shift the Labour Supply Curve

Any factor that changes the amount of labour supplied at a given level of the current real wage shifts the labour supply curve. Let's look at the effects on labour supply of changes in wealth and in the expected future real wage.

Wealth. The effect of wealth on labour supply is most easily illustrated by an extreme example. A person is working two jobs to make ends meet when she learns that she has won the the top prize in the National Lottery. Although predicting exactly how the person will use the lottery winnings is impossible, she will probably no longer do two jobs and in fact may choose not to work at all. In any case, she will reduce the amount of labour she supplies. This extreme example illustrates a general point: because a person who is wealthier can afford to enjoy more leisure, an increase in wealth tends to reduce the

Figure 3.7
The labour supply curve of an individual worker
The horizontal axis shows the amount of labour that a worker will supply for any given current real wage on the vertical axis. The labour supply curve slopes upward, indicating that—with other factors including the expected future real wage held constant—an increase in the current real wage raises the amount of labour supplied.

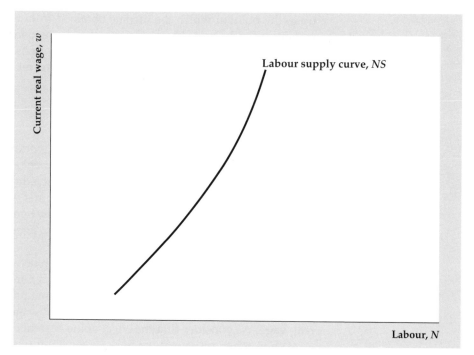

amount of labour supplied at any level of the current real wage. Thus an increase in wealth shifts the labour supply curve to the left, as in Figure 3.8.

The Expected Future Real Wage. An increase in the real wage that a worker expects to receive in the future makes that person effectively wealthier and thus reduces the amount of labour supplied at any current real wage. For example, a recent college graduate who has been promised a highly paid job starting in the autumn is less likely to take a low-paying summer job than is another graduate without such good prospects. Thus an increase in the expected future real wage causes the labour supply curve to shift to the left, as in Figure 3.8.

Aggregate Labour Supply

As we mentioned earlier, the aggregate supply of labour is the total amount of labour supplied by everyone in the economy. Just as the quantity of labour supplied by an individual rises when the person's current real wage rises, the aggregate quantity of labour supplied increases when the economy-wide real wage rises. An increase in the current economy-wide real wage raises the aggregate quantity of labour supplied for two reasons. First, when the real wage rises, people who are already working may supply even more hours – by offering to work overtime, by changing from part-time to full-time work, or by taking a second job. Second, a higher real wage may entice some people who are not currently in the labour force to decide to look for work. Because higher current real wages induce people to want to work more, the aggregate labour supply curve – which shows the relation between the aggregate amount of labour supplied and the current real wage – slopes upward.

Figure 3.8
The effect on labour supply of an increase in wealth
An increase in wealth reduces the amount of labour supplied at any real wage. Therefore, an increase in wealth causes the labour supply curve to shift to the left. Similarly, an increase in the expected future real wage, which has the effect of making the worker wealthier, reduces the amount of labour supplied at any given current real wage and shifts the labour supply curve to the left.

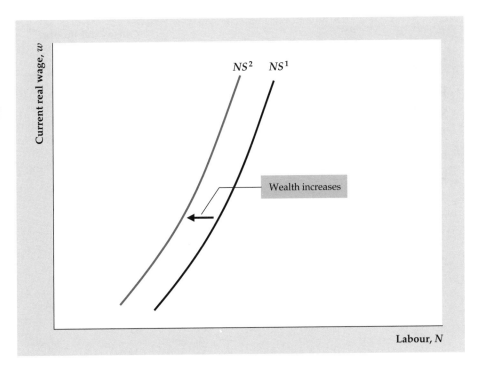

Factors other than the current real wage that change the amount of labour that people want to supply cause the aggregate labour supply curve to shift. Summary table 4 lists the factors that shift aggregate labour supply. We discussed the first two factors in the table, wealth and the expected future real wage, when we considered the individual's labour supply decision. Aggregate labour supply will also increase if the country's working-age population increases (for example, because of an increased birth rate or immigration), or if changes in the social or legal environment cause a greater proportion of the working-age population to enter the labour force (increased labour force participation). For example, evolving attitudes about the role of women in society contributed to a large increase in the number of women in labour markets across Europe during the 1970s and 1980s.

3.4 LABOUR MARKET EQUILIBRIUM

Equilibrium in the labour market requires that the aggregate quantity of labour demanded equals the aggregate quantity of labour supplied. The basic supply–demand model of the labour market introduced here (called the *classical model of the labour market*) is based on the assumption that the real wage adjusts reasonably quickly to equate labour supply and labour demand. Thus, if labour supply is less than labour demand, firms competing for scarce workers bid up the real wage, whereas if many workers are competing for relatively few jobs, the real wage will tend to fall.

SUMMARY 4	An increase in	Causes the labour supply curve to shift	Reason
Factors that Shift the Aggregate Labour Supply Curve	Wealth	Left	Increase in wealth increases amount of leisure workers can afford.
	Expected future real wage	Left	Increase in expected future real wage increases amount of leisure workers can afford.
	Working-age population	Right	Increased number of potential workers increases amount of labour supplied.
	Participation rate	Right	Increased number of people wanting to work increases amount of labour supplied.

Labour market equilibrium is represented graphically by the intersection of the aggregate labour demand curve and the aggregate labour supply curve at point E in Figure 3.9. The equilibrium level of employment, achieved after the complete adjustment of wages and prices, is known as the **full-employment level of employment**, $\overline{N}$. The corresponding market-clearing real wage is $\overline{w}$.

Factors that shift either the aggregate labour demand curve or the aggregate labour supply curve affect both the equilibrium real wage and the full-employment level of employment. An example of such a factor is a temporary adverse supply shock. A temporary adverse supply shock – because of, say, a spell of unusually bad weather – decreases the marginal product of labour at every level of employment. As Figure 3.10 shows, this decrease causes the labour demand curve to shift to the left, from ND^1 to ND^2. Because the supply shock is temporary, however, it is not expected to affect future marginal products or the future real wage, so the labour supply curve does not shift. Equilibrium in the labour market moves from point A to point B. Thus the model predicts that a temporary supply shock will lower both the current real wage (from $\overline{w}_1$ to $\overline{w}_2$) and the full-employment level of employment (from $\overline{N}_1$ to $\overline{N}_2$).

The classical supply–demand model of the labour market has the virtue of simplicity and is quite useful for studying how economic disturbances or changes in economic policy affect employment and the real wage. However, a significant drawback of this basic model is that it cannot be used to study unemployment. Because it assumes that any worker who wants to work at the equilibrium real wage can find a job, the model implies zero unemployment, which never occurs.

**Figure 3.9
Labour market equilibrium**
The quantity of labour demanded equals the quantity of labour supplied at point *E*. The equilibrium real wage is $\overline{w}$, and the corresponding equilibrium level of employment is $\overline{N}$, the full-employment level of employment.

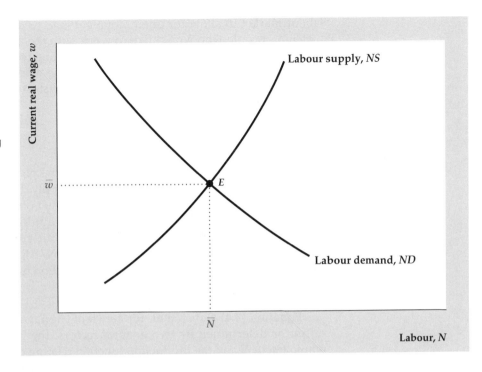

**Figure 3.10
Effects of a temporary adverse supply shock on the labour market**
An adverse supply shock that lowers the marginal product of labour (see Fig. 3.4) reduces the quantity of labour demanded at any real wage level. Thus the labour demand curve shifts left, from ND^1 to ND^2, and the labour market equilibrium moves from point *A* to point *B*. The adverse supply shock causes the real wage to fall from $\overline{w}_1$ to $\overline{w}_2$ and reduces the full-employment level of employment from $\overline{N}_1$ to $\overline{N}_2$.

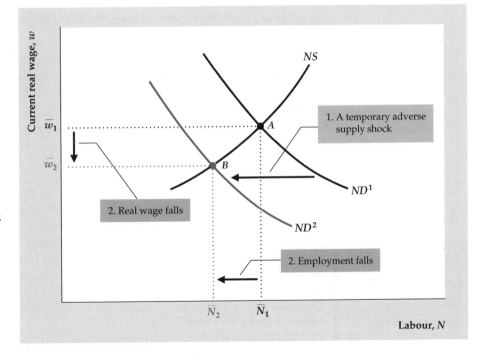

One way to get unemployment into the model is to drop the assumption that the real wage adjusts rapidly to equate supply and demand. The assumption that the real wage is slow to adjust underlies the Keynesian approach to business cycle analysis (Chapter 12). Another way to extend the model of the labour market to allow for unemployment is to recognize that the process of matching people who would like to work with the appropriate available jobs is not immediate but takes time. Because matching workers with jobs is a time-consuming process, at any particular time some workers will be without jobs. We discuss the matching process and its relationship to unemployment later in this chapter.

Full-Employment Output

By combining labour market equilibrium and the production function, we can determine how much output firms want to supply. **Full-employment output,** $\overline{Y}$, sometimes called *potential output,* is the level of output that firms in the economy supply when wages and prices have fully adjusted. Equivalently, full-employment output is the level of output supplied when aggregate employment equals its full-employment level $\overline{N}$. Algebraically, we can define full-employment output $\overline{Y}$ by using the production function (equation 3.1):

$$\overline{Y} = AF(K, \overline{N}) \qquad (3.4)$$

Equation (3.4) shows that, for constant capital stock K, full-employment output is determined by two general factors: the full-employment level of employment $\overline{N}$ and the production function relating output to employment.

Anything that changes either the full-employment level of employment $\overline{N}$ or the production function will change full-employment output $\overline{Y}$. For example, an adverse supply shock that reduces the *MPN* (Figure 3.10) works in two distinct ways to lower full-employment output:

1. The adverse supply shock lowers output directly, by reducing the quantity of output that can be produced with any fixed amounts of capital and labour. This direct effect can be thought of as a reduction in the productivity measure A in equation (3.4).

2. The adverse supply shock reduces the demand for labour and thus lowers the full-employment level of employment $\overline{N}$, as Figure 3.10 shows. A reduction in $\overline{N}$ also reduces full-employment output $\overline{Y}$, as equation (3.4) confirms.

APPLICATION

Output, Employment, and the Real Wage During Oil Price Shocks

Among the most severe supply shocks hitting European and other economies since World War II were sharp increases in the prices of oil and other energy products. Figure 3.11 shows how the price of energy paid by firms on average in Europe, measured relative to the GDP deflator (the general price level of all output) again calculated for the whole of the EU, varied during the period 1965–95. Two adverse oil price shocks stand out: one in 1973–74, when the Organization of Petroleum Exporting Countries (OPEC) first imposed an oil embargo and then greatly increased crude oil prices; and a second in 1979–80, after the Iranian revolution disrupted oil supplies. The 1979–80 oil price shock turned out to be temporary, as energy prices subsequently fell. A third increase in oil prices followed Iraq's invasion of Kuwait in August 1990. However, the 1990 shock had less of an impact on overall energy prices than the previous two oil price shocks and thus does not appear as much more than a blip in Figure 3.11.

When energy prices rise, firms cut back on energy use, implying that less output is produced at any particular levels of capital and labour. Thus an increase in energy prices is an adverse supply shock. How important were these supply shocks? James Hamilton[12] of the University of California at San Diego has found that seven of the first eight postwar recessions in the United States have been preceded, and probably caused, by oil price shocks. In an empirical study of eight major OECD countries for the period 1955–81, Michael Bruno of the Hebrew University of Jerusalem and Jeffrey Sachs of Harvard University[13] found that higher real factor prices, including higher oil prices, contributed to the slowdown in economic activity during 1973–75 and 1979–81.

Our analysis predicts that an adverse supply shock will lower labour demand, reducing employment and the real wage, as well as reducing the supply of output. In fact, many European economies went into a recession following the 1973–74, the 1979–80, and the 1990 oil shocks, with negative GDP growth. Each time the fraction of the adult population employed and the real wage fell. Care must be taken in interpreting these results because macroeconomic policies and other factors were changing at the same time; however, our model appears to account for the response to the recent oil price shocks.

12. 'Oil and the Macroeconomy since World War II', *Journal of Political Economy*, 1983, pp. 228–48.
13. *Economics of Worldwide Stagflation* (Basil Blackwell, 1985).

Figure 3.11
Relative price of energy, EU average (1965–95)
The figure shows the producer price index of fuels and related products and power (an index of energy prices paid by producers) relative to the GDP deflator. Note the impact of the 1973–74 and 1979–80 oil shocks and the decline in energy prices in the first half of the 1980s. The 1990 Iraqi invasion of Kuwait also increased this price index.

Source: Average price of petroleum (crudo) converted to index (1990 = 100) from *International Financial Statistics Yearbook 1996* and *Volume L*, June 1997, table of Commodity prices table; GDP deflator (1990 = 100) from *European Economy 1996, op cit. Table 1.1(b)*, Table 24.

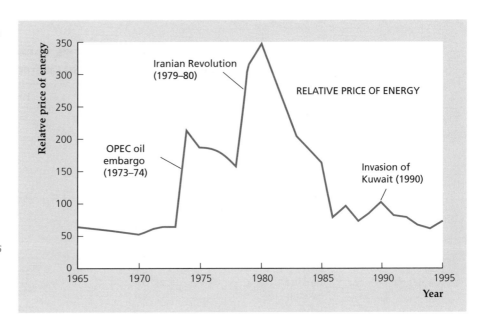

APPLICATION

Technical Change and Wage Inequality

Because many families have little income other than wage income, trends in real wages have important implications for the standard of living of a large segment of society. During the twenty-five years after World War II, real wages in all European countries grew strongly. Since about 1970, however, real wage growth has slowed considerably. This trend is illustrated in Table 3.4, which shows the growth in real wages for EU member countries for the periods 1961–70, 1971–80, and 1981–90. In the 1960s, real wages increased, on average, by 4.5% across Europe though real wage growth was especially strong among the Mediterranean countries. During the 1970–79 period real wage growth dropped to 2.9% on average with the slowdown being especially significant in Sweden and Denmark, Germany, the Netherlands, Italy and the UK. It is during the 1980s, however, that the decline in the growth of real earnings is most significant, falling to less than 1% on average for Europe as a whole.[14] The notable exception to the trend is the UK, where real earnings actually increased faster during the 1980s than during the previous decade.

A second disturbing trend that is observed in a number of European countries during the 1980s is that real wages became more unequal, with the wages of the lowest-paid workers in some countries actually falling in real terms. This disturbing trend is in sharp contrast to what was happening to real wages in Europe during the 1970s when there was a movement towards greater equality.[15] The increase in inequality was most evident in the UK and, to a lesser extent, in France and Sweden. Not all Western European countries followed this trend, however, and wage inequality in Italy, the Netherlands and Germany actually fell during the 1980s.[16]

---

14. This trend was not confined to Europe but was also observed in North America and in Japan.
15. The trends to slower and more unequal wage growth has been observed in most industrialized countries, see Steven Davis, 'Cross-Country Patterns of Change in Relative Wages' in Olivier Blanchard and Stanley Fischer (eds), *NBER Macroeconomic Annual* (MIT Press, 1992).
16. Andrew Glyn, 'The Assessment: Unemployment and Inequality', *Oxford Review of Economic Policy*, 1995, pp. 1–25.

Table 3.4 Growth in Real Wages, 1961–90 (average percentage growth)

	1961–70	1971–80	1981–90
Belgium	4.2	4.7	0.6
Denmark	3.9	1.6	0.7
Germany	4.6	2.9	0.8
Greece	6.1	4.0	1.0
Spain	7.1	4.6	0.6
France	4.9	3.5	1.0
Ireland	4.1	4.2	2.4
Italy	6.0	3.1	1.3
Luxembourg	2.5	3.9	1.1
Netherlands	5.1	3.0	0.1
Austria	4.8	3.6	1.2
Portugal	6.6	5.6	1.6
Finland	3.7	3.5	2.6
Sweden	4.1	1.6	0.7
UK	2.8	1.8	2.2
EU	4.5	2.9	0.9

Source: *European Economy*, 1996 *op cit. Table 1.1(b)*, Table 30.

The upward trend in the UK in both real wages and wage inequality is illustrated in Figure 3.12, which is drawn from a study by the OECD. It shows how real wages of different groups of British workers have changed over time. In the diagram, real wages are measured in index form with 1980 = 100. The line marked 1–10 shows the trend in real earnings of workers whose wages are in the bottom 10% of the distribution each year and the line marked 91–100 shows the trend in the average real earnings of the best-paid workers, whose wages are in the top 10% of the wage distribution. The line marked 50 shows the trend in average (median) earnings. Figure 3.12 shows that there has been an improvement in real wages since 1980 for all groups of workers, especially for women. However, the improvements in the real wage of the lowest paid has been modest when compared with that of the best-paid workers. A useful indicator of wage inequality is the ratio of the average wage of highest-paid workers (the 91–100 group) to that of the lowest-paid workers (the 1–10 group). In 1973 this ratio was 2.5 but it had risen to 3.4 by 1992.[17]

The explanations offered by most economists for both the slowdown in overall real wage growth and the increase in real wage inequality focus on the pattern of technological change. The overall slowdown in real wage growth is generally attributed to the slowdown in productivity growth over the past two decades. Because of slow productivity growth, the marginal product of labour, *MPN*, and thus labour demand, have grown slowly. Coupled with a relatively stable labour supply, slow growth in labour demand, has held down the growth of real wages. The growth in real wage inequality in the UK, on the other hand, has been associated with strong productivity growth throughout most of the 1980s (discussed in the Application, 'The Production Function of an Economy and Productivity Growth', earlier in the chapter). Chapter 6 discusses further the general slowdown in productivity growth across Europe and its implications.

Some economists link the rising inequality in real wages to the character, not the pace, of technical change. In particular, they argue that technical change during the past two decades has been *skill-biased*, meaning that it has raised the productivity of highly trained or educated workers more than that of the less skilled.[18] For example, some new manufacturing techniques rely considerably more on worker initiative and problem solving than did the traditional assembly-line approach and thus require better-skilled workers. Computerization is another development that has in many cases increased the productivity of more skilled workers while squeezing out those without the education or training to use this new tool effectively. For example, a study by

---

17. A third trend that is evident in Figure 3.12 is the relative improvement in women's wages compared to men's wages. Most explanations for this trend to greater equality in male–female earnings focus on changes in labour supply, and particularly the increased participation of women in full-time employment. While an increase in labour supply tends to lower the real wage, increased full-time job experience tends to raise the real wage by raising productivity.

18. This conclusion is drawn by, among others, John Bound and George Johnson, 'Changes in the Structure of Wages in the 1980s: An Evaluation of Alternative Explanations'. *American Economic Review*, June 1992, pp. 371–92; Paul Gregg and Stephen Machin, 'Is the UK Rise in Inequality Different?', in Ray Barrel (ed.), *The UK Labour Market* (Cambridge University Press, 1994); and Stephen Nickell and Brian Bell, 'The Collapse in the Demand for the Unskilled and Unemployment across the OECD', *Oxford Review of Economic Policy*, 1996, pp. 40–62.

Figure 3.12 The increase in real wage equality in the UK 1973–92

The figures show the real hourly wage of different groups of male and female workers, measured relative to real wages paid in 1980. The lines marked 1–10 show the average real wage of workers who are in the bottom 10% of the distributions of male and female wages. The lines marked 50 show the average (median) real wage, and the line marked 91–100 shows the average real wage of workers whose wages are in the top 10% of the wage distribution. Note both the faster growth of wages since 1980 and the trend toward greater inequality, especially among female workers (the distance between the top and bottom lines has increased).

Source: 'Earnings and Inequality: Changes During the 1980s', *Economic Outlook* (OECD, 1996).

(a) women

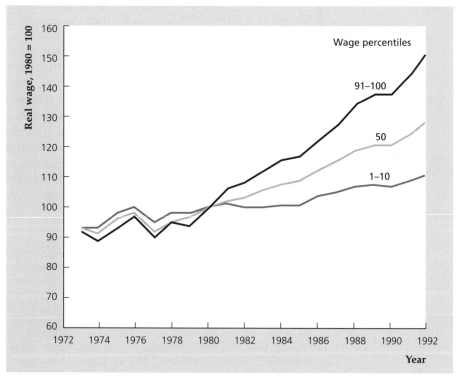

(b) men

Alan Krueger of Princeton University found that workers who are able to use computers in their jobs enjoy a 10–15% wage premium over similar workers who are not trained to use computers.[19]

Figure 3.13 illustrates the labour market effects of a skill-biased technical change. Here we drop the simplifying assumption made earlier that all workers are identical and instead allow for two types of worker, skilled and unskilled.[20] Supply and demand for each type of worker are shown separately, with the market for skilled workers shown in Figure 3.13(a) and the market for unskilled workers shown in Figure 3.13(b). The supply of each type of worker

---

19. 'How Computers Have Changed the Wage Structure: Evidence from Microdata, 1984–89', *Quarterly Journal of Economics*, February 1993, pp. 33–60.

20. With two types of worker, there are three factors of production: capital, skilled labour, and unskilled labour. The production function thus becomes $Y = AF(K, N_{sk}, N_{unsk})$, where N_{sk} is the number of skilled and N_{unsk} the number of unskilled workers employed. A skill-biased technical change changes the function F so that the marginal product of skilled workers rises relative to the marginal product of unskilled workers.

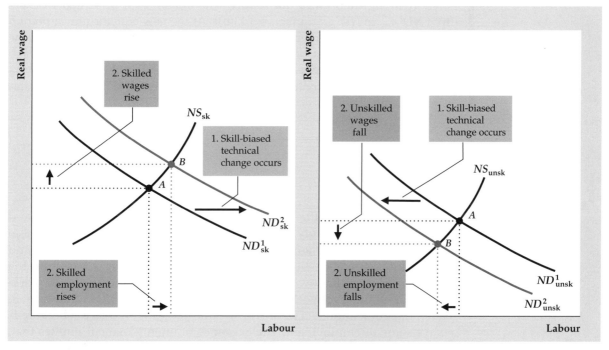

(a) Skilled workers **(b) Unskilled workers**

Figure 3.13
The effects of skill-biased technical change on wage inequality
The supply and demand for skilled labour is shown in (a), and the supply and demand for unskilled labour is shown in (b). The initial equilibrium is shown as point *A* in both parts. Because skilled workers have a higher *MPN* than unskilled workers, their real wage is higher.

A skill-biased technical change increases the *MPN* of skilled workers relative to the *MPN* of unskilled workers. A rise in the *MPN* of skilled workers raises the demand, from ND^1_{sk} to ND^2_{sk} in (a). If the *MPN* of unskilled workers actually falls, demand for unskilled labour falls, from ND^1_{unsk} to ND^2_{unsk} in (b). At the new equilibrium, point *B* in both parts, the wages of skilled workers have risen relative to those of unskilled workers.

reflects the number of people in the labour force with each level of skills. For simplicity, and to focus on the effects of a skill-biased technical change, we ignore population growth and changing participation rates and assume that the labour supply curves are fixed. The demand for each type of worker depends on the *MPN* of that type of worker, for constant capital stock and number of employed workers of the other type.

The initial labour demand curves are ND^1_{sk} in Figure 3.13(a) and ND^1_{unsk} in Figure 3.13(b), and the initial labour market equilibrium is at point *A* in both parts. The real wages of skilled workers are higher than those of unskilled workers (i.e., the equilibrium real wage at point *A* in Figure 3.13(a) is higher than the equilibrium real wage at point *A* in Figure 3.13(b). This difference reflects the higher *MPN* and lower supply of skilled workers, relative to unskilled workers.

A skill-biased technical change, such as the introduction of computers, raises the *MPN* of skilled workers (who can accomplish more with the aid of a computer than they could without one) but reduces the *MPN* of unskilled workers (who do not have the training to be productive in a computerized workplace). Because the *MPN* curve and the demand curve for labour are the same, this technical change raises the demand for skilled workers (from ND^1_{sk} to ND^2_{sk} in Figure 3.13(a)) but reduces the demand for unskilled workers (from ND^1_{unsk} to ND^2_{unsk} in Figure 3.13(b)). At the new equilibrium, at point *B* in both parts, skilled workers' real wages and employment have risen, and the wages and employment of the unskilled have fallen. The increased wage inequality predicted by this analysis is consistent with the facts. It also appears to be true that the fraction of employment composed of skilled workers has increased while the fraction composed of unskilled workers has decreased. [21]

3.5   UNEMPLOYMENT

Our classical model of the labour market, which relies on supply–demand analysis, is useful for studying the wage rate and the level of employment in an economy and for showing how these variables are linked to output and productivity. However, this model of the labour market is based on the strong assumption that, when the labour market is in equilibrium, all workers who are willing to work at the prevailing wage are able to find jobs. In reality, of course, not everyone who would like to work has a job; there is always some unemployment. The existence of unemployment implies that, at any time, not all of society's labour resources are actively involved in producing goods and services.

---

21. A complication not shown in Figure 3.13 arises if workers expect the skill bias of technical change to be permanent. In that case, skilled workers expect both their current and future wage to rise, which shifts their labour supply curve left; expected declines in the future wage of the unskilled shifts their labour supply curve to the right. This complication may reverse the predictions of the analysis about employment but only reinforces the main conclusion drawn here, that skilled workers' wages rise relative to those of unskilled workers.

We discuss the problem of unemployment several times in this book, notably in Chapter 13. Here we introduce the topic by presenting some basic facts about unemployment and then turning to a preliminary economic analysis of it.

Measuring Unemployment

There are a number of different ways in which European governments estimate the unemployment rate in their countries. In the UK, the official measure is based on those people eligible for and in receipt of unemployment and social security benefits. Other countries base their measures on a survey of households. Because governments use different methods for estimating the unemployment rate, the measures they produce are not strictly comparable. One source of information that does contain comparable data on employment, unemployment and related variables is the *Labour Force Survey* undertaken by EU governments using a common methodology. Each quarter government statistical departments (such as the Office for National Statistics in the UK) surveys thousands of households. Each person over age fifteen in the surveyed household is assigned to one of three categories:

1. *employed*, if the person worked full-time or part-time during the past week (or was on sick leave or vacation from a job);

2. *unemployed*, if the person did not work during the past week but looked for work during the past four weeks; or

3. *not in the labour force*, if the person did not work during the past week and did not look for work during the past four weeks (examples are full-time students, homemakers, and retirees).

Table 3.5 shows the number of people in each category for several European countries and for the EU as a whole in 1994. (Good sources for these and other data about the labour market are described in the box 'In Touch with The Macroeconomy: Labour Market Data', p. 99.) In that year there were 146.2 million employed and 18.5 million unemployed workers in the EU. The **labour force** consists of all employed and unemployed workers, so in 1994 it totalled 164.7 million workers (146.2 million employed plus 18.5 million unemployed). The working-age population in 1994 was 249.2 million, which leaves 84.5 million adults not in the labour force (total population of 249.2 million less 164.7 million in the labour force).

Some useful measures of the labour market are the unemployment rate, the participation rate, and the employment ratio. The **unemployment rate** is the fraction of the labour force that is unemployed. In 1994 the unemployment rate was 11.2% (18.5 million divided by 164.7 million in the labour force). This is the average for the EU as a whole and member states have very different unemployment rates. In the Netherlands, for example, unemployment in 1994 averaged 7.0% while in France it was 12.3%. Figure 1.2 shows the unemployment rate for a number of European countries for the period since 1920.

The fraction of the working-age population in the labour force is the **participation rate**. Of the 249.2 million working-age people in the EU in 1994, 164.7 million were in the labour force, so the participation rate was 66.1%.

Table 3.5 Employment Status of Adult Population in Selected EU
Countries, 1994

	Employed Workers	Unemployed Workers	Labour Force	Not in Labour Force	Adult Population
EU (millions)	146.2	18.5	164.7	84.5	249.2
Share of labour force (%)	88.8	11.2	100		
Share of adult population (%)	58.7	7.4	66.1	33.9	100
UK (millions)	25.1	2.6	27.7	10.4	38.1
Share of labour force (%)	90.6	9.4	100		
Share of adult population (%)	65.9	6.8	72.7	27.3	100
Netherlands (millions)	6.7	0.5	7.2	3.3	10.5
Share of labour force (%)	93.0	7.0	100		
Share of adult population (%)	63.8	4.8	68.6	31.4	100
Sweden (millions)	4.0	0.4	4.4	1.2	5.6
Share of labour force (%)	90.1	9.9	100		
Share of adult population (%)	71.4	7.1	78.6	21.4	100
Italy (millions)	19.9	2.5	22.4	17.0	39.4
Share of labour force (%)	88.8	11.2	100		
Share of adult population (%)	50.5	6.3	56.9	43.1	100
Germany (millions)	34.9	3.3	38.2	17.6	55.8
Share of labour force (%)	91.4	8.6	100		
Share of adult population (%)	62.5	5.9	68.5	31.5	100
France (millions)	22.1	3.1	25.2	12.7	37.9
Share of labour force (%)	87.7	12.3	100		
Share of adult population (%)	58.3	8.2	66.5	33.5	100

Source: *Employment in Europe*, 1996 Employment and Social Affairs, European Commission.

Again, we find that some European countries have much lower participation
rates, such as in Italy where it is only 56.9%, compared with, say, Sweden
where 78.6% of the working-age population are in the labour force.

The **employment ratio** is the employed fraction of the working population. In 1994 the employment ratio was 58.7% (146.2 million employed
divided by the working-age population of 249.2 million). With an employment ratio of 58.7%, 41.3% of the adult population was not employed in
1994. Of this 41.3%, 7.4% reflected unemployment and the remaining 33.9%
reflected people not in the labour force. Thus a large majority of working-age
people who are not employed at any given time are not in the labour force
rather than unemployed.

Changes in Employment Status

The labour market is in a constant state of flux. Even when the unemployment
rate remains unchanged from one month to the next, during the month many
thousands of European workers become unemployed and many thousands
become employed.

IN TOUCH *WITH THE MACROECONOMY*

LABOUR MARKET DATA

In all European countries, government agencies collect and distribute a remarkable variety of data pertaining to the labour market. In the UK, a useful summary of labour market data can be found in *Labour Market Trends*, a monthly publication of the Office for National Statistics. This publication includes data for the previous month or quarter on employment, unemployment, average earnings, industrial disputes and government-financed training. Historical data over the previous three or four years is also provided. The data are presented for the aggregate UK economy and for various categories of workers based on age, gender, occupation industry, and region. Detailed information on average weekly and hourly earnings and hours of work are published in the annual *New Earnings Survey* which includes a detailed breakdown of average earnings and hours of work by occupation, industry and region.

Labour Market Trends also reports information from the *Labour Force Survey*. The *Labour Force Survey* includes labour market data for all EU Member States and it has the advantage that it adopts a common methodology and common defin-

itions for all countries. Data for the *Labour Force Survey* are obtained from household surveys carried out quarterly by the national statistics offices of each country. In the UK, the survey covers around 60,000 households. Households provide information on employment, unemployment, reasons for inactivity and earnings. Data collected in each member state are analyzed by the Statistical Office of the European Union (Eurostat) in order to assist the EU in matters such as the allocation of the European Social Fund. Many of the data are later reprinted in aggregate country-by-country form in *Employment in Europe* published by the Employment and Social Affairs Department of the European Commission. *Employment in Europe* also provides commentary and analysis on developments in the European Labour Market.

Labour market data for OECD countries are available in *Quarterly Labour Force Statistics* published by the OECD. Data on employment and unemployment disaggregated by age, gender and industry is presented for OECD countries using common definitions which allows country-by-3 country comparisons.

Figure 3.14 shows how workers change their employment status (that is, whether they are employed, unemployed, or not in the labour force) in a typical three-month period in the UK. The arrows between each pair of boxes represent a change from one employment status to another, and the number on the arrow shows the fraction of the people in one status that switch to the other status in a typical quarter. Thus, for example, the arrow from the employed box to the unemployed box has the label 4%, indicating that 4% of employed workers in a typical quarter will become unemployed by the following quarter.

What are the employment prospects of an unemployed worker? Figure 3.14 shows that 34% of the unemployed people in a typical quarter will be employed the following quarter and that 21% of the unemployed people will be out of the labour force the next quarter. The remaining 45% of the unemployed people will still be unemployed the following quarter. Of the 21% of the unemployed who leave the labour force each quarter, some are **discouraged workers**, or people who have become so discouraged by lack of success at finding a job that they stop searching. Other unemployed workers leave the labour force to engage in some activity outside the labour market, such as homemaking or going to college.

Figure 3.14
Changes in employment status in the UK in a typical quarter
The arrow between two boxes represents a change from one employment status to another; the label on the arrow shows the fraction of the people in one status that switch to the other status in a typical quarter. For example, the arrow from the unemployed box to the employed box indicates that 34% of unemployed workers become employed the following quarter; the arrow from the employed box to the unemployed box indicates that 4% of employed workers become unemployed the following quarter.

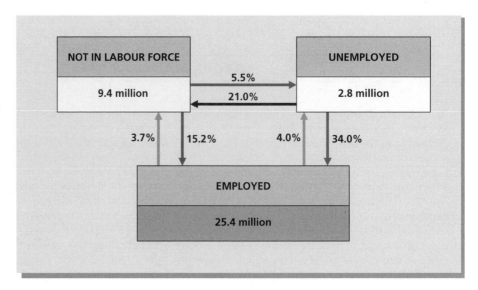

How Long Are People Unemployed?

Of the 45% of those unemployed in a typical quarter who remain unemployed the following quarter, some may remain unemployed for a considerable period of time. The length of time that an individual is continuously unemployed is called an **unemployment spell**. The length of time that an unemployment spell lasts is called its **duration**. The duration of an unemployment spell determines in large part the degree of hardship suffered by an unemployed worker. At one extreme, a one-week unemployment spell will cost a worker a week's pay but probably will not seriously affect the worker's standard of living. At the other extreme, an unemployment spell that lasts for several months may force an unemployed worker to exhaust his or her life savings or to sell the car or house.

The duration of unemployment spells in many countries is characterized by two seemingly contradictory statements:

1. Most unemployment spells are of short duration, about four months or less.

2. Most people who are unemployed on a given date are experiencing unemployment spells with long duration.

To understand how both of these statements can be true, consider an economy with 100 people in the labour force. Suppose that at the beginning of every month, two workers become unemployed and remain unemployed for one month before finding a new job. In addition, at the beginning of every year four workers become unemployed and remain unemployed for the entire year.

In this example there are twenty-eight spells of unemployment during a year: twenty-four spells that last one month, and four spells that last one year. Thus twenty-four of twenty-eight, or 86%, of the spells last only one month, which is consistent with the first statement: most spells are short.

How many people are unemployed on a given day, say, on 15 May? There are six unemployed workers on 15 May: two unemployed workers who began one-month spells of unemployment on 1 May, and four unemployed workers who began one-year spells of unemployment on 1 January. Thus four of six, or 67%, of the workers unemployed on 15 May are experiencing one-year spells of unemployment, which is consistent with the second statement: most people who are unemployed on a given date are experiencing long spells of unemployment.

One of the most striking differences between Europe and other countries such as the USA and Japan is the relative importance of long-term unemployment. Data collected by the OECD indicates that in 1993, 12.2% of the unemployed in the USA had been out of work for more than twelve months (the usual definition of long-term unemployment). In Italy the long-term unemployed represented 57.7% of total unemployment, while in both the UK and Germany it was in excess of 40%. Only in Sweden was the relative importance of long-term unemployment approaching that found in the USA, and even here it was 17.3%.

Why There Always Are Unemployed People

Even when the economy is growing vigorously and many new jobs are being created, some people remain unemployed. Why is unemployment apparently a permanent feature of the economy? Here we discuss frictional unemployment and structural unemployment, two types of unemployment that always exist in the labour market and thus prevent the unemployment rate from ever reaching zero.

Frictional Unemployment. The labour market is characterized by a great deal of searching by both workers and firms. Unemployed workers search for suitable jobs, and firms with vacancies search for suitable workers. If all workers were identical and all jobs were identical, these searches would be short and easy: unemployed workers would simply have to find firms that had vacancies and they would immediately be hired. The problem, of course, is that neither jobs nor workers are identical. Workers vary in their talents, skills, experience, goals, and geographic location (and willingness to move), and in the amount of time and energy they are willing to commit to their job. Similarly, jobs vary in the skills and experience required, working conditions, location, hours, and pay. Because of these differences, an unemployed worker may search for several weeks or more before finding a suitable job; similarly, a firm may search for a considerable time before it is able to hire a suitable worker.

The unemployment that arises as workers search for suitable jobs and firms search for suitable workers is called **frictional unemployment**. Because the economy is dynamic, with jobs continually being created and destroyed and workers continually entering and exiting the labour force, there is always some frictional unemployment as workers are matched with appropriate jobs.

Structural Unemployment. In addition to those suffering long spells of unemployment, many people are chronically unemployed. Although their unemployment spells may be broken by brief periods of employment or being out of the labour force, workers who are **chronically unemployed** are unemployed a large part of the time. Long spells of unemployment and chronic unemployment cannot be attributed primarily to the matching process. People in these situations do not seem to search for work very intensively and do not generally find stable employment. The long-term and chronic unemployment that exists even when the economy is not in a recession is called **structural unemployment**.

Structural unemployment occurs for two primary reasons. First, unskilled or low-skilled workers often are unable to obtain desirable, long-term jobs. The jobs available to them typically offer relatively low wages and little chance for training or advancement. Most directly related to the issue of structural unemployment is the fact that jobs held by low-skilled workers often do not last long. After a few months the job may end, or the worker may quit or be fired, thus entering another spell of unemployment. Some workers with low skill levels eventually get enough training or experience to obtain more secure, long-term jobs. Because of factors such as inadequate education, discrimination, and language barriers, however, some unskilled workers never make the transition to long-term employment and remain chronically unemployed.

The second source of structural unemployment is the reallocation of labour from industries that are shrinking, or regions that are depressed, to areas that are growing. When industries find that their product is no longer in demand (for example, gas lamp manufacturers) or that they are no longer competitive (for example, European producers of colour television sets who lost much of the market to the Japanese), workers in these industries lose their jobs. At the same time, some industries will be growing (for example, health care providers and computer software developers). To prevent unemployment from rising requires that workers who lose jobs in declining industries be matched somehow with jobs in growing industries. This matching may involve a long period of unemployment, especially if workers need to relocate or be trained for a new job.

The Natural Rate of Unemployment. Because of the combination of frictional and structural unemployment, an economy's unemployment rate is never zero, even when the economy is at its full-employment level. The rate of unemployment that prevails when output and employment are at the full-employment level is called the **natural rate of unemployment,** $\bar{u}$. The natural rate of unemployment reflects unemployment owing to frictional and structural causes. Although there is no single official measure of the natural rate of unemployment, many economists believe that the natural rate in Europe was around 2% during the 1950s and increased to over 7% in the 1980s. Chapter 13 discusses the reasons for the increase in the natural rate.

As output fluctuates around its full-employment level, the unemployment rate fluctuates around the natural rate. The difference between the actual unemployment rate and the natural rate of unemployment is called **cyclical unemployment**. Specifically, cyclical unemployment = $u - \bar{u}$, where u is the actual unemployment rate and $\bar{u}$ is the natural rate. Cyclical unemployment is positive whenever the economy's output and employment are below full-employment levels; it is negative when output and employment exceed full-employment levels.

3.6 RELATING OUTPUT AND UNEMPLOYMENT: OKUN'S LAW

Earlier in this chapter we said that many short-run output fluctuations result from changes in employment. When employment falls and unemployment rises, the reduction in the number of people working leads to a decline in the quantity of goods and services produced. We can use the concept of cyclical unemployment to provide a more precise link between the state of the labour market and aggregate output.

The quantitative impact on aggregate output of a change in the unemployment rate is described by Okun's law, a rule of thumb (rather than a 'law') first stated by Arthur Okun, chairman of the Council of Economic Advisers in the 1960s during President Johnson's administration in the United States. According to **Okun's law,** the gap between an economy's full-employment output and its actual level of output increases by 2.5 percentage points for each percentage point the unemployment rate increases.[22, 23] We express Okun's law algebraically as

$$\frac{\overline{Y} - Y}{\overline{Y}} = 2.5(u - \overline{u}) \tag{3.5}$$

The left-hand side of equation (3.5) equals the amount by which actual output Y falls short of full-employment output $\overline{Y}$, expressed as a percentage of $\overline{Y}$. Thus equation (3.5) says that the percentage gap between potential and actual output equals 2.5 times the cyclical unemployment rate.

Let us apply Okun's law by supposing that the natural rate of unemployment is 6% and the full-employment level of output is 6000 billion ECU. If the actual unemployment rate is 7%, or 1 percentage point above the natural rate, cyclical unemployment, $u - \overline{u}$, equals 1%. If cyclical unemployment is 1%, Okun's law predicts that actual output Y will be 2.5% (2.5 times 1%) lower than full-employment output $\overline{Y}$. Because $\overline{Y}$ equals 6000 billion ECU, Okun's law says that actual output will be 150 billion ECU below the full-employment level (2.5% times 6000 billion).

You may wonder why a 1 percentage point increase in the unemployment rate, which reduces employment by about 1%, leads (according to Okun's law) to a drop in output that is about two and a half times as large in percentage terms. The reason is that when cyclical unemployment increases, other factors that determine output – the number of people in the labour force, the number of hours each worker works per week, the average productivity of labour – also fall, which magnifies the effect of the increase in unemployment. Numerical Problem 10 at the end of this chapter illustrates this point.

Sometimes we express Okun's law in a slightly different form:

$$\frac{\Delta Y}{Y} = \frac{\Delta \overline{Y}}{\overline{Y}} - 2.5 \; \Delta u, \tag{3.6}$$

where $\Delta Y / Y$ is the percentage growth rate of output, $\Delta \overline{Y} / \overline{Y}$ is the percentage growth rate of full-employment output, and Δu is the change in the actual unemployment rate from one year to the next. Equation (3.6) says that when unemployment is rising ($\Delta u > 0$), actual output Y is growing more slowly than full-employment output $\overline{Y}$. Equation (3.6), which requires the assumption that

22. When the unemployment rate increases (for example, from 6% to 9%), we say that it increases by 3 percentage points (9% – 6%), or that it increases by 50 per cent (3% is 50 per cent of 6%).

23. In Okun's original work ('Potential GNP: Its Measurement and Significance', reprinted in Arthur Okun, *The Political Economy of Prosperity*, Brookings Institution, pp. 132–45), the 'Okun's law coefficient' was 3.0 rather than 2.5, so each percentage point of cyclical unemployment was associated with a difference between actual output and full-employment output of 3 percentage points. Current estimates put the Okun's law coefficient closer to 2.5 for EU countries.

Figure 3.15
Okun's law in the EU, 1960–96

This figure shows the relation between the growth rate of real GDP (vertical axis) and the change in the unemployment rate (horizontal axis). Line OL is a graph of Okun's law (equation 3.6). The slope of this line is −2.5, indicating that a 1 percentage point change in the unemployment rate changes the growth rate of output by 2.5 percentage points in the opposite direction. The horizontal line at $3^3/_4$% shows the approximate average growth rate of full-employment output, equalling the rate at which actual output would grow if there were no change in the unemployment rate ($\Delta u = 0$).

Source: Civilian unemployment rate from *European Economy 1996, op cit. Table 1.1 (b)*, Table 3; Growth in real GDP constructed from *European Economy 1996*, Table 10 'GDP at current market prices (annual percentage charge)' and Table 24 'GDP deflator'.

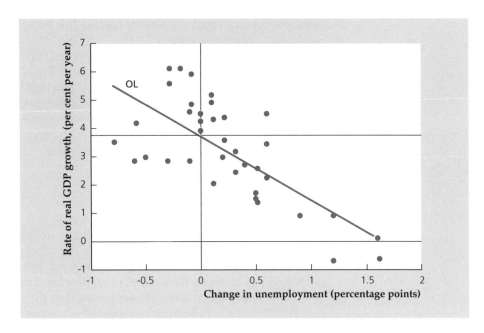

the natural rate of unemployment is constant, is called the growth rate form of Okun's law. See Appendix 3.A at the end of this chapter for a derivation of equation (3.6).

Figure 3.15 illustrates the growth rate form of Okun's law. The figure shows the relation between the annual change in the unemployment rate (measured on the horizontal axis) and the annual growth rate of output (measured on the vertical axis) for the period 1960–96 for Europe as a whole. Line OL in this figure represents Okun's law. Its slope is −2.5, indicating that a 1 percentage point increase in the unemployment rate is associated with a 2.5% drop in output. The vertical line rising from 0 on the horizontal axis intersects OL at $3\frac{3}{4}$%. This intercept indicates that, when there is no change in the unemployment rate, the growth rate of actual output is $3\frac{3}{4}$%, or the approximate average growth rate of full-employment output in Europe.

CHAPTER SUMMARY

1. The production function tells us the amount of output that can be produced with any given quantities of capital and labour. The production function can be graphed as a relationship between output and capital, holding labour fixed, or as a relationship between output and labour, holding capital fixed. In either case the production function slopes upward, implying that greater use of capital or labour leads to more output. A shift in the production function, which indicates a change in the amount of output that can be produced with given amounts of capital and labour, is called a supply shock.

2. The extra output that can be produced when the capital stock is increased by one unit, with labour held constant, is called the marginal product of capital (*MPK*). In a graph of the pro-

duction function relating output to capital, the *MPK* can be measured as the slope of the production function. The *MPK* falls as the capital stock increases, reflecting the diminishing marginal productivity of capital. Similarly, the marginal product of labour (*MPN*) is the extra output that can be produced when labour increases by one unit, with capital held constant. The *MPN* – which can be measured as the slope of the production function relating output to labour – falls as employment rises, indicating that labour also has diminishing marginal productivity.

3. To maximize profits, firms demand labour to the point that the marginal revenue product of labour (*MRPN*) equals the nominal wage, *W*; or, equivalently, to the point that the *MPN* equals the real wage, *w*.

4. The labour demand curve is identical to the *MPN* curve. Because an increase in the real wage causes firms to demand less labour, the labour demand curve slopes downward. Factors that increase the amount of labour demanded at any real wage, such as a beneficial supply shock or an increase in the capital stock, shift the labour demand curve to the right. Aggregate labour demand is the sum of the labour demands of firms in the economy.

5. An individual's decision about how much labour to supply reflects a trade-off between income and leisure. Labour is supplied to the point where the income received for working an extra hour just compensates the worker for giving up an extra hour of leisure.

6. The labour supply curve relates the amount of labour supplied to the current real wage. The labour supply curve slopes upward, indicating that an increase in the current real wage – with other factors, including the expected future real wage, held fixed – raises the amount of labour supplied. Factors that decrease the quantity of labour supplied at the current real wage, and thus shift the labour supply curve to the left, include an increase in wealth and an increase in the expected future real wage. Aggregate labour supply, which is the sum of labour supplies of the individuals in the economy, is also influenced by changes in the working-age population and social or legal factors that affect the number of people participating in the labour market.

7. The classical supply–demand model of the labour market is based on the assumption that the real wage adjusts relatively quickly to equalize the quantities of labour demanded and supplied. The equilibrium level of employment, which arises when wages and prices in the economy have fully adjusted, is called the full-employment level of employment. Fluctuations in employment and the real wage are the result of factors that shift the labour supply curve and/or the labour demand curve.

8. Full-employment output, or potential output, is the amount of output produced when employment is at its full-employment level. Increases in the full-employment level of employment or beneficial supply shocks increase the full-employment level of output.

9. Working-age people without jobs are classified as unemployed if they looked for work during the preceding four weeks; they are classified as not in the labour force if they have not been looking for work. The labour force consists of all employed workers plus all unemployed workers. The unemployment rate is the fraction of the labour force that is unemployed.

10. Frictional unemployment reflects the time required for potential workers to find suitable jobs and for firms with vacancies to find suitable workers. Structural unemployment – long-term and chronic unemployment that exists even when the economy is not in recession – occurs because some workers do not have the skills needed to obtain long-term employment, or because of delays in reallocating workers from economically depressed areas to those that are growing. Frictional and structural unemployment together account for the natural rate of unemployment, which is the unemployment rate that exists when employment is at its full-employment level. Cyclical unemployment is the excess of the actual unemployment rate over the natural rate of unemployment.

11. According to Okun's law, a 1 percentage point increase in the rate of cyclical unemployment reduces output by 2.5 percentage points.

KEY DIAGRAM   1

The Production Function

The production function indicates how much output an economy or a firm can produce with any given quantities of capital and labour.

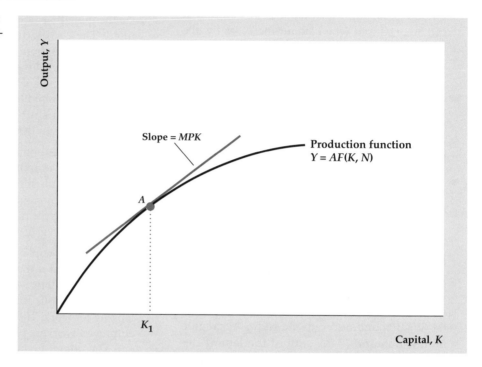

Diagram Elements

■ The production function graphed here has the amount of output produced, Y, on the vertical axis and the quantity of capital used, K, on the horizontal axis, with labour, N, held constant. It can also be drawn as a relationship between output and labour, with capital held constant. The production function relating output to labour looks like the graph shown here.

■ The equation for the production function is $Y = AF(K, N)$, where A (total factor productivity, or simply productivity) measures how effectively the economy uses capital and labour.

Analysis

■ The production function slopes upward, reflecting the fact that an increase in the quantity of capital will allow more output to be produced.

■ The production function becomes flatter from left to right, implying that the larger the capital stock already is, the less extra output is gained by adding another unit of capital. The fact that extra capital becomes

less productive as the capital stock grows is called diminishing marginal productivity of capital.

■ With labour held constant, if an increase in capital of ΔK leads to an increase in output of ΔY, then $\Delta Y / \Delta K$ is called the marginal product of capital, or MPK. The MPK is measured graphically by the slope of the line tangent to the production function. For example, in the diagram the MPK when the capital stock is K_1 equals the slope of the line tangent to the production function at point A.

Factors that Shift the Curve

■ Any change that allows more output to be produced for given quantities of capital and labour – a beneficial supply shock – shifts the production function upward. Examples of beneficial supply shocks include new inventions and improved management techniques.

■ Any change that reduces the amount of output that can be produced for given quantities of capital and labour – an adverse supply shock – shifts the production function downward. Examples of adverse supply shocks include bad weather and the depletion of natural resources.

KEY DIAGRAM   2

The Labour Market

An economy's level of employment and the real wage are determined in the labour market.

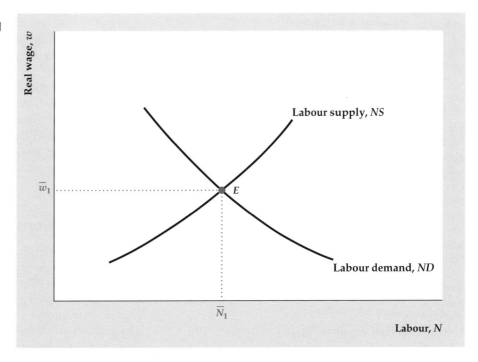

Diagram Elements

■ The current real wage, w, is on the vertical axis, and the level of employment, N, is on the horizontal axis. The variable N may also represent alternative measures of labour, such as total hours worked.

■ The labour demand curve, ND, shows the amount of labour that firms want to employ at each current real wage. The labour demand curve slopes downward because firms find hiring more labour profitable when the real wage falls. The labour demand curve for an individual firm is the same as the MPN curve, which shows the marginal product of labour at each level of employment.

■ The labour supply curve, NS, shows the amount of labour offered by workers at each current real wage. The labour supply curve slopes upward because an increase in the current real wage, with other factors held constant, increases the amount of labour supplied.

Analysis

■ Equilibrium in the labour market occurs when the quantity of labour demanded equals the quantity of labour supplied. In the figure equilibrium employment is $\overline{N}_1$, and the equilibrium real wage is $\overline{w}_1$. The equilibrium level of employment, which occurs after wages and prices have fully adjusted, is called the full-employment level of employment.

Factors that Shift the Curves

■ Any factor that increases the amount of labour demanded at a given current real wage shifts the labour demand curve to the right. Such factors include an increase in the marginal product of labour at any given level of employment and an increase in the capital stock. See Summary table 3.

■ Any factor that increases the amount of labour supplied at a given current real wage shifts the labour supply curve to the right. Such factors include a decline in wealth, a drop in the expected future real wage, a rise in the working-age population, and an increase in labour force participation. See Summary table 4.

Key Terms

aggregate demand for labour, p. 83
aggregate supply of labour, p. 84
chronically unemployed, p. 101
cyclical unemployment, p. 102
diminishing marginal productivity, p. 73
discouraged workers, p. 99
duration, p. 100
employment ratio, p. 98
factors of production, p. 68
frictional unemployment, p. 101
full-employment level of employment, p. 88
full-employment output, p. 90
labour force, p. 97
Labour Force Survey, p. 97
leisure, p. 84
marginal product of capital (*MPK*), p. 72
marginal product of labour (*MPN*), p. 74
marginal revenue product of labour (*MRPN*), p. 77
natural rate of unemployment, p. 102
Okun's law, p. 103
participation rate, p. 97
production function, p. 69
productivity, p. 67
real wage, p. 79
structural unemployment, p. 101
supply shock, p. 74
unemployment rate, p. 97
unemployment spell, p. 100

Key Equations

$$Y = AF(K, N) \qquad (3.1)$$

The *production function* indicates how much output Y can be produced for given quantities of capital K and labour N and for a given level of total factor productivity A.

$$\overline{Y} = AF(K, \overline{N}) \qquad (3.4)$$

Full-employment output $\overline{Y}$ is the quantity of output supplied by firms when wages and prices have fully adjusted, and employment equals its equilibrium value $\overline{N}$.

$$\frac{\overline{Y} - Y}{\overline{Y}} = 2.5(u - \overline{u}) \qquad (3.5)$$

Okun's law states that a 1 percentage point increase in the unemployment rate u reduces output Y by 2.5% of the full-employment level of output $\overline{Y}$. When the unemployment rate equals the natural rate of unemployment $\overline{u}$, output equals its full-employment level.

$$\frac{\Delta Y}{Y} = \frac{\Delta \overline{Y}}{\overline{Y}} - 2.5 \, \Delta u \qquad (3.6)$$

The growth rate form of Okun's law relates the growth rate of output $\Delta Y/Y$ to the growth rate of full-employment output $\Delta \overline{Y}/\overline{Y}$ and the change in the unemployment rate Δu. According to equation (3.6), output grows more slowly than full-employment output when unemployment is rising and more quickly than full-employment output when unemployment is falling. This version of Okun's law is based on the assumption that the natural rate of unemployment is constant.

Review Questions

1. What is a production function? What are some factors that can cause a nation's production function to shift over time? What do you have to know besides an economy's production function to know how much output the economy can produce?
2. The production function slopes upward, but its slope declines from left to right. Give an economic interpretation of each of these properties of the production function.
3. Define *marginal product of capital,* or *MPK*. How can the *MPK* be shown graphically?
4. Explain why the profit-maximizing level of employment for a firm occurs when the marginal revenue product of labour equals the nominal wage. How can this profit-maximizing condition be expressed in real terms?
5. What is the *MPN* curve? How is the *MPN* curve related to the production function? How is it related to labour demand?
6. What two variables are related by the aggregate labour supply curve? What are some factors that cause the aggregate labour supply curve to shift?
7. Define *full-employment output.* How is full-employment output affected by an increase in labour supply? By a beneficial supply shock?
8. Why is the classical model of the labour market discussed in this chapter not very useful for studying unemployment?
9. Define the following: *labour force, unemployment rate, participation rate,* and *employment ratio.*

10. Define *unemployment spell* and *duration*. What are the two seemingly contradictory facts about unemployment spells? Why are the two facts not actually contradictory?

11. What is frictional unemployment? Why is a certain amount of frictional unemployment probably necessary in a well-functioning economy?

12. What is structural unemployment? What are the two principal sources of structural unemployment?

13. Define the *natural rate of unemployment* and *cyclical unemployment*. What does negative cyclical unemployment mean?

14. What is Okun's law? If the unemployment rate increases by 2 percentage points between this year and next year, by how much will output change during the same period? Assume that the natural unemployment rate and full-employment output are constant.

Numerical Problems

1. The following data give real GDP, Y, capital, K, and labour, N, for the UK economy in various years.

Year	Y	K	N
1960	239	386	22.7
1970	314	629	22.4
1980	423	1095	23.0
1990	551	1157	22.9

Units and sources are the same as in Table 3.1. Assume that the production function is $Y = AK^{0.3}N^{0.7}$.

a. How much did UK total factor productivity grow between 1960 and 1970? Between 1970 and 1980? Between 1980 and 1990?

b. What happened to the marginal product of labour between 1960 and 1990? Calculate the marginal product numerically as the extra output gained by adding 1 million workers in each of the two years. (The data for employment, N, are measured in millions of workers, so an increase of one million workers is an increase of 1.0.)

2. An economy has the production function

$$Y = 0.2(K + \sqrt{N})$$

In the current period $K = 100$ and $N = 100$.

a. Graph the relationship between output and capital, holding labour constant at its current value. What is the MPK? Does the marginal productivity of capital diminish?

b. Graph the relationship between output and labour, holding capital constant at its current value. Find the MPN for an increase of labour from 100 to 110. Compare this result with the MPN for an increase in labour from 110 to 120. Does the marginal productivity of labour diminish?

3. Acme Widget, Inc., has the following production function.

Number of Workers	Number of Widgets Produced
0	0
1	8
2	15
3	21
4	26
5	30
6	33

a. Find the MPN for each level of employment.

b. Acme can get 5 kronor for each widget it produces. How many workers will it hire if the nominal wage is 38 kronor? If it is 27 kronor? If it is 22 kronor?

c. Graph the relationship between Acme's labour demand and the nominal wage. How does this graph differ from a labour demand curve? Graph Acme's labour demand curve.

d. With the nominal wage fixed at 38 kronor, the price of widgets doubles from 5 kronor each to 10 kronor each. What happens to Acme's labour demand and production?

e. With the nominal wage fixed at 38 kronor and the price of widgets fixed at 5 kronor, the introduction of a new automatic widget maker doubles the number of widgets that the same number of workers can produce. What happens to labour demand and production?

f. What is the relationship between your answers to part (d) and part (e)? Explain.

4. The marginal product of labour (measured in units of output) for a certain firm is

$$MPN = A(100 - N)$$

where A measures productivity and N is the number of labour hours used in production. The price of output is £2.00 per unit.

a. If $A = 1.0$, what will be the demand for labour if the nominal wage is £10? If it is £20? Graph the demand curve for labour. What is the equilibrium real wage if the supply of labour is fixed at 95?

b. Repeat part (a) for $A = 2.0$.

5. For an economy the *MPN* is

$$MPN = 500 - 0.5N$$

where N is aggregate employment. The aggregate quantity of labour supplied is $400 + 8(1 - t)w$, where w is the real wage and t is the income tax rate. The expression for labour supply reflects the fact that workers care about their after-tax real wage, $(1 - t)w$, rather than their before-tax real wage, w. Employers are not taxed.

a. Find the before-tax real wage and employment when $t = 0.50$.

b. Find the before-tax real wage and employment when $t = 0.25$. Compare the result with that in part (a). Explain why the cut in the income tax rate has the effect that it does on the labour market.

6. In this problem you are to find the effects of a legal minimum wage on the labour income of unskilled workers. Assume that the marginal product of labour for unskilled labour is

$$MPN = 100 - 0.2N$$

The supply of unskilled labour is $80 + 2w$, where w is the real wage received by unskilled labour.

a. If there is no minimum wage, find the equilibrium values of the real wage, employment, and labour income for unskilled workers.

b. Now suppose that a minimum wage that sets the real wage at 70 is instituted. What are the new levels of employment and total labour income for unskilled workers?

c. Repeat parts (a) and (b) for $MPN = 100 - 0.9N$. How does the imposition of a minimum real wage of 70 affect labour income now? How does the impact of a minimum wage on labour income depend on the sensitivity of labour demand to the real wage?

7. Consider an economy with 500 people in the labour force. At the beginning of every month 5 people lose their jobs and remain unemployed for exactly one month; one month later, they find new jobs and become employed. In addition, on 1 January of each year 20 people lose their jobs and remain unemployed for six months before finding new jobs. Finally, on 1 July of each year 20 people lose their jobs and remain unemployed for six months before finding new jobs.

a. What is the unemployment rate in this economy in a typical month?

b. What fraction of unemployment spells lasts for one month? What fraction lasts for six months?

c. What is the average duration of an unemployment spell?

d. On any particular date, what fraction of the unemployed are suffering a long spell (six months) of unemployment?

8. Use the data in Figure 3.14 to calculate how many people become unemployed during a typical quarter. How many become employed? How many leave the labour force?

9. You are given the following data on the unemployment rate and output.

Year	1	2	3	4
Unemployment rate	8%	6%	7%	5%
Output	950	1030	1033.5	1127.5

a. Assume that the natural rate of unemployment is 6% and that $(\bar{Y} - Y)/\bar{Y} = 2.5(u - \bar{u})$. Find the full-employment level of output in each year.

b. Calculate the growth rate of full-employment output in years 2, 3, and 4 two different ways. First, calculate the growth rates by using the values for full-employment output that you found in part (a). Then calculate the growth rate of full-employment output by using only the change in the unemployment rate, the growth rate of output, and the growth rate version of Okun's law, equation (3.6). Compare your answers from the two sets of calculations.

10. Consider an economy that initially has a labour force of 2000 workers. Of these workers, 1900 are employed and each works 40 hours per week. Ten units of output are produced by each hour of labour.

a. What is the total number of hours worked per week in the economy? What is the total output per week in the economy?

b. The economy enters a recession. Employment falls by 4%, and the number of hours per week worked by each employed worker falls by 2.5%. In addition, 0.2% of the labour force becomes discouraged at the prospect of finding a job and leaves the labour force. Finally, suppose that whenever total hours fall by 1%, total output falls by 1.4%.

After the recession begins, what is the size of the labour force? How many workers are unemployed and what is the unemployment rate? What is the total output per week in the economy?

By what percentage has total output fallen relative to the initial situation? What is the value of the Okun's law coefficient relating the loss of output to the increase in the unemployment rate?

Analytical Problems

1. **a.** A technological breakthrough raises a country's total factor productivity A by 10%. Show how this change affects the graphs of both the production function relating output to capital and the production function relating output to labour.

   b. Show that a 10% increase in A also increases the MPK and the MPN by 10% at any level of capital and labour. (*Hint:* What happens to ΔY for any increase in capital ΔK or for any increase in labour ΔN?)

   c. Can a beneficial supply shock leave the MPK and MPN unaffected? Show graphically.

2. How would each of the following affect the current level of full-employment output? Explain.

   a. A large number of immigrants enter the country.

   b. Energy supplies become depleted.

   c. New teaching techniques improve the educational performance of secondary school students.

   d. A new law mandates the shutdown of some unsafe forms of capital.

3. During the 1980s the average rate of unemployment in Europe was high. Some economists claimed that this rate was in part the result of 'real-wage rigidity', a situation in which unions kept real wages above their market-clearing levels.

   a. Accepting for the sake of argument that real wages were too high in Europe in the 1980s, show how this would lead to unemployment (a situation where people who would like to work at the going wage cannot find jobs).

   b. What is the effect of real-wage rigidity on the output actually supplied by firms, relative to the output they would supply if there were no real-wage rigidity?

4. How would each of the following affect Heather Handbasket's supply of labour?

   a. The value of Heather's home triples in an unexpectedly hot property market.

   b. Originally an unskilled worker, Heather acquires skills that give her access to a higher-paying job. Assume that her preferences about leisure are not affected by the change in jobs.

   c. A temporary income tax surcharge raises the percentage of her income that she must pay in taxes, for the current year only. (Taxes are proportional to income in Heather's country.)

5. Suppose that under a new law all businesses must pay a tax equal to 6% of their sales revenue. Assume that this tax is not passed on to consumers. Instead, consumers pay the same prices after the tax is imposed as they did before. What is the effect of this tax on labour demand? If the labour supply curve is unchanged, what will be the effect of the tax on employment and the real wage?

6. Can the unemployment rate and the employment ratio rise during the same month? Can the participation rate fall at the same time that the employment ratio rises? Explain.

APPENDIX 3.A

THE GROWTH RATE FORM OF OKUN'S LAW

To derive the growth rate form of Okun's law, equation (3.6), we start with the basic form of Okun's law, equation (3.5):

$$\frac{\overline{Y} - Y}{\overline{Y}} = 2.5(u - \overline{u}) \tag{3.5}$$

After multiplying by -1, we rewrite equation (3.5) as

$$-1 + \frac{Y}{\overline{Y}} = -2.5u + 2.5\overline{u}$$

We now calculate the change from the previous year to the current year for each side of this equation. Setting the change on the left-hand side equal to the change on the right-hand side, and assuming that $\overline{u}$ is constant (so that $\Delta \overline{u} = 0$), we get

$$\Delta(Y/\overline{Y}) = -2.5\, \Delta u$$

The left-hand side of this equation, which is the change in $Y/\overline{Y}$, is very close to the growth rate of $Y/\overline{Y}$, which is $\Delta(Y/\overline{Y})/(Y/\overline{Y})$. (To go from the change to the growth rate, we divide by $Y/\overline{Y}$, which is a number close to 1.) Approximating the change in $Y/\overline{Y}$ by the growth rate, and using the formula that states that the growth rate of a ratio is the growth rate of the numerator minus the growth rate of the denominator (Appendix A, Section A.7), we rewrite the equation once more as

$$\frac{\Delta Y}{Y} - \frac{\Delta \overline{Y}}{\overline{Y}} = -2.5\, \Delta u$$

Rearranging this equation gives the growth rate form of Okun's law, equation (3.6).

CHAPTER 4

CONSUMPTION, SAVING, AND INVESTMENT

Chapter 3 focused on some of the factors determining the amount of output produced, or *supplied,* in the economy. This chapter considers the factors that underlie the economy-wide *demand* for goods and services. In other words, we move from examining how much is produced to examining how that production is used.

Recall from Chapter 2 that aggregate demand (spending) in the economy has four components: the demand for consumer goods and services by households (consumption), the demand for new capital goods by firms (investment), government purchases of goods and services, and the net demand for domestic goods by foreigners (net exports). Because the level of government purchases is determined primarily by the political process, macroeconomic analysis usually treats that component of spending as given. For this chapter we also assume that the economy is closed so that net exports are zero (we drop the closed-economy assumption in Chapter 5). That leaves two major components of spending – consumption and investment – to be discussed in this chapter. Section 4.1 presents the factors that determine how much households choose to consume, and Section 4.2 looks at the decision by firms about how much to invest.

We have said that this chapter is about the aggregate demand for goods and services. However, we could just as easily say that it is about a seemingly very different (but equally important) topic: the determination of saving and capital formation. Studying the aggregate demand for goods and services is the same as studying the factors that determine saving and capital formation for the following reasons. First, saving is simply what is left after an economic unit (say, a household) decides how much of its income to consume. Thus the decision about how much to consume is the same as the decision about how much to save. Second, investment spending is part of the aggregate demand for goods and services, but it also represents the acquisition of new capital goods by firms; and so, in studying investment spending, we are also looking at the factors that lead an economy to acquire new factories, machines, and housing. In effect, we do two things at once in this chapter:

■ We explore the determinants of the aggregate demand for goods, which prepares you for future discussions of topics such as the role of spending fluctuations in business cycles.

■ While exploring aggregate demand we also examine the factors affecting saving and capital formation, which prepares you for future discussions of the sources of economic growth and other issues.

In making many economic decisions, including those we consider in this chapter, people must trade off the present against the future. In deciding how much to consume and save, for example, a household must weigh the benefits of enjoying more consumption today against the benefits of putting aside some of its income as saving for the future. Similarly, in deciding how much to invest, a firm's manager must determine how much to spend today in order to increase the firm's productive capacity one, five, or even twenty years from now. In making these trade-offs, households and firms must take into account their expectations about the future of the economy, including expectations about government policy.

In Chapter 3 we asked: what forces act to bring the labour market into equilibrium? We close this chapter by asking the same question for the goods market. The goods market is in equilibrium when the quantity of goods and services that producers want to supply (discussed in Chapter 3) equals the quantity of goods and services demanded by households, firms, and the government (discussed in this chapter). Equivalently, the goods market is in equilibrium when desired saving in the economy equals desired investment. We show that the real interest rate plays a key role in bringing the goods market into equilibrium.

4.1   CONSUMPTION AND SAVING

We begin consideration of the demand for goods and services by discussing the factors that affect consumer spending. Because consumption spending by households is by far the largest component of the demand for goods and services – accounting for about two-thirds of total spending – changes in consumers' willingness to spend have major implications for the behaviour of the economy.

Besides the sheer size of consumption spending, another reason to study consumption is that the individual's or household's decision about how much to consume is closely linked to another important economic decision, the decision about how much to save. Indeed, for given levels of disposable income, the decision about how much to consume and the decision about how much to save are really the same decision. For example, a university student with a part-time job that pays £2000 per year after taxes might decide to spend £1750 per year on clothes, food, entertainment, and other consumption. If she does consume this amount, her saving will automatically be £250 (£2000 minus £1750) per year. Equivalently, she might decide to save £250 per year. If she succeeds in saving £250, her consumption is automatically £1750 (£2000 minus £250) per year. Because the decision about how much to consume and the decision about how much to save actually are two sides of the same coin, we analyse them together.

What determines how much of their current income people choose to consume and how much they choose to save? An important insight is that, in making their economic decisions, most people think about the future as well as the present. They save part of their current income – instead of immediately spending everything they receive – because they care not only about the consumption they get to enjoy today but also about the consumption they hope to enjoy next week, next year, and when they retire. By limiting their current consumption and saving more, people hope to improve their standard of living in the future. Thus consumers face a trade-off between the present and the future: greater current consumption means less saving and (all else being equal) less consumption in the future.

Recognizing that people save now primarily to consume in the future, we can identify the major factors determining current consumption and saving. Here we describe these factors in general terms. We present a more detailed analysis based on a formal model of household decision making in Chapter 8.

Current Income

If you received a one-off bonus at work that raised your current income by £2000, what would you do with it? You would probably spend part of the extra income on consumption goods, perhaps a vacation or a new CD player. You might save the rest – for example, by increasing the balance in your bank account or paying off some debts (a form of saving, because it reduces your liabilities and therefore increases your wealth). Thus the increase in your current income would raise both your total consumption and your total saving.

This response to an increase in current income makes good economic sense: when a person's current income rises, that person feels better off and will thus want to consume more today. But one benefit of a rise in current income is that, in addition to enjoying more consumption today, an individual can also plan for greater future consumption by saving part of the current increase in income. Thus *both consumption and saving should rise when current income rises.* Note that the increases in consumption and in saving must sum to the increase in income, so each separately is less than the increase in income.

The same argument works in reverse if current income falls. Because a decline in income makes an individual worse off, that person will respond both by consuming less today and by putting less aside for future consumption. In response to a decline in current income, therefore, both consumption and saving will fall (although each separately must fall by less than income does).

To demonstrate what these observations about individual behaviour imply about consumption and saving at the macroeconomic level, we first have to define two terms: desired consumption and desired national saving.

- *Desired consumption, C^d,* is the aggregate quantity of goods and services that households want to consume, given income and other factors affecting households' economic opportunities.

- *Desired national saving, S^d,* is the level of national saving that occurs when consumption is at its desired level.

Recall from Chapter 2 that, if net factor payments from abroad (*NFP*) equal zero (as must be true in a closed economy), national saving S equals $Y - C - G$ (equation 2.8), where Y is output, C is consumption, and G is government purchases. Because desired national saving S^d is the level of national saving S that occurs when consumption equals the desired level, we obtain an expression for desired national saving by substituting desired consumption C^d for consumption C in the definition of national saving. This substitution yields

$$S^d = Y - C^d - G \tag{4.1}$$

We use equation (4.1), which defines desired national saving, to look at the effects of an increase in current income at the aggregate level. In macroeconomic terms, a rise in current income corresponds to an increase in total output Y. Our preceding discussion of the effect of current income on an individual's consumption and saving suggests that, when current output Y rises, desired current consumption C^d also rises, but not by as much as the increase in output. Desired consumption rises less than output increases, so desired national saving $Y - C^d - G$ also must rise when output rises.

The relationship between desired consumption C^d and aggregate output Y is sometimes expressed as

$$C^d = c_0 + c_Y Y \tag{4.2}$$

where c_0 and c_Y are constants. Equation (4.2) simply says that desired consumption depends on current aggregate output. This relationship is called the **Keynesian consumption function** because Keynes wrote about it in his *General Theory*. The parameter c_Y is called the marginal propensity to consume. The **marginal propensity to consume**, or *MPC*, is the amount by which desired consumption rises when current output rises by one unit. Because an increase in current output causes desired consumption to rise, but by less than the increase in output, the *MPC* lies between 0 and 1.

The Keynesian consumption function is useful for building simple models of the economy, but it leaves out some important factors besides current output that affect desired consumption. We look at some of these additional influences on consumption next.

Expected Future Income

Suppose that, instead of receiving the £2000 bonus in your current pay cheque, you are told that you will receive the bonus next year. This bonus is legally guaranteed and you have no doubt that you will receive it as promised. What will happen to your current (this year's) consumption and saving? Most likely, *the increase in expected future income will cause your current consumption to rise and your current saving to fall*. Because you know that you will receive the bonus next year, you have less need to save for the future and can enjoy more current consumption instead. Similarly, a drop in expected future income – for example, you learn that your employer is going out of business, which will cost you your job – should make you want to save more and consume less today.

In macroeconomic terms, a rise in expected future income or output raises today's desired consumption C^d. If we assume that today's output Y is unchanged, an increase in C^d will lower desired national saving $Y - C^d - G$.

Economists cannot measure expected future income directly, so how do they take this variable into account when predicting consumption and saving behaviour? As the following application discusses, one approach is to survey consumers and ask them about their expectations.

The theory of consumer behaviour tells us that consumers' decisions on how much to consume and how much to save should depend on their expectations about the economy's future. When consumers are generally optimistic about the future, they consume more and save less than when they are pessimistic about it. Thus economic forecasters and other analysts may find it useful to know what consumers are thinking about the future at any particular time.

Various surveys regularly try to measure consumers' expectations. In this application we focus on the European Union's 'consumer confidence indicator' which was started in 1972 and which is constructed on the basis of surveys of consumer opinion carried out in all member states except Greece and Luxembourg. The indicator of consumer sentiment is based on the responses of roughly 2,500 households per country to questions about their household's current and expected financial situation over the next twelve months, about any major purchases recently made by the household or any which they expect to make in the near future, about their holiday spending intentions, and about their car ownership and the ownership of certain other consumer durables. They are also asked about the current economic state of the country as reflected in their views about inflation and unemployment. The indicator is a weighted total of the percentage responses to the various questions and the weighting scheme is such that the possible values for the series lie within the range −100 to +100, with positive values corresponding to greater consumer optimism. The indicator is published in a detailed monthly report called *European Economy Consumer Survey Results*.

Historically, the indicator has been a sensitive indicator of recessions and other macroeconomic shocks. Figure 4.1(a) shows quarterly data for the consumer confidence indicator for the period from 1978 to 1996 for the UK and the Netherlands. Figure 4.1(b) shows quarterly real consumption data for the same period for both countries.

The consumer confidence indicator in both the Netherlands and the UK dropped sharply during the 1980–81 recession, but it also recovered quickly in the UK with consumer confidence rising again by the end of 1981. In the Netherlands consumer confidence did not start to recover until 1984. Note that the stock market crash of October 1987 caused a drop in the indicator of consumer confidence in both countries, but one that was quickly reversed. In the Netherlands, real consumption also fell.

In the UK, the indicator took its sharpest decline, however, in 1988, which coincided with a marked increase in domestic interest rates, and continued to fall through the 1990–91 recession. As Figure 4.1(b) shows, consumer spending in the UK declined when the consumer confidence indicator was at its lowest. In contrast, the decline in consumer confidence in the Netherlands came later and was more gradual, reflecting both the timing of the recession in most European countries compared with its timing in the UK and the fact that the recession was less severe in the Netherlands than it was in the UK.

Wealth

Another factor that affects consumption and saving is the stock of wealth. Recall from Chapter 2 that the wealth of any entity, such as a household or an entire nation, equals its assets minus its liabilities.

**Figure 4.1(a)
Consumer confidence,
Netherlands and the
UK 1978–96**
The index of consumer
confidence is based on
what consumers tell
interviewers about their
expectations for the
future of the economy.
The index of consumer
sentiment dipped sharply
in both the Netherlands
and the UK in the
recession years of the
early 1980s and again
during the stock market
crash in October 1987.

Source: Data for the period
1978–82 from *European
Economy Supplement C,
Consumer Survey Results*,
European Commission, Brussels
(revised historical series), 1983;
Data for the period 1983–96
from *European Economy,
Supplement B, Business and
Consumer Survey Results*,
European Commission, Brussels
(various issues).

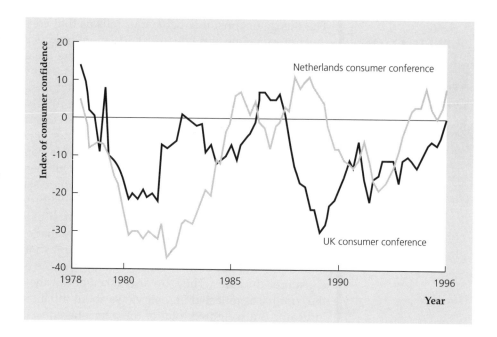

**Figure 4.1(b)
Consumption,
Netherlands and the
UK 1978–96**
The figure shows real
consumption
expenditures from the
first quarter of 1978
through the last quarter
of 1996. Consumption
in the Netherlands
declined after the stock
market crash of 1987.
In the UK consumption
growth fell slightly in
1987 and consumption
fell sharply along with
the index of consumer
confidence in the
recession which started
in the second quarter of
1990.

Source: *Datastream* Private
Consumption Expenditures
(Netherlands); Consumer
Expenditure (UK).

To see the effect of wealth on consumption and saving, imagine that you
learn that your old stamp collection (which you had always thought to be of
no value) is worth £2000. You sell the collection and deposit the money in your
bank account. How does this £2000 increase in wealth affect your economic
behaviour? In terms of your economic well-being, receiving this unexpected
windfall of £2000 is effectively the same as receiving a £2000 bonus at work; as

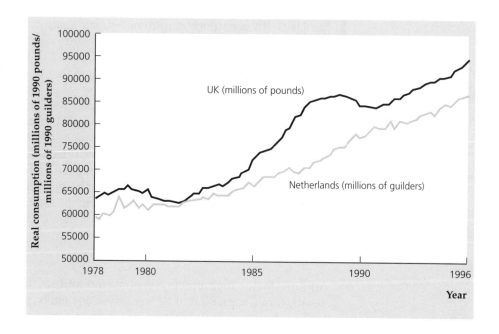

when you received the bonus at work, you would probably use some of the £2000 to increase current consumption. What about saving? Because your current income has not changed,[1] the increase in current consumption necessarily implies that your saving is lower. Generally, when wealth increases there is less need to save for the future out of current income. Hence *an increase in wealth raises current consumption and lowers current saving.*

In macroeconomic terms, the results are analogous: an increase in aggregate wealth increases desired consumption C^d. However, if we assume that current output Y is unchanged by the increase in wealth, the increase in wealth reduces desired national saving $Y - C^d - G$. Similarly, if wealth decreases, desired consumption will fall and desired national saving will rise. The next application illustrates the effects of a change in wealth on consumer behaviour.

APPLICATION
The 1987 Stock Market Crash and Consumer Spending

On 19 October, 1987 stock market prices on Wall Street took their biggest ever one-day plunge and this was followed by a sharp fall in prices on European stock markets as part of a world-wide decline in stock prices. The downward trend in stock prices on European stock markets continued for three weeks, by which time stock prices in London, Paris, and Frankfurt had fallen by over 30%. Although estimates differ, in the three weeks following 19 October about £100 billion of financial wealth (equal in value to more than three months' GDP) was eliminated through declining stock values in the UK alone.

According to economic theory, how should a stock market crash affect consumers' spending? There are two possible channels.

First, the crash reduced households' wealth, which should have reduced consumption. According to theory, however, the effect on current consumption should have been much smaller than the reduction in wealth; the reason is that consumers would be expected to spread the effects of their losses in wealth over a long period of time, reducing the consumption they had planned for future years as well as current consumption. We can get a quick estimate of the effect of a drop in stock values on current consumption by supposing that consumers spread their reduction in consumption over 25 years. Also, for simplicity, let's assume that the real interest rate is zero.[2] Hence, in response to a £100 billion loss in wealth, consumers would plan to reduce their consumption in each of the next 25 years by 1/25 of £100 billion, or £4 billion per year. This number is consistent with an estimate presented in the London Business School Centre for Economic Forecasting's October 1987 *Economic Outlook* of the likely effects of the stock market crash on current consumption. To the extent that current income was unaffected by the crash, saving would have to rise by the same amount that consumption fell.

---

1. An increase in the value of assets that you own, such as the stamp collection, is an increase in wealth but is not counted as an increase in income. Analogously, for the economy as a whole, an increase in stock prices raises national wealth but the increase in stock values is not counted as part of income.
2. If the real interest rate were positive, in calculating the effect on consumption we would have to take into account the interest that the lost £100 billion would have earned in future years.

The second way a crash could affect consumption is that it might lead consumers to expect bad economic times ahead and falling future incomes. As discussed previously, a reduction in expected future income tends to reduce current consumption and raise current saving. Surveys of consumer attitudes did find significant declines in consumer confidence about the future in the months following the crash (see the preceding Application, 'Consumer Confident and Recessions'). This effect appeared to be temporary, however; by early 1988, consumer confidence had recovered completely (see Figure 4.1(a)).

What, then, was the actual effect of the October stock market crash on consumption? Consumption behaviour is affected by many factors, and isolating the influence of any single factor is not easy. C. Alan Garner[3] of the Kansas City Federal Reserve Bank estimated that the crash led to a $7.5–10 billion shortfall in US consumption between October 1987 and January 1988, or $30–40 billion at an annual rate. The crash is estimated to have cut financial wealth in the USA by $1 trillion. If we again assume a zero rate of interest and that the reduction in wealth is spread over 25 years, consumption would thus fall by $40 billion in each of the next 25 years. So Garner's estimates are reasonably close to this calculation of the direct impact of the change in wealth on consumption, but they leave no room for an impact on expected future incomes. David Runkle[4] of the Minneapolis Federal Reserve Bank argued that the overall effect of the crash on the US economy was surprisingly small, probably less than the $40 billion predicted. Moreover, it seems that the decline in stock prices had very little effect on consumer spending in many European countries. For the UK, researchers at the Bank of England in early 1988 noted that 'Although it is too early to assess properly the effect of the decline in share price activity, there are signs that it has had only a limited impact so far.'[5] This was an opinion shared by economic analysts at the OECD.[6]

The theory was correct, then, in predicting that the loss of financial wealth in the crash should reduce consumption and increase saving, but the effects on consumption and saving appeared to be even smaller than the small effect predicted by the theory. Why? One possible explanation is connected with the unusually erratic behaviour of stock prices during 1987. The tremendous decline in stock prices late in the year mirrored equally impressive gains earlier in the year. Because the earlier increase of stock prices was so rapid, it is possible that by August 1987 stockholders had not yet fully adjusted their consumption and saving behaviour to their higher level of wealth. Thus when the market fell, consumption did not have to decline by very much in order to fall back into line with wealth.

Other explanations for the small effect of the crash on consumption in the UK focus on the steep rise in real earnings through 1987 and on the sharp fall in interest rates which followed the crash, both of which may have had offsetting effects on consumption. In Europe generally, the small impact of the fall in stock prices on consumer spending is probably a reflection of the limited extent of personal-sector share holdings in many European countries.

---

3. 'Has the Stock Market Crash Reduced Consumer Spending?' Federal Reserve Bank of Kansas City, *Economic Review,* April 1988, pp. 3–16.
4. 'Why No Crunch from the Crash?' Federal Reserve Bank of Minneapolis, *Quarterly Review,* Winter 1988, pp. 2–7. Interestingly, when the Japanese stock market fell sharply in early 1990, the effect on consumption again appeared to be quite small.
5. Bank of England, *Quarterly Bulletin,* February 1988, p. 10.
6. OECD, *Economic Outlook,* June 1988, p. 2.

The Expected Real Interest Rate

An important aspect of saving is that the funds people put aside usually earn interest or some other form of return. We showed in Chapter 2 that the rate at which the real value of a financial investment is expected to grow over time is the expected real interest rate, or the nominal interest rate minus the expected rate of inflation.

Suppose that the real interest rate that people expect to earn on their saving increases. How will this higher real interest rate affect the amount of saving that people do (and hence the amount that they consume)?

Economists have pointed out that a higher real interest rate affects people's incentive to save in two opposite ways. On the one hand, a higher real interest rate means that saving today will have a larger pay-off in the future, in terms of the goods and services the accumulated saving will be able to buy. This greater future reward for saving tends to make people more eager to save when the real interest rate rises.

On the other hand, a higher real interest rate means that less saving has to be done today to achieve any future savings target. Consider the doting parents of a young genius who know that they have to accumulate 100,000 French francs (in 1994 francs) by the year 2005 to pay university fees, etc. The higher the real interest rate, the faster their savings will grow and the less they will have to put aside each month to achieve their long-run goal. Thus to the extent that some people are 'target savers,' a higher real interest rate will depress saving.

Economic theory does not indicate whether the positive or the negative effect on saving of a higher real interest rate is the stronger, so we must rely on empirical studies (studies that examine this relationship by using actual data). Unfortunately, interpretation of the empirical evidence from the many studies done is still disputed. The most widely accepted conclusion seems to be that an increase in the real interest rate reduces consumption and increases saving but that this effect is not very strong.

Taxes and the Real Return to Saving. In discussing the real return that savers earn, we have not yet mentioned an important practical consideration: interest earnings (and other returns on savings) are taxed. Because part of interest earnings must be paid as taxes, the real return earned by savers is actually less than the difference between the nominal interest rate and expected inflation.

A useful measure of the returns received by savers that recognizes the effects of taxes is the *expected after-tax real interest rate*. To define this concept, we let i represent the nominal interest rate and t the rate at which interest income is taxed. In Europe, for example, most interest earnings are taxed as ordinary income, so t is the income tax rate. Savers retain a fraction $(1 - t)$ of total interest earned so that the after-tax *nominal* interest rate, received by savers after payment of taxes, is $(1 - t)i$. The **expected after-tax real interest rate**, $r_{a\text{-}t}$, is the after-tax nominal interest rate minus the expected inflation rate π^e, or

$$r_{a\text{-}t} = (1 - t)i - \pi^e \tag{4.3}$$

The expected after-tax real interest rate is the appropriate interest rate for consumers to use in making consumption and saving decisions because it measures the increase in the purchasing power of their saving after payment of taxes.

IN TOUCH *WITH THE MACROECONOMY*

INTEREST RATES

Although in our theoretical discussions we refer to 'the' interest rate, as if there were only one, actually there are many different interest rates, each of which depends on the identity of the borrower and the terms of the loan. Shown here are some interest rates (the bank or prime rate, and the yield on ten year and corporate bonds) that appeared in *The Economist* for 19–26 October, 1996 for four countries, France, Germany, the Netherlands and the UK. The figures for the other rates are taken from *Datastream*.

	Bank/ prime	Inter- bank rate	3-month treasury bills	10-year government bonds	Corporate bonds
France	6.55	3.41	n.a.	5.93	6.01
Germany	5.50	3.11	n.a.	5.95	5.35
Netherlands	4.25	2.86	n.a.	5.85	6.08
United Kingdom	6.75	5.97	5.66	7.54	8.26

The bank or prime rate (called the base rate in the UK) is the basic rate that commercial banks charge on loans to their best customers. The inter-bank rate is the rate at which banks make loans (typically overnight, but they can be up to one year) to each other. Treasury bills and government bonds are each country's government debt, and corporate bonds are the debt of private issuers. With the exception of the bank/prime rates, these interest rates vary continuously as financial market conditions change.

The interest rates charged on these different types of loan need not be the same. One reason for this variation is differences in the risk of non-repayment, or default. Government debt is believed to be free from default risk, but there is always a chance that a business or bank may not be able to repay what it borrowed. Lenders charge risky borrowers extra interest to compensate themselves for the risk of default. Thus bank and prime rates, and rates on corporate bonds, tend to be higher than they would be if there were no default risk.

A second factor affecting interest rates is the length of time for which the funds are borrowed. Comparing the different government obligations, you can see that generally (although not always) lenders charge a higher interest rate on long-term loans than on short-term loans. Thus the interest rate on UK Treasury bills repayable in three months was about 5.66% (annual rate) at that time and the interest rate on ten-year loans to the government was more than 7%. The inter-bank rate, the rate on overnight loans between banks, is one of the lowest of the interest rates in the table, even though this rate reflects some default risk.

Although the levels of the various interest rates are quite different, interest rates tend to go up and down together. For example, all the interest rates in the table had fallen from a year earlier (although by different amounts). Because interest rates tend to move together, it is reasonable to talk about a change in 'the' interest rate in our economic analyses.

Table 4.1 shows how to calculate the after-tax nominal interest rate and the expected after-tax real interest rate. Note that, given the nominal interest rate and expected inflation, a reduction in the tax rate on interest income increases the nominal and real after-tax rates of return that a saver receives. Thus, by reducing the rate at which it taxes interest, the government can increase the real rate of return earned by savers and (possibly) increase the rate of saving in the economy. The stimulation of saving is the motivation for tax provisions such as tax exempt savings accounts (TESSAs in the UK), which allow savers to shelter part of their interest earnings from taxes and thus earn higher after-tax rates of return. Unfortunately, because economists disagree about the effect of higher real interest rates on saving, the effectiveness of TESSAs and similar tax breaks for saving is also in dispute.

Table 4.1   Calculating After-Tax Interest Rates

---

i = nominal interest rate = 5% per year
π^e = expected inflation rate = 2% per year

Example 1
t = tax rate on interest income = 30%
After-tax nominal interest rate = $(1 - t)i = (1 - 0.30)5\% = 3.5\%$
Expected after-tax real interest rate = $(1 - t)i - \pi^e = (1 - 0.30)5\% - 2\% = 1.5\%$

Example 2
t = tax rate on interest income = 20%
After-tax nominal interest rate = $(1 - t)i = (1 - 0.20)5\% = 4\%$
Expected after-tax real interest rate = $(1 - t)i - \pi^e = (1 - 0.20)5\% - 2\% = 2\%$

Fiscal Policy

We have just demonstrated how government tax policies can affect the real return earned by savers and thus, perhaps, the saving rate. However, even when government fiscal policies – its decisions about spending and taxes – are not intentionally directed at affecting the saving rate, these policies have important implications for the amount of consumption and saving that takes place in the economy. Although understanding the links between fiscal policy and consumer behaviour requires some difficult economic reasoning, these links are so important that we introduce them here. We discuss several of these issues further in this book, particularly in Chapters 8 and 16.

To make the discussion of fiscal policy effects as straightforward as possible, we take the economy's aggregate output Y as a given. That is, we ignore the possibility that the changes in fiscal policy that we consider affect the aggregate supply of goods and services. This assumption is valid if the economy is at full employment (as we are assuming throughout Part II of this book) and if the fiscal policy changes do not significantly affect the capital stock or labour supply. Later we relax the fixed-output assumption and discuss both the classical and Keynesian views about how fiscal policy changes can affect output.

In general, fiscal policy affects *desired consumption* C^d primarily by affecting households' current and expected future incomes. More specifically, fiscal changes that increase the tax burden on the private sector, either by raising current taxes or by leading people to expect that taxes will be higher in the future, will cause people to consume less.

For a given level of output Y, government fiscal policies affect *desired national saving* S^d, or $Y - C^d - G$, in two basic ways. First, as we just noted, fiscal policy can influence desired consumption: for any levels of output Y and government purchases G, a fiscal policy change that reduces desired consumption C^d by one pound will at the same time raise desired national saving S^d by one pound. Second, for any levels of output and desired consumption, increases in government purchases directly lower desired national saving, as is apparent from the definition of desired national saving, $S^d = Y - C^d - G$.

To illustrate these general points, we consider how desired consumption and desired national saving would be affected by two specific fiscal policy changes: an increase in government purchases and a tax cut.

Government Purchases. Suppose that current government purchases in France, G, increase by FFr20 billion, say, because the government increases military spending. Assume that this increase in G is temporary so that plans for future government purchases are unchanged. (Analytical Problem 5 at the end of this chapter looks at the case of a permanent increase in government purchases.) For any level of output Y, how will this change in fiscal policy affect desired consumption and desired national saving in the economy?

Let's start by finding the effect of the increased government purchases on consumption. As already mentioned, changes in government purchases affect consumption because they affect private-sector tax burdens. Suppose, for example, that the government pays for the extra FFr20 billion in military spending by raising current taxes by FFr20 billion. For given total (before-tax) output Y, this tax increase implies a FFr20 billion decline in consumers' current (after-tax) incomes. We know that consumers respond to a decline in their current incomes by reducing consumption, although by less than the decline in current income.[7] So, in response to the FFr20 billion tax increase, consumers might reduce their current consumption by FFr12 billion.

What happens to consumption if the government does not raise current taxes when it increases its purchases? The analysis in this case is more subtle. If the government does not raise current taxes, it will have to borrow the FFr20 billion to pay for the extra spending. The government will have to repay the FFr20 billion it borrows, plus interest, sometime in the future, implying that future taxes will have to rise.[8] If taxpayers are clever enough to understand that increased government purchases today mean higher taxes in the future, households' expected future (after-tax) incomes will fall, and again they will reduce desired consumption. For the sake of illustration, we can imagine that they again reduce their current consumption by FFr12 billion, although the reduction in consumption might be less if some consumers do not understand that their future taxes are likely to rise.

What about the effects on desired national saving? The increase in government purchases affects desired national saving, or $Y - C^d - G$, directly by increasing G and indirectly by reducing desired consumption C^d. In our example, the increase in government purchases reduces desired consumption by FFr12 billion, which by itself would raise national saving by FFr12 billion. However, this effect is outweighed by the increase in G of FFr20 billion so that overall desired national saving $Y - C^d - G$ falls by FFr8 billion, with output Y held constant.[9] More generally, because the decline in desired consumption can be expected to be less than the initial increase in government purchases, a temporary increase in government purchases will lower desired national saving.

To summarize, for the current level of output Y, we conclude that a temporary increase in government purchases reduces both desired consumption and desired national saving.

7. Recall that the marginal propensity to consume out of current income is positive but less than 1.
8. For example, the government may increase taxes to help control the government budget deficit, much of which reflects interest on earlier government borrowings.
9. Note that national saving would fall by even more than FFr8 billion if consumers ignored the prospect of future tax increases and thus did not reduce their current consumption.

Taxes. Now suppose that government purchases G remain constant but that the government reduces current taxes T by FFr20 billion. To keep things as simple as possible, we suppose that the tax cut is a *lump sum,* giving each taxpayer the same amount. With government purchases G and output Y held constant, desired national saving $Y - C^d - G$ will change only if desired consumption C^d changes. So the question is, how will desired consumption respond to the cut in current taxes?

Again the key issue is: how does the tax cut affect people's current and expected future incomes? The FFr20 billion current tax cut directly increases current (after-tax) incomes by FFr20 billion, so the tax cut should increase desired consumption (by somewhat less than FFr20 billion). However, the FFr20 billion current tax cut should also lead people to expect *lower* after-tax incomes in the future. The reason is that, because the government has not changed its spending, to cut taxes by FFr20 billion today the government must also increase its current borrowing by FFr20 billion. Because the extra FFr20 billion of government debt will have to be repaid with interest in the future, future taxes will have to be higher, which in turn implies lower future disposable incomes for households. All else being equal, the decline in expected future incomes will cause people to consume less today, offsetting the positive effect of increased current income on desired consumption. Thus, in principle, a current tax cut – which raises current incomes but lowers expected future incomes – could either raise or lower current desired consumption.

Interestingly, some economists argue that the positive effect of increased current income and the negative effect of decreased future income on desired consumption should exactly cancel so that the overall effect of a current tax cut on consumption is zero! The idea that tax cuts do not affect desired consumption and (therefore) also do not affect desired national saving,[10] is called the **Ricardian equivalence proposition.**[11]

The Ricardian equivalence idea can be briefly explained as follows (see Chapter 16 for a more detailed discussion). In the long run, all government purchases must be paid for by taxes. Thus if the government's current and planned purchases do not change, a cut in current taxes can affect the *timing* of tax collections but (advocates of Ricardian equivalence emphasize) not the ultimate tax burden borne by consumers. A current tax cut with no change in government purchases does not really make consumers any better off (any reduction in taxes today is balanced by tax increases in the future), so they have no reason to respond to the tax cut by changing their desired consumption.

---

10. In this example, private disposable income rises by FFr20 billion, so if desired consumption does not change, desired private saving rises by FFr20 billion. However, the government deficit also rises by FFr20 billion because of the tax cut, so government saving falls by FFr20 billion. Therefore desired national saving – private saving plus government saving – does not change.
11. The argument was first advanced by the nineteenth-century economist David Ricardo, although he expressed some reservations about its applicability to real-world situations. The word 'equivalence' refers to the idea that, if Ricardian equivalence is true, taxes and government borrowing have equivalent effects on the economy. For a recent discussion, see *Journal of Eoncomic Perspectives*, Spring 1989, pp. 17–94.

Although the logic of the Ricardian equivalence proposition is sound, many economists question whether it makes sense in practice. Most of these sceptics argue that, even though the proposition predicts that consumers will not increase consumption when taxes are cut, in reality lower current taxes will probably lead to increased desired consumption and thus reduced desired national saving. One reason that consumption may rise after a tax cut is that many, perhaps most, consumers do not understand that increased government borrowing today is likely to lead to higher taxes in the future. Thus consumers may simply respond to the current tax cut, as they would to any other increase in current income, by increasing their desired consumption.

The effects of a tax cut on consumption and saving may be summarized as follows. According to the Ricardian equivalence proposition, with no change in current or planned government purchases, a tax cut does not change desired consumption and desired national saving. However, the Ricardian equivalence proposition may not apply if consumers fail to take account of possible future tax increases in their planning; in that case, a tax cut will increase desired consumption and reduce desired national saving.

The factors that affect consumption and saving are listed in Summary table 5.

SUMMARY 5	An increase in	Causes desired national saving to	Reason
Determinants of Desired National Saving	Current output, Y	Rise	Part of the extra income is saved to provide for future consumption.
	Expected future output	Fall	Anticipation of future income raises current desired consumption, lowering current desired saving.
	Wealth	Fall	Some of the extra wealth is consumed, which reduces saving for given income.
	Expected real interest rate, r	Probably rise	An increased return makes saving more attractive, probably outweighing the fact that less must be saved to reach a specific savings target.
	Government purchases, G	Fall	Higher government purchases directly lower desired national saving.
	Taxes, T	Stay the same or rise	Saving does not change if consumers take into account an offsetting future tax cut; saving rises if consumers do not take into account a future tax cut and thus reduce current consumption.

4.2 INVESTMENT

Let us now turn to a second major component of spending: investment spending by firms. Like consumption and saving decisions, the decision about how much to invest depends largely on expectations about the economy's future. Investment also shares in common with saving and consumption the idea of a trade-off between the present and the future. In making a capital investment, a firm commits its current resources (which could otherwise be used, say, to pay increased dividends to shareholders) to increasing its capacity to produce and earn profits in the future.

Recall from Chapter 2 that investment refers to the purchase or construction of capital goods, including residential and non-residential buildings, machines and equipment used in production, and additions to inventory stocks. From a macroeconomic perspective, there are two main reasons to study investment behaviour. First, more so than the other components of aggregate spending, investment spending fluctuates sharply over the business cycle, falling in recessions and rising in booms. Even though investment is only about one-sixth of GDP, in the typical recession half or more of the total decline in spending is reduced investment spending. Hence explaining the behaviour of investment is important for understanding the business cycle, which we explore further in Part III.

The second reason for studying investment behaviour is that investment plays a crucial role in determining the long-run productive capacity of the economy. Because investment creates new capital goods, a high rate of investment means that the capital stock is growing quickly. As discussed in Chapter 3, capital is one of the two most important factors of production (the other is labour). All else being equal, output will be higher in an economy that has invested rapidly and thus built up a large capital stock than in an economy that has not acquired much capital.

The Desired Capital Stock

To understand what determines the amount of investment, we must consider how firms decide how much capital they want. If firms attempt to maximize profit, as we assume, a firm's **desired capital stock** is the amount of capital that allows the firm to earn the largest expected profit. Managers can determine the profit-maximizing level of the capital stock by comparing the costs and benefits of using additional capital – a new machine, for example. If the benefits outweigh the costs, expanding the capital stock will raise profits. But if the costs outweigh the benefits, the firm should not increase its planned capital stock and may even want to reduce it. As you might infer from this brief description, the economic logic underlying a firm's decision about how much capital to use is similar to the logic of its decision about how many workers to employ, discussed in Chapter 3.

In real terms, the benefit to a firm of having an additional unit of capital is the marginal product of capital, *MPK*. Recall from Chapter 3 that the *MPK* is the increase in output that a firm can obtain by adding a unit of capital, holding constant the firm's workforce and other factors of production. Because lags occur in obtaining and installing new capital, the expected *future* marginal product of capital, MPK^f, is the benefit from increasing investment today by one unit of capital. This expected future benefit must be compared to the expected cost of using that extra unit of capital, or the user cost of capital.

The User Cost of Capital. To make the discussion of the user cost of capital more concrete, let us consider the case of Jack's Bakery, a company that produces speciality biscuits. Jack, the bakery's owner–manager, is considering investing in a new solar-powered oven that will allow him to produce more biscuits in the future. If he decides to buy such an oven, he must also determine its size. In making this decision, Jack has the following three items of information:

1. A new oven can be purchased in any size at a price of £1000 per cubic metre, measured in real (base-year) pounds.

2. Because the oven is solar powered, using it does not involve energy costs. The oven also does not require maintenance expenditures.[12] However, the oven becomes less efficient as it ages: With each year that passes, the oven produces 10% fewer biscuits. Because of this depreciation, the real value of an oven falls 10% per year. For example, after one year of use, the real value of the oven is £900 per cubic metre.

3. Jack can borrow (from a bank) or lend (to the government, by buying a one-year government bond) at the prevailing expected real interest rate of 8% per year.

In calculating the user cost of capital, we use the following symbols (the numerical values are from the example of Jack's Bakery):

$$p_K = \text{real price of capital goods (£1000 per cubic metre);}$$
$$d = \text{rate at which capital depreciates (10\% per year);}$$
$$r = \text{expected real interest rate (8\% per year).}$$

The **user cost of capital** is the expected real cost of using a unit of capital for a specified period of time. For Jack's Bakery, we consider the expected costs of purchasing a new oven, using it for a year, then selling it. The cost of using the oven has two components: a depreciation cost and an interest cost.

In general, the depreciation cost of using capital is the value lost as the capital wears out. Because of depreciation, after one year the oven that Jack pays £1000 per cubic metre for when new will be worth only £900 per cubic metre. The £100-per-cubic-metre loss that Jack suffers over the year is the depreciation cost of using the oven. Even if Jack does not sell the oven at the end of a year, he suffers this loss because at the end of the year the asset's (the oven's) economic value will be 10% less.

The interest cost of using capital equals the expected real interest rate times the price of the capital. As the expected real interest rate is 8%, Jack's interest cost of using the oven for a year is 8% of £1000 per cubic metre, or £80 per cubic metre. To see why the interest cost is a cost of using capital, imagine first that Jack must borrow the funds necessary to buy the oven; in this case, the interest cost of £80 per cubic metre is the interest he pays on the

---

12. These assumptions simplify the example. If there were operating costs, such as fuel and maintenance costs, we would subtract them from the expected future marginal product of capital when calculating the benefit of using the machine.

loan, which is obviously part of the total cost of using the oven. Alternatively, if Jack uses profits from the business to buy the oven, he gives up the opportunity to use those funds to buy an interest-bearing asset, such as a government bond. For every £1000 that Jack puts into the oven, he is sacrificing £80 in interest that he would have earned by purchasing a £1000 government bond. This forgone interest is a cost to Jack of using the oven. Thus the interest cost is part of the true economic cost of using capital, whether the capital's purchase is financed with borrowed funds or with the firm's own retained profits.

The user cost of capital is the sum of the depreciation cost and the interest cost. The interest cost is rp_K, the depreciation cost is dp_K, and the user cost of capital, uc, is

$$uc = rp_K + dp_K = (r + d)p_K \qquad (4.4)$$

In the case of Jack's Bakery,

$$uc = 0.08(\text{£1000 per cubic metre}) + 0.10(\text{£1000 per cubic metre})$$
$$= \text{£180 per cubic metre}$$

Thus Jack's user cost of capital is £180 per cubic metre per year.

Determining the Desired Capital Stock. Now we can find a firm's profit-maximizing capital stock, or desired capital stock. A firm's desired capital stock is the capital stock at which the expected future marginal product of capital equals the user cost of capital.

Figure 4.2 shows the determination of the desired capital stock for Jack's Bakery. The capital stock K, expressed as cubic metres of oven capacity, is measured along the horizontal axis. Both the MPK^f and the user cost of capital are measured along the vertical axis.

Figure 4.2
Determination of the desired capital stock
The desired capital stock (50 cubic metres of oven capacity in this example) is the capital stock that maximizes profits. When the capital stock is 50 cubic metres, the expected future marginal product of capital MPK^f is equal to the user cost of capital uc. If the MPK^f is larger than uc, as it is when the capital stock is 40 cubic metres, the benefit of extra capital exceeds the cost, and the firm should increase its capital stock. If the MPK^f is smaller than uc, as it is at 60 cubic metres, the cost of extra capital exceeds the benefit, and the firm should reduce its capital stock.

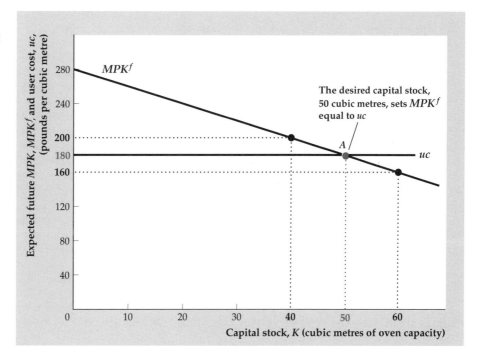

BOX 4.1

Investment and the Stock Market

Fluctuations in the stock market can have important macroeconomic effects. We saw earlier in this chapter that changes in stock prices may cause households to change how much they consume and save (see the Application, 'The 1987 Stock Market Crash and Consumer Spending', p. 119). Similarly, economic theory suggests that rises and falls in the stock market should lead firms to change their rates of capital investment in the same direction. The relationship between stock prices and firms' investments in physical capital is captured by the '*q* theory of investment', developed by Nobel laureate James Tobin of Yale University.

The *q* theory can be illustrated by an example from another market, the property market. Suppose that homes in a particular town are selling for £100,000 (that is, £100,000 is a typical home's *market value*). However, construction firms determine that they can build a home in this town for a total cost (inclusive of the cost of land and the user cost of the builder's capital equipment) of £80,000. We refer to the £80,000 as the *replacement cost* of a typical home. Since it costs £80,000 to build a home that can then be sold for £100,000, giving the builder a clear profit of £20,000, we would expect to see a lot of home building (a high rate of investment in residential capital) taking place in this town.

More generally, Tobin argued that the rate of investment in any particular type of capital can be predicted by looking at the ratio of the capital's market value to its replacement cost. (In the property example, this ratio is £100,000/£80,000 = 1.25.) Tobin dubbed this ratio *q*, or as we call it today in his honour, *Tobin's q*. When Tobin's *q* for a specific type of capital greatly exceeds 1, so that the capital good can be sold for much more than its cost of production, we should expect to see a high rate of investment in that type of capital. When Tobin's *q* for a specific type of capital is low, the rate of investment in that type of capital should be lower. If Tobin's *q* is below 1, so that the cost of building the capital good exceeds its market value, then we should see no investment at all in that particular type of capital.

To see how Tobin's theory relates to the stock market, recall that the stock price of a firm multiplied by the number of shares of stock outstanding equals the market value of the firm. Much of the value of firms comes from the capital that they own. Thus when stock prices rise, it is likely that the market value of firms' capital also rises; and, similarly, when the stock market falls, the market value of firms' capital is likely to fall. If we let V stand for the stock market value of a firm (which for the moment we assume to be the same as the market value of the firm's capital), K be the amount of capital the firm owns, and p_K be the price of new capital goods, then Tobin's q for an individual firm can be defined by

$$\text{Tobin's } q = V/(p_K K)$$

where $p_K K$ is the replacement cost of the firm's capital stock. Assuming that the replacement cost of capital is not changing too much, a boom in the stock market (increases in V) will cause Tobin's q to rise for most firms, leading to increased rates of investment. Essentially, when the stock market is high, firms find it profitable to expand, since the increase in market value achieved by adding new capital exceeds the cost of the new factories and machines.

Empirically, researchers have found that investment in new capital goods does tend to rise when the stock market rises and fall when the market falls, although the relationship is not always strong. Part of the problem is that, in practice, share prices reflect many firm assets besides capital, such as the patents it holds or the reputation of its products. Thus changes in stock prices are imperfect measures of the changes in the market value of capital.

Although it may seem different, the q theory of investment is very similar to the theory of investment discussed in the text. In the theory developed in the text, we identified three main factors affecting the desired capital stock: the expected future marginal product of capital MPK^f, the real interest rate r, and the purchase price of new capital p_K. Each of these factors also affects Tobin's q: (1) An increase in the expected marginal product of capital tends to increase the expected future earnings of the firm, which raises the stock market value of the firm and thus increases q. (2) A reduction in the real interest rate also tends to raise stock prices (and hence q), as financial investors substitute away from low-yielding bonds and bank deposits and buy stocks instead. (3) A decrease in the purchase price of capital reduces the denominator of the q ratio and thus increases q. Because all three of these changes increase Tobin's q, they also increase the desired capital stock and investment, just as predicted by our analysis in the text.

The downward-sloping curve shows the value of the MPK^f for different sizes of the capital stock K; at each level of K, the MPK^f equals the expected real value of the extra biscuits that could be produced if oven capacity were expanded an additional cubic metre. The MPK^f curve slopes downward because the marginal product of capital falls as the capital stock is increased (we discussed reasons for the diminishing marginal productivity of capital in Chapter 3). The user cost (equal to £180 per cubic metre in the example) does not depend on the amount of capital and is represented by a horizontal line.

The amount of capital that maximizes the expected profit of Jack's Bakery is 50 cubic metres, represented by point A in Figure 4.2. At A, the expected benefit of an additional unit of capital, MPK^f, equals the user cost, uc. For any amount of oven capacity of less than 50 cubic metres, Jack's Bakery could increase its expected profit by increasing oven capacity. For example, Figure 4.2 shows that at a planned capacity of 40 cubic metres the MPK^f of an additional cubic metre is £200 worth of biscuits per year, which exceeds the £180 expected cost of using the additional cubic metre of capacity. Starting from a planned capacity of 40 cubic metres, if Jack adds an extra cubic metre of capacity, he will gain an additional £200 worth of future output while incurring only £180 in expected future costs. Thus expanding beyond 40 cubic metres is profitable for Jack. Similarly, Figure 4.2 shows that at an oven capacity of more than 50 cubic metres, the expected future marginal product of capital, MPK^f, is less than the user cost, uc; in this case Jack's Bakery could increase expected profit by reducing its capital stock. Only when $MPK^f = uc$ will the capital stock be at the level that maximizes expected profit.

As mentioned earlier, the determination of the desired capital stock is similar to the determination of the firm's labour demand, described in Chapter 3. Recall that the firm's profit-maximizing level of employment is the level at which the marginal product of labour equals the wage. Analogously, the firm's profit-maximizing level of capital is the level at which the expected future marginal product of capital equals the user cost, which can be thought of as the 'wage' of capital (the cost of using capital for one period). The desired capital stock can be derived in other ways, as well. In Box 4.1 on the previous page, we discuss the relationship of the desired capital stock to share prices.

Changes in the Desired Capital Stock

Any factor that shifts the MPK^f curve or changes the user cost of capital changes the firm's desired capital stock. For Jack's Bakery, suppose that the real interest rate falls from 8% to 6%. If the real interest rate r is 0.06 and the depreciation rate d and the price of capital p_K remain at 0.10 and £1000 per cubic metre, respectively, the decline in the real interest rate reduces the user cost of capital $(r + d)p_K$ from £180 per cubic metre to $(0.06 + 0.10)$£1000 per cubic metre, or £160 per cubic metre.

This decline in the user cost is shown as a downward shift of the user cost line, from uc^1 to uc^2 in Figure 4.3. After that shift, the MPK^f at the original desired capital stock of 50 cubic metres (point A), or £180 per cubic metre, exceeds the user cost of capital, now £160 per cubic metre (point B). Jack's Bakery can increase its profit by raising planned oven capacity to 60 cubic metres, where the MPK^f equals the user cost of £160 per cubic metre (point C). This example illustrates that a decrease in the expected real interest rate – or any other change that lowers the user cost of capital – increases the desired capital stock.

Figure 4.3
A decline in the real interest rate raises the desired capital stock
For the Jack's Bakery example, a decline in the real interest rate from 8% to 6% reduces the user cost uc of a cubic metre of oven capacity from £180 to £160 per cubic metre and shifts the user cost line down from uc^1 to uc^2. The desired capital stock rises from 50 (point A) to 60 (point C) cubic metres of oven capacity. At 60 cubic metres the MPK^f and the user cost of capital again are equal, at £160 per cubic metres.

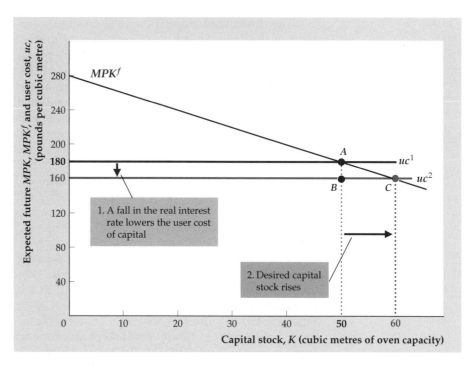

Technological changes that affect the MPK^f curve also affect the desired stock of capital. Suppose that Jack invents a new type of biscuit dough that requires less baking time, allowing 12.5% more biscuits to be baked daily. Such a technological advance would cause the MPK^f curve for ovens to shift upward by 12.5% at each value of the capital stock. Figure 4.4 shows this effect as a shift of the MPK^f curve from MPK^{f1} to MPK^{f2}. If the user cost remains at £180 per cubic metre, the technological advance causes Jack's desired capital stock to rise from 50 to 60 cubic metres. At 60 cubic metres (point D) the MPK^f again equals the user cost of capital. In general, with the user cost of capital held constant, an increase in the expected future marginal product of capital at any level of capital raises the desired capital stock.

Taxes and the Desired Capital Stock. So far we have ignored the role of taxes in the investment decision. But Jack is interested in maximizing the profit his firm gets to keep after paying taxes. Thus he must take into account taxes in evaluating the desirability of an additional unit of capital.

Suppose that Jack's Bakery pays 20% of its revenues in taxes. In this case extra oven capacity that increases the firm's future revenues by, say, £200 will raise Jack's after-tax revenue by only £160, with £40 going to the government. To decide whether to add this extra capacity, Jack should compare the after-tax MPK^f of £160 – not the before-tax MPK^f of £200 – with the user cost. In general, if τ is the tax rate on firm revenues, the after-tax future marginal product of capital is $(1 - \tau)MPK^f$. The desired capital stock is the one for which the after-tax future marginal product equals the user cost, or

$$(1 - \tau)MPK^f = uc$$

Figure 4.4
An increase in the expected future *MPK* raises the desired capital stock

A technological advance raises the expected future marginal product of capital, *MPK*^{f}, shifting the *MPK*^{f} curve upward from *MPK*^{f1} to *MPK*^{f2}. The desired capital stock increases from 50 (point *A*) to 60 (point *D*) cubic metres of oven capacity. At 60 cubic metres the *MPK*^{f} equals the user cost of capital *uc* at £180 per cubic metre.

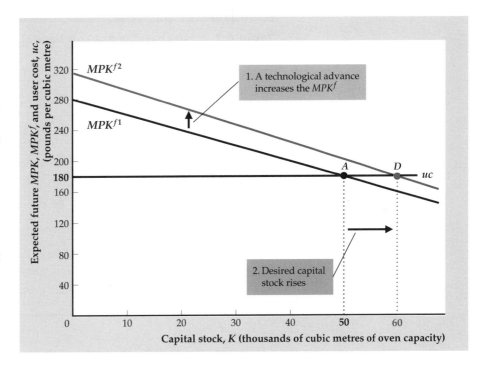

Dividing both sides of this equation by $1 - \tau$, we obtain

$$MPK^f = \frac{uc}{1-\tau} = \frac{(r+d)p_K}{1-\tau} \tag{4.5}$$

In equation (4.5), the term $uc/(1 - \tau)$ is called the tax-adjusted user cost of capital. The **tax-adjusted user cost of capital** shows how large the before-tax future marginal product of capital must be for a firm willingly to add another unit of capital. An increase in the tax rate τ raises the tax-adjusted user cost and thus reduces the desired stock of capital.

To derive the tax-adjusted user cost we assumed that taxes are levied as a proportion of firms' revenues. However, actual corporate taxes in European and other countries are much more complicated. Firms generally pay taxes on their profits rather than on their revenues, and the part of profit that is considered taxable may depend on how much the firm invests. For example, when a firm purchases some capital, it is allowed to deduct part of the purchase price of the capital from its taxable profit in both the year of purchase and subsequent years. By reducing the amount of profit to be taxed, these deductions, known as *depreciation allowances,* allow the firm to reduce its total tax payment.

Another important tax provision, which has been used at various times in most European countries, is the *investment tax credit.* An investment tax credit permits the firm to subtract a percentage of the purchase price of new capital directly from its tax bill. So, for example, if the investment tax credit is 10%, a firm that purchases a £15,000 piece of equipment can reduce its taxes by £1500 (10% of £15,000) in the year the equipment is purchased.

Economists summarize the many provisions of the tax code affecting investment by a single measure of the tax burden on capital called the **effec-**

Table 4.2   Effective Tax Rate on Capital, 1990, Selected Countries

Country	Effective Tax Rate on Capital %
Australia	14.6
Canada	25.9
France	−33.4[†]
Germany	4.6
Italy	−72.8[†]
Japan	6.1
Sweden	1.0
UK	28.0
USA	24.0

[†] A negative effective tax rate indicates that the tax system subsidizes investment.

Source: Dale Jorgenson, 'Tax Reform and the Cost of Capital: An International Comparison', *Tax Notes International*, 19 April, 1993, Table 1.

tive tax rate. Essentially, the idea is to ask: what tax rate τ on a firm's revenue would have the same effect on the desired capital stock as do the actual provisions of the tax code? The hypothetical tax rate that answers this question is the effective tax rate. Changes in the tax law that, for example, raise the effective tax rate are equivalent to an increased tax on firm revenue and a rise in the tax-adjusted user cost of capital. Thus, all else being equal, an increase in the effective tax rate lowers the desired capital stock.

Table 4.2 shows effective tax rates on capital for several countries in 1990. The highest effective tax rates were in the United Kingdom (28.0%), Canada (25.9%), and the United States (24.0%). Although other factors besides the effective tax rate affect investment, investment-to-GDP ratios in these countries are generally lower than in the other countries listed (see the Application 'An International Comparison of National Saving and Investment Rates' in Chapter 2, p. 47). In contrast, 1990 effective tax rates on capital in France and Italy were actually negative, reflecting tax systems that subsidize investment in those countries.

APPLICATION

Measuring the Effects of Taxes on Investment

Does the effective tax rate significantly affect investment patterns? Determining the empirical relationship between tax rates and investment is not easy. One problem is that the factors other than taxes that affect the desired capital stock – such as the expected future marginal product of capital and real interest rates – are always changing, so that it is difficult to isolate the 'pure' effects of tax changes. Another problem is that changes in the tax code do not happen randomly, but reflect the government's assessment of economic conditions. For example, a government is more likely to reduce taxes on investment when investment spending is expected to be unusually low. But if governments behave in this way, then low taxes on capital will tend to be associated with periods of low investment, and the econometrician might mistakenly conclude that tax cuts reduce rather than increase investment spending.

An interesting study that attempted to solve both of these problems was carried out by Jason Cummins and R. Glenn Hubbard of Columbia University and Kevin Hassett of the Board of Governors of the Federal Reserve System.[13] To get around the problem that factors other than taxes are always changing, Cummins, Hubbard, and Hassett focused their attention on the periods around major tax reforms in fourteen OECD countries. The authors' idea was that by looking at occasions in which the tax code changed sharply in a short period of time, they could reasonably assume that most of the ensuing change in investment was due to the tax change rather than other factors. To get around the second problem, that tax cuts tend to take place when aggregate investment is low, Cummins and his co-authors did not look at the behaviour of aggregate investment at all; instead, they compared the investment responses of a large number of individual corporations to each tax reform. Since the tax laws treat different types of capital differently (for example, a machine is taxed differently than a factory), and since companies use capital in different combinations, then observing how different companies changed their investment after each tax reform should provide information on the effectiveness of the tax changes. For example, if a tax reform cuts taxes on machines relative to taxes on factories, and taxes are an important determinant of investment, then we should see companies whose investment is concentrated in machinery respond relatively more strongly to the tax change than companies who invest primarily in factories.

Cummins, Hubbard, and Hassett found considerably stronger effects of tax changes on investment than previous studies, possibly because earlier studies did not deal effectively with the two problems discussed above. These authors found an empirical elasticity that was very similar across most of the countries they examined. For the Netherlands and the UK the elasticity was about –0.6. That is, according to their estimates, a tax change that lowers the user cost of capital by 10% would raise aggregate investment by about 6.0%, a significant amount. Somewhat smaller values were found for Sweden, Italy and France, where the estimated elasticity was between –0.2 and –0.4. For Germany, the authors calculated an elasticity of about –0.8.

From the Desired Capital Stock to Investment

Now let us look at the link between a firm's desired capital stock and the amount it invests. In general, the capital stock (of a firm or of a country) changes over time through two opposing channels. First, the purchase or construction of new capital goods increases the capital stock. We have been calling the total purchase or construction of new capital goods that takes place each year 'investment', but its precise name is **gross investment**. Second, the capital stock depreciates or wears out, which reduces the capital stock.

Whether the capital stock increases or decreases over the course of a year depends on whether gross investment is greater or less than depreciation during the year; when gross investment exceeds depreciation, the capital stock grows. The change in the capital stock over the year – or, equivalently, the difference between gross investment and depreciation – is **net investment**.

---

13. 'Tax Reforms and Investment: A Cross Country Comparison', *Journal of Public Economics*, October 1996, pp. 237–77.

We express these concepts algebraically with the symbols:

I_t = gross investment during year t,
K_t = capital stock at the beginning of year t, and
K_{t+1} = capital stock at the beginning of year $t + 1$ (equivalently, at the end of year t).

Net investment, the change in the capital stock during period t, equals $K_{t+1} - K_t$. The amount of depreciation during year t is dK_t, where d is the fraction of capital that depreciates each year. The relationship between net and gross investment is

$$\text{net investment} = \text{gross investment} - \text{depreciation};$$
$$K_{t+1} - K_t = I_t - dK_t \qquad (4.6)$$

In most but not all years, gross investment is larger than depreciation so that net investment is positive and the capital stock increases. Figure 4.5 shows the behaviour since 1920 of gross and net investment in the United Kingdom, expressed as percentages of GDP; the difference between gross and net investment is depreciation. Note the occasional large swings in both gross and net investment that occurred in several years especially during the 1970s and the negative rates of net investment during World War II (1939–45).

We can use equation (4.6) to illustrate the relationship between the desired capital stock and investment. First, rewriting equation (4.6) gives

$$I_t = K_{t+1} - K_t + dK_t$$

which states that gross investment equals net investment plus depreciation.

Now suppose that firms use information available at the beginning of year t about the expected future marginal product of capital and the user cost of capital and determine the desired capital stock K^* they want by the end of year t (beginning of year $t + 1$). For the moment, suppose also that capital is easily obtainable so that firms can match the actual capital stock at the end of year t,

Figure 4.5
Gross and net investment UK, 1920–96

Gross and net investment in the United Kingdom are shown as percentages of GDP. During World War II net investment was negative, implying that the capital stock was shrinking.

Source: Data for the period 1920–65, gross investment and net investment from Feinstein, *op cit. Figure 1.4*, Tables 40 and 48 respectively; Data for the period 1965–96 from *UK National Accounts, The Blue Book*, London, HMSO (various issues)

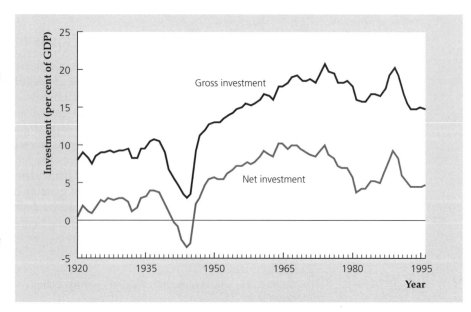

K_{t+1}, with the desired capital stock K^*. Substituting K^* for K_{t+1} in the preceding equation yields

$$I_t = K^* - K_t + dK_t \qquad (4.7)$$

Equation (4.7) shows that firms' gross investment, I_t, during a year has two parts: (1) the desired net increase in the capital stock over the year, $K^* - K_t$; and (2) the investment needed to replace worn-out or depreciated capital, dK_t. The amount of depreciation that occurs during a year is determined by the depreciation rate and the initial capital stock. However, the desired net increase in the capital stock over the year depends on the factors – such as taxes, interest rates, and the expected future marginal product of capital – that affect the desired capital stock. Indeed, equation (4.7) shows that any factor that leads to a change in the desired capital stock K^* results in an equal change in gross investment I_t.

Lags and Investment. The assumption just made, that firms can obtain capital quickly enough to match actual capital stocks with desired levels each year, is not realistic in all cases. Although most types of equipment are readily available, a skyscraper or a nuclear power plant may take years to construct. Thus, in practice, a £1 million increase in a firm's desired capital stock may not translate into a £1 million increase in gross investment within the year; instead, the extra investment may be spread over several years as planning and construction proceed. Despite this qualification, factors that increase firms' desired capital stocks also tend to increase the current rate of investment. Summary table 6 brings together the factors that affect investment.

Investment in Inventories and Housing

Our discussion so far has emphasized what is called business fixed investment, or investment by firms in structures (such as factories and office buildings) and equipment (such as drill presses and jetliners). However, there are two other components of investment spending: inventory investment and residential investment. As discussed in Chapter 2, inventory investment equals the increase in firms' inventories of unsold goods, unfinished goods, or raw materials. Residential investment is the construction of housing, such as single-family homes or blocks of flats.

Fortunately, the concepts of future marginal product and the user cost of capital, which we used to examine business fixed investment, apply equally well to inventory investment and residential investment. Consider, for example, a new-car dealer trying to decide whether to increase the number of cars she normally keeps in her showroom from 100 to 150: that is, to make an inventory investment of 50 cars. The benefit of having more cars to show is that potential car buyers will have a greater variety of models to select from and may not have to wait for delivery, enabling the car dealer to sell more cars. The increase in sales commissions the car dealer expects to make, measured in real terms and with the same sales force, is the expected future marginal product of the increased inventory. The cost of holding more cars reflects (1) depreciation of the cars sitting in the showroom, and (2) the interest the car dealer must pay on the loan obtained to finance the higher inventory. The car dealer will make the inventory investment if the expected benefits of increasing her inventory, in terms of increased sales, are at least as great as the

SUMMARY 6	An increase in	Causes desired investment to	Reason
Determinants of Desired Investment	Real interest rate, r	Fall	The user cost increases, which reduces desired capital stock.
	Effective tax rate	Fall	The tax-adjusted user cost increases, which reduces desired capital stock.
	Expected future MPK	Rise	The desired capital stock increases.

interest and depreciation costs of adding 50 cars. This principle is the same one that applies to business fixed investment.

We can also use this same approach to analyse residential investment. The expected future marginal product of an apartment building, for example, is the real value of rents that can be collected from the tenants, minus taxes and operating costs. The user cost of capital for an apartment building during a year is its depreciation, or loss of value from wear and tear, plus the interest cost (reflected in mortgage payments, for example). As for other types of capital, constructing an apartment building is profitable only if its expected future marginal product is at least as great as its user cost.

4.3   GOODS MARKET EQUILIBRIUM

In Chapter 3 we showed that the quantity of goods and services supplied in an economy depends on the level of productivity – as determined, for example, by the technology used – and on the quantity of inputs, such as the capital and labour used. In this chapter we have discussed the factors that affect the demand for goods and services, particularly the demand for consumption goods by households and the demand for investment goods by firms. But how do we know that the amount of goods and services that consumers and investors want to buy will be the same as the amount that producers are willing to provide? Putting the question another way: what economic forces bring the goods market into equilibrium, with quantities demanded equal to quantities supplied? In this section, we show that the real interest rate is the key economic variable whose adjustments help bring the quantities of goods supplied and demanded into balance; thus a benefit of our analysis is an explanation of what determines interest rates. Another benefit is that, by adding the analysis of goods market equilibrium to the analysis of labour market equilibrium in Chapter 3, we take another large step toward constructing a complete model of the macroeconomy.

The goods market is in equilibrium when the aggregate quantity of goods supplied equals the aggregate quantity of goods demanded. (For brevity, we refer only to 'goods' rather than to 'goods and services,' but services are always included.) Algebraically, this condition is

$$Y = C^d + I^d + G \tag{4.8}$$

The left-hand side of equation (4.8) is the quantity of goods Y supplied by firms, which is determined by the factors discussed in Chapter 3. The right-hand side of equation (4.8) is the aggregate demand for goods. If we continue to assume no foreign sector, so that net exports are zero, the quantity of goods demanded is the sum of desired consumption by households, C^d, desired investment by firms, I^d, and government purchases, G.[14] Equation (4.8) is called the goods market equilibrium condition.

The goods market equilibrium condition is different in an important way from the income–expenditure identity for a closed economy, $Y = C + I + G$ (this identity is equation (2.3), with $NX = 0$). The income–expenditure identity is a relationship between actual income (output) and actual spending, which, by definition, is always satisfied. In contrast, the goods market equilibrium condition does not always have to be satisfied. For example, firms may produce output faster than consumers want to buy it so that undesired inventories pile up in firms' warehouses. In this situation the income–expenditure identity is still satisfied (because the undesired additions to firms' inventories are counted as part of total spending – see Chapter 2); but the goods market would not be in equilibrium because production exceeds *desired* spending (which does *not* include the undesired increases in inventories). Although in principle the goods market equilibrium condition need not always hold, strong forces act to bring the goods market into equilibrium fairly quickly.

A different, but equivalent, way to write the goods market equilibrium condition emphasizes the relationship between desired saving and desired investment. To obtain this alternative form of the goods market equilibrium condition, we first subtract $C^d + G$ from both sides of equation (4.8):

$$Y - C^d - G = I^d$$

The left-hand side of this equation, $Y - C^d - G$, is desired national saving, S^d (see equation 4.1). Thus the goods market equilibrium condition becomes

$$S^d = I^d \qquad (4.9)$$

This alternative way of writing the goods market equilibrium condition says that the goods market is in equilibrium when desired national saving equals desired investment.

Because saving and investment are central to many issues we present in this book, and because the desired-saving-equals-desired-investment form of the goods market equilibrium condition is often is easier to work with, we utilize equation (4.9) in most of our analyses. However, we emphasize once again that equation (4.9) is equivalent to the condition that the supply of goods equals the demand for goods, equation (4.8).

The Saving–Investment Diagram

For the goods market to be in equilibrium, then, the aggregate supply of goods must equal the aggregate demand for goods, or equivalently, desired national saving must equal desired investment. We demonstrate in this section that adjustments of the real interest rate allow the goods market to attain equilibrium.[15]

---

14. We assume that G always equals the level desired by the government and so do not distinguish between desired and actual G.

15. Strictly speaking, we should refer to the expected real interest rate rather than simply the real interest rate. The two are the same if expected inflation and actual inflation are equal.

The determination of goods market equilibrium can be shown graphically with a saving–investment diagram (Figure 4.6). The real interest rate is measured along the vertical axis, and national saving and investment are measured along the horizontal axis. The saving curve, S, shows the relationship between desired national saving and the real interest rate. The upward slope of the saving curve reflects the empirical finding (Section 4.1) that a higher real interest rate raises desired national saving. The investment curve, I, shows the relationship between desired investment and the real interest rate. The investment curve slopes downward because a higher real interest rate increases the user cost of capital and thus reduces desired investment.

Goods market equilibrium is represented by point E, at which desired national saving equals investment, as required by equation (4.9). The real interest rate corresponding to E (6% in this example) is the only real interest rate that clears the goods market. When the real interest rate is 6%, both desired national saving and desired investment equal 1000.

How does the goods market come to equilibrium at E, where the real interest rate is 6%? Suppose instead that the real interest rate is 3%. As Figure 4.6 shows, when the real interest rate is 3%, the amount of investment that firms want to do (1500) exceeds desired national saving (850). With investors wanting to borrow more than savers want to lend, the 'price' of saving – the real interest rate that lenders receive – will be bid up. The return to savers will rise until it reaches 6%, and desired national saving and desired investment are equal. Similarly, if the real interest rate exceeds 6%, the amount that savers want to lend will exceed what investors want to borrow, and the real return paid to savers will be bid down. Thus adjustments of the real interest rate, in response to an excess supply or excess demand for saving, bring the goods market into equilibrium.

Figure 4.6
Goods market equilibrium
Goods market equilibrium occurs when desired national saving equals desired investment. In the figure equilibrium occurs when the real interest rate is 6% and both desired national saving and desired investment equal 1000. If the real interest rate were, say, 3%, desired investment (1500) would not equal desired national saving (850), and the goods market would not be in equilibrium. Competition among borrowers for funds would then cause the real interest rate to rise until it reaches 6%.

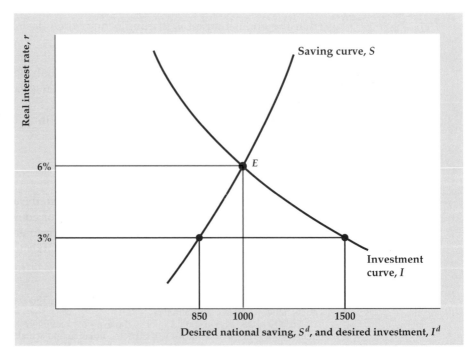

Although Figure 4.6 shows goods market equilibrium in terms of equal saving and investment, keep in mind that an equivalent way to express goods market equilibrium is that the supply of goods, Y, equals the demand for goods, $C^d + I^d + G$ (equation 4.8). Table 4.3 illustrates this point with a numerical example consistent with the values shown in Figure 4.6. Here the assumption is that output Y and government purchases G are fixed at values of 4500 and 1500, respectively. Desired consumption C^d and desired investment I^d depend on the real interest rate. Desired consumption depends on the real interest rate because a higher real interest rate raises desired saving, which necessarily reduces desired consumption. Desired investment depends on the real interest rate because an increase in the real interest rate raises the user cost of capital, which lowers desired investment.

In the example in Table 4.3, when the real interest is 6%, desired consumption $C^d = 2000$. Therefore desired national saving $S^d = Y - C^d - G = 4500 - 2000 - 1500 = 1000$. Also, when the real interest rate is 6%, desired investment $I^d = 1000$. As desired national saving equals desired investment when $r = 6\%$, the equilibrium real interest rate is 6%, as in Figure 4.6.

Note, moreover, that when the real interest rate is at the equilibrium value of 6%, the aggregate supply of goods, Y, which is 4500, equals the aggregate demand for goods, $C^d + I^d + G = 2000 + 1000 + 1500 = 4500$. Thus both forms of the goods market equilibrium condition, equations (4.8) and (4.9), are satisfied when the real interest rate equals 6%.

Table 4.3 also illustrates how adjustments of the real interest rate bring about equilibrium in the goods market. Suppose that the real interest rate initially is 3%. Both components of private-sector demand for goods (C^d and I^d) are higher when the real interest rate is 3% than when it is 6%. The reason is that consumers save less and firms invest more when real interest rates are relatively low. Thus, at a real interest of 3%, the demand for goods ($C^d + I^d + G = 2150 + 1500 + 1500 = 5150$) is greater than the supply of goods ($Y = 4500$). Equivalently, at a real interest rate of 3%, Table 4.3 shows that desired investment ($I^d = 1500$) exceeds desired saving ($S^d = 850$). As Figure 4.6 shows, an increase in the real interest rate to 6% eliminates the disequilibrium in the goods market by reducing desired investment and increasing desired national saving. An alternative explanation is that the increase in the real interest rate eliminates the excess of the demand for goods over the supply of goods by reducing both consumption demand and investment demand.

Table 4.3   Components of Aggregate Demand for Goods (An example)

Real Interest Rate, r	Output, Y	Desired Consumption, C^d	Desired Investment, I^d	Government Purchases, G	Desired National Saving, $S^d = Y - C^d - G$	Aggregate Demand for Goods, $C^d + I^d + G$
3%	4500	2150	1500	1500	850	5150
6%	4500	2000	1000	1500	1000	4500

Shifts of the Saving Curve. For any real interest rate, a change in the economy that raises desired national saving shifts the saving curve to the right, and a change that reduces desired national saving shifts the saving curve to the left. (Summary table 5 lists the factors affecting desired national saving.)

A shift of the saving curve leads to a new goods market equilibrium with a different real interest rate and different amounts of saving and investment. Figure 4.7 illustrates the effects of a decrease in desired national saving – resulting, for example, from a temporary increase in current government purchases. The initial equilibrium point is at E, where (as in Figure 4.6) the real interest rate is 6% and desired national saving and desired investment both equal 1000. When current government purchases increase, the resulting decrease in desired national saving causes the saving curve to shift to the left, from S^1 to S^2. At the new goods market equilibrium point, F, the real interest rate is 7%, reflecting the fact that at the initial real interest rate of 6% the demand for funds by investors now exceeds the supply of saving.

Figure 4.7 also shows that, in response to the increase in government purchases, national saving and investment both fall, from 1000 to 850. Saving falls because of the initial decrease in desired saving, which is only partially offset by the increase in the real interest rate. Investment falls because the higher real interest rate raises the user cost of capital that firms face. When increased government purchases cause investment to decline, economists say that investment has been *crowded out*. The crowding out of investment by increased government purchases occurs, in effect, because the government is using more real resources, some of which would otherwise have gone into investment.

Figure 4.7
A decline in desired saving
A change that reduces desired national saving, such as a temporary increase in current government purchases, shifts the saving curve to the left, from S^1 to S^2. The goods market equilibrium point moves from E to F. The decline in desired saving raises the real interest rate, from 6% to 7%, and lowers saving and investment, from 1000 to 850.

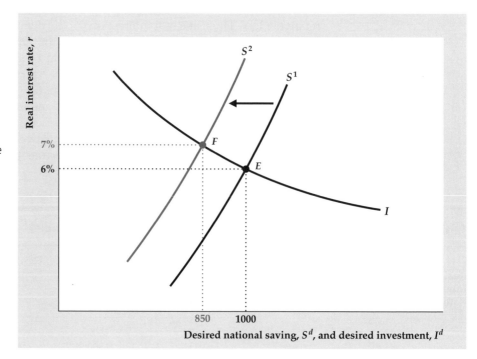

APPLICATION

The Effect of Wars on Investment and the Real Interest Rate

Economically, an important aspect of war and military build-ups in general is that government purchases rise sharply as expenditures on military pay and equipment increase. Also, to a greater degree than other types of increase in government purchases, increases owing to military build-ups are temporary because military expenditures tend to return to lower peacetime levels after a war. Thus thinking of a war as a largely temporary increase in current government purchases is reasonable. Our model predicts that a temporary increase in government purchases associated with a war will increase the real interest rate and reduce investment.

How well do these predictions hold up? Historically, wars (especially large ones) have often had negative effects on investment. Figure 4.8 shows UK real investment spending and real government purchases, measured relative to real GDP, for the period 1925–96. During World War II a large decline in private investment spending mirrored the sharp increase in government purchases. A similar pattern developed during the Korean War in the early 1950s.

Besides predicting that military build-ups will crowd out investment, our analysis also implies that real interest rates will be higher during wars. Robert Barro[16] of Harvard University has studied the behaviour of real interest rates during wars. He found that this prediction of the model does not fit the data well for the United States: although real interest rates were slightly above normal during the Korean and Vietnam wars, they were below normal during the Civil War, World War I, and World War II.

For the US case, especially during the two world wars, government price controls, rationing, and control of production decisions may have prevented the private economy from functioning normally. As an alternative test of the theory, Barro used British data for the period 1730–1913. The British fought many wars,

16. 'The Neoclassical Approach to Fiscal Policy', in Robert Barro (ed), *Modern Business Cycle Theory*, (Harvard University Press, 1989).

Figure 4.8
Shares of government purchases and investment in UK GDP, 1925–96
The graph shows the percentages of UK GDP devoted to government purchases and to investment since 1925. Note the sharp increases in government purchases during World War II when investment's share of GDP fell sharply.

Sources: Investment, as in Figure 4.6; GDP and government purchases, from Table 1.3 *Economic Trends Annual Supplement 1997*, 1997, London, HMSO.

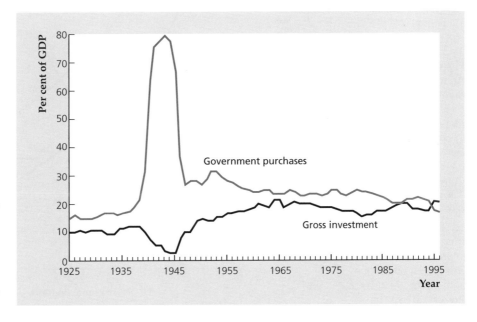

both large and small, during that period, and they rarely invoked price or production controls. Thus the British data should provide a good test of the theory.

Barro found evidence in the British data that real interest rates do rise during wars. Long-term nominal interest rates (which, because inflation was essentially zero over this period, were about the same as real rates) were normally about 3.5% in Britain for this time span. During the American Revolution, however, British rates rose to about 5.5%, and they reached 6% during the Napoleonic Wars. This effect is not huge, but it is statistically significant. For the British case, at least, Barro's evidence is consistent with the prediction that wars raise real interest rates.

Shifts of the Investment Curve. Like the saving curve, the investment curve can shift. For any real interest rate, a change in the economy that raises desired investment shifts the investment curve to the right, and a change that lowers desired investment shifts the investment curve to the left. (See Summary table 6 for the factors affecting desired investment.)

The effects on goods market equilibrium of an increase in desired investment – as from an invention that raises the expected future marginal product of capital – are shown in Figure 4.9. The increase in desired investment shifts the investment curve to the right, from I^1 to I^2, changing the goods market equilibrium point from E to G. The real interest rate rises from 6% to 8% because the increased demand for investment funds causes the real interest rate to be bid up. Saving and investment also increase, from 1000 to 1100, with the higher saving reflecting the willingness of savers to save more when the real interest rate rises.

In these last two chapters we have presented supply–demand analyses of the labour and goods markets and developed tools needed to understand the

Figure 4.9
An increase in desired investment
A change in the economy that increases desired investment, such as an invention that raises the expected future *MPK*, shifts the investment curve to the right, from I^1 to I^2. The goods market equilibrium point moves from E to G, The real interest rate rises form 6% to 8%, and saving and investment also rise, from 1000 to 1100.

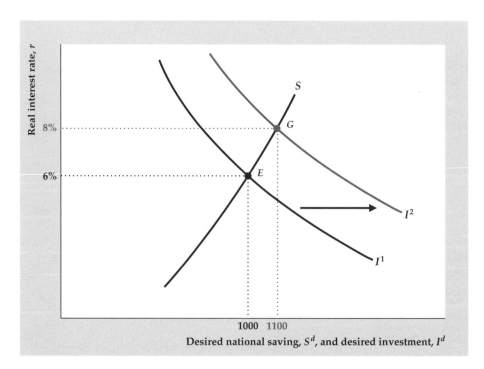

behaviour of various macroeconomic variables, including employment, the real wage, output, saving, investment, and the real interest rate. These concepts – and a few more developed in the study of asset markets in Chapter 7 – form the basis for the economic analysis presented in the rest of this book. In Chapter 5 we use the concepts developed so far to examine the determinants of trade flows and international borrowing and lending. In Chapter 6 we use them to tackle the fundamental question of why some countries' economies grow more quickly than others'.

CHAPTER SUMMARY

1. Because saving equals income minus consumption, a household's decisions about how much to consume and how much to save are really the same decision. Individuals and households save because they value both future consumption and current consumption; for the same amount of income, an increase in current saving reduces current consumption but increases the amount that the individual or household will be able to consume in the future.

2. For an individual or household, an increase in current income raises both desired consumption and desired saving. Analogously, at the national level, an increase in current output raises both desired consumption and desired national saving. At both the household and national levels, an increase in expected future income or in wealth raises desired consumption; however, because these changes raise desired consumption without affecting current income or output, they cause desired saving to fall.

3. An increase in the expected real interest rate has two contradictory effects on saving: an increase in the real interest rate increases the reward to saving but also reduces the amount of saving that must be done to reach a specific target. Empirical estimates suggest that an increase in the real interest rate raises desired national saving (and thus reduces desired consumption)—but not by very much. The expected after-tax real interest rate is the real return that savers expect to earn after paying a portion of interest received in taxes.

4. With total output held constant, a temporary increase in government purchases reduces desired consumption. The reason is that higher government purchases imply increases in present or future taxes, which makes consumers feel poorer. However, the decrease in desired consumption is smaller than the increase in government purchases, so that desired national saving, $Y - C^d - G$, falls as a result of a temporary increase in government purchases.

5. According to the Ricardian equivalence proposition, a current lump-sum tax cut should have no effect on desired consumption or desired national saving. The reason is that, if there is no change in current or planned government purchases, a tax cut that increases current income must be offset by future tax increases that lower expected future income. If consumers do not take account of expected future tax changes, however, the Ricardian equivalence proposition will not hold and a tax cut is likely to raise desired consumption and lower desired national saving.

6. The desired capital stock is the level of capital that maximizes expected profits. At the desired capital stock, the expected future marginal product of capital equals the user cost of capital. The user cost of capital is the expected real cost of using a unit of capital for a period of time; it is the sum of the depreciation cost (the loss in value because the capital wears out) and the interest cost (the interest rate times the price of the capital good).

7. Any change that reduces the user cost of capital or increases the expected future marginal product of capital increases the desired capital stock. A reduction in the taxation of capital, as measured by the effective tax rate, also increases the desired capital stock.

8. Gross investment is spending on new capital goods. Gross investment minus depreciation (worn-out or scrapped capital) equals net investment, or the change in the capital stock. Firms invest in order to achieve their desired level of capital stock; when the desired capital stock increases, firms invest more.

9. The goods market is in equilibrium when the aggregate quantity of goods supplied equals the aggregate quantity of goods demanded, which (in a closed economy) is the sum of desired consumption, desired investment, and government purchases of goods and services. Equivalently,

the goods market is in equilibrium when desired national saving equals desired investment. For any given level of output, the goods market is brought into equilibrium by changes in the real interest rate.

10. The determination of goods market equilibrium, for any supply of output Y, is represented graphically by the saving–investment diagram. The saving curve slopes upward because empirical evidence suggests that a higher real interest rate raises desired saving. The investment curve slopes downward because a higher real interest rate raises the user cost of capital, which lowers firms' desired capital stocks and thus the amount of investment they do. At constant output, changes in variables that affect desired saving or investment shift the saving or investment curves and change the real interest rate that clears the goods market.

KEY DIAGRAM   3

The Saving–Investment Diagram

In an economy with no foreign trade the goods market is in equilibrium when desired national saving equals desired investment. Equivalently, the goods market is in equilibrium when the aggregate quantity of goods supplied equals the aggregate quantity of goods demanded.

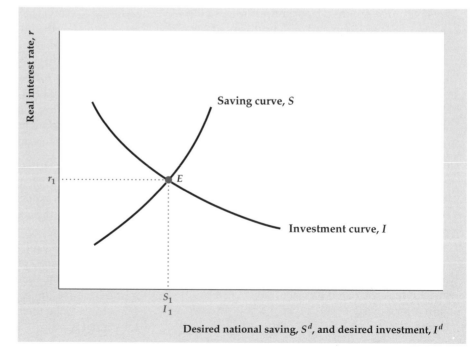

Diagram Elements

■ The real interest rate r is on the vertical axis; desired national saving S^d and desired investment I^d are on the horizontal axis.

■ The saving curve, S, shows the level of desired national saving at each real interest rate. The saving curve slopes upward because a higher real interest rate increases the reward for saving and causes households to save more. (Empirically, this effect outweighs the tendency of a higher real interest rate to lower saving by reducing the amount of saving necessary to reach any specified target.) Desired national saving is defined as $S^d = Y - C^d - G$, where Y is output, C^d is desired consumption, and G is government purchases.

■ The investment curve, I, shows the amount that firms want to invest in new capital goods at each real interest rate. The investment curve slopes downward because a higher real interest rate raises the user cost of capital and thus lowers the amount of capital that firms want to use.

Analysis

■ Goods market equilibrium requires that desired national saving equal desired investment, or $S^d = I^d$.

■ Goods market equilibrium occurs in the diagram at point E, where the saving curve and investment curve intersect. At E desired national saving equals S_1, desired investment equals I_1, and $S_1 = I_1$. The real interest rate at E, r_1, is the real interest rate that clears the goods market.

■ An alternative way to express the goods market equilibrium condition is as follows: the quantity of goods supplied, Y, equals the quantity of goods demanded by households, C^d, firms, I^d, and the government, G, or $Y = C^d + I^d + G$. As $S^d = Y - C^d - G$, this condition is equivalent to $S^d = I^d$.

Factors that Shift the Curves

■ Any factor that raises desired national saving at a given real interest rate shifts the saving curve to the right; similarly, any factor that lowers desired national saving shifts the saving curve to the left. Factors that affect desired national saving are listed in Summary table 5. Similarly, factors that change desired investment for a given real interest rate shift the investment curve; see Summary table 6 for factors that affect desired investment. Shifts of either curve change the goods market equilibrium point and thus change national saving, investment, and the real interest rate.

Key Terms

desired capital stock, p. 127
effective tax rate, p. 133
expected after-tax real interest rate, p. 121
gross investment, p. 135
Keynesian consumption function, p. 116
marginal propensity to consume, p. 116
net investment, p. 135
Ricardian equivalence proposition, p. 125
tax-adjusted user cost of capital, p. 133
user cost of capital, p. 129

Key Equations

$$S^d = Y - C^d - G \qquad (4.1)$$

Desired national saving, S^d, is the level of national saving that occurs when consumption is at its desired level. Equation (4.1) is obtained by substituting desired

consumption C^d for actual consumption C in the definition of national saving.

$$r_{\text{a-t}} = (1 - t)i - \pi^e \qquad (4.3)$$

The expected after-tax real interest rate, $r_{\text{a-t}}$, is the after-tax nominal interest rate, $(1 - t)i$, minus the expected rate of inflation π^e. The expected after-tax real interest rate is the real return expected by a saver when a portion t of interest income must be paid as taxes.

$$uc = rp_K + dp_K = (r + d)p_K \qquad (4.4)$$

The user cost of capital, uc, is the sum of the interest cost, rp_K, and the depreciation cost, dp_K, where d is the depreciation rate and p_K is the price of a new capital good.

$$MPK^f = \frac{uc}{1 - \tau} = \frac{(r + d)p_K}{1 - \tau} \qquad (4.5)$$

The desired capital stock, or the capital stock that maximizes the firm's expected profits, is the capital stock for which the expected future marginal product of capital, MPK^f, equals the tax-adjusted user cost of capital, $uc/(1 - \tau)$, where τ is the tax rate on firm revenues (equivalently, the effective tax rate).

$$Y = C^d + I^d + G \qquad (4.8)$$

The *goods market equilibrium condition* says that the goods market is in equilibrium when the aggregate quantity of goods supplied, Y, equals the aggregate quantity of goods demanded, $C^d + I^d + G$.

$$S^d = I^d \qquad (4.9)$$

Another way of stating the goods market equilibrium condition is that desired national saving, S^d, must equal desired investment, I^d. This equation is equivalent to equation (4.8).

Review Questions

1. Given income, how are consumption and saving linked? What is the basic motivation for saving?
2. How are desired consumption and desired saving affected by increases in current income, expected future income, and wealth? Why is the effect on desired saving of an increase in the expected real interest rate potentially ambiguous?
3. What effect does a temporary increase in government purchases – for example, to fight a war – have on desired consumption and desired national saving, for a constant level of output? What is the effect on desired national saving of a lump-sum tax increase? Why is the effect of a lump-sum tax increase controversial?
4. What are the two components of the user cost of capital? Explain why each is a cost of using a capital good.
5. What is the desired capital stock? How does it depend on the expected future marginal product of capital, the user cost of capital, and the effective tax rate?
6. What is the difference between gross investment and net investment? Can gross investment be positive when net investment is negative?
7. Give two equivalent ways of describing equilibrium in the goods market. Use a diagram to show how goods market equilibrium is attained.
8. Explain why the saving curve slopes upward and the investment curve slopes downward in the saving–investment diagram. Give two examples of changes that would shift the saving curve to the right, and two examples of changes that would shift the investment curve to the right.

Numerical Problems

1. A consumer is making saving plans for this year and next. She knows that her real income after taxes will be £10,000 in both years. Any part of her income saved this year will earn a real interest rate of 10% between this year and next year. Currently, the consumer has no wealth (no money in the bank or other financial assets, and no debts). There is no uncertainty about the future.

   The consumer wants to save an amount this year that will allow her to (1) make university tuition payments next year equal to £2520 in real terms; (2) enjoy exactly the same amount of consumption this year and next year, not counting tuition payments as part of next year's consumption; and (3) have neither assets nor debts at the end of next year.

   a. How much should the consumer save this year? How much should she consume?

   How are the amounts that the consumer should save and consume affected by each of the following changes (taken one at a time, with other variables held at their original values)?

   b. Her current income rises from £10,000 to £10,840.

   c. The income she expects to receive next year rises from £10,000 to £10,840.

   d. During the current year she receives an inheritance of £210 (an increase in wealth, not income).

   e. The expected tuition payment for next year rises from £2520 to £2940.

   f. The real interest rate rises from 10% to 25%.

2. Hula hoop fabricators cost 10,000 kronor each. The Hi-Ho Hula Hoop Company is trying to decide how many of these machines to buy. HHHHC expects to produce the following number of hoops each year for each level of capital stock shown.

Number of Fabricators	Number of Hoops Produced per Year
0	0
1	100
2	150
3	180
4	195
5	205
6	210

Hula hoops have a real value of 100 kronor. HHHHC has no other costs besides the cost of fabricators.

a. Find the expected future marginal product of capital (in terms of kronor) for each level of capital. The MPK^f for the third fabricator, for example, is the real value of the extra output obtained when the third fabricator is added.

b. If the real interest rate is 12% per year and the depreciation rate of capital is 20% per year, find the user cost of capital (in kronor per fabricator per year). How many fabricators should HHHHC buy?

c. Repeat part (b) for a real interest rate of 8% per year.

d. Repeat part (b) for a 40% tax on HHHHC's sales revenues.

e. A technical innovation doubles the number of hoops a fabricator can produce. How many fabricators should HHHHC buy when the real interest rate is 12% per year? 8% per year? Assume that there are no taxes and that the depreciation rate is still 20% per year.

3. You have just taken a job that requires you to move home. In relocating, you face the decision of whether to buy or rent a house. A suitable house costs £200,000 and you have saved enough for the downpayment. The (nominal) mortgage interest rate is 10% per year, and you can also earn 10% per year on savings. Mortgage interest payments are tax deductible, interest earnings on savings are taxable, and you are in a 30% tax bracket. Interest is paid or received, and taxes are paid, on the last day of the year. The expected inflation rate is 5% per year.

The cost of maintaining the house (replacing worn-out roofing, painting, and so on) is 6% of the value of the house. Assume that these expenses are also paid entirely on the last day of the year. If the maintenance is done, the house retains its full real value. There are no other relevant costs or expenses.

a. What is the expected after-tax real interest rate on the house mortgage?

b. What is the user cost of the house?

c. If all you care about is minimizing your living expenses, at what (annual) rent level would you be just indifferent between buying a house and renting a house of comparable quality? Rent is also paid on the last day of the year.

4. Consider a firm that faces the following expected future marginal product of capital:

$$MPK^f = 1000 - 2K$$

where MPK^f is the expected future marginal product of capital and K is the capital stock. The price of capital, p_K, is 1000, the real interest rate, r, is 10%, and the depreciation rate, d, is 15%.

a. What is the user cost of capital?

b. What is the value of the firm's desired capital stock?

c. Now suppose that the firm must pay a 50% tax on its revenue. What is the value of the desired capital stock?

d. Now suppose that in addition to the 50% tax rate on revenue, the firm can take advantage of a 20% investment tax credit, which allows it to reduce its taxes paid by 20% of the value of new capital purchased. What is the firm's desired capital stock now? (*Hint:* An investment tax credit effectively reduces the price of capital to the firm.)

5. An economy has full-employment output of 9000, and government purchases are 2000. Desired consumption and desired investment are as follows:

Real interest rate (%)	Desired consumption	Desired investment
2	6100	1500
3	6000	1400
4	5900	1300
5	5800	1200
6	5700	1100

a. Why do desired consumption and desired investment fall as the real interest rate rises?

b. Find desired national saving for each value of the real interest rate.

c. If the goods market is in equilibrium, what are the values of the real interest rate, desired national saving, and desired investment? Show that both forms of the goods market equilibrium condition, equations (4.8) and (4.9), are satisfied at the equilibrium. Assume that output is fixed at its full-employment level.

d. Repeat part (c) for the case in which government purchases fall to 1600. Assume that the amount people desire to consume at each real interest rate is unchanged.

6. An economy has full-employment output of 6000. Government purchases, G, are 1200. Desired consumption and desired investment are

$$C^d = 3600 - 2000r + 0.10Y$$
and $$I^d = 1200 - 4000r$$

where Y is output and r is the real interest rate.

a. Find an equation relating desired national saving S^d to r and Y.

b. Using both versions of the goods market equilibrium condition, equations (4.8) and (4.9), find the real interest rate that clears the goods market. Assume that output equals full-employment output.
c. Government purchases rise to 1440. How does this increase change the equation describing desired national saving? Show the change graphically. What happens to the market-clearing real interest rate?

Analytical Problems

1. Use the saving–investment diagram to analyse the effects of the following on national saving, investment, and the real interest rate. Explain your reasoning.
   a. Consumers become more future-oriented and thus decide to save more.
   b. The government announces a large, one-off bonus payment to veterans returning from a war. The bonus will be financed by additional taxes levied on the general population over the next five years.
   c. The government introduces an investment tax credit (offset by other types of tax, so total tax collections remain unchanged).
   d. A large number of accessible oil deposits are discovered, which increases the expected future marginal product of oil rigs and pipelines. It also causes an increase in expected future income.
2. A country loses much of its capital stock to a war.
   a. What effects should this event have on the country's current employment, output, and real wage?
   b. What effect will the loss of capital have on desired investment?
   c. The effects on desired national saving of the wartime losses are ambiguous. Give one reason for desired saving to rise and one reason for it to fall.
   d. Assume that desired saving does not change. What effect does the loss of capital have on the country's real interest rate and the quantity of investment?
3. **a.** Analyse the effects of a temporary increase in the price of oil (a temporary adverse supply shock) on current output, employment, the real wage, national saving, investment, and the real interest rate. Because the supply shock is temporary, you should assume that the expected future MPK and

households' expected future incomes are unchanged. Assume throughout that output and employment remain at full-employment levels (which may change).
   b. Analyse the effects of a permanent increase in the price of oil (a permanent adverse supply shock) on current output, employment, the real wage, national saving, investment, and the real interest rate. Show that in this case, unlike the case of a temporary supply shock, the real interest rate need not change. (*Hint:* A permanent adverse supply shock lowers the current productivity of capital and labour, just as a temporary supply shock does. In addition, a permanent supply shock lowers both the expected future MPK and households' expected future incomes.)
4. Economists often argue that a temporary increase in government purchases, say, for military purposes, will crowd out private investment. Use the saving–investment diagram to illustrate this point, explaining why the curve(s) shift. Does it matter whether the temporary increase in military spending is funded by taxes or by borrowing?
   Alternatively, suppose that the temporary increase in government purchases is for infrastructure (roads, sewers, bridges) rather than for military purposes. The government spending on infrastructure makes private investment more productive, increasing the expected future MPK at each level of the capital stock. Use the saving–investment diagram to analyse the effects of government infrastructure spending on current consumption, national saving, investment, and the real interest rate. Does investment by private firms get crowded out by this kind of government investment? If not, what kind of spending, if any, does get crowded out? Assume that there is no change in current productivity or current output and assume also (for simplicity) that households do not expect a change in their future incomes.
5. 'A permanent increase in government purchases has a larger effect than a temporary increase of the same amount.' Use the saving–investment diagram to evaluate this statement, focusing on effects on consumption, investment, and the real interest rate for a fixed level of output. (*Hint:* The permanent increase in government purchases implies larger increases in current and future taxes.)

5

SAVING AND INVESTMENT IN THE OPEN ECONOMY

With virtually no exceptions, modern economies are open economies, which means that they engage in international trade of goods and services and in international borrowing and lending. Economic openness is of tremendous benefit to the average person. Because Western European countries are open economies, European consumers can enjoy products both from their European neighbours and from around the world (Japanese videocassette recorders, American soya beans, Brazilian coffee) and European businesses can find new markets abroad for their products (computers, beef, financial services). Similarly, the internationalization of financial markets means that savers have the opportunity to purchase government bonds or shares in foreign companies as well as domestic assets, and firms who want to finance investment projects can borrow in London, Paris, Frankfurt, New York or Tokyo.

Beyond the economic diversity and opportunity it creates, economic openness carries another important implication: in an open economy, *a country's spending need not equal its production in every period,* as would be required in a closed economy with no foreign trade and no international borrowing and lending. In particular, by importing more than they export and borrowing from abroad to pay for the difference, the residents of an open economy can temporarily spend more than they produce.

The ability of an open economy to spend more than it produces is both an opportunity and a potential problem. For example, by borrowing abroad, the UK was able to finance a large excess of imports over exports during the 1980s and early 1990s. As a result, Britons enjoyed higher levels of consumption, investment, and government purchases than they could have otherwise. At the same time, however, they incurred foreign debts that may be a future burden to the UK economy. Similarly, by borrowing heavily from abroad during the 1970s, some less developed countries (LDCs) were able to avoid large reductions in domestic spending even though the two oil price shocks of that decade caused sharp declines in their output. During the 1980s, however, many LDC borrowers were unable to cope with the burden of their foreign debts – a situation that became known as the LDC debt crisis – and perhaps as a result suffered severely reduced economic growth.

Why do countries sometimes borrow abroad to pay for an excess of imports over exports but at other times export more than they import and lend the difference to other countries? Why doesn't each country just balance its books and import as much as it exports each year? As this chapter explains, the fundamental determinants of a country's trade position are the country's saving and investment decisions. Thus, although the issues of trade balances and international lending introduced here may seem at first to be unrelated to the topics covered in Chapter 4, the two sets of questions are actually closely related.

To explore how desired national saving and desired investment help determine patterns of international trade and lending, we extend the idea of goods market equilibrium, described by the saving–investment diagram, to include a foreign sector. We show that, unlike the situation in a closed economy, in an open economy desired national saving and desired investment do not have to be equal. Instead, we show that, when a country's desired national saving exceeds its desired investment, the country will be a lender in the international capital market and will have a current account surplus. Similarly, when a country's desired national saving is less than its desired investment, the country will be an international borrower and will have a current account deficit.

In its emphasis on saving and investment, this chapter develops an important theme of this part of the book. However, in order to focus on the role of saving and investment, we ignore some other factors that also influence international trade and lending. The most important of these factors is the exchange rate, or the rate at which domestic currency can be exchanged for foreign currency. We discuss exchange rates and their role in the open economy fully in Chapter 14.

5.1   BALANCE OF PAYMENTS ACCOUNTING

Examining the factors that affect international trade and lending first requires an understanding of the basics of balance of payments accounting. The **balance of payments accounts**, which are part of the national income accounts discussed in Chapter 2, are the record of a country's international transactions. (The box 'In Touch with the Macroeconomy: The Balance of Payments Accounts,' p. 154, contains information about how the balance of payments accounts are constructed and where to find these data.) As you read this section, you should refer to Table 5.1, which presents balance of payments data for the Netherlands for 1995; note that some of the numbers are positive and that others are negative. To sort out which international transactions are entered with a plus sign and which are entered with a minus sign, keep the following principle in mind: any transaction that involves a flow of funds *into* the Netherlands is a *credit* item and is entered with a plus sign; any transaction that involves a flow of funds *out of* the Netherlands is a *debit* item and is entered with a minus sign. We illustrate this principle as we discuss the various components of the balance of payments accounts.

Table 5.1   **The Balance of International Payments for the Netherlands, 1995 (billions of guilders)**

CURRENT ACCOUNT			
Net exports		**34.3**	
Exports			
Merchandise	278.3		
Services	77.6		
Imports			
Merchandise	−247.3		
Services	−74.3		
Net income from assets		**2.6**	
Income receipts	45.9		
Income payments	−43.3		
Net transfers		**−10.9**	
Current account balance (*CA*)			**26.0**
CAPITAL ACCOUNT			
Increase in Dutch-owned assets abroad		**−70.3**	
Official reserve assets	3.1		
Other Dutch assets	−73.4		
Increase in foreign-owned assets in the Netherlands		**59.4**	
Capital account balance (*KA*)			**−10.9**
Statistical discrepancy			**−15.1**

Source: *Balance of Payments Statistics Yearbook 1996*, IMF

The Current Account

The **current account** measures a country's trade in currently produced goods and services, along with unilateral transfers between countries. For convenience we divide the current account into three separate components: (1) net exports of goods and services, (2) investment income from assets abroad, and (3) net unilateral transfers.

Net Exports of Goods and Services. We discussed the concept of net exports, *NX*, or exports minus imports, as part of the expenditure approach to measuring GDP in Chapter 2. Here we point out that net exports often are broken into two categories: merchandise (goods) and services.

Merchandise consists of currently produced goods, such as British apples, French perfume, Belgian chocolates and German cars. When a Dutchman buys a German car, for example, the transaction is recorded as a merchandise import for the Netherlands (a debit item for the Netherlands, because funds flow out of the Netherlands to pay for the car) and a merchandise export for Germany (a credit item for Germany because funds flow into Germany to pay for the car). The difference between a country's merchandise exports and its merchandise imports is called the **merchandise trade balance**, or simply the trade balance. The merchandise trade balance receives

IN TOUCH *WITH THE MACROECONOMY*

THE BALANCE OF PAYMENTS ACCOUNTS

The introduction of a Single Market caused customs frontiers between Member States to be abolished. Goods were now able to flow freely without regard to any customs formalities. However, the main information on trade flows had been provided by customs services from declarations made by individual companies. The abolition of frontiers therefore also abolished the means of measuring trade flows within the EU.

To maintain information on trade flows, EU Member States adopted a new system (INTRASTAT) of collecting information on exports and imports with their European partners. This involves collecting monthly data as a summary declaration which businesses send to the relevant government department in their own country. Each Member State then adjusts the data to compensate for the failure of some companies to respond (either by not completing their declaration or because the enterprise is below the size threshold for the system). Quality checks are also carried out by each Member State using a VAT declaration sysem for intra-EU trade. This system contains information on which companies engage in intra-EU trade and the total number of transactions.

The INTERSTAT system is now a number of years old, but concerns remain about the quality and speed of availability of information. The volume of trade between Member States following the introduction of the system fell sharply, only partly due to changes in economic acitvity.

To assess the INTRASTAT system intra-EU imports and exports are compared. Export and import figures for intra-EU transactions should agree, but the total figures for imports and exports have differed by up to 4% (up to 30% for a more detailed breakdown of goods). One reason is delays in availability of data in some countries. The non-response of companies and errors in reporting the exact nature of goods have also contributed. Several countries have started to compare and align their results, and the EU is seeking to identify countries with the largest discrepancies, to improve their data collection. Also, the data required is being reduced, which may improve the provision of trade data.

---

a lot of attention from the public and the press.[1] This attention does not seem entirely warranted, however, because merchandise trade is only one component of the current account.

Internationally traded services include transportation, tourism, insurance, education, and financial services, among others. When a Dutch family spends a week's vacation in France, for example, the family's expenditures for accommodation, food, sight-seeing tours, and so on, are counted in the Dutch current account as an import of tourism services (a debit item for the Netherlands because funds are flowing out of the country). The family's expenditures count as an export of tourism services for France (a credit item in the French current account). Similarly, when a foreign student attends college in the Netherlands, her tuition payments are included as an export of services for the Netherlands and an import of services for her home country.

Investment Income from Assets Abroad. Investment income received from assets abroad includes interest payments, dividends, royalties, and other

---

1. This attention may in part reflect the availability of merchandise trade data monthly, whereas most balance of payments data are available only quarterly. See the box 'In Touch with the Macroeconomy: The Balance of Payments Accounts'.

returns that residents of a country receive from assets (such as bonds, stocks, or patents) that they own outside their own country. For example, the interest that a Dutch saver receives from a French government bond he owns, or the profits a Dutch company receives from a foreign subsidiary, are income receipts from assets abroad. These are credit items in the current account because the receipts are payments from foreigners to domestic residents.

Payment of investment income to foreign owners of assets in a country are debit items because they represent funds that flow out of the country. *Net investment income from assets abroad* equals investment income received from assets abroad minus investment income paid to foreign owners of domestic assets.

For the Netherlands, net investment income from assets abroad is quantitatively almost the same as net factor payments from abroad, *NFP,* discussed in Chapter 2. The difference between the two concepts is that net factor payments from abroad also include wages and salaries of people from the Netherlands working outside the country, less the wages and salaries of foreigners working in the Netherlands. In practice, the wage and salary component of *NFP* is very small, so we ignore it and treat *NFP* and net investment income from abroad as equivalent concepts.

Net Transfers. **Unilateral transfers** are payments from one country to another that do not correspond to the purchase of any good, service, or asset. Examples are official foreign aid (a payment from one government to another) or a gift of money from a resident of one country to family members living in another country. When the Netherlands makes a transfer to another country, the amount of the transfer is a debit item because funds flow out of the Netherlands. A country's net unilateral transfers equal unilateral transfers received by the country minus unilateral transfers flowing out of the country. The negative value of net unilateral transfers in Table 5.1 shows that the Netherlands is a net donor to other countries.

Current Account Balance. Adding all the credit items and subtracting all the debit items in the current account yields a number called the **current account balance.** If the current account balance is positive – with the value of credit items exceeding the value of debit items – the country has a current account surplus. If the current account balance is negative – with the value of debit items exceeding the value of credit items – the country has a current account deficit. As Table 5.1 shows, in 1995 the Netherlands had a 26 billion guilders current account surplus, equal to the sum of net exports ($NX = 34.3$ billion guilders), net investment income from abroad ($NFP = 2.6$ billion guilders), and net unilateral transfers (–10.9 billion guilders).

The Capital Account

Not all transactions with foreign countries are tallied in the current account. If a Dutch investor purchases a ten-year-old vacation house in France, for example, the purchase is *not* included in the current account of either the Netherlands or France. The reason is that the current account includes only the trade of currently produced goods and services. A ten-year-old house is an existing asset rather than a currently produced good or service, so its sale is not part of the current account.

Trade between countries in existing assets, either real or financial, is recorded in the **capital account**. When the home country sells an asset to another country, the transaction is recorded as a **capital inflow** for the home country and as a credit item in the capital account. So, for example, if a Dutch hotel is sold to Italian investors, the transaction is counted as a capital inflow to the Netherlands and as a credit item in the Dutch capital account. (Why is a capital inflow a credit item? Because when someone from the Netherlands sells an asset to a foreigner, funds flow *into* the Netherlands.) Similarly, when the home country buys an asset from abroad – say, someone from the Netherlands obtains a Swiss bank account – the transaction is a **capital outflow** from the home country (the Netherlands in this example) and a debit item in the home country's capital account (funds are flowing *out of* the Netherlands).

The **capital account balance** equals the value of capital inflows (credit items) minus the value of capital outflows (debit items). When residents of a country sell more assets to foreigners than they buy from foreigners, the capital account balance is positive, creating a capital account surplus. When residents of the home country purchase more assets from foreigners than they sell, the capital account balance is negative, creating a capital account deficit. Table 5.1 shows that in 1995 the Dutch increased their holdings of foreign assets by 70.3 billion guilders while foreigners increased their holdings of Dutch assets by 59.4 billion guilders. Thus the Netherlands had a capital account deficit (a net capital outflow) of 10.9 billion guilders in 1995.

The Official Settlements Balance. In Table 5.1 one set of capital account transactions, transactions in official reserve assets, has been broken out separately. These transactions differ from other capital account transactions in that they are conducted by central banks (such as De Nederlandsche Bank in the Netherlands), which are the official institutions that determine national money supplies. Held by central banks, **official reserve assets** are assets, other than domestic money or securities, that can be used in making international payments. Historically, gold was the primary official reserve asset, but now the official reserves of central banks also include government securities of major industrialized economies, foreign bank deposits, and special assets created by the International Monetary Fund (an international agency that facilitates trade and financial relationships among countries).

Central banks can change the quantity of official reserve assets they hold by buying or selling reserve assets on open markets. For example, De Nederlandsche Bank could increase its reserve assets by using guilders to buy gold. According to Table 5.1 (see the line 'official reserve assets'), in 1995 the Netherlands central bank sold 3.1 billion guilders of its official reserve assets.[2] The **official settlements balance** – also called the **balance of payments** – is the net increase (domestic less foreign) in a country's official reserve assets. A country that increases its net holdings of reserve assets during a year has a balance of payments surplus, and a country that reduces its net holdings of reserve assets has a balance of payments deficit.

---

2. Remember that a positive number in the capital account indicates a capital inflow, or a sale of assets.

For the issues we discuss in this chapter, the balances on current account and capital account play a much larger role than the balance of payments. The macroeconomic significance of the balance of payments is explained in Chapter 14, when we discuss the determination of exchange rates.

The Relationship between the Current Account and the Capital Account

The logic of balance of payments accounting implies a close relationship between the current account and the capital account. Except for errors arising from problems of measurement, *in each period the current account balance and the capital account balance must sum to zero.* That is, if

$$CA = \text{current account balance,}$$
$$KA = \text{capital account balance,}$$

then

$$CA + KA = 0 \tag{5.1}$$

The reason that equation (5.1) holds is that every international transaction involves a swap of goods, services, or assets between countries. The two sides of the swap always have offsetting effects on the sum of the current and capital account balances, $CA + KA$. Thus the sum of the current and capital account balances must equal zero.

Table 5.2 helps clarify this point. Suppose that someone in the Netherlands buys an imported British sweater, paying 300 guilders for it. This transaction is an import of goods to the Netherlands and thus reduces the Dutch current account balance by 300 guilders. However, the British exporter who sold the sweater now holds 300 guilders. What will he do with it? There are several possibilities, any of which will offset the effect of the purchase of the sweater on the sum of the current and capital account balances.

The Briton may use the 300 guilders to buy a Dutch product, say, electrical goods. This purchase is a 300 guilders export for the Netherlands. This Dutch export together with the original import of the sweater into the Netherlands results in no net change in the Dutch current account balance CA. The Dutch capital account balance KA has not changed, as no assets have been traded. Thus the sum of CA and KA remains the same.

A second possibility is that the Briton will use the 300 guilders to buy a Dutch asset, say, a bond issued by a Dutch corporation. The purchase of this bond is a capital inflow to the Netherlands. This 300 guilders increase in the Dutch capital account offsets the 300 guilders reduction in the Dutch current account caused by the original import of the sweater. Again, the sum of the current and capital account balances, $CA + KA$, is unaffected by the combination of transactions.

Finally, the Briton may decide to go to his bank and trade his guilders for UK pounds. If the bank sells these guilders to another Briton for the purpose of buying Dutch exports or assets, or if it buys Dutch assets itself, one of the previous two cases is repeated. Alternatively, the bank may sell the guilders to De Nederlandsche Bank in exchange for pounds. But in giving up 300 guilders worth of UK pounds, De Nederlandsche Bank reduces its holdings of official

---

Table 5.2   Why the Current Account Balance and the Capital Account Balance Sum to Zero: An Example (Balance of Payments Data Refer to the Netherlands)

Case I: **The Netherlands imports 300 guilder sweater from the UK; the UK imports 300 guilders of Electrical Goods from the Netherlands**

Current account
Exports	+300
Imports	−300
Current account balance, CA	0

Capital account
No transaction	
Capital account balance, KA	0
Sum of current and capital account balances, $CA + KA$	0

Case II: **The Netherlands imports 300 guilder sweater from the UK; the UK buys 300 guilder bond from the Netherlands**

Current account
Imports	−300
Current account balance, CA	−300

Capital account
Capital inflow	+300
Capital account balance, KA	+300
Sum of current and capital account balances, $CA + KA$	0

Case III: **The Netherlands imports 300 guilder sweater from the UK; De Nederlandsche Bank sells 300 guilders of UK pounds to UK bank**

Current Account
Imports	−300
Current account balance, CA	−300

Capital Account
Capital inflow (reduction in Dutch official reserve assets)	+300
Capital account balance, KA	+300
Sum of current and capital account balances, $CA + KA$	0

---

reserve assets by 300 guilders, which counts as a capital inflow. As in the previous case, the capital account balance rises by 300 guilders, offsetting the decline in the current account balance caused by the import of the sweater.[3]

This example shows why, conceptually, the current account balance and capital account balance must always sum to zero. In practice, problems in

---

3. In this case the balance of payments falls by 300 guilders, reflecting De Nederlandsche Bank's loss of official reserves. We did not consider the possibility that the Briton would just hold 300 guilders in Dutch currency. As guilders are an obligation of the Netherlands (in particular, of De Nederlandsche Bank), the Briton's acquisition of guilders would be a credit item in the Dutch capital account, which would offset the effect of the sweater import on the Dutch current account.

measuring international transactions prevent this relationship from holding exactly. The amount that would have to be added to the sum of the current and capital account balances for this sum to reach its theoretical value of zero is called the **statistical discrepancy**. As Table 5.1 shows, in 1995 the statistical discrepancy was about –15.1 billion guilder. Box 5.1 discusses a puzzle that arises because of statistical discrepancies in the balance of payments accounts.

Net Foreign Assets and the Balance of Payments Accounts

In Chapter 2 we defined the net foreign assets of a country as the foreign assets held by the country's residents (including, for example, foreign stocks, bonds, or property) minus the country's foreign liabilities (domestic physical and financial assets owned by foreigners). Net foreign assets are part of a country's national wealth, along with the country's domestic physical assets, such as land and the capital stock. The total value of a country's net foreign assets can change in two ways: (1) the value of existing foreign assets and foreign liabilities can change, as when stock held by someone in the Netherlands in a foreign corporation increases in value or the value of Dutch farmland owned by a foreigner declines; and (2) the country can acquire new foreign assets or incur new foreign liabilities.

What determines the quantity of new foreign assets that a country can acquire? In any period *the net amount of new foreign assets that a country acquires equals its current account surplus*. For example, suppose a country exports £10 million more in goods and services than it imports and thus runs

---

BOX 5.1

Does Mars Have a Current Account Surplus?

The exports and imports of any individual country need not be equal in value. However, as every export is somebody else's import, for the world as a whole exports must equal imports and the current account surplus must be zero.

Or must it? When official current account figures for all nations are added up, the result is a current account deficit for the world. For example, International Monetary Fund (IMF) projections for 1993 were that industrial countries would have a collective $35.6 billion current account deficit, developing countries would have a $52.9 billion deficit, and former centrally planned economies would have a $24.6 billion deficit, all of which adds up to a current account deficit for the world as a whole of $113.1 billion. Is planet Earth a net importer, and does Mars have a current account surplus?

Since extraterrestrial trade seems unlikely, the explanation of the Earth's current account deficit must lie in statistical and measurement problems. A study by the IMF concluded that the main problem is the misreporting of income from assets held abroad. For example, interest earned by an American on a foreign bank account should in principle be counted as a credit item in the US. current account and a debit item in the current account of the foreign country. However, if the American fails to report this interest income to the US government, it may show up only as a debit to the foreign current account, leading to a measured Earth-wide current account deficit. The fact that the world's current account deficit is generally larger during periods of high interest rates provides some support for this explanation.

Sources: International Monetary Fund, *Report on the World Current Account Discrepancy*, September 1987; and IMF, *World Economic Outlook*, October 1992, Table A30.

a £10 million current account surplus (assuming that net investment income from abroad and net unilateral transfers are both zero). The country must then use this £10 million to acquire foreign assets or reduce foreign liabilities. In this case we say that the country has undertaken net foreign lending of £10 million.

Similarly, if a country has a £10 million current account deficit, it must cover this deficit either by selling assets to foreigners or borrowing from foreigners. Either action reduces the country's net foreign assets by £10 million. We describe this situation by saying that the country has engaged in net foreign borrowing of £10 million.

Equation (5.1) emphasizes the link between the current account and the acquisition of foreign assets. Because $CA + KA = 0$, if a country has a current account surplus, it must have an equal capital account deficit. In turn, a capital account deficit implies that the country is experiencing capital outflows, or a net increase in holdings of foreign assets. Similarly, a current account deficit implies a capital account surplus and a decline in the country's net holdings of foreign assets. Summary table 7 presents some equivalent ways of describing a country's current account position and its acquisition of foreign assets.

SUMMARY 7

Equivalent Measures of a Country's International Trade and Lending

Each Item Describes the Same Situation

A current account surplus of £10 million

A capital account deficit of £10 million

Net acquisition of foreign assets of £10 million

Net foreign lending of £10 million

Net exports of £10 million (if net factor payments, *NFP*, and net unilateral transfers equal zero)

APPLICATION

Is the United States the World's Largest International Debtor?

From about World War I until the 1980s, the USA was a net creditor internationally, in that it had more foreign assets than liabilities. However, beginning in the early 1980s the USA ran up large annual current account deficits, which had to be financed by net foreign borrowing.[4]

According to official statistics released at the time by the Bureau of Economic Analysis (BEA), US foreign obligations drew level with its foreign assets in 1984; by the end of the decade foreign liabilities exceeded foreign assets by nearly $700 billion. Journalists and others often cited the implication of these numbers: that during the 1980s the USA had become the world's largest international debtor and was in economic decline.

---

4. Keep in mind that we have defined net foreign borrowing broadly to include the sale of US foreign and domestic assets as well as the incurring of new foreign debts.

It is certainly true that years of current account deficits have eroded America's net foreign assets. However, the claim that the USA is the world's largest debtor needs to be put into perspective. First, the economic burden created by any debt depends not on the absolute size of the debt but on its size relative to the debtor's economic resources. Even if the $700 billion estimate for US net foreign debt in the late 1980s were correct (and there are reasons to question this number), that debt would have represented about 13% of American annual GDP – a much smaller share of national output than the debt of countries such as Mexico (debt equals 78% of output), Chile (125%), Nigeria (123%), and Jamaica (176%),[5] although larger than the debt-to-GDP ratio of most other industrial countries. Thus the actual burden of foreign debt borne by the USA is surely smaller than that of many nations, particularly developing nations.

Second, the official estimates of the USA's foreign debt that circulated in the 1980s have not gone unchallenged. The main point raised by critics was that, in calculating American net foreign assets, the BEA valued many assets and liabilities at their original cost, or book value, rather than at their current market value. So, for example, a company purchased for $10,000,000 ten years ago would still have been valued at $10,000,000 in the BEA's calculation, even though inflation and economic growth might mean that the company's dollar value is much greater today. Because many US investments abroad were made years ago, but many foreign investments in the USA were made relatively recently, the BEA's valuing of investments at original cost understated the value of American investments abroad more than it understated the value of foreign investments in the USA.

Studies that have attempted to correct for measurement problems have generally obtained more optimistic results for the US net foreign asset position. For example, Michael Ulan and William G. Dewald,[6] economists at the US Department of State, estimated that as late as 1989, the USA's foreign assets and liabilities were of approximately equal value. Another piece of evidence in favour of the view that the USA is not a large net debtor is that US receipts from assets abroad remain about the same size as payments made to foreign holders of US assets. Recently, the BEA modified its methods to allow for changes in market values, obtaining estimates of the USA's foreign debt much closer to those calculated by Ulan and Dewald and others.[7]

In evaluating the significance of a nation's foreign debt, you must also remember that net foreign assets are only one component of national wealth, the other being domestic physical assets. If national wealth is growing at a healthy rate overall, there is not much reason to be concerned if one of its components is falling. For example, if a country were to incur large foreign debts in order to build up its capital stock, and if the new capital were highly pro-

---

5. These data, which are for 1987, are from Kenneth Rogoff, 'Symposium on New Institutions for Developing Country Debt', *Journal of Economic Perspectives*, Winter 1990, pp. 3–6, Table 1.

6. 'Appreciating America's Foreign Investments', *The American Enterprise,* September/October 1990, pp. 73–5.

7. See Russell B. Scholl, Raymond J. Mataloni, Jr, and Steve D. Bezirganian, 'The International Investment Position of the United States in 1991', *Survey of Current Business,* June 1992, pp. 46–59. Scholl *et al.* find that the USA became a net foreign debtor in 1987 or 1988, depending on the method of estimation used.

ductive, the foreign debt would not be an economic burden. Unfortunately, this scenario does not apply to the USA or to Western Europe: although our measurements are imprecise, the national wealth of the USA and of European countries has apparently grown relatively slowly in real terms over the past decade,[8] reflecting low rates of national saving (see Figure 2.2). This relatively slow growth of total national wealth should be of greater concern to policy-makers than the behaviour of net foreign assets viewed in isolation.

5.2   GOODS MARKET EQUILIBRIUM IN AN OPEN ECONOMY

We are now ready to investigate the economic forces that determine international trade and borrowing. In the remainder of this chapter we demonstrate that a country's current account balance and foreign lending are closely linked to its domestic spending and production decisions. Understanding these links first requires developing the open-economy version of the goods market equilibrium condition.

In Chapter 4 we derived the goods market equilibrium condition for a closed economy. We showed that this condition can be expressed either as desired national saving equals desired investment or, equivalently, as the aggregate supply of goods equals the aggregate demand for goods. With some modification, we can use these same two conditions to describe goods market equilibrium in an open economy.

Let's begin with the open-economy version of the condition that desired national saving equals desired investment. In Chapter 2 we derived the national income accounting identity (equation 2.9):

$$S = I + CA = I + (NX + NFP) \tag{5.2}$$

Equation (5.2) is a version of the uses-of-saving identity. It states that national saving S has two uses: (1) to increase the nation's stock of capital by funding investment I, and (2) to increase the nation's stock of net foreign assets by lending to foreigners (recall that the current account balance CA equals the amount of funds that the country has available for net foreign lending). Equation (5.2) also reminds us that (assuming no net unilateral transfers) the current account, CA, is the sum of net exports, NX, and net factor payments from abroad, NFP.

Because equation (5.2) is an identity, it must always hold (by definition). For the economy to be in goods market equilibrium, actual national saving and investment must also equal their desired levels. If actual and desired levels are equal, equation (5.2) becomes

$$S^d = I^d + CA = I^d + (NX + NFP) \tag{5.3}$$

where S^d and I^d represent desired national saving and desired investment, respectively. Equation (5.3) is the goods market equilibrium condition for an

---

8. According to Federal Reserve estimates, real US national wealth grew 2.0% per year during the period 1980–91, compared to 3.5% per year during 1970–80 and 3.3% per year during 1960–70. See the *Economic Report of the President*, February 1993, Table B-110.

open economy, in which the current account balance CA equals net lending to foreigners, or capital outflows. Hence equation (5.3) states that *in goods market equilibrium in an open economy, the desired amount of national saving S^d must equal the desired amount of domestic investment I^d plus the amount lent abroad CA.* Note that the closed-economy equilibrium condition is a special case of equation (5.3), with $CA = 0$.

In general, net factor payments, NFP, are determined by past investments and are not much affected by current macroeconomic developments. If for simplicity we assume that net factor payments are zero, the current account equals net exports and the goods market equilibrium condition, equation (5.3), becomes

$$S^d = I^d + NX \tag{5.4}$$

Equation (5.4) is the form of the goods market equilibrium condition that we will work with. Under the assumption that net factor payments are zero, we can refer to the term NX interchangeably as net exports or as the current account balance.

As for the closed economy, we can also write the goods market equilibrium condition for the open economy in terms of the aggregate supply and aggregate demand for goods. In an open economy, where net exports, NX, are part of the aggregate demand for goods, this alternative condition for goods market equilibrium is

$$Y = C^d + I^d + G + NX \tag{5.5}$$

where Y is output, C^d is desired consumption spending, and G is government purchases. This way of writing the goods market equilibrium condition is equivalent to the condition in equation (5.4).[9]

We can rewrite equation (5.5) as

$$NX = Y - (C^d + I^d + G) \tag{5.6}$$

Equation (5.6) states that in goods market equilibrium the amount of net exports a country sends abroad equals the country's total output (gross domestic product) Y less total desired spending by domestic residents, $C^d + I^d + G$. Total spending by domestic residents is called **absorption**. Thus equation (5.6) states that an economy in which output exceeds absorption will send goods abroad ($NX > 0$) and have a current account surplus and that an economy that absorbs more than it produces will be a net importer ($NX < 0$), with a current account deficit.

5.3 SAVING AND INVESTMENT IN A SMALL OPEN ECONOMY

To show how saving and investment are related to international trade and lending, we first present the case of a small open economy. A **small open economy** is an economy that is too small to affect the world real interest rate.

---

9. To see that equation (5.5) is equivalent to equation (5.4), subtract $C^d + G$ from both sides of equation (5.5) to obtain $Y - C^d - G = I^d + NX$. The left-hand side of this equation equals desired national saving S^d, so it is the same as equation (5.4).

The **world real interest rate** is the real interest rate that prevails in the international capital market, the market in which individuals, businesses, and governments borrow and lend across national borders. Because changes in saving and investment in the small open economy are not large enough to affect the world real interest rate, this interest rate is fixed in our analysis, which is a convenient simplification. Later in this chapter we consider the case of an open economy, such as the US or German economy, that is large enough to affect the world real interest rate.

As with the closed economy, we can describe the goods market equilibrium in a small open economy by using the saving–investment diagram. The important new assumption that we make is that residents of the economy can borrow or lend in the international capital market at the (expected) world real interest rate r^w, which for now we assume is fixed. If the world real interest rate is r^w, the domestic real interest rate must be r^w as well, as no domestic borrower with access to the international capital market would pay more than r^w to borrow, and no domestic saver with access to the international capital market would accept less than r^w to lend.[10]

Figure 5.1 shows the saving and investment curves for a small open economy. In a closed economy, goods market equilibrium would be represented by point E, the intersection of the curves. The equilibrium real interest rate in the closed economy would be 4% (per year), and national saving and investment would be £3 million (per year). In an open economy, however, desired national saving need not equal desired investment. If the small open economy faces a fixed world real interest rate r^w higher than 4%, desired national saving will be greater than desired investment. For example, if r^w is 6%, desired national saving is £5 million and desired investment is £1 million, so desired national saving exceeds desired investment by £4 million.

Can the economy be in equilibrium when desired national saving exceeds desired investment by £4 million? In a closed economy it could not. The excess saving would have no place to go, and the real interest rate would have to fall to bring desired saving and desired investment into balance. However, in the open economy the excess £4 million of saving can be used to buy foreign assets. This capital outflow uses up the excess national saving, so that there is no disequilibrium. Instead, the goods market is in equilibrium with desired national saving of £5 million, desired investment of £1 million, and net foreign lending of £4 million (see equation (5.4) and recall that net exports NX and net foreign lending are the same).

Alternatively, suppose that the world real interest rate r^w is 2% instead of 6%. As Figure 5.2 shows, in this case desired national saving is £1 million and desired investment is £5 million so that desired investment exceeds desired saving by £4 million. Now firms desiring to invest will have to borrow £4 billion in the international capital market. Is this also a goods market equilibrium? Yes it is, because desired national saving (£1 million) again equals desired investment (£5 million) plus net foreign lending (minus £4 million). Indeed, a small open economy can achieve goods market equilibrium for any value of the world real interest rate. All that is required is that

---

10. For simplicity we ignore factors such as differences in risk or taxes that might cause the domestic real interest rate to differ from the world rate. We also assume that there are no legal barriers to international borrowing and lending (when they exist, such barriers are referred to as capital controls).

Figure 5.1
A small open economy that lends abroad
The graph shows the saving–investment diagram for a small open economy. The country faces a fixed world real interest rate of 6%. At this real interest rate national saving is £5 million (point *B*) and investment is £1 million (point *A*). The part of national saving not used for investment is lent abroad, so foreign lending is £4 million (distance *AB*).

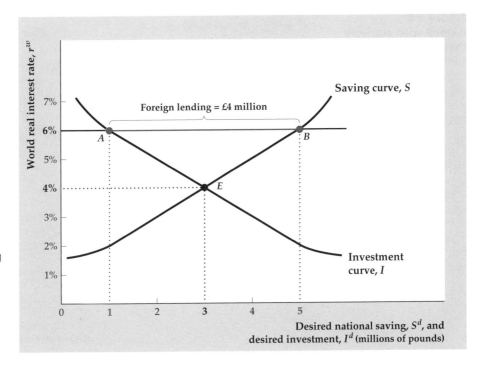

net foreign lending equal the difference between the country's desired national saving and its desired investment.

A more detailed version of the example illustrated in Figures 5.1 and 5.2 is presented in Table 5.3. As shown in the top panel, we assume that in this small country, gross domestic product Y is fixed at its full-employment value of £20 million and government purchases G are fixed at £4 million. The middle panel shows three possible values for the world real interest rate r^w and the assumed levels of desired consumption and desired investment at each of these values of the real interest rate. Note that higher values of the world real interest rate imply lower levels of desired consumption (because people choose to save more) and lower desired investment. The bottom panel shows the values of various economic quantities implied by the assumed values in the top two panels.

The equilibrium in this example depends on the value of the world real interest rate r^w. Suppose that $r^w = 6\%$, as shown in Figure 5.1. Column (3) of Table 5.3 shows that, if $r^w = 6\%$, desired consumption C^d is £11 million (row 2) and that desired investment I^d is £1 million (row 3). With C^d at £11 million, desired national saving, $Y - C^d - G$, is £5 million (row 5). Desired net foreign lending, $S^d - I^d$, is £4 million (row 7) – the same result as illustrated in Figure 5.1.

If $r^w = 2\%$, as in Figure 5.2, column (1) of Table 5.3 shows that desired national saving is £1 million (row 5) and that desired investment is £5 million (row 3). Thus desired foreign lending, $S^d - I^d$, equals –£4 million (row 7) – that is, foreign borrowing totals £4 million. Again, the result is the same as illustrated in Figure 5.2.

An advantage of working through the numerical example in Table 5.3 is that we can also use it to demonstrate how the goods market equilibrium,

Figure 5.2
A small open economy that borrows abroad
The same small open economy shown in Fig. 5.1 now faces a fixed world real interest rate of 2%. At this real interest rate national saving is £1 million (point C) and investment is £5 million (point D). Foreign borrowing of £4 million (distance CD) makes up the difference between what investors want to borrow and what domestic savers want to lend.

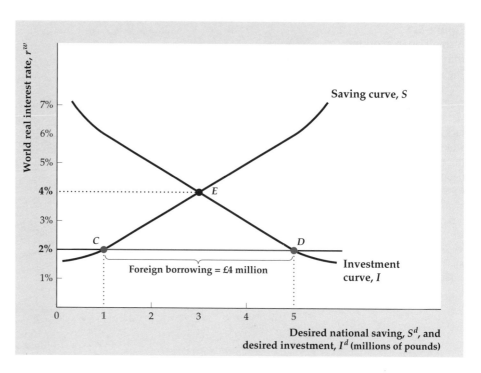

which we have been interpreting in terms of desired saving and investment, can be interpreted in terms of output and absorption. Suppose again that $r^w = 6\%$, giving a desired consumption C^d of £11 million and a desired investment I^d of £1 million. Government purchases G are fixed at £4 million. Thus when r^w is 6%, desired absorption (the desired spending by domestic residents), $C^d + I^d + G$, totals £16 million (row 4, column 3).

In goods market equilibrium a country's net exports – the net quantity of goods and services that it sends abroad – equal gross domestic product Y minus desired absorption (equation 5.6). When r^w is 6%, Y is £20 million and desired absorption is £16 million so that net exports NX are £4 million. Net exports of £4 million imply that the country is lending £4 million abroad, as in Figure 5.1. If the world real interest rate drops to 2%, desired absorption rises (because people want to consume more and invest more) from £16 million to £24 million (row 4, column 1). Because in this case absorption (£24 million) exceeds domestic production (£20 million), the country has to import goods and services from abroad ($NX = -£4$ million). Note that desired net imports of £4 million imply net foreign borrowing of £4 million, as shown in Figure 5.2.

The Effects of Economic Shocks in a Small Open Economy

The saving–investment diagram can be used to determine the effects of various types of economic disturbance in a small open economy. Briefly, any change that increases desired national saving relative to desired investment at a given world real interest rate will increase net foreign lending, the current account

Table 5.3 Goods Market Equilibrium in a Small Open Economy: An Example (millions of pounds)

Given

Gross domestic product, Y	20
Government purchases, G	4

Effect of real interest rate on desired consumption and investment

	(1)	(2)	(3)
(1) World real interest rate, r^w (%)	2	4	6
(2) Desired consumption, C^d	15	13	11
(3) Desired investment, I^d	5	3	1

Results

	(1)	(2)	(3)
(4) Desired absorption, $C^d + I^d + G$	24	20	16
(5) Desired national saving, $S^d = Y - C^d - G$	1	3	5
(6) Net exports, $NX = Y -$ desired absorption	-4	0	4
(7) Desired foreign lending, $S^d - I^d$	-4	0	4

Note: We assume that net factor payments, *NFP*, equal zero.

balance, and net exports (which are all equivalent[11]). A decline in desired national saving relative to desired investment reduces those quantities. Let's look at two examples, both of which are useful in the application that follows.

Example 1: A Temporary Adverse Supply Shock.

Suppose that a small open economy is hit with a severe drought – an adverse supply shock – that temporarily lowers output. The effects of the drought on the nation's saving, investment, and current account are shown in Figure 5.3. The initial saving and investment curves are S^1 and I^1. For the world real interest rate r^w, national saving equals the distance OB and investment equals distance OA. Initial net foreign lending (equivalently, net exports or the current account balance) is length AB.

The drought brings with it a temporary decline in income. A drop in current income causes people to reduce their saving at any prevailing real interest rate, so the saving curve shifts left, from S^1 to S^2. If the supply shock is temporary, as we have assumed, the expected future marginal product of capital is unchanged. As a result, desired investment at any real interest rate is unchanged, and the investment curve does not shift. The world real interest rate is given and does not change.

In the new equilibrium, national saving has decreased to distance OD and net foreign lending and the current account have shrunk to length AD. The current account shrinks because the country saves less and thus is not able to lend abroad as much as before.

---

11. Remember that we are assuming that net factor payments from abroad and net unilateral transfers are zero, so that net exports equal the current account balance.

Figure 5.3

A temporary adverse supply shock in a small open economy

Curve S^1 is the initial saving curve, and curve I^1 is the initial investment curve of a small open economy. With a fixed world real interest rate of r^w, national saving equals the distance OB and investment equals distance OA. The current account surplus (equivalently, net foreign lending) is the difference between national saving and investment, shown as distance AB. A temporary adverse supply shock lowers current output and causes consumers to save less at any real interest rate, which shifts the saving curve left, from S^1 to S^2. National saving decreases to distance OD, and the current account surplus decreases to distance AD.

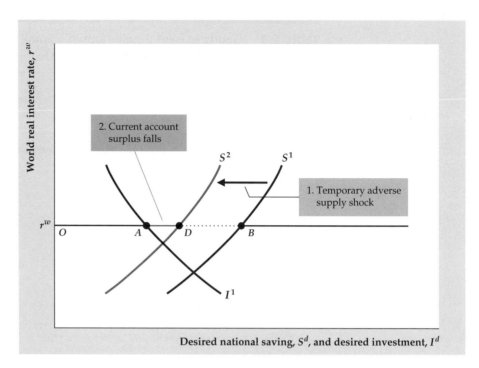

In this example we assumed that the country started with a current account surplus, which is reduced by the drought. If, instead, the country had begun with a current account deficit, the drought would have made the deficit larger. In either case the drought reduces (in the algebraic sense) net foreign lending and the current account balance.

Example 2: An Increase in the Expected Future Marginal Product of Capital.

Suppose that technological innovations increase the expected future marginal product MPK^f of current capital investments. The effects on a small open economy are shown in Figure 5.4. Again, the initial national saving and investment curves are S^1 and I^1 so that the initial current account surplus equals length AB.

An increase in the MPK^f raises the capital stock that domestic firms desire to hold so that desired investment rises at every real interest rate. Thus the investment curve shifts right, from I^1 to I^2, causing investment to increase from distance OA to distance OF. The current account and net foreign lending shrink from distance AB to distance FB. Why does the current account fall? Because building capital has become more profitable in the home country, more of the country's output is absorbed by domestic investment, leaving less to send abroad.[12]

---

12. A possibility that we have neglected so far is that technological innovations also cause savers to expect a higher future income, which would reduce current saving at every level of the world real interest rate. A leftward shift of the saving curve would further reduce the current account balance. This effect would only reinforce the effect on the country's current account of the rightward shift of the investment curve, so for simplicity we continue to ignore this potential change in desired saving.

Figure 5.4
An increase in the expected future *MPK* in a small open economy
As in Fig. 5.3, the small open economy's initial national saving and investment curves are S^1 and I^1. At the fixed world real interest rate of r^w, there is an initial current account surplus equal to the distance *AB*. An increase in the expected future marginal product of capital (MPK^f) shifts the investment curve right, from I^1 to I^2, causing investment to increase from distance *OA* to distance *OF*. The current account surplus, which is national saving minus investment, decreases from distance *AB* to distance *FB*.

APPLICATION:

The LDC Debt Crisis

During the 1970s less developed countries (LDCs) greatly increased their international borrowing. Table 5.4 presents data for a group of fifteen developing countries, ten of which are in Latin America, that had become heavily indebted by the early 1980s. Over the 1972–81 period, these countries ran current account deficits averaging more than 18% of their exports of goods and services (column 1). These current account deficits were financed by borrowing abroad, primarily from private commercial banks in Europe, the United States, and Japan. By 1982 – the year in which the LDC debt crisis became generally recognized – foreign debt was 41% of the gross domestic product of the fifteen countries.

During 1982, for reasons that we discuss shortly, banks began to lose confidence that their LDC loans would be repaid as promised and refused to make new loans. Unable to obtain new credit to replace maturing loans or to make planned investments, dozens of countries came under intense financial pressure. Negotiations with the banks and international agencies such as the International Monetary Fund and the World Bank resulted in some modest reductions in outstanding LDC debt, as did some unilateral decisions by debtor countries to reduce or delay payments to the banks. Mainly, though, the debtors did not default on (refuse to repay) their debts and attempted to keep making interest payments.

In the years following, interest payments on international debt were a serious burden on LDC economies. Column (2) of Table 5.4 shows that for the fifteen heavily indebted countries, interest payments during 1982–89 were between a quarter and a third of the total value of those countries' exports. In the balance of payments accounts, payments of interest on debt (which are part of investment income paid to foreigners) are debit items in the current

Table 5.4   Macroeconomic Data for Fifteen Heavily
Indebted Countries

Year	(1) Current Account Balance[a]	(2) Interest Payments on Debt[a]	(3) Balance on Merchandise Trade[a]	(4) Per Capita Real GDP Growth
1972–81	−18.2%	—	—	2.2%
1982	−35.7	32.0%	3.1%	−2.6
1983	−11.3	30.3	21.1	−4.9
1984	−1.5	30.8	28.8	0.2
1985	−0.5	30.1	27.6	1.6
1986	−14.5	30.9	16.2	1.1
1987	−6.2	26.0	18.0	0.7
1988	−5.9	25.5	18.0	−0.8
1989	−3.6	24.4	16.4	−0.9
1990	−2.2	21.8	16.0	−2.2
1991	−11.8	20.7	8.5	−0.5
1992	−16.2	13.2	4.2	−1.7
1993	−21.5	17.2	3.6	1.6
1994	−20.9	17.3	–	–

[a] As a percentage of exports of goods and services.

Source: International Monetary Fund, *World Economic Outlook,* October 1992, Tables A6, A35, and A39, and May 1994, Tables A29 and A41. The fifteen heavily indebted countries are Argentina, Bolivia, Brazil, Chile, Colombia, Côte d'Ivoire, Ecuador, Mexico, Morocco, Nigeria, Peru, the Philippines, Uruguay, Venezuela, and Yugoslavia. Data for 1993 and part of 1992 are IMF estimates.

account. Because the LDC debtors could not get new loans (capital inflows) for use in making interest payments, they were forced to expand exports and cut imports of goods and services. In particular, merchandise exports for LDC debtors substantially exceeded merchandise imports throughout the decade (column 3). Lower imports, especially reductions in imports of capital goods and intermediate goods, contributed to poor growth performance during the 1980s (column 4), with living standards in some countries falling sharply.

In March 1989 US Treasury Secretary Nicholas Brady announced what has become known as the Brady plan. It amounted to a three-way deal among the commercial banks holding LDC debt, the international agencies such as the World Bank that make loans to poor countries, and the debtor nations themselves. The Brady plan called on the commercial banks to accept significant reductions in the interest and principal owed to them by developing countries, in exchange for guarantees that the reduced LDC obligations would in fact be met. The role of the international agencies was to help the debtor nations meet their reduced debt payments by providing loans and other assistance. For their part, besides making continued debt payments, the LDC debtors were required to undertake reforms to improve the performance of their economies.

The Brady plan, together with falling world interest rates, contributed to a reduced burden of LDC debt after 1989. Table 5.4, column (2) shows that, between 1986 and 1994, the ratio of interest payments to exports had been approximately halved. Unfortunately, the economic troubles of these countries continued. The world-wide recession of the early 1990s reduced demand for LDC exports, leading both their trade balances and GDP growth rates to deteriorate (columns 3 and 4).

The LDC debt crisis raises several important questions:

1. *Why did the LDCs borrow so much in the first place, and why were lenders willing to lend?* There were two main causes of the increase in LDC debt, both of which can be analysed with our model of the small open economy. The first cause is that heavy foreign borrowing is a normal part of the process of economic development. The United States and Canada, for example, both piled up large international debts during their early growth. Figure 5.5 illustrates the reasons. In a developing economy the capital stock is low, whereas other types of resources (labour, land, minerals) may be relatively abundant. As a result, the expected future marginal product of capital investments is potentially high. This high expected future *MPK* is reflected by a desired investment curve that is quite far to the right.

At the same time, at early stages of development a country's income is low, so desired national saving is low. Reflecting this low desired saving, the saving curve is far to the left. The combination of high desired investment and low desired national saving at the given world real interest rate results in large capital inflows, or foreign borrowing, represented by length *AB*. Corresponding to the capital inflows are current account deficits, which arise because the developing country is importing large quantities of capital goods and other supplies without yet producing much for export. In a growing LDC attractive investment opportunities exceed the domestic population's capacity to save, so borrowing abroad is profitable for domestic investors, and lending is profitable for foreign lenders.

The second cause of the increase in LDC debt was specific to the 1970s. The oil shocks of 1973–74 and 1979–80 represented severe adverse supply shocks, which sharply depressed income in non-oil-exporting LDCs. Presumably because they thought that these shocks would be temporary, consumers in non-oil-exporting LDCs responded by reducing saving, so they would not have to reduce current consumption by as much as the current drop in output. Lower desired saving at given values of the world real interest rate led to increased current account deficits and foreign borrowing. Our analysis of a temporary adverse supply shock in Figure 5.3 predicts such a result.

Ironically, the ultimate source of a significant portion of the funds borrowed by LDCs was the oil-exporting countries themselves, which needed somewhere to invest the huge increase in their oil revenues created by the higher prices. In practice, the oil exporters lent to banks in industrialized countries, who then re-lent the funds to LDCs in a process known as 'recycling petro-dollars'.

2. *If the LDC lending was justified, why did the loans go bad?* Various adverse macroeconomic developments, not foreseen when most of the LDC loans were made, caused problems for the LDC debtors. Among these developments was a world-wide recession in 1979–82 that lowered the demand for LDC exports. Reduced export sales kept LDC borrowers from achieving the large surpluses on the merchandise and services portion of the current account that they

Figure 5.5
International borrowing in a developing economy
In a small developing economy income and desired national saving are low, so the saving curve S is far to the left. Investment opportunities are good (the expected future *MPK* is high), so the investment curve *I* is far to the right. At the world real interest rate of r^w, investment (distance *OB*) greatly exceeds national saving (distance *OA*). To fund its desired investment, the country must borrow abroad. Distance *AB* is the developing country's foreign borrowing or, equivalently, its current account deficit.

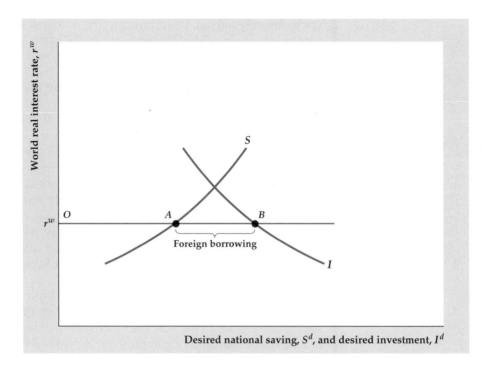

needed to pay interest on their debts.[13] Another adverse macroeconomic development of the early 1980s was sharp increases in interest rates. Because most LDC debt was in the form of floating-rate loans, whose required interest payments rise automatically when current interest rates rise, the interest obligations of the LDC debtors increased greatly.

Although the macroeconomic problems that arose were generally unexpected, it is probably also true that many of the loans made to the LDCs in the 1970s were not adequately researched by lenders, and some borrowing firms and governments wasted or mismanaged the funds they received. The rapidity with which lending was expanded in the 1970s may have been one reason that careless lending and investment decisions were made.

3. *Why has the LDC debt crisis taken so long to be resolved?* Because the true economic values of LDC loans fell dramatically below their 'paper' values, someone had to bear large losses; the long delay in resolving the crisis was (and remains) a result of continuing disagreement over how the losses should be shared. The borrowers, of course, could have escaped their debts by defaulting. However, default itself may impose sufficient economic and political costs on the borrowers to make it unattractive (see the box 'The Political Environment: Default and Sovereign Debt,' p. 173). The banks that made the LDC loans had little incentive to make concessions, particularly when their own financial health was at serious risk early in the decade. Only over a long period of time, as the costs of an ongoing debt crisis have become clear, have political leaders begun to take steps toward finding a comprehensive resolution of the debt problem.

---

13. The open-economy macroeconomic model used in this chapter is too simplified to explain the effects of a decline in demand for a country's exports. We incorporate this type of effect into the model in Chapter 14.

THE POLITICAL ENVIRONMENT

DEFAULT AND SOVEREIGN DEBT

If an individual consumer defaults on a loan, the creditors have well-established legal means to try to force repayment. For example, they may be able to seize the consumer's assets, or a court may rule that part of the consumer's future wages may be attached in repayment. In contrast, default on sovereign debt, or debt owed by an independent nation, leaves creditors with limited options. There is no international authority to enforce repayment of sovereign debts, and creditors can neither seize the debtors' domestic assets nor "attach" its income.

With this lack of legal enforceability, why do sovereign debtors usually try to repay what they owe, even when doing so imposes economic hardship on their people? Some researchers emphasize that defaulting countries may face significant economic costs. Such costs may include seizure of the country's assets held abroad, disruption of international trade (as creditors interfere with shipments or payments), and denial of future international loans.

Although the economic costs of default are part of the reason that international debtors usually repay, key political considerations are equally important:

1. *Creditors' political power within their own country.* When there were widespread defaults on foreign bonds during the Great Depression, the American holders of the foreign bonds were politically unorganized and received little help from the US government (well-organized British bondholders got much more help from their government in the 1930s).* In the 1980s, in contrast, concern about the health of the domestic banking system (which stood to suffer from LDC defaults) prompted the United States to put diplomatic and political pressures on the debtor countries to repay.

2. *Relations between creditor and debtor countries.* History has shown that debtors are more likely to repay when they value the political, economic, and military relations they have with creditors. A debt-laden Australia did not default during the Great Depression because it wanted good relations with its main creditor, the UK. At the opposite extreme, in 1990 Iraq tried to 'solve' its foreign debt problems by invading a principal creditor, Kuwait. Similarly, creditors are less likely to be tough when they value their relationships with the debtors. The United States has forgiven many of the war debts owed it by its military allies, for example.

3. *Relations among the debtor countries.* If many LDC debtors defaulted simultaneously, the creditor countries would have much greater difficulty punishing them. Enforcing trade sanctions against one country is easier than enforcing them against thirty countries, for example. For this reason some LDC leaders have called for the formation of a 'debtors' cartel', an organization of debtor countries that would negotiate with the creditors as a bloc. The feasibility of such debtor cooperation depends on the ability of the debtors to get along and cooperate politically. So far, differing goals and animosities among debtors, and political pressures from the creditor nations, have prevented the emergence of a debtors' cartel.

---

* For an interesting discussion of the debt crisis in historical perspective, see Barry Eichengreen, 'Historical Research on International Lending and Debt', *Journal of Economic Perspectives*, Spring 1991, pp. 149–69.

5.4 SAVING AND INVESTMENT IN LARGE OPEN ECONOMIES

Although the model of a small open economy facing a fixed real interest rate is appropriate for studying many of the countries in the world, it is not the right model to use for analysing the world's major developed economies. The problem is that significant changes in the saving and investment patterns of a major economy can and do affect the world real interest rate, which violates the assumption made for the small open economy that the world real interest rate is fixed. Fortunately, we can readily adapt the analysis of the small open economy to the case of a **large open economy**: that is, an economy large enough to affect the world real interest rate.

To begin, let's think of the world as comprising only two large economies: (1) the home or domestic economy, and (2) the foreign economy (representing the economies of the rest of the world combined). Figure 5.6 shows the saving–investment diagram that applies to this case. Figure 5.6(a) shows the saving curve S and the investment curve I of the home economy. Figure 5.6(b) displays the saving curve S_{For} and the investment curve I_{For} of the foreign economy. These saving and investment curves are just like those for the small open economy.

Instead of taking the world real interest rate as given, as we did in the model of a small open economy, we determine the world real interest rate within the model for a large open economy. What determines the value of the world real interest rate? Remember that for the closed economy, the real interest rate was set by the condition that the amount that savers want to lend must equal the amount that investors want to borrow. Analogously, in the case of two large open economies, *the world real interest rate will be such that desired international lending by one country equals desired international borrowing by the other country.*

To illustrate the determination of the equilibrium world real interest rate, we return to Figure 5.6. Suppose, arbitrarily, that the world real interest rate r^w is 6%. Does this rate result in a goods market equilibrium? Figure 5.6(a) shows that, at a 6% real interest rate, in the home country desired national saving is DM450 billion and desired investment is DM150 billion. Because desired national saving exceeds desired investment by DM300 billion, the amount that the home country would like to lend abroad is DM300 billion.

To find how much the foreign country wants to borrow, we turn to Figure 5.6(b). When the real interest rate is 6%, desired national saving is DM550 billion and desired investment is DM650 billion in the foreign country. Thus at a 6% real interest rate the foreign country wants to borrow DM100 billion (DM650 billion less DM550 billion) in the international capital market. Because this amount is less than the DM300 billion the home country wants to lend, 6% is *not* the real interest rate that is consistent with equilibrium in the international capital market.

At a real interest rate of 6%, desired international lending exceeds desired international borrowing, so the equilibrium world real interest rate must be less than 6%. Let's try a real interest rate of 5%. Figure 5.6(a) shows that at that interest rate desired national saving is DM400 billion and desired investment is DM200 billion in the home country, so the home country wants to lend DM200 billion abroad. In Figure 5.6(b), when the real interest rate is 5%, desired national saving in the foreign country is DM500 billion and desired investment is DM700 billion, so the foreign country's desired international borrowing is DM200 billion. At a 5% real interest rate, desired international borrowing and desired international lending are equal (both are DM200 billion), so the equilibrium world real interest rate is 5% in this example.

Graphically, the home country's desired lending when r^w equals 5% is length AB in Figure 5.6(a), and the foreign country's desired borrowing is length DE in Figure 5.6(b). Because length AB equals length DE, desired international lending and borrowing are equal when the world real interest rate is 5%.

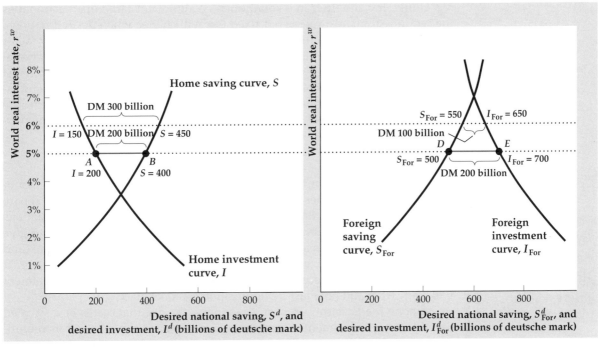

(a) Home country

(b) Foreign country

Figure 5.6
The determination of the world real interest rate with two large open economies
The equilibrium world real interest rate is the real interest rate at which desired international lending by one country equals desired international borrowing by the other country. In the figure, when the world real interest rate is 5%, desired international lending by the home country is DM200 billion (DM400 billion desired national saving less DM200 billion desired investment, or distance *AB*), which equals the foreign country's desired international borrowing of DM200 billion (DM700 billion desired investment less DM500 billion desired national saving, or distance *DE*). Thus 5% is the equilibrium world real interest rate. Equivalently, when the interest rate is 5%, the current account surplus of the home country equals the current account deficit of the foreign country (both are DM200 billion).

We defined international equilibrium in terms of desired international lending and borrowing. Equivalently, we can define equilibrium in terms of international flows of goods and services. The amount the lending country desires to lend (distance *AB* in Figure 5.6(a) is the same as its current account surplus. The amount the borrowing country wants to borrow (distance *DE* in Figure 5.6(b) equals its current account deficit. Thus saying that desired international lending must equal desired international borrowing is the same as saying that the desired net outflow of goods and services from the lending country (its current account surplus) must equal the desired net inflow of goods and services to the borrowing country (its current account deficit).

In summary, for a large open economy the equilibrium world real interest rate is the rate at which the desired international lending by one country equals the desired international borrowing of the other country. Equivalently, it is the real interest rate at which the lending country's current account surplus equals the borrowing country's current account deficit.

Unlike the situation in a small open economy, for large open economies the world real interest rate is not fixed but will change when desired national saving or desired investment changes in either country. Generally, any factor that increases desired international lending relative to desired international borrowing at the initial world real interest rate causes the world real interest rate to fall. Similarly, a change that reduces desired international lending relative to desired international borrowing at the initial world real interest rate will cause the world real interest rate to rise. We illustrate this principle further in an application.

APPLICATION

German Reunification and the World Real Interest Rate

The collapse of communism in Eastern Europe in 1989 revealed a legacy of economic decay. Factories and equipment were outmoded and in poor repair, infrastructure (roads, utilities, and communications systems) was inadequate, and substantial environmental problems had to be addressed. Clearly, to give market-oriented reforms a chance to work, large infusions of capital were (and are) needed to modernize the Eastern European economies. Among the great uncertainties for those economies are where the funds needed for investment will come from and how fast modernization can take place.

Among the Eastern European economies, the one that seems best situated to receive new investment is the former East Germany's, because of its reunification with West Germany. The new, united Germany has announced plans for major infrastructure spending in the east, and private firms, attracted by the former East Germany's educated labour force and its new attachment to capitalism, have expressed interest in making capital investments there. The question we address here is: assuming that substantial new investment does occur in eastern Germany and Eastern Europe generally, what will be the effect on international capital markets and trade patterns in the rest of the world? More narrowly, what would be the effect of an investment boom in eastern Germany and Eastern Europe on the world real interest rate?

Figure 5.7 shows an analysis of this issue. The home economy, shown in Figure 5.7(a), is a united Germany. We label the foreign economy in Figure 5.7(b) as the rest of the EU, although the foreign economy might more accurately be taken to represent all of Germany's trading partners as a group.

In Figure 5.7 the initial (before reunification) equilibrium world real interest rate is r_1^w. At that interest rate Germany has a current account surplus, represented by length AB, and the rest of the EU has a current account deficit, represented by length DE. As required for equilibrium, before reunification the current account deficit for the rest of the EU equals the German current account surplus. That is, lengths AB and DE are equal.

Two likely results of reunification are (1) temporarily increased German government purchases as the infrastructure in eastern Germany is rebuilt; and (2) an increase in the expected future marginal product MPK^f for German investment, resulting from eastern Germany's switch to a capitalist system and the opening up of the economy. To determine the impact of reunification, we consider how these two factors should affect desired national saving and desired investment in a united Germany.

Recall that a temporary increase in government purchases lowers desired national saving at any real interest rate. Thus the German saving curve shifts left, from S^1 to S^2 in Figure 5.7(a). The effect of the increase in the MPK^f in east-

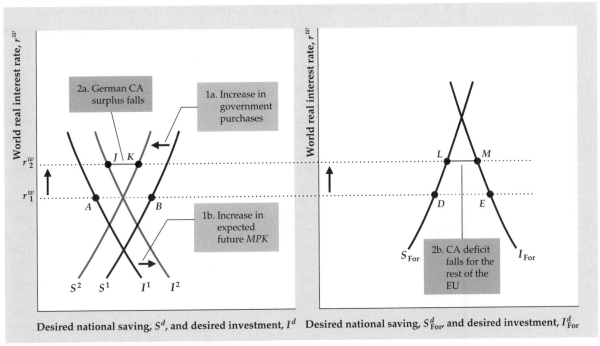

Desired national saving, S^d, and desired investment, I^d

(a) Home country (Germany)

Desired national saving, S^d_{For}, and desired investment, I^d_{For}

(b) Foreign country (rest of EU)

Figure 5.7

German reunification and the world real interest rate

The figure represents two large open economies, Germany (the home economy) and the rest of the EU (the foreign economy). Before reunification, the German saving and investment curves are S^1 and I^1. The equilibrium world real interest rate, r^w_1, is the real interest rate at which the German current account surplus AB just equals the current account deficit DE of the rest of the EU. Reunification raises government purchases in Germany, which shifts the German saving curve left from S^1 to S^2, and also improves investment opportunities in Germany, which shifts the German investment curve right from I^1 to I^2. The saving and investment curves of the rest of the EU do not shift. The new world real interest rate is r^w_2, where the German current account surplus JK again equals the current account deficit LM for the rest of the EU. Reunification raises the world real interest rate, lowers the German current account surplus, and lowers the current account deficit in the rest of the EU.

ern Germany is to raise desired investment at any real interest rate, leading the German investment curve to shift right, from I^1 to I^2. There is no reason to expect any change in desired national saving or desired investment in the rest of the EU at any given world real interest rate.

Because of the reduction in desired national saving and the increase in desired investment in Germany, the international capital market is no longer in equilibrium at the original world real interest rate r^w_1. At that real interest rate the amount the Germans want to lend abroad has fallen, so desired international borrowing exceeds desired international lending. Thus the world real interest rate must rise. Figure 5.7 shows that the new equilibrium interest rate is r^w_2. When the real interest rate is r^w_2, desired international lending by Germany, distance JK, equals desired international borrowing by the rest of the EU, distance LM. Because r^w_2 is greater than r^w_1, we conclude that German reunification will tend to raise the world real interest rate.

Other possible effects of reunification shown in Figure 5.7 include:

- a lower German current account surplus (length *JK* is shorter than length *AB*);

- a lower current account deficit in the rest of the EU (length *LM* is shorter than length *DE*); and

- more national saving and less investment in the rest of the EU.

The German current account surplus falls in this analysis because new investment opportunities in eastern Germany raise German desired investment at the same time that increased government purchases reduce German desired national saving. The increase in national saving and the drop in investment in the rest of the EU, which imply a smaller current account deficit in the EU, are responses by savers and investors in the rest of the EU to the higher world real interest rate.

We cannot yet say whether these predictions are on target. As the analysis suggests, since reunification the German current account balance has declined significantly, from a surplus exceeding 4% of German output in 1989 to a deficit greater than 1% of output in 1992. However, because of uncertainties about the outcomes of the ongoing reforms, capital inflows to eastern Germany and to Eastern Europe more generally have not yet been very large, and they probably have not yet had much impact on the world real interest rate.[14] No doubt additional developments will affect the pace of investment in Eastern Europe, and many other types of shock may affect international capital markets. Nevertheless, this analysis provides a way to think about these questions; and indeed, our results are consistent with projections made by economists in both the private and the public sectors.[15]

5.5 FISCAL POLICY AND THE CURRENT ACCOUNT

During the period from the late 1970s, through to the early 1990s, many economies, both in Europe and elsewhere, experienced large government budget deficits at the same time as having large current account deficits. Were these two phenomena related? Many economists and other commentators argue that they were, suggesting that in fact the budget deficit was the primary cause of the current account deficit. Those supporting this view often use the phrase 'twin deficits' to convey the idea that the government budget deficit and the current account deficit were closely linked. Not all economists agree with this interpretation, however; some argue that the two deficits were largely unrelated. In this section we briefly discuss what the theory has to say about this issue and then turn to the evidence.

---

14. See International Monetary Fund, *World Economic Outlook,* Table A51 for data on international saving and investment flows. Data on the German current account are from Table A31 of the same publication.

15. See, for example, Alessandro Giustiniani, Francesco Papadia, and Daniela Porciani, 'Growth and Catch-up in Central and Eastern Europe: Macroeconomic Effects on Western Countries', Princeton Essays in International Finance no. 186, April 1992; see also 'Economic Reform in Eastern Europe and the USSR', in IMF, *World Economic Outlook,* May 1990, particularly the box on the effects of German reunification.

The Critical Factor: The Response of National Saving

In theory, the issue of whether there is a link between the government budget deficit and the current account deficit revolves around the following proposition: *an increase in the government budget deficit will raise the current account deficit only if the increase in the budget deficit reduces desired national saving.*

Let's first look at why the link to national saving is crucial. Figure 5.8 shows the case of the small open economy. The world real interest rate is fixed at r^w. We draw the initial saving and investment curves S^1 and I so that, at the world real interest rate r^w, the country is running a current account surplus, represented by length AB. Now suppose that the government budget deficit rises. For simplicity, we assume throughout this section that the change in fiscal policy does not affect the tax treatment of investment so that the investment curve does not shift. Hence, as Figure 5.8 shows, the government deficit increase will change the current account balance only if it affects desired national saving.

The usual claim made by supporters of the twin-deficits idea is that an increase in the government budget deficit reduces desired national saving. If it does, the increase in the government deficit shifts the desired national saving curve left, from S^1 to S^2. The country still has a current account surplus, now equal to distance AC, but it is less than the original surplus AB.

We conclude that in a small open economy an increase in the government budget deficit reduces the current account balance by the same amount that it reduces desired national saving. By reducing saving, the increased budget deficit reduces the amount that domestic residents want to lend abroad at the world real interest rate, thus lowering capital outflows. Equivalently, reduced national saving means that a greater part of domestic output is absorbed at

Figure 5.8
The government budget deficit and the current account in a small open economy
An increase in the government budget deficit affects the current account only if the increased budget deficit reduces national saving. Initially, the saving curve is S^1 and the current account surplus is distance AB. If an increase in the government deficit reduces national saving, the saving curve shifts left, from S^1 to S^2. With no change in the effective tax rate on capital, the investment curve I doesn't move. Thus the increase in the budget deficit causes the current account surplus to decrease from distance AB to distance AC. In contrast, if the increase in the budget deficit has no effect on national saving, the current account is also unaffected and remains equal to distance AB.

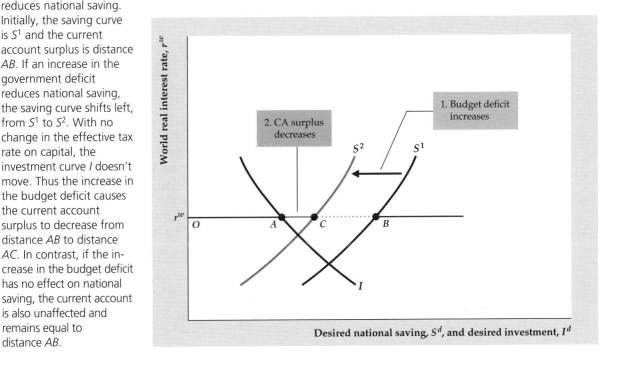

home; with less output to send abroad, the country's current account falls. Similar results hold for the large open economy (you are asked to work out this case in Analytical Problem 4 at the end of the chapter).

The Government Budget Deficit and National Saving

Let's now turn to the link between the budget deficit and saving and consider two cases: a budget deficit arising from an increase in government purchases and a deficit rising from a cut in taxes.

A Deficit Caused by Increased Government Purchases.

Suppose that the source of the government budget deficit is a temporary increase in government purchases, perhaps owing to a military build-up. In this case there is no controversy: recall (Chapter 4) that, with output, Y, held constant at its full-employment level, an increase in government purchases, G, directly reduces desired national saving, $S^d = Y - C^d - G$.[16, 17] Because economists agree that a deficit owing to increased government purchases reduces desired national saving, they also agree that a deficit resulting from increased government purchases reduces the nation's current account balance.

A Deficit Resulting from a Tax Cut.

Suppose instead that the government budget deficit is the result of a cut in current taxes, with current and planned future government purchases unchanged. With government purchases, G, unchanged and with output, Y, held constant at its full-employment level, the tax cut will cause desired national saving, $S^d = Y - C^d - G$, to fall only if it causes desired consumption, C^d, to rise.

Will a tax cut cause people to consume more? As we discussed in Chapter 4, believers in the Ricardian equivalence proposition argue that a lump-sum tax change (with current and future government purchases held constant) will not affect desired consumption or desired national saving. These economists point out that a cut in taxes today forces the government to borrow more to pay for its current purchases; when this extra borrowing plus interest is repaid in the future, future taxes will have to rise. Thus, although a tax cut raises consumers' current after-tax incomes, the tax cut creates the need for higher future taxes and lowers the after-tax incomes that consumers can expect to receive in the future. Overall, according to this argument, a tax cut does not benefit consumers and thus will not increase their desired consumption.

If the Ricardian equivalence proposition is true, a budget deficit resulting from a tax cut will have no effect on the current account because it does not affect desired national saving. However, as we noted in Chapter 4, many economists argue that – despite the logic of Ricardian equivalence – in practice many consumers do respond to a current tax cut by consuming more. For example, consumers simply may not understand that a higher deficit today makes higher taxes tomorrow more likely. If for any reason consumers do

---

16. Because the increase in government purchases also means that taxes may be raised in the future, lowering consumers' expected future income, desired consumption, C^d, may fall. However, because the increase in G is temporary so that the future tax increase need not be too large, this drop in C^d should not offset the effect of increased G on desired national saving.

17. In general, in an open economy, $S^d = Y + NFP - C^d - G$, but we are assuming that $NFP = 0$ so that $S^d = Y - C^d - G$.

respond to a tax cut by consuming more, the deficit resulting from a tax cut will reduce national saving and thus also will reduce the current account balance.

APPLICATION

The Twin Deficits

The relationship between the government budget deficit and the current account deficit – the twin deficits – for Germany, the Netherlands, Sweden and the UK is shown in Figure 5.9 for the period 1970–96. Here, fiscal policy is measured by government expenditures (including transfers and interest paid) and government total receipts, in both cases relative to GDP. The difference between government purchases and receipts is the government budget deficit, shown in pink. Figure 5.9 also shows the current account balance. Negative values of the current account balance indicate a current account deficit.

The apparently close relationship of the government budget deficit and current account deficit at certain times during the past 25 years is evidence in favour of the twin-deficits idea, that budget deficits cause current account deficits.

However, the evidence from other episodes is less supportive of this hypothesis. For example, during the 1990s, Sweden's government budget deficit increased sharply but the current account was improving. The Netherlands simultaneously ran large government budget deficits and large current account

Figure 5.9
The government budget deficit and the current account in selected European countries 1970–96
Shown are government expenditures, (including interest payments), total current government tax receipts, and the current account balance for Germany, the Netherlands, Sweden, and the UK for 1970–96, with all series measured as a percentage of GDP. The government deficit is the difference between government expenditures and current receipts. Note the government deficit in Germany, Sweden and the UK in the 1990s coincided with current account deficit, which in the United States has been called the twin-deficits phenomenon.

Source: *European Economy 1996, op cit Table 1.1(b)*, Table 4.4 'Balance of transactions with rest of world'; Table 62 'Total current receipts: general government'; Table 71 'Total current expenditure by general government'.

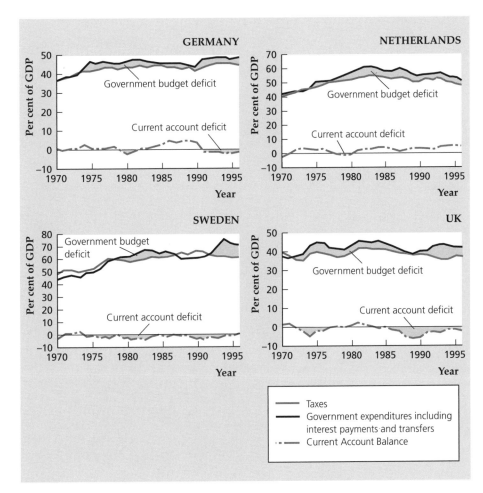

surpluses during the 1980s as did the USA during both world wars. During the mid-1980s Canada and Italy both ran large government budget deficits without experiencing severe current account problems. Because of the lack of clear evidence, a good deal of disagreement remains among economists about the relationship between government budget deficits and the current account.[18] What we can say for sure (because it is implied by the uses-of-saving identity, equation 2.11) is that, if an increase in the government budget deficit is not offset by an equal increase in private saving, the result must be a decline in domestic investment or a rise in the current account deficit, or both.

---

18. For a review of this debate, including useful references, see Ellis Tallman and Jeffrey Rosensweig, 'Investigating US Government and Trade Deficits', in Federal Reserve Bank of Atlanta, *Economic Review*, May/June 1991, pp. 1–11. Evidence for a number of European (and other) countries can be found in Colin Kearney and Mehdi Monadjemi, 'Fiscal Policy and Current Acccount Performance: International Evidence on the Twin Deficits', *Journal of Macoeconomics*, Spring 1990, pp. 197–219.

CHAPTER SUMMARY

1. The balance of payments accounts consist of the current account and the capital account. The current account records trade in currently produced goods and services, investment income from assets held abroad, and transfers between countries. The capital account records trade in existing assets, both real and financial.

2. In the current account, exports of goods and services, receipts of investment income from assets held abroad, and unilateral transfers received from abroad count as credit (plus) items. Imports of goods and services, payments of investment income to foreigners holding assets in the home country, and unilateral transfers sent abroad are debit (minus) items in the current account. The current account balance, *CA*, equals the value of credit items less debit items in the current account. Setting net factor payments and net unilateral transfers to zero makes the current account balance the same as net exports, *NX*. The capital account balance, *KA*, is the value of assets sold to foreigners (capital inflows) minus the value of assets purchased from foreigners (capital outflows).

3. In each period, except for measurement errors, the current account balance and the capital account balance must sum to zero. The reason is that any international transaction amounts to a swap of goods, services, or assets between countries; the two sides of the swap always have offsetting effects on the sum of the current account and capital account balances.

4. In an open economy, goods market equilibrium requires that the desired amount of national saving equal the desired amount of domestic investment plus the amount the country lends abroad. Equivalently, net exports must equal the country's output (gross domestic product) less desired total spending by domestic residents (absorption).

5. A small open economy faces a fixed real interest rate in the international capital market. In goods market equilibrium in a small open economy, national saving and investment equal their desired levels at the prevailing world real interest rate; foreign lending, net exports, and the current account all equal the excess of national saving over investment. Any factor that increases desired national saving or reduces desired investment at the world real interest rate will increase the small open economy's foreign lending (equivalently, its current account balance).

6. The levels of saving and investment of a large open economy affect the world real interest rate. In a model of two large open economies, the equilibrium real interest rate in the international capital market is the rate at which desired international lending by one country equals desired international borrowing by the other country. Equivalently, it is the rate at which the lending country's current account surplus equals the borrowing country's current account deficit. Any factor that increases desired national saving or reduces desired investment at the initial interest rate for either large country will increase the supply of international loans relative to the demand and cause the world real interest rate to fall.

7. According to the 'twin-deficits' hypothesis, large government budget deficits during the past 25 years helped cause the increased current account deficits during that time. Whether budget deficits cause current account deficits is the subject of disagreement. In theory, and if we assume no change in the tax treatment of investment, an increase in the government budget deficit will raise the current account deficit only if it reduces national saving. Economists generally agree that an increase in the budget deficit caused by a temporary increase in government purchases will reduce national saving, but whether an increase in the budget deficit caused by a tax cut reduces national saving is controversial.

National Saving and Investment in a Small Open Economy

This open-economy version of the saving–investment diagram shows the determination of national saving, investment, and the current account balance in a small open economy that takes the world real interest rate as given.

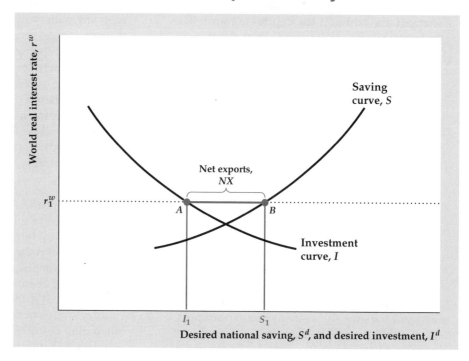

Diagram Elements

■ The world real interest rate is measured on the vertical axis, and the small economy's desired national saving S^d and desired investment I^d are measured on the horizontal axis.

■ The world real interest rate r^w is fixed, as indicated by the horizontal line.

■ The saving curve S and the investment curve I are the same as in the closed-economy saving–investment diagram, Key Diagram 3 (p. 146).

Analysis

■ Goods market equilibrium in a small open economy requires that desired national saving equal desired investment plus net exports (equation 5.4). In the diagram when the world real interest rate is r_1^w desired national saving is S_1 and desired investment is I_1. The country's net exports NX and current account balance CA, or $S_1 - I_1$, is distance AB. Equivalently, distance AB, the excess of desired national saving over desired

investment, is the amount that the small open economy is lending abroad, or its capital account deficit.

Factors that Shift the Curves

■ Anything that increases desired national saving in the small open economy, for a fixed value of the world real interest rate, shifts the saving curve right. Factors that shift the saving curve right (see Summary table 5, p. 126) include

an increase in current output, Y,
a decrease in expected future output,
a decrease in wealth,
a decrease in current government purchases, G, and
an increase in current taxes, T, if Ricardian equivalence does not hold and taxes affect saving.

■ Anything that increases desired investment at the prevailing real interest rate shifts the investment curve right. Factors that shift the investment curve right (see Summary table 6, p. 138) include an increase in the expected future marginal product of capital, MPK^f, and a decrease in the effective tax rate on capital.

■ An increase in desired national saving shifts the saving curve right and raises net exports and the current account balance. Equivalently, an increase in desired national saving raises the country's net foreign lending, which equals its capital account deficit. Similarly, an increase in desired investment shifts the investment curve right and lowers net exports, the current account balance, net foreign lending, and the capital account deficit.

■ An increase in the world real interest rate r^w raises the horizontal line in the diagram. Because an increase in the world real interest rate increases national saving and reduces investment, it raises net foreign lending, net exports, the current account surplus, and the capital account deficit.

KEY DIAGRAM 5

National Saving and Investment in Large Open Economies

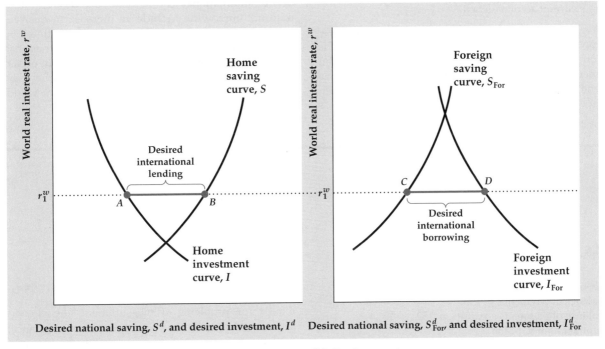

(a) **Home country**

(b) **Foreign country**

This diagram shows the determination of national saving, investment, and the current account balance in large open economies, economies large enough to affect the world real interest rate.

Diagram Elements

■ The figure consists of two saving–investment diagrams, one for the home country and one for the foreign country (representing the rest of the world).

■ The world real interest rate r^w, measured on the vertical axis, is the real interest rate faced by both countries in the international capital market.

■ The saving and investment curves in the home country (S and I) and in the foreign country (S_{For} and

I_{For}) are the same as the saving and investment curves presented before (Key Diagram 3, p. 146, and Key Diagram 4).

Analysis

■ This case differs from the case of the small open economy (Key Diagram 4) in that the world real interest rate r^w is determined within the model, not given.

■ Goods market equilibrium for large open economies requires that the desired international lending of one country equal the desired international borrowing of the other. Equivalently, because a country's international lending equals its current account balance, goods market equilibrium requires that one country's current account surplus equal the other country's current account deficit.

■ The world real interest rate adjusts to achieve goods market equilibrium. In the diagram r_1^w is the equilibrium world real interest rate, because at that interest rate the home country's desired international lending (its desired national saving less desired investment, or distance AB) equals the foreign country's

desired international borrowing (its desired investment less desired national saving, or distance CD).

Factors that Shift the Curves

■ The saving and investment curves in the two countries are shifted by the same factors as in Key Diagram 3, p. 146, and Key Diagram 4.

■ The world real interest rate changes when desired national saving or desired investment changes in either country. Any change that increases desired international lending relative to desired international borrowing at the initial world real interest rate will cause the world real interest rate to fall to restore equilibrium in the international capital market. Changes that increase desired international lending relative to desired international borrowing include an increase in desired national saving or a decrease in desired investment in either country. Similarly, a decrease in desired national saving or an increase in desired investment in either country reduces desired international lending relative to desired international borrowing and raises the world real interest rate.

Key Terms

Key Equations

$$CA + KA = 0 \qquad (5.1)$$

Except for problems of measurement, the current account balance, CA, and the capital account balance, KA, always sum to zero. The reason is that every international transaction involves a swap of goods, services, or assets; and the two sides of the swap always have offsetting effects on $CA + KA$.

$$S^d = I^d + NX \qquad (5.4)$$

The goods market equilibrium condition in an open economy holds that desired national saving, S^d, must equal desired investment, I^d, plus the amount lent abroad. The amount lent abroad equals the current account balance, which (if we assume that net factor payments and unilateral transfers are zero) also equals net exports, NX.

$$NX = Y - (C^d + I^d + G) \qquad (5.6)$$

An alternative way of writing the goods market equilibrium condition, this equation states that net exports must equal the country's output, Y, less its desired absorption, $C^d + I^d + G$.

Review Questions

1. List the categories of credit items and debit items that appear in a country's current account. What is the current account balance? What is the relationship between the current account balance and net exports?

2. What is the key difference that determines whether an international transaction appears in the current account or the capital account?

3. A French publisher sells 1000 francs worth of books to a resident of Brazil. By itself, this item is a credit item in the French current account. Describe some offsetting transactions that could ensure that the French current and capital account balances would continue to sum to zero.

4. How do a country's current and capital account balances affect its net foreign assets? If country A has greater net foreign assets per citizen than does country B, is country A necessarily better off than country B?

5. Explain why, in a small open economy, (a) national saving does not have to equal investment, and (b) output does not have to equal absorption.

6. Generally, what types of factor will cause a small open economy to run a large current account deficit and thus borrow abroad? More specifically, what two major factors contributed to heavy LDC borrowing in the 1970s?

7. In a world with two large open economies, what determines the world real interest rate? What relationship between the current accounts of the two countries is satisfied when the world real interest rate is at its equilibrium value?

8. How does an increase in desired national saving in a large open economy affect the world real interest rate? How does an increase in desired investment affect it? Why do changes in desired saving or investment in large open economies affect the world real interest rate but changes in desired saving or investment in small open economies do not?

9. Under what circumstances will an increase in the government budget deficit affect the current account balance in a small open economy? In the cases in which the current account balance changes, by how much does it change?

10. What are the twin deficits? What is the connection between them?

Numerical Problems

1. Here are some balance of payments data (without pluses and minuses):

   Merchandise exports, 100
   Merchandise imports, 125
   Service exports, 90
   Service imports, 80
   Investment income receipts from assets, 110
   Investment income payments on assets, 140
   Transfers from home country to other countries, 10
   Increase in home country's ownership of assets abroad, 160
   Increase in foreign ownership of assets in home country, 200
   Increase in home reserve assets, 30
   Increase in foreign reserve assets, 35

   Find the merchandise trade balance, net exports, the current account balance, the capital account balance, the official settlements balance, and the statistical discrepancy.

2. In a small open economy output (gross domestic product) is £250 million, government purchases are £60 million, and net factor payments from abroad are zero. Desired consumption and desired investment are related to the world real interest rate in the following manner:

World Real Interest Rate	Desired Consumption	Desired Investment
5%	£120 million	£30 million
4%	£130 million	£40 million
3%	£140 million	£50 million
2%	£150 million	£60 million

   For each value of the world real interest rate, find national saving, foreign lending, and absorption. Calculate net exports as the difference between output and absorption. What is the relationship between net exports and foreign lending?

3. In a small open economy,

   desired national saving, $S^d = £10 \text{ billion} + (£100 \text{ billion})r^w$;

   desired investment, $I^d = £15 \text{ billion} - (£100 \text{ billion})r^w$;

output, $Y = £50$ billion;

government purchases, $G = £10$ billion;

world real interest rate, $r^w = 0.03$.

a. Find the economy's national saving, investment, current account surplus, net exports, desired consumption, and absorption.

b. Owing to a technological innovation, the country's desired investment rises by £2 billion at each level of the world real interest rate. Repeat part (a).

4. Consider two large open economies, the home economy and the foreign economy. In the home country the following relationships hold:

desired consumption, $C^d = 320 + 0.4(Y - T) - 200r^w$;

desired investment, $I^d = 150 - 200r^w$;

output, $Y = 1000$;

taxes, $T = 200$;

government purchases, $G = 275$.

In the foreign country the following relationships hold:

desired consumption, $C^d_{For} = 480 + 0.4(Y_{For} - T_{For}) - 300r^w$;

desired investment, $I^d_{For} = 225 - 300r^w$;

output, $Y_{For} = 1500$;

taxes, $T_{For} = 300$;

government purchases, $G_{For} = 300$.

a. What is the equilibrium interest rate in the international capital market? What are the equilibrium values of consumption, national saving, investment, and the current account balance in each country?

b. Suppose that in the home country government purchases increase by 50 to 325. Taxes also increase by 50 to keep the deficit from growing. What is the new equilibrium interest rate in the international capital market? What are the new equilibrium values of consumption, national saving, investment, and the current account balance in each country?

5. A small island nation is endowed with indestructible coconut trees. These trees live for ever and no new trees can be planted. Every year 1 million kronor worth of coconuts fall off the trees and can be eaten locally or exported to other countries. In past years the island nation ran current account surpluses and capital account deficits, acquiring foreign bonds. It now owns 500,000 kronor of foreign bonds. The

interest rate on these bonds is 5% per year. The residents of the island nation consume 1,025,000 kronor per year. What are the values of investment, national saving, the current account balance, the capital account balance, net exports, GDP, and GNP in this country?

Analytical Problems

1. Explain how each of the following transactions would enter the French balance of payments accounts. Discuss only the transactions described. Do not be concerned with possible offsetting ransactions.

   a. The French government sells fighter planes to a foreign government.

   b. A London bank sells yen to, and buys French Francs from, a Swiss bank.

   c. The Central bank of France sells yen to, and buys francs from, a Swiss bank.

   d. A Paris bank receives the interest on its loans to Brazil.

   e. A French collector buys some ancient artifacts from a collection in Egypt.

   f. A French oil company buys insurance from Lloyds of London to insure its oil rigs in the Gulf of Mexico.

   g. A French company borrows from a British bank.

2. For each transaction described in Analytical Problem 1 that by itself changes the sum of the French current account balance, CA, and the French capital account balance, KA, give an example of an offsetting transaction that would leave $CA + KA$ unchanged.

3. A large country imposes capital controls that prohibit foreign borrowing and lending by domestic residents. Analyse the effects on the country's current account balance, national saving, and investment, and on domestic and world real interest rates. Assume that, before the capital controls were imposed, the large country was running a capital account surplus.

4. The text showed, for a small open economy, that an increase in the government budget deficit raises the current account deficit only if it affects desired national saving in the home country. Show that this result is true also for a large open economy. Then assume that an increase in the government budget deficit does affect desired national saving in the home country. What effects will the increased budget deficit have on the foreign country's current

account, investment in both countries, and the world real interest rate?

5. How would each of the following affect national saving, investment, the current account balance, and the real interest rate in a large open economy?

a. An increase in the domestic willingness to save (which raises desired national saving at any given real interest rate).

b. An increase in the willingness of foreigners to save.

c. An increase in foreign government purchases.

d. An increase in foreign taxes (consider both the case in which Ricardian equivalence holds and the case in which it does not hold).

6. Analyse the effects on a large open economy of a temporary adverse supply shock that hits only the foreign economy. Discuss the impact on the home country's national saving, investment, and current account balance – and on the world real interest rate. How does your answer differ if the adverse supply shock is worldwide?

CHAPTER **6**

LONG-RUN ECONOMIC GROWTH

A nation's ability to provide improving standards of living for its people depends crucially on its long-run rate of economic growth. Over a long period of time even an apparently small difference in the rate of economic growth can translate into a large difference in the income of the average person.

Compare, for example, the historical experiences of Australia and Japan. In 1870 real GDP per person was about five times greater in Australia than in Japan, as the data on national growth performances in Table 6.1 show. Indeed, of sixteen major economies considered by British economist Angus Maddison in his important research on long-run growth (and from whose work the data in Table 6.1 are taken), Australia was the richest and Japan the poorest in 1870. Australia's economy did not stand still after 1870. Over the next 119 years, according to Maddison's data, Australian real GDP per person grew by 1.2%

Table 6.1 **Economic Growth in Nine Major Countries, 1870–1989**

Country	Levels of Real GDP per Capita				Annual growth rate (%),
	1870	1913	1950	1989	1870–1989
Australia	3123	4523	5931	13584	1.2%
France	1571	2734	4149	13837	1.8
Germany	1300	2606	3339	13989	2.0
Italy	1210	2087	2819	12955	2.0
Japan	618	1114	1563	15101	2.7
Netherlands	2064	3178	4706	12737	1.5
Sweden	1316	2450	5331	14912	2.1
United Kingdom	2610	4024	5651	13468	1.4
United States	2247	4854	8611	18317	1.8

Note: Figures are in US dollars at 1985 prices, adjusted for differences in the purchasing power of the various national currencies.

Source: Angus Maddison, *Dynamic Forces in Capitalist Development: A Long-Run Comparative View* (Oxford University Press, 1991), Table 1.1.

per year, so that by 1989 the real income of the average Australian was more than four times higher than it had been in 1870. However, during the same period Japanese real GDP per person grew at a rate of 2.7% per year, reaching a level in 1989 that was more than twenty-four times larger than it had been in 1870.

The Japanese growth rate of 2.7% per year may not seem dramatically greater than the Australian growth rate of 1.2% per year. Yet by 1989 Japan, which had been far poorer than Australia a century earlier, had surpassed its Pacific neighbour in per capita GDP. Other, similar comparisons can be drawn from Table 6.1; compare, for example, the long-term growth performance of the United Kingdom against that of Italy or Sweden. Note, however, that even those countries that grew relatively slowly have dramatically increased their output per person during the past century.

Although the comparisons highlighted by Table 6.1 span a long period of time, a change in the rate of economic growth can have important effects over even a decade or two. For example, since about 1973 industrialized countries in Europe and elsewhere have experienced a sustained slowdown in their rates of growth. So, for example, between 1947 and 1973, total (not per capita) real GDP in the Netherlands grew by more than 5.6% per year, but between 1973 and 1996 the Netherlands' real GDP grew by only 2.2% per year. To appreciate the significance of this slowdown, imagine that the 1947–73 growth trend had continued – that is, suppose that real GDP in the Netherlands had continued to grow at 5.6% per year instead of at the 2.2% per year rate actually achieved. Then in 1996 real GDP would have been more than double its actual value. Surely, if this growth had occurred, many of Europe's pressing economic problems would be far less severe. Just to give one (very speculative) example, if government tax collections in 1996 had reflected tax bases that were double their actual size, average European government budgets would have shown healthy surpluses instead of the deficits most have reported.

No one understands completely why economies grow, and no one has a magic formula for inducing rapid growth. Indeed, if such a formula existed, there would be no poor nations. Nevertheless, economists have gained useful insights about the growth process. In this chapter we identify the forces that determine the growth rate of an economy over long periods of time and examine various policies that governments may use to try to influence the rate of growth. Once again, saving and investment decisions play a central role in the analysis. Along with changes in productivity, the rates at which a nation saves and invests – and thus the rate at which it accumulates capital goods – are important factors in determining the standard of living that the nation's people can attain.

6.1 THE SOURCES OF ECONOMIC GROWTH

An economy's output of goods and services depends on the quantities of available inputs, such as capital and labour, and on the productivity of those inputs. The relationship between output and inputs is described by the production function, introduced in Chapter 3:

$$Y = AF(K, N) \tag{6.1}$$

Equation (6.1) relates total output Y to the economy's use of capital K and labour N and to productivity A.

The production function states that if inputs and productivity are constant, output will also be constant – there will be no economic growth. For the quantity of output to grow, either the quantity of inputs must grow or productivity must improve, or both. The relationship between the rate of output growth and the rates of input growth and productivity growth is

$$\frac{\Delta Y}{Y} = \frac{\Delta A}{A} + a_K \frac{\Delta K}{K} + a_N \frac{\Delta N}{N} \tag{6.2}$$

where

$$\frac{\Delta Y}{Y} = \text{rate of output growth};$$

$$\frac{\Delta K}{K} = \text{rate of capital growth};$$

$$\frac{\Delta N}{N} = \text{rate of labour growth};$$

$$\frac{\Delta A}{A} = \text{rate of productivity growth};$$

$a_K = $ elasticity of output with respect to capital;

$a_N = $ elasticity of output with respect to labour.

In equation (6.2) the elasticity of output with respect to capital, a_K, is the percentage increase in output resulting from a 1% increase in the capital stock, and the elasticity of output with respect to labour, a_N, is the percentage increase in output resulting from a 1% increase in the amount of labour used. The elasticities a_K and a_N are numbers between 0 and 1 that must be estimated from historical data.[1]

Equation (6.2), called the **growth accounting equation**, is the production function (equation 6.1) written in growth rate form. Some examples will be helpful for understanding the growth accounting equation.

Suppose that a new invention allows firms to produce 10% more output for the same amount of capital and labour. In terms of the production function, equation (6.1), for constant capital and labour inputs, a 10% increase in productivity A raises output Y by 10%. Similarly, from the growth accounting equation, equation (6.2), if productivity growth $\Delta A/A$ equals 10% and capital and labour growth are zero, output growth $\Delta Y/Y$ will be 10%. Thus the production function and the growth accounting equation give the same result, as they should.

Now suppose that firms' investments cause the economy's capital stock to rise by 10% ($\Delta K/K$ = 10%) while labour input and productivity remain unchanged. What will happen to output? The production function shows that, if the capital stock grows, output will increase. However, because of the diminishing marginal productivity of capital (see Chapter 3), the extra capital

---

1. Elasticities and growth rate formulas such as equation (6.2) are discussed further in Appendix A, Sections A.3 and A.7.

will be less productive than that used previously, so the increase in output will be less than 10%. Diminishing marginal productivity of capital is the reason that the growth rate of capital, $\Delta K/K$, is multiplied by a factor less than 1 in the growth accounting equation. For most European countries this factor, a_K, the elasticity of output with respect to capital, is about 0.3. Thus the growth accounting equation, equation (6.2), indicates that a 10% increase in the capital stock, with labour and productivity held constant, will increase average output by about 3%, or (0.3)(10%).

Similarly, the elasticity of output with respect to labour a_N is about 0.7 in European countries. Thus, according to equation (6.2), a 10% increase in the amount of labour used ($\Delta N/N = 10\%$), with no change in capital or productivity, will raise output by about 7%, or (0.7)(10%).[2]

Growth Accounting

According to equation (6.2), output growth $\Delta Y/Y$ can be broken into three parts:

1. that resulting from productivity growth, $\Delta A/A$,
2. that resulting from increased capital inputs, $a_K \Delta K/K$, and
3. that resulting from increased labour inputs, $a_N \Delta N/N$.

Growth accounting measures empirically the relative importance of these three sources of output growth. A typical growth accounting analysis involves the following four steps (see Table 6.2 on the next page for a summary and numerical example).

■ *Step 1.* Obtain measures of the growth rates of output, $\Delta Y/Y$, capital, $\Delta K/K$, and labour, $\Delta N/N$, for the economy over any period of time. In the calculation of growth rates for capital and labour, more sophisticated analyses make adjustments for changing quality as well as quantity of inputs. For example, to obtain a quality-adjusted measure of N, an hour of work by a skilled worker is counted as more labour than an hour of work by an unskilled worker. Similarly, to obtain a quality-adjusted measure of K, a machine that can turn fifty bolts a minute is treated as being more capital than a machine that can turn only thirty bolts a minute.

■ *Step 2.* Estimate values for the elasticities a_K and a_N from historical data. Keep in mind the estimates for European countries of 0.3 for a_K and 0.7 for a_N.

■ *Step 3.* Calculate the contribution of capital to economic growth as $a_K \Delta K/K$ and the contribution of labour to economic growth as $a_N \Delta N/N$.

■ *Step 4.* The part of economic growth assignable to neither capital growth nor labour growth is attributed to improvements in total factor productivity. The rate of productivity change $\Delta A/A$ is calculated from the formula

$$\frac{\Delta A}{A} = \frac{\Delta Y}{Y} - a_K \frac{\Delta K}{K} - a_N \frac{\Delta N}{N}$$

2. Chapter 3 examined the production function for the UK economy, $Y = AK^{0.3}N^{0.7}$. In that production function, called a Cobb–Douglas production function, the exponent on the capital stock K, 0.3, equals the elasticity of output with respect to capital, and the exponent on the quantity of labour input N, 0.7, equals the elasticity of output with respect to labour. See Appendix A, Section A.7.

**Table 6.2   The Steps of Growth Accounting:
A Numerical Example**

Step 1. Obtain measures of output growth, capital growth, and labour growth over the period to be studied.

Example:

$$\text{Output growth} = \frac{\Delta Y}{Y} = 40\%$$

$$\text{Capital growth} = \frac{\Delta K}{K} = 20\%$$

$$\text{Labour growth} = \frac{\Delta N}{N} = 30\%$$

Step 2. Using historical data, obtain estimates of the elasticities of output with respect to capital and labour, a_K and a_N.

Example: $a_K = 0.3$ and $a_N = 0.7$

Step 3. Find the contributions to growth of capital and labour.

Example:

$$\begin{array}{l}\text{Contribution to output growth}\\\text{of growth in capital}\end{array} = a_K \frac{\Delta K}{K} = (0.3)(20\%) = 6\%$$

$$\begin{array}{l}\text{Contribution to output growth}\\\text{of growth in labour}\end{array} = a_N \frac{\Delta N}{N} = (0.7)(30\%) = 21\%$$

Step 4. Find productivity growth as the residual (the part of output growth not explained by capital or labour).

Example: $$\text{Productivity growth} = \frac{\Delta A}{A} = \frac{\Delta Y}{Y} - a_K \frac{\Delta K}{K} - a_N \frac{\Delta N}{N}$$

$$= 40\% - 6\% - 21\% = 13\%$$

---

which is the growth accounting equation, equation (6.2), rewritten with $\Delta A/A$ on the left-hand side. Thus the growth accounting technique treats productivity change as a residual, that is, the portion of growth not otherwise explained.[3]

---

3. The growth accounting method for calculating productivity growth is similar to the method we used to find productivity growth in Section 3.2, where we also determined productivity growth as the part of output growth not explained by increases in capital and labour. The differences are that growth accounting uses the growth accounting equation, which is the production function in growth rate form, instead of using the production function directly, as we did in Chapter 3; and growth accounting analyses usually adjust measures of capital and labour for changes in quality, which we did not do in Chapter 3.

APPLICATION

Growth accounting and the east Asian 'miracle'

Over the past quarter of a century, several east Asian countries – sometimes known as the east Asian 'tigers' – have exhibited remarkable rates of economic growth. Between 1966 and the early 1990s, Hong Kong averaged real GDP growth of over 7% per year, and Singapore, South Korea, and Taiwan maintained real GDP growth rates of over 8% per year. An 8% per year growth rate over 25 years translates into a level of real output nearly seven times as great at the end of the period as at the beginning. Not surprisingly, this east Asian 'growth miracle' is of great interest not only to economists, but also to political leaders and business people who would like to find some way to create a similar miracle in their own countries.

What caused the east Asian miracle? And will it continue? To address these questions, Alwyn Young of Boston University applied the methodology of growth accounting in a particularly careful study of east Asian growth.[*] Young used a variety of data sources to develop comprehensive measures of the growth of output, capital, and labour for each of the four east Asian countries mentioned above. He found that, to a surprising degree, the rapid economic growth of the east Asian tigers has resulted from rapid growth in capital and labour inputs rather than improvements in total factor productivity. For example, all four countries experienced remarkable increases in labour-force participation rates, as well as general population growth. Similarly, extremely high rates of national saving in east Asia (in some cases, enforced by government regulations) led to rapid growth in capital stocks.

After accounting for increases in inputs, Young found that rates of growth in total factor productivity in the east Asian countries were not so high as many people had thought; he found annual TFP growth rates of 2.3% for Hong Kong, 1.7% for South Korea, 2.6% for Taiwan, and only 0.2% for Singapore! These are good rates of TFP growth (except for Singapore's) but not 'miraculous' ones: for example, over approximately the same period Italy enjoyed TFP growth of about 2.0% per year.

As we shall discuss in more detail in this chapter, because of diminishing marginal productivity, it is difficult to sustain growth over the very long term by means of increasing inputs alone. At some point, only advances in total factor productivity can keep an economy on a rapid growth path. Thus, an implication of Young's research is that the period of rapid economic growth in east Asia may soon be coming to an end – unless those countries can find ways to stimulate growth in total factor productivity.

Growth Accounting and the Productivity Slowdown. What does growth accounting say about the sources of economic growth in Europe and elsewhere? Table 6.3 summarizes Maddison's findings for the period 1913–87 for six countries.

---

* Alwyn Young, 'Tyranny of Numbers: Confronting the Statistical Realities of the East Asian Growth Experience', *Quarterly Journal of Economics*, August 1995, pp. 641–80.

**Table 6.3   Sources of Economic Growth (Maddison)
            (average annual growth rates)**

	(1) 1913–50	(2) 1950–73	(3) 1973–87
France			
Source of growth			
Labour input	−0.17	0.18	−0.25
Capital input	0.65	1.84	1.49
Total input growth	0.48	2.02	1.24
Productivity growth	0.67	3.02	0.92
Total output growth	**1.15**	**5.04**	**2.16**
Germany			
Source of growth			
Labour input	0.38	0.15	−0.49
Capital input	0.62	2.27	1.28
Total input growth	1.00	2.42	0.79
Productivity growth	0.28	3.50	1.01
Total output growth	**1.28**	**5.92**	**1.80**
Japan			
Source of growth			
Labour input	0.36	2.51	0.67
Capital input	1.21	2.93	2.28
Total input growth	1.57	5.44	2.95
Productivity growth	0.67	3.83	0.78
Total output growth	**2.24**	**9.27**	**3.73**
Netherlands			
Source of growth			
Labour input	1.04	0.36	0.09
Capital input	1.05	1.96	1.21
Total input growth	2.09	2.32	1.30
Productivity growth	0.34	2.42	0.60
Total output growth	**2.43**	**4.74**	**1.78**
UK			
Source of growth			
Labour input	0.12	0.01	−0.19
Capital input	0.82	1.75	1.12
Total input growth	0.94	1.76	0.93
Productivity growth	0.35	3.50	1.01
Total output growth	**1.28**	**5.92**	**1.80**
USA			
Source of growth			
Labour input	0.60	1.17	1.31
Capital input	0.93	1.37	1.24
Total input growth	1.53	2.54	2.55
Productivity growth	1.26	1.11	−0.04
Total output growth	**2.79**	**3.65**	**2.51**

Source: Angus Maddison, *Dynamic Forces in Capitalist Development: A Long-Run Comparative View* (Oxford University Press, 1991), Tables 5.10 and 5.19.

Looking at the data for Germany, the last entry in column (1) shows for example that, over the 1913–50 period, output grew at an average rate of 1.28% per year. According to Maddison's measurements, the growth of labour accounted for output growth of 0.38% per year. The growth of labour in turn resulted primarily from an increase in population, an increase in the percentage of the population in the labour force, and higher educational levels, which raised workers' skills. (Offsetting these trends to a degree was a decline in the number of hours worked per person.) According to Maddison, the growth of the capital stock accounted for output growth of 0.62% per year. So, together, labour and capital growth contributed 1.00% to the annual growth rate of output.

Note, however, that for some countries the contribution of labour to economic growth is negative. This reflects the move towards a shorter working week and longer vacations, which were discussed in Chapter 3. In many countries, the impact of these reductions in the average number of hours worked per worker on GDP offset the positive effects of higher labour force participation rates and the improvement in workers' skills.

The difference between total growth (1.28%) and the amount of growth attributed to capital and labour growth (1.00%) is 0.28%. By the growth accounting method, this remaining 0.28% per year of growth is attributed to increases in productivity. Thus, according to Maddison, increased quantities of factors of production and improvements in the effectiveness with which those factors were used both played an important role in German growth prior to 1950.

Data for three periods are given in columns (1)–(3) of Table 6.3. This breakdown highlights a striking conclusion: productivity growth during 1973–87 was much lower than it had been during the 1950–73 period, and in the USA it was actually negative. In other words, for the USA Maddison estimated that any combination of capital and labour would have produced less output in 1987 than it could have in 1973! Comparing columns (2) and (3) for each country reveals the extent to which productivity growth fell between 1950–73 and 1973–87.

The finding of a significant slowdown in productivity growth beginning in the early 1970s has been confirmed by many more recent studies, for European and other industrialized countries. Table 6.4 reports some results from a

Table 6.4   Growth Rates of Output and Productivity Before and After 1973 (% per year)

	Output growth		Productivity growth	
	1960–73	1973–90	1960–73	1973–90
Europe	4.9	2.3	3.2	1.3
USA	4.0	2.5	1.6	0.0
Japan	10.0	4.0	5.9	1.8
OECD	5.3	2.7	2.8	0.7

Notes: Output is business-sector output, and productivity growth refers to total factor productivity. OECD refers to members of the Organization for Economic Cooperation and Development, a group of 25 industrialized countries. 'Europe' refers to European members of the OECD.

Source: Kumiharu Shigehara, 'Causes of Declining Growth in Industrialized Countries', in Federal Reserve Bank of Kansas City, *Policies for Long-Run Economic Growth*, 1992, Table 1.

study by Kumiharu Shigehara, head of the Department of Economics and Statistics for the Organization for Economic Cooperation and Development (OECD), an organization of the major industrialized countries. The table updates the measurement of productivity growth to 1990 and includes results for the USA, Japan, Europe, and the OECD membership as a whole. It shows that European and other industralized countries experienced slower growth after 1973 and that much of the reduction in output growth is attributable to slower rates of productivity improvement.

The widespread slowdown in productivity growth of the past two decades is a major economic concern and has a direct impact on living standards, real wages, and other basic economic issues. Unfortunately, the source of the worldwide slowdown remains something of a puzzle, as the next Application discusses.

APPLICATION

The Post–1973 Slowdown in Productivity Growth

Since about 1973, the rate of economic growth has declined significantly. This slowdown has had significant consequences for real wages and living standards. Growth accounting was useful in showing that the slowdown in output growth primarily reflects reduced growth of productivity, rather than slower growth in the amount of capital and labour available. But this finding only pushes the puzzle back one step. The obvious next question is: what caused productivity performance to deteriorate so sharply? In this application we discuss some alternative explanations, including possible measurement problems, deterioration in the legal and human environment, reduced rates of technological innovation, and the effects of high oil prices.

Measurement. Interestingly, several economists have suggested that the productivity slowdown really is not a genuine economic problem. Instead, they argue, the slowdown is an illusion, the result of measurement problems that have overstated the extent of the decline.

The key issue in productivity measurement is whether the official output statistics adequately capture changes in quality. Consider the case of a firm producing air conditioners. Using unchanged quantities of capital and labour, it makes the same number of air conditioners this year as last year. However, this year's air conditioners are of much higher quality than last year's because they are more reliable and energy-efficient. The firm's output this year has a greater real economic value than last year's output, so the true productivity of the firm's capital and labour has risen over the year, even though the firm produces the same *number* of air conditioners as before. However, if statisticians measuring the firm's output counted only the *number* of air conditioners produced and failed to adjust for quality change, they would miss this improvement in productivity. (Numerical Problem 3 at the end of this chapter illustrates the proper way to measure productivity when the quality of goods is changing.) Similar issues arise in the constructions of price indexes; see Box 2.2, 'Does CPI Inflation Overstate Increases in the Cost of Living', p.55.

In fact, official output measures do try to account for quality improvements – for example, by counting a more energy-efficient air conditioner as contributing more to output than a less efficient model. However, measuring quality change is difficult, and to the extent that improvements are not fully accounted for in the data, productivity growth will be underestimated.

A careful study of the measurement issue was done for the Brookings Institution by Martin N. Baily and Robert J. Gordon.[4] They found that measurement problems may be important for explaining the productivity slowdown in some industries. A striking example is the US construction industry: according to the official data, productivity in the construction industry *declined* by 40% between 1967 and 1986! Baily and Gordon argue that this result is implausible and point to various quality improvements in residential construction (such as more frequent installation of central air-conditioning, more custom woodwork, and better insulation and landscaping), which official measures of construction output do not recognize.

However, Baily and Gordon also point out that measurement problems are not new, that they also existed before 1973. For inadequate measurement to explain the post-1973 productivity decline, we must show not only that current measurement procedures understate productivity growth but also that recent productivity growth is understated by much more than it was before 1973. Overall, Baily and Gordon conclude that measurement problems could explain at most a third of the reported post-1973 slowdown. Thus the productivity slowdown is not, for the most part, simply a measurement problem.

The Legal and Human Environment. One explanation given for the low productivity growth during 1973–87 is the change in what has been called *the legal and human environment*, which includes several diverse factors. For example, since 1973 a cleaner environment and worker safety and health have been emphasized. To the extent that capital and labour resources are devoted to these goals, measured output and productivity will decline.[5]

In addition to pollution control and improvements in worker health and safety, changes in the legal and human environment include factors that reduce productivity but do not yield any benefit to society. For example, it has been estimated that increased dishonesty and crime reduced the annual growth rate of output in the USA by 0.05% per year, because productive resources were diverted to protection against crime or were lost to theft, arson, or vandalism. A potentially more important problem was an apparent decline in educational quality during the 1970s, which led to slower improvement in workers' skills. A study by John H. Bishop of Cornell University found that some slowdown in productivity growth could be attributed to declines in student achievement, as measured by standardized tests, that took place primarily between 1967 and 1980.[6]

The evidence presented by Maddison, however, supports the view that education has had a positive impact on the growth of output, at least in some countries. Maddison finds that improvements in educational standards contributed more to output growth after 1973 than during the 1950–73 period in France, the Netherlands and the UK, though education does have a smaller impact on growth after 1973 in Germany, the USA and Japan.

---

4. 'The Productivity Slowdown, Measurement Issues, and the Explosion of Computer Power', *Brookings Papers on Economic Activity*, 1988:2, pp. 347–420.
5. See Edward F. Denison, *Trends in American Economic Growth*, 1929–1982 (Brookings Institute, 1985).
6. 'Is the Test Score Decline Responsible for the Productivity Growth Decline?' *American Economic Review*, March 1989, pp. 178–97.

Technological Depletion and Slow Commercial Adaptation.
Improvements in technology are a fundamental source of productivity growth and economic growth. The production processes used and the products and services available today are vastly different from those of 50 years ago. One explanation of the productivity slowdown is that the major technological advances of the past have now been largely exploited, but commercially significant new technologies have not arrived fast enough to maintain earlier rates of productivity growth. The idea that technological innovation has at least temporarily dried up is part of the 'depletion hypothesis' suggested by William Nordhaus[7] of Yale University.

Why should the pace of technological innovation have slowed down since 1973? One argument is that the high rate of innovation in the decades following World War II was abnormal, reflecting a backlog of technological opportunities that were not exploited earlier because of the Great Depression and World War II. In addition, the rapid productivity growth observed for many countries compared with the United States in the early postwar period was a result of the massive reconstruction programme in Europe and Japan, some of which was linked to the transfer of US technology to these countries. Another possibility is that this time was also one of structural change for many industrial economies, which saw the decline of agriculture and the growth of new industries and products. According to this view, in recent years we have simply returned to a more normal rate of innovation. Some economists also point out that nothing requires economically valuable inventions to arrive at a steady rate. Perhaps some of the recent scientific and engineering breakthroughs in computerization and gene splicing, for example, have not yet produced the expected payoffs for those countries which have invested heavily in them.

A variation of the technological depletion hypothesis holds that there is no shortage of breakthroughs in basic science. Instead, the problem is that European and US corporations have been slow or unable to adapt the most recent breakthroughs to commercial uses. In contrast, studies have found that Japanese firms do a much better job of maintaining communication and cooperation between the laboratory and the shop floor and of bringing new scientific results quickly into the marketplace – even when the original scientific breakthroughs occurred in other countries.[8]

The Oil Price Explanation. A popular explanation for the productivity slowdown is the large increase in energy prices that followed the OPEC oil embargo in 1973. The idea is that, as companies responded to high energy prices by using less energy, the amount of output they could produce with the same amount of capital and labour declined, reducing productivity. What makes this explanation plausible is not only that the timing is right – the pro-

---

7. 'Economic Policy in the Face of Declining Productivity Growth', *European Economic Review*, May/June 1982, pp. 131–58.
8. See Edwin Mansfield, 'Industrial R&D in Japan and the United States: A Comparative Study', *American Economic Review*, May 1988, pp. 223–8; Nathan Rosenberg and W. Edward Steinmueller, 'Why Are Americans Such Poor Imitators?' *American Economic Review*, May 1988, pp. 229–34. The argument that the US problem is slow commercial adaptation of new scientific findings is also made by an influential MIT study; see MIT Commission on Industrial Productivity, *Made in America: Regaining the Productive Edge* (MIT Press, 1989).

ductivity decline appears to have begun in earnest in about 1973 – but that, unlike several of the other explanations, the oil price story explains why all major industrial countries experienced a slowdown.

Pinning the blame for the productivity slowdown on oil price increases is not easy, though. For many industries energy costs are a relatively small part of total costs. Why then should energy price increases have had such dramatic effects? One answer, proposed by Martin N. Baily,[9] is that the rise in oil prices may have made many older, more energy-intensive machines and factories unprofitable to operate, thus effectively reducing the nation's capital stock. Such a decline in the 'true' capital stock below the measured capital stock would show up in the data as a drop in productivity. If Baily's explanation were correct, however, the prices of used capital goods should have dropped sharply when oil prices rose, reflecting their diminished economic value. Generally, though, the predicted decline in the prices of used capital goods did not happen.[10]

Maddison's growth accounting analysis is one of a number of studies which support the oil price explanation, especially for the Netherlands, where the discovery of cheap natural gas before 1973 encouraged a more energy-intensive economy, and for Japan.[11] Moreover, low energy prices during the 1960s might also account for rapid productivity growth during that period. Despite these points, however, proponents of the oil price explanation face the problem of explaining why productivity growth did not resurge when oil prices fell in real terms in the 1980s.

Conclusion. The problem involved in explaining the post-1973 slowdown in productivity growth may not be a lack of reasonable explanations but too many. We should not dismiss the possibility that there was no single cause of the slowdown but that many factors contributed to it. Unfortunately, if there are multiple explanations for the slowdown, no single policy action by itself is likely to rev up the productivity engine. Instead, policies to improve productivity growth will have to address many problems at the same time.

6.2   GROWTH DYNAMICS: THE NEOCLASSICAL GROWTH MODEL

Although growth accounting provides useful information about the sources of economic growth, it does not completely explain a country's growth performance. Because growth accounting takes the economy's rates of input growth as given, it cannot explain why capital and labour grow at the rates that they do. The growth of the capital stock in particular is the result of the myriad saving and investment decisions of households and firms. By taking the

---

9. 'Productivity and the Services of Capital and Labour', *Brookings Papers on Economic Activity*, 1982:2, pp. 423–54.

10. See Charles R. Hulten, James W. Robertson, and Frank C. Wykoff, 'Energy, Obsolescence, and the Productivity Slowdown', NBER working paper no. 2404, October 1987.

11. See, Dale Jorgenson, 'Productivity and Economic Growth', Harvard Institute of Economic Research discussion paper no. 1487, June 1990, which provides an industry-by-industry analysis of productivity growth.

growth of the capital stock as given, the growth accounting method leaves out an important part of the story.

In this section we take·a closer look at the dynamics of economic growth, or how the growth process evolves over time. In doing so, we drop the assumption made in Chapter 3 that the capital stock is fixed and study the factors that cause the economy's stock of capital to grow. Our analysis is based on a famous model of economic growth developed in the late 1950s by Nobel laureate Robert Solow of MIT and Trevor Swan of the Australian National University, a model that has become the basic framework for most subsequent research on growth[12]. Besides clarifying how capital accumulation and economic growth are interrelated, the model is useful for examining three basic questions about growth:

1. What is the relationship between a nation's long-run standard of living and fundamental factors such as its saving rate, its population growth rate, and its rate of technical progress?

2. How does a nation's rate of economic growth evolve over time? Will economic growth stabilize, accelerate, or stop?

3. Do economic forces exist that will ultimately allow poorer countries to catch up with the richest countries in terms of living standards?

Set-up of the Neoclassical Growth Model

The neoclassical growth model examines an economy as it evolves over time. In order to analyse the effects of labour force growth as well as changes in capital, we assume that the population is growing and that at any particular time a fixed share of the population is of working age. For any year t,

$$N_t = \text{the number of workers available}$$

We assume that the population and workforce both grow at fixed rate n. So, if $n = 0.05$, the number of workers in any year is 5% greater than in the previous year.

At the beginning of each year t the economy has´available a capital stock K_t. (We demonstrate shortly how this capital stock is determined.) During each year t capital, K_t, and labour, N_t, are used to produce the economy's total output, Y_t. Part of the output produced each year is invested in new capital or in replacing worn-out capital. We further assume that the economy is closed and that there are no government purchases,[13] so the uninvested part of output is consumed by the population. If

$$Y_t = \text{output produced in year } t,$$
$$I_t = \text{gross (total) investment in year } t, \text{ and}$$
$$C_t = \text{consumption in year } t,$$

12. The original articles are Robert M. Solow, 'A Contribution to the Theory of Economic Growth', *Quarterly Journal of Economics*, February 1956, pp. 65–94, and Trevor Swan, 'Economic Growth and Capital Accumulation', *Economic Record*, November 1956, pp. 334–61. For this reason the neo-classical growth model is often called the Solow–Swan model of economic growth.
13. Analytical Problem 3 at the end of this chapter adds government purchases to the model.

the relationship among consumption, output, and investment in each year is

$$C_t = Y_t - I_t \qquad (6.3)$$

Equation (6.3) states that the uninvested part of the economy's output is consumed.

Because the population and the labour force are growing in this economy, focusing on output, consumption, and the capital stock *per worker* is convenient. Hence we use the following notation:

$$y_t = \frac{Y_t}{N_t} = \text{output per worker in year } t$$

$$c_t = \frac{C_t}{N_t} = \text{consumption per worker in year } t$$

$$k_t = \frac{K_t}{N_t} = \text{capital stock per worker in year } t$$

The capital stock per worker, k_t, is also called the **capital–labour ratio.** An important goal of the model is to understand how output per worker, consumption per worker, and the capital–labour ratio change over time.[14]

The Per-Worker Production Function. In general, the amount of output that can be produced by specific quantities of inputs is determined by the production function. Until now we have written the production function as a relationship between total output Y and the total quantities of capital and labour inputs K and N. However, we can also write the production function in per-worker terms as

$$y_t = f(k_t) \qquad (6.4)$$

Equation (6.4) indicates that, in each year t, output per worker y_t depends on the amount of available capital per worker k_t.[15] Here we use a small f instead of a capital F for the production function to emphasize that the measurement of output and capital is in *per-worker* terms. For the time being we focus on the role of the capital stock in the growth process by assuming no productivity growth and thus leaving the productivity term out of the production function, equation (6.4).[16] We bring productivity growth back into the model later.

The per-worker production function is graphed in Figure 6.1. The capital–labour ratio (the amount of capital per worker) k_t is measured on the horizon-

14. For purposes of analysis, discussing output and consumption per worker is more convenient than discussing output and consumption per member of the population as a whole. Under the assumption that the workforce is a fixed fraction of the population, anything we say about the growth rate of output or consumption per worker will also be true of the growth rate of output or consumption per member of the population.

15. To write the production function in the form of equation (6.4) requires the assumption of constant returns to scale, which means that an equal percentage increase in both capital and labour inputs results in the same percentage increase in total output. So, for example, with constant returns to scale, a 10% increase in both capital and labour raises output by 10%. In terms of the growth accounting equation, equation (6.2), constant returns to scale requires that $a_K + a_N = 1$. See Analytical Problem 6 at the end of this chapter.

16. More precisely, we set the total factor productivity term A at 1.

Figure 6.1
The per-worker production function
The per-worker production function, $y_t = f(k_t)$, relates the amount of output produced per worker, y_t, to the capital–labour ratio, k_t. For example, when the capital–labour ratio is k_1, output per worker is y_1. The per-worker production function slopes upward from left to right because an increase in the capital–labour ratio raises the amount of output produced per worker. The bowed shape of the production function reflects the diminishing marginal productivity of capital.

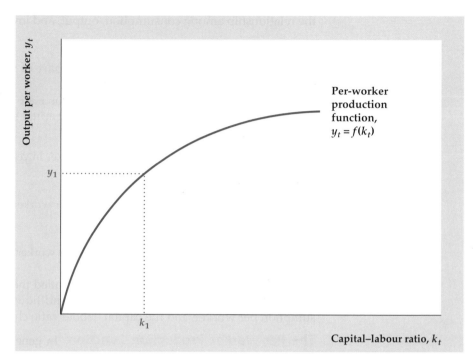

tal axis, and output per worker y_t is measured on the vertical axis. For example, when the capital–labour ratio is k_1, output per worker is y_1. The production function slopes upward from left to right because an increase in the amount of capital per worker allows each worker to produce more output. As with the standard production function, the bowed shape of the per-worker production function reflects the diminishing marginal productivity of capital. Thus when the capital–labour ratio is already high, an increase in the capital–labour ratio has a relatively small effect on output per worker.

Steady States. One of the most striking conclusions obtained from the neoclassical growth model is that in the absence of productivity growth the economy reaches a steady state in the long run. A **steady state** is a situation in which the economy's output per worker, consumption per worker, and capital stock per worker are constant – that is, in the steady state, y_t, c_t, and k_t do not change over time.[17] To explain how the neoclassical growth model works, we first examine the characteristics of a steady state and then discuss how the economy might attain it.

Let us begin by looking at investment in a steady state. In general, gross (total) investment in year t, I_t, is devoted to two purposes: (1) replacing worn-out or depreciated capital, and (2) expanding the size of the capital stock. If d is the capital depreciation rate, or the fraction of capital that wears out each year, the total amount of depreciation in year t is dK_t. The amount by which the capital stock is increased is net investment. What is net investment in a steady state? Because capital per worker, K_t/N_t, is constant in a steady state,

17. Note that if output, consumption, and capital per worker are constant, then total output, consumption, and capital all are growing at rate n, the rate of growth of the workforce.

the total capital stock grows at the same rate as the labour force, that is, at rate n. Net investment is therefore nK_t in a steady state.[18] To obtain steady-state investment we add net investment nK_t and depreciation dK_t:

$$I_t = (n + d)K_t \quad \text{(in a steady state)} \tag{6.5}$$

To obtain steady-state consumption (output less investment), we substitute equation (6.5) into equation (6.3):

$$C_t = Y_t - (n + d)K_t \quad \text{(in a steady state)} \tag{6.6}$$

Equation (6.6) measures consumption, output, and capital as economy-wide totals rather than in per-worker terms. To put them in per-worker terms, we divide both sides of equation (6.6) by the number of workers N_t, recalling that $c_t = C_t/N_t$, $y_t = Y_t/N_t$, and $k_t = K_t/N_t$. Then we use the per-worker production function, equation (6.4), to replace y_t with $f(k_t)$ and obtain

$$c = f(k) - (n + d)k \quad \text{(in a steady state)} \tag{6.7}$$

Equation (6.7) shows the relationship between consumption per-worker c and the capital–labour ratio k in the steady state. Because consumption per-worker and the capital–labour ratio are constant in the steady state, we dropped the time subscripts, t.

Equation (6.7) shows that an increase in the steady-state capital–labour ratio k has two opposing effects on steady-state consumption per worker c. First, an increase in the steady-state capital–labour ratio raises the amount of output each worker can produce, $f(k)$. Second, an increase in the steady-state capital–labour ratio also increases the amount of output per worker that must be devoted to investment, $(n + d)k$. More goods devoted to investment leaves fewer goods to consume.

Figure 6.2 shows the trade-off between these two effects. In Figure 6.2(a) different possible values of the steady-state capital–labour ratio k are measured on the horizontal axis. The curve is the per-worker production function, $y = f(k)$, as in Figure 6.1. The straight line shows steady-state investment per worker, $(n + d)k$. Equation (6.7) indicates that steady-state consumption per worker c equals the height of the curve $f(k)$ minus the height of the straight line $(n + d)k$. For example, if the capital–labour ratio is k_1, steady-state consumption per worker is c_1.

The relationship between consumption per worker and the capital–labour ratio in the steady state is shown more explicitly in Figure 6.2(b). For each value of the steady-state capital–labour ratio k, steady-state consumption per worker c is the difference between the production function and investment in Figure 6.2(a). Note that starting from low and medium values of k (values less than k_1 in Figure 6.2(b)), increases in the steady-state capital–labour ratio lead to greater steady-state consumption per worker. However, for high values of k (values greater than k_1), increases in the steady-state capital–labour ratio actually result in lower steady-state consumption per worker because so much investment is needed to maintain the high level of capital per worker. In the

---

18. Algebraically, net investment in year t is $K_{t+1} - K_t$. If total capital grows at rate n, then $K_{t+1} = (1 + n)K_t$. Substituting for K_{t+1} in the definition of net investment, we find that net investment $= (1 + n)K_t - K_t = nK_t$ in a steady state.

Figure 6.2
The relationship of consumption per worker to the capital–labour ratio in the steady state
(a) For each value of the capital–labour ratio, k, steady-state output per worker, y, is given by the per-worker production function, $f(k)$. Steady-state investment per worker, $(n + d)k$, is a straight line with slope $n + d$. Steady-state consumption per worker, c, is the difference between output per worker and investment per worker (the shaded area). For example, if the capital–labour ratio is k_1, steady-state consumption per worker is c_1.
(b) For each value of the steady-state capital–labour ratio, k, steady-state consumption per worker, c, is derived in (a) as the difference between output per worker and investment per worker. Thus the shaded area (green) in (b) corresponds to the shaded area in (a). Note that, starting from a low value of the capital–labour ratio, an increase in the capital–labour ratio raises steady-state consumption per worker. However, starting from a capital–labour ratio greater than k_1, an increase in the capital–labour ratio actually lowers consumption per worker. When the capital–labour ratio equals k_{max}, all output is devoted to investment, and steady-state consumption per worker is zero.

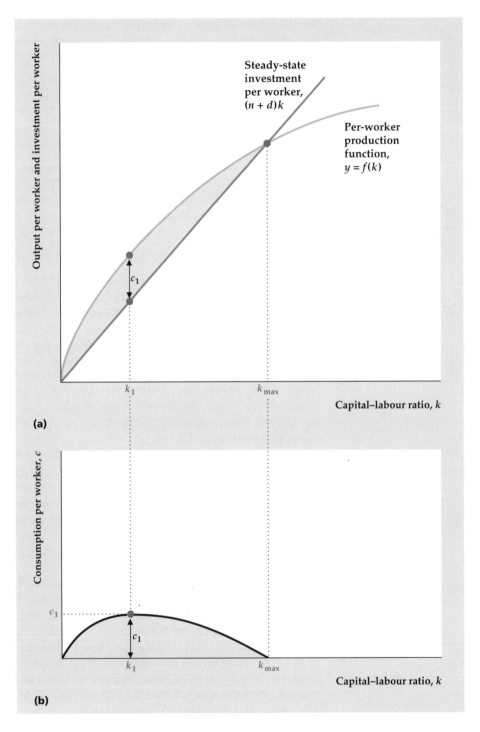

extreme case, where $k = k_{max}$ in Figure 6.2, all output has to be devoted to replacing and expanding the capital stock, with nothing left to consume!

Policymakers often try to improve long-run living standards with policies aimed at stimulating saving and investment – and thus increasing the rate of capital formation. Figure 6.2 shows the limits to this strategy. A country with a low amount of capital per worker may hope to improve long-run (steady-state) living standards substantially by increasing rates of saving and investment. However, a country that already has a high level of capital per worker may find that further increases in saving and investment fail to raise steady-state consumption much. The fundamental reason for this outcome is the diminishing marginal productivity of capital – that is, the larger the capital stock already is, the smaller the benefit from expanding the capital stock still further. Indeed, Figure 6.2 shows that, theoretically, capital per worker can be so high that further increases will actually *lower* steady-state consumption per worker. The level of the capital stock that maximizes consumption per worker in the steady state, shown as k_1 in Figure 6.2, is known as the **Golden Rule** level of the capital stock, so called because it maximizes the economic welfare of future generations. [19]

In any economy in the world today, could a higher capital stock lead to less consumption in the long run? A recent study of seven advanced industrial countries concluded that the answer is 'no'. Even for high-saving Japan, further increases in capital per worker would lead to higher steady-state consumption per worker.[20] Thus in our analysis we will always assume that an increase in the steady-state capital–labour ratio raises steady-state consumption per worker.

Reaching the Steady State. Our discussion of steady states leaves two loose ends. First, we need to say something about why an economy like the one we describe here will eventually reach a steady state, as we claimed earlier. Second, we have not yet shown *which* steady state the economy will reach: that is, we would like to know the steady-state level of consumption per worker and the steady-state capital–labour ratio that the economy will eventually attain.

To tie up these loose ends, we need one more piece of information: the rate at which people save. To keep things as simple as possible, suppose that saving in this economy is proportional to current income:

$$S_t = sY_t \qquad (6.8)$$

where S_t is national saving[21] in year t and s is the saving rate, which we assume to be constant. Because a £1 increase in current income raises saving, but by less than £1 (see Chapter 4), we take s to be a number between 0 and 1. Equation (6.8) ignores some other determinants of saving discussed in earlier chapters, such as the real interest rate. However, including these other factors would not change our basic conclusions, so for simplicity we omit them.

In every year, national saving S_t equals investment I_t. Therefore

$$sY_t = (n + d)K_t \quad \text{(in a steady state)}, \qquad (6.9)$$

where the left-hand side of equation (6.9) is saving (see equation 6.8) and the right-hand side of equation (6.9) is steady-state investment (see equation 6.5).

---

19. Readers familiar with calculus might try to use Equation (6.7) to show that, at the Golden Rule level of the capital stock, the marginal product of capital equals $n + d$.
20. See Andrew B. Abel, N. Gregory Mankiw, Lawrence H. Summers, and Richard J. Zeckhauser, 'Assessing Dynamic Efficiency: Theory and Evidence', *Review of Economic Studies,* January 1989, pp. 1–20.
21. With no government in this model, national saving and private saving are the same.

Equation (6.9) shows the relation between total output Y_t and the total capital stock K_t that holds in the steady state. To determine steady-state capital per worker, we divide both sides of equation (6.9) by N_t. We then use the production function, equation (6.4), to replace y_t with $f(k_t)$:

$$sf(k) = (n + d)k \quad \text{(in the steady state)} \tag{6.10}$$

Equation (6.10) indicates that saving per worker $sf(k)$ equals steady-state investment per worker $(n + d)k$. Because the capital–labour ratio k is constant in the steady state, we again drop the subscripts t from the equation.

With equation (6.10) we can now determine the steady-state capital–labour ratio that the economy will attain, as shown in Figure 6.3. The capital–labour ratio is measured along the horizontal axis. Saving per worker and investment per worker are measured on the vertical axis.

The bowed curve shows how the amount of saving per worker $sf(k)$ is related to the capital–labour ratio. This curve slopes upwards because an increase in the capital–labour ratio implies higher output per worker and thus more saving per worker. The saving-per-worker curve has the same general shape as the per-worker production function, because saving per worker equals the per-worker production function $f(k)$ multiplied by the fixed saving rate s.

The line in Figure 6.3 represents steady-state investment per worker $(n + d)k$. The steady-state investment line slopes upwards because, as the capital–labour ratio rises, more investment per worker is required to replace depreciating capital and equip new workers with the same high level of capital.

According to equation (6.10), the steady-state capital–labour ratio must ensure that saving per worker and steady-state investment per worker are equal. The one level of the capital–labour ratio for which this condition is satisfied is shown in Figure 6.3 as k^*, the value of k at which the saving curve

Figure 6.3
Determining the capital–labour ratio in the steady state
The steady-state capital–labour ratio, k^*, is determined by the condition that saving per worker, $sf(k)$, equals steady-state investment per worker, $(n + d)k$. The steady-state capital–labour ratio k^* corresponds to point A, where the saving curve and the steady-state investment line cross. From any starting point, eventually the capital–labour ratio reaches k^*. If the capital–labour ratio happens to be below k^*, say, at k_1, saving per worker, $sf(k_1)$, exceeds the investment per worker, $(n + d)k_1$, needed to maintain the capital–labour ratio at k_1. As this extra saving is converted into capital, the capital–labour ratio will rise, as indicated by the arrows. Similarly, if the capital–labour ratio is greater than k^*, say, at k_2, saving is too low to maintain the capital–labour ratio, and it will fall over time.

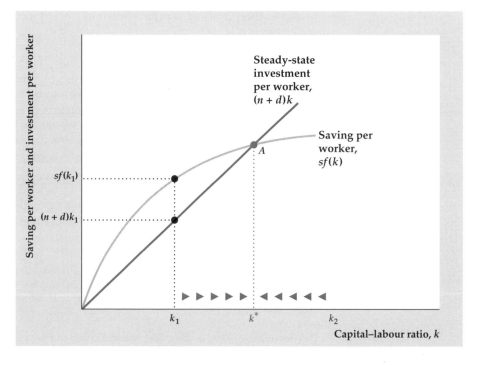

and the steady-state investment line cross (at point A). For any other value of k, saving will not be equal to steady-state investment. Thus k^* is the only possible steady-state capital–labour ratio for this economy.[22]

With the unique steady-state capital–labour ratio k^*, we can also find steady-state output and consumption per worker. From the per-worker production function, equation (6.4), if the steady-state capital–labour ratio is k^*, steady-state output per worker y^* is

$$y^* = f(k^*)$$

From equation (6.7) steady-state consumption per worker, c^*, equals steady-state output per worker, $f(k^*)$, minus steady-state investment per worker, $(n + d)k^*$:

$$c^* = f(k^*) - (n + d)k^*$$

Recall that, in the empirically realistic case, a higher value of the steady-state capital–labour ratio k^* implies greater steady-state consumption per worker c^*.

Using the condition that in a steady state, national saving equals steady-state investment, we found the steady-state capital–labour ratio k^*. When capital per worker is k^*, the amount that people choose to save will just equal the amount of investment necessary to keep capital per worker at k^*. Thus when the economy's capital–labour ratio reaches k^*, it will remain there for ever.

But is there any reason to believe that the capital–labour ratio will ever reach k^* if it starts at some other value? Yes, there is. Suppose that the capital–labour ratio happens to be less than k^*: for example, it equals k_1 in Figure 6.3. When capital per worker is k_1, the amount of saving per worker, $sf(k_1)$, is greater than the amount of investment needed to keep the capital–labour ratio constant, $(n + d)k_1$. When this extra saving is converted into capital, the capital–labour ratio will rise. As indicated by the arrows on the horizontal axis, the capital–labour ratio will increase from k_1 towards k^*.

If capital per worker is initially greater than k^* – for example, if k equals k_2 in Figure 6.3 – the explanation of why the economy converges to a steady state is similar. If the capital–labour ratio exceeds k^*, the amount of saving that is done will be less than the amount of investment that is necessary to keep the capital–labour ratio constant. (In Figure 6.3 when k equals k_2, the saving curve lies below the steady-state investment line.) Thus the capital–labour ratio over time will fall from k_2 towards k^*, as indicated by the arrows. Output per worker will also fall until it reaches its steady-state value.

To summarize, if we assume no productivity growth, the economy must eventually reach a steady state. In this steady state the capital–labour ratio, output per worker, and consumption per worker remain constant over time. (However, total capital, output, and consumption grow at rate n, the rate of growth of the labour force.) This conclusion might seem gloomy, since it implies that living standards must eventually stop improving. However, we shall see that this conclusion can be avoided if, in fact, productivity continually increases.

---

22. Actually, there is also a steady state at the point $k = 0$, at which the capital stock, output, and consumption are zero forever. However, as long as the economy starts out with a positive amount of capital, it will never reach the zero-capital steady state.

The Fundamental Determinants of Long-Run Living Standards

What determines how well off the average person in an economy will be in the long run? If we measure long-run well-being by the steady-state level of consumption per worker, we can use the neoclassical growth model to answer this question. Here, we discuss three factors that affect long-run living standards: the saving rate, population growth, and productivity growth (see Summary table 8).

The Saving Rate. According to the neoclassical growth model, a higher saving rate implies higher living standards in the long run, as illustrated in Figure 6.4. Suppose that the economy's initial saving rate is s_1 so that saving per worker is $s_1 f(k)$. The saving curve when the saving rate is s_1 is labelled 'Initial saving per worker'. The initial steady-state capital–labour ratio k_1^* is the capital–labour ratio at which the initial saving curve and the investment line cross (point A).

Suppose now that, say, because the government introduces policies that strengthen the incentives for saving, the country's saving rate rises from s_1 to s_2. The increased saving rate raises saving at every level of the capital–labour ratio. Graphically, the saving curve shifts upwards from $s_1 f(k)$ to $s_2 f(k)$. The new steady-state capital–labour ratio k_2^* corresponds to the intersection of the new saving curve and the investment line (point B). Because k_2^* is larger than k_1^*, the higher saving rate has increased the steady-state capital–labour ratio. Gradually, this economy will move to the higher steady-state capital–labour ratio, as indicated by the arrows on the horizontal axis. In the new steady state, output per worker and consumption per worker will be higher than in the original steady state.

An increased saving rate leads to higher output, consumption, and capital per worker in the long run, so it seems that a policy goal should be to make the country's saving rate as high as possible. However, this conclusion is not necessarily correct: although a higher saving rate raises consumption per

SUMMARY 8	An Increase in	Causes Long-Run Output, Consumption, and Capital per Worker to	Reason
The Fundamental Determinants of Long-Run Living Standards	The saving rate, s	Rise	Higher saving allows for more investment and a larger capital stock.
	The rate of population growth, n	Fall	With higher population growth more output must be used to equip new workers with capital, leaving less output available to increase capital per worker.
	Productivity	Rise	Higher productivity directly increases output; by raising incomes, it also raises saving and the capital stock.

Figure 6.4
The effect of an increased saving rate on the steady-state capital–labour ratio
An increase in the saving rate from s_1 to s_2 raises the saving curve from $s_1f(k)$ to $s_2f(k)$. The point where saving per worker equals steady-state investment per worker moves from point A to point B, and the corresponding capital–labour ratio rises from k_1^* to k_2^*. Thus a higher saving rate raises the steady-state capital–labour ratio.

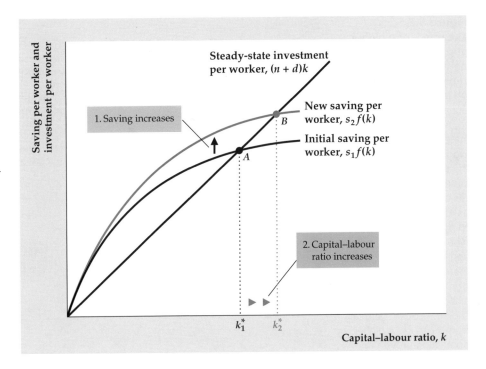

worker in the long run, an increase in the saving rate initially causes consumption to fall. This decline occurs because, at the initial level of output, increases in saving and investment leave less available for current consumption. Thus higher future consumption has a cost in terms of lower present consumption. Society's choice of a saving rate should take into account this trade-off between current and future consumption. Beyond a certain point the cost of reduced consumption today will outweigh the long-run benefits of a higher saving rate.

Population Growth. In many developing countries a high rate of population growth is considered to be a major problem, and reducing it is a primary policy goal. What is the relationship between population growth and a country's level of development, as measured by output, consumption, and capital per worker?

The neoclassical growth model's answer to this question is shown in Figure 6.5. An initial steady-state capital–labour ratio k_1^* corresponds to the intersection of the steady-state investment line and the saving curve at point A. Now suppose that the rate of population growth, which is the same as the rate of labour force growth, rises from an initial level of n_1 to n_2. What happens?

An increase in the population growth rate means that workers are entering the labour force more rapidly than before. These new workers must be equipped with capital. Thus to maintain the same steady-state capital–labour ratio, the amount of investment per current member of the workforce must rise. Algebraically, the rise in n increases steady-state investment per worker from $(n_1 + d)k$ to $(n_2 + d)k$. This increase in the population growth rate causes the steady-state investment line to pivot up and to the left, as its slope rises from $(n_1 + d)$ to $(n_2 + d)$.

Figure 6.5
The effect of a higher population growth rate on the steady-state capital–labour ratio

An increase in the population growth rate from n_1 to n_2 increases steady-state investment per worker from $(n_1 + d)k$ to $(n_2 + d)k$. The steady-state investment line pivots up and to the left as its slope rises from $n_1 + d$ to $n_2 + d$. The point where saving per worker equals steady-state investment per worker shifts from point A to point B, and the corresponding capital–labour ratio falls from k_1^* to k_2^*. A higher population growth rate therefore causes the steady-state capital-labour ratio to fall.

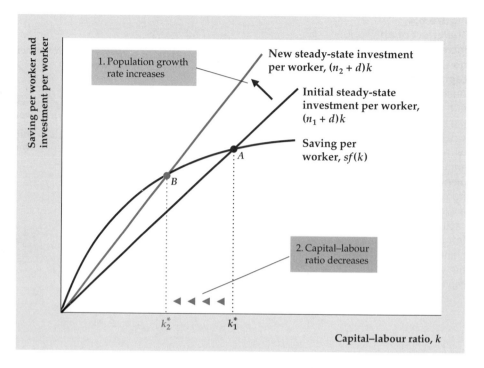

After the pivot of the steady-state investment line, the new steady state is at point B. The new steady-state capital–labour ratio is k_2^*, which is lower than the original capital–labour ratio k_1^*. Because the new steady-state capital–labour ratio is lower, the new steady-state output per worker and consumption per worker will be lower as well.

Thus the neoclassical growth model implies that increased population growth will lower living standards. The basic problem is that when the workforce is growing rapidly, a large part of current output must be devoted just to providing capital for the new workers to use. This result suggests that policies to control population growth will indeed improve living standards.

There are some counterarguments to the conclusion that policy should aim to reduce population growth. First, although a reduction in the rate of population growth n raises consumption *per worker*, it also reduces the growth rate of *total* output and consumption, which grow at rate n in the steady state. Having fewer people means more for each person but also less total productive capacity. For some purposes (military, political) a country may care about its total output as well as output per person. Thus, for example, some countries of Western Europe are concerned about projections that their populations will actually shrink in the next century, possibly reducing their ability to defend themselves or influence world events.

Second, an assumption in the neoclassical growth model is that the proportion of the total population that is of working age is fixed. When the population growth rate changes dramatically, this assumption may not hold. For example, declining birth rates in many European countries imply that the ratio of working-age people to retirees will become unusually low early in the twenty-first century, a development that may cause problems for social security funding and other areas such as health care.

Productivity Growth. A significant aspect of the basic neoclassical growth model is that, ultimately, the economy reaches a steady state in which output per capita is constant. But in the introduction to this chapter we described how Japanese output per person has grown by a factor of 24 since 1870! How can the neoclassical growth model account for that sustained growth? The key is a factor that we have not yet made part of the analysis: productivity growth.

The effects of a productivity improvement – the result of, say, a new technology – are shown in Figures 6.6 and 6.7. An improvement in productivity corresponds to an upward shift in the per-worker production function because, at any prevailing capital–labour ratio, each worker can produce more output. Figure 6.6 shows a shift from the original production function $y = f_1(k)$ to a 'new, improved' production function $y = f_2(k)$. More output per worker y can be produced at any capital–labour ratio k. The productivity improvement corresponds to a beneficial supply shock, as explained in Chapter 3.

Figure 6.7, on the next page, shows the effects of this productivity improvement in the neoclassical growth model. As before, the initial steady state is determined by the intersection of the saving curve and the steady-state investment line at point A; the corresponding steady-state capital–labour ratio is k_1^*. The productivity improvement raises output per worker for any level of the capital–labour ratio. As saving per worker is a constant fraction s of output per worker, saving per worker also rises at any capital–labour ratio. Graphically, the saving curve shifts upwards from $sf_1(k)$ to $sf_2(k)$, now intersecting the steady-state investment line at point B. The new steady-state capital–labour ratio is k_2^*, which is higher than the original steady-state capital–labour ratio k_1^*.

Overall, a productivity improvement raises steady-state output and consumption per worker in two ways. First, it directly increases the amount that can be produced at any capital–labour ratio. Second, as Figure 6.7 shows, by

Figure 6.6
An improvement in productivity

An improvement in productivity shifts the per-worker production function upward from the initial production function $y = f_1(k)$ to the new production function $y = f_2(k)$. After the productivity improvement, more output per worker y can be produced at any capital–labour ratio k.

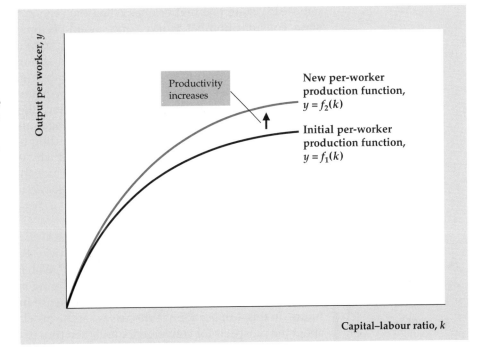

Figure 6.7
The effect of a productivity improvement on the steady-state capital–labour ratio

A productivity improvement shifts the production function upward from $f_1(k)$ to $f_2(k)$, raising output per worker for any capital–labour ratio. Because saving is proportional to output, saving per worker also rises, from $sf_1(k)$ to $sf_2(k)$. The point where saving per worker equals steady-state investment per worker shifts from point A to point B, and the corresponding steady-state capital–labour ratio rises from k_1^* to k_2^*. Thus a productivity improvement raises the steady-state capital–labour ratio.

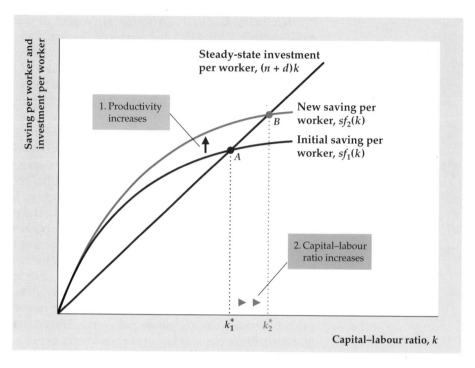

raising the supply of saving, a productivity improvement also causes the long-run capital–labour ratio to rise. Thus a productivity improvement has a doubly beneficial impact on the standard of living.

Like a one-off increase in the saving rate or decrease in the population growth rate, a one-off productivity improvement shifts the economy only from one steady state to a higher one. When the economy reaches the new steady state, consumption per worker once again becomes constant. Is there some way to keep consumption per worker growing indefinitely?

In reality, there are limits to how high the saving rate can rise (it certainly cannot exceed 100%!) or how low the population growth rate can fall. Thus higher saving rates or slower population growth are not likely sources of continually higher living standards. However, since the Industrial Revolution, if not before, people have shown remarkable ingenuity in becoming more and more productive. In the very long run, according to the neoclassical growth model, only these continuing increases in productivity hold the promise of perpetually better living standards. Thus we conclude that, in the long run, *the rate of productivity improvement is the dominant factor determining how quickly living standards rise.*

APPLICATION

Do Economies Converge?

A wide gulf separates living standards in the richest and the poorest nations of the world. Will this difference persist for ever? Will, indeed, the 'rich get richer and the poor get poorer'? Or will national living standards ultimately converge? These questions are obviously of immense importance for humanity's future. In this Application we discuss what the neoclassical growth model says about the prospects for convergence and then turn to the empirical evidence.

There are at least three possible scenarios for the evolution of living standards throughout the world: we will refer to them as unconditional convergence, conditional convergence, and no convergence.

By **unconditional convergence** we mean that the poor countries will eventually catch up with the rich countries so that in the long run living standards around the world become more or less the same. The neoclassical growth model predicts unconditional convergence under certain special conditions. For example, let us suppose that the world's economies differed principally in terms of their capital–labour ratios, with rich countries having high capital–labour ratios and high levels of output per worker, and poor countries having low capital–labour ratios and low levels of output per worker. Suppose, however, that on other dimensions – specifically in terms of saving rates, population growth rates, and the production functions to which they had access – rich and poor countries were the same. If each of a group of countries has the same saving rate, population growth rate, and production function, the neoclassical growth model predicts that – despite any differences in initial capital–labour ratios – these countries will all eventually reach the same steady state. In other words, according to the neoclassical growth model, if countries have the same fundamental characteristics, capital–labour ratios and living standards will unconditionally converge, even though some countries may start from way behind.

To see what this involves let us compare one of the former communist countries, the Czech Republic, with Germany. In 1995, Germany's real GDP per capita was roughly DM40,000 whereas that in the Czech Republic was only a little over DM6000. It would take 25 years for the Czech Republic to converge to the same real GDP per capita as that enjoyed by the Germans in 1995 if the growth rate in real GDP in the Czech Republic were about 8% per year. If, on the other hand, the growth rate in real GDP per capita in the Czech Republic were only 2% per year, then it would take nearly 100 years for living standards there to converge to what they were in Germany in 1995.

But if countries differ in characteristics such as their saving rates, population growth rates, and access to technology, according to the neoclassical growth model they will converge to different steady states, with different capital–labour ratios and different living standards in the long run. If countries differ in fundamental characteristics, the neoclassical growth model predicts **conditional convergence**, by which we mean that living standards will converge only within groups of countries having similar characteristics. For example, if there is conditional convergence, a poor country with a low saving rate may catch up some day with a richer country that also has a low saving rate, but it will never catch up with a rich country that has a high saving rate.

For a variety of reasons (such as different cultures, political systems, and economic policies), countries do differ in characteristics such as saving rates, so conditional convergence seems to be the most likely outcome. However, our discussion so far assumes that these economies are all closed economies. According to the neoclassical growth model, if economies are open and international borrowing and lending flow freely, some additional economic forces support unconditional convergence. In particular, as poor countries have less capital per worker and thus higher marginal products of capital than do rich countries, savers in all countries will be able to earn the highest return by investing in poor countries. Thus foreign investment should cause capital stocks in poor countries to grow rapidly, even if domestic saving rates are low. Eventually, borrowing abroad should allow initially poor countries' capital–labour ratios and output per worker to be the same as in initially rich countries.[23]

The third possibility is *no convergence,* by which we mean that poor countries do not catch up over time. Living standards may even diverge (the poor get poorer and the rich get richer). Although reconciling no convergence with the neoclassical growth model is not impossible (for example, permanent differences in productivity growth rates across countries could lead to divergence), this outcome would be inconsistent with the spirit of that model, which tends to favour the general idea of convergence.

What is the evidence? Unfortunately (from the perspective of the world's poor countries), there is little empirical support for unconditional convergence: most studies have uncovered little tendency for poor countries to catch up with rich ones. For example, in a study of seventy-two countries over the period 1950–85, William Baumol[24] of Princeton University and New York University found no overall tendency towards convergence. Using data beginning in 1870, Baumol did find some evidence for convergence among a group of sixteen major free-market economies, with the countries in the sample that were relatively poorest in 1870 growing somewhat faster over the period. However, J. Bradford DeLong[25] of the University of California at Berkley pointed out that the countries that Baumol studied were the richest countries as of 1980. In choosing this set of countries, DeLong argued, Baumol created a bias in favour of finding convergence, because countries that failed to converge to high levels of output per hour would not be included among the sample of currently rich countries. DeLong showed that if Baumol's sample were expanded to include countries that were relatively rich in 1870 but are not among the richest countries today – countries such as Argentina, Chile, the former East Germany, Ireland, New Zealand, Portugal, and Spain – Baumol's evidence for convergence disappears.

The evidence for conditional convergence, however, seems much better. For example, an article by N. Gregory Mankiw of Harvard University, David Romer of University of California at Berkeley, and David Weil[26] of Brown University examined a sample of 98 countries for the period 1960–1985. While finding no evidence for unconditional convergence in their data, Mankiw, Romer, and Weil showed that the failure of poor countries to catch up reflected high rates of population growth and low rates of saving (defined broadly to include resources devoted to education along with those devoted to accumulation of physical capital). After correcting for differences in national saving rates and population growth rates, Mankiw, Romer, and Weil found strong tendencies for countries with similar characteristics to converge. Similar results were obtained by Robert Barro of Harvard University and Xavier Sala-i-Martín[27] of Yale University, who also demonstrated a convergence of living

---

23. Although output per worker in poor countries converges to that of rich countries, consumption per worker will remain at a lower level in poor countries because part of output must be used to repay foreign investors.

24. 'Productivity Growth, Convergence, and Welfare: What the Long-Run Data Show', *American Economic Review,* December 1986, pp. 1072–85.

25. 'Productivity Growth, Convergence and Welfare: Comment', *American Economic Review,* December 1988, pp. 1138–54.

26. 'A Contribution to the Empirics of Economic Growth', *Quarterly Journal of Economics,* May 1992, pp. 407–38.

27. 'Convergence', *Journal of Political Economy,* April 1992, pp. 223–51.

standards among the states of the United States. Because the states are similar in fundamental economic characteristics, such as saving rates and access to technology, this result also is consistent with conditional convergence.

The findings in support of conditional convergence are encouraging for the neoclassical growth model, and they provide some empirical confirmation that factors such as the saving rate (including the provision of resources for education) are important for growth. These results also suggest that international capital markets linking rich and poor countries are not as efficient as we might hope, since evidently foreign investment in poor countries has been insufficient to overcome the problem of low domestic saving rates. Possibly, political barriers such as legal limits or high taxes on foreign investment prevent enough foreign lending from flowing into poor countries. Alternatively, potential lenders in rich nations may not be able to obtain adequate information about investment opportunities in countries that are both physically distant and also have different languages, cultures, and legal systems.

The New Growth Theory

The traditional neoclassical growth model has proved to be quite useful. However, it does have one serious shortcoming: it takes the rate of productivity growth as given, providing no explanation for why productivity improvements are sometimes rapid and sometimes slow. We have argued that the rate of productivity growth is the most important determinant of long-run living standards, so treating this important variable as a 'black box' is not very satisfying. Instead, a better understanding of how economic forces affect the evolution of productivity would be desirable.

In recent years, researchers have tried to expand the neoclassical growth framework to include explanations of productivity change within the model. This so-called **new growth theory** has two principal strands.[28]

First, some new growth theorists have focused on the role of **human capital**, the economist's term for the knowledge, skills, and training of individuals. The links between human capital and growth flow two ways. On the one hand, as economies become richer, they become more likely to 'invest in people', through improved nutrition, schooling, and on-the-job training. On the other hand, a healthier and more highly skilled labour force is more productive, which leads to improved living standards. New growth theorists have examined the implications of adding human capital formation to the neoclassical growth growth model. They found that it better describes the actual process of economic growth. In particular, many empirical studies reveal strong links between educational and literacy levels in the population and the rate at which the economy is able to grow subsequently.[29]

---

28. Two important early articles in the new growth theory are Paul Romer, 'Increasing Returns and Long-Run Growth', *Journal of Political Economy*, October 1986, pp. 1002–37 and Robert E. Lucas, Jr, 'On the Mechanics of Economic Development', *Journal of Monetary Economics*, July 1988, pp. 3–42. For a recent discussion of the 'old' and 'new' growth theories, see Gene Grossman and Elhanan Helpman, 'Endogenous Innovation in the Theory of Growth', *Journal of Economic Perspectives*, Winter 1994, pp. 23–44.

29. Two such studies are the Mankiw–Romer–Weil article cited earlier and Robert Lucas, 'Making a Miracle', *Econometrica*, March 1993, pp. 251–72, which considers economic growth in South Korea and the Philippines.

A second strand of the new growth theory emphasizes the importance of *technological innovation by private firms* as a source of productivity growth. Firms improve product design and production efficiency in various ways. Some innovation takes place in formal research and development programmes, as when a cosmetics company's laboratory works on a better shampoo or an underarm deodorant that will not stick to your clothes. Much innovation also takes place informally, as when workers on the shop floor suggest a better production method or feedback from customers leads to a change in product design. Economists refer to innovations that arise in the process of making and marketing a good or service as *learning by doing*.[30] New growth theorists have studied the economic incentives that lead firms to innovate and have tried to incorporate the process of innovation by firms into the neoclassical growth growth model. Clearly, this strand of the new growth theory is closely related to the strand that emphasizes human capital formation, as the development and use of technological innovations often requires a skilled workforce.

The new growth theory is promising. Although drawing strong policy lessons from this work may be premature, one implication is worth mentioning. In the traditional neoclassical growth model, the ability of government policies to influence long-run living standards is limited. For example, if policy succeeded in raising the saving rate, according to the neoclassical growth model the result would be a one-off improvement in living standards, as the economy moves to a new, higher steady state. In some new growth theory models, in contrast, a rise in the saving rate can result in a permanent rise in the *growth rate* of output, leading to ongoing improvements in living standards. The reason for the ongoing effect is that, according to the new growth theory, more output not only raises living standards but also leads to more human capital formation and innovation, which increase productivity and output, which increase human capital and innovation again, and so on in a 'virtuous circle'. Thus, in the new growth theory models, the impact of an increase in the saving rate in the long run can be much greater than that predicted by the traditional neoclassical growth model.

6.3   GOVERNMENT POLICIES TO RAISE LONG-RUN LIVING STANDARDS

Increased growth and a higher standard of living in the long run are often cited by political leaders as primary policy goals. Let us take a closer look at government policies that may be useful in raising a country's long-run standard of living. (The Political Environment: Economic Growth and Democracy, p. 219, discusses whether the *form* of government – democratic or non-democratic – affects the long-run growth rate of an economy.)

---

30. The term is originally from Kenneth Arrow, 'The Economic Implications of Learning by Doing', *Review of Economic Studies*, June 1962, pp. 155–73.

Policies to Affect the Saving Rate

The neoclassical growth model suggests that the rate of national saving is a principal determinant of long-run living standards. However, this conclusion does not necessarily mean that policymakers should try to force the saving rate upwards because more saving means less consumption in the short run. Indeed, if the 'invisible hand' of free markets is working well, the saving rate freely chosen by individuals should be the one that optimally balances the benefit of saving more (higher future living standards) against the cost of saving more (less present consumption).

The Political Environment

ECONOMIC GROWTH AND DEMOCRACY

Economic growth is an important social goal, but it is certainly not the only one. Most people also value political freedom and a democratic political process highly. Are these two goals conflicting or mutually supporting? If the citizens of poor countries succeed in achieving democracy, as many did during the 1980s and early 1990s, can they expect to enjoy faster economic growth as well? Or does increased political freedom involve economic sacrifice?

There are several reasons to believe that democracy may promote growth. Relative to dictatorships, democratic governments that command popular support might be expected to be more stable, to be less likely to start wars, and to have better relations with the advanced industrial nations, most of which are democracies. Constitutional protections of both human and property rights should increase the willingness of both foreigners and residents to invest in the country, and freedoms of speech and expression are probably essential for the full development of a nation's educational and scientific potential. However, the ability of a democratic government to undertake unpopular but necessary economic reforms or make other tough choices may be hampered by pressures of interest groups or fluctuations of public opinion. Similarly, a dictatorial government may be better able than a democratic one to enforce a high national saving rate and keep government spending under control.

What does empirical evidence show about the relationship between democracy and economic growth? A simple fact is that, for the most part, the richest countries of the world are democratic, and the poorest nations are non-democratic. (There are exceptions: India is poor but is more democratic than wealthy Saudi Arabia or Singapore.) Not too much should be read into this fact, however, because many wealthy nations that are currently democratic initially achieved economic leadership under kings, princes, or emperors.

A more relevant empirical test is to compare the current economic growth rates (rather than the current levels of output) of democratic and non-democratic countries. Here the findings of recent research have been generally good news for democracy. In a study of 115 market economies over the period 1960–80, Gerald Scully[*] of the University of Texas at Dallas found that 'politically open' societies grew at an average of 2.7% per year, compared to only 0.9% per year for repressive societies. Other researchers found a somewhat smaller advantage for democracy or even a slight edge for non-democratic economies. For example, a study of 98 countries over the period 1960–85 by John Helliwell[†] of Harvard University found essentially no statistical link between democracy and subsequent economic growth, although he did find that democracy promoted improved education and raised investment rates. There seems to be no support, however, for the view that adopting democratic institutions imposes high costs in terms of lost economic growth.[‡]

---

[*] 'The Institutional Framework and Economic Development', *Journal of Political Economy*, June 1988, pp. 652–62.
[†] 'Empirical Linkages Between Democracy and Economic Growth', NBER working paper no. 4066, May 1992.
[‡] Jakub de Haan and Clemens Sierman, 'New Evidence on the Relationship between Democracy and Economic Growth', *Public Choice*, January 1996, pp. 175–98.

Despite the argument that saving decisions are best left to private individuals and the free market, some people claim that Europeans save too little and that government policy should aim at raising the saving rate. One possible justification for this claim is that existing tax laws discriminate against saving by taxing away part of the returns to saving; a 'pro-saving' policy is thus necessary to offset this bias. Another, stronger view is that many Europeans are just too shortsighted in their saving decisions and must be encouraged to save more.

What policies can be used to increase saving? If saving were highly responsive to the real interest rate, tax breaks that increase the real return that savers receive would be effective. For example, some economists advocate taxing households on how much they consume rather than on how much they earn, thereby exempting from taxation the income that is saved. But as Chapter 4 noted, although saving appears to increase when the expected real return available to savers rises, most studies find this response to be small.

An alternative and perhaps more direct way to increase the national saving rate is by increasing the amount that the government saves: in other words, the government should try to reduce its deficit or increase its surplus. Our analysis of the 'twin deficits' debate (Chapter 5) indicated that reducing the deficit by reducing government purchases will lead to more national saving. Many economists also argue that raising taxes to reduce the deficit will also increase national saving by leading people to consume less. However, believers in Ricardian equivalence contend that tax increases without changes in current or planned government purchases will not affect consumption or national saving.

Policies to Raise the Rate of Productivity Growth

Of the factors affecting long-run living standards, the rate of productivity growth may well be the most important in that – according to the neoclassical growth model – only ongoing productivity growth can lead to continuing improvement in output and consumption per worker. Government policy can attempt to increase productivity in several ways.

Improving Infrastructure. Some research findings suggest a significant link between productivity and the quality of a nation's infrastructure – its highways, bridges, utilities, dams, airports, and other publicly owned capital.[31] The construction of motorway systems across Europe, for example, significantly reduced the cost of transporting goods and stimulated tourism and other industries. In the past two decades the rate of government investment in infrastructure has fallen, leading to a decline in the quality and quantity of public capital. Reversing this trend, some economists argue, might help achieve higher productivity.[32] However, not everyone agrees that more infrastructure investment is needed. For example, some critics have pointed out

31. See, for example, David A. Aschauer, 'Rx for Productivity: Build Infrastructure', *Chicago Fed Letter*, Federal Reserve Bank of Chicago, September 1988, and Alicia Munnell, 'Infrastructure and Economic Growth', *Journal of Economic Perspectives*, Fall 1992, pp. 189–98.
32. The European Union has introduced a programme of projects to develop a Trans-European transport network which it is claimed will boost European productivity.

that the links between productivity growth and infrastructure are not clear. If rich countries are more likely to build roads and hospitals, perhaps higher productivity growth leads to more infrastructure, rather than vice versa. Others worry that infrastructure investments by governments may involve political considerations more than promoting economic efficiency.

Building Human Capital. Recent research findings point to a strong connection between productivity growth and human capital. The government affects human capital development through educational policies, worker training or relocation programmes, health programmes, and in other ways. Specific programmes should be examined carefully to see whether benefits exceed costs, but a case may be made for greater commitment to human capital formation as a way to fight productivity slowdown.

One crucial form of human capital, which we have not yet mentioned, is entrepreneurial skill. People with the ability to build a successful new business or to bring a new product to market play a key role in economic growth. Productivity growth might increase if the government were to remove unnecessary barriers to entrepreneurial activity (such as excessive red tape) and give people with entrepreneurial skills greater incentives to use those skills productively.[33]

Encouraging Research and Development. It may also be possible to stimulate productivity growth by affecting rates of scientific and technical progress. Individual European governments, as well as the EU, directly support much basic scientific research. Most economists agree with this type of policy because the benefits of scientific progress, like those of human capital development, spread throughout the economy. Basic scientific research may thus be a good investment from society's point of view, even if no individual firm finds such research profitable. Some economists would go further and say that even more applied, commercially oriented research deserves government aid.

Industrial Policy

Beyond support for basic science and technology, an aggressive approach that has been proposed for encouraging technological development is industrial policy. Generally, **industrial policy** is a growth strategy in which the government – using taxes, subsidies, or regulation – attempts to influence the nation's pattern of industrial development. More specifically, some advocates of industrial policy argue that the government should subsidize and promote 'high-tech' industries, in order to try to achieve or maintain national leadership in technologically dynamic areas.

The idea that the government should try to determine the nation's mix of industries is controversial. Economic theory and practice suggest that under normal circumstances the free market can allocate resources well without government assistance. This approach underlies the EU Treaty provisions on

---

33. For a discussion of the importance of entrepreneurial activity and how it is affected by government policy and the social environment, see William J. Baumol, 'Entrepreneurship: Productive, Unproductive, and Destructive', *Journal of Political Economy*, October 1990 (part 1), pp. 893–921.

industrial policy, which call upon member states to establish the conditions necessary for promoting competitiveness. Thus advocates of industrial policy must explain why the free market fails in the case of high technology. Two possible sources of market failure that have been suggested are borrowing constraints and spillovers.

Borrowing constraints are limits imposed by lenders on the amounts that individuals or small firms can borrow.[34] Because of borrowing constraints, private companies, especially start-up firms, may have difficulty obtaining enough financing for some projects. Development of a new supercomputer, for example, is likely to require heavy investment in research and development and involve a long period during which expenses are high and no revenues are coming in.

Spillovers occur when a given company's innovation – say, the development of an improved computer memory chip – stimulates a flood of related innovations and technical improvements by other companies and industries. The innovative company thus may enjoy only some of the total benefits of its breakthrough while bearing the full development cost. Without a government subsidy (argue advocates of industrial policy), such companies may not have a sufficiently strong incentive to innovate.

A third argument for industrial policy has less to do with market failure and more to do with nationalism. In some industries (such as aerospace) the efficient scale of operation is so large that the world market has room for only a few firms. For the world, the most desirable outcome is that those few firms be the most efficient, lowest-cost producers. However, in terms of a single country, say, France, at least some of the firms in the market should be French so that profits from the industry will accrue to France. Moreover, having French firms in the market may enhance French prestige and yield military advantages. These perceived benefits might lead France to subsidize its firms in that industry, helping them to compete with the firms of other nations in the race to capture the world market. Of course, other nations may well retaliate by introducing or increasing existing subsidies to their own firms.

These theoretical arguments for government intervention all assume that the government is skilled at picking 'winning' technologies and that its decisions about which industries to subsidize would be free from purely political considerations. However, both assumptions are questionable. A danger of industrial policy is that the favoured industries would be those with the most powerful political supporters, rather than those with the most economic promise.

The available evidence on the arguments for industrial policy has been surveyed by Gene Grossman[35] of Princeton University. Grossman concludes that, in general, industrial policy is not desirable because, in choosing industries to target, governments have frequently 'backed the wrong horse'; the costly attempt of European governments to develop the supersonic transport (SST) and other new types of commercial aeroplane is a case in point. Grossman also points out that alternative policies – such as a tax break for all

---

34. Chapter 8 presents further discussion of borrowing constraints.
35. 'Promoting New Industrial Activities: A Survey of Recent Arguments and Evidence', *OECD Economic Studies*, Spring 1990, pp. 87–125.

research and development spending – promote technology without requiring the government to target specific industries.

However, Grossman also concedes that government intervention may be desirable in some cases, notably in the early development stages of technologically innovative products, such as computers and CAT scanners. Empirically, the potential for beneficial spillovers in these cases appears so large that government intervention may be justified, even though many projects that the government may choose to support will ultimately not prove worthwhile.

CHAPTER SUMMARY

1. Economic growth is the principal source of improving standards of living over time. Over long periods even small differences in growth rates can have a large effect on nations' standards of living.

2. Growth accounting is a method for breaking total output growth into the portions resulting from growth in capital inputs, growth in labour inputs, and growth in productivity. All three factors have contributed to long-run economic growth in Europe. However, the slowdown in European output growth after 1973 (and in other countries such as the United States) primarily reflects a sharp decline in productivity growth. This decline in productivity growth in turn is the result of various factors, including problems in the legal and human environment, slower technical progress, and increased oil prices.

3. The neoclassical growth model examines the interaction of growth, saving, and capital accumulation over time. It predicts that in the absence of productivity growth the economy will reach a steady state in which output, consumption, and capital per worker are constant.

4. According to the neoclassical growth model, each of the following leads to higher output, consumption, and capital per worker in the long run: an increase in the saving rate, a decline in the population growth rate, and an increase in productivity.

5. The neoclassical growth model implies that living standards of countries with similar saving rates, population growth rates, and production functions will tend to converge over time (conditional convergence). Empirical evidence tends to support conditional convergence. Unconditional convergence – the idea that living standards in most poor countries will eventually catch up with those of rich countries – is not supported by the data.

6. The new growth theory incorporates explanations of productivity growth into the neoclassical growth model. One strand of the new growth theory emphasizes the formation of human capital, including the acquisition of skills and training by workers. A second strand focuses on the economic incentives for technological innovation by private firms.

7. Government policies to raise long-run living standards include raising the rate of saving and increasing productivity. Possible ways of increasing productivity involve investing in public capital (infrastructure), encouraging the formation of human capital, and increasing research and development. A more aggressive strategy is industrial policy, in which the government uses subsidies and other tools to influence the nation's pattern of industrial development – and, in particular, to stimulate high-tech industries. Theoretical arguments for the use of industrial policy include the possible existence of borrowing constraints and spillovers. Critics of this approach contend that in practice the government cannot successfully pick and subsidize only 'winning' technologies.

Key Terms

capital–labour ratio, p. 203
conditional convergence, p. 215
Golden Rule, p. 207
growth accounting, p. 193
growth accounting equation, p. 192
human capital, p. 217
industrial policy, p. 221
new growth theory, p. 217
steady state, p. 204
unconditional convergence, p. 215

Key Equations

$$\frac{\Delta Y}{Y} = \frac{\Delta A}{A} + a_K \frac{\Delta K}{K} + a_N \frac{\Delta N}{N} \qquad (6.2)$$

The growth accounting equation states that output growth, $\Delta Y/Y$, depends on the growth rate of productivity, $\Delta A/A$, the growth rate of capital, $\Delta K/K$, and the growth rate of labour, $\Delta N/N$. The elasticity of output with respect to capital, a_K, gives the percentage increase in output that results when capital increases by 1%. The elasticity of output with respect to labour, a_N, gives the percentage increase in output that results when labour increases by 1%.

$$y_t = f(k_t) \qquad (6.4)$$

For any year t the per-worker production function relates output per worker, y_t, to capital per worker (also called the capital–labour ratio), k_t.

$$c = f(k) - (n + d)k \qquad (6.7)$$

Steady-state consumption per worker c equals steady-state output per worker $f(k)$ minus steady-state investment per worker $(n + d)k$. Steady-state output per worker is determined by the per-worker production $f(k)$, where k is the steady-state capital–labour ratio. Steady-state investment per worker has two parts: equipping new workers with the per-worker capital stock, nk, and replacing worn-out or depreciated capital, dk.

$$sf(k) = (n + d)k \qquad (6.10)$$

The steady state is determined by the condition that saving per worker $sf(k)$ equals steady-state investment per worker $(n + d)k$. Saving per worker equals the saving rate s times output per worker $f(k)$.

Review Questions

1. According to the growth accounting approach, what are the three sources of economic growth? From what basic economic relationship is the growth accounting approach derived?
2. Of the three sources of growth identified by growth accounting, which one is primarily responsible for the slowdown in economic growth after 1973? What explanations have been given for the decline in this source of growth?
3. According to the neoclassical growth model of economic growth, if there is no productivity growth, what will happen to output per worker, consumption per worker, and capital per worker in the long run?
4. True or false? The higher the steady-state capital–labour ratio is, the more consumption each worker can enjoy in the long run. Explain your answer.
5. What effect should each of the following have on long-run living standards, according to the neoclassical growth model?
   a. An increase in the saving rate.
   b. An increase in the population growth rate.
   c. A one-off improvement in productivity.
6. What is *convergence*? Explain the difference between *unconditional convergence* and *conditional convergence*. What prediction does the neoclassical growth model make about convergence? What does the evidence say?
7. What two explanations of productivity growth does the new growth theory offer?
8. What types of policy are available to a government that wants to promote economic growth? For each type of policy you identify, explain briefly how the policy is supposed to work and list its costs or disadvantages.

Numerical Problems

1. Two economies, Hare and Tortoise, each start with a real GDP per person of $5000 in 1950. Real GDP per person grows by 3% a year in Hare and 1% a year in Tortoise. In the year 2000, what will be real GDP per person in each economy? Make a guess first; then use a calculator to get the answer.

2. Over the past twenty years an economy's total output has grown from 1000 to 1300, its capital stock has risen from 2500 to 3250, and its labour force has increased from 500 to 575. All measurements are in real terms. Calculate the contributions to economic growth of growth in capital, labour, and productivity
   a. assuming that $a_K = 0.3$ and $a_N = 0.7$.
   b. assuming that $a_K = 0.5$ and $a_N = 0.5$.

3. This problem illustrates how allowing for quality change can affect estimates of labour productivity and other variables.

   An economy with four workers produces only pizzas and six-packs of beer. Quantities of each product and the prices they sold for in two different years were as follows:

Year		Quantity	Price
1987	Pizza	5000	£4.00
1987	Beer	5000	£2.00
1997	Pizza	7000	£6.00
1997	Beer	6000	£2.50

   a. Calculate nominal GDP and real GDP for both years, assuming that 1987 is the base year. What is average labour productivity (real GDP per worker) in each of the two years? What is the total percentage change in the GDP deflator between 1987 and 1997?

   b. Pizzas produced in 1997 contain more anchovies than 1987 pizzas did. Indeed, a taste test study concludes that one-and-a-half 1987-style pizzas are needed to produce as much consumer satisfaction as a 1997-style pizza. To adjust for this quality change, restate the number of pizzas produced in 1997 as the number of '1987 pizza equivalents' produced in 1997. Also restate the 1997 pizza price so that it is the cost of the amount of 1997 pizza needed to give the same satisfaction obtained from a 1987 pizza. (*Hint:* These two adjustments should not affect total nominal spending on pizzas for 1997.) Now recalculate real GDP and average labour productivity for 1997 and the percentage change in the GDP deflator from 1987 to 1997. How does the quality adjustment affect these variables?

4. For a particular economy, the following capital input K and labour input N were reported in four different years.

Year	K	N
1	200	1000
2	250	1000
3	250	1250
4	300	1200

   The production function in this economy is

   $$Y = K^{0.3}N^{0.7}$$

   where Y is total output.

   a. Find total output, the capital–labour ratio, and output per worker in each year. Compare year 1 with year 3 and year 2 with year 4. Can this production function be written in per-worker form? If so, write algebraically the per-worker form of the production function.

   b. Repeat part (a) but assume now that the production function is $Y = K^{0.3}N^{0.8}$.

5. Use the data from Table 6.1 to calculate annual growth rates of GDP per capita for each country listed over the period 1950–89. (*Note:* The annual growth rate z will satisfy the equation $(1 + z)^{39} =$ GDP$_{1989}$/GDP$_{1950}$. To solve this equation for z using a calculator, take logs of both sides of the equation.) You will find that Germany and Japan, two countries that suffered extensive damage in World War II, had the two highest growth rates after 1950. Give a reason, based on the analysis of the neoclassical growth model, for these countries' particularly fast growth during this period.

6. An economy has the per-worker production function

   $$y_t = 3k_t^{0.5}$$

   where y_t is output per worker and k_t is the capital–labour ratio. The depreciation rate is 0.1, and the population growth rate is 0.05. Saving is

   $$S_t = 0.3Y_t$$

   where S_t is total national saving and Y_t is total output.

   a. What are the steady-state values of the capital–labour ratio, output per worker, and consumption per worker?

   The rest of the problem shows the effects of changes in the three fundamental determinants of long-run living standards.

   b. Repeat part (a) for a saving rate of 0.4 instead of 0.3.

   c. Repeat part (a) for a population growth rate of 0.08 (with a saving rate of 0.3).

d. Repeat part (a) for a production function of

$$y_t = 4k_t^{0.5}$$

Assume that the saving rate and population growth rate are at their original values.

Analytical Problems

1. According to the neoclassical growth model, how would each of the following affect consumption per worker in the long run (that is, in the steady state)? Explain.

   a. The destruction of a portion of the nation's capital stock in a war.

   b. A permanent increase in the rate of immigration (which raises the overall population growth rate).

   c. A permanent increase in energy prices.

   d. A temporary rise in the saving rate.

   e. A permanent increase in the fraction of the population in the labour force (the population growth rate is unchanged).

2. An economy is in a steady state with no productivity change. Because of an increase in acid rain, the rate of capital depreciation rises permanently. Determine the effects on steady-state capital per worker, output per worker, and consumption per worker. Is the long-run growth rate of the total capital stock affected? If so, in what way?

3. This problem adds the government to the neoclassical growth model. Suppose that a government purchases goods in the amount of g per worker every year; with N_t workers in year t, total government purchases are gN_t. The government has a balanced budget so that its tax revenue in year t, T_t, equals total government purchases. Total national saving S_t is

$$S_t = s(Y_t - T_t)$$

where Y_t is total output and s is the saving rate.

   a. Graphically show the steady state for the initial level of government purchases per worker.

   b. Suppose that the government permanently increases its purchases per worker. What are the effects on the steady-state levels of capital per worker, output per worker, and consumption per worker? Does your result imply that the optimal level of government purchases is zero?

4. In a neoclassical growth-type economy total national saving S_t is

$$S_t = sY_t - hK_t.$$

The extra term, $-hK_t$, reflects the idea that when wealth (as measured by the capital stock) is higher, saving is lower. (Wealthier people have less need to save for the future.)

   Find the steady-state values of per-worker capital, output, and consumption. What is the effect on the steady state of an increase in h?

5. Two countries are identical in every way except that one has a much higher capital–labour ratio than the other. According to the neoclassical growth model, which country's total output will grow more quickly? Does your answer depend on whether one country or the other is in a steady state? In general terms, how will your answer be affected if the two countries are allowed to trade with each other?

6. Suppose that total capital and labour both increase by the same percentage amount, so that the amount of capital per worker k does not change. Writing the production function in per-worker terms, $y = f(k)$, requires that this increase in capital and labour must not change the amount of output produced per worker y. Use the growth accounting equation to show that equal percentage increases in capital and labour will leave output per worker unaffected only if $a_K + a_N = 1$.

7

THE ASSET MARKET, MONEY, AND PRICES

Chapters 3 and 4 discussed the labour market and the goods market, two of the three markets in our model of the macroeconomy. In this chapter we consider the third market, the asset market. By *asset market* we mean the entire set of markets in which people buy and sell real and financial assets, including, for example, gold, houses, stocks, and bonds.

A type of asset that has long been believed to have special macroeconomic significance is money. Money is the economist's term for assets that can be used in making payments, such as cash and cheque accounts. One reason that money is important is that most prices are expressed in units of money, such as francs, pounds or dollars. Because prices are measured in money terms, understanding the role of money in the economy is basic to studying issues related to the price level, such as inflation and its causes. In addition, many economists believe that the amount of money in the economy affects real economic variables, such as output and employment. If it does, then it may be possible to use monetary policy to promote stable output growth and fight unemployment, as we discuss in Part III.

Because money is such an important asset, it is the focus of our discussion of the asset market. The first part of the chapter explains what money is and why people choose to hold it. We show that a person's decision about how much money to hold (his or her money demand) is part of a broader decision about how to allocate wealth among the various assets that are available. We then bring together the demand for money and the supply of money (which is determined by the central bank) to analyse equilibrium in the asset market. This analysis demonstrates that the price level in an economy is closely related to the amount of money in the economy. Thus high rates of inflation – that is, rapid increases in prices – are likely when the money supply is growing rapidly.

7.1

WHAT IS MONEY?

In economics the meaning of the term 'money' is different from its everyday meaning. People often say 'money' when they mean *income* or *wealth*, as in 'That job pays good money', or 'Her family has a lot of money'. In economics, however, **money** refers specifically to assets that are widely used and accepted as payment. Historically, the forms of money have ranged from beads and shells to gold and silver – and even to cigarettes (see Box 7.1). In modern economies the most familiar forms of money are coins and paper money, or currency. Another common form of money is chequable deposits, or bank accounts on which cheques can be written for making payments.

The Functions of Money

Since the earliest times almost all societies – from the most primitive to the most sophisticated and with many types of political and economic systems – have used money. Money has three useful functions in an economy: it is a medium of exchange, a unit of account, and a store of value.

Medium of Exchange. In an economy with no money, trading takes the form of barter, or the direct exchange of certain goods for other goods. Even today some people belong to barter clubs, in which members swap goods and services among themselves. Generally, though, barter is an inefficient way to trade, because finding someone who has the item you want and is willing to exchange that item for something you have is both difficult and time consuming. In a barter system, if one of the authors of this book wanted a restaurant meal, he would first have to find a restaurateur willing to trade his blue-plate special for an economics lecture – which might not be easy to do.

Money makes searching for the perfect trading partner unnecessary. In an economy that utilizes money, the economics professor does not have to find a restaurant owner who is hungry for knowledge. Instead, he can first exchange his economics lecture to students for money and then use the money to buy a meal. In functioning as a **medium of exchange**, or a device for making transactions, money permits people to trade at less cost in time and effort. Having a medium of exchange also raises productivity by allowing people to specialize in economic activities at which they are most skilled. In an economy with money, specialized producers have no problem trading their goods or services for the things they need. In a barter economy, though, the difficulty of trading would leave people no choice but to produce most of their own food, clothing, and shelter. Thus in a barter economy the opportunity to specialize is greatly reduced.

Unit of Account. As a **unit of account**, money is the basic unit for measuring economic value. In Sweden, for example, virtually all prices, wages, asset values, and debts are expressed in kronor, whereas in the UK they will be in pounds. Having a single, uniform measure of value is convenient. For example, pricing all goods in Sweden in kronor – instead of some goods being priced in yen, some in gold, and some in Volvo shares – simplifies comparison among different goods.

The medium-of-exchange and unit-of-account functions of money are closely linked. Because goods and services are most often exchanged for

BOX 7.1

Money in a Prisoner-of-War Camp

Among the Allied soldiers liberated from German prisoner-of-war (POW) camps at the end of World War II was a young man named R. A. Radford. Radford had been trained in economics, and shortly after his return home he published an article entitled 'The Economic Organisation of a POW Camp'.* This article, a minor classic in the economics literature, is a fascinating account of the daily lives of soldiers in several POW camps. It focuses particularly on the primitive 'economies' that grew up spontaneously in the camps.

The scope for economic behaviour in a POW camp might seem severely limited, and to a degree that's so. There was little production of goods within the camps, although there was some trade in services, such as laundry or tailoring services and even portraiture. However, prisoners were allowed to move around freely within the compound, and they actively traded goods obtained from the Red Cross, the Germans, and other sources. Among the commodities exchanged were tinned milk, jam, butter, biscuits, chocolate, sugar, clothing, and toilet articles. In one particular camp, which at various times had up to fifty thousand prisoners of many nationalities, active trading centres were run entirely by the prisoners.

A key practical issue was how to organize the trading. At first, the camp economies used barter, but it proved to be slow and inefficient. Then the prisoners hit on the idea of using cigarettes as money. Soon prices of all goods were quoted in terms of cigarettes, and cigarettes were accepted as payment for any good or service. Even non-smoking prisoners would happily accept cigarettes as payment, because they knew that they could easily trade the cigarettes for other things they wanted. The use of cigarette money greatly simplified the problem of making trades and helped the camp economy function much more smoothly.

Why were cigarettes, rather than some other commodity, used as money by the POWs? Cigarettes satisfied a number of criteria for a good money. A cigarette is a fairly standardized commodity whose value was easy for both buyers and sellers to ascertain. An individual cigarette is low enough in value that making 'change' was not a problem. Cigarettes are portable, are easily passed from hand to hand, and do not spoil quickly.

A drawback was that, as a commodity money (a form of money with an alternative use), cigarette money had a resource cost: cigarettes that were being used as money could not simultaneously be smoked. In the same way, the traditional use of gold and silver as money was costly, in that it diverted these metals – and the labour and capital used to locate and mine them – from alternative uses.

The use of cigarettes as money is not restricted to POW camps. Just before the collapse of communism in Eastern Europe, cigarette money was reportedly used in Romania and other countries instead of the nearly worthless official money.

_____

* *Economica*, November 1945, pp. 189–201.

money (the medium-of-exchange function), expressing economic values in money terms (the unit-of-account function) is natural. Otherwise, we could just as well express economic values in terms of, say, bushels of wheat. However, the medium of exchange and the unit of account are not always the same. In countries with high and erratic inflation, for example, fluctuating currency value makes money a poor unit of account because prices must be changed frequently. In such cases, economic values are commonly stated in terms of a more stable unit of account, such as US dollars or ounces of gold, even though transactions may continue to be carried out in the local currency.

Store of Value. As a **store of value**, money is a way of holding wealth. An extreme example is a miser who keeps his life's savings in cash under the mattress. But even someone who spends his cash wages fifteen minutes after receiving them is using money as a store of value for that short period.

In most cases, only money functions as a medium of exchange or a unit of account, but any asset – for example, stocks, bonds, or property – can be a store of value. As these other types of asset normally pay the holder a higher return than money does, why do people use money as a store of value? The answer is that money's usefulness as a medium of exchange makes it worthwhile to hold, even though its return is relatively low.

Measuring Money: The Monetary Aggregates

Money is defined as those assets that are widely used and accepted in payment. This definition suggests a hard-and-fast line between assets that should be counted as money and those that should not. Actually, the distinction between monetary assets and non-monetary assets is not so clear.

Consider, for example, money market funds (MMFs), which first became popular in Germany in the late 1980s. MMFs are organizations that sell shares to the public and invest the proceeds in short-term government and corporate debt. MMFs strive to earn a high return for their shareholders. At the same time, MMFs typically allow their shareholders to write a small number of cheques each month against their accounts, perhaps for a fee. Thus, although MMF shares can be used to make payments, they are not as convenient as cash or regular cheque accounts for this purpose. Should MMF shares be counted as money or not? There is no definitive answer.

Because assets differ in their 'moneyness,' no single measure of the amount of money in the economy – or the money stock, as it is often called – is likely to be completely satisfactory. For this reason, in most countries economists and policymakers use several different measures of the money stock, though the ones actually used differ between countries. These official measures are known as **monetary aggregates**. The various monetary aggregates differ in how narrowly they define the concept of money. Because the financial and banking systems of countries are also different, exactly what is included in a particular monetary aggregate will also vary among countries. In Germany, for example, the two most widely used monetary aggregates are called M1 and M2, whereas in the United Kingdom M0 and M4 are the monetary aggregates monitored, and in Sweden M0 and M3 are the two definitions used. A number of countries, including Germany, France and the Netherlands, also monitor a broader definition of money (for these countries it is M3 or M3H) because broad monetary aggregates are subject to fewer fluctuations over time and provide a more predictable basis for monetary policy. Summary definitions and data for the monetary aggregates used in Germany are given in Table 7.1. Information about where to find data on the monetary aggregates in the UK is presented in the box 'In Touch with the Macroeconomy: The Monetary Aggregates'.

The M0 and M1 Monetary Aggregates. The most narrowly defined official money measure used in Germany and adopted by most European countries, **M1**, consists of currency plus balances held in cheque accounts. More precisely, M1 is made up of currency held by the public and demand or sight deposits (non-interest-bearing cheque accounts). Most European countries also include in their measurement of M1 some form of interest-bearing chequable deposits. M1 is perhaps the closest counterpart to the theoretical definition of

IN TOUCH *WITH THE MACROECONOMY*

THE MONETARY AGGREGATES IN THE UK

The official UK monetary aggregates – currently M0 and M4 – are compiled and reported by the Bank of England in London. Over time, the definitions of the monetary aggregates have changed several times, reflecting the evolution of the financial system, and a number of monetary aggregates, including M1 and M3, have been discontinued.

The Bank of England reports estimates of the aggregates monthly using data supplied by banks, building societies and other sources. Provisional figures for M0 are announced three or four working days after the end of the month to which they relate although information on notes and coins in circulation is available from the Bank on a weekly basis. Provisional figures for M4 are released three weeks after the end of the month to which they relate. These announcements are regularly reported by the business media. More detailed information on both monetary aggregates, including a limited amount of historical data, is subsequently published by the Bank in the following month's *Monetary and Financial Statistics*, and in various other publications including the Bank of England's *Quarterly Bulletin* and the Office for National Statistics' *Financial Statistics*. Historical data over a longer period are available in *Economic Trends: Annual Abstract* published by the Office for National Statistics.

Publication of the monetary aggregates helps keep the public, economic commentators, and politicians informed about what is happening to the nation's money supply. Although the Bank of England does not directly control the monetary aggregates, they are an indicator both of current monetary policy and of future changes in real GDP and inflation. As such they play a key role in the monthly discussions between the Chancellor of the Exchequer and the Governor of the Bank of England.

* Further details are given in Bank of England, Quarterly Bulletin, February 1996.

Table 7.1 **The German Monetary Aggregates (January 1997)**

	DM billion
M1	848.2
Currency in circulation	246.2
Sight deposits	612.9
M2	1260.3
Components of M1	848.2
Time deposits for less than 4 years	412.0
M3	2139.2
Components of M2	1260.3
Savings deposits at three months' notice	879.0
M3 extended	2444.5
Components of M3	2139.2
Euro-deposits, short-term debt securities, and certificates of domestic and foreign money market funds	305.3

Source: Deutsche Bundesbank, *Monthly Report*, June 1997, Table II.2. Components do not sum exactly to the aggregates due to rounding.

money because all its components are actively used and widely accepted for making payments. In the UK the narrowest monetary aggregate is **M0**, which consists of notes and coins in circulation, currency held by commercial banks and building societies, and some deposits held by commercial banks at the Bank of England.

The M2 Monetary Aggregate. Everything in M1 plus other assets that are somewhat less 'money-like' comprise **M2**. The main additional assets in M2 typically include savings deposits at banks and other financial institutions and small-denomination time deposits, although the actual measurement of M2 varies from country to country depending upon the nature of their financial institutions. Time deposits are interest-bearing deposits with a fixed term (early withdrawal usually involves a penalty). As Table 7.1 shows, M2 in Germany includes time deposits held by domestic non-banks for less than four years with domestic credit institutions. Short-term foreign currency deposits are also included in M2.

Other Monetary Aggregates. Two additional aggregates are **M3** and **M4**. These are broader definitions of money than M2 and generally include other assets such as large-denomination time deposits, deposits with restricted access, commercial paper (the short-term debt of large corporations), certificates of deposit, short-term Treasury debt, and deposits at other financial institutions in addition to everything in M2. In the German monetary aggregates shown in Table 7.1, M3 is equal to M2 plus savings deposits held at three months' notice, while **M3 extended** includes Euro-deposits, short-term bank debt securities, and certificates of domestic and foreign money market funds.

Because definitions of the different monetary aggregates differ so much among EU countries, the central banks of the EU countries have produced a 'harmonized' broad monetary aggregate which is applicable to each country and which can be used for comparisons between EU economies. The Netherlands is one of a number of EU countries that have adopted this as the main monetary aggregate to be monitored.

Many of the assets included in M3 and M4 (as well as some that are in M2) are not money in the strict sense of being directly acceptable in payment. For example, assets such as Treasury bills or commercial paper, which are part of the broadest monetary aggregate, cannot be used directly for making purchases. However, because these assets can be quickly and cheaply converted into currency or chequable deposits, economists include them in the broader measures of money.

Weighted Monetary Aggregates. The monetary aggregates are constructed by simply adding the outstanding amounts of various types of asset. Thus a pound, franc, or kronor of currency contributes no more to the measured money stock than does a pound, franc, or kronor of savings deposits. This standard way of measuring the money stock ignores the fact that some assets, such as currency, are more money-like than others. Recently, some economists have experimented with weighted monetary aggregates. In this approach a pound, say, of a very money-like asset such as currency is given a greater weight in the total than is a pound of a less money-like asset such as a savings deposit. Several studies conclude that weighted monetary aggregates are more useful measures of money than are the standard aggregates.[1] Disagreements about the best way to weight the various monetary assets remain, however, and so far this approach has not been officially adopted.

The Money Supply

The **money supply** is the amount of money available in an economy.[2] In modern economies the money supply is determined by the central bank, such as the Deutsche Bundesbank in Germany, De Nederlandsche Bank in the Netherlands, and the Bank of England in the UK. A detailed explanation of how central banks control the money supply raises issues that would take us too far afield at this point, so we defer that discussion to Chapter 15. To grasp the basic idea, however, let us consider the simple hypothetical situation in which the only form of money is currency. In this case to increase the money supply the central bank only needs to increase the amount of currency in circulation. How can it do so?

One way – which is close to what happens in practice – is for the central bank to use newly minted currency to buy financial assets, such as government bonds, from the public. In making this swap, the public increases its holdings of money, and the amount of money in circulation rises. When the central bank uses money to purchase government bonds from the public, thus raising the money supply, it is said to have conducted an *open-market purchase*.

To reduce the money supply, the central bank can make this trade in reverse, selling government bonds that it holds to the public in exchange for currency. After the central bank removes this currency from circulation, the money supply is lower. When the central bank sells government bonds to the public to reduce the money supply, the transaction is an *open-market sale*. Open-market purchases and sales together are called **open-market operations**.

In addition to buying government bonds from the public, the central bank can also increase the money supply by buying newly issued government bonds directly from the government itself. For example, if a country's treasury needs DM10 million to pay for some new fighter planes, it might give an IOU for DM10 million (government bonds) to the central bank in exchange for DM10 million in newly minted currency. The treasury then gives the DM10 million of currency to the manufacturer of the fighter planes. After the treasury has distributed this currency, the amount of money in circulation – the money supply – will be higher by DM10 million. Effectively, this second way of increasing the money supply amounts to the government financing its expenditures by printing money.[3] This practice is most common in poor countries or in countries wracked by war or natural disaster, in which

---

1. For two recent technical discussions of weighted aggregates, see William A. Barnett, Douglas Fisher, and Apostolos Serletis, 'Consumer Theory and the Demand for Money', *Journal of Economic Literature*, December 1992, pp. 2086–119, and 'The Demand for Divisia Money by the Personal Sector and by Industrial and Commercial Companies', Bank of England, *Quarterly Bulletin*, November 1996, pp. 405–11.

2. The terms 'money supply' and 'money stock' are used interchangeably.

3. In Chapter 2 we said that the portion of government outlays not covered by taxes had to be borrowed from the private sector. Is this still true when the government has the option of paying for its outlays by printing money? Yes; for national income accounting purposes, the central bank is treated as part of the private sector. So when the treasury sells government bonds to the central bank in exchange for currency, it is still technically borrowing from the private sector.

government spending often greatly exceeds the amount that can be raised through taxes.[4]

For the rest of this chapter we assume that the economy has a money supply of M pounds, francs, kronor, or whatever, which is determined by the central bank. The term M may represent M1, M2, or some other measure of money. For the purpose of developing the theoretical model, which measure of money M refers to does not matter.

7.2   PORTFOLIO ALLOCATION AND THE DEMAND FOR ASSETS

Our next goal is to understand how people determine the amount of money they choose to hold. We begin by considering the broader question of how people allocate their wealth among the many different assets that are available, of which money is only one example.

A consumer, a business, a pension fund, a university, or any other holder of wealth must decide how to distribute that wealth among many types of asset. The set of assets that a holder of wealth chooses to own is called a *portfolio*. The decision about which assets and how much of each asset to hold is called the **portfolio allocation decision**.

The portfolio allocation decision can be complex. Many people make their living by giving financial advice to holders of wealth, and a major branch of economics, called financial economics, is devoted largely to the study of the portfolio allocation decision. But, fundamentally, only three characteristics of assets matter for the portfolio allocation decision: expected return, risk, and liquidity.

Expected Return

The rate of return to an asset is the rate of increase in its value per unit of time. For example, the return on a bank account is the interest rate on the account. The return on a share of stock is the dividend paid by the stock plus any increase in the stock's price. Clearly, a high return is a desirable feature for an asset to have: all else being equal, the higher the return a wealth holder's portfolio provides, the more consumption she can enjoy in the future for any given amount of saving done today.

Of course, the return on an asset is not always known in advance. Stock prices may go up or down, for example. Thus holders of wealth must base their portfolio allocation decisions on **expected returns**, or their best guesses about returns on assets. Everything else being equal, the higher an asset's expected return (after subtracting taxes and fees such as brokers' commissions), the more desirable the asset is and the more of it holders of wealth will want to own.[5]

---

4. The financing of government spending through money created is discussed further in Chapter 16.

5. For the purpose of comparing expected returned among assets, returns may be expressed in either real or nominal terms. For any expected rate of inflation, if asset A's nominal return is 1% higher than asset B's nominal return, asset A's expected real return (its nominal return minus expected inflation) will also be 1% higher than asset B's expected real return.

Risk

The uncertainty about the return an asset will earn relates to the second important characteristic of assets – riskiness. An asset or a portfolio of assets has high **risk** if there is a significant chance that the actual return received will be very different from the expected return. An example of a risky asset is a share in a start-up gene-splicing company that will be worthless if the company fails but will triple in value if the company succeeds. Because most people do not like risk, they hold risky assets only if the expected return is higher than that on relatively safe assets, such as government bonds.

Liquidity

Besides risk and return a third characteristic, liquidity, affects the desirability of assets. The **liquidity** of an asset is the ease and quickness with which it can be exchanged for goods, services, or other assets. Because it is accepted directly in payment, money is a highly liquid asset. An example of an illiquid asset is your car: time and effort are required to exchange a used car for other goods and services; you must find someone interested in buying the car and arrange legal transfer of ownership. Between liquid money and illiquid cars are many assets, such as stocks and bonds, of intermediate liquidity. A share of stock, for example, cannot be used directly to pay for groceries as cash can, but stock can be transformed into cash with a short delay and at the cost of a broker's fee.

In addition to making transactions easier and cheaper, liquidity provides flexibility to the holder of wealth. A liquid asset can easily be disposed of if there is an emergency need for funds or if an unexpectedly good financial investment opportunity arises. Thus, everything else being equal, the more liquid an asset is, the more attractive it will be to holders of wealth.

Asset Demands

Typically, there is a trade-off among the three characteristics that make an asset desirable: a high expected return, safety (low risk), and liquidity. For example, a safe and liquid asset, such as a cheque account, is likely to have a low expected return. The essence of the portfolio allocation decision is determining which assets, taken together, achieve the wealth holder's preferred combination of expected return, safety, and liquidity.

The amount of each particular asset that a holder of wealth desires to include in her portfolio is called her demand for that asset. Because all wealth must be held as some type of asset, the sum of a wealth holder's asset demands must equal her total wealth. For example, suppose that you have wealth of £10,000 and decide to hold £5000 in stock, £4000 in bonds, and £1000 in cash. The sum of your three asset demands must equal your total wealth of £10,000.

7.3   THE DEMAND FOR MONEY

The **demand for money** is the quantity of monetary assets, such as cash and bank and other cheque accounts, that people choose to hold in their portfolios. Choosing how much money to demand is thus a part of the broader portfolio allocation decision. In general, the demand for money – like the demand for any other asset – will depend on the expected return, risk, and liquidity of money and of other assets.

In practice, two features of money are particularly important. First, money is the most liquid asset. This liquidity is the primary benefit of holding money.[6] Second, money pays a low return (indeed, currency pays a zero nominal return). The low return earned by money, relative to other assets, is the major cost of holding money. People's demand for money is determined by how they trade off their need for liquidity against the cost of a lower return.

In this section we look at how some key macroeconomic variables affect the demand for money. Although we primarily consider the aggregate, or total, demand for money, the same economic arguments apply to individual money demands. This relation is to be expected, as the aggregate demand for money is the sum of all individual money demands.

The macroeconomic variables that have the greatest effects on money demand are the price level, real income, and interest rates. Higher prices or incomes increase people's need for liquidity and thus raise the demand for money. Interest rates affect money demand through the expected return channel: the higher the interest rate on money, the more money people will demand; however, the higher the interest rate paid on alternative assets to money, the more people will want to switch from money to those alternative assets.

The Price Level

The higher the general level of prices, the more pounds, francs, or kronor people need to conduct transactions and thus the more currency people will want to hold. For example, 30 years ago the price level in the United Kingdom was about one-tenth of its level today; in 1965 a good restaurant meal in London cost a pound. Because less money was needed for transactions, the number of pounds that a person held in the form of currency or cheque accounts – their nominal demand for money – was probably much smaller than the amount of money you hold today. The general conclusion is that a higher price level, by raising the need for liquidity, increases the nominal demand for money. In fact, because prices are ten times higher today than they were in 1965, an identical transaction takes ten times as many pounds today as it did back then. Thus, everything else being equal, the nominal demand for money is *proportional* to the price level.

Real Income

The more transactions that individuals or businesses conduct, the more liquidity they need and the greater is their demand for money. An important factor determining the number of transactions is real income. For example, a large,

---

6. Money also has low risk, but many alternative assets (such as short-term government bonds) are no riskier than money and pay a higher return.

high-volume supermarket has to deal with a larger number of customers and suppliers and pay more employees than does a corner grocery shop. Similarly, a high-income individual makes more and larger purchases than a low-income individual. Because higher real income means more transactions and a greater need for liquidity, the amount of money demanded should increase when real income increases.

Unlike the response of money demand to changes in the price level, the increase in money demand need not be proportional to an increase in real income. Actually, a 1% increase in real income usually leads to less than a 1% increase in money demand. One reason that money demand grows more slowly than income is that higher-income individuals and firms typically use their money more efficiently. For example, a high-income individual may open a special cash management account in which money not needed for current transactions is automatically invested in non-monetary assets paying a higher return. Because of minimum-balance requirements and fees, such an account might not be worthwhile for a lower-income individual.

Another reason that money demand grows more slowly than income is that nations' financial sophistication tends to increase as national income grows. In poor countries people may hold much of their saving in the form of money, for lack of anything better; in richer countries people have many attractive alternatives to money. Money substitutes such as credit cards also become more common as a country becomes richer, again leading to aggregate money demand's growing more slowly than income.

Interest Rates

The theory of portfolio allocation implies that, with risk and liquidity held constant, the demand for money depends on the expected returns of both money and alternative, non-monetary assets. An increase in the expected return on money increases the demand for money, and an increase in the expected return on alternative assets causes holders of wealth to switch from money to higher-return alternatives, thus lowering the demand for money.

For example, suppose that, of your total wealth of £10,000, you have £8000 in government bonds earning 8% interest and £2000 in an interest-bearing cheque account earning 3%. You are willing to hold the cheque account at a lower return because of the liquidity it provides. But if the interest rate on bonds rises to 10%, and the cheque account interest rate remains unchanged, you may decide to switch £1000 from the cheque account into bonds. In making this switch, you reduce your holding of money (your money demand) from £2000 to £1000. Effectively, you have chosen to trade some liquidity for the higher return offered by bonds.

Similarly, if the interest rate paid on money rises, holders of wealth will choose to hold more money. In the example, if the cheque account begins paying 5% instead of 3%, with bonds still at 8%, you may sell £1000 of your bonds, lowering your holdings of bonds to £7000 and increasing your cheque account to £3000. The sacrifice in return associated with holding money is less than before, so you increase your cheque account balance and enjoy the flexibility and other benefits of extra liquidity. Thus a higher interest rate on money makes the demand for money rise.

In principle, the interest rate on each of the many alternatives to money should affect money demand. However, as previously noted, the many interest rates in the economy generally tend to move up and down together. For the purposes of macroeconomic analysis, therefore, assuming that there is just one nominal interest rate, i, which measures the nominal return on non-monetary assets, is simpler and not too misleading. The nominal interest rate i minus the expected inflation rate π^e gives the expected real interest rate r that is relevant to saving and investment decisions, as discussed in Chapter 4.

Also, in reality, various interest rates are paid on money. For example, currency pays zero interest, but different types of chequable accounts pay varying rates. Again for simplicity, let's assume that there is just one nominal interest rate for money, i^m. The key conclusions are that an increase in the interest rate on non-monetary assets, i, reduces the amount of money demanded, and an increase in the interest rate on money, i^m, raises the amount of money demanded.

The Money Demand Function

We express the effects of the price level, real income, and interest rates on money as

$$M^d = PL(Y, i) \tag{7.1}$$

where

> M^d = the aggregate demand for money, in nominal terms;
> P = the price level;
> Y = real income or output;
> i = the nominal interest rate earned by alternative, non-monetary assets;
> L = a function relating money demand to real income and the nominal interest rate.

Equation (7.1) holds that nominal money demand M^d is proportional to the price level P. Hence, if the price level P doubles (and real income and interest rates do not change), nominal money demand M^d also will double, reflecting the fact that twice as much money is needed to conduct the same real transactions. Equation (7.1) also indicates that, for any price level P, money demand depends (through the function L) on real income Y and the nominal interest rate on non-monetary assets i. An increase in real income Y raises the demand for liquidity and thus increases money demand. An increase in the nominal interest rate i makes non-monetary assets more attractive, which reduces money demand.

We could have included the nominal interest rate on money, i^m, in equation (7.1), because an increase in the interest rate on money makes people more willing to hold money and thus increases money demand. Historically, however, the nominal interest rate on money has varied much less than the nominal interest rate on non-monetary assets (for example, currency and a proportion of cheque accounts have always paid zero interest) and thus has been ignored by many statistical studies of equation (7.1). Thus for simplicity we do not explicitly include i^m in the equation.

An equivalent way of writing the demand for money expresses the nominal interest rate i in terms of the expected real interest rate and the expected rate of inflation. Recall from equation (2.13) that the expected real interest rate r equals the nominal interest rate i minus the expected rate of inflation π^e. Therefore the nominal interest rate i equals $r + \pi^e$. Substituting $r + \pi^e$ for i in equation (7.1) yields

$$M^d = PL(Y, \ r + \pi^e) \tag{7.2}$$

Equation (7.2) shows that, for any expected rate of inflation π^e, an increase in the real interest rate increases the nominal interest rate and reduces the demand for money. Similarly, for any real interest rate, an increase in the expected rate of inflation increases the nominal interest rate and reduces the demand for money.

Nominal money demand M^d measures the demand for money in terms of pounds, francs, lira, kronor or whatever the local currency. But, sometimes, measuring money demand in real terms is more convenient. If we divide both sides of equation (7.2) by the price level P, we get

$$\frac{M^d}{P} = L(Y, \ r + \pi^e) \tag{7.3}$$

The expression on the left-hand side of equation (7.3), M^d/P, is called real money demand or, sometimes, the demand for real balances. Real money demand is the amount of money demanded in terms of the goods it can buy. Equation (7.3) states that real money demand M^d/P depends on real income (or output) Y and on the nominal interest rate, which is the sum of the real interest rate r and expected inflation rate π^e. The function L that relates real money demand to output and interest rates in equation (7.3) is called the **money demand function**.

Other Factors Affecting Money Demand

The money demand function in equation (7.3) captures the main macroeconomic determinants of money demand, but some other factors should be mentioned. Besides the nominal interest rate on money, which we have already discussed, additional factors influencing money demand include wealth, risk, liquidity of alternative assets, and payment technologies. Summary table 9 contains a comprehensive list of variables that affect the demand for money.

Wealth. When wealth increases, part of the extra wealth may be held as money, increasing total money demand. However, with income and the level of transactions held constant, a holder of wealth has little incentive to keep extra wealth in money rather than in higher-return alternative assets. Thus the effect of an increase in wealth on money demand is likely to be small.

Risk. Money usually pays a fixed nominal interest rate (zero in the case of cash), so holding money itself usually is not risky. However, if the risk of alternative assets such as stocks and property increases greatly, people may demand safer assets, including money. Thus increased riskiness in the economy may increase money demand.[7]

---

7. For some evidence that this effect occurred in the United States in the early 1980s, see James M. McGibany and Farrokh Nourzad, 'Interest Rate Volatility and the Demand for Money', *Quarterly Review of Economics and Business*, Autumn 1986, pp. 73–83.

SUMMARY 9	An Increase in	Causes Money Demand to	Reason
Macroeconomic Determinants of the Demand for Money	Price level, P	Rise proportionally	A doubling of the price level doubles the amount of a currency needed for transactions.
	Real income, Y	Rise less than proportionally	Higher real income implies more transactions and thus a greater demand for liquidity.
	Real interest rate, r	Fall	Higher real interest rate means a higher return on alternative assets and thus a switch away from money.
	Expected inflation, π^e	Fall	Higher expected inflation means a higher return on alternative assets and thus a switch away from money.
	Nominal interest rate on money, i^m	Rise	A higher return on money makes people more willing to hold money.
	Wealth	Rise	Part of an increase in wealth may be held in the form of money.
	Risk	Rise, if risk of alternative asset increases	Higher risk of alternative asset makes money more attractive.
		Fall, if risk of money increases	Higher risk of money makes it less attractive.
	Liquidity of alternative assets	Fall	Higher liquidity of alternative assets makes these assets more attractive.
	Efficiency of payments technologies	Fall	People can operate with less money.

However, money does not always carry a low risk. In a period of erratic inflation, even if the nominal return on money is fixed, the real return on money (the nominal return minus inflation) may become quite uncertain, making money risky. Money demand will then fall as people switch to inflation hedges (assets whose real returns are less likely to be affected by erratic inflation) such as gold, consumer durable goods, and property.

Liquidity of Alternative Assets. The more quickly and easily alternative assets can be converted into cash, the less need there is to hold money. In recent years the joint impact of deregulation, competition, and innovation in financial markets has made alternatives to money more liquid. For example, with a home equity line of credit, a family can now write cheques that are backed by the value of its home. We have mentioned individual cash management accounts whose introduction allowed individuals to switch wealth easily between high-return assets, such as stocks, and more liquid forms. As alternative assets become more liquid, the demand for money declines.

Payment Technologies. A last factor affecting money demand is the technologies available for making and receiving payments. For example, the introduction of credit cards allowed people to make transactions without money – at least until the end of the month, when a cheque must be written to pay the credit card bill. Automatic teller (or cash) machines (ATMs) have probably reduced the demand for cash because people know that they can obtain cash quickly whenever they need it. In the future more innovations in payment technologies will undoubtedly help people operate with less and less money. Some experts even predict that ultimately we will live in a 'cashless society', in which almost all payments will be made through immediately accessible computerized accounting systems, and that the demand for money will be close to zero.

Elasticities of Money Demand

The theory of portfolio allocation helps economists identify factors that should affect the aggregate demand for money. However, for many purposes – such as forecasting and quantitative analyses of the economy – economists need to know not just which factors affect money demand but also how strong the various effects are. This information can be obtained only through statistical analysis of the data.

Over the past three decades, economists have performed hundreds of statistical studies of the money demand function. The results of these studies are often expressed in terms of elasticities, which measure the change in money demand resulting from changes in factors affecting the demand for money. Specifically, the **income elasticity of money demand** is the percentage change in money demand resulting from a 1% increase in real income. Thus, for example, if the income elasticity of money demand is 2/3, a 3% increase in real income will increase money demand by 2% ($2/3 \times 3\% = 2\%$). Similarly, the **interest elasticity of money demand** is the percentage change in money demand resulting from a 1% increase in the interest rate.

When we work with the interest elasticity of money demand, some care is needed to avoid a potential pitfall. To illustrate, suppose that the interest rate increases from 5% per year to 6% per year. To describe this increase in the interest rate as a 1% increase in the interest rate is tempting (but incorrect). In fact, it is a 20% increase in the interest rate, because 6 is 20% larger than 5.[8] If the interest elasticity of money demand is −0.1, for example, an increase in the interest rate from 5% to 6% reduces money demand by 2% ($-0.1 \times 20\% = -2\%$). Note that, if the interest elasticity of money demand is negative, as in this example, an increase in the interest rate reduces money demand.

What are the actual values of the income elasticity and interest elasticity of money demand? Although the many statistical studies of money demand provide a range of answers, some common results emerge. First, there is

---

8. The change from 5% to 6% can be described as 'a one *percentage point* increase' or as 'a twenty *per cent* increase'.

widespread agreement that the income elasticity of money demand is positive. For example, in his classic 1973 study of M1 money demand in the USA, which established the framework for many later studies, Stephen Goldfeld of Princeton University found this elasticity to be about 2/3.[9] A study by Ray Fair of Yale University[10] found quite large differences among European countries in the income elasticity of money demand. For a number of Scandinavian countries, the UK and Italy, Fair reported income elasticities that were larger than 1, while in the Netherlands, Belgium and France, they were less than 1. For Germany the income elasticity of money demand was about 1. A positive income elasticity of money demand implies that money demand rises when income rises, as predicted by our theory. The finding that the income elasticity of money demand is less than 1 in some of the countries studied by Fair is similar to that of many other empirical analyses. An income elasticity of money demand smaller than 1 implies that money demand rises less than proportionally with income. Earlier in the chapter we discussed some reasons why, as an individual or nation becomes richer, the demand for money might be expected to grow more slowly than income.

Second, for the interest elasticity of money demand, most studies for European countries find a large negative value. For example, Fair found the interest elasticity of money demand in the UK to be –6.14, in the Netherlands –1.51 and in Germany –1.83. Of the thirteen European countries Fair considered, only one (France) had an interest elasticity of demand for money that was less (in absolute value) than –1, although some studies (including work undertaken at the Bank of England) have found values for this elasticity as small as –1[11]. A negative value for the interest elasticity of money demand implies that when interest rates on non-monetary assets rise, people reduce their holdings of money, again as predicted by the theory.

Finally, Goldfeld's study and others have confirmed empirically that the nominal demand for money is proportional to the price level. Again, this result is consistent with the theory, as reflected in the money demand equation (equation 7.3).

APPLICATION

Financial Innovation and the 'Case of the Missing Money'

In the early 1970s, studies for a number of European countries showed that a money demand function in a form similar to equation (7.3) fitted the existing data well. By the mid-1970s, however, problems arose in a number of countries, although the problem was especially striking in the UK where the demand for M1 was much lower than predicted by its principal macroeconomic determinants – the price level, income, and interest rates. Goldfeld referred to this puzzle as the 'case of the missing money' when describing similar results for the United States.[12] In the early 1980s, the relationship between money demand

---

9. 'The Demand for Money Revisited', *Brookings Papers on Economic Activity*, 1973:4, pp. 577–638. Goldfeld reported elasticities of money demand that applied to the short run and the long run. The figures we present here are long-run elasticities.

10. 'International Evidence on the Demand for Money', *Review of Economics and Statistics*, 1987, pp. 473–80.

11. A summary of the evidence on this and other aspects of the demand for money can be found in David Laidler, *The Demand for Money*, 4th edn (HarperCollins, 1993).

12. 'The Case of the Missing Money', *Brookings Papers on Economic Activity*, 1976:3, pp. 683–730. For an example of European results see F.A.G. den Butter, and M.M.G. Fase, 'The Demand for Money in EEC Countries', *Journal of Monetary Economics*, 1981, pp. 221–30.

and its macroeconomic determinants again shifted erratically, although this time the demand for money was *higher* than predicted on the basis of the price level, income, and interest rates – the case of 'too much money'.

Numerous explanations have been offered for the instability of money demand in the UK.[13] One factor emphasized by many economists was an increased pace of innovation and change in the financial system during the 1970s and 1980s. Spurred by deregulation and intense competition during this period, banks and other financial institutions provided the public with many new financial assets to choose from, as well as a variety of new portfolio management techniques. Most of these innovations reduced the demand for money, although some increased it.

From the mid-1970s, several important advances in payments technologies have been identified which tended to reduce the demand for narrow money in the UK, including a switch away from the system by which employees are paid in cash, improved access to cash from financial institutions, mainly through the introduction of ATMs, and an increased availability of non-cash methods of payment for goods and services, such as credit and debit cards.[14] It was suggested by some economists that the unpredictable nature of money demand in the UK at this time was one reason for the failure of the Thatcher government's attempt to control inflation by announcing targets for monetary growth. Section 7.5 explains the economic theory behind these ideas. The relative experiences of Germany and the UK during the 1970s and 1980s seem to support this view. At this time, Germany also pursued a policy of monetary targeting with considerable success. Money demand in Germany was much more stable and predictable than it was in the UK. However, the German financial system had not been subject to the sort of rapid transformation that had taken place in the UK. This suggests that the conduct and success of monetary policy depends upon the financial environment in which it operates.[15]

Velocity and the Quantity Theory of Money

A concept related to money demand, which at times is used in discussions of monetary policy, is velocity. It measures how often the money stock 'turns over' each period. Specifically, **velocity** is nominal GDP (the price level P times real output Y) divided by the nominal money stock M. If we let V represent velocity,

$$V = \frac{\text{nominal GDP}}{\text{nominal money stock}} = \frac{PY}{M} \qquad (7.4)$$

If velocity rises, each unit of the money stock is being used in a greater volume of transactions in each period, assuming that the volume of transactions is pro-

---

13. The problems associated with estimating stable money demand relationships have recently been examined in a paper by David Laidler, 'Notes on the Microfoundation of Monetary Economics', *The Economic Journal*, July 1997, pp. 1213–1235.

14. N. Janseen, 'Can We Explain the Shift in M0 Velocity? Some Time-Series and Cross-Section Evidence', Bank of England, *Quarterly Review*, 1961:1 pp. 39–48.

15. See Iris Biefang-Frisancho Mariscal, Hans-Michael Trautwein, Peter Howells, Philip Arestis, and Harald Hagemann, 'Financial Innovation and the Long-Run Demand for Money in the United Kingdom and in West Germany', *Weltwirtschaftliches Archiv*, 1995, pp. 305–25.

portional to GDP. Figure 7.1 shows the velocities for Germany and the UK for the period 1965–96 for both narrow and broad definitions of money.

The concept of velocity comes from one of the earliest theories of money demand, the quantity theory of money.[16] The **quantity theory of money** asserts that real money demand is proportional to real income, or

$$\frac{M^d}{P} = kY \tag{7.5}$$

16. The quantity theory of money was developed by several classical economists, notably Irving Fisher, in the late nineteenth and early twentieth centuries. A famous statement of the theory is contained in Fisher's book *The Purchasing Power of Money* (Macmillan, 1911).

Figure 7.1
Velocity of M0, M1 and M2, UK and Germany 1965–1996

M0 velocity is nominal GDP divided by M0 (UK only), M1 velocity is nominal GDP divided by M1, M2 velocity is nominal GDP divided by M2 (Germany only) and M4 velocity is nominal GDP divided by M4 (UK only). M1 velocity in the UK moved steadily upward until about 1980 when it fell sharply. In contrast, M0 velocity increased throughout the period. M4 velocity has no clear trend and is more stable than either M0 or M1. Both M1 and M2 velocity in Germany have fallen during the period though M1 velocity has behaved more erratically than M2 velocity and M1 velocity in the UK.

Source: Money stock and GDP variables from *International Financial Statistics Yearbook*, International Monetary Fund, Washington D.C., various issues

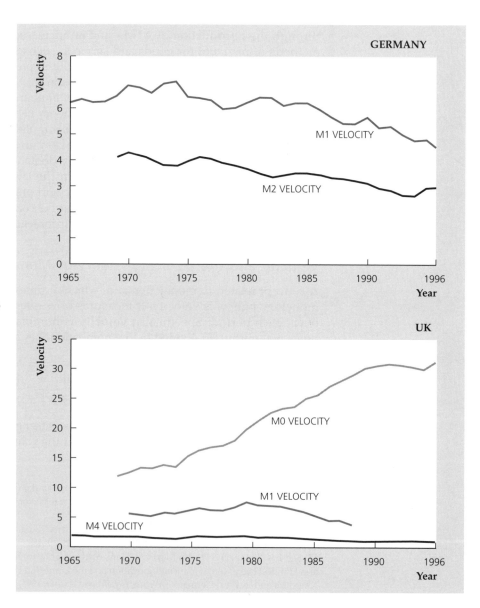

where M^d/P is real money demand, Y is real income, and k is a constant. In equation (7.5) the real money demand function $L(Y, r + \pi^e)$ takes the simple form kY. This way of writing money demand is based on the strong assumption that velocity is a constant, $1/k$, and does not depend on income or interest rates.[17]

Is velocity actually a constant? As Figure 7.1 shows, both M0 and M1 velocity in the UK are clearly not constant: M0 velocity has increased steadily since 1975, whereas M1 velocity increased until about 1980 then fell sharply in the early 1980s, and it continued to fall until the publication of data on M1 was discontinued in 1989. Financial innovation has played a role in the increase in M0 velocity. As discussed, the payment of interest on sight deposits and innovations in payment methods have both reduced the demand for currency, thus increasing M0 velocity. An additional factor which also reduced the demand for currency was a marked shift away from the system whereby workers are paid in cash to one in which wages and salaries are paid into their bank or building society accounts. M1 velocity fell sharply after 1980 due to the popularity of new interest-bearing cheque accounts during this period, which raised the demand for M1 at any level of GDP and thereby lowered its velocity. But in addition, departures from the quantity theory's assumption that interest rates do not affect money demand – an assumption contradicted by most empirical studies – probably contributed to the fall in the demand for M1. Lower interest rates on non-monetary assets in the 1980s increased people's willingness to hold low-interest or zero-interest money, which raised the demand for M1 at any level of GDP, and thus reduced M1 velocity.

M4 velocity, also shown in Figure 7.1, is closer to being a constant. It shows a slight downward trend but does not exhibit the instability of either M0 or M1 velocities. Also shown in Figure 7.1 are the M1 and M2 velocities for Germany. Both show a downward trend and M1 velocity exhibits more instability than M2 velocity.

7.4 ASSET MARKET EQUILIBRIUM

Recall that the asset market is actually a set of markets, in which real and financial assets are traded. The demand for any asset (say, government bonds) is the quantity of the asset that holders of wealth want in their portfolios. The demand for each asset depends on its expected return, risk, and liquidity relative to other assets. The supply of each asset is the quantity of that asset that is available. At any particular time the supplies of individual assets are typically fixed, although over time asset supplies change (the government may issue more bonds, firms may issue new shares, more gold may be mined, and so on).

The asset market is in equilibrium when the quantity of each asset that holders of wealth demand equals the (fixed) available supply of that asset. In

---

17. To derive velocity under the quantity theory, we must assume that nominal money demand M^d equals the actual money stock M, an assumption that we justify later in the chapter. Under this assumption, you should verify that $V = 1/k$.

this section we examine asset market equilibrium, focusing on the role of money. We then show how asset market equilibrium is linked to the price level.

Asset Market Equilibrium: An Aggregation Assumption

In analysing the labour market in Chapter 3 and the goods market in Chapter 4, we relied on aggregation to keep things manageable. That is, instead of looking at the supply and demand for each of the many different types of labour and goods in the economy, we studied the supply and demand for both labour and goods in general. Aggregating in this way allowed us to analyse the behaviour of the economy as a whole without getting lost in the details.

Because there are many different types of asset, aggregation is equally necessary for studying the asset market. Thus we adopt an aggregation assumption for the asset market that economists often make for macroeconomic analysis: we assume that all assets may be grouped into two categories, money and non-monetary assets. Money includes assets that can be used in payment, such as currency and cheque accounts. All money is assumed to have the same risk and liquidity and to pay the same nominal interest rate, i^m. The fixed nominal supply of money is M. Non-monetary assets include all assets other than money, such as stocks, bonds, land, and so on. All non-monetary assets are assumed to have the same risk and liquidity and to pay a nominal interest rate of $i = r + \pi^e$, where r is the expected real interest rate and π^e is the expected rate of inflation. The fixed nominal supply of non-monetary assets is NM.

Although the assumption that assets can be aggregated into two types ignores many interesting differences among assets, it greatly simplifies our analysis and has proved to be very useful. One immediate benefit of making this assumption is that, if we allow for only two types of asset, *asset market equilibrium reduces to the condition that the quantity of money supplied equals the quantity of money demanded.*

To demonstrate this point, let's look at the portfolio allocation decision of an individual named Erik. Erik has a fixed amount of wealth that he allocates between money and nonmonetary assets. If m^d is the nominal amount of money and nm^d is the nominal amount of non-monetary assets that Erik wants to hold, the sum of Erik's desired money holdings and his desired holdings of non-monetary assets must be his total wealth, or

$$m^d + nm^d = \text{Erik's total nominal wealth}$$

This equation has to be true for every holder of wealth in the economy.

Suppose that we sum this equation across all holders of wealth in the economy. Then the sum of all individual money demands m^d equals the aggregate demand for money M^d. The sum of all individual demands for non-monetary assets is the aggregate demand for non-monetary assets, NM^d. Finally, adding nominal wealth for all holders of wealth gives the aggregate nominal wealth of the economy, or

$$M^d + NM^d = \text{aggregate nominal wealth} \tag{7.6}$$

Equation (7.6) states that the total demand for money in the economy plus the total demand for non-monetary assets must equal the economy's total nominal wealth.

Next, we relate the total supplies of money and non-monetary assets to aggregate wealth. Because money and non-monetary assets are the only assets in the economy, aggregate nominal wealth equals the supply of money M plus the supply of non-monetary assets NM, or

$$M + NM = \text{aggregate nominal wealth} \tag{7.7}$$

Finally, we subtract equation (7.7) from equation (7.6) to obtain

$$(M^d - M) + (NM^d - NM) = 0 \tag{7.8}$$

The term $M^d - M$ in equation (7.8) is the *excess demand for money*, or the amount by which the total amount of money demanded exceeds the money supply. Similarly, the term $NM^d - NM$ in equation (7.8) is the *excess demand for non-monetary assets*.

Now suppose that the demand for money M^d equals the money supply M so that the excess demand for money $M^d - M$ is zero. Equation (7.8) shows that, if $M^d - M$ is zero, $NM^d - NM$ must also be zero: that is, if the amounts of money supplied and demanded are equal, the amounts of non-monetary assets supplied and demanded must also be equal. By definition, if quantities supplied and demanded are equal for each type of asset, the asset market is in equilibrium.

If we make the simplifying assumption that assets can be lumped into monetary and non-monetary categories, the asset market is in equilibrium only if the quantity of money supplied equals the quantity of money demanded. This result is convenient, because it means that in studying asset market equilibrium we only have to look at the supply and demand for money and can ignore non-monetary assets. As long as the amounts of money supplied and demanded are equal, the entire asset market will be in equilibrium.

The Asset Market Equilibrium Condition

Equilibrium in the asset market occurs when the quantity of money supplied equals the quantity of money demanded. This condition is valid whether money supply and demand are expressed in nominal terms or real terms. We work with this condition in real terms, or

$$\frac{M}{P} = L(Y, \ r + \pi^e) \tag{7.9}$$

The left-hand side of equation (7.9) is the nominal supply of money M divided by the price level P, which is the supply of money measured in real terms. The right-hand side of the equation is the same as the real demand for money M^d/P, as in equation (7.3). Equation (7.9), which states that the real quantity of money supplied equals the real quantity of money demanded, is called the *asset market equilibrium condition*.

The asset market equilibrium condition involves five variables: the nominal money supply M, the price level P, real income Y, the real interest rate r, and the expected rate of inflation π^e. The nominal money supply M is determined by the central bank through its open-market operations. For now, we treat the expected rate of inflation π^e as fixed (we return to the determination of expected inflation later in the chapter). That leaves three variables in the asset market equilibrium condition whose values we have not yet specified: output Y, the real interest rate r, and the price level P.

In this part of the book we have made the assumption that the economy is at full employment or, equivalently, that all markets are in equilibrium. Both classical and Keynesian economists agree that the full-employment assumption is reasonable for analysing the long-term behaviour of the economy. If we continue to assume full employment,[18] we can use the analysis from previous chapters to describe how output and the real interest rate are determined. Recall from Chapter 3 that if the labour market is in equilibrium – with employment at its full-employment level – output equals full-employment output $\overline{Y}$. Chapter 4 showed that, for any level of output, the real interest rate must take the value that makes desired national saving and desired investment equal (the goods market equilibrium condition).

With the values of output and the real interest rate established by equilibrium in the labour and goods markets, the only variable left to be determined by the asset market equilibrium condition is the price level P. To emphasize that the price level is the variable determined by asset market equilibrium, we multiply both sides of equation (7.9) by P and divide both sides by real money demand, $L(Y, r + \pi^e)$, to obtain

$$P = \frac{M}{L(Y,\ r + \pi^e)} \tag{7.10}$$

According to equation (7.10), the economy's price level P equals the ratio of the nominal money supply M to the real demand for money $L(Y, r + \pi^e)$. For given values of real output Y, the real interest rate r, and the expected rate of inflation π^e, the real demand for money $L(Y, r + \pi^e)$ is fixed. Thus equation (7.10) states that the price level is proportional to the nominal money supply. A doubling of the nominal money supply M, for instance, would double the price level P, with other factors held constant. The existence of a close link between the price level and the money supply in an economy is one of the oldest and most reliable conclusions about macroeconomic behaviour, having been recognized in some form for hundreds if not thousands of years. We discuss the empirical support for this link in Section 7.5.

What forces lead the price level to its equilibrium value, equation (7.10)? A complete description of how the price level adjusts to its equilibrium value involves an analysis of the goods market as well as the asset market. We leave this task until Chapter 10, where we discuss the links among the three main markets of the economy in more detail. Briefly, in Chapter 10 we show that an increase in the money supply leads people to increase their nominal spending on goods and services; this increased nominal demand for output leads prices to rise. Prices continue to rise until people are content to hold the increased nominal quantity of money in their portfolios, satisfying the asset market equilibrium condition (rewritten as equation 7.10).

7.5 MONEY GROWTH AND INFLATION

In Section 7.4 we established that, when the markets for labour, goods, and assets are all in equilibrium, the price level P is proportional to the nominal money supply M. However, the price level itself is generally of less concern to

---

18. We relax this assumption in Part III when we discuss short-run economic fluctuations.

policymakers and the public than is the rate of inflation, or the percentage rate of increase of the price level. In this section we extend our analysis of the price level to show how inflation is determined. We conclude that the inflation rate, which is the growth rate of the price level, is closely related to the growth rate of the nominal money supply.

To obtain an equation for the rate of inflation in a full-employment economy, we set the growth rate of the left-hand side of equation (7.10) equal to the growth rate of its right-hand side to obtain

$$\frac{\Delta P}{P} = \frac{\Delta M}{M} - \frac{\Delta L(Y, \ r + \pi^e)}{L(Y, \ r + \pi^e)} \tag{7.11}$$

where the symbol Δ indicates the change in a variable from one year to the next. The left-hand side of equation (7.11) is the growth rate of the price level, $\Delta P/P$, which is the same as the inflation rate π. The right-hand side of equation (7.11) expresses the growth rate of the ratio on the right-hand side of equation (7.10) as the growth rate of the numerator, M, minus the growth rate of the denominator, $L(Y, r + \pi^e)$. (Appendix A, Section A.7 provides some useful formulas for calculating growth rates.) Equation (7.11) shows that, if the asset market is in equilibrium, *the rate of inflation equals the growth rate of the nominal money supply minus the growth rate of real money demand.*

Equation (7.11) highlights the point that the rate of inflation is closely related to the rate of growth of the nominal money supply. However, to use equation (7.11) to predict the behaviour of inflation we must also know how quickly real money demand is growing. The money demand function, equation (7.3), focused on two macroeconomic variables with significant effects on real money demand: income (or output) Y and the nominal interest rate $r + \pi^e$. We show later in this section that, in a long-run equilibrium with a constant growth rate of money, the nominal interest rate will be constant. Therefore here we look only at growth in income as a source of growth in real money demand.

Earlier we defined the income elasticity of money demand to be the percentage change in money demand resulting from a 1% increase in real income. If $\Delta Y/Y$ is the percentage change in real income from one year to the next and η_Y is the income elasticity of money demand, $\eta_Y \Delta Y/Y$ is the resulting increase in the real demand for money, with other factors affecting money demand held constant. Substituting π for $\Delta P/P$ and $\eta_Y \Delta Y/Y$ for the growth rate of real money demand in equation (7.11) yields

$$\pi = \frac{\Delta M}{M} - \eta_Y \frac{\Delta Y}{Y} \tag{7.12}$$

Equation (7.12) is a useful simple expression for the rate of inflation. According to equation (7.12), the rate of inflation equals the growth rate of the nominal money supply minus an adjustment for the growth rate of real money demand arising from growth in real output. For example, suppose that nominal money supply growth is 10% per year, real income is growing by 3% per year, and the income elasticity of money demand is 2/3. Then equation (7.12) predicts that the inflation rate will be 10% − (2/3)(3%), or 8% per year.

Money Growth and Inflation in the Formerly Communist Countries of Eastern Europe

The fall of communism in Eastern Europe and the break-up of the Soviet Union led to economic, political, and social upheaval. All of these countries, to varying degrees, have introduced reforms intended to make their economies more market oriented, and many (particularly the new countries formed from the break-up of the Soviet Union) have introduced new currencies. However, Russia and many of the Eastern European economies have continued to face serious problems, including very high rates of inflation. In this box we will see that the main reason for these high inflation rates is the rapid rates of money growth in these countries.

In general, both the growth of the nominal money supply and the growth of real money demand (resulting from real income growth, for example) affect the rate of inflation (see equation 7.12). In countries with high inflation, however, the growth of the nominal money supply is usually the much more important of these two factors. To illustrate, if the income elasticity of money demand in a country is 2/3, and real output were to grow at the stunning rate of 15% per year, then according to equation (7.12) real money demand would grow at 10% per year (2/3 × 15%) in that country. If a second country also has an income elasticity of 2/3, but its income is falling at the painful rate of 15% per year, the rate of growth of real money demand is −10% per year. Thus, even with the radically different income growth rates in this example, the difference in the growth rates of real money demand is only 20% per year.

In contrast to the relatively modest differences among countries in the growth rates of real money demand, rates of growth of nominal money supplies may vary among countries by hundreds of percentage points per year. Thus large differences in inflation rates among countries are almost always the result of large differences in rates of money growth.

The link between money growth and inflation is illustrated in Figure 7.2, which shows the 1995 values of these variables in the formerly communist countries of Eastern Europe. The three countries that had inflation rates above

Figure 7.2
Money growth and inflation in selected Eastern European countries, 1995
The countries included in the figure are those in the group of developing countries in Europe for which 1995 data are available on money growth and inflation, excluding Cyprus, Malta, and Turkey, which were not formerly communist.

Source: *International Financial Statistics*, International Monetary Fund, Washington D.C., December 1996, pp.70–1.

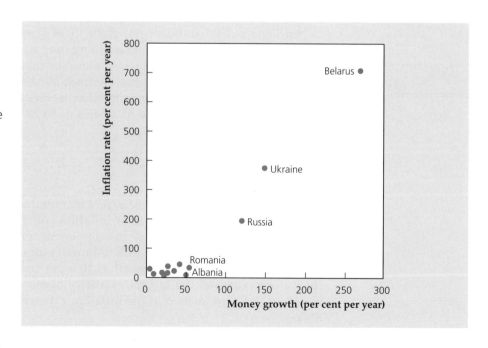

100% per year – Belarus, Ukraine, and Russia – also had money growth rates above 100% per year. Whether we compare inflation rates among these three countries, or compare the high inflation rates of these countries with the relatively low inflation rates of the remaining ten countries, it is clear that large differences in inflation rates are associated with large differences in rates of money growth.

If rapid money growth causes inflation, why do countries allow their money supplies to grow so quickly? As we discussed earlier, governments sometimes find that printing money (borrowing from the central bank) is the only way that they can finance their expenditure. This situation is most likely to occur in poor countries or countries that undergo economic upheavals associated with war, natural disaster, or (as in the case of the Eastern European countries) major political and economic change. Unfortunately, the almost inevitable result of financing government expenditures in this way is increased inflation.

The Expected Inflation Rate and the Nominal Interest Rate

In our earlier discussion of asset market equilibrium, we made the assumption that the expected inflation rate is fixed. For a given real interest rate r (which is determined by the goods market equilibrium condition), if the expected inflation rate π^e is fixed, so is the nominal interest rate, at $r + \pi^e$. We close the chapter with a brief look at the factors that determine the expected inflation rate and the nominal interest rate.

What should holders of wealth and others expect the inflation rate to be in the future? As we demonstrated, equation (7.12), which relates inflation to the growth rates of the nominal money supply and real income, is useful for predicting inflation. For expected values of money growth (based, for example, on plans announced by the central bank) and real income growth, as well as an estimate of the income elasticity of money demand, equation (7.12) can be used to calculate the expected inflation rate. Suppose that people in a particular country expect their nation's money supply to grow much more rapidly over the next two years because the government is committed to large military expenditures and can pay for these expenditures only by printing money. In this case, equation (7.12) shows that people should expect much higher inflation rates in the future.

The inflation prediction equation, equation (7.12), is particularly easy to apply when the growth rates of the nominal money supply and real income are constant over time. In this case, the expected growth rates of the nominal money supply and real income equal their current growth rates, and (from equation 7.12) the expected inflation rate equals the current inflation rate (assuming no change in the income elasticity of money demand). In practice, the current inflation rate often approximates the expected inflation rate, as long as people do not expect money or income growth to change too much in the near future.

The public's expected inflation rate is not directly observable, except perhaps through surveys and similar methods. However, an observable economic variable that is strongly affected by expected inflation is the nominal interest rate. At any real interest rate r, which is determined by the goods market equilibrium condition that desired national saving equals desired investment, the nominal interest rate $r + \pi^e$ changes one-for-one with changes in the expected inflation rate π^e. Thus policy actions (such as rapid expansion of the money supply) that cause people to fear future increases in inflation should cause nominal interest rates to rise, all else being equal.

But, as already noted, if people do not expect large changes in the growth rates of the money supply or real income, expected inflation will not be much different from current inflation. In this case, nominal interest rates and current inflation rates should move together. If current inflation is high, for example, expected inflation is also likely to be high; but high expected inflation also causes nominal interest rates to be high, all else being equal.

The historical relationship between nominal interest rates and inflation is illustrated by Figure 7.3, which shows the nominal interest rate and the annual inflation rate measured by the GDP deflator in a number of European countries from 1965 to 1996. In general, nominal interest rates and inflation rates have tended to move together, rising during the 1960s and 1970s and then falling sharply after reaching a peak in 1981. However, movements in the inflation rate are not perfectly matched by movements in the nominal interest rate because the real interest rate has not been constant over this period. In particular, during the late 1970s and early 1980s, the rise in the nominal interest rate was much greater than the rise in the inflation rate, reflecting in some countries an increase in the real interest rate from a negative value in the mid 1970s to much higher, positive values in the 1980s.

Figure 7.3
Inflation and the nominal interest rates in France, Germany, Italy, Netherlands, Sweden and UK 1965–96
The figures show nominal short-term interest rates and the annual rates of inflation as measured by the GDP deflator. The nominal interest rate tends to move together with inflation in most of the countries shown, though there are periods in all of them when the two variables diverge.

Source: *European Economy 1996 op cit. Table 1.1(b)*, Table 24 'Price deflator gross domestic production'; Table 51 'Nominal short-term interest rates'.

(a) In Germany, the nominal interest rate moves closely with inflation until the mid-1970s when the two variables start to diverge. In particular, the nominal interest rate increased sharply in the early 1980s, and early 1990s following unification, while inflation showed more modest increases during both periods.

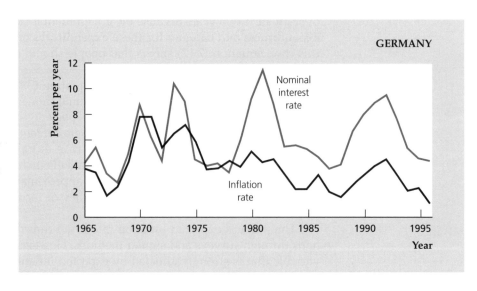

(b) The nominal interest rate in France moves closely with inflation up until 1980, when the two variables diverge. Most striking, is the period during the late 1980s and early 1990s when nominal interest rates rose, but inflation continued to fall.

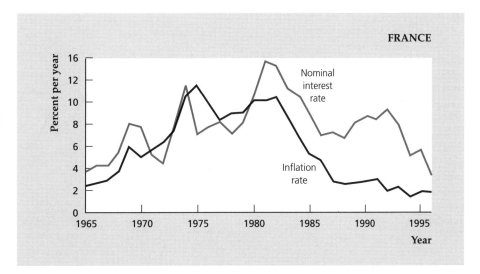

(c) The nominal interest rate and inflation have moved together in Italy for much of the 1965–96 period. They diverged significantly in the mid-1970s when inflation rose much faster than nominal interest rates, resulting in negative real interest rates. Since the mid-1980s the nominal interest rate and inflation have moved in the same direction but the gap between them has increased.

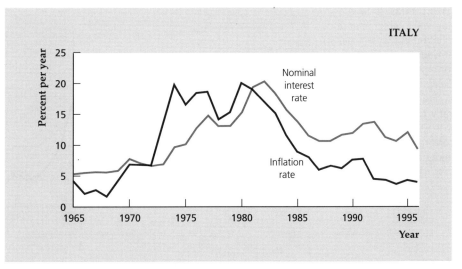

(d) The nominal interest rate and inflation in the Netherlands, in contrast to France, have hardly moved since the early 1970s. The nominal interest rate is seen to be especially volatile in the mid-1970s when inflation was high but falling. During the mid-1980s and early 1990s, the two variables diverge significantly, with the Netherlands having very high real interest rates during this period.

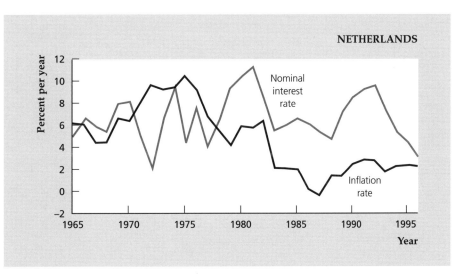

(e) Since 1965, the nominal interest rate and inflation in Sweden have followed very different paths. Nominal interest rates hardly changed during the sharp fall in inflation during the late 1960s and the sharp rise in inflation during the mid-1970s. Since then, both variables show a downward trend but little evidence of moving together.

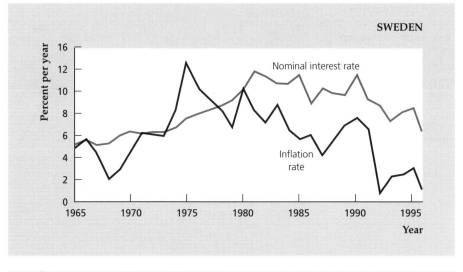

(f) In contrast to Sweden, nominal interest rates and inflation in the UK have moved closely together for much of the period. Exceptions to this are during the mid-1970s and early 1980s when inflation rose sharply without a corresponding increase in nominal interest rates.

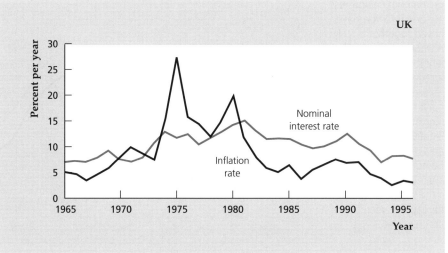

CHAPTER SUMMARY

1. Money is the set of assets that are widely used and accepted as payment, such as currency and cheque accounts. Money functions as a medium of exchange, a unit of account, and a store of value.

2. The supply of money is set by the central bank. The central bank's official measures of money are called the monetary aggregates. M1, which is made up primarily of currency and cheque accounts, and M2, which includes a broader set of monetary assets, are the monetary aggregates that are widely watched in many European countries. In the UK the two monetary aggregates monitored are M0 which is currency, and M4 a broad monetary aggregate, whilst in Sweden, M0 and M3 are the two monetary aggregates that are watched.

3. A portfolio allocation decision is made by a holder of wealth when determining which assets and how much of each asset to hold. The three characteristics of assets that most affect their desirability are expected return, risk, and liquidity.

4. Money demand is the total amount of money that people choose to hold in their portfolios. The principal macroeconomic variables that affect money demand are the price level, real income, and interest rates. Nominal money demand is proportional to the price level. Higher real income increases the number of transactions and thus raises real money demand. A higher interest rate on alternative, non-monetary assets lowers real money demand by making the alternative assets more attractive than money. The money demand function measures the relationship between real money demand and these macroeconomic variables.

5. Velocity is the ratio of nominal GDP to the nominal money stock. The quantity theory of money is an early theory of money demand that assumes that velocity is constant, so that money demand is proportional to income. Historically, in the UK M4 has been more stable than M0 and M1, whereas in Germany, the velocity of narrow and broad money aggregates have fallen over time, though the former exhibits more instability.

6. Under the simplifying assumption that assets can be grouped into two categories – money and non-monetary assets – the asset market is in equilibrium if the quantity of money supplied equals the quantity of money demanded. When all markets are in equilibrium (the economy is at full employment), the level of output is determined by equilibrium in the labour market, the real interest rate is determined by equilibrium in the goods market, and the price level is determined by equilibrium in the asset market. The equilibrium price level is proportional to the nominal money supply.

7. When all markets are in equilibrium, the inflation rate equals the growth rate of the nominal money supply minus the growth rate of real money demand. The growth rate of real money demand in turn depends primarily on the real income growth rate. Expected inflation depends on expected growth rates of the nominal money supply and real income. For a given real interest rate, the nominal interest rate responds one-for-one to changes in expected inflation.

Key Terms

money demand function, p. 239
money supply, p. 233
open-market operations, p. 233
portfolio allocation decision, p. 234
quantity theory of money, p. 244
risk, p. 235
store of value, p. 229
unit of account, p. 228
velocity, p. 243

Key Equations

$$\frac{M^d}{P} = L(Y,\ r + \pi^e) \qquad (7.3)$$

According to the money demand function, the real quantity of money demanded, M^d/P, depends on output and the nominal interest rate on alternative, non-monetary assets. An increase in output, Y, raises the number of transactions people make and thus raises the demand for money. An increase in the nominal interest rate on non-monetary assets, i (which equals the real interest rate, r, plus the expected rate of inflation, π^e) raises the attractiveness of alternative assets and thus reduces the demand for money.

$$V = \frac{\text{nominal GDP}}{\text{nominal money supply}} = \frac{PY}{M} \qquad (7.4)$$

Velocity V is nominal GDP, or P times Y, divided by the nominal money stock, M. Velocity is assumed to be constant by the quantity theory of money.

$$\frac{M}{P} = L(Y,\ r + \pi^e) \qquad (7.9)$$

The asset market equilibrium conditions states that the real supply of money, M/P, and the real demand for money, $L(Y, r + \pi^e)$, are equal.

$$\pi = \frac{\Delta M}{M} - \eta_Y \frac{\Delta Y}{Y} \qquad (7.12)$$

The inflation rate, π, equals the growth rate of the nominal money supply, $\Delta M/M$, minus the growth rate of real money demand. The growth rate of real money demand equals the income elasticity of money demand, η_Y, times the growth rate of real income or output, $\Delta Y/Y$.

Review Questions

1. Define *money*. How does the economist's use of this term differ from its everyday meaning?
2. What are the three functions of money? How does each function contribute to a more smoothly operating economy?
3. Who determines the nation's money supply? Explain how the money supply could be expanded or reduced in an economy in which all money is in the form of currency.
4. What are the three characteristics of assets that are most important to holders of wealth? How does money compare with other assets for each characteristic?
5. List and discuss the macroeconomic variables that affect the aggregate demand for money.
6. Define *velocity*. Discuss the role of velocity in the quantity theory of money.
7. Why is equilibrium in the asset market described by the condition that real money supply equal real money demand? What is the aggregation assumption that is needed to allow ignoring the markets for other assets?
8. What is the relationship between the price level and the nominal money supply when all markets are in equilibrium? What is the relationship between inflation and the nominal money supply?
9. Give an example of a factor that would increase the public's expected rate of inflation. All else being equal, how would this increase in the expected inflation rate affect interest rates?

Numerical Problems

1. Money demand in an economy in which no interest is paid on money is

$$\frac{M^d}{P} = 500 + 0.2Y - 1000i.$$

   a. You know that $P = 100$, $Y = 1000$, and $i = 0.10$. Find real money demand, nominal money demand, and velocity.
   b. The price level doubles from $P = 100$ to $P = 200$. Find real money demand, nominal money demand, and velocity.
   c. Starting from the values of the variables given in part (a) and assuming that the money demand

function as written holds, determine how velocity is affected by an increase in real income; by an increase in the nominal interest rate; by an increase in the price level.

2. Mr Midas has wealth of £100,000 that he invests entirely in money (a cheque account) and government bonds. Mr Midas instructs his broker to invest £50,000 in bonds, plus £5000 more in bonds for every percentage point that the interest rate on bonds exceeds the interest rate on his cheque account.

   a. Write an algebraic formula that gives Mr Midas's demand for money as a function of bond and cheque account interest rates.

   b. Write an algebraic formula that gives Mr Midas's demand for bonds. What is the sum of his demand for money and his demand for bonds?

   c. Suppose that all holders of wealth in the economy are identical to Mr Midas. Fixed asset supplies per person are £80,000 of bonds and £20,000 of cheque accounts. Cheque accounts pay no interest. What is the interest rate on bonds in asset market equilibrium?

3. Assume that the quantity theory of money holds and that velocity is constant at 5.0. Output is fixed at its full-employment value of 10,000, and the price level is 2.0.

   a. Determine the real demand for money and the nominal demand for money.

   b. In this same economy the government fixes the nominal money supply at 5000. With output fixed at its full-employment level and with the assumption that prices are flexible, what will be the new price level? What happens to the price level if the nominal money supply rises to 6000?

4. Consider an economy with a constant nominal money supply, a constant level of real output $Y = 100$, and a constant real interest rate $r = 0.10$. Suppose that the income elasticity of money demand is 0.5 and the interest elasticity of money demand is -0.1.

   a. By what percentage does the equilibrium price level differ from its initial value if output increases to $Y = 106$ (and r remains at 0.10)? (*Hint:* Use equation 7.11.)

   b. By what percentage does the equilibrium price level differ from its initial value if the real interest increases to $r = 0.11$ (and Y remains at 100)?

   c. Suppose that the real interest rate increases to $r = 0.11$. What would real output have to be in order for the equilibrium price level to remain at

its initial value?

5. Suppose that the real money demand function is

$$L(Y, \ r + \pi^e) = \frac{0.01Y}{(r + \pi^e)},$$

where Y is real output, r is the real interest rate, and π^e is the expected rate of inflation. Real output is constant over time at $Y = 150$. The real interest rate is fixed in the goods market at $r = 0.05$ per year.

   a. Suppose that the nominal money supply is growing at the rate of 10% per year and that this growth rate is expected to persist for ever. Currently, the nominal money supply is $M = 300$. What are the values of the real money supply and the current price level? (*Hint:* What is the value of the expected inflation rate that enters the money demand function?)

   b. Suppose that the nominal money supply is $M = 300$. The central bank announces that from now on the nominal money supply is going to grow at the rate of 5% per year. If everyone believes this announcement, and if all markets are in equilibrium, what are the values of the real money supply and the current price level? Explain the effects on the real money supply and the current price level of a slowdown in the rate of money growth.

Analytical Problems

1. All else being equal, how would each of the following affect the demand for M1? The demand for M3? Explain.

   a. The maximum number of cheques per month that can be written on money market mutual funds and money market deposit accounts is raised from three to thirty.

   b. Home equity lines of credit that allow homeowners to write cheques against the value of their homes are introduced.

   c. The stock market crashes, and further sharp declines in the market are widely feared.

   d. Banks introduce overdraft protection, under which funds are automatically transferred from savings to cheque accounts as needed to cover cheques.

   e. A crackdown reduces the illegal drug trade (which is carried out largely in currency).

2. Figure 7.1 shows that, before the 1980s, M1

velocity in the UK generally rose over time. Suggest some explanations for this upward trend.

3. The prisoner-of-war camp described by Radford (Box 7.1) periodically received large shipments of cigarettes from the Red Cross or other sources.

   a. How did cigarette shipments affect the price level (the prices of goods in terms of cigarettes) in the POW camp?

   b. (More difficult) On some occasions the prisoners knew in advance when the cigarette shipments were to arrive. What happened to the demand for cigarette money and the price level in the camp in the days just before an anticipated shipment?

4. Assume that prices and wages adjust rapidly so that the markets for labour, goods, and assets are always in equilibrium. What are the effects of each of the following on output, the real interest rate, and the current price level?

   a. A temporary increase in government purchases.

   b. A reduction in expected inflation.

   c. A temporary increase in labour supply.

   d. An increase in the interest rate paid on money.

CHAPTER 8

HOUSEHOLD DECISIONS TO CONSUME, SAVE, AND WORK: A MORE FORMAL TREATMENT[1]

The focus of macroeconomics is on aggregate quantities such as GDP, national saving, investment, and employment. However, you must not lose sight of the fact that these aggregate quantities reflect the individual decisions of millions of people, from assembly-line workers to corporate executives to homemakers to government officials. One useful strategy for trying to understand the behaviour of aggregate quantities is to think about the forces that affect the economic behaviour of individuals and firms.

We have already analysed the economic behaviour of firms. In Chapter 3 we looked at firms' decisions about how much labour to employ and how much output to produce; in Chapter 4 we examined firms' decisions about how much capital to use. In this chapter we focus on the economic behaviour of households (individuals and families). Although we discussed household economic behaviour in general terms earlier, here we use some tools from microeconomics to examine certain aspects of household decision making in greater detail. These decisions are the ones having the greatest macroeconomic significance: the household's choices about how much to consume, how much to save, and how much to work.

As you might expect, the main conclusions that we draw in this chapter about household economic behaviour are not much different from those reached in our earlier, briefer discussions. The principal benefit of this chapter's more formal approach is not a new set of conclusions but rather a deeper insight into the factors affecting household economic behaviour and clarification of some ongoing controversies. The chapter will also give you a sense of

---

1. This chapter is optional; it can be used alone or to supplement Chapters 3 and 4. See the Preface for additional information and suggestions.

some of the methods that professional economists use in economic analysis and research, and as a basis for policy advice.

8.1 CONSUMPTION AND SAVING: THE PRESENT VERSUS THE FUTURE

Let us begin by taking a closer look at the household's decision about how much of its income to consume and how much to save. (Recall from Chapter 4 that, because saving is the portion of income left after the household decides how much to consume, the decisions about how much to consume and how much to save are really two aspects of the same decision.) We have already stressed the significance of the consumption–saving decision from the macro-economic perspective. For example, in Chapter 5 we discussed the close link between national saving and the trade balance. In Chapter 6 we demonstrated that the national saving rate is one of the primary factors that determines a country's long-run standard of living.

Why do people save? Recall from Chapter 4 that the benefit of saving is that, by putting some of its income aside today, a household increases its ability to consume in the future. The cost of saving is that the household must reduce the amount of consumption that it presently enjoys. Thus, fundamentally, in choosing how much to consume and save today the household is making a trade-off between the present and the future. In this section we present an economic model of this trade-off. To illustrate how the model works, we follow the fortunes of an individual consumer named Prudence.

To keep the analysis of the model manageable, we make three simplifying assumptions. (At various points in the chapter we discuss the implications for our analysis of dropping each of these assumptions.)

1. We assume that the time horizon over which Prudence makes her plans (her 'lifetime') consists of only two periods: the present, or current, period and the future period. You might think of the two periods as corresponding to Prudence's working years and her retirement years, for example. A two-period model is the simplest framework that captures the essential idea of a trade-off between the present and the future.

2. We assume that Prudence takes her current and future income and her wealth as given, ignoring the possibility that, by working overtime or taking on a second job, she might be able to increase her income. In Section 8.4 we discuss what happens when Prudence can vary the amount of labour she supplies.

3. We assume that Prudence can choose how much to borrow or save at a given real interest rate. For now we ignore the facts that consumers typically have to pay a higher real interest rate to borrow than they can earn on their savings and that in practice lenders may restrict the amount that consumers can borrow. Later we discuss how Prudence's behaviour might change when limits are placed on how much she can borrow.

How Much Can the Consumer Afford? The Budget Constraint

To analyse Prudence's decision about how much to consume and save, we first examine how her economic resources determine the choices available to her. To have some specific numbers to work with, let's suppose that Prudence receives a fixed after-tax income, measured in real terms[2], of 14,000 in the current period and expects to receive a real income of 11,000 in the future period. In addition, she begins the current period with real wealth of 6000 in a savings account.

Next, we list the symbols used to represent Prudence's situation. We used capital letters as symbols for aggregate variables in earlier chapters, so we use lower-case letters for an individual's variables:

y = Prudence's current real income (14,000);
y^f = Prudence's future real income (11,000);
a = Prudence's real wealth (assets) at the beginning of the current period (6000);
a^f = Prudence's real wealth at the beginning of the future period (not yet determined);
c = Prudence's current real consumption (not yet determined);
c^f = Prudence's future real consumption (not yet determined).

Many different combinations of current and future consumption – that is, of c and c^f – are available to Prudence. Here is one possibility: in the current period she could consume all her initial wealth (6000) plus all her current income (14,000), for a total (real) consumption of 20,000. If she did so, in the future period Prudence would be able to consume 11,000, her future income. Thus one consumption combination available to Prudence is

$$c = 20,000 \quad \text{and} \quad c^f = 11,000$$

If Prudence makes this particular consumption choice, how much does she save in the first period? Saving, s, is current income minus current consumption, or

$$s = y - c$$
$$= 14,000 - 20,000 = -6000 \qquad (8.1)$$

Hence Prudence's saving (−6000) is negative; the term for negative saving is *dissaving*. Here, Prudence dissaves by spending her initial wealth *and* all her current income. She could have consumed even more – and dissaved even more – in the current period by borrowing and repaying the loan in the future.

In general, any amount of current consumption c that Prudence chooses will determine the amount of future consumption c^f that she will be able to enjoy. To work out the relationship between Prudence's current consumption and her future consumption, we note first that the funds that Prudence has on hand in the current period are her current income y and her initial wealth a. If her current consumption is c, at the end of the current period she has $y + a - c$ left.

---

2. The units in which Prudence's income is measured are base-year currency units. Or you can think of a world in which there is only one good, say hamburgers, which provides the unit of measurement.

Prudence can put these leftover current resources in the bank to earn interest. If the real interest rate that Prudence can earn on her deposit is r, the real value of her bank account (principal plus interest) in the future period will be $(y + a - c)(1 + r)$. The amount $(y + a - c)(1 + r)$ corresponds to a^f, Prudence's assets at the beginning of the future period.

In the future period the funds available to Prudence consist of her assets a^f plus the income she receives in the future period y^f, for a total of $(y + a - c)(1 + r) + y^f$. Because the future period is the last period of Prudence's 'life' (and there is no one whom she wants to leave an inheritance to), she spends all her remaining resources on consumption. Thus Prudence's future consumption c^f is

$$c^f = (y + a - c)(1 + r) + y^f \qquad (8.2)$$

Equation (8.2) is called the consumer's budget constraint. For any level of current consumption c, the **budget constraint** indicates how much future consumption c^f Prudence can afford, based on her current and future income and initial wealth.[3]

Some sample calculations using the budget constraint, under the assumption that the real interest rate r equals 10%, are shown in Table 8.1. Column (1) shows different values of current consumption c that Prudence might choose.

---

3. In our derivation of equation (8.2), we assumed that Prudence's current consumption was less than her total current resources so that she had some resources left to deposit in the bank. However, the budget constraint, equation (8.2), still works if Prudence's current consumption exceeds her total current resources so that she must borrow from the bank. See Analytical Problem 2 at the end of the chapter.

Table 8.1   Consumption Combinations Available to Prudence

y = current real income = 14,000.
y^f = expected future real income = 11,000.
a = initial real wealth or assets = 6000.
r = real interest rate = 10%.

(1) Current Consumption, c	(2) Saving, $s = y - c$	(3) Leftover Current Resources, $y - c + a$	(4) Future Assets, $a^f = (y - c + a) \times (1 + r)$	(5) Future Consumption, $c^f = a^f + y^f$	
0	14,000	20,000	22,000	33,000	A
5,000	9,000	15,000	16,500	27,500	B
10,000	4,000	10,000	11,000	22,000	C
15,000	−1,000	5,000	5,500	16,500	D
20,000	−6,000	0	0	11,000	E
25,000	−11,000	−5,000	−5,500	5,500	F
30,000	−16,000	−10,000	−11,000	0	G

The letters in the final column correspond to the lettered points in Figure 8.1.

Column (2) shows the implied level of current saving s, or current income y minus current consumption c. Column (3) gives the total amount of current resources left, $y - c + a$, after Prudence enjoys her current consumption. Prudence's wealth at the beginning of period 2, a^f (column 4), equals leftover current resources times $1 + r$ (negative values of a^f imply that Prudence enters the second period in debt). Finally, future consumption (column 5) equals Prudence's wealth at the beginning of the future period a^f, plus future income y^f.[4] Future consumption can be calculated directly from the budget constraint, equation (8.2).

The Budget Line

The **budget line** is the graph of the budget constraint, equation (8.2); it shows the combinations of current and future consumption that Prudence can afford, based on her current and future income, her initial level of wealth, and the real interest rate. Figure 8.1 shows Prudence's budget line, with current consumption c on the horizontal axis and future consumption c^f on the vertical axis. The possible consumption combinations calculated in Table 8.1 appear as points A–G on the budget line.

Figure 8.1 shows that the budget line slopes downwards, which reflects the trade-off between current and future consumption. If Prudence increases her current consumption by one unit, her saving falls by one unit; and because

---

4. We do not include in future income y^f the interest that Prudence earns on her saving. Future income y^f includes only labour income or transfers received, such as social security payments.

Figure 8.1
The budget line
The budget line shows the combinations of current and future consumption c and c^f available to Prudence, as presented in Table 8.1. Each lettered point corresponds to a consumption combination in Table 8.1. The slope of the budget line is $-(1 + r)$ $= -1.10$. The slope equals $-(1 + r)$ because each extra unit of current consumption implies one less unit of saving; savings earn interest at rate r, so each unit reduction in saving in turn implies a reduction of $1 + r$ units in Prudence's future consumption.

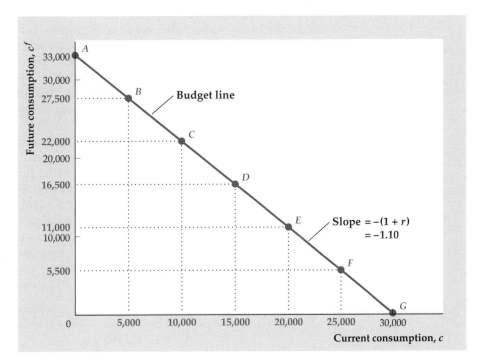

saving earns interest at rate r, a one-unit decline in saving today implies that Prudence's future wealth – and thus her future consumption – will be lower by $1 + r$ units. Because an increase in current consumption by one unit lowers future consumption by $1 + r$ units, the slope of the budget line is $-(1 + r)$. In our numerical example the real interest rate is 10%, so the slope of the budget line in Figure 8.1 is -1.10.

Present Values

To describe Prudence's budget constraint seemingly requires four separate quantities: Prudence's current income y, her future income y^f, her initial wealth a, and the real interest rate r. However, by using the present value concept, we can conveniently summarize Prudence's economic resources, both current and future, with a single number.

Present value measures the value of payments to be made in the future in terms of today's currency or goods. To illustrate, suppose that you know that you must make a payment of £13,200 one year from now. How much money would you have to put aside today so that you could make that future payment? The answer to this question is the present value of £13,200.

The present value of a future payment depends on the interest rate. If the current nominal interest rate i is 10% per year, the present value of £13,200 to be paid one year from now is £12,000. The reason is that £12,000 deposited in the bank today at a 10% interest rate will earn £1200 (10% of £12,000) of interest in one year, which added to the initial £12,000 equals £13,200. Therefore at an interest rate of 10%, having £13,200 one year from now is economically equivalent to having £12,000 today.

More generally, if the nominal interest rate is i per year, each pound in the bank today is worth $1 + i$ pounds one year from now. To have £13,200 one year from now requires £13,200/$(1 + i)$ in the bank today; thus the present value of £13,200 to be paid one year from now is £13,200/$(1 + i)$. So, as we have already shown, if $i = 10\%$ per year, the present value of £13,200 one year from now is £13,200/1.10 = £12,000. If $i = 20\%$ per year, the present value of £13,200 one year in the future is £13,200/1.20 = £11,000. Hence an increase in the interest rate reduces the present value of a future payment; the higher the interest rate is, the less must be put aside today to attain that amount in the future.[5]

In this discussion we have measured future payments in nominal, or currency, terms. When future payments are measured in nominal terms, the appropriate interest rate for calculating present values is the nominal interest rate i. If future payments are measured in real terms, present values are calculated exactly the same way, except that the real interest rate r rather than the nominal interest rate i is used. In analysing Prudence's consumption–saving decision, we are measuring everything in real terms, so we use the real interest rate r to calculate the present values of Prudence's future income and consumption.

---

5. Our examples consider only payments due in one year, but present values can be calculated for payments at any time in the future. See Numerical Problem 2 at the end of the chapter.

Present Value and the Budget Constraint

We now use the concept of present value to restate Prudence's budget constraint in a convenient form. We define the **present value of lifetime resources (PVLR)** as the present value of the income the consumer expects to receive in current and future periods plus initial wealth. In the two-period case the present value of lifetime resources is

$$PVLR = y + \frac{y^f}{1+r} + a \tag{8.3}$$

which is the sum of Prudence's current income, y,[6] the present value of her future income, $y^f/(1+r)$, and her current wealth, a.

Using the $PVLR$ concept, we restate the budget constraint as follows: the present value of lifetime consumption ($PVLC$) must equal the present value of lifetime resources ($PVLR$).

Let us show that this restatement of the budget constraint holds for our example. Recall that Prudence has $y = 14,000$, $y^f = 11,000$, and $a = 6000$. With a real interest rate r of 10%, Prudence's $PVLR$ is $14,000 + 11,000/1.10 + 6000$, or 30,000 (see equation 8.3). According to the budget constraint, therefore, the present value of current and future consumption at any point on her budget line is 30,000. At point E in Figure 8.1, for example, $c = 20,000$ and $c^f = 11,000$. The present value of c is 20,000 and the present value of c^f is $11,000/1.10 = 10,000$; thus the present value of lifetime consumption at E is $20,000 + 10,000 = 30,000$, the same as Prudence's $PVLR$. As you may verify, the present value of lifetime consumption equals 30,000 at every point along the budget line in Figure 8.1.

The restatement of the budget constraint in terms of present values may also be shown algebraically. First, we divide both sides of equation (8.2) by $(1 + r)$ and then add c to both sides to get

$$c + \frac{c^f}{1+r} = y + \frac{y^f}{1+r} + a \tag{8.4}$$

$$PVLC = PVLR.$$

Equation (8.4) states that the present value of lifetime consumption, $c + c^f/(1 + r)$, equals the present value of lifetime resources, $y + y^f/(1 + r) + a$.

In terms of Figure 8.1, and indeed for any graph of the budget line, the $PVLR$ equals the value of current consumption, c, at the horizontal intercept of the budget line. To understand why, note that the horizontal intercept is the point on the budget line at which future consumption c^f equals zero. Setting future consumption c^f at zero in equation (8.4) yields current consumption c on the left-hand side, which must equal the $PVLR$ on the right-hand side. Thus $c = PVLR$ at the horizontal intercept of the budget line. In our numerical example the budget line's horizontal intercept (point G in Figure 8.1) occurs at $c = 30,000$, which is the same as the value of Prudence's $PVLR$.

---

6. Note that the present value of current income is just current income.

What Does the Consumer Want? Consumer Preferences

The budget constraint, represented graphically as the budget line, shows the combinations of current and future consumption *available* to Prudence. To determine which of the many possible consumption combinations Prudence will actually choose, we need to know something about Prudence's preferences for current versus future consumption.

Economists use the term **utility** to describe the satisfaction or well-being of an individual. Preferences about current versus future consumption are summarized by how much utility a consumer obtains from each combination of current and future consumption.

We can graphically represent Prudence's preferences for current versus future consumption by using indifference curves. An **indifference curve** shows all consumption combinations that yield the same level of utility. Because Prudence is equally happy with all consumption combinations on an indifference curve, she does not care (that is, she is indifferent) about which combination she actually gets. Figure 8.2 shows two of Prudence's indifference curves. Because the consumption combinations corresponding to points X, Y, and Z are all on the same indifference curve (IC^1), Prudence would obtain the same level of utility at X, Y, and Z.

Indifference curves have three important properties, each of which has an economic interpretation, and each of which appears in Figure 8.2.

1. *Indifference curves slope downward from left to right.* To understand why, let us suppose that Prudence has selected the consumption combination at point Y, where $c = 15,000$ and $c^f = 15,000$.[7] Now suppose that Prudence must reduce her current consumption to $c = 13,000$. Clearly, if she reduces current consumption while maintaining future consumption, she will suffer a reduction in utility. However, Prudence can be compensated for this reduction in current consumption by increasing her future consumption. Suppose that, if her future consumption is increased to $c^f = 21,000$ while her current consumption is reduced to $c = 13,000$ so that she moves to point X, her level of utility remains unchanged. If this is true, she is indifferent between the consumption combinations at X and Y because the higher level of future consumption at X makes up for the lower level of current consumption at X. In general, any change in the level of current consumption must be accompanied by a change in the *opposite* direction in the level of future consumption in order to keep Prudence's level of utility unchanged. Thus indifference curves, which represent consumption combinations with equal levels of utility, must slope downwards from left to right.

2. *Indifference curves that are farther up and to the right represent higher levels of utility.* Consider for example point W, which lies above and to the right of point Y in Figure 8.2. Both current consumption and future consumption are higher at W than at Y. Because Prudence obtains utility from both current and

---

7. Point Y lies below Prudence's budget line shown in Figure 8.1, which means that not only could Prudence afford this consumption combination, but she would have resources left over at the end of the future period. Unless she wants to leave a bequest, she would not actually choose such a combination for the resources shown in Figure 8.1.

Figure 8.2
Indifference curves
All points on an indifference curve represent consumption combinations that yield the same level of utility. Indifference curves slope downward because a consumer can be compensated for a reduction in current consumption by an appropriate increase in future consumption. All points on IC^2 represent consumption combinations that are preferred to all consumption combinations represented by points on IC^1. Indifference curves are bowed toward the origin to reflect the consumption-smoothing motive. Prudence prefers the consumption combination at point W, which is an average of the combinations at points X and Z because W represents a smoother pattern of consumption. Thus the indifference curve containing W (IC^2) lies above and to the right of the indifference curve containing X, Y, and Z (IC^1).

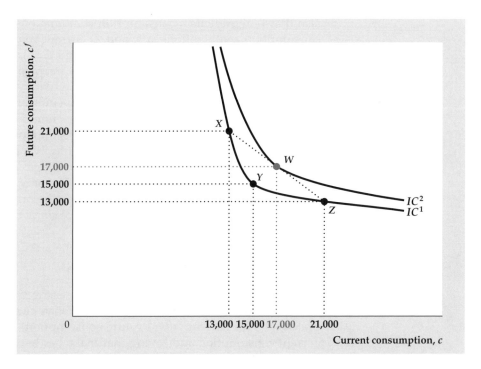

future consumption, W offers a higher level of utility than does Y: that is, Prudence prefers W to Y. In fact, as all points on the indifference curve IC^1 yield the same level of utility as Y, Prudence prefers W to all points on the indifference curve IC^1. Furthermore, as all points on indifference curve IC^2 yield the same level of utility as W, Prudence prefers all points on IC^2 to all points on IC^1. In general, for any two indifference curves, consumers prefer consumption combinations on the indifference curve that is above and to the right of the other indifference curve.

3. *Indifference curves are bowed towards the origin.* This characteristic shape of indifference curves for current and future consumption captures the common-sense idea that most consumers prefer relatively smooth consumption over time to having large amounts of consumption in one period and small amounts in the other. For example, most people would rather have a moderate lunch on both Tuesday and Wednesday to the alternative of stuffing themselves on Tuesday and having only a slice of bread on Wednesday. Similarly, most people would prefer a moderate living standard during both their working lives and their retirement to an alternative of opulence during their working lives and poverty during retirement. This preference for relatively smooth consumption is known as the **consumption-smoothing motive.**

We can illustrate the link between the shape of indifference curves and the consumption-smoothing motive by considering the following three consumption combinations in Figure 8.2: point X ($c = 13,000$; $c^f = 21,000$), point W ($c = 17,000$; $c^f = 17,000$), and point Z ($c = 21,000$; $c^f = 13,000$). Note that W corresponds to complete consumption smoothing, with equal consumption in both periods. In contrast, X and Z represent consumption combinations with large changes in consumption between the first period and the second period. Note also that W represents a consumption combination that is the average of the consumption combinations at X and Z: current consumption at W, 17,000, is the average of current consumption at X and Z (13,000 and 21,000); similarly, future consumption at W, also 17,000, is the average of future consumption at X and Z (21,000 and 13,000).

Even though point W is essentially an average of points X and Z, and Prudence is indifferent between X and Z, she prefers W to X and Z because W represents much 'smoother' (more even) consumption. Graphically, Prudence's preference for W over X and Z is indicated by W's position above and to the right of indifference curve IC^1 (which runs through X and Z). Note that W lies on a straight line drawn between X and Z. The only way that W can lie above and to the right of IC^1 is if IC^1 bows towards the origin, as depicted in Figure 8.2. Thus the bowed shape of the indifference curve captures the consumption-smoothing motive.

The Optimal Level of Consumption

Combining Prudence's budget line (which describes Prudence's available consumption combinations) and her indifference curves (which describe her preferences for current versus future consumption), we can find the levels of current consumption and saving that make her happiest. This best available, or *optimal,* level of current consumption and saving is represented graphically by the point at which Prudence's budget line is tangent to an indifference curve, shown as point D in Figure 8.3.

How do we know that Prudence achieves her highest possible level of satisfaction, or utility, at point D? First, note that D lies on indifference curve IC^*, which means that all consumption combinations on IC^* yield the same level of

**Figure 8.3
The optimal consumption combination**

The optimal (highest-utility) combination of current and future consumption is represented by the point of tangency between the budget line and an indifference curve (point D). All other points on the budget line, such as B and E, lie on indifference curves below and to the left of indifference curve IC^* and thus yield lower utility than the consumption combination at D, which lies on IC^*. Prudence would prefer the consumption combination at point T to the one at D, but as T lies above the budget line she can't afford the consumption combination that T represents.

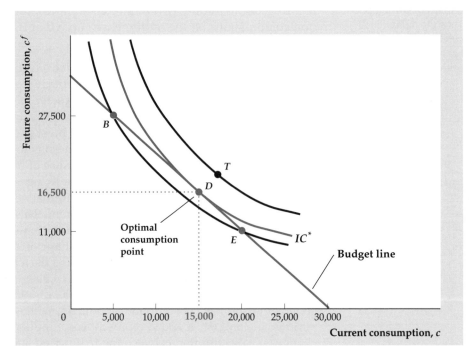

utility as D. All points on Prudence's budget line other than point D – points such as B and E – lie on indifference curves that are below and to the left of IC^*. Thus the consumption combinations represented by all these other points yield a lower level of utility than the consumption combination at D. Prudence would prefer the consumption combination represented by a point such as T in Figure 8.3 to the consumption combination represented by D, because T lies on an indifference curve above and to the right of IC^*; however, because T also lies above the budget line, Prudence cannot afford the consumption combination represented by that point. With her budget constraint, Prudence cannot do any better than D.

We conclude that Prudence's utility-maximizing consumption and saving choice is represented by point D, where her budget line is tangent to an indifference curve. Here, her optimal level of current consumption is 15,000, and her optimal level of future consumption is 16,500. Prudence's choice of current consumption automatically determines her current saving. Her optimal saving s equals her current income (14,000) minus her optimal current consumption:

$$s = y - c = 14,000 - 15,000 = -1000$$

Thus Prudence chooses to dissave (decrease her initial assets) by 1000. As Table 8.1 shows, if Prudence dissaves 1000 in the current period, she will be able to consume 16,500 in the future period, consistent with her consumption plan, represented by point D.

8.2 THE EFFECTS OF CHANGES IN INCOME AND WEALTH ON CONSUMPTION AND SAVING

Two key factors that affect consumption and saving are the levels of income and wealth in an economy. In Chapter 4 we discussed generally the linkage between these variables and household decisions. In this section we use our model of consumer behaviour to examine it further. The formal model provides a helpful insight: *the effect on consumption of a change in current income, expected future income, or wealth depends only on how that change affects the consumer's present value of lifetime resources, or PVLR.*

An Increase in Current Income

Let's begin by analysing the effects on consumption and saving of a change in *current income*. Suppose that Prudence receives a bonus at work of 4000, which raises her current real income from 14,000 to 18,000. Her initial assets (6000), future income (11,000), and the real interest rate (10%) are unchanged; hence the increase of 4000 in current income implies an equal increase in Prudence's present value of lifetime resources, or *PVLR*. If she has not yet committed herself to her original consumption–saving plan, how might Prudence revise that plan in light of her increased current income?

We use the graph in Figure 8.4 to answer this question. In Figure 8.4, BL^1 is Prudence's original budget line, and point D, where $c = 15,000$ and $c^f = 16,500$, represents Prudence's original, pre-bonus consumption plan. Prudence's bonus will allow her to consume more, both currently and in the future, so the increase in her income causes her budget line to shift. To see exactly how the budget line shifts, note that the increase of 4000 in Prudence's current income implies that her *PVLR* also increases by 4000. Because the horizontal intercept of the budget line occurs at $c = PVLR$, the bonus shifts the horizontal intercept to the right by 4000. The slope of the budget line, $-(1 + r)$, remains unchanged because the real interest rate r is unchanged. Thus the increase in current income of 4000 causes a parallel shift of the budget line to the right by 4000, from BL^1 to BL^2.

That shift demonstrates graphically that, after receiving her bonus, Prudence can enjoy greater current and future consumption. Two particular consumption combinations now available are represented by points H and K on the new budget line BL^2. At H, which lies directly above point D, Prudence's current consumption is unchanged from what it was at D, but her future consumption is higher by 4400. To reach H, Prudence must save all of her bonus, then use both the bonus and the interest of 400 earned on the bonus to increase future consumption. An alternative possibility is represented by K, where future consumption is unchanged from that at D but current consumption has risen by 4000. To reach K, Prudence must spend all of her bonus on current consumption, saving none of it for the future.

Both H (save all of the bonus) and K (save none of the bonus) represent extreme strategies for Prudence. If Prudence has a consumption-smoothing motive, she will use her bonus *both* to increase her current consumption and (by saving part of her bonus) to increase future consumption. If her indifference curves are as shown in Figure 8.4, she will move to J, where her new budget line, BL^2, is tangent to the indifference curve IC^{**}. At J, current consumption $c = 17,000$, future consumption $c^f = 18,700$, and saving $s = 18,000 - 17,000 = 1000$. Both current and future consumption are higher at J than at D (where $c = 15,000$ and

Figure 8.4
An increase in income or wealth
An increase in current income, future income, and/or initial wealth that raises Prudence's *PVLR* by 4000 causes the budget line to make a parallel shift to the right by 4000, from BL^1 to BL^2. If Prudence's original consumption plan was to consume at point D, she could move to point H by spending all the increase on future consumption and none on current consumption; or she could move to point K by spending all the increase on current consumption and none on future consumption. However, if Prudence has a consumption-smoothing motive she will move to point J, which has both higher current consumption and higher future consumption than D. Point J is optimal because it lies where the new budget line BL^2 is tangent to an indifference curve, IC^{**}.

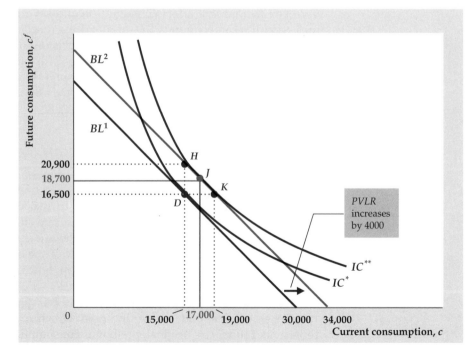

$c^f = 16,500$). Prudence's current saving of 1000 at J is higher than her saving was at D (where she dissaved by 1000) because the increase in her current consumption of 2000 is less than the increase in her current income of 4000. This example demonstrates the conclusion of Chapter 4 – that an increase in current income raises both current consumption and current saving.

An Increase in Future Income

Suppose that Prudence does not get her bonus of 4000 in the current period, so that her current income y remains at its initial level of 14,000. Instead, because of an improved company pension plan, she learns that her future income will increase by 4400, so y^f rises from 11,000 to 15,400. How will this good news affect Prudence's current consumption and saving?

At a real interest rate of 10%, the improvement in the pension plan increases the present value of Prudence's future income by 4400/1.10, or 4000. So, as in the case of the current-period bonus just discussed, the improved pension plan raises Prudence's $PVLR$ by 4000 and causes a parallel shift of the budget line to the right by that amount. The effects on current and future consumption are therefore exactly the same as they were for the increase of 4000 in current income (and Figure 8.4 applies equally well here).

Although increases in current income and expected future income that are equal in present value will have the same effects on current and planned future consumption, the effects of these changes on current saving are different. We showed that an increase in current income raises current saving. In contrast, because the increase in future income raises current consumption (by 2000, in this example) but does not affect current income, it causes saving to fall (by 2000, from −1000 to −3000). Prudence knows that she will be receiving more income in the future, so she has less need to save today.

An Increase in Wealth

Changes in wealth also affect consumption and saving. Suppose that, while rummaging through her attic, Prudence unexpectedly finds a passbook for a savings account that her grandmother had opened for her. When Prudence checks with the bank, she learns that the real value of the account is 4000. How will this unexpected increase in wealth affect Prudence's consumption and saving?

Our work so far makes this analysis easy. As in the cases of current and future income, the effect of a change in wealth on consumption depends only on how much the $PVLR$ changes. In this example, the increase in wealth of 4000 raises the $PVLR$ by 4000; thus its effect on consumption must be the same as that of an increase in current income of 4000 or that of an increase in future income of 4400, each of which also raises the $PVLR$ by 4000. Again, we use Figure 8.4. Prudence's increase in wealth raises her $PVLR$ by 4000 and thus shifts the budget line to the right by 4000, from BL^1 to BL^2. As before, her optimal consumption choice goes from point D (before she finds the passbook) to point J (after her increase in wealth). Because the increase in wealth raises current consumption (from 15,000 at D to 17,000 at J) but leaves current income (14,000) unchanged, it results in a decline in current saving (from −1000 at D to −3000 at J). Being wealthier, Prudence does not have to save as much of her current income (actually, she is increasing her dissaving) in order to provide for the future.

The preceding analyses show that changes in current income, future income, and initial wealth all lead to parallel shifts of the budget line by the amount that they change the *PVLR*. Thus the effect of any of these changes on current and future consumption may be summarized by their effect on the *PVLR*. Economists use the term **income effect** to describe the impact of any change that causes a parallel shift of the budget line. Because increases in current income, future income, or wealth raise current and future consumption, the income effect on current and future consumption is positive.

The Permanent Income Theory

Some increases in income – winning money in a competition or getting a one-off bonus at work – are purely one-shot, or temporary, increases. Other increases in income, such as finding a new long-term job at a higher salary, are permanent. Our analysis implies that consumption and saving will react differently to these two types of change.

In terms of our model, a temporary increase in income represents a rise in current income y, with future income y^f held constant. In contrast, a permanent increase in income raises *both* current income y *and* future income y^f. Therefore a permanent one-unit increase in income leads to a larger increase in the *PVLR* than does a temporary one-unit increase in income.

Because income changes affect consumption only to the extent that they lead to changes in the *PVLR*, our theory predicts that a permanent one-unit increase in income will raise current and future consumption more than a temporary one-unit increase in income will. Equivalently, because current consumption rises more when an income increase is permanent, the amount saved from a permanent increase in income will be less than the amount saved from a temporary increase in income.

This distinction between the effects of permanent and temporary income changes is emphasized in the **permanent income theory** of consumption and saving, developed in the 1950s by Nobel laureate Milton Friedman.[8] He pointed out that income should affect consumption only through the *PVLR* in a many-period version of the model we present here. Thus permanent changes in income, because they last for many periods, may have much larger effects on consumption than temporary changes in income. As a result, temporary income increases would be mostly saved, and permanent income increases would be mostly consumed.

Friedman also provided some of the first empirical evidence for this theory. For example, he found that the consumption of farm families on average responded less to changes in income than did the consumption of non-farm families. Friedman's explanation was that, as farm incomes depend heavily on weather and crop prices, both of which are volatile, changes in farm incomes are much more likely to be temporary than are changes in non-farm incomes. Current changes in farm incomes have a smaller effect on the *PVLR* and therefore have a smaller effect on current consumption.

8. Friedman, *A Theory of the Consumption Function,* (Princeton University Press, 1957).

APPLICATION

Aggregate Consumption During Recessions

Recessions are periods during which real GDP declines (or grows very slowly) so that consumers' real incomes also decline. However, recessions are usually short-lived, and the losses in income suffered by consumers are to some degree temporary.[9] If the declines in GDP during recessions are at least partly temporary, the permanent income theory predicts that aggregate consumption should fall by less than GDP falls when the economy turns down. More generally, if output fluctuations are partly temporary, the theory predicts that aggregate consumption should be 'smoother' than real GDP, reflecting the consumption-smoothing motive of consumers.

Figure 8.5 shows the behaviour of real GDP and real aggregate consumption, excluding spending on consumer durables, in France and the UK for the

9. There is some debate about how much of the decline in income in a typical recession is temporary and how much is permanent. See Box 9.1.

Figure 8.5
Consumption during recessions in France and the UK
The figure shows real GDP and aggregate real consumption, excluding expenditure on consumer durables in France and in the UK. Because of the consumption-smoothing motive, the path of consumption is generally smoother than that of output, and consumption does not fall as sharply as output during recessions.

Source: Data on GDP and consumers expenditure on non-durable goods from *Datastream*.

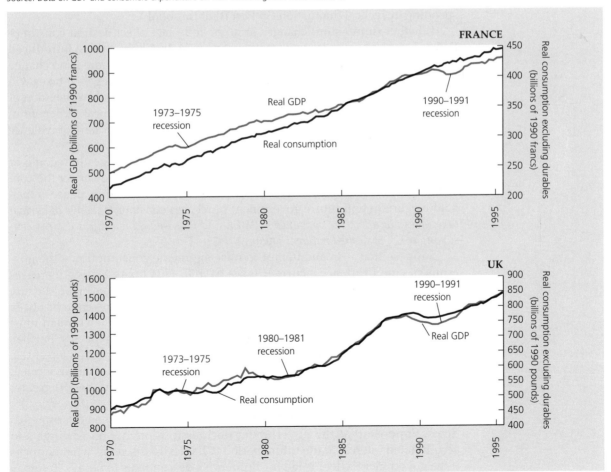

period 1970–96. (We exclude spending on consumer durables from the consumption measure because items such as cars or furniture are not completely consumed during the period in which they are purchased, but instead are used over many years.) The period 1970–96 included three major recessions, in the mid 1970s, in the early 1980s, and in the early 1990s. Figure 8.5 generally confirms the predictions of the permanent income theory that consumption is smoother than output and does not plunge sharply in recessions. Because consumption drops less in recessions than income does, saving must decline during recessions.

Ricardian Equivalence

Although consumption and saving decisions are made by households, there are times when policymakers would like to influence these decisions. For example, as we pointed out in Chapter 6, some economists argue that in both the UK and Scandanavia consumption is 'too high' and national saving is 'too low' relative to what is needed to provide a high living standard in the long run. Many of those who make this argument go on to suggest that higher taxes are needed to depress desired consumption, C^d, and raise desired national saving, $Y - C^d - G$. At times, such as during recessions, others have proposed that taxes be cut to stimulate consumer spending (we discuss the role of spending in cyclical fluctuations in Part III of this book).

Whether (lump-sum) changes in taxes do in fact affect desired consumption is a controversial issue in macroeconomics. In Chapter 4 we introduced the Ricardian equivalence proposition, which states that, if there is no change in current or planned government purchases, lump-sum changes in taxes will *not* affect desired consumption or desired national saving. Our explanation of this proposition in Chapter 4 was intuitive rather than analytical. A benefit of the analysis of this chapter is that we can now explain Ricardian equivalence both precisely and simply.

The most significant result of this analysis is that changes in income or wealth affect desired consumption only to the extent that they affect the consumer's *PVLR*. The point made by advocates of Ricardian equivalence is that, holding current and future government purchases constant, *a change in current taxes does not affect the consumer's PVLR and thus should not affect desired consumption, C^d, or desired national saving, $Y - C^d - G$.*

Suppose that – in an attempt to raise aggregate consumption – the government cuts Prudence's current taxes by 100. This tax reduction increases Prudence's current income by 100, which (all else being equal) would cause her to consume more. However, because the government's revenue has been reduced by 100 and its expenditures have not changed, the government must increase its current borrowing from the public by 100 (per taxpayer). Further, the government must pay interest on its borrowings. So if the real interest rate that the government must pay on its debt is 10%, as we have been assuming, in the future period the government's outstanding debt will be 110 greater than it would have been without the tax cut.

As a taxpayer, Prudence is ultimately responsible for the government's debts. Suppose that the government decides to repay its borrowings and accumulated interest in the future period (Chapter 16 discusses what happens if the government's debt is left for Prudence's descendants to repay). To repay its debt plus interest the government must raise taxes in the future period by 110, so Prudence's expected future income falls by 110. Overall, then, the government's tax policy has raised Prudence's current income by 100 but reduced her future income by 110. At a real interest rate of 10%, the present value of the future income change is −100, which cancels out the increase in current income of 100. Thus Prudence's *PVLR* is unchanged by the tax cut, and (as the Ricardian equivalence proposition implies) she should not change her current consumption.

Ricardian equivalence is closely linked to the consumer model presented in this chapter and, in particular, to the idea that consumption should depend only on the *PVLR*. To assess the practical validity of Ricardian equivalence, we need to know how well our model fits the empirical evidence.

Excess Sensitivity and Borrowing Constraints

Many-period versions of our two-period model of consumer behaviour, such as the permanent-income theory, have been extensively tested with empirical data.[10] In general, the model has held up well. A variety of studies confirm that consumption is affected by current income, expected future income, and wealth, and that permanent income changes have larger effects on consumption than do temporary income changes – all of which are implied by the model.

However, not all researchers have accepted a more specific prediction of the model – that the impact of a change in income or wealth on consumption depends only on the change in the *PVLR*. In particular, some studies show that the response of consumption to a change in current income is greater than would be expected based on the effect of the current income change on the *PVLR*. This tendency of consumption to respond to current income more strongly than the model predicts is called the *excess sensitivity* of consumption to current income.[11]

If consumption is in fact 'excessively' sensitive to current income, what is the explanation? One possibility is that people are more short-sighted than assumed for the model and do not always think about their future prospects when making current consumption and saving decisions. Another possibility, which is more in the spirit of the model, is that the amount that people can borrow is limited.

In developing our two-period model of consumption and saving, we assumed that consumers can borrow and lend as much as they desire at a single real interest rate. Realistically, though, banks and other lenders typically restrict the amount that a consumer may borrow.[12] Sometimes they deny credit altogether because they believe that a heavily indebted consumer is

---

10. An extensive survey of the literature is provided by Angus Deaton, *Understanding Consumption* (Oxford University Press, 1992).

11. An important early article that found excess sensitivity was Marjorie Flavin, 'The Adjustment of Consumption to Changing Expectations About Future Income', *Journal of Political Economy*, October 1981, pp. 974–1009.

12. Most consumer borrowing is used to finance purchases of housing or consumer durables. In those cases the consumer has an asset – the house or the durable goods – that the bank can seize if payments are not made on time. In contrast, if the reason for borrowing is to finance a level of current consumption that exceeds current income and assets, the bank may have no assets to take if the payments are not made.

likely to go bankrupt or fail to repay the loan. A restriction imposed by lenders on the amount that someone can borrow against future income is called a **borrowing constraint**.

The effect of a borrowing constraint on a consumer's consumption–saving decision depends on whether the consumer would want to borrow in the absence of a borrowing constraint. If the consumer would not want to borrow even if borrowing were possible, the borrowing constraint is said to be *non-binding*. A non-binding borrowing constraint has no effect on a consumer's consumption or saving behaviour because the consumer does not want to borrow anyway. In contrast, when a consumer wants to borrow but is prevented from doing so, the borrowing constraint is said to be *binding*. In this case, the consumer will spend all available current income and wealth on current consumption in order to come as close as possible to the consumption combination desired in the absence of borrowing constraints.

Now consider the effect on consumption of an increase in current income. Because a consumer facing a binding borrowing constraint spends all her current income and wealth on current consumption, she consumes all of any increase in current income, whether the increase is temporary or permanent. An unconstrained consumer saves part of an increase in current income. Thus the effect of an increase in current income on current consumption is greater for a constrained consumer than for an unconstrained consumer. In macroeconomic terms this result implies that – if a significant number of consumers face binding borrowing constraints – the response of aggregate consumption to an increase in aggregate income (output) will be greater than implied by the basic theory in the absence of borrowing constraints. In other words, if there are borrowing constraints, consumption may be excessively sensitive to current income.

Empirically, how prevalent are borrowing constraints in Europe? We have no direct way of counting how many consumers are constrained from borrowing. However, several studies estimate that, to account for the observed relationship between aggregate consumption and current income, during any one year the percentage of consumers facing binding borrowing constraints ranges from 30% in Sweden to around 90% in France and that differences across countries appear to reflect differences in the development of the market for consumer credit.[13]

8.3   CONSUMPTION AND SAVING OVER MANY PERIODS: THE LIFE-CYCLE MODEL

The two-period model suggests that a significant part of saving is done to pay for retirement. However, the two-period model does not reflect other important aspects of the consumer's lifetime income and consumption patterns. For example, income typically rises over most of a person's working life, and people save for reasons other than retirement. The **life-cycle model** of consumption and

---

13. See, for example, John Y. Campbell and N. Gregory Mankiw, 'The Response of Consumption to Income: A Cross-Country Investigation', *European Economic Review*, 1991, pp. 723–56.

saving, originated in the 1950s by Nobel laureate Franco Modigliani[14] and his associates, extends the two-period model to many periods and focuses on the patterns of income, consumption, and saving throughout an individual's life.

The essence of the life-cycle model is shown in Figure 8.6. In Figure 8.6(a) the typical consumer's patterns of income and consumption are plotted against the consumer's age, from age 20 (the approximate age of economic independence) to age 80 (the approximate age of death). Two points about Figure 8.6(a) are significant.

First, the average worker experiences steadily rising real income, with peak earnings typically occurring between the ages of 50 and 60. After retirement, income (excluding interest earned from previous saving) drops fairly sharply.

---

14. A review of the life-cycle theory is provided by Franco Modigliani, 'Life Cycle, Individual Thrift, and the Wealth of Nations', *American Economic Review*, June 1986, pp. 297–313.

Figure 8.6
Life-cycle consumption, income, and saving
(a) Income and consumption are plotted against age. Income typically rises gradually throughout most of a person's working life and peaks shortly before retirement. The desire for a smooth pattern of consumption means that consumption varies less than income over the life cycle. Consumption here is constant.
(b) Saving is the difference between income and consumption; the saving pattern is hump-shaped. Early in a person's working life consumption is larger than income, so saving is negative. In the middle years saving is positive; the excess of income over consumption is used to repay debts incurred earlier in life and to provide for retirement. During retirement people dissave.

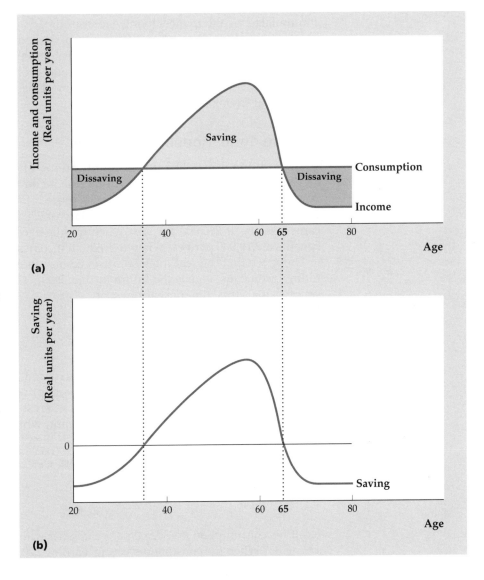

Second, the lifetime pattern of consumption is much smoother than the pattern of income over time, which is consistent with the consumption-smoothing motive discussed earlier. Because consumers do not like large changes in their consumption levels, they spread their lifetime resources to maintain a fairly even standard of living over time. Although shown as perfectly flat in Figure 8.6(a), consumption, in reality, varies somewhat by age: for example, it will be higher during years of high child-rearing expenses. An advantage of using the life-cycle model to study consumption and saving is that it may be easily modified to allow for various patterns of lifetime income and consumption.

The lifetime pattern of saving, shown in Figure 8.6(b), is the difference between the income and consumption curves in Figure 8.6(a). This overall hump-shaped pattern has been confirmed empirically. Saving is minimal or even negative during the early working years, when income is low. Maximum saving occurs when the worker is between 50 and 60, when income is highest. Finally, during retirement there is dissaving, as the consumer draws down accumulated wealth to meet living expenses.

An important implication of the hump-shaped pattern of saving is that national saving rates depend on the age distribution of a country's population. Countries with unusually young or unusually old populations have low saving rates, and countries with relatively more people in their middle years have higher saving rates.

The Life-Cycle Model: An Example

Some additional insight into the implications of the life-cycle model can be gained from a simple example. Imagine a consumer who is 'young' for 20 years, 'middle-aged' for 20 years, and 'retired' for 20 years (after which he dies). He has no initial wealth, earns a salary of £20,000 per year when young, earns a salary of £60,000 per year when middle-aged, and receives retirement benefits of £10,000 per year when retired (all incomes are in real terms).

Suppose that the real interest rate is zero so that the present value of any future income just equals the future income itself. Then the consumer's *PVLR* simply equals total lifetime earnings, or

$$PVLR = \text{total lifetime income}$$
$$= (20 \times £20,000) + (20 \times £60,000) + (20 \times £10,000)$$
$$= £1,800,000$$

Suppose also that the consumer is an extreme 'consumption-smoother': that is, he tries to keep his annual real consumption *c* at a constant level for each of his 60 adult years. With a zero real interest rate, the present value of his consumption is 60*c*. The budget constraint, which states that the present value of consumption must equal the *PVLR*, is therefore

$$\text{present value of consumption} = 60c = PVLR = £1,800,000$$

or, solving for *c*,

$$c = £30,000$$

If his consumption is £30,000 per year, what will the consumer's pattern of saving be? When the consumer is young, earning £20,000 per year and consuming £30,000 per year, his saving will be –£10,000 per year (he will dissave, borrowing to do so). During middle age, he will save £60,000 – £30,000 = £30,000 per year. Finally, during retirement, the consumer will dissave at the rate of £20,000 per year (his saving will be £10,000 – £30,000 = –£20,000 per year).

Bequests and Saving

In both the two-period model and the life-cycle model, we assumed that the consumer plans to spend all his wealth and income during his lifetime, leaving nothing to heirs. Empirically, however, many people leave bequests, or inheritances, to children, charities, and others. What effect does a **bequest motive**, or a desire to leave inheritances, have on saving behaviour?

Let us return to the life-cycle example. Suppose that the consumer does not plan to spend all his economic resources but wants to leave £120,000 to his heirs. Because the consumer's adult life spans 60 years, he can achieve this bequest by reducing consumption and increasing saving by £2000 per year. (Remember that the real interest rate is zero.) We conclude that, to the extent that consumers desire to leave bequests, they will consume less and save more than when they simply consume all their resources during their lifetimes.

APPLICATION

Why Do the Japanese Save So Much?

The Japanese are known for their high saving rate, especially in comparison with the saving rate in most European countries. To some extent, the perceived difference between Japan and Europe may reflect different accounting practices. For example, the Japanese count government investment projects, such as roads, as part of national saving, but European countries do not. Even with corrections, though, the Japanese saving rate seems to be significantly higher.

Numerous explanations for high Japanese saving were examined by Fumio Hayashi of the University of Pennsylvania.[15] Several of these explanations were related to life-cycle factors, including the following:

1. *Population age structure.* The Japanese have among the world's highest life expectancies and thus long expected retirements. To finance these long retirements, they must save more during their working years. The Japanese also had a postwar baby boom, followed by a population growth slowdown, which means that a relatively large proportion of the population is now middle-aged, the peak saving period.

2. *High income growth.* Because of Japan's rapid economic growth during the past 40 years, current Japanese workers earn much higher real incomes than their now-retired parents did when they were working in the 1950s or 1960s. Thus current workers can plan to consume more when they retire than their parents did. This rise in incomes implies that current workers will save much more than current retirees are dissaving, leading to a high aggregate saving rate for the country as a whole.[16]

---

15. 'Why Is Japan's Saving Rate So Apparently High?', in Stanley Fischer, ed., *NBER Macroeconomics Annual* (MIT Press, 1986).
16. Numerical Problem 6 at the end of the chapter further develops the relationship of income growth and saving.

3. *High housing and land prices, including high required downpayments.* Despite recent decreases, Japanese housing prices are fantastically high. Potential home buyers not only must face these high prices but also must make downpayments that in percentage terms are much higher than in most European countries. Thus young people frequently must save for years to buy a home.

4. *High bequests.* Japanese customarily leave large bequests, perhaps because many elderly Japanese live with their children. To be able to leave large bequests, the Japanese must save more during their working lives.

Hayashi's paper discusses these factors in detail. Although all may contribute, his tentative conclusion is that the desire to leave large bequests may be the single most important cause of high Japanese saving.

8.4   THE REAL INTEREST RATE AND THE CONSUMPTION–SAVING DECISION

Until now, we have focused on the effects of changes in income and wealth on consumption and saving, holding constant the real interest rate. Actually, the real interest rate may change sharply, as when it rose from negative values in the late 1970s to over 5% in the early 1980s in some European countries. Government policies, such as tax breaks designed to encourage saving, may also lead to changes in the after-tax real interest rate faced by households, even when the real interest rate itself does not change. Building on our more general discussion in Chapter 4, we now use our model of consumer behaviour to analyse the link between the real interest rate and the amounts that households choose to consume and save.

The Real Interest Rate and Saving in the Two-Period Model

To explore the effects of a change in the real interest rate on consumption and saving, let's return to the two-period model and Prudence's situation. Recall that Prudence initially has current real income y of 14,000, future income y^f of 11,000, initial wealth a of 6000, and faces a real interest rate r of 10% (which should be thought of as the after-tax real interest rate; see Section 4.1). At this real interest rate Prudence's present value of lifetime resources, *PVLR*, is 30,000. Her budget line, which is the same as in Figure 8.1, is shown in Figure 8.7 as BL^1. Now let us see what happens when for some reason the real interest rate jumps from 10% to 76%.[17]

The Real Interest Rate and the Budget Line. To see how Prudence's budget line is affected when the real interest rate rises, let's first consider point E

---

17. A 76% real interest rate is not realistic, but assuming this large a change makes its effects more obvious.

Figure 8.7
The effect of an increase in the real interest rate on the budget line

The figure shows the effect on Prudence's budget line of an increase in the real interest rate r from 10% to 76%. Because the slope of a budget line is $-(1 + r)$ and the initial real interest rate is 10%, the slope of Prudence's initial budget line BL^1 is −1.10. The initial budget line BL^1 also passes through the no-borrowing, no-lending point E, which represents the consumption combination that Prudence obtains by spending all her current income and wealth on current consumption. Because E can still be obtained when the real interest rate rises, it also lies on the new budget line BL^2. However, the slope of BL^2 is −1.76, reflecting the rise in the real interest rate to 76%. Thus the higher real interest rate causes the budget line to pivot clockwise around the no-borrowing, no-lending point.

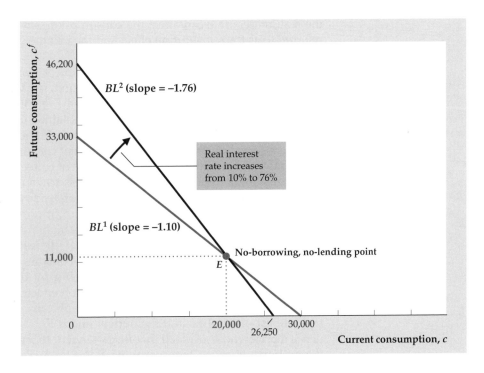

on the budget line BL^1. Point E is special in that it is the only point on the budget line at which current consumption equals current income plus initial wealth ($c = y + a = 20{,}000$) and future consumption equals future income ($c^f = y^f = 11{,}000$). If she chooses this consumption combination, Prudence does not need to borrow (her current income and initial wealth are just enough to pay for her current consumption) nor does she have any current resources left to deposit in (lend to) the bank. Thus E is the **no-borrowing, no-lending point**. Because E involves neither borrowing nor lending, the consumption combination it represents is available to Prudence regardless of the real interest rate. Thus the no-borrowing, no-lending point remains on the budget line when the real interest rate changes.

Next, recall that the budget line's slope is $-(1 + r)$, reflecting the fact that sacrificing one unit of current consumption allows Prudence to increase her future consumption by $(1 + r)$ units. When the real interest rate r jumps from 10% to 76%, the slope of the budget line changes from −1.10 to −1.76: that is, the new budget line is steeper. Knowing one point on the new budget line (E) and the slope of the new budget line (−1.76) is enough information to draw the new budget line, BL^2. Comparing BL^2 to BL^1 shows that an increase in the real interest rate causes the budget line to pivot clockwise around the no-borrowing, no-lending point, E.

The Substitution and Income Effects of a Change in the Real Interest Rate

Because an increase in the real interest rate changes the budget line and thus the combinations of current and future consumption available to Prudence, she may respond by altering the amounts consumed and saved. A change in the real interest rate can affect the consumption–saving decision in two ways, referred to as the substitution effect and the income effect.

The Substitution Effect. If Prudence reduces her consumption by one unit today, thereby increasing her saving by one unit, she will be able to consume $1 + r$ additional units in the future. Thus when the real interest rate r increases, the amount of future consumption that can be obtained in exchange for giving up a unit of current consumption rises. In effect, a higher real interest rate makes future consumption cheaper, relative to current consumption.

In the same way that a drop in the price of coffee relative to the price of tea leads consumers to buy more coffee and less tea, a drop in the price of future consumption relative to current consumption leads consumers to switch from current consumption toward future consumption – that is, they save more. The tendency to save more in response to a higher reward for saving is called the **substitution effect**, because a higher real interest rate causes consumers to substitute future consumption for current consumption. When people argue that a higher real interest rate raises saving by increasing the reward for saving, they are talking about the substitution effect.

The substitution effect is illustrated graphically in Figure 8.8. Initially, the real interest rate is 10% and the budget line is BL^1. Suppose for now that Prudence's preferences are such that BL^1 is tangent to an indifference curve, IC^1, at the no-borrowing, no-lending point, E.[18] At a real interest rate of 10%, then, Prudence chooses the consumption combination at E.

When the real interest rate rises from 10% to 76%, the budget line pivots clockwise to BL^2. Because Prudence's original consumption point, the no-borrowing, no-lending point, E, also lies on the new budget line BL^2, she has the option of remaining at E and enjoying the same combination of current and future consumption after the real interest rate rises. But note that points along BL^2 immediately above and to the left of E lie above and to the right of IC^1. These points represent consumption combinations that are available to Prudence and yield a higher level of utility than the consumption combination at E. Prudence can attain the highest level of utility along BL^2 at point V, where indifference curve IC^2 is tangent to BL^2. In response to the increased incentive to save, Prudence reduces her current consumption, from 20,000 to 17,000, and moves from E to V on BL^2. Prudence's reduction of 3000 in current consumption between E and V is equivalent to an increase of 3000 in saving. The increase in saving between E and V reflects the substitution effect on saving of a higher real interest rate.

The Income Effect. If Prudence's current consumption initially equals her current resources (current income plus initial wealth) so that she is neither a lender nor a borrower, a change in the real interest rate has only a substitution effect on her saving, as shown in Figure 8.8. However, if Prudence's current consumption is initially less than her current resources (so that she has resources to lend), or if her current consumption initially exceeds her current resources (so that she must borrow to pay for her current consumption), a change in the real interest rate has an additional effect (the income effect) on her saving decision.

---

18. Note that Prudence's indifference curves in Figure 8.8 are different from those in Figure 8.4.

Figure 8.8
The substitution effect of an increase in the real interest rate
We assume that Prudence's preferences are such that when the real interest rate is 10% she chooses the consumption combination at the no-borrowing, no-lending point, point E, on the initial budget line BL¹. Point E lies on the indifference curve IC¹. An increase in the real interest rate to 76% causes the budget line to pivot clockwise from BL¹ to BL², as in Fig. 8.7. By substituting future consumption for current consumption along the new budget line BL², Prudence can reach points that lie above and to the right of IC¹; these points represent consumption combinations that yield higher utility than the consumption combination at E. Her highest utility is achieved by moving to point V, where the new budget line BL² is tangent to indifference curve IC². The drop in current consumption (by 3000) and the resulting equal rise in saving that occur in moving from E to V reflect the substitution effect of the increase in the real interest rate.

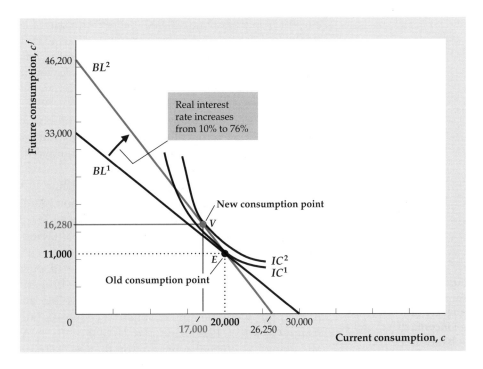

We can illustrate the income effect by supposing that Prudence plans to consume only part of her current income and wealth in the first period, leaving some resources to be deposited in the bank. When the real interest rate rises, as a lender Prudence will be able to earn a higher return, which makes her better off. More precisely, an increase in the real interest rate increases the amount of current and future consumption that a lender can enjoy. Because she is made economically better off by the increase in the real interest rate, Prudence will tend to increase her current consumption and thus save less when the real interest rate rises.

But, if Prudence initially is a borrower, an increase in the real interest rate makes her worse off, because she must pay more interest on any loans that she takes out. Because she is made worse off by the increase in the real interest rate, Prudence will choose to consume less in the first period and thus increase her saving (actually, reduce the amount she dissaves). The tendency of lenders to consume more and save less in response to being economically better off, and of borrowers to consume less and save more in response to being economically worse off, is called the **income effect** of an increase in the real interest rate. For a lender note that the income effect of an increase in the real interest rate works in the opposite direction to the substitution effect, whereas for a borrower the income and substitution effects work in the same direction.

The full impact of an increase in the real interest rate on Prudence's saving, including the substitution and income effects – assuming that Prudence is initially a lender – is shown in Figure 8.9. As before, Prudence's original budget line is BL^1 when the real interest rate is 10%. However, we now assume that Prudence's preferences are such that BL^1 is tangent to an indifference curve, IC^1, at point D. Thus, at a 10% real interest rate, Prudence plans current consumption of 15,000 and future consumption of 16,500. Prudence's current resources equal 20,000 (current income of 14,000 plus initial assets of 6000), so if she enjoys current consumption of 15,000 she will have resources of 5000 to lend. Her chosen point, D, being to the left of the no-borrowing, no-lending point, E (current consumption is lower at D than at E) shows that Prudence is a lender.

The increase in the real interest rate from 10% to 76% causes Prudence's budget line to pivot clockwise through the no-borrowing, no-lending point, E, ending at BL^2 as before. To separate the substitution and income effects of the increase in the real interest rate, think of the movement of the budget line from BL^1 to BL^2 as taking place in two steps.

First, imagine that the original budget line BL^1 pivots clockwise around Prudence's original consumption combination, point D, until it is parallel with the new budget line BL^2 (that is, its slope is -1.76). The resulting intermediate budget line is the dashed line BL^{int}. Second, imagine that BL^{int} makes a parallel shift to the right to BL^2.

The response of Prudence's saving and current consumption to the increase in the real interest rate can also be broken into two steps. First, consider her response to the pivot of the budget line through point D, from BL^1 to BL^{int}. If this were the only change in Prudence's budget line, she would move from D to P ($c = 12,200$ and $c^f = 21,428$) on BL^{int}. At P, she would save more and enjoy less current consumption than at D. The increase in saving between D and P, similar to Prudence's shift from E to V in Figure 8.8, measures the substitution effect on Prudence's saving of the increase in the real interest rate.

Second, consider the effect of the parallel shift from BL^{int} to BL^2. The new budget line BL^2 is tangent to an indifference curve, IC^3, at point Q, so Prudence will choose the consumption combination at Q. Current and future

Figure 8.9
An increase in the real interest rate with both an income effect and a substitution effect
We assume that Prudence initially consumes at point D on the original budget line BL^1. An increase in the real interest rate from 10% to 76% causes the budget line to pivot clockwise from BL^1 to the new budget line BL^2. We break the overall shift of the budget line into two parts: (1) a pivot around the original consumption point, D, to yield an intermediate budget line BL^{int}, and (2) a parallel shift from BL^{int} to the final budget line BL^2. The substitution effect is measured by the movement from the original consumption point, D, to point P on BL^{int}, and the income effect is measured by the movement from P to Q on BL^2. As drawn, the substitution effect is larger than the income effect so that the overall effect is for current consumption to fall and saving to rise.

consumption are higher, and saving is lower, at Q than at P. The increase in current consumption and the decrease in saving between P and Q reflect the income effect of the increase in the real interest rate. Thus, as discussed earlier, income effects occur when a change in some variable causes a parallel shift of the budget line. Because it corresponds to a parallel shift of the budget line, the income effect of a change in the real interest rate on consumption and saving is the same as the effect of a change in income or wealth.

The total change in Prudence's consumption and saving resulting from the rise in the real interest rate is shown in Figure 8.9 as the change in saving between point D and point Q. This change is the sum of the substitution effect, measured by the increase in saving in moving from D to P, and the income effect, measured by the decline in saving in moving from P to Q. As Figure 8.9 is drawn, current consumption is lower and saving is higher at the final point, Q, than at the original point, D. However, we could just as easily draw it so that saving is less at the final point, Q, than at the initial point, D. Thus the theory fails to predict whether Prudence's saving will rise or fall in response to an increase in the real interest rate.

The reason that we cannot say for sure how Prudence's saving will change is that, for the case of a lender analysed in Figure 8.9, the income and substitution effects work in opposite directions; the final result depends on which effect is stronger. In contrast, for a borrower the income and substitution effects work in the same direction (you are asked to show this result in Analytical Problem 5 at the end of the chapter). A higher real interest rate increases a borrower's reward for saving, which tends to make him save more (the substitution effect); and, because a borrower pays rather than receives interest, a higher real interest rate also makes him poorer, leading him to consume less and save more.

To summarize, the two-period model implies that an increase in the real interest rate increases saving by borrowers. However, because of conflicting income and substitution effects, economic theory is not decisive about the effect of the real interest rate on the saving of lenders. In European economies, which of course include both borrowers and lenders, empirical studies show that an increase in the real interest rate tends to increase aggregate saving, although the effect is often found to be relatively small.

APPLICATION

Tax Policy and the Divergence of Canadian and US Private Saving

Because Canada and the USA have similar and closely integrated economies, you might expect private saving in the two countries to be similar. However, an interesting study of aggregate saving behaviour in Canada and the USA by Chris Carroll of the Federal Reserve Board and Lawrence Summers of Harvard University[19] found that, although private saving rates in the two countries moved in parallel over much of the post-World War II period, beginning in about 1971 private saving behaviour in the USA and Canada began to diverge. During the 1970s and early 1980s Canadian private saving surged, but US private saving declined. By the mid 1980s the Canadian private saving rate was substantially higher than the US rate.[20]

---

19. 'Why Have Private Savings Rates in the United States and Canada Diverged?', *Journal of Monetary Economics*, September 1987, pp. 249–79.

Carroll and Summers concluded that differences in general macroeconomic conditions could not explain the differences in saving behaviour between Canada and the USA. Instead, they argued that, relative to US policies, Canadian tax policies have been more favourable towards saving by leading to a higher after-tax real interest rate. They focused on two differences in tax policy.

First, Canada has tax-favoured saving plans (including employer-sponsored Registered Pension Plans, or RPPs, and individual Registered Retirement Savings Plans, or RRSPs), which were expanded substantially in the early 1970s. The Canadian plans allow a significant portion of interest income to go untaxed. The USA has had similar 'tax-sheltered' saving plans, such as Individual Retirement Accounts (IRAs), but these plans were not made widely available until 1981 and were limited after 1986. Because before-tax real interest rates in the USA and Canada were similar in the 1970s and 1980s, the differences in tax policy implied that Canadian savers were able to obtain higher after-tax real interest rates than US savers were, which may help explain why the Canadians saved more.

Second, compared to the Canadian tax system, the US tax system encourages borrowing and consumption, which, of course, reduces saving. In contrast to Canada, where consumers who borrow are not allowed to deduct their interest payments from their taxable incomes, in the USA prior to 1986 all consumer interest payments were tax-deductible.[21] We can demonstrate the effect of this difference in tax laws by comparing two borrowers (one in the USA and one in Canada) both of whom have borrowed $10,000 at a 10% rate of interest and assuming that the US borrower is in a 30% tax bracket. Both borrowers pay $1000 each year in interest, but the US borrower gets to deduct the $1000 from his taxable income, which saves him $300 (30% of $1000) in taxes. After taxes, the US borrower's interest cost is $700 ($1000 less $300 in reduced taxes), for an after-tax nominal interest rate of 7% ($700 divided by the principal of $10,000). The Canadian borrower gets no tax break, so the after-tax interest rate she pays on her loan equals her before-tax interest rate of 10% – three percentage points higher than that of the US borrower. Further, the benefit of tax deductibility of interest to the borrower is highest when interest rates are high, so that the difference in borrowing costs between Canadians and US citizens was greatest in the high-interest-rate periods of the 1970s and early 1980s, when the saving rates diverged most.

In the case of borrowers, the substitution and income effects work in the same direction, and the theory tells us unambiguously that higher after-tax borrowing rates should reduce borrowing and consumption and increase aggregate saving. Thus it is likely that the different tax treatment of borrowers' interest payments contributed to the difference in aggregate saving between the United States and Canada.

---

20. The private saving measure used by Carroll and Summers is net private saving, or private saving less depreciation of capital, divided by GNP. Using this measure, they found that the private saving rate in Canada rose from 7.8% in the 1971–75 period to 11.9% in the 1981–85 period; between the same two periods the US private saving rate fell from 8.7% to 6.2%.

21. The US Tax Reform Act of 1986 began a phase-out of some types of consumer interest deduction. However, mortgage interest is still deductible, as is interest paid on home equity lines of credit.

8.5 THE SUPPLY OF LABOUR: THE INCOME–LEISURE TRADE-OFF

The decision about how much to consume and save is not the only decision made by households that has macroeconomic significance. Equally important is the household's decision about whether and how much to work – that is, how much labour to supply. In Chapter 3 we introduced the concept of labour supply and showed that the amount of labour that people choose to supply helps determine the level of real wages, employment, and output in the economy.

Here, we re-examine some of the factors that affect labour supply. Although the labour supply decision can be analysed in the same formal model as consumption and saving,[22] for simplicity and to conserve space we stay with a less formal discussion here. Nevertheless, concepts from the earlier part of this chapter – in particular, the ideas of income and substitution effects – are quite useful in our analysis of labour supply.

To illustrate the key issues in the determination of labour supply with an example, let us look at how Prudence decides how much to work. Suppose that, having played on the professional golf tour when she was younger, Prudence's best job opportunity is to work as a golf instructor. After paying taxes and job-related expenses, she finds that by giving golf lessons she can earn a real income of 100 per day. Furthermore, by varying the number of students she allows to sign up for lessons, she can work anywhere from 0 to 365 days this year. Prudence is reluctant to work too much, though, because every day she spends on the golf course means one less day available to devote to her real passion, skydiving. The decision Prudence faces is how many days to work this year – or, in other words, how much labour to supply.

Prudence approaches this question by asking herself: 'Economically speaking, what really makes me happy?' After a little reflection, she concludes that her level of satisfaction, or utility, depends on the amount of goods and services she consumes (in the present and in the future) and on the amount of leisure time she has available to jump out of aeroplanes. Her question can thus be recast as: 'How much should I work this year in order to obtain the highest possible level of utility?'

To find the level of labour supply that maximizes her utility, Prudence must compare the costs and benefits of working an extra day. The cost of an extra day of work is the loss of a day of leisure; this cost can be measured as the loss in utility that Prudence experiences when she has to work for a day instead of skydiving. The benefit of working an extra day is an increase of 100 in real income, which allows Prudence to enjoy more current and future consumption. Specifically, the benefit of the extra day of work is the increase in utility that results when Prudence optimally distributes her extra real income of 100 between current and future consumption.[23]

---

22. To do so, the necessary change is to drop the assumption that incomes are given and allow current and future incomes to depend on the amount that Prudence chooses to work.
23. Another benefit of increased income in the present is that it would allow Prudence to work less in the future.

If the benefit of working an extra day (utility gained from extra income) exceeds the cost (utility lost by reducing leisure), Prudence should work the extra day. In fact, she should continue to increase her time at work until the utility she receives from extra real income of 100 just equals the loss of utility associated with missing a day of leisure. Prudence's labour supply at that point is the one that maximizes her utility.[24] Using the idea that the labour supply decision results from a trade-off of leisure against income, we can discuss factors that influence the amount of labour Prudence supplies.

Real Wages and Labour Supply

The real wage is the amount of real income that a worker receives in exchange for giving up a unit of leisure (an hour, day, or week, for example) for work. It is thus an important determinant of the quantity of labour that is supplied.

Generally, as discussed in Chapter 3, an increase in the real wage affects the labour supply decision in two ways. First, an increase in the real wage raises the benefit (in terms of extra real income) of working an extra day and thus tends to make the worker want to supply more labour. The tendency of workers to supply more labour in response to a higher reward for working is called the **substitution effect** of a higher real wage on the quantity of labour supplied.

Second, an increase in the real wage also makes workers effectively wealthier because for the same amount of work they now earn a higher real income. Someone who is wealthier will be more able to afford extra leisure and, as a result, will supply less labour. The tendency of workers to supply less labour in response to becoming wealthier is called the **income effect** of a higher real wage on the quantity of labour supplied. Note that the substitution and income effects of a higher real wage work in opposite directions, with the substitution effect tending to raise the quantity of labour supplied and the income effect tending to reduce it.

A Pure Substitution Effect: A One-Day Rise in the Real Wage. We can illustrate the substitution effect by supposing that, after some consideration, Prudence decides to work six days per week, leaving every Wednesday free to go skydiving. She could work and earn real income of 100 each Wednesday, but her highest utility is obtained by taking leisure on that day instead.

Now imagine that one Tuesday, an eccentric golfer calls Prudence and requests a lesson on Wednesday to help him prepare for a weekend amateur tournament. He offers Prudence her regular wage of 100 per day, but Prudence declines, explaining that she is going skydiving on Wednesday. Not willing to take no for an answer, the golfer then offers to pay a fee of 1000 for an all-day lesson on Wednesday. When Prudence hears this offer to work for ten times her usual wage rate, she thinks: 'I do not get offers like this every day. I'll go skydiving some other day, but this Wednesday, I'm going to work.'

Prudence's decision to work rather than skydive (that is, to substitute labour for leisure) on this one Wednesday is a response to a very high reward,

---

24. Not everyone can choose his or her labour supply as flexibly as Prudence: for example, some jobs are available for 40 hours a week or not at all. Still, by choosing to work overtime, part-time, or at a second job, or by varying the number of family members who are working, households do have a significant amount of latitude over how much labour to supply.

in terms of extra income, that the extra day of work will bring. Thus her decision to work the extra day is the result of the substitution effect. Because receiving a very high wage for only one day does not make Prudence substantially wealthier, the income effect of the one-day wage increase is negligible. Thus the effect of a one-day increase in the real wage on the quantity of labour supplied by Prudence is an almost pure example of the substitution effect.

A Pure Income Effect: A Gift. By the next week Prudence has forgotten all about the eccentric golfer. But then she hears that he managed to win his amateur tournament. Furthermore, in gratitude he sends Prudence a cheque worth 30,000, or nearly a year's pay. Prudence's response is to reduce the amount she works from six to five days a week.

Why did Prudence reduce the quantity of labour she supplied when she received the unexpected gift? Prudence treasures the time she spends skydiving but decided to work six days per week to pay for food, clothes, rent, and skydiving trips. However, when the large cheque arrives, suddenly she can afford to take more time off from work – and so she does. Because the gift made her wealthier, she reduces her labour supply. This is an example of a pure income effect.

In Chapter 3 we concluded that either an increase in wealth or an increase in the expected future real wage would reduce current labour supply. Both results are examples of pure income effects. An increase in wealth – say, winning a lottery prize – is like the gift that Prudence received from the golfer; a wealthier worker can afford more leisure – and more consumption – and thus will supply less labour. Similarly, an increase in the expected future real wage raises the worker's present value of lifetime resources, *PVLR*, by raising expected future income; so again, the worker is better off and will choose more current leisure. Neither an increase in wealth nor an increase in the expected future real wage has any effect on the current reward for working, so neither change has any substitution effect on labour supply.

The Substitution Effect and the Income Effect Together: A Long-Term Increase in the Real Wage. Now imagine that, some weeks following her windfall, Prudence receives a call from a nearby country club offering her a long-term position as the resident golf pro. She will receive a wage of 200 per day (twice her previous wage) and will continue to be free to set the number of days she works. Prudence accepts the offer immediately.

On her new job, will Prudence work more days or fewer days than she did before? In this case, two effects work in opposite directions. On the one hand, because the reward for working is greater, she will be tempted to work more than she did previously. This tendency to increase labour supply in response to a higher real wage is the substitution effect. On the other hand, at double her original wage Prudence can pay for food, rent, and skydiving expenses by working only three or four days a week, tempting her to work less and spend more time skydiving. This tendency to reduce labour supply because she is wealthier is the income effect.

Which effect wins? One factor that will influence Prudence's decision is the length of time she expects her new, higher wage to last. The longer the higher wage is expected to last, the larger its impact is on Prudence's lifetime resources, and the stronger the income effect is. Thus, if Prudence expects to hold the new job until she retires, the income effect is strong (she is much wealthier) and she is more likely to reduce the amount she works. If Prudence believes that the job may not last very long, the income effect is weak (the increase in her lifetime resources is small) and she may choose to work more to take advantage of the higher wage while she can. In general, the longer an increase in the real wage is expected to last, the larger the income effect is and the more likely it is that the quantity of labour supplied will be reduced.

Empirical Evidence on Real Wages and Labour Supply. Because of conflicting income and substitution effects, there is some ambiguity about how a real-wage change will affect labour supply. What is the empirical evidence?

In his book on labour supply Mark Killingsworth[25] of Rutgers University surveyed the results of more than 60 studies of the labour supply decision in the United States, the United Kingdom, Canada, West Germany, Japan, and Taiwan. Although the studies differed in many respects and did not all yield precisely the same results, generally they showed that the aggregate amount of labour supplied rises in response to a temporary increase in the real wage but falls in response to a permanent increase in the real wage. The finding that a temporary increase in the real wage raises the amount of labour supplied confirms the substitution effect: if the reward for working rises for a short period, people will take advantage of the opportunity to work more. The result that a permanent increase in the real wage lowers the aggregate amount of labour supplied indicates that for long-lived increases in the real wage the income effect outweighs the substitution effect: if permanently higher wages make workers much better off, they will choose to work less. The effect of permanent increases in real wages is further illustrated in the following Application.

APPLICATION

Weekly Hours of Work and the Wealth of Nations

In 1870 a typical European worker worked about 56 hours per week. However, as shown in Table 8.2, the average hours worked each year in the main European economies declined into the 1930s. Although various forces contributed to the shortening of the working week before 1930, the major reason was sharply rising real wages. Increases in real wages during the late nineteenth and early twentieth centuries in Europe were driven by technological innovation and increased productivity and thus were largely permanent. In response to permanent increases in the real wage, workers reduced the amount of labour they supplied.

The response of labour supply to increases in real wages does not explain all of the changes in weekly hours worked. For example, the relatively low number of hours worked per year during the 1930s, especially in France and Italy, reflects primarily the general economic collapse that occurred during the Great Depression. Since World War II, the quantity of labour supplied across Europe has declined, partly resulting from the increase in real wages during the 1950s and 1960s. This decline in labour supply is refected in a shift towards both shorter working weeks and longer vacation times.

The historical data in Table 8.2 provide some evidence that, in response to a permanent increase in the real wage, workers choose to have more leisure and to work fewer hours per week. Figure 8.10 presents additional evidence,

---

25. *Labor Supply*, (Cambridge University Press, 1983). See especially Tables 3.1–3.5 and 4.2–4.4.

drawn from 36 nations. Each point in the diagram represents a different country. The horizontal axis measures real gross domestic product (GDP) per person, and the vertical axis measures the average number of hours worked per week by production workers in manufacturing. Workers in richer countries with higher wage rates (United States, Sweden) tend to work fewer hours per week than workers in poorer countries with lower wage rates (South Korea, Bolivia). Because the differences in wages among countries reflect long-term differences in productivity, the fact that high-wage countries have shorter working weeks provides further support for the finding that permanent increases in the real wage cause workers to supply less labour.

Table 8.2 Average Annual Hours of Work, 1870–1987

	France	Germany	Italy	Netherlands	Sweden	UK
1870	2945	2941	2886	2964	2945	2984
1913	2588	2584	2536	2605	2588	2634
1929	2297	2284	2228	2260	2283	2286
1938	1848	2316	1927	2244	2204	2267
1950	1926	2316	1997	2208	1951	1958
1960	1919	2081	2059	2051	1823	1911
1973	1771	1804	1612	1751	1571	1688
1987	1543	1620	1528	1387	1466	1577

Source: Angus Maddison, *Dynamic Forces in Capitalist Development: A Long-Run Comparative View* (Oxford University Press, 1991), Table C9.

Figure 8.10
The working week and real GDP per person in 36 countries, 1980
The point corresponding to each country shows the country's real GDP per person in 1980 on the horizontal axis and the average number of hours worked per week in manufacturing on the vertical axis. Because of the income effect on labour supply, richer countries tend to have short work weeks.

Source: Average hours per week: *United Nations Statistical Yearbook,* 1985–86, p. 89; real GDP per capita (in 1975 dollars): Robert Summers and Alan Heston, 'Improved International Comparisons of Real Product and Its Components: 1950–1980', *Review of Income and Wealth,* June 1984, pp. 259–61.

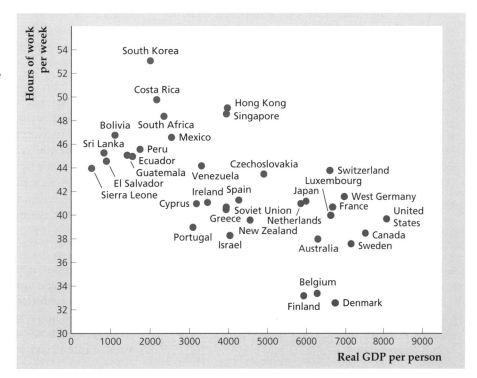

CHAPTER SUMMARY

1. In deciding how much to consume and to save, households trade off present consumption against future consumption. This trade-off can be analysed most simply in a two-period model of consumer behaviour.

2. For any possible level of current consumption, the budget constraint shows how much future consumption an individual can afford, based on the individual's economic resources. The graph of the budget constraint, in a diagram with current consumption on the horizontal axis and future consumption on the vertical axis, is called the budget line. The budget line slopes downwards (with slope = $-(1 + r)$, where r is the real interest rate) because an increase in current consumption implies less saving and thus less consumption in the future.

3. Present values measure payments to be made in the future in terms of today's money. The budget constraint can be expressed in terms of present values. The present value of an individual's lifetime consumption, $PVLC$, equals that person's present value of lifetime resources, $PVLR$. Thus a change in income or wealth affects an individual's consumption opportunities only to the extent that it changes the $PVLR$.

4. Preferences about current and future consumption are represented by indifference curves. All combinations of current and future consumption on an indifference curve yield the same level of utility, or economic satisfaction. Indifference curves slope downwards, and indifference curves that are higher and to the right represent higher levels of utility. Indifference curves are bowed toward the origin, which indicates that households prefer relatively even consumption over time (the consumption-smoothing motive).

5. Consumers choose the available combination of current and future consumption that yields the highest level of utility. Graphically, this consumption combination is represented by the point at which the budget line is tangent to an indifference curve.

6. An increase in current income, expected future income, or initial wealth raises the $PVLR$ and shifts the budget line parallel and to the right by an amount equal to the increase in the $PVLR$. This rise in economic resources increases both current and future consumption. An increase in current income raises saving, but increases in future income or initial wealth – because they increase current consumption without raising current income – reduce saving. The effects of any parallel shift in the budget line are called income effects.

7. Friedman's permanent income theory of consumption and saving predicts that permanent increases in income, because they have a larger effect on the individual's $PVLR$, should have a larger effect on current consumption than do temporary increases in income.

8. Empirically, some studies show that current consumption responds more strongly to current income than the theory predicts (the excess sensitivity phenomenon). Borrowing constraints – limits imposed by lenders on the amounts that households can borrow – may help explain why consumption responds so strongly to changes in current income.

9. Modigliani's life-cycle model of consumption and saving focuses on patterns of income, consumption, and saving throughout an individual's life. Because income is highest during an individual's middle years and because people try to keep consumption relatively constant over time, the life-cycle model predicts that middle-aged people will have high saving rates and people in their early working years or in retirement will have low or negative saving rates.

10. An increase in the real interest rate has two effects on saving. First, a higher real interest rate makes future consumption cheaper in terms of current consumption, which causes people to want to save more; this effect is called the substitution effect. Second, an increase in the real interest rate makes lenders better off (inducing

them to save less) and makes borrowers worse off (inducing them to save more); this effect is called the income effect. The income and substitution effects work in opposite directions for lenders so that their saving may either rise or fall when the real interest rate rises. For borrowers, the income and substitution effects work in the same direction so that a borrower always increases saving when the real interest rate rises. The empirical evidence is not conclusive but suggests that aggregate saving rises modestly in response to a higher real interest rate.

11. The benefit of working an extra hour is the extra real income earned, which can be used to increase current and future consumption. The cost of working an extra hour is the loss of an hour's leisure. Utility is highest when labour is supplied to the point where the cost of working an extra hour (utility lost because of reduced leisure) equals the benefit (utility gained because of increased income).

12. An increase in the real wage has competing substitution and income effects on the amount of labour supplied. The substitution effect of a higher real wage increases the amount of labour supplied, as the worker responds to the increased reward for working. The income effect reduces the amount of labour supplied, as the higher real wage makes the worker wealthier and thus able to afford a greater amount of leisure. The longer an increase in the real wage is expected to last, the stronger is the income effect. Thus permanent increases in the real wage typically reduce the quantity of labour supplied.

Key Terms

bequest motive, p. 279
borrowing constraint, p. 276
budget constraint, p. 262
budget line, p. 263
consumption-smoothing motive, p. 267
income effect, p. 272
income effect (of the real interest rate on saving), p. 283
income effect (of the real wage on labour supply), p. 288
indifference curve, p. 266
life-cycle model, p. 276
no-borrowing, no-lending point, p. 281
permanent income theory, p. 272

present value, p. 264
present value of lifetime resources (*PVLR*), p. 265
substitution effect (of the real interest rate on saving), p. 282
substitution effect (of the real wage on labour supply), p. 288
utility, p. 266

Key Equations

$$c^f = (y + a - c)(1 + r) + y^f \qquad (8.2)$$

For any possible level of current consumption, c, the budget constraint shows how much future consumption, c^f, the consumer can afford, given current real income, y, expected future real income, y^f, and initial wealth (assets), a.

$$c + \frac{c^f}{1 + r} = y + \frac{y^f}{1 + r} + a \qquad (8.4)$$

$$PVLC = PVLR$$

An alternative way to state the budget constraint is that the present value of lifetime consumption (*PVLC*), $c + c^f/(1 + r)$, equals the present value of lifetime resources (*PVLR*), $y + y^f/(1 + r) + a$.

Review Questions

1. Explain how, in choosing how much to consume and how much to save out of current income, an individual or household is making a trade-off between the present and the future.

2. Without using numbers or equations, sketch a consumer's budget line, labelling the axes of the graph. What can be said about points that lie on the budget line? Why does the budget line slope the way it does? If the budget line you have drawn were to shift to the left, would the consumer be better off or worse off? Why?

3. How is the present value of a given future payment affected if the interest rate rises? In words, how can the consumer's budget constraint be expressed in terms of present values?

4. Sketch an indifference curve. Why does it have the slope that it does? Why does it have the shape that it does? What is the relationship between one indifference curve and another that lies below and to the left of the first?

5. What are the effects on current consumption and saving of an increase in current income? An increase in expected future income? An increase in wealth? Explain in words (without using a diagram).

6. Compare the effects of a £1000 permanent increase in income on current consumption, future consumption, and saving to the effects of a £1000 temporary increase in income. Explain your answer by using the concept of the *PVLR*.

7. Define *borrowing constraint,* and distinguish between binding and non-binding borrowing constraints. Does your answer to Review Question 6 change if there is a binding borrowing constraint? If there is a non-binding borrowing constraint?

8. According to the life-cycle model, when during a consumer's life is saving likely to be high? When is saving likely to be low? Explain.

9. What are the two effects that an increase in the real interest rate has on desired saving? Describe each effect briefly. What is the overall effect of an increase in the real interest rate on saving? How does your answer depend on whether the consumer is a borrower or a lender?

10. What two effects does an increase in the real wage have on the amount of labour supplied? What determines which effect is the stronger?

11. Using the concepts of income and substitution effects, discuss how the amount of labour a household supplies should react to (a) a decline in wealth and (b) an increase in the real wage that household members expect to earn in the future.

Numerical Problems

1. A consumer has initial real wealth of 20, current real income of 90, and future real income of 110. The real interest rate is 10% per period.
   a. Find the consumer's *PVLR*.
   b. Write the equation for the consumer's budget constraint (using the given numerical values) and graph the budget line.
       Suppose that the consumer's goal is to smooth consumption completely. That is, he wants to have the same level of consumption in both the current and future periods.
   c. How much will he save and consume in the current period?
   d. How will his current saving and consumption be affected by an increase of 11 in current income?

e. How will his current saving and consumption be affected by an increase of 11 in future income?
f. How will his current saving and consumption be affected by an increase of 11 in his initial wealth?

2. a. The present value of a nominal payment P one year from now is $P/(1 + i)$, where i is the (annual) nominal interest rate. If the nominal interest rate i is constant, show that the present value of a payment P to be received in n years is $P/(1 + i)^n$. (*Hint:* If the nominal interest rate is i, how much would you have to put in the bank today in order to have P pounds in n years?)
   b. When taking out a £100,000 mortgage you are offered two options: First, you can repay £10,000 at the end of each of the first four years after you get the loan, then repay £110,000 at the end of the fifth year. Or second, you can repay £12,000 at the end of each of the first four years, then repay £100,000 at the end of the fifth year. At a 10% constant annual interest rate, which option is the better deal in present value terms? (To find the present value of a series of payments, add the present values of the individual payments.)

3. Bill Melater has a current real income after taxes of 300, an expected future real income after taxes of 360, and no initial wealth. The real interest rate is fixed at 20% throughout the problem. Bill always consumes an amount equal to half his *PVLR* in the current period.
   a. What are Bill's *PVLR*, current-period consumption, and current-period saving?
   b. The government raises Bill's current taxes by 30 but does not change its spending. Assuming that future taxes are adjusted to offset the effect of the current tax increase on the government debt, does Ricardian equivalence hold in this example? Explain.
   c. Repeat part (b) under the assumption that Bill is not allowed to borrow against future income.
   d. Repeat part (b) under the assumption that the current tax increase is accompanied by an equal increase in the government's current-period foreign aid programme.

4. In a particular town each of its 2000 residents makes consumption and saving plans over a current period and a future period. All want to smooth consumption completely (that is, make current and future consumption equal), if possible. For 1000 of the residents current income is 120 and future income is 100. For the remaining 1000 residents

current income is 100 and future income is 120. None has any initial wealth. The real interest rate is zero (and is unaffected by decisions made by the residents). The residents can freely borrow from and lend to people in other towns at the fixed real interest rate.

a. What is the town's aggregate consumption in the current period?

b. What is the effect on aggregate consumption if all consumers receive a temporary (current-period-only) increase in income of 10?

c. What is the effect on aggregate consumption if all consumers receive a permanent (both current- and future-period) income increase of 10?

Suppose that consumers are not allowed to borrow, but they may save if they want.

d. Now what is the town's aggregate consumption in the current period?

e. What is the effect on aggregate consumption if all consumers receive a temporary increase in income of 10?

f. Comparing the change in aggregate consumption in part (e) to the change that occurred in part (b), can you conclude that the presence of borrowing constraints makes consumption 'excessively sensitive' to current income? Why or why not?

5. A consumer lives three periods, called the learning period, the working period, and the retirement period. Her income is 200 during the learning period, 800 during the working period, and 200 again during the retirement period. The consumer's initial assets are 300. The real interest rate is zero. The consumer desires perfectly smooth consumption over her lifetime.

a. What are consumption and saving in each period, assuming no borrowing constraints? What happens if the consumer faces a borrowing constraint that prevents her from borrowing?

b. Assume that the consumer's initial wealth is zero instead of 300. Repeat part (a). Does being borrowing constrained mean that her consumption is lower in all three periods of her life than it would be if there were no borrowing constraints?

6. This problem analyses the relationship between the rate of income growth in a country and its rate of saving. (See item 2 in the application 'Why Do the Japanese Save So Much?' p. 279.)

An economy lasts three periods. One hundred people called 'parents' live during the first and second periods. Each parent earns a real income of 10,000 in

the first period and earns nothing (is retired) in the second period. Parents desire to have equal consumption during their working lives and retirement. The real interest rate is zero in all periods.

One hundred people called 'children' live during the second and third periods. Children each earn a real income of $(1 + g)$ times 10,000 in the second period, where g is the real growth rate of the economy. Children earn no income (are retired) in the third period. Children also desire perfectly even consumption over their lives.

Calculate total saving (adding the saving of parents and children) during the second period, assuming a growth rate of $g = 0$. (*Hint:* Remember that parents dissave during retirement.) What happens if $g = 0.10$? If $g = 0.50$? How is saving in the second period related in general to the growth rate of the economy?

7. Rudy Day has current real income of 12,000, has initial real wealth of 2000, and expects future real income of 12,000. The real interest rate is 20%.

a. Draw Rudy's budget line, and give numerical values for the budget line's horizontal intercept and its slope.

b. The real interest rate rises to 50%. Repeat part (a).

c. Initially, Rudy's current consumption is 12,000. Show diagrammatically the substitution and income effects of the increase in the real interest rate on Rudy's saving. Do you have enough information to know whether his saving will increase or decrease? Explain.

d. Suppose that initially Rudy's current consumption is 16,000 rather than 12,000. Repeat part (c).

Analytical Problems

1. If you are a utility-maximizing consumer with no borrowing constraints, how would each of the following affect your current consumption and saving?

a. You are informed that a long-lost relative has left you a large bequest. However, the bequest is to be kept in a trust, and you will not be able to withdraw any of the money for ten years.

b. Your doctor tells you that you have an amazingly healthy constitution and that you should easily live to the age 90. This prediction does not change your plan to retire at age 65 in order to perfect your fishing skills.

c. You are a taxpayer, and you read in the paper that your state government's deficit is much worse than thought. A tax increase next year now seems inevitable.

d. You work in the car industry and read in the newspaper that a serious recession and tough foreign competition are predicted to drive down car sales.

e. Your son's dentist tells you that in three or four years he will need a very expensive set of braces.

f. After several years of litigation you receive an insurance award compensating you for losses incurred in a fire. Though fairly large, the award is less than what you had been expecting.

2. To derive the budget constraint, equation (8.2), we assumed that Prudence's current consumption was less than her current resources so that she had some resources to put in the bank until the future period. Show that equation (8.2) still holds if Prudence's current consumption exceeds her current resources. (*Hint:* In this case Prudence must borrow an amount equal to the difference between her consumption and her resources in the current period and then repay this amount with interest in the future period. Her future consumption then equals her future income less her loan repayment.)

3. Many taxpayers have more income withheld from their pay cheques in the USA than they owe in taxes, with the result that after filing their tax returns, they receive refund cheques from the Internal Revenue Service. In early 1985 the installation of a new computer system at the IRS delayed the processing of individual income tax returns. During February and March, a period in which many refund cheques are usually mailed out, relatively few were processed. However, as the new computer came on line, the IRS moved to catch up. Refunds were above normal in April and much higher than normal in May. By June nearly all refunds had been mailed out, as is usually the case. Thus the aggregate income of US consumers, including tax refunds, was noticeably below normal in February and March and higher than normal in April, May, and June.

Some economic forecasters predicted that the IRS's computer problems would lead to a weakening in February and March consumer purchases. Discuss this prediction, using the concept of *PVLR*. What happens if many consumers have binding borrowing constraints?[26]

4. One of the many innovations in US financial markets during the past fifteen years has been the increased availability of home equity lines of credit (HELs). Home equity lines (technically a form of second mortgage, usually offered by a bank or savings and loan association) allow homeowners to borrow against the value of the equity in their house, often just by writing a cheque when funds are needed.[27] This contrasts with earlier periods, when borrowing against a home at any time other than the initial purchase date was typically a complex and costly process. What effect should the increased availability of HELs have on household consumption and saving? Discuss.[28]

5. Draw a budget line and indifference curves for a consumer who is initially a borrower. Be sure to indicate the no-borrowing, no-lending point and the optimal consumption point. Then show the effect on the budget line and the consumer's optimal consumption of an increase in the real interest rate. Using an intermediate budget line, show the income effect and the substitution effect. Do they work in the same direction or in opposite directions? Explain.

6. Consumers typically pay a higher real interest rate to borrow than they receive when they lend (by making bank deposits, for example). Draw a consumer's budget line under the assumption that the real rate of return earned on funds lent, r_l, is lower than the real interest rate paid to borrow, r_b. Show how the budget line is affected by an increase in r_l, an increase in r_b, or an increase in the consumer's initial wealth.

---

26. This problem is based on David W. Wilcox, 'Income Tax Refunds and the Timing of Consumption Expenditure', Board of Governors of the Federal Reserve System, revised May 1990. Wilcox found that, empirically, the delay in making refunds did not affect the timing of consumer purchases.

27. A homeowner's equity in her house is the value of the house minus the value of any mortgage she owes against the house. Consumer use of home equity lines was particularly stimulated by tax law changes in 1986, which eliminated the tax deductibility of interest on most types of consumer debt but not on home equity lines and other mortgages. However, growth in this type of borrowing had been strong even before 1986.

28. In a study of individual families ('Second Mortgages and Household Saving', *Regional Science and Urban Economics*, May 1989, pp. 325–46) Joyce Manchester of Dartmouth and James Poterba of the Massachusetts Institute of Technology found that with family characteristics held constant, each extra dollar of second-mortgage borrowing was associated with about 75 cents less total saving by the family.

Show that changes in r_l and r_b may leave current and future consumption unchanged. (*Hint:* Draw the consumer's indifference curves so that the consumer initially chooses the no-borrowing, no-lending point.)

7. Repeat Analytical Problem 4 in Chapter 3, p. 111. Discuss each part in terms of income and substitution effects.

8. John Doe learns that the percentage of his wages paid into the Social Security fund has been permanently raised.

a. Suppose that John's expected Social Security benefits are not changed; instead, the increase in his Social Security tax is used to make up some unexpected shortfalls in the current Social Security programme. John also does not expect his before-tax real wages in the future to change. John is well below the Social Security 'cap': that is, none of his labour earnings is exempt from the Social Security tax. What will be the effect of the increase in the Social Security tax on the amount of labour that John supplies?

b. Repeat part (a), but assume that John's extra Social Security taxes all go directly to increase his expected retirement benefits. Assume also that John will get the full increase in retirement benefits whether or not he keeps working at his present rate. What happens to John's labour supply now?

PART

BUSINESS
CYCLES
AND
MACROECONOMIC
POLICY

CHAPTER 9

BUSINESS CYCLES

Since the Industrial Revolution, the economies of Europe and many other countries have grown tremendously. That growth has transformed economies and greatly improved living standards. Yet even in prosperous countries, economic expansion has been periodically interrupted by episodes of declining production, income, and spending and rising unemployment. Sometimes – fortunately, not very often – episodes have been severe and prolonged. But whether brief or more extended, declines in economic activity have been followed almost invariably by a resumption of economic growth.

This repeated sequence of economic expansion giving way to temporary decline followed by recovery is known as the *business cycle*. The business cycle is a central concern in macroeconomics because business cycle fluctuations – the ups and downs in overall economic activity – are felt throughout the economy. When the economy is growing strongly, prosperity is shared by most of the nation's industries and their workers and owners of capital. When the economy weakens, many sectors of the economy experience declining sales and production, and the number of unemployed workers increases. Because the effects of business cycles are so widespread, and because economic downturns can cause great hardship, economists have tried to find the causes of these episodes and to determine what, if anything, can be done to counteract them. The two basic questions of (1) what causes business cycles and (2) how policymakers should respond to cyclical fluctuations are the main concern of Part III of this book.

The answers to these two questions remain highly controversial. Much of this controversy involves the proponents of the classical and Keynesian approaches to macroeconomics, introduced in Chapter 1. In brief, classical economists view business cycles as generally representing the economy's best response to disturbances in production or spending. Thus classical economists do not see much, if any, need for government action to counteract these fluctuations. In contrast, Keynesian economists argue that, because wages and prices adjust slowly, disturbances in production or spending may drive the economy away from its most desirable level of output and employment for long periods of time. According to the Keynesian view, government should intervene to smooth business cycle fluctuations.

We explore the debate between classical economists and Keynesians, and the implications of that debate for economic analysis and macroeconomic policy, in Chapters 10–12. In this chapter we provide essential background for that discussion by presenting the basic features of the business cycle. We begin with a definition and a brief history of the business cycle in France, Germany and the UK. We then turn to a more detailed discussion of business cycle characteristics, or 'business cycle facts.' We conclude the chapter with a brief preview of the alternative approaches to the analysis of business cycles.

9.1   WHAT IS A BUSINESS CYCLE?

Countries have experienced ups and downs in overall economic activity since they began to industrialize. Economists have measured and studied these fluctuations for more than a century. Marx and Engels referred to 'commercial crises', an early term for business cycles, in their Communist Manifesto in 1848. In the United States, the National Bureau of Economic Research (NBER), a private non-profit organization of economists founded in 1920, pioneered business cycle research. The NBER developed and continues to update the **business cycle chronology**, a detailed history of business cycles in the United States and other countries. The NBER has also sponsored many studies of the business cycle. One landmark study was the 1946 book *Measuring Business Cycles*, by Arthur Burns (who served as Federal Reserve chairman from 1970 until 1978) and Wesley Mitchell (a principal founder of the NBER). This work was among the first to document and analyse the empirical facts about business cycles. It begins with the following definition:

> Business cycles are a type of fluctuation found in the aggregate economic activity of nations that organize their work mainly in business enterprises. A cycle consists of expansions occurring at about the same time in many economic activities, followed by similarly general recessions, contractions, and revivals which merge into the expansion phase of the next cycle; this sequence of changes is recurrent but not periodic; in duration business cycles vary from more than one year to ten or twelve years.[1]

Five points in this definition should be clarified and emphasized.

1. *Aggregate economic activity.* Business cycles are defined broadly as fluctuations of 'aggregate economic activity' rather than as fluctuations in a single, specific economic variable such as real GDP. Although real GDP may be the single variable that most closely measures aggregate economic activity, Burns and Mitchell also thought it important to look at other indicators of activity, such as employment and financial market variables.

2. *Expansions and contractions.* Figure 9.1 – a diagram of a typical business cycle – helps explain what Burns and Mitchell meant by expansions and contractions. The dashed line shows the average, or normal, growth path of aggregate economic activity, and the solid curve shows the rises and falls of actual business activity. The period of time during which aggregate economy activity is falling is a **contraction** or **recession**. If the recession is particularly

---

1. Burns and Mitchell, *Measuring Business Cycles* (National Bureau of Economic Research, 1946), p. 1.

Figure 9.1
A business cycle
The solid curve graphs the behaviour of aggregate economic activity over a typical business cycle. The dashed line shows the economy's normal growth path. During a contraction aggregate economic activity falls until it reaches a trough, *T*. The trough is followed by an expansion during which economic activity increases until it reaches a peak, *P*. A complete cycle is measured from peak to peak or trough to trough.

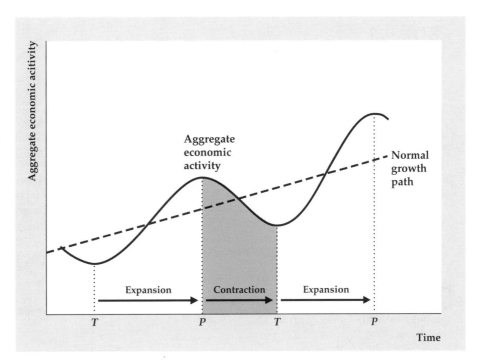

severe, it becomes a **depression**. After reaching the low point of the contraction, the **trough** (T), economic activity begins to increase. The period of time during which aggregate economic activity grows is an **expansion** or a **boom**. After reaching the high point of the expansion, the **peak** (P), aggregate economic activity begins to decline again. The entire sequence of decline followed by recovery, measured from peak to peak or trough to trough, is a **business cycle**.

Figure 9.1 suggests that business cycles are purely temporary deviations from the economy's long-run growth path. However, part of the output losses and gains that occur during a business cycle may become permanent (see Box 9.1).

Peaks and troughs in the business cycle are known collectively as **turning points**. One goal of business cycle research is to identify when turning points occur. Aggregate economic activity is not measured directly by any single variable, so there is no simple formula that tells economists when a peak or trough has been reached.[2] In practice, economists examine a variety of economic data to determine whether a peak or trough has been reached and, if so, the month it happened. However, precise dating of turning points usually comes well after a peak or trough occurs, so these judgements are more useful for historical analysis of business cycles than as a guide to current policy making.

---

2. A conventional definition used by the media – that a recession has occurred when there are two consecutive quarters of negative real GDP growth – is not widely accepted by economists. The reason that economists tend not to like this definition is that real GDP is only one of many possible indicators of economic activity.

BOX 9.1

Temporary and Permanent Components of Recessions

Until the 1980s, economists generally believed that business cycles are temporary events. According to this view, after the economy recovers from a recession, it returns to the level it would have reached had the recession not occurred. Thus, although a recession creates short-run problems, it has no important long-run effects on a country's standard of living.

However, in a 1982 article* Charles Nelson of the University of Washington and Charles Plosser of the University of Rochester showed that business cycles are not entirely temporary events. Instead, some permanent reduction in output is associated with the typical recession. Nelson and Plosser examined many macroeconomic variables, including measures of output and employment. Using statistical techniques, they found that for every variable except the unemployment rate, part of a typical cyclical fluctuation represents a permanent change. Only in the unemployment rate did they find fluctuations to be completely transitory.

The severe recession of 1973–75 illustrates the potential permanence of cyclical changes in output. The solid curve in the accompanying figures shows

Permanent components of the business cycle

The figures show actual French and UK real GDP (measured quarterly) and trend lines based on real GDP growth from 1967 to 1973. Both economies did not return to the earlier trend after the 1973–75 recession. Hence much of the output loss of the 1973–75 recession was permanent.

Source: GDP data taken from *Datastream*

(Continued)

actual real GDP in France since 1967 and the UK from 1960 to the first quarter of 1997. The dashed curve in the figures shows the trend in real output, based on the period to 1973 and extended to 1997.[†] In the 1980s and 1990s GDP remained well below the levels it would have reached on the basis of the earlier trend, suggesting that the 1973–75 recession was associated with a permanent reduction in real GDP. Of course, we cannot conclude that the 1973–75 recession directly caused the subsequent slowdown. External factors, such as OPEC's quadrupling of oil prices, may have caused both the recession and the subsequent slowdown. Alternatively, the slowdown of growth after 1973 may have been purely coincidental and unrelated to the 1973–75 recession. Whatever the reason, at least part of the 1973–75 drop in output became permanent.

In a typical recession, what fraction of the decline in output is permanent? This question is not easily answered. One problem is that the nature of a decline in output – temporary or permanent – cannot be determined until several years afterward. Another problem is that all cyclical output changes may not be alike in their degree of permanence. For example, we have seen that a portion of the output decline during the 1973–75 recession turned out to be permanent, because that recession was associated with a large and long-lasting change in the economy: a fourfold increase in the price of oil. Output declines in recessions not associated with long-lasting supply shocks, in contrast, may well be less permanent than the

1973–75 decline. Indeed, one recent statistical analysis – by Pierre Perron[‡] of Princeton University – concluded that, of post-World War II US recessions, only the 1973–75 downturn had a significant permanent effect on the level of output.

Another interesting statistical study of the degree of permanence of cycles for a number of European countries was carried out by Gabriel Sterne and Tamin Bayoumi[§] of the Bank of England and the IMF respectively. Sterne and Bayoumi examined fluctuations in output growth and found that about 50% of the changes in real output are permanent and 50% are temporary. They find, however, that in some European countries changes in real output are more likely to be permanent while others are characterized more by temporary fluctuations in real output. For example, in the Netherlands and Germany around 75% of changes in real output are permanent, whereas in the UK and Italy the figure is roughly 30%.

---

[*] 'Trends and Random Walks in Macroeconomic Time Series: Some Evidence and Implications', *Journal of Monetary Economics,* September 1982, pp. 139–62.
[†] The trend line in the figure curves upward slightly because it is based on the assumption of a constant growth rate. The graph of a variable that grows by the same percentage every year will curve upward over time, rather than being a straight line.
[‡] 'The Great Crash, the Oil Price Shock and the Unit Root Hypothesis', *Econometrica,* November 1989, pp. 1361–401.
[§] 'Temporary Cycles or Volatile Trends? Economic Fluctuations in 21 OECD Economies', *Manchester School of Economic and Social Studies,* March 1995, pp. 23–51.

3. *Co-movement.* Business cycles do not occur in just a few sectors or in just a few economic variables. Instead, expansions or contractions 'occur at about the same time in many economic activities'. Thus, although some industries are more sensitive to the business cycle than others, output and employment in most industries tend to fall in recessions and rise in expansions. Many other economic variables, such as prices, productivity, investment, and government purchases, also have regular and predictable patterns of behaviour over the course of the business cycle. This tendency is called **co-movement**.

4. *Recurrent but not periodic.* The business cycle is not periodic, in that it does not occur at regular, predictable intervals and does not last for a fixed or predetermined length of time. (Box 9.2, p. 329, discusses the seasonal cycle – or economic fluctuations over the seasons of the year – which, unlike the business cycle, is periodic.) Although the business cycle is not periodic, it is recurrent: that is, the standard pattern of contraction–trough–expansion–peak recurs again and again in industrial economies.

5. *Persistence.* The duration of a complete business cycle can vary greatly, from about a year to more than a decade, and predicting it is extremely difficult. However, once a recession begins, the economy tends to keep contracting for a period of time, perhaps for a year or more. Similarly, an expansion once begun usually lasts a while. This tendency for declines in economic activity to be followed by further declines, and for growth in economic activity to be followed by more growth, is called **persistence**. Because movements in economic activity have some persistence, economic forecasters are always on the lookout for turning points, which are likely to indicate a change in the direction of economic activity.

9.2 THE EUROPEAN BUSINESS CYCLE: THE HISTORICAL RECORD

An overview of the business cycle history of the three largest European economies, Germany, France, and the UK, is provided by the monthly business cycle chronology,[3] as summarized in Table 9.1. It gives the dates of the troughs and peaks of the complete business cycles that each economy has experienced since 1868 for France and the UK and since 1879 for Germany. Also shown are the number of months that each contraction and expansion lasted.

The Pre-World War I Period

The period between 1870 and World War I (1914–18) was one of economic growth in Europe. Nevertheless, as Table 9.1 shows, recessions were a serious problem during that time. For example, the longest contraction on record in the UK is the 81-month-long decline between September 1872 and June 1879, a contraction that was worldwide in scope and is referred to by economic historians as the Depression of the 1870s. Overall, during the pre-World War I period France, Germany and the UK suffered nearly as many months of contraction as months of expansion. In contrast, from 1950 to January 1997 the number of months of expansion outnumbered months of contraction by more than seven to one in the UK and by about three to one in France and Germany.

The Great Depression and World War II

The interwar period was a very turbulent time for most European countries. The years immediately following World War I were a period of general prosperity as industrial activity expanded and reconstruction took place. Following this brief period of postwar prosperity, economic activity in many European

---

3. The dates of turning points for the three countries up to 1945 are presented in Geoffrey H. Moore and Victor Zarnowitz, 'The NBER's Business Cycle Chronologies', in Robert J. Gordon, ed., *The American Business Cycle: Continuity and Change* (University of Chicago Press, 1986). Data on turning points since 1950 were kindly provided by Geoffrey H. Moore and Anirvan Banerji of the Economic Cycle Research Institute (ECRI) in New York and are based on the NBER methodology.

Table 9.1 Business Cycle Turning Points and Durations in France, Germany and the UK

Trough		Expansion (Months from trough to peak)	Peak		Contraction (Months from peak to trough)
France					
October	1868	22	August	1870	18
February	1872	19	September	1873	35
August	1876	20	April	1878	17
September	1879	27	December	1881	68
August	1887	41	January	1891	48
January	1895	62	March	1900	30
September	1902	8	May	1903	17
October	1904	33	July	1907	19
February	1909	52	June	1913	14
August	1914	46	June	1918	10
April	1919	17	September	1920	10
July	1921	39	October	1924	8
June	1925	16	October	1926	8
June	1927	33	March	1930	28
July	1932	12	July	1933	21
April	1935	26	June	1937	14
August	1938				
April[a]	1959	87	July	1966	22
May	1968	74	July	1974	11
June	1975	82	April	1982	32
December	1984	86	February	1992	9
November	1993				
Germany					
February	1879	35	January	1882	55
August	1886	41	January	1890	61
February	1895	61	March	1900	24
March	1902	17	August	1903	18
February	1905	29	July	1907	17
December	1908	52	April	1913	16
August	1914	46	June	1918	12
June	1919	35	May	1922	18
November	1923	16	March	1925	12
March	1926	37	April	1929	40
August	1932				
May[b]	1967	75	August	1973	24
August	1975	54	February	1980	31
November	1982	98	January	1991	39
April	1994				
United Kingdom					
March	1868	54	September	1872	81
June	1879	42	December	1882	42
June	1886	51	September	1890	53
February	1895	64	June	1900	15
September	1901	21	June	1903	17
November	1904	31	June	1907	17
November	1908	49	December	1912	21
September	1914	49	October	1918	6
April	1919	11	March	1920	15
June	1921	41	November	1924	20
July	1926	8	March	1927	18
September	1928	10	July	1929	37
August	1932	61	September	1937	12
September	1938				
August[a]	1952	265	September	1974	11
August	1975	46	June	1979	23
May	1981	108	May	1990	21
February	1992				

[a] Data start in 1955.
[b] Data start in 1952.
Source: 1868–1938, Geoffrey H. Moore and Victor Zarnowitz, op. cit.; 1938–93, Geoffrey H. Moore and Anirvan Banerji, Economic Cycle Research Institute, New York.

countries slumped in the early 1920s, although the downturn began at different times and came about for different reasons. The economic contraction was especially severe in the UK, where output fell by over 16% between 1919 and 1921. It was in Germany, however, that the drop in economic activity was most dramatic. The German economy enjoyed a period of expansion between 1921 and 1922 but this came to a dramatic end in 1923 when French and Belgian troops entered the Ruhr to enforce payment of war reparations. German output fell by around 20% from its 1922 level as German workers adopted a policy of 'passive resistance' (basically a general strike). The workers and their families were supported by the German government, which financed this sudden increase in expenditure by printing money on a massive scale.[4] As the government sought to control the hyperinflation which resulted, economic activity fell dramatically and unemployment soared. It was not until the end of the decade that prosperity began to return to Europe, although unemployment in most countries remained high.

For most European countries, the worst economic contraction in the interwar period was the Great Depression of the 1930s. This hit European countries at different times and some much harder than others. Although economic historians identify various sources of the Depression, events in the USA at the time played a crucial part in explaining the recession in Europe. The USA was a major importer of European goods and was the most important foreign lender to European countries. The sharp downturn in economic activity in the USA – real GDP fell by nearly 30% between 1929 and 1933 – thus had major knock-on effects for European economies. Between 1929 and 1932, real GDP in Germany fell by more than 20%, in France by roughly 16% and in the UK, where the level of economic activity had only just recovered to what it was before World War I, by around 6%.

To appreciate how severe the Great Depression was, compare it with the three worst post-World War II recessions of 1973–75, 1980–82 and 1990–91. In contrast to the 20% real GDP decline in Germany, in the 1973–75 recession German real GDP fell by 1.3% and only in one year (1975); in the 1980–82 recession German real GDP fell by only 0.9% (in 1982). In the UK, which has suffered some of the largest falls in real GDP experienced by European countries in the post-World War II period, real GDP fell by 2.4% in the 1974–75 recession, by 1.3% in the 1980–82 recession and by 2.5% in the 1990–91 recession.

Although no sector escaped the Great Depression, some were particularly hard hit. Economic development and reconstruction during the 1920s had relied on money and capital from the USA, increasingly in the form of short-term or 'on call' loans. In the latter part of 1928 and early 1929, US banks began calling in their loans, putting pressure on the European banking system. This pressure was felt especially in Germany, Austria, and France. In the financial sector stock prices across Europe continued to collapse after the stock market crash in the USA in October 1929. Stock prices fell by around 60% in Germany, France, and

---

4. Frank Tipton and Robert Aldrich in their book *An Economic and Social History of Europe, 1890–1939*, state that at one time 30 paper mills and 150 printing firms were working 24 hours a day to meet the demand for Mark notes. The value of the Mark fell to such an extent that at the end one US dollar could buy 4,200,000,000,000 Marks.

the Netherlands, by 45% in the UK, and by 30% in Sweden. Depositors withdrew their money from banks, and borrowers, unable to repay their bank loans, were forced to default. Although bank failures were not the common occurrence in Europe that they were in the USA, a number of large and important European banks, including the Credit-Anstalt in Austria and the Banque Nationale de Credit in Paris, collapsed. The crisis also led to the UK coming off the Gold Standard. Investment, both business and residential, fell to extremely low levels, and a 'trade war' – in which countries competed in erecting barriers to imports – virtually halted international trade.

The Great Depression ended dramatically with the advent of World War II. Even before Britain and France delared war on Germany in September 1939, all three economies were gearing up for increased armaments production. As the demand for armaments and other supplies for the war effort increased, real GDP rose sharply.

Post-World War II European Business Cycles

As World War II was ending in 1945, economists and policymakers were concerned that the economy would relapse into depression. As an expression of this concern, governments in many countries committed themselves to fight recessions and depressions with macroeconomic policies and to avoid the tariff wars and other protectionist policies of the 1930s. But instead of falling into a new depression as feared, European economies began to grow strongly. As a result only a few relatively brief and mild recessions interrupted the economic expansion of the early postwar period.

Because no serious recession occurred between 1945 and 1970, some economists suggested that the business cycle had been 'tamed', or even that it was 'dead'. This view was especially popular during the 1960s – a period of near continuous expansion in many European countries, which was widely attributed to the macroeconomic policies pursued by European governments. Some economists argued that policymakers should stop worrying about recessions and focus their attention on inflation, which had been gradually increasing during the 1960s.

Unfortunately, reports of the business cycle's death proved premature. Shortly after the Organization of Petroleum Exporting Countries (OPEC) succeeded in quadrupling oil prices in the fall of 1973, the majority of European economies and those of many other nations fell into a severe recession. In the 1973–75 recession, real GDP for the EU as a whole fell by less than 1%, although the impact of the sharp rise in oil prices was more severe in the UK and in Italy where real GDP fell by around 2.5%. OPEC's decision had much less impact in Sweden, where real output continued to grow, and in the Netherlands where real GDP fell by only 0.1%. Most European unemployment rates did increase sharply, more than doubling in a number of countries (Sweden is again an exception to this trend). However, despite these sharp rises, European unemployment rates remained, with one or two exceptions, below 5%. The 1973–75 recession was therefore a serious downturn rather than a depression, but one that was associated with another disturbing development. Inflation, which had fallen during most previous recessions, shot up to unprecedented double-digit levels in every European country except Germany. Inflation continued to be a problem for the rest of the 1970s, even as Europe recovered from the 1973–75 recession.

More evidence that the business cycle was not dead came with the sharp recession in the early 1980s. This contraction hit all European countries with recession being especially hard in the UK, the Netherlands, and Germany. Unemployment rates across Europe increased sharply, reaching postwar highs in many countries. Many economists claim that central banks knowingly created this contraction to reduce inflation. Inflation did drop dramatically: in the UK, for example, inflation fell from over 16% in 1980 to less than 4% in 1984. The recovery from this recession was strong, however, and the ensuing expansion continued until the early 1990s.

For a number of countries, the period of expansion came to an end in 1990. Sweden and the UK were among those economies which entered a recession, which in the case of Sweden was quite prolonged (it lasted until 1994) and severe (real GDP fell by more than 5%). Several other countries also entered a recession in 1993 – including Germany and Italy – although these were relatively short lived. Economic activity in Europe generally was curtailed up to 1994 and unemployment rates increased markedly. One disturbing feature of the late 1990s is that unemployment in Europe has remained high despite the recovery from the earlier downturn (we consider this in more detail in Chapter 13).

Have Business Cycles Become Less Severe?

Until recently, macroeconomists believed that, over the long sweep of history, business cycles have generally become less severe. Obviously, no recession in Europe since World War II can begin to rival the severity of the recession in the 1920s or of the Great Depression. Even putting aside those episodes, economists generally believed that business downturns before 1929 were longer and deeper than those since 1945. According to the business cycle chronology (Table 9.1), for example, the average contraction before 1929 lasted about 28 months and the average expansion lasted slightly more than 30 months. Since 1950, contractions have shortened to an average of less than 18 months in France and the UK, and expansions have lengthened to an average of 80 months for France and Germany and more than 100 months for the UK. Standard measures of economic fluctuations, such as real GDP growth and the unemployment rate, also show considerably less volatility since 1950, relative to data available for the pre-1929 era.

Since World War II a major goal of economic policy has been to reduce the size and frequency of recessions. If researchers found – contrary to the generally accepted view – that business cycles had *not* moderated in the postwar period, serious doubt would be cast on the ability of economic policymakers to achieve this goal. For this reason, although the question of whether the business cycle has moderated over time may seem to be a matter of interest only to economic historians, this issue is of great practical importance.

Thus Christina Romer, now at the University of California at Berkeley, sparked a heated controversy by writing a series of articles denying the claim that the business cycle has moderated over time.[5] Romer's main point con-

---

5. The articles included 'Is the Stabilization of the Postwar Economy a Figment of the Data?', *American Economic Review*, June 1986, pp. 314–34; 'The Prewar Business Cycle Reconsidered: New Estimates of Gross National Product, 1869–1908', *Journal of Political Economy*, February 1989, pp. 1–37; and 'The Cyclical Behaviour of Individual Production Series, 1889–1984', *Quarterly Journal of Economics*, February 1991, pp. 1–31.

cerned the dubious quality of the pre-1929 data. Unlike today, in earlier periods governments did not collect comprehensive data on economic variables such as GDP. Instead, economic historians, using whatever fragmentary information they could find, have had to estimate historical measures of these variables.

Romer argued that methods used for estimating historical data typically overstated the size of earlier cyclical fluctuations. For example, the widely accepted estimates of pre-1929 US GNP compiled by Nobel laureate Simon Kuznets made heavy use of data, originally collected by William Shaw, on the economy's total output of 'commodities' during those years. Shaw's commodity output data measured the output of the goods-producing sectors of the economy (agriculture, mining, manufacturing, and to some extent construction) but left out important components of GNP such as wholesale and retail distribution, transportation, and services. Because manufacturing and construction are among the most cyclically volatile components of the modern economy – and distribution, transportation, and services are much less volatile – Romer argued that basing GNP estimates only on commodity output tends to overstate the size of business cycle fluctuations. She used statistical methods to create new estimates of GNP that showed much less volatility in the pre-Depression economy than implied by Kuznets's work. Indeed, she concluded that pre-Depression business cycles, on average, were only about 25% larger than post-1945 cycles, rather than roughly twice as severe, as Kuznets's figures implied.

Since Romer raised the issue, much new research has been done, including work on the historical experience of countries other than the United States. Some of this research has supported Romer's view that cycles have not moderated. For example, Steven Sheffrin[6] of the University of California at Davis looked at historical data for six European countries (United Kingdom, Denmark, Sweden, Italy, France, and Norway) and found evidence for post-war moderation of the business cycle only in Sweden.

But the traditional view that the cycle has moderated also has defenders. For example, David Backus of New York University and Patrick Kehoe of the University of Minnesota have studied business cycle fluctuations for ten countries, comparing the pre-World War I, interwar and post-World War II periods.[7] They found that, in general, output growth is less volatile since World War II than in either of the two earlier periods, although the extent of the difference varies between countries. They also found that that business fluctuations in the interwar period were larger than before World War I. The notable exception to this general pattern is Japan.

9.3 BUSINESS CYCLE FACTS

Although no two business cycles are identical, all (or most) cycles have features in common. This point has been made strongly by a leading business cycle theorist, Nobel Laureate Robert E. Lucas, Jr, of the University of Chicago:

---

6. 'Have Economic Fluctuations Been Dampened? A Look at Evidence Outside the United States', *Journal of Monetary Economics,* January 1988, pp. 73–83.

7. 'International Evidence on the Historical Properties of Business Cycles', *American Economic Review,* September 1992, pp. 864–88.

Though there is absolutely no theoretical reason to anticipate it, one is led by the facts to conclude that, with respect to the qualitative behaviour of co-movements among series [that is, economic variables], *business cycles are all alike*. To theoretically inclined economists, this conclusion should be attractive and challenging, for it suggests the possibility of a unified explanation of business cycles, grounded in the *general* laws governing market economies, rather than in political or institutional characteristics specific to particular countries or periods.[8]

Lucas's statement that business cycles are all alike (or more accurately, that they have many features in common) is based on examinations of co-movements among economic variables over the business cycle. In this section, we study these co-movements, which we call business cycle facts, for the post-World War II period using data for France, Germany, and the UK. Knowing these business cycle facts is useful for interpreting economic data and evaluating the state of the economy. In addition, they provide guidance and discipline for developing economic theories of the business cycle. When we discuss alternative theories of the business cycle in Chapters 11 and 12, we evaluate the theories principally by determining how well they account for business cycle facts. To be successful, a theory of the business cycle must explain the cyclical behaviour not just of a few variables, such as output and employment, but of a wide range of key economic variables.

The Cyclical Behaviour of Economic Variables: Direction and Timing

Two characteristics of the cyclical behaviour of macroeconomic variables are important to our discussion of the business cycle facts. The first is the *direction* in which a macroeconomic variable moves, relative to the direction of aggregate economic activity. An economic variable that moves in the same direction as aggregate economic activity (up in expansions, down in contractions) is **procyclical**. A variable that moves in the opposite direction to aggregate economic activity (up in contractions, down in expansions) is **countercyclical**. Variables that do not display a clear pattern over the business cycle are **acyclical**.

The second characteristic is the *timing* of the variable's turning points (peaks and troughs) relative to the turning points of the business cycle. An economic variable is a **leading variable** if it tends to move in advance of aggregate economic activity. In other words, the peaks and troughs in a leading variable occur before the corresponding peaks and troughs in the business cycle. A **coincident variable** is one whose peaks and troughs occur at about the same time as the corresponding business cycle peaks and troughs. Finally, a **lagging variable** is one whose peaks and troughs tend to occur later than the corresponding peaks and troughs in the business cycle.

The fact that some economic variables consistently lead the business cycle suggests that they might be used to forecast the future course of the economy. This idea is behind the **index of leading indicators,** discussed in the box, 'In Touch with the Macroeconomy: The OECD Composite Leading Index', p. 313.

---

8. Robert E. Lucas, Jr., "Understanding Business Cycles," in K. Brunner and A. H. Meltzer, eds., *Carnegie-Rochester Conference Series on Public Policy*, vol. 5, Autumn, 1977, p. 10.

IN TOUCH *WITH THE MACROECONOMY*

THE OECD COMPOSITE LEADING INDEX

The OECD index of leading indicators (the Composite Leading Index) is a weighted average of a number of economic variables that lead the business cycle.[*] The index is constructed for all 22 member countries and its purpose is to aid in forecasting their future economic activity. The index is modelled on the US index of leading indicators first developed in 1938 at the National Bureau of Economic Research by Wesley Mitchell and Arthur Burns.[†] The OECD index of leading indicators is currently updated by members of the Economics and Statistics Department of the OECD in cooperation with the statistics departments of member countries and is published in the OECD's *Main Economic Indicators* for each member country.

The variables that make up the index vary from country to country due to differences in their economic structures and in the statistical systems they use. Also, variables that are good predictors of economic activity in one country may not be so useful in others. The variables used in the index of leading indicators for France, Germany and the UK are listed in the accompanying table. The variables chosen have a tendency to predict (lead) economic activity and data on them are frequently and promptly reported. This second characteristic is important because a variable cannot be of much help in forecasting if accurate data on the variable arrive only after a long delay.

Although the components are varied, there are good economic reasons why each component helps predict economic activity. For example, the inflow of new orders is a direct measure of the amount of future production being planned in the economy. Business surveys and the index of stock prices reflect the optimism or pessimism of businesspeople and stock market participants respectively about the economy's future.

The percentage change in the index of leading indicators is reported monthly, with two or three consecutive declines being regarded as the warning sign that a recession is on the way. The behaviour of the index of leading indicators during the period 1961–94 for France, Germany, Italy, the UK, the USA, and Japan is shown in the accompanying figures. Note how the index tends to turn down in advance of cyclical peaks. On the whole the index is a valuable and much watched forecasting device, correctly predicting a large majority of economic turning points for more than 30 years. However, the index is not without problems, including the following:

1. Despite the emphasis on the use of data that are promptly available, the data on the various components of the index and thus the index of leading indicators itself are usually revised during the first

Components of the Composite Leading Index

	France	Germany	UK
Inflow of new orders		✓	
Sales or registrations of new motor cars	✓		✓
Wages and salaries per unit of ouput		✓	
Price indices	✓		
Profits, flow of funds, net acquisition of financial assets			✓
Credit			✓
Money supply	✓	✓	
Interest rates	✓	✓	✓
Stock prices	✓	✓	✓
Terms of trade	✓		
Business survey of economy	✓	✓	
Business survey of production	✓		✓
Business survey of new orders		✓	
Business survey of sales		✓	✓
Business survey of stocks of raw materials			✓
Business survey of stocks of finished goods	✓	✓	✓

IN TOUCH *WITH THE MACROECONOMY*

(Continued)

three months after their initial release. As a result, an early signal of recession or recovery may be reversed when the revised data become available. A typical revision is about 0.2%, although they are rather higher for France and Japan (about 0.4%).

2. On several occasions the index has given false warnings, predicting a recession when in fact no recession occurred in the months following the drop in the index, or failed to forecast a turning point.

3. Although it may forecast that a recession is coming, the index does not provide much information about how far in the future the recession is or how severe it will be when it arrives.

4. Changes in the structure of the economy over time may cause some variables to become better predictors of the economy and others to become worse. For this reason, the index of leading indicators must be revised periodically, either to change the list of component indicators or to change the weights of the components.

The OECD Composite Leading Index

Used for forecasting, the composite leading index is a weighted average of up to sixteen economic variables that typically lead the business cycle. The index turns down in advance of business cycle peaks, signalling the onset of recession. Also shown is the index of industrial production for each country and the peaks (P) and troughs (T) in industrial production.

Source: OECD composite leading index from M.J. Artis, R.C. Bladen Hovell and W. Zhang, 'Turning Points in the International Business Cycle: An Analysis of the OECD Leading Indicators for the G-7 countries', *OECD Economic Studies*, 1995, pp 125–165, Annex 1.

IN TOUCH *WITH THE MACROECONOMY*

(Continued)

A recent evaluation of the OECD index of leading indicators[‡] found that the index performed better in predicting turning points in the US, Canadian, and Japanese economies than for European countries. For France, Germany, and the UK, the error rate in terms of the number of early, false, or missed signals was 40% for predicting peaks in economic activity and, for France and the UK, 20% in predicting troughs. The authors suggest the relatively better predictive performance for North America and Japan may be a reflection of their larger and more diversified economies, which also make output less volatile and easier to predict. Alternatively, it may simply be an indication that the Burns–Mitchell methodology upon which the index is modelled is suitable for tracking economic activity in these countries.

---

[*] Historical data are available in *Leading Indicators: OECD Leading Indicators and Business Cycles in Member Countries 1960–1985*, January 1987. For an accessible discussion of the OECD's index of leading indicators, see Ronny Nilsson, 'OECD Leading Indicators', *OECD Economic Studies*, Autumn 1987.
[†] Wesley Mitchell and Arthur Burns, *Statistical Indicators of Cyclical Revivals* (NBER, 1938).
[‡] Michael Artis, Robin Bladen-Hovell and W. Zhang, 'Turning Points in the International Business Cycle: An Analysis of the OECD Leading Indicators for the G-7 Countries', *OECD Economic Studies*, 1995, pp. 125–65.

Let us now examine the cyclical behaviour of some key macroeconomic variables. We showed the historical behaviour of several of these variables in Figures 1.1–1.4. Those figures covered a long time period and were based on annual data. We can get a better view of short-run cyclical behaviour by looking at quarterly or monthly data. The direction and timing of the variables considered are presented in Summary table 10 on page 319.

Production

Because the level of production is a basic indicator of aggregate economic activity, peaks and troughs in production tend to occur at about the same time as peaks and troughs in aggregate economic activity. Thus production is a coincident and procyclical variable. Figure 9.2 shows the behaviour of the industrial production index in France, Germany, and the UK since 1970. This index is a broad measure of production in manufacturing, mining, and utilities. The vertical lines P and T in Figures 9.2–9.10 indicate the dates of business cycle peaks and troughs, as determined by the ECRI (see Table 9.1). The turning points in industrial production correspond closely to the turning points of the cycle.

Although almost all types of production rise in expansions and fall in recessions, the cyclical sensitivity of production in some sectors of the economy is greater than in others. Industries that produce relatively durable, or long-lasting, goods – houses, consumer durables (refrigerators, cars, washing machines), or capital goods (drill presses, computers, factories) – respond strongly to the business cycle, producing at high rates during expansions and at much lower rates during recessions. In contrast, industries that produce relatively non-durable or short-lived goods (foods, paper products) or services (education, insurance) are less sensitive to the business cycle.

Expenditure

For components of expenditure, as for types of production, durability is the key to determining sensitivity to the business cycle. Figure 9.3 shows the cyclical behaviour of consumption spending and investment. Investment is made up primarily of spending on durable goods and is strongly procyclical. However, consumption expenditures, which include expenditures on non-durable goods and services, in addition to consumer durables, are relatively smoother. A breakdown of consumption into its components would show that spending on consumer durables is strongly procyclical (sales of cars, furniture, and washing machines go up sharply during an economic expansion) but that consumption of non-durable goods and services is much less affected by the business cycle. With respect to timing, consumption and investment are generally coincident with the business cycle, although individual components of fixed investment vary in their cyclical timing.[9]

One component of spending that seems to follow its own rules is inventory investment, or changes in business inventories (not shown), which

---

9. Summary table 10 shows that residential investment leads the cycle.

Figure 9.2
Cyclical behaviour of the index of industrial production in France, Germany and the UK
The index of industrial production, a broad measure of production in manufacturing, mining, and public utilities, is procyclical and coincident. The peaks and troughs of the business cycle are shown by the vertical lines *P* and *T*. The shaded areas represent recessions.

Source: Data on industrial production from *Datastream*.

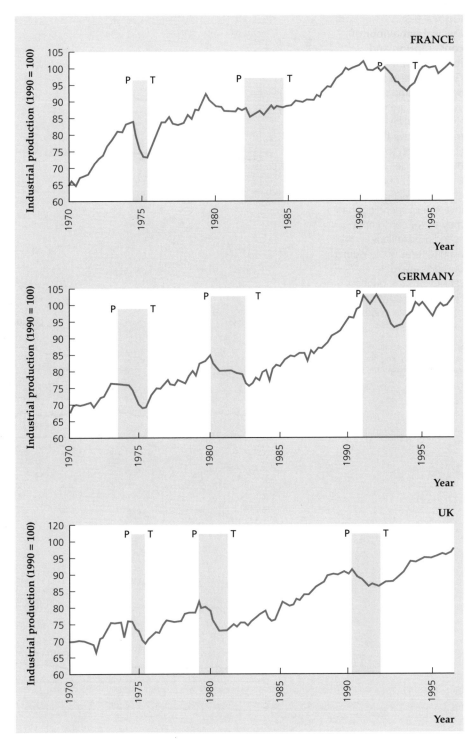

Figure 9.3
Cyclical behaviour of consumption and investment In France, Germany and the UK
Both consumption and investment are procyclical. However, investment is more sensitive than consumption to the business cycle, reflecting the fact that durable goods are a larger part of investment spending than they are of consumption spending. Similarly, expenditures on consumer durables are more sensitive to the business cycle than is consumption of nondurable goods and services.

Source: Data on consumers expenditure and gross fixed investment from *Datastream*.

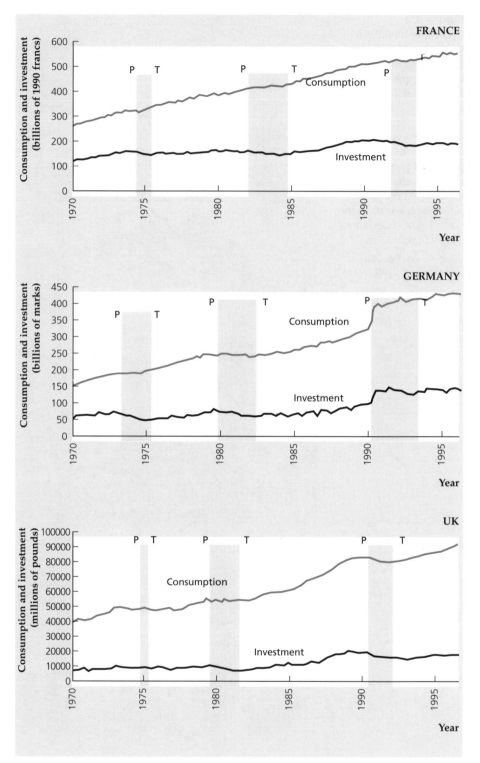

SUMMARY 10	Variable	Direction	Timing
The Cyclical Behaviour of Key Macroeconomic Variables (The Business Cycle Facts)	**Production**		
	Industrial production	Procyclical	Coincident
	Durable goods industries are more volatile than non-durable goods and services		
	Expenditure		
	Consumption	Procyclical	Coincident
	Business fixed investment	Procyclical	Coincident
	Residential investment	Procyclical	Leading
	Inventory investment	Procyclical	Leading
	Government purchases	Procyclical	?
	Investment is more volatile than consumption		
	Labour Market Variables		
	Employment	Procyclical	Coincident
	Unemployment	Countercyclical	Unclassified
	Average labour productivity	Procyclical	Leading
	Real wage	Procyclical	?
	Money Growth and Inflation		
	Money growth	Procyclical	Leading
	Inflation	Procyclical	Lagging
	Financial Variables		
	Stock prices	Procyclical	Leading
	Nominal interest rates	Procyclical	Lagging
	Real interest rates	Acyclical	?

often displays large fluctuations that are not associated with business cycle peaks and troughs. In general, however, inventory investment is procyclical and leading. Even though goods kept in inventory need not be durable, inventory investment is also very volatile. Athough, on average, inventory investment is a small part (about 1%) of total spending, sharp declines in inventory investment represented a large part of the total decline in spending in some recessions, most notably those of 1973–75, the early 1980s, and the early 1990s.

Government purchases of goods and services are generally procyclical (see Figure 4.8). Rapid military build-ups, as during World War II, are usually associated with economic expansions.

Employment and Unemployment

Business cycles are strongly felt in the labour market. In a recession, employment grows slowly or falls, many workers are laid off, and jobs become more difficult to find.

Figure 9.4 shows the number of civilians employed for France, Germany and the UK. Employment is clearly procyclical, as more people have jobs in booms than in recessions, and is also coincident with the cycle.

Figure 9.4
Cyclical behaviour of civilian employment in France, Germany and the UK
Civilian employment is procyclical and coincident with the business cycle.

Source: Data on total employment (France and the UK) and total wage and salary earners (Germany) from *Datastream*.

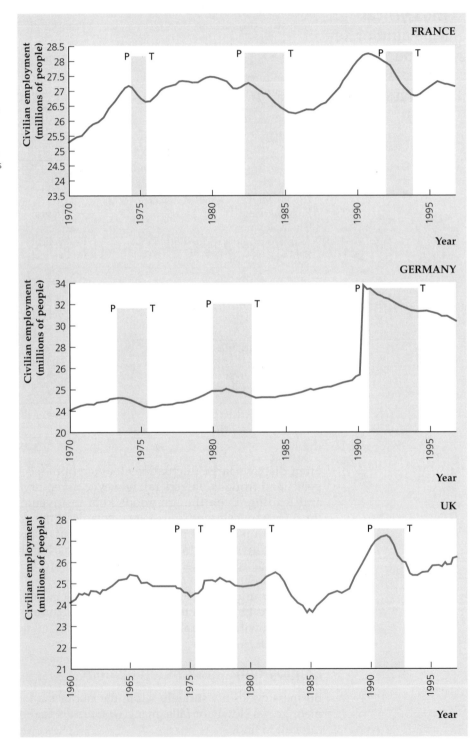

Figure 9.5 shows the civilian unemployment rate, which is the fraction of the civilian labour force (the number of people who are available for work and want to work) that is unemployed.[10] The civilian unemployment rate is strongly countercyclical, rising sharply in contractions but falling more slowly in expansions. Figure 9.5 illustrates a somewhat unusual aspect of both the 1980–81 and 1990–91 recessions in the UK: the unemployment rate continued to climb for several months after the recession's trough was reached. Similarly the unemployment rate in Germany continued to increase despite the recovery in economic activity following the 1980–81 recession.

Average Labour Productivity and the Real Wage

Two other significant labour market variables are average labour productivity and the real wage. As discussed in Chapter 1, average labour productivity is output per unit of labour input. Figure 9.6 shows average labour productivity measured as total real output in the German and UK economies (excluding farms) divided by the total number of hours worked to produce that output. Average labour productivity, in general, tends to be procyclical: in booms, workers produce more output during each hour of work than they do in recessions.[11] Average labour productivity also tends to lead the business cycle.

Recall from Chapter 3 that the real wage is the compensation received by workers per unit of time (such as an hour or a week) measured in real, or purchasing-power, terms. The real wage, as shown in Figure 9.7 for France and the UK, is an especially important variable in the study of business cycles because it is one of the main determinants of the amount of labour supplied by workers and demanded by firms. Most of the evidence points to the conclusion that real wages are mildly procyclical, but there is some controversy on this point.[12]

Money Growth and Inflation

Another variable whose cyclical behaviour is somewhat controversial is the money supply. Figure 9.8, shows the behaviour of the growth in the money supply.[13] Note that (nominal) money growth fluctuates a great deal and does not always display an obvious cyclical pattern. However, as Figure 9.8

---

10. Quarterly unemployment data for France are available only from 1980.

11. The Application in Chapter 3, 'The Production Function of an Economy and Productivity Growth', p. 69, made the point that total factor productivity A also tends to be procyclical.

12. See, for example, Mark Mitchell, Myles Wallace, and John Warner, 'Real Wages Over the Business Cycle: Some Further Evidence', *Southern Economic Journal*, April 1985, pp. 1162–73; and Michael Keane, Robert Moffitt, and David Runkle, 'Real Wages Over the Business Cycle: Estimating the Impact of Heterogeneity with Micro Data', *Journal of Political Economy*, December 1988, pp. 1232–66. Stronger procyclicality for the real wage is claimed by Gary Solon, Robert Barsky, and Jonathan Parker, 'Measuring the Cyclicality of Real Wages: How Important Is Composition Bias?', *Quarterly Journal of Economics*, February 1994, pp. 1–25.

13. To reduce the effect of high month-to-month volatility in money growth, Figure 9.8 presents a six-month moving average of money growth rates: that is, the reported growth rate in each month is actually the average of the growth rate in the current month and in the previous five months.

Figure 9.5
Cyclical behaviour of unemployment in France, Germany and the UK

The unemployment rate is countercyclical and very sensitive to the business cycle. Its timing pattern relative to the cycle is unclassified, meaning that it has no definite tendency to lead, be coincident, or lag.

Source: Data on total unemployment rates from *Datastream*.

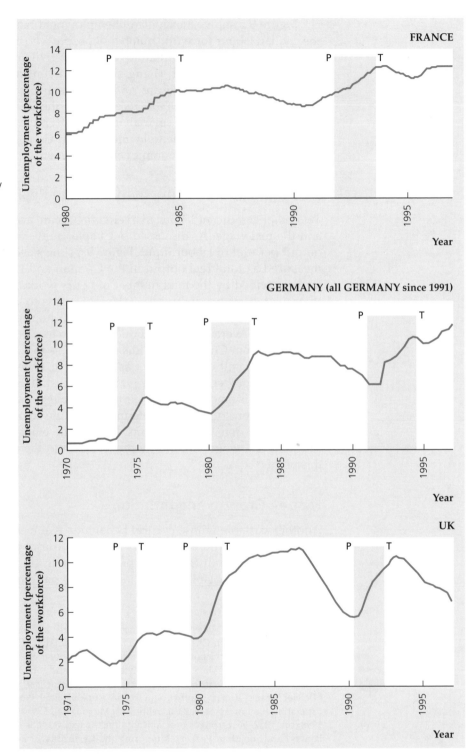

**Figure 9.6
Cyclical behaviour of
average labour
productivity in
Germany and the UK**
Average labour
productivity, measured as
real output per employee
hour, is procyclical and
leading.

Source: Data on output per
person-hour from *Datastream*.

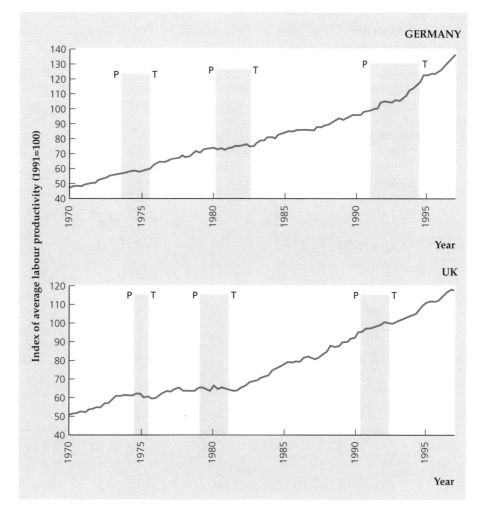

shows, money growth often falls sharply at or just before the onset of a recession. Moreover, many statistical and historical studies – including a classic work by Milton Friedman and Anna J. Schwartz[14] that used data back to 1867 – demonstrate that money growth is procyclical and leads the cycle.

The cyclical behaviour of inflation, shown in Figure 9.9, presents a somewhat clearer picture. Inflation is procyclical but with some lag. Inflation typically builds during an economic expansion, peaks slightly after the business cycle peak, and then falls until some time after the business cycle trough is reached.

---

14. *A Monetary History of the United States, 1867–1960* (Princeton University Press for NBER, 1963). We discuss this study further in Chapter 11.

Figure 9.7
Cyclical behaviour of the real wage in France and the UK
The economywide average real wage is mildly procyclical. Note how sharply real wage growth has slowed since 1973 in France but increased in the UK.

Source: Data on index of real hourly wages from *Datastream*.

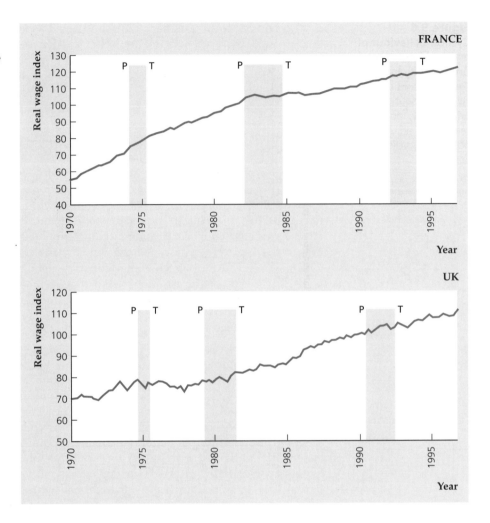

Financial Variables

Financial variables are another class of economic variables that are sensitive to the cycle. For example, stock prices are generally procyclical (stock prices rise in good economic times) and leading (stock prices usually fall in advance of a recession).

Nominal interest rates are procyclical and lagging. The nominal interest rate shown in Figure 9.10 is the rate on three-month Treasury bills. However, other interest rates, such as the prime rate charged by banks to their best customers, are also procyclical and lagging. Note that nominal interest rates have the same general cyclical pattern as inflation; in Chapter 7 we discussed why nominal interest rates tend to move up and down with the inflation rate.

The real interest rate does not have an obvious cyclical pattern. For instance, the real interest rate was actually negative during the 1973–75 recession but was very high during the 1981–82 recession. (Annual values of the real interest rate are shown in Figure 2.4.) The acyclicality of the real interest rate does not necessarily mean its movements are unimportant over the business cycle. Instead, the lack of a stable cyclical pattern may reflect the facts that individual business cycles have different causes and that these different sources of cycles have different effects on the real interest rate.

**Figure 9.8
Cyclical behaviour of
nominal money growth
in France, Germany and
the UK**
Nominal money growth,
here measured as the
six-month moving average
of monthly growth rates
in M0 (UK) and M2
(France and Germany), all
expressed as annual rates,
are volatile. However, the
figures show that money
growth often falls at or
just before a cyclical peak.
Statistical and historical
studies suggest that,
generally, money growth
is procyclical and leading.

Source: Data on M2 (France and
Germany) and M0 (UK) from
Datastream.

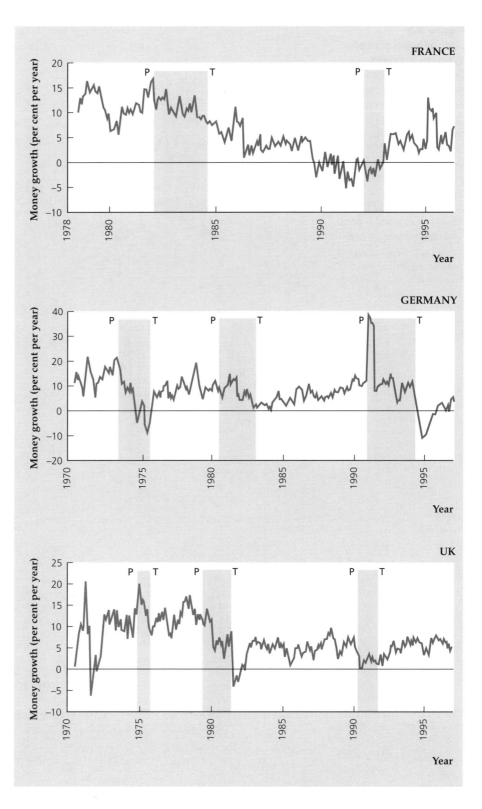

Figure 9.9
Cyclical behaviour of inflation in France, Germany and the UK
Inflation, here measured as the six-month moving average of monthly growth rates of the CPI (expressed in annual rates), is procyclical and lags the business cycle. A typical pattern is for inflation to build up during the expansion and then to fall after the cyclical peak.

Source: Dat on CPI (France and Germany) and RPI (UK) from *Datastream*.

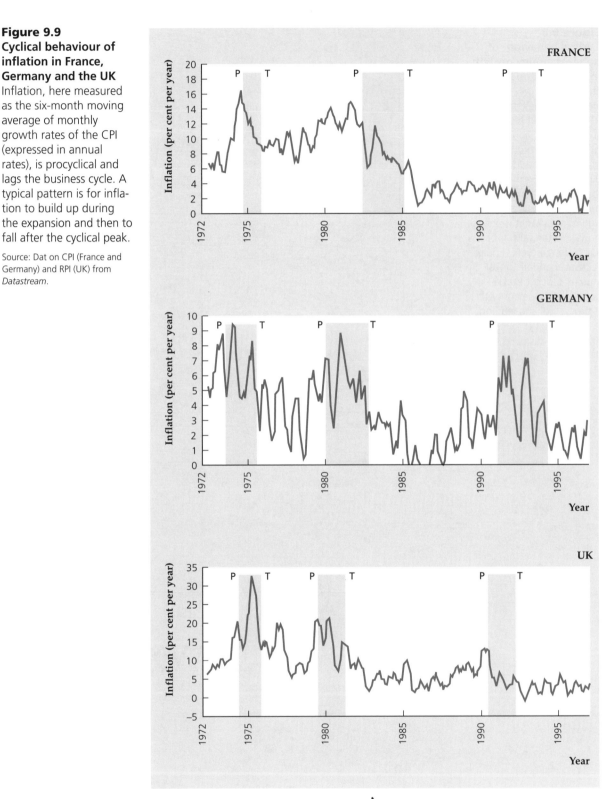

**Figure 9.10
Cyclical behaviour of
the nominal interest
rate in France, Germany
and the UK**
The nominal interest
rate, measured here as
the interest rate on
three-month Treasury bills
(France and the UK) and
on the three-month
Frankfurt Interbank
offered rate, is procyclical
and lagging.

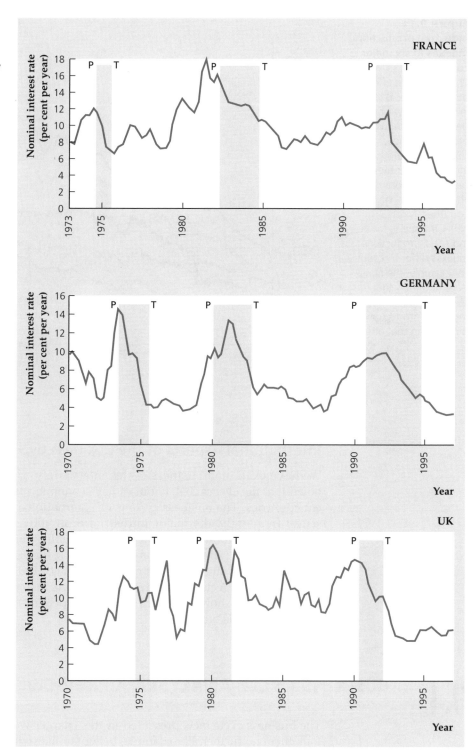

**Figure 9.11
Industrial production
indexes in six major
countries**
The worldwide effect of
business cycles is reflected
in the similarity of the
behaviour of industrial
production in each of the
six countries shown. But
individual countries also
have fluctuations not
shared with other
countries.
Note: the scales for the
industrial production
indexes differ by country:
for example, the figure
does not imply that the
United Kingdom's total
industrial production is
higher than that of Japan.

Source: The Conference Board
(with scales adjusted for clarity).

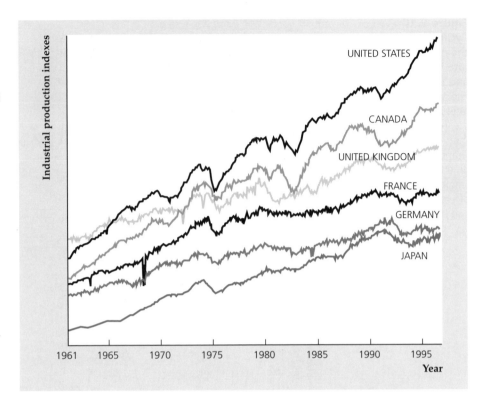

International Aspects of the Business Cycle

We have examined business cycles in a variety of countries, and we have
noted that the cyclical behaviour of key economic variables is similar in different countries. The business cycle is an international phenomenon in another
sense: frequently, the major industrial economies undergo recessions and
expansions at about the same time, suggesting that they share a common
cycle. Figure 9.11 illustrates this common cycle by showing the index of industrial production since 1961 for each of six major industrial countries. Note in
particular the effects of worldwide recessions in about 1975, 1982, and 1991.
Figure 9.11 also shows that each economy experiences many small fluctuations
not shared by the others.

9.4   BUSINESS CYCLE ANALYSIS: A PREVIEW

The business cycle facts presented in this chapter would be useful even if we
took them no further: For example, being familiar with the typical cyclical patterns of key macroeconomic variables helps forecasters project the course of
the economy, as we showed when discussing the index of leading indicators.
Knowing the facts about cycles is also important for businesspeople making
investment and hiring decisions and for financial investors trying to choose

BOX 9.2

The Seasonal Cycle and the Business Cycle

Did you know that all European countries have a large economic boom, followed by a deep recession, every year? The boom always occurs in the fourth quarter of the year (October through December). During this quarter output is 5% higher than in the third quarter (July–September) and about 8% higher than in the following first quarter (January–March). Fortunately, the first-quarter recession is always a short one, with output rising by almost 4% in the second quarter (April–June). This regular seasonal pattern, known as the seasonal cycle, actually accounts for more than 85% of the total fluctuation in the growth rate of real output!

Why don't large seasonal fluctuations appear in Figures 9.2–9.11? Normally, macroeconomic data are seasonally adjusted, meaning that regularly recurring seasonal fluctuations are removed from the data. Seasonal adjustment allows users of economic data to ignore seasonal changes and focus on business cycle fluctuations and longer-term movements in the data. However, Robert Barsky of the University of Michigan and Jeffrey Miron of Boston University* argue that the practice of seasonally adjusting macroeconomic data may throw away information that could help economists better understand the business cycle. Using data that had not been seasonally adjusted, Barsky and Miron determined that the co-movements of variables over the seasonal cycle are similar to their co-movements over the business cycle. Specifically, they obtained the following results:

1. Of the types of expenditure, expenditures on durable goods vary most over the seasonal cycle and expenditures on services vary least.

2. Government spending is seasonally procyclical.
3. Employment is seasonally procyclical, and the unemployment rate is seasonally countercyclical.
4. Average labour productivity is seasonally procyclical, and the real wage hardly varies over the seasonal cycle.
5. The nominal money stock is seasonally procyclical.

Each observation appears to be true for both the business cycle and the seasonal cycle (although, as discussed, there is some controversy about the cyclical behaviour of the real wage). However, the seasonal fluctuations of inventory investment, the price level, and the nominal interest rate are much smaller than their fluctuations over the business cycle.

The seasonal cycle illustrates three potential sources of aggregate economic fluctuations: (1) changes in consumer demand, as at Christmas time; (2) changes in productivity, as when construction workers become less productive because of winter weather in the first quarter; and (3) changes in labour supply, as when people take summer vacations or students enter the labour force in the third quarter. Each of these three sources of fluctuation may also contribute to the business cycle.

As we discuss in Chapter 11, classical economists believe that business cycles generally represent the economy's best response to changes in the economic environment, a response that macroeconomic policy need not try to eliminate. Although it does not necessarily confirm this view, the seasonal cycle shows that large economic fluctuations may be desirable responses to various factors (Christmas, the weather) and do not need to be offset by government policy.

---

* 'The Seasonal and the Business Cycle', *Journal of Political Economy*, June 1989, pp. 503–34.

portfolios that provide the desired combinations of risk and return. However, macroeconomists are interested not only in *what* happens during business cycles but also in *why* it happens. This desire to understand cycles is not just idle intellectual curiosity. For example, as we demonstrate in Chapters 10–12, the advice that macroeconomists give to policymakers about how to respond to a recession depends on what they think is causing the recession. Thus, with the business cycle facts as background, in the rest of Part III we describe the primary alternative explanations of business cycle fluctuations, as well as policy recommendations based on these explanations.

In general, theories of the business cycle have two main components. The first is a description of the types of factor that have major impacts on the economy – wars, new inventions, harvest failures, and changes in government policy are examples. Economists often refer to these (typically unpredictable) forces hitting the economy as *shocks*. The other component of a business cycle theory is a *model* of how the economy responds to the various shocks. Think of the economy as a car moving down a poorly maintained highway: the shocks can be thought of as the potholes and bumps in the road; the model describes how the components of the car (its tyres and shock absorbers) act to smooth out or amplify the effects of the shocks on the passengers.

The two principal business cycle theories that we discuss in this book are the *classical* and the *Keynesian*. Fortunately, to present and discuss these two theories we do not have to develop two completely different models. Instead, both can be considered within a general framework called the *aggregate demand–aggregate supply*, or *AD–AS, model*. To introduce some of the key differences between the classical and Keynesian approaches to business cycle analysis, in the rest of this chapter we preview the *AD–AS* model and how it is used to analyse business cycles.

Aggregate Demand and Aggregate Supply: A Brief Introduction

We develop and apply the *AD–AS* model, and a key building block of the *AD–AS* model, the *IS–LM* model, in Chapters 10–12. Here, we simply introduce and briefly explain the basic components of the *AD–AS* model. The *AD–AS* model has three components, as illustrated in Figure 9.12: (1) the aggregate demand curve, (2) the short-run aggregate supply curve, and (3) the long-run aggregate supply curve. Each curve represents a relationship between the aggregate price level, P, measured on the vertical axis in Figure 9.12, and output, Y, measured along the horizontal axis.

The *aggregate demand (AD) curve* shows for any price level, P, the total quantity of goods and services, Y, *demanded* by households, firms, and governments. The *AD* curve slopes downwards in Figure 9.12, implying that, when the general price level is higher, people demand fewer goods and services. We give the precise explanation for this downward slope in Chapter 10. The intuitive explanation for the downward slope of the *AD* curve – that when prices are higher people can afford to buy fewer goods – is *not* correct. The problem with the intuitive explanation is that, although an increase in the general price level does reflect an increase in the prices of most goods, it also implies an increase in the incomes of the people who produce and sell those goods. Thus to say that a higher price level reduces the quantities of goods and services that people can afford to buy is not correct, because their incomes, as well as prices, have gone up.

The *AD* curve relates the amount of output demanded to the price level, if we hold other economic factors constant. However, for a specific price level, any change in the economy that increases the aggregate quantity of goods and services demanded will shift the *AD* curve to the right (and any change that decreases the quantity of goods and services demanded will shift the *AD* curve to the left). For example, a sharp rise in the stock market, by making consumers wealthier, would probably increase households' demand for goods

Figure 9.12
The aggregate demand–aggregate supply model
The aggregate demand (*AD*) curve slopes downward, reflecting the fact that the aggregate quantity of goods and services demanded, *Y*, falls when the price level, *P*, rises. The short-run aggregate supply (*SRAS*) curve is horizontal, reflecting the assumption that, in the short run, prices are fixed and firms simply produce whatever quantity is demanded. In the long run, firms produce their normal levels of output, so the long-run aggregate supply (*LRAS*) curve is vertical at full-employment level of output, $\overline{Y}$. The economy's short-run equilibrium is at the point where the *AD* and *SRAS* curves intersect, and its long-run equilibrium is where the *AD* and *LRAS* curves intersect. In this example the economy is in both short-run and long-run equilibrium at point *E*.

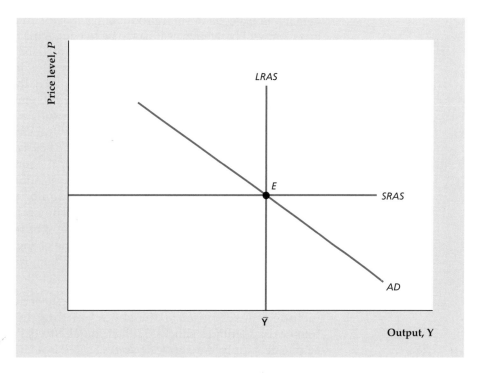

and services, shifting the *AD* curve to the right. Similarly, the development of more efficient capital goods would increase firms' demand for new capital goods, again shifting the *AD* curve to the right. Government policies also can affect the *AD* curve. For example, a decline in government spending on military hardware reduces the aggregate quantity of goods and services demanded and shifts the *AD* curve to the left.

An aggregate supply curve indicates the amount of output producers are willing to *supply* at any particular price level. Two aggregate supply curves are shown in Figure 9.12 – one that holds in the short run and one that holds in the long run. The *short-run aggregate supply (SRAS) curve*, shown in Figure 9.12, is a horizontal line. The horizontal *SRAS* curve captures the ideas that in the short run the price level is fixed and that firms are willing to supply any amount of output at that price. If the short run is a very short period of time, such as a day, this assumption is realistic. For instance, an ice cream shop posts the price of ice cream in the morning and sells as much ice cream as is demanded at that price (up to its capacity to produce ice cream). During a single day, the owner typically will not raise the price of ice cream if the quantity demanded is unusually high; nor does the owner lower the price of ice cream if the quantity demanded is unusually low. The tendency of a producer to set a price for some time and then supply whatever is demanded at that price is represented by a horizontal *SRAS* curve.

However, suppose that the quantity of ice cream demanded remains high day after day, to the point that the owner is straining to produce enough ice cream to meet demand. In this case, the owner may raise her price in order to reduce the quantity of ice cream demanded to a more manageable level. The owner will keep raising the price of ice cream as long as the quantity demanded exceeds normal production capacity. In the long run, the price of ice cream will be whatever it has to be to equate the quantity demanded to the owner's normal level of output. Similarly, in the long run, all other firms in the economy will adjust their prices as necessary so as to be able to produce their normal level of output. As discussed in Chapter 3, the normal level of production for the economy as a whole is called the full-employment level of output, denoted $\bar{Y}$. In the long run, then, when prices fully adjust, the aggregate quantity of output supplied will simply equal the full-employment level of output $\bar{Y}$. Thus the *long-run aggregate supply (LRAS) curve is* vertical, as shown in Figure 9.12, at the point that output supplied, Y, equals $\bar{Y}$.

Figure 9.12 represents an economy that is simultaneously in short-run and long-run equilibrium. The short-run equilibrium is represented by the intersection of the AD and $SRAS$ curves, shown as point E. The long-run equilibrium is represented by the intersection of the AD and $LRAS$ curves, also shown as point E. However, when some change occurs in the economy, the short-run equilibrium can differ from the long-run equilibrium.

Aggregate Demand Shocks. Recall that a theory of business cycles has to include a description of the shocks hitting the economy. The AD–AS framework identifies shocks by their initial effects – on aggregate demand or aggregate supply. An *aggregate demand shock* is a change in the economy that shifts the AD curve. For example, a negative aggregate demand shock would occur if consumers became more pessimistic about the future and thus reduced their current consumption spending, shifting the AD curve to the left.

To analyse the effect of an aggregate demand shock, let's suppose that the economy initially is in both short-run and long-run equilibrium at point E in Figure 9.13. We assume that, because consumers become more pessimistic, the aggregate demand curve shifts down and to the left from AD^1 to AD^2. In this case, the new short-run equilibrium (the intersection of AD^2 and $SRAS$) is at point F, where output has fallen to Y_2 and the price level remains unchanged at P_1. Thus the decline in household consumption demand causes a recession, with output falling below its normal level. However, the economy will not stay at point F forever, because firms will not be content to keep producing below their normal capacity. Eventually firms will respond to lower demand by adjusting their prices – in this case downwards – until the economy reaches its new long-run equilibrium at point H, the intersection of AD^2 and $LRAS$. At point H, output is at its original level, $\bar{Y}$, but the price level has fallen to P_2.

Our analysis shows that an adverse aggregate demand shock, which shifts the AD curve down, will cause output to fall in the short run but not in the long run. How long does it take for the economy to reach the long run? This question is crucial to economic analysis and is one to which classical economists and Keynesian economists have very different answers. Their answers help explain why classical economists and Keynesians have different views about the appropriate role of government policy in fighting recessions.

The classical answer is that prices adjust quite rapidly to imbalances in quantities supplied and demanded so that the economy gets to its long-run equilibrium quickly – in a few months or less. Thus a recession caused by a downward shift of the AD curve is likely to end rather quickly, as the price level falls and the economy reaches the original level of output $\bar{Y}$. In the

Figure 9.13
An adverse aggregate demand shock

An adverse aggregate demand shock reduces the aggregate quantity of goods and services demanded at a given price level; an example is that consumers become more pessimistic and thus reduce their spending. This shock is represented by a shift to the left of the aggregate demand curve from AD^1 to AD^2. In the short run, the economy moves to point F. At this short-run equilibrium, output has fallen to Y_2 and the price level is unchanged. Eventually, price adjustment causes the economy to move to the new long-run equilibrium at point H, where output returns to its full-employment level, $\overline{Y}$, and the price level falls to P_2. In the strict classical view, the economy moves almost immediately to point H, so the adverse aggregate demand shock essentially has no effect on output in both the short run and the long run. Keynesians argue that the adjustment process takes longer so that the adverse aggregate demand shock may lead to a sustained decline in output.

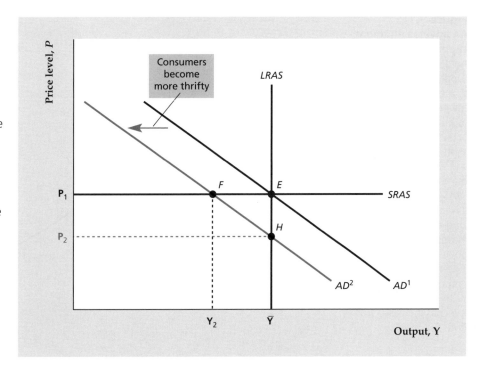

strictest versions of the classical model, the economy is assumed to reach its long-run equilibrium essentially immediately, implying that the short-run aggregate supply curve is irrelevant and that the economy always operates on the long-run aggregate supply (*LRAS*) curve. Because the adjustment takes place quickly, classical economists argue that little is gained by the government actively trying to fight recessions. Note that this conclusion is consistent with the 'invisible hand' argument described in Chapter 1, according to which the free market and unconstrained price adjustments are sufficient to achieve good economic results.

In contrast to the classical view, Keynesian economists argue that prices (and wages, which are the price of labour) do not necessarily adjust quickly in response to shocks. Hence the return of the economy to its long-run equilibrium may be slow, taking perhaps years rather than months. In other words, although Keynesians agree with classical economists that the economy's level of output will eventually return from its recessionary level (represented by Y_2 in Figure 9.13) to its full-employment level, $\overline{Y}$, they believe that this process may be slow. Because they lack confidence in the self-correcting powers of the economy, Keynesians tend to see an important role for the government in fighting recessions. For example, Keynes himself originally argued that government could fight recessions by increasing spending. In terms of Figure 9.13, an increase in government spending could in principle shift the *AD* curve to the right, from AD^2 back to AD^1, restoring the economy to full employment.

Aggregate Supply Shocks. Because classical economists believe that aggregate demand shocks do not cause sustained fluctuations in output, they generally view aggregate supply shocks as the major force behind changes in

Figure 9.14
An adverse aggregate supply shock
An adverse aggregate supply shock, such as a drought, reduces the full-employment level of output from $\overline{Y}_1$ to $\overline{Y}_2$. Equivalently, the shock shifts the long-run aggregate supply curve the left, from $LRAS^1$ to $LRAS^2$. As a result of the adverse supply shock, the long-run equilibrium moves from point E to point F. In the new long-run equilibrium, output has fallen from $\overline{Y}_1$ to $\overline{Y}_2$ and the price level has increased from P_1 to P_2.

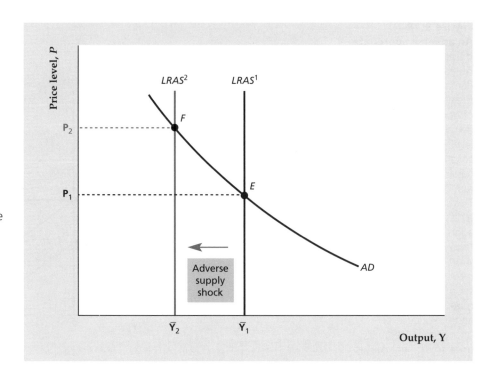

output and employment. An *aggregate supply shock* is a change in the economy that causes the long-run aggregate supply (*LRAS*) curve to shift. The position of the *LRAS* curve depends only on the full-employment level of output, $\overline{Y}$, so aggregate supply shocks can also be thought of as factors – such as changes in productivity or labour supply – that lead to changes in $\overline{Y}$.

Figure 9.14 illustrates the effects of an adverse supply shock: that is, a shock that reduces the full-employment level of output (an example would be a severe drought that greatly reduces crop yields). Suppose that the economy is initially in long-run equilibrium at point E in Figure 9.14, where the initial long-run aggregate supply curve, $LRAS^1$, intersects the aggregate demand curve AD. Now imagine that the adverse supply shock hits, reducing full-employment output from $\overline{Y}_1$ to $\overline{Y}_2$ and causing the long-run aggregate supply curve to shift to the left from $LRAS^1$ to $LRAS^2$. The new long-run equilibrium occurs at point F, where the level of output is lower than at point E. According to the classical view, the economy moves quickly from point E to point F and then remains at point F. The drop in output as the economy moves from point E to point F is a recession. Note that the new price level, P_2, is higher than the initial price level, P_1, so adverse supply shocks cause prices to rise during recessions. We return to this implication for the price level and discuss its relation to the business cycle facts in Chapter 11.

Although classical economists first emphasized supply shocks, Keynesian economists also recognize the importance of supply shocks in accounting for business cycle fluctuations in output. Keynesians agree that an adverse supply shock will reduce output and increase the price level in the long run. In Chapter 12, we discuss the Keynesian view of the process by which the economy moves from the short run to the long run in response to a supply shock.

CHAPTER SUMMARY

1. A business cycle consists of a period of declining aggregate economic activity (a contraction or recession) followed by a period of rising economic activity (an expansion or a boom). The low point of the contraction is called the trough, and the high point of the expansion is called the peak. Business cycles have been observed in market economies since the beginning of industrialization.

2. Many economic variables have regular and predictable patterns of behaviour over the course of the cycle. That tendency is called comovement. We refer to the typical cyclical patterns of key macroeconomic variables as the 'business cycle facts'.

3. The fluctuations in aggregate economic activity that constitute business cycles are recurrent, having been observed again and again in industrialized market economies. However, they are not periodic, in that they do not occur at regular or predictable intervals. Business cycle fluctuations are also persistent, which means that once a recession or expansion begins, it usually lasts for a while.

4. Economists believe that European economies before 1929 had longer recessions and more cyclical volatility than the post-World War II economy. However, data problems prevent precise measurements of how much more cyclical pre-World War I economies were. The Great Depression that began in 1929 and did not end until 1933 was the most severe cyclical decline in the history of many European countries. Moderation of the business cycle after World War II led to premature pronouncements that the cycle was 'dead'. However, many European economies suffered severe recessions in 1973–75, 1981–82, and the early 1990s.

5. The direction of a variable relative to the business cycle can be procyclical, countercyclical, or acyclical. A procyclical variable moves in the same direction as aggregate economic activity, rising in booms and falling in recessions. A countercyclical variable moves oppositely to aggregate economic activity, falling in booms and rising in recessions. An acyclical variable has no clear cyclical pattern.

6. The timing of a variable relative to the business cycle may be coincident, leading, or lagging. A coincident variable's peaks and troughs occur at about the same time as peaks and troughs in aggregate economic activity. Peaks and troughs in a leading variable come before, and peaks and troughs in a lagging variable come after, the corresponding peaks and troughs in aggregate economic activity.

7. The cyclical direction and timing of major macroeconomic variables – the business cycle facts – are described in Summary table 10. In brief, production, consumption, and investment are procyclical and coincident. Investment is much more volatile over the business cycle than consumption is. Employment is procyclical, but the unemployment rate is countercyclical. Average labour productivity and the real wage are procyclical, although according to most studies the real wage is only mildly so. Money and stock prices are procyclical and lead the cycle. Inflation and nominal interest rates are procyclical and lagging. The real interest rate is acyclical.

8. A theory of business cycles consists of (1) a description of shocks that affect the economy and (2) a model, such as the aggregate demand–aggregate supply (AD–AS) model, that describes how the economy responds to these shocks. In the AD–AS model, shocks to the aggregate demand (AD) curve cause ouput to change in the short run, but output returns to its full-employment level, $\bar{Y}$ in the long run. Shocks to the aggregate supply curve can affect output both in the long run and the short term.

9. Classical economists argue that the economy reaches its long-run equilibrium quickly, because prices adjust rapidly. This view implies that aggregate demand shocks have only very short-lived effects on real variables such as output;

instead, classical economists emphasize aggregate supply shocks as the source of business cycles. Classical economists also see little role for government policies to fight recessions. Keynesian economists, in contrast, believe that it takes a long time for the economy to reach long-run equilibrium. They conclude, therefore, that aggregate demand shocks can affect ouput for substantial periods of time. Further, they believe that government policies may be useful in speeding the economy's return to full employment.

Key Terms

acyclical, p. 312
boom, p. 303
business cycle, p. 303
business cycle chronology, p. 302
coincident variable, p. 312
co-movement, p. 305
contraction, p. 302
countercyclical, p. 312
depression, p. 303
expansion, p. 303
index of leading indicators, p. 312
lagging variable, p. 312
leading variable, p. 312
peak, p. 303
persistence, p. 306
procyclical, p. 312
recession, p. 302
trough, p. 303
turning points, p. 303

Review Questions

1. Draw a diagram showing the phases and turning points of a business cycle. Using the diagram, illustrate the concepts of recurrence and persistence.
2. What is *co-movement*? How is co-movement related to the business cycle facts presented in this chapter?
3. What is the evidence for the view that the business cycle has become less severe over time? Why is the question of whether the cycle has moderated over time an important one?
4. What terms are used to describe the way a variable moves when economic activity is rising or falling? What terms are used to describe the timing of cyclical changes in economic variables?

5. If you knew that the economy was falling into a recession, what would you expect to happen to production during the next few quarters? To investment? To average labour productivity? To the real wage? To the unemployment rate?
6. How is the fact that some economic variables are known to lead the cycle used in macroeconomic forecasting?
7. What are the two components of a theory of business cycles?
8. How do Keynesian and classical economists differ in their beliefs about how long it takes the economy to reach long-run equilibrium? What implications do these differences in beliefs have for Keynesian and classical views about the usefulness of anti-recessionary policies? About the types of shock that cause most recessions?

Analytical Problems

1. Figure 9.1 shows that business cycle peaks and troughs are identified with peaks and troughs in the level of aggregate economic activity. However, for business cycles before 1927, the identified business cycle peaks and troughs with peaks and troughs in *detrended* aggregate economy activity (aggregate economic activity minus the 'normal growth path' shown in Figure 9.1). Show that this alternative methodology implies that peaks occur earlier and that troughs occur later than you would find when using the current methodology. Compared to the current methodology, does the alternative methodology increase or decrease the computed length of contractions and expansions? How might this change in measurement account for the differences in the average measured lengths of expansions and contractions since World War II compared to the period before World War I?[15]
2. Consumer expenditures on durable goods such as cars and furniture, as well as purchases of new houses, fall much more than expenditures on non-durable goods and services during recessions. Why do you think that is?

---

15. For further discussion of these issues, see Christina D. Romer, 'Remeasuring Business Cycles', *Journal of Economic History*, September 1994, pp. 573–709; and Randall E. Parker and Philip Rothman, 'Further Evidence on the Stabilization of Postwar Economic Fluctuations', *Journal of Macroeconomics*, Spring 1996, pp. 289–98. Romer was the first to emphasize the potential importance of the change in business cycle dating methodology.

3. Output, total hours worked, and average labour productivity all are procyclical.

    a. Which variable, output or total hours worked, increases by a larger percentage in expansions and falls by a larger percentage in recessions? (*Hint:* Average labour productivity = output ÷ total hours worked so that the percentage change in average labour productivity equals the percentage change in output minus the percentage change in total hours worked.)

    b. How is the procyclical behaviour of average labour productivity related to Okun's Law, discussed in Chapter 3?

3. During the period 1973–75 the United Kingdom experienced a deep recession with a simultaneous sharp rise in the price level. Would you conclude that the recession was the result of a supply shock or a demand shock? Illustrate, using *AD–AS* analysis.

CHAPTER 10

THE *IS–LM/AD–AS* MODEL: A GENERAL FRAMEWORK FOR MACROECONOMIC ANALYSIS

The main goal of Chapter 9 was to *describe* business cycles by presenting the business cycle facts. This and the following two chapters *explain* business cycles and how policymakers should respond to them. First, we must develop a macroeconomic model that we can use to analyse cyclical fluctuations and the effects of policy changes on the economy. By examining the labour market in Chapter 3, the goods market in Chapter 4, and the asset market in Chapter 7, we have already identified the three components of a complete macroeconomic model. Now we put these three components together into a single framework that allows us to analyse them simultaneously. This chapter, then, consolidates our previous analyses to provide the theoretical structure for the rest of the book.

The macroeconomic model developed in this chapter is known as the *IS–LM* model. (As we discuss later, this name originates in two of its basic equilibrium conditions: that investment, *I*, must equal saving, *S*, and that money demanded, *L*, must equal money supplied, *M*.) The *IS–LM* model was developed in 1937 by Nobel laureate Sir John Hicks,[1] who intended it as a graphical representation of the ideas presented by Keynes in his famous 1936 book, *The General Theory of Employment, Interest, and Money*. Reflecting Keynes's belief that wages and prices do not adjust quickly to clear markets (see Section 1.3), in his original *IS–LM* model Hicks assumed that the price level was fixed, at least temporarily. Since Hicks, several generations of economists have worked to refine the *IS–LM* model, and it has been widely applied in analyses of cyclical fluctuations and macroeconomic policy, and in forecasting.

---

1. Hicks outlined the *IS–LM* framework in an article entitled 'Mr Keynes and the Classics: A Suggested Interpretation', *Econometrica*, April 1937, pp. 137–59.

Because of its origins, the *IS–LM* model is commonly identified with the Keynesian approach to business cycle analysis. Classical economists – who believe that wages and prices move rapidly to clear markets – would reject Hicks's *IS–LM* model because of his assumption that the price level is fixed. However, the conventional *IS–LM* model may be easily adapted to allow for rapidly adjusting wages and prices. Thus the *IS–LM* framework, although originally developed by Keynesians, may also be used to present and discuss the classical approach to business cycle analysis. In addition, the *IS–LM* model is equivalent to the *AD–AS* model that we previewed in Section 9.4. We show how the *AD–AS* model is derived from the *IS–LM* model and illustrate how the *AD–AS* model can be used with either a classical or a Keynesian perspective.

Using the *IS–LM* model (and the equivalent *AD–AS* model) as a framework for both classical and Keynesian analyses has several practical benefits: First, it avoids the need to learn two different models. Second, utilizing a single framework emphasizes the large areas of agreement between the Keynesian and classical approaches while showing clearly how the two approaches differ. Moreover, because versions of the *IS–LM* model (and its concepts and terminology) are so often applied in analyses of the economy and macroeconomic policy, studying this framework will help you understand and participate more fully in current economic debates.

We use a graphical approach to develop the *IS–LM* model. Appendix 10.A, presents the identical analysis in algebraic form. If you have difficulty understanding why the curves used in the graphical analysis have the slopes they do or why they shift, you may find the algebra in the appendix helpful.

To keep things as simple as possible, in this chapter we assume that the economy is closed. In Chapter 14 we show how to extend the analysis to allow for a foreign sector.

10.1 THE *FE* LINE: EQUILIBRIUM IN THE LABOUR MARKET

Previous chapters discussed the three main markets of the economy: the labour market, the goods market, and the asset market. We also identified some of the links among these markets, but now we want to be more precise about how they fit into a complete macroeconomic system.

Let us turn first to the labour market and recall from Chapter 3 the concepts of the full-employment level of employment and full-employment output. The *full-employment level of employment* $\overline{N}$ is the equilibrium level of employment reached after wages and prices have fully adjusted so that the quantity of labour supplied equals the quantity of labour demanded. *Full-employment output,* $\overline{Y}$, is the amount of output produced when employment is at its full-employment level, for the current level of the capital stock and the production function. Algebraically, full-employment output $\overline{Y}$ equals $AF(K, \overline{N})$, where K is the capital stock, A is productivity, and F is the production function (see equation 3.4).

Our ultimate goal is a diagram that has the real interest rate on the vertical axis and output on the horizontal axis. In such a diagram equilibrium in the labour market is represented by the **full-employment line**, or *FE*, in Figure 10.1.

Figure 10.1
The *FE* line
The full-employment (*FE*) line represents labour market equilibrium. When the labour market is in equilibrium, employment equals its full-employment level, $\bar{N}$, and output equals its full-employment level, $\bar{Y}$, regardless of the value of the real interest rate. Thus the *FE* line is vertical at $Y = \bar{Y}$.

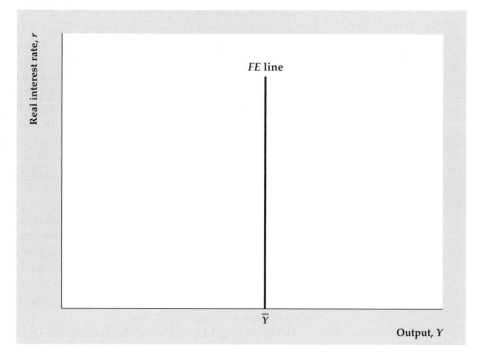

The *FE* line is vertical at $Y = \bar{Y}$ because, when the labour market is in equilibrium, output equals its full-employment level, regardless of the interest rate.[2]

Factors that Shift the *FE* Line

The full-employment level of output is determined by the full-employment level of employment and the current levels of capital and productivity. Any change that affects the full-employment level of output $\bar{Y}$ will cause the *FE* line to shift. Recall that full-employment output $\bar{Y}$ increases – and thus the *FE* line shifts to the right – when the labour supply increases (which raises equilibrium employment $\bar{N}$) or when there is a beneficial supply shock. Similarly, a drop in the labour supply or an adverse supply shock lowers full-employment output $\bar{Y}$ and shifts the *FE* line to the left. Summary table 11 lists the factors that shift the *FE* line.

10.2 THE *IS* CURVE: EQUILIBRIUM IN THE GOODS MARKET

The second of the three markets in our model is the goods market. Recall from Chapter 4 that the goods market is in equilibrium when desired investment and desired national saving are equal or, equivalently, when the aggregate

---

2. The real interest rate affects investment and thus the amount of capital that firms will have in the future, but it does not affect the current capital stock, and hence does not affect current output.

SUMMARY 11	A(n)	Shifts the *FE* Line	Reason
Factors that Shift the Full-Employment (*FE*) Line	Beneficial supply shock	Right	1. More output can be produced for the same amount of capital and labour. 2. If the *MPN* rises, labour demand increases and raises employment. Full-employment output increases for both reasons.
	Increase in labour supply	Right	Equilibrium employment rises, raising full-employment output.
	Increase in the capital stock	Right	More output can be produced with the same amount of labour. In addition, increased capital may increase the *MPN*, which increases labour demand and equilibrium employment.

quantity of goods supplied equals the aggregate quantity of goods demanded. In Chapter 4 we demonstrated that adjustments in the real interest rate help bring about equilibrium in the goods market.

In a diagram with the real interest rate on the vertical axis and real output on the horizontal axis, equilibrium in the goods market is described by a curve called the *IS* curve. Specifically, for any level of output (or income) *Y*, the *IS* **curve** shows the real interest rate *r* for which the goods market is in equilibrium. The *IS* curve is so named because at all points on the curve desired investment, *I*, equals desired national saving, *S*.

Figure 10.2 shows the derivation of the *IS* curve from the saving–investment diagram introduced in Chapter 4 and used extensively in Chapters 4 and 5 (see Key Diagram 3, p. 146). Figure 10.2(a) shows the saving–investment diagram drawn for two randomly chosen levels of output, 4000 and 5000. Corresponding to each level is a saving curve, with the value of output indicated in parentheses next to it. Each saving curve slopes upward because an increase in the real interest rate causes households to increase their desired level of saving. An increase in current output (income) leads to more desired saving at any real interest rate, so the saving (*S*) curve for *Y* = 5000 lies to the right of the saving (*S*) curve for *Y* = 4000.

Also shown in Figure 10.2(a) is an investment curve. Recall from Chapter 4 that the investment curve slopes downwards because an increase in the real interest rate increases the user cost of capital, which reduces the desired capital stock and hence desired investment. Desired investment is not affected by current output, so the investment curve is the same whether *Y* = 4000 or *Y* = 5000.

Each level of output implies a different market-clearing real interest rate. When output is 4000, goods market equilibrium is at point *D* and the market-clearing real interest rate is 7%. When output is 5000, goods market equilibrium occurs at point *F* and the market-clearing real interest rate is 5%.

Figure 10.2(b) shows the *IS* curve for this economy, with output on the horizontal axis and the real interest rate on the vertical axis. For any level of output, the *IS* curve shows the real interest rate that clears the goods market. Thus $Y = 4000$ and $r = 7\%$ at point D on the *IS* curve. (Note that point D in Figure 10.2(b) corresponds to point D in Figure 10.2(a) Similarly, when output is 5000, the real interest rate that clears the goods market is 5%. This combination of output and the real interest rate occurs at point F on the *IS* curve in Figure 10.2(b), which corresponds to point F in Figure 10.2(a). In general, because a rise in output increases desired national saving, thereby reducing the real interest rate that clears the goods market, the *IS* curve slopes downwards.

The slope of the *IS* curve may also be interpreted in terms of the alternative (but equivalent) version of the goods market equilibrium condition, which states that in equilibrium the aggregate quantity of goods demanded must equal the aggregate quantity of goods supplied. To illustrate, let us suppose

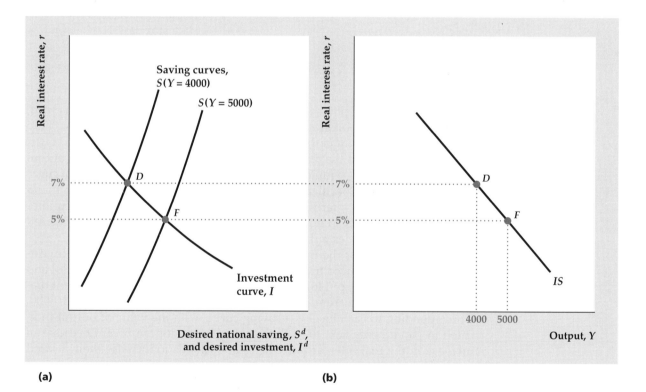

(a)   **(b)**

Figure 10.2
Deriving the *IS* curve
(a) The graph shows the goods market equilibrium for two different levels of output: 4000 and 5000 (the output corresponding to each saving curve is indicated in parentheses next to the curve). Higher levels of output (income) increase desired national saving and shift the saving curve to the right. When output is 4000, the real interest rate that clears the goods market is 7% (point *D*). When output is 5000, the market-clearing interest rate is 5% (point *F*).

(b) For each level of output the *IS* curve shows the corresponding real interest rate that clears the goods market. Thus each point on the *IS* curve corresponds to an equilibrium point in the goods market. As in (a), when output is 4000, the real interest rate that clears the goods market is 7% (point *D*); when output is 5000, the market-clearing interest rate is 5% (point *F*). Because higher output raises saving and leads to a lower market-clearing interest rate, the *IS* curve slopes downward.

that the economy is initially at point *F* in Figure 10.2(b). The aggregate quantities of goods supplied and demanded are equal at point *F*, because *F* lies on the *IS* curve, which means that the goods market is in equilibrium at that point.[3]

Now suppose that for some reason the real interest rate *r* rises from 5% to 7%. Recall from Chapter 4 that an increase in the real interest rate reduces both desired consumption C^d (because people desire to save more when the real interest rate rises) and desired investment I^d, thereby reducing the aggregate quantity of goods demanded. If output, *Y*, remained at its initial level of 5000, the increase in the real interest rate would imply that more goods were being supplied than demanded. For the goods market to reach equilibrium at the higher real interest rate, the quantity of goods supplied has to fall. At point *D* in Figure 10.2(b), output has fallen enough (from 5000 to 4000) that the quantities of goods supplied and demanded are equal, and the goods market has returned to equilibrium.[4] Again, higher real interest rates are associated with less output in goods market equilibrium, so the *IS* curve slopes downwards.

Factors that Shift the *IS* Curve

For any level of output, the *IS* curve shows the real interest rate needed to clear the goods market. With output held constant, any economic disturbance or policy change that changes the value of the goods-market-clearing real interest rate will cause the *IS* curve to shift. More specifically, for constant output, *any change in the economy that reduces desired national saving relative to desired investment will increase the real interest rate that clears the goods market and thus shifts the IS curve up.* Similarly, for constant output, changes that increase desired saving relative to desired investment, thereby reducing the market-clearing real interest rate, shift the *IS* curve down. Factors that shift the *IS* curve are described in Summary table 12.

We can use a change in current government purchases to illustrate *IS* curve shifts in general. The effects of a temporary increase in government purchases on the *IS* curve are shown in Figure 10.3 on page 345. Figure 10.3(a) shows the saving–investment diagram, with an initial saving curve S^1 and an initial investment curve *I*. The S^1 curve represents saving when output (income) is fixed at *Y* = 4500. Figure 10.3(b) shows the initial *IS* curve, IS^1. The initial goods market equilibrium when output *Y* equals 4500 is represented by point *E* in both (a) and (b). At *E*, the initial market-clearing real interest rate is 6%.

Now suppose that the government increases its current purchases of goods, *G*. Desired investment at any level of the real interest rate is not affected by the increase in government purchases, so the investment curve

---

3. We have just shown that desired national saving equals desired investment at point *F*, or $S^d = I^d$. Substituting the definition of desired national saving, $Y - C^d - G$, for S^d in the condition that desired national saving equals desired investment shows also that $Y = C^d + I^d + G$ at *F*.

4. Although a drop in output *Y* obviously reduces the quantity of goods supplied, it also reduces the quantity of goods demanded. The reason is that a drop in output is also a drop in income, which reduces desired consumption. However, although a drop in output of one unit reduces the supply of output by the same amount, a drop in income of one unit reduces desired consumption C^d by *less* than that amount (that is, the marginal propensity to consume, defined in Chapter 4, is less than 1). Thus a drop in output *Y* reduces goods supplied more than goods demanded and therefore reduces the excess supply of goods.

does not shift. However, as discussed in Chapter 4, a temporary increase in government purchases reduces desired national saving, $Y - C^d - G$ (see Summary table 5, p. 126), so the saving curve shifts to the left from S^1 to S^2 in Figure 10.3(a). As a result of the reduction in desired national saving, the real interest rate that clears the goods market when output equals 4500 increases from 6% to 7% (point F in Figure 10.3(a)).

The effect on the IS curve is shown in Figure 10.3(b). With output constant at 4500, the real interest rate that clears the goods market increases from 6% to 7%, as shown by the shift from point E to point F. The new IS curve, IS^2, passes through F and lies above and to the right of the initial IS curve, IS^1. Thus a temporary increase in government purchases shifts the IS curve up.

SUMMARY 12	An Increase in	Shifts the *IS* Curve	Reason
Factors that Shift the *IS* Curve	Expected future output	Up	Desired saving falls (desired consumption rises), raising the real interest rate that clears the goods market.
	Wealth	Up	Desired saving falls (desired consumption rises), raising the real interest rate that clears the goods market.
	Government purchases, G	Up	Desired saving falls (demand for goods rises), raising the real interest rate that clears the goods market.
	Taxes, T	No change or Down	No change, if consumers take into account an offsetting future tax cut and do not change consumption (Ricardian equivalence); down, if consumers do not take into account a future tax cut and reduce desired consumption, increasing desired national saving and lowering the real interest rate that clears the goods market.
	Expected future marginal product of capital, MPK^f	Up	Desired investment increases, raising the real interest rate that clears the goods market.
	Effective tax rate on capital	Down	Desired investment falls, lowering the real interest rate that clears the goods market.

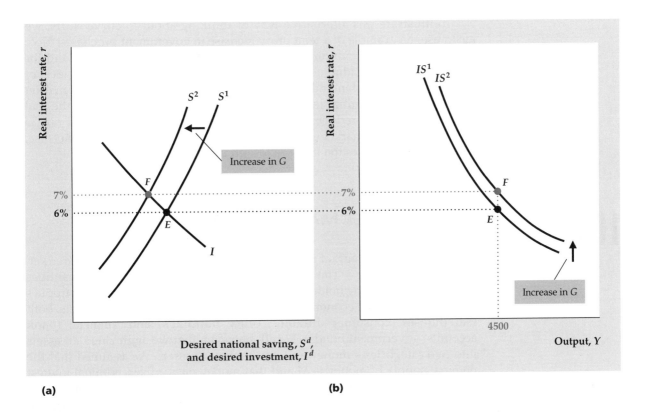

(a)   **(b)**

Figure 10.3
Effect on the *IS* curve of a temporary increase in government purchases
(a) The saving–investment diagram shows the effects of a temporary increase in government purchases, *G*, with output, *Y*, constant at 4500. The increase in *G* reduces desired national saving and shifts the saving curve to the left, from S^1 to S^2. The goods market equilibrium point

moves from point *E* to point *F*, and the real interest rate rises from 6% to 7%.
(b) The increase in *G* raises the real interest rate that clears the goods market for any level of output. Thus the *IS* curve shifts upward from IS^1 to IS^2. In this example, with output held constant at 4500, an increase in government purchases raises the real interest rate that clears the goods market from 6% (point *E*) to 7% (point *F*).

So far our discussion of *IS* curve shifts has focused on the goods market equilibrium condition that desired national saving must equal desired investment. However, factors that shift the *IS* curve may also be described in terms of the alternative (but equivalent) goods market equilibrium condition – that the aggregate quantities of goods demanded and supplied are equal. In particular, for a given level of output, *any change that increases the aggregate demand for goods shifts the IS curve up.*

This rule works because, for the initial level of output, an increase in the aggregate demand for goods causes the quantity of goods demanded to exceed the quantity supplied. Goods market equilibrium can be restored at the same level of output by an increase in the real interest rate, which reduces desired consumption C^d and desired investment I^d. For any level of output, an increase in aggregate demand for goods raises the real interest rate that clears the goods market, so we conclude that an increase in the aggregate demand for goods shifts the *IS* curve up.

To illustrate this alternative way of thinking about *IS* curve shifts, we again use the example of a temporary increase in government purchases. Note that an increase in government purchases, *G*, directly raises the demand for goods, $C^d + I^d + G$, leading to an excess demand for goods at the initial level of output. The excess demand for goods can be eliminated and goods market equilibrium at the initial level of output restored by an increase in the real interest rate, which reduces C^d and I^d. Because a higher real interest rate is required for goods market equilibrium when government purchases increase, an increase in *G* causes the *IS* curve to shift up.

10.3 THE *LM* CURVE: ASSET MARKET EQUILIBRIUM

The third and final market in our macroeconomic model is the asset market, presented in Chapter 7. The asset market is in equilibrium when the quantities of assets demanded by holders of wealth for their portfolios equal the supplies of those assets in the economy. In reality, there are many different assets, both real (houses, consumer durables, office buildings) and financial (bank accounts, government bonds). Recall, however, that we aggregated all assets into two categories – money and non-monetary assets. We assumed that the nominal supply of money is *M* and that money pays a fixed nominal interest rate i^m. Similarly, we assumed that the nominal supply of non-monetary assets is *NM* and that these assets pay a nominal interest rate *i* and (given expected inflation π^e) an expected real interest rate *r*.

With this aggregation assumption, we showed that the asset market equilibrium condition reduces to the requirement that the quantities of money supplied and demanded be equal. In this section we show that asset market equilibrium can be represented by the *LM* curve. However, in order to discuss how the asset market comes into equilibrium – a task that we did not complete in Chapter 7 – we first introduce an important relationship used every day by traders in financial markets: the relationship between the *price* of a non-monetary asset and the *interest rate* on that asset.

The Interest Rate and the Price of a Non-monetary Asset

The price of a non-monetary asset, such as a government bond, is what a buyer has to pay for it. Its price is closely related to the interest rate that it pays (sometimes called its *yield*). To illustrate this relationship with an example, let us consider a bond that matures in one year. At maturity, we assume, the bondholder will redeem it and receive FFr10,000; the bond does not pay any interest before it matures.[5] Suppose that this bond can now be purchased for FFr9615. At this price, over the coming year the bond will increase in value by FFr385 (FFr10,000 – FFr9615), or approximately 4% of its current price of FFr9615. Therefore the nominal interest rate on the bond, or its yield, is 4% per year.

---

5. A bond that does not pay any interest before maturity is called a *discount bond*.

Now suppose that for some reason the current price of a FFr10,000 bond that matures in one year drops to FFr9524. The increase in the bond's value over the next year will be FFr476 (FFr10,000 − FFr9524), or approximately 5% of the purchase price of FFr9524. Therefore, when the current price of the bond falls to FFr9524, the nominal interest rate on the bond increases to 5% per year. More generally, given the promised schedule of repayments of a bond or other non-monetary asset, the higher the price of the asset, the lower is the nominal interest rate that the asset pays. Thus a media report that, in yesterday's trading, the bond market 'strengthened' (bond prices rose), is equivalent to saying that nominal interest rates fell.

We have just indicated why the price of a non-monetary asset and its nominal interest rate are negatively related. For a given expected rate of inflation, π^e, movements in the nominal interest rate are matched by equal movements in the real interest rate, so the price of a non-monetary asset and its *real* interest rate are also inversely related. This relationship is a key to deriving the *LM* curve and explaining how the asset market comes into equilibrium.

The Equality of Money Demanded and Money Supplied

To derive the *LM* curve, which represents asset market equilibrium, recall that the asset market is in equilibrium only if the quantity of money demanded equals the currently available money supply. We depict the equality of money supplied and demanded using the *money supply–money demand diagram*, shown in Figure 10.4(a) overleaf. The real interest rate is on the vertical axis and money, measured in real terms, is on the horizontal axis.[6] The *MS* line shows the economy's real money supply, M/P. The nominal money supply M is set by the central bank. Thus, for a given price level P, the real money supply M/P is a fixed number and the *MS* line is vertical. For example, if $M = 2000$ and $P = 2$, the *MS* line is vertical at $M/P = 1000$.

Real money demand at two different levels of income, Y, is shown by the two *MD* curves in Figure 10.4(a). Recall from Chapter 7 that a higher real interest rate, r, increases the relative attractiveness of non-monetary assets and causes holders of wealth to demand less money. Thus the money demand curves slope downwards. The money demand curve, *MD*, for $Y = 4000$ shows the real demand for money when output is 4000; similarly, the *MD* curve for $Y = 5000$ shows the real demand for money when output is 5000. Because an increase in income increases the amount of money demanded at any real interest rate, the money demand curve for $Y = 5000$ is farther to the right than the money demand curve for $Y = 4000$.

Graphically, asset market equilibrium occurs at the intersection of the money supply and money demand curves, where the real quantities of money supplied and demanded are equal. For example, when output is 4000, so that the money demand curve is *MD* ($Y = 4000$), the money demand and money supply curves intersect at point *A* in Figure 10.4(a). The real interest rate at *A*

---

6. Asset market equilibrium may be expressed as either nominal money supplied equals nominal money demanded, or as real money supplied equals real money demanded. As in Chapter 7, we work with the condition expressed in real terms.

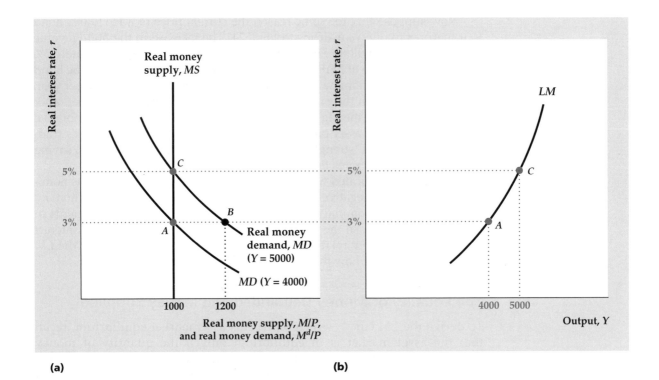

Figure 10.4
Deriving the *LM* curve
(a) The curves show real money demand and real money
supply. Real money supply is fixed at 1000. When output
is 4000, the real money demand curve is *MD* (*Y* = 4000);
the real interest rate that clears the asset market is
3% (point *A*). When output is 5000, more money is
demanded at the same real interest rate, so the real money
demand curve shifts to the right to *MD* (*Y* = 5000). In this
case the real interest rate that clears the asset market is
5% (point *C*).

(b) The graph shows the corresponding *LM* curve. For
each level of output the *LM* curve shows the real
interest rate that clears the asset market. Thus when
output is 4000, the *LM* curve shows that the real
interest rate that clears the goods market is 3% (point
A). When output is 5000, the *LM* curve shows a market-
clearing real interest rate of 5% (point *C*). Because
higher output raises money demand, and thus raises the
real interest rate that clears the asset market, the *LM*
curve slopes upward.

is 3%. Thus when output is 4000, the real interest rate that clears the asset
market (equalizes the quantities of money supplied and demanded) is 3%. At
a real interest rate of 3% and an output of 4000, the real quantity of money
demanded by holders of wealth is 1000, which equals the real money supply
made available by the central bank.

What happens to the asset market equilibrium if output rises from 4000 to
5000? People need to conduct more transactions, so their real money demand
increases at any real interest rate. As a result, the money demand curve shifts
to the right, to *MD* for *Y* = 5000. If the real interest rate remained at 3%, the
real quantity of money demanded would exceed the real money supply. At
point *B* in Figure 10.4(a) the real quantity of money demanded is 1200, which
is greater than the real money supply of 1000. To restore equality of money
demanded and supplied and thus bring the asset market back into equilib-

rium, the real interest rate must rise to 5%. When the real interest rate is 5%, the real quantity of money demanded declines to 1000, which is equal to the fixed real money supply (point *C* in Figure 10.4(a)).

How does an increase in the real interest rate eliminate the excess demand for money, and what causes this increase in the real interest rate? Recall that the prices of non-monetary assets and the interest rates they pay are negatively related. At the initial real interest rate of 3%, the increase in output from 4000 to 5000 causes people to demand more money (the *MD* curve shifts to the right in Figure 10.4(a)). To satisfy their desire to hold more money, people will try to sell some of their non-monetary assets for money. But when people rush to sell a portion of their non-monetary assets, the prices of these assets will fall, which will cause the real interest rates on these assets to rise. Thus it is the public's attempt to increase its holdings of money by selling non-monetary assets that causes the real interest rate to rise.

Because the real supply of money in the economy is fixed, the public as a whole cannot increase the amount of money it holds. As long as people attempt to do so by selling non-monetary assets, the real interest rate will continue to rise. But the increase in the real interest rate paid by non-monetary assets makes those assets more attractive relative to money, reducing the real quantity of money demanded (here the movement is *along* the *MD* curve for *Y* = 5000, from point *B* to point *C* in Figure 10.4(a)). The real interest rate will rise until the real quantity of money demanded again equals the fixed supply of money and restores asset market equilibrium. The new asset market equilibrium is at *C*, where the real interest rate has risen from 3% to 5%.

The preceding example shows that when output rises, increasing real money demand, a higher real interest rate is needed to maintain equilibrium in the asset market. In general, the relationship between output and the real interest rate that clears the asset market is expressed graphically by the *LM* curve. For any level of output, the **LM curve** shows the real interest rate for which the asset market is in equilibrium, with equal quantities of money supplied and demanded. The term *LM* comes from the asset market equilibrium condition that the real quantity of money demanded, as determined by the real money demand function *L*, must equal the real money supply *M*/*P*.

The *LM* curve corresponding to our numerical example is shown in Figure 10.4(b), with the real interest rate *r* on the vertical axis and output *Y* on the horizontal axis. Points *A* and *C* lie on the *LM* curve. At *A*, which corresponds to point *A* in the money supply–money demand diagram of Figure 10.4(a), output, *Y*, is 4000 and the real interest rate, *r*, is 3%. Because *A* lies on the *LM* curve, when output is 4000 the real interest rate that clears the asset market is 3%. Similarly, because *C* lies on the *LM* curve, when output is 5000 the real interest rate that equalizes money supplied and demanded is 5%; this output–real interest rate combination corresponds to the asset market equilibrium at point *C* in Figure 10.4(a).

Figure 10.4(b) illustrates the general point that the *LM* curve always slopes upwards from left to right. It does so because increases in output, by raising money demand, also raise the real interest rate on non-monetary assets needed to clear the asset market.

Factors that Shift the *LM* Curve

In deriving the *LM* curve we varied output but held constant other factors, such as the price level, that affect the real interest rate that clears the asset market. Changes in any of these other factors will cause the *LM* curve to shift. In particular, for constant output, *any change that reduces real money supply relative to real money demand will increase the real interest rate that clears the asset market and cause the LM curve to shift up.* Similarly, for constant output, anything that raises real money supply relative to real money demand will reduce the real interest rate that clears the asset market and shift the *LM* curve down. Here we discuss in general terms how changes in real money supply or demand affect the *LM* curve. Summary table 13 describes the factors that shift the *LM* curve.

Changes in the Real Money Supply.   An increase in the real money supply *M/P* will reduce the real interest rate that clears the asset market and shift the *LM* curve down. Figure 10.5 illustrates this point and extends our previous numerical example.

SUMMARY 13	An Increase in	Shifts the *LM* Curve	Reason
Factors that Shift the *LM* Curve	Nominal money supply, M	Down	Real money supply increases, lowering the real interest rate that clears the asset market (equates money supplied and money demanded).
	Price level, P	Up	Real money supply falls, raising the real interest rate that clears the asset market.
	Expected inflation, π^e	Down	Demand for money falls, lowering the real interest rate that clears the asset market.
	Nominal interest rate on money, i^m	Up	Demand for money increases, raising the real interest rate that clears the asset market.

In addition, for constant output, any factor that increases real money demand raises the real interest rate that clears the asset market and shifts the *LM* curve up. Other factors that increase real money demand (see Summary table 9, p. 240) include

- an increase in wealth;
- an increase in the risk of alternative assets relative to the risk of holding money;
- a decline in the liquidity of alternative assets; and
- a decline in the efficiency of payment technologies.

Figure 10.5(a) contains the money supply–money demand diagram. Initially, suppose that the real money supply M/P is 1000 and output is 4000, so the money demand curve is MD ($Y = 4000$). Then equilibrium in the asset market occurs at point A with a market-clearing real interest rate of 3%. The LM curve corresponding to the real money supply of 1000 is shown as LM ($M/P = 1000$) in Figure 10.5(b). At point A on this LM curve, as at point A in the money supply–money demand diagram in Figure 10.5(a), output is 4000 and the real interest rate is 3%. Because A lies on the initial LM curve, when output is 4000 and the money supply is 1000, the real interest rate that clears the asset market is 3%.

Now suppose that, with output constant at 4000, the real money supply rises from 1000 to 1200. This increase in the real money supply causes the vertical money supply curve to shift to the right, from MS^1 to MS^2 in Figure 10.5(a). The asset market equilibrium point is now point D, where, with output remaining at 4000, the market-clearing real interest rate has fallen to 2%.

Why has the real interest rate that clears the asset market fallen? At the initial real interest rate of 3%, there is an excess supply of money – that is, holders

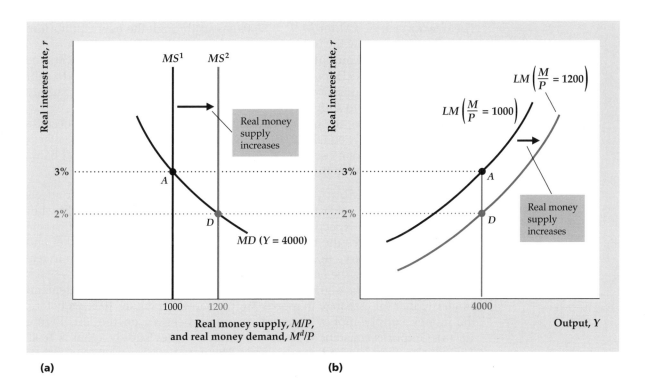

(a)   **(b)**

Figure 10.5
An increase in the real money supply shifts the *LM* curve down
(a) An increase in the real supply of money shifts the money supply curve to the right, from MS^1 to MS^2. For a constant level of output, the real interest rate that clears the asset market falls. If output is fixed at 4000, for example, the money demand curve is MD ($Y = 4000$) and the real interest rate that clears the asset market falls from 3% (point A) to 2% (point D).

(b) The graph shows the effect of the increase in real money supply on the *LM* curve. For any level of output, the increase in the real money supply causes the real interest rate that clears the asset market to fall. So, for example, when output is 4000, the increase in the real money supply causes the real interest rate that clears the asset market to fall from 3% (point A) to 2% (point D). Thus the *LM* curve shifts down, from *LM* for $M/P = 1000$ to *LM* for $M/P = 1200$.

of wealth have more money in their portfolios than they want to hold and, consequently, they have a smaller share of their wealth than they would like in non-monetary assets. To eliminate this imbalance in their portfolios, holders of wealth will want to use some of their money to buy non-monetary assets. However, when holders of wealth as a group try to purchase non-monetary assets, the price of non-monetary assets is bid up and hence the real interest rate paid on these assets declines. As the real interest rate falls, non-monetary assets become less attractive relative to money. The real interest rate continues to fall until it reaches 2% at point D in Figure 10.5(a), where the excess supply of money and the excess demand for non-monetary assets are eliminated and the asset market is back in equilibrium.

The effect of the increase in real money supply on the LM curve is illustrated in Figure 10.5(b). With output constant at 4000, the increase in the real money supply lowers the real interest rate that clears the asset market, from 3% to 2%. Thus point D, where $Y = 4000$ and $r = 2\%$, is now a point of asset market equilibrium, and point A no longer is. More generally, for any given level of output, an increase in the real money supply lowers the real interest rate that clears the asset market. Therefore the entire LM curve shifts down. The new LM curve, LM for $M/P = 1200$, passes through the new equilibrium point D and lies below the old LM curve, LM for $M/P = 1000$.

Thus, with fixed output, an increase in the real money supply lowers the real interest rate that clears the asset market and causes the LM curve to shift down. A similar analysis would show that a drop in the real money supply causes the LM curve to shift up.

What might cause the real money supply to increase? In general, because the real money supply equals M/P, the real money supply will increase whenever the nominal money supply M, which is controlled by the central bank, grows more quickly than the price level P.

Changes in Real Money Demand. A change in any variable that affects real money demand, other than output or the real interest rate, will also shift the LM curve. More specifically, with output constant, an increase in real money demand raises the real interest rate that clears the asset market and thus shifts the LM curve up. Analogously, with output constant, a drop in real money demand shifts the LM curve down.

Figure 10.6 shows a graphical analysis of an increase in money demand similar to that for a change in money supply shown in Figure 10.5. As before, the money supply–money demand diagram is shown on the left, Figure 10.6(a). Output is constant at 4000, and the real money supply again is 1000. The initial money demand curve is MD^1. The initial asset market equilibrium point is at A, where the money demand curve MD^1 and the money supply curve MS intersect. At initial equilibrium, point A, the real interest rate that clears the asset market is 3%.

Now suppose that, for a fixed level of output, a change occurs in the economy that increases real money demand. For example, if banks decided to increase the interest rate paid on money, i^m, the public would want to hold more money at the same levels of output and the real interest rate. Graphically, the increase in money demand shifts the money demand curve to the right, from MD^1 to MD^2 in Figure 10.6(a). At the initial real interest rate of 3% the real quantity of money demanded is 1300, which exceeds the available supply of 1000; so 3% is no longer the value of the real interest rate that clears the asset market.

How will the real interest rate that clears the asset market change after the increase in money demand? If holders of wealth want to hold more money, they will exchange non-monetary assets for money. Increased sales of non-monetary assets will drive down their price and thus raise the real interest rate that they pay. The real interest rate will rise, reducing the attractiveness of holding money, until the public is satisfied to hold the available real money supply (1000). The real interest rate rises from its initial value of 3% at *A* to 6% at *G*.

Figure 10.6(b) shows the effect of the increase in money demand on the *LM* curve. The initial *LM* curve, LM^1, passes through point *A*, showing that when output is 4000 the real interest rate that clears the asset market is 3%. (Point *A* in Figure 10.6(b) corresponds to point *A* in Figure 10.6(a)). Following the increase in money demand, with output fixed at 4000, the market-clearing real interest rate rises to 6%. Thus the new *LM* curve must pass through point *G* (corresponding to point *G* in Figure 10.6(a)), where $Y = 4000$ and $r = 6\%$. The new *LM* curve, LM^2, is higher than LM^1 because the real interest rate that clears the asset market is now higher for any level of output.

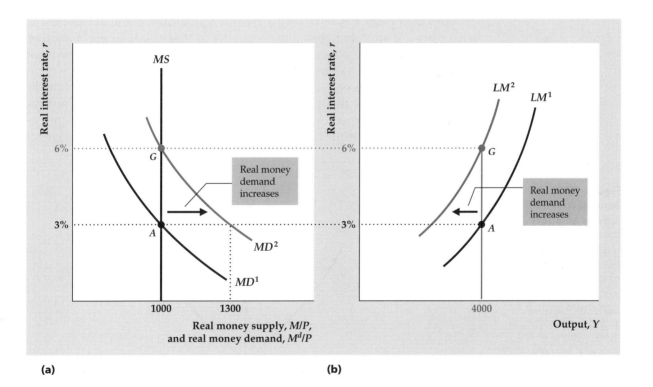

(a)

(b)

Figure 10.6
An increase in real money demand shifts the *LM* curve up
(a) With output constant at 4000 and the real money supply at 1000, an increase in the interest rate paid on money raises real money demand. The money demand curve shifts to the right, from MD^1 to MD^2, and the real interest rate that clears the asset market rises from 3% (point *A*) to 6% (point *G*).

(b) The graph shows the effect of the increase in real money demand on the *LM* curve. When output is 4000, the increase in real money demand raises the real interest rate that clears the asset market from 3% (point *A*) to 6% (point *G*). More generally, for any level of output, the increase in real money demand raises the real interest rate that clears the asset market. Thus the *LM* curve shifts up, from LM^1 to LM^2.

10.4 GENERAL EQUILIBRIUM IN THE COMPLETE *IS–LM* MODEL

The next step is to put the labour market, the goods market, and the asset market together and examine the equilibrium of the economy as a whole. A situation in which all markets in an economy are simultaneously in equilibrium is called a **general equilibrium**. Figure 10.7 shows the complete *IS–LM* model, illustrating how the general equilibrium of the economy is determined. Shown are

- the full-employment, or *FE*, line, along which the labour market is in equilibrium;
- the *IS* curve, along which the goods market is in equilibrium; and
- the *LM* curve, along which the asset market is in equilibrium.

The three curves intersect at point *E*, indicating that all three markets are in equilibrium at that point. Therefore *E* represents a general equilibrium and, because it is the only point that lies on all three curves, it represents the only general equilibrium for this economy.

Although point *E* is obviously a general equilibrium point, not so clear is what forces, if any, act to bring the economy to that point. To put it another way, although the *IS* curve and *FE* line must intersect somewhere, we have not explained why the *LM* curve must pass through that same point. In Section 10.5 we discuss the economic forces that lead the economy to general equilibrium. There we show that (1) the general equilibrium of the economy always occurs at the intersection of the *IS* curve and the *FE* line; and (2) adjustments of the price level cause the *LM* curve to shift until it passes through the general

Figure 10.7
General equilibrium in the *IS–LM* model
The economy is in general equilibrium when quantities supplied equal quantities demanded in every market. The general equilibrium point, *E*, lies on the *IS* curve, the *LM* curve, and the *FE* line. Thus at *E*, and only at *E*, the goods market, the asset market, and the labour market are simultaneously in equilibrium.

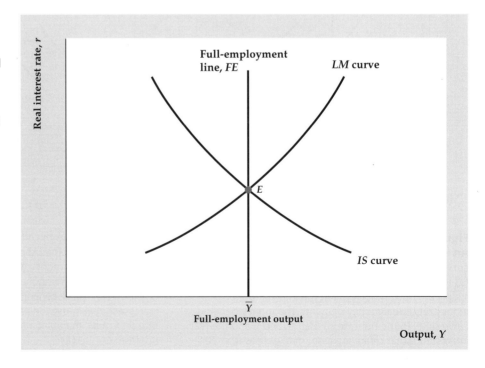

equilibrium point defined by the intersection of the *IS* curve and the *FE* line. Before discussing the details of this adjustment process, however, let us consider an example that illustrates the use of the complete *IS–LM* model.

Applying the *IS–LM* Framework: A Temporary Adverse Supply Shock

An economic shock relevant to business cycle analysis is an adverse supply shock. Specifically, suppose that (because of bad weather or a temporary increase in oil prices) the productivity parameter A in the production function drops temporarily.[7] We can use the *IS–LM* model to analyse the effects of this shock on the general equilibrium of the economy and the general equilibrium values of economic variables such as the real wage, employment, output, the real interest rate, the price level, consumption, and investment.

Suppose that the economy is initially in general equilibrium at point E in Figure 10.8(a), where the initial *FE* line, FE^1, *IS* curve, and *LM* curve, LM^1, for this economy intersect. To determine the effects of a temporary supply shock on the general equilibrium of this economy, we must consider how the temporary drop in productivity A affects the positions of the *FE* line and the *IS* and *LM* curves.

The *FE* line describes equilibrium in the labour market. Hence to find the effect of the supply shock on the *FE* line we must start by looking at how the shock affects labour supply and labour demand. In Chapter 3 we demonstrated that an adverse supply shock reduces the marginal product of labour and thus shifts the labour demand curve down (see Figure 3.10). Because the supply shock is temporary, we assume that it does not affect workers' wealth or expected future wages and so does not affect labour supply. As a result of the decline in labour demand, the equilibrium values of the real wage and employment, $\overline{N}$, fall.

The *FE* line shifts only to the degree that full-employment output $\overline{Y}$ changes. Does $\overline{Y}$ change? Yes. Recall from Chapter 3 that an adverse supply shock reduces full-employment output $\overline{Y}$, which equals $AF(K, \overline{N})$, for two reasons: (1) as we just mentioned, the supply shock reduces the equilibrium level of employment $\overline{N}$, which lowers the amount of output that can be produced; and (2) the drop in productivity A directly reduces the amount of output produced by any combination of capital and labour. The reduction in $\overline{Y}$ is represented by a shift to the left of the *FE* line, from FE^1 to FE^2 in Figure 10.8(b).

Now consider the effects of the temporary adverse supply shock on the *IS* curve. Recall that we derived the *IS* curve by changing the level of current output in the saving–investment diagram (Figure 10.2) and finding for each level of current output the real interest rate for which desired saving equals desired investment. A *temporary* adverse supply shock reduces current output but does not change any other factor affecting desired saving or investment (such as wealth, expected future income, or the future marginal product of capital). Therefore a temporary supply shock is just the sort of change in current output that we used to trace out the *IS* curve. We conclude that a

---

7. Recall that the production function, equation (3.1), is $Y = AF(K, N)$, so a drop in A reduces the amount of output that can be produced for any quantities of capital K and labour N.

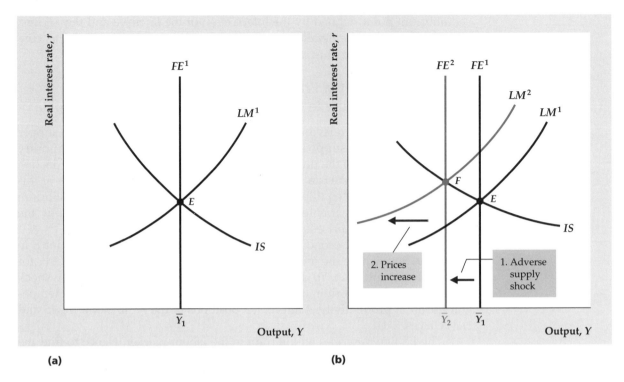

(a)

(b)

Figure 10.8
Effects of a temporary adverse supply shock
(a) Initially, the economy is in general equilibrium at point E, with output at its full-employment level $\overline{Y}_1$.
(b) A temporary adverse supply shock reduces full-employment output from $\overline{Y}_1$ to $\overline{Y}_2$ and shifts the FE line to the left from FE^1 to FE^2. The new general equilibrium is

represented by point F, where FE^2 intersects the unchanged IS curve. The price level increases and shifts the LM curve up and to the left, from LM^1 to LM^2, until it passes through F. At the new general equilibrium point, F, output is lower, the real interest rate is higher, and the price level is higher than at the original general equilibrium point, E.

temporary adverse supply shock is a movement *along* the *IS* curve, *not a shift* of the *IS* curve, leaving it unchanged.[8]

Finally, we consider the *LM* curve. A temporary supply shock has no direct effect on the demand or supply of money and thus does not shift the *LM* curve.

We now look for the new general equilibrium of the economy. In Figure 10.8(b), there is no point at which FE^2 (the new FE line), IS, and LM^1 all intersect. As we mentioned – and demonstrate in Section 10.5 – when the FE line, the IS curve, and the LM curve do not intersect at a common point, the LM curve shifts until it passes through the intersection of the FE line and IS curve. This shift in the LM curve is caused by changes in the price level, P, which change the real money supply, M/P, and thus affect the equilibrium of the asset market. As Figure 10.8(b) shows, to restore general equilibrium at point F, the LM curve must shift up and to the left, from LM^1 to LM^2. For it to do so the real money supply M/P must fall (see Summary table 13) and thus the price level P must rise. We infer (although we have not yet given an economic explanation) that an adverse supply shock will cause the price level to rise.

---

8. Analytical Problem 2 at the end of the chapter examines the effect of a permanent adverse supply shock and identifies factors that shift the *IS* curve in that case.

What is the effect of a temporary supply shock on the inflation rate, as distinct from the price level? As the inflation rate is the growth rate of the price level, during the period in which prices are rising to their new, higher level, a burst of inflation will occur. However, after the price level stabilizes at its higher value (and is no longer rising), inflation subsides. Thus a temporary supply shock should cause a temporary rather than a permanent increase in the rate of inflation.

Let us pause and review our results.

1. As we had already shown in Chapter 3, a temporary adverse supply shock lowers the equilibrium values of the real wage and employment.

2. Comparing the new general equilibrium, point *F*, to the old general equilibrium, point *E*, in Figure 10.8(b), we see that the supply shock lowers output and raises the real interest rate.

3. The supply shock raises the price level and causes a temporary burst in inflation.

4. Because in the new general equilibrium the real interest rate is higher and output is lower, consumption must be lower than before the supply shock. The higher real interest rate also implies that investment must be lower after the shock.

In the Application 'Oil Price Shocks Revisited' we check out how well our model explains the historical behaviour of the economy. However, note that economic models, such as the *IS–LM* model, are also used extensively in forecasting economic conditions (Box 10.1, p. 361).

APPLICATION

Oil Price Shocks Revisited

In Chapter 3 we pointed out that an increase in the price of oil is an example of an adverse supply shock, and we looked at the effects of the 1973–74 and 1979–80 oil price shocks on the European economy (see the Application, 'Output, Employment, and the Real Wage During Oil Price Shocks', p. 90). The theory's predictions – that adverse supply shocks reduce output, employment, and the real wage – were confirmed for those two episodes. Our analysis using the complete *IS–LM* model is consistent with that earlier discussion. However, it adds the predictions that, following an oil price shock, consumption and investment decline, inflation increases, and the real interest rate rises.

Figure 9.3 shows that in the UK and Germany consumption fell slightly and that investment fell sharply immediately after these oil price shocks, as did consumption and investment in France following the 1973–74 oil price shock. From the beginning of the recession in the fourth quarter of 1973 until the fourth quarter of 1975, real consumption in the UK fell by 2.3% and real investment by 6.5%. Following the onset of the recession in the first quarter of 1980, real consumption in the UK fell by 2.6% and real investment by 3.6% in just one quarter. The fall in real consumption was especially severe in Scandinavia: in Sweden, for example, real consumption fell by around 4% in the same one quarter period. Across Europe most countries experienced a drop in real consumption for one or two quarters, though the fall was more prolonged in Germany and the Netherlands. Real investment also fell in most European countries in 1980, most notably in Germany where it declined by over 15%. Inflation also behaved as predicted by our analysis, surging temporarily in the mid 1970s and again in the early 1980s.

Our analysis also predicted that an oil price shock will cause the real interest rate to rise. However, this result depends somewhat on the assumption we made that people expected the oil price shock to be temporary. In Analytical Problem 2 at the end of the chapter, you will find that, if the adverse supply shock is expected to be permanent, the rise in the real interest rate will be less than when the adverse supply shock is expected to be temporary (and the real interest rate may not rise). However, we do not really know what people's expectations were about the duration of the two major oil price shocks. Therefore we cannot state with confidence what the effect of such a shock on the real interest rate should have been. Actually, the real interest rate rose during the 1979–80 shock but not during the 1973–74 shock (see Figure 2.4(b)). On the basis of these data only, our model suggests that people expected the 1973–74 oil shock to be permanent and the 1979–80 shock to be temporary. Interestingly, those expectations were essentially correct: Figure 3.11 shows that the oil price increase of 1979–80 was reversed rather quickly but that the price increase of 1973–74 was not.

10.5 PRICE ADJUSTMENT AND THE ATTAINMENT OF GENERAL EQUILIBRIUM

We now explain the economic forces that lead prices to change and shift the *LM* curve until it passes through the intersection of the *IS* curve and the *FE* line. In discussing the role of price adjustments in bringing the economy back to general equilibrium, we also show the basic difference between the two main approaches to business cycle analysis, classical and Keynesian.

To illustrate the adjustment process, let us use the complete *IS–LM* model to consider what happens to the economy if the nominal money supply increases. This analysis allows us to discuss monetary policy (the control of the money supply) and to introduce some ongoing controversies about the effects of monetary policy on the economy.

The Effects of a Monetary Expansion

Suppose that the central bank decides to raise the nominal money supply M by 10%. For now we hold the price level P constant so that the real money supply M/P also increases by 10%. What effects will this monetary expansion have on the economy? Figure 10.9, on page 360, helps us answer this question with the complete *IS–LM* model.

The three parts of Figure 10.9 show the sequence of events involved in the analysis. For simplicity, suppose that the economy is initially in general equilibrium so that in Figure 10.9(a) the *IS* curve, the *FE* line, and the initial *LM* curve, LM^1, all pass through the general equilibrium point, E. At E output equals its full-employment value of 1000, and the real interest rate is 5%. Both the *IS* and *LM* curves pass through E, so we know that 5% is the market-clearing real interest rate in both the goods and asset markets. For the moment the price level, P, is fixed at its initial level of 100.

The 10% increase in the real supply of money, M/P, does not shift the *IS* curve or the *FE* line because, with output and the real interest rate held constant, a change in M/P does not affect desired national saving, desired investment, labour demand, labour supply, or productivity. However, Figure 10.5 showed that an increase in the real money supply does shift the *LM* curve down, which we show here as a shift of the *LM* curve from LM^1 to LM^2, in Figure 10.9(b). The *LM* curve shifts down because, at any level of output, an increase in the money supply lowers the real interest rate needed to clear the asset market.

Note that, after the *LM* curve has shifted down to LM^2, there is no point in Figure 10.9(b) at which all three curves intersect. In other words, the goods market, the labour market, and the asset market are no longer simultaneously in equilibrium. We must now make some assumptions about how the economy behaves when it is not in general equilibrium.

Of the three markets in the *IS–LM* model, the asset market (represented by the *LM* curve) undoubtedly adjusts the most quickly, because financial markets can respond within minutes to changes in economic conditions. The labour market (the *FE* line) is probably the slowest to adjust, because the process of matching workers and jobs takes time and wages may be renegotiated only periodically. The adjustment speed of the goods market (*IS* curve) is probably somewhere in the middle. We assume that, when the economy is not in general equilibrium, the asset market and the goods market are in equilibrium so that *output and the real interest rate are given by the intersection of the IS and LM curves.* Note that, when the economy is not in general equilibrium, the *IS–LM* intersection does not lie on the *FE* line, so the labour market is not in equilibrium.

Immediately after the increase in the nominal money supply, therefore, the economy is out of general equilibrium with the level of output and the real interest rate represented by point *F* in Figure 10.9(b), where the new *LM* curve, LM^2, intersects the *IS* curve. At *F*, output (1200) is higher and the real interest rate (3%) is lower than at the original general equilibrium, point *E*. We refer to *F*, the point at which the economy comes to rest before any adjustment occurs in the price level, as the *short-run equilibrium* point. (Although we refer to *F* as a short-run equilibrium point, keep in mind that only the asset and goods markets are in equilibrium there – the labour market is not.)

In economic terms, why does the increase in the money supply shift the economy to point *F*? The sequence of events can be described as follows. After the increase in the money supply, holders of wealth are holding more money in their portfolios than they desire at the initial values of output and the real interest rate. To bring their portfolios back into balance, they will try to use their excess money to buy non-monetary assets. However, as holders of wealth bid for non-monetary assets, they put upward pressure on the price of those assets, which reduces their interest rate. Thus, after an increase in the money supply, wealth-holders' attempts to achieve their desired mix of money and non-monetary assets cause the interest rate to fall.

The drop in the real interest rate is not the end of the story, however. Because the lower real interest rate increases the demand by households for consumption, C^d, and the demand by firms for investment, I^d, the aggregate demand for goods rises. Here we make a fundamental assumption, to which we return shortly: when demanders increase their spending on goods, firms

Figure 10.9
Effects of a monetary expansion
(a) The economy is in general equilibrium at point *E*. Output equals the full-employment level of 1000, the real interest rate is 5%, and the price level is 100.
(b) With the price level fixed, a 10% increase in the nominal money supply *M* raises the real money supply, *M/P*, and shifts the *LM* curve down from *LM*^{1} to *LM*^{2}. At point *F*, the intersection of the *IS* curve and the new *LM* curve, *LM*^{2}, the real interest rate has fallen to 3%, which raises the aggregate demand for goods. If firms produce extra output to meet the increase in aggregate demand, output rises to 1200 (higher than full-employment output of 1000).
(c) Because aggregate demand exceeds full-employment output at point *F*, firms raise prices. A 10% rise in *P*, from 100 to 110, restores the real money supply to its original level and shifts the *LM* curve back to its original position at *LM*^{1}. This returns the economy to point *E*, where output again is at its full-employment level of 1000, but the price level has risen 10% from 100 to 110.

(a)

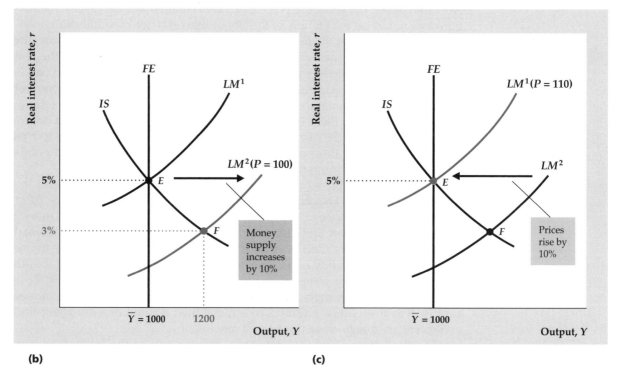

(b)   **(c)**

BOX 10.1

Econometric Models and Macroeconomic Forecasts

The *IS–LM* model developed in this chapter is a relatively simple example of a macroeconomic model. Much more complicated models of the economy, (many though not all of them based on the *IS–LM* framework) are used in applied macroeconomic research and analysis.

A common use of macroeconomic models is to help economists forecast the course of the economy. In general, using a macroeconomic model to obtain quantitative economic forecasts involves three steps. First, numerical values for the parameters of the model (such as the income elasticity of money demand) must be obtained. In *econometric* models, these values are estimated through statistical analyses of the data. Second, projections must be made of the likely behaviour of relevant *exogenous* variables, or variables whose values are not determined within the model. Examples of exogenous variables include policy variables (such as government spending and the money supply), oil prices, and changes in productivity. Third, based on the expected path of the exogenous variables and the model parameters, the model can be solved (usually on a computer) to give forecasts of variables determined within the model (such as output, employment, and interest rates). Variables determined within the model are *endogenous* variables.

Although a relatively simple model like the *IS–LM* model developed in this chapter could be used to create real forecasts, the results would probably not be very good. Because real-world economies are complex, macroeconomic models actually used in forecasting tend to be much more detailed than the *IS–LM* model presented here. For example, instead of a single aggregate production function, an econometric model used for forecasting might include production functions estimated separately for many individual industries. The complexity of models used in forecasting is illustrated by the accompanying table, taken from a book by John Whitley of the Centre for Economic Forecasting at the London Business School.*

Despite the amount of detail in some econometric models, they typically do not capture all information relevant to forecasting the economy. Most forecasters, therefore, also combine the results from their econometric models with other forecasting techniques, including personal judgement, time-series methods (statistical methods that attempt to extrapolate economic trends without the explicit use of an economic model), and detailed analysis of current data (including partial and preliminary data). Studies have shown that combining several different forecasting methods usually provides more accurate forecasts than relying on a single approach.

_____

* *A Course in Macroeconomic Modelling and Forecasting*, Harvester Wheatsheaf, 1994

Forecaster	Model Name	Number of Equations/ Variables	Region
UK			
HM Treasury	–	509 variables	UK
National Institute for Economic and Social Research	–	586 variables	UK
NIESR and London Business School	GEM	750 variables	16 countries (G7, OECD)
France			
INSEE	Metric	950 equations	France
Ministry of Finance	ATLAS	1450 equations	
Netherlands			
Central Bank	MORKMON	360 equations	Netherlands
Central Planning Bureau	FREIA-KOMPAS	620 variables	Netherlands
Sweden			
National Institute of Economic Research	KOSMOS	467 equations	Sweden
Other			
European Commission	QUEST	2500 equations	EU
OECD	INTERLINK	4200 equations	large OECD countries

are willing (at least temporarily) to produce enough to meet the extra demand for their output. After the decline in the real interest rate raises the aggregate demand for goods, therefore, we assume that firms respond by increasing production, leading to higher output at the short-run equilibrium point, F.

To summarize, with the price level constant, an increase in the nominal money supply takes the economy to the short-run equilibrium point, F, in Figure 10.9(b), at which the real interest rate is lower and output is higher than at the initial general equilibrium point, E. We made two assumptions: (1) when the economy is not in general equilibrium, the economy's short-run equilibrium occurs at the intersection of the *IS* and *LM* curves; and (2) when the aggregate demand for goods rises, firms are willing (at least temporarily) to produce enough extra output to meet the expanded demand.

The Adjustment of the Price Level. So far we have simply taken the price level, P, as fixed. In reality, prices respond to conditions of supply and demand in the economy. The price level, P, refers to the price of output (goods), so to think about how prices are likely to adjust in this example, let us reconsider the effects of the increase in the money supply on the goods market.

In Figure 10.9(b), the short-run equilibrium point, F, lies on the *IS* curve, implying that the goods market is in equilibrium at that point with equal aggregate quantities of goods supplied and demanded. Recall our assumption that firms are willing to meet any increases in aggregate demand by producing more. In that sense, then, the aggregate quantity of goods supplied equals the aggregate quantity of goods demanded. However, in another sense the goods market is *not* in equilibrium at point F. The problem is that, in order to meet the aggregate demand for goods at F, firms have to produce more output than their full-employment level of output, $\overline{Y}$. Full-employment output, $\overline{Y}$, is the level of output that maximizes firms' profits because that level of output corresponds to the profit-maximizing level of employment (Chapter 3). Therefore, in meeting the higher level of aggregate demand, firms are producing more output than they would like. In the sense that, at point F, the production of goods by firms is *not* the level of output that maximizes their profits, the goods market is not truly in equilibrium.

At point F the aggregate demand for goods exceeds firms' desired supply of output, $\overline{Y}$, so we can expect firms to begin raising their prices, causing the price level, P, to rise. With the nominal money supply, M, set by the central bank, an increase in the price level, P, lowers the real money supply, M/P, which in turn causes the *LM* curve to shift up. Indeed, as long as the aggregate quantity of goods demanded exceeds what firms want to supply, prices will keep rising. Thus the *LM* curve will keep shifting up and to the left until the aggregate quantity of goods demanded equals full-employment output. Aggregate demand equals full-employment output only when the *LM* curve has returned to its initial position, LM^1 in Figure 10.9(c), where it passes through the original general equilibrium point, E. At E all three markets of the economy are again in equilibrium, with output at its full-employment level.

Compare Figure 10.9(c) to the initial situation in Figure 10.9(a) and note that after the adjustment of the price level the 10% increase in the nominal money supply has had no effect on output or the real interest rate. Employment is also unchanged from its initial value, as the economy has returned to its original level of output. However, as a result of the 10% increase in the nominal money supply, the price level is 10% higher (so that $P = 110$). How do we know that the price level changes by exactly 10%? To return the LM curve to its original position, the increase in the price level had to return the real money supply, M/P, to its original value. Because the nominal money supply, M, was raised by 10%, to return M/P to its original value, the price level, P, had to rise by 10% as well. Thus the change in the nominal money supply causes the price level to change proportionally. This result is the same result obtained in Chapter 7 (see equation 7.10), where we assumed that all markets are in equilibrium.

Note that, because in general equilibrium the price level has risen by 10% but real economic variables are unaffected, all nominal economic variables must also rise by 10%. In particular, for the real wage to have the same value after prices have risen by 10% as it did before, the nominal wage must rise by 10%. Thus the return of the economy to general equilibrium requires adjustment of the nominal wage (the price of labour) as well as the price of goods.

Trend Money Growth and Inflation. In Figure 10.9 we analysed the effects of a one-off 10% increase in the nominal money supply, followed by a one-off 10% adjustment in the price level. In reality, in most countries the money supply and the price level grow continuously. Our framework easily handles this situation. Suppose that in some country both the nominal money supply M and the price level, P, are growing steadily at 7% per year, which implies that the real money supply, M/P, is constant. The LM curve depends on the real money supply, M/P, so in this situation the LM curve will not shift, even though the nominal money supply and prices are rising.

Now suppose that for one year the money supply of this country is increased an additional 3% − for a total of 10% − while prices rise 7%. Then the real money supply, M/P, grows by 3% (10% minus 7%), and the LM curve shifts down and to the right. Similarly, if for one year the nominal money supply increased by only 4%, with inflation still at 7% per year, the LM curve would shift up, reflecting the 3% drop ($-3\% = 4\% - 7\%$) in the real money supply.

This example illustrates that changes in M or P *relative to the expected or trend rate of growth of money and inflation* (7% in this example) shift the LM curve. Thus, when we analyse the effects of 'an increase in the money supply', we have in mind an increase in the money supply relative to the expected, or trend, rate of money growth (for example, a rise from 7% to 10% growth for one year); by a 'decrease in the money supply', we mean a drop relative to a trend rate (such as a decline from 7% to 4% growth in money). Similarly, if we say something like 'the price level falls to restore general equilibrium', we do not necessarily mean that the price level literally falls but only that it rises by less than its trend or expected rate of growth would suggest.

Classical versus Keynesian Versions of the *IS–LM* Model

Our diagrammatic analysis of the effects of a change in the money supply highlights two questions that are central to the debate between the classical and Keynesian approaches to macroeconomics: (1) How rapidly does the economy reach general equilibrium? and (2) What are the effects of monetary policy on the economy? We previewed the first of these questions in Section 9.4, using the *AD–AS* model. Now we examine both questions, using the *IS–LM* model.

Price Adjustment and the Self-Correcting Economy. In our analysis of the effects of a monetary expansion, we showed that *the economy is brought into general equilibrium by adjustment of the price level.* In graphical terms, if the intersection of the *IS* and *LM* curves lies to the right of the *FE* line – so that the aggregate quantity of goods demanded exceeds full-employment output, as in Figure 10.9(b) – the price level will rise. The increase in *P* shifts the *LM* curve up, reducing the quantity of goods demanded, until all three curves intersect at the general equilibrium point, as in Figure 10.9(c). Similarly, if the *IS–LM* intersection lies to the left of the full-employment line – so that desired spending on goods is below firms' profit-maximizing level of output – firms will cut prices. A decrease in the price level raises the real money supply and shifts the *LM* curve down, until all three curves again intersect, returning the economy to general equilibrium.

There is little disagreement about the idea that, after some sort of economic disturbance, price level adjustments will eventually restore the economy to general equilibrium. However, as discussed in Section 9.4, the *speed* at which this process takes place is a controversial issue in macroeconomics. Under the classical assumptions that prices are flexible the adjustment process is rapid. When prices are flexible, the economy is effectively self-correcting, automatically returning to full employment after a shock moves it away from general equilibrium.[9] Indeed, if firms respond to increased demand by raising prices rather than by temporarily producing more (as we earlier assumed), the adjustment process will be almost immediate.

According to the opposing Keynesian view, however, sluggish adjustment of prices (and of wages, the price of labour) might prevent general equilibrium from being attained for a much longer period, perhaps even several years. While the economy is not in general equilibrium, Keynesians argue, output is determined by the level of aggregate demand, represented by the intersection of the *IS* and *LM* curves; the economy is not on the *FE* line, and the labour market is not in equilibrium. This assumption of sluggish price adjustment, and the consequent disequilibrium in the labour market, distinguishes the Keynesian version of the *IS–LM* model from the classical version.

Monetary Neutrality. Closely related to the issue of how fast the economy reaches general equilibrium is the question of how a change in the nominal money supply affects the economy. We showed that, after the economy reaches its general equilibrium, an increase in the nominal money supply has no effect on real variables such as output, employment, or the real interest rate but raises the price level. Economists say that there is **monetary neutrality**, or simply that money is neutral, if a change in the nominal money supply changes the price level proportionally but has no effect on real variables. Our analysis shows that, after the complete adjustment of prices, money is neutral in the *IS–LM* model.

The practical relevance of monetary neutrality is much debated by classical and Keynesian economists. The basic issue again is the speed of price adjustment. In the classical view a monetary expansion is rapidly transmitted into prices and has, at most, a transitory effect on real variables: that is, the

---

9. The proposition that a free-market economy with flexible prices is automatically self-correcting is consistent with Adam Smith's invisible hand idea, discussed in Chapter 1.

economy moves quickly from the situation shown in Figure 10.9(a) to the situation shown in Figure 10.9(c), spending little time in the position shown in Figure 10.9(b). Keynesians agree that money is neutral after prices fully adjust but believe that, because of slow price adjustment, the economy may spend a long time in disequilibrium. During this period the increased money supply causes output and employment to rise and the real interest rate to fall (compare Figure 10.9(b) with Figure 10.9(a)).

In brief, Keynesians believe in monetary neutrality in the long run (after prices adjust) but not in the short run. Classical economists are more accepting of the view that money is neutral even in the relatively short run. We return to the issue of monetary neutrality when we develop the classical and Keynesian models of the business cycle in more detail in Chapters 11 and 12.

10.6 THE AGGREGATE DEMAND–AGGREGATE SUPPLY MODEL

The *IS–LM* model introduced in this chapter is a complete model representing the general equilibrium of the economy. In this section we use the *IS–LM* model to develop the aggregate demand–aggregate supply (*AD–AS*) model, which we previewed in Chapter 9. The *AD–AS* model appears to be different from the *IS–LM* model, but in fact the two models are equivalent. They are based on the same assumptions about economic behaviour and price adjustment, and they give the same answers when used to analyse the effects of various shocks on the economy. Why then do we bother to present both models? The reason is that, depending on the issue being addressed, one way of representing the economy may be more convenient than the other. The *IS–LM* model relates the real interest rate to output, and the *AD–AS* model relates the price level to output. Thus the *IS–LM* model is more useful for examining the effect of various shocks on the real interest rate and on variables, such as saving and investment, that depend on the real interest rate. In Chapter 14, for example, when we discuss international borrowing and lending in open economies, the behaviour of the real interest rate is crucial; and so, in that chapter, we emphasize the *IS–LM* approach. However, for issues related to the price level, or inflation, use of the *AD–AS* model is more convenient. For example, we rely on the *AD–AS* framework in Chapter 13 when we describe the relationship between inflation and unemployment. Keep in mind, though, that the choice of the *IS–LM* framework or the *AD–AS* framework is a matter of convenience; the two models express the same basic macroeconomic theory.

The Aggregate Demand Curve

The **aggregate demand curve** shows the relation between the aggregate quantity of goods demanded, $C^d + I^d + G$, and the price level, P. The aggregate demand curve slopes downwards, as does the demand curve for a single product (apples, for example). Despite the superficial similarity between the *AD* curve and the demand curve for a specific good, however, there is an important difference between these two types of curve. The demand curve for apples relates the demand for apples to the price of apples *relative to the prices of other goods*. In contrast, the *AD* curve relates the aggregate quantity of output demanded to the *general price level*. If the prices of all goods increase by 10%, the price level, P, also increases by 10%, even though all relative prices of goods remain unchanged. Nevertheless, the increase in the price level reduces the aggregate quantity of goods demanded.

The reason that an increase in the price level, P, reduces the aggregate quantity of output demanded is illustrated in Figure 10.10. Recall that, for a *given price level*, the aggregate quantity of output that households, firms, and the government choose to demand is where the *IS* curve and the *LM* curve intersect. Suppose that the nominal money supply is M and that the initial price level is P_1. Then the real money supply is M/P_1, and the initial *LM* curve is LM^1 in Figure 10.10(a). The *IS* and LM^1 curves intersect at point E, where the amount of output that households, firms, and the government want to buy is Y_1. Thus we conclude that, when the price level is P_1, the aggregate amount of output demanded is Y_1.

Now suppose that the price level increases to P_2. With a nominal money supply of M, this increase in the price level reduces the real money supply from M/P_1 to M/P_2. Recall (Summary table 13, p. 350) that a decrease in the real money supply shifts the *LM* curve up and to the left, to LM^2. The *IS* and LM^2 curves intersect at point F, where the aggregate quantity of output demanded is Y_2. Thus the increase in the price level from P_1 to P_2 reduces the aggregate quantity of output demanded from Y_1 to Y_2.

This negative relation between the price level and the aggregate quantity of output demanded is shown as the downward-sloping *AD* curve in Figure 10.10(b). Points E and F in Figure 10.10(b) correspond to points E and F in Figure 10.10(a). The *AD* curve slopes downwards because an increase in the price level reduces the real money supply, which shifts the *LM* curve up and to the left; the reduction in the real money supply increases the real interest rate, which reduces the demand for goods by households and firms.

Factors that Shift the *AD* Curve. The *AD* curve relates the aggregate quantity of output demanded to the price level. For a constant price level, any factor that changes the aggregate demand for output will cause the *AD* curve to shift, with increases in aggregate demand shifting the *AD* curve to the right and decreases in aggregate demand shifting it to the left. Aggregate demand is determined by the intersection of the *IS* and *LM* curves, so we can also say that, holding the price level constant, any factor that causes the intersection of the *IS* curve and the *LM* curve to shift to the right raises aggregate demand and shifts the *AD* curve to the right. Similarly, for a constant price level, any factor that causes the intersection of the *IS* and *LM* curves to shift to the left shifts the *AD* curve to the left.

An example of a factor that shifts the *AD* curve to the right, which we have considered before, is a temporary increase in government purchases. The effect of the increase in government purchases on the *AD* curve is illustrated in Figure 10.11. The initial *IS* curve, IS^1, intersects the *LM* curve at point E in Figure 10.11(a) so that the initial aggregate quantity of output demanded is Y_1. As we have shown, a temporary increase in government purchases shifts the

IS curve to the right to *IS²*. With the price level held constant at its initial value of P_1, the intersection of the *IS* and *LM* curves moves to point *F* so that the aggregate quantity of output demanded increases from Y_1 to Y_2.

**Figure 10.10
Derivation of the aggregate demand curve**

For a given price level, the aggregate quantity of output demanded is determined where the *IS* and *LM* curves intersect. If the price level, *P*, is P_1 and the initial *LM* curve is *LM¹*, the initial aggregate quantity of output demanded is Y_1, corresponding to point *E* in both (a) and (b). To derive the aggregate demand curve, we examine what happens to the quantity of output demanded when the price level changes.
(a) An increase in the price level from P_1 to P_2 reduces the real money supply and the shifts the *LM* curve up and to the left, from *LM¹* to *LM²*. Therefore the aggregate quantity of output demanded, represented by the intersection of the *IS* and *LM* curves, falls from Y_1 to Y_2.
(b) The increase in the price level from P_1 to P_2 reduces the aggregate quantity of output demanded from Y_1 to Y_2, so the aggregate demand curve slopes downward.

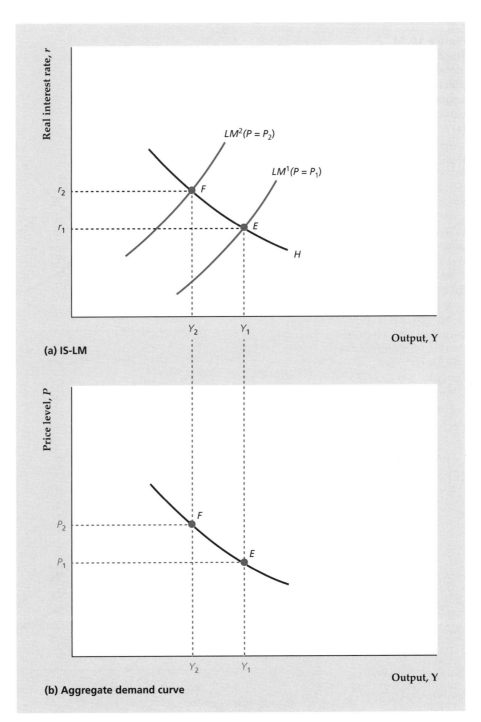

(a) IS-LM

(b) Aggregate demand curve

The shift of the *AD* curve resulting from the increase in government purchases is shown in Figure 10.11(b). The increase in the aggregate quantity of output demanded at price level P_1 is shown by the movement from point E to point F. Because the increase in government purchases raises the aggregate

Figure 10.11
The effect of an increase in government purchases on the aggregate demand curve
(a) An increase in government purchases shifts the *IS* curve up and to the right, from IS^1 to IS^2. At price level P_1, the aggregate quantity of output demanded increases from Y_1 to Y_2, as shown by the shift of the *IS–LM* intersection from point E to point F.
(b) Because the aggregate quantity of output demanded rises at any price level, and *AD* curve shifts to the right. Points E and F in part (b) correspond to points E and F in part (a).

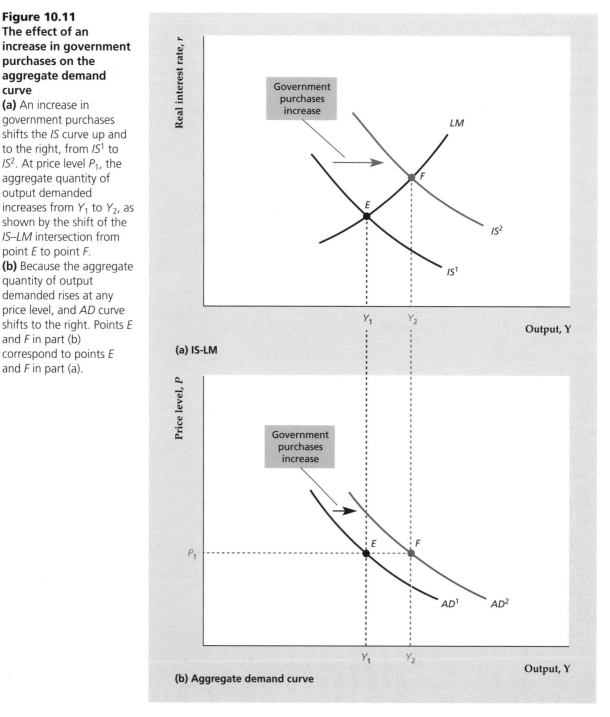

SUMMARY 14

Factors that Shift the *AD* Curve

For a constant price level, any factor that shifts the intersection of the *IS* and *LM* curves to the right increases aggregate output demanded and shifts the *AD* curve to the right.

Factors that shift the *IS* curve up and to the right, and thus shift the *AD* curve to the right (see Summary table 12, p. 344) include
- an increase in expected future output;
- an increase in wealth;
- an increase in government purchases, *G*;
- a reduction in taxes, *T* (assuming no Ricardian equivalence so that consumers respond by raising desired consumption);
- an increase in the expected future *MPK*; and
- a reduction in the effective tax rate on capital.

Factors that shift the *LM* curve down and to the right, and thus shift the *AD* curve to the right (see Summary table 13, p. 350) include

- an increase in the nominal money supply, *M*;
- a rise in expected inflation, π^e.
- a decrease in the nominal interest rate on money, i^m; and
- any other change that reduces the real demand for money.

quantity of output demanded at any price level, the entire *AD* curve shifts to the right, from AD^1 to AD^2. Other factors that shift the *AD* curve are listed in Summary table 14 and an algebraic derivation of the *AD* curve is presented in Appendix 10.A.

The Aggregate Supply Curve

The **aggregate supply curve** shows the relation between the price level and the aggregate amount of output that firms supply. Recall from the preview in Chapter 9 and our discussion of the *IS–LM* model that firms are assumed to behave differently in the short run and in the long run. That is, the assumption is that prices remain fixed in the short run and that firms supply the quantity of output demanded at this fixed price level. Thus the **short-run aggregate supply curve**, or *SRAS*, is a horizontal line, as shown in Figure 10.12.

In the long run, prices and wages adjust to clear all markets in the economy. In particular the labour market clears so that employment equals $\overline{N}$, which is the level of employment that maximizes firms' profits. When employment equals $\overline{N}$, the aggregate amount of output supplied is the full-employment level, $\overline{Y}$, which equals $AF(K, \overline{N})$, regardless of the price level. In the long run firms supply $\overline{Y}$ at any price level, so the **long-run aggregate supply curve**, or *LRAS*, is a vertical line at $Y = \overline{Y}$, as shown in Figure 10.12.

Factors that Shift the Aggregate Supply Curves. Any factor that increases the full-employment level of output, $\overline{Y}$, shifts the long-run aggregate supply (*LRAS*) curve to the right, and any factor that reduces $\overline{Y}$ shifts the *LRAS*

Figure 10.12
The short-run and long-run aggregate supply curves
In the short run firms supply the amount of output demanded at the fixed price, so the short-run aggregate supply (*SRAS*) curve is a horizontal line. In the long run, when the labour market clears, firms supply the full-employment level of output, $\bar{Y}$ regardless of the price level. Thus the long-run aggregate supply (*LRAS*) curve is a vertical line at $Y = \bar{Y}$.

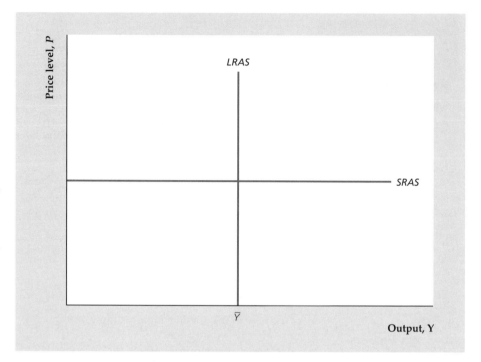

curve to the left. Thus any change that shifts the *FE* line to the right in the *IS–LM* diagram also shifts the *LRAS* curve to the right. For instance, an increase in the labour force raises the full-employment levels of employment and output, shifting the *LRAS* curve to the right.

The short-run aggregate supply curve shifts whenever firms change their prices in the short run. Any factor, such as an increase in costs, that leads firms to increase prices in the short run will shift the *SRAS* curve up, and any factor that leads firms to decrease prices in the short run will shift the *SRAS* curve down.

Equilibrium in the *AD–AS* Model

When we previewed the *AD–AS* model in Section 9.4, we introduced the distinction between short-run equilibrium (equilibrium when prices are fixed) and long-run equilibrium (equilibrium when prices have fully adjusted). Short-run equilibrium is represented by the intersection of the *AD* and *SRAS* curves, as at point *E* in Figure 10.13. Long-run equilibrium is represented by the intersection of the *AD* and *LRAS* curves, which is also at point *E* in Figure 10.13. Thus point *E* represents both the short-run and long-run equilibrium of the economy. When the economy is in long-run equilibrium, output equals its full-employment level, $\bar{Y}$. Long-run equilibrium is the same as general equilibrium, because in long-run equilibrium all markets clear.

When the economy reaches general, or long-run, equilibrium, all three curves – *AD*, *SRAS*, and *LRAS* – intersect at a common point, as in Figure 10.13. This condition is not a coincidence. As with the *IS* curve, the *LM* curve, and the *FE* line, strong economic forces lead the economy to arrive eventually

Figure 10.13
Equilibrium in the
***AD–AS* model**
Short-run equilibrium is represented by the intersection of the *AD* and *SRAS* curves at point *E*. At short-run equilibrium, prices are fixed and firms meet demand at those prices. Long-run equilibrium, which occurs after prices have fully adjusted, is represented by the intersection of the *AD* and *LRAS* curves, also at point *E*. Long-run equilibrium is the same as general equilibrium, because in long-run equilibrium all markets clear.

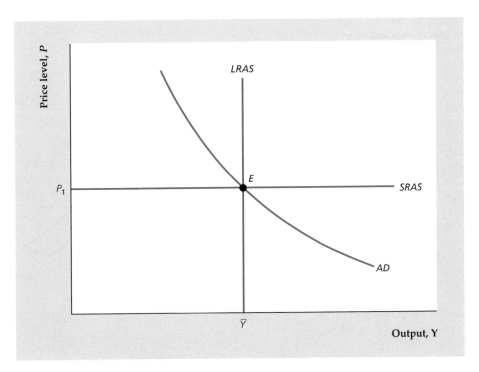

at a common point of intersection of the three curves. Indeed, the forces leading the *AD, SRAS,* and *LRAS* curves to intersect at a common point are the same as the forces leading the *IS* curve, the *LM* curve, and the *FE* line to intersect at a common point. To illustrate, we use the *AD–AS* framework to examine the effects on the economy of an increase in the money supply, which we previously analysed with the *IS–LM* model.

Monetary Neutrality in the *AD–AS* Model

Suppose that the economy is initially in equilibrium at point *E* in Figure 10.14, where the level of output is $\bar{Y}$ and the price level is P_1, and that the money supply then increases by 10%. In the *IS–LM* model an increase in the money supply shifts the *LM* curve down and to the right, raising the aggregate quantity of output demanded at any particular price level. Thus an increase in the money supply also shifts the *AD* curve up and to the right, from AD^1 to AD^2.

Moreover, *when the money supply rises by 10%, the AD curve shifts vertically upward by 10% at each level of output demanded.* To see why, compare points *E* and *H*. Because *H* lies on AD^2 and *E* lies on AD^1, the nominal money supply, *M*, is 10% higher at *H* than at *E*. However, the aggregate quantity of output demanded is the same ($\bar{Y}$) at *H* and *E*. The aggregate quantity of output demanded can be the same at *H* and *E* only if the real money supply, *M/P*, which determines the position of the *LM* curve and hence the aggregate quantity of output demanded, is the same at *H* and *E*. With the nominal money supply 10% higher at *H*, for the real money supply to be the same at the two points the price level at *H* must be 10% higher than at *E*. Therefore P_2 is 10% higher than P_1. Indeed, for every level of output the price level is 10% higher on AD^2 than on AD^1.

Figure 10.14
Monetary neutrality in the *AD–AS* framework
If we start from general equilibrium at point *E*, a 10% increase in the nominal money supply shifts the *AD* curve up by 10% at each level of output, from *AD*¹ to *AD*². The *AD* curve shifts up by 10% because at any given level of output, a 10% increase in the price level is needed to keep the real money supply, and thus the aggregate quantity of output demanded, unchanged. In the new short-run equilibrium at point *F*, the price level is unchanged, and output is higher than its full-employment level. In the new long-run equilibrium at point *H*, output is unchanged at $\overline{Y}$, and the price level P_2 is 10% higher than the initial price level P_1. Thus money is neutral in the long run.

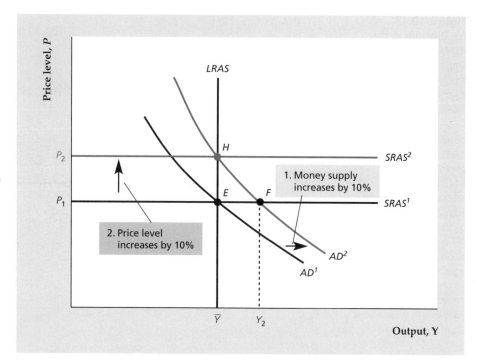

In the short run, the price level remains fixed, and the increase in the nominal money supply shifts the aggregate demand curve from AD^1 to AD^2. The short-run equilibrium moves from point *E* to point *F* (which corresponds to the movement from point *E* to point *F* in the *IS–LM* diagram in Figure 10.9(b). Thus in the short run the increase in the nominal money supply increases output from $\overline{Y}$ to Y_2, causing an economic boom.

However, the economy will not remain at point *F* indefinitely. Because the amount of output, Y_2, is higher than the profit-maximizing level of output, $\overline{Y}$, firms will eventually increase their prices. Rising prices cause the short-run aggregate supply curve to shift up from $SRAS^1$. Firms will increase their prices until the quantity of output demanded falls to the profit-maximizing level of output, $\overline{Y}$. The new long-run equilibrium is represented by point *H*, where the *AD* curve, the *LRAS* curve, and the new short-run aggregate supply curve, or $SRAS^2$, all intersect. In the new long-run equilibrium, the price level has increased by 10%, which is the same amount that the nominal money supply has increased. Output is the same in the new long-run equilibrium at point *H* as at point *E*. Thus we conclude that money is neutral in the long run, as we did when using the *IS–LM* model.

Our analysis highlights the distinction between the short-run and long-run effects of an increase in the money supply, but it leaves open the crucial question of how long it takes the economy to reach long-run equilibrium. As we have emphasized in both Chapter 9 and this chapter, classical and Keynesian economists have very different answers to this question. Classical economists argue that the economy reaches its long-run equilibrium quickly. Indeed, in its strictest form, the classical view is that the economy reaches long-run equilibrium almost immediately so that the long-run aggregate supply (*LRAS*) curve is the only aggregate supply curve that matters (the short-run aggregate supply (*SRAS*) curve is irrelevant). However, Keynesians argue that the economy may take years to reach long-run equilibrium and that in the meantime output will differ from its full-employment level. We elaborate on these points of view in Chapter 11, which is devoted to the classical model, and in Chapter 12, which is devoted to the Keynesian model.

CHAPTER SUMMARY

1. The *IS–LM* model represents the three main markets of the economy – the labour market, the goods market, and the asset market – simultaneously, in a diagram that has the real interest rate on the vertical axis and output on the horizontal axis. Although the *IS–LM* model was originally developed by Keynesians, it may be used to illustrate both classical and Keynesian analyses of the economy.

2. In the *IS–LM* model, equilibrium in the labour market is represented graphically by the full-employment, or *FE*, line, which is vertical at full-employment output. Factors that raise full-employment output shift the *FE* line to the right, and factors that reduce full-employment output shift the *FE* line to the left.

3. For any level of output, the *IS* curve shows the value of the real interest rate that clears the goods market. The *IS* curve slopes downwards because higher output leads to more desired saving and thus a lower goods-market-clearing real interest rate. For constant output, any change that reduces desired national saving relative to desired investment increases the real interest rate that clears the goods market and shifts the *IS* curve up. Equivalently, for constant output, any change that increases the aggregate demand for goods increases the real interest rate that clears the goods market and shifts the *IS* curve up.

4. For any level of output, the *LM* curve identifies the real interest rate that equates the quantities of money supplied and demanded and thus clears the asset market. The *LM* curve slopes upwards because an increase in output raises money demand, implying that a higher real interest rate is needed to clear the asset market.

With output fixed, any change that reduces the money supply relative to money demand increases the real interest rate that clears the asset market and causes the *LM* curve to shift up.

5. General equilibrium in the macroeconomy occurs when all markets are in equilibrium. Graphically, the general equilibrium point is where the *IS* curve, the *FE* line, and the *LM* curve intersect. Price-level adjustments push the economy towards general equilibrium. Specifically, changes in the price level, *P*, change the real money supply, M/P, which causes the *LM* curve to shift until it passes through the point at which the *FE* line and the *IS* curve intersect.

6. A temporary adverse supply shock causes the general equilibrium levels of the real wage, employment, output, consumption, and investment to fall, and the general equilibrium levels of the real interest rate and price level to increase.

7. A change in the money supply is neutral if it leads to a proportional change in the price level but does not affect real variables. In the *IS–LM* model, money is neutral after prices have adjusted and the economy has returned to general equilibrium.

8. The aggregate demand–aggregate supply (*AD–AS*) model is based on the *IS–LM* model and in fact is equivalent to it. However, the two models allow us to focus on the behaviour of different macroeconomic variables: the *IS–LM* model is most useful for studying the relationship between the real interest rate and the level of output, whereas the *AD–AS* model focuses on the relation between the price level and the level of output.

9. The aggregate demand (*AD*) curve relates the aggregate quantity of output demanded – the level of output at the intersection of the *IS* and *LM* curves – to the price level. An increase in the price levels reduces the real money supply and shifts the *LM* curve up and to the left, thereby reducing the aggregate quantity of output demanded. Because an increase in the price level reduces the aggregate quantity of goods demanded, the aggregate demand curve slopes downwards. Factors that increase the aggregate quantity of output demanded at a given price level, such as increases in government purchases or the money supply, shift the *AD* curve to the right.

10. The aggregate supply curve relates the quantity of output supplied to the price level. In the short run, the price level is fixed and firms supply whatever level of output is demanded, so the short-run aggregate supply (*SRAS*) curve is horizontal. In the long run, after prices and wages have fully adjusted and all markets are in equilibrium, firms produce the profit-maximizing level of output. Hence in the long run aggregate output, Y, equals its full-employment level, $\overline{Y}$. In the long run firms supply $\overline{Y}$ regardless of the price level, so the long-run aggregate supply (*LRAS*) curve is a vertical line at $Y = \overline{Y}$.

11. Classical macroeconomists argue that prices and wages adjust rapidly in response to changes in supply or demand. This argument implies that, following shocks or changes in policy, the economy quickly reaches its general equilibrium, represented by the *IS–LM–FE* intersection or, equivalently, by the intersection of the *AD* and *LRAS* curves. In contrast, Keynesian macroeconomists argue that prices and wages adjust slowly enough that the economy can remain away from its general equilibrium (long-run equilibrium) for a prolonged period of time. Keynesians agree with classicals, however, that eventually prices and wages fully adjust so that the economy reaches its general equilibrium.

12. Classical and Keynesian economists agree that money is neutral in the long run, after the economy has reached its general equilibrium. Because classical economists believe that long-run equilibrium is reached quickly, they dismiss the short-run equilibrium in which money is not neutral as essentially irrelevant. Keynesians, who believe that it may take several years for the economy to reach general equilibrium, ascribe much more importance to the short-run period in which money is not neutral.

KEY DIAGRAM 6

The *IS–LM* diagram

The *IS–LM* model shows general equilibrium in the goods, asset, and labour markets. It can be used to analyse the effects of economic shocks on output, the real interest rate, the price level, and other macroeconomic variables.

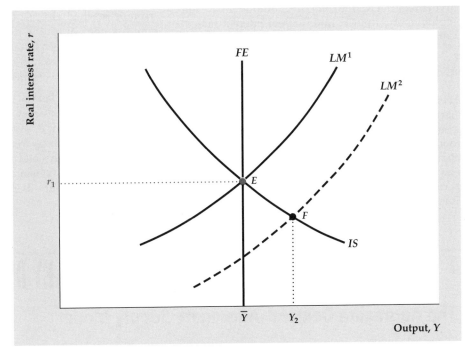

Diagram Elements

■ The real interest rate, r, is on the vertical axis, and output, Y, is on the horizontal axis.

■ The full-employment line, *FE*, is vertical at full-employment output. Full-employment output, $\overline{Y}$, is the level of output that firms supply when wages and prices have fully adjusted, so employment is at its full-employment level, $\overline{N}$. Full-employment output is determined by the equation $\overline{Y} = AF(K, \overline{N})$.

■ For any level of output Y, the *IS* curve gives the real interest rate r that clears the goods market – or, in other words, the rate that equalizes desired national saving, S^d, and desired investment, I^d. Because higher output raises desired saving and lowers the real interest rate that clears the goods market, the *IS* curve slopes downward. Equivalently, the *IS* curve gives combinations of output Y and the real interest rate r that equalize the aggregate quantities of goods supplied and demanded, $Y = C^d + I^d + G$.

■ For given values of the price level and output, the *LM* curve gives the real interest rate that clears the asset market, making the real money supply, M/P, and the real quantity of money demanded, $L(Y, r + \pi^e)$, equal. Because an increase in income raises real money demand, which raises the real interest rate that clears the asset market, the *LM* curve slopes upwards.

Factors that Shift the Curves

■ Any factor that raises full-employment output shifts the *FE* line to the right. See Summary table 11 (p. 341).

■ For constant output, any change that reduces desired national saving relative to desired investment increases the real interest rate that clears the goods market and shifts the *IS* curve up. Equivalently, any change that increases the aggregate demand for goods at a specific level of income raises the real interest rate that clears the goods market and shifts the *IS* curve up. See Summary table 12 (p. 344).

■ For constant output, any change that reduces real money supply relative to real money demand increases the real interest rate that clears the asset market and shifts the *LM* curve up. See Summary table 13 (p. 350).

Analysis

■ If we assume that the *LM* curve is LM^1, the economy is in general equilibrium at point *E*, which lies on all three curves. At *E* the labour market (*FE* line), the goods market (*IS* curve), and the asset market (*LM* curve) are all in equilibrium. At *E* output equals full-employment output $\overline{Y}$; and the real interest rate, r_1, clears both the goods and asset markets.

■ If we assume that the *LM* curve is LM^2, the *FE* line and *IS* and *LM* curves do not all intersect, and the economy is out of general equilibrium. We assume that, when the economy is out of general equilibrium, the short-run equilibrium of the economy occurs at the intersection of the *IS* and *LM* curves (point *F*), where the goods and asset markets are in equilibrium but the labour market is not. If we further assume that (at least temporarily) firms produce enough output to meet the increased aggregate demand at *F*, in short-run equilibrium the economy's output is Y_2.

■ At the short-run equilibrium point, *F*, output Y_2 is greater than firms' profit-maximizing level of output $\overline{Y}$. Because aggregate demand at *F* exceeds what firms want to produce, they raise prices. An increase in the price level *P* lowers the real money supply M/P and shifts the *LM* curve up to LM^1, and general equilibrium is reached at *E*. At *E* output again equals full-employment output $\overline{Y}$. Similarly, if the short-run equilibrium had been to the left of the *FE* line, declines in the price level *P* would have shifted the *LM* curve to the right and restored general equilibrium at *E*.

■ According to classical economists, the price adjustment process quickly restores the economy to general equilibrium at point *E*, so the economy spends little or no time at point *F* away from full employment. Keynesians argue that prices and wages are slow to adjust, so the economy may remain at the short-run equilibrium point, *F*, with output different from $\overline{Y}$, for an extended period of time.

KEY DIAGRAM | 7

The Aggregate Demand–Aggregate Supply Model

The *AD–AS* model shows the determination of the price level and output. In the short run, before prices adjust, equilibrium occurs at the intersection of the *AD* and *SRAS* curves. In the long run, equilibrium occurs at the intersection of the *AD* and *LRAS* curves.

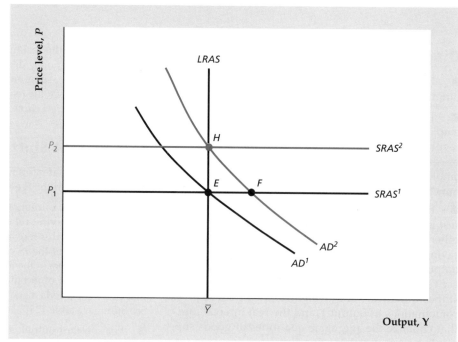

Diagram Elements

■ The price level, P, is on the vertical axis, and the level of output, Y, is on the horizontal axis.

■ The aggregate demand (AD) curve shows the aggregate quantity of output demanded at each price level. The aggregate amount of output demanded is determined by the intersection of the IS and LM curves (see Figure 10.10). An increase in the price level, P, reduces the real money supply, shifting the LM curve up and to the left, and reduces the aggregate quantity of output demanded. Thus the AD curve slopes downwards.

■ The aggregate supply curves show the relationship between the price level and the aggregate quantity of output supplied in the short run and in the long run. In the short run, the price level is fixed at $\bar{P}$, and firms supply whatever level of output is demanded. Thus the short-run aggregate supply (SRAS) curve is horizontal at $P = \bar{P}$. In the long run firms produce the amount of output that maximizes their profits, which is the full employment level of output, $\bar{Y}$. Because aggregate output in the long run equals $\bar{Y}$ regardless of the price level, P, the long-run aggregate supply (LRAS) curve is a vertical line at $Y = \bar{Y}$.

Factors that Shift the Curves

■ The aggregate quantity of output demanded is determined by the intersection of the IS and the LM curves. At a constant price level, any factor that shifts the IS–LM intersection to the right increases the aggregate quantity of goods demanded and thus also shifts the AD curve to the right. Factors that shift the AD curve are listed in Summary table 14.

■ Any factor, such as an increase in the costs of production, that leads firms to increase prices in the short run will shift the short-run aggregate supply (SRAS) curve up. Any factor that increases the full-employment level of output, $\bar{Y}$, shifts the long-run aggregate supply (LRAS) curve to the right. Factors that increase $\bar{Y}$ include beneficial supply shocks and an increase in labour supply

Analysis

■ The economy's short-run equilibrium is represented by the intersection of the AD and $SRAS$ curves, as at point E. The long-run equilibrium of the economy is represented by the intersection of the AD curve and $LRAS$ curve, also at point E. In the long run, output equals its full-employment level, $\bar{Y}$.

■ The short-run equilibrium can temporarily differ from the long-run equilibrium as a result of shocks or policy changes that affect the economy. For instance, an increase in the nominal money supply shifts the aggregate demand curve up from AD^1 to AD^2. The new short-run equilibrium is represented by point F, where output is higher than its full-employment level, $\bar{Y}$. At point F, firms produce an amount of output that is greater than the profit-maximizing level, and they begin to increase prices. In the new long-run equilibrium at point H, output is at its full-employment level and the price level is higher than its initial value, $\bar{P}$. Because the new price level is P_2, the short-run aggregate supply curve shifts up to $SRAS^2$, which is a horizontal line at $P = P_2$.

Key Terms

Review Questions

1. What determines the position of the FE line? Give two examples of changes in the economy that would shift the FE line to the right.
2. What relationship does the IS curve capture? Derive the IS curve graphically and show why it slopes as it does. Give two examples of changes in the economy that would cause the IS curve to shift down and to the left.

3. What relationship does the *LM* curve capture? Derive the *LM* curve graphically and show why it slopes as it does. Give two examples of changes in the economy that would cause the *LM* curve to shift down and to the right.

4. For constant output, if real money supply exceeds the real quantity of money demanded, what will happen to the real interest rate that clears the asset market? In describing the adjustment of the real interest rate, use the relationship that exists between the price of a non-monetary asset and the interest rate that it pays.

5. Define *general equilibrium* and show the general equilibrium point in the *IS–LM* diagram. If the economy is not in general equilibrium, what determines output and the real interest rate? What economic forces act to bring the economy back to general equilibrium?

6. Define *monetary neutrality*. Show that, after prices adjust completely, money is neutral in the *IS–LM* model. What are the classical and Keynesian views about whether money is neutral in the short run? In the long run?

7. What two variables are related by the aggregate demand (*AD*) curve? Why does the *AD* curve slope downward? Give two examples of changes in the economy that shift the *AD* curve to the right and explain why the shifts occur.

8. Describe the short-run aggregate supply (*SRAS*) curve and the long-run aggregate supply (*LRAS*) curve. Why is one of these curves horizontal and the other vertical?

9. Use the *AD–AS* framework to analyse whether money is neutral in the short run and whether it is neutral in the long run.

Numerical Problems

1. Desired consumption and investment are
$$C^d = 3600 - 2000r + 0.10Y$$
$$I^d = 1200 - 4000r$$

As usual, *Y* is output and *r* is the real interest rate. Government purchases, *G*, are 1200.
a. Find an equation relating desired national saving, S^d, to *r* and *Y*.
b. What value of the real interest rate clears the goods market when *Y* = 6000? Use both forms of the goods market equilibrium condition. What value of

the real interest rate clears the goods market when *Y* = 6400? Graph the *IS* curve.
c. Government purchases rise to 1320. How does this increase change the equation for national saving in part (a)? What value of the real interest rate clears the goods market when *Y* = 6000? Use both forms of the goods market equilibrium condition. How is the *IS* curve affected by the increase in *G*?

2. In a particular economy the real money demand function is

$$\frac{M^d}{P} = 2000 + 0.2Y - 20{,}000i$$

Assume that *M* = 3000, *P* = 2.0, and $\pi^e = 0.05$.
a. What is the real interest rate *r* that clears the asset market when *Y* = 5000? When *Y* = 6000? Graph the *LM* curve.
b. Repeat part (a) for *M* = 3600. How does the *LM* curve in this case compare with the *LM* curve in part (a)?
c. Use *M* = 3000 again and repeat part (a) for $\pi^e = 0.04$. Compare the *LM* curve in this case with the one in part (a).

3. An economy has full-employment output of 1000. Desired consumption and desired investment are

$$C^d = 200 + 0.8(Y - T) - 500r$$
$$I^d = 200 - 500r$$

Government purchases are 196 and taxes are

$$T = 20 + 0.25Y$$

Money demand is

$$\frac{M^d}{P} = 0.5Y - 250(r + \pi^e)$$

where the expected rate of inflation $\pi^e = 0.10$. The nominal supply of money *M* = 9890.
a. What are the general equilibrium values of the real interest rate, price level, consumption, and investment?
b. Suppose that government purchases are increased to *G* = 216. What are the new general equilibrium values of the real interest rate, the price level, consumption, and investment?

4. The production function in an economy is

$$Y = A(5N - 0.0025N^2)$$

where *A* is productivity. With this production function, the marginal product of labour is

$$MPN = 5A - 0.005AN$$

Suppose that $A = 2$. The labour supply curve is

$$NS = 55 + 10(1 - t)w$$

where NS is the amount of labour supplied, w is the real wage, and t is the tax rate, which is 0.5.

Desired consumption and investment are

$$C^d = 300 + 0.8(Y - T) - 200r$$
$$I^d = 258.5 - 250r$$

Taxes and government purchases are

$$T = 20 + 0.5Y$$
$$G = 50$$

Money demand is

$$\frac{M^d}{P} = 0.5Y - 250(r + \pi^e)$$

The expected rate of inflation π^e is 0.02, and the nominal money supply M is 9150.

a. What are the general equilibrium levels of the real wage, employment, and output?

b. For any level of output Y, find an equation that gives the real interest rate r that clears the goods market; this equation describes the IS curve. (*Hint:* Write the goods market equilibrium condition and solve for r in terms of Y and other variables.) What are the general equilibrium values of the real interest rate, consumption, and investment?

c. For any level of output Y, find an equation that gives the real interest rate that clears the asset market; this equation describes the LM curve. (*Hint:* As in part (b), write the appropriate equilibrium condition and solve for r in terms of Y and other variables.) What is the general equilibrium value of the price level?

d. Suppose that government purchases increase to $G = 72.5$. Now what are the general equilibrium values of the real wage, employment, output, the real interest rate, consumption, investment, and the price level?

5. Consider the following economy.
Desired consumption $C^d = 1275 + 0.5(Y - T) - 200r$
Desired investment $I^d = 900 - 200r$
Real money demand $L = 0.5Y - 200i$
Full-employment output $\bar{Y} = 4600$
Expected inflation $\pi^e = 0$

a. Suppose that $T = G = 450$ and that $M = 9000$. Find an equation describing the IS curve. (*Hint:* Set

desired national saving and desired investment equal, and solve for the relationship between r and Y.) Find an equation describing the LM curve. (*Hint:* Set real money supply an real money demand equal, and again solve for the relationship between r and Y, given P.) Finally, find an equation for the aggregate demand curve. (*Hint:* Use the IS and LM equations to find a relationship between Y and P.) What are the equilibrium values of output, consumption, investment, the real interest rate, and the price level?

b. Suppose that $T = G = 450$ and that $M = 4500$. What is the equation for the aggregate demand curve now? What are the equilibrium values of output, consumption, investment, the real interest rate, and the price level? Assume that full-employment output $\bar{Y}$ is fixed.

c. Repeat part (b) for $T = G = 330$ and $M = 9000$.

6. (Appendix). This question asks you to use the formulas in Appendix 10.A to find the general equilibrium values of variables for the economy described in Numerical Problem 4. Assume that $G = 50$.

a. Use the data from Numerical Problem 4 to find the numerical values of the parameters $A, f_1, f_2, n_0, n_w, c_0, c_Y, c_r, t_0, t, i_0, i_r, \ell_0, \ell_Y,$ and ℓ_r defined in Appendix 10.A.

b. Substitute the values of these behavioural parameters into the relevant equations in Appendix 10.A to compute the general equilibrium values of the real wage, employment, output, the real interest rate, and the price level.

c. Assume that government purchases G increase to 72.5, and repeat part (b).

Analytical Problems

1. Use the IS–LM model to determine the effects of each of the following on the general equilibrium values of the real wage, employment, output, the real interest rate, consumption, investment, and the price level.

a. A reduction in the effective tax rate on capital that increases desired investment.

b. The expected rate of inflation rises.

c. An influx of working-age immigrants increases labour supply (ignore any other possible effects of increased population).

d. The introduction of automatic teller machines reduces the demand for money.

2. Use the *IS–LM* model to analyse the general equilibrium effects of a permanent increase in the price of oil (a permanent adverse supply shock) on current output, employment, the real wage, national saving, consumption, investment, the real interest rate, and the price level. Assume that, besides reducing the current productivity of capital and labour, the permanent supply shock lowers both the expected future *MPK* and households' expected future incomes. (Assume that the rightward shift in labour supply is smaller than the leftward shift in labour demand.) Show that, if the real interest rate rises at all, it will rise less than in the case of a temporary supply shock that has an equal effect on current output.

3. Suppose that the price level is fixed in the short run so that the economy does not reach general equilibrium immediately after a change in the economy. For each of the following changes, what are the short-run effects on the real interest rate and output? Assume that, when the economy is in disequilibrium, only the labour market is out of equilibrium; assume also that for a short period firms are willing to produce enough output to meet the aggregate demand for output.

   a. A decrease in the expected rate of inflation.

   b. An increase in consumer optimism that increases desired consumption at each level of income and the real interest rate.

   c. An increase in government purchases.

   d. An increase in lump-sum taxes, with no change in government purchases (consider both the case in which Ricardian equivalence holds and the case in which it does not).

e. A scientific breakthrough increases the expected future *MPK*.

4. (Appendix) In some macroeconomic models, desired investment depends on the current level of output and the real interest rate. One possible reason that desired investment may depend on output is that, when current production and sales are high, firms may expect continued strong demand for their products in the future, which leads them to want to expand capacity.

   Algebraically, we can allow for a link between desired investment and current output by replacing equation (10.A.10) with

   $$I^d = i_0 - i_r r + i_Y Y$$

   where i_Y is a positive number. Use this alternative equation for desired investment to derive the algebraic expressions for the general equilibrium values of employment, the real wage, output, the real interest rate, and the price level.

5. (Appendix) Recall from Chapter 7 that an increase in i^m, the nominal interest rate on money, increases the demand for money. To capture that effect, let us replace equation (10.A.17) with

   $$\frac{M^d}{P} = \ell_0 + \ell_Y Y - \ell_r (r + \pi^e - i^m).$$

   How does this modification change the solutions for the general equilibrium values of the variables discussed in Appendix 10.A, including employment, the real wage, output, the real interest rate, and the price level?

APPENDIX 10.A

ALGEBRAIC VERSIONS OF THE *IS-LM* AND THE *AD–AS* MODELS

This appendix presents an algebraic version of the *IS–LM* and *AD–AS* models. For each of the three markets – labour, goods, and assets – we first present equations that describe demand and supply in that market, then find the market equilibrium. After considering each market separately, we solve for the general equilibrium of the complete *IS–LM* model. We use the *IS–LM* model to derive the aggregate demand (*AD*) curve and then introduce the short-run and long-run aggregate supply curves to drive the short-run and long-run equilibria.

The Labour Market

The demand for labour is based on the marginal product of labour, as determined by the production function. Recall from Chapter 3 (equation 3.1) that the production function can be written as $Y = AF(K, N)$, where Y is output, K is the capital stock, N is labour input, and A is productivity. Holding the capital stock K fixed, we can write the production function with output Y as a function only of labour input N and productivity A. A useful specific production function is

$$Y = A\left(f_1 N - \frac{1}{2} f_2 N^2\right) \tag{10.A.1}$$

where f_1 and f_2 are positive numbers.

The marginal product of labour, MPN, is the slope of the production function. The slope of the production function in equation (10.A.1) at any level of employment N equals[10] $A(f_1 - f_2 N)$, so the marginal product of labour is

$$MPN = A(f_1 - f_2 N) \tag{10.A.2}$$

Firms hire labour to the point at which the marginal product of labour equals the real wage. Thus, the relation between the real wage w and the amount of labour demanded ND is

$$w = A(f_1 - f_2 ND) \tag{10.A.3}$$

The supply of labour is an increasing function of the current, after-tax real wage. If t is the tax rate on wage income (we assume that $0 \le t < 1$) so that $(1 - t)w$ is the after-tax real wage, a simple form of the labour supply curve is

$$NS = n_0 + n_w(1 - t)w \tag{10.A.4}$$

where NS is the amount of labour supplied, and n_0 and n_w are positive numbers. Factors other than the after-tax real wage that affect labour supply, such

---

10. Students who know calculus can derive the slope of the production function by taking the derivative of equation (10.A.1) with respect to N.

as wealth or the working-age population, are captured by the constant term n_0 in equation (10.A.4).

Equilibrium in the Labour Market. In equilibrium, the amounts of labour demanded *ND* and supplied *NS* are equal; their common value is the full-employment level of employment $\overline{N}$. If we substitute $\overline{N}$ for *NS* and *ND* in equations (10.A.3) and (10.A.4), we have two linear equations in the two variables $\overline{N}$ and *w*. Solving these equations for *w* and $\overline{N}$ yields[11]

$$w = A\left[\frac{f_1 - f_2 n_0}{1 + (1-t)Af_2 n_w}\right] \tag{10.A.5}$$

and

$$\overline{N} = \frac{n_0 + (1-t)Af_1 n_w}{1 + (1-t)Af_2 n_w}. \tag{10.A.6}$$

Using the full-employment level of employment $\overline{N}$ in equation (10.A.6), we obtain the full-employment level of output $\overline{Y}$ by substituting $\overline{N}$ into the production function (10.A.1):

$$\overline{Y} = A\left[f_1\overline{N} - \frac{1}{2}f_2\overline{N}^2\right], \; FE \text{ line} \tag{10.A.7}$$

The value of full-employment output in equation (10.A.7) is the horizontal intercept of the *FE* line.

We can use these equations to analyse the effects on the labour market of changes in productivity and in labour supply. First consider an increase in productivity *A*. Equation (10.A.5) shows that an increase in *A* leads to an increase in the equilibrium real wage (an increase in *A* raises the ratio $A/[1 + (1-t)Af_2 n_w]$). Although not directly evident from equation (10.A.6), an increase in *A* also increases $\overline{N}$.[12] To see why, note first that an increase in *A* does not affect the labour supply curve, equation (10.A.4). Second, an increase in *A* raises the real wage. Hence the implication is that an increase in *A* raises the equilibrium amount of labour supplied and thus also the full-employment level of employment, $\overline{N}$. Because an increase in *A* raises $\overline{N}$, it must also raise full-employment output $\overline{Y}$ (see equation 10.A.7) and shift the *FE* line to the right.

Now consider an increase in the amount of labour supplied at each level of the after-tax real wage, represented algebraically as an increase in n_0 in equation (10.A.4). Equations (10.A.5) and (10.A.6) show that an increase in n_0 reduces the equilibrium real wage and increases employment, $\overline{N}$. Because an increase in labour supply raises $\overline{N}$, it also raises full-employment output, $\overline{Y}$, and shifts the *FE* line to the right.

---

11. We assume that the constants f_1, f_2, and n_0 are such that $f_1 - f_2 n_0 > 0$. This assumption is needed to guarantee that the marginal product of labour and the equilibrium real wage are positive.
12. Students who know calculus can compute the derivative of $\overline{N}$ with respect to *A* in equation (10.A.6) and will find that the sign of this derivative is positive only if $f_1 - f_2 n_0 > 0$. As we have assumed that $f_1 - f_2 n_0 > 0$ (see preceding footnote), an increase in *A* does indeed increase $\overline{N}$.

The Goods Market

To find equilibrium in the goods market, we start with equations describing desired consumption and desired investment. Desired consumption is

$$C^d = c_0 + c_Y (Y - T) - c_r r \qquad (10.A.8)$$

where $Y - T$ is disposable income (income Y minus taxes T), r is the real interest rate, and c_0, c_Y, and c_r are positive numbers. The number c_Y in equation (10.A.8) is the marginal propensity to consume, as defined in Chapter 4; because people consume only part of an increase in disposable income, saving the rest, a reasonable assumption is that $0 < c_Y < 1$. According to equation (10.A.8), an increase in disposable income causes desired consumption to increase, and an increase in the real interest rate causes desired consumption to fall (and desired saving to rise). Other factors that affect desired consumption, such as wealth or expected future income, are included in the constant term c_0.[13]

Taxes in equation (10.A.8) are

$$T = t_0 + tY \qquad (10.A.9)$$

where t is the tax rate on income (the same tax rate that is levied on wages) and t_0 is a lump-sum tax. As mentioned earlier, $0 \leq t < 1$, so an increase in income Y increases total taxes T and also increases disposable income $Y - T$, thereby increasing consumption.

Desired investment is

$$I^d = i_0 - i_r r \qquad (10.A.10)$$

where i_0 and i_r are positive numbers. Equation (10.A.10) indicates that desired investment falls when the real interest rate rises. Other factors affecting desired investment, such as the expected future marginal product of capital, are included in the constant term i_0.

Equilibrium in the Goods Market. The goods market equilibrium condition in a closed economy is given by equation (4.8), which we repeat here:

$$Y = C^d + I^d + G \qquad (10.A.11)$$

Equation (10.A.11) is equivalent to the goods market equilibrium condition, $S^d = I^d$, which could be used equally well here.

If we substitute the equations for desired consumption (equation 10.A.8, with taxes T as given by equation 10.A.9) and desired investment (equation 10.A.10) into the goods market equilibrium condition (equation 10.A.11), we get

$$Y = c_0 + c_Y(Y - t_0 - tY) - c_r r + i_0 - i_r r + G \qquad (10.A.12)$$

---

13. Because an increase in taxes, T, reduces desired consumption in equation (10.A.8), this formulation of desired consumption appears, at first glance, to be inconsistent with the Ricardian equivalence proposition discussed in Chapter 4. However, essential to the idea of Ricardian equivalence is that consumers expect an increase in current taxes, T, to be accompanied by lower taxes in the future. This decrease in expected future taxes would increase desired consumption, which would be captured in equation (10.A.8) as an increase in c_0. According to the Ricardian equivalence proposition, after an increase in T with no change in current or planned government purchases, an increase in c_0 would exactly offset the reduction in $c_Y(Y - T)$ so that desired consumption would be unchanged.

Collecting the terms that multiply Y on the left-hand side yields

$$[1 - (1 - t)c_Y]Y = c_0 + i_0 + G - c_Y t_0 - (c_r + i_r)r \qquad (10.A.13)$$

Equation (10.A.13) relates output Y to the real interest rate, r, that clears
the goods market. This relationship between Y and r defines the *IS* curve.
Because the *IS* curve is graphed with r on the vertical axis and Y on the horizontal axis, we rewrite equation (10.A.13) with r on the left-hand side and Y
on the right-hand side. Solving equation (10.A.13) for r gives

$$r = \alpha_{IS} - \beta_{IS}Y, \qquad \text{IS curve} \qquad (10.A.14)$$

In equation (10.A.14), α_{IS} and β_{IS} are positive numbers defined as

$$\alpha_{IS} = \frac{c_0 + i_0 + G - c_Y t_0}{c_r + i_r} \qquad (10.A.15)$$

and

$$\beta_{IS} = \frac{1 - (1 - t)c_Y}{c_r + i_r} \qquad (10.A.16)$$

Equation (10.A.14) yields the graph of the *IS* curve. In equation (10.A.14),
the coefficient of Y, or $-\beta_{IS}$, is the slope of the *IS* curve; because this slope is
negative, the *IS* curve slopes downwards. Changes in the constant term α_{IS} in
equation (10.A.14), which is defined in equation (10.A.15), shift the *IS* curve.
Anything that increases α_{IS} – such as (1) an increase in consumer optimism
that increases desired consumption by increasing c_0; (2) an increase in the
expected future marginal product of capital MPK^f that raises desired investment by raising i_0; or (3) an increase in government purchases G – shifts the *IS*
curve up. Similarly, anything that decreases α_{IS} shifts the *IS* curve down.

The Asset Market

In general, the real demand for money depends on real income, Y, and on the
nominal interest rate on non-monetary assets i, which in turn equals the
expected real interest rate r plus the expected rate of inflation π^e. We assume
that the money demand function takes the form

$$\frac{M^d}{P} = \ell_0 + \ell_Y Y - \ell_r (r + \pi^e) \qquad (10.A.17)$$

where M^d is the nominal demand for money, P is the price level, and ℓ_0, ℓ_Y, and
ℓ_r are positive numbers. The constant term ℓ_0 includes factors other than output
and the interest rate that affect money demand, such as the liquidity of alternative assets. The real supply of money equals the nominal supply of money M,
which is determined by the central bank, divided by the price level, P.

Equilibrium in the Asset Market. As we showed in Chapter 7, if we
assume that there are only two types of asset (money and non-monetary assets),
the asset market is in equilibrium when the real quantity of money demanded
equals the real money supply M/P. Using the money demand function in equation (10.A.17), we write the asset market equilibrium condition as

$$\frac{M}{P} = \ell_0 + \ell_Y Y - \ell_r (r + \pi^e) \tag{10.A.18}$$

For fixed levels of the nominal money supply, M, price level P, and expected rate of inflation π^e, equation (10.A.18) relates output, Y, and the real interest rate, r, that clears the asset market. Thus equation (10.A.18) defines the *LM* curve. To get equation (10.A.18) into a form that is easier to interpret graphically, we rewrite the equation with r alone of the left-hand side:

$$r = \alpha_{LM} - \left(\frac{1}{\ell_r}\right)\left(\frac{M}{P}\right) + \beta_{LM}Y, \qquad LM \text{ curve} \tag{10.A.19}$$

where

$$\alpha_{LM} = \left(\frac{\ell_0}{\ell_r}\right) - \pi^e \tag{10.A.20}$$

and

$$\beta_{LM} = \left(\frac{\ell_Y}{\ell_r}\right). \tag{10.A.21}$$

The graph of equation (10.A.19) is the *LM* curve. In equation (10.A.19), the coefficient of Y, or β_{LM}, is the slope of the *LM* curve; because this coefficient is positive, the *LM* curve slopes upwards. Variables that change the intercept of the equation in equation (10.A.19), $\alpha_{LM} - (1/\ell_r)(M/P)$, shift the *LM* curve. An increase in the real money supply, M/P, reduces this intercept and thus shifts the *LM* curve down and to the right. An increase in the expected rate of inflation π^e reduces α_{LM} and shifts the *LM* curve down. An increase in real money demand arising from (for example) reduced liquidity of alternative assets raises ℓ_0, which raises α_{LM} and shifts the *LM* curve up.

General Equilibrium in the *IS–LM* Model

From the supply and demand relationships and equilibrium conditions in each market, we can calculate the general equilibrium values for the most important macroeconomic variables. We have already solved for the general equilibrium levels of the real wage, employment, and output in the labour market: the real wage is given by equation (10.A.5); employment equals its full-employment level $\overline{N}$, given by equation (10.A.6); and, in general equilibrium, output equals its full-employment level $\overline{Y}$, as given by equation (10.A.7).

Turning to the goods market, we obtain the general equilibrium real interest rate by substituting $\overline{Y}$ for Y in equation (10.A.14):

$$r = \alpha_{IS} - \beta_{IS}\overline{Y} \tag{10.A.22}$$

Having output $\overline{Y}$ and the real interest rate, r (determined by equation 10.A.22), we use equations (10.A.9), (10.A.8), and (10.A.10) to find the general equilibrium values of taxes, T, consumption, C, and investment, I, respectively.

The final important macroeconomic variable whose equilibrium value needs to be determined is the price level, P. To find the equilibrium price level, we work with the asset market equilibrium condition, equation (10.A.18). In equation (10.A.18), we substitute full-employment output $\overline{Y}$ for Y and use equation (10.A.22) to substitute the equilibrium value of the real interest rate for r. Solving equation (10.A.18) for the price level gives

$$P = \frac{M}{\ell_0 + \ell_Y \, \overline{Y} - \ell_r \, (\alpha_{IS} - \beta_{IS}\overline{Y} + \pi^e)} . \tag{10.A.23}$$

Equation (10.A.23) confirms that the equilibrium price level, P, is proportional to the nominal money supply, M.

We can use these equations to analyse the effects of an adverse productivity shock on the general equilibrium, as in the text. We have already shown that an increase in the productivity parameter A increases the equilibrium real wage, the full-employment level of employment, and the full-employment level of output. Thus an adverse productivity shock (a reduction in A) reduces the general equilibrium levels of the real wage, employment, and output. Equation (10.A.22) indicates that an adverse productivity shock, because it reduces $\overline{Y}$, must increase the equilibrium real interest rate. Lower output and a higher real interest rate imply that both consumption and investment must decline (equations 10.A.8 and 10.A.10). Finally, the decrease in $\overline{Y}$ resulting from an adverse productivity shock reduces the denominator of the right-hand side of equation (10.A.23), so the price level, P, must rise. All these results are the same as those found by graphical analysis.

The *AD–AS* Model

Building on the algebraic version of the *IS-LM* model just derived, we now derive an algebraic version of the *AD–AS* model presented in this chapter. We present algebraic versions of the aggregate demand (*AD*) curve, the short-run aggregate supply (*SRAS*) curve, and the long-run aggregate supply (*LRAS*) curve and then solve for short-run and long-run equilibrium.

The Aggregate Demand curve

Aggregate output demanded at any price level, P, is the amount of output coresponding to the intersection of the *IS* and *LM* curves. We find the value of Y at the intersection of the *IS* and *LM* curves by setting the right-hand sides of equations (10.A.14) and (10.A.19) equal and solving for Y:

$$Y = \frac{\alpha_{IS} - \alpha_{LM} + (1/\ell_r) \, (M/P)}{\beta_{IS} + \beta_{LM}} \tag{10.A.24}$$

Equation (10.A.24) is the aggregate demand curve. For constant nominal money supply, M, equation (10.A.24) shows that the aggregate quantity of goods demanded, Y, is a decreasing function of the price level, P, so that the *AD* curve slopes downwards. Note that the numerator of the right-hand side of equation (10.A.24) is the intercept of the *IS* curve minus the intercept of the *LM* curve. Thus, for a constant price level, any change that shifts the *IS* curve up (such as an increase in government purchases) or shifts the *LM* curve down (such as an increase in the nominal money supply) increases aggregate ouput demand and shifts the *AD* curve to the right.

The Aggregate Supply Curve

In the short run, firms supply the output demanded at the fixed price level, which we denote as $\bar{P}$. Thus the short-run aggregate supply (*SRAS*) curve is a horizontal line:

$$P = \bar{P}, \quad SRAS. \tag{10.A.25}$$

The long-run aggregate supply curve is a vertical line at the full-employment level of output, $\bar{Y}$ or

$$Y = \bar{Y}, \quad LRAS. \tag{10.A.26}$$

Short-Run and Long-Run Equilibrium

The short-run equilibrium of the economy is represented by the intersection of the aggregate demand (*AD*) curve and the short-run aggregate supply (*SRAS*) curve. We find the quantity of output in short-run equilibrium simply by substituting the equation of the *SRAS* curve (equation 10.A.25) into the equation of the *AD* curve (equation 10.A.24) to obtain

$$Y = \frac{\alpha_{IS} - \alpha_{LM} + (1/\ell_r)\,(M/\bar{P})}{\beta_{IS} + \beta_{LM}} \tag{10.A.27}$$

The long-run equilibrium of the economy, which is reached when the labour, goods, and asset market are all in equilibrium, is represented by the intersection of the aggregate demand curve and the long-run aggregate supply curve. Thus $Y = \bar{Y}$ in long-run equilibirum, from the *LRAS* curve in equation (10.A.26). We find the price level in long-run equilibrium by setting the left-hand sides of the equation of the *AD* curve (equation 10.A.24) and the equation of the *LRAS* curve (equation 10.A.26) equal and solving for P to obtain

$$P = \frac{M}{\ell_r[\alpha_{LM} - \alpha_{IS} + (\beta_{IS} + \beta_{LM})\bar{Y}]} \tag{10.A.28}$$

The long-run equilibrium price level in equation (10.A.28) is the same as that at the *IS–LM–FE* intersection in equation (10.A.23). You can verify that the price level is the same in both equations by substituting the definitions of α_{LM} and β_{LM} from equations (10.A.20) and (10.A.21), respectively, into equation (10.A.28).

11

CLASSICAL BUSINESS CYCLE ANALYSIS: MARKET-CLEARING MACROECONOMICS

Economists generally agree about the basic business cycle facts outlined in Chapter 9. They know that economic growth is not necessarily smooth and that occasionally there are periods of recession in which output declines and unemployment rises. They know that recessions are typically followed by periods of recovery in which the economy grows more strongly than normal. And they also know a great deal about how other macroeconomic variables – such as productivity, interest rates, and inflation – behave during recessions.

Recall that recessions and booms in the economy raise two basic questions: (1) What are the underlying economic causes of these business cycles? and (2) What, if anything, should government policymakers do about them? Unfortunately, economists agree less about the answers to these two questions than about the basic business cycle facts.

The main disagreements about the causes and cures of recessions are between two broad groups of macroeconomists, the classical economists and the Keynesians. As discussed first in Chapter 1 and again in Chapters 9 and 10, classical and Keynesian economists – although agreeing on many points – differ primarily in their views on how rapidly prices and wages adjust to restore general equilibrium after an economic shock. Classical macroeconomists assume that prices and wages adjust quickly to equate quantities supplied and demanded in each market; as a result, they argue, a market economy is largely 'self-correcting', with a strong tendency to return to general equilibrium on its own when it is disturbed by an economic shock or a change in public policy. Keynesians usually agree that prices and wages *eventually* change as needed to clear markets; however, they believe that *in the short run* price and wage adjustment is likely to be incomplete. That is, in the short run quantities supplied and demanded need not be equal and the economy may remain out of general equilibrium. Although this difference in views may seem purely theoretical, it has a practical implication: because Keynesians are sceptical about the economy's ability to reach equilibrium rapidly on its own, they are much more inclined than are classical economists to recommend that government act to raise output and employment during recessions and to moderate economic growth during booms.

In this chapter and Chapter 12 we develop and compare the classical and Keynesian theories of the business cycle and the policy recommendations of the two groups, beginning with the classical perspective in this chapter. Conveniently, both the classical and Keynesian analyses can be expressed in terms of a common analytical framework, the *IS–LM/AD–AS* model. In this chapter we use the classical (or market-clearing) version of the *IS–LM/AD–AS* model, comprising the *IS–LM/AD–AS* model and the assumption that prices and wages adjust rapidly. The assumption that prices and wages adjust rapidly implies that the economy is always in or near general equilibrium and therefore that variables such as output and employment are always close to their general equilibrium levels.

In comparing the principal competing theories of the business cycle, we are particularly interested in how well the various theories explain the business cycle facts. The classical theory is consistent with many of the most important facts about the cycle. However, one business cycle fact that challenges the classical theory is the observation that changes in the money stock lead the cycle. Recall the implication of the classical assumption that wages and prices adjust quickly to clear markets so that the economy reaches long-run equilibrium quickly. Money is neutral, which means that changes in the money supply do not affect output and other real variables. However, most economists interpret the fact that money leads the cycle as evidence that money is *not* neutral in all situations. If money is not neutral, we must either modify the basic classical model to account for monetary non-neutrality or abandon the classical model in favour of alternative theories (such as the Keynesian approach) that are consistent with non-neutrality. In Section 11.3 we extend the classical model to allow for non-neutrality of money. We then examine the implications of this extended classical approach for macroeconomic policy.

11.1 BUSINESS CYCLES IN THE CLASSICAL MODEL

We have identified two basic questions of business cycle analysis: What causes business cycles? and What can (or should) be done about them? Let's examine the classical answers to these questions, beginning with what causes business cycles.

The Real Business Cycle Theory

Recall from Section 9.4 that a complete theory of the business cycle must have two components. The first is a description of the types of shock or disturbance believed to affect the economy the most. Examples of economic disturbances emphasized by various theories of the business cycle include supply shocks, changes in monetary or fiscal policy, and changes in consumer spending. The second component is a model that describes how key macroeconomic variables, such as output, employment, and prices, respond to economic shocks. The model preferred by classical economists is the market-clearing version of the *IS–LM* model or some similar framework. However, the issue of which shocks are crucial in driving cyclical fluctuations remains.

An influential group of classical macroeconomists, led by Edward Prescott of the University of Minnesota and Finn Kydland of Carnegie Mellon University, developed a theory that takes a strong stand on the sources of shocks that cause cyclical fluctuations. This theory, the **real business cycle theory** (or RBC theory), argues that real shocks to the economy are the primary cause of business cycles.[1] **Real shocks** are disturbances to the 'real side' of the economy, such as shocks that affect the production function, the size of the labour force, the real quantity of government purchases, and the spending and saving decisions of consumers. Economists contrast real shocks with **nominal shocks**, or shocks to money supply or money demand. In terms of the *IS–LM* model, real shocks directly affect only the *IS* curve or the *FE* line, whereas nominal shocks directly affect only the *LM* curve.

Although many types of real shock could contribute to the business cycle, RBC theorists give the largest role to production function shocks – what we have called supply shocks and what the RBC theorists usually refer to as **productivity shocks**. Productivity shocks include the development of new products or production methods, the introduction of new management techniques, changes in the quality of capital or labour, changes in the availability of raw materials or energy, unusually good or unusually bad weather, changes in government regulations affecting production, and any other factor affecting productivity. According to RBC theorists, most economic booms result from beneficial productivity shocks, and most recessions are caused by adverse productivity shocks.

The Recessionary Impact of an Adverse Productivity Shock.

Does the RBC theorists' idea that adverse productivity shocks lead to recessions (and, similarly, that beneficial productivity shocks lead to booms) make sense? We examined the theoretical effects on the economy of a temporary adverse productivity shock in Chapters 3, 9, and 10.[2] In Chapter 3 we showed that an adverse productivity shock (or supply shock), such as an increase in the price of oil, reduces the marginal product of labour (*MPN*) and the demand for labour at any real wage. As a result, the equilibrium values of the real wage and employment both fall (see Figure 3.10). The equilibrium level of output (the full-employment level of output $\overline{Y}$) also falls, both because equilibrium employment declines and because the adverse productivity shock reduces the amount of output that can be produced by any amount of capital and labour.

We later used the complete *IS–LM* model (Figure 10.8) to explore the general equilibrium effects of a temporary adverse productivity shock. We

---

1. For a more detailed introduction to real business cycles, see Charles Plosser, 'Understanding Real Business Cycles', *Journal of Economic Perspectives*, Summer 1989, pp. 51–78.
2. RBC theorists analyse permanent as well as temporary productivity shocks; we focus on temporary shocks because it is the slightly easier case.

confirmed our earlier conclusion that an adverse productivity shock lowers the general equilibrium levels of the real wage, employment, and output. In addition, we showed that an adverse productivity shock raises the real interest rate, depresses consumption and investment, and raises the price level.

Broadly, then, our earlier analyses of the effects of an adverse productivity shock support the RBC theorists' claim that such shocks are recessionary, in that they lead to declines in output. Similar analyses show that a beneficial productivity shock leads to a rise in output (a boom). Note that, in the RBC approach, output declines in recessions and rises in booms because the general equilibrium (or full-employment) level of output has changed and because rapid price adjustment ensures that actual output always equals full-employment output. As classical economists, RBC theorists would reject the Keynesian view (discussed in Chapter 12) that recessions and booms are periods of disequilibrium, during which actual output is below or above its general equilibrium level for a protracted period of time.

Real Business Cycle Theory and the Business Cycle Facts. Although the RBC theory – which combines the classical, or market-clearing, version of the *IS–LM* model with the assumption that productivity shocks are the dominant form of economic disturbance – is relatively simple, it is consistent with many of the basic business cycle facts. First, under the assumption that the economy is being continuously buffeted by productivity shocks, the RBC approach predicts recurrent fluctuations in aggregate output, which actually occur. Second, the RBC theory correctly predicts that employment will move procyclically – that is, in the same direction as output. Third, the RBC theory predicts that real wages will be higher during booms than during recessions (procyclical real wages), as also occurs.

A fourth business cycle fact explained by the RBC theory is that average labour productivity is procyclical: that is, output per worker is higher during booms than during recessions. This fact is consistent with the RBC theorists' assumption that booms are periods of beneficial productivity shocks, which tend to raise labour productivity, whereas recessions are the result of adverse productivity shocks, which tend to reduce labour productivity. The RBC theorists point out that without productivity shocks – allowing the production function to remain stable over time – average labour productivity would not be procyclical. With no productivity shocks, the expansion of employment that occurs during booms would tend to reduce average labour productivity because of the principle of diminishing marginal productivity of labour. Similarly, without productivity shocks, recessions would be periods of relatively higher labour productivity, instead of lower productivity as observed. Thus RBC theorists regard the procyclical nature of average labour productivity as strong evidence supporting their approach.

A business cycle fact that does *not* seem to be consistent with the simple RBC theory is that inflation tends to slow during or immediately after a recession. The theory predicts that an adverse productivity shock will both cause a recession and increase the general price level. Thus, according to the RBC approach, periods of recession should also be periods of inflation, contrary to the business cycle fact.

Some RBC theorists have responded by taking issue with the conventional view that inflation is procyclical. For example, in a study of business cycle facts in six European countries and in the USA and Japan between 1960 and 1990, Peter Van Els found that the price level was countercyclical.[3] RBC proponents Finn Kydland and Edward Prescott[4] have shown for the USA that the finding of procyclical inflation is somewhat sensitive to the statistical methods used to calculate the trends in inflation and output. Using a different method of calculating these trends, Kydland and Prescott found evidence that, when aggregate output has been above its long-run trend, the price level has tended to be below its long-run trend, a result more nearly consistent with the RBC prediction about the cyclical behaviour of prices. The view that inflation is procyclical does seem to hold for the period before World War II, and especially during the Great Depression, when the world economy had a different structure and was subject to different types of shock than has been the case in more recent years. For example, many economists believe that the Great Depression – the most important macroeconomic event between the two world wars – resulted from a sequence of large, adverse aggregate demand shocks. As we illustrated in Figure 9.13, an adverse aggregate demand shock shifts the *AD* curve down and to the left, leading first to a decline in output and then to a decline in prices; this pattern is consistent with the conventional business cycle fact that inflation is procyclical and lagging. Kydland and Prescott argue, however, that since World War II large adverse supply shocks have caused the price level to rise while output fell. Most notably, inflation surged during the recessions that followed the oil price shocks of 1973–74 and 1979–80. The issue of the cyclical behaviour of prices remains controversial, however.

The RBC theory has been able to explain facts about international business cycles. One such fact is that saving and investment tend to move together closely in most European countries, even though (as we saw in Chapter 5) they need not be equal in an open economy. Evidence for Europe is able to account for this fact by showing that productivity shocks in many European countries are fairly similar and tend to move together.[5] If, for example, two countries both experience an adverse productivity shock then saving and investment will fall in both countries and they will tend to move together country by country. Researchers also use real business cycle models to account for similarities in movements in consumption, output and the current account.

| APPLICATION | If we put aside the debate about price-level behaviour, the RBC theory can account for some of the business cycle facts, including the procyclical behaviour of employment, productivity, and real wages. However, real business cycle theorists argue that an adequate theory of the business cycle should be *quantitative* as well as *qualitative*. In other words, in addition to predicting generally how key macroeconomic variables move throughout the business cycle, |

Calibrating the Business Cycle

3. 'Real Business Cycle Models and Money: A Survey of Theories and Stylized Facts', *Weltwirtschaftliches Archiv*, 1995, vol. 131, pp. 223–64.
4. 'Business Cycles: Real Facts and a Monetary Myth', *Quarterly Review*, Federal Reserve Bank of Minneapolis, Spring 1990, pp. 3–18.
5. See Nicos Christodoulakis, Sophia Dimelis, and Tryphon Kollintzas, 'Comparisons of Business Cycles in the EC: Idiosyncrasies and Regularities', *Economica*, 1995, pp. 1–27.

the theory should predict numerically the size of economic fluctuations and the strength of relationships among the variables.

To examine the quantitative implications of their theories, RBC theorists developed a method called *calibration*. The idea is to work out a detailed numerical example of a more general theory. The results are then compared to macroeconomic data to see whether model and reality broadly agree.

The first step in calibration is to write down a model of the economy – such as the classical version of the *IS–LM* model – except that specific functions replace general functions. For example, instead of representing the production function in general terms as

$$Y = AF(K, N)$$

the person doing the calibration uses a specific algebraic form for the production function, such as[6]

$$Y = AK^a N^{1-a}$$

where a is a number between 0 and 1. Similarly, specific functions are used to describe the behaviour of consumers and workers.

Next, the specific functions chosen are made even more specific by expressing them in numerical terms. For example, for $a = 0.3$, the production function becomes

$$Y = AK^{0.3} N^{0.7}$$

In the same way, specific numbers are assigned to the functions describing the behaviour of consumers and workers. Where do these numbers come from? Generally, they are *not* estimated from macroeconomic data but are based on other sources. For example, the numbers assigned to the functions in the model may come from previous studies of the production function or of the saving behaviour of individuals and families.

The third step, which must be carried out on a computer, is to find out how the numerically specified model behaves when it is hit by random shocks, such as productivity shocks. The shocks are created on the computer with a random number generator, with the size and persistence of the shocks (unlike the numbers assigned to the specific functions) being chosen to fit the actual macroeconomic data. For these shocks, the computer tracks the behaviour of the model over many periods and reports the implied behaviour of key macroeconomic variables such as output, employment, consumption, and investment. The results are then compared to the behaviour of the actual economy to determine how well the model fits reality.

Edward Prescott[7] performed an early and influential calibration exercise. He used a model similar to the RBC model we present here, the main difference being that our version of the RBC model is essentially a two-period

---

6. This production function is the Cobb–Douglas production function (Chapter 3). As we noted, although it is relatively simple, it fits the data quite well.

7. 'Theory Ahead of Business Cycle Measurement', *Carnegie-Rochester Conference Series on Public Policy*, Volume 25, Autumn 1986, pp. 11–39. Reprinted in *Quarterly Review*, Federal Reserve Bank of Minneapolis, Fall 1986, pp. 9–22. For a critical assessment of this approach see Kevin D. Hoover, 'Facts and Artifacts: Calibration and the Empirical Assessment of Real Business Cycle Models', *Oxford Economic Papers*, 1995, pp. 24–44.

model (the present and the future), and Prescott's model allowed for many periods. The results of his computer simulations are shown in Figures 11.1 and 11.2.

Figure 11.1 compares the actually observed volatilities of six macroeconomic variables, as calculated from post–World War II US data, with the volatilities predicted by Prescott's calibrated RBC model.[8] Prescott set the size of the random productivity shocks in his simulations so that the volatility of GNP in his model would match the actual volatility in US GNP.[9] That choice explains why the actual and simulated volatilities of GNP are equal in Figure 11.1. But he did nothing to guarantee that the simulation would match the actual volatilities of the other five variables. Note, however, that the simulated and actual volatilities for the other variables in most cases are quite close.

Figure 11.2 compares the actual US economy with Prescott's calibrated model in another respect: how closely important macroeconomic variables move with GNP over the business cycle. The statistical measure of how closely variables move together is called *correlation*. If a variable's correlation with GNP is positive, the variable tends to move in the same direction as GNP over the business cycle (that is, the variable is procyclical). A correlation with GNP of 1.0 indicates that the variable's movements track the movements of GNP

---

8. The measure of volatility used is called the *standard deviation*. The higher the standard deviation, the more volatile is the variable being measured.

9. At the time of Prescott's study, the national income and product accounts of the United States focused on GNP rather than GDP, so Prescott also focused on GNP.

Figure 11.1
Actual versus simulated volatilities of key US macroeconomic variables

The figure compares the actual volatilities of key macroeconomic variables observed in post–World War II US data with the volatilities of the same variables predicted by computer simulations of Edward Prescott's calibrated RBC model. Prescott set the size of the random productivity shocks in his simulations so that the simulated volatility of GNP would match the actually observed volatility of GNP exactly. For these random productivity shocks, the simulated volatilities of the other five macroeconomic variables (with the possible exception of consumption) match the observed volatilities fairly well.

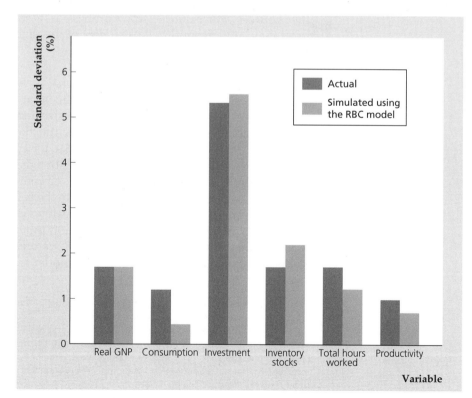

perfectly (thus the correlation of GNP with itself is 1.0), and a correlation with GNP of 0 indicates no relationship to GNP. Correlations with GNP between 0 and 1.0 reflect relationships with GNP of intermediate strength. Figure 11.2 shows that Prescott's model generally accounts well for the strength of the relationships between some of the variables and GNP, although the correlation of productivity and GNP predicted by Prescott's model is noticeably larger than the actual correlation.

The degree to which relatively simple calibrated RBC models can match the actual data is impressive. In addition, the results of calibration exercises help guide further development of the model. For example, the version of the RBC model discussed here has been modified to improve the match between the actual and predicted correlations of productivity with GNP.

Are Productivity Shocks the Only Source of Recessions? Although RBC theorists agree in principle that many types of real shock buffet the economy, in practice much of their work rests on the assumption that productivity shocks are the dominant, or even the only, source of recessions. Many economists, including both classical and Keynesian, have criticized this assumption as being unrealistic. For example, some economists challenged the RBC theorists to identify the specific productivity shocks that they believe caused each of the recessions since World War II. The critics argue that, except for the oil price shocks of 1973, 1979, and 1990, historical examples of economy-wide productivity shocks are virtually non-existent.

Figure 11.2
Actual versus simulated correlations of key US macroeconomic variables with GNP
How closely a variable moves with GNP over the business cycle is measured by its correlation with GNP, with higher correlations implying a closer relationship. The figure compares the correlations of key variables with GNP that were actually observed in the post-World War II US economy with the correlations predicted by computer simulations of Prescott's calibrated RBC model. Except for productivity, whose predicted correlation with GNP is too high, the simulations predicted correlations of macroeconomic variables with GNP that closely resemble the actual correlations of these variables with GNP.

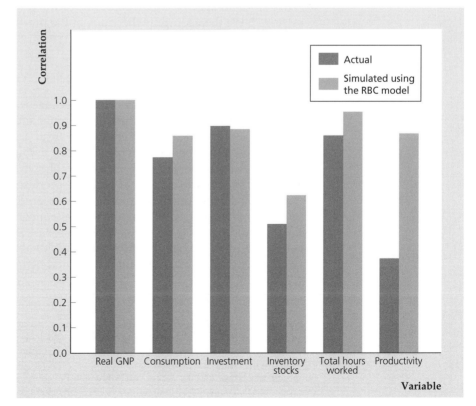

An interesting RBC response to that argument is that, in principle, economy-wide fluctuations could also be caused by the cumulative effects of a series of small productivity shocks. To illustrate the point that small shocks can cause large fluctuations, Figure 11.3 shows the results of a computer simulation of productivity shocks and the associated behaviour of output for a simplified RBC model. In this simple RBC model the change in output from one month to the next has two parts: (1) a fixed part that arises from normal technical progress or from a normal increase in population and employment; and (2) an unpredictable part that reflects a random shock to productivity during the current month.[10] The random, computer-generated productivity shocks are shown at the bottom of Figure 11.3, and the implied behaviour of output is displayed above them. Although none of the individual shocks is large, the cumulative effect of the shocks causes large fluctuations in output that look something like business cycles. Hence business cycles may be the result of productivity shocks, even though identifying specific, large shocks is difficult.

Does the Solow Residual Measure Technology Shocks? Because productivity shocks are the primary source of business cycle fluctuations in RBC models, RBC theorists have attempted to measure the size of these shocks. The most common measure of productivity shocks is known as the **Solow residual**, which is an empirical measure of total factor productivity, A. The Solow residual is named after one of the originators of modern growth theory Robert Solow, who used this measure in the 1950s.[11]

Recall from Chapter 3 that, to measure total factor productivity A, we need data on output, Y, and the inputs of capital, K, and labour, N. In addition, we need to use a specific algebraic form for the production function, such as $Y = AK^aN^{1-a}$. We then compute the value of the productivity parameter, A, also known as the Solow residual, as

$$\text{Solow residual} = \frac{Y}{K^aN^{1-a}} = A \tag{11.1}$$

The Solow residual is called a 'residual' because it is the part of output that cannot be directly explained by measured capital and labour inputs.

When the Solow residual is computed from actual data, using equation (11.1), it turns out to be strongly procyclical, rising in economic expansions and falling in recessions (as we have already shown in Chapters 3 and 9). This procyclical behaviour is consistent with the premise of RBC theory that cyclical fluctuations in aggregate output are driven largely by productivity shocks.

Recently, however, some economists have questioned whether the Solow residual should be interpreted solely as a measure of technology, as RBC proponents tend to do. If changes in the Solow residual reflect only changes in the technologies available to an economy, it should be unrelated to factors such as

---

10. Specifically, the model is $Y_t = Y_{t-1} + 0.01 + e_t$, where Y_t is output in month t, Y_{t-1} is output in the previous month, and e_t is the random productivity shock in month t. The productivity shocks are randomly chosen numbers between -1.0 and 1.0. A similar example is given in Numerical Problem 5 at the end of this chapter.
11. 'Technical Change and the Aggregate Production Function', *Review of Economics and Statistics*, 1957, pp. 312–20. In Chapter 6 we described Solow's contributions to growth theory.

Figure 11.3
Small shocks and large cycles

A computer simulation of a simple RBC model is used to find the relationship between computer-generated random productivity shocks (shown at the bottom of the figure) and aggregate output (shown in the middle of the figure). Even though all the productivity shocks are small, the simulation produces large cyclical fluctuations in aggregate output. Thus large productivity shocks are not necessary to generate large cyclical fluctuations.

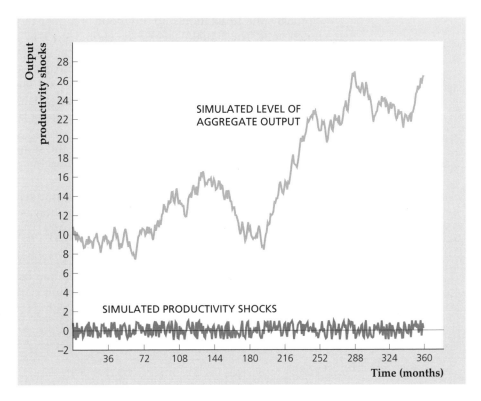

government purchases or monetary policy that do not directly affect scientific and technological progress (at least in the short run). However, statistical studies reveal that the Solow residual is in fact correlated with factors such as government expenditures, suggesting that movements in the Solow residual may also reflect the impacts of other factors.[12]

To understand why measured productivity can vary, even if the actual technology used in production does not change, we need to recognize that capital and labour are sometimes used more intensively than at other times and that more intensive use of inputs leads to higher output. For instance, a printing press used full time contributes more to production than an otherwise identical printing press used half the time. Similarly, workers working fast (for example, restaurant workers during a busy lunch hour) will produce more output and revenue than the same number of workers working more slowly (the same restaurant workers during the afternoon lull). To capture the idea that capital and labour resources can be used more or less intensively at different times, we define the *utilization rate of capital*, u_K, and the *utilization rate of labour*, u_N. The utilization rate of a factor measures the intensity at which it is being used. For example, the utilization rate of capital for the printing press run full time would be twice as high as for the printing press used half time;

---

12. Changes in technology might well be correlated with changes in government spending on research and development (R&D). However, the Solow residual is also highly correlated with non-R&D government spending and with lags too short to be accounted for by the effects of spending on the rate of invention.

similarly, the utilization rate of labour is higher in the restaurant during the lunch hour. The actual usage of the capital stock in production, which we call *capital services*, equals the utilization rate of capital times the stock of capital, or $u_K K$. Capital services are a more accurate measure of the contribution of the capital stock to output than is the level of capital itself, because the definition of capital services adjusts for the intensity at which capital is used. Similarly, we define *labour services* to be the utilization rate of labour times the number of workers (or hours) employed by the firm, or $u_N N$. Thus the labour services received by an employer are higher when the same number of workers are working hard and fast than when they are working slowly (that is, the utilization of labour is higher).

Recognizing that capital services and labour services go into the production of output, we rewrite the production function as

$$Y = AF(u_K K, u_N N) = A(u_K K)^a (u_N N)^{1-a} \tag{11.2}$$

where we have replaced the capital stock, K, with capital services, $u_K K$, and labour, N, with labour services, $u_N N$. Now we can use the production function in equation (11.2) to substitute for Y in equation (11.1) to obtain an expression for the Solow residual that incorporates utilization rates for capital and labour:

$$\text{Solow residual} = \frac{A(u_K K)^a (u_N N)^{1-a}}{K^a N^{1-a}} \quad A u_K^a u_N^{1-a} \tag{11.3}$$

Equation (11.3) shows that the Solow residual, as conventionally measured, includes not only parameter A (which reflects technology and perhaps other factors affecting productivity) but also utilization rates of capital and labour, u_K and u_N. Thus, even if technology were unchanging, the calculated Solow residual would be procyclical if the utilization rates of capital and labour were procyclical.

There is evidence that utilization is procyclical (so that capital and labour are worked harder in boom periods than in economic slumps). For example, Craig Burnside of the University of Pittsburgh, Martin Eichenbaum of Northwestern University, and Sergio Rebelo of the University of Rochester studied the cyclical behaviour of capital utilization by using data on the amount of electricity used by producers.[13] Their rationale for using data on electricity is that additional electricity is needed to increase capital utilization, whether the increased utilization is achieved by operating capital for an increased number of hours per day or by increasing the speed at which the capital is operated. This study revealed that electricity used per unit of capital rises in economic upturns, leading the authors to conclude that capital utilization is strongly procyclical. In addition, this study showed that a measure of technology, analogous to the term A in equation (11.2), is much less procyclical than is the Solow residual.

Measuring the cyclical behaviour of labour utilization is more difficult, but various studies have found evidence that the utilization rate of labour is also procyclical. For example, Jon Fay and James Medoff[14] of Harvard University

---

13. 'Capital Utilization and Returns to Scale', in B. Bernanke and J. Rotemberg, eds., NBER, *Macroeconomics Annual*, 1995.
14. 'Labour and Output Over the Business Cycle', *American Economic Review*, September 1985, pp. 638–55.

sent questionnaires to large manufacturing enterprises, asking about employment and production during the most recent downturn experienced at each plant. Fay and Medoff found that during a downturn the average plant surveyed cut production by 31% and cut its total use of blue-collar hours to 23% below the normal level. Plant managers estimated that total hours could have been reduced by an additional 6% of the normal level without further reducing output. Of this 6% of normal hours, about half (3% of normal hours) were typically assigned to various types of useful work, including equipment maintenance and overhaul, painting, cleaning, reworking output, and training. The remaining 3% of normal hours were assigned to 'make-work' and other unproductive activities. These numbers suggest that firms utilize labour less intensively during recessions.

Further evidence that labour utilization is procyclical has been presented in a study of US car assembly plants by Ana Aizcorbe[15] of the US Bureau of Labor Statistics. Aizcorbe found that during off-peak periods the extent to which labour was being underutilized was equivalent to 5% of average plant employment. Another interesting study, by John Shea[16] of the University of Maryland, examined the cyclical behaviour of industrial injury rates. Shea reasoned that, if manufacturing workers work harder and more quickly during booms than during recessions, more workers should suffer injuries during booms. Shea found that, consistent with procyclical labour utilization, industrial injury rates are procyclical.

It seems, however, that there has been a decline in procyclical labour utilization across a number of European countries in more recent years. A study of Dutch companies found that labour under-utilization was at a maximum in the mid 1970s when it amounted to 7% of employment, falling to 0.5% in the mid 1980s.[17] Evidence presented by the OECD[18] for several European countries shows that firms reduced their demand for workers more rapidly during the period 1986–90 in response to falling output than had previously been the case, suggesting that firms are now utilizing labour more intensively during downturns.

The tendency to use workers less intensively in recessions than in expansions has been referred to as labour hoarding. **Labour hoarding** occurs when, because of the costs of firing and hiring workers, firms retain some workers in a recession that they would otherwise lay off. Firms keep these workers on the payroll to avoid costs of laying off workers and then rehiring them or hiring and training new workers when the economy revives. Hoarded labour either works less hard during the recession (there is less to do) or is put to work doing tasks, such as maintaining equipment, that are not measured as part of the firm's output. When the economy revives, the hoarded labour goes back to working in the normal way. In much the same way, it may not pay the restaurant owner to send her workers home between the lunch and dinner rush hours, with the result that restaurant workers are less productive during the

15. 'Procyclical Labor Productivity, Increasing Returns to Labor and Labor Hoarding in US Assembly Plant Employment', *Economic Journal*, July 1992, pp. 860–73.
16. 'Accident Rates, Labor Effort and the Business Cycle', SSRI working paper 9028, November 1990.
17. Peter Van Els and Linda Keijzer, 'Labour Hoarding in a Disequilibrium Model of the Dutch Labour Market', *De-Economist*, 1993, pp. 256–78.
18. OECD, *Economic Outlook*, June, 1994, pp. 102–8.

slow afternoon period. This lower rate of productivity during recessions (or during the afternoon slow period, in the restaurant) does not reflect changes in the available technology, but only changes in the rate at which firms utilize capital and labour. Hence you should be cautious about interpreting cyclical changes in the Solow residual (equivalently, total factor productivity, A) as solely reflecting changes in technology.

Although changes in technology or the utilization rates of capital and labour can cause aggregate cyclical fluctuations, history suggests that shocks other than productivity shocks also affect the economy; wars and military build-ups are but one obvious example. Thus many classical economists favour a broader definition of classical business cycle theory that allows for both productivity and other types of shock to have an impact on the economy.

The macroeconomic effects of shocks other than productivity shocks can be analysed with the classical *IS–LM* model. Let us use it to examine the effects of a fiscal policy shock.

Fiscal Policy Shocks in the Classical Model

Another type of shock that can be a source of business cycles in the classical model is a change in fiscal policy, such as an increase or decrease in real government purchases of goods and services.[19] Examples of shocks to government purchases include military build-ups (or more recently, build-downs) and the initiation of large road-building or other public works programmes. Because government purchases are procyclical – and in particular, because national output tends to be above normal during wars and at other times when military spending is high – we need to explore how shocks to government purchases affect aggregate output and employment.

Let us consider what happens when the government purchases more goods, as it would, for example, when the country is at war. (Think of the increase in government purchases as temporary. Analytical Problem 2 at the end of the chapter asks you to work out what happens if the increase in government purchases is permanent.)

Figure 11.4 illustrates the effects of an increase in government purchases in the classical *IS–LM* model. Before the fiscal policy change, the economy's general equilibrium is represented by point E in both (a) and (b). To follow what happens after purchases rise, we start with the labour market in Figure 11.4(a). The change in fiscal policy does not affect the production function or the marginal product of labour (the *MPN* curve), so the labour demand curve does not shift.

However, classical economists argue that an increase in government purchases will affect labour supply by reducing workers' wealth. People are made less wealthy because, if the government increases the amount of the nation's output that it takes for military purposes, less output will be left for private

---

19. Another important example of a change in fiscal policy is a change in the structure of the tax code. Classical economists argue that the greatest effects of tax changes are those that affect people's incentives to work, save, and invest and thus affect full-employment output. Because most classical economists accept the Ricardian equivalence proposition, they would not expect lump-sum changes in taxes without accompanying changes in government purchases to have much effect on the economy, however.

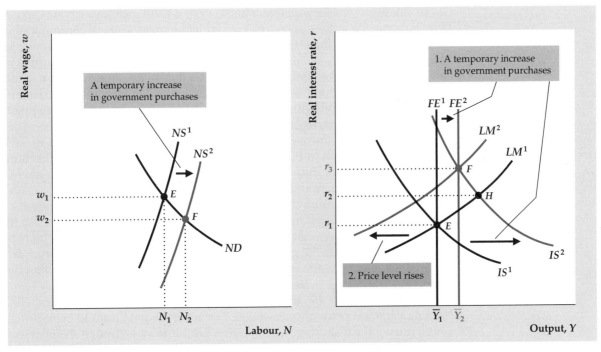

(a) Labour market

(b) General equilibrium

Figure 11.4
Effects of a temporary increase in government purchases

Initial equilibrium is at point E in both (a) and (b).
(a) A temporary increase in government purchases raises workers' current or future taxes. Because workers feel poorer, they supply more labour and the labour supply curve shifts to the right, from NS^1 to NS^2. The shift in the labour supply curve reduces the real wage and increases employment, as indicated by point F.
(b) The increase in employment raises full-employment output and shifts the FE line to the right, from FE^1 to FE^2.

The increase in government purchases also reduces desired national saving and shifts the IS curve up, from IS^1 to IS^2. Because the intersection of IS^2 and LM^1 is to the right of FE^2, the aggregate quantity of output demanded is higher than the full-employment level of output $\bar{Y}_2$, so the price level rises. The rise in the price level reduces the real money supply and shifts the LM curve up, from LM^1 to LM^2, until the new general equilibrium is reached at point F. The effect of the increase in government purchases is to increase output, the real interest rate, and the price level.

consumption and investment. This negative impact of increased government purchases on private wealth is most obvious if the government pays for its increased military spending by raising current taxes.[20] However, even if the government does not raise current taxes to pay for the extra military spending and borrows the funds it needs, taxes will still have to be raised in the future to pay the principal and interest on this extra government borrowing. So, whether or not taxes are currently raised, under the classical assumption that output is always at its full-employment level, an increase in government military spending effectively makes people poorer.

---

20. For simplicity, we assume that the tax increase is a lump sum. A tax increase that is not a lump sum – for example, one that changes the effective tax rate on capital – has complicating effects.

In Chapter 3 we showed that a decrease in wealth increases labour supply because someone who is poorer can afford less leisure. Thus, according to the classical analysis, an increase in government purchases – which makes people financially worse off – should lead to an increase in aggregate labour supply.[21] The increase in government purchases causes the labour supply curve to shift to the right, from NS^1 to NS^2 in Figure 11.4(a). Following the shift of the labour supply curve, the equilibrium in the labour market shifts from point E to point F, with employment increasing and the real wage decreasing.[22]

The effects of the increase in government purchases in the classical IS–LM framework are shown in Figure 11.4(b). First, note that, because equilibrium employment increases, full-employment output $\overline{Y}$ also increases. Thus the FE line shifts to the right, from FE^1 to FE^2.

In addition to shifting the FE line to the right, the fiscal policy change also shifts the IS curve. Recall that, at any level of output, a temporary increase in government purchases reduces desired national saving and raises the real interest rate that clears the goods market. Thus the IS curve shifts up, from IS^1 to IS^2. (See also Summary table 12, p. 344.) The LM curve is not directly affected by the change in fiscal policy.

The new IS curve, IS^2, the initial LM curve, LM^1, and the new FE line, FE^2, have no common point of intersection. For general equilibrium to be restored, prices must adjust, shifting the LM curve until it passes through the intersection of IS^2 and FE^2 (point F). Will prices rise or fall? The answer to this question is ambiguous because the fiscal policy change has increased both the aggregate demand for goods (by reducing desired saving and shifting the IS curve up) and the full-employment level of output (by increasing labour supply and shifting the FE line to the right). If we assume that the effect on labour supply and full-employment output of the increase in government purchases is not too large (probably a reasonable assumption), after the fiscal policy change the aggregate quantity of goods demanded is likely to exceed full-employment output. In Figure 11.4(b) the aggregate quantity of goods demanded (point H at the intersection of IS^2 and LM^1) exceeds full-employment output, $\overline{Y}_2$. Thus the price level must rise, shifting the LM curve to the left and causing the economy to return to general equilibrium at F. At F both output and the real interest rate are higher than at the initial equilibrium point, E.

Therefore the increase in government purchases increases output, employment, the real interest rate, and the price level. Because the increase in employment is the result of an increase in labour supply rather than an increase in labour demand, real wages fall when government purchases rise. Because of diminishing marginal productivity of labour, the increase in employment also implies a decline in average labour productivity when government purchases rise.

---

21. In theory the effect on labour supply of an increase in government purchases should be the strongest for spending, such as military spending, that extracts resources without providing any direct benefits to the private sector. Government purchases that effectively replace private consumption expenditures – for example, purchases of medical services, roads, or playgrounds – should in principle have a smaller negative impact on people's economic well-being and thus a smaller positive effect on labour supply.

22. Note that this labour supply effect was omitted from our discussion of the impact of increased government purchases in Chapter 4, as illustrated in Figure 4.8.

That fiscal shocks play some role in business cycles seems reasonable, which is itself justification for including them in the model. However, including fiscal shocks along with productivity shocks in the RBC model has the additional advantage of improving the match between model and data. We previously noted that government purchases are procyclical, which is consistent with the preceding analysis. Another advantage of adding fiscal shocks to a model that also contains productivity shocks is that it improves the model's ability to explain the behaviour of labour productivity.

Refer back to Figure 11.2 to recall a weakness of the RBC model with only productivity shocks: it predicts that average labour productivity and GNP are highly correlated. In fact, RBC theory predicts a correlation that is more than twice the actual correlation. However, as we have just shown, a classical business cycle model with shocks to government purchases predicts a negative correlation between labour productivity and GNP because a positive shock to government purchases raises output but lowers average productivity. A classical business cycle model that includes *both* shocks to productivity *and* shocks to government purchases can match the empirically observed correlation of productivity and GNP well, without reducing the fit of the model in other respects.[23] Thus adding fiscal shocks to the real business cycle model seems to improve its ability to explain the actual behaviour of the economy.

Should Fiscal Policy Be Used to Dampen the Cycle?

Our analysis shows that changes in government purchases can have real effects on the economy. Changes in the tax laws can also have real effects on the economy in the classical model, although these effects are more complicated and depend mainly on the nature of the tax, the type of income or revenue that is taxed, and so on. Potentially, then, changes in fiscal policy could be used to offset cyclical fluctuations and stabilize output and employment: for example, the government could increase its purchases during recessions. This observation leads to the second of the two questions posed in the introduction to the chapter: should policymakers use fiscal policy to smooth business cycle fluctuations?

Recall that classical economists generally oppose active attempts to dampen cyclical fluctuations because of Adam Smith's invisible hand argument that free markets produce efficient outcomes without government intervention. The classical view holds that prices and wages adjust fairly rapidly to bring the economy into general equilibrium, allowing little scope for the government to improve the macroeconomy's response to economic disturbances. Therefore, although in principle fiscal policy could be used to fight recessions and reduce output fluctuations, classical economists advise against using this approach. Instead, they argue that not interfering in the economy's adjustment to disturbances is better.

This scepticism about the value of active anti-recessionary policies does *not* mean that classical economists do not regard recessions as a serious problem. If an adverse productivity shock causes a recession, for example, real

---

23. See Lawrence Christiano and Martin Eichenbaum, 'Current Real-Business-Cycle Theories and Aggregate Labor-Market Fluctuations', *American Economic Review*, June 1992, pp. 430–50. The analysis of this paper is technically complex but it gives a flavour of much recent work in classical business cycle analysis.

wages, employment, and output all fall, which means that many people experience economic hardship. But would offsetting the recession by, for example, increasing government purchases help? In the classical analysis, a rise in government purchases increases output by raising the amount of labour supplied, and the amount of labour supplied is increased by making workers poorer (as a result of higher current or future taxes). Thus, under the classical assumption that the economy is always in general equilibrium, increasing government purchases for the sole purpose of increasing output and employment makes people worse off rather than better off. Classical economists conclude that government purchases should be increased only if the benefits of the expanded government programme – in terms of improved military security or public services, for example – exceed the costs to taxpayers. They apply this criterion for useful government spending – that the benefits should exceed the costs – whether or not the economy is currently in recession.

So far we have assumed that, because fiscal policy affects the equilibrium levels of employment and output, the government is capable of using fiscal policy to achieve the levels of employment and output it chooses. In fact, the legislative process can lead to lengthy delays, or *lags,* between the time that a fiscal policy change is proposed and the time that it is enacted. Additional lags occur in implementing the new policies and in the response of the economy to the policy changes. Because of these lags, fiscal policy changes contemplated today should be based on where the economy will be several quarters in the future; but, unfortunately, forecasting the future of the economy is an inexact art at best. Beyond the problems of forecasting, policymakers also face uncertainties about how and by how much to modify their policies to get the desired output and employment effects. Classical economists cite these practical difficulties as another reason for not using fiscal policy to fight recessions.

Unemployment in the Classical Model

A major weakness of the classical model is that it does not explain why unemployment rises during business downturns. Indeed, in the simple classical, or supply and demand, model of the labour market, unemployment is literally zero: anyone who wants to work at the market-clearing wage can find a job. Of course, in reality unemployment is never zero. Furthermore, the sharp increases in unemployment that occur during recessions are a principal reason that policymakers and the public are so concerned about economic downturns.

Classical economists are perfectly aware of this issue, and they have developed more sophisticated versions of the classical business cycle model to account for unemployment. The main modification they make to the simple supply and demand model of the labour market is to drop the model's implicit assumption that all workers and jobs are the same. Rather than all being the same, workers in the real world have different abilities, skills, and interests, among other things; jobs entail different skill requirements, work environments, locations, and other characteristics. Because workers and jobs both vary in so many ways, matching workers to jobs is not instantaneous and free, but time consuming and costly. The fact that someone who has lost a job or has just entered the labour force must spend time and effort to find a new job helps explain why there always are some unemployed people.

Some classical economists suggest that differences among workers and among jobs explain not only why the unemployment rate is always greater than zero, but also why unemployment rises so sharply in recessions. They argue that productivity shocks and other macroeconomic disturbances that cause recessions also often increase the degree of mismatch between workers and firms.[24] Thus a major adverse productivity shock might affect the various industries and regions within the country differently, with jobs being destroyed in some sectors but new opportunities emerging in others. An oil price shock, for example, would eliminate jobs in energy-intensive industries but create new opportunities in industries that supply energy or are light energy users.

Following such a shock, workers in industries and regions where labour demand has fallen will be induced to search elsewhere for jobs, which raises the frictional component of unemployment. Some of these workers will find that their skills do not match the requirements of industries with growing labour demand; these workers may become chronically unemployed, raising structural unemployment.[25] With many unemployed workers looking for jobs, and because creating new jobs takes a while, the time necessary to find a new job is likely to increase. For all these reasons, an adverse productivity shock may raise unemployment as well as reduce output and employment. Note that this predicted rise in frictional and structural unemployment during recessions is the same as an increase in the natural rate of unemployment (the sum of frictional and structural unemployment rates).

What is the evidence of worker–job mismatch and unemployment? The process of job creation and job destruction in several European countries has been studied in some detail by the OECD.[26] They showed that, during the period 1983–92, between 6% and 16% of all existing jobs disappeared, on average, each year, reflecting plant closures and cutbacks. During a typical year, however, these lost jobs were more than replaced by newly created jobs elsewhere in the economy. Thus the OECD study confirmed that a great deal of 'churning' of jobs and workers occurs in the economy. They also showed that much of this churning (about 90%) reflected closing of old plants and opening of new ones *within the same industries,* rather than a general decline in some industries and growth in others. Thus reallocation of workers within industries seems to be as important as movement of workers between industries as a source of unemployment.

Table 11.1 shows the rates of job creation and destruction from a sample of countries used in the OECD study. Note that in recession years, such as during the early 1990s, many more jobs were lost than created; but a significant number of new jobs were created even in recession years, reflecting shifts of workers in the labour market.

It seems clear that increased mismatches between workers and jobs cannot account for *all* the increase in unemployment that occurs during recessions. Much of that increase is in the form of temporary layoffs; rather than search for new jobs, many workers who are temporarily laid off simply wait until

---

24. This idea was proposed in David Lilien, 'Sectoral Shifts and Cyclical Unemployment', *Journal of Political Economy,* August 1982, pp. 777–93.
25. See Chapter 3 for definitions and discussion of frictional and structural unemployment.
26. OECD, *Economic Outlook,* June 1994, pp. 102–8.

Table 11.1   Rates of Job Creation and Destruction in Selected European Countries

	France		Germany		Italy		Sweden		UK	
	1984–89	1989–92	1983–89	1989–90	1984–89	1989–92	1985–89	1989–92	1985–89	1989–91
Gross job creation	**13.9**	**13.7**	**8.7**	**10.2**	**12.7**	**11.8**	**16.1**	**12.6**	**9.1**	**8.0**
Openings of new plants	7.3	6.9	2.4	2.8	4.1	3.6	7.3	5.6	3.1	1.9
Expansion of employment in existing plants	6.6	6.8	6.4	7.4	8.6	8.2	8.8	7.0	6.0	6.1
Gross job destruction	**12.8**	**13.9**	**7.7**	**6.6**	**10.5**	**11.9**	**13.2**	**16.1**	**6.7**	**6.4**
Closures of existing plants	6.9	7.1	2.0	1.8	3.6	4.0	5.2	4.9	4.2	3.4
Contraction of employment in existing plants	5.9	6.8	5.7	4.8	7.0	7.9	8.1	11.3	2.5	3.0
Net employment change	**1.2**	**–0.2**	**1.1**	**3.6**	**2.2**	**–0.1**	**2.9**	**–3.5**	**2.4**	**1.6**
Net entry of new plants (openings of new plants *less* plants closing)	0.5	–0.2	0.4	1.0	0.6	–0.4	2.1	0.8	–1.1	–1.5
Net expansion of employment in existing plants (expansion *less* contraction)	0.7	–0.1	0.6	2.6	1.6	0.3	0.8	–4.2	3.5	3.1
Job turnover (gross creation plus destruction)	**26.7**	**27.6**	**16.4**	**16.8**	**23.3**	**23.7**	**29.4**	**28.7**	**15.8**	**14.4**
Base period employment (thousands)	12,778	13,594	16,350	17,400	8381	9347	2306	2588	16,744	15,835

Source: OECD, *Employment Outlook*, 1994, pp. 102–8.

they are called back by their old firm. Moreover, if recessions were times of increased mismatch in the labour market, more postings of vacancies and help-wanted ads during recessions would be expected; but, in fact, both vacancies and new job openings fall in recessions.[27] Despite these objections, however, economists generally agree that the dynamic reallocation of workers from shrinking to growing sectors is an important source of unemployment.

Modifying the classical model to allow for unemployment does not change the classical view that fiscal policy should not be actively used to combat recessions. Classical economists point out that raising the aggregate demand for goods (by increasing government purchases, for example) does not directly address the problem of unemployment arising from the mismatch that exists at the microeconomic level between workers and jobs. A better approach, in the classical view, is to eliminate barriers to labour market adjustment, such as high legal minimum wages that price low-skilled workers out of the labour market or burdensome regulations that raise businesses' costs of employing additional workers.

11.2   MONEY IN THE CLASSICAL MODEL

So far we have focused on real shocks to the economy, such as productivity shocks and changes in government purchases. However, many macroeconomists believe that nominal shocks – shocks to money supply and money demand – also affect the business cycle. In the rest of the chapter we discuss the role of money and monetary policy in the classical approach to the business cycle.

---

27. See Katharine Abraham and Lawrence Katz, 'Cyclical Unemployment: Sectoral Shifts or Aggregate Disturbances?', *Journal of Political Economy*, June 1986, pp. 507–22.

Monetary Policy and the Economy

Monetary policy refers to the central bank's decisions about how much money to supply to the economy (Chapter 7). Recall that the central bank can control the money supply through open market operations, in which it sells government bonds to the public in exchange for money (to reduce the money supply) or uses newly created money to buy bonds from the public (to increase the money supply).

In Chapter 10 we examined the effects of changes in the money supply, using the *IS–LM* model (Figure 10.9) and the *AD–AS* model (Figure 10.14). With both models we found that, after prices fully adjust, changes in the money supply are *neutral*: a change in the nominal money supply, *M*, causes the price level, *P*, to change proportionally, but a change in the money supply has no effect on real variables, such as output, employment, or the real interest rate. Our analysis left open the possibility that a change in the money supply would affect real variables, such as output, in the short run before prices had a chance to adjust. However, because classical economists believe that the price adjustment process is rapid, they view the period of time during which the price level is fixed – and money is not neutral – to be too short to matter. That is, for practical purposes, they view money as neutral for any relevant time horizon.

Monetary Non-Neutrality and Reverse Causation

The prediction that money is neutral is a striking result of the classical model, but it seems inconsistent with the business cycle fact that money is a leading, procyclical variable. If an expansion of the money supply has no effect, why are expansions of the money supply typically followed by increased rates of economic activity? And, similarly, why are reductions in the money supply often followed by recessions?

Some classical economists have responded to these questions by pointing out that, although increases in the money supply tend to *precede* expansions in output, this fact does not necessarily prove that economic expansions are *caused* by those increases. After all, just because people put storm windows on their houses before winter begins does not mean that winter is caused by putting on storm windows. Rather, people put storm windows on their houses because they know that winter is coming.

Many classical economists, including RBC theorists in particular, argue that the link between money growth and economic expansion is like the link between putting on storm windows and the onset of winter, a relationship they call reverse causation. Specifically, **reverse causation** means that expected future increases in output cause increases in the current money supply and that expected future decreases in output cause decreases in the current money supply, rather than the other way around. Reverse causation explains how money could be a procyclical and leading variable even if the classical model is correct and changes in the money supply are neutral and have no real effects.[28]

---

28. Robert King and Charles Plosser, 'Money, Credit, and Prices in a Real Business Cycle', *American Economic Review*, June 1984, pp. 363–80, explain reverse causation and present supporting evidence for the idea.

Reverse causation might arise in one of several ways. One possibility (which you are asked to explore in more detail in Analytical Problem 4 at the end of the chapter) is based on the idea that money demand depends on both expected future output and current output. Suppose that a firm's managers expect business to pick up considerably in the next few quarters. To prepare for this expected increase in output, the firm may need to increase its current transactions (for example, to purchase raw materials, hire workers, and so on) and thus it will demand more money now. If many firms do so, the aggregate demand for money may rise in advance of the actual increase in output.

Now suppose that the central bank observes this increase in the demand for money. If it does nothing, leaving the money supply unchanged, the increase in money demand will cause the equilibrium value of the price level to fall. As one of the central bank's objectives is stable prices, it will not like this outcome; to keep prices stable, instead of doing nothing, the central bank should provide enough extra money to the economy to meet the higher money demand. But if it does so, the money supply will rise in advance of the increase in output, consistent with the business cycle fact – even though money is neutral.

Undoubtedly, reverse causation explains at least some of the tendency of money to lead output (see Box 11.1 for a seasonal example). However, this explanation does not rule out the possibility that changes in the money supply also sometimes cause changes in output so that money is non-neutral. That is, a combination of reverse causation and monetary non-neutrality could account for the procyclical behaviour of money.

The Non-Neutrality of Money: Additional Evidence

Because of reverse causation, the leading and procyclical behaviour of money cannot by itself establish that money is non-neutral. To settle the issue of whether money is neutral, we need additional evidence. One useful source is a historical analysis of monetary policy. The classic study is Milton Friedman and Anna J. Schwartz's, *A Monetary History of the United States, 1867–1960*.[29] Using a variety of sources, including Federal Reserve policy statements and the journals and correspondence of monetary policymakers, Friedman and Schwartz carefully described and analysed the causes of money supply fluctuations and the interrelation of money and other economic variables. They concluded:

Throughout the near-century examined in detail we have found that:

1. Changes in the behavior of the money stock have been closely associated with changes in economic activity, [nominal] income, and prices.

2. The interrelation between monetary and economic change has been highly stable.

3. Monetary changes have often had an independent origin; they have not been simply a reflection of changes in economic activity. (p. 676)

---

29. Princeton University Press for NBER, 1963. See also, Robert Lucas's Nobel Lecture, 'Monetary Neutrality', *Journal of Political Economy*, August 1996, pp. 661–82.

BOX 11.1

Money and Economic Activity at Christmas

According to the reverse causation argument, the association of higher than normal money growth with economic booms and lower than normal money growth with recessions occurs because money growth *responds* to changes in output, not because money growth *causes* changes in output. An example of reverse causation is provided by the behaviour of money and economic activity at Christmas: in Europe both the money supply and retail sales grow faster in the fourth quarter of the year than in any other quarter, as shown in the accompanying table which gives data for 1996. Clearly, the sharp increase in fourth-quarter retail sales (measured in real terms) results from Christmas gift buying and not from the fourth-quarter increase in the money supply. Thus at Christmas higher economic activity must cause a higher money supply, rather than vice versa. Where does the extra money come from? Central banks regularly increase the money supply in the fourth quarter to meet the demands of merchants and shoppers for more money.

The existence of reverse causation from output to money in the fourth quarter does not rule out monetary non-neutrality, but it does mean that we have to be cautious in interpreting the positive association between money and output over the course of the business cycle. This association could arise because of monetary non-neutrality, reverse causation, or both. The relationship between money and economic activity at Christmas shows that reverse causation does in fact occur and can be important.

Quarter	Germany		Italy		Sweden		UK	
	Growth of Money Supply	Growth of Real Retail Sales	Growth of Money Supply	Growth of Real Retail Sales	Growth of Money Supply	Growth of Real Retail Sales	Growth of Money Supply	Growth of Real Retail Sales
Jan.–Mar.	−5.3	−11.2	−9.4	−19.9	3.6	−20.3	1.7	−17.1
Apr.–June	3.0	5.5	2.2	6.4	1.0	8.5	1.2	5.3
July–Sept.	1.6	3.4	0.8	−4.3	2.2	1.0	0.8	1.5
Oct.–Dec.	13.3	12.0	12.0	22.6	4.1	13.6	1.5	18.9

Note: *Growth rates are measured quarter to quarter.*

Source: *OECD Main Economic Indicators*, November 1997, country tables. Money supply Germany and Italy (M1, seasonally unadjusted), UK (M0, seasonally unadjusted), and Sweden (M3, seasonally unadjusted); retail sales, total (seasonally unadjusted), and deflator, Germany, Italy and Sweden (CPI), UK (RPI).

The first two conclusions restate the basic business cycle fact that money is procyclical. The third conclusion states that reverse causation cannot explain the entire relationship between money and real income or output. Friedman and Schwartz focused on historical episodes in which changes in the supply of money were not (they argued) responses to macroeconomic conditions but instead resulted from other factors such as gold discoveries (which affected money supplies under the gold standard), changes in monetary institutions, or changes in the leadership of the Federal Reserve. In the majority of these cases, 'independent' changes in money growth were followed by changes in the same direction in real output. This evidence suggests that money is not neutral.

More recently, Christina Romer and David Romer,[30] of the University of California at Berkeley, reviewed and updated the Friedman–Schwartz analysis. Although they disputed some of Friedman and Schwartz's interpretations, they generally agreed with the conclusion that money is not neutral. In particular, they argued that since 1960 half a dozen additional episodes of monetary non-neutrality have occurred. Probably the most famous one occurred in the UK in 1979, when Margaret Thatcher's government announced that money supply procedures would change and that the money growth rate would be reduced to fight inflation. A severe downturn in 1980–81 followed the Thatcher government's change in monetary policy. An economic boom followed relaxation of the anti-inflationary monetary policy in 1983.

Because of the Friedman–Schwartz evidence and episodes such as the Thatcher government's policy of 1979–83 (and a similar experience in the United States at the same time), most economists now believe that money is *not* neutral. If we accept that evidence, contrary to the prediction of the classical model, we are left with two choices: either we must adopt a different framework for macroeconomic analysis, or we must modify the classical model. In Section 11.3 we take the second approach and consider how monetary non-neutrality can be explained in a classical model.

11.3 THE MISPERCEPTIONS THEORY AND THE NON-NEUTRALITY OF MONEY

According to the classical model, prices do not remain fixed for any substantial period of time, so the horizontal short-run aggregate supply curve developed in Chapter 10 is irrelevant. The only relevant aggregate supply curve is the long-run aggregate supply curve. As we showed in Figure 10.14, changes in the money supply cause the *AD* curve to shift; but, because the aggregate supply curve is vertical, the effect of the *AD* shift is simply to change prices without changing the level of output. Thus money is neutral in the classical model.

For money to be non-neutral, the relevant aggregate supply curve must not be vertical. In this section, we extend the classical model to incorporate the assumption that producers have imperfect information about the general price level and thus sometimes misinterpret changes in the general price level as changes in the relative prices of the goods that they produce. We demonstrate that the assumption that producers may misperceive the aggregate price level – the *misperceptions theory* – implies a short-run aggregate supply curve that is not vertical. Unlike the short-run aggregate supply curve developed in Chapter 10, however, the short-run aggregate supply curve based on the misperceptions theory does not require the assumption that prices are slow to adjust. Even though prices may adjust instantaneously, the short-run aggregate supply curve slopes upwards, so money is non-neutral in the short run.

---

30. 'Does Monetary Policy Matter? A New Test in the Spirit of Friedman and Schwartz', in Olivier Blanchard and Stanley Fischer, eds., NBER, *Macroeconomics Annual* (MIT Press, 1989).

The misperceptions theory was originally proposed by Nobel laureate Milton Friedman and then was rigorously formulated by another Nobel laureate, Robert E. Lucas, Jr, of the University of Chicago.[31] According to the **misperceptions theory**, the *aggregate quantity of output supplied rises above the full-employment level, $\bar{Y}$, when the aggregate price level, P, is higher than expected.* Thus for any expected price level, the aggregate supply curve relating the price level and the aggregate quantity of output supplied slopes upwards.

If you took a course in the principles of economics, you learned that supply curves generally slope upwards, with higher prices leading to increased production. However, just as the demand curves for individual goods differ from the aggregate demand curve, so the supply curves for individual goods differ from the aggregate supply curve. An ordinary supply curve relates the supply of some good to the price of that good *relative to other prices*. In contrast, the aggregate supply curve relates the aggregate amount of output produced to the *general price level*. Changes in the general price level can occur while the relative prices of individual goods remain unchanged.

To understand the misperceptions theory and why it implies an upward-sloping aggregate supply curve, let's think about an individual producer of a particular good, say bread. For simplicity, consider a bakery owned and operated by one person, a baker. The baker devotes all his labour to making bread and earns all his income from selling bread. Thus the price of bread is effectively the baker's nominal wage, and the price of bread relative to the general price level is the baker's real wage. When the relative price of bread increases, the baker responds to this increase in his current real wage by working more and producing more bread. Similarly, when the price of bread falls relative to the other prices in the economy, the baker's current real wage falls and he decreases the amount of bread he produces.

But how does an individual baker know whether the relative price of bread has changed? To calculate the relative price of bread, the baker needs to know both the nominal price of bread and the general price level. The baker knows the nominal price of bread because he sells bread every day and observes the price directly. However, the baker is probably not as well informed about the general price level, because he observes the prices of the many goods and services he might want to buy less frequently than he observes the price of bread. Thus in calculating the relative price of bread, the baker cannot use the actual current price level. The best he can do is to use his previously formed expectation of the current price level to estimate the actual price level.

Suppose that before he observes the current market price of bread the baker expected an overall inflation rate of 5%. How will he react if he then observes that the price of bread increases by 5%? The baker reasons as follows: I expected the overall rate of inflation to be 5%, and now I know that the price of bread has increased by 5%. This 5% increase in the price of bread is consistent with what I had expected. My best estimate is that all prices increased by 5%, and thus I think that the relative price of bread is unchanged. There is no reason to change my output.

31. See Friedman, 'The Role of Monetary Policy', *American Economic Review*, March 1968, pp. 1–17. Lucas's formalization of Friedman was first presented in Lucas's article, 'Expectations and the Neutrality of Money', *Journal of Economic Theory*, April 1972, pp. 103–24.

The baker's logic applies equally to suppliers of output in the aggregate. Suppose that all suppliers expected the nominal price level to increase by 5% and that in fact all prices do increase by 5%. Then all suppliers will estimate that their relative price has not changed and will not change their output. Hence, if expected inflation is 5%, an actual increase in prices of 5% will not affect aggregate output.

For a change in the nominal price of bread to affect the quantity of bread produced, the increase in the nominal price of bread must differ from the *expected* increase in the general price level. For example, suppose that the baker expected the general price level to increase by 5% but then observes that the price of bread rises by 8%. The baker then estimates that the relative price of bread has increased so that the real wage he earns from baking is higher. In response to the perceived increase in the relative price, he increases the production of bread.

Again, the same logic applies to the economy in the aggregate. Suppose that everyone expects the general price level to increase by 5%, but instead it actually increases by 8%, with the prices of all goods increasing by 8%. Now all producers will estimate that the relative prices of the goods they make have increased, and hence the production of all goods will increase. Thus a greater than expected increase of the price level will tend to raise output. Similarly, if the price level actually increases by only 2% when all producers expected a 5% increase, producers will think that the relative prices of their own goods have declined; in response, all suppliers reduce their output.

Thus, according to the misperceptions theory, the amount of output that producers choose to supply depends on the actual general price level compared to the expected general price level. When the price level exceeds what was expected, producers are fooled into thinking that the relative prices of their own goods have risen, and they increase their output. Similarly, when the price level is lower than expected, producers believe that the relative prices of their goods have fallen, and they reduce their output. This relation between output and prices is captured by the equation

$$Y = \overline{Y} + b(P - P^e) \qquad (11.4)$$

where b is a positive number that describes how strongly output responds while the actual price level exceeds the expected price level. Equation (11.4) summarizes the misperceptions theory by showing that output, Y, exceeds full-employment output, $\overline{Y}$, when the price level, P, exceeds the expected price level, P^e.

To obtain an aggregate supply curve from the misperceptions theory, we graph equation (11.4) in Figure 11.5. Given full-employment output, $\overline{Y}$, and the expected price level, P^e, the aggregate supply curve slopes upwards, illustrating the relation between the amount of output supplied, Y, and the actual price level, P. Because an increase in the price level of ΔP increases the amount of the output supplied by $\Delta Y = b\Delta P$, the slope of the aggregate supply curve is $\Delta P / \Delta Y = 1/b$. Thus the aggregate supply curve is steep if b is small and is relatively flat if b is large.

Point E helps us locate the aggregate supply curve. At E the price level, P, equals the expected price level, P^e, so that (from equation 11.4) the amount of output supplied equals full-employment output, $\overline{Y}$. When the actual price level is higher than expected ($P > P^e$), the aggregate supply curve shows that the amount of output supplied is greater than $\overline{Y}$; when the price level is lower than expected ($P < P^e$), output is less than $\overline{Y}$.

Figure 11.5

The aggregate supply curve in the misperceptions theory

The misperceptions theory holds that, for a given value of the expected price level, P^e, an increase in the actual price level, P, fools producers into increasing output. This relationship between output and the price level is shown by the short-run aggregate supply ($SRAS$) curve. Along the $SRAS$ curve, output equals $\bar{Y}$ when prices equal their expected level ($P = P^e$, at point E), output exceeds $\bar{Y}$ when the price level is higher than expected ($P > P^e$), and output is less than $\bar{Y}$ when the price level is lower than expected ($P < P^e$). In the long run, the expected price level equals the actual price level so that output equals $\bar{Y}$. Thus the long-run aggregate supply ($LRAS$) curve is vertical at $Y = \bar{Y}$.

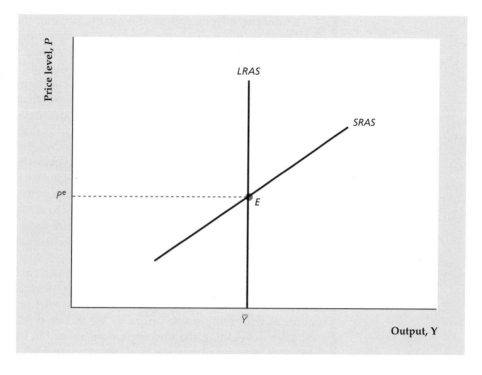

The aggregate supply curve in Figure 11.5 is called the short-run aggregate supply ($SRAS$) curve because it applies only to the short period of time that P^e remains unchanged. In the long run people learn what is actually happening to prices, and the expected price level adjusts to the actual price level ($P = P^e$). When the actual price level equals the expected price level, no misperceptions remain and producers supply the full-employment level of output. In terms of equation (11.4), in the long run P equals P^e, and output, Y, equals full-employment output, $\bar{Y}$. In the long run, then, the supply of output does not depend on the price level. Thus, as in Chapters 9 and 10, the long-run aggregate supply ($LRAS$) curve is vertical at the point where output equals $\bar{Y}$.

APPLICATION

International Evidence on the Slope of the Short-Run Aggregate Supply Curve

According to the misperceptions theory, when the actual price level, P, is higher than the expected price level, P^e, output is higher than the full-employment level $\bar{Y}$. Extra output is produced because all producers believe (mistakenly) that the relative prices of the goods they produce have increased. The *amount* by which producers increase their output when the general price level rises depends on how much they believe that their relative prices have increased. For example, when the general price level increases, if producers believe that the increase in their individual relative prices is small, they will not increase output by much. In this case the coefficient b in the equation for the $SRAS$ curve, equation (11.4), which measures the response of output to changes in $P - P^e$, will be small; the slope of the $SRAS$ curve, $1/b$, will be steep. Alternatively, if producers interpret a rise in the price level as meaning that their individual relative prices have increased a lot, they will increase their output substantially so that the coefficient b is large; the $SRAS$ cure will be relatively flat (its slope, $1/b$, is small).

Under the misperceptions theory, the slope of the *SRAS* curve depends on the degree to which producers tend to interpret increases in the price level above its expected value as changes in their own relative prices. But what determines whether producers believe that a positive value of $P - P^e$ represents a large or small increase in relative prices? Robert E. Lucus, Jr, was the first to argue that, if the aggregate price level in a country is generally stable, when producers perceive increases in the prices of their own goods, they are likely to conclude that the overall price level has changed little and thus that the relative prices of their individual goods must have increased. Lucas concluded that, in countries with stable prices, an unanticipated increase in the prices will lead output to increase by a large amount, and so the short-run aggregate supply curve will be relatively flat. However, in countries with highly variable price levels (for example, high-inflation countries), producers are more likely to attribute increases in the prices of their own goods to a rise in the general price level, implying that the relative prices of their own goods have probably not changed much. Thus, in countries with unstable price levels, output will increase only a little in response to a general increase in prices, and the aggregate supply curve will be relatively steep.

One way to test the misperceptions theory is to compare the *SRAS* curves in different countries, to determine whether the *SRAS* curves are indeed flatter in countries with more stable prices, as the theory predicts. Lucas performed this test after developing the misperceptions theory in the early 1970s.[32] He examined aggregate supply curves in eighteen countries. Of these eighteen countries, sixteen had relatively stable inflation rates and thus relatively predictable price levels, and two – Argentina and Paraguay – had unstable inflation rates and hence unpredictable price levels. Lucas found that the *SRAS* curves in Argentina and Paraguay were more than ten times as steep as the short-run aggregate supply curves in any of the other sixteen countries. The finding that countries with unpredictable prices have steep *SRAS* curves is exactly what the misperceptions theory predicts.

Monetary Policy and the Misperceptions Theory

Let us now re-examine the neutrality of money in the extended version of the classical model based on the misperceptions theory. This framework highlights an important distinction between anticipated and unanticipated changes in the money supply: unanticipated changes in the nominal money supply have real effects, but anticipated changes are neutral and have no real effects.

Unanticipated Changes in the Money Supply. Suppose that the economy is initially in general equilibrium at point *E* in Figure 11.6, where AD^1 intersects $SRAS^1$. Here, output equals the full-employment level $\overline{Y}$, and the price level and the expected price level both equal P_1. Suppose that everyone expects the money supply and the price level to remain constant but that the central bank unexpectedly and without publicity increases the money supply by 10%. A 10% increase in the money supply shifts the *AD* curve up to AD^2, increasing the price level at each level of output by 10%. Given the expected price level P_1 the *SRAS* curve remains unchanged, still passing through point *E*.

32. 'Some International Evidence on Output–Inflation Tradeoffs', *American Economic Review*, June 1973, pp. 326–34.

The increase in aggregate demand bids up the price level to the new equilibrium level P_2, where AD^2 intersects $SRAS^1$ (point F). In the new short-run equilibrium at F, the actual price level exceeds the expected price level and output exceeds $\overline{Y}$. Because the increase in the money supply leads to a rise in output, money is not neutral in this analysis.

The reason is that producers are fooled. Each producer misperceives the higher nominal price of his or her output as an increase in its relative price, rather than as an increase in the general price level. Although output increases in the short run, producers are not better off. They end up producing more than they would have if they had known the true relative prices.

The economy cannot stay long at the equilibrium represented by point F because at F the actual price level, P_2, is higher than the expected price level, P_1. Over time, people obtain information about the true level of prices and adjust their expectations accordingly. The only equilibrium that can be sustained in the long run is one in which people do not permanently underestimate or overestimate the price level so that the expected price level and the actual price level are equal. Graphically, when people learn the true price level, the relevant aggregate supply curve is the long-run aggregate supply ($LRAS$) curve, along which P always equals P^e. In Figure 11.6 the long-run equilibrium is point H, the intersection of AD^2 and $LRAS$. At H output equals its full-employment level $\overline{Y}$, and the price level, P_3, is 10% higher than the initial price level, P_1. Because everyone now expects the price level to be P_3, a new $SRAS$ curve, with $P^e = P_3$, $SRAS^2$, passes through H.

Thus, according to the misperceptions theory, an unanticipated increase in the money supply raises output and is not neutral *in the short run*. However, an unanticipated increase in the money supply *is* neutral in the long run, after people have learned the true price level.

Figure 11.6
An unanticipated increase in the money supply
If we start from the initial equilibrium at point E, an unanticipated 10% increase in the money supply shifts the AD curve up by 10% at each level of output, from AD^1 to AD^2. The short-run equilibrium is located at point F, the intersection of AD^2 and the short-run aggregate supply curve $SRAS^1$, where prices and output are both higher than at point E. Thus an unanticipated change in the money supply isn't neutral in the short run. In the long run, people learn the true price level and the equilibrium shifts to point H, the intersection of AD^2 and the long-run aggregate supply curve $LRAS$. In the long-run equilibrium at H, the price level has risen by 10% but output returns to its full-employment level, $\overline{Y}$, so that money is neutral in the long run. As expectations of the price level rise from P_1 to P_3, the $SRAS$ curve also shifts up until it passes through H.

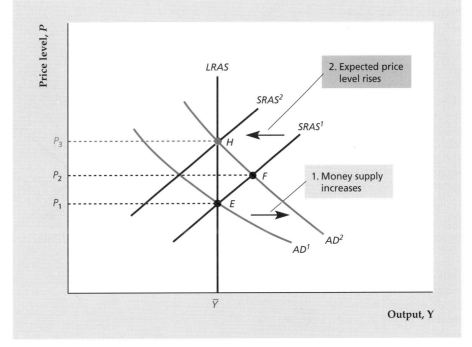

Anticipated Changes in the Money Supply. In the extended classical model based on the misperceptions theory, the effects of an anticipated money supply increase are different from the effects of a surprise money supply increase. Figure 11.7 illustrates the effects of an anticipated money supply increase. Again, the initial general equilibrium point is at E, where output equals its full-employment level and the actual and expected price levels both equal P_1. Suppose that the central bank announces that it is going to increase the money supply by 10% and that the public believes this announcement.

As we have shown, a 10% increase in the money supply shifts the AD curve up by 10% at each level of output, from AD^1 to AD^2. However, in this case the $SRAS$ curve also shifts up. The reason is that the public's expected price level rises as soon as people learn of the increase in the money supply. Suppose that people expect – correctly – that the price level will also rise by 10% so that P^e rises by 10%, from P_1 to P_2. Then the new $SRAS$ curve, $SRAS^2$, passes through point F in Figure 11.7, where Y equals $\overline{Y}$ and both the actual and expected price levels equal P_2. The new equilibrium is also at F, where AD^2 and $SRAS^2$ intersect. At the new equilibrium, output equals its full-employment level, and prices are 10% higher than they were initially. The anticipated increase in the money supply has not affected output but has raised prices proportionally. Similarly, an anticipated drop in the money supply would lower prices but not affect output or other real variables. Thus *anticipated changes in the money supply are neutral in the short run as well as in the long run.* The reason is that, if producers know that increases in the nominal prices of their products are the result of an increase in the money supply and do not reflect a change in relative prices, they will not be fooled into increasing production when prices rise.

Figure 11.7
An anticipated increase in the money supply
The economy is in initial equilibrium at point E. when the central bank publicly announces a 10% increase in the money supply. When the money supply increases, the AD curve shifts up by 10%, from AD^1 to AD^2. But in addition, because the increase in the money supply is anticipated by the public, the expected price level increases by 10%, from P_1 to P_2. Thus the short-run aggregate supply curve shifts up from $SRAS^1$ to $SRAS^2$. The new short-run equilibrium, which is the same as the long-run equilibrium, is at point F. At F output is unchanged at $\overline{Y}$ and the price level is 10% higher than in the initial equilibrium at E. Thus an anticipated increase in the money supply is neutral in the short run as well as in the long run.

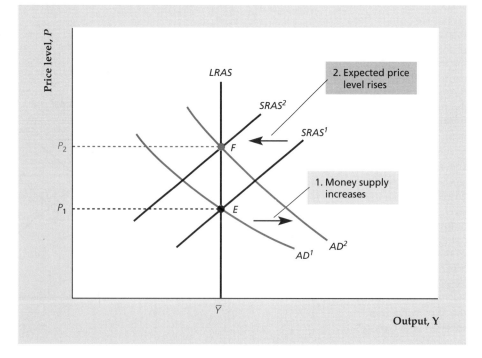

Rational Expectations and the Role of Monetary Policy

In the extended classical model based on the misperceptions theory, *unanticipated* changes in the money supply affect output, but *anticipated* changes in the money supply are neutral. Thus, if the central bank wanted to use monetary policy to affect output, it seemingly should use only unanticipated changes in the money supply. So, for example, when the economy is in recession, the central bank would try to use surprise increases in the money supply to raise output; when the economy is booming, the central bank would try to use surprise decreases in the money supply to slow the economy.

A serious problem for this strategy is the presence of private economic forecasters in financial markets. These people spend a good deal of time and effort trying to forecast macroeconomic variables such as the money supply and the price level, and their forecasts are well publicized. If the central bank began a pattern of raising the money supply in recessions and reducing it in booms, forecasters and central bank watchers would quickly understand and report this fact. As a result, the central bank's manipulations of the money supply would no longer be unanticipated, and the changes in the money supply would have no effect other than possibly causing instability in the price level. More generally, according to the misperceptions theory, to achieve any systematic change in the behaviour of output, the central bank must conduct monetary policy in a way that systematically fools the public. But there are strong incentives in the financial markets and elsewhere for people to try to figure out what the central bank is doing. Thus most economists believe that attempts by the central bank to surprise the public in a systematic way cannot be successful.

The idea that the central bank cannot systematically surprise the public is part of a larger hypothesis that the public has rational expectations. The hypothesis of **rational expectations** states that the public's forecasts of various economic variables, including the money supply, the price level, and GDP, are based on reasoned and intelligent examination of available economic data.[33] (The evidence for rational expectations is discussed in Box 11.2.) If the public has rational expectations, it will eventually understand the central bank's general pattern of behaviour. If expectations are rational, purely random changes in the money supply may be unanticipated and thus non-neutral. However, because the central bank will not be able to surprise the public systematically, it cannot use monetary policy to stabilize output. Thus, even if smoothing business cycles were desirable, according to the combination of the misperceptions theory and rational expectations, the central bank could not systematically use monetary policy to do so.

**Propagating the Effects of Unanticipated Changes in the Money
Supply.** The misperceptions theory implies that unanticipated changes in the money supply are non-neutral because individual producers are temporarily fooled about the price level. However, money supply data are available weekly

---

33. The idea of rational expectations was first discussed by John F. Muth in his classic 1961 paper, 'Rational Expectations and the Theory of Price Movements', *Econometrica*, July 1961, pp. 315–35. However, this idea was not widely used in macroeconomics until the new classical 'revolution' of the early 1970s.

and price-level data are reported monthly, suggesting that any misperceptions about monetary policy or the price level – and thus any real effects of money supply changes – should be quickly eliminated.

To explain how changes in the money supply can have real effects that last more than a few weeks, classical economists stress the role of propagation mechanisms. A **propagation mechanism** is an aspect of the economy that allows short-lived shocks to have relatively long-term effects on the economy.

BOX 11.2

Are Price Forecasts Rational?

Most classical economists assume that people have rational expectations about future economic variables: that is, people make intelligent use of available information in forecasting variables that affect their economic decisions. The rational expectations assumption has important implications. For example, as we have demonstrated, if monetary non-neutrality is the result of temporary misperceptions of the price level and people have rational expectations about future prices, monetary policy is not able to affect the real economy systematically.

The rational expectations assumption is attractive to economists – including many Keynesian as well as classical economists – because it fits well economists' presumption that people intelligently pursue their economic self-interests. If people's expectations are not rational, the economic plans that individuals make will not generally be as good as they could be. But the theoretical attractiveness of rational expectations obviously is not enough; economists would like to know whether people really do have rational expectations about important economic variables.

The rational expectations idea can be tested with data from surveys, in which people are asked their opinions about the future of the economy. To illustrate how such a test would be conducted, suppose that we have data from a survey in which people were asked to make a prediction of the price level one year in the future. Imagine that this survey is repeated each year for several years. Now suppose that, for each individual in the survey, we define

$P_t^e =$ the individual's forecast, made in year $t - 1$, of the price level in year t

Suppose also that we let P_t represent the price level that actually occurs in year t. Then the individual's *forecast error* for year t is the difference between the actual price level and the individual's forecast:

$P_t - P_t^e =$ the individual's forecast error in year t

If people have rational expectations, these forecast errors should be unpredictable random numbers. However, if forecast errors are consistently positive or negative – meaning that people systematically tend to underpredict or overpredict the price level – expectations are not rational. If forecast errors have a systematic pattern – for example, if people tend to overpredict the price level when prices have been rising in the recent past – again, expectations are not rational.

Many statistical studies of price level forecasts made by consumers, journalists, academic economists, and others reject the rational expectations theory. A common finding is that people are too slow to incorporate new information into their forecasts. However, supporters of the rational expectations idea argue that typical survey respondents are not likely to think very hard about the forecast they give to the survey-taker because they have little or no economic stake in the quality of their answer. They argue that a fairer test of rational expectations is to examine the expectations of people who do have a real stake in the quality of their forecasts – namely, professional economic forecasters. Michael Keane and David Runkle* of the Federal Reserve Bank of Minneapolis studied the price level forecasts of a panel of professional forecasters who have been surveyed by the American Statistical Association and the National Bureau of Economic Research since 1968. Perhaps not too surprisingly, Keane and Runkle found no evidence to refute the hypothesis that the professional forecasters had rational expectations. A plausible conclusion to draw from the research is that, the greater a person's economic incentives to make good forecasts about the future, the more likely that person is to have rational expectations.

_____

* 'Are Economic Forecasts Rational?' *Quarterly Review*, Federal Reserve Bank of Minneapolis, Spring 1989, pp. 26–33.

An important example of a propagation mechanism is the behaviour of inventories. Consider a manufacturing firm that has both a normal level of monthly sales and a normal amount of finished goods in inventory that it tries to maintain. Suppose that an unanticipated rise in the money supply increases aggregate demand and raises prices above their expected level. Because increasing production sharply in a short period of time is costly, the firm will respond to the increase in demand partly by producing more goods and partly by selling some finished goods from inventory, thus depleting its inventory stocks below their normal level.

Next month suppose that everyone learns the true price level and that the firm's rate of sales returns to its normal level. Despite the fact that the monetary shock has passed, the firm may continue to produce for a while at a higher than normal rate. The reason for the continued high level of production is that besides meeting its normal demand, the firm wants to replenish its inventory stock. The need to rebuild inventories illustrates a propagation mechanism that allows a short-lived shock (a monetary shock, in this case) to have a longer-term effect on the economy.

CHAPTER SUMMARY

1. Classical business cycle analysis utilizes the classical *IS–LM* model along with the assumption that wages and prices adjust quickly to bring the economy into general equilibrium.

2. The real business cycle (RBC) theory is a version of the classical theory that emphasizes productivity shocks (shocks to the production function) as the source of business cycle fluctuations. In the classical *IS–LM* model, a temporary decline in productivity reduces the real wage, employment, and output, while raising the real interest rate and the price level. The RBC theory can account for the observed procyclical behaviour of employment, real wages, and labour productivity. However, the prediction of the RBC theory that prices are countercyclical is viewed by some as a failing.

3. The Solow residual is an empirical measure of total factor productivity, A, in the production function. It increases as a result of technical progress that increases the amount of output that can be produced with the same amounts of labour and capital services (inputs). However, the Solow residual also changes as a result of changes in the utilization rates of capital and

labour. The Solow residual is procyclical, at least partly because the utilization rates of capital and labour are procyclical. The procyclical behaviour of the utilization rate of labour may reflect labour hoarding, which occurs when firms continue to employ workers during recessions but use them less intensively or on tasks, such as maintenance, that do not contribute directly to measured output.

4. Classical business cycle analysis allows for other shocks to the economy besides changes in productivity, including changes in fiscal policy. According to the classical *IS–LM* model, an increase in government purchases raises employment, output, the real interest rate, and the price level. Including both fiscal and productivity shocks in the classical model improves its ability to fit the data. Although fiscal policy can affect employment and output, classical economists argue that it should not be used to smooth the business cycle because the invisible hand leads the economy to an efficient outcome without government interference. Instead, decisions about government purchases should be based on comparisons of costs and benefits.

5. In the basic classical model (which includes RBC theory), money is neutral, which means that changes in the nominal money supply change the price level proportionally but do not affect real variables such as output, employment, and the real interest rate.

6. The basic classical model can account for the procyclical and leading behaviour of money if there is reverse causation: that is, if anticipated changes in output lead to changes in the money supply in the same direction. For example, if firms increase their money demand in anticipation of future output increases, and if the central bank (to keep the price level stable) supplies enough extra money to meet the increase in money demand, increases in the money stock precede increases in output. This result holds even though changes in the money stock do not *cause* subsequent changes in output.

7. Examination of historical monetary policy actions suggests that money is not neutral. Friedman and Schwartz identified occasions when the money supply changed for independent reasons, such as gold discoveries or changes in monetary institutions, and changes in output followed these changes in the money supply in the same direction. More recent experiences, such as the severe economic slowdown that followed the Thatcher government's decision to reduce money growth in 1979, also provide evidence for the view that money is not neutral.

8. The misperceptions theory is based on the idea that producers have imprecise information about the current price level. According to the misperceptions theory, the amount of output supplied equals the full-employment level of output $\overline{Y}$, only if the actual price level equals the expected price level. When the price level is higher than expected, suppliers are fooled into

thinking that the relative prices of the goods they supply have risen, so they supply a quantity of output that exceeds $\overline{Y}$. Similarly, when the price level is lower than expected, the quantity of output supplied is less than $\overline{Y}$.

The short-run aggregate supply (*SRAS*) curve, based on the misperceptions theory, slopes upwards in describing the relation between output and the actual price level, with the expected price level held constant. In the long run the price level equals the expected price level so that the supply of output equals $\overline{Y}$; thus the long-run aggregate supply (*LRAS*) curve is a vertical line at the point where output equals $\overline{Y}$.

9. With the upward-sloping *SRAS* curve based on the misperceptions theory, an *unanticipated* increase in the money supply increases output (and is thus non-neutral) in the short run. However, because the long-run aggregate supply curve is vertical, an unanticipated increase in the money supply does not affect output (and so is neutral) in the long run. An *anticipated* increase in the money supply causes price expectations to adjust immediately and leads to no misperceptions about the price level; thus an anticipated increase in the money supply is neutral in both the short and long runs.

10. According to the extended classical model based on the misperceptions theory, only surprise changes in the money supply can affect output. If the public has rational expectations about macroeconomic variables, including the money supply, the central bank cannot systematically surprise the public because the public will understand and anticipate the central bank's pattern of behaviour. Thus classical economists argue that the central bank cannot systematically use changes in the money supply to affect output.

The Misperceptions Version of the *AD–AS* Model

The misperceptions version of the *AD–AS* model shows how the aggregate demand for output and the aggregate supply of output interact to determine the price level and output in the classical model in which producers misperceive the aggregate price level.

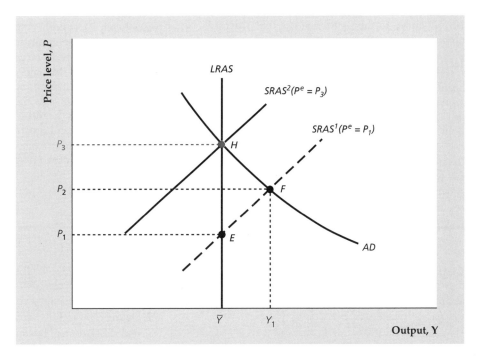

Diagram Elements

■   The price level, P, is on the vertical axis, and the level of output, Y, is on the horizontal axis.

■   The aggregate demand (*AD*) curve shows the aggregate quantity of output demanded at each price level. It is identical to the *AD* curve in Key Diagram 7, p. 376. The aggregate amount of output demanded is determined by the intersection of the *IS* and *LM* curves (see Figure 10.10). An increase in the price level, P, reduces the real money supply, shifting the *LM* curve up and to the left and reducing the aggregate quantity of output demanded. Thus the *AD* curve slopes downwards.

■   The misperceptions theory is based on the assumption that producers have imperfect information about the general price level and hence do not know precisely the relative prices of their products. When producers misperceive the price level, an increase in the general price level above the expected price level fools suppliers into thinking that the relative prices of their goods have increased, so all suppliers increase output. The

short-run aggregate supply (*SRAS*) curve shows the aggregate quantity of output supplied at each price level, with the expected price level held constant. Because an increase in the price level fools producers into supplying more output, the short-run aggregate supply curve slopes upwards, as shown by $SRAS^1$.

■   The short-run aggregate supply curve $SRAS^1$ is drawn so that the expected price level, P^e, equals P_1. When the actual price level equals the expected price level, producers are not fooled and so supply the full-employment level of output, $\overline{Y}$. Therefore at point E, where the actual price level equals the expected price level (both equal P_1), the short-run aggregate supply curve, $SRAS^1$, shows that producers supply $\overline{Y}$.

■   In the long run producers learn about the price level and adjust their expectations until the actual price level equals the expected price level. Producers then supply the full-employment level of output, $\overline{Y}$, regardless of the price level. Thus, the long-run aggregate supply (*LRAS*) curve is vertical at $Y = \overline{Y}$, just as in the basic *AD–AS* model in Key Diagram 7.

Factors that Shift the Curves

■   The aggregate quantity of output demanded is determined by the intersection of the *IS* curve and the *LM* curve. At a constant price level, any factor that shifts the *IS*–*LM* intersection to the right increases the aggregate quantity of goods demanded and thus also shifts the *AD* curve to the right. Factors that shift the *AD* curve are listed in Summary table 14.

■   Any factor that increases full-employment output, $\overline{Y}$, shifts both the short-run and the long-run aggregate supply curves to the right. Factors that increase full-employment output include beneficial supply shocks or an increase in labour supply. An increase in government purchases, because it induces workers to supply more labour, also shifts the short-run and long-run aggregate supply curves to the right in the classical model.

■   An increase in the expected price level shifts the short-run aggregate supply curve up.

Analysis

■   The short-run equilibrium is at the intersection of the *AD* curve and the *SRAS* curve. For example, if the expected price level is P_1, the *SRAS* curve is $SRAS^1$, and the short-run equilibrium is at point *F*. At *F* output, Y_1, is higher than the full-employment level, $\overline{Y}$, and the price level, P_2, is higher than the expected price level, P_1. As producers obtain information about the price level, the expected price level is revised upwards, which shifts the *SRAS* curve up. The long-run equilibrium is at point *H*, where the long-run aggregate supply (*LRAS*) curve intersects the *AD* curve. In the long run (1) output equals $\overline{Y}$, and (2) the price level equals the expected price level (both equal P_3). In the long run, when the expected price level has risen to P_3, the short-run aggregate supply curve, $SRAS^2$, passes through *H*.

Key Terms

labour hoarding, p. 399
misperceptions theory, p. 411
nominal shocks, p. 390
productivity shocks, p. 390
propagation mechanism, p. 418
rational expectations, p. 417
real business cycle theory, p. 390
real shocks, p. 390
reverse causation, p. 407
Solow residual, p. 396

Key Equation

$$Y = \overline{Y} + b(P - P^e) \qquad (11.4)$$

The short-run aggregate supply curve, based on the misperceptions theory, indicates that the aggregate amount of output supplied, Y, equals full-employment output, $\overline{Y}$, when the price level, P, equals the expected price level, P^e. When the price level is higher than expected ($P > P^e$), output exceeds $\overline{Y}$; when the price level is lower than expected ($P < P^e$), output is less than $\overline{Y}$.

Review Questions

1. What main feature of the classical *IS*–*LM* model distinguishes it from the Keynesian *IS*–*LM* model? Why is the distinction of practical importance?

2. What are the two main components of any theory of the business cycle? Describe these two components for the real business cycle theory.

3. Define *real shock* and *nominal shock*. What type of real shock do real business cycle theorists consider the most important source of cyclical fluctuations?

4. What major business cycle facts does the RBC theory explain successfully? Does it explain any business cycle facts less well?

5. What is the Solow residual and how does it behave over the business cycle? What factors cause the Solow residual to change?

6. What effects does an increase in government purchases have on the labour market, according to the classical theory? What effects does it have on output, the real interest rate, and the price level? According to classical economists, should fiscal policy be used to smooth out the business cycle? Why or why not?

7. In the context of the relationship between the money supply and real economic activity, what is meant by *reverse causation*? Explain how reverse causation could occur. What business cycle fact is it intended to explain?

8. According to the misperceptions theory, what effect does an increase in the price level have on the amount of output supplied by producers? Explain. Does it matter whether the increase in the price level was expected?

9. What conclusion does the basic classical model (with no misperceptions of the price level) allow about the neutrality or non-neutrality of money? In what ways is this conclusion modified by the extended classical model based on the misperceptions theory?

10. Define *rational expectations*. According to the classical model, what implications do rational expectations have for the ability of the central bank to use monetary policy to smooth business cycles?

Numerical Problems

1. In a certain economy the production function is

$$Y = A(100N - 0.5N^2)$$

where Y is output, A is productivity, and N is total hours worked. The marginal product of labour associated with this production function is

$$MPN = A(100 - N)$$

Initially, $A = 1.0$, but a beneficial productivity shock raises A to 1.1.

a. The supply of labour is

$$NS = 45 + 0.1w$$

where w is the real wage. Find the equilibrium levels of output, hours worked, and the real wage before and after the productivity shock. Recall (Chapter 3) that the MPN curve is the same as the labour demand curve, with the real wage replacing the MPN.

b. Repeat part (a) if the labour supply is

$$NS = 10 + 0.8w$$

c. Some studies show that the real wage is only slightly procyclical. Assume for the sake of argument that this finding is correct. Would a calibrated RBC model fit the facts better if the labour supply were relatively insensitive to the real wage, or if it were relatively sensitive? Justify your answer diagrammatically and relate it to your answers to parts (a) and (b).

2. An economy is described as follows.

Desired consumption	$C^d = 600 + 0.5(Y - T) - 50r$
Desired investment	$I^d = 450 - 50r$
Real money demand	$L = 0.5Y - 100i$
Full-employment output	$\overline{Y} = 2210$
Expected inflation	$\pi^e = 0.05$

In this economy the government always has a balanced budget, so $T = G$, where T is total taxes collected.

a. Suppose that $M = 4320$ and $G = 150$. Use the classical IS–LM model to find the equilibrium values of output, the real interest rate, the price level, consumption, and investment. (*Hint:* In the classical model, output always equals its full-employment level.)

b. The money supply rises to 4752. Repeat part (a). Is money neutral?

c. With the money supply back at 4320, government purchases and taxes rise to 190. Repeat part (a). Assume for simplicity that $\overline{Y}$ is fixed (unaffected by G). Is fiscal policy neutral in this case? Explain.

3. Consider the following economy.

Desired consumption	$C^d = 250 + 0.5(Y - T) - 500r$
Desired investment	$I^d = 250 - 500r$
Real money demand	$L = 0.5Y - 500i$
Full-employment output	$\overline{Y} = 1000$
Expected inflation	$\pi^e = 0$

a. Suppose that $T = G = 200$ and that $M = 7650$. Find an equation describing the IS curve. Find an equation describing the LM curve. Finally, find an equation for the aggregate demand curve. What are the equilibrium values of output, consumption, investment, the real interest rate, and the price level? Assume that there are no misperceptions about the price level.

b. Suppose that $T = G = 200$ and that $M = 9000$. What is the equation for the aggregate demand curve now? What are the equilibrium values of output, consumption, investment, the real interest rate, and the price level? Assume that full-employment output $\overline{Y}$ is fixed.

c. Repeat part (b) for $T = G = 300$ and $M = 7650$.

4. An economy has the following AD and AS curves.

AD curve	$Y = 300 + 30(M/P)$
AS curve	$Y = \overline{Y} + 10(P - P^e)$

Here, $\overline{Y} = 500$ and $M = 400$

a. Suppose that $P^e = 60$. What are the equilibrium values of the price level, P, and output, Y? (*Hint:* The solutions for P in this part and in part (b) are multiples of 10.)

b. An unanticipated increase raises the money supply to $M = 700$. Because the increase is unanticipated, P^e remains at 60. What are the equilibrium values of the price level, P, and output, Y?

c. The central bank announces that the money supply will be increased to $M = 700$, which the public believes. Now what are the equilibrium values of the price level, P, the expected price level, P^e, and output, Y?

5. Try the following experiment. Toss a coin fifty times, keeping track of the results. Think of each 'heads' as a small positive shock that increases output by one unit; similarly, think of each 'tails' as a small negative shock that reduces output by one unit. Let the initial value of output, Y, be 50, and graph the level of output over time as it is hit by the 'positive' and 'negative' shocks (tosses of the coin). For example, if your first four tosses are three heads and a tail, output takes the values 51, 52, 53, 52. After fifty flips, have your small shocks produced any large cycles in output?

6. In a particular economy the labour force (the sum of employed and unemployed workers) is fixed at 100 million. In this economy, each month 1% of the workers who were employed at the beginning of the month lose their jobs, and 19% of the workers who were unemployed at the beginning of the month find new jobs.
   a. The January unemployment rate is 5%. For the rates of job loss and job finding given, what will the unemployment rate be in February? In March?
   b. In April an adverse productivity shock raises the job loss rate to 3% of those employed. The job loss rate returns to 1% in May, while the job finding rate remains unchanged at 19% throughout. Find the unemployment rate for April, May, June, and July.

7. (Appendix) Consider the following economy.
   IS curve $r = 2.47 - 0.0004Y$
   Real money demand $L = 0.5Y - 500(r + \pi^e)$
   Short-run aggregate supply $Y = \overline{Y} + 100(P - P^e)$
   Here, r is the real interest rate, Y is output, and P is the price level. Assume that expected inflation, π^e, is 0, nominal money supply, M is 88,950, and full-employment output, $\overline{Y}$ is 6000.
   a. Use the notation of Appendixes 10.A and 11.A. What are the values of the parameters α_{IS}, β_{IS}, α_{LM}, β_{LM}, ℓ_r, and b? (*Hint:* Solve for asset market equilibrium to obtain the coefficients of the LM equation.)
   b. What is the equation of the aggregate demand curve?
   c. Suppose that the expected price level, P^e, is 29.15. What are the short-run equilibrium values of the price level, P, and output Y?
   d. What are the long-run equilibrium values of the price level, P, and output, Y?

Analytical Problems

1. The discovery of a new technology increases the expected future marginal product of capital.
   a. Use the classical $IS–LM$ model to determine the effect of the increase in the expected future MPK on current output, the real interest rate, employment, real wages, consumption, investment, and the price level. Assume that expected future real wages and future incomes are unaffected by the new technology. Assume also that current productivity is unaffected.
   b. Find the effects of the increase in the expected future MPK on current output and prices from the $AD–AS$ diagram based on the misperceptions theory. What accounts for the difference with part (a)?

2. Use the classical $IS–LM$ model to analyse the effects of a permanent increase in government purchases of 100 per year (in real terms). The increase in purchases is financed by a permanent increase in lump-sum taxes of 100 per year.
   a. Begin by finding the effects of the fiscal change on the labour market. How does the effect of the permanent increase in government purchases of 100 compare with the effect of a temporary increase in purchases of 100?
   b. Because the tax increase is permanent, assume that at any constant levels of output and the real interest rate consumers respond by reducing their consumption each period by the full amount of the tax increase. Under this assumption, how does the permanent increase in government purchases affect desired national saving and the IS curve?
   c. Use the classical $IS–LM$ model to find the effects of the permanent increase in government purchases and taxes on output, the real interest rate, and the price level in the current period. What happens if consumers reduce their current consumption by less than 100 at any level of output and the real interest rate?

3. Consider a business cycle theory that combines the classical $IS–LM$ model with the assumption that temporary changes in government purchases are the main source of cyclical fluctuations. How well would this theory explain the observed cyclical behaviour of each of the following variables? Give reasons for your answers.

a. Employment
b. The real wage
c. Average labour productivity
d. Investment
e. The price level

4. This problem asks you to work out in more detail the example of reverse causation described in the text. Suppose that firms that expect to increase production in the future have to increase their current transactions (for example, they may need to purchase more raw materials). For this reason, current real money demand rises when expected future output rises.

a. Under the assumption that real money demand depends on expected future output, use the classical *IS–LM* model to find the effects of an increase in expected future output on the current price level. For simplicity, assume that any effects of the increase in expected future output on the labour market or on desired saving and investment are small and can be ignored.

b. Suppose that the central bank wants to stabilize the current price level. How will the central bank respond to the increase in expected future output? Explain why the central bank's response is an example of reverse causation.

5. Two countries called East and West agree to unify. The real value of full-employment output in East is 1 trillion widgets, and in West it is 2 trillion widgets. The combined full-employment output of the unified country is expected to be the sum of the two full-employment outputs, or 3 trillion widgets.

Real money demand in the West is 10% of West's real output and will remain so after unification. In the East people do not have access to financial instruments, such as stocks and bonds, and so are forced to save in the form of money. As a result, real money demand in the East is 40% of East's real output. However, after unification easterners will have access to a full range of financial assets, and thus their real money demand will drop to 10% of output.

The unified country will use only the West's currency. As part of the unification plan, the West central bank has agreed to print new western currency and trade it for eastern currency, which will be destroyed. At the initial price levels the total real value of the western currency received by easterners equals the total real value of the eastern currency they give up.

Use the classical *IS–LM* model to find the effects on post-unification output and prices of the currency swap. Give a quantitative estimate of the effect on the price level (measured in the western currency). Qualitatively, does your answer change if you use the *AD–AS* model based on the misperceptions theory? What can West's central bank do to offset the effects of the currency swap on the price level?

6. Starting from a situation with no government spending and no taxes, the government introduces a foreign aid programme (in which domestically produced goods are shipped abroad) and pays for it with a temporary 10% tax on current wages. Future wages are untaxed.

What effects will the temporary wage tax have on labour supply? Use the classical *IS–LM* model to find the effects of the fiscal change on output, employment, the (before-tax) real wage, the real interest rate, and the price level.

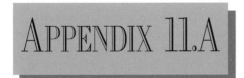

AN ALGEBRAIC VERSION OF THE CLASSICAL *AD–AS* MODEL WITH MISPERCEPTIONS

Building on the algebraic version of the *AD–AS* model developed in Appendix 10.A, in this appendix we derive an algebraic version of the classical *AD–AS* model with misperceptions. We present algebraic versions of the aggregate demand (*AD*) curve and the aggregate supply (*AS*) curve and then solve for the general equilibrium.

The Aggregate Demand Curve

Because misperceptions by producers do not affect the demand for goods, the aggregate demand curve is the same as in Appendix 10.A. Recall from equation (10.A.27) that the equation of the aggregate demand (*AD*) curve is

$$Y = \frac{\alpha_{IS} - \alpha_{LM} + (1/\ell_r)(M/P)}{\beta_{IS} + \beta_{LM}} \qquad (11.A.1)$$

where the coefficients of the *IS* curve, α_{IS} and β_{IS}, are given by equations (10.A.15) and (10.A.16), respectively, the coefficients of the *LM* curve, α_{LM} and β_{LM}, are given by equations (10.A.20) and (10.A.21), respectively, and ℓ_r is the coefficient of the nominal interest rate in the money demand equation, equation (10.A.17).

The Aggregate Supply Curve

The short-run aggregate supply curve based on the misperceptions theory is represented by equation (11.4), which, for convenience, we repeat here:

$$Y = \overline{Y} + b(P - P^e) \qquad (11.A.2)$$

where b is a positive number.

General Equilibrium

For a given expected price level, P^e, the short-run equilibrium value of the price level is determined by the intersection of the aggregate demand curve (equation 11.A.1) and the short-run aggregate supply curve (equation 11.A.2). Setting the right-hand sides of equations (11.A.1) and (11.A.2) equal and multiplying both sides of the resulting equation by P yields a quadratic equation for the price level P:

$$a_2 P^2 + a_1 P - a_0 = 0 \qquad (11.A.3)$$

where

$$a_2 = (\beta_{IS} + \beta_{LM})b;$$

$$a_1 = (\beta_{IS} + \beta_{LM})(\overline{Y} - bP^e) - \alpha_{IS} + \alpha_{LM};$$

$$a_0 = \frac{M}{\ell_r}.$$

The coefficients a_2 and a_0 are positive, and the coefficient a_1 could be positive, negative, or zero. Because both a_2 and a_0 are positive, the solution of equation (11.A.3) yields one positive value of P and one negative value of P. The price level cannot be negative, so the short-run equilibrium price level is the positive solution of this equation. Using the standard quadratic formula, we find the positive solution of equation (11.A.3) to be

(11.A.4)

$$P = \frac{-a_1 + \sqrt{a_1^2 + 4a_2a_0}}{2a_2}.$$

(11.A.6)

We obtain the short-run equilibrium level of output by substituting the value of the price level from equation (11.A.4) into either the aggregate demand curve equation (11.A.1) or the aggregate supply curve equation (11.A.2).

Note that an increase in the nominal money supply, M, increases the constant a_0 and thus, according to equation (11.A.4), it increases the equilibrium price level. Because an increase in M does not affect the aggregate supply curve but does increase the equilibrium price level, equation (11.A.2) shows that it increases output.

We focused on short-run equilibrium in this appendix. In the long run, the actual price level equals the expected price level so that, according to equation (11.A.2), output equals its full-employment level, $\overline{Y}$. In the long run the economy reaches the general equilibrium described in Appendix 10.A.

12

KEYNESIANISM: THE MACROECONOMICS OF WAGE AND PRICE RIGIDITY

Chapter 11 presented the classical, or market-clearing, approach to business cycle analysis. In the classical approach wages and prices are assumed to adjust quickly so that markets are almost always in equilibrium. Classical economists argue that business cycles represent the economy's best response to disturbances, such as productivity shocks, so there is little justification for government attempts to smooth the cycle.

In contrast to the classical economists, Keynesians are less optimistic about the ability of free-market economies to respond quickly and efficiently to shocks. One of the central ideas of Keynesianism is that wages and prices are 'rigid' or 'sticky' and do *not* adjust quickly to market-clearing levels. Wage and price rigidity implies that the economy can be away from its general equilibrium for significant periods of time. Thus a deep recession is not an optimal response of the free market to outside shocks; rather, it is a disequilibrium situation in which high unemployment reflects an excess of labour supplied over labour demanded. Keynesians believe that the government should act to eliminate – or at least minimize – these periods of low output and high unemployment.

As wage and price rigidity is the basis for Keynesian theory and policy recommendations, understanding the potential causes of rigidity is important. A telling criticism that the classical economists aimed at the Keynesians in the early 1970s was that the Keynesians simply assumed that wages and prices are rigid, without giving a good economic explanation of why these rigidities occur. After all, argued the classical economists, wages and prices are not simply 'given' to the economy but are the results of decisions made by millions of individuals and firms. If excessively high wages are causing unemployment, why do unemployed workers not offer to work for lower wages until firms are willing to hire them? If prices are not at the levels at which quantities supplied equal quantities demanded, why do firms not just change their prices? In effect, the classical economists challenged the Keynesians to show how wage and price rigidity could be consistent with the idea – basic to almost all of economics – that individuals and firms are economically rational: that is, they do the best they can for themselves when making economic decisions.

Keynesian researchers accepted this challenge and have made progress in explaining wage and price rigidity in terms consistent with economic rationality. In the first part of this chapter we discuss some leading Keynesian explanations for wage and price rigidity. We then show how slow adjustment of wages and prices can be incorporated into the *IS–LM* model, converting it from a classical model to a Keynesian model. Using this model, we discuss the Keynesian answers to the two central questions about business cycles: namely, what causes business cycles and what should policymakers do about them?

12.1 REAL-WAGE RIGIDITY

Because Keynesian analysis and policy prescriptions depend so greatly on the assumption that wages and prices do not move rapidly to clear markets, we begin by discussing in some detail the possible economic reasons for slow or incomplete adjustment. In this section we focus on the rigidity of real wages, and in Section 12.2 we look at the slow adjustment of prices.

The main reason that Keynesians bring wage rigidity into their analysis is their dissatisfaction with the classical explanation of unemployment. Recall that classical economists believe that most unemployment, including the increases in unemployment that occur during recessions, arises from mismatches between workers and jobs (frictional or structural unemployment). Keynesians do not dispute that mismatch is a major source of unemployment, but they are sceptical that it explains all unemployment.

Keynesians are particularly unwilling to accept the classical idea that recessions are periods of increased mismatch between workers and jobs. If higher unemployment during downturns reflected increased mismatch, Keynesians argue, recessions should be periods of particularly active search by workers for jobs and by firms for new employees. However, surveys suggest that unemployed workers spend relatively little time searching for work (many are simply waiting, hoping to be recalled to their old jobs), and help-wanted advertising and vacancy postings by firms fall rather than rise during recessions. Rather than times of increased worker–job mismatch, Keynesians believe that recessions are periods of generally low demand for both output and workers throughout the economy.

To explain the existence of unemployment without relying solely on worker–job mismatch, Keynesians argue for rejecting the classical assumption that real wages adjust relatively quickly to equate the quantities of labour supplied and demanded. In particular, if the real wage is above the level that clears the labour market, unemployment (an excess of labour supplied over labour demanded) will result. From the Keynesian perspective, the idea that the real wage moves 'too little' to keep the quantity of labour demanded equal to the quantity of labour supplied is called **real-wage rigidity**.

Some Reasons for Real-Wage Rigidity

For a rigid real wage to be the source of unemployment, the real wage that firms are paying must be higher than the market-clearing real wage, at which quantities of labour supplied and demanded are equal. But if the real wage is higher than necessary to attract workers, why do firms not save labour costs by simply reducing the wage that they pay, as suggested by the classical analysis?

Various explanations have been offered for why real wages might be rigid, even in the face of an excess supply of labour. One possibility is that there are legal and institutional factors that keep wages high, such as labour market regulations, including minimum wage legislation, unemployment benefits and trade union contracts and bargaining behaviour. It is interesting to note that trade union membership and the extent of labour market regulation are more dominant features of European labour markets than in either the USA or Japan. This lends some support to the view that European labour markets are characterized by greater real-wage rigidity, and therefore higher unemployment, than is the case in the USA and Japan.[1]

Another explanation for why a firm might pay a higher real wage than it 'has' to is that this policy might reduce the firm's **turnover costs**, or the costs associated with hiring and training new workers. By paying a high wage, the firm can keep more of its current workers, which saves the firm the cost of hiring and training replacements. Similarly, by developing a reputation for paying well, the firm can assure itself of more and better applicants for any position that it may have to fill.

A third reason that firms might pay real wages above market-clearing levels is that workers who are paid well may have greater incentives to work hard and effectively. If highly paid workers are more productive, the firm may profit from paying its employees well, even though it could attract all the workers it needs at a lower real wage. The idea that a worker's productivity depends on the real wage received, and that therefore firms may pay wages above the market-clearing level, is the essence of the **efficiency wage model**.[2] Because this model of wage determination has played a key role in recent Keynesian analyses and because it has several interesting aspects, we focus on it for the remainder of this section.

The Efficiency Wage Model

If better-paid workers are more productive, firms may gain by paying wages higher than the minimum necessary to attract workers. But why might a worker's productivity depend on the real wage received? The answer has both 'carrot' and 'stick' aspects.

---

1. This will be discussed in more detail in Chapter 13.
2. See Janet Yellen, 'Efficiency Wage Models of Unemployment', *American Economic Review*, May 1984, pp. 200–5.

The *carrot* or positive incentive is based on the idea that workers who feel well treated will work harder and more efficiently. George Akerlof of the University of California at Berkeley argued that workers who believe that their employer is treating them fairly – say, by paying higher wages than required to retain them and by not cutting wages in slack times – will in turn want to treat the employer fairly by doing a good job. Akerlof called this motivation the *gift exchange motive*[3] because it is similar to the one that leads people to exchange gifts.

The *stick* or threat aspect of why a firm would pay a higher wage than necessary has been analysed in an economic model called the 'shirking' model of wage determination.[4] According to the *shirking model,* if workers are paid only the minimum amount needed to attract them to a particular job, they will not be too concerned about the possibility of being fired if they do not perform well. After all, if the job pays the minimum amount necessary to induce them to take the job, they are not much happier with the job than without the job. In this case workers will be more inclined to take it easy at work and shirk their duties, and the employer will have to bear the cost either of the shirking or of paying supervisors to make sure that the work gets done. In contrast, workers receiving a higher wage will place a greater value on keeping their job (it is not that easy to find another job as good) and will work hard to avoid being fired for shirking.

The gift exchange idea and the shirking model both imply that workers' efforts on the job depend on the real wages they receive. Graphically, the relation between the real wage and the level of effort is shown by the **effort curve** in Figure 12.1. The real wage w is measured along the horizontal axis, and the level of effort E is measured along the vertical axis. The effort curve passes through points O, A, and B. When real wages are higher, workers choose to work harder, for either 'carrot' or 'stick' reasons; therefore the effort curve slopes upwards. We assume that the effort curve is S-shaped. At the lowest levels of the real wage, workers make hardly any effort, and effort rises only slowly as the real wage increases. At higher levels of the real wage, effort rises sharply, as shown by the steeply rising portion of the curve. The curve flattens at very high levels of the real wage because there is some maximum level of effort that workers really cannot exceed no matter how motivated they are.

Wage Determination in the Efficiency Wage Model

The effort curve shows that effort depends on the real wage, but what determines the real wage? To make as much profit as possible, *firms will choose the level of the real wage that gets the most effort from workers for each unit of real wages paid.* The amount of effort per unit of real wages equals the amount of effort E divided by the real wage w. The ratio of E to w can be found graphically from Figure 12.1. Consider, for example, point A on the effort curve, at which the

3. See George Akerlof, 'Labour Contracts as Partial Gift Exchange', *Quarterly Journal of Economics,* November 1982, pp. 543–69.
4. See Carl Shapiro and Joseph E. Stiglitz, 'Equilibrium Unemployment as a Worker Discipline Device,' *American Economic Review,* June 1984, pp. 433–44.

**Figure 12.1
Determination of the
efficiency wage**
The effort curve shows
the relation between
worker effort, E, and the
real wage workers receive,
w. A higher real wage
leads to more effort, but
above a certain point
higher wages are unable
to spur effort much, so
the effort curve is
S-shaped. For any point
on the curve, the amount
of effort per unit of real
wage is the slope of the
line from the origin to
that point. At point A,
effort per unit of real
wage is E_A/w_A. The
highest level of effort per
unit of real wage is at
point B, where the line
from the origin is tangent
to the curve. The real
wage rate at B is the
efficiency wage w^*, and
the corresponding level of
effort is E^*.

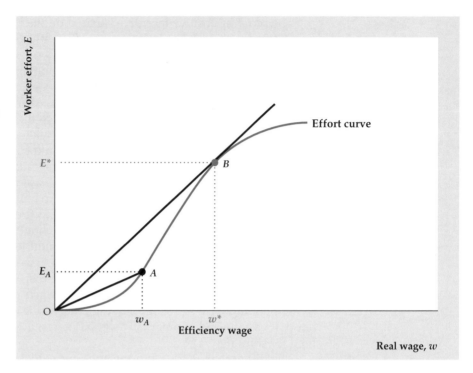

real wage w_A induces workers to supply effort E_A. The slope of the line from the origin to A equals the height of the curve at point A, E_A, divided by the horizontal distance, w_A. Thus the slope of the line from the origin to A equals the amount of effort per unit of real wage at A.

The real wage that achieves the highest effort per unit of wages is at point B. The slope of the line from the origin to B, which is the amount of effort per unit of real wage at B, is greater than the slope of the line from the origin to any other point on the curve. In general, to locate the real wage that maximizes effort per unit of real wage, draw a line from the origin tangent to the effort curve; the real wage at the tangency point maximizes effort per unit of real wage. We call the real wage that maximizes effort or efficiency per unit of real wages the **efficiency wage**. In Figure 12.1 the efficiency wage is w^*, and the corresponding level of effort is E^*.

The efficiency wage theory helps explain real-wage rigidity. Because the employer chooses the real wage that maximizes effort received per unit of real wage paid, as long as the effort curve does not change, the employer will not change the real wage. Therefore the theory implies that the real wage is permanently rigid and equals the efficiency wage.

Employment and Unemployment in the Efficiency Wage Model

According to the efficiency wage theory, the real wage is rigid at the level that maximizes effort per unit of real wage paid. We now consider how the levels of employment and unemployment in the labour market are determined.

The workings of the labour market when there is an efficiency wage are shown in Figure 12.2. The efficiency wage w^* is indicated by a horizontal line. Because the efficiency wage is determined solely by the effort curve, for the purpose of analysing the labour market we can take w^* to be fixed. Similarly, we can take the level of effort E^* induced by the efficiency wage w^* as fixed at this stage of the analysis.

The upward-sloping curve is the standard labour supply curve, NS. As in the classical model, this curve shows the number of hours of work that people would like to supply at each level of the real wage.[5]

The downward-sloping curve is the demand curve for labour in the efficiency wage model. Recall from Chapter 3 that the amount of labour demanded by a firm depends on the marginal product of labour, or MPN. Specifically, the labour demand curve is identical to the MPN curve, which in turn relates the marginal product of labour MPN to the quantity of labour input N being used. The MPN curve – and hence the labour demand curve – slopes down because of the diminishing marginal productivity of labour.

In the classical model, the marginal product of labour depends only on the production function and the capital stock. A complication of the efficiency wage model is that the amount of output produced by an extra worker (or hour of work) also depends on the worker's effort. Fortunately, as we noted, the efficiency wage w^* and the effort level induced by that wage, E^*, are fixed at this stage of the analysis. Thus the labour demand curve in Figure 12.2, ND^*, reflects the marginal product of labour *when worker effort is held fixed at* E^*. As

---

5. For simplicity we assume that the number of hours of labour that people want to supply does not depend on the effort they must exert while on the job.

Figure 12.2
Excess supply of labour in the efficiency wage model
When the efficiency wage w^* is paid, the firm's demand for labour is $\bar{N}$, represented by point A. However, the amount of labour that workers want to supply at a real wage of w^* is NS_1. The excess supply of labour equals distance AB. We assume that the efficiency wage w^* is higher than the market-clearing wage w_E that would prevail if the supply of labour equalled the demand for labour at point E.

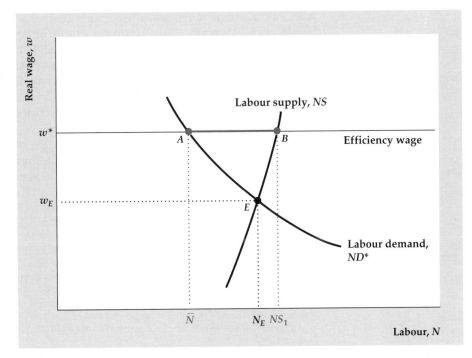

in the classical case, an increase in productivity or in the capital stock shifts the labour demand curve ND^* to the right. In addition, any change in the effort curve that led to an increase in the optimal level of effort E^* would raise the MPN and the labour demand curve ND^* would again shift to the right.

Now we can put the elements of Figure 12.2 together to show how employment is determined. Point A on the labour demand curve ND^* indicates that, when the real wage is fixed at w^*, firms want to employ $\overline{N}$ hours of labour. Point B on the labour supply curve indicates that, when the real wage is fixed at w^*, workers want to supply NS_1 hours of labour, which is greater than the amount demanded by firms. At the efficiency wage the quantity of labour supplied is greater than the quantity demanded,[6] so the level of employment is determined by the labour demand of firms and hence equals $\overline{N}$. The demand-determined level of employment is labelled $\overline{N}$ because it represents the full-employment level of employment for this model: that is, $\overline{N}$ is the level of employment reached after full adjustment of wages and prices. (Note that the value of $\overline{N}$ in the efficiency wage model differs from the full-employment level of employment in the classical model of the labour market, which would correspond to N_E in Figure 12.2.) Because the efficiency wage is rigid at w^*, in the absence of shocks the level of employment in this economy remains at $\overline{N}$ indefinitely.

Perhaps the most interesting aspect of Figure 12.2 is that it provides a new explanation of unemployment. It shows that, even when wages have adjusted as much as they are going to and the economy is technically at 'full employment,' an excess supply of labour, $NS_1 - \overline{N}$ remains.[7]

Why do the unemployed not bid down the real wage and thus gain employment, as they would in the classical model of the labour market? Unlike the classical case, in a labour market with an efficiency wage the real wage cannot be bid down by people offering to work at lower wages because employers will not hire them. Employers know that people working at lower wages will not put out as much effort per unit of real wage as workers receiving the higher efficiency wage. Thus the excess supply of labour shown in Figure 12.2 will persist indefinitely. The efficiency wage model thus implies that unemployment will exist even if there is no mismatch between jobs and workers.

The efficiency wage model is an interesting theory of real wages and unemployment, but does it explain actual behaviour? Box 12.1 interprets a famous episode in labour history in terms of efficiency wage theory. In addition to this anecdotal evidence, studies of wages and employment in various firms and industries provide some support for the efficiency wage model. For example, Sushil Wadhawani and Martin Wall[8] found that, consistent with one aspect of the theory, firms that paid higher wages to workers, or were in industries where unemployment had increased, experienced less shirking, measured by the level of productivity in the firm.

---

6. The result that there is an excess supply of labour requires the assumption that the efficiency wage w^* is higher than the real wage that would clear the labour market, shown as w_E in Figure 12.2. We always assume that the efficiency wage is higher than the market-clearing wage; if it were not, firms would have to pay the market-clearing wage to attract workers.

7. Because the unemployment represented by the excess supply of labour persists even when the economy is at full employment, it is considered part of structural unemployment.

8. 'A Direct Test of the Efficiency Wage Model using UK Micro Data', *Oxford Economic Papers*, October 1991, pp. 529–48.

BOX 12.1

Henry Ford's Efficiency Wage

During 1908–14 Henry Ford instituted at Ford Motor Company a radically new way of producing motor cars.* Prior to Ford's innovations, car components were not produced to uniform specifications. Instead, cars had to be assembled one by one by skilled craftsmen, who could make the parts fit even if sizes or shapes were off by fractions of an inch. Ford introduced a system of assembly-line production in which a standardized product, the Model T, was produced from precisely made, interchangeable components. The production process was also broken into numerous small, simple steps, replacing the skilled craftsmen who had built cars from start to finish with unskilled workers who performed only a few operations over and over again.

The high speed at which Ford ran the assembly line and the repetitiveness of the work were hard on the workers. As one labourer said, 'If I keep putting on Nut No. 86 for about 86 more days, I will be Nut No. 86 in the Pontiac bughouse.'[†] As a result, worker turnover was high, with the typical worker lasting only a few months on the job. Absenteeism was also high – about 10% on any given day – and morale was low. Worker slowdowns and even sabotage occurred.

In January 1914 Ford announced that the company would begin paying $5 a day to workers who met certain criteria, one being that the worker had been with the company at least six months. Five dollars a day was more than double the normal wage for production workers at the time. Although the motivation for Ford's announcement has been debated, its effect was stunning: thousands of workers lined up outside the plant, hoping for jobs. Within the plant the number of people quitting dropped by 87%, absenteeism dropped by 75%, and productivity rose by 30% or more. The productivity increases helped increase Ford's profits, despite the higher wage bill and a cut in the price of a Model T.

Many results of Ford's $5 day can be predicted by the efficiency wage model, including improved efficiency and higher profits. As other car makers adopted Ford's technological innovations, they also adopted his wage policies. By 1928, before unions were important in the industry, car industry wages were almost 40% higher than those in the rest of manufacturing.

---

* The source for this box is Daniel M. G. Raff and Lawrence H. Summers, 'Did Henry Ford Pay Efficiency Wages?', *Journal of Labour Economics*, October 1987, pp. S57–S86.
[†] This quote is originally from Stephen Meyer, *The Five-Dollar Day: Labour Management and Social Control in the Ford Motor Company, 1908–1921* (State University of New York Press, 1981).

A criticism of the efficiency wage model presented here is that it predicts that the real wage is literally fixed (for no change in the effort curve). Of course, this result is too extreme because the real wage does change over time (and over the business cycle, as demonstrated in Chapter 9). However, the basic model can be extended to allow for changes in the effort curve that bring changes in the efficiency wage over time. For example, a reasonable assumption would be that workers are more concerned about losing their jobs during recessions, when finding a new job is more difficult, than during booms. Under this assumption, the real wage necessary to obtain any specific level of effort will be lower during recessions; hence the efficiency wage paid in recessions may also be lower. This extension may help the efficiency wage model match the business cycle fact that real wages are lower in recessions than in booms (procyclical real wages).

Efficiency Wages and the *FE* Line

In the Keynesian version of the *IS–LM* model, as in the classical version, the *FE* line is vertical, showing the full-employment level of output $\overline{Y}$. If we assume that employers pay efficiency wages, full-employment output $\overline{Y}$ in turn is the output produced when employment is at the full-employment level of employment $\overline{N}$, as shown in Figure 12.2, and the level of worker effort is E^*.

As in the classical model, anything that changes full-employment output $\overline{Y}$ shifts the *FE* line. The classical model emphasizes two factors that shift the *FE* line: changes in the supply of labour and changes in productivity. In the efficiency wage model, however, labour supply does not affect employment, so *changes in labour supply do not affect the FE line in the Keynesian model* with efficiency wages. A change in productivity, however, *does* affect the *FE* line in the Keynesian model, as in the classical model. A drop in productivity reduces full-employment output $\overline{Y}$ and shifts the *FE* line to the left, for two reasons. First, by reducing the marginal product of labour at any given level of employment, a drop in productivity reduces the demand for labour at any fixed real wage. With the real wage fixed at w^*, the full-employment level of employment $\overline{N}$ falls. Second, a drop in productivity reduces the amount of output that can be produced with any particular amount of capital, labour, and effort.

12.2 PRICE STICKINESS

The rigidity created by efficiency wages is a *real* rigidity in that the real wage, rather than the nominal wage, remains fixed. Keynesian theories also emphasize *nominal* rigidities that occur when a price or wage is fixed in nominal, or money, terms and does not readily change in response to changes in supply or demand. Keynesians often refer to rigidity of nominal prices – a tendency of prices to adjust only slowly to changes in the economy – as **price stickiness**.

We explained in Section 12.1 that Keynesians introduced real-wage rigidity because of their dissatisfaction with the classical explanation of unemployment. Similarly, the assumption of price stickiness addresses what Keynesians believe is another significant weakness of the basic classical model: the classical prediction that monetary policy is neutral.

Recall that, in the basic classical model without misperceptions, the assumption that wages and prices adjust quickly implies that money is neutral. If money is neutral, an increase or decrease in the money supply changes the price level by the same proportion but has no effect on real variables, such as output, employment, or the real interest rate. However, recall also that empirical studies – including analyses of historical episodes – have led most economists to conclude that money is probably not neutral in the real world.

One approach to accounting for monetary non-neutrality (pursued in Chapter 11) is to extend the classical model by assuming that workers and firms have imperfect information about the current price level (the misperceptions theory). However, Keynesians favour an alternative way to explain monetary non-neutrality: modify the classical assumption that prices adjust quickly. If prices are sticky, the price level cannot adjust immediately to offset changes in the money supply, and money is not neutral. Thus for Keynesians, the importance of price stickiness is that it helps explain monetary non-neutrality.

Although we focus on nominal-price rigidity in this section, a long Keynesian tradition emphasizes nominal-wage rigidity instead of nominal-price rigidity. An alternative version of the Keynesian model that rests on the assumption of nominal-wage rigidity is discussed in Appendix 12.A. This alternative model has similar implications to the Keynesian model with price rigidity: in particular, that money is not neutral.

Sources of Price Stickiness: Monopolistic Competition and Menu Costs

To say that price stickiness gives rise to monetary non-neutrality does not completely explain non-neutrality because it raises another question: why are prices sticky? The Keynesian explanation for the existence of price rigidity relies on two main ideas: (1) most firms actively *set* the prices of their products rather than taking the prices of their output as given by the market; and (2) when firms change prices, they incur a cost, known as a menu cost.

Monopolistic Competition. Talking about price stickiness in a highly competitive, organized market – such as the market for wheat or the stock exchange – would not make much sense. In these markets, prices adjust rapidly to reflect changes in supply or demand. Principal reasons for price flexibility in these competitive, highly organized markets include standardization of the product being traded (one kilogram of wheat, or one share of British Airways stock, is much like any other) and the large number of actual or potential market participants. These two factors make it worthwhile to organize a centralized market (such as the London, Paris and Frankfurt Stock Exchanges) in which prices can react swiftly to changes in supply and demand. These same two factors also promote keen competition among buyers and sellers, which greatly reduces the ability of any individual to affect prices.

Most participants in the wheat market or stock market think of themselves as price takers. A *price taker* is a market participant who takes the market price as given. For example, a small farmer correctly perceives that the market price of wheat is beyond his control. In contrast, a *price setter* has some power to set prices.

Markets having fewer participants and less standardized products than the wheat or stock markets may exhibit price-setting rather than price-taking behaviour. For example, consider the market for films in a medium-sized city. This market may be fairly competitive, with many different cinemas, each trying to attract customers from other cinemas, home video stores, and so on. Although the market for films is competitive, it is not competitive to the same degree as the wheat market. If a farmer tried to raise the price of a kilogram of his wheat by a small amount above the market price, he would sell no wheat; but a cinema that raised its ticket prices by the small amount above its competitors' prices would not lose all its customers. Because the cinema's product is not completely standardized (it is showing a different film than other cinemas, its location is better for some people, it has different chocolate bars in the concession stand, a larger screen, or more comfortable seats, and so on), the cinema has some price-setting discretion. It is a price setter, not a price taker.

Generally, a situation in which all buyers and sellers are price takers (such as the market for wheat) is called **perfect competition**. In contrast, a situation in which there is some competition, but in which a smaller number of sellers and imperfect standardization of the product allow individual producers to act as price setters, is called **monopolistic competition**.

Perfect competition is the model underlying the classical view of price determination, and as we have said, price rigidity or stickiness is extremely unlikely in a perfectly competitive market. Keynesians agree that price rigidity would not occur in a perfectly competitive market but point out that a relatively small part of the economy is perfectly competitive. Keynesians argue that price rigidity is possible, even likely, in a monopolistically competitive market.

To illustrate the issues, let us return to the example of the competing cinemas. If the market for cinema tickets were perfectly competitive, how would tickets be priced? Presumably, there would be some central meeting place where buyers and sellers of tickets would congregate. Market organizers would call out 'bids' (prices at which they are willing to buy) and 'asks' (prices at which they are willing to sell). Prices would fluctuate continuously as new information hit the market, causing supplies and demands to change. For example, a favourable review would instantly drive up the price of tickets to that film, but news of a prospective shortage of baby-sitters would cause all cinema ticket prices to fall.

Obviously, though, this is not how cinema tickets are priced. Actual pricing by most cinemas has the following three characteristics, which are also common to most price-setting markets:

1. Rather than accept the price of films as completely determined by the market, a cinema *sets* the price of tickets (or a schedule of prices), in *nominal* terms, and maintains the nominal price for some period of time.

2. At least within some range, the cinema *meets the demand* that is forthcoming at the fixed nominal price. By 'meets the demand' we mean that the cinema will sell as many tickets as people want to buy at its fixed price, to the point that all its seats are filled.

3. The cinema readjusts its price from time to time, generally when its costs or the level of demand changes significantly.

Can this type of pricing behaviour maximize profits? Keynesian theory suggests that it can, if there are costs associated with changing nominal prices, and if the market is monopolistically competitive.

Menu Costs and Price Setting. The classic example of a cost of changing prices is the cost that a restaurant faces when it has to reprint its menu to show changes in the prices of its offerings. Hence the cost of changing prices is called a **menu cost**. More general examples of menu costs (which can apply to any kind of firm) include costs of remarking merchandise, reprinting price lists and catalogues, and informing potential customers. Clearly, if firms incur costs when changing prices, they will change prices less often than they would otherwise, which creates a certain amount of price rigidity.

A potential problem with the menu cost explanation for price rigidity is that these costs seem to be rather small. How, then, can they be responsible for an amount of nominal rigidity that could have macroeconomic significance?

Here is the first point at which the monopolistic competition assumption is important. For a firm in a perfectly competitive market, getting the price 'a little bit wrong' has serious consequences: The farmer who prices his wheat a small amount per kilogram above the market price sells no corn. Therefore the existence of a menu cost would not prevent the farmer from pricing his product at precisely the correct level. However, the demand for the output of a monopolistically competitive firm responds much less sharply to changes in its price; the cinema does not lose many of its customers if its ticket price is slightly higher than its competitors'. Thus as long as the monopolistic competitor's price is in the right general range, the loss of profits from not getting the price exactly right is not too great. If the loss in profits is less than the cost of changing prices – the menu costs – the firm will not change its price.

Over time, the production function and the demand curve that the firm faces will undergo a variety of shocks so that eventually the profit-maximizing price for a firm may be significantly different from the preset price. When the profits lost by having the 'wrong' price clearly exceed the cost of changing the price, the firm will change its nominal price. Thus cinemas periodically raise their ticket and popcorn prices to reflect general inflation and other changes in market conditions.

Empirical Evidence on Price Stickiness. Several studies have examined the degree of rigidity or stickiness in actual prices. Using data first collected by Nobel laureate George Stigler and James Kindahl for the low-inflation period 1957–66, Dennis Carlton[9] of the University of Chicago documented that US industrial prices can be very sticky. Table 12.1, taken from Carlton's study, shows the average number of months between price changes for various industrial product groups. Note that for three of eleven groups the average time between price changes is more than a year. Using a statistical analysis, Carlton also found that prices were less rigid in relatively more competitive industries, a finding that fits the theory.

There is also some evidence that prices of consumer goods can be sticky. Stephen Cecchetti,[10] now of Ohio State University, studied the price changes of

---

9. 'The Rigidity of Prices', *American Economic Review*, September 1986, pp. 637–58.
10. 'The Frequency of Price Adjustment: A Study of the Newsstand Prices of Magazines', *Journal of Econometrics*, April 1986, pp. 255–74.

Table 12.1   Average Times Between Price Changes for Various Industries

Product Group (most to least rigid)	Average Time Between Price Changes (months)
Cement	13.2
Steel	13.0
Chemicals	12.8
Glass	10.2
Paper	8.7
Rubber tyres	8.1
Petroleum	5.9
Truck motors	5.4
Plywood	4.7
Non-ferrous metals	4.3
Household appliances	3.6

Source: Dennis W. Carlton, 'The Rigidity of Prices', *American Economic Review*, September 1986, pp. 637–58, Table 1.

38 newsstand magazines during the period 1953–79. He found that magazine prices are remarkably sticky. During the low-inflation period 1953–65 magazines changed their prices on average only once every seven and a half years. Even during the inflationary 1970s, price changes occurred on average less than once every three years. This degree of stickiness is probably greater than can be explained by simple menu costs. The direct cost of changing a magazine's price is virtually zero (a new cover that states the price must be printed for each issue anyway), and it is not very expensive to inform newsstands and subscribers of a price change. However, most magazine revenue comes from advertisers and subscribers (who usually do not pay the newsstand price). Hence publishers may not have found it profitable to review their pricing policies frequently. Perhaps more likely, publishers may have feared that raising prices before their close competitors did would cause them to lose customers. Thus neither *Time* nor *Newsweek* may have been willing to move first to raise its price, until it was obvious to customers as well as newsstands that a price increase was appropriate.

In another study of price stickiness Anil Kashyap,[11] now of the University of Chicago, examined the prices of twelve individual items listed in the catalogues of L.L. Bean, Orvis, and Recreational Equipment, Inc., over a 35-year period. Changing the prices listed in a new catalogue is virtually costless, yet Kashyap found that the nominal prices of many goods remained fixed in successive issues of the catalogue. When nominal prices were changed, Kashyap found both large and small changes. He interpreted the combination of small price changes and long periods of unchanged prices as evidence against menu costs. If menu costs are the reason that prices are not changed frequently, prices should be changed only when they are relatively far out of line, and the price changes should be large; small changes seem to contradict this implication of menu costs. Even if menu costs are not the underlying cause of pricing behaviour, however, Kashyap's study confirms the findings by Carlton and Cecchetti of substantial nominal-price rigidity in the economy.

Meeting the Demand at the Fixed Nominal Price. When prices are sticky, firms react to changes in demand by changing the amount of production rather than by changing prices. According to Keynesians, why are firms willing to meet demand at a fixed nominal price? To answer this question, we again rely on the assumption of monopolistic competition. We have stated that a monopolistically competitive firm can raise its price some without risk of losing all its customers. The profit-maximizing strategy for a monopolistically competitive firm is to charge a price higher than its **marginal cost**, or the cost of producing an additional unit of output. The excess of the price over the marginal cost is the **mark-up**. For example, if a firm charges a price 15% above its marginal cost, the firm has a mark-up of 15%. More generally, if the firm charges a constant mark-up of η over marginal cost, the following mark-up rule describes its price:

$$P = (1 + \eta)MC \tag{12.1}$$

11. 'Sticky Prices: New Evidence from Retail Catalogs', *Quarterly Journal of Economics*, February 1995, pp. 245–74.

where P is the nominal price charged by the firm and MC is the nominal marginal cost.[12]

When the firm sets its price according to equation (12.1), it has an idea of how many units will sell. Now suppose that, to the firm's surprise, customers demand several more units than the firm expected to sell at that price. Will it be profitable for the firm to meet the demand at this price?

The answer is 'yes.' Because the price the firm receives for each extra unit exceeds its cost of producing that extra unit (its marginal cost), the firm's profits increase when it sells additional units at the fixed price. Thus, as long as the marginal cost remains below the fixed price of its product, the firm gladly supplies more units at this fixed price. Furthermore, if the firm is paying an efficiency wage, it can easily hire more workers to produce the units needed to meet the demand, because there is an excess supply of labour.

The macroeconomic importance of firms' meeting demand at the fixed nominal price is that *the economy can produce an amount of output that is not on the full-employment line.* Recall that the *FE* line shows the amount of output that firms would produce after complete adjustment of all wages and prices. However, with nominal-price stickiness the prices of goods do not adjust rapidly to their general equilibrium values. During the period in which prices have not yet completely adjusted, the amount of output produced need not be on the *FE* line. Instead, as long as marginal cost is below the fixed price, monopolistically competitive firms will produce the level of output demanded.

Effective Labour Demand. When a firm meets the demand for its output at a specific price, it may produce a different amount of output and employ a different amount of labour than it had planned. How much labour will a firm actually employ when it meets the demand? The answer is given by the effective labour demand curve, $ND^e(Y)$, shown in Figure 12.3. For any amount of output Y, the **effective labour demand curve** indicates how much labour is needed to produce that output, with productivity, the capital stock, and effort held constant.

We already have a concept that expresses the relationship between the amount of labour used and the amount of output produced: the production function. Indeed, the effective labour demand curve in Figure 12.3 is simply a graph of the production function relating output and labour input, except that output Y is measured on the horizontal axis and labour N is measured on the vertical axis. (Reversing the units on the axes is convenient later.) The effective labour demand curve slopes upwards from left to right because a firm needs more labour in order to produce more output.

We use the effective labour demand curve to determine the level of employment in the Keynesian model in Section 12.3. When the economy is not on the *FE* line and the price level is fixed, the effective labour demand curve gives the level of employment. Then, after complete adjustment of wages and

---

12. Technical note: For a monopolistically competitive firm that faces a demand curve with a constant price elasticity and a fixed wage, the constant mark-up rule in equation (12.1) will maximize profit. Also, in this case the labour demand curve is proportional to (rather than equal to) the marginal product of labour curve. Specifically, to maximize profits the firm equates the MPN to $(1 + \eta)w^*$, where w^* is the efficiency wage, rather than equating the MPN to w^* itself. This qualification does not affect any conclusions presented in this chapter.

Figure 12.3
The effective labour demand curve
When a firm meets the demand for its output, it employs just the amount of labour needed to produce the quantity of output demanded. Because more labour is required to produce more output, firms must employ more labour when the demand for output is high. This relation between the amount of output demanded and the amount of labour employed is the effective labour demand curve. The effective labour demand curve is the same as the production function relating output and labour, except that labour is plotted on the vertical axis and output is plotted on the horizontal axis.

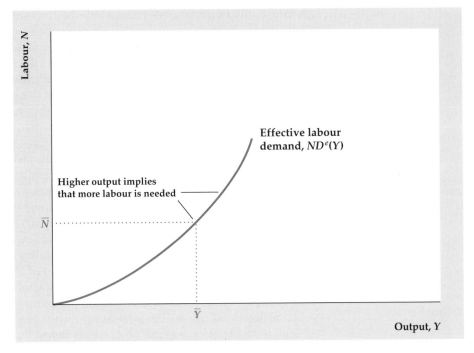

prices, the economy returns to the *FE* line and the level of employment is given by the labour demand curve *ND** (Figure 12.2). After wages and prices have completely adjusted, with output at its full-employment level $\overline{Y}$, the effective labour demand curve indicates that employment equals $\overline{N}$, as shown in Figure 12.3.

12.3   MONETARY AND FISCAL POLICY IN THE KEYNESIAN MODEL

Let us now consider the complete Keynesian model. Like the classical model, the Keynesian model can be expressed in terms of the *IS–LM* diagram, or alternatively, in terms of the *AD–AS* diagram. Rather than describe the Keynesian model in the abstract, we put it to work analysing the effects of monetary and fiscal policy. Appendix 12.B presents an algebraic analysis of the short-run behaviour of the economy in the Keynesian model.

Monetary Policy

The main reason for introducing nominal-price stickiness into the Keynesian model was to explain monetary non-neutrality. We examine the link between price stickiness and monetary non-neutrality first in the Keynesian *IS–LM* framework and then in the *AD–AS* version of the Keynesian model.

Monetary Policy in the Keynesian *IS–LM* Model. The Keynesian version of the *IS–LM* model is quite similar to the *IS–LM* model discussed in Chapters 10 and 11. In particular, the *IS* curve and the *LM* curve are the same as in our earlier analyses. The *FE* line in the Keynesian model is also similar to the *FE* line used earlier. The Keynesian *FE* line is vertical at the full-employment level of output $\overline{Y}$, which in turn depends on the full-employment level of employment determined in the labour market. However, the Keynesian and classical *FE* lines are different in two respects. First, in the Keynesian model the full-employment level of employment is determined at the intersection of the labour demand curve and the efficiency wage line, not at the point where the quantities of labour demanded and supplied are equal, as in the classical model. Second, because labour supply does not affect employment in the efficiency wage model, changes in labour supply do not affect the Keynesian *FE* line, although changes in labour supply do affect the classical *FE* line.

Because of price stickiness, in the Keynesian model the economy does not have to be in general equilibrium in the short run. However, in the long run when prices adjust, the economy reaches its general equilibrium at the intersection of the *IS* curve, the *LM* curve, and the *FE* line, as in the classical model.

According to Keynesians, what happens to the economy in the short run, if sticky prices prevent it from reaching general equilibrium? Keynesians assume that the asset market clears quickly and that the level of output is determined by aggregate demand. Thus, according to Keynesians, *the economy always lies at the intersection of the IS and LM curves.* However, because monopolistically competitive firms are willing to meet the demand for goods at fixed levels of prices, output can differ from full-employment output and the economy may not be on the *FE* line in the short run. When the economy is off the *FE* line, firms use just enough labour to produce the output needed to meet demand. Under the assumption that the efficiency wage is higher than the market-clearing real wage, there are always unemployed workers who want to work, and firms are able to change employment as needed to meet the demand for output without changing the wage.

Figure 12.4 analyses the effect of a decrease in the nominal money supply in the Keynesian *IS–LM* model. We assume that the economy starts at its general equilibrium point, *E*. Recall that a decrease in the money supply shifts the *LM* curve up and to the left, from LM^1 to LM^2 (Figure 12.4(a)). Because a decrease in the money supply does not directly affect the goods or labour market, the *IS* curve and the *FE* line are unaffected. So far this analysis is like that of the classical model.

Unlike the classical model, however, the Keynesian model assumes temporarily fixed prices (because of menu costs) so that the general equilibrium at *E* is not restored immediately. Instead, the short-run equilibrium of the economy – that is, the resting point of the economy at the fixed price level – lies at the intersection of *IS* and LM^2 (point *F*), where output drops to Y_2 and the real interest rate rises to r_2.

Because the *IS–LM* intersection at point *F* is to the left of the *FE* line, aggregate output demanded, Y_2, is less than the full-employment level of output, $\overline{Y}$. Monopolistically competitive firms facing menu costs do not cut their prices in the short run, as competitive firms do. Instead they cut production to Y_2 to satisfy the lower level of demand. To reduce production, firms cut employment – for example, by laying off workers or putting some employees on part-time schedules. The level of employment is given by the effective labour demand curve in Figure 12.4(b). Because the level of output falls from $\overline{Y}$ to Y_2 in the short run, the level of employment falls from $\overline{N}$ to N_2.

**Figure 12.4
A decrease in the
money supply**
(a) If we start from an
initial general equilibrium
at point E, a decrease in
the money supply shifts
the LM curve up and to
the left, from LM^1 to LM^2;
the IS curve and the FE
line remain unchanged.
Because prices are fixed
and firms meet the
demand for output in the
short run, the economy
moves to point F, which is
to the left of the FE line.
Output falls to Y_2 and the
real interest rate rises.
(b) Because firms produce
less output, employment
falls to N_2, as shown by
the effective labour
demand curve.

In the long run, the price
level falls in the same
proportion as the money
supply, the real money
supply returns to its initial
level, and the LM curve
returns to its initial
position, LM^1, in (a). The
economy returns to E in
both (a) and (b), and
money is neutral in the
long run.

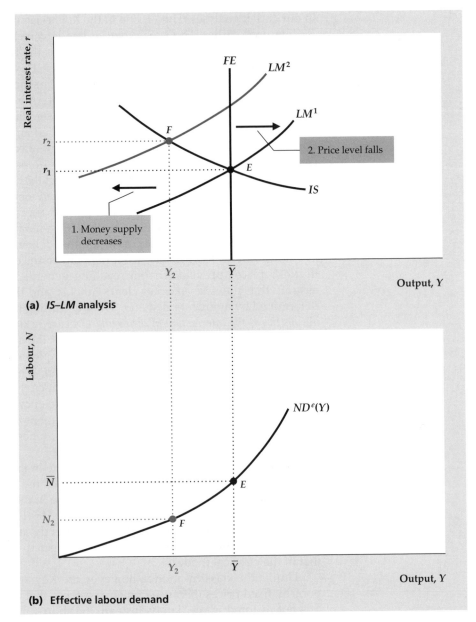

(a) *IS–LM analysis*

(b) **Effective labour demand**

We refer to a monetary policy that shifts the LM curve up and to the left –
and thus reduces output and employment – as a contractionary monetary
policy, or 'tight' money. Analogously, an expansionary monetary policy, or
'easy' money, is an increase in the money supply that shifts the LM curve
down and to the right, raising output and employment.

Why does tight money reduce output in the Keynesian model? In the Keynesian model prices are fixed in the short run, so a reduction in the nominal
money supply M also is a reduction in the real money supply M/P. Recall
that, for holders of wealth to be willing to hold more non-monetary assets and

less real money, the real interest rate must rise.[13] Finally, the higher interest rate reduces both consumption spending (because saving rises) and investment spending. With less demand for their output, firms cut production and lay off workers, taking the economy to point F in Figure 12.4.

The rigidity of the price level is not permanent. Eventually, firms will review and readjust their prices, allowing the economy to reach its long-run equilibrium. In the case of monetary contraction, firms find that demand for their products in the short run is less than they had planned (aggregate output demanded Y_2 is less than full-employment output $\overline{Y}$), so eventually they lower their prices. The decline in the price level returns the real money supply to its initial level, which shifts the LM curve back to LM^1 and restores the general equilibrium at point E in Figure 12.4(a). This adjustment process is exactly the same as in the classical model, but it proceeds more slowly.

Thus, the Keynesian model predicts that *money is not neutral in the short run but is neutral in the long run*. In this respect the predictions of the Keynesian model are the same as those of the extended classical model with misperceptions. In the Keynesian model short-run price stickiness prevents the economy from reaching its general equilibrium, but in the long run prices are flexible, ensuring general equilibrium.

The Keynesian *AD–AS* Framework

Macroeconomic behaviour in the Keynesian model can also be represented in terms of aggregate demand and aggregate supply. The aggregate demand (*AD*) curve in the Keynesian model (Figure 12.5) is the same as that in the classical model (see Figure 11.5). The *AD* curve relates the aggregate quantity of output demanded to the price level. Recall that an increase in the price level P reduces the real money supply M/P and shifts the LM curve up and to the left. Because the aggregate demand for goods corresponds to the intersection of the IS curve and the LM curve, a shift of the LM curve to the left reduces the aggregate quantity of output demanded. Because an increase in the price level reduces the aggregate quantity of output demanded, the *AD* curve slopes downwards.

In the Keynesian model the short-run aggregate supply curve, *SRAS*, is a horizontal line, as shown in Figure 12.5. The reason is that, with monopolistic competition and menu costs, firms hold the price level P fixed in the short run and produce the level of output needed to satisfy demand. Thus the *SRAS* curve is horizontal at the initial price level. However, in the long run, after complete price adjustment, firms produce the full-employment level of output $\overline{Y}$ regardless of the price level P. Because the amount of output supplied by firms does not depend on the price level in the long run, the long-run aggregate supply curve, *LRAS*, is a vertical line at $Y = \overline{Y}$, as in the classical version of the model. The economy's long-run equilibrium is at the intersection of the *AD* curve and the *LRAS* curve, or point E in Figure 12.5. At the long-run equilibrium point, output equals its full-employment level, and the price level equalizes the aggregate quantities of output demanded and supplied.

---

13. As we discussed in Chapter 10, the real interest rate is driven up by wealth-holders' attempts to exchange non-monetary assets for money. The selling of non-monetary assets drives down their prices, which is the same as increasing the real interest rate that they pay.

Figure 12.5
**The Keynesian *AD–AS*
framework**
The aggregate demand
(*AD*) curve slopes
downward in the
Keynesian model for the
same reason it slopes
downward in the classical
model: an increase in the
price level reduces the real
money supply, which
shifts the *LM* curve up and
to the left and reduces the
aggregate quantity of
output demanded. The
short-run aggregate
supply (*SRAS*) curve is
horizontal in the
Keynesian model because
firms meet the demand
for their output at a fixed
price. In the long run,
prices adjust completely
so that firms produce the
full-employment level of
output $\overline{Y}$ regardless of
the price level. Thus the
long-run aggregate supply
(*LRAS*) curve is vertical at
$Y = \overline{Y}$.

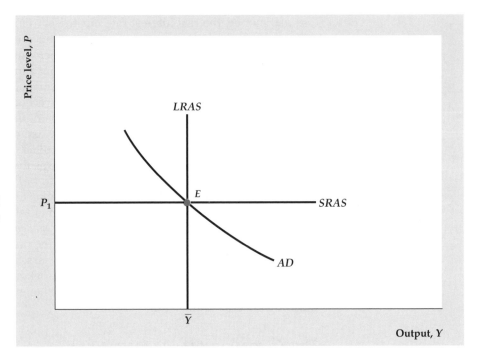

Let us examine monetary neutrality in the Keynesian *AD–AS* framework by supposing that the economy is initially in long-run equilibrium at point *E* in Figure 12.6, that output equals $\overline{Y}$, that the price level equals P_1, and that the central bank then reduces the money supply by 10%. As in the classical model, the reduction in the money supply shifts the *AD* curve down by 10% at each level of output, from AD^1 to AD^2. The short-run equilibrium is at point *F*, where AD^2 intersects the short-run aggregate supply curve $SRAS^1$. At *F* the price level is unchanged from its initial value of P_1, and output equals the aggregate quantity of output demanded at that price level, Y_2. Point *F* is analogous to point *F* in the *IS–LM* diagram in Figure 12.4, where the price level also equalled its initial value and output also equalled the quantity of output demanded at that price level.

The economy does not stay at point *F* for ever. Because the quantity of output demanded, Y_2, is smaller than the full-employment level of output, $\overline{Y}$, firms eventually reduce their prices. The *SRAS* curve gives the price level at which firms are willing to meet the demand; thus as the prices set by firms fall, the *SRAS* curve moves down. In the long run the price level falls by 10%, and the economy reaches general equilibrium at point *H*, where the aggregate demand curve AD^2 intersects the long-run aggregate supply curve *LRAS*. The drop in the price level shifts the short-run aggregate supply curve down to $SRAS^2$, so that it too passes through *H* in the long run.

Because the *AD–AS* framework and the *IS–LM* model are equivalent, they lead to the same conclusions about monetary neutrality. In the short run the Keynesian *AD–AS* framework implies that money is not neutral because the reduction in money supply causes output to fall (point *F* in Figure 12.6). However, as in the *IS–LM* model, money is neutral in the long run in the

Figure 12.6
A decrease in the money supply in the Keynesian *AD–AS* framework

If we start from the full-employment general equilibrium at point *E*, a 10% reduction in the money supply shifts the *AD* curve down by 10% at each level of output, from AD^1 to AD^2. In the short run, the economy moves to point *F*, where the new aggregate demand curve AD^2 intersects the short-run aggregate supply curve $SRAS^1$. At *F* output has fallen to Y_2. Because aggregate output demanded is less than $\overline{Y}$, the price level falls. In the long run the economy returns to full-employment general equilibrium at point *H*, where AD^2 intersects the vertical long-run aggregate supply curve *LRAS*. Output returns to $\overline{Y}$, and the new price level P_2 is 10% lower than the initial price level P_1. Thus, again, money is neutral in the long run. As a result of the drop in the price level, the short-run aggregate supply curve shifts down, to $SRAS^2$.

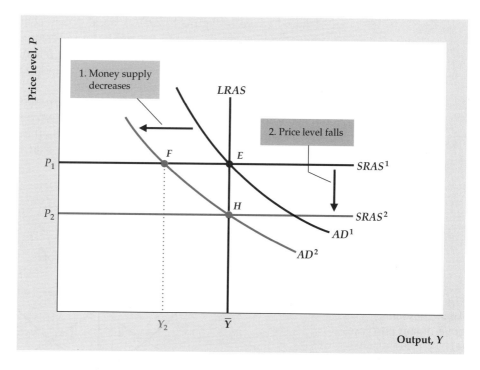

AD–AS framework. Changes in the money supply leave output unchanged and affect only the price level (point *H* in Figure 12.6).

Fiscal Policy

The Keynesian model was initially developed during the Great Depression as economists struggled to explain the worldwide economic collapse and find policies to help the economy return to normal. The early Keynesians stressed that fiscal policy, the government's decisions about government purchases and taxes, can significantly affect output and employment levels. Let's look at the Keynesians' conclusion that both increased government purchases and lower taxes can be used to raise output and employment.

The Effect of Increased Government Purchases. The Keynesian analysis of how increased government purchases affect the economy is shown in Figure 12.7. Again, we assume that the economy starts from full employment (later we discuss what happens if the economy starts from a recession). Point *E* represents the initial equilibrium in both (a) and (b). As before, a temporary increase in government purchases increases the demand for goods and reduces desired national saving at any level of the real interest rate, so that the *IS* curve shifts up and to the right, from IS^1 to IS^2 (see Summary table 12, p. 344). In the short run, before prices can adjust, the economy moves to point *F* in Figure 12.7(a), where the new *IS* curve, IS^2, and LM^1 intersect. At *F* both output and the real interest rate have increased, to Y_2 and r_2 respectively. Because firms meet the higher demand at the fixed price level, employment also rises, from $\overline{N}$ to N_2, as shown by the movement from point *E* to point *F* along the effective labour demand curve in Figure 12.7(b). A fiscal policy change, such as this one, that shifts the *IS* curve up and to the right and raises output and employment is an expansionary change. Similarly, a fiscal policy (such as a reduction in government purchases) that shifts the *IS* curve down and to the left and reduces output and employment is a contractionary change.

In discussing the effects of increased government purchases or other types of spending, Keynesians often use the multiplier concept. The **multiplier** associated with any particular type of spending is the short-run change in total output resulting from a one-unit change in that type of spending. So, for

Figure 12.7
An increase in government purchases
(a) If we start from the general equilibrium at point *E*, an increase in government purchases reduces desired national saving and shifts the *IS* curve up and to the right, from IS^1 to IS^2. The short-run equilibrium is at point *F*, with output increasing to Y_2 and the real interest rate rising to r_2.
(b) As firms increase production to meet the demand, employment increases from $\bar{N}$ to N_2, as shown by the effective labour demand curve. However, the economy does not remain at point *F*. Because aggregate output demanded exceeds $\bar{Y}$ in the short run, the price level increases, reducing the real money supply and shifting the *LM* curve up and to the left, from LM^1 to LM^2. In the long run, with equilibrium at point *H*, output returns to $\bar{Y}$ and employment returns to $\bar{N}$, but the real interest rate rises further to r_3.

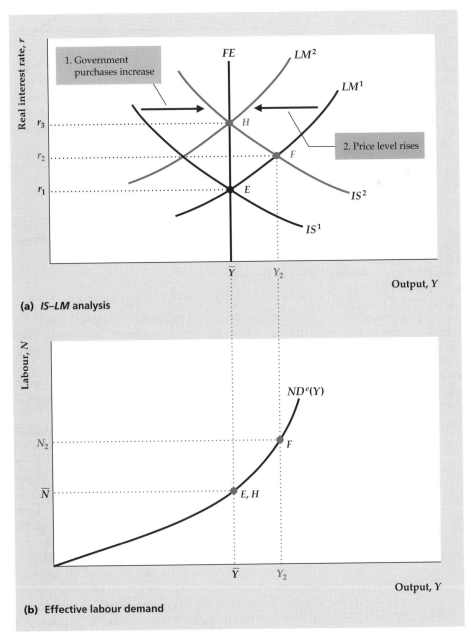

(a) *IS–LM* analysis

(b) **Effective labour demand**

example, if the increase in government purchases analysed in Figure 12.7 is ΔG and the resulting short-run increase in output between points E and F in Figure 12.7 is ΔY, the multiplier associated with government purchases is $\Delta Y / \Delta G$. Keynesians usually argue that the fiscal policy multiplier is greater than 1, so that if government purchases rise by DM1 billion, output will rise by more than DM1 billion. Unlike the classical analysis, which indicates that government spending diverts resources from the private-sector, Keynesian analysis indicates that fiscal expansion can actually increase private sector resources in the short run, if the government purchases multiplier is greater than 1. We derive an algebraic expression for the government purchases multiplier in Appendix 12.B.

Recall that the classical version of the $IS–LM$ model also predicts that a temporary increase in government purchases increases output, but in a different way. The classical analysis focuses on the fact that increased government purchases require higher current or future taxes to pay for the extra spending. Higher taxes make workers (who are taxpayers) effectively poorer, which induces them to supply more labour. This increase in labour supply shifts the FE line to the right and causes output to rise in the classical model. In contrast, the FE line in the Keynesian model does not depend on labour supply (because of efficiency wages) and thus is unaffected by the increase in government purchases. Instead, the increase in government purchases affects output by raising aggregate demand (that is, by shifting the $IS–LM$ intersection to the right). Output increases above its full-employment level in the short run as firms satisfy extra demand at the initial price level.

The effect of increased government purchases on output in the Keynesian model lasts only as long as needed for the price level to adjust. (However, many Keynesians believe that price adjustment is sufficiently slow that this effect could be felt for several years.) In the long run, when firms adjust their prices, the LM curve moves up and to the left, from LM^1 to LM^2 in Figure 12.7(a), and the economy reaches general equilibrium at point H, with output again at $\overline{Y}$ and employment at $\overline{N}$. Thus an increase in government purchases does not raise output in the long run. However, the real interest rate further to r_3.

The effects of more government purchases also appear in the Keynesian $AD–AS$ framework (Figure 12.8). Increased government purchases shift the IS curve up and to the right and raise the aggregate demand for output at any given price level. Thus as a result of expansionary fiscal policy, the aggregate demand curve shifts to the right, from AD^1 to AD^2. The increase in aggregate demand raises output from $\overline{Y}$ to Y_2, as shown by the shift from the initial equilibrium at point E to the short-run equilibrium at point F. At F the aggregate demand for output is greater than full-employment output, so firms eventually raise their prices. In the long run the economy reaches the full-employment general equilibrium at point H, with output again at $\overline{Y}$ and with a higher price level at P_2. These results are identical to those we obtained using the Keynesian $IS–LM$ framework.

The Effect of Lower Taxes.
Keynesians generally believe that, like an increase in government purchases, a lump-sum reduction in current taxes is expansionary. In other words, they expect that a tax cut will shift the IS curve up and to the right, raising output and employment in the short run. Similarly, they expect a tax increase to be contractionary, shifting the IS curve down and to the left.

Figure 12.8
An increase in government purchases in the Keynesian *AD–AS* framework
An increase in government purchases raises the aggregate demand for output at any price level (see Fig. 12.7). Thus the aggregate demand curve shifts to the right, from AD^1 to AD^2. In the short run the increase in aggregate demand increases output to Y_2 (point F) but does not affect the price level, because prices are sticky in the short run. Because aggregate output demanded Y_2 exceeds $\overline{Y}$ at F, firms eventually raise their prices. The long-run equilibrium is at H, where AD^2 intersects the long-run aggregate supply curve *LRAS*. At H, output has returned to $\overline{Y}$ and the price level has risen from P_1 to P_2. The higher price level raises the short-run aggregate supply curve, from $SRAS^1$ to $SRAS^2$.

APPLICATION

Macroeconomic Policy and the Real Interest Rate in the UK in the Early 1980s and the Early 1990s

Why does a tax cut affect the *IS* curve, according to Keynesians? The argument is that if consumers receive a tax cut, they will spend part of it on increased consumption. For any output Y and level of government purchases G, an increase in desired consumption arising from a tax cut will lower desired national saving, $Y - C^d - G$. A drop in desired saving raises the real interest rate that clears the goods market and shifts the *IS* curve up.[14]

If a tax cut raises desired consumption and shifts the *IS* curve upwards, as Keynesians claim, the effects on the economy are similar to the effects of increased government purchases (Figures 12.7 and 12.8). In the short run a tax cut raises aggregate demand and thus output and employment at the initial price level. In the long run, after complete price adjustment, the economy returns to full employment with a higher real interest rate than in the initial general equilibrium. The only difference between the tax cut and the increase in government purchases is that, instead of raising the portion of full-employment output devoted to government purchases, a tax cut raises the portion of full-employment output devoted to consumption.

In the early 1980s both UK monetary and fiscal policy changed significantly. The shift actually began in May 1979 with the election of the Thatcher government and its announcement that it was committed to bringing down inflation, which was running at nearly 17% per year at the time, by tightening monetary

14. In arguing that a tax cut raises desired consumption and lowers desired national saving, Keynesian economists reject the Ricardian equivalence proposition (Chapter 4), which states that a lump-sum tax cut should *not* affect consumption or national saving. Ricardian equivalence is discussed further in Chapter 16.

policy. Fiscal policy also became more contractionary. In 1980 the Thatcher government introduced the Medium-Term Financial Strategy (MTFS), which represented a fundamental change in macroeconomic policy formulation. The main element of the MTFS was that it set targets to bring down the growth in the money supply over a four-year period. Fiscal policy was to be used in association with the tight monetary policy to offset excessive increases in the rate of interest.

The combined effects of tight money and a contractionary fiscal policy are illustrated in Figure 12.9. The economy was essentially at full employment in 1979 (unemployment was 4.0% of the labour force, close to its normal level, and the business cycle reached a peak in late 1979), so the initial situation in 1979 is represented by the full-employment general equilibrium at point E. Following the Thatcher government's commitment to bring down inflation, money growth fell below its previous trend, causing the LM curve to shift up and to the left, from LM^1 to LM^2. The contractionary fiscal policy shifted the IS curve down and to the left, from IS^1 to IS^2. As a result of the two policy changes, the economy shifted from point E to a short-run equilibrium at point F.

What effects did this policy mix have on the economy? According to the Keynesian analysis in Figure 12.9, the effect on the interest rate is ambiguous, because tight monetary policy tends to raise the real interest rate but a tight fiscal policy tends to reduce it. In other words, whether the government can achieve its aim of holding down the rate of interest is unclear. Actually, the real interest rate rose in the early 1980s to its highest level since the 1930s.

Although the effect on the interest rate is unclear, the combination of tight monetary and contractionary fiscal policies has an unambiguous impact in reducing output. In fact, the UK economy went into recession in the early 1980s.

Figure 12.9
Tight money and a contractionary fiscal policy

The UK economy was essentially at full employment in 1979 (point E), and late in the year the government tightened monetary growth in an attempt to reduce inflation. The reduction in monetary growth shifted the LM curve up and to the left, from LM^1 to LM^2. In addition, the government reduced government purchases, shifting the IS curve down and to the left, from IS^1 to IS^2. With tight money and a tight fiscal policy, the economy moved to point F with a lower level of output causing a recession. Point F is drawn so that it lies above point E, indicating that the contractionary effects of tight money on the rate of interest outweighed the impact of the reduction in government purchases which push the rate of interest down.

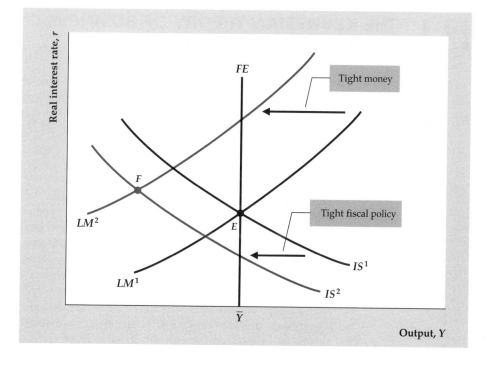

As the 1990s began, the UK economy was again at full employment (the business cycle reached a peak in May 1990) and again received doses of monetary and fiscal medicine. However, this time the policy changes were not in the same direction as those at the beginning of the 1980s. On the monetary side, the upsurge in inflation during the period 1988–90, when it went above 10%, led the government to tighten monetary policy during 1989–91. On the fiscal side, the government leaned towards an easing of fiscal policy, with general government expenditures on both defence and housing increasing. The Keynesian model predicts that this combination of easy fiscal policy and tight money should increase the real interest rate, and interest rates did indeed rise. For example, between early 1988 and early 1990, the three-month Treasury bill interest rate rose from almost 9% to more than 15%. However, interest rates then started to fall again despite the tight monetary policy and easy fiscal policy. One reason for this may be the dramatic fall in consumer confidence during 1989 and 1990 (see Figure 4.1(a)). As Figure 12.9 illustrates, the Keynesian model predicts that a fall in consumer sentiment causes the *IS* curve to shift downwards, reducing the real interest rate. The impact of a decline in consumer confidence on the rate of interest thus works in the opposite direction to both the expansionary fiscal policy and tight monetary policy, and may explain why interest rates did not rise as much as one might have expected.

As often happens, reality was more complicated than suggested by these simple analyses. One important complication was that oil price shocks occurred both during 1979–80 and in 1990 (see Figure 3.11). Nevertheless, a Keynesian interpretation that focuses on the role of the policy mix seems to explain the behaviour of at least one important macroeconomic variable, the real interest rate, fairly well.

12.4   THE KEYNESIAN THEORY OF BUSINESS CYCLES AND MACROECONOMIC STABILIZATION

Recall that there are two basic questions about business cycles that a macroeconomic theory should try to answer: (1) What causes recurrent fluctuations in the economy? and (2) What, if anything, should policymakers try to do about cycles? We are now ready to give the Keynesian answers to these two questions.

Keynesian Business Cycle Theory

An explanation of the business cycle requires not only a macroeconomic model but also some assumptions about the types of shock hitting the economy. For example, RBC theorists believe that productivity shocks, which directly shift the *FE* line, are the most important type of macroeconomic shock.

In contrast to RBC theorists, most Keynesians believe that aggregate demand shocks are the primary source of business cycle fluctuations. **Aggregate demand shocks** are shocks to the economy that shift *either* the *IS* curve or the *LM* curve and thus affect the aggregate demand for output. Examples of aggregate demand shocks affecting the *IS* curve are changes in fiscal policy, changes in desired investment arising from changes in the expected future

marginal product of capital,[15] and changes in consumer confidence about the
future that affect desired saving. Examples of aggregate demand shocks affecting the *LM* curve are changes in the demand for money or changes in the
money supply. The Keynesian version of the *IS–LM* model, combined with the
view that most shocks are aggregate demand shocks, constitutes the Keynesian theory of business cycles.

Figure 12.10 uses the Keynesian model to illustrate a recession caused by
an aggregate demand shock. The economy starts at general equilbrium at
point *E*. Suppose that consumers become pessimistic about the long-term
future of the economy and thus reduce their current desired consumption;
equivalently, they raise their current desired saving. For any level of income,
an increase in desired saving lowers the real interest rate that clears the goods
market and thus shifts the *IS* curve down, from IS^1 to IS^2. The economy goes
into recession at point *F*, and, as prices do not adjust immediately to restore
full employment, it remains in recession for some period of time with output
below its full-employment level $\overline{Y}$. Because firms face below-normal levels of
demand, they also cut employment.

Note that a decline in investment spending (reflecting, for example, pessimism of business investors) or reduced government purchases would have
similar recessionary effects to the decline in consumer spending analysed in
Figure 12.10. Alternatively, a shift to the left of the *LM* curve (because of

---

15. A change in the expected future *MPK* might also be thought of as a technological shock
because it involves a change in the future production function. However, because a change in the
future *MPK* shifts the *IS* curve but does not affect the current *FE* line, Keynesians classify it as an
aggregate demand shock.

**Figure 12.10
A recession arising
from an aggregate
demand shock**
The figure illustrates how
an adverse aggregate
demand shock can cause
a recession in the
Keynesian model. The
economy starts at general
equilibrium at point *E*. A
decline in consumer
confidence about the
future of the economy
reduces desired
consumption and raises
desired saving so that the
IS curve shifts down, from
IS^1 to IS^2. The economy
falls into recession at
point *F*, with output
below its full-employment
level $\overline{Y}$.

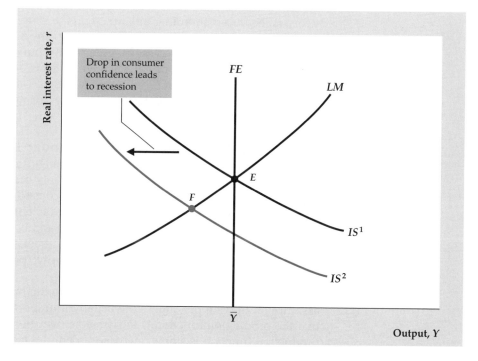

either increased money demand or reduced money supply) could also cause a recession in the Keynesian framework; in this case, high real interest rates caused by the 'shortage' of money would cause the declines in consumer spending and investment. Thus Keynesians attribute recessions to 'not enough demand' for goods, in contrast to classical economists who attribute recessions to 'not enough supply.'

Like the real business cycle theory, the Keynesian theory of cycles can account for several of the business cycle facts: (1) in response to occasional aggregate demand shocks, the theory predicts recurrent fluctuations in output; (2) the theory correctly implies that employment will fluctuate in the same direction as output; and (3) because it predicts that shocks to the money supply will be non-neutral, the theory is consistent with the business cycle fact that money is procyclical and leading.

A business cycle fact that we previously emphasized (Chapter 9) is that spending on investment goods and other durable goods is strongly procyclical and volatile. This cyclical behaviour of durable goods spending can be explained by the Keynesian theory if shocks to durable goods demand are themselves a main source of cycles. The demand for durable goods would be a source of cyclical fluctuations if, for example, investors frequently reassessed their expectations of the future *MPK*. Keynes himself thought that waves of investor optimism and pessimism, which he called 'animal spirits,' were a significant source of cyclical fluctuations. A rise in the demand for investment goods or consumer durables (at fixed levels of output and the real interest rate) is expansionary because it shifts the *IS* curve to the right. Investment will also be procyclical in the Keynesian model whenever cycles are caused by fluctuations in the *LM* curve: for example, an increase in the money supply that shifts the *LM* curve down and to the right both increases output and (by reducing the real interest rate) increases investment.

Another important business cycle fact that is consistent with the Keynesian theory is the observation that inflation tends to slow during or just after recessions (inflation is procyclical and lagging). In the Keynesian view, as Figure 12.10 illustrates, during a recession aggregate output demanded is less than the full-employment level of output. Thus when firms do adjust their prices, they will be likely to cut them in order to increase their sales. According to the Keynesian model, because demand pressure is low during recessions, inflation will tend to subside when the economy is weak.

Procyclical Labour Productivity and Labour Hoarding. Although the Keynesian model is consistent with many of the business cycle facts, one fact – that labour productivity is procyclical – presents problems for this approach. Recall that procyclical labour productivity is consistent with the real business cycle assumption that cycles are caused by productivity shocks – that recessions are times when productivity is unusually low and booms are times when productivity is unusually high. Unlike the RBC theorists, however, Keynesians assume that demand shocks rather than supply (productivity) shocks cause most cyclical fluctuations.

Because supply shocks are shifts of the production function, the Keynesian assumption that supply shocks are usually unimportant is the same as saying that the production function is fairly stable over the business cycle. But if the production function is stable, increases in employment during booms should *reduce* average labour productivity because of the diminishing marginal productivity of labour. Thus the Keynesian model predicts that average labour productivity is countercyclical, contrary to the business cycle fact.

To explain the procyclical behaviour of average labour productivity, Keynesians have modified their models to include labour hoarding. As discussed in Section 11.1, **labour hoarding** occurs if firms retain, or 'hoard', labour in a recession rather than laying off or firing workers. The reason that firms might hoard labour during a recession is to avoid the costs of letting workers go and then having to rehire them or hire and train new workers when the recession ends. Thus hoarded labour may be used less intensively (for example, shop assistants may wait on fewer customers in a day) or be assigned to activities such as painting, cleaning, maintaining equipment, and training. If labour is utilized less intensively during a recession, or workers spend time on activities such as maintenance that do not directly contribute to measured output, labour productivity may fall during a recession even though the production function is stable. Thus labour hoarding provides a way of explaining the procyclical behaviour of average labour productivity without assuming that recessions and expansions are caused by productivity shocks.

Macroeconomic Stabilization

From the Keynesian explanation of why business cycles occur we turn to the Keynesian view on how policymakers should respond to recessions and booms. Briefly, Keynesians – unlike classical economists – generally favour policy actions to 'stabilize' the economy by eliminating large fluctuations in output and employment. Keynesian support of more active policy measures follows from the theory's characterization of business cycle expansions and contractions as periods in which the economy is temporarily away from its general equilibrium (or not at the *IS–LM–FE* intersection). According to Keynesians, recessions are particularly undesirable because in a recession employment may be far below the amount of labour that workers want to supply, which leads to hardships for the unemployed and to output that is 'too low'. Keynesians therefore argue that average economic well-being would be increased if governments tried to reduce cyclical fluctuations, especially recessions.

The Keynesian analysis of monetary and fiscal policies suggests that these policies could be used to smooth the business cycle. To understand how, consider Figure 12.11. Suppose that the economy, initially in general equilibrium at point *E*, has been driven into recession at point *F*. Various types of shock could have caused this recession. In Figure 12.10, for example, we considered a drop in consumer confidence about the future of the economy. A drop in confidence would reduce current desired consumption and increase current desired saving, thereby shifting the *IS* curve down from IS^1 to IS^2 (See Box 12.2).

How might policymakers respond to this recession? We consider three possibilities: (1) no change in monetary or fiscal policy; (2) an increase in the money supply; and (3) an increase in government purchases.

■ *Scenario 1: No change in macroeconomic policy.* One policy option is to do nothing. With no government intervention, the economy will eventually correct itself. At point *F* in Figure 12.11 aggregate output demanded is below the full-employment level of output $\overline{Y}$. Therefore, over time, prices will begin to

BOX 12.2

The Role of a Credit Crunch in the 1990–91 Recession

In early 1990, both the UK and US economies reached business cycle peaks before entering recessions that lasted until the last quarter of 1991 in the case of the UK and eight months in the USA. A major factor contributing to these recessions was increased consumer pessimism in both countries, caused possibly by the Iraqi invasion of Kuwait and the resulting increase in oil prices. The index of consumer sentiment for the UK, shown in Figure 4.1(a), fell sharply through 1989, reaching its lowest point for more than ten years in the first quarter of 1990. Similarly, the US index of consumer sentiment dropped from a value of 88.2 in July 1990 to only 63.9 three months later. As illustrated in Figure 12.10, a decline in consumer sentiment (resulting in lower consumer expenditure) causes the IS curve to shift downwards from IS^1 to IS^2, thereby causing both output and the real interest rate to fail.

Besides the decline in consumer sentiment, a second factor that was widely cited as a possible cause of the 1990–91 recession in the USA was the 'credit crunch'.* A *credit crunch* is a reduction in the supply of loans made available by banks and other lenders (such as savings and loan associations and credit unions) at any given real interest rate. During the 1980s and early 1990s many US banks, and especially savings and loan associations, suffered losses on their loans, and some of these institutions went bankrupt. Many observers argued that these widespread problems reduced the supply of loans by banks and other lenders. One reason for the reduced supply was that US regulators imposed tougher standards on banks, forcing them to reduce the riskiness of their lending and limiting the share of their assets that they could lend; as a result, banks were able to make fewer loans, particularly to consumers and builders. Banks also adopted more conservative lending policies on their own without being compelled by regulators, in the hope of avoiding more financial problems of the type that plagued them during the 1980s. During the late 1980s and early 1990s, the profitability of UK banks was also hit by a sharp rise in bad debts, especially in the corporate sector, which resulted in banks adopting much more cautious lending criteria. A reduction in the supply of loans at any given interest rate makes it more difficult

for consumers and others to finance planned purchases, reducing the effective demand for goods and services by potential borrowers. In terms of the IS–LM model, a credit crunch can therefore be interpreted as a shift of the IS curve down and to the left. A leftward shift of the IS curve caused by a credit crunch would act to reinforce the effect of a decline in consumer sentiment shown in Figure 12.10.

Hard evidence that the credit crunch played a major role in the 1990–91 recessions on either side of the Atlantic is lacking. Bank loans did fall significantly in both the UK and USA during the recession, which is consistent with a decline in the supply of loans, but this could also be explained by a falling demand for loans. Indeed, there is evidence that the demand for loans fell unusually sharply during this recession. For example, large corporations borrow from banks but are also able to borrow by selling short-term bonds known as commercial paper. Typically, during recessions, banks reduce their lending but the amount of commercial paper outstanding increases as large borrowers turn to this alternative source of credit. However, during the 1990–91 recession, the amount of borrowing in the commercial paper market actually fell, suggesting that corporations chose to reduce their borrowing from all sources (that is, credit demand declined). With respect to consumers, we know from past experience that consumer demand for credit falls when consumer sentiment falls, as it did during the 1990–91 recession. In the UK, the domestic property market declined sharply from around 1985 with house prices in some parts of the country falling.

The fact that many consumers and businesses had built up large amounts of debt during the 1980s meant that they were reluctant to borrow further, given the uncertain economic climate. We conclude, therefore, that the fall in bank lending during the recession was due as much, if not more, to a drop in loan demand as to a credit crunch. However, whether the ultimate sources of the decline in lending came from the demand side or the supply side of the credit market is not so important for macroeconomic purposes. In either case, the factors which slowed bank lending also reduced spending by consumers and firms, causing the IS curve to shift down and to the left and worsening the recession.

---

* For a discussion of the credit crunch in the USA, see Ben S. Bernanke and Cara Lown, 'The Credit Crunch', *Brookings Papers on Economic Activity*, 1991:2, pp. 205–48

fall, increasing the real money supply and shifting the *LM* curve down and
to the right. In the long run price declines shift the *LM* curve from *LM*[1] to
LM[2], restoring the economy to general equilibrium at point *H*. However, a
disadvantage of this strategy is that, during the (possibly lengthy) price
adjustment process, output and employment remain below their full-
employment levels.

■ *Scenario 2: An increase in the money supply.* Instead of waiting for the economy
to reach general equilibrium through price adjustment, the central bank
could increase the money supply, which would also shift the *LM* curve from
LM[1] to *LM*[2] in Figure 12.11. If prices adjust slowly, this expansionary policy
would move the economy to general equilibrium at point *H* more quickly
than would doing nothing.

■ *Scenario 3: An increase in government purchases.* An alternative policy of raising government purchases will shift the *IS* curve up and to the right, from
IS[2] to *IS*[1]. This policy also takes the economy to full employment, although
at point *E* in Figure 12.11 rather than at point *H*.

In all three scenarios the economy eventually returns to full employment.
However, the use of monetary or fiscal policy to achieve full employment
leads to two important differences from the scenario in which no policy action
is taken. First, if the government uses monetary or fiscal expansion to end the
recession, the economy returns directly to full employment; if policy is not
changed, the economy remains in recession in the short run, returning to full
employment only when prices have fully adjusted. Second, if there is no
policy change (scenario 1), in the long run the price level falls relative to the
nominal money supply. Indeed, the drop in the price level relative to the
money supply increases the real money supply, shifts the *LM* curve down and

**Figure 12.11
Stabilization policy in
the Keynesian model**
From point *E* the economy
is driven into a recession
at point *F* by a drop in
consumer confidence and
spending, which shifts the
IS curve down, from *IS*[1] to
IS[2]. If the government
took no action, in the
long run price adjustment
would shift the *LM* curve
from *LM*[1] to *LM*[2] and
restore general equilibrium
at point *H* (scenario 1).
Alternatively, the
government could try to
offset the recession
through stabilization
policy. For example, the
central bank could in-
crease the money supply,
which would shift the *LM*
curve directly from *LM*[1] to
LM[2], speeding the recovery in output (scenario 2).
Another possibility is a
fiscal expansion, such as
an increase in government
purchases, which would
shift the *IS* curve from *IS*[2]
back to *IS*[1], again
restoring full employment
at *E* (scenario 3).
Compared to a strategy
of doing nothing,
expansionary monetary
or fiscal policy helps the
economy recover more
quickly but leads to a
higher price level in the
long run.

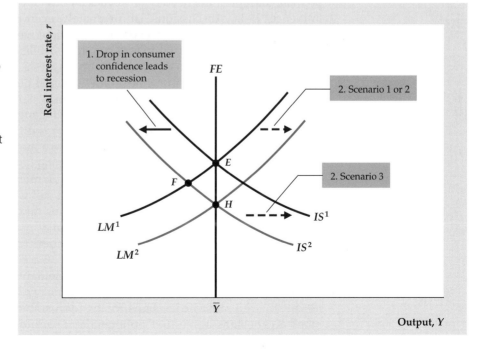

to the right, and restores full employment at point H. In contrast, when monetary or fiscal policy is used to restore full employment (scenarios 2 and 3), the
downward adjustment of the price level does not occur because expansionary
policy returns aggregate demand directly to the full-employment level. Thus
according to the Keynesian analysis, using expansionary monetary or fiscal
policy has the advantage of bringing the economy back to full employment
more quickly but the disadvantage of leading to a higher price level than if no
policy action is undertaken.

Either monetary or fiscal policy can be used to bring the economy back to
full employment. Does it matter which policy is used? Yes, there is at least one
basic difference between the outcomes of the two policies: monetary and fiscal
policies affect the composition of spending (the amount of output that is
devoted to consumption, the amount to investment, and so on) differently. In
Figure 12.11, although total output is the same at the alternative general equilibrium points E and H, at E (reached by an increase in government purchases)
government purchases are higher than at H (reached by an increase in the
money supply). Because government purchases are higher at E, the remaining
components of spending – in a closed economy, consumption and investment
– must be lower at E than at H. Relative to a monetary expansion, an increase
in government purchases crowds out consumption and investment by raising
the real interest rate, which is higher at E than at H. In addition, increased government purchases imply higher current or future tax burdens, which also
reduce consumption relative to what it would be with monetary expansion.

Difficulties of Macroeconomic Stabilization. The use of monetary and
fiscal policies to smooth or moderate the business cycle is called **macroeconomic
stabilization**. Using macroeconomic policies to try to smooth the cycle is also
sometimes called **aggregate demand management** because monetary and fiscal
policies shift the aggregate demand curve. Macroeconomic stabilization was a
popular concept in the heyday of Keynesian economics in the 1960s, and it still
influences policy discussions. Unfortunately, even putting aside the debates
between classical and Keynesian economists about whether smoothing the business cycle is sensible, actual macroeconomic stabilization has been much less
successful than the simple Keynesian theory suggests.

As discussed earlier in connection with fiscal policy, attempts to stabilize
the economy run into some technical problems. First, because the ability to
measure and analyse the economy is imperfect, gauging how far the economy
is from full employment at any particular time is difficult. Second, the precise
amount that output will increase in response to a monetary or fiscal expansion
is not known. These uncertainties make assessing how much of a monetary or
fiscal change is needed to restore full employment difficult. Finally, even
knowing the size of the policy change needed still would not provide enough
information. Because macroeconomic policies take time to implement and
more time to affect the economy, their optimal use requires knowledge of
where the economy will be six months or a year from now. But such knowledge is, at best, very imprecise.

Because of these problems, aggregate demand management has been
likened to trying to hit a moving target in a heavy fog. These problems have
not persuaded most Keynesians to abandon stabilization policy; however,
many Keynesians agree that policymakers should concentrate on fighting

major recessions and not try to 'fine-tune' the economy by smoothing every bump and wiggle in output and employment.

Beyond the technical problems associated with trying to find the right policies to stabilize the economy, economists also face the practical problem of convincing policymakers to take their advice.

Supply Shocks in the Keynesian Model

Until the 1970s the Keynesian business cycle theory focused almost exclusively on aggregate demand shocks as the source of business cycle fluctuations. Because aggregate demand shocks lead to procyclical movements in inflation, however, the Keynesian theory failed to account for the stagflation – high inflation together with a recession – that hit many European and other economies following the 1973–75 oil price shock. This experience led to much criticism of the traditional theory by both economists and policymakers, so Keynesians recast the theory to allow for both supply and demand shocks. Although Keynesians would not go so far as to agree with RBC theorists that supply (productivity) shocks are a factor in most recessions, they now concede that there have been occasional episodes – the oil price shocks of the 1970s being the leading examples – in which supply shocks have played a primary role in an economic downturn.

Figure 12.12 shows a Keynesian analysis of the effects of a sharp temporary increase in the price of oil (a similar analysis would apply to other supply shocks, such as a drought). As we showed in Chapter 3, if firms respond to an increase in the price of oil by using less energy, the amount of output that can be produced with the same amount of capital and labour falls. Thus the increase in the price of oil is an adverse supply shock, which reduces the full-employment level of output and shifts the FE line to the left, from FE^1 to FE^2. After complete wage and price adjustment, which occurs virtually immediately in the basic classical model but only in the long run in the Keynesian model, output falls to its new full-employment level $\overline{Y}_2$, the LM curve is at LM^3 and equilibrium is at point H. Thus in the long run (after full wage and price adjustment), the Keynesian analysis and the classical analysis of a supply shock are the same.

However, the Keynesian analysis of the short-run effects of an oil price shock is slightly different from the classical analysis. To understand the short-term effects of the oil price shock in the Keynesian model, first think about the effects of the increase in the oil price on the general price level. Recall that firms facing menu costs will not change their prices if the 'right' prices are only a little different from the preset prices. However, if the right prices are substantially different from the preset prices, so that firms would lose considerable profits by maintaining the preset prices, they will change their prices. In the case of a large increase in the price of oil, firms whose costs are strongly affected by the price of oil – including petrol stations, suppliers of home heating oil, and airlines, for example – find that the right prices for their products are substantially higher than the preset prices. These oil-dependent firms increase their prices quickly, whereas firms in other sectors maintain their preset prices in the short run. Thus there is price stickiness in the sense that not all prices adjust to their equilibrium values, and yet the average price level rises in the short run.

Figure 12.12
**An oil price shock in
the Keynesian model**
An increase in the price of
oil is an adverse supply
shock that reduces
full-employment output
from $\overline{Y}_1$ to $\overline{Y}_2$ and thus
shifts the *FE* line to the
left. In addition, the increase in the price of oil
increases prices in sectors
that depend heavily on
oil, whereas prices in
other sectors remain fixed
in the short run. Thus the
average price level rises,
which reduces the real
money supply *M/P* and
shifts the *LM* curve up
and to the left, from LM^1
to LM^2. In the short run,
the economy moves to
point *F*, with output
falling below the new,
lower value of full-
employment output and
the real interest rate
increasing. Because the
aggregate quantity of
goods demanded at *F* is
less than the full-
employment level of
output $\overline{Y}_2$, in the long run
the price level falls,
partially offsetting the
initial increase in prices.
The drop in the price level
causes the *LM* curve to
shift down and to the
right, from LM^2 to LM^3,
moving the economy to
full-employment
equilibrium at point *H*.

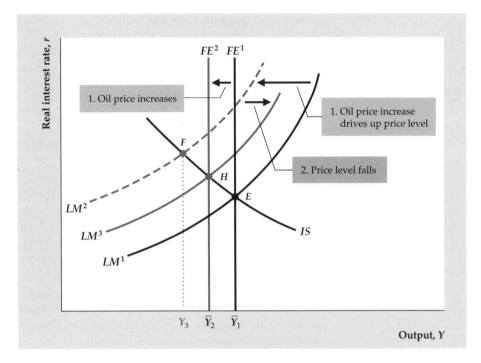

Because a sharp increase in the price of oil raises the price level P in the
short run, it also reduces the real money supply M/P. A decline in the real
money supply shifts the LM curve to left, from LM^1 to LM^2 in Figure 12.12. As
drawn, the LM curve shifts farther to the left than the FE line shifts, though
this outcome is not logically necessary. The short-run equilibrium is at point F,
where LM^2 intersects the IS curve. Because F is to the left of the FE line, the
economy is in a recession at F, with output (at Y_3) below the new value of full-
employment output, $\overline{Y}_2$, and the real interest rate increasing. In the short run
the economy experiences stagflation, with both a drop in output *and* a burst of
inflation. Note that, according to this analysis, the short-run decline in output
has two components: (1) the drop in full-employment output from $\overline{Y}_1$ to $\overline{Y}_2$;
and (2) the drop in output below the new full-employment level arising from
the shift to the left of the LM curve (the difference between $\overline{Y}_2$ and Y_3).

Supply shocks of the type analysed in Figure 12.12 pose tremendous difficulties for Keynesian stabilization policies. First, monetary or fiscal policy can
do little about the portion of the decline in output resulting from the shift of the
FE line; attempts to expand the economy beyond the new full-employment
output level $\overline{Y}_2$ will increase output only temporarily and worsen inflation. In
contrast, the portion of the output decline arising from the shift to the left of the
LM curve (the difference between $\overline{Y}_2$ and Y_3) represents an output level below
the full-employment level and could, in principle, be eliminated by expansionary monetary or fiscal policies that raise output to $\overline{Y}_2$. However, by using
expansionary policies at point F, rather than doing nothing, the government
risks worsening the already-high rate of inflation. Hence in the face of a shock
that induces stagflation like the one shown in Figure 12.12, macroeconomic
policy can neither avoid a sharp decline in output, nor restore output even to
its new, lower full-employment level without potentially worsening inflation.

CHAPTER SUMMARY

1. Keynesians are sceptical that a mismatch between workers and jobs can explain all unemployment. They argue that some unemployment is caused by real wages that are rigid and above the level at which the quantities of labour demanded and supplied are equal.

2. One explanation for real-wage rigidity is based on the efficiency wage model, which assumes that workers work harder in response to an increase in the real wage. Firms can attain the highest level of profit by paying the real wage, known as the efficiency wage, that elicits the most worker effort per unit of wages. If the effort curve relating effort provided by workers to the real wage does not change, the efficiency wage, and hence the real wage actually paid, is rigid.

3. At the efficiency wage, firms demand the level of employment $\overline{N}$ at which the marginal product of labour equals the efficiency wage. If the efficiency wage is above the market-clearing real wage, employment is determined by labour demand. The difference between the quantity of labour supplied and the quantity of labour demanded at the efficiency wage represents unemployment.

4. Full-employment output $\overline{Y}$ is the output that can be produced when employment is at its full-employment level $\overline{N}$ and worker effort is at the level induced by the efficiency wage. The *FE* line in the Keynesian *IS–LM* model is vertical where output equals its full-employment level. In the Keynesian model, full-employment output and the *FE* line are affected by productivity shocks but not by changes in labour supply because changes in labour supply do not affect employment in the efficiency wage model.

5. Keynesians attribute the non-neutrality of money to price stickiness, which means that some firms may not change their prices in the short run even though the demand for or supply of their product has changed. Price stickiness is contrary to the assumption of the basic classical model that prices and wages are completely flexible.

6. Price stickiness can arise from the profit-maximizing behaviour of monopolistically competitive firms that face menu costs, or costs of changing prices. Such firms are price setters rather than price takers, and once they set their prices they meet customer demand at that fixed price. These firms readjust prices only occasionally, generally when costs or demand have changed significantly.

7. In the Keynesian model with sticky prices, output is determined in the short run at the intersection of the *IS* and *LM* curves. The economy can be off the *FE* line in the short run because firms are willing to meet demand at predetermined prices. The level of employment in the short run is given by the effective labour demand curve, which shows the amount of labour needed to produce any given amount of output. In the long run, after prices and wages have completely adjusted, the *LM* curve moves to restore general equilibrium with full employment.

8. As in the classical model, the aggregate demand (*AD*) curve slopes downwards in the Keynesian model. The reason is that an increase in the price level reduces the real money supply and shifts the *LM* curve up and to the left, which reduces aggregate demand. The Keynesian short-run aggregate supply (*SRAS*) curve is horizontal because in the short run the price level is fixed and firms supply the amount of output demanded. In the long run, after complete wage and price adjustment, firms supply the full-employment level of output $\overline{Y}$, regardless of the price level; so the long-run aggregate supply (*LRAS*) curve is vertical.

9. In the Keynesian model an increase in the money supply shifts the *LM* curve down and to the right, raising output and lowering the real interest rate in the short run. Thus money is not neutral in the short run. In the long run, however, money is neutral; monetary expansion raises the price level proportionally but has no real effects.

10. In the Keynesian model an increase in government purchases or a cut in taxes shifts the *IS*

curve up and to the right, raising output and the real interest rate in the short run. In the long run, output returns to the full-employment level but the real interest rate increases. Fiscal policy is not neutral in the long run because it affects the composition of output among consumption, investment, and government purchases.

11. Keynesians attribute most business cycles to aggregate demand shocks. These shocks hit the *IS* curve (changes in government purchases, desired consumption, or desired investment) or the *LM* curve (changes in money supply or money demand). Keynesian business cycle theory, which has traditionally emphasized the importance of aggregate demand shocks, can account for the procyclical behaviour of employment, money, inflation, and investment. To explain the procyclical behaviour of average labour productivity, the Keynesian theory must include the additional assumption that firms

hoard labour – that is, they employ more workers than necessary during recessions.

12. Macroeconomic stabilization, also called aggregate demand management, is the use of monetary or fiscal policy to try to eliminate recessions and keep the economy at full employment. The Keynesian theory suggests that macroeconomic stabilization is both desirable and possible. However, practical problems include the difficulty of measuring and forecasting the state of the economy and determining how much monetary and fiscal stimulus is needed at any particular time. Keynesian anti-recessionary policies also lead to a higher price level than would occur in the absence of policy changes.

13. Following the oil price shocks of the 1970s, the Keynesian theory was modified to allow for supply shocks. Adverse supply shocks lead to stagflation (a combination of inflation and recession) and pose great difficulties for stabilization policy.

Key Terms

aggregate demand management, p. 457
aggregate demand shocks, p. 452
effective labour demand curve, p. 441
efficiency wage, p. 432
efficiency wage model, p. 430
effort curve, p. 431
labour hoarding, p. 455
macroeconomic stabilization, p. 457
marginal cost, p. 440
mark-up, p. 440
menu cost, p. 438
monopolistic competition, p. 437
multiplier, p. 448
perfect competition, p. 437
price stickiness, p. 436
real-wage rigidity, p. 430
turnover costs, p. 430

Review Questions

1. Define *efficiency wage*. What assumption about worker behaviour underlies the efficiency wage theory? Why does it predict that the real wage will remain rigid even if there is an excess supply of labour?

2. How is full-employment output $\bar{Y}$ determined in the Keynesian model with efficiency wages? In this model, how is full-employment output affected by changes in productivity (supply shocks)? How is it affected by changes in labour supply?

3. What is price stickiness? Why do Keynesians believe that allowing for price stickiness in macroeconomic analysis is important?

4. Define *menu cost*. Why might small menu costs lead to price stickiness in monopolistically competitive markets but not in perfectly competitive markets? Why can a monopolistically competitive firm profitably meet demand at its fixed price when actual demand is greater than the firm anticipated?

5. What does the Keynesian model predict about monetary neutrality (both in the short run and in the long run)? Compare the Keynesian predictions about neutrality with those of the basic classical model and the extended classical model with misperceptions.

6. In the Keynesian model, how do increased government purchases affect output and the real interest rate in the short run? In the long run? How do increased government purchases affect the composition of output in the long run?

7. Describe three alternative responses available to policymakers when the economy is in recession. What are the advantages and disadvantages of each strategy? Be sure to discuss the effects on employment, the price level, and the composition of output. What are some of the practical difficulties in using macroeconomic stabilization policies to fight recessions?

8. Use the Keynesian model to explain the procyclical behaviour of employment, money, inflation, and investment.

9. What does the Keynesian model predict about the cyclical behaviour of average labour productivity? How does the idea of labour hoarding help bring the prediction of the model into conformity with the business cycle facts?

10. According to the Keynesian analysis, in what two ways does an adverse supply shock reduce output? What problems do supply shocks create for Keynesian stabilization policies?

Numerical Problems

1. A firm identifies the following relationship between the real wage it pays and the effort exerted by its workers.

Real Wage	Effort
8	7
10	10
12	15
14	17
16	19
18	20

The marginal product of labour for this firm is

$$MPN = \frac{E(100 - N)}{15}$$

where E is the effort level and N is the number of workers employed. If the firm can pay only one of the six wage levels shown, which should it choose? How many workers will it employ?

There are 200 workers in the town where the firm is located, all willing to work at a real wage of 8. Does this change your answer to the first part of this question? If so, how?

2. An economy is described by the following equations.

Desired consumption	$C^d = 130 + 0.5(Y - T) - 500r$
Desired investment	$I^d = 100 - 500r$
Government purchases	$G = 100$
Taxes	$T = 100$
Real money demand	$L = 0.5Y - 1000r$
Money supply	$M = 1320$
Full-employment output	$\overline{Y} = 500$

Assume that expected inflation is zero so that money demand depends directly on the real interest rate.

a. Write the equations for the *IS* and *LM* curves. (These equations express the relationship between r and Y when the goods and asset markets are in equilibrium.)

b. Calculate the full-employment values of output, the real interest rate, the price level, consumption, and investment.

c. Now suppose that, because of investor optimism about the future marginal product of capital, the investment function becomes

$$I^d = 200 - 500r$$

Assuming that the economy was initially at full employment, what are the new values of output, the real interest rate, the price level, consumption, and investment in the short run? In the long run? Show your results graphically.

3. Consider the following economy.

Desired consumption	$C^d = 325 + 0.5(Y - T) - 500r$
Desired investment	$I^d = 200 - 500r$
Government purchases	$G = 150$
Taxes	$T = 150$
Real money demand	$L = 0.5Y - 1000r$
Money supply	$M = 6000$
Full-employment output	$\overline{Y} = 1000$

a. Calculate the full-employment values of the real interest rate, the price level, consumption, and investment.

b. Now suppose that government purchases are increased to 250, with no change in current taxes. Assuming that the economy was initially at full employment, what are the new values of output, the real interest rate, the price level, consumption, and investment in the short run? In the long run?

c. Repeat part (b) for an increase in the money supply to 7200. Assume that $G = 150$.

4. An economy is described by the following equations.

Desired consumption	$C^d = 300 + 0.5(Y - T) - 300r$
Desired investment	$I^d = 100 - 100r$
Government purchases	$G = 100$
Taxes	$T = 100$
Real money demand	$L = 0.5Y - 200r$
Money supply	$M = 6300$
Full-employment output	$\bar{Y} = 700$

a. Write the equation for the aggregate demand curve. (*Hint:* Find the equations describing goods market equilibrium and asset market equilibrium. Use these two equations to eliminate the real interest rate. For any given price level the equation of the aggregate demand curve gives the level of output that satisfies both goods market equilibrium and asset market equilibrium.)

b. Suppose that $P = 15$. What are the short-run values of output, the real interest rate, consumption, and investment?

c. What are the long-run equilibrium values of output, the real interest rate, consumption, investment, and the price level?

5. (Appendix 12.A) Consider an economy in which all workers are covered by contracts that specify the nominal wage and give the employer the right to choose the amount of employment. The production function is

$$Y = 20\sqrt{N}$$

and the corresponding marginal product of labour is

$$MPN = \frac{10}{\sqrt{N}}$$

Suppose that the nominal wage $W = 20$.

a. Derive an equation that relates the real wage to the amount of labour demanded by firms (the labour demand curve).

b. For the nominal wage of 20, what is the relation between the price level and the amount of labour demanded by firms?

c. What is the relation between the price level and the amount of output supplied by firms? Graph this relation.

Now suppose that the *IS* and *LM* curves of the economy (the goods market and asset market equilibrium conditions) are described by the following equations:

IS curve	$Y = 120 - 500r$
LM curve	$M/P = 0.5Y - 500r$

d. The money supply M is 300. Use the *IS* and *LM* equations to derive a relation between output Y and the price level P. This relation is the equation for the aggregate demand curve. Graph this relation on the same axis as the relation between the price level and the amount of output supplied by firms (the aggregate supply curve) from part (c).

e. What are the equilibrium values of the price level, output, employment, the real wage, and the real interest rate?

f. Now suppose that the money supply M is 135. What are the equilibrium values of the price level, output, employment, the real wage, and the real interest rate?

6. (Appendix 12.B) Consider the economy described in Numerical Problem 3.

a. What are the values of α_{IS}, β_{IS}, α_{LM}, β_{LM} and ℓ_r for this economy? (You will have to refer back to Appendix 10.A for definitions of these coefficients.)

b. Suppose that the price level is fixed at $\bar{P} = 15$. What are the short-run equilibrium values of output and the real interest rate?

c. With the price level still fixed at $\bar{P} = 15$, suppose that government purchases increase from $G = 150$ to $G = 250$. What are the new values of α_{IS} and the short-run equilibrium level of output?

d. Use equation (12.B.10) to compute the government purchases multiplier. Use your answer to compute the short-run change in Y resulting from an increase in government purchases from $G = 150$ to $G = 250$. How does your answer here compare to your answer in part (c)?

Analytical Problems

1. According to the Keynesian *IS–LM* model, what is the effect of each of the following on output, the real interest rate, employment, and the price level? Distinguish between the short run and the long run.

a. Increased tax incentives for investment (the tax breaks for investment are offset by lump-sum tax increases that keep total current tax collections unchanged).

b. Increased tax incentives for saving (as in part (a), lump-sum tax increases offset the effect on total current tax collections).

c. A wave of investor pessimism about the future profitability of capital investments.

d. An increase in consumer confidence, as consumers expect that their incomes will be higher in the future.

2. According to the Keynesian *IS–LM* model, what is the effect of each of the following on output, the real interest rate, employment, and the price level? Distinguish between the short run and the long run.

a. Financial deregulation allows banks to pay a higher interest rate on cheque accounts.

b. The introduction of sophisticated credit cards greatly reduces the amount of money that people need for transactions.

c. A severe water shortage causes sharp declines in agricultural output and increases in food prices.

d. A temporary beneficial supply shock affects most of the economy, but no individual firm is affected sufficiently to change its prices in the short run.

3. Suppose that the central bank has a policy of increasing the money supply when it observes that the economy is in recession. However, suppose that about six months are needed for an increase in the money supply to affect aggregate demand, which is about the same amount of time needed for firms to review and reset their prices. What effects will the central bank policy have on output and price stability? Does your answer change if (a) the central bank has some ability to forecast recessions or (b) price adjustment takes longer than six months?

4. Classical economists argue that using fiscal policy to fight a recession does not make workers better off. Suppose, however, that the Keynesian model is correct. Relative to a policy of doing nothing, does an increase in government purchases that brings the economy to full employment make workers better off? In answering the question, discuss the effects of the fiscal expansion on the real wage, employment, consumption, and current and future taxes. How does your answer depend on (a) the direct benefits of the government spending programme and (b) the speed with which prices adjust in the absence of fiscal stimulus?

5. Some labour economists argue that it is useful to think of the labour market as being divided into two sectors: a primary sector, where 'good' (high-paying, long-term) jobs are located, and a secondary sector, which has 'bad' (low-paying, short-term) jobs. Suppose that the primary sector has a high marginal product of labour and (because effort is costly for firms to monitor) firms pay an efficiency wage. The secondary sector has a low marginal product of labour and no efficiency wage; instead, the real wage in the secondary sector adjusts so that the quantities of labour demanded and supplied are equal in that sector. Workers are alike, and all would prefer to work in the primary sector. However, workers who cannot find jobs in the primary sector work in the secondary sector.

What are the effects of each of the following on the real wage, employment, and output in both sectors?

a. Expansionary monetary policy increases the demand for primary-sector output.

b. Immigration increases the labour force.

c. The effort curve changes so that a higher real wage is needed to elicit the greatest effort per unit of wages in the primary sector. Effort exerted at the higher real wage is the same as before the change in the effort curve.

d. There is a temporary productivity improvement in the primary sector.

e. There is a temporary productivity improvement in the secondary sector.

LABOUR CONTRACTS AND NOMINAL-WAGE RIGIDITY

In the Keynesian theory the non-neutrality of money is a consequence of nominal rigidity. In this chapter we emphasized nominal-*price* rigidity. An alternative nominal rigidity that could account for the non-neutrality of money, which many Keynesians emphasize, is nominal-*wage* rigidity. Nominal-wage rigidity could reflect long-term labour contracts between firms and unions in which wages are set in nominal terms (the case we study here). In terms of the *AD–AS* framework the difference between nominal-price rigidity and nominal-wage rigidity is that nominal-price rigidity implies a horizontal short-run aggregate supply curve, whereas nominal-wage rigidity implies a short-run aggregate supply curve that slopes upwards. However, this difference does not really affect the results obtained from the Keynesian model. In particular, in the Keynesian model with nominal-wage rigidity, money remains non-neutral in the short run and neutral in the long run.

The Short-Run Aggregate Supply Curve with Labour Contracts

In many countries most labour contracts specify employment conditions and nominal wages for a number of years. Although labour contracts specify the nominal wage rate, they usually do not specify the total amount of employment. Instead, employers unilaterally decide how many hours will be worked and whether workers will be laid off. These factors imply that the short-run aggregate supply curve slopes upwards.

We can see why the short-run aggregate supply curve slopes upwards when labour contracts prespecify the nominal wage by considering what happens when the price level increases. With the nominal wage W already determined by the contract, an increase in the price level P reduces the real wage w, or W/P. In response to the drop in the real wage, firms demand more labour. Because firms unilaterally choose the level of employment, the increase in the amount of labour demanded leads to an increase in employment and therefore an increase in output. Thus an increase in the price level leads to an increase in the amount of output supplied, as shown by the *SRAS* curves in Figure 12.A.1.

Non-neutrality of Money

Money is non-neutral in the short run in the model with long-term labour contracts, as illustrated in Figure 12.A.1. The initial general equilibrium is at point E, where the initial aggregate demand curve AD^1 intersects the short-run aggregate supply curve $SRAS^1$. A 10% increase in the money supply shifts the AD curve up to AD^2. (For any level of output the price level is 10% higher on AD^2 than on AD^1.) In the short run the rise in the money supply increases the price level to P_2 and output to Y_2 at point F. Output is higher than its full-

**Figure 12.A.1
Monetary
non-neutrality with
long-term contracts**
With long-term labour
contracts that fix the
nominal wage in the short
run, an increase in the
price level lowers the real
wage and induces firms to
employ more labour and
produce more output.
Thus the short-run aggre-
gate supply curve $SRAS^1$
slopes upward. When
nominal wages are rigid,
money is not neutral.
From the initial equilibrium point E a 10%
increase in the money
supply shifts the AD curve
up, from AD^1 to AD^2. In
the short run both output
and the price level in-
crease, as shown by point
F. Over time, contracts are
renegotiated and nominal
wages rise
to match the increase in
prices. As wages rise, the
short-run aggregate sup-
ply curve shifts up, from
$SRAS^1$ to $SRAS^2$, so that
general equilibrium is restored at H. At H both
the price level P and the
nominal wage W have
risen by 10%, so the real
wage is the same as it was
initially, and firms supply
the full-employment level
of output $\overline{Y}$.

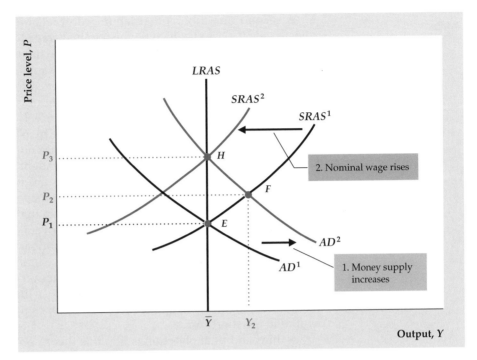

employment level at F because the rise in prices lowered the real wage, which
leads firms to employ more labour and produce more output.

At the short-run equilibrium point, F, however, workers will be dissatisfied because their real wages are lower than they had expected. Over time, as
contracts are renewed or renegotiated, nominal wages will rise to offset the
increase in prices. At any price level a rise in the nominal wage also raises the
real wage, inducing firms to employ less labour and produce less output. Thus
rising nominal wages cause the short-run aggregate supply curve to shift up,
from $SRAS^1$ to $SRAS^2$. Eventually, general equilibrium is restored at point H.

In the long run at point H, the price level rises to P_3, which is 10% higher
than its initial value P_1. At H the nominal wage W has also increased by 10%
so that the real wage W/P has returned to its initial value. With the real wage
back at its original value, firms employ the same amount of labour and produce the same amount of output ($\overline{Y}$) as they did at the initial equilibrium
point, E. Thus, as in the Keynesian model based on efficiency wages and price
stickiness, in the Keynesian model with nominal-wage rigidity, money is neutral in the long run but not in the short run.

Although nominal-wage rigidity arising from labour contracts can explain
short-run monetary non-neutrality, some economists object to this explanation.
One objection is that in many European countries less than half the workforce
is unionized and covered by long-term labour contracts. However, many non-
union workers receive wages similar to those set in union contracts. For
example, although most non-union workers do not have formal wage contracts, they may have 'implicit contracts' with their employers, or informal
unwritten arrangements for comparable wages.

A second objection is that labour contracts often contain cost-of-living adjustments (COLAs), which tie the nominal wage to the overall price level, as measured, for example, by the consumer price index. Contracts with *complete* indexation increase the nominal wage by the same percentage as the increase in the price level. If wages are completely indexed to the price level, the short-run aggregate supply curve is vertical and money is neutral. To show why, let's suppose that the price level increases by 6%. If labour contracts are completely indexed, nominal wages also increase by 6% and the real wage W/P remains unchanged. Because the real wage does not change, firms choose the same levels of employment and output independent of the price level.

However, in most labour contracts wages are not completely indexed to prices. Most contracts with COLA provisions have partial rather than complete indexation. For example, under a contract that calls for 50% indexation, the nominal wage will increase by 50% of the overall rate of increase in prices. Thus, if the price level increases by 6%, the nominal wage increases by 3%. As a result, the real wage falls by 3% (a 3% increase in the nominal wage W minus a 6% increase in the price level P). The reduction in the real wage induces firms to increase employment and production. Thus with partial indexation the short-run aggregate supply curve again slopes upwards, and money is not neutral in the short run.

A third and final objection is that this theory predicts that real wages will be countercyclical, contrary to the business cycle fact that real wages are procyclical. For example, at point F in Figure 12.A.1 output is higher than the full-employment level, but the real wage is lower than at full employment (indeed, the low real wage induces firms to produce the extra output). Thus the theory holds that real wages will fall in booms – that is, the real wage is countercyclical – which is inconsistent with the evidence.

However, perhaps both supply shocks and aggregate demand shocks affect real wages. For the real business cycle theory we showed that, if productivity shocks cause cyclical fluctuations, the real wage should be procyclical, perhaps strongly so. A combination of supply shocks (which cause the real wage to move procyclically) and aggregate demand shocks (which, as in Figure 12.A.1, cause the real wage to move countercyclically) might average out to a real wage that is at least mildly procyclical. Some evidence for this view was provided in a study by Scott Sumner of Bentley College and Stephen Silver of Virginia Military Institute, which shows that the real wage has been procyclical during periods dominated by supply shocks but has been countercyclical during periods in which aggregate demand shocks were more important.[16]

---

16. 'Real Wages, Employment and the Phillips Curve', *Journal of Political Economy*, June 1989, pp. 706–20.

APPENDIX 12.B

AN ALGEBRAIC VERSION OF THE SHORT-RUN KEYNESIAN MODEL

Further extending the algebraic analysis of Appendices 10.A and 11.A, this appendix examines short-run macroeconomic behaviour in the Keynesian model. In the long run, the Keynesian model predicts that the economy reaches a general equilibrium much like that described in Appendix 10.A. Long-run equilibrium in the Keynesian model differs from the classical general equilibrium in only one respect: the full-employment level of employment $\overline{N}$ lies at the intersection of the labour demand curve and the efficiency wage line, rather than at the intersection of the labour demand and labour supply curves.

In the short run, the Keynesian model holds that prices are fixed and that output is determined by aggregate demand. Aggregate output demanded in turn is at the intersection of the *IS* and *LM* curves. Earlier we derived algebraic expressions for the *IS* and *LM* curves, equations (10.A.14) and (10.A.19), as follows:

$$r = \alpha_{IS} - \beta_{IS}Y, \qquad IS \text{ curve} \tag{12.B.1}$$

$$r = \alpha_{LM} - \left(\frac{1}{\ell_r}\right)\left(\frac{M}{P}\right) + \beta_{LM}Y, \qquad LM \text{ curve} \tag{12.B.2}$$

In equations (12.B.1) and (12.B.2), r is the real interest rate, Y is output, M/P is the real money supply, and α_{IS}, α_{LM}, β_{IS}, β_{LM} and ℓ_r are positive numbers defined in Appendix 10.A. The terms α_{IS} and α_{LM} capture factors that shift the *IS* curve (such as government purchases) and the *LM* curve (such as expected inflation), respectively.

As in Appendix 10.A, to find the aggregate quantity of output demanded, we set the right-hand sides of equations (12.B.1) and (12.B.2) equal and solve for Y:

$$Y = \frac{\alpha_{IS} - \alpha_{LM} + (1/\ell_r)(M/P)}{\beta_{IS} + \beta_{LM}} \tag{12.B.3}$$

In equation (12.B.3), which is the same as equation (10.A.24), Y is the aggregate quantity of output demanded at the intersection of the *IS* and *LM* curves. Equation (12.B.3) is also the equation for the aggregate demand curve; it states that, for constant money supply M, aggregate output demanded Y is a decreasing function of the price level P. Thus the aggregate demand curve slopes downwards.

In the short-run Keynesian model, the price level is fixed at some initial level $\overline{P}$, so the Keynesian short-run aggregate supply curve is simply

$$P = \overline{P} \tag{12.B.4}$$

We find the short-run equilibrium level of output by substituting the fixed price level $\overline{P}$ for the price level P in the aggregate demand curve, equation (12.B.3), to get

$$Y = \frac{\alpha_{IS} - \alpha_{LM} + (1/\ell_r)(M/\bar{P})}{\beta_{IS} + \beta_{LM}} \qquad (12.B.5)$$

Equation (12.B.5) shows that the short-run equilibrium value of output in the Keynesian model increases in response to an increase in the nominal money supply M, or in response to any factor that shifts the IS curve up (an increase in α_{IS}) or the LM curve down (a decrease in α_{LM}).

To obtain the short-run equilibrium value of the real interest rate we substitute the short-run equilibrium level of output, from equation (12.B.5), into the IS curve, equation (12.B.1):

$$r = \frac{\alpha_{IS}\beta_{LM} + \beta_{IS}\alpha_{LM} - (\beta_{IS}/\ell_r)(M/\bar{P})}{\beta_{IS} + \beta_{LM}} \qquad (12.B.6)$$

According to equation (12.B.6), the short-run equilibrium real interest rate in the Keynesian model increases in response to a decline in the nominal money supply M, or in response to any factor that shifts the IS curve up (an increase in α_{IS}) or the LM curve up (an increase in α_{LM}).

The Multiplier

In this chapter we defined the multiplier associated with any particular type of spending as the short-run change in total output resulting from a one-unit change in that type of spending. Here we derive the multiplier associated with government purchases G. We proceed in three steps. First, we calculate the effect on α_{IS} (the intercept of the IS curve in equation 12.B.1) of an increase in G. Then, we calculate the effect on the short-run equilibrium value of Y, shown by equation (12.B.5), of an increase in α_{IS}. Finally, we combine these two effects to calculate the effect on output Y of an increase in G.

To calculate the effect on α_{IS} of an increase in G, we repeat the definition of α_{IS}, equation (10.A.15):

$$\alpha_{IS} = \frac{c_0 + i_0 + G - c_Y t_0}{c_r + i_r} \qquad (12.B.7)$$

where c_0, i_0, c_Y, c_r, i_r, and t_0 are parameters that determine desired consumption and desired investment (see Appendix 10.A). If G increases by ΔG, then α_{IS} increases by $\Delta G/(c_r + i_r)$, so

$$\Delta\alpha_{IS} = \frac{\Delta G}{c_r + i_r} \qquad (12.B.8)$$

Next, observe from equation (12.B.5) that, if α_{IS} increases by $\Delta\alpha_{IS}$, output Y increases by $\Delta\alpha_{IS}/(\beta_{IS} + \beta_{LM})$, or

$$\Delta Y = \frac{\Delta\alpha_{IS}}{\beta_{IS} + \beta_{LM}} \qquad (12.B.9)$$

Finally, if we substitute the right-hand side of equation (12.B.8) for $\Delta\alpha_{IS}$ on the right-hand side of equation (12.B.9) and then divide both sides of the resulting equation by ΔG, we obtain

$$\frac{\Delta Y}{\Delta G} = \frac{1}{(c_r + i_r)(\beta_{IS} + \beta_{LM})} \tag{12.B.10}$$

The right-hand side of equation (12.B.10) is the increase in short-run equilibrium output Y that occurs for each one-unit increase in government purchases G. In other words, it is the government purchases multiplier. Similar calculations show that changes in desired consumption or desired investment (as reflected in the terms c_0 and i_0) have the same multiplier as government purchases.

Because c_r, i_r, β_{IS}, and β_{LM} are all positive, the multiplier is positive. However, depending on the specific values of those parameters, the multiplier may be greater or less than 1. A case in which the multiplier is likely to be large occurs when the LM curve is horizontal (that is, when the slope of the LM curve β_{LM} is 0). If the LM curve is horizontal, shifts in the IS curve induced by changes in spending have relatively large effects on output. Recall that equation (10.A.16) gives the slope of the IS curve β_{IS} as $[1 - (1 - t)c_Y]/(c_r + i_r)$. Making this substitution and setting the slope of the LM curve $\beta_{LM} = 0$ yield a simple form of the multiplier:

$$\frac{\Delta Y}{\Delta G} = \frac{1}{1 - (1 - t)c_Y} \tag{12.B.11}$$

For example, suppose that the marginal propensity to consume $c_Y = 0.8$ and that the tax rate $t = 0.25$. Then the multiplier defined in equation (12.B.11) is $1/[(1 - (0.75)(0.8)] = 1/0.4$, or 2.5.

PART IV

MACROECONOMIC POLICY: ITS ENVIRONMENT AND INSTITUTIONS

CHAPTER 13

UNEMPLOYMENT AND INFLATION

The last several chapters focused on the concepts of the business cycle, macro-economic stabilization, and classical and Keynesian approaches to business cycle analysis. Although these concepts are central to today's macroeconomics, actual policy discussions rarely involve such abstract terms. Policy debates tend to focus on highly publicized economic statistics such as inflation and unemployment. To make a stronger connection between business cycle theories and policy debates, we now take a closer look at unemployment and inflation, first together and then separately.

Unemployment and inflation – sometimes referred to as the 'twin evils' of macroeconomics – are among the most difficult and politically sensitive economic issues that policymakers face. High rates of unemployment and inflation generate intense public concern because their effects are direct and visible: almost everyone is affected by rising prices, and few workers can be confident that they will never lose their jobs.

Moreover, there is a long-standing idea in macroeconomics that unemployment and inflation are somehow related. In the first part of this chapter we discuss in some detail the concept of the Phillips curve – an empirical relationship between inflation and unemployment. According to the Phillips curve, inflation tends to be low when unemployment is high and high when unemployment is low. The Phillips curve relationship raises some important questions about how the economy works and how macroeconomic policies should be used.

We then look at unemployment and inflation separately. We examine the costs that each imposes on society and consider the options that policymakers have for dealing with these problems.

This chapter begins Part IV of the book, the purpose of which is to explore macroeconomic policy making in greater detail. Following the discussion of inflation and unemployment in this chapter, Chapter 14 addresses the issue of how economic openness – as reflected in the trading and financial links among countries – affects macroeconomic policy. Chapter 15 takes a closer look at institutions and debates related to the making of monetary policy, and Chapter 16 provides a similar overview of fiscal policy.

13.1 UNEMPLOYMENT AND INFLATION: IS THERE A TRADE-OFF?

Newspaper editorials and public discussions about economic policy often refer to the 'trade-off' between inflation and unemployment. The idea is that, to reduce inflation, the economy must tolerate high unemployment; or alternatively that, to reduce unemployment, more inflation must be accepted. This section examines the idea of an inflation–unemployment trade-off and its implications for macroeconomic policy.

The origin of the idea of a trade-off between inflation and unemployment was a 1958 article by economist A. W. Phillips.[1] Phillips examined 97 years of British data on unemployment and nominal wage growth data; he found that, historically, unemployment tended to be low in years when nominal wages grew rapidly and high in years when nominal wages grew slowly. Economists who built on Phillips's work shifted its focus slightly by looking at the link between unemployment and inflation – that is, the growth rate of prices – rather than the link between unemployment and the growth rate of wages. During the late 1950s and the 1960s, many statistical studies examined inflation and unemployment data for numerous countries and time periods, in many cases finding a negative relationship between the two variables. This negative empirical relationship between unemployment and inflation is known as the **Phillips curve**.

Two striking examples of Phillips curves, shown in Figure 13.1, occurred in the UK and USA during the 1960s. The US economy expanded throughout most of the 1960s, with unemployment falling and inflation rising steadily, where as the UK economy expanded in the early parts of the decade but then the economy declined again. In Figure 13.1, the inflation rate is measured on the vertical axis, and the unemployment rate is measured on the horizontal axis. Note that years that had high unemployment also had low inflation, and that years that had high inflation also had low unemployment. The data produce an almost perfect downward-sloping relation between inflation and unemployment – that is, a Phillips curve, for both countries. The experience of the UK and USA in the 1960s, which came after Phillips's article had been published and widely disseminated, as well as that for many other European countries, was viewed by many as a confirmation of his basic finding.

The policy implications of these findings were much debated. Initially, the Phillips curve seemed to offer policymakers a 'menu' of combinations of inflation and unemployment from which they could choose. Indeed, during the 1960s some economists argued that, by accepting a modest amount of inflation, macroeconomic policymakers could keep the unemployment rate low indefinitely. This belief seemed to be borne out in the USA during the 1960s, when rising inflation was accompanied by falling unemployment.

In the following decades, however, this relationship between inflation and unemployment failed to hold: Figure 13.2 shows inflation and unemployment for both countries for the period 1973–92. During those years, unlike the

---

1. 'The Relation Between Unemployment and the Rate of Change of Money Wage Rates in the United Kingdom, 1861–1957,' *Economica*, November 1958, pp. 283–99.

**Figure 13.1
The Phillips curve and the UK and US economies during the 1960s**
During the 1960s rates of unemployment and inflation seemed to lie along a Phillips curve. In the US inflation rose and unemployment fell fairly steadily during this decade. The UK economy was more erratic though, as in the US, policymakers apparently had to decide to live with higher inflation in order to reduce unemployment.

Source: (a) Richard Layard, Stephen Nickell and Richard Jackman, *Unemployment: Macroeconomic Performance and the Labour Market*, Oxford, Oxford University Press, 1991, Annexe 1.6, Table A3 'Civilian unemployment rate' and Table A4 'GDP deflator inflation rate, year to year'. (b) USA *Economic Report of the President*, February 1993; Table B-59 'CPI inflation rate, year to year'; Table B-30 'Civilian unemployment rate'.

(a)

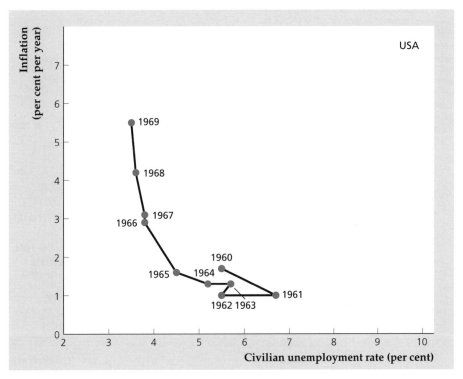

(b)

Figure 13.2
Inflation and unemployment in the United Kingdom and United States, 1973–95
The figure shows the combinations of inflation and unemployment experienced in the United Kingdom and the United States each year from 1973 to 1992. Unlike during the 1960s (see Fig. 13.1), after 1973 a clear negative relationship between inflation and unemployment did not seem to exist in either country.

Sources: (a) For data up to 1990, Richard Layard, Stephen Nickell and Richard Jackman, *Unemployment: Macroeconomic Performance and the Labour Market*, Oxford, Oxford University Press, 1991. For data since 1990, *European Economy, 1996 op cit. Table 1.1(b)*, Table 3 'Civilian unemployment rate' (Eurostat definition) and Table 26 'GDP deflator inflation rate, year to year'. (b) USA *Economic Report of the President,* February 1993; Table B-59 'CPI inflation rate, year to year' (1992 rate from *Survey of Current Business*); Table B-30 'Civilian unemployment rate'.

(a)

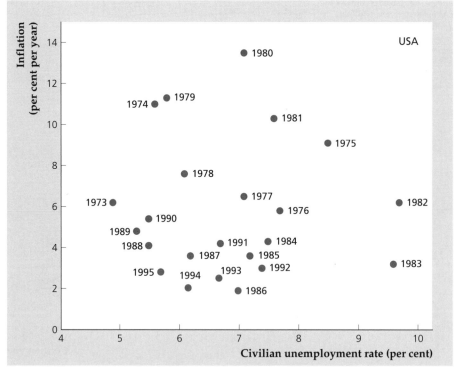

(b)

1960s, there seemed to be no reliable relationship between unemployment and inflation, and this applied equally to other European countries. From the perspective of the Phillips curve the most puzzling periods were the mid 1970s and early 1980s, during which many countries experienced high inflation and high unemployment simultaneously (stagflation). In 1975, for example, unemployment in the USA reached 8.5% of the labour force and the annual inflation rate was 9.1%. In 1981, the unemployment rate in the UK was nearly 10% and the annual inflation rate was 11.7%. High unemployment, together with high inflation, is inconsistent with the Phillips curve.

The original empirical results of Phillips and others who extended his work, together with the unexpected experience of many economies after 1970, raises at least three important questions:

■ Why was the original Phillips curve relationship between inflation and unemployment frequently observed historically, as in the cases of Great Britain in the century before 1958 and most of Europe and the United States in the 1960s?

■ Why did the simple negative relationship between inflation and unemployment that seemed to exist during the 1960s vanish after 1970? In other words, was there in fact no systematic relationship between inflation and unemployment after 1970?

■ Does the Phillips curve actually provide a menu of choices from which policymakers can choose? For example, by electing to maintain a high inflation rate can policymakers guarantee a *permanently* low rate of unemployment?

Economic theory provides reasonable answers to these questions; in particular, it explains the collapse of the Phillips curve after 1970. Interestingly, the key economic analysis of the Phillips curve – which predicted that this relationship would not be stable – was done during the 1960s, *before* the Phillips curve had actually broken down. Thus we have at least one example of economic theorists predicting an important development in the economy that policymakers and the public did not anticipate.

The Expectations-Augmented Phillips Curve

Although the Phillips curve seemed to describe adequately the unemployment–inflation relationship in the 1960s, during the second half of the decade some economists, notably Milton Friedman[2] of the University of Chicago and Edmund Phelps[3] of Columbia University, questioned the logic of the Phillips curve. Friedman and Phelps argued – purely on the basis of economic theory – that there should not be a stable negative relationship between inflation and unemployment. Instead, a negative relationship should exist between *unanticipated* inflation (the difference between the actual and expected inflation rates) and *cyclical* unemployment (the difference between the actual and natural

---

2. 'The Role of Monetary Policy,' *American Economic Review*, March 1968, pp. 1–17.
3. 'Money Wage Dynamics and Labour Market Equilibrium,' in Edmund Phelps, ed., *Microeconomic Foundations of Employment and Inflation Theory* (W.W. Norton, 1970) pp. 124–66.

unemployment rates).[4] Although these distinctions appear to be merely technical, they are crucial in understanding the relationship between the actual rates of inflation and unemployment.

Before discussing the significance of their analyses, we need to explain how Friedman and Phelps arrived at their conclusions. To do so we use the extended classical model, which includes the misperceptions theory. (Analytical Problem 3 at the end of the chapter asks you to perform a similar analysis using the Keynesian model.) We proceed in two steps, first considering an economy at full employment with steady, fully anticipated inflation. In this economy, both unanticipated inflation and cyclical unemployment are zero. Second, we consider what happens when aggregate demand growth increases unexpectedly. In this case both positive unanticipated inflation (inflation greater than expected) and negative cyclical unemployment (actual unemployment lower than the natural rate) occur. This outcome confirms the Friedman–Phelps point that a negative relationship exists between unanticipated inflation and cyclical unemployment.

We develop the first step of this analysis by using the extended classical model to analyse an economy with steady inflation (see Figure 13.3). We assume that this economy is in full-employment equilibrium in which the money supply has been growing at 10% per year for many years and is expected to continue to grow at this rate indefinitely. With the money supply growing by 10% per year, the aggregate demand curve shifts up by 10% each year, from AD^1 in year 1 to AD^2 in year 2, and so on. For simplicity we assume that full-employment output $\overline{Y}$ is constant, but relaxing that assumption would not affect our basic conclusions.

In Figure 13.3 the short-run aggregate supply ($SRAS$) curve shifts up by 10% each year. Why? With the growth in money supply fully anticipated, there are no misperceptions. Instead, people expect the price level to rise by 10% per year (a 10% inflation rate), which in turn causes the $SRAS$ curve to shift up by 10% per year. With no misperceptions, the economy remains at full employment with output at $\overline{Y}$. For example, when the expected price level is 100 in year 1, the $SRAS$ curve is $SRAS^1$. At point E the price level is 100 (the same as the expected price level) and output is $\overline{Y}$. In year 2 the expected price level is 110, and the $SRAS$ curve is $SRAS^2$. In year 2 equilibrium occurs at point F, again with output of $\overline{Y}$ and equal expected and actual price levels. Each year, both the AD curve and the $SRAS$ curve shift up by 10%, increasing the actual price level and expected price level by 10% and maintaining output at its full-employment level.

What happens to unemployment in this economy? Because output is continuously at its full-employment level $\overline{Y}$, unemployment remains at the natural rate $\bar{u}$. With unemployment at its natural rate, cyclical unemployment is zero. Hence this economy has zero unanticipated inflation *and* zero cyclical unemployment.

Against this backdrop of 10% monetary growth and 10% inflation, suppose now that in year 2 the money supply grows by 15% rather than by the expected 10% (Figure 13.4). In this case, instead of being 10% higher than AD^1 (as shown

4. In Chapter 3 we defined cyclical unemployment. Recall that the natural rate of unemployment is the unemployment rate that exists when output is at its full-employment level. The natural rate exceeds zero because of frictional and structural unemployment, also defined in Chapter 3.

Figure 13.3
Ongoing inflation in the extended classical model
If the money supply grows by 10% every year, the AD curve shifts up by 10% every year, from AD^1 in year 1 to AD^2 in year 2, and so on. If the money supply has been growing by 10% per year for some time and the rate of inflation has been 10% for some time, the expected rate of inflation is also 10%. Thus the expected price level also grows by 10% each year, from 100 in year 1 to 110 in year 2, and so on. The 10% annual increase in the expected price level shifts the $SRAS$ curve up by 10% each year, for example, from $SRAS^1$ in year 1 to $SRAS^2$ in year 2. The economy remains in full-employment equilibrium at the intersection of the AD curve and the $SRAS$ curve in each year (point E in year 1 and point F in year 2), with output at $\overline{Y}$, unemployment at the natural rate of unemployment $\overline{u}$, and inflation and expected inflation both at 10% per year.

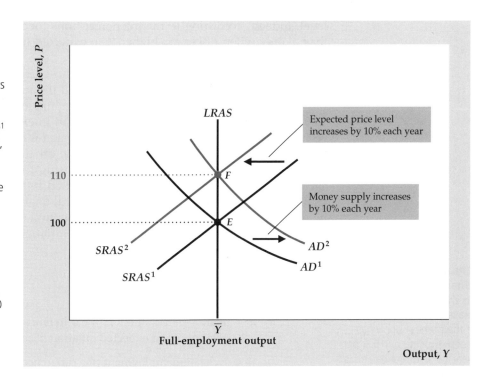

by $AD^{2,old}$), the aggregate demand curve in year 2 will be 15% higher than AD^1 (as shown by $AD^{2,new}$). If this increase in the rate of monetary growth is *unanticipated* at the beginning of year 2, the expected price level in year 2 remains at 110, and the short-run aggregate supply curve is $SRAS^2$, as before. The short-run equilibrium in year 2 is at point G, the intersection of the $AD^{2,new}$ and $SRAS^2$ curves. At G the price level is 113, so the actual rate of inflation in year 2 is 13%. Because the expected rate of inflation was 10%, the 13% inflation rate implies unanticipated inflation of 3% in year 2. Further, because output is above its full-employment level $\overline{Y}$ at G, the actual unemployment rate is below the natural rate and cyclical unemployment is negative.

Why is output above its full-employment level in year 2? Note that, in year 2, the 13% rate of inflation is less than the 15% rate of money growth but greater than the 10% expected rate of inflation. Because the price level grows by less than does the nominal money supply in year 2, the real money supply M/P increases, lowering the real interest rate and raising the aggregate quantity of goods demanded above $\overline{Y}$. At the same time, because the price level grows by more than expected, the aggregate quantity of goods supplied is also greater than $\overline{Y}$ as producers are fooled into thinking that the relative prices of their products have increased.

Producers cannot be fooled about price behaviour indefinitely, however. In the long run producers learn the true price level, the economy returns to full employment, and the inflation rate again equals the expected inflation rate, as in Figure 13.3. In the meantime, however, as long as actual output is higher than full-employment output $\overline{Y}$, and actual unemployment is below the natural rate $\overline{u}$, the actual price level must be higher than the expected price level. Indeed, according to the misperceptions theory, output can be higher than $\overline{Y}$ only when prices are higher than expected (and therefore when inflation is also higher than expected).

Thus in this economy, when the public correctly predicts aggregate demand growth and inflation, unanticipated inflation is zero, actual unemployment equals the natural rate, and cyclical unemployment is zero (Figure 13.3). However, if aggregate demand growth unexpectedly speeds up, the economy faces a period of positive unanticipated inflation and negative cyclical unemployment (Figure 13.4). Similarly, an unexpected slowdown in aggregate demand growth could occur, causing the AD curve to rise more slowly than expected; for a time unanticipated inflation would be negative (actual inflation less than expected) and cyclical unemployment would be positive (actual unemployment greater than the natural rate).

The relationship between unanticipated inflation and cyclical unemployment implied by this analysis is

$$\pi - \pi^e = -h(u - \overline{u})$$

where

$\pi - \pi^e$ = unanticipated inflation (the difference between actual inflation π and expected inflation π^e);

$u - \overline{u}$ = cyclical unemployment (the difference between the actual unemployment rate u and the natural unemployment rate $\overline{u}$);

h = a positive number that measures the strength of the relationship between unanticipated inflation and cyclical unemployment.

Figure 13.4
Unanticipated inflation in the extended classical model
If the money supply has been growing by 10% per year for a long time and is expected to continue growing by 10%, the expected price level increases by 10% each year. The 10% increase in the expected price level shifts the SRAS curve up from $SRAS^1$ in year 1 to $SRAS^2$ in year 2. Then, if the money supply actually increases by 15% in year 2 rather than by the expected 10%, the AD curve is $AD^{2,\text{new}}$ rather than $AD^{2,\text{old}}$. As a result of higher-than-expected money growth, output increases above $\overline{Y}$ in year 2 and the price level increases to 113, at point G. Because the price level rises by 13% rather than the expected 10%, unanticipated inflation is 3% in year 2. This unanticipated inflation is associated with output higher than $\overline{Y}$ and unemployment below the natural rate $\overline{u}$ (negative cyclical unemployment).

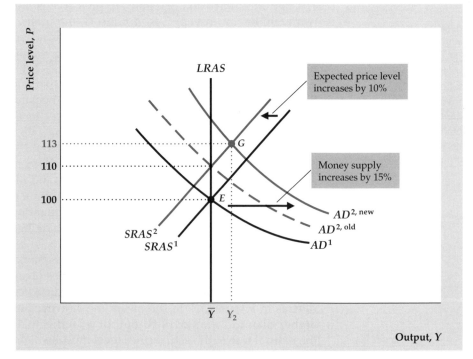

The preceding equation expresses mathematically the idea that unanticipated inflation will be positive when cyclical unemployment is negative, negative when cyclical unemployment is positive, and zero when cyclical unemployment is zero.[5] If we add π^e to both sides of the equation, it becomes

$$\pi = \pi^e - h(u - \bar{u}) \tag{13.1}$$

Equation (13.1) describes the expectations-augmented Phillips curve. According to the **expectations-augmented Phillips curve**, actual inflation π exceeds expected inflation π^e if the actual unemployment rate u is less than the natural rate $\bar{u}$; and actual inflation is less than expected inflation if the unemployment rate exceeds the natural rate.

The Shifting Phillips Curve

Let us return to the original Phillips curve, which links the levels of inflation and unemployment in the economy. The insight gained from the Friedman–Phelps analysis is that the relationship illustrated by the Phillips curve depends on the expected rate of inflation and the natural rate of unemployment. If either factor changes, the Phillips curve will shift.

Changes in the Expected Rate of Inflation. Figure 13.5 shows how a change in the expected inflation rate affects the relationship between inflation and unemployment, according to the Friedman–Phelps theory. The curve PC^1 is the Phillips curve for an expected rate of inflation of 3%. What identifies the expected rate of inflation as 3% along PC^1? Equation (13.1) indicates that, when the actual unemployment rate equals the natural rate (6% in this example), the actual inflation rate equals the expected inflation rate. Thus to determine the expected inflation rate on a Phillips curve, we find the inflation rate at the point where the actual unemployment rate equals the natural rate. For instance, at point A on curve PC^1 the unemployment rate equals the natural rate, and the actual and expected rates of inflation both equal 3%. As long as the expected inflation rate remains at 3% (and the natural unemployment rate remains at 6%), the Phillips curve PC^1 will describe the relationship between inflation and unemployment.

Now suppose that the expected rate of inflation increases from 3% to 12%. Figure 13.5 shows that this 9 percentage point increase in the expected rate of inflation shifts the Phillips curve up by 9 percentage points at each level of the unemployment rate, from PC^1 to PC^2. When the actual unemployment rate equals the natural rate on PC^2 (at point B), the inflation rate is 12%, confirming that the expected inflation rate is 12% along PC^2. Comparing PC^2 and PC^1 reveals that an increase in the expected inflation rate shifts the Phillips curve relationship between inflation and unemployment up and to the right.

---

5. The equation also implies that the relationship between unanticipated inflation and cyclical unemployment is linear, but this is for convenience only. The relationship of the two variables might as easily be a curve as a line.

Figure 13.5
The shifting Phillips curve: an increase in expected inflation
The Friedman–Phelps theory implies that there is a different Phillips curve for every expected inflation rate. For example, PC^1 is the Phillips curve when the expected rate of inflation is 3%. To verify this claim, note from Eq. (13.1) that, when the actual unemployment rate equals the natural rate $\bar{u}$ (6% here), the actual inflation rate equals the expected inflation rate. At point A, the unemployment rate equals the natural rate and the inflation rate equals 3% on PC^1, so the expected inflation rate is 3% on PC^1. Similarly, at point B on PC^2, where the unemployment rate equals its natural rate, the inflation rate is 12%, so the expected inflation rate is 12% along PC^2. Thus an increase in the expected inflation rate from 3% to 12% shifts the Phillips curve up and to the right, from PC^1 to PC^2.

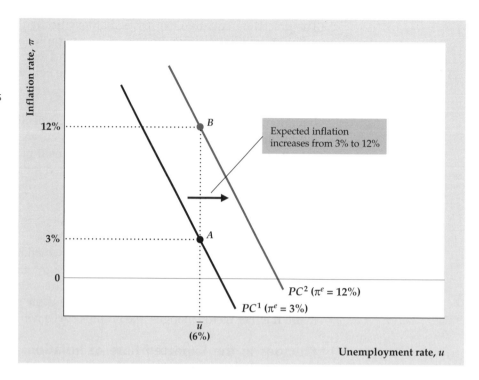

Changes in the Natural Rate of Unemployment.

The Phillips curve relationship between inflation and unemployment is also shifted by changes in the natural unemployment rate, as illustrated by Figure 13.6. The Phillips curve PC^1 shows a natural unemployment rate at 6% and an expected inflation rate at 3% (PC^1 in Figure 13.6 is the same as PC^1 in Figure 13.5). Now suppose that the natural unemployment rate increases to 7% but that the expected inflation rate remains unchanged at 3%. As Figure 13.6 shows, the increase in the natural unemployment rate causes the Phillips curve to shift, from PC^1 to PC^3.

To confirm that the natural unemployment rate corresponding to Phillips curve PC^3 in Figure 13.6 is 7%, look at point C on PC^3: at C, where the actual and expected inflation rates are equal, the unemployment rate is 7%. Thus the natural unemployment rate associated with Phillips curve PC^3 is 7%. This example illustrates that – like an increase in expected inflation – an increase in the natural unemployment rate causes the Phillips curve relationship between inflation and unemployment to shift up and to the right.

Supply Shocks and the Phillips Curve.

The Friedman–Phelps theory holds that changes in either expected inflation or the natural unemployment rate will shift the Phillips curve. One type of economic disturbance that is likely to affect both factors is a supply shock. Recall that an adverse supply shock causes a burst of inflation, which may lead people to expect higher inflation.[6]

---

6. The inflationary impact of a supply shock will be reinforced if, in an attempt to moderate the rise in unemployment caused by the shock, the central bank increases the money supply.

Figure 13.6
The shifting Phillips curve: an increase in the natural unemployment rate
According to the Friedman–Phelps theory, an increase in the natural unemployment rate shifts the Phillips curve up and to the right. At point A on PC^1, the actual inflation rate and the expected inflation rate are equal at 3%, so the natural unemployment rate equals the actual unemployment rate at A, or 6%. Thus PC^1 is the Phillips curve when the natural unemployment rate is 6% and the expected inflation rate is 3%, as in Fig. 13.5. If the natural unemployment rate increases to 7%, with expected inflation unchanged, the Phillips curve shifts to PC^3. At point C on PC^3, both expected and actual inflation equal 3%, so the natural unemployment rate equals the actual unemployment rate at C, or 7%.

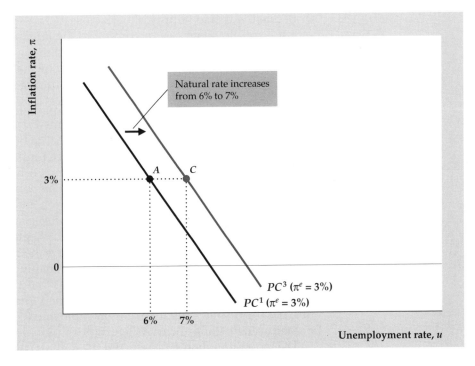

An adverse supply shock also tends to increase the natural unemployment rate, although the reasons for this effect are different for the classical and Keynesian models.

Recall that, from the classical perspective, an adverse supply shock raises the natural rate of unemployment by increasing the degree of mismatch between workers and jobs. For example, an oil price shock eliminates jobs in heavy-energy-using industries but increases employment in energy-providing industries.

In the Keynesian model, recall that much of the unemployment that exists even when the economy is at the full-employment level is blamed on rigid real wages. In particular, if the efficiency wage is above the market-clearing real wage, the amount of labour supplied at the efficiency wage will exceed the amount of labour demanded at that wage (Figure 12.2), leading to persistent structural unemployment. An adverse supply shock has no effect on the supply of labour,[7] but it does reduce the marginal product of labour and thus labour demand. With a rigid efficiency wage, the drop in labour demand increases the excess of labour supplied over labour demanded, raising the amount of unemployment that exists when the economy is at full employment. Thus, as in the classical model, the Keynesian model predicts that an adverse supply shock will raise the natural unemployment rate.

---

7. This statement is strictly true only for a temporary adverse supply shock. A permanent adverse supply shock, if it reduces expected future wages, would increase labour supply and thus cause an even larger rise in the natural rate of unemployment.

Because adverse supply shocks raise both expected inflation and the natural unemployment rate, according to the Friedman–Phelps analysis they should cause the Phillips curve to shift up and to the right. Similarly, beneficial supply shocks should shift the Phillips curve down and to the left. Overall, the Phillips curve should be particularly unstable during periods of supply shocks.

The Shifting Phillips Curve in Practice. Our analysis of the shifting Phillips curve (Figures 13.5 and 13.6) helps answer the basic questions about the Phillips curve raised earlier in the chapter. The first question was: why did the original Phillips curve relationship between inflation and unemployment apply to many historical cases, including the UK and most other European economies during the 1960s? The Friedman–Phelps analysis shows that a negative relationship between the levels of inflation and unemployment holds *as long as expected inflation and the natural unemployment rate are approximately constant.* As shown in Figure 13.10 later in this chapter, the natural unemployment rate changes relatively slowly, and during the 1960s it was approximately constant. Expected inflation was also probably nearly constant in most European economies in the 1960s, because at that time people were used to low and stable inflation and inflation remained low for most of the decade. Thus, not surprisingly, inflation and unemployment data for the 1960s seem to lie along a single Phillips curve (Figure 13.1).

The second question was: why did the Phillips curve relationship, so apparent in the the United Kingdom and United States in the 1960s, seem to disappear after 1970 (Figure 13.2)? The answer suggested by the Friedman–Phelps analysis is that, in the two decades after 1970, the expected inflation rate and the natural unemployment rate varied considerably more than they had in the 1960s, causing the Phillips curve relationship to shift erratically.

Contributing to the shifts of the Phillips curve after 1970 were the two large supply shocks associated with sharp increases in the price of oil that hit European economies in 1973–74 and 1979–80. Recall that adverse supply shocks are likely to increase both expected inflation and the natural rate of unemployment, shifting the Phillips curve up and to the right. Oil prices also varied considerably during the 1980s, declining precipitously in the middle of the decade and then temporarily rising again after the Iraqi invasion of Kuwait in August 1990.

Beyond the direct effects of supply shocks, other forces may have increased the variability of expected inflation and the natural unemployment rate after 1970. As we discuss later in the chapter, the natural unemployment rate also rose during this period.

Expected inflation probably varied more after 1970 because actual inflation varied more (see Figure 2.3 for the inflation rate for a representative selection of European countries for 1961–96). After being relatively low for a long time, inflation, driven by monetary and fiscal policies that had probably been over-expansionary for several years, emerged as a problem at the end of the 1960s. The 1970s were a period of high and erratic inflation, the result of the oil price shocks and macroeconomic policies that again were probably too expansionary, especially in the latter part of the decade. In contrast, following the tough anti-inflationary policies of many European governments, particularly the Thatcher government in the UK during 1979–82, inflation returned to a relatively low level during the 1980s. To the extent that expected inflation followed the path of actual inflation – high and erratic in the 1970s, low in the 1980s – our analysis suggests that the Phillips curve relationship between inflation and unemployment would not have been stable over the period.

Does the unstable Phillips curve in the decades after 1970 imply that there was no systematic relationship between inflation and unemployment during that period? The answer is no. According to the Friedman–Phelps analysis, a negative relationship between *unanticipated* inflation and *cyclical* unemployment should appear in the data, even if expected inflation and the natural unemployment rate are changing. Measures of unanticipated inflation and cyclical unemployment for each year during the period 1973–92 are shown in Figure 13.7 for both the UK and USA. These measures are approximate because we cannot directly observe either expected inflation (needed to calculate unanticipated inflation) or the natural unemployment rate (needed to find cyclical unemployment). We assumed that expected inflation for each year was the average inflation rate of the previous two years, and we used estimates of the natural unemployment rate presented later in the chapter in Figure 13.9.[8]

Figure 13.7 suggests that, despite the instability of the traditional Phillips curve relationship between inflation and unemployment, a negative relationship between *unanticipated* inflation and *cyclical* unemployment did exist during the period 1973–92, as predicted by the Friedman–Phelps analysis (compare Figure 13.7 to Figure 13.2).[9] In particular, note that inflation was much lower than expected and that cyclical unemployment was high in both the UK and the USA during 1982 and 1983, years that both countries reduced inflation through tight monetary policy.

Macroeconomic Policy and the Phillips Curve

We have addressed two of the questions about the Phillips curve raised earlier in the chapter – the questions of why the Phillips curve was observed in historical data and why it seemed to shift after 1970. We still must answer the third question: can the Phillips curve be thought of as a 'menu' of inflation–unemployment combinations from which policymakers can choose? For example, can policymakers reduce the unemployment rate by increasing the rate of inflation (moving up and to the left along the Phillips curve)?

According to the expectations-augmented Phillips curve, unemployment will fall below the natural rate only when inflation is unanticipated. So the question becomes: can macroeconomic policy be used systematically to create unanticipated inflation?

---

8. The values for the UK are actually an average of the natural rate of unemployment in the UK, France, Germany, Belgium, and Denmark.
9. In Figure 13.7, the points corresponding to the years 1975 for the UK and 1974, 1975, and 1980 for the USA lie somewhat above the curve defined by the rest of the points. Note that all of those years follow oil price shocks, which were largely unexpected when they occurred. Our estimates of expected inflation for those years – based on inflation rates in the previous two years – may be too low, resulting in estimates of unanticipated inflation for those years that are too high. The years 1974 and 1975 also follow the 1971–74 price control period in the USA, during which inflation was kept artificially low by government restrictions on price increases, so that again we may have underestimated the inflation rate actually expected in 1974 and 1975.

**Figure 13.7
The expectations-augmented Phillips curve in the United Kingdom and the United States, 1973–92**

The expectations-augmented Phillips curve is a negative relationship between unanticipated inflation and cyclical unemployment. Shown is this relationship for the years 1973–92 in the United Kingdom and the United States. Unanticipated inflation equals actual minus expected inflation, where expected inflation in any year is measured here as the average inflation rate for the preceding two years. Cyclical unemployment for each year is actual unemployment minus an estimate of the natural unemployment rate for that year (see Fig. 13.10). Note that years in which unanticipated inflation is high usually are years in which cyclical unemployment is low.

Source: (a) Unemployment rate and inflation rate, 1973–90 from Layard *et al. op cit. Figure 13.2(a).* Data for the period 1991–92 from *Economic Trends Annual Supplement, 1997,* Table 3.3 (unemployment) and Table 2.1 (inflation) natural rate is taken from *OECD Jobs Study, Part 1,* Paris, OECD, 1994, Chart 2.4 p. 68; inflation, see Figure 13.2(a). (b) Unemployment rate, all civilian workers, 1993 *Economic Report of the President,* Table B-37; natural rate of unemployment: see Figure 13.9; CPI inflation rate, year to year, all items (CPI-U): 1973–91 from 1993 *Economic Report of the President,* Table B-59, 1992 value from *Survey of Current Business.*

(a)

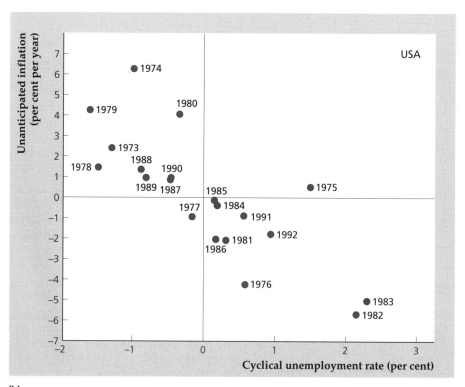

(b)

Classical and Keynesian economists disagree on the answer to this question. Classical economists argue that wages and prices adjust quickly in response to new economic information, including information about changes in government policies. Furthermore, they believe that people have rational expectations, meaning that they make intelligent forecasts of future policy changes. Because prices and price-level expectations respond quickly to new information, the government cannot keep actual inflation above expected inflation – as would be needed to drive unemployment below the natural rate – except perhaps for a very short time. According to classical economists, policies (such as more rapid monetary expansion) that increase the growth rate of aggregate demand act primarily to raise actual *and* expected inflation and so do not lead to a sustained reduction in unemployment. Because any systematic attempt to affect the unemployment rate will be thwarted by the rapid adjustment of inflation expectations, they conclude that the Phillips curve does *not* represent a usable trade-off for policymakers. (Box 13.1, explores a general lesson for policymakers of the shifting Phillips curve.)

In contrast, Keynesians contend that policymakers do have some ability – in the short run, at least – to create unanticipated inflation and thus to bring unemployment below the natural rate.[10] Although many Keynesians accept the notion that people have rational expectations, they argue that the expected rate of inflation that should be included in the expectations-augmented Phillips curve is the forecast of inflation made at the time that the oldest sticky prices in the economy were set. Because of price stickiness, when policymakers cause aggregate demand to rise above the expected level, time is needed for prices fully to reflect this new information. In the meantime some prices reflect older information, and the rate of inflation is higher than the expected inflation rate based on this older information. In response to increased inflation, therefore, unemployment may remain below the natural rate for a while.

The Long-Run Phillips Curve

Although classical and Keynesian economists disagree about whether the Phillips curve relationship can be exploited to reduce unemployment temporarily, they agree that policymakers cannot keep the unemployment rate *permanently* below the natural rate by maintaining a high rate of inflation. Expectations about inflation will eventually adjust so that the expected and actual inflation rates are equal, or $\pi^e = \pi$. The expectations-augmented Phillips curve (equation 13.1) implies that, when $\pi^e = \pi$, the actual unemployment rate u equals the natural unemployment rate $\bar{u}$. Thus the actual unemployment rate equals the natural rate in the long run regardless of the inflation rate maintained.

---

10. As we discussed in Chapter 12, Keynesian economists also believe that macroeconomic policy can be used to return the unemployment rate to its natural level, if the economy starts out in a recession or a boom.

BOX 13.1

The Lucas Critique

Suppose that you observed, in a particular season, that Manchester United made a shot directly on goal 100% of the time when given a free kick just outside their opponent's penalty area. Could you safely conclude, based on this empirical evidence, they would shoot directly at goal from free kicks next season? In most cases, you could safely make this prediction, even if you did not know anything about soccer. But what if, during the off-season, the rules are changed to allow opposition players to stand only one metre from where the free kick is taken? Would you expect Manchester United to follow the same tactics? Certainly no one familiar with soccer would expect them to follow their old strategy, which would be foolish under the new rules. The simple lesson to be learned from this example is that, when the rules of the game change, people's behaviour also changes.

In an influential article,* Nobel Laureate Robert E. Lucas, Jr. of the University of Chicago, applied this lesson to macroeconomic policy making. Frequently, in attempting to forecast the effects of a new set of policies, economists and policymakers assume that historical relationships between macroeconomic variables will continue to hold after the new policies are in place. Lucas objected to this assumption, asserting what has become known as the *Lucas critique*.

According to the Lucas critique, because new policies change the economic 'rules' and thus affect economic behaviour, no one can safely assume that historical relationships between variables will hold when policies change.

A good example of the Lucas critique in action is the shifting Phillips curve. Historically, there seemed to be a stable relationship between inflation and unemployment, which led some policymakers to believe that they could permanently reduce unemployment by increasing inflation. However, as we have discussed, when policymakers allowed inflation to rise, the public's inflation expectations also rose. As a result, the Phillips curve shifted and the historical relationship between inflation and unemployment broke down.

The main message of the Lucas critique for economists is that, in order to predict the effects of policy changes on the economy, they must understand how economic behaviour will change under the new policies. Understanding the impact of policy changes on behaviour – particularly the introduction of policies that have not been tried before – requires the use of economic theory as well as empirical analysis.

_____

* 'Econometric Policy Evaluation: A Critique', in K. Brunner and A. H. Meltzer, eds., *Carnegie-Rochester Conference Series on Public Policy*, vol. 1, 1976.

The long-run relationship of unemployment and inflation is shown by the **long-run Phillips curve**. In the long run, because unemployment equals the natural rate regardless of the inflation rate, the long-run Phillips curve is a vertical line at $u = \bar{u}$, as shown in Figure 13.8.

The vertical long-run Phillips curve is related to the long-run neutrality of money, discussed in Chapters 11 and 12. Classical and Keynesian economists agree that changes in the money supply will have no long-run effects on real variables, including unemployment. The vertical long-run Phillips curve carries the notion of monetary neutrality one step further by indicating that changes in the *growth rate* of money, which lead to changes in the inflation rate, also have no real effects in the long run.

At best, the Phillips curve can be exploited only temporarily, so why would policymakers attempt to reduce unemployment by creating surprise inflation? One possibility is that stimulating the economy may help the incumbent political party win elections; see the box 'The Political Environment: Government Elections and Macroeconomic Policy', p. 492.

Figure 13.8
The long-run Phillips curve
Because people will not permanently overestimate or underestimate the rate of inflation, in the long run the expected and actual inflation rates are equal and the actual unemployment rate equals the natural unemployment rate. Because in the long run actual unemployment equals the natural rate regardless of the inflation rate, the long-run Phillips curve is vertical.

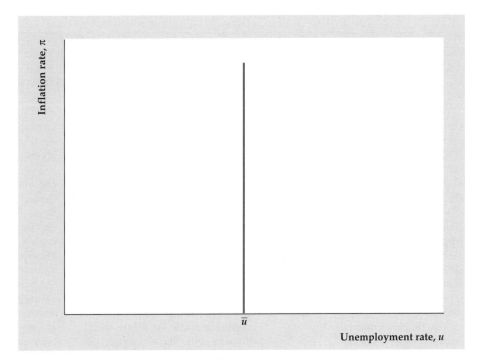

13.2 THE PROBLEM OF UNEMPLOYMENT

In the rest of the chapter we look more closely at unemployment and inflation, beginning with unemployment in this section. We start by discussing the costs of unemployment, then consider the factors that determine the long-run unemployment level, and conclude by exploring some ways in which macro-economic policy can address unemployment.

The Costs of Unemployment

There are two principal costs of unemployment. The first is the loss of output that occurs because fewer people are productively employed. This cost is borne disproportionately by unemployed workers themselves, in terms of the income they lose because they are out of work. However, because the unemployed may stop paying taxes and instead receive unemployment benefits or other government payments, society (in this case, taxpayers) also bears some of the output cost of unemployment.

How big is the output cost of unemployment? One estimate is provided by Okun's law (see equation 3.5), which states that each percentage point of *cyclical* unemployment is associated with a loss equal to 2.5% of full-employment output. Thus if full-employment output is £600 billion, Okun's law indicates that each percentage point of unemployment sustained for one year reduces output by £15 billion.

The loss of output predicted by Okun's law reflects not only the direct impact of increased unemployment, but also other labour market changes that

THE POLITICAL ENVIRONMENT

GOVERNMENT ELECTIONS AND MACROECONOMIC POLICY

Among the many issues affecting government elections in any European country, macroeconomic policy and performance are always among the most important. Concern about how the French economy was performing underlay Lionel Jospin's defeat of Alain Juppé in the 1997 French parliamentary elections. More generally, statistical studies of election results confirm that a growing economy and falling unemployment during an election year significantly improve the election prospects of the incumbent party.*

Of course, governments are aware that an improving economy helps their re-election chances, and they undoubtedly consider these political benefits when planning macroeconomic policy. According to the theory of 'political business cycles' introduced by William Nordhaus[†] of Yale University, we should expect incumbent Prime Ministers to use expansionary aggregate demand policies to stimulate the economy during election years. Anecdotal evidence, at least, supports this theory: For example, many observers claimed that Nigel Lawson, the then Chancellor of the Exchequer, used expansionary aggregate demand

policies to improve the re-election chances of the Thatcher government in 1987.

Despite this anecdotal evidence, the data do not consistently support Nordhaus's political business cycle theory. One problem with the theory is the assumption that incumbents are motivated only by the prospects of re-election, which ignores the possibility that politicians have other goals, such as promoting policies that they favour. For example, an implication of the political business cycle theory is that the Prime Minister's political party should not matter in terms of the economy's performance, as the Prime Minister will simply do what is needed to win re-election regardless of party affiliation. However, in general, economic performance under conservatives and socialists is not the same: historically, conservatives have been more successful than socialists at reducing inflation, but socialists have done a better job at moderating unemployment.

To explain the difference in macroeconomic behaviour during socialist and conservative administrations, Douglas Hibbs[‡] of Harvard University proposed a 'partisan theory' of macroeconomic policy in which socialists, who typically have greater support

among less affluent voters, are assumed to care relatively more about unemployment and relatively less about inflation than conservatives do. The partisan theory accounts for the fact that unemployment is more likely to fall and inflation is more likely to rise during socialist administrations than during conservative administrations. A problem with the partisan theory is its assumption that a stable Phillips curve gives policymakers a choice among fixed combinations of unemployment and inflation. However, as we demonstrated, changes in the expected inflation rate shift the Phillips curve so that policymakers do *not* face a stable trade-off between inflation and unemployment.

Most recently, Alberto Alesina[§] of Harvard University has combined the partisan theory with rational expectations and an expectations-augmented Phillips curve to examine the effects of aggregate demand policy in socialist and conservative administrations. The importance of rational expectations and an expectations-augmented Phillips curve is that only surprises in policy can affect real variables such as output and unemployment.

occur during recessions, such as shorter working weeks, reduced labour force participation, and lower productivity (Numerical Problem 10 in Chapter 3 illustrates these effects). Thus the output cost of unemployment estimated by Okun's law is probably too high. Nevertheless, an output loss that was only one-quarter of that predicted by Okun's law would still be a significant cost, particularly if it were borne largely by the relatively poor and disadvantaged members of society.

THE POLITICAL ENVIRONMENT

(Continued)

Alesina argues that surprises arising from electoral uncertainty occur only at the beginning of an administration because, when expectations of future inflation are formed before an election, the outcome of the election is unknown. Therefore the expected inflation rate is an average of the higher inflation that would prevail under a socialist Prime Minister and the lower inflation that would occur if a conservative is elected. If a socialist wins the election, inflation is higher than expected and unemployment falls; if a conservative wins, inflation is lower than expected and unemployment rises. After expectations have completely adjusted to take into account the election outcome, however, aggregate demand policy does not yield systematically different results for socialists and conservatives.

An important implication of Alesina's theory is thus that output and inflation will be higher and unemployment lower in the couple of years immediately following the election of a socialist government than in either the preceding one or two years or when compared with the government's entire term of office. The election of a conservative government, on the other hand,

will result in lower output and inflation and higher unemployment in the first few years after an election. The accompanying table shows the number of cases when these predictions are correct for a number of different countries. Alesina's predictions, in fact, turn out to be generally correct in nearly three quarters of the elections he considered. The one exception is the Netherlands which does not exhibit the pattern predicted by the theory.

* An early study is Ray Fair, 'The Effects of Economic Events on votes for President', *The Review of Economics and Statistics*, May 1978, pp. 159–172.
† For a survey, see William Nordhaus, 'Alternative Approaches to the Political Business Cycle,' *Brookings Papers on Economic Activity*, 1989:2, pp. 1–49.
‡ 'Political Parties and Macroeconomic Policy,' *American Political Science Review*, December 1977, pp. 1467–87.
§ 'Politics and Business Cycles in Industrial Democracies', *Economic Policy*, 1989, pp. 55–89.

Indicators	Output growth		Unemployment		Inflation		Total	
Correct outcome	Yes	No	Yes	No	Yes	No	Yes	No
Austria	4	0	3	1	0	1	7	2
Belgium	5	4	8	1	1	2	14	7
Denmark	6	0	4	2	3	0	13	2
Finland	3	0	2	1	0	1	5	2
France	2	0	2	0	n.a	n.a	4	0
Germany	4	2	5	1	1	1	10	4
Netherlands	2	5	1	6	3	0	6	11
Norway	5	2	4	3	2	1	11	6
Sweden	4	0	3	1	1	0	8	1
UK	5	1	4	2	2	0	11	3
USA	5	1	5	1	2	0	12	2
Total	45	15	41	19	15	6	101	40
% of Yes	75		68		71		72	

Source: Constructed from data presented in Alesina, *op. cit.*, p. 70.

The other substantial cost of unemployment is the personal or psychological cost faced by unemployed workers and their families. This cost is especially important for workers suffering long spells of unemployment and for the chronically unemployed. Workers without steady employment for long periods lose job skills and self-esteem, and suffer from stress.[11]

11. See, for example, Andrew Clarke and Andrew Oswald, 'Unhappiness and Unemployment', *Economic Journal*, May 1994, pp. 648–59.

The costs of unemployment are real and serious, but two offsetting factors should be noted. First, to the extent that unemployed workers engage in economically productive activities such as searching for a job or acquiring new skills, the loss of output arising from current unemployment may be compensated for by increased output in the future. In particular, frictional unemployment – the result of workers and firms seeking appropriate matches – raises future productivity and output and thus may impose little net economic cost, or even lead to an economic gain.

A second offsetting factor is that unemployed people have more leisure time – to spend with family and friends, work around the house, and so on. However, the benefits of extra leisure time decrease as the amount of leisure increases, and most unemployed workers would not feel that increased leisure was adequate compensation for their lost income.

The Long-Term Behaviour of the Unemployment Rate

Classical and Keynesian economists agree that, although the actual unemployment rate may deviate from the natural unemployment rate in the short run, in the long run the actual rate equals the natural rate. Thus understanding the behaviour of unemployment in all but the short run requires identifying the determinants of the natural rate of unemployment. In Chapter 3 we discussed the reasons for the natural unemployment rate always being greater than zero; here we focus more narrowly on the reasons for a rising natural rate in recent years in Europe and the United States.

For thirty years after World War II many European countries maintained low unemployment rates. Then, after the oil price shocks and worldwide recessions of the 1970s, unemployment rates in those countries rose sharply. (See Figure 13.9.) The unemployment rate in the United States also rose to high levels during the 1970s but fell quickly during the recovery that followed

Figure 13.9
Unemployment in Europe and the US
Unemployment rates in many European countries rose from less than 3% in the early 1970s to around 10% in the mid 1980s. The unemployment rate in Italy, which was more than double that in other European countries during the 1960s and 1970s, also increased though the rise was less dramatic. The exception to this trend is Sweden, where the unemployment rate was stable at around 2% until 1990 when it rose sharply. Unlike the US, the persistence of high unemployment in many European countries suggests that the natural unemployment rate also increased. The increase in the natural rate, in response to actual unemployment, is an example of hysteresis.

Source: *European Economy, 1996 op.cit. Table 1.1(b).*

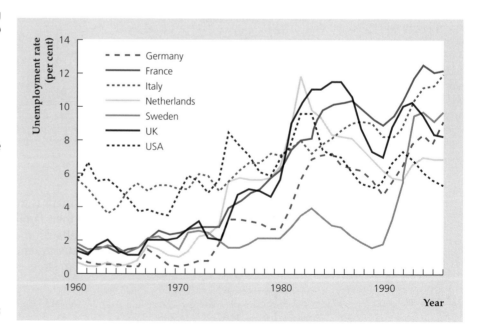

the 1981–82 recession. In contrast, unemployment rates in Europe remained high throughout most of the decade, falling temporarily during the late 1980s but rising again in the early 1990s. This long-term increase in the European unemployment rate from only 1%–3% of the labour force in the early 1970s to much higher levels in the 1980s reflects an increase in the natural unemployment rate of six percentage points or more, according to some estimates. What accounts for this apparent large increase in the natural unemployment rate in Europe?[12]

12. Two excellent accounts of the rising unemployment rate in Europe compared with what has happened in other countries are Richard Layard, Stephen Nickell and Richard Jackman, *Unemployment: Macroeconomic Performance and the Labour Market* (Oxford University Press, 1992) and Charles Bean 'European Unemployment: A Survey', *Journal of Economic Literature*, June 1994, pp. 573–619.

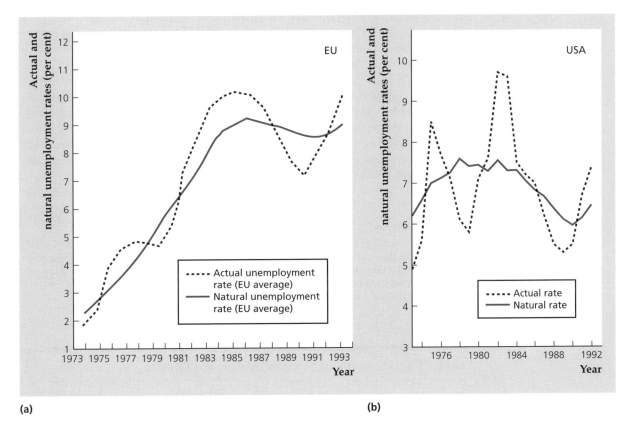

(a)   (b)

Figure 13.10
Actual and natural unemployment rates in the EU and USA

The figure shows the actual unemployment rate and an estimate of the natural rate of unemployment in the EU for the period 1973–93 and in the United States for the period 1973–1992. The difference between the actual and natural unemployment rates is the cyclical unemployment rate. Note that the natural rate of unemployment has risen over this period.

Sources: (a) Unemployment rate, all civilian workers from *European Economy 1996, op cit. Table 1.1(b)*, Table 3; natural rate of unemployment from *OECD Jobs Study* (see Figure 13.7(a)): (b) Unemployment rate, all civilian workers, 1993 *Economic Report of the President*, Table B-37; natural rate of unemployment: 1973–86 from Ellen Rissman, Federal Reserve Bank of Chicago, private communication; 1987–92, estimated by the authors as a weighted average of the actual unemployment rate and the previous natural rate.

The Rising Natural Rate. The natural unemployment rate corresponds to full-employment output. Unfortunately, because we cannot be sure when the economy is at full employment, we cannot directly observe the natural rate and so must estimate it. Inevitably, therefore, there is some uncertainty about the value of the natural rate at any particular time. Figure 13.10 shows estimated values of the natural unemployment rate, along with the actual unemployment rate for the EU during 1973–93 and for the USA during 1973–92. The estimates of the natural unemployment rate for the EU were produced by the OECD and are based on data for Germany, France, Belgium, Denmark, and the United Kingdom.[13] Ellen Rissman of the Federal Reserve Bank of Chicago provided the estimated levels of the US natural rate before 1987; based on her research, we estimated the levels of the natural rate since 1987.[14] Most current estimates, including those in Figure 13.10, suggest a natural unemployment rate of about 9% of the labour force in Europe and 6% in the USA. In comparison, most estimates of the natural rate for the 1950s and 1960s were in the range of 2%–3% in Europe and 4%–5% in the USA. Hence the natural unemployment rate in Europe has apparently risen by six percentage points and in the USA by one or two percentage points over the last thirty years.

Giving a fully satisfactory explanation of the rise in the natural rate of unemployment is difficult, especially when no one cause by itself can explain the sharp rise in the natural unemployment rate across the whole of Europe and when one factor which may be important in, say, the Netherlands is of less significance in, say, the UK or Sweden. One suggestion is that the increase has been the result of demographic changes. Table 13.1 shows unemployment rates for workers in different demographic groups for a number of countries.

---

13. OECD, *The OECD Jobs Study*: Part 1, 1994, p. 68.

14. See Rissman, 'Wage Growth and Sectoral Shifts: Phillips Curve Redux,' *Journal of Monetary Economics*, June 1993, pp. 395–416 for a discussion of issues in estimating the natural unemployment rate. Unlike those in Rissman's article, estimates of the natural rate shown in Figure 13.9 have not been adjusted for changing demographics. We estimated the natural rate since 1987 as a weighted average of the actual unemployment rate and the year-earlier natural rate.

Table 13.1 Unemployment Rates by Age and Gender

	Adult Male		Adult Female		Young People	
	1975	**1995**	**1975**	**1995**	**1985**	**1995**
France	2.7	9.5	5.8	13.8	25.4	27.0
Germany	3.2	7.1	3.9	9.8	10.3	8.8
Italy	3.2	9.2	8.7	16.4	29.4	33.2
Netherlands	3.8	6.0	3.5	9.1	13.1	12.5
Sweden	1.5	10.1	2.2	8.2	7.1	19.4
UK	3.8	10.1	1.8	7.0	18.5	15.9

Source: *Employment in Europe*, 1996.

Young people (aged sixteen to twenty-four) have higher unemployment rates than adults, and for much of the post-World War II period (but not recently in Sweden and the UK) women have had a higher unemployment rate than men. A principal reason for this is that these workers are less likely than adult males to hold long-term, stable jobs and are more likely to hold temporary or 'dead-end' jobs, with little prospect for advancement or long-term employment. Because these jobs do not last long, young people and women are frequently unemployed and must spend a relatively large amount of time looking for work. A cause of the historically higher unemployment rate for women is that, traditionally, women have spent more time than men in taking care of children and thus have had more interruptions in their careers. For women, moving in and out of the labour force often involves periods of unemployment. Young people have high unemployment rates both because they move in and out of the labour force frequently while they are at college or university and also because many young people work at low-skill jobs that do not provide long-term employment.

Since World War II, young people and women have emerged as a large portion of the labour force in many European countries. This shift in the composition of the labour force towards groups that have higher unemployment rates may have raised the overall unemployment rate.

The demographic explanation of the increase in the natural unemployment rate has some merit but is incomplete for two reasons. First, the changes in labour force composition account only for a portion – probably less than one percentage point – of the increase in the natural rate. Indeed, some demographic changes – such as the relative increase in university-educated workers, who typically have low unemployment rates – work in the direction of reducing the natural rate. Second, the unemployment rate in most countries has risen *within* each demographic category. Thus even if there had been no change in labour force composition, the overall unemployment rate would have risen.

Another factor that may have contributed to the increase in the natural unemployment rate is a faster pace of structural change in the economy, which has taken several forms. Technological changes have increased the skill levels that firms demand from workers, reducing the employment opportunities for low-skilled or poorly educated workers (see the Application, 'Technical Change and Wage Inequality', p. 92). Also, some industries and regions have grown significantly while others were suffering long-term declines; notably, the share of jobs in manufacturing has fallen while that in services has risen. Both changes worsen the problem of mismatch between jobs and workers, raising frictional and structural unemployment and hence the natural rate.[15]

A third factor which may have resulted in an increase in the natural unemployment rate in many European countries is the behaviour of trade unions. Table 13.2 (overleaf) shows trade union density (trade union membership as a

15. Richard Jackman, Richard Layard, and S. Savouri construct a number of mismatch indexes for both occupational and regional labour markets but find no evidence that the level of mismatch is increasing in Europe apart from in Sweden. See 'Mismatch: A Framework for Thought', in F. Padoa-Schioppa, ed., *Mismatch and the Labour Market* (Cambridge University Press, 1991).

percentage of total employment) for a number of European countries and does indeed show that trade union membership increased during the 1970s in many European countries. However, during the 1980s when union density started to fall, unemployment continued to rise, which casts some doubt on the view that the rising natural unemployment rate in Europe was primarily driven by more aggressive behaviour on the part of trade unions. Nor does the Swedish experience fit well with this explanation. During the 1970s, trade union density increased in Sweden, along with that in other European countries, but it did so without a corresponding increase in unemployment. Rather unemployment rose sharply in Sweden during the 1990s, at a time when union density was actually falling there.

Wage setting is, of course, a complex matter and involves not just trade unions but also management and government. The extent to which these three work together in setting wages in an economy is called **corporatism**. Lars Calmfors of the University of Stockholm and John Driffill of the University of Southampton examined the nature of wage bargaining in a number of OECD countries to see if there is a relationship between the extent to which wage-setting arrangements are centralized and economic performance.[16] The authors find large differences in the extent to which wage bargaining is centralized. Austria and Sweden and the other Scandinavian countries have very centralized wage bargaining in which powerful union and employer organizations set wages. At the other extreme are countries, such as the UK, Italy, France, the USA, and Japan, where wage setting takes place at the firm, and sometimes at the industry, level. Most European countries lie between these extremes. Calmfors and Driffill find that the most favourable forms of wage setting in terms of macroeconomic performance involve either a high degree of corporatism – because wage bargaining directly takes into account macroeconomic considerations – or a decentralized system of wage setting, where workers can appreciate the direct impact of wage settlements on the performance of the firm they work for.

---

16. Lars Calmfors and John Driffill, 'Bargaining Structure, Corporatism and Macroeconomic Performance', *Economic Policy*, April 1988, pp. 14–61.

Table 13.2 Trade Union Density

	1970	1980	1988
Germany	33.0	37.0	33.7
France	22.3	19.0	12.0
Italy	36.3	49.3	39.6
Netherlands	50.6	56.9	57.1
Sweden	67.7	80.0	85.3
UK	44.8	50.7	41.5

Source: 'Trends in the Trade Union Membership' *OECD Employment Outlook*, July 1991, pp. 97–120.

Hysteresis in Unemployment. Although economists would like to understand why the natural unemployment rate has risen, a more serious and puzzling change is that the natural unemployment rate, after increasing sharply, has remained high in Europe, in marked contrast to what happened in the USA and a number of other industrialized countries. It is the persistence of high rates of unemployment, associated with high levels of long-term unemployment, which many economists believe is the most serious problem.

Some economists use a term taken from physics, hysteresis, to describe the behaviour of European unemployment. Applied to unemployment, **hysteresis** means that the natural unemployment rate changes in response to the actual unemployment rate, rising if the actual rate is above the natural rate and falling if the actual rate is below the natural rate. According to the proponents of hysteresis theory, the rise in European unemployment in the mid 1970s, originally because of factors such as rising oil prices and contractionary macroeconomic policies, also increased the natural unemployment rate. This increase in turn helps account for the continued high actual unemployment rate in these countries. When these countries return to long-run equilibrium with full employment, the actual rate equals the new higher natural rate.

Some economists use the example of the UK in the early 1980s as an example of hysteresis to show how a recession can have long-term effects on the natural rate of unemployment. In the late 1970s, the Thatcher government's contractionary monetary policy resulted in an increase in unemployment accompanied by a falling rate of inflation. However, unemployment remained high even after inflation had stabilized at a lower level by the mid 1980s and the UK had adopted an easier monetary policy.

There are several explanations of hysteresis in European unemployment. First, some economists suggest that, when a high unemployment rate idles workers for a long period of time, their skills deteriorate (or the workers fail to get training in the first place). Lower skill levels increase the mismatch between workers and firms and raise the natural unemployment rate.

Workers who have been unemployed also lose heart in looking for work and as a result become less effective in job search.[17] Moreover, the long-term unemployed are less attractive to potential employers, who will often use unemployment history as a criterion when hiring labour.[18] The incidence of long-term unemployment (the percentage of unemployed workers who have been out of work for more than twelve months) is shown in Table 13.3 (overleaf). The most striking feature of the data shown in the table is the difference between the incidence of long-term unemployment in most European countries and that found in Sweden, a country which adopts a very interventionist approach to unemployment, and in the USA.

---

17. See, for example, Gordon Hughes and Barry McCormick, 'Hidden Unemployment and Suppressed Labour Mobility in the British Labour Market', mimeo, University of Southampton, 1989, who find that job search activity falls sharply after one year of unemployment.
18. See, for example, Nigel Meager and Hilary Metcalf, *Recruitment of the Long-term Unemployed* (Institute of Manpower Studies, Brighton, 1987).

Second, some economists argue that the bureaucratic aspects of firms and unions, as well as government regulation, interfere with the adjustment of the labour market in Europe. For example, in some European countries the government severely restricts the ability of firms to fire workers. Because firms know that firing workers is difficult, they are reluctant to hire additional workers unless they are confident that they will not have to reduce their work forces for a long time. Thus after many workers were laid off in the mid 1970s, firms were reluctant to rehire them or to hire new workers.[19]

Minimum wage legislation is another way in which government regulation can interfere with the adjustment of the labour market. Many European countries already have some form of minimum wage legislation (minimum wages are also a central feature of the Social Charter) which sets wages at a level well above those applied in the USA.[20] Can this help to explain the persistence of high unemployment rates in Europe compared with the USA? It appears not, for two reasons. In the first place, it is argued that the percentage of workers employed at the minimum in most countries is small and so minimum wages cannot explain the sharp rise in unemployment. More importantly, the statistical evidence for a number of European countries and for the USA about the impact of minimum wage legislation is far from supportive of this view. Although some studies have indeed shown that such legislation does increase unemployment, many have found that minimum wage legislation has no impact on either employment or unemployment.[21]

Table 13.3 The Incidence of Long-Term Unemployment

	1985	1995
Germany	53.7	48.7
France	46.8	40.2
Italy	65.8	63.6
Netherlands	58.8	46.7
Sweden	11.7	20.2
UK	48.1	43.5
USA	n.a.	12.2*

Note: Incidence of long-term unemployment measured as the number of workers unemployed for at least twelve months as a percentage of total unemployment.

* 1994.

Source: *Employment in Europe*, 1996.

19. See, for example, Edward Lazear, 'Job Security Provisions and Employment', *Quarterly Journal of Economics*, August 1990, pp. 699–726 and George Alogoskoufis and Alan Manning, 'Wage Setting and the Persistence of Unemployment in Europe, Japan and the USA, *European Economic Review*, March 1988, pp. 698–706. Evidence that hiring costs have also reduced job creation in Europe is presented in a paper by Simon Burgess, 'Where did Europe Fail? A Disaggregated Comparison of Net Job Creation in Europe and the US', Centre for Economic Performance, Discussion Paper No. 192, 1994, London School of Economics.

20. See, Richard Freeman, 'Minimum Wages – Again!', *International Journal of Manpower*, 1994, pp. 8–25.

21. One example of a positive effect of minimum wage legislation on employment is the impact minimum wages have had on youth unemployment in the Netherlands, which was found to be lower as a result of government intervention in the Dutch labour market. See Arthur van Soest, 'Youth Minimum Wage Rates: The Dutch Experience, *International Journal of Manpower*, 1994, pp. 100–17.

BOX 13.2

The Effect of Unemployment Benefits on Unemployment

Most countries have unemployment benefits that provide income to unemployed workers. The purpose of benefit systems is to soften the economic hardship associated with unemployment, but benefits have an additional effect: because unemployed workers who receive benefits can afford to be more choosy when searching for a job, the availability of benefits may tend to increase the length of unemployment spells and the unemployment rate.

Some economists have suggested that the generous UI benefits in Europe are at least partly responsible for the persistent increase in unemployment that began there during the mid 1970s (see Figure 13.9). Gary Burtless* of the Brookings Institution compared unemployment rates and the generosity of benefit systems for the period 1966–85 in Britain, France, Germany, Sweden, and the United States. To measure the generosity of benefit systems, he focused on three factors:

1. the *replacement ratio*, which measures the size of unemployment benefits relative to lost wages (a replacement ratio of 2/3, as in the French, German, and Swedish systems, means that benefits are 2/3 of an unemployed worker's lost wages);
2. the *benefit duration*, which measures the amount of time that an unemployed worker may receive benefits; and
3. *eligibility requirements*, which specify who can collect benefits.

Burtless did not find much evidence that more generous benefit systems lead directly to higher unemployment rates. For example, the benefit system in the United States historically has been less generous than the four European systems, having a lower replacement ratio, a substantially shorter benefit duration, and more stringent eligibility requirements than its European counterparts. Nevertheless, before 1973 the US unemployment rate was higher than the European unemployment rates, despite a relatively more restrictive benefit system. Similarly, according to Burtless, changes in unemployment benefits cannot explain increases in European unemployment rates after the mid 1970s, except possibly in the case of France where a sharp increase in unemployment followed a liberalization of the system.

Although the generosity of unemployment benefits does not seem closely related to unemployment rates, the *duration* of individual spells of unemployment – the length of time that an unemployed worker remains unemployed – is apparently affected by the generosity of benefits. Burtless found that unemployment spells were much longer in Europe (where benefit systems were much more generous) than in the United States (see Table 13.3), even during the late 1960s and early 1970s when European unemployment rates overall were lower than in the United States. In particular, the longer benefit duration of European systems seems to account for the longer spells of unemployment in Europe.

---

* 'Jobless Pay and High European Unemployment,' in R. Lawrence and C. Schultze, eds., *Barriers to European Growth: A Transatlantic View* (Brookings Institution, 1987). For a recent description of the different benefit systems adopted across Europe and elsewhere see OECD, *The OECD Jobs Study*, 1994, Part II, Chapter 8.

Third, the **insider–outsider theory** suggests that, when a union negotiates a labour contract with a firm, it seeks the highest real wage (including fringe benefits) possible without causing the firm to cut employment.[22] This union behaviour is in the best interests of currently employed workers, or insiders. But think about what happens if a contract is negotiated when unemployment is high. If the union succeeds in getting the highest wage consistent with continued employment of the insiders, the wage will be too high for the firm to increase employment and hire outsiders. Thus outsiders will remain unemployed.

---

22. See Assar Lindbeck and Dennis Snower, *The Insider–Outsider Theory of Employment and Unemployment* (MIT Press, 1989).

The insider–outsider theory applies in a unionized setting. Because European labour markets are much more highly unionized than the US labour market, the insider–outsider theory predicts that hysteresis is quantitatively more important in Europe than in the USA. This prediction is consistent with the fact that during the 1980s unemployment rates in Europe came down much more slowly than they did in the USA. Another difference is that unemployment benefits are more generous in Europe than in the USA. Box 13.2 discusses the implications of this difference for the behaviour of the natural rate of unemployment.

Policies to Reduce the Natural Rate of Unemployment

Although we call the rate of unemployment towards which the economy gravitates in the long run the 'natural' rate of unemployment, we do not mean to imply that it is necessarily desirable or optimal. Many people would argue that, for both economic and social reasons, economic policies should be used to try to lower the natural unemployment rate. Although no certain method for reducing the natural rate exists, several strategies have been suggested:

1. *Government support for job training and worker relocation.* Firms have strong incentives to find and train capable workers, and unemployed workers have equally strong incentives to find productive jobs. However, some economists argue that the private incentives to match workers and jobs still are not as strong as they should be. For example, firms may be reluctant to train workers if they fear that, once trained, the workers will leave for other firms. Similarly, in deciding whether to retrain for a new job, unemployed workers will not take into account the gain of their re-employment to taxpayers, who will no longer be responsible for financing their unemployment benefits. Thus a case can be made for policy measures such as tax breaks or subsidies for training or relocating unemployed workers. If these measures had their desired effect, the mismatch between workers and jobs would be eliminated more quickly and the natural unemployment rate would fall.

2. *Increased labour market flexibility.* Currently, government regulations mandate minimum wages, working conditions, workers' fringe benefits, conditions for firing a worker, and many other terms of employment. Such regulations may be well intentioned but they also increase the cost of hiring additional workers, particularly workers with limited skills and experience. New and existing labour market regulations should be carefully reviewed to ensure that their benefits outweigh the costs they impose in higher unemployment.

3. *Unemployment insurance reform.* Although unemployment benefits provide essential support for the unemployed, they may also increase the natural unemployment rate by increasing the time that the unemployed spend looking for work (see Box 13.2) and by increasing the incentives for firms to lay off workers during slack times. Reforms to benefit systems that preserve the function of supporting the unemployed but reduce incentives for increased unemployment are needed. For example, taxes on employers might be changed to force employers that use temporary layoffs extensively to bear a greater portion of the unemployment benefits that their workers receive.

4. *A high-pressure economy?* Classical and Keynesian economists generally agree that macroeconomic stabilization policies cannot be used to affect the natural rate of unemployment; in other words, the long-run Phillips curve is vertical. However, some proponents of the hysteresis theory take issue with this view. They argue that if monetary and fiscal policy are used aggressively to keep unemployment as low as possible – a 'high-pressure economy' – then, following the principle of hysteresis, the natural rate will eventually fall. So, for example, if current employment is stimulated by monetary expansion, workers may be able to acquire more on-the-job training, which reduces mismatch and lowers the natural unemployment rate in the long run. Opponents of this suggestion point out that there is much less evidence of hysteresis in the United States than in Europe. Opponents also express concern that a high-pressure strategy would reignite inflation.

13.3 THE PROBLEM OF INFLATION

In the 1960s and 1970s many European governments instituted wage and price controls in an attempt to reduce inflation. These strong measures were taken even though the inflation rate was only about 5% at the time in most countries. During the late 1970s, when the inflation rate reached 'double digits' across Europe, surveys of voters found that they thought inflation was 'public enemy number one'. The British Prime Minister in the early 1980s, Mrs Thatcher, once suggested that it was her 'moral duty' to control inflation, and her success in achieving this contributed to her re-election in 1983 and 1987 despite high levels of unemployment in the UK at the time. In this section we look at inflation, beginning with a discussion of inflation costs and then turning to the question of what can be done to control inflation.

The Costs of Inflation

The costs of inflation depend primarily on whether consumers, investors, workers, and firms are able to predict the inflation before it occurs. To illustrate this point, we discuss two extreme cases: an inflation that everyone is able to predict and an inflation that comes as a complete surprise.

Perfectly Anticipated Inflation. Let's first consider the case of an inflation that is perfectly anticipated by the public. Imagine, for example, that everyone knew that the inflation rate would be 4% per year. To keep things simple, assume also no change in relative prices so that the prices of all individual goods and services are also rising at the rate of 4% per year.

Why then does a fully anticipated inflation impose any costs? The prices you pay for groceries, cinema tickets, and other goods would increase by 4% per year but so would your nominal wage or the nominal value of the goods or services you produce. Because your nominal income is rising along with prices, your purchasing power is not hurt by the perfectly anticipated inflation.[23]

---

23. It may be true that, psychologically, people think of increases in their wages arising from ongoing inflation as being earned and thus 'fair,' but that increases in the prices they pay because of inflation are 'unfair.' This is a confusion, although one that may have real political consequences if it causes the public to demand strong action on inflation.

What about the money that you hold in your savings account? Although inflation reduces the purchasing power of money, perfectly anticipated inflation would not hurt the value of your savings account. The reason is that the nominal interest rate would adjust to offset the drop in the purchasing power of money. For instance, with a zero inflation rate and a nominal interest rate on savings deposits of 3%, the real interest rate is also 3% per year. If inflation rises to a perfectly anticipated rate of 4% per year, an increase in the nominal interest rate to 7% per year will leave the real interest rate unchanged at 3%. Because both savers and banks care only about the real interest rate, when inflation rises to 4% banks should be willing to offer 7% nominal interest, and savers should be willing to accept that nominal return. Thus neither banks nor savers are hurt by an anticipated increase in inflation.[24]

The suggestion that perfectly anticipated inflation imposes no economic costs is not quite correct. Inflation erodes the value of currency, which leads people to keep less currency on hand – for example, by going to the bank or the automatic teller machine to make withdrawals every week instead of twice a month. Similarly, inflation may induce firms to reduce their cash holdings by introducing computerized cash management systems or adding staff to the accounting department. The costs in time and effort incurred by people and firms who are trying to minimize their holdings of cash are called **shoe leather costs**. For modest inflation rates, shoe leather costs are small but not completely trivial. For example, the shoe leather costs of a 10% perfectly anticipated inflation have been estimated to be about 0.3% of GNP.[25]

A second cost of perfectly anticipated inflation arises from menu costs, or the costs of changing nominal prices. When there is inflation and prices are continually rising, sellers of goods and services must use resources to change nominal prices. For instance, mail-order firms have to print and mail catalogues frequently to report the increases in prices. Although some firms face substantial menu costs, for the economy as a whole these costs are probably small. Furthermore, technological progress, such as the introduction of electronic scanners in supermarkets, reduces the cost of changing prices.

Unanticipated Inflation. Much of the public's aversion to inflation is aversion to unanticipated inflation – inflation that is different from the rate expected. For example, if everyone expects the inflation rate to be 4% per year, but it is actually 6% per year, unanticipated inflation is 2% per year.

What is the effect of 6% inflation if (1) you expected 4% inflation and (2) your savings account pays 7% interest? When inflation is 6% per year instead of 4% per year, the actual real interest rate on your savings account is only 1% per year (the nominal interest rate of 7% minus the inflation rate of 6%) instead of the 3% per year that you expected. By earning a lower actual real interest rate, you lose as a result of the unanticipated inflation. However, your loss is the bank's gain because the bank pays a lower real interest rate than it expected. Note that the roles would have been reversed if the actual inflation

---

24. This argument ignores the fact that interest is taxed on a nominal basis. If the after-tax real interest rate is to be kept constant, the nominal interest rate will have to rise by somewhat more than the increase in inflation.

25. See Stanley Fischer, 'Towards an Understanding of the Costs of Inflation: II,' in K. Brunner and A.H. Meltzer, eds., *Carnegie-Rochester Conference Series on Public Policy*, vol. 15, Autumn 1981.

rate had been lower than expected; in that case the real interest rate that you earn, and that the bank has to pay, will be higher than anticipated.

Similarly, suppose that your nominal salary is set in advance. If inflation is higher than expected, the real value of your salary is less than you expected, and your loss is your employer's gain. If inflation is lower than expected, however, you benefit and your employer loses.

These examples show that a primary effect of unanticipated inflation is to transfer wealth from one person or firm to another. People who lend or save at fixed interest rates (creditors) and those with incomes set in nominal terms are hurt by unanticipated inflation, whereas people who borrow at fixed interest rates (debtors) or who must make fixed nominal payments are helped by unanticipated inflation.

For the economy as a whole, a transfer of wealth from one group to another is not a net loss of resources and hence does not represent a true cost. However, from the viewpoints of individual people and firms in the economy, the *risk* of gaining or losing wealth as a result of unanticipated inflation is unwelcome. Because most people do not like risk, the possibility of significant gains or losses arising from unexpected inflation makes people feel worse off and hence is a cost of unanticipated inflation. Furthermore, any resources that people use in forecasting inflation and trying to protect themselves against the risks of unanticipated inflation represent an additional cost. However, some of these costs of unanticipated inflation can be eliminated by contracts that are indexed to the price level (see Box 13.3).

Another cost of unanticipated inflation relates to the fact that prices serve as signals in a market economy. For example, if wheat becomes more expensive than corn, that is a signal to consumers to switch from wheat to corn and to farmers to produce more wheat and less corn. However, the prices that act as signals in the economy are *relative* prices, such as the price of wheat relative to the price of corn. Knowing that wheat costs so much per kilogram does not help the consumer and farmer make good economic decisions unless they also know the price of corn. When inflation is unanticipated, particularly if it is erratic, people may confuse changes in prices arising from changes in the general price level with changes in prices arising from shifts in the supply or demand for individual goods. Because the signals provided by prices may be distorted by unanticipated inflation, the market economy works less efficiently. In addition, when there is a great deal of uncertainty about the true inflation rate, people must spend time and effort learning about different prices, by comparison shopping, for example.

The Costs of Hyperinflation. **Hyperinflation** occurs when the inflation rate is extremely high for a sustained period of time.[26] We have already mentioned the German hyperinflation of 1922–23 and there are many other examples. During a twelve-month period beginning in August 1945, the average rate of inflation in Hungary was 19,800% *per month*.[27] In the more recent

---

26. Philip Cagan, in his classic study of hyperinflation ('The Monetary Dynamics of Hyperinflation', in Milton Friedman, ed., *Studies in the Quality Theory of Money*, University of Chicago Press, 1956) defined a hyperinflation as beginning in the month in which the rate of inflation first exceeds 50% *per month*.
27. *Ibid.*, Table 1.

BOX 13.3

Indexed Contracts

In principle, much of the risk of gains and losses associated with unanticipated inflation can be eliminated by using contracts in which payments are indexed to inflation. If a bank wanted to offer a guaranteed 3% real interest rate on savings accounts, for instance, it could index the nominal interest rate to the rate of inflation by offering to pay a nominal interest rate equal to 3% plus whatever the rate of inflation turns out to be. Then if the actual inflation rate is 6%, the bank will end up paying a nominal interest rate of 9% – giving the depositor the promised 3% real interest rate. Similarly, other financial contracts, such as loans, mortgages, and bonds, can be indexed to protect the real rate of return against unanticipated inflation. Wage payments set by labour contracts can also be indexed to protect workers and employers against unanticipated inflation (we discussed the macroeconomic effects of wage indexation in Appendix 12.A).

How widespread is indexing? Most financial contracts in Europe are not indexed to the rate of inflation, although a number of government and savings institutions offer savings accounts which provide returns that are linked to the rate of inflation, such as National Savings certificates in the UK. Payments on some long-term financial contracts (adjustable-rate mortgages, for example) are indexed to nominal interest rates such as the prime rate charged by banks or the Treasury bill interest rate. Because nominal interest rates move roughly in step with inflation, these long-term financial contracts are to some extent indexed to inflation.

Labour contracts in Europe tend not to be completely index linked, though this was common in a number of countries, including the Netherlands, during the 1970s. In Germany, indexation has been illegal since the 1920s when the country was hit by hyperinflation.

Many labour contracts in the United States are indexed to the rate of inflation through provisions called cost-of-living adjustments, or COLAs. They provide for some increase in nominal wages if inflation is higher than expected, but usually a 1% increase in unanticipated inflation results in somewhat less than a 1% adjustment of wages. Because the public often expresses concern about inflation, economists are puzzled that indexed contracts are not more widely used in the United States.

In contrast, in countries that have experienced high and unpredictable inflation rates, indexed contracts are common. A case in point is Israel, which had a CPI inflation rate of 445% per year in 1984. At that time over 80% of liquid financial assets in Israel were indexed: for example, long-term government bonds were indexed to the CPI, and banks offered short-term deposits whose purchasing power was tied to that of the US dollar. However, the fraction of financial assets that were indexed decreased after the Israeli hyperinflation ended in the second half of 1985.*

---

* See Stanley Fischer, 'Israeli Inflation and Indexation', in J. Williamson, ed., *Inflation and Indexation: Argentina, Brazil, Israel,*, (Institute for International Economics, 1985), reprinted in Stanley Fischer, *Indexing, Inflation, and Economic Policy* (MIT Press, 1986); and Zalman F. Shiffer, 'Adjusting to High Inflation: The Israeli Experience,' Federal Reserve Bank of St Louis *Review,* May 1986, pp. 18–29.

---

hyperinflation in Bolivia, the annual rate of inflation was 1281% in 1984, and soared to 11,750% in 1985, before dropping to 276% in 1986.[28] The costs of inflation during these hyperinflations were much greater than the costs associated with moderate inflation. For example, when prices are increasing at such mind-boggling rates, the incentives to minimize holdings of currency are powerful and the resulting shoe leather costs are enormous. In severe hyperinflations workers are paid much more frequently – perhaps even more than once a day – and they rush out to spend their money (or to convert their

---

28. See Table 7.3, Juan-Antonio Morales, 'Inflation Stabilization in Bolivia' in Michael Bruno, Guido De Tella, Rudiger Dornbusch, and Stanley Fischer, eds., *Inflation Stabilization: The Experience of Israel, Argentina, Brazil. Bolivia, and Mexico* (MIT Press, 1988).

money into some other form, such as a foreign currency) before prices rise even further. The time and energy devoted to getting rid of currency as fast as possible wastes resources and disrupts production.

One early casualty of hyperinflations is the government's ability to collect taxes. In a hyperinflation taxpayers have an incentive to delay paying their taxes as long as possible. Because tax bills are usually set in nominal terms, the longer the taxpayer delays, the less the real value of that obligation is. The real value of taxes collected by the government falls sharply during hyperinflations, with destructive effects on the government's finances and its ability to provide public services.

Finally, the disruptive effect of inflation on market efficiency that we discussed earlier becomes most severe in the case of a hyperinflation. If prices change so often that they cease to be reliable indicators of the supply and demand for different goods and services, the invisible hand of the free market cannot allocate resources efficiently.

Fighting Inflation: The Role of Inflationary Expectations

Basically, inflation occurs when the aggregate quantity of goods demanded at any particular price level is rising more quickly than the aggregate quantity of goods supplied at that price level. (Figure 13.3 illustrates such a situation.) Many factors can cause rapid increases in the aggregate quantity of goods demanded relative to the aggregate quantity supplied. Among these sources of inflation are increases in consumption or investment spending, expansionary fiscal policies, and adverse supply shocks. However, as discussed in Chapter 7, in general the only factor that can create *sustained* rises in aggregate demand, and thus ongoing inflation, is a high rate of money growth.

If rapid money growth is inflationary, why do central banks permit rapid monetary expansion? As mentioned in Chapter 7 (and discussed in more detail in Chapter 16), in developing or war-torn countries governments may not be able to raise enough revenue by taxing or borrowing, so they print money to finance their spending. However, in industrialized countries not engaged in or recovering from a war, governments are usually able either to tax or to borrow enough to cover their expenditures. In these countries, rapid money growth is usually the result of past attempts to use expansionary monetary policy to fight recessions, not balanced by tighter monetary policies in periods when output is above the full-employment level.

Because ongoing inflation is generally the result of rapid money growth, the prescription for stopping inflation appears to be simple: reduce the rate of money growth. Unfortunately, the process of **disinflation** – the reduction of the inflation rate – by slowing money growth may lead to a serious recession. In terms of the expectations-augmented Phillips curve, equation (13.1), if macroeconomic policy succeeds in reducing inflation below the expected rate, unemployment will rise above the natural rate. Unemployment will remain above the natural rate until expected inflation falls to the new, lower actual inflation rate.

Is there some way to reduce inflation without incurring serious unemployment costs? The expectations-augmented Phillips curve suggests one possibility: if the public's expected rate of inflation could be lowered as actual inflation was being brought down, unemployment would not have to rise above the natural rate. (You should confirm that, in equation (13.1), if actual inflation π and expected inflation π^e fall by the same amount, cyclical unemployment $u - \bar{u}$ does not increase.) That is, if *expected* inflation can be reduced, the original Phillips curve relating inflation and unemployment can be shifted down and to the left, reducing the rate of inflation associated with any level of unemployment.

But how can policymakers reduce the public's inflationary expectations? In the rest of this section we discuss some suggested approaches for reducing both inflation and inflationary expectations.

Rapid Versus Gradual Disinflation. Some classical economists have proposed that disinflation should be implemented quickly by a rapid and decisive reduction in the growth rate of the money supply – a strategy sometimes referred to as **cold turkey**. Because a cold-turkey disinflation is dramatic and highly visible to the public, proponents of this policy argue that it will quickly and substantially reduce inflationary expectations, particularly if the policy is announced well in advance. If expected inflation falls sufficiently, the expectations-augmented Phillips curve implies that the unemployment costs of the disinflation will be minimal.

However, most Keynesian economists disagree with the idea that rapid disinflation can be achieved without significant costs in terms of increased cyclical unemployment. They argue that because of factors such as menu costs and nominal wage contracts, several years may be required for prices and wages to adjust to a disinflationary policy; during the adjustment period cyclical unemployment could be high. Further, Keynesians point out that the cold-turkey strategy may not lower inflation expectations, because people may expect the government to abandon the policy if the resulting unemployment reaches politically intolerable levels.

Because they fear the possible unemployment consequences of the cold-turkey strategy, many Keynesians recommend a policy of **gradualism**, or reducing the rate of money growth and inflation gradually over a period of years. Keynesians argue that a gradual approach, which gives prices, wages, and expectations more time to adjust to the disinflation, will raise the unemployment rate by less than the cold-turkey strategy – although the period during which unemployment exceeds the natural rate may be longer. They further argue that, because the policy will be viewed as sustainable politically, gradualism may be as effective as the cold-turkey approach at reducing inflationary expectations. The results of one study comparing cold turkey and gradualism are discussed in Box 13.4.

Wage and Price Controls. Frustrated by the costs and difficulties of reducing inflation by reducing money growth, policymakers in some countries have taken a more direct approach and imposed wage and price controls – legal limits on the ability of firms to raise wages or prices. Supporters of wage–price controls (or of *incomes policies,* as wage–price controls are also called) argue that by using the force of law to stop price increases the government can 'break the back' of inflationary expectations, allowing the disinflation to proceed without serious unemployment consequences.

Critics of price controls make two points. First, price controls are likely to cause shortages. In a free market the ever-changing forces of supply and demand lead to changes in relative prices, with the prices of some products rising more rapidly than the prices of others. If price controls prevent the price of a product from rising to the level at which quantity supplied equals quantity demanded, there will be excess demand for the product: that is, a shortage. These shortages and the disruptions they cause are a major cost of price controls.

Second, critics dispute that wage–price controls have a major effect on the public's inflation expectations. Although controls stop inflation for the moment, because they cause shortages and disrupt the economy they eventually have to be removed. Knowing that the controls are temporary, people may expect even greater inflation in the future.

One factor that may affect expectations of inflation during the period of controls is how the government handles monetary and fiscal policy. If macroeconomic policies allow aggregate demand to continue to grow rapidly, people may expect renewed inflation when the controls are lifted (see Analyti-

BOX 13.4

The Sacrifice Ratio

To reduce inflation, tight monetary and fiscal policies must be used to slow down the rate of growth aggregate demand. However, if these policies are not perfectly anticipated, they will also cause output and employment to fall below their full-employment levels, at least for a time. This loss of output and jobs is an important cost that must be weighed against the benefits of inflation-reducing policies.

Economists sometimes measure the cost of lowering the inflation rate by the **sacrifice ratio**, which is the amount of output that is lost for each percentage point by which the inflation rate is reduced. For example, according to a study by Laurence Ball of Johns Hopkins University,[*] during the disinflation of the early 1980s the rate of inflation in the United States fell by 8.83 percentage points (from a rate of 12.10% per year to 3.27% per year). For the fifteen quarters of this disinflation, Ball estimated the total loss in output caused by inflation-reducing policies to be 16.18% of one year's potential GDP. Dividing the output loss of 16.18% of potential GDP by the 8.83 percentage point reduction in inflation yields a sacrifice ratio of 1.832 for this episode. We can interpret this result as saying that each percentage point by which US inflation was reduced during the early 1980s cost the country 1.832% of a year's potential GDP.

Using quarterly data for nine countries, Ball calculated the sacrifice ratio for 28 disinflations occurring during the 1960s, 1970s, and 1980s. The table in this box reports the average sacrifice ratio he found for each country. As you can see, the output cost of reducing inflation may vary considerably. The average sacrifice ratio ranges from less than 1.0 in France, the United Kingdom, and Japan, to almost 3.0 in Germany. In other words, reducing inflation in Germany is three times more expensive, in terms of lost output, than it is in some other industrialized countries. What accounts for these differences?

By comparing the characteristics of the different countries in his sample, Ball found that one factor affecting the sacrifice ratio is the flexibility of the labour market. Countries in which wages adjust relatively slowly to changes in the supply of and demand for labour – owing, for example, to heavy government regulation of the labour market – tend to have higher sacrifice ratios. This finding makes sense, since countries with inflexible labour markets should take longer to reach long-run equilibrium following an unexpected slowdown in the growth of aggregate demand. Ball also found that rapid disinflations tend to have lower sacrifice ratios than slow disinflations, which is a bit of evidence in favour of the cold-turkey approach, rather than gradualism.

Ball's results are interesting but should be interpreted with some caution. One problem is that it is not easy to determine exactly how much output loss can be attributed to a particular set of anti-inflationary policies, a number that is needed to calculate the sacrifice ratio. For example, to calculate the output loss due to disinflation it is necessary to estimate what ouput would have been if there had been no disinflation, which is difficult. Factors like supply shocks, which affect both output and inflation, can also distort the calculation of sacrifice ratios. Thus, calculated sacrifice ratios provide, at best, a rough measure of the costs of reducing inflation.

Average Sacrifice Ratios by Country	
Australia	1.00
Canada	1.50
France	0.75
Germany	2.92
Italy	1.74
Japan	0.93
Switzerland	1.57
United Kingdom	0.79
United States	2.39

[*] 'What Determines the Sacrifice Ratio?' in N. Gregory Mankiw, ed., *Monetary Policy* (University of Chicago Press, 1994), pp. 155–88.

cal Problem 5 at the end of the chapter). This failure to reduce aggregate demand growth appears to have been the problem with the US wage–price controls that began in 1971 (see the following Application). But if controls are accompanied by tight monetary and fiscal policy, the idea that inflation will not resume when controls are lifted is more plausible.

<table>
<tr><td>

APPLICATION

Wage–Price Controls

</td></tr>
</table>

Following World War II, many European countries adopted policies aimed at directly restraining price and wage increases, although such policies were especially popular during the 1960s and 1970s. After increasing steadily in the 1960s, the inflation rate in the early 1970s hovered around 6% in many European countries. Attempts to control inflation using tighter monetary and fiscal policies were not successful and most governments turned to some form of price controls and/or incomes policy to combat their inflation problem. These policies primarily involved government intervention in the labour market (that is, they were incomes policies), although price controls were an important feature of the French, Dutch, UK, and Swedish efforts to hold down the rate of inflation.

Despite their extensive usage, there is not a great deal of evidence to suggest that wage and price controls achieved anything more than temporary success in restraining inflation. A detailed analysis of US price controls imposed by President Nixon during 1971–74 highlights the problems encountered by government intervention in wage and price setting.

On 15 August, 1971, in a surprise announcement, President Nixon instituted a programme of price controls. The controls began with a 90-day price freeze, known as Phase I, that prevented any prices from increasing. The programme evolved haphazardly in response to economic events, reaching Phase IV before the programme was finally terminated in April 1974.

As predicted by the basic economics of supply and demand, shortages developed during the period of price controls. To try to prevent shortages, the government exempted some prices, including the prices of raw agricultural products – feed grains, for example – from controls. But prices of final products, such as 'broilers' (chickens sold to consumers in grocery stores), remained subject to controls. As feed grain prices increased, broiler producers could no longer make a profit by paying for feed grain at an uncontrolled price while selling broilers at a controlled price. When this profit squeeze caused broilers to disappear from grocery shelves, the government reclassified broilers as a raw agricultural product so that the price of broilers was no longer controlled. Broilers reappeared on the shelves but at 50% higher prices.[29] Shortages of other goods, including lumber and various steel products, also developed.

To study whether price controls succeeded in reducing inflation after the controls were lifted, Robert J. Gordon[30] conducted a statistical analysis of inflation in the United States during and after the period of price controls. He concluded that price controls reduced the rate of inflation during the period they were in effect (August 1971–April 1974). However, after the price controls

29. See George P. Shultz and Kenneth W. Dam, 'The Life Cycle of Wage and Price Controls' in G. Shultz and K. Dam, eds., *Economic Policy Beyond the Headlines* (Stanford Alumni Association, 1977).
30. 'The Impact of Aggregate Demand on Prices', *Brookings Papers on Economic Activity*, 1975:3, pp. 613–55.

were eliminated in April 1974, Gordon found that prices rose rapidly so that by the third quarter of 1975 the price level had reached the same level that it would have attained had there been no controls. In other words, the reduction in the rate of inflation during the period of controls was completely offset by an acceleration of inflation after price controls were removed. A probable reason that inflation accelerated after the removal of controls is that for political reasons the Nixon administration continued to use expansionary monetary and fiscal policy during the period of controls.

Further evidence on the effects of wage and price controls is presented in a study by the National Institute for Economic and Social Research, which examined the impact of UK incomes policies for the period 1961–77, and a study of price controls in Sweden for the period 1970–72 by Ingemar Hansson of the University of Lund.[31] The UK study examined the various incomes policies which had been implemented by the British government between 1961 and 1977 and found that wage controls did indeed hold down the level of wage increases while the policy was in effect. However, this dampening down of wage inflation was completely offset by an acceleration of wage rises immediately after the policy was removed. The Swedish experience with price controls is very different. Swedish price controls were introduced for most goods in the latter part of 1970 but abolished in 1971. They were then reintroduced in early 1973 on a selective basis up until 1982. Hansson finds that the controls were effective in bringing down inflation during 1971 and during 1973 and 1974, and that there were no compensating price rises during 1972.

Credibility and Reputation. Classical and Keynesian economists agree that, for disinflation to be achieved without high unemployment costs, reducing the public's expected inflation rate is important. Perhaps the most important factor determining how quickly expected inflation adjusts is the credibility, or believability, of the government's announced disinflationary policy. If the government announces a policy to reduce the inflation rate – and if workers, consumers, and firms believe that the government means what it says – expected inflation should drop fairly rapidly.

How can a government improve its credibility with the public? One desirable way would be for the government to develop a reputation for carrying out its promises; then when it announced a disinflation programme, people would likely take this announcement seriously. Unfortunately, time is needed to develop such a reputation, and changes in administration may lead to relatively frequent changes in the people who make policy decisions.

Another strategy is to organize policy-making institutions in ways that create credibility with the public. For example, a strong and independent central bank, run by someone with well-known anti-inflation views, may have credibility with the public when it announces a disinflationary policy. However, if the central bank is controlled directly by the executive branch – and is therefore exposed to intense political pressure when unemployment rises – an announced disinflationary programme is likely to be less credible. We explore the relationship among institutional structure, government credibility, and inflation expectations in greater detail in Chapter 15.

---

31. S.G.B. Henry and Paul Ormerod, 'Incomes Policy and Wage Inflation: Empirical Evidence for the UK 1961–1977', *National Institute Economic Review*, 1978, pp. 31–9; and Ingemar Hansson, 'Inflation and Price Controls in Sweden', *Scandinavian Journal of Economics*, 1983, pp. 415–23.

CHAPTER SUMMARY

1. Following the famous 1958 article by A. W. Phillips, empirical studies often showed that inflation is high when unemployment is low and low when unemployment is high. This negative empirical relationship between inflation and unemployment is called the Phillips curve. Inflation and unemployment in European economies conformed to the Phillips curve during the 1960s but not during the 1970s and 1980s.

2. Economic theory suggests that, in general, the negative relationship between inflation and unemployment should not be stable. Instead, in an economy in which there are unanticipated changes in the growth rate of aggregate demand, there should be a negative relationship between *unanticipated* inflation and *cyclical* unemployment. In particular, when actual and expected inflation are equal (so that unanticipated inflation is zero), the actual unemployment rate will equal the natural unemployment rate (so that cyclical unemployment is zero). This negative relationship between unanticipated inflation and cyclical unemployment is called the expectations-augmented Phillips curve.

3. According to the theory of the expectations-augmented Phillips curve, a stable negative relationship between inflation and unemployment (a Phillips curve) will be observed only if expected inflation and the natural unemployment rate are constant. An increase in expected inflation or an increase in the natural unemployment rate shifts the Phillips curve up and to the right. Adverse supply shocks typically increase both expected inflation and the natural unemployment rate and also shift the Phillips curve up and to the right. Major supply shocks during the 1970s, a rising natural unemployment rate, and highly variable expected inflation rates explain why the Phillips curve shifted erratically after about 1970.

4. According to the expectations-augmented Phillips curve, macroeconomic policy can reduce unemployment below the natural rate only by surprising the public with higher-than-expected inflation. Classical economists argue that, because of rational expectations and rapid price adjustment, policy cannot be used systematically to create inflation higher than expected; thus policymakers cannot usefully exploit the Phillips curve relationship by trading higher inflation for lower unemployment. Keynesians believe that, because not all prices adjust rapidly to reflect new information, policymakers are able to create surprise inflation temporarily and thus trade off inflation and unemployment in the short run.

5. Classical and Keynesian economists agree that, in the long run, expected and actual inflation rates are equal. Thus in the long run the actual unemployment rate equals the natural rate, regardless of the inflation rate. Reflecting the fact that there is no long-run trade-off between inflation and unemployment, the long-run Phillips curve is vertical at the natural unemployment rate.

6. The costs of unemployment include output lost when fewer people are working and the personal or psychological costs for unemployed workers and their families.

7. In the long run the unemployment rate is determined by the natural unemployment rate. According to some estimates, the natural unemployment rate in Europe and in the United States has risen over time. Explanations for this increase include demographic changes in the labour force and more rapid structural change in the economy.

8. The actual unemployment rate displays hysteresis if the natural rate increases whenever the actual rate is above the natural rate and decreases whenever the actual unemployment rate is below the natural rate. Hysteresis is thought to be a particularly serious problem in Europe. Explanations for hysteresis include loss of skills by the unemployed, bureaucratic and legal barriers to labour market adjustment, and wage-setting practices by unions that favour the currently employed (insiders) over those who are currently unemployed (outsiders).

9. Policies to reduce the natural unemployment rate include government support for job training and worker relocation, policies to increase labour market flexibility, and unemployment benefit reform. Some proponents of the hysteresis theory argue that pushing down the actual unemployment rate by means of expansionary policies (a 'high-pressure' economy) will ultimately reduce the natural rate as well.

10. The costs of inflation depend on whether the inflation was anticipated or unanticipated. The costs of anticipated inflation, which (except in extreme inflations) are relatively minor, include shoe leather costs (resources used by individuals and firms to reduce their holdings of currency) and menu costs (costs of changing posted prices during an inflation). Unanticipated inflation causes unpredictable transfers of wealth among individuals and firms. The risk of unpredictable gains and losses, and the resources that people expend in trying to reduce this risk, are costs of unanticipated inflation. Unanticipated inflation may also reduce the efficiency of the market system by making it more difficult for people to observe relative prices.

11. Disinflation is a reduction in the rate of inflation. Attempts to disinflate by slowing money growth will cause cyclical unemployment to rise if actual inflation falls below expected inflation. To reduce the unemployment cost of disinflation, the public's expected inflation rate should be brought down along with the actual inflation rate. Strategies for reducing expected inflation include rapid and decisive reduction in the growth rate of the money supply (the cold-turkey approach), wage and price controls, and taking measures to improve the credibility of government policy announcements.

Key Terms

cold turkey, p. 508
corporatism, p. 498
disinflation, p. 507
expectations-augmented Phillips curve, p. 483
gradualism, p. 508
hyperinflation, p. 505
hysteresis, p. 498
insider–outsider theory, p. 501
long-run Phillips curve, p. 490

Phillips curve, p. 476
sacrifice ratio, p. 509
shoe leather costs, p. 504

Key Equation

$$\pi = \pi^e - h(u - \bar{u}) \qquad (13.1)$$

The expectations-augmented Phillips curve states that unanticipated inflation, $\pi - \pi^e$, is negatively related to cyclical unemployment, $u - \bar{u}$. The expectations-augmented Phillips curve also implies that inflation, π, is negatively related to unemployment, u, only if the expected inflation rate π^e and the natural unemployment rate $\bar{u}$ are constant. Changes in the expected inflation rate or in the natural unemployment rate cause the relationship between inflation and unemployment – the traditional Phillips curve – to shift.

Review Questions

1. What is the Phillips curve? Does the Phillips curve relationship hold for European data? Explain.

2. How does the expectations-augmented Phillips curve differ from the traditional Phillips curve? According to the theory of the expectations-augmented Phillips curve, under what conditions should the traditional Phillips curve relationship appear in the data?

3. How do changes in the expected inflation rate account for the behaviour of the Phillips curve in the 1960s, 1970s, and 1980s in Europe? What role do supply shocks play in explaining the behaviour of the Phillips curve in the Europe?

4. Can policymakers exploit the Phillips curve relationship by trading more inflation for less unemployment in the short run? In the long run? Explain both the classical and Keynesian points of view.

5. Why is the natural unemployment rate an important economic variable? What factors explain the changes in the natural rate over time in Europe and in the United States? What government policies, if any, might be used to reduce the natural unemployment rate?

6. Give two costs of anticipated inflation and two costs of unanticipated inflation. How is the magnitude of each affected if, instead of a moderate inflation, hyperinflation occurs?

7. What is the greatest potential cost associated with disinflation? How does the responsiveness of the public's inflation expectations affect the size of this potential cost?

8. Discuss at least two strategies for reducing expected inflation rapidly. What are the pros and cons of these strategies?

Numerical Problems

1. Consider an economy in long-run equilibrium with an inflation rate π of 12% (0.12) per year and a natural unemployment rate $\bar{u}$ of 6% (0.06). The expectations-augmented Phillips curve is

$$\pi = \pi^e - 2(u - \bar{u})$$

Assume that Okun's law holds so that a 1 percentage point increase in the unemployment rate maintained for one year reduces GDP by 2.5% of full-employment output.

a. Consider a two-year disinflation. In the first year $\pi = 0.04$ and $\pi^e = 0.08$. In the second year $\pi = 0.04$ and $\pi^e = 0.04$. In the first year, what is the unemployment rate? By what percentage does output fall short of full-employment output? In the second year, what is the unemployment rate? By what percentage does output fall short of full-employment output?

b. Now consider a four-year disinflation according to the following table.

Year	1	2	3	4
π	0.08	0.04	0.04	0.04
π^e	0.10	0.08	0.06	0.04

What is the unemployment rate in each of the four years? By what percentage does output fall short of full-employment output each year?

2. Consider the following extended classical economy.

AD	$Y = 300 + 10(M/P)$
SRAS	$Y = \bar{Y} + P - P^e$
Okun's law	$(Y - \bar{Y})/\bar{Y} = -2.5(u - \bar{u})$
Full-employment output	$\bar{Y} = 500$
Natural unemployment rate	$\bar{u} = 0.06$

a. Suppose that the money supply $M = 1000$ and that the expected price level $P^e = 50$. What are the short-run equilibrium values of output Y, the price level P, and the unemployment rate u? What are the long-run equilibrium values of these three variables?

b. Now suppose that an unanticipated increase raises the nominal money supply to $M = 1260$. What are the new short-run equilibrium values of output Y, the price level P, and the unemployment rate u? What are the new long-run equilibrium values of these three variables? In general, are your results consistent with an expectations-augmented Phillips curve?

3. In a certain economy the expectations-augmented Phillips curve is

$$\pi = \pi^e - 2(u - \bar{u})$$

and

$$\bar{u} = 0.06$$

a. Graph the Phillips curve of this economy for an expected inflation rate of 0.10. If the central bank chooses to keep the actual inflation rate at 0.10, what will be the unemployment rate?

b. An aggregate demand shock (resulting from increased military spending) raises expected inflation to 0.12 (the natural unemployment rate is unaffected). Graph the new Phillips curve and compare it with the curve you drew in part (a). What happens to the unemployment rate if the central bank holds actual inflation at 0.10? What happens to the Phillips curve and the unemployment rate if the central bank announces that it will hold inflation at 0.10 after the aggregate demand shock, and this announcement is fully believed by the public?

c. Suppose that a supply shock (a drought) raises expected inflation to 0.12 *and* raises the natural unemployment rate to 0.08. Repeat part (b).

4. Consider the following extended classical economy.

AD	$Y = 400 + 5(M/P)$
SRAS	$Y = \bar{Y} + 40(P - P^e)$
Okun's law	$(Y - \bar{Y})/\bar{Y} = -2.5(u - \bar{u})$
Full-employment output	$\bar{Y} = 800$
Natural unemployment rate	$\bar{u} = 0.08$

a. Suppose that the nominal money supply has been constant for many years at $M = 2000$ and is expected to remain constant for ever. What are the equilibrium values of the price level P, the expected price level P^e, output Y, and the unemployment rate u?

b. Suppose that as a complete surprise the nominal money supply increases to $M = 2912$. What are the short-run equilibrium values of the price level P (Hint: It is a whole number), the expected price level

P^e, output Y, and the unemployment rate u? What are the values of cyclical unemployment and unanticipated inflation?

c. What is the slope of the expectations-augmented Phillips curve? (*Hint:* The slope of the expectations-augmented Phillips curve is $-h$ in equation (13.1).)

Analytical Problems

1. Suppose that the government institutes a programme to help unemployed workers learn new skills, find new jobs, and relocate as necessary to take the new jobs.

   a. If this programme reduces structural unemployment, what is the effect on the expectations-augmented Phillips curve and the long-run Phillips curve?

   b. The government programme is expensive, and critics argue that a cheaper way to cut unemployment would be by monetary expansion. Comment.

2. Two extended classical economies (in which the misperceptions theory holds) differ only in one respect: in economy A money growth and inflation have been low and stable for many years, but in economy B money growth and inflation have fluctuated erratically between very low and very high levels. When producers in economy B observe changes in the prices of the goods they produce, from past experience they usually attribute these changes to fluctuations in the overall price level rather than to changes in the relative prices of their goods.

   Will the slope of the short-run aggregate supply curve for economy B be flatter or steeper than the slope of the curve for economy A? What about the slope of the Phillips curve?

3. In this problem you are asked to show that the expectations-augmented Phillips curve (derived in the text using the extended classical model) can be derived using the Keynesian model.

   Consider a Keynesian economy in which full-employment output is constant, and in which the nominal money supply has been growing at 10% per year for some time and is expected to keep growing at that rate in the future. To avoid some technical complications, suppose that, instead of growing continuously over time, the money supply is increased by 10% each 31 December and then

held constant until the next 31 December. Monopolistically competitive firms reset their prices on 31 December of each year at the level that they expect will allow them to sell the full-employment level of output during the coming year. Inflation is measured as the percentage change in prices between 1 January and 31 December of each year.

   a. Show how the *AD* curve, *SRAS* curve, output, the price level, and the expected price level evolve over time in this economy. What are the values of unanticipated inflation and cyclical unemployment?

   b. Now suppose that on 30 June, 1997, the money supply is unexpectedly raised by an additional 5%. However, the central bank announces – and is believed by firms – that this extra increase in the money supply is a one-off increase and that next 31 December the central bank will return to its policy of increasing the money supply by 10%. (Thus the total increase in the money supply between 1 January, 1997, and 31 December, 1997, is 15%.) Firms do not change prices until 31 December, as usual, but when they do they respond fully to the new information about money supply growth.

   What are the actual and unanticipated inflation rates during 1997? Is cyclical unemployment positive, negative, or zero (on average) during 1997? Relate your results to the expectations-augmented Phillips curve.

4. Some economists have suggested that some day we will live in a 'cashless society' in which all businesses (including shops) and banks will be linked to a centralized accounting system. In this system you will be able to pay for purchases directly from your bank account without using cash. What are the costs of anticipated inflation in a cashless society? What are the costs of unanticipated inflation?

5. To fight an ongoing 10% inflation, the government makes raising wages or prices illegal. However, the government continues to increase the money supply (and hence aggregate demand) by 10% per year. The economy starts at full-employment output, which remains constant.

   a. Using the Keynesian *AD–AS* framework, show the effects of the government's policies on the economy. Assume that firms meet the demand at the fixed price level.

   b. After several years in which the controls have kept prices from rising, the government declares victory over inflation and removes the controls. What happens.

CHAPTER 14

EXCHANGE RATES, BUSINESS CYCLES, AND MACROECONOMIC POLICY IN THE OPEN ECONOMY

In Chapters 10–13 we focused on a closed economy, or one that does not interact with other economies. For some purposes ignoring the foreign sector simplifies the analysis. But the reality is that today, more than ever, we live in a highly interdependent world economic system. This is especially so in Europe where economies are more closely linked together in the European Monetary System.

There are two primary aspects of the interdependence of the world's economies. The first is international trade in goods and services, which has increased steadily in volume since World War II. Today firms produce goods and services with an eye on foreign *and* domestic markets, and they obtain many raw materials from distant sources. Expanded international trade has increased productivity by allowing economies to specialize in producing the goods and services best suited to their natural and human resources. However, expanded trade also implies that national economies are more dependent on what happens in other countries. For example, because the Netherlands sells so much of its output to Germany, a German recession or macroeconomic policy change may affect the Dutch economy as well.

The second is the worldwide integration of financial markets, which allows borrowers to obtain funds and savers to look for their best lending opportunities almost anywhere in the world, not just in their own countries. By allowing savings to flow to the highest-return uses regardless of where savers and investors happen to live, the integration of world financial markets increases worldwide productivity, as does the development of an integrated world trading system. But financial market linkages, like trade linkages, increase the sensitivity of individual economies to developments abroad. For example, because of closely connected financial markets, macroeconomic policies that change the real interest rate in one country may affect real interest rates and economic activity in other countries.

In this chapter we build on earlier analyses of the open economy (Chapter 5) and cyclical fluctuations (Chapters 9–12) to examine the macroeconomic implications of trading and financial links among countries. We are particularly concerned in this chapter with how economic openness affects fiscal and monetary policies and how macroeconomic policy changes affect the economies of a country's trading partners. We begin our discussion by introducing two new variables that play central roles in the international economy: the nominal exchange rate and the real exchange rate.

14.1 EXCHANGE RATES

In discussing exchange rates, we must distinguish between nominal and real exchange rates. Briefly stated, the nominal exchange rate is the answer to the question: how many units of a foreign *currency* can I get in exchange for one unit of my domestic *currency*? The real exchange rate is the answer to the question: how many units of the foreign *good* can I get in exchange for one unit of my domestic *good*?

Nominal Exchange Rates

Virtually all countries have their own national currencies:[1] the US dollar, the Japanese yen, the British pound, the German mark, and the French franc are but a few well-known currencies. If someone in one country wants to buy goods, services, or assets from someone in another country, normally she will first have to exchange her country's currency for that of her trading partner's country.

The rate at which two currencies can be traded is the nominal exchange rate between the two currencies. For example, if the nominal exchange rate between the French franc and the Japanese yen is 20 yen per franc, a franc can buy 20 yen (ignoring transaction fees) in the **foreign exchange market**, which is the market for international currencies. Equivalently, 20 yen can buy 1 franc in the foreign exchange market. More precisely, the **nominal exchange rate** between two currencies, e_{nom}, is the number of units of foreign currency that can be purchased with one unit of the domestic currency. For residents of France the domestic currency is the French franc, and the nominal exchange rate between the French franc and the Japanese yen is expressed as $e_{nom} = 20$ yen per franc. The nominal exchange rate often is simply called the **exchange rate**, so whenever someone mentions the exchange rate without specifying real or nominal, the reference is taken to mean the *nominal* exchange rate.

The franc–yen exchange rate is not constant. The franc might trade for 20 yen one day, but the next day it might rise in value to 21 yen or fall in value to 19 yen. Such changes in the exchange rate are normal under a flexible exchange rate system, the type of system in which many of the world's major currencies (including the franc and the yen) are currently traded. In a **flexible exchange rate system**, or **floating exchange rate system**, exchange rates are

---

1. An exception is Panama, in which US dollars are the official currency (some Panamanian coins are also used).

not officially fixed but are determined by conditions of supply and demand in the foreign exchange market. Under a flexible exchange rate system, exchange rates move continuously and respond quickly to any economic or political news that might influence the supplies and demands for various currencies. The box 'In Touch with the Macroeconomy: Exchange Rates', p. 528, discusses exchange rate data.

The values of currencies have not always been determined by a flexible exchange rate system. In the past, some type of **fixed exchange rate system**, under which exchange rates were set at officially determined levels, often operated. Usually, these official rates were maintained by the commitment of nations' central banks to buy and sell their own currencies at the fixed exchange rate. For example, under the international gold standard system that operated in the late 1800s and early 1900s, the central bank of each country maintained the value of its currency in terms of gold by agreeing to buy or sell gold in exchange for currency at a fixed rate of exchange. The gold standard was suspended during World War I, was temporarily restored in the late 1920s, and then collapsed during the economic and financial crises of the 1930s.

A more recent example of a fixed exchange rate system was the Bretton Woods system, named after the town in New Hampshire in the United States where the 1944 conference establishing the system was held. Under the Bretton Woods system the values of various currencies were fixed in terms of the US dollar, and the value of the dollar was set at $35 per ounce of gold. The Bretton Woods system functioned until the early 1970s, when inflation in the United States made keeping the price of gold from rising above $35 per ounce virtually impossible (see the Application, 'Policy Coordination Failure...', p. 557, for a further discussion of the collapse of the Bretton Woods system). Since the breakdown of the Bretton Woods system, no fixed-exchange-rate system has encompassed all the world's major currencies.

Although no worldwide system of fixed exchange rates currently exists, fixed exchange rates have not disappeared entirely. Some groups of countries, called **exchange rate unions,** have agreed to try to fix exchange rates among themselves, while allowing their currencies to fluctuate against those of countries outside the union. The most significant example of an exchange rate union is the European Monetary System (EMS), founded in 1979, whose members include most of the European countries. The members of the EMS agreed to form an exchange rate union, the Exchange Rate Mechanism, as part of a larger plan to increase economic integration among the countries of Europe (we discuss the EMS further in Section 14.5). Also many individual countries, especially smaller ones, attempt to fix their exchange rates against a major currency. For example, several African countries tie their currencies to the French franc. By doing so, these countries hope to stabilize their own currencies and reduce the sharp swings in import and export prices that may result from exchange rate fluctuations.

Real Exchange Rates

The nominal exchange rate does not tell you all you need to know about the purchasing power of a currency. If you were told, for example, that the nominal exchange rate between the French franc and the Japanese yen is 20 yen per franc, but you did not know anything else about the French or Japanese economies, you might be tempted to conclude that someone from Paris could visit Tokyo very cheaply – after all, 20 yen for just 1 franc seems like a good deal. But even at 20 yen per franc, Japan is an expensive place to visit. The reason is that although 1 franc can buy a lot of yen, it also takes a lot of yen (thousands or hundreds of thousands) to buy everyday goods in Japan.

Suppose, for example, that you want to compare the price of hamburgers in Tokyo and Paris. Knowing that the exchange rate is 20 yen per franc does not help much. But if you also know that a hamburger costs 20 francs in Paris and 600 yen in Tokyo, you can compare the price of a hamburger in the two cities by asking how many francs are needed to buy a hamburger in Japan. Because a hamburger costs 600 yen in Tokyo, and 20 yen cost 1 franc, the price of a hamburger in Tokyo is 30 francs (calculated by dividing the price of a Japanese hamburger, ¥600, by ¥20/franc, to obtain 30 francs per hamburger). The price of a French hamburger relative to a Japanese hamburger is therefore (20 francs per French hamburger)/(30 francs per Japanese hamburger) = 2/3 Japanese hamburgers per French hamburger. The Japanese hamburger is expensive in the sense that (in this example) one French hamburger equals only two-thirds of a Japanese hamburger.

The price of domestic goods relative to foreign goods–equivalently, the number of foreign goods someone gets in exchange for one domestic good–is called the **real exchange rate**. In the hamburger example the real exchange rate between France and Japan is 0.67 Japanese hamburgers per French hamburger.

In general, the real exchange rate is related to the nominal exchange rate and to prices in both countries. To write this relation we use the following symbols:

e_{nom} = the nominal exchange rate
(20 yen per franc);
P_{For} = the price of foreign goods, measured in the foreign currency
(600 yen per Japanese hamburger);
P = the price of domestic goods, measured in the domestic currency
(20 francs per French hamburger).

The real exchange rate e is the number of foreign goods (Japanese hamburgers) that can be obtained in exchange for one unit of the domestic good (French hamburgers). The general formula for the real exchange rate is

$$e = \frac{e_{nom}P}{P_{For}}$$

$$= \frac{(¥20/\text{franc})(20 \text{ franc}/\text{French hamburger})}{¥600/\text{Japanese hamburger}} \quad (14.1)$$

= 0.67 Japanese hamburgers per French hamburger.

In defining the real exchange rate as the number of foreign goods that can be obtained for each domestic good, we assume that each country produces a single, unique good. (Think of Italy producing only bottles of wine and Saudi Arabia producing only barrels of oil; then the Italian real exchange rate with respect to Saudi Arabia is the number of barrels of oil that can be purchased for one bottle of wine.) The assumption that each country produces a single good (which is different from the good produced by any other country) simplifies the theoretical analysis in this chapter.[2]

Of course, in reality countries produce thousands of different goods, so real exchange rates must be based on price indexes (such as the GDP deflator or the CPI) to measure P and P_{For}. Thus the real exchange rate is not actually the rate of exchange between two specific goods but instead is the rate of exchange between a typical basket of goods in one country and a typical basket of goods in the other country. Changes in the real exchange rate over time indicate that, on average, the goods of the country whose real exchange rate is rising are becoming more expensive relative to the goods of the other country.

Appreciation and Depreciation

When the nominal exchange rate e_{nom} falls so that, say, a franc buys fewer units of foreign currency, we say that the franc has undergone a **nominal depreciation**. This is the same as saying that the franc has become 'weaker.' If the franc's nominal exchange rate e_{nom} rises, then the franc has had a **nominal appreciation**. When the franc appreciates, it can buy more units of foreign currency and thus has become 'stronger.'[3] The terms 'appreciation' and 'depreciation' are associated with flexible exchange rates. Under a fixed-exchange-rate system, in which exchange rates are changed only by official government action, different terms are used. Instead of a depreciation, a weakening of the currency is called a **devaluation**. A strengthening of the currency under fixed exchange rates is called a **revaluation**, rather than an appreciation. These terms are listed for convenience in Summary table 15.

An increase in the real exchange rate e is called a **real appreciation**. With a real appreciation, the same quantity of domestic goods can be traded for more of the foreign good than before because e, the price of domestic goods relative

---

2. The assumption that different countries produce different goods is a change from Chapter 5, where we implicitly assumed that all countries produce an identical good that can be used for all purposes (consumption, investment, etc.). The assumption that all countries produce the same good implied that, in the analysis of that chapter, the real exchange rate was always equal to 1.

3. You will sometimes see the exchange rate defined as the number of units of domestic currency per unit of foreign currency, which is the reciprocal of how we have defined it. Under this alternative definition an appreciation corresponds to a fall in the nominal exchange rate. The two ways of defining the exchange rate are equally valid, as long as consistency is maintained. We have chosen to define the exchange rate as the number of units of foreign currency per unit of home currency because it is easier to remember that an appreciation (when the value of the currency goes up) is associated with a rise in the exchange rate.

SUMMARY 15	Type of Exchange Rate System	Exchange Rate Increases (Currency Strengthens)	Exchange Rate Decreases (Currency Weakens)
Terminology for Changes in Exchange Rates	Flexible exchange rates	Appreciation	Depreciation
	Fixed exchange rates	Revaluation	Devaluation

to the price of foreign goods, has risen. A drop in the real exchange rate, which decreases the quantity of foreign goods that can be purchased with the same quantity of domestic goods, is called a **real depreciation**.

Purchasing Power Parity

How are nominal exchange rates and real exchange rates related? A simple hypothetical case that allows us to think about this question is when all countries produce the same good (or same set of goods), and goods are freely traded among countries. In this case, no one would trade domestic goods for foreign goods except on a one-for-one basis, and so (ignoring transportation costs), the real exchange rate e would always equal 1. If $e = 1$, then using equation (14.1) we can write

$$P = \frac{P_{For}}{e_{nom}}. \tag{14.2}$$

Equation (14.2) says that the price of the domestic good must equal the price of the foreign good, when the price of the foreign good is expressed in terms of the domestic currency. (To express the foreign price in terms of the domestic currency, divide by the exchange rate). The idea that similar foreign and domestic goods, or baskets of goods, should have the same price when priced in terms of the same currency is called **purchasing power parity**, or *PPP* for short. Equivalently, as you can see from equation (14.2), purchasing power parity says that the nominal rate, e_{nom}, should equal the foreign price level divided by the domestic price level, $\frac{P_{For}}{P}$.

There is some empirical evidence that *PPP* holds in the very long run, but (as Box 14.1 suggests) over shorter periods the *PPP* hypothesis does not describe exchange rate behaviour very well. The failure of *PPP* in the short to medium run occurs for a number of reasons, including the fact that countries produce very different baskets of goods and services, not the same goods as assumed by *PPP*; that some types of goods, and most services, are not internationally traded at all; and that transportation costs and legal barriers to trade may prevent the prices of traded goods and services from being equalized in different countries.

To find a relationship between real and nominal exchange rates that holds more generally, we can use the definition of the real exchange rate in equation (14.1), $e = e_{nom}P/P_{For}$, to calculate $\Delta e/e$, the percentage change in the real exchange rate. Because the real exchange rate is expressed as a ratio, its percentage change equals the percentage change in the numerator minus the percentage change in the denominator.[4] The percentage change in the numerator of the expression for the real exchange rate[5] is $\Delta e_{nom}/e_{nom} + \Delta P/P$, and the percentage change in the denominator is $\Delta P_{For}/P_{For}$. Thus the percentage change in the real exchange rate is

$$\frac{\Delta e}{e} = \frac{\Delta e_{nom}}{e_{nom}} + \frac{\Delta P}{P} - \frac{\Delta P_{For}}{P_{For}} \tag{14.3}$$

---

4. Appendix A, Section A.7, describes how to calculate growth rates of products and ratios.
5. This result is obtained by using the rule that the percentage change in a product XY is the percentage change in X plus the percentage change in Y. See Appendix A, Section A.7.

In equation (14.3) the term $\Delta P/P$, the percentage change in the domestic price level, is the same as the domestic rate of inflation π, and the term $\Delta P_{\text{For}}/P_{\text{For}}$, the percentage change in the foreign price level, is the same as the foreign rate of inflation π_{For}. Making these substitutions and rearranging the equation, we rewrite equation (14.3) as

$$\frac{\Delta e_{\text{nom}}}{e_{\text{nom}}} = \frac{\Delta e}{e} + \pi_{\text{For}} - \pi \qquad (14.4)$$

Equation (14.4) is purely definitional and thus must always be satisfied. It states that the rate of nominal exchange rate appreciation $\Delta e_{\text{nom}}/e_{\text{nom}}$ equals the rate of real exchange rate appreciation $\Delta e/e$ plus the excess of foreign inflation over domestic inflation, $\pi_{\text{For}} - \pi$. Hence two factors contribute to strengthening a currency (a nominal appreciation): (1) an increase in the relative price of a country's exports (a real appreciation), which might occur if, for

BOX 14.1

McParity

If purchasing power parity holds, similar goods produced in different countries should cost about the same, when their prices are expressed in a common currency, say US dollars. As a test of this hypothesis, *The Economist* magazine has long recorded the prices of Big Mac hamburgers in different countries. The dollar prices of Big Macs in selected countries, as reported by the magazine on 15 April 1995, are shown in the table.[*]

Country	Dollar price of a Big Mac
Switzerland	5.20
Denmark	4.92
Japan	4.65
Germany	3.48
United States	2.32
Canada	1.99
Hong Kong	1.23
China	1.05

Big Macs are not exactly the same product the world over: for example, in Italy and Holland, ketchup is about 50 cents extra, instead of being free as in the United States and Canada. Nevertheless, the table shows that *PPP* definitely does not hold for Big Macs.

Even though *PPP* fails to hold at a given point in time, it might still be the case that there is some tendency for Big Mac prices in different countries to come gradually closer together. One way in which such a convergence could occur would be for countries in which Big Macs are relatively expensive to experience some depreciation of their exchange rates, relative to the currencies of countries in which Big Macs are cheap. Robert Cumby of Georgetown University[†] studied *The Economist*'s data on Big Mac prices to see if they could be used to forecast the behaviour of exchange rates. He found that part of the differential in Big Mac prices across countries is essentially permanent; it will be a very long time, if ever, before Big Macs are as cheap in Switzerland as they are in China. However, he also found that, if the ratio of Big Mac prices in Switzerland and China exceeds its normal level, that is an indication that the Swiss franc will depreciate relative to the Chinese yuan.

Cumby concluded his article, written in mid-1996, with forecasts of how thirteen exchange rates would change over the succeeding year, as predicted by relative prices of Big Macs. When we compared the forecasts in Cumby's paper to the actual behaviour of exchange rates a year later, we found that he got the direction of change (appreciation or depreciation) right in nine of the thirteen cases, but tended to forecast larger changes than actually occurred. We leave it to you to decide whether that is a good forecasting record.

---

[*] The numbers in the table are taken from Kenneth Rogoff, 'The Purchasing Power Parity Puzzle', *Journal of Economic Literature*, June 1996, pp. 647–68. Rogoff's article provides a comprehensive survey of the evidence for and against purchasing power parity.
[†] 'Forecasting Exchange Rates and Relative Prices with the Hamburger Standard: Is What You Want What You Get with McParity?', NBER working paper no. 5675, 1996.

example, foreign demand for those exports rises; and (2) a rate of domestic inflation π lower than that of the country's trading partners π_{For}.

A special case of equation (14.4) occurs when the real exchange rate is constant, so that $\frac{\Delta e}{e} = 0$. In that case, equation (14.4) expresses a relationship called relative purchasing power parity. According to **relative purchasing power parity**, the rate of appreciation of the nominal exchange rate equals the foreign inflation rate minus the domestic inflation rate. Relative purchasing power parity usually works well for high-inflation countries, since in those countries changes in relative inflation rates are usually much larger than changes in the real exchange rate.

The Real Exchange Rate and Net Exports

We have defined the real exchange rate, but so far we have not indicated why it is important in macroeconomic analysis. One reason that policymakers and the public should care about the real exchange rate is that it represents the rate at which domestic goods and services can be traded for those produced abroad. An increase in the real exchange rate – also sometimes referred to as the **terms of trade** – is good for a country in the sense that its citizens are able to obtain more foreign goods and services in exchange for a given amount of domestic production.

A second reason is that the real exchange rate affects a country's net exports, or exports less imports. Changes in net exports in turn have a direct impact on the domestic industries that produce for export or that compete with imported goods in the domestic market. In addition, as we discuss later in the chapter, changes in net exports affect a country's overall level of economic activity and are a primary channel through which business cycle disturbances and macroeconomic policy changes are transmitted internationally.

What is the link between the real exchange rate and net exports? A basic determinant of the demand for any good or service – say, coffee or taxi rides – is the price of that good or service relative to alternatives. If the price of coffee is too high, some people will switch to tea; if taxi fares rise, more people will take the bus. Similarly, the real exchange rate – the price of domestic goods relative to foreign goods – helps determine the demand for domestic goods both in home and foreign markets.

Suppose that the real exchange rate is high so that a unit of the domestic good can buy relatively many units of the foreign good. For example, let's say that a domestically produced car costs twice as much as a comparable foreign car (both prices are measured in terms of the same currency). Domestic residents will then find that foreign cars are less expensive than domestic cars, so (all else being equal) their demand for imported cars will be high. Foreign residents, in contrast, will find that the domestic country's cars are more expensive than their own, so they will want to purchase relatively few of the domestic country's exports. With few cars being sold abroad and many cars being imported, the country's net exports of cars will be low, probably even negative.

Conversely, suppose that the real exchange rate is low: for example, imagine that a domestically produced car costs only half what a comparable foreign car costs. Then, all else being equal, the domestic country will be able to export relatively large quantities of cars and will import relatively few, so that its net exports of cars will be high.

The general conclusion, then, is that *the higher the real exchange rate is, the lower a country's net exports will be,* holding constant other factors affecting export and import demand. The reason for this result is the same reason that higher prices reduce the amount of coffee people drink or the number of taxi rides they take. Because the real exchange rate is the relative price of a country's goods and services, an increase in the real exchange rate induces both foreigners and domestic residents to consume less domestic production and more goods and services produced abroad, which lowers net exports.

The J Curve. Although the conclusion that (holding other factors constant) a higher real exchange rate depresses net exports is generally valid, there is one important qualification: depending on how quickly importers and exporters respond to changes in relative prices, the effect of a change in the real exchange rate on net exports may be weak in the short run and may even go the 'wrong' way.

To understand why, consider a country that imports most of its oil and suddenly faces a sharp increase in world oil prices. Because the country's domestic goods can now buy less of the foreign good (oil), the country's real exchange rate has fallen. In the long run, this decline in the real exchange rate may increase the country's net exports because high oil prices will lead domestic residents to reduce oil imports and the relative cheapness of domestic goods will stimulate exports (to oil-producing countries, for example). In the short run, however, switching to other fuels and increasing domestic oil production are difficult, so the number of barrels of oil imported may drop only slightly. For this reason, and because the real cost of each barrel of oil (in terms of the domestic good) has risen, for some period of time after the oil price increase the country's total real cost of imports (measured in terms of the domestic good) may rise. Thus in the short run a decline in the real exchange rate might be associated with a *drop* rather than a rise in net exports, contrary to our earlier conclusion. (Numerical Problem 2 at the end of the chapter provides an example of how a real depreciation can cause net exports to fall.)

Figure 14.1 shows the typical response pattern of a country's net exports to a drop in the real exchange rate (a real depreciation). The economy initially has negative net exports when the real exchange rate depreciates. In the short run the real depreciation reduces rather than increases net exports because the drop in the real exchange rate forces the country to pay more for its imports. Over time, however, as the lower real exchange rate leads to larger export quantities and smaller import quantities, net exports begin to rise (even taking into account the higher relative cost of imports). Eventually, the country's net exports rise relative to the initial situation. This typical response pattern of net exports to a real depreciation is called the **J curve** because the graph of net exports against time looks like the letter J lying on its back.

The macroeconomic analyses in this chapter are based on the assumption that the time period is long enough that (all else being equal) a real depreciation increases net exports and that a real appreciation reduces net exports. Keep in mind, though, that this assumption may not be valid for shorter periods – and in some cases, even for several years – as the following Application demonstrates.

Figure 14.1
The J curve
The J curve shows the response pattern of net exports to a real depreciation. Here, net exports are negative at time zero, when the real exchange rate depreciates. In the short run net exports become more negative, as the decline in the real exchange rate raises the real cost of imports (measured in terms of the export good). Over time, however, increased exports and reduced quantities of imports more than compensate for the increased cost of imports, and net exports rise above their initial level.

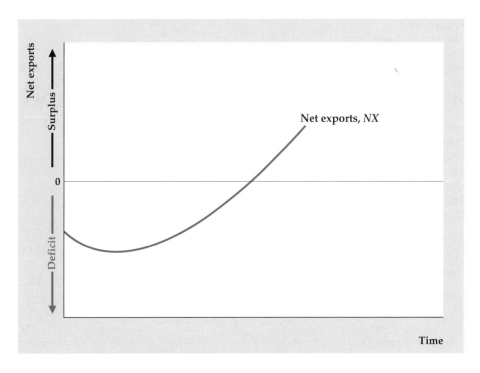

APPLICATION

Currency Values and Net Exports in the 1970s and 1980s

In the early 1970s the major industrialized countries of the world switched from fixed to flexible exchange rates, although the establishment of the European Monetary System (EMS) in 1979 has resulted in an increasing number of European countries fixing their exchange rates with their EU partners as part of the Exchange Rate Mechanism (ERM). Figure 14.2 shows the real exchange rate ('the real value of a currency') and real net exports for several European countries and for the USA since 1975. Although some of these countries have exchange rates fixed within the ERM, most real exchange rates have actually fluctuated markedly over time. The most striking example of this is the French franc. France was a member of the ERM from its inception in 1979, as were the Netherlands and Italy. However, the real value of the franc has proved to be much more volatile than either the guilder or the lira. The real value of the British pound has also been subject to dramatic movements, appreciating more than 50% between 1977 and 1981.

Because the real exchange rate is the relative price of a country's goods, the real value of a country's currency and its net exports should move in opposite directions (assuming that changes in the real exchange rate are the primary source of changes in net exports). Some confirmation that the real exchange rate and net exports move in opposite directions is evident from the experiences of the countries we are considering. From 1980 to 1985 the real value of the US dollar increased by about 50%. This sharp increase was followed, with a brief delay, by a large decline in US exports. Similarly, the real value of the franc, the Swedish krona and the lira all fell sharply in value in the early 1990s. This was good news for firms in these countries, making their goods more competitive in foreign markets and, by making foreign goods more expensive, also increasing their sales at home. As a result, net exports increased.

Figure 14.2
**The real exchange rate
and net exports of
selected European
countries and USA,
1975–96**
Net exports are measured
along the left vertical axes
(in millions of 1990 US
dollars) and real exchange
rates (the real value of the
domestic currency) are
measured along the right
vertical axes (1990 =100).

Source: For Europe, real exchange
rate; real effective exchange rate
of currency in question, 1990 =
100, measured against the
currencies of selected other
countries. *International Financial
Statistics*, International Monetary
Fund, country tables (various
issues); net exports, *European
Economy* (various issues). For
USA, real exchange rate: real
narrow effective exchange rate,
1980–2 = 100, measured against
15 industrial country currencies,
courtesy of J.P. Morgan
Economic research; net exports,
Survey of Current Business,
various issues.

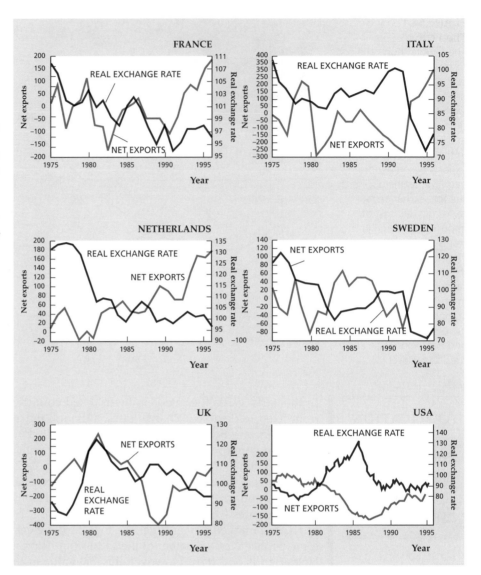

However, sharp declines in the real value of a currency do not always
have a positive impact on net exports, as was the case in the UK during the
period 1979–81. Nor do large changes in the real exchange rate always have an
immediate impact on a country's net exports. Beginning in March 1985, the
real value of the dollar fell sharply for almost three years. Despite this precipi-
tous decline, US net exports continued to fall until late in 1987, when they
finally began to increase. During the two and a half years in which US net
exports continued to decline despite the rapid depreciation of the dollar, the
public and policymakers expressed increasing scepticism about economists'
predictions that the depreciation would lead to more net exports. Initially,
economists responded by saying that, because of the J curve, there would be
some delay between the depreciation of the dollar and the improvement in net
exports. By 1987, however, even the strongest believers in the J curve had

begun to wonder whether net exports would ever begin to rise. Finally, US real net exports did recover substantially, although they remained negative.

What took so long? One explanation suggests that, because the dollar was so strong in the first half of the 1980s (which made US goods very expensive relative to foreign goods), US firms lost many of their foreign customers. Once these foreign customers were lost, regaining them or adding new foreign customers was difficult, especially as many US exporters reduced production capacity and cut back foreign sales operations when the value of the dollar was high. Similarly, the strong dollar gave foreign producers, including some who had not previously sold their output to the United States, a chance to make inroads into the US domestic market. Having established sales networks and customer relationships in the United States, these foreign companies were better able than before to compete with US firms when the dollar began its decline in 1985.

The idea that the strong dollar permanently increased the penetration of the US market by foreign producers, while similarly reducing the capability of American firms to sell in foreign markets, has been called the 'beachhead effect.'[6] After recovering from 1987 to 1992, US net exports began falling again. One explanation for this decline is that, as the US economy recovered from the 1990–91 recession, consumers began to increase their spending on imports. We discuss the effects of income on net exports in the next section.

14.2 HOW EXCHANGE RATES ARE DETERMINED: A SUPPLY-AND-DEMAND ANALYSIS

In flexible exchange rate systems, exchange rates change constantly. In fixed exchange rate systems, by definition, exchange rates are stable most of the time; but even under a fixed-rate system, large devaluations or revaluations are not uncommon. What economic forces cause a nation's exchange rate to rise or fall? In this section we address this question by using supply and demand to analyse the determination of exchange rates in a flexible exchange rate system (we return to fixed exchange rates in Section 14.5).

For clarity our supply-and-demand analysis focuses on the nominal exchange rate rather than the real exchange rate. However, recall from equation (14.1) that, for given levels of domestic and foreign prices, the real exchange rate and the nominal exchange rate are proportional. Because we hold price levels constant in this section, *all our conclusions about the nominal exchange rate apply equally to the real exchange rate.*

The nominal exchange rate e_{nom} is the value of a currency, say, the franc. The value of the franc, like that of any asset, is determined by supply and demand in the relevant market. For francs the relevant market is the foreign exchange market, where banks and currency traders continuously trade francs for other currencies.

---

6. Empirical support for the beachhead effect is presented in Richard E. Baldwin, 'Hysteresis in Import Prices: The Beachhead Effect,' *American Economic Review,* September 1988, pp. 773–85.

IN TOUCH *WITH THE MACROECONOMY*

EXCHANGE RATES

Exchange rates are determined in foreign exchange markets, in which the currencies of different countries are traded. Principal foreign exchange markets are located in New York, London, Tokyo, Frankfurt, Paris and other financial centres. Because foreign exchange markets are in widely separated time zones, at least one of the markets is open at almost any time of the day, so trading in currencies essentially takes place around-the-clock.

Exchange rates among major currencies are often reported daily on radio and television, and daily quotations of exchange rates are printed in major newspapers and financial dailies. The exchange rates in the accompanying table were reported in the 'Currencies and Money' section of the *Financial Times* on 21 March 1997, and apply to transactions of 20 March 1997.

Four exchange rates relative to the US dollar are reported in the table for each country: a spot rate and three forward rates. All are expressed as units of foreign currency per US dollar. The spot rate is the rate at which foreign currency can be traded immediately for US dollars. For instance, the spot exchange rate for France, 5.6900, means that on 19 March 1997, one US dollar could buy 5.6900 francs for immediate delivery.

Forward exchange rates are prices at which you can agree now to buy foreign currency at a specified date in the future. For example, on 19 March 1997, you could have arranged to buy or sell German marks one month later at an exchange rate

of 1.6835 marks per dollar. Note that for each of the currencies listed, except for the Italian lira and the British pound, the one-month forward exchange rate is lower than the spot exchange rate and that forward exchange rates decrease for dates farther into the future (three months and one year). This pattern of falling forward rates indicates that, as of 19 March 1997, participants in the foreign exchange market expected the value of the dollar relative to the other currencies (except the lira and pound) to fall over the next twelve months. For the Italian lira (and British poind), the forward rates against the dollar are higher than the spot rate, indicating that the lira–dollar exchange rate was expected to rise in the future.

Exchange Rate Against US Dollar

	Spot	One Month Forward	Three Months Forward	One Year Forward
France (francs per US dollar)	5.6900	5.6793	5.6583	5.55
Germany (marks per US dollar)	1.6867	1.6835	1.677	1.6433
Italy (lira per US dollar)	1690.70	1693.70	1698.55	1708.35
Netherlands (guilder per US dollar)	1.8986	1.8948	1.8868	1.8513
Sweden (krona per US dollar)	7.6564	7.6536	7.6437	7.5964
UK (pounds per US dollar)	0.6273	0.6276	0.6283	0.6308

Figure 14.3 shows the supply and demand for francs. The horizontal axis of the diagram measures the quantity of francs supplied or demanded, and the vertical axis measures the value of the franc in terms of other currencies, or the nominal exchange rate e_{nom}. The supply curve for francs, S, shows the number of francs that people want to supply to the foreign exchange market at each 'price' (nominal exchange rate). To supply francs to the foreign exchange market means to offer to exchange francs for some other currency. When the franc's value in terms of other currencies is high, people are more willing to supply francs to the market; thus the supply curve slopes upwards. Similarly, the demand curve for francs, D, shows the quantity of francs that people want to buy in the foreign exchange market at each exchange rate. When the franc is

Figure 14.3
The supply of and demand for the franc
The figure shows the determination of the value of the franc in the foreign exchange market. The supply curve for francs, S, indicates the number of francs that people are willing to sell in the foreign exchange market at each value of the French nominal exchange rate e_{nom}. The demand curve for francs, D, shows the number of francs that people want to buy at each nominal exchange rate. At equilibrium, point E, the value of the franc, e_{nom}^1, is the nominal exchange rate at which the quantity of francs supplied equals the quantity of francs demanded.

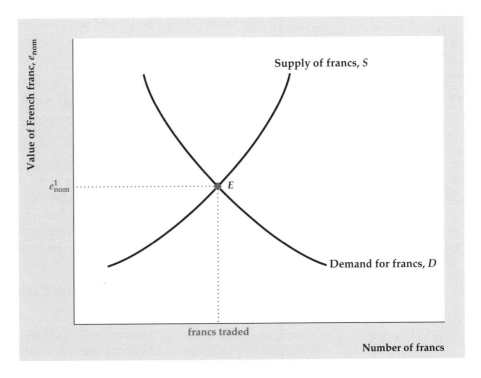

more expensive in terms of other currencies, people demand fewer francs, so the demand curve slopes downwards. The equilibrium value of the franc at point E is e_{nom}^1, the exchange rate at which the quantity of francs supplied and the quantity of francs demanded are equal.

Figure 14.3 aids in understanding the forces that determine the value of the franc, or any other currency. To go any further, though, we must ask why people decide to demand or supply francs. Unlike apples or haircuts, francs are not demanded because people value them in themselves; rather, people value francs because of what they can buy. Specifically, foreign individuals or firms demand francs in the foreign exchange market for two reasons:

1. to be able to buy French goods and services (French exports), and

2. to be able to buy French real and financial assets (French capital inflows).

Note that the two types of transaction for which foreigners need francs (to purchase French exports and French assets) correspond to the two components of the balance of payments accounts: the current account and the capital account.[7]

Similarly, the French supply francs to the foreign exchange market, thereby acquiring foreign currencies, for two reasons:

---

7. The current account and the capital account are defined and discussed in Chapter 5. The idea that foreigners must hold francs to buy French goods or assets is not completely accurate, because many transactions between the French and foreigners are done without anyone ever literally holding a supply of francs or the foreign currency. Nevertheless, this way of thinking about the determination of exchange rates is fairly simple and gives the same answers as would a more complex analysis.

1. to be able to buy foreign goods and services (French imports), and

2. to be able to buy real and financial assets in foreign countries (French capital outflows).

Thus factors that increase foreigners' demand for French exports and assets will also increase the foreign exchange market demand for francs, raising the franc exchange rate. Likewise, the value of the franc will rise if French demand for foreign goods and assets declines, so the French supply fewer francs to the foreign exchange market.

As an example, suppose that French goods improve in quality, so that foreigners demand more of them. This increase in the demand for French exports would translate into an increase in the demand for francs. In Figure 14.4 the demand for francs shifts to the right, from D^1 to D^2, and the equilibrium value of the franc rises from e^1_{nom} to e^2_{nom}. All else being equal, then, improvements in the quality of French goods would lead to an appreciation of the franc.

Macroeconomic Determinants of the Exchange Rate and Net Export Demand

In our previous *IS–LM* analyses we emphasized two key macroeconomic variables: real output (income) Y and the real interest rate r. In anticipation of the open-economy version of the *IS–LM* model presented in Section 14.3, we now consider how changes in real output or the real interest rate (either at home or abroad) are linked to the exchange rate and net exports. Again, because we are holding domestic and foreign price levels constant, the results we discuss here apply equally to the nominal exchange rate and the real exchange rate.

Figure 14.4
The effect of increased export quality on the value of the franc
An increase in the quality of French exports raises foreigners' demands for French goods and hence their demand for French francs, which are needed to buy French goods. The demand curve for francs shifts, from D^1 to D^2, raising the value of the franc (the nominal exchange rate) from e^1_{nom} to e^2_{nom}.

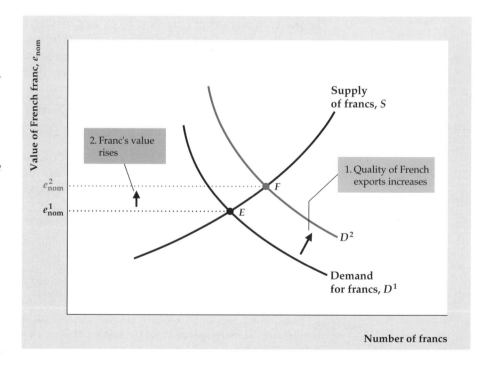

Effects of Changes in Output (Income). Imagine that domestic output (equivalently, domestic income) Y increases but that other factors (such as the real interest rate) remain unchanged. How would the increase in Y affect the exchange rate and net exports?

To consider the effect on net exports first is easier. We know that spending by consumers depends in part on their current incomes. When domestic income rises, consumers will spend more on all goods and services, *including imports.* Thus when domestic output (income) rises, net exports (exports minus imports) must fall, other factors held constant.[8]

To determine the effect of increased domestic output on the exchange rate, recall that, in order to increase their purchases of imports, domestic residents must obtain foreign currencies. Equivalently, domestic residents must supply more domestic currency to the foreign exchange market. An increased supply of domestic currency causes its value to fall: that is, the exchange rate depreciates.

We can also analyse the effects of an increase in the real output of the country's trading partners, Y_{For} (foreign output or income). An increase in Y_{For} leads foreign consumers to increase their spending on all goods and services, including the exports of the domestic country. Thus an increase in the income of Germany and Japan, for example, would increase those nations' demand for French exports and raise French net exports. The increase in foreign demand for French goods also would increase foreigners' demand for francs, raising the value of the franc. Note that the effects of changes in foreign income are the opposite of the effects of changes in domestic income.

Effects of Changes in Real Interest Rates. A second key macroeconomic variable to be considered is the real interest rate. Imagine that the domestic country's real interest rate r rises, with other factors (including the foreign real interest rate) held constant.[9] In this case, the country's real and financial assets will become more attractive to foreign savers seeking the highest return on their funds. Because domestic currency can be used to buy domestic assets, a rise in the domestic real interest rate also increases the demand for domestic currency. An increased demand for domestic currency in turn leads to exchange rate appreciation.

A rise in the domestic real interest rate r has no *direct* effect on net exports, but it does have an *indirect* effect through the exchange rate. An increase in r raises the exchange rate so that domestic exports become more expensive and imports from abroad become cheaper. Thus, other factors being constant, an increase in r reduces the domestic country's net exports.

---

8. The conclusion that an increase in output reduces net exports seems to contradict a result obtained in Chapter 5 – that an increase in output owing to a beneficial supply shock raises net exports. There is no contradiction because a supply shock does not hold variables other than output constant as we are assuming here. See Analytical Problem 5 at the end of the chapter.

9. Note that, by holding the foreign real interest rate constant, we no longer assume (as we did in Chapter 5) that the domestic and foreign countries face the same world real interest rate. In general, real interest rates in different countries need not be the same when countries produce different goods, as we assume in this chapter. The reason is that real interest rates in different countries measure different things. For example, the Japanese real interest rate measures the growth of an asset's purchasing power in terms of Japanese goods, whereas the German real interest rate measures the growth of an asset's purchasing power in terms of German goods. If the Japanese–German real exchange rate is changing, the two need not be the same.

The effects of a change in the foreign real interest rate, r_{For}, are the opposite of the effects of a change in the domestic real interest rate. If the foreign real interest rate rises, for example, foreign assets will become more attractive to domestic savers. To get the foreign currency needed to buy foreign assets, domestic savers will supply domestic currency to the foreign exchange market. The increased supply of domestic currency will lead to a depreciation of the exchange rate. The depreciation of the exchange rate caused by the rise in r_{For} in turn raises the domestic country's net exports.

Summary tables 16 and 17 list the effects of the various macroeconomic factors on the exchange rate and net exports.

14.3   THE *IS–LM* MODEL FOR AN OPEN ECONOMY

Now we are ready to explore how exchange rates and international trade interact with the behaviour of the economy as a whole. To do so, we extend the *IS–LM* model to allow for trade and lending among nations. An algebraic version of this analysis is presented in Appendix 14.A. We use the *IS–LM* diagram rather than the *AD–AS* diagram because we want to focus on the real interest rate, which plays a key role in determining exchange rates and the flows of goods and services.

Recall that the components of the *IS–LM* model are the *IS* curve, which describes goods market equilibrium; the *LM* curve, which describes asset market equilibrium; and the *FE* line, which describes labour market equilibrium. Nothing discussed in this chapter affects our analysis of the supply of or demand for money; so, in developing the open-economy *IS–LM* model, we use the same *LM* curve that we used for the closed economy model. Similarly, the labour market and the production function are not directly affected by international factors, so the *FE* line is also unchanged.[10]

However, because net exports are part of the demand for goods, we have to modify the *IS* curve in order to describe the open economy. Three main points need to be made about the *IS* curve in the open economy:

1. Although the open-economy *IS* curve is derived somewhat differently than the closed-economy *IS* curve, it is a downward-sloping relationship between output and the real interest rate, as the closed-economy *IS* curve is.

2. All factors that shift the *IS* curve in the closed economy shift the *IS* curve in the open economy in the same way.

3. In an open economy factors that change net exports also shift the *IS* curve. Specifically, for given values of domestic output and the domestic real interest rate, factors that raise a country's net exports shift the open-economy *IS* curve up; and factors that lower a country's net exports shift the *IS* curve down.

---

10. A case in which the *FE* line does depend on international considerations is when some raw materials (such as oil) are imported. In this book we have modelled oil price shocks as productivity shocks, which captures the main domestic macroeconomic effects. A full analysis that includes all the international aspects of an oil price shock is complex, so we do not present it here.

SUMMARY 16	An Increase in	Causes the Exchange Rate to	Reason
Determinants of the Exchange Rate (Real or Nominal)	Domestic output (income), Y	Fall	Higher domestic output raises demand for imports and increases supply of domestic currency.
	Foreign output (income), Y_{For}	Rise	Higher foreign output raises demand for exports and increases demand for domestic currency.
	Domestic real interest rate, r	Rise	Higher real interest rate makes domestic assets more attractive and increases demand for domestic currency.
	Foreign real interest rate, r_{For}	Fall	Higher foreign real interest rate makes foreign assets more attractive and increases supply of domestic currency.
	World demand for domestic goods	Rise	Higher demand for domestic goods increases demand for domestic currency.

SUMMARY 17	An Increase in	Causes Net Exports to	Reason
Determinants of Net Exports	Domestic output (income), Y	Fall	Higher domestic output raises demand for imports.
	Foreign output (income), Y_{For}	Rise	Higher foreign output raises foreign demand for exports.
	Domestic real interest rate, r	Fall	Higher real interest rate appreciates the real exchange rate and makes domestic goods more expensive relative to foreign goods.
	Foreign real interest rate, r_{For}	Rise	Higher foreign real interest rate depreciates the real exchange rate and makes domestic goods cheaper relative to foreign goods.
	World demand for domestic goods	Rise	Higher demand for domestic goods directly increases net exports.

After discussing each point, we use the open-economy $IS–LM$ model to analyse the international transmission of business cycles and the operation of macroeconomic policies in an open economy.

The Open-Economy IS Curve

For any level of output the IS curve gives the real interest rate that brings the goods market into equilibrium. In a closed economy the goods market equilibrium condition is that desired national saving S^d must equal desired investment I^d, or $S^d – I^d = 0$. In an open economy, as we showed in Chapter 5, the goods market equilibrium condition is that desired saving S^d must equal desired investment I^d plus net exports NX. Writing the goods market equilibrium condition for an open economy, we have

$$S^d – I^d = NX \qquad (14.5)$$

To interpret equation (14.5), recall that $S^d – I^d$, the excess of national saving over investment, is the amount that domestic residents desire to lend abroad. Recall also that net exports NX (which, if net factor payments are zero, is the same as the current account balance) equals the amount that foreigners want to borrow from domestic savers. Thus equation (14.5) indicates that, for the goods market to be in equilibrium, desired foreign lending must equal desired foreign borrowing.

An equivalent way to write the goods market equilibrium condition is as follows:

$$Y = C^d + I^d + G + NX \qquad (14.6)$$

We obtained equation (14.6) from equation (14.5) by replacing desired saving, S^d, with its definition, $Y – C^d – G$, and rearranging. Equation (14.6) states that the goods market is in equilibrium when the supply of goods, Y, equals the demand for goods, $C^d + I^d + G + NX$. Note that in an open economy the total demand for goods includes spending on net exports.

Figure 14.5 illustrates goods market equilibrium in an open economy. The horizontal axis measures desired saving minus desired investment, $S^d – I^d$, and net exports NX. Note that the horizontal axis includes both positive and negative values. The vertical axis measures the domestic real interest rate, r.

The upward-sloping curve, $S – I$, shows the difference between desired national saving and desired investment for each value of the real interest rate r. This curve slopes upwards because, with output held constant, an increase in the real interest rate raises desired national saving and reduces desired investment, raising the country's desired foreign lending.

The downward-sloping curve in Figure 14.5, NX, shows the relationship between the country's net exports and the domestic real interest rate, other factors held constant. As discussed in Section 14.2, a rise in the real interest rate causes the exchange rate to appreciate, which in turn reduces net exports (see Summary table 17). Hence the NX curve slopes downwards.

Goods market equilibrium requires that the excess of desired saving over desired investment equal net exports (equation 14.5). This condition is satisfied at the intersection of the $S – I$ and NX curves at point E. Thus the domestic real interest rate that clears the goods market is the interest rate at E, or r_1.

Figure 14.5
Goods market equilibrium in an open economy

The upward-sloping curve shows desired saving S^d less desired investment I^d. This curve slopes upward because a higher domestic real interest rate increases the excess of desired saving over desired investment. The *NX* curve relates net exports to the domestic real interest rate. This curve slopes downward because a higher domestic real interest rate causes the real exchange rate to appreciate, reducing net exports. Goods market equilibrium occurs at point *E*, where the excess of desired saving over desired investment equals net exports (equivalently, where desired lending abroad equals desired borrowing by foreigners). The real interest rate that clears the goods market is r_1.

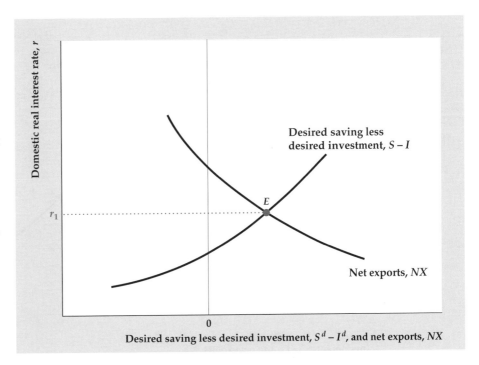

To derive the open-economy *IS* curve, we need to know what happens to the real interest rate that clears the goods market when the current level of domestic output rises (see Figure 14.6). Suppose that domestic output initially equals Y_1 and that goods market equilibrium is at point *E*, with a real interest rate of r_1. Now suppose that output rises to Y_2. An increase in current output raises desired national saving but does not affect desired investment, so the excess of desired saving over desired investment rises at any real interest rate. Thus the curve measuring the excess of desired saving over desired investment shifts to the right, from $(S - I)^1$ to $(S - I)^2$ in Figure 14.6(a).

What about the *NX* curve? An increase in domestic income causes domestic consumers to spend more on imported goods, which (other factors held constant) reduces net exports (Summary table 17). Thus when output rises from Y_1 to Y_2, net exports fall, and the *NX* curve shifts to the left, from NX^1 to NX^2.

After the increase in output from Y_1 to Y_2, the new goods market equilibrium is at point *F* in Figure 14.6(a), with the real interest rate at r_2. The *IS* curve in Figure 14.6(b) shows that, when output equals Y_1, the real interest rate that clears the goods market is r_1; and that when output equals Y_2, the real interest rate that clears the goods market is r_2. Because higher current output lowers the real interest rate that clears the goods market, the open-economy *IS* curve slopes downwards, as for a closed economy.

Factors that Shift the Open-Economy *IS* Curve

As in a closed economy, in an open economy any factor that raises the real interest rate that clears the goods market at a constant level of output shifts the *IS* curve up. This point is illustrated in Figure 14.7, which shows the effects on

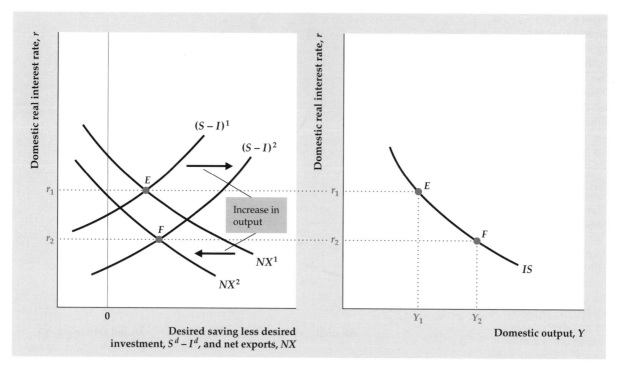

(a) Goods market equilibrium

(b) Open-economy *IS* curve

Figure 14.6
Derivation of the *IS* curve in an open economy
The initial equilibrium in the goods market is represented
by point *E* in both (a) and (b).
(a) At point *E*, domestic output is Y_1 and the domestic
real interest rate is r_1. An increase in domestic output
from Y_1 to Y_2 raises desired national saving at each real
interest rate and doesn't affect desired investment.

Therefore the $S - I$ curve shifts to the right, from $(S - I)^1$
to $(S - I)^2$. The increase in output also raises domestic
spending on imports, reducing net exports and causing
the *NX* curve to shift to the left, from NX^1 to NX^2. At the
new equilibrium point, *F*, the real interest rate is r_2.
(b) Because an increase in output from Y_1 to Y_2 lowers
the real interest rate that clears the goods market from r_1
to r_2, the *IS* curve slopes downwards.

the open-economy *IS* curve of a temporary increase in government purchases.
With output held constant at Y_1, the initial equilibrium is at point *E*, where the
real interest rate is r_1. A temporary increase in government purchases lowers
desired national saving at every level of output and the real interest rate. Thus
the $S - I$ curve shifts to the left, from $(S - I)^1$ to $(S - I)^2$, as shown in Figure
14.7(a). The new goods market equilibrium is at point *F*, where the real interest
rate is r_2.

Figure 14.7(b) shows the effect on the *IS* curve. For output Y_1, the increase
in government purchases raises the real interest rate that clears the goods
market from r_1 to r_2. Thus the *IS* curve shifts up and to the right, from IS^1 to IS^2.

In general, any factor that shifts the closed-economy *IS* curve up does so
by reducing desired national saving relative to desired investment. Because a
change that reduces desired national saving relative to desired investment
shifts the $S - I$ curve to the left (Figure 14.7(a)), such a change also shifts the
open-economy *IS* curve up.

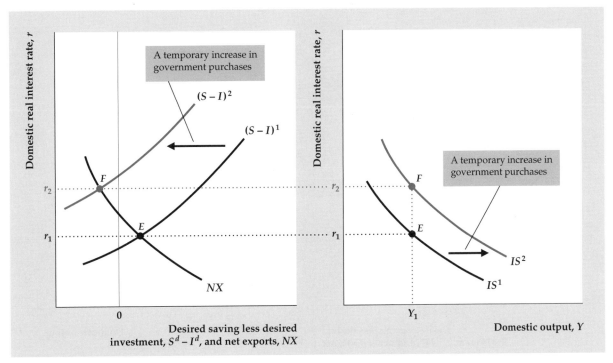

(a) Goods market equilibrium   **(b)** Open-economy *IS* curve

Figure 14.7
Effect of an increase in government purchases on the open-economy *IS* curve
Initial equilibrium is at point *E*, where output is Y_1 and the real interest rate is r_1, in both (a) and (b).
(a) A temporary increase in government purchases lowers desired national saving at every level of output and the

real interest rate. Thus the $S - I$ curve shifts to the left, from $(S - I)^1$ to $(S - I)^2$.
(b) For output Y_1, the real interest rate that clears the goods market is now r_2, at point *F* in both (a) and (b). Because the real interest rate that clears the goods market has risen, the *IS* curve shifts up and to the right, from IS^1 to IS^2.

In addition to the standard factors that shift the *IS* curve in a closed economy, some new factors affect the position of the *IS* curve in an open economy. In particular, anything that raises a country's net exports, given domestic output and the domestic real interest rate, will shift the open-economy *IS* curve up. This point is illustrated in Figure 14.8.

At the initial equilibrium point, *E*, in both Figure 14.8(a) and (b), domestic output is Y_1 and the domestic real interest rate is r_1. Now suppose that some change raises the country's net exports at any level of domestic output and the domestic real interest rate. This increase in net exports is shown as a shift to the right of the *NX* curve in Figure 14.8(a), from NX^1 to NX^2. At the new goods market equilibrium point, *F*, the real interest rate has risen to r_2. Because the real interest rate that clears the goods market has risen for constant output, the *IS* curve shifts up and to the right, as shown in Figure 14.8(b), from IS^1 to IS^2.

What might cause a country's net exports to rise, for any given domestic output and domestic real interest rate? We have discussed three possibilities at various points in this chapter: an increase in foreign output, an increase in the

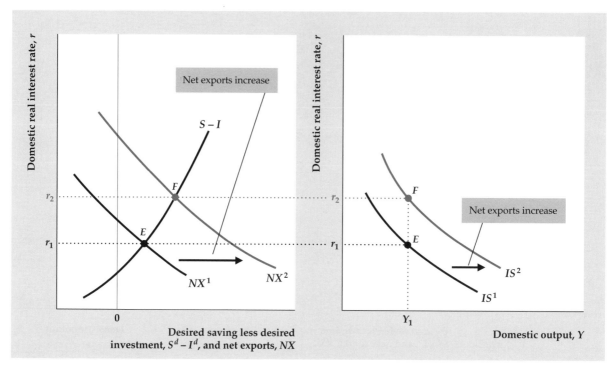

(a) Goods market equilibrium

(b) Open-economy *IS* curve

Figure 14.8
Effect of an increase in net exports on the open-economy *IS* curve
In both (a) and (b), at the initial equilibrium point, E, output is Y_1 and the real interest rate that clears the goods market is r_1.
(a) If some change raises the country's net exports at any

given domestic output and domestic real interest rate, the *NX* curve shifts to the right, from NX^1 to NX^2.
(b) For output Y_1, the real interest rate that clears the goods market has risen from r_1 to r_2, at point F in both (a) and (b). Thus the *IS* curve shifts up and to the right, from IS^1 to IS^2.

foreign real interest rate, and a shift in world demand toward the domestic country's goods (see Summary table 17).

■ *An increase in foreign output,* Y_{For}, increases purchases of the domestic country's goods by foreigners, directly raising the domestic country's net exports and shifting the *IS* curve up.

■ *An increase in the foreign real interest rate,* r_{For}, makes foreign assets relatively more attractive to domestic savers, increasing the supply of domestic currency and causing the exchange rate to depreciate. A lower real exchange rate stimulates net exports, shifting the domestic country's *IS* curve up.

■ *A shift in world demand toward the domestic country's goods,* as might occur if the quality of domestic goods improved, raises net exports and thus also shifts the *IS* curve up. A similar effect would occur if, for example, the domestic country imposed trade barriers that reduced imports (thereby increasing net exports); see Analytical Problem 1 at the end of the chapter. Summary table 18 lists factors that shift the open-economy *IS* curve.

SUMMARY 18	An Increase in	Shifts the *IS* Curve	Reason
International Factors that Shift the *IS* Curve	Foreign output, Y_{For}	Up	Higher foreign output raises demand for home country exports.
	Foreign real interest rate, r_{For}	Up	Higher foreign real interest rate depreciates the real exchange rate and raises net exports.
	Demand for domestic goods relative to foreign goods	Up	Higher demand for domestic goods raises net exports.

The International Transmission of Business Cycles

In the introduction to this chapter we discussed briefly how trade and financial links among countries transmit cyclical fluctuations across borders. The analysis here shows that the impact of foreign economic conditions on the real exchange rate and net exports is one of the principal ways by which cycles are transmitted internationally.

For example, consider the impact of a recession in Germany on the economies for which Germany is a major export market, say, the Netherlands. In terms of the *IS–LM* model a decline in German output lowers the demand for Dutch net exports, which shifts the Dutch *IS* curve down. In the Keynesian version of the model this downward shift of the *IS* curve throws the Dutch economy into a recession, with output below its full-employment level, until price adjustment restores full employment (see, for example, Figure 12.10). Dutch output is also predicted to fall in the classical model with misperceptions because the drop in net exports implies a decline in the Dutch aggregate demand (*AD*) curve and the short-run aggregate supply (*SRAS*) curve slopes upwards. However, in the basic classical model without misperceptions, in which the aggregate supply curve is vertical at full-employment output, the decline in net exports would not affect Dutch output.

Similarly, a country's domestic economy can be sensitive to shifts in international tastes for various goods. For example, a shift in demand away from Dutch goods – induced perhaps by trade restrictions against Dutch products – would shift the Dutch *IS* curve down, with the same contractionary effects as the decrease in foreign (German) output had.

14.4 MACROECONOMIC POLICY IN AN OPEN ECONOMY WITH FLEXIBLE EXCHANGE RATES

A primary reason for developing the *IS–LM* model for the open economy is to determine how borrowing and trading links among countries affect fiscal and monetary policies. When exchange rates are flexible, the effects of macroeconomic

policy on domestic variables such as output and the real interest rate are largely
unchanged when foreign trade is added. However, adding foreign trade does
raise two new questions: (1) How do fiscal and monetary policy affect a country's
real exchange rate and net exports? and (2) How do the macroeconomic policies
of one country affect the economies of other countries? With the open-economy
IS–LM model, we can answer both of these questions.

To examine the international effects of various domestic macroeconomic
policies, we proceed as follows:

1. We use the *IS–LM* diagram for the domestic economy to determine the effects
    of the policies on domestic output and the domestic real interest rate. This
    step is the same as in our analyses of closed economies in Chapters 10–12.

2. We apply the results of Section 14.2 (see in particular Summary tables 16
    and 17) to determine how changes in domestic output and the domestic
    real interest rate affect the exchange rate and net exports.

3. We use the *IS–LM* diagram for the foreign economy to determine the
    effects of the domestic policies on foreign output and the foreign real
    interest rate. Domestic policies that change the demand for the foreign
    country's net exports will shift the foreign *IS* curve.

A Fiscal Expansion

To consider the effects of fiscal policy in an open economy, let us look again at
a temporary increase in domestic government purchases. In analysing this
policy change we use the classical version of the *IS–LM* model (with no misperceptions) but also discuss the results that would be obtained in the
Keynesian framework.

Figure 14.9 shows two *IS–LM* diagrams, one for the domestic country
(where the fiscal policy change is taking place) and one for the foreign country,
representing the domestic country's major trading partners. Suppose that the
original equilibrium is at point E in Figure 14.9(a). As usual, the increase in
government purchases shifts the domestic *IS* curve up and to the right, from IS^1 to
IS^2. In addition, in the classical model the *FE* line shifts to the right, from FE^1 to
FE^2. The reason for this shift is that the increase in government purchases raises
present or future tax burdens; because higher taxes make workers poorer, they
increase their labour supply, which raises full-employment output. The new
equilibrium is represented by point F, the intersection of IS^2 and FE^2. The
domestic price level rises, shifting the domestic *LM* curve to the left, from LM^1
to LM^2, until it passes through F. Comparing point F with point E reveals that
the increase in government purchases increases both output Y *and* the real
interest rate r in the domestic country. So far the analysis is identical to the
classical analysis for a closed economy (Chapter 11). Note also that fiscal
expansion raises output and the real interest rate – the same results that we
would get from the Keynesian model.

To examine the role of international trade, we first consider the effects on
the exchange rate of the increases in domestic output and the domestic real
interest rate. Recall that an increase in output Y causes domestic residents
to demand more imports and thus to supply more currency to the foreign
exchange market. The increase in domestic output therefore causes the

Figure 14.9
Effects of an increase in domestic government purchases
(a) In the classical *IS–LM* model, an increase in domestic government purchases shifts the domestic *IS* curve to the right, from IS^1 to IS^2. It also shifts the domestic *FE* line to the right, from FE^1 to FE^2. Therefore domestic output and the domestic real interest rate both increase. These increases reduce net exports but have an ambiguous effect on the real exchange rate. The results are similar in the Keynesian model.
(b) Because the domestic country's exports are the foreign country's imports and vice versa, the decrease in the domestic country's net exports is equivalent to a rise in the foreign country's net exports. This increase shifts the foreign *IS* curve up, from IS^1_{For} to IS^2_{For}. In the classical model, prices adjust rapidly, shifting the *LM* curve from LM^1_{For} to LM^2_{For}. The new equilibrium is at point *F*, where the foreign real interest rate and price level are higher but foreign output is unchanged. In the Keynesian model, price stickiness would cause a temporary increase in foreign output at *H* before price adjustment restores general equilibrium at *F*.

(a) Domestic country

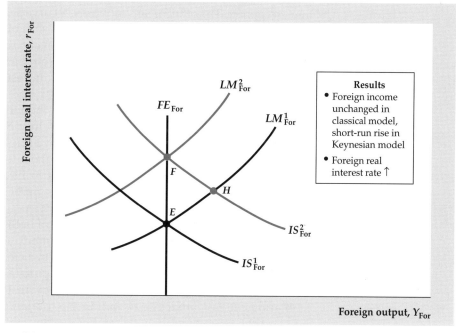

(b) Foreign country

exchange rate to depreciate. However, the rise in the domestic real interest rate makes domestic assets more attractive, causing foreign savers to demand the domestic currency and causing the exchange rate to appreciate. The overall effect of the increase in government purchases on the exchange rate is ambiguous: we cannot be sure whether the increase in government purchases will raise or lower the exchange rate.

The effect of the fiscal expansion on the country's net export demand is not ambiguous. Recall that the increase in domestic output (which raises domestic consumers' demand for imports) and the increase in the real interest rate (which tends to cause the exchange rate to appreciate) both cause net exports to fall. Thus the overall effect of the fiscal expansion is clearly to move the country's trade balance towards deficit. This result is consistent with the analysis of the 'twin deficits' (the government budget deficit and the trade deficit) of Chapter 5.

In an interconnected world, the effects of macroeconomic policies in one country are not limited to that country but are also felt abroad. Based on the analysis we have just finished, taking the extra step and finding out how the domestic fiscal expansion affects the economies of the domestic country's trading partners is not difficult.

The effects of the domestic fiscal expansion on the rest of the world – represented by the foreign country IS–LM diagram in Figure 14.9(b) – are transmitted through the change in net exports. Because the domestic country's imports are the foreign country's exports and vice versa, the decline in net exports of the domestic country is equivalent to an increase in net exports for the foreign country. Thus the foreign country's IS curve shifts up, from IS^1_{For} to IS^2_{For}.

In the classical IS–LM model, the upward shift of the foreign IS curve does not affect foreign output; instead the price level rises immediately to restore general equilibrium (the LM curve shifts up from LM^1_{For} to LM^2_{For}). The foreign economy ends up at point F, with the real interest rate and the price level higher than they were initially.

If prices were sticky, as in the Keynesian model, the effects of the shift of the foreign country's IS curve would be slightly different. If prices do not adjust in the short run, the shift of the IS curve implies that the foreign economy would have *temporarily* higher output at the intersection of the IS and LM curves at point H in Figure 14.9(b); only after firms adjust their prices would the economy arrive at point F. Otherwise, the implications of the classical and Keynesian analyses are the same.[11]

Therefore, in the open-economy versions of both the classical and Keynesian models, a temporary increase in government purchases raises domestic income and the domestic real interest rate, as in a closed economy. In addition, net exports fall; thus increased government purchases reduce, or crowd out, both investment and net exports. The effect on the real exchange rate is ambiguous: It can either rise or fall. In the foreign economy the real interest rate and the price level rise. In the Keynesian version of the model foreign output also rises, but only in the short run.

---

11. In principle, we could continue the analysis by discussing how changes in foreign output and real interest rates in turn affect the domestic economy. However, these so-called *feedback effects* are generally small and thus do not reverse any of our conclusions, so we omit this discussion.

A Monetary Contraction

We can also use the open-economy IS–LM model to study the effects of monetary policy when exchange rates are flexible. For the Keynesian version of the IS–LM model we analyse the effects of a drop in the money supply in both the short and long run. Because the effects of monetary policy are the same in the basic classical model (without misperceptions) and the long-run Keynesian model, our analysis applies to the classical model as well.

Short-Run Effects on the Domestic and Foreign Economies. The effects of a monetary contraction are shown in Figure 14.10, which shows IS–LM diagrams corresponding to both the domestic and foreign countries. Suppose that the initial equilibrium is represented by point E and that a decrease in the money supply shifts the domestic LM curve up and to the left, from LM^1 to LM^2, in Figure 14.10(a). In the Keynesian model, the price level is rigid in the short run, so the short-run equilibrium is at point F, the intersection of the IS and LM^2 curves. Comparing points F and E reveals that in the short run domestic output falls and the domestic real interest rate rises. This result is the same as for the closed economy (Chapter 12).

After the monetary contraction, the exchange rate appreciates in the short run, for two reasons. First, the drop in domestic income reduces the domestic demand for imports, leading domestic consumers to demand less foreign currency to buy imported goods. Second, the rise in the domestic real interest rate makes domestic assets relatively more attractive to foreign savers, increasing foreign savers' demand for the domestic currency.

What happens to the country's net exports? Here there are two competing effects: (1) the drop in domestic income created by the monetary contraction reduces the domestic demand for foreign goods and thus tends to increase the country's net exports; but (2) the rise in the real interest rate, which leads to exchange rate appreciation, tends to reduce net exports. The theory does not indicate for certain which way net exports will change. In our earlier discussion of the J curve, however, we noted that the effects of changes in the real exchange rate on net exports may be weak in the short run. Based on that analysis, we assume that in the short run exchange rate effects on net exports are weaker than the effects of changes in domestic income so that overall the country's net exports will increase.

The next question is: how does the domestic monetary contraction affect the economies of the country's trading partners? The effects on the typical foreign economy are illustrated by Figure 14.10(b). If the domestic country's net exports are increased by the monetary contraction, the foreign country's net exports must decrease because the domestic country's exports are the foreign country's imports. Thus the IS curve of the foreign country shifts to the left, from IS_{For}^1 to IS_{For}^2. The short-run equilibrium is at point F, where the IS_{For}^2 and LM_{For} curves intersect. Output in the foreign country declines, and the foreign real interest rate falls.

These results show that a domestic monetary contraction also leads to a recession abroad. This transmission of recession occurs because the decline in domestic output also reduces domestic demand for foreign goods. The appreciation of the domestic real exchange rate works in the opposite direction by making foreign goods relatively cheaper, which tends to increase the net exports of the foreign country. However, we have assumed that the negative

Figure 14.10
Effects of a decrease in the domestic money supply
(a) A decrease in the domestic money supply shifts the domestic *LM* curve up, from *LM*¹ to *LM*². The short-run equilibrium in the Keynesian model is at point *F*, the intersection of the *IS* and *LM*² curves. The decline in the money supply reduces domestic output and increases the domestic real interest rate. The drop in domestic output and the rise in the real interest rate cause the real exchange rate to appreciate. The effect on net exports is potentially ambiguous; if we assume that the effect on net exports of the drop in domestic income is stronger than the effect of the appreciation of the exchange rate, net exports increase as domestic residents demand fewer goods from abroad.
(b) Because the domestic country's net exports increase, the foreign country's net exports fall and the foreign *IS* curve shifts down, from *IS*¹₍For₎ to *IS*²₍For₎ Thus output and the real interest rate fall in the foreign country in the short run.

In the long run, domestic prices fall and both economies return to equilibrium at point *E*. Thus in the long run money is neutral.

(a) Domestic country

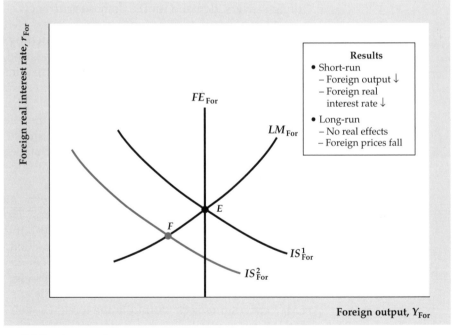

(b) Foreign country

effect of declining domestic income on the foreign country's net exports is stronger than the positive effect of the appreciating domestic exchange rate. Thus a domestic monetary contraction leads to a recession in both the foreign country and the domestic country.

Long-Run Effects on the Domestic and Foreign Economies. In the long run after a monetary contraction, wages and prices decline in the domestic country, as firms find themselves selling less output than they desire. The domestic country's LM curve returns to its initial position, LM^1 in Figure 14.10(a), so that money is neutral in the long run. As all real variables in the domestic economy return to their original levels, the real exchange rate and the domestic demand for foreign goods also return to their original levels. As a result, the foreign country's IS curve shifts back to its initial position, IS^1_{For} in Figure 14.10(b), and the foreign country's economy also returns to its initial equilibrium point, E. At E, all foreign macroeconomic variables (including the price level) are at their original levels. Hence, in the long run, the change in the domestic money supply does not affect any real variables, either domestically or abroad. In particular, the real exchange rate and net exports are not affected by the monetary contraction in the long run.

Although monetary neutrality holds in the long run in the Keynesian model, it holds immediately in the basic classical model. So, in the basic classical model, monetary policy changes have no effect on real exchange rates or trade flows; they affect only the price level. In a monetary contraction, the domestic price level will fall (the foreign price level does not change).

Although money cannot affect the *real* exchange rate in the long run, it does affect the *nominal* exchange rate by changing the domestic price level. (This is one case where the responses of the real and nominal exchange rates to a change in macroeconomic conditions differ.) As we have shown, the long-run neutrality of money implies that a 10% decrease in the nominal money supply will decrease the domestic price level by 10%. Recall (equation 14.1) that the nominal exchange rate e_{nom} equals eP_{For}/P, where e is the real exchange rate, P_{For} is the foreign price level, and P is the domestic price level. Because the real exchange rate e and the foreign price level P_{For} are unchanged in the long run by a domestic monetary contraction, the 10% drop in the domestic price level P raises the nominal exchange rate e_{nom} by (approximately) 10%. Thus a monetary contraction reduces the domestic price level and causes the nominal exchange rate to appreciate by the same percentage as the drop in money supply.

APPLICATION

Why the Dollar Rose So High and Fell So Far in the 1980s

As Figure 14.2 shows, the US dollar appreciated strongly during the first half of the 1980s. Then after reaching its peak in March 1985, the dollar fell precipitously for nearly three years before stabilizing at a level close to where it had been in 1980. Associated with the rise in the dollar was a sharp decline in US net exports, as Figure 14.2 also shows. What were the ultimate causes of these fluctuations?

To explain these fluctuations Keynesians focus on the effects of macroeconomic policies during that decade – specifically, a combination of tight monetary policy and expansionary fiscal policy. The tight-money policy began in October 1979 when Federal Reserve Chairman Paul Volcker announced that money growth rates would be reduced to fight inflation, which at that time was causing concern. Contractionary monetary policy contributed to a short recession in 1980 and a deep recession in 1981–82. Fiscal policy became expansionary in about 1981, when the tax cuts mandated by the Economic Recovery Tax Act (ERTA) began to be phased in. Military expenditures also increased, and the government's budget deficit rose significantly.

In the Keynesian analysis the effects on output of tight money and expansionary fiscal policy tend to cancel out, and, indeed, by 1983 the economy had begun a strong recovery from the 1981–82 recession. However, the tight money and expansionary fiscal combination also led to a higher real interest rate, reaching record levels in the early 1980s. The high real interest rate in the United States attracted foreign investors; as foreigners demanded dollar-denominated assets, the real value of the dollar rose sharply. According to the Keynesians, because the dollar was so strong, US net exports fell sharply in 1983 and 1984.

By the mid 1980s some of the factors keeping the dollar high had begun to reverse. Although budget deficits remained high, the ebbing of inflation reduced the need for tight money and the US real interest rate declined. In 1985 and 1986 some major foreign countries, notably Japan and Germany, agreed to cooperate with the United States to help bring the value of the dollar down. At the same time, foreign savers, who had acquired large quantities of US assets during the early 1980s, became reluctant to hold more dollar assets. Hence the dollar declined, ultimately bringing some improvement in the US net export position.

An alternative (and to some degree complementary) explanation of the dollar's rise has been offered by some classical economists. Their explanation is based on the idea that during the early 1980s the United States became a relatively more attractive place to make real and financial investments. The argument is based on both a 'push' and a 'pull'. The pull came from the liberalization of US tax laws pertaining to investment and the generally pro-business attitude of the Reagan administration, both of which increased the profitability of investing in the United States. The push came from the failure of many developing countries to repay their international debts fully and on schedule. Savers both in the United States and abroad began to shy away from lending to these countries, preferring instead the safe haven of US assets. According to the classical argument, the increased desirability of US assets relative to foreign assets increased the demand for the dollar and raised the US real exchange rate, which in turn reduced US net exports.[12] Again, however, as the decade progressed foreign savers became 'satiated' with US assets, setting the stage for the ultimate decline in the value of the dollar.

14.5   FIXED EXCHANGE RATES

Following the abandonment of the Bretton Woods system of fixed exchange rates during the early 1970s, many industrialized countries opted for a flexible exchange rate. However, fixed exchange rate systems – in which exchange rates are officially set by international agreement – have been important histor-

---

12. Analytical Problem 3 at the end of the chapter asks you to work out this argument in more detail.

ically and are still used by many countries. From the point of view of European economies, the consequences of adopting a fixed exchange rate, at least with their EU trading partners, are particularly significant. Let us now consider fixed exchange rate systems and address two questions: (1) How does the use of a fixed exchange rate system affect an economy and macroeconomic policy? and (2) Ultimately, which is the better system, flexible or fixed exchange rates?

Fixing the Exchange Rate

In contrast to flexible exchange rate systems – where exchange rates are determined by supply and demand in foreign exchange markets – in a fixed exchange rate system the value of the nominal exchange rate is officially set by the government, perhaps in consultation or agreement with other countries. For example, as members of the EMS, France and Germany have agreed on the exchange rate between French francs and German marks; similar agreements govern the rates at which francs and marks will trade for the currencies of other EMS members.[13] This system of fixed exchange rates is one of the key elements of the movement towards monetary union in Europe.

---

13. Not all members of the EMS have their currencies fixed within the ERM. The UK, for example, was a member of the EMS from 1979 but did not join the ERM until 1990. It then came out again in 1992 in dramatic fashion, as we discuss later in the chapter.

BOX 14.2

Optimal Currency Areas

The move towards monetary unification in Europe raises a number of issues about the costs and benefits of countries forgoing their own national currencies in favour of a single currency, and we consider these in Chapter 15. However, one way of approaching this problem is to ask: what determines the optimal area for a single currency?[*] A number of criteria have been suggested as necessary for an optimal currency area. First, factors of production should be mobile and able to move easily within the area. If, for example, productivity is increasing faster in one location, adjustments can take place within the area as labour and capital move to where they are most productive. Where there are constraints on mobility and factors of production cannot move freely within the area, separate currencies and exchange rate changes provide an alternative adjustment mechanism.

The second criterion necessary for an optimal currency area is that there should be an integrated fiscal system. Fiscal transfers can then be used to offset imbalances in income levels, etc. within the area. Finally, different locations within the area should face similar external shocks or disturbances. If the two areas have separate currencies then a depreciation of the exchange rate would stabilize demand. If these disturbances are similar then there would be no need for exchange rate changes and the two locations could adopt a single currency.

An interesting study by Tamin Bayoumi and Barry Eichengreen[†] compared the shocks experienced by EU countries with those experienced by US states. The authors find that the shocks affecting EU countries are, on average, smaller than those which hit US states, but that they are more dissimilar. For example, the shocks which affect Germany are not the same as those which affect France, Belgium, and the Netherlands – Germany's closest neighbours. Those affecting the UK and Italy were even less like those in Germany. It would therefore appear that the EU is less of an optimal currency area than the USA.

---

[*] The idea of an optimal currency area was first developed by Robert Mundell, 'A Theory of Optimal Currency Areas', *American Economic Review*, September 1961.
[†] 'Shocking Aspects of European Monetary Union', NBER working paper no. 3949, 1992.

A potential problem with fixed exchange rate systems is that the value of the exchange rate set by the government may not be the exchange rate determined by the supply and demand for currency. Figure 14.11 shows a situation in which the official exchange rate, $\bar{e}_{nom}$, is higher than the **fundamental value of the exchange rate**, e^1_{nom}, or the value that would be determined by free market forces without government intervention. When an exchange rate is higher than its fundamental value, it is an **overvalued exchange rate** (often referred to as an overvalued currency).

How can a country deal with a situation in which its official exchange rate is different from the fundamental value of its exchange rate? There are several possible strategies. First, the country can simply change the official value of its exchange rate so that it equals, or is close to, its fundamental value. For example, in the case of overvaluation shown in Figure 14.11, the country could simply devalue (lower) its nominal fixed exchange rate from $\bar{e}_{nom}$ to e^1_{nom}. However, although occasional devaluations or revaluations can be expected under fixed exchange rate systems, if a country continuously adjusts its exchange rate it might as well switch to a flexible rate system.

Second, the government could restrict international transactions – for example, by limiting or taxing imports or capital outflows. Such policies reduce the supply of the domestic currency to the foreign exchange market, thus raising the fundamental value of the exchange rate toward its fixed value. Some countries go even further and prohibit people from trading the domestic currency for foreign currencies without government approval; a currency that cannot be freely traded for other currencies is said to be an **inconvertible currency**. However, direct government intervention in international transactions has many economic costs, including reduced access to foreign goods and credit.

**Figure 14.11
An overvalued exchange rate**
The figure shows a situation in which the officially fixed nominal exchange rate, $\bar{e}_{nom}$, is higher than the fundamental value of the exchange rate, e^1_{nom} as determined by supply and demand in the foreign exchange market. In this situation the exchange rate is said to be overvalued. The country's central bank can maintain the exchange rate at the official rate by using its reserves to purchase its own currency in the foreign exchange market, in the amount of *AB* in each period. This loss of reserves also is referred to as the country's balance of payments deficit.

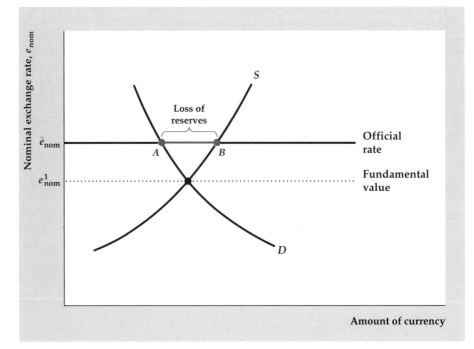

Third, the government itself may become a demander or supplier of its currency in the foreign exchange market, an approach used by most of the industrialized countries having fixed exchange rates. For example, in the case of overvaluation shown in Figure 14.11, the supply of the country's currency to the foreign exchange market (point B) exceeds private demand for the currency (point A) at the official exchange rate by the amount AB. To maintain the value of the currency at the official rate, the government could buy back its own currency in the amount AB in each period.

Usually, these currency purchases are made by the nation's central bank using official reserve assets. Recall that official reserve assets are assets other than domestic money or securities that can be used to make international payments (examples are gold, foreign bank deposits, or special assets created by international agencies such as the International Monetary Fund). During the gold standard period, for example, gold was the basic form of official reserve asset, and central banks offered to exchange gold for their own currencies at a fixed price. If Figure 14.11 represented a gold standard country, AB would represent the amount of gold that the central bank would have to use to buy back its currency in each period to equalize the quantities of its currency supplied and demanded at the official exchange rate. Recall also that the decline in a country's official reserve assets during a year equals its *balance of payments deficit*. Thus amount AB measures the reserves that the central bank must use to support the currency and corresponds to the country's balance of payments deficit.

Although a central bank can maintain an overvalued exchange rate for a time by offering to buy back its own currency at a fixed price, it cannot do so forever because it has only a limited supply of official reserve assets. During the gold standard period, for example, central banks did not own unlimited amounts of gold. Attempting to support an overvalued currency for a long period of time would have exhausted a central bank's limited gold reserves, leaving the country no choice but to devalue its currency.

A central bank's attempts to support an overvalued currency can be ended quickly and dramatically by a speculative run. A **speculative run** occurs when financial investors begin to fear that an overvalued currency may soon be devalued, reducing the value of assets denominated in that currency relative to assets denominated in other currencies. To avoid losses, financial investors frantically sell assets denominated in the overvalued currency. The panicky sales of domestic assets associated with a speculative run on a currency shift the supply curve for that currency sharply to the right, from S^1 to S^2 in Figure 14.12, increasing the gap between the quantities supplied and demanded of the currency from amount AB to amount AC. This widening gap increases the rate at which the central bank has to spend its official reserve assets to maintain the overvalued exchange rate, speeding devaluation and confirming the financial investors' expectations.

Without strong restrictions on international trade and finance (themselves economically costly), we conclude that an overvalued exchange rate is not sustainable for long. If the exchange rate is overvalued, the country must either devalue its currency or make some policy change to raise the fundamental value of the exchange rate. We show in the next section that the basic tool for changing the fundamental value of the exchange rate is monetary policy.

Figure 14.12

A speculative run on an overvalued currency

Initially, the supply curve of the domestic currency is S^1 and, to maintain the fixed exchange rate, the central bank must use amount AB of its reserves each period to purchase its own currency in the foreign exchange market. A speculative run occurs when holders of domestic assets begin to fear a devaluation, which would reduce the values of their assets (measured in terms of foreign currency). Panicky sales of domestic-currency assets lead to more domestic currency being supplied to the foreign exchange market, which shifts the supply curve of the domestic currency to the right, from S^1 to S^2. The central bank must now purchase its currency and lose reserves in the amount AC. This more rapid loss of reserves may force the central bank to stop supporting the overvalued currency and to devalue it, confirming the market's expectations.

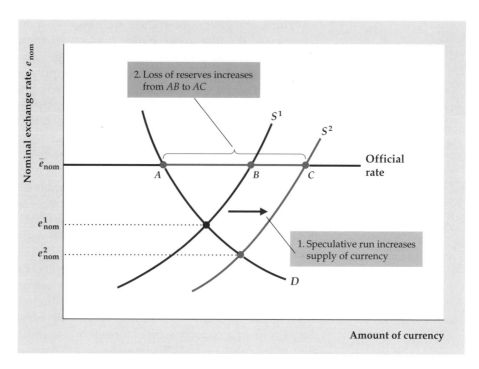

We have focused on overvaluation, but an exchange rate could also be undervalued. As illustrated in Figure 14.13, an **undervalued exchange rate** (or undervalued currency) exists if the officially fixed value is less than the value determined by supply and demand in the foreign exchange market. In this case, instead of buying its own currency, the central bank sells its currency to the foreign exchange market and accumulates reserves in the amount AB each period. With no limit to the quantity of reserve assets (gold, for example) that a central bank could accumulate, an undervalued exchange rate could apparently be maintained indefinitely. However, a country with an undervalued exchange rate can accumulate reserves only at the expense of trading partners who have overvalued exchange rates and are therefore losing reserves. Because the country's trading partners cannot continue to lose reserves indefinitely, eventually they will put political pressure on the country to bring the fundamental value of its exchange rate back in line with the official rate.

Monetary Policy and the Fixed Exchange Rate

Suppose that a country wants to eliminate currency overvaluation by raising the fundamental value of its nominal exchange rate until it equals the fixed value of the exchange rate. How can it achieve this goal? Economists have long recognized that the best way for a country to do so is through contraction of its money supply.

To demonstrate why a monetary contraction raises the fundamental value of the nominal exchange rate, we first rewrite equation (14.1), which defined the relationship of the real and nominal exchange rates:

Figure 14.13
An undervalued exchange rate
The exchange rate is undervalued when the officially determined nominal exchange rate, $\bar{e}_{nom}$, is less than the fundamental value of the exchange rate as determined by supply and demand in the foreign exchange market, e^1_{nom}. To maintain the exchange rate at its official level, the central bank must supply its own currency to the foreign exchange market in the amount AB each period, thereby accumulating foreign reserves.

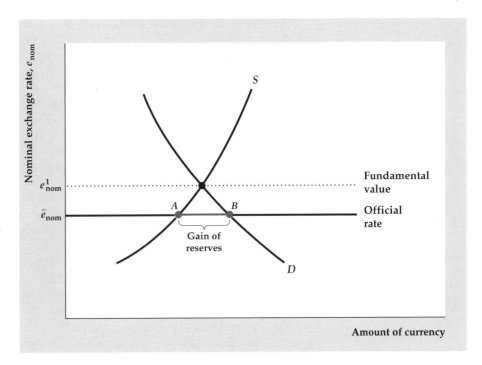

$$e_{nom} = \frac{eP_{For}}{P} \qquad (14.7)$$

Equation (14.7) states that, for any foreign price level P_{For}, the nominal exchange rate e_{nom} is proportional to the real exchange rate e and inversely proportional to the domestic price level P.

In our earlier discussion of monetary policy in the Keynesian model with flexible exchange rates, we showed that a monetary contraction causes the real exchange rate to appreciate in the short run by reducing domestic output and increasing the real interest rate. Because short-run domestic and foreign price levels are fixed in the Keynesian model, equation (14.7) indicates that the short-run appreciation of the real exchange rate also implies a short-run appreciation of the nominal exchange rate. In the long run money is neutral; hence a monetary contraction has no effect on the real exchange rate, but it does cause the domestic price level to fall. In the long run the domestic price level P falls but the real exchange rate e is unaffected, so equation (14.7) implies that the nominal exchange rate rises (appreciates) both in the long run and in the short run. Thus in both the short and long run a monetary contraction increases the fundamental value of the nominal exchange rate, or the value of the nominal exchange rate determined by supply and demand in the foreign exchange market.[14] Conversely, a monetary easing reduces the fundamental value of the nominal exchange rate in both the short and long run.

---

14. Because money is neutral in both the short and long run in the basic classical model, a monetary contraction increases the fundamental value of the nominal exchange rate in both the short and long run in the basic classical model too.

Figure 14.14 illustrates the relationship between the nominal exchange rate and the money supply in a country with a fixed exchange rate.[15] The downward-sloping curve shows the relationship of the money supply to the fundamental value of the nominal exchange rate. This curve slopes downwards because, other factors being equal, an increase in the money supply reduces the fundamental value of the nominal exchange rate. The horizontal line in Figure 14.14 is the officially determined exchange rate. The value of M_1 on the horizontal axis is the money supply that equalizes the fundamental value of the exchange rate and its officially fixed value. If the money supply is more than M_1, the country has an overvaluation problem (the fundamental value of the exchange rate is below the official value), and if the money supply is less than M_1 the country has an undervaluation problem.

Figure 14.14 suggests that, in a fixed exchange rate system, individual countries are typically *not* free to expand their money supplies in order to try to raise output and employment. Instead, the money supply is governed by the condition that the official and fundamental values of the exchange rate be the same. If the country represented in Figure 14.14 wanted to expand its money supply to fight a recession, for example, it could do so only by creating an overvaluation problem (probably leading to a future devaluation) or by devaluing its currency immediately. Under fixed exchange rates, then, a central bank cannot use monetary policy to pursue macroeconomic stabilization goals.

Although one member of a group of countries in a fixed exchange rate system is generally not free to use monetary policy by itself, the group *as a*

15. The country's money supply is the amount of money in circulation domestically, as in previous chapters. It is *not* the supply of currency to foreign exchange markets, which depends only on domestic residents' demands for foreign goods and assets.

**Figure 14.14
Determination of the
money supply under
fixed exchange rates**
The downward-sloping
fundamental value curve
shows that a higher
domestic money supply
causes a lower fundamental
value of the exchange
rate. The horizontal line
shows the officially fixed
nominal exchange rate.
Only when the country's
money supply equals M_1
does the fundamental val-
ue of the exchange rate
equal the official rate. If
the central bank increased
the money supply above
M_1, the exchange rate
would become overvalued.
A money supply below M_1
would result in an under-
valued currency.

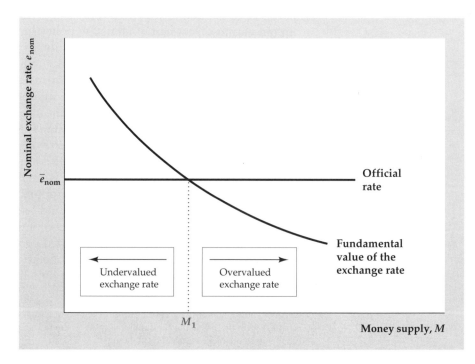

Figure 14.15
Coordinated monetary expansion

Suppose that Spain and Portugal are members of a fixed-exchange-rate system and that both are suffering from recessions. Initially, the fundamental value of Portugal's exchange rate as a function of the country's money supply is FV^1, and its money supply level consistent with maintenance of the official exchange rate is M_1. If Portugal raises its money supply to M_2 in an attempt to stimulate its economy, the fundamental value of its exchange rate will fall below the official fixed rate, and Portugal's currency will be overvalued.

Now suppose that Spain also expands its money supply in a coordinated effort to stimulate both economies. For any level of Portugal's money supply, the increase in Spain's money supply will cause the fundamental value of Spain's exchange rate to depreciate and the fundamental value of Portugal's exchange rate to appreciate. The fundamental value curve of Portugal's exchange rate shifts up from FV^1 to FV^2. Portugal can now increase its money supply to M_2 without creating an overvaluation problem. Thus Spain and Portugal have achieved a coordinated monetary expansion.

whole may be able to do so, *if* they coordinate their policies. For example, suppose that Spain and Portugal have a fixed exchange rate between their two currencies and that, because of a recession in both countries, both want to expand their money supplies. If Portugal attempts a monetary expansion on its own, from M_1 to M_2 in Figure 14.15, its exchange rate will become overvalued (its fundamental value, at the intersection of M_2 and FV^1, would be lower than the official exchange rate). As a result, the Bank of Portugal would lose reserves, ultimately forcing Portugal to undo its attempted expansion.[16]

Suppose, however, that Spain goes ahead with its own money supply expansion. If Portugal's money supply remains constant, an increase in Spain's money supply reduces Spain's (nominal) exchange rate, which is equivalent to raising Portugal's exchange rate. In terms of Figure 14.15, the increase in Spain's money supply increases the fundamental value of Portugal's exchange rate at any level of its money supply. The fundamental value curve in Figure 14.15 shifts up from FV^1 to FV^2. Now Portugal can expand its money supply, from M_1 to M_2, without creating an overvaluation problem (the fundamental value of the Portuguese exchange rate, at the intersection of M_2 and FV^2, is the same as the official exchange rate). Thus if Spain and Portugal cooperate by changing their money supplies in the same direction, both countries can achieve their stabilization goals without either country experiencing overvaluation.

---

16. This does not, of course mean that countries do not attempt to gain an advantage by devaluing their currencies. During the Great Depression a number of countries devalued in an attempt to boost domestic demand at the expense of that in other countries. Such 'begger-thy-neighbour' policies typically result in retaliatory action by those countries adversely affected either in the form of offsetting devaluations or restrictions on trade.

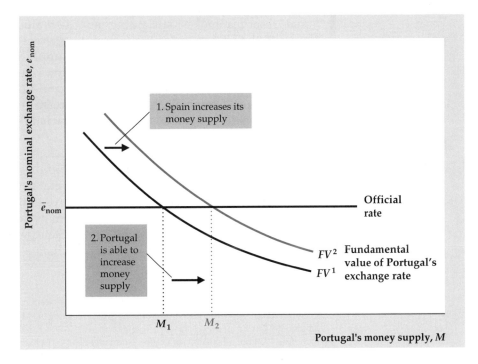

1. Spain increases its money supply

2. Portugal is able to increase money supply

$\bar{e}_{nom}$

Official rate

FV^2 Fundamental value of Portugal's exchange rate

FV^1

M_1 M_2

Portugal's nominal exchange rate, e_{nom}

Portugal's money supply, M

As this example shows, fixed exchange rates are most likely to work well when the countries in the system have similar macroeconomic goals and can cooperate on monetary policies. As the following application illustrates, the failure of nations to cooperate within a fixed exchange rate system can lead to severe problems, including the potential breakdown of the system.

APPLICATION

Policy Coordination Failure and the Collapse of Fixed Exchange Rates: The Cases of Bretton Woods and the EMS

Towards the end of World War II, the world's industrialized nations established the Bretton Woods system, under which exchange rates were fixed (with occasional adjustments).[17] The USA, by far the world's largest economy at the time, played a central role in the system and US dollars were widely used by other countries as official reserve assets. Other countries were willing to do so because the USA pledged to maintain the exchange rate between dollars and gold at $35 per ounce. In other words, the US dollar was 'as good as gold'. All in all, the Bretton Woods system seemed to perform well. While the system was fully operational (1959–71)[18] most countries recorded solid macroeconomic growth and stability. However, the inability of the principal member countries to coordinate their monetary policies created severe strains in the system and eventually led to its collapse.

Several international disputes erupted over monetary policy during the Bretton Woods era, but the one that ultimately proved fatal was triggered by American monetary policy during the 1960s. The US money supply grew more and more rapidly, reflecting the Federal Reserve's aggressive attempts to promote growth in output and employment and its desire to keep interest rates low despite expansionary fiscal policies. (US government spending increased significantly during the 1960s because of the Vietnam War and the expansion of Great Society social programmes.) Increasing money growth and the inflation that followed caused the dollar to become increasingly overvalued.

Normally, in a fixed exchange rate system, a country's loss of international reserves makes sustaining an overvalued currency impossible. However, the USA avoided the loss of its reserves for a time by persuading foreign central banks to buy the excess supply of dollars in the foreign exchange market. Foreign central banks at first were willing to use their own currencies to buy US dollars because they could use the dollars as international reserves. Ultimately, however, the foreign central banks grew tired of accumulating dollars and complained about what they considered to be overexpansionary US monetary policy.

The solution suggested by US policymakers was for the other Bretton Woods members to increase their money supplies, thereby eliminating the dollar overvaluation problem. However, several countries, notably Germany, refused to accept the inflationary consequences of this proposal and began to demand instead that the United States redeem its dollars with gold. Fearing a huge drain on its gold reserves, the United States was reluctant to redeem its dollars. A series of crises in the foreign exchange markets followed, and in

17. For a detailed recent study of the Bretton Woods system, see Michael D. Bordo and Barry Eichengreen, eds., *A Retrospective on the Bretton Woods System* (University of Chicago Press for NBER), 1993.
18. Before 1959 not all currencies in the system were convertible.

August 1971 President Nixon announced that the United States would no longer exchange gold for dollars. This announcement effectively ended the Bretton Woods system and left the world's major currencies to float freely against each other.

Two decades later a different kind of dispute over monetary policy threatened the European Monetary System (EMS) and the Exchange Rate Mechanisam (ERM) a system of fixed exchange rates that operated among a number of European nations. Because of its large economy, Germany was the most influential country in the EMS. In 1992, concerned about increased inflation after German reunification, the Bundesbank tightened Germany's monetary policy, raising interest rates significantly. This action undervalued the mark and overvalued other EMS currencies, putting considerable pressure on other members of the EMS to tighten monetary policies as well. However, the UK, Italy, and other countries at the time were mired in serious recessions and did not want to go along with German contractionary policies.

In September 1992, participants in the foreign exchange market became convinced that the UK and Italy would not tighten monetary policy and that, as a result, they would eventually have to devalue the pound and the lira respectively. This fear led to a speculative run on both currencies. After losing large quantities of reserves in attempts to maintain their value relative to other currencies in the ERM, they decided to leave the fixed exchange rate system and allowed the value of the pound and lira to fall. Several other countries refused to match Germany's tight monetary policies and were forced to devalue. The French franc came under heavy pressure in August 1993 but the French government resisted pressure to devalue. Instead, the bands within which the franc was allowed to fluctuate were widened to ± 15% around its central value. The 1992 EMS crisis substantially delayed progress toward the ultimate goal of a single European currency although by 1994 some credibility was restored to the ERM and most currencies remain fairly close to their central rates.

In the Bretton Woods case, the dominant country in the system followed a monetary policy that was more expansionary than the other members wanted; in the EMS case, the dominant country followed a monetary policy that was tighter than the other members preferred. In both instances, however, international disagreements about the appropriate rate of monetary growth posed a severe threat to the very existence of the fixed exchange rate system.

Fixed Versus Flexible Exchange Rates

We have discussed some of the problems that arose in the Bretton Woods and EMS fixed exchange rate systems. However, flexible exchange rate systems have problems of their own, primarily the volatility of exchange rates, which introduces uncertainty for people and businesses in their transactions with other countries. Each type of system has its problems, so which is preferable?

Proponents of fixed exchange rate systems stress two major benefits. First, relative to a situation in which exchange rates fluctuate continuously, stable exchange rates make trading goods and assets among countries easier and less costly. Thus a system of fixed rates may promote economic and financial integration and improve economic efficiency. Second, fixed exchange rates may improve monetary policy 'discipline', in the sense that countries with fixed exchange rates are typically less able to carry out highly expansionary monetary policies; the result may be lower inflation in the long run.

The other side of the monetary discipline argument is that fixed exchange rates take away a country's ability to use monetary policy flexibly to deal with recessions.[19] This inability is particularly serious if the different countries in the fixed exchange rate system have different policy goals and face different types of economic shock. As the preceding Application illustrated, disagreements among countries in a fixed exchange rate system about the conduct of monetary policy may even lead to the breakdown of the system.

Which system is better depends on the circumstances. Fixed exchange rates (or even a common currency) among a group of countries are useful when large benefits can be gained from increased trade and integration and when the countries in the system coordinate their monetary policies closely, as in the EMS. Countries that value the ability to use monetary policy independently – perhaps because they face different macroeconomic shocks than other countries or hold different views about the relative costs of unemployment and inflation – should retain a floating exchange rate.

Currency Unions

An alternative to fixing exchange rates is for a group of countries to form a **currency union**, under which they agree to share a common currency. Members of a currency union also typically cooperate economically and politically. The agreement among the original thirteen American colonies, enshrined in the US Constitution, to abandon their individual currencies and create a single money, may be thought of as an early example of currency union.

An effective currency union usually requires more than just cooperation of national central banks; for the currency union to work, the common monetary policy must be controlled by a single institution. Because countries are typically reluctant to give up having their own currencies and monetary policies, currency unions have been rare. However, if politically feasible, a currency union has several advantages over fixed exchange rates. First, the costs of trading goods and assets among countries are even lower with a single currency than under fixed exchange rates. Second, if national currencies are eliminated in favour of the common currency, speculative attacks on the national currencies can obviously no longer occur.

However, a currency union shares the major disadvantage of a fixed exchange rate system, which is that it requires all its members to share a common monetary policy. Thus if one member of a currency union is in a recession while another is concerned about inflation, the common monetary policy cannot deal with both countries' problems simultaneously. In contrast, under flexible exchange rates, each country could set its own monetary policy independently.

---

19. Keynesians consider this a cost, but classical economists do not.

14.6 EUROPEAN MONETARY UNIFICATION

In December 1991, at a summit meeting at Maastricht in the Netherlands, the member countries of the European Community (EC) adopted the Treaty on European Union, usually called the Maastricht Treaty. The treaty took effect in November 1993, after being ratified (not without some resistance) by popular votes in the member countries. One of the most important provisions of the treaty is that the member countries will attempt to adopt a common currency, to be called the Euro, beginning (at the time of this writing) on 1 January, 1999. A European Central Bank (ECB), to be located in Frankfurt, Germany, will determine the common monetary policy for all countries joining in the currency union.

The European Monetary System and the Exchange Rate Mechanism

The establishment of a currency union would represent the final stage in a process of monetary integration in Europe which began in the early 1970s. Following the collapse of the Bretton Woods Agreement (see the Application on page 554), most European countries adopted flexible exchange rates. Turbulent foreign exchange markets, however, encouraged a number of European countries to adopt a system of 'fixed but adjustable' exchange rates (called the European 'snake'), in which member states agreed to limit fluctuations in the exchange rates of their currencies to +/– 2.25%. However, the 'snake' system was beset with problems, and currencies often entered and left the system, causing uncertainty in trade relations within Europe.

The failure of the 'snake' system to achieve foreign exchange stability encouraged a number of governments (most notably France and Germany) to propose even greater monetary integration. The outcome was the European Monetary System (EMS), which came into operation in March 1979.

In order to achieve exchange rate stability, the EMS imposed a system of fixed exchange rates on member states: a system called the Exchange Rate Mechanism (ERM). The ERM requires participating countries to keep the exchange rate of their currencies within specified bounds around an official central rate with respect to the currencies of other member states and to the ECU. The ECU, a second important feature of the EMS, is the official unit of account in the EU and is used in transactions between central banks within the EU. The bands set within the ERM were originally +/– 2.25% around the official central value, although these were widened in August 1993 following a speculative crisis, discussed in the Application on page 554. If any two currencies reach the upper or lower limit, the monetary authorities of the countries involved are required to intervene in the foreign exchange market to support the weaker currency.

The ECU is not itself a currency but a basket of all the currencies of the EMS member states, and its value is calculated by summing specified amounts of each currency. The amounts of each currency are based on a country's economic performance, so that currencies of stronger economies figure more prominently in the ECU than those of weaker economies. Since the German economy has had the strongest record in terms of economic performance, the German mark has been dominant in determining the value of the ECU. Indeed, the dominance of the mark has meant that countries in the ERM have in effect fixed their currencies to the mark. As discussed in the Application on page 554, this created problems for a number of countries when Germany adopted a very tight monetary policy following German unification, and it resulted in both the UK and Italy leaving the ERM, although Italy has since rejoined.

Although the ERM has come under considerable pressure on a number of occasions – several EMS member states are not members of the ERM – intergovernmental discussions about the movement towards further full monetary unification have proceeded. The negotiations resulted in the Maastricht Treaty, which set out the stages and timetable for the transition to European Monetary Union (EMU).

The Convergence Criteria

European countries will not automatically be allowed to join the EMU. According to the provisions of the Maastricht Treaty, to be eligible to join, countries must achieve certain specified standards in maintaining low inflation, low fiscal deficits, and a stable exchange rate. Because of these restrictions, it remains very uncertain how many countries will be allowed to adopt the Euro in 1999, or whether in fact the target date of 1999 will be achieved at all.

The four main criteria are:

- *Price stability*: an average rate of inflation in the twelve months prior to joining EMU that is not more than 1.5 percentage points above the average for the three EU economies with the best inflation records.

- *Interest rates*: a rate of interest that is not more than 2 percentage points above the average of the three EU economies with the lowest long-run interest rates.

- *Exchange rate stability*: an exchange rate that has remained within the 'normal' band within the ERM for at least two years prior to entry to the EMU.

- *Fiscal criteria*: public debt no greater than 60% of GDP and a government budget deficit of no more than 3% of GDP.

These criteria are designed to ensure that countries joining the EMU have and are able to maintain a low-inflation economy. However, many economists believe that the 1 January 1999 deadline set for full monetary integration in the Maastricht Treaty was far too optimistic and that it could be met only if the convergence criteria are relaxed. Indeed, very few countries have succeeded in actually meeting the convergence criteria. Even Germany, with its record of monetary stability, has found it difficult to meet the fiscal criteria due to the impact that unification has had on the budget deficit. The German government's efforts to reduce the deficit brought it into conflict with the German central bank, the Bundesbank. The German government sought to revalue its gold reserves held at the Bundesbank to generate income which would transfer to the government and thus ease its own fiscal problems. The Bundesbank accused the German government of 'cooking the books' and operating in a way that was not in the 'spirit of Maastricht'.

The Costs and Benefits of a European Currency Union

The proposed European Monetary Union is a very interesting, but risky, experiment. Possible advantages include the elimination of the transaction costs associated with buying and selling foreign currency that arise from trade between European countries.

A single currency would also eliminate uncertainty about foreign exchange movements, giving firms greater confidence in the environment in which they operate, which could encourage trade and investment decisions. A single currency would also reduce the need for foreign currency reserves for cross-border trade, providing additional resources that could be put to other uses. The EU has estimated these savings to be around $200 billion.

Another possible advantage of a European currency union is that it could enable all European countries to achieve lower inflation rates. The creation of a European Central Bank, tasked with promoting price stability and determining a common monetary policy, would promote monetary stability and impose on all member states a commitment to low rates of inflation. An integrated European market would rival that of the USA in scope and wealth, and the Euro could become a preferred currency for international transactions (as the dollar is today). European securities denominated in Euros may also prove more attractive to international investors.

A major risk of a common currency and EMU is that countries could have very different views about the priority of economic variables, such as inflation and unemployment, and strongly disagree about whether the common monetary policy should be contractionary or expansionary at a given time. This risk would be increased if fluctuations in economic activity did not coincide country by country. Countries with 'strong' currencies, like Germany, also fear that the Euro might not be as stable and resistant to inflation as their own national currencies have been.

CHAPTER SUMMARY

1. The nominal exchange rate is the number of units of foreign currency that can be obtained for one unit of domestic currency. The real exchange rate is the number of units of foreign goods that can be obtained for one unit of the domestic good. The idea that similar foreign and domestic goals should have the same prices in terms of the same currency is called purchasing power parity (*PPP*)

2. There are two major types of exchange rate system: flexible or floating exchange rate systems, in which the value of the nominal exchange rate is determined by market forces; and fixed exchange rate systems, in which the value of the exchange rate is officially set by a government or group of governments. In a flexible exchange rate system, an exchange rate increase is called an appreciation, and an exchange rate decrease is called a depreciation.

3. The real exchange rate is important because it affects net exports, or exports minus imports. Other factors held constant, a decline in the real exchange rate makes domestic goods cheaper relative to foreign goods and thus tends to increase net exports in the long run. Because a drop in the real exchange rate raises the cost of imports, however, it may cause net exports to fall in the short run before physical flows of exports and imports have had time to adjust. The characteristic pattern of the response of net exports to a drop in the real exchange rate – falling net exports in the short run but rising net exports in the long run – is called the J curve.

4. In a flexible exchange rate system, the value of the (nominal) exchange rate is determined by supply and demand in the foreign exchange market. Foreigners demand the domestic currency to buy domestic goods and assets. Domestic residents supply the domestic currency to obtain the foreign currency needed to buy foreign goods and assets.

5. Other factors held constant, an increase in domestic output leads domestic residents to demand more imports, reducing the country's net exports and depreciating its exchange rate. An increase in the domestic real interest rate makes domestic assets more attractive, increasing the demand for the domestic currency and causing the exchange rate to appreciate; the higher exchange rate in turn reduces net exports. The effects of changes in foreign output and the foreign real interest rate on the domestic country's net exports and exchange rate are the opposite of the effects of changes in domestic output and the domestic real interest rate.

6. The *IS–LM* model for an open economy is similar to that for the closed economy. The principal difference is that, in the open-economy *IS–LM* model, factors (other than output or the real interest rate) that increase a country's net exports cause the *IS* curve to shift up. Among the factors that increase net exports are a rise in foreign output, an increase in the foreign real interest rate, and a shift in world demand toward the domestic country's goods. Economic shocks or policy changes are transmitted from one country to another by changes in net exports that lead to *IS* curve shifts.

7. In an open economy with flexible exchange rates, a fiscal expansion increases domestic output, domestic prices, and the domestic real interest rate, as in a closed economy. The effect on the exchange rate is ambiguous. The increase in output raises the demand for imported goods, which weakens the exchange rate, but the higher real interest rate makes domestic assets more attractive, which strengthens the exchange rate. Because increased output raises the demand for imports, net exports fall. The fiscal expansion is transmitted to the foreign country by the increase in demand for the foreign country's exports.

8. In an open economy with flexible exchange rates, changes in the money supply are neutral in the basic classical model. Changes in the money supply are also neutral in the long run in the Keynesian model. In the short run in the Keynesian model, however, a decrease in the domestic money supply reduces domestic output and raises the domestic real interest rate, causing the current real exchange rate to appreciate. Net exports by the domestic country increase, if the effect of lower output (which increases net exports) is stronger than the effect of the rise in the real exchange rate (which tends to reduce net exports). The monetary contraction is transmitted to the foreign country by the effect on the foreign country's net exports, which decline.

9. In a fixed exchange rate system, nominal exchange rates are officially determined. If the officially determined exchange rate is greater than the fundamental value of the exchange rate as determined by supply and demand in the foreign exchange market, the exchange rate is said to be overvalued. The central bank can maintain the exchange rate at an overvalued level for a time by using official reserves (such as gold or foreign-currency bank deposits) to buy its own currency in the foreign exchange market. A country that tries to maintain an overvalued exchange rate for too long will run out of reserves and be forced to devalue its currency. If financial investors expect a devaluation, they may sell large quantities of domestic assets (a speculative run). A speculative run increases the supply of the domestic currency in the foreign exchange market and increases the rate at which the central bank must pay out its reserves.

10. To raise the fundamental value of its exchange rate, the central bank can tighten monetary policy. There is only one value of the domestic money supply at which the fundamental value of the exchange rate equals its officially fixed rate. With fixed exchange rates, individual countries are not free to use expansionary monetary policies to fight recessions because such policies result in an overvalued exchange rate. However, a group of countries in a fixed exchange rate system can use expansionary monetary policies effectively if they coordinate their policies.

11. The advantages of a fixed exchange rate system are that it may promote economic and financial integration among countries and that it imposes discipline on the monetary policies of individual countries. A fixed exchange rate system will not work well if member countries have different macroeconomic policy goals or face different macroeconomic disturbances and thus are unable or unwilling to coordinate their monetary policies.

12. An alternative to fixing exchange rates is for a group of countries to form a currency union, under which they share a common currency. To work successfully, a currency union requires member countries to adopt a common monetary policy, which can be a disadvantage when their economies are facing different economic problems and require conflicting policy responses. A currency union has two main advantages: the cost of trading goods and assets between member countries is reduced and speculative attacks on the national currencies are eliminated.

13. The European Monetary Union is an example of a currency union and the euro will be the single currency which member states will adopt when the union is established. The transition to monetary union and a single currency has involved member states joining a system of fixed exchange rates (the European Monetary Union) and meeting several convergence criteria designed to ensure that countries which join are able to maintain low rates of inflation, low fiscal deficits and a stable exchange rate.

Key Terms

currency union, p. 556
devaluation, p. 520
exchange rate, p. 517
exchange rate unions, p. 518
fixed exchange rate system, p. 518
flexible exchange rate system, p. 517
floating exchange rate system, p. 517
foreign exchange market, p. 517
fundamental value of the exchange rate, p. 548
incovertible currency, p. 548
J curve, p. 524
nominal appreciation, p. 520
nominal depreciation, p. 520
nominal exchange rate, p. 517
overvalued exchange rate, p. 548
purchasing power parity, p. 521
real appreciation, p. 520
real depreciation, p. 521
real exchange rate, p. 519
relative purchasing power parity, p. 523
revaluation, p. 520
speculative run, p. 549
terms of trade, p. 523
undervalued exchange rate, p. 550

Key Equations

$$e = \frac{e_{\text{nom}} P}{P_{\text{For}}} \tag{14.1}$$

The real exchange rate, e, or the number of foreign goods that can be obtained for one domestic good, is defined in terms of the nominal exchange rate e_{nom} (the amount of foreign currency that can be obtained for one unit of domestic currency), the domestic price level P, and the foreign price level P_{For}.

$$\frac{\Delta e_{\text{nom}}}{e_{\text{nom}}} = \frac{\Delta e}{e} + \pi_{\text{For}} - \pi \tag{14.4}$$

The percentage change in the nominal exchange rate, $\Delta e_{\text{nom}}/e_{\text{nom}}$, equals the percentage change in the real exchange rate, $\Delta e/e$, plus the excess of the foreign rate of inflation over the domestic rate of inflation, $\pi_{\text{For}} - \pi$.

$$S^d - I^d = NX \qquad (14.5)$$

In an open economy, goods market equilibrium (the *IS* curve) requires that the excess of desired national saving over desired investment equal net exports. Equation (14.5) is equivalent to the condition that output, *Y*, must equal the aggregate demand for goods, $C^d + I^d + G + NX$, equation (14.6).

Review Questions

1. Define *nominal exchange rate* and *real exchange rate*. How are changes in the real exchange rate and the nominal exchange rate related?
2. What are the two main types of exchange rate system? Currently, which type of system determines the values of the major currencies, such as the mark, the franc, the dollar, and the yen?
3. What is the J curve? What explains the behaviour of net exports represented by the J curve?
4. For a given real exchange rate, how are a country's net exports affected by an increase in domestic income? An increase in foreign income? How does an increase in the domestic real interest rate affect the real exchange rate and net exports? Explain.
5. Why do foreigners demand francs in the foreign exchange market? Why do the French supply francs to the foreign exchange market? Give two examples of changes that would lead to an increased demand for francs and two examples of changes that would lead to an increased supply of francs in the foreign exchange market.
6. How does the *IS–LM* model for an open economy differ from the *IS–LM* model for a closed economy? Illustrate the use of the open-economy *IS–LM* model in describing how a recession in one country may be transmitted to other countries.
7. How are net exports affected by expansionary fiscal policy? By expansionary monetary policy? What is the potential ambiguity in determining these effects?
8. What effects does expansionary monetary policy have on the nominal exchange rate in both the short and long run? Explain.
9. What is the *fundamental value* of a currency? What does saying that a currency is *overvalued* mean? Why is an overvalued currency a problem? What can a country do about an overvalued currency?
10. Why is a country limited in changing its money supply under a fixed exchange rate system? Explain

how policy coordination among countries on a fixed exchange rate system can increase the degree to which monetary policy may be used to pursue macroeconomic goals.

Numerical Problems

1. West Bubble makes ordinary soap bars that are sold for 5 guilders each. East Bubble makes deluxe soap bars that are sold for 100 florins each. The real exchange rate between West and East Bubble is two ordinary soap bars per deluxe soap bar.
   a. What is the nominal exchange rate between the two countries?
   b. During the following year West Bubble has 10% domestic inflation and East Bubble has 20% domestic inflation. Two ordinary soap bars are still traded for a deluxe soap bar. At the end of the year what has happened to the nominal exchange rate? Which country has had a nominal appreciation? Which has had a nominal depreciation?
2. Japan produces and exports only cameras, and Saudi Arabia produces and exports only barrels of oil. Initially, Japan exports 40 cameras to Saudi Arabia and imports 64 barrels of oil. The real exchange rate is 4 barrels of oil per camera. Neither country has any other trading partners.
   a. Initially, what is the real value of Japan's net exports, measured in terms of its domestic good? (*Hint:* You have to use the real exchange rate to express Japan's oil imports in terms of an equivalent number of cameras. Then calculate Japan's net exports as the number of cameras exported minus the real value of its imports in terms of cameras.)
   b. The real exchange rate falls to 3 barrels of oil per camera. Although the decline in the real exchange rate makes oil more expensive in terms of cameras, in the short run there is relatively little change in the quantities of exports and imports, as Japan's exports rise to 42 cameras and its imports fall to 60 barrels of oil. What has happened to the real value of Japan's net exports?
   c. In the longer run, quantities of exports and imports adjust more to the drop in the real exchange rate from 4 to 3, and Japan's exports rise to 45 cameras and its imports of oil fall to 54 barrels. What are Japan's real net exports now?
   d. Relate your answers to parts (b) and (c) to the J-curve concept.

3. Consider the following classical economy.

Desired consumption	$C^d = 300 + 0.5Y - 200r$
Desired investment	$I^d = 200 - 300r$
Government purchases	$G = 100$
Net exports	$NX = 150 - 0.1Y - 0.5e$
Real exchange rate	$e = 20 + 600r$
Full-employment output	$\overline{Y} = 900$

a. What are the equilibrium values of the real interest rate, the real exchange rate, consumption, investment, and net exports?

b. Now suppose that full-employment output increases to 940. What are the equilibrium values of the real interest rate, the real exchange rate, consumption, investment, and net exports?

c. Suppose that full-employment output remains at 940 and that government purchases increase to 132. What are the equilibrium values of the real interest rate, the real exchange rate, consumption, investment, and net exports?

4. Consider the following Keynesian economy.

Desired consumption	$C^d = 200 + 0.6(Y - T) - 200r$
Desired investment	$I^d = 300 - 300r$
Taxes	$T = 20 + 0.2Y$
Government purchases	$G = 152$
Net exports	$NX = 150 - 0.08Y - 500r$
Money demand	$L = 0.5Y - 200r$
Money supply	$M = 924$
Full-employment output	$\overline{Y} = 1000$

a. What are the general equilibrium (that is, long-run) values of output, the real interest rate, consumption, investment, net exports, and the price level?

b. Starting from full employment, government purchases are increased by 62, to 214. What are the effects of this change on output, the real interest rate, consumption, investment, net exports, and the price level in the short run? In the long run?

c. With government purchases at their initial value of 152, net exports increase by 62 at any income and real interest rate so that $NX = 212 - 0.08Y - 500r$. What are the effects of this change on output, the real interest rate, consumption, investment, net exports, and the price level in the short run? In the long run? Compare your answer to that for part (b).

5. Consider the following classical economy.

AD	$Y = 400 + 50\,M/P$
AS	$Y = \overline{Y} = 1000$

This economy produces only wine, its output is measured in terms of wine, and its currency is francs. It trades with a country that produces only cheese, and the currency of that country is crowns. The real exchange rate e equals 5 wedges of cheese per bottle of wine. The foreign price level is 20 crowns per wedge of cheese, and the domestic money supply is 48 francs.

a. What is the domestic price level? What is the fundamental value of the (nominal) exchange rate?

b. Suppose that the domestic country fixes its exchange rate at 50 crowns per franc. Is its currency overvalued, undervalued, or neither? What will happen to the domestic central bank's stock of official reserve assets if it maintains the exchange rate at 50 crowns per franc?

c. Suppose that the domestic country wants a money supply level that equalizes the fundamental value of the exchange rate and the fixed rate of 50 crowns per franc. What level of the domestic money supply achieves this goal? (*Hint:* For the given real exchange rate and foreign price level, what domestic price level is consistent with the official rate? What domestic money supply level will yield this price level?)

Analytical Problems

1. Recessions often lead to calls for protectionist measures to preserve domestic jobs. Suppose that a country that is in a recession imposes restrictions that sharply reduce the amount of goods imported by the country.

a. Using the Keynesian $IS–LM$ model, analyse the effects of import restrictions on the domestic country's employment, output, real interest rate, and real exchange rate, keeping in mind that the country is initially in a recession.

b. What are the effects of the country's action on foreign employment, output, real interest rates, and real exchange rate? What happens if the foreign country retaliates by imposing restrictions on goods exported by the domestic country?

c. Suppose that the domestic economy is at full employment when it imposes restrictions on imports. Using the basic classical model without misperceptions, find the effects on the country's employment, output, real interest rate, and real exchange rate.

2. 'US government budget deficits not only crowd out investment in the United States but also reduce capital formation in other countries.'

Is this statement true? To analyse it, use the Keynesian model to work out the effects on investment, both at home and abroad, of a government budget deficit. Assume that the deficit was the result of a large tax cut and assume also that households respond to the tax cut by increasing desired consumption (Ricardian equivalence did not hold). Consider both the short and long run. Does your answer change if Ricardian equivalence holds so that desired consumption is unaffected by the tax cut?

3. The Application at the end of Section 14.4 discussed the idea that the United States became a relatively more attractive place to invest in the early 1980s. Analyse this argument by using the classical *IS–LM* model for two countries. Assume that because of more favourable tax laws, the user cost of capital falls in the domestic country and that, because of the LDC debt crisis, the expected future marginal product of capital falls in the foreign country. Show that these changes lead to an appreciation of the home country's real exchange rate and a drop in the domestic country's net exports. Assume no change in current productivity or current labour supply in either country. What is happening to capital flows? Why?

4. East Bubble's main trading partner is West Bubble. To fight inflation, West Bubble undertakes a contractionary monetary policy.

a. What is the effect of West Bubble's contractionary monetary policy on East Bubble's real exchange rate in the short run, assuming no change in East Bubble's policies? In the long run? Use the Keynesian model with flexible exchange rates.

b. What is the effect of West Bubble's monetary contraction on East Bubble's *nominal* exchange rate in the short run and in the long run?

c. Suppose now that East Bubble has fixed its exchange rate with West Bubble. If East Bubble wants to keep the exchange rate equal to its fundamental value, how will East Bubble have to respond to West Bubble's monetary tightening? What will happen to East Bubble's output, real exchange rate, and net exports in the short run if it maintains the fixed exchange rate at its fundamental value? Compare your answer to that for part (a).

d. Suppose that, after West Bubble's monetary tightening, East Bubble decides not to change any of its own macroeconomic policies (the exchange rate is still fixed). What will happen? Describe some alternative scenarios.

5. Use a diagram like Figure 14.6 to analyse the effect on a country's net exports of a beneficial supply shock that temporarily raises full-employment output by 100 per person. Assume that the basic classical model applies so that income is always at its full-employment level.

a. Suppose that, in response to the temporary increase in income, the residents of the country do not change the amount they desire to spend at any real interest rate (on either domestic or foreign goods). What is the effect of the supply shock on the country's net exports? (*Hint:* What is the effect of the increase in income on the curve representing desired saving minus desired investment? What is the effect on the curve representing net exports?)

b. Now suppose that, in response to a temporary increase in income, the residents of the country increase their desired spending at any real interest rate by 100 per person. A portion of this increased spending is for foreign-produced goods. What is the effect on the country's net exports?

c. More difficult: If the increase in income is temporary, would the spending behaviour assumed in part (a) or the spending behaviour assumed in part (b) be more likely to occur? Based on your answer, do the results of this problem confirm or contradict the prediction of the model in Chapter 5 of the response of net exports to a supply shock? Explain.

AN ALGEBRAIC VERSION OF THE OPEN-ECONOMY *IS–LM* MODEL

The *IS–LM* model for the open economy is basically the same as the closed-economy *IS–LM* model derived in Appendix 10.A, with the exception that the goods market equilibrium condition (the *IS* curve) is expanded to include net exports. The *LM* curve and the *FE* line are unchanged from previous analyses.

To derive the *IS* curve for the open economy, we begin with the equations describing desired consumption and desired investment, equations (10.A.8) and (10.A.10):

$$C^d = c_0 + c_Y[Y - (t_0 + tY)] - c_r r \tag{14.A.1}$$

$$I^d = i_0 - i_r r. \tag{14.A.2}$$

Equation (14.A.1) shows that desired consumption depends positively on disposable income, $Y - T$, and negatively on the real interest rate, r. (In equation (14.A.1) we used equation (10.A.9) to substitute for taxes, T.) Equation (14.A.2) states that desired investment depends negatively on the real interest rate r. Other factors influencing desired consumption and desired investment are included in the constant terms c_0 and i_0, respectively.

In an open economy net exports are also a source of demand for domestic output. We assume that net exports are

$$NX = x_0 - x_Y Y + x_{YF} Y_{\text{For}} - x_r r + x_{rF} r_{\text{For}} \tag{14.A.3}$$

where x_0, x_Y, x_{YF}, x_r, and x_{rF} are positive numbers. According to equation (14.A.3), a country's net exports depend negatively on domestic income Y (increased domestic income raises spending on imports) and positively on foreign income Y_{For} (increased foreign income raises spending on exports). Net exports also depend negatively on the domestic real interest rate r (a higher real interest rate causes the real exchange rate to appreciate, making domestic goods relatively more expensive) and positively on the foreign real interest rate r_{For} (a higher foreign real interest rate causes the domestic country's real exchange rate to depreciate). Other factors influencing net exports, such as the qualities of domestic and foreign goods, are reflected in the constant term x_0 in equation (14.A.3).

The goods market equilibrium condition for an open economy, equation (5.5), is

$$Y = C^d + I^d + G + NX. \tag{14.A.4}$$

The alternative version of the open-economy goods market equilibrium condition, $S^d = I^d + NX$, which is emphasized in the text, could be used equally well.

If we substitute the equations for desired consumption, equation (14.A.1), desired investment, equation (14.A.2), and net exports, equation (14.A.3), into the goods market equilibrium condition, equation (14.A.4), we get

$$Y = c_0 + c_Y(Y - t_0 - tY) - c_r r + i_0 - i_r r + G + x_0 - x_Y Y + x_{YF} Y_{\text{For}} - x_r r + x_{rF} r_{\text{For}}. \tag{14.A.5}$$

Collecting the terms that multiply Y on the left-hand side yields

$$[1 - (1-t)c_Y + x_Y]Y = c_0 + i_0 + G - c_Y t_0 + x_0 + x_{YF} Y_{\text{For}} + x_{rF} r_{\text{For}} - (c_r + i_r + x_r)r. \quad (14.A.6)$$

Equation (14.A.6) relates output Y to the real interest rate r that clears the goods market and thus defines the open-economy IS curve. To put equation (14.A.6) in a form that is easier to interpret graphically, we rewrite it with r on the left-hand side and Y on the right side to obtain

$$r = \alpha'_{IS} - \beta'_{IS} Y, \qquad \text{open-economy } IS \text{ curve.} \quad (14.A.7)$$

Here, α'_{IS} and β'_{IS} are positive numbers defined as

$$\alpha'_{IS} = \frac{c_0 + i_0 + G - c_Y t_0 + x_0 + x_{YF} Y_{\text{For}} + x_{rF} r_{\text{For}}}{c_r + i_r + x_r} \quad (14.A.8)$$

and

$$\beta'_{IS} = \frac{1 - (1-t)c_Y + x_Y}{c_r + i_r + x_r}. \quad (14.A.9)$$

If there are no net exports, so that $x_0 = x_Y = x_{YF} = x_r = x_{rF} = 0$, the coefficients α'_{IS} and β'_{IS} reduce to the coefficients of the closed-economy IS curve, α_{IS} and β_{IS} (compare equations (14.A.8) and (14.A.9) to equations (10.A.15) and (10.A.16)).

We use the open-economy IS curve equation, equation (14.A.7), to confirm the three points made about the curve in the text. First, it slopes downwards (the slope of the IS curve is $-\beta'_{IS}$ which is negative). Second, any factor that shifts the closed-economy IS curve also shifts the open-economy IS curve (any factor that changes the intercept α_{IS} also changes the intercept α'_{IS} in the same direction). Finally, for a given output and real interest rate, any factor that increases net exports shifts the open-economy IS curve up. That is, an increase in Y_{For} or r_{For}, or some other change that increases the demand for net exports as reflected in an increase in x_0, raises the intercept term α'_{IS} and thus shifts the IS curve up.

General equilibrium in the open-economy IS–LM model is determined as in the closed-economy model, except that the open-economy IS curve (equation 14.A.7) replaces the closed-economy IS curve (equation 10.A.14). Similarly, classical and Keynesian AD–AS analysis in the open economy is the same as in the closed economy (Appendix 10.A), except that the coefficients α_{IS} and β_{IS} in the equation for the aggregate demand curve, equation (10.A.27), are replaced by their open-economy analogues, α'_{IS} and β'_{IS}.

For values of output Y, the real interest rate r, and the price level P determined by the open-economy IS–LM or AD–AS model, exchange rates can be determined from:

$$e = e_0 - e_Y Y + e_{YF} Y_{\text{For}} + e_r r - e_{rF} r_{\text{For}} \quad (14.A.10)$$

where e_0, e_Y, e_{YF}, e_r, and e_{rF} are positive numbers; and

$$e_{\text{nom}} = \frac{e P_{\text{For}}}{P}. \quad (14.A.11)$$

According to equation (14.A.10), an increase in foreign income Y_{For} or the domestic interest rate r, either of which raises the demand for the domestic currency, causes the real exchange rate e to appreciate. Also, an increase in domestic income Y or the foreign real interest rate r_{For}, either of which increases the supply of domestic currency, causes the real exchange rate to depreciate. Equation (14.A.11), which is the same as equations (14.1) and (14.6), states that the nominal exchange rate e_{nom} depends on the real exchange rate e and the foreign and domestic price levels, P_{For} and P.

To illustrate the use of equations (14.A.10) and (14.A.11), let us consider the effects of a monetary expansion in the Keynesian model. In the short run, an increase in the money supply raises domestic output Y, lowers the domestic real interest rate r, and leaves the domestic price level P unchanged. For these changes equations (14.A.10) and (14.A.11) – holding constant foreign output Y_{For} and the foreign real interest rate r_{For} – imply a lower real exchange rate e and a lower nominal exchange rate e_{nom} (both a real and a nominal depreciation). In the long run, money is neutral, so Y and r return to their original levels. Equation (14.A.10) indicates, therefore, that the real exchange rate e also returns to its original value in the long run. However, a monetary expansion leads to a long-run increase in the domestic price level P. Hence from equation (14.A.11) we see that the nominal exchange rate e_{nom} also depreciates in the long run.

CHAPTER

15

MONETARY POLICY AND THE CENTRAL BANK

Monetary policy – the government's decisions about how much money to supply to the economy – is one of the two principal tools available for affecting macroeconomic behaviour. (The other, fiscal policy, is discussed in Chapter 16.) Monetary policy decisions have widespread implications for the economy. The macroeconomic models that we have presented predict that changes in the money supply will affect nominal variables such as the price level and the nominal exchange rate. In addition, theories that allow for non-neutrality (including the extended classical theory with misperceptions and the Keynesian theory) imply that, in the short run, monetary policy also affects real variables such as real GDP, the real interest rate, and the unemployment rate. Because monetary policy has such pervasive economic effects, the central bank's announcements and actions are closely monitored by the media, financial market participants, and the general public.

In this chapter we look more closely at monetary policy, concentrating first on the basic question of how the nation's money supply is determined. We demonstrate that, although a nation's central bank can exert strong influence over the level of the money supply, the money supply is also affected by the banking system's behaviour and the public's decisions.

In the second part of the chapter, we explore the question: how should the central bank conduct monetary policy? Not surprisingly, because of classical and Keynesian differences over the effects of monetary policy and the desirability of trying to smooth the business cycle (Chapters 11 and 12), the question is controversial. Keynesians usually argue that monetary authorities should have considerable latitude to try to offset cyclical fluctuations. Opposing the Keynesian view, both classical economists and a group of economists called *monetarists* believe that monetary policy should not be left to the discretion of the central bank but instead should be governed by simple rules. Although establishing rules for monetary policy might seem to tie policymakers' hands unnecessarily, monetarists and classicals argue that the use of rules would lead to a more stable and less inflationary economy in the long run. After examining the arguments for and against the use of rules, we compare the performances of rules-based monetary policies in the United States, Germany, and Japan. We also discuss how the debate about rules is related to questions of how monetary policy-making institutions should be designed. For example, should the central bank be largely independent from the rest of the government, as in Germany and the United Kingdom, or should it be more directly controlled by the executive and legislative branches? Finally, we examine how the movement towards monetary union in Europe will affect the conduct of monetary policy.

15.1 PRINCIPLES OF MONEY SUPPLY DETERMINATION

How is the nation's money supply determined? So far we have assumed that the money supply, M, is controlled directly by the central bank. Although this assumption is a useful simplification, it is not literally true. The central bank's control of the money supply is only indirect and depends to some extent on the structure of the economy.

Most generally, three groups affect the money supply: the central bank, depository institutions, and the public.

1. In nearly all countries the **central bank** is the governmental institution responsible for monetary policy.[1] Examples of central banks are the Bank of England in the UK, the Riksbank in Sweden, the Bundesbank in Germany, and the Federal Reserve System in the United States.

2. **Depository institutions** are privately owned banks and credit institutions (such as building societies and other savings and loan associations) that accept deposits from and make loans directly to the public. We refer to depository institutions as banks, for short.

3. The public includes every person or firm (except banks) that holds money, either as currency and coin or as deposits in banks – in other words, virtually the whole private economy outside of the banking system.

Before investigating how these groups interact to set the money supply in financially complex European countries, we begin with an example of a primitive agricultural economy, which we call Agricola. Examining the introduction of money and the development of banking in Agricola identifies clearly the factors involved in the determination of the money supply. Additionally, the development of the monetary and banking systems in fictitious Agricola loosely parallels the actual evolution of such systems over the centuries in many countries.

The Money Supply in an All-Currency Economy

The imaginary country of Agricola is an agricultural nation that produces a variety of fruits, nuts, vegetables, and grains. Initially, Agricola has no money supply, so all trading is done by barter, or the direct trading of goods for goods. Recall, however, that a trading system based on barter is extremely

---

1. Most industrialized countries established central banks in the nineteenth century or early twentieth century. Prior to the establishment of central banks, national Treasury Departments were often responsible for currency issue and other matters pertaining to the money supply.

inconvenient (Chapter 7). Under a barter system a farmer who wants to trade barley for pomegranates must find someone willing to exchange pomegranates for barley, which involves a costly and time-consuming search.

The benevolent leader of Agricola recognizes this inconvenience and decides to create a national money to ease trade among the people. The first step in establishing a national money is to create a government agency called the Agricolan Central Bank. The Central Bank then prints paper certificates[2] and decrees the value of each certificate to be one florin (abbreviated fl), which becomes the national currency of Agricola. The government of Agricola prohibits anyone other than the Agricolan Central Bank from printing these certificates.

To get the florins into general circulation, the Central Bank uses them to buy some real assets from the public. In the agricultural economy of Agricola real assets are storable agricultural products such as coconuts, so the Central Bank uses newly printed florins to buy coconuts from the public. Why do people in Agricola willingly surrender valuable coconuts in exchange for paper certificates? In general, people accept paper money in payment for goods, services, or assets because they expect to be able to use it to buy other goods, services, or assets in the future. In other words, people accept paper money because they believe that other people also will accept it. The belief that money has value becomes self-justifying: if most people believe that money has value, then it has value.[3] The government helps convince the public that paper money has value, usually by decreeing that the money is *legal tender* – that is, creditors are required to accept the money in settlement of debts – and by stating its own willingness to accept money from the public in payment of taxes.

Suppose that the people of Agricola accept the new currency and that the Central Bank trades 1 million florins to the public for 1 million coconuts. The balance sheet of the Agricolan Central Bank is

Agricolan Central Bank			
ASSETS		LIABILITIES	
Coconuts	1,000,000 fl	Currency	1,000,000 fl

On the left-hand side of the balance sheet are the Central Bank's assets – what it owns or is owed: in this case, the coconuts. On the right-hand side are the bank's liabilities – what it owes to others. Because the florins are technically debt obligations of the Central Bank, they are entered as liabilities in the balance sheet. The liabilities of the Central Bank that are usable as money are called the **monetary base**, or, equivalently, **high-powered money**. The monetary base of Agricola is thus 1 million florins.

Assume that Agricola initially has no banking system. With no banks and hence no bank deposits, the total money supply is the currency held by the public. That is, the paper certificates distributed by the Agricolan Central Bank are used directly as money. Thus the money supply in Agricola equals 1 million

---

2. In most countries the actual printing of paper money is done by a separate agency, not by the central bank itself.

3. Also possible is that no one believes that money has value, which would again be a self-justifying belief because no one would then accept money in payment.

florins, which in turn equals the monetary base (the liabilities of the Agricolan Central Bank). Hence *in an all-currency economy (one with no bank deposits) the money supply equals the monetary base.*

The Money Supply Under Fractional Reserve Banking

As the people of Agricola become financially more sophisticated, a system of private banks emerges. The banks announce their willingness to accept deposits from the public.

For the time being, let's assume that, because currency is easily lost or stolen, Agricolans want to hold *all* their money in bank deposits rather than in currency. After the Agricolans deposit all their currency (1 million florins) in banks, the combined, or consolidated, balance sheet of all the banks is

Consolidated Balance Sheet of Banks			
ASSETS		LIABILITIES	
Currency	1,000,000 fl	Deposits	1,000,000 fl

The banking system's assets are the 1,000,000 paper florins in bank vaults. The banking system's liabilities are the deposits, which are the banks' debts or obligations to the public. The balance sheet of the Central Bank remains the same.

Liquid assets held by banks to meet the demands for withdrawals by depositors or to pay the cheques drawn on depositors' accounts are called **bank reserves**. In general, bank reserves comprise currency held by private banks in their vaults and deposits held by private banks at the Central Bank. Here, all bank reserves are held as currency in the banks' vaults. Note that the bank reserves equal total deposits of 1,000,000 fl. This type of banking system is called **100% reserve banking** because bank reserves equal 100% of deposits. Under 100% reserve banking, banks are nothing more than a safekeeping service for the public's currency. Indeed, the only way that banks could cover their expenses and make a profit under 100% reserve banking would be to charge depositors a fee for holding their money for them (that is, to pay negative interest on deposits).

However, one day an enterprising Agricolan banker notices that the paper florins that the bank has accepted from depositors are just sitting idly in neat stacks in the bank's vault. True, a few florins flow out when a depositor writes a cheque to someone who banks elsewhere, or when a depositor switches an account to another bank. However, this outflow is balanced by a roughly equivalent inflow, when the bank's depositors receive cheques drawn on other banks or the bank attracts a depositor away from another bank. The banker calculates that keeping florins in the vault equal to, say, 20% of outstanding deposits would more than cover this random ebb and flow. The remaining 80% of the florins on deposit could be lent to earn interest for the bank!

Under the Agricolan banker's scheme the reserves held by the bank will equal only a fraction of the bank's outstanding deposits. In this case, the **reserve–deposit ratio**, or reserves divided by deposits, equals 20%. A banking system in which banks hold only a fraction of their deposits in reserve, so that the reserve–deposit ratio is less than 1, is called **fractional reserve banking**.

Fractional reserve banking is profitable for banks because, instead of sitting in the vault earning no interest for the bank, a portion of the funds received from depositors can be used to make interest-earning loans.

All the bankers of Agricola quickly grasp the idea of fractional reserve banking, and decide to hold reserves of 20% of deposits and lend the other 80% (800,000 fl) to farmers. The farmers use the loans to buy fertilizer for their farms. The sellers of the fertilizer receive 800,000 fl in payment, and, because everyone prefers having bank deposits to holding currency, they deposit the 800,000 fl in the banking system. After these deposits are made all of the florins are back in the banks, and the consolidated balance sheet of the banking system is

Consolidated Balance Sheet of Banks			
ASSETS		**LIABILITIES**	
Currency (reserves)	1,000,000 fl	Deposits	1,800,000 fl
Loans to farmers	800,000 fl		
Total	1,800,000 fl	Total	1,800,000 fl

The banks' assets now include the 800,000 fl in loans to farmers (the loans are owed to the banks, so they are assets of the banks). The banks' assets also include 1,000,000 paper florins: 200,000 fl originally kept in reserve plus the 800,000 fl deposited by the sellers of the fertilizer.

The banks' consolidated liabilities equal 1,800,000 fl in deposits: the 1,000,000 fl in original deposits and the 800,000 fl in new deposits from the fertilizer sellers.

At this point, as the bankers examine their balance sheets, they note that their reserves (holdings of paper florins) are back up to 1,000,000 fl. Their deposits equal 1,800,000 fl. Based on the principle that reserves need be only 20% of deposits, their reserves of 1,000,000 fl are too high. The bankers need to hold only 360,000 fl, or 0.20(1,800,000 fl). The other 640,000 fl, or 1,000,000 fl – 360,000 fl, can be lent again to earn more interest.

So the banks make additional interest-bearing loans in the amount of 640,000 fl. The banks' borrowers use the funds to make purchases. As before, these florins are eventually redeposited in the banking system. At this point the consolidated balance sheet of all the banks is

Consolidated Balance Sheet of Banks			
ASSETS		**LIABILITIES**	
Currency (reserves)	1,000,000 fl	Deposits	2,440,000 fl
Loans to farmers	1,440,000 fl		
Total	2,440,000 fl	Total	2,440,000 fl

The assets of the banks now include 1,000,000 paper florins (the 360,000 fl kept as reserves and the 640,000 fl redeposited by the public) and 1,440,000 fl in loans (the 800,000 fl of first-round loans and the 640,000 fl of second-round loans). The liabilities are 2,440,000 fl in deposits (the 1,800,000 fl from earlier deposits and the 640,000 fl in new deposits).

The process does not stop here. Checking their balance sheets after this latest round of loans and redeposits, the bankers find that their reserves (1,000,000 fl) still exceed 20% of their deposits, or 0.20(2,440,000 fl) = 488,000 fl. So yet another round of loans and redeposits of loaned funds will occur.

This process of **multiple expansion of loans and deposits**, in which fractional reserve banking increases an economy's loans and deposits, will stop only when the reserves of the banking system equal 20% of its deposits. The reserves of the banks always equal 1,000,000 fl (the entire supply of paper florins) at the end of each round, so the process will stop when total bank deposits equal 1,000,000 fl/0.20, or 5,000,000 fl. At this final point the consolidated balance sheet of the banks is

---

Consolidated Balance Sheet of Banks

ASSETS		LIABILITIES	
Currency (reserves)	1,000,000 fl	Deposits	5,000,000 fl
Loans to farmers	4,000,000 fl		
Total	5,000,000 fl	Total	5,000,000 fl

At this final stage the ratio of reserves to deposits equals the ratio desired by banks (20%). No further expansion of loans and deposits can occur after this point because the ratio of reserves to deposits is at its minimum acceptable level.

What is the money supply in Agricola at the end of this process? Recall that the public does not hold any currency but, instead, deposits any currency received in the banking system, where it is held in the form of bank reserves. The reserves in the banks' vaults are not available for transactions and thus are not counted as money. However, the public *is* holding deposits. Because they are liquid and can be used for transactions, bank deposits are counted as part of the money supply.[4] Indeed, as there is no public holding of currency in Agricola, bank deposits *are* the money supply. Therefore the money supply equals 5,000,000 fl, or the total quantity of deposits.

What is the relationship between the money supply and the monetary base with fractional reserve banking and no holding of currency by the public? We use the following variables to answer this question algebraically:

M = the money supply;
$BASE$ = the monetary base;
DEP = total bank deposits;
RES = total bank reserves;
res = the banks' desired reserve–deposit ratio = RES/DEP.

With no currency being held by the public, the money supply equals the quantity of bank deposits:

$$M = DEP \tag{15.1}$$

For any level of deposits DEP, the amount of reserves that banks want to hold is $(res)(DEP)$. At the end of the multiple-expansion process, bank reserves

---

4. Recall from Chapter 7 that the most narrowly defined monetary aggregate after M0 (notes and coins) is M1, which includes demand deposits and other chequable deposits. Slightly less liquid deposits, such as savings deposits and time deposits, are included in broader monetary aggregates.

must equal the amount of currency distributed by the Central Bank (the monetary base). Therefore

$$(res)(DEP) = BASE \tag{15.2}$$

Solving equation (15.2) for deposits yields $DEP = BASE/res$. Because the money supply equals deposits in this example,

$$M = DEP = \frac{BASE}{res} \tag{15.3}$$

Hence *in an economy with fractional reserve banking and no currency held by the public, the money supply equals the monetary base divided by the reserve–deposit ratio.* In Agricola the monetary base is 1,000,000 fl, and the reserve–deposit ratio chosen by the banks is 0.20. The money supply is therefore 1,000,000 fl/0.20, or 5,000,000 fl, as we have already shown.

The multiple expansion of loans and deposits allows the economy to create a money supply that is much larger than the monetary base. Each unit of monetary base allows $1/res$ units of money to be created, leading to a money supply that is a multiple of the monetary base. Because each unit of monetary base permits creation of several units of money supply, the base is also called *high-powered money*.

Bank Runs

Fractional reserve banking works on the assumption that outflows and inflows of reserves will roughly balance, and in particular that a large fraction of a bank's depositors will never want to withdraw their funds at the same time. If a large number of depositors attempt to withdraw currency simultaneously (more than 20% of the bank's deposits in Agricola), the bank will run out of reserves and be unable to meet all its depositors' demands for cash.

Historically in many countries, there were episodes in which rumours circulated that a particular bank had made some bad loans and was at risk of becoming bankrupt. On the principle of 'better safe than sorry,' the bank's depositors lined up to withdraw their money. From the depositors' perspective withdrawal avoided the risk that the bank would fail and not be able to pay off depositors in full. A large-scale, panicky withdrawal of deposits from a bank is called a **bank run**. Even if the rumours about the bank's loans proved untrue, a large enough run could exhaust the bank's reserves and force it to close.[5] We discuss the link between bank runs and the money supply in the Application 'The Money Multiplier in the USA During the Great Depression', p. 578.

The Money Supply with both Public Holdings of Currency and Fractional Reserve Banking

In most economies the public holds some currency (as at first in Agricola) and there is also a fractional reserve banking system (as later in Agricola). Currency in the public's hands and bank deposits both may be used for transactions, so

---

5. To stop a run, a bank had to convince customers that it was 'sound' – financially solvent – and had plenty of funds available. This was James Stewart's strategy in the film *It's A Wonderful Life*.

both are forms of money. When the public holds both currency, *CU*, and bank deposits, *DEP*, the money supply *M* is

$$M = CU + DEP \tag{15.4}$$

In this situation the monetary base has two uses: some of the monetary base is held as currency by the public, and the rest is held as reserves by banks. Therefore the monetary base equals the sum of the two, or

$$BASE = CU + RES \tag{15.5}$$

The central bank controls the amount of monetary base but does not directly control the money supply. To relate the money supply to the monetary base, we first divide the money supply, equation (15.4), by the monetary base, equation (15.5), to get

$$\frac{M}{BASE} = \frac{CU + DEP}{CU + RES} \tag{15.6}$$

Next, we divide both the numerator and the denominator on the right-hand side of equation (15.6) by *DEP* to obtain

$$\frac{M}{BASE} = \frac{(CU/DEP) + 1}{(CU/DEP) + (RES/DEP)} \tag{15.7}$$

The right-hand side of equation (15.7) contains two important ratios. The first is the **currency–deposit ratio** (*CU/DEP*, or *cu*), which is the ratio of the currency held by the public to the public's deposits in banks. The currency–deposit ratio is determined by the public and depends on the amount of money the public wants to hold as currency versus the amount it wants to hold as deposits. The public can raise the currency–deposit ratio to any level that it wants by withdrawing currency from banks (which increases currency held and reduces deposits); similarly, by depositing currency in banks, the public can lower the currency–deposit ratio.

The second important ratio on the right-hand side of equation (15.7) is the reserve–deposit ratio (*RES/DEP*, or *res*), which we have already discussed. The reserve–deposit ratio is determined by banks' decisions about how much of their deposits to lend.[6]

When the process of multiple expansion of loans and deposits is complete, the currency–deposit ratio equals the ratio desired by the public, *cu*, and the reserve–deposit ratio equals the ratio desired by the banks, *res*. Substituting *cu* for *CU/DEP* and *res* for *RES/DEP* in equation (15.7) and multiplying both sides of equation (15.7) by *BASE*, we obtain

$$M = \left(\frac{cu + 1}{cu + res}\right) BASE \tag{15.8}$$

---

6. As we discuss later in this chapter, government regulations may set minimum levels for banks' reserve–deposit ratios. However, not all European governments impose minimum reserves and among those that do the reserve requirement varies significantly. For example, in Italy the minimum requirement is around 15% whereas in the UK it is less than 0.5%.

Equation (15.8) states that the money supply is a multiple of the monetary base. The relation of the money supply to the monetary base depends on the currency–deposit ratio chosen by the public and the reserve–deposit ratio chosen by banks. The factor $(cu + 1)/(cu + res)$, which is the number of units of money supply that can be created from each unit of monetary base, is called the **money multiplier**. The money multiplier will be greater than 1 as long as res is less than 1 (that is, with fractional reserve banking). Note that if the public holds no currency ($cu = 0$), the money multiplier equals $1/res$, or the same value as that in Agricola when all money was held as bank deposits (equation 15.3).

Table 15.1 uses German data to illustrate the money multiplier and the relation among currency, reserves, monetary base, and the money supply. With these data, you can verify that the currency–deposit ratio is 0.4015 and that the reserve–deposit ratio is 0.1115. Thus the money multiplier, $(cu + 1)/(cu + res)$, equals 2.73. You may verify this formula by dividing the money supply (DM848.2 billion) by the monetary base (DM310.5 billion) to obtain 2.73. The money multiplier is smaller in Germany than in some other European countries including France, where it is about 5.0, and the UK, where it is around 10.0.

It can be shown algebraically that the money multiplier decreases when either the currency–deposit ratio cu or the reserve–deposit ratio res increases.[7] Recall that the reason that the monetary base gets 'multiplied' is that, under fractional reserve banking, banks use some of the currency received as deposits to make loans to the public. The public can either hold the money it borrows from banks as currency or redeposit its borrowings in the banking system, but in either case the result is a higher total money supply than existed before the loans were made. When the reserve–deposit ratio rises, banks lend a smaller fraction of each mark of deposits, creating less money for the same amount of monetary base; thus an increase in the reserve–deposit ratio lowers

---

7. That the money multiplier decreases when cu increases is not obvious, as cu appears in both the numerator and the denominator of the money multiplier. However, as you can confirm by trying numerical examples or by taking a derivative, an increase in cu reduces the money multiplier as long as res is less than 1, which must always be the case under fractional reserve banking.

Table 15.1 The Monetary Base, the Money Multiplier, and the Money Supply in Germany

Currency in circulation, CU	DM 243.0 bn
Bank reserves, RES	DM 67.5 bn
Monetary base, $BASE$ (=$CU + RES$)	DM 310.5 bn
Deposits, DEP	DM 605.2 bn
Money supply, M (=$CU + DEP$)	DM 848.2 bn
Reserve–deposit ratio, res (=RES/DEP)	0.1115
Currency–deposit ratio, cu (=CU/DEP)	0.4015
Money multiplier, $(cu + 1)/(cu + res)$	2.73
Ratio of money supply to base, $M/BASE$	2.73

Source: *Deutsche Bundesbank Monthly Report,* April 1997, Tables II.2, III.2, IV.1. The money supply is M1. Data are for January 1997.

the money multiplier. When the currency–deposit ratio rises, the public puts a smaller fraction of its money in banks, which means that banks have less money to loan. With banks lending less, less money is created from the same amount of monetary base, again reducing the money multiplier.

Open-Market Operations

We have shown how the monetary base and the money multiplier determine the money supply. To change the level of the money supply, a central bank must change the amount of monetary base or change the money multiplier. In Section 15.2 we discuss how the central bank can affect the money multiplier. For now we focus on the most direct and frequently used way of changing the money supply: raising or lowering the monetary base. For any value of the money multiplier, equation (15.8) indicates that a change in the monetary base will cause a proportional change in the money supply.

Suppose that the Agricolan Central Bank decides to increase the monetary base by 10%, from 1,000,000 to 1,100,000 fl. How would it actually do so? First, the Central Bank has to print the extra 100,000 fl. Then it can use the 100,000 new florins to buy assets (coconuts) from the public. After purchasing the additional coconuts, the Agricolan Central Bank's balance sheet is

Agricolan Central Bank			
ASSETS		LIABILITIES	
Coconuts	1,100,000 fl	Currency	1,100,000 fl

By purchasing 100,000 fl of coconuts, the Central Bank puts 100,000 more paper certificates (florins) into circulation. The monetary base, which is the same as the total liabilities of the Central Bank, rises to 1,100,000 fl. If the money multiplier remains unchanged, the money supply also increases by 10%.

Suppose, instead, that the Agricolan Central Bank wanted to reduce the monetary base by 10%. To do so it would sell 100,000 fl of coconuts to the public for 100,000 fl in currency. The 100,000 florins collected by the Central Bank are retired from circulation. (The retired florins are not treated as assets of the Central Bank; if you paid off a debt and retrieved your IOU, you would not consider the IOU to be an asset.) The Agricolan Central Bank's balance sheet is now

Agricolan Central Bank			
ASSETS		LIABILITIES	
Coconuts	900,000 fl	Currency	900,000 fl

The Agricolan Central Bank's liabilities outstanding (the monetary base) have been reduced to 900,000 fl. With a constant money multiplier the money supply will fall proportionately.

Recall (Chapter 7) that a purchase of assets by the central bank is called an **open-market purchase**.[8] It increases the monetary base and thus the money

---

8. The term 'open market' refers to the fact that the central bank's transactions with the public take place in regular asset markets that are open to and used by the public.

supply. A sale of assets to the public by the central bank is called an **open-market sale**. It reduces the monetary base and the money supply. A form of open-market operations commonly used by European central banks is called **open-market repurchase agreements**. Whereas an open-market transaction involves a straightforward purchase or sale of an asset, repurchase agreements involve an arrangement whereby the seller of the asset agrees to buy it back from the central bank at a higher price some time in the future. That is, it agrees to repurchase it. The difference between the price paid by the central bank for the asset and the price at which it sells it back is the interest rate that the central bank is charging. This rate is often called the 'repo rate'. Open-market purchases and sales and repurchase agreements are collectively called open-market operations. Open-market operations are the most direct way for central banks to change their national money supplies.

APPLICATION

The Money Multiplier in the USA During the Great Depression

The money multiplier usually is relatively stable, but not always as this example from the USA demonstrates. During 1930–33, in the early part of the Great Depression, the money multiplier in the United States fell sharply, creating serious problems for US monetary policy.

The source of the instability in the money multiplier, as discussed in detail by Milton Friedman and Anna Schwartz in their *Monetary History of the United States, 1867–1960*,[9] was a series of severe banking panics. A banking panic is an episode in which many banks suffer runs by depositors, with some banks being forced to close. The US panics resulted from both financial weakness in the banking system and the arrival of bad economic and financial news. Among the causes of banking panics emphasized by Friedman and Schwartz were: (1) the effects of falling agricultural prices on the economies of farm states in the autumn of 1930; (2) the failure of a large New York bank called the Bank of the United States, in December 1930 (a private bank, despite its name); (3) the failure in May 1931 of Austria's largest bank, which led to a European financial crisis; and (4) Great Britain's abandonment of the gold standard in September 1931. The most severe banking panic began in January 1933 and was halted only when the newly inaugurated President Roosevelt proclaimed a 'bank holiday' that closed all US banks in March 1933. By that time more than a third of the banks in the United States had failed or been taken over by other banks. Banking reforms that were passed as part of Roosevelt's New Deal legislation restored confidence in the banking system and halted bank runs after March 1933.

The banking panics affected the money multiplier in two ways. First, people became very distrustful of banks, fearing that their banks might suddenly fail and not be able to pay them the full amounts of their deposits. (These events occurred before deposits were insured by the US government, as they are today.) Instead of holding bank deposits, people felt safer holding currency, perhaps under the mattress or in coffee cans buried in the backyard. Conversion of deposits into currency caused the currency–deposit ratio to rise, as shown in Figure 15.1, with a spectacular rise in the first quarter of 1933.

Second, in anticipation of possible runs, banks began to hold more reserves (including vault cash) to back their deposits, as shown by the behaviour of the reserve–deposit ratio. Banks hoped to convince depositors that

9. Princeton University Press for NBER, 1963.

Figure 15.1
The currency–deposit ratio and the reserve–deposit ratio in the United States during the Great Depression
During the Great Depression people worried about the safety of their money in banks and increased the ratio of currency in circulation to deposits. In anticipation of possible bank runs banks increased the ratio of reserves to deposits.

Source: Milton Friedman and Anna Schwartz, *A Monetary History of the United States, 1867–1960:* Currency—Table A-1, column (1); deposits, total commercial banks (demand and time)—Table A-1, column (4); bank reserves—Table A-2, column (3).

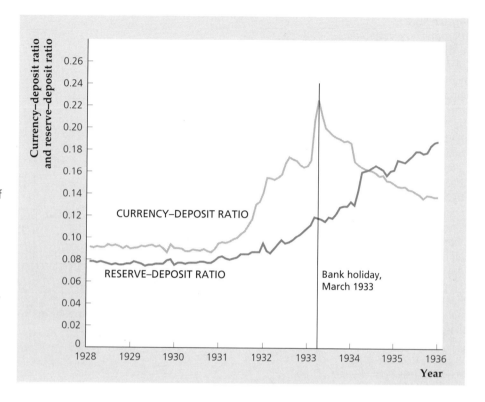

there was enough cash in the banks' vaults to satisfy withdrawals so that the depositors would not be tempted to start a run.

As discussed earlier, increases in either the currency–deposit ratio or the reserve–deposit ratio cause the money multiplier to fall. As shown in Figure 15.2(a), as a result of the banking panics, the money multiplier fell precipitously, from 6.6 in March 1930 to 3.6 by the bank holiday in March 1933. Thus, even though the monetary base grew by 20% during that three-year period, the money multiplier fell by so much that the money supply fell by 35%, as shown in Figure 15.2(b). There is some controversy about whether the drop in the money supply was a primary cause of the decline in output during 1930–33 (Friedman and Schwartz argue that it was), but there is general agreement that the drastic decline in the price level (by about a third) in this period was the result of the plunge in the money supply.

15.2 MONETARY CONTROL IN GERMANY

The principles of money supply determination developed in the Agricola example can be applied directly to actual economies by adding a few institutional details. In this section we link these general principles to monetary institutions in Germany. The German mark plays a central role in the EMS, and monetary policy in Germany has achieved considerable success in promoting monetary stability. The institutional framework of the Bundesbank will also form the basis for the European Central Bank, which will determine monetary policy in the European Monetary Union.

Figure 15.2
US monetary variables in the Great Depression
(a) As a result of the increases in the currency–deposit ratio and the reserve–deposit ratio, the money multiplier fell sharply during the Great Depression. The monetary base rose during the Great Depression.
(b) Although the monetary base rose during the Great Depression, the money multiplier fell so much that the money supply—the product of the money multiplier and the monetary base—declined sharply.

Source: Milton Friedman and Anna Schwartz, *A Monetary History of the United States, 1867–1960:* Currency – Table A-1, column (1); deposits, total commercial banks (demand and time) – Table A-1, column (4); bank reserves – Table A-2, column (3); base = currency + reserves; money multiplier = (currency + deposits)/base; money = currency + deposits.

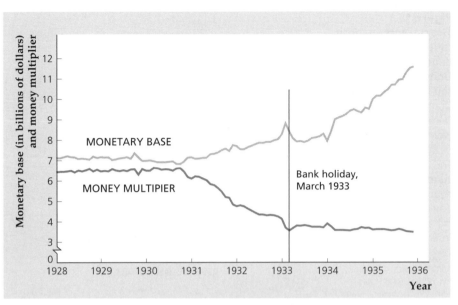

(a) The monetary base and the money multiplier in the Great Depression

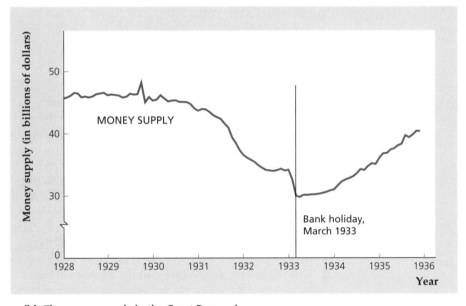

(b) The money supply in the Great Depression

The German Bundesbank

The central bank in Germany is the Bundesbank (or federal bank). The Bundesbank was created by The Bundesbank Act of 1957 and replaced the two-tier central bank system put in place by the Allies in 1948 following the collapse of the German currency and financial system after World War II. This two-tier system was modelled on the US Federal Reserve System and comprised the Land (or regional) central banks and the Bank deutscher Länder. The Land central banks operated in each Land and acted as independent central banks in their own regions. The Bank deutscher Länder was responsible for the issue of bank notes and for the coordination of central bank policy. Following the 1957 Bundesbank Act, the Land central banks and the Bank deutscher Länder were amalgamated to form the Deutscher Bundesbank, though the Land central banks continued to operate as regional offices of the Bundesbank.

The Bundesbank Act set out the principal functions of the Bundesbank. As with all central banks, this included both the right to issue bank notes and the Bundesbank's duties and responsibilities within the German monetary and financial system, including its relationship with credit institutions (private banks and other loans and savings associations). However, the Act also required that the work of the Bundesbank should always meet its primary responsibility to maintain monetary stability and therefore avoid the severe crises associated with accelerating inflation experienced during the hyperinflation of the 1920s. To ensure that the Bundesbank conducted monetary policy with the exclusive aim of achieving monetary stability free from political pressures, it was established as independent of government. From time to time this has led to conflict between the Bundesbank and the Federal government on those occasions when the goal of monetary stability (the concern of the Bundesbank) does not coincide with the wishes of the Federal government. (See Section 14.6 for a recent example of this.)

The leadership of the Bundesbank is provided by the Central Bank Council, which meets fortnightly and is the main policy-making body of the bank. The Central Bank Council comprises the Directorate of the Bundesbank and the nine Presidents of the Land central banks. The Directorate includes the President and Vice-president of the Bundesbank plus up to six other members, who are all nominated by the Federal Cabinet, appointed by the President of the Federal Republic and who have a term of office of up to eight years. Besides having considerable influence over monetary policy, the President of the Bundesbank is an important figure in financial markets (the Bundesbank has responsibility for regulating securities markets and the banking sector) and is often consulted by the Federal government on matters of economic policy.

The Bundesbank's Balance Sheet and Open-Market Operations

The balance sheet of the Bundesbank as of January 1997 is shown in Table 15.2. The Bundesbank's largest asset is its holdings of securities, or government bonds. It also owns gold and makes loans to credit institutions, which count as assets for the Bundesbank. The category 'Other assets' includes foreign exchange, bonds issued by public agencies and departments, and other relatively small items.

The largest liability of the Bundesbank is currency outstanding. Some of this currency (DM23.9 billion) is held in the vaults of private banks and is known as **cash in hand**. The remainder of currency outstanding, DM243.0 billion, is in circulation (that is, held by the public) and corresponds to what we label *CU*.

The other principal liability of the Bundesbank is deposits made by credit institutions. Credit institutions are depository institutions in Germany which carry out all types of banking business. In accepting deposits from credit

Table 15.2   The Balance Sheet of the Bundesbank (DM billions)

Assets		Liabilities		
Gold	13.7	Currency		266.9
		Cash in hand[a]	23.9	
Loans to credit		In circulation[b]	243.0	
institutions	64.4			
Securities purchased in	147.4	Deposits of credit		
open-market operations		institutions[c]		43.6
Other assets	123.6			
		Other liabilities and		
		net worth[d]		38.6
Total	349.1	Total		349.1

Addenda
Reserves = deposits of credit institutions + vault cash = DM67.5 billion.
Monetary base = currency in circulation + reserves = DM310.5 billion.

[a]Table IV. 1.
[b]Table III.2.
[c]Table III.2.
[d]Calculated as total minus the sum of the other figures in the column.
Source: Deutsche Bundesbank. Data are for January 1997.

institutions, the Bundesbank acts as the 'banks' bank.' Credit institutions make deposits at the Bundesbank because it is a convenient way of holding reserves. These accounts at the Bundesbank (DM43.6 billion), together with cash in hand (DM23.9 billion), equal the total reserves of the banking system (DM67.5 billion), what we call *RES*.

Recall from equation (15.5) that the monetary base equals bank reserves (DM67.5 billion) plus currency in circulation (DM243.0 billion), or DM310.5 billion. As shown in Figure 15.3, the monetary base can be calculated equivalently as the sum of total currency outstanding (DM266.9 billion) plus deposits of credit institutions at the Bundesbank (DM43.6 billion), which again is DM310.5 billion.[10]

Like the Agricolan Central Bank, if the Bundesbank wants to change the money supply, its primary tool is open-market operations. To increase the money supply, for example, the Bundesbank could conduct an open-market purchase, in which it would buy securities (instead of coconuts, as in Agricola) from the public. A purchase of DM10 billion in securities would increase the Bundesbank's assets by DM10 billion. To pay for these securities, the Bundesbank would write a cheque on itself, redeemable by a bank either as a deposit at the Bundesbank or as currency. In either case the monetary base would rise by DM10 billion. Because of the money multiplier, an increase in the monetary base translates into a proportional increase in the money supply.

---

10. The Bundesbank also has other liabilities, including accounts held by the German Treasury and by foreign central banks. Because these accounts are not owned by the public or the German banking sector, they are not counted as part of the monetary base.

Figure 15.3
Components of the monetary base
The monetary base equals currency in circulation, *CU* plus bank reserves, *RES*. The monetary base also may be expressed as the sum of deposits at the central bank by credit institutions and total currency outstanding (currency in circulation and vault cash).

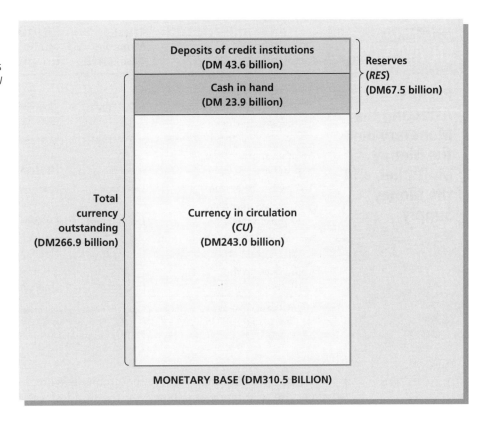

To reduce the money supply, the Bundesbank could use an open-market sale. The Bundesbank could sell DM10 billion of securities to the public, receiving cheques drawn on banks in exchange. The Bundesbank's assets would fall by DM10 billion (it owns DM10 billion less in securities). The Bundesbank would use the DM10 billion in cheques it receives to eliminate DM10 billion in deposits of credit institutions, so that the monetary base would fall by DM10 billion.

Other Means of Controlling the Money Supply

Although open-market operations are the main way that the Bundesbank affects the money supply, it has two other methods available: changes in reserve requirements and refinancing. The effects of these and other factors on the money supply are listed in Summary table 19.

Reserve Requirements. The Bundesbank sets the minimum fraction of each type of deposit that credit institutions must hold as reserves. An increase in reserve requirements forces banks to hold more reserves and increases the reserve–deposit ratio. A higher reserve–deposit ratio reduces the money multiplier, so an increase in reserve requirements reduces the money supply for any level of the monetary base.

Traditionally, the Bundesbank has set minimum reserve requirements that were high compared with those in other European countries. In 1978, for

SUMMARY 19	Factor	Effect on Monetary Base, *BASE*	Effect on Money Multiplier, (*cu* + 1)/(*cu* + *res*)	Effect on Money Supply, *M*
Factors Affecting the Monetary Base, the Money Multiplier, and the Money Supply	An increase in the reserve–deposit ratio, *res*	Unchanged	Decrease	Decrease
	An increase in the currency–deposit ratio, *cu*	Unchanged	Decrease	Decrease
	An open-market purchase	Increase	Unchanged	Increase
	An open-market sale	Decrease	Unchanged	Decrease
	An increase in reserve requirements	Unchanged	Decrease	Decrease
	An increase in borrowing from the central bank	Increase	Unchanged	Increase
	An increase in the discount rate	Decrease	Unchanged	Decrease

Note: The relationship among the money supply, the money multiplier, and the monetary base is $M = [(cu + 1)/(cu + res)]BASE$.

example, the minimum reserve requirements were set at between 6% and 14%. Over the past few years, however, the Bundesbank has sought to restructure German minimum reserve regulations and to lower the required reserve ratios considerably. As of August 1995, credit institutions were required to hold reserves equal to 2% of sight and time deposits and 1.5% of savings deposits. This move, in part, reflects the fact that international financial markets are now closely linked, which provides private banks and other credit institutions in Germany with access to funds in other countries, thereby avoiding German minimum reserve regulations.

Refinancing Policy. Although financial panics and bank runs are no longer a feature of the German financial and money markets, the Bundesbank still lends reserves to banks and other credit institutions, which affects the monetary base. For example, if banks borrow DM10 billion from the Bundesbank and deposit these borrowings in their reserve accounts at the Bundesbank, the Bundesbank's balance sheet is affected in two ways: (1) on the asset side, loans to credit institutions rise by DM10 billion; and (2) on the liability side, deposits held by credit institutions also rise by DM10 billion, increasing the monetary base by DM10 billion. Thus an increase in borrowing from the central bank raises the monetary base, and a decrease in central bank borrowing lowers the monetary base.

The system under which the Bundesbank lends reserves to credit institutions is called **refinancing** and involves two types of loan. The first is **rediscount credit** which is when the Bundesbank purchases bills of exchange from credit institutions. Bills of exchange are the security used by commercial enterprises when they borrow from credit institutions. Credit institutions, in turn, are able to sell these bills of exchange to the Bundesbank and thus increase their own reserves. The rate of interest charged by the Bundesbank on rediscount credit is called the **discount rate** and is traditionally the lowest rate of interest at which credit institutions can borrow reserves. Indeed, because the rate is so favourable the amount of rediscount credit is limited by quota.

The second way the Bundesbank lends to credit institutions is in the form of **lombard loans**. The rate of interest charged on these loans, the **lombard rate**, is the highest rate of interest set by the Bundesbank and as a result credit institutions will only use lombard loans in emergencies. Lombard loans are, in principle, designed to be for emergency funding when credit institutions have temporary liquidity problems.

Until 1967, other rates of interest in the German money and financial markets, such as the rate at which customers borrow from credit institutions and the inter-bank rate (the rate at which commercial banks borrow and lend to each other) were directly tied to the discount and lombard rates. Since 1967, bank lending and deposit rates have been determined by market conditions, although they still largely follow the discount and, more especially, the lombard rates. By changing the discount and/or the lombard rates, the Bundesbank is able to influence what is happening in the money market. An increase in the discount rate makes borrowing more costly. If banks reduce their borrowing in response to the higher discount rate, the monetary base falls. For a constant money multiplier, a drop in the monetary base implies a decline in the money supply as well.

Credit institutions may also borrow reserves from other banks that have extra reserves at the inter-bank rate. This is a market interest rate determined by the forces of supply and demand and changes much more frequently than either the discount rate or the lombard rate, which the Bundesbank sets. The inter-bank rate usually exceeds the discount rate, because banks are willing to pay a premium to avoid borrowing from the Bundesbank. Figure 15.4 shows the behaviour of the lombard and discount rates together with two money market rates, the inter-bank rate and the call-money rate.

Intermediate Targets

In conducting monetary policy, the Bundesbank has certain goals, or ultimate targets, such as price stability and stable economic growth. In trying to reach these goals, the Bundesbank can use the monetary policy tools, or **instruments**, that we have discussed: reserve requirements, the discount and lombard rates, and especially open-market operations. The problem the Bundesbank faces is how to use the instruments that it controls directly, particularly open-market operations, to achieve its goals. Because there are several steps between open-market operations and the ultimate behaviour of prices and economic activity – and because these steps often cannot be predicted accurately – the Bundesbank uses intermediate targets to guide monetary policy. **Intermediate targets**, also sometimes called indicators, are macroeconomic variables that the Bundesbank cannot control directly but can influence fairly predictably, and that in turn are related to the goals the Bundesbank is trying to achieve.[11]

11. For a discussion of the use of intermediate targets and further references, see Richard Davis, 'Intermediate Targets and Indicators for Monetary Policy: An Introduction to the Issues', in Federal Reserve Bank of New York, *Quarterly Review,* Summer 1990, pp. 71–82, and Merih Uctum, 'Money Markets and Common Monetary Policy in France, Germany and Italy', Federal Reserve Bank of New York, Research Paper 9212, July 1992.

Figure 15.4
The discount, lombard, inter-bank and call-money rates
Banks can borrow reserves from the Bundesbank and pay the discount rate, or they can borrow reserves from other banks and pay the inter-bank rate. In emergencies, banks can also borrow from the Bundesbank at the lombard rate which is usually higher than other interest rates.

Source: **Data Stream and** *Deutsche Bundesbank Monthly Report,* **April 1997.**

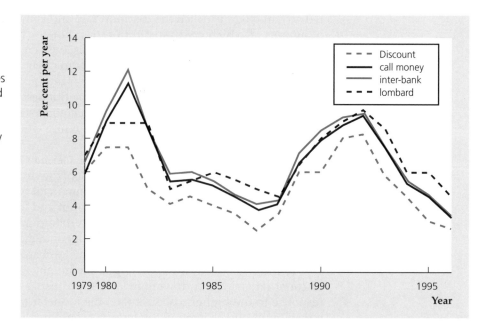

The most important and frequently used intermediate targets are monetary aggregates, such as M3, and short-term interest rates.[12] By using open-market operations, the Bundesbank can directly control the level of the monetary base, which influences the monetary aggregates. Fluctuations in the money supply in turn affect interest rates, at least temporarily, by causing the *LM* curve to shift. Neither monetary aggregates nor short-term interest rates are important determinants of economic welfare in and of themselves, but both influence the state of the macroeconomy. Because monetary aggregates and short-term interest rates are affected in a predictable way by the Bundesbank's policies and both in turn affect the economy, these variables qualify as intermediate targets.

At various times the Bundesbank has guided monetary policy by attempting to keep either monetary growth rates or short-term interest rates at or near pre-established target ranges (the Application 'Money-Growth Targeting and Inflation Targeting', p. 600, discusses the historical experience with money-growth targets). Note that, although the Bundesbank may be able to stabilize one or the other of these variables, it cannot target both simultaneously. For example, suppose that the Bundesbank were trying to target both the money supply and the lombard rate and that the pre-established target ranges called for an increase in both variables. How could the Bundesbank meet these targets simultaneously? If it raised the monetary base in order to raise the money supply, in the short run the increase in money supply would shift the *LM*

---

12. Other intermediate targets that have been suggested include the extent of bank lending to commercial enterprises, the exchange rate, the price level, and nominal GDP. The latter two pose problems because the control of the Bundesbank over prices and nominal GDP is indirect and operates only with a lag. In recent years, a number of European central banks, including those in the UK and Finland, have abandoned the use of intermediate targets.

curve down and to the right, which would lower rather than raise the lombard rate. Alternatively, if the Bundesbank lowered the monetary base in order to try to increase the lombard rate, the money supply would fall instead of rising, as required. Thus, in general, the Bundesbank cannot simultaneously meet targets for *both* interest rates and the money supply, unless those targets are set to be consistent with each other.

In recent years – and during much of the 1970s – the short-term monetary policies of many European countries often involved attempts to stabilize the rate of interest at a target level. Figure 15.5 shows a situation in which this strategy is useful. When the *LM* curve is LM^1, the economy is at full-employment equilibrium at point E, with output at $\overline{Y}$ and a real interest rate of r_1. Suppose that most of the shocks hitting the economy are nominal shocks, including shocks to money supply (perhaps because of changes in the money multiplier) and to money demand. Without intervention by the central bank, these nominal shocks cause the *LM* curve to shift between LM^2 and LM^3, leading aggregate demand to shift erratically between Y_2 and Y_3. In either the extended classical model or the Keynesian model, random shifts in aggregate demand cause undesirable cyclical fluctuations in the economy.

The central bank could reduce the instability caused by nominal shocks by using monetary policy to hold the real interest rate at r_1.[13] In other words, whenever the *LM* curve shifted up to LM^2, the central bank could increase the money supply to restore the *LM* curve to LM^1; similarly, shifts of the *LM* curve to LM^3 could be offset by reductions in the money supply to return the

---

13. The central bank actually targets nominal interest rates. Over a short period of time, in which expected inflation is constant, targeting nominal interest rates and targeting real interest rates are the same.

Figure 15.5
Interest rate targeting
The figure shows an economy that is buffeted by nominal shocks. Changes in money supply or money demand cause the *LM* curve to shift between LM^2 and LM^3 and aggregate demand to move erratically between Y_2 and Y_3. A central bank policy of keeping the real interest rate at r_1, by raising the monetary base whenever the interest rate exceeds r_1 and lowering the base whenever the interest rate falls below r_1, will keep the economy at full employment at E.

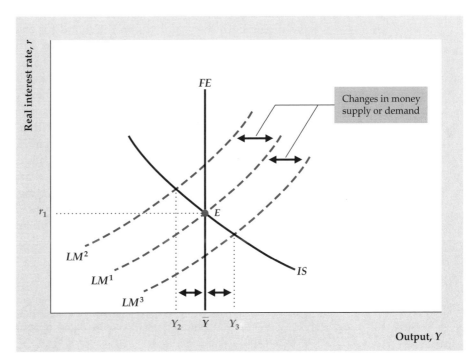

LM curve to *LM*^{1}. In this case stabilizing the intermediate target, the interest rate, would also stabilize output at its full-employment level. For interest rate targeting to be a good strategy, however, nominal shocks must be the main source of instability. As discussed in Analytical Problem 2 at the end of the chapter, if other types of shock to the economy are more important than nominal shocks, the use of monetary policy to stabilize the interest rate could instead destabilize output.

The Channels of Monetary Policy Transmission

Another difficulty faced by monetary policymakers in practice is determining exactly how monetary policy has its effects on the economy. In this book we have so far identified two major ways in which monetary policy affects economic activity and prices.

First, according to the Keynesian *IS–LM* analysis (see Chapter 12), a reduction in the money supply raises *real interest rates*, which in turn reduces aggregate demand (spending by consumers and firms). Declining aggregate demand leads to falling output and prices. The effects of monetary policy on the economy that work through changes in real interest rates are termed the **interest rate channel** of monetary policy.

Second, in open economies, a tightening of monetary policy raises the *real exchange rate* (see Chapter 14). A higher real exchange rate, by making domestic goods more expensive for foreigners and foreign goods cheaper for domestic residents, reduces the demand for the home country's net exports. All else equal, this reduced demand for net exports also reduces aggregate demand, depressing output and prices.[21] The effects of monetary policy working through changes in the real exchange rate are called the **exchange rate channel**.

According to some economists, a tightening of monetary policy also works by reducing both the supply of and demand for credit, a mechanism referred to as the **credit channel** of monetary policy. Box 15.1 provides a brief description of this potential channel.

There are ongoing empirical controversies about the relative importance of these different channels of monetary policy. These controversies increase the difficulty that policymakers have in judging how 'tight' or 'easy' monetary policy is at a given time. For example, suppose that the Bundesbank observes that real interest rates are currently high, but that the mark has been falling. Is monetary policy tight or not? It is hard to tell, unless one knows the relative strengths of the interest rate channel and the exchange rate channel. Similarly, suppose that the real interest rate is low (suggesting easy policy) but that borrowing and lending have been unusually weak (suggesting tight policy). Again, the signals are conflicting, and the judgement about whether monetary policy is expansionary or contractionary depends on the relative strength of the different channels.

---

21. As we discussed in Chapter 14, actual net exports need not decline following a tightening of monetary policy, since the effect of falling domestic income on import demand may outweigh the real exchange rate effects. However, the effect of the higher real exchange rate taken by itself is to reduce net exports.

BOX 15.1

The Credit Channel of Monetary Transmission

According to some economists, besides working through interest rates and exchange rates, monetary policy also has effects on the supply and demand for credit. These effects have been termed the *credit channel* of monetary policy.[*] On the supply of the credit market, according to this theory, tight monetary policy leads to reduced lending by banks. The reason is that, as we saw earlier in the chapter, a tightening of monetary policy reduces bank reserves and thus the quantity of customer deposits that banks can accept. With fewer deposits on hand, banks have a smaller quantity of funds available to lend. As banks cut back on their lending, the argument goes, borrowers who depend on banks for credit, such as consumers and small firms, are unable to obtain the credit they need to make planned purchases. The resulting decline in spending depresses aggregate demand and thus economic activity.

On the demand side of the credit market, according to proponents of the credit channel, tight monetary policy has the effect of making potential borrowers less 'credit-worthy', or less eligible for loans. Consider, for example, a firm that has a substantial amount of floating-rate debt, or debt whose interest rate is tied to the current interest rate in the market. If a tightening of monetary policy raises interest rates, the firm will find that its interest costs have risen substantially, reducing its profitability. The reduced profitability of the firm makes lending to the firm riskier (since the firm is more likely to go bankrupt), so that it is more difficult for the firm to obtain credit. Alternatively, consider a consumer who wishes to use some stocks that she owns as collateral for a bank loan. Tighter monetary policy reduces the value of those stocks (as financial investors, lured by higher interest rates, switch from stocks to bonds). With reduced collateral, the consumer will be able to borrow less. In either example, the reduction in credit available to the borrower is likely to lead to reduced spending (a shift to the left of the IS curve) and thus a weaker economy.

What is the evidence for the credit channel? On the supply side of the credit market, many econo-

mists would argue that the credit channel was powerful in the UK and the USA in the 1960s and 1970s, but has been less so recently. The reason for this weakening is that the deregulation of the banking sector and elimination of reserve requirements for some types of large deposit have made it easier for banks to maintain their lending, despite a reduction in bank reserves caused by tight money. For example, today (unlike twenty years ago), a bank that loses deposits can replace them by selling certificates of deposit (CDs) to corporations or wealthy individuals. A certificate of deposit is a large fixed-term debt obligation of the bank, against which no reserves need to be held. Since the bank does not need to back its CD issuances with reserves, a tightening of monetary policy does not affect its ability to raise funds in this way (except, perhaps, by raising the interest rate that the bank must pay).

The evidence that monetary policy has effects on the demand side of the credit market is stronger. For example, it has been shown that the spending of consumers and small firms is more sensitive to monetary policy than the spending of large firms.[†] A likely explanation of this finding is that consumers and small firms are financially riskier than large firms to begin with, and so when monetary policy tightens they are much more likely to find themselves disqualified for loans. Bankruptcies do increase among small firms and consumers following a tightening of monetary policy, and small firms and consumers also receive less credit after monetary policy tightens, relative to that received by large firms.

The quantitative importance of the credit channel, relative to the other two channels of monetary policy, remains controversial. However, since credit factors appeared to play an important role in the 1990–91 recession in the United Kingdom and the United States (see Box 12.2 'The Role of a Credit Crunch in the 1990–91 Recession, p. 456), interest in this channel has increased.

---

[*] For a survey of the theory and evidence for the credit channel, see Ben Bernanke and Mark Gertler, 'Inside the Black Box: The Credit Channel of Monetary Policy Transmission', *Journal of Economic Perspectives*, vol. 9, Fall 1995, pp. 27–48.

[†] See, for example, Mark Gertler and Simon Gilchrist, 'Monetary Policy, Business Cycles, and the Behavior of Small Manufacturing Firms', *Quarterly Journal of Economics*, vol. 109, May 1994, pp. 309–40.

15.3   THE CONDUCT OF MONETARY POLICY: RULES VERSUS DISCRETION

How should monetary policy be used? On some aspects of this question, there is broad agreement. Most classical and Keynesian economists agree that money is neutral in the long run so that changes in money growth affect inflation but not real variables in the long run. Therefore most would accept that the main long-run goal of monetary policy should be to maintain a low and stable inflation rate. However, there is much less agreement about the effects of monetary policy and its appropriate use in the short run (Chapters 11 and 12). Most Keynesians believe that monetary policy can and should be used to smooth the business cycle, but most classical economists do not. In this section we revisit the debate about the appropriate use of monetary policy by addressing a long-standing question in macroeconomics: should monetary policy be conducted according to fixed rules or at the discretion of the central bank?

The use of rules in monetary policy has been advocated primarily by a group of economists called monetarists and by classical macroeconomists. Supporters of **rules** believe that monetary policy should be essentially automatic. In particular, in its control of the money supply, the central bank should be required to follow a set of simple, prespecified, and publicly announced rules. Many such rules can be imagined. For example, the central bank might be instructed to increase the monetary base by 1% each quarter. An alternative rule, which has been used historically, is to require the central bank to conduct monetary policy to keep the price of gold at a predetermined level (this rule was the essence of the gold standard).

Although the exact form of the rule chosen is not crucial, supporters of the rules-based approach emphasize that the monetary rule should be simple; there cannot be dozens of exceptions and conditions. Furthermore, the rule should be stated in terms of variables that the central bank can control directly or nearly directly. Because the central bank can control the monetary base precisely, a prespecified growth rate for the monetary base is acceptable as a rule. But as the central bank's control over, say, the national unemployment rate is indirect and imperfect, an instruction to the central bank to 'keep the unemployment rate at 4%' is not acceptable to advocates of a rules-guided monetary policy.

The opposite of the rules approach, which has been supported by most (though not all) Keynesian economists, is called **discretion**. The idea behind discretion is that the central bank should be free to conduct monetary policy in any way that it believes will advance the ultimate objectives of low and stable inflation, high economic growth, and low unemployment. In particular, the central bank should continuously monitor the economy and, using the advice of economic experts, should change the money supply as needed to best achieve its goals. For example, if inflation is currently low and economic indicators suggest that the economy is slipping into recession, under a strategy of discretion the central bank would be free to increase the money supply to try to stimulate the economy. In contrast, under an approach based on rules the central bank would have to follow its preannounced policy and would not be free to apply such a stimulus. Because a strategy of discretion involves active responses by the central bank to changes in economic circumstances, such a strategy sometimes is called *activist*.

From this description of rules and discretion, you may have trouble understanding why many economists advocate the use of rules. After all, why should anyone arbitrarily and unnecessarily tie the hands of the central bank? The idea that giving the central bank the option of responding to changing economic conditions is always better than putting monetary policy in a strait-jacket dictated by rules is the essence of the Keynesian case for discretion.

This basic argument for discretion is sound, but a strong case may also be made for rules. Next we discuss the traditional monetarist argument for rules. We then consider a relatively new argument for rules: that the use of rules increases the credibility of the central bank.

In discussing the many problems of practical monetary policy making, we do not want to claim that good monetary policy is impossible. Indeed, many countries have had quite good results from monetary policy in the last fifteen years or so, in that both inflation and unemployment have been relatively low and stable. However, this discussion does illustrate why making monetary policy has been called 'more an art than a science'.

The Monetarist Case for Rules

Monetarism emphasizes the importance of monetary factors in the macroeconomy. Although monetarists have included numerous outstanding economists, the dominant figure and leader of the group is Milton Friedman. For many years Friedman has argued that monetary policy should be conducted by rules, and this idea has become an important part of monetarist doctrine.[14]

Friedman's argument for rules may be broken down into a series of propositions.

Proposition 1. *Monetary policy has powerful short-run effects on the real economy. In the longer run, however, changes in the money supply have their primary effect on the price level.*

Friedman's research on US monetary history (with Anna Schwartz) provided some of the earliest and best evidence that changes in the money supply can be non-neutral in the short run (Chapter 11). Friedman and other monetarists believe that fluctuations in the money supply historically have been one of the most significant – if not the most significant – sources of business cycle fluctuations. On long-run neutrality Friedman (along with Edmund Phelps) was one of the first to argue that, because prices eventually adjust to changes in the money supply, the effect of money on real variables can only be temporary (Chapter 13).

Proposition 2. *Despite the powerful short-run effect of money on the economy, there is little scope for using monetary policy actively to try to smooth business cycles.*

Friedman backs this proposition with several points (several of which we discussed in connection with macroeconomic policy more generally in earlier chapters). First, time is needed for the central bank and other agencies to gather and process information about the current state of the economy. These

---

14. Friedman's book, *A Program for Monetary Stability* (Fordham University Press, 1959) presents a clear early statement of his views.

information lags may make it difficult for the central bank to determine whether the economy is actually in a recession and whether a change in policy is appropriate.

Second, there is considerable uncertainty about how much effect a given change in the money supply will have on the economy and how long the effect will take to occur. Friedman has emphasized that there are *long and variable lags* between monetary policy actions and their economic results. From his empirical research Friedman claims that, on average, monetary changes take about a year to have a significant impact on the economy (that is, the lag is long). Furthermore, the time required for policy to have an effect is unpredictable and may vary from as little as six months to as much as eighteen months (the lag is variable).

Third, wage and price adjustment, although not instantaneous, is fast enough that, by the time the central bank recognizes that the economy is in a recession and increases the money supply, the economy may already be heading out of the recession. If the expansion in the money supply stimulates the economy with a lag of about a year, the stimulus may take effect when output has already recovered and the economy is in a boom. In this case the monetary expansion will cause the economy to overshoot full employment and cause prices to rise. Thus the monetary increase, intended to fight the recession, may actually be destabilizing (causing more variability of output than there would have been otherwise), as well as inflationary.

> Proposition 3. *Even if there is some scope for using monetary policy to smooth business cycles, central banks cannot be relied on to do so effectively.*

One reason that Friedman does not trust central banks to manage an activist monetary policy effectively is political. He believes that despite the supposed independence of many central banks, they are susceptible to short-run political pressures from governments. For example, the central bank might be pressured to stimulate the economy during an election year. If timed reasonably well, an election-year monetary expansion could expand output and employment just before voters go to the polls, with the inflationary effects of the policy not being felt until after the incumbents were safely re-elected (see the box 'The Political Environment: Government Elections and Macroeconomic Policy', p. 492).

More fundamentally, though, monetarist scepticism about discretion arises from their interpretation of macroeconomic history. From his work with Anna Schwartz, Friedman concludes that for whatever reason – incompetence, shortsightedness, or bad luck – monetary policy historically has been a greater source of economic instability than of stability. The primary example cited by Friedman is the 1929–33 period, when the Federal Reserve system was unable or unwilling to stop the money supply from falling by one-third in the wake of widespread runs on banks. Friedman and Schwartz argued that this monetary contraction was one of the main causes of the Great Depression. Thus Friedman concludes that eliminating monetary policy as a source of instability would substantially improve macroeconomic performance.

How could central banks be removed as a source of instability? This question leads to Friedman's policy recommendation, the last proposition:

Proposition 4. *A central bank should choose a specific monetary aggregate (such as M1 or M2) and commit themselves to making that aggregate grow at a fixed percentage rate, year in and year out.*

For monetarists the crucial step in eliminating central banks as a source of instability is to get them to give up activist, or discretionary, monetary policy and to commit themselves – publicly and in advance – to following some rule. Although the exact choice of a rule is not critical, monetarists believe that a constant-money-growth rule would be a good choice for two reasons. First, central banks have considerable influence, though not complete control, over the rate of money growth. Thus if money growth deviated significantly from its target, central banks could not easily blame the deviation on forces beyond their control. Second, monetarists argue that steady money growth would lead to smaller cyclical fluctuations than the supposedly 'countercyclical' monetary policies utilized historically. They conclude that a constant money growth rate would provide a 'stable monetary background' that would allow economic growth to proceed without concern about monetary instability.

Monetarists do not advocate a sudden shift from discretionary monetary policy to a low, constant rate of money growth. Instead, they envision a transition period in which central banks, by gradual preannounced steps, would steadily reduce the growth rate of money. Ultimately, the growth rate of the monetary aggregate selected would be consistent with an inflation rate near zero. Importantly, after the constant growth rate has been attained, central banks would not respond to modest economic downturns by changing money growth but would continue to follow the policy of maintaining a fixed rate of money growth. However, in some of their writings monetarists appear to leave open the possibility that the monetary rule could be temporarily suspended in the face of major economic crises, such as a depression.

Rules and Central Bank Credibility

Much of the monetarist argument for rules rests on pessimism about the competence or political reliability of central banks. Economists who are more optimistic about the ability of the government to intervene effectively in the economy (which includes many Keynesians) question the monetarist case for rules. A 'policy optimist' could argue as follows:

> Monetary policy may have performed badly in the past. However, as time passes, we learn more about the economy and the use of policy gets better. For example, UK monetary policy was clearly handled better after World War II than during the Great Depression. Imposing rigid rules just as we are beginning to learn how to use activist policy properly would be foolish. As to the issue of political reliability, that problem affects fiscal policymakers and indeed all our branches of government. We just have to trust in the democratic process to ensure that policymakers will take actions that for the most part are in the best interests of the country.

For policy optimists this reply to the monetarist case for rules seems perfectly satisfactory. During the past two decades, however, a new argument for rules has been developed that applies even if the central bank knows exactly how monetary changes affect the economy and is completely public-spirited. Thus the new argument for rules is a challenge even to policy optimists. It holds that the use of monetary rules can improve the **credibility** of the central bank, or the degree to which the public believes central bank announcements about future policy, and that the credibility of the central bank influences how well monetary policy works.

Dad, the Kids, and the Game: Credible Threats and Commitment.

To help explain what credibility is, why it may be enhanced by rules, and why it may be important to monetary policy, let us look at a simple example drawn from family life. Knowing that Mum will be going to a business meeting, Dad has bought tickets to a football match for himself and the two kids, Jason and Sarah. Dad likes football, as do the kids. Unfortunately, the kids also like to fight with each other. Dad has warned the kids: 'Don't fight. If you do, we just won't go to the football match.' Dad cannot go to the match without both kids because Mum will not be home to baby-sit and at such short notice he will not be able to find a sitter. We are interested in the following questions about the behaviour of Dad and the kids: (1) Will the kids fight? and (2) Will Dad take the kids to the football match?

Before we analyse this situation, let us discuss it informally. The kids know that, because Dad wants to go to the game himself, he will be reluctant to impose the punishment he has threatened. That is, Dad's threat is not credible (believable) to the kids. Therefore the kids will fight anyway, assuming that when push comes to shove, Dad will not be able to bring himself to waste the tickets and they will go to the match.

Figure 15.6 illustrates this situation. The two columns of the diagram correspond to the two possible actions that the kids can take: *fight* and *don't fight*. The two rows correspond to the two actions that Dad can take: *go to match* and *do not go to match*. Each of the four squares in the diagram thus refers to a possible outcome: square A corresponds to the outcome *kids fight and Dad takes kids to match;* square B refers to *kids don't fight and Dad takes kids to match;* and so on.

Dad and the kids each have preferences about the four possible outcomes. Let us measure preferences in terms of points: the more points someone assigns to an outcome, the more he or she likes it. Dad likes football, so let us assume that he assigns 2 points to going to the match. Also, he assigns 1 point to having the kids not fight. The total number of points Dad assigns to each outcome is shown in each square. Dad's preferred outcome (worth 3 points) is B, in which the kids do not fight and they all go to the match. Dad's worst outcome is C, in which the kids fight and no one goes to the match, an outcome that gets 0 points from Dad.

The kids also like football, and they also assign 2 points to going to the match. However, they also like to fight, and they assign 1 point to fighting. The kids' point totals for each outcome are also shown in each box. The kids' favourite outcome, worth 3 points, is A (they fight and still get to go to the match). Their least favourite outcome, worth 0 points, is D (no fight and no match).

The sequence of actions is as follows. First, the kids decide whether to fight (after hearing the warning), and then Dad decides whether to take the kids to the match. In terms of Figure 15.6 the kids get to pick the column (*fight* or *do not fight*). After the kids pick the column, Dad gets to pick whether they

Figure 15.6
The game between Dad and the kids
Each square represents a combination of an action by the kids and an action by Dad. The points assigned to each combination of actions (shown in each square) measure how much each set of players likes each outcome. The kids 'move' first by picking a column; then Dad 'moves' by picking a row. The equilibrium is outcome A, in which the kids fight and still get to go to the match.

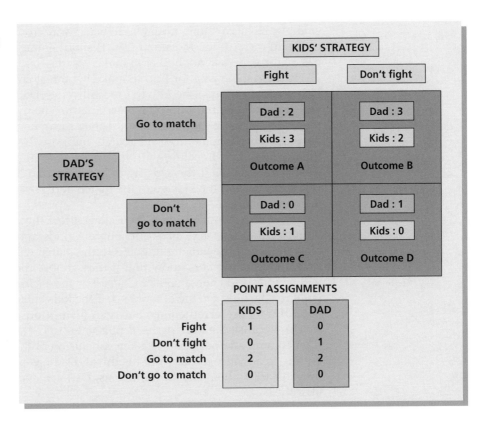

will be in the top square (*go to match*) or the bottom square (*do not go to match*). We assume that at each stage both the kids and Dad make the choices that attain their preferred outcome.

The kids reason as follows:

Suppose we pick *fight* (the left column). That leaves Dad with the choice of A (*go to match*) or C (*do not go to match*). Outcome A is worth 2 points to Dad; C is worth 0 points. So Dad will pick A over C and, if we fight, we still get to go to the match. If we pick *do not fight* (the right column), Dad will pick B over D, so we also go to the match in that case. But because we like to fight, and we get to go to the match in either case, we might as well fight.

In terms of Figure 15.6, the kids know that once they factor in their Dad's response, they effectively have a choice between A and B. They prefer A to B, so they pick the left column (that is, they fight).

This type of diagram is a standard tool from a branch of mathematics, much used in economics, called game theory. **Game theory** explores situations (games) in which strategy is used by individuals (players) to achieve their goals, possibly at the expense of the other players. An equilibrium of a game is an outcome that occurs if all players do the best they can for themselves.

In the game here, the 'players' are Dad and the kids. The equilibrium of the game is outcome A, in which the kids fight and still go to the match. Outcome A is the equilibrium because the kids recognize that Dad's threat is not credible; he has a strong incentive to back away from his threat when the time comes to carry it out. Indeed, if Dad is smart enough to realize that his threat has no force, he will not bother to make it in the first place.

Is there some way for Dad to make his threat credible and thereby get the kids to behave? Yes; the key to credibility for Dad is to find some way by which he can commit himself to carrying out the threat. In other words, Dad must convince the kids that, should they fight, he will have *no choice* but to keep everybody home from the match. Suppose, for example, that Dad gives the match tickets to Mum, with instructions to hide them and not to reveal their whereabouts if the kids fight. Suppose that Mum is indifferent about whether Dad and the kids go to the match and can be counted on to carry out these instructions.

How does Mum's hiding the tickets affect the equilibrium of the game? Formally, the effect is to cross out square A (kids fight, go to match) as a possible outcome. If the kids fight, going to the match will not be a possible choice for Dad. Thus the kids know that if they choose the left column (*fight*), Dad will be forced to choose square C (*don't go to match*), an outcome that yields 1 point for the kids. On the other hand, if the kids choose the right column (*don't fight*), Dad's preferred choice between his options B and D will be B (*go to match*). Because the kids prefer B (2 points) to C (1 point), they will pick the right column and not fight. The key conclusion of this analysis is that by committing in advance to carry out his threat, Dad has made his threat credible. If the kids act in their own best interests, Dad achieves the outcome (B) that he likes the best.

A Game Between the Central Bank and Firms. We can use game theory to think about the credibility of the central bank. Consider a situation in which the macroeconomy is in general equilibrium so that the *IS* and *LM* curves cross at the *FE* line (point *E* in Figure 15.7(a)). Initially, suppose that both the money supply and the price level are growing steadily at 10% per year. As *M* and *P* are growing at the same rate, the real money supply M/P is constant, and the *LM* curve, LM^1, remains fixed and passes through *E*. Thus the economy is initially at full employment with the unemployment rate at the natural rate, say, 6%, and inflation equal to 10% per year.

The central bank wants to reduce the inflation rate to zero without increasing the unemployment rate. Suppose that the central bank makes the following announcement to all the firms in the economy:

> There is no reason why we should be suffering from this 10% inflation. Let's make a deal. If you businesses hold prices *P* constant this period, rather than raising them by 10%, we will hold the money supply *M* constant. With *M* and *P* both constant, the real money supply M/P will not change and the *LM* curve will not shift. Thus the economy will remain at full employment, with an unemployment rate of 6%, but we will all be better off with no inflation. However, if you insist on raising prices, we will still keep the money supply constant. In this case the real money supply M/P will fall by 10%, the *LM* curve will shift up and to the left to LM^2, and we will all suffer from both high unemployment and continued inflation (point *F*).

How will the firms respond to this statement by the central bank? As we show, the central bank's threat to reduce the real money supply if firms raise

Figure 15.7
The game between the central bank and the firms

(a) This part of the figure shows the possible outcomes of the game between the central bank and the firms. Initially, the economy is at point *E* (full employment) with 10% inflation. The real money supply *M/P* depends both on the price level *P* chosen by firms and the money supply *M* chosen by the central bank. If the real money supply doesn't change, the economy remains at full employment at *E*. If the real money supply falls, the *LM* curve shifts from *LM*¹ to *LM*², and the economy goes into a recession with 9% unemployment at point *F*. If the real money supply increases, the *LM* curve shifts from *LM*¹ to *LM*³, and the economy goes into a boom with 3% unemployment at point *H*.

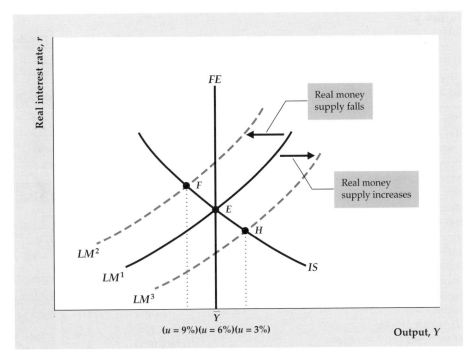

prices is not credible because the central bank does not want a recession. As a result, the firms will go ahead and raise prices.

The game between the central bank and the firms is analysed formally in Figure 15.7(b). The firms' choices, *raise P* (by 10%) and *don't raise P*, correspond to the two columns of the diagram. The central bank's two choices, *increase M* (by 10%) and *don't increase M* correspond to the two rows. Square A represents the outcome *firms raise P and central bank raises M*; square B represents the outcome *firms do not raise P and central bank raises M*; and so on.

What happens to the economy in each case? Determining what happens to inflation is easy: in squares A and C, firms raise prices by 10%, so inflation π is 10%; in squares B and D firms do not raise prices, so $\pi = 0$.

What about unemployment? In square A both money and prices rise by 10%, so M/P is unchanged and the economy remains at full employment (point *E* in Figure 15.7(a)). Similarly, in square D neither *M* nor *P* changes, so M/P is unchanged and the economy remains at full employment. Thus in squares A and D the unemployment rate *u* remains at the natural rate of 6%. In square C, *P* rises but *M* does not. Thus M/P falls, the *LM* curve shifts up and to the left to LM^2, and the economy goes into recession at point *F* in Figure 15.7(a), with the unemployment rate increasing to 9%. Finally, in square B, *M* rises but *P* does not, so M/P rises and the *LM* curve shifts down and to the right to LM^3. In this case the economy goes into a boom (point *H* in Figure 15.7(a)), and the unemployment rate falls to 3%.

The next step is to determine the points that each player assigns to each outcome. Let us start with the central bank, which does not like inflation. It assigns 1 point to zero inflation (B and D) and no points to a positive rate of inflation (A and C). However, the central bank also does not like unemploy-

Figure 15.7
(b) This part of the figure shows the possible moves in the game between the central bank and the firms. The firms move first by deciding whether to raise the price level *P*, choosing the column. Then the central bank moves by deciding whether to increase the money supply *M*, choosing the row. If *M* and *P* both rise (outcome A) or both stay the same (outcome D), the real money supply is unchanged, and the economy remains at full employment at point *E* in (a). In outcome B, *M* increases and *P* remains the same; thus the real money supply rises and unemployment falls as at point *H* in (a). In outcome C, *M* remains the same and *P* increases, so the real money supply falls and unemployment increases as at point *F* in (a). Point assignments show the preferences of the central bank and firms for each outcome. The equilibrium of the game is outcome A, in which the firms raise prices and the central bank increases the money supply.

ment. It assigns 0 points to the natural unemployment rate (A and D), 1 point to unemployment below the natural rate (B), and –1 point to unemployment above the natural rate (C). The total point scores for the central bank are shown in each square. The central bank's preferred outcome is B, with no inflation and 3% unemployment; its least favourite outcome is C, with 10% inflation and 9% unemployment.

The firms' profits are maximized on the *FE* line: that is, when the economy is at full employment. Therefore the firms assign 2 points to the natural unemployment rate (A and D). Firms prefer zero inflation to positive inflation, so they assign 1 point to zero inflation (B and D). Total scores for firms are also shown in each box.

Now let us find the equilibrium, assuming that firms first decide whether to raise prices and then the central bank decides whether to increase the money supply. The firms reason as follows:

Suppose that we raise prices. This action leaves the central bank the choice between outcomes A and C. The central bank does not want a recession, so it will choose A: that is, it will increase the money supply. If we don't raise prices, the central bank has a choice of B or D. The central bank prefers B to D because, with no inflation, it prefers unemployment below the natural rate to unemployment at the natural rate. In this case the central bank will also increase the money supply. Therefore, no matter what we do, the central bank will increase the money supply. The central bank claim that it will maintain a constant money supply if we raise prices just isn't credible. If we raise prices we get outcome A, and if we don't raise prices we get outcome B. We prefer A to B (we'd rather be at full employment than off the *FE* line and above full employment), so we will raise prices.

The equilibrium of the game is therefore outcome A, in which the firms raise prices and the central bank (failing to carry out its threat) raises the money supply. Because the central bank's threat is not credible, the firms ignore it. Note that *both the central bank and the firms prefer outcome D (full employment and no inflation) to the equilibrium outcome A.* Yet because the central bank's promise to hold the money supply constant is not credible, the economy does not attain outcome D.

In contrast, suppose that the central bank could credibly promise not to increase the money supply under any circumstances and that the firms believed this promise. The firms would reason: 'If we raise prices, the central bank will pick outcome C (inflation and a recession). If we don't raise prices, the central bank will pick D (no inflation and no recession). We prefer D to C, so we won't raise prices.'

The equilibrium in this case would be outcome D, which is preferred by everyone to the no-credibility outcome A. In outcome D disinflation is achieved without increasing unemployment because the central bank is credible.

Rules, Commitment, and Credibility. The formal analysis shows why central bank credibility is important. If a central bank is credible, it can reduce money growth and inflation without incurring high unemployment. But how can a central bank achieve credibility?

One possibility is for the central bank to develop a reputation for carrying out its promises. Suppose that in the preceding example firms raise their prices, fully expecting the central bank to increase the money supply. However, the central bank holds the money supply constant, causing a recession. The next time, the firms may take the central bank's promises more seriously, and the economy may attain outcome D. Similarly, if Dad refuses to take the kids to the match after they fight, he will improve his reputation for carrying out his threats; the next time, the kids may take him seriously.

The problem with this strategy is that it may involve serious costs while the reputation is being established: the economy suffers a recession while the central bank establishes its reputation; Dad and the kids miss the match while Dad establishes his. Is there some less costly way to achieve credibility?

Advocates of rules suggest that, by forcing the central bank to keep its promises, rules may substitute for reputation in establishing credibility. Suppose that there is an ironclad rule – ideally, enforced by some outside agency – that the central bank must gradually reduce the growth of the money supply. Observing the existence of this rule, the firms might well believe that money supply growth is going to decline no matter what, and painless disinflation (outcome D) can be achieved. Similarly, in the case with Dad and the kids, if there is an unbreakable family rule that fighting suspends all privileges – and Mum is there to help enforce it – Dad's threat not to go to the match might be more credible. Note that if it increases credibility, a rule improves central bank performance even if the central bank is competent and public-spirited. Hence this reason for monetary policy rules is different from the monetarists' argument presented earlier.

How do advocates of discretion respond to the credibility argument for rules? Keynesians argue that there may be a trade-off between credibility and flexibility. For a rule to establish credibility, it must be virtually impossible to change – otherwise, no one will believe that the central bank will stick to it. In the extreme, the monetary growth rule would be added as an amendment to the constitution, which could then be changed only at great cost and with long delays. But if a rule is completely unbreakable, what happens (ask the Keynesians) if some unexpected crisis arises – for example, a new depression? In that case the inability of the central bank to take corrective action – that is, its lack of flexibility – could prove disastrous. Therefore, Keynesians argue, establishing a rule ironclad enough to create credibility for the central bank would, by eliminating policy flexibility, also create unacceptable risks.

APPLICATION

Money-Growth Targeting and Inflation Targeting

The decade of the 1970s, with its combination of high unemployment and high inflation, led many central banks around the world to wonder whether monetary policy could not be handled in a more effective manner. Since that period there has been considerable experimentation with alternative strategies for conducting monetary policy, in the hope of improving macroeconomic performance. In response to the arguments made by economists for the importance of credibility, many of these strategies have involved public announcements by central banks of their goals, accompanied by attempts to convince the public that monetary policymakers were committed to those goals. In this Application we discuss the experience with two such strategies, money-growth targeting and inflation targeting.[15]

Money-growth targeting is the older of the two strategies. The Bundesbank introduced money growth targets in 1975, following a run-up in inflation, and Germany has adhered to this strategy ever since. The UK, the USA, and many other countries adopted some form of money-growth targeting during the 1970s.

Under a strategy of *money-growth targeting*, the central bank announces in advance the rate of growth of money that it will try to achieve over the next year (or perhaps longer). In principle, the target growth rate of money is set so as to be consistent with the central bank's desired levels of inflation and real output growth, and hitting the targeted rate of growth of money is understood to be the central bank's most important objective. Initially, Germany targeted the growth of a broad money aggregate called central bank money (CBM), a weighted sum of currency, cheque accounts, savings accounts, and time deposits. In most years, the Bundesbank came reasonably close to achieving its stated targets, although there were exceptions, such as in 1978 when the Bundesbank overshot its money-growth targets as part of an international effort to strengthen the US dollar.

The USA also began to experiment with money-growth targeting in 1975, when the Federal Reserve (the central bank of the USA) announced target

---

15. For discussions and historical analyses of these approaches, see Ben Bernanke and Frederic Mishkin, 'Central Bank Behavior and the Strategy of Monetary Policy: Observations from Six Industrialized Countries', in Olivier Blanchard and Stanley Fischer, eds., NBER, *Macroeconomics Annual*, 1992, as well as 'Inflation Targeting: A New Strategy for Monetary Policy?' by the same two authors, in *Journal of Economic Perspectives*, Spring 1997.

growth ranges for three different monetary aggregates: M1, M2, and M3. Since the Fed (as the Federal Reserve is often known), like any central bank, has only one instrument at its disposal – the control of the monetary base – attempting to control the growth rate of three separate monetary aggregates at the same time was not realistic; and indeed the Fed was not able to accomplish this feat, often badly missing its announced targets. Monetarists have argued that, in choosing three different monetary aggregates to target simultaneously, the Fed revealed that it was not very serious about adhering to a money growth rule.

According to the arguments advance by Friedman, maintaining a low and steady growth rate of money should lead to low inflation and stable output and employment growth. Most countries did experience a substantial reduction in inflation during the early 1980s. However, output and employment growth were often unstable. For example, Germany, the UK, and the USA all suffered sharp increases in unemployment in the early 1980s, during the period of their money-growth targeting experiments. In the USA, the Fed became so dissatisfied with money-growth targeting that it de-emphasized money-growth targets in 1982 in favour of targeting interest rates. In 1993 the Fed dropped the use of money-growth targets entirely. Many other countries also abandoned or weakened their reliance on money-growth targeting during the 1980s, the principal exceptions being Germany and Switzerland, which have continued to announce money-growth targets.

Why was money-growth targeting abandoned? One explanation was that, because of rapid changes in financial systems of many countries, at times during the 1970s and 1980s the demand for money was quite unstable and unpredictable (see the Application, 'Financial Innovation and the "Case of the Missing Money"', pp. 242). Recall that, if money demand is so unstable that the *LM* curve moves randomly back and forth, varying the money supply to keep interest rates constant leads to more stable aggregate demand than does holding the money stocks to a fixed level (see Figure 15.5). According to this view, sharp changes in the demand for money (unstable velocity) made money growth targeting an ineffective strategy. Instability of money demand contributed to the abandonment of money-growth targets in both the United Kingdom and the United States. Germany's more tightly regulated financial system changed less during the 1980s than those of other countries, reducing the Bundesbank's problems with unstable money demand. But even the Bundesbank was forced to switch from targeting central bank money to targeting M3 in 1987, because the relationship between the former aggregate and the economy appeared to have become too unstable.

The end of money-growth targeting in many countries left cental banks groping for a new strategy. Since 1990 a number of countries have adopted an alternative strategy called inflation targeting. The pioneer of this new approach was New Zealand, which, as part of a package of economic reforms, announced a set of inflation targets that the Reserve Bank (the central bank of New Zealand) would have to meet. Under the law passed by New Zealand, if the Reserve Bank failed to meet its inflation targets, the Governor of the Bank could be fired. Numerous other countries have adopted inflation targeting in recent years, including the United Kingdom, Sweden and Spain. In the United States, the Fed has increased its emphasis on maintaining low and stable inflation, but at the time of writing it had not officially adopted a strategy of inflation targeting.

Under a strategy of *inflation targeting*, as the name implies, the central bank (usually together with the executive branch of the government) announces the inflation rate that it will try to achieve over the subsequent one to four years. Thus, rather than targeting an intermediate variable (money growth), the central bank targets one of its ultimate goals, the rate of inflation. A strategy of inflation targeting does not preclude the use of monetary policy to help stabilize output or other macroeconomic variables in the short run, but in announcing an inflation target the central bank signals that hitting that target in the longer run is its number-one priority.

Relative to money-growth targeting, inflation targeting has advantages and disadvantages. One clear advantage is that inflation targeting sidesteps the problem of money demand instability. Under an inflation-targeting strategy, if money demand changes, there is nothing to prevent the central bank from adjusting the money supply to compensate.[16] Another advantage of inflation targeting is that it is easier to explain to the public that the central bank is trying to achieve a certain rate of inflation (which most people understand) than that it is trying to achieve a certain growth rate of M3 (which most people do not understand). Better communication of the central bank's goals should make the public and the financial markets less uncertain about what the central bank is going to do, and may increase the democratic accountability of the central bank.

A major disadvantage of inflation targeting is that inflation responds to policy actions only with a long lag. As a result, it is hard for the central bank to judge what policy actions are needed in order to hit the inflation target, and equally hard for the public to tell if the central bank is living up to its promises. Thus it is possible that inflation-targeting central banks may badly miss their targets, losing credibility as a result. It remains to be seen whether inflation targeting will be the preferred strategy for monetary policy in the twenty-first century.

Other Ways to Achieve Central Bank Credibility

The preceding Application suggests that adopting money-growth targets does not generally give the central bank credibility, possibly because central banks are unwilling or unable to commit to meeting those targets. Are there other ways to increase the central bank's credibility and thus improve the performance of monetary policy? Three possibilities have been suggested: to appoint a 'tough' central banker; to change central bankers' incentives; and to increase the central bank's independence.

1. *Appointing a 'tough' central banker.* By definition, a credible central bank is one that will be believed by the public when it states its intention to reduce money growth and inflation. One way to increase credibility is for the government to appoint a central bank chairman who strongly dislikes inflation and who people believe is willing to accept increased unemployment if necessary

---

16. As Figure 15.5 shows, this compensation for money demand shocks occurs automatically when interest rates are used as intermediate targets. Most central banks that set inflation targets for the longer run also use interest rates as their intermediate target in the short run. There is no conflict between short-run interest rate targeting and long-run inflation targeting, as long as the interest rate is periodically adjusted in a way consistent with the long-run inflation target.

to bring inflation down. Thus, when US President Jimmy Carter faced a serious inflation problem in 1979, he appointed Paul Volcker – an imposing individual with a strong anti-inflation reputation – to be chairman of the Federal Reserve System. In appointing a 'tough' central banker, Carter hoped to convince the financial markets and the public that he was serious about reducing inflation. Volcker succeeded in getting rid of inflation, but, because unemployment rose significantly in the process, his appointment did not completely solve the credibility problem.[17]

2. *Changing central bankers' incentives.* A second way to enhance the central bank's credibility is to give its leadership strong incentives to be 'tough' on inflation (and to ignore any unemployment costs associated with disinflation).[18] If the incentives are strong enough and are publicly known, people may find the central bank's anti-inflation pronouncements to be credible. An interesting recent example of this approach is the law passed in New Zealand that sets explicit inflation targets for the central bank and provides for the replacement of the head of the central bank if those targets are not met. Inflation has come down significantly in New Zealand, but unemployment has risen. Again, credibility problems have not been completely solved.

3. *Increasing central bank independence.* A third strategy is to increase the independence of the central bank from the other parts of the government – for example, by limiting the legal ability of the executive and legislative branches to interfere in monetary policy decisions. An important feature in the movement towards monetary union in Europe is an independent European System of Central Banks. The rationale is that a more independent central bank will be less subject to short-term political pressures to try to expand output and employment (say, before an election) and will be more strongly committed to maintaining a low long-run inflation rate. Because the public will recognize that an independent central bank is less subject to political pressures, announcements made by the central bank should be more credible.

Considerable evidence supports the idea that independent central banks are more credible. Figure 15.8, taken from a study by Alberto Alesina and Lawrence Summers[19] of Harvard University, shows the relationship between central bank independence and inflation in sixteen industrialized countries. The vertical axis measures average inflation for each country for the period 1955–88. The horizontal axis shows an index of central bank independence (based on factors such as the ease with which the government can dismiss the head of the central bank or reverse central bank decisions). Countries

---

17. The point that appointing a tough central banker may improve central bank credibility was made by Kenneth Rogoff, 'The Optimal Degree of Commitment to an Intermediate Monetary Target', *Quarterly Journal of Economics*, November 1985, 1169–89. Keynesians might argue that Volcker was credible but that long-lived stickiness in wages and prices led unemployment to increase in 1981–82 anyway.
18. An analysis of central bankers' incentives is Carl Walsh, 'Optimal Contracts for Central Bankers', unpublished paper, University of California-Santa Cruz and Federal Reserve Bank of San Francisco, 1992.
19. 'Central Bank Independence and Macroeconomic Performance', *Journal of Money, Credit and Banking*, May 1993, pp. 151–62.

**Figure 15.8
Central bank
independence and
inflation**

The figure compares
average inflation to an
index of central bank
independence from the
rest of the government
(higher values of the index
imply that the central
bank is more indepen-
dent) for each of sixteen
countries for the period
1955–1988. It shows that
countries with more
independent central
banks have lower average
inflation rates.

Source: Alberto Alesina and
Lawrence Summers, 'Central
Bank Independence and Macroeconomic Performance', *Journal
of Money, Credit and Banking*,
May 1993, pp. 151–62, Table A1
and Fig. 1a.

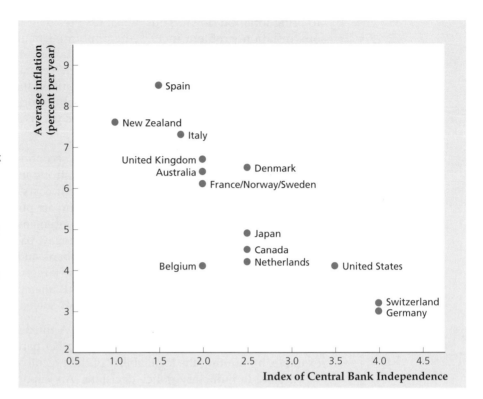

with relatively independent central banks, such as Germany, Switzerland, and the United States, have clearly had lower long-run inflation rates than countries without independent central banks, such as, New Zealand,[20] Italy, and Spain. A similar figure in the Alesina–Summers study shows that countries with independent central banks do not have higher long-run rates of unemployment. This evidence supports the idea that increased central bank independence raises credibility and thus lowers the unemployment cost of keeping inflation low. Reflecting growing acceptance of the idea that increased central bank independence improves macroeconomic performance, in 1993 France took several steps expressly designed to increase the independence of its central bank, the Bank of France. Similarly, in June 1997, the Bank of England became independent when it took over responsibility for setting interest rates. The Bank will set interest rates in order to meet an inflation target set by the government, and the performance of the Bank will be measured against how well it achieves that target.

---

20. The evaluation of the independence of New Zealand's central bank preceded the recent reforms in New Zealand's central banking laws mentioned earlier.

15.4 EUROPEAN MONETARY UNION AND THE CONDUCT OF MONETARY POLICY

As discussed in Chapter 14, the Maastricht Treaty set out the stages and timetable for the transition to monetary union. The main elements of the treaty were a total commitment by member states to the ERM system of fixed exchange rates, the establishment of the European Monetary Institute as the first step in the move towards a European System of Central Banks, and the adoption of a single currency on 1 January 1999. We have considered the role of the central bank in determining monetary policy in one country. Will a European Central Bank set monetary policy on an EMU-wide basis in just the same way, or are there further issues about the conduct of monetary policy which have to be addressed?

The European System of Central Banks

The conduct of monetary policy in most industrialized countries is carried out by their central banks, whether independently of government or not. As European economies move towards full monetary union, this will change. The 1992 Maastricht Treaty led to the creation of the European Monetary Institute (EMI). The EMI is located in Frankfurt and comprises the central banks of each of the EU member states. The EMI has two primary tasks: to coordinate monetary policy within the EU and to put in place an operational framework for the **European System of Central Banks (ESCB)** and for the establishment of a **European Central Bank (ECB)** which will begin operation in mid 1998. The ECB will represent the final stage in the transition to monetary union and it will be charged with determining and implementing monetary policy with respect to the single currency within the EMU.

The ECB has been modelled on the Bundesbank and key features of the way it will operate reflect the Bundesbank's constitution. The ECB will be independent of political control and pressure from either national governments or the European Union. Its primary task is to maintain monetary stability in order that inflation in the EMU will be kept low. ECB policy will be set by an Executive Board and the heads of the central banks of those countries which join the EMU. The ECB will operate in just the same way as any other central bank does, using open-market operations, interest rates, and minimum reserve ratios to control the money supply.

The key feature of the way that the ECB will operate involves a sale and repurchasing system along the lines of the German system discussed earlier (page 579). There remains some disagreement, however, about the role of minimum reserve ratios. The Bundesbank favours minimum reserve requirements as a means of controlling the money supply, although in recent years it has cut its reserve ratios. The majority of European central banks, however, have only token reserve requirements and would fight hard against these being increased or reinstated.

Monetary Policy in the EMU

The ECB has been charged with setting monetary policy in order to maintain price stability. We have discussed some of the problems that central banks face when they attempt to set policy to achieve low inflation. The difficulties encountered by the ECB in setting policy and achieving inflation targets on an EMU-wide basis are no less problematic. Indeed, they are, if anything, significantly increased.

Consider, for example, the information that central banks use when formulating policy. Data on a range of economic indicators will be analysed to determine the most appropriate policy. Yet within the EU there are major differences in the way statistics are collected and indicators constructed. For example, a key indicator will be a measure of inflation, but countries differ in the way they put together their consumer price indexes, the basket of goods they include, and how frequently they change the basket to reflect changing consumer trends. Countries also differ in the priority they give to the various economic indicators and in terms of the actual measures they favour. Germany, for example, along with several other European countries, monitors the M3 monetary aggregate, whereas the UK favours M0 and Sweden favours M1.

A further problem is that European economies differ in the strategies that monetary policymakers adopt to promote public credibility in their commitment to fighting inflation. Some, like Germany, have opted for money-growth targeting, whereas others, including the UK and Sweden, favour an inflation target. It is not clear yet whether the ECB will choose money growth or inflation as its intermediate target, or whether either alone will be satisfactory in setting policy on an EMU-wide basis. One reason that some countries abandoned money-growth targeting was that changes in their financial systems affected the stability and predictability of money demand. Yet not all countries were affected by financial innovations, and the stability and predictability of money demand did not undermine money growth targeting to the same extent in many European countries as it did in, say, the UK. Setting a common monetary policy is further complicated by the fact that a particular monetary policy will have a different impact country by country.

The unwillingness of national governments to give up sovereignty over the control of their own monetary policy remains one of the main stumbling blocks in the move towards EMU. A monetary policy determined by the ECB with regard to conditions within the EMU and not in response to particular problems encountered in any one country faces many difficulties. This is why the convergence criteria are so important, since they seek to ensure that economic conditions across member states are similar. A common monetary policy for each country aimed at monetary stability should not then create any problems. However, how the system will deal with weaker economies which are not able to achieve the same level of economic performance has led some economists to question whether the EMU and a single currency will ever be seen in all European countries.

CHAPTER SUMMARY

1. Three groups help determine the money supply: the central bank, private banks, and the general public. The central bank sets the monetary base, which is the quantity of central bank liabilities that can be used as money. The monetary base equals the sum of bank reserves (deposits by banks at the central bank plus currency in the vaults of banks) and currency in circulation. Private banks and the general public interact to determine the money multiplier, which is the ratio of the money supply to the monetary base.

2. In an all-currency economy the monetary base consists entirely of currency in circulation. Therefore the money supply equals the monetary base, and the money multiplier equals 1.

3. In an economy with fractional reserve banking and no currency held by the public, the money supply is $1/res$ times the monetary base, where res is the ratio of reserves to deposits desired by banks. The money supply is greater than the monetary base in this case because banks lend part of the deposits they receive. When those funds are redeposited in the banking system, bank deposits and thus the money supply increase.

4. In an economy with both fractional reserve banking and currency in circulation, the money multiplier equals $(cu + 1)/(cu + res)$, where cu is the public's desired ratio of currency to deposits. The money supply equals deposits plus currency in circulation and also equals the money multiplier times the monetary base. An increase in the desired currency–deposit ratio cu or in the desired reserve–deposit ratio res reduces the money multiplier. During the Great Depression, banking panics caused both cu and res to increase, and the money multiplier and the money supply both fell sharply.

5. The central bank can affect the size of the monetary base and thus the money supply through open-market operations. An open-market sale (in which central bank assets are sold for currency or bank reserves) reduces the monetary base. An open-market purchase (in which the central bank uses money to buy assets, such as govern-ment securities, from the public) increases the monetary base.

6. The central bank of Germany is called the Bundesbank. The leadership of the Bundesbank is the Central Bank Council which meets several times each year to set monetary policy.

7. The Bundesbank affects the German money supply primarily through open-market operations. Lending and changes in reserve requirements can also be used to affect the money supply. An increase in lending raises the monetary base and thus the money supply. An increase in reserve requirements raises the reserve–deposit ratio, lowering the money multiplier and the money supply.

8. Central banks often focus on intermediate targets such as the money supply or short-term interest rates to guide monetary policy. Stabilizing interest rates is a useful strategy when fluctuations in money supply or demand would otherwise cause the LM curve to shift randomly back and forth.

9. Monetary policy may be conducted either by rules or by discretion. Under rules the central bank is required to follow a simple predetermined rule for monetary policy, such as a requirement for constant money growth, and is not allowed to respond to current economic conditions. Under discretion the central bank is expected to monitor the economy and use monetary policy actively to maintain full employment and to keep inflation low. Discretion for monetary policy is favoured by Keynesians, who argue that it gives the central bank maximum flexibility to stabilize the economy.

10. Monetarists, led by Milton Friedman, argue that, because of information problems and lags between the implementation of policy changes and their effects, the scope for using monetary policy to stabilize the economy is small. Furthermore, they argue, central banks cannot be relied on to use active monetary policy wisely and in the public interest. Monetarists advocate a constant-

growth-rate rule for the money supply in order to discipline central banks and keep monetary fluctuations from destabilizing the economy.

11. An additional argument for rules is that they increase central bank credibility. Supporters of rules claim that the use of ironclad rules will cause the public to believe the central bank if it says (for example) that money supply growth will be reduced, with the implication that inflation can be reduced without a large increase in unemployment.

12. Although some countries have experimented with money-growth targets – similar in spirit to the monetarists' constant-growth-rate rule – central banks have not been willing or able to make strong commitments to meet their targets. One reason for their reluctance is that fluctuations in the demand for money have led the relationship between specific monetary aggregates and the macroeconomy to be unstable or unpredictable at times. The use of money-growth targets seems to have helped central banks bring inflation under control, but there is not much evidence that money targeting has reduced the unemployment cost of disinflation.

13. Possible alternatives for increasing a central bank's credibility are to appoint a central banker who is 'tough' on inflation; to increase central bankers' incentives to reduce inflation; and to increase the central bank's independence from other parts of the government.

14. Monetary policy in the European Monetary Union will be determined by the European Central Bank, which is modelled on the Bundesbank. The ECB will set monetary policy across the EMU in order to achieve price stability. Setting a common monetary policy for countries whose economies are performing differently and when there are differences in the relationships between key economic variables may prove a stumbling block to the establishment of a wider monetary union in Europe.

Key Terms

bank reserves, p. 571
bank run, p. 574
cash in hand, p. 581

central bank, p. 569
credibility, p. 594
credit channel, pp. 588
currency–deposit ratio, p. 575
depository institutions, p. 569
discount rate, p. 585
discretion, p. 590
European Central Bank, pp. 605
European System of Central Banks, p. 605
exchange rate channel, p. 588
fractional reserve banking, p. 572
game theory, p. 593
high-powered money, p. 570
instruments, p. 585
intermediate targets, p. 585
interest rate channel, p. 605
lombard loans, p. 585
lombard rate, p. 585
monetarism, p. 591
monetary base, p. 570
money multiplier, p. 576
multiple expansion of loans and deposits, p. 573
100% reserve banking, p. 571
open-market purchase, p. 577
open-market-repurchase agreements, p. 578
open-market sale, p. 578
rediscount credit, p. 584
refinancing, p. 584
reserve–deposit ratio, p. 571
rules, p. 590

Key Equations

$$M = CU + DEP \qquad (15.4)$$

The money supply, M, is the sum of currency in circulation, CU, and deposits held by the public at banks, DEP.

$$BASE = CU + RES \qquad (15.5)$$

The monetary base, or the liabilities of the central bank that are usable as money, equals the sum of currency in circulation, CU, and bank reserves, RES.

$$M = \left(\frac{cu + 1}{cu + res} \right) BASE \qquad (15.8)$$

The money supply, M, equals the monetary base times the money multiplier, $(cu + 1)/(cu + res)$, where cu is the currency–deposit ratio chosen by the public and res is the reserve–deposit ratio chosen by banks.

Review Questions

1. Define *monetary base*. What is the relationship between the monetary base and the money supply in an all-currency economy?
2. Define *money multiplier*. What is the value of the money multiplier in a system of 100% reserve banking? What is the value of the money multiplier in a system of fractional reserve banking, if all money is held in the form of deposits? Why is the money multiplier higher under fractional reserve banking than under 100% reserve banking?
3. Discuss how actions of the public and banks can cause the money multiplier to rise or fall. Does the fact that the public and banks can affect the money multiplier imply that the central bank cannot control the money supply? Why or why not?
4. What is the effect on the monetary base of an open-market purchase of securities? What other means do the central banks have for controlling the money supply?
5. What are intermediate targets? How do they differ from monetary policy goals? List the two principal types of intermediate target that have been used.
6. 'It is plain to see that discretion is a better way to run monetary policy than following a rule because a policy of discretion gives the central bank the ability to react to news about the economy.' What is the monetarist response to the statement? What is the more recent argument for using rules rather than discretion?
7. Has the use of money-growth targets significantly improved central bank credibility? Besides adopting money-growth targets, what other actions can a country take to increase the credibility of its central bank?
8. What will be the role of a European Central Bank in determining monetary policy for member states which participate in the European Monetary Union? What problems might the Bank encounter in its role of setting monetary policy?

Numerical Problems

1. The Agricolan monetary base is 1,000,000 florins. The public always holds half its money supply as currency and half as deposits. Banks hold 20% of deposits in the form of reserves. Starting with the initial creation of a monetary base that accompanies the purchase by the central bank of 1,000,000 fl worth of coconuts from the public, show the consolidated balance sheet of the banks after they first receive deposits, after a first round of loans and redeposits, and after a second round of loans and redeposits. (*Hint:* Don't forget that the public keeps only half its money in the form of bank deposits.)

Show the balance sheets of the central bank, the banking system, and the public at the end of the process of multiple expansion of loans and deposits. What is the final value of the money supply?

2. **a.** The money supply is DM6,000,000, currency held by the public is DM2,000,000, and the reserve–deposit ratio is 0.25. Find deposits, bank reserves, the monetary base, and the money multiplier.
   b. In a different economy cash in hand is DM1,000,000, deposits by depository institutions at the central bank are DM4,000,000, the monetary base is DM10,000,000, and bank deposits are DM20,000,000. Find bank reserves, the money supply, and the money multiplier.
3. When the real interest rate increases, banks have an incentive to lend a greater portion of their deposits, which reduces the reserve–deposit ratio. In particular, suppose that

$$res = 0.4 - 2r$$

where *res* is the reserve–deposit ratio and r is the real interest rate. The currency–deposit ratio is 0.4, the price level is fixed at 1.0, and the monetary base is 60. The real quantity of money demanded is

$$L(Y, i) = 0.5Y - 10i$$

where Y is real output and i is the nominal interest rate. Assume that expected inflation is zero so that the nominal interest rate and the real interest rate are equal.
a. If $r = i = 0.10$, what are the reserve–deposit ratio, the money multiplier, and the money supply? For what real output Y does a real interest rate of 0.10 clear the asset market?
b. Repeat part (a) for $r = i = 0.05$.
c. Suppose that the reserve–deposit ratio is fixed at the value you found in part (a) and is not affected by interest rates. If $r = i = 0.05$, for what output Y does the asset market clear in this case?
d. Is the *LM* curve flatter or steeper when the reserve–deposit ratio depends on the real interest

rate than when the reserve–deposit ratio is fixed? Explain your answer in economic terms.

4. This question asks you to analyse a game played by two players, player I and player II. Player I can choose one of two actions, A and B. Player II also has two actions to choose from, a and b. Both players are affected by their own action and by the action of the other player. The points that each player assigns to each possible outcome (combination of actions) are shown in the following table.

Outcome	Points for Player I	Points for Player II
(A, a)	2	2
(A, b)	5	0
(B, a)	0	5
(B, b)	3	3

The first row indicates that, if player I chooses action A and player II chooses action a, player I gets 2 points and player II gets 2 points. The more points a player gets, the happier she is with the outcome. Players do not care about how many points the other player gets.

a. If player I moves (chooses an action) first and then player II moves, what action will each player take? (Set up a game theory diagram like Figure 15.6.) What is the outcome of the game? Does your answer change if player II moves first?

b. Suppose that player I moves first, but before player I moves, player II announces which action (a or b) she will take when it is her turn. Player II's announcement is legally binding. What is the outcome of the game now?

c. Before player I makes the first move, player II is allowed to make a threat, telling player I what action she will take on her turn if player I chooses A and what action she will take if player I chooses B. Player II's threats are legally binding. What is the outcome of the game now? Is player I made worse off or better off by player II's ability to threaten her?

Analytical Problems

1. How would each of the following affect the money supply? Explain.
   a. Banks decide to hold more excess reserves. (Excess reserves are reserves over and above what banks are legally required to hold against deposits.)

   b. People withdraw cash from their bank accounts for Christmas shopping.

   c. The central bank sells gold to the public.

   d. The central bank begins to pay interest on deposits of depository institutions held at the bank (it currently does not pay interest).

   e. The introduction of automatic teller machines, which allow people to withdraw cash from the bank as needed, makes deposits relatively more convenient.

   f. The government covers part of its fiscal deficit by selling bonds to the central bank. The proceeds of the sale are used to pay government employees.

   g. The central bank sells some of its government securities in Tokyo for yen.

2. Suppose that the central bank strictly followed a rule of keeping the real interest rate at 3% per year. That rate happens to be the real interest rate consistent with the economy's initial general equilibrium.
   a. Assume that the economy is hit only by money demand shocks. Under the central bank's rule, how will the money supply respond to money demand shocks? Will the rule make aggregate demand more stable or less stable than it would be if the money supply were constant?

   b. Assume that the economy is hit only by *IS* shocks. Under the central bank's interest rate rule, how will the money supply behave? Will the interest rate rule make aggregate demand more stable or less stable than it would be if the money supply were constant? Will the central bank be able to follow its rule in the long run?

   c. Assume that the economy is hit only by supply shocks (shocks to the *FE* line). Repeat part (b).

3. In the game between the central bank and the firms shown diagrammatically in Figure 15.7(b), what happens if the central bank does not value having the unemployment rate below the natural rate $\bar{u}$? Specifically, assume that the central bank assigns 0 points to a situation in which u equals $\bar{u}$ and assigns −1 points to a situation in which u is either above or below $\bar{u}$. How does this modification affect the outcome of the game? (Assume that if the central bank is indifferent between two actions, it chooses the one that makes the firms better off.)

4. Why do many governments have policies against negotiating with hostage-taking terrorists? Under what conditions, if any, are such policies likely to reduce hostage taking? Discuss the analogy to monetary rules.

16

GOVERNMENT SPENDING AND ITS FINANCING

At every level of government, fiscal policy – government decisions about how much to spend, what to spend for, and how to finance its spending – is of central importance. Politicians and the public understand that the government's fiscal choices have a direct impact on the 'bread and butter' issues of how much they pay in taxes and what government benefits and services they receive. Equally important are the effects of fiscal policy on the economy. In recent years people have become more aware of the macroeconomic effects of fiscal policy as the economic implications of government budget deficits, tax reform, and other aspects of fiscal policy have been extensively debated. This debate is of particular significance for EU countries as participation in the European Monetary Union and the single currency is conditional upon tight control over government spending. The electorate in a number of countries, including France and Sweden, have shown reluctance to embrace these constraints, especially when faced with rising unemployment.

This chapter takes a closer look at fiscal policy and its macroeconomic effects. To provide some background, we begin with definitions and facts about the UK government's budget. We then discuss some basic fiscal policy issues, including the effects of government spending and taxes on economic activity, the burden of government debt, and the link between budget deficits and inflation. Finally we look at some of the problems encountered as European economies prepare for monetary union and the single currency.

16.1 THE GOVERNMENT BUDGET: SOME FACTS AND FIGURES

Before getting into the analytical issues of fiscal policy, we set the stage by looking at the components of the government budget and their recent trends. We discuss three main aspects of the budget: (1) spending, or outlays; (2) tax revenues, or receipts; and (3) the budget deficit. Our discussion reviews and builds on Chapter 2, which introduced basic budget concepts.

Government Outlays

Government outlays, the total spending by the government during a period of time, are divided into three primary categories: government purchases, transfer payments, and net debt interest payments.[1]

1. *Government purchases* (G) are government spending on currently produced goods and services. Examples are spending on military hardware or road repairs and government workers' salaries.

2. *Transfer payments* (TR) are payments made to individuals for which the government does not receive *current* goods or services in exchange. Examples of transfers are social security payments, military and civil service pensions, unemployment benefits, and welfare payments (such as child allowances).

3. *Net debt interest payments* (INT) are the interest paid to the holders of government bonds less the interest received by the government – for example, on outstanding government loans to students or farmers.

In addition there is a minor category called *subsidies*. Subsidies are government payments that are intended to affect the production or prices of various goods. Examples are price support payments to farmers and fare subsidies for public transport systems. This category of outlays is relatively small, so for simplicity we ignore it in the equations later in this chapter.

In the United Kingdom total government outlays (central and local) are about 40% of GDP. Figure 16.1 shows the trends since 1930 in the three main categories of government outlay, expressed as a percentage of GDP. The most obvious feature of Figure 16.1 is the enormous increase in government purchases during World War II: in 1943 and 1944, when the war effort was at its peak, government purchases exceeded 45% of GDP. After falling to about 15% of GDP in the late 1940s, the share of GDP devoted to government consumption has risen to a little over 20% in recent years.

Figure 16.1 also shows that transfer payments rose slightly in the early 1930s during the Great Depression and then again in the years following the end of World War II in 1945. Transfer payments then rose steadily as a share of GDP from the early 1950s until the early 1980s, nearly doubling their share of GDP during that 30-year period. Transfers have increased in the 1990s and are currently about 15%–16% of GDP. The long-term increase in transfer payments is the result of the creation of new social programmes (such as family income supplement), the expansion of benefits under existing programmes (such as unemployment benefits), and the increased number of people covered by the various programmes. The rising cost of the welfare system in many European countries has led them to examine the possibility of how the system can be reformed. Such reforms may ultimately have significant effects on the level of transfer payments.

Finally, Figure 16.1 shows how net debt interest payments – interest payments, for short – have evolved. Because interest payments are much smaller

---

1. The names of the categories of government expenditure and tax receipts vary by country. For example, these three categories in the UK are: final government consumption, current grants, and debt interest. For simplicity we shall use the general terms to describe these different types of outlay.

Figure 16.1

Government purchases, transfer payments and interest payments in the UK, 1930–96

The figure shows the behavior since 1930 of the three major components of government outlays, for all levels of government and measured as a percentage of GDP. Government purchases rose most sharply during World War II (1939–1945). Transfer payments increased sharply in the immediate post-war period and have risen steadily as a share of GDP since then. Interest payments declined during the 1930s but then rose most sharply during World War II and again in the early 1980s.

Source: Data for the period 1930–65: Feinstein, *op cit. Figure 1.4*, Table 14 (current account of combined public authorities), Table 3 (GDP). Data for the period 1966–96: *European Economy 1996*, *op cit.* Table 1.1(b), Table 68 (consumption of general government), Table 67 (actual interest payments), Table 63 (current transfers paid by general government).

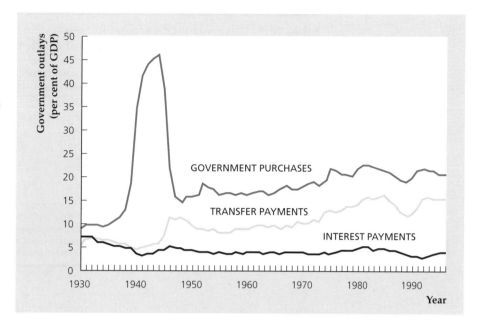

than the other two categories of government outlay, they appear to fluctuate less. However, interest payments rose sharply as a percentage of GDP in three periods. First, interest payments were very high as a percentage of GDP in the 1930s (and, for that matter, through the 1920s although this is not shown), reflecting the high levels of borrowing that had previously been undertaken by the British government to finance the war effort during World War I. High unemployment levels during the 1920s and 1930s also contributed to the government's debts. At this time, interest payments were roughly 8% of GDP. Second, interest payments rose to over 5% of GDP in 1946, again because of wartime borrowing.[2] Third, interest payments as a percentage of GDP increased to around 5% in 1980–81. This increase reflected both higher rates of borrowing, mainly as a result of the recession in the UK at that time, and the generally high level of interest rates during the early 1980s.

How does the rate of government expenditure in the United Kingdom compare with rates in Europe and in other countries with similar living standards? Because official accounting rules for measuring the government budget vary widely among countries, the answer is not as straightforward as you might think. Nevertheless, Table 16.1 compares the ratios of government spending to GDP for seven industrialized countries. Shown are ratios for both central government spending and total government spending. Both Japan and the United States have lower rates of government spending than European countries. The lower rate of government spending in the United States relative to European countries largely reflects the more extensive government-financed social welfare programmes (such as national health insurance) in those

---

2. Interestingly, during World War II, the government relied more heavily on taxation, as opposed to borrowing, to fund the war effort than had been the case during World War I. This change in policy was significantly influenced by J. M. Keynes, who was employed at the Treasury during World War II.

Table 16.1 Government Spending in Seven Industrialized Countries (% of GDP), 1994

Country	Central Government	All Government
Italy	30.7	50.6
France	19.1	51.5
Netherlands	29.1	52.0
Germany	15.4	45.4
United Kingdom	29.9	40.7
United States	17.4	34.6
Japan	13.9	26.2

Sources: *European Economy 1996; op cit. Table 1.1(b), OECD, National Accounts*, 1978–1990. All data are for 1994 except for Japan (1990) and the USA (1989). Data for the 'Central Government' in the USA, Japan, Germany, France, and the UK exclude social security payments, but these payments are included in the 'All Government' category. Data for 'Central Government' in Italy include some social security benefits.

countries. These programmes are particularly significant in Italy and France, where transfer payments now account for about one-third of GDP.

Tax Receipts

On the revenue side of the government's budget are tax receipts. There are four principal categories of tax receipt in the UK: taxes on income, taxes on expenditure, social security contributions and a number of smaller taxes such as the gross trading surplus of government-run enterprises.[3] Figure 16.2 shows the history of revenues from these four major categories of tax in the United Kingdom, all expressed as a percentage of GDP. Note that the share of taxes in GDP has risen steadily, nearly doubling from 21% of GDP in 1930 to 37% of GDP in 1996.

The largest category of tax receipts is *taxes on expenditure,* which are mainly sales taxes such as excise duties and value added tax. These increased as a share of GDP after World War II but have not shown any long-term increase or decrease since. The second largest category of tax receipts, *taxes on income,* are divided into the tax paid by persons on their income and those paid by corporations. Personal income tax represents about four-fifths of taxes on income compared with the one-fifth paid by corporations. Income tax was first introduced in Britain in 1799 to finance the Napoleonic War but was abolished in 1815 when peace was finally established. The tax was reintroduced on a permanent basis in 1842 as part of Robert Peel's economic reforms.

Taxes on income took their biggest jump during World War II, rising from 6.9% of GDP in 1939 to 18% of GDP in 1945. The slight upward drift in taxes on income tax receipts since 1945 has been interrupted by several major tax reforms, most notably the tax cuts introduced by Mrs Thatcher during the 1980s.

Figure 16.2 shows that a large share of the increase in tax receipts since World War II reflects the increase in the third category of taxes, *social security*

---

3. The two categories listed in official UK publications are: gross trading surplus, rent and royalties; and interest, dividends and miscellaneous current transfers.

Figure 16.2
UK government tax receipts by category of tax, 1930–96
Shown is the history of revenues collected from various types of taxes, for all levels of government and measured as a percentage of GDP. Total taxes increased sharply during World War II and have drifted upwards since then. Most of this increase in taxes is accounted for by increases in social security contributions and in taxes on income.

Source: Data for the period 1930–65: Feinstein, *op cit. Table 1.1(b)*, Table 14 (current account of combined public authorities), Table 3 (GDP). Data for the period 1966–96: *Public Finance Trends 96*, London, HMSO, August 1996, Table 21 (current account general government); *UK National Accounts, The Blue Book*, London, HMSO, various issues (GDP)

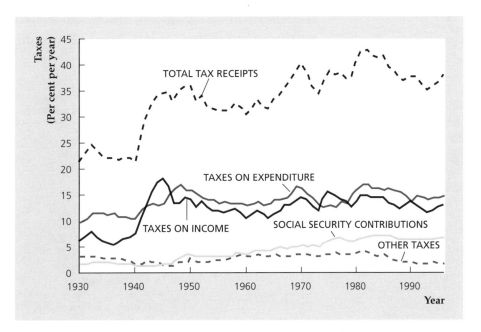

contributions. Social security contributions are usually levied as a fixed percentage of a worker's salary, up to a ceiling; income above that ceiling is not taxed. In most cases the worker's contributions are at least matched by the employer so that the deduction appearing on the worker's pay cheque reflects less than half the total tax levied. Increases in social security contributions are the result of increases in the contribution rate and higher ceilings on the amount of income subject to the tax.

The fourth category of taxes includes those on the gross trading surplus of government enterprises and a number of small tax receipts such as interest, dividends and miscellaneous current transfers. Gross trading surpluses are the profits of government-run organizations such as the Post Office. These tax receipts increased as a share of GDP after 1945, rising from less than 1% of GDP to nearly 4% in 1980. They have since fallen back to under 2% of GDP. During the 1980s, the UK, along with France and Sweden, embarked on privatization programmes under which government-run enterprises were sold into private ownership. Privatization was especially extensive in the UK, where the public utilities and rail services were among the industries that went from public to private ownership. As more government-run enterprises are privatized, this component of tax receipts as a proportion of total tax receipts will fall further.

The Composition of Outlays and Taxes: Central Government Versus Local Governments. The components of government spending shown in Figure 16.1 and the components of taxes shown in Figure 16.2 lump together central and local governments. For most purposes of macroeconomic analysis, combining central and local fiscal policy is the most sensible course. The macroeconomic effect of a new road-building programme, for example, should not depend on whether the new roads are financed from the central or local budget

Table 16.2 UK Government Outlays and Receipts, 1995

Outlays	Central — Billions of Pounds	Central — Percentage of Outlays	Local — Billions of Pounds	Local — Percentage of Outlays
Final consumption	95.83	34.9	52.81	74.2
(of which national defence)	(23.15)	(8.4)	–	–
Transfer payments	83.02	30.2	13.47	18.9
Debt interest	25.36	9.2	4.2	6.0
Subsidies	6.26	2.3	0.7	0.9
Current grants to local authorities	57.07	20.8	–	–
Current grants paid abroad	7.18	2.6	–	–
Total outlays	274.72	100	71.18	100

Receipts	Central — Billions of Pounds	Central — Percentage of Receipts	Local — Billions of Pounds	Local — Percentage of Receipts
Taxes on incomes	90.67	36.2	–	–
Taxes on expenditure	103.44	41.4	–	–
Social security contributions	44.25	17.8	–	–
Cross trading surplus	0.25	0.1	0.36	0.5
Other	11.49	4.6	7.09	9.6
Transfers from central government	–	–	57.07	77.5
Rates and council tax	–	–	9.14	12.4
Total receipts	250.11	100	73.66	100
Deficit (outlays less receipts: surplus if negative)	24.61		–2.48	
Primary deficit	–0.75		–6.68	

Source: *Public Finance Trends* (HMSO) August 1996, Table 10.31 (current account summary of receipts, central government), Table 10.33 (current account summary of expenditure, central government), Table 10.41 (current account summary of receipts, local authorities), Table 10.42 (current account summary of expenditure, local authorities).

– or from a combination of those budgets. In this respect the tendency of many news stories about fiscal policy to focus exclusively on the central government's budget can be misleading.

Nevertheless, it is useful to know that in the United Kingdom central government budgets have a much different composition, on both the expenditure and the revenue sides, from those of local governments. A summary of the major components of both the central and the local government budgets for 1995 is given in Table 16.2. Note in particular the following points:

1. *Goods and services.* By far the largest part of local outlays (about three-quarters) is for goods and services. In contrast, just over a third of central government outlays is for goods and services, and 25% of this amount is for national defence.

2. *Transfer payments.* The central government budget is more heavily weighted toward transfer payments (particularly, benefits from social security and related programmes) than local budgets are.

3. *Current grants to local authorities.* Grants to local government authorities are payments made by central government to help support education, law and order, transportation, and those welfare programmes organized by local rather than national government. They appear as an expenditure for central government and as a receipt for local government. In 1995 these grants made up nearly 80% of local government receipts, highlighting the fact that local government in the UK, unlike in some European countries and in North America, has very little revenue-raising power in its own right.

4. *Net debt interest paid.* Because of the large quantity of central government bonds outstanding, net interest payments are an important component of central government spending, accounting for nearly 10% of total expenditure in 1995. Net interest payments for local governments are smaller as a proportion of GDP, though they still take up 6% of total outlays of local government.

5. *Composition of taxes.* Over 95% of central government receipts come from taxes (on income and expenditure) and from contributions for social security. As already mentioned, local government counts as revenue the grants it receives from central government, which is its main source of receipts.

Deficits

Government outlays need not equal tax revenues in each period. In Chapter 2 we showed that, when government outlays exceed revenues, there is a government budget deficit (or simply a deficit); and when revenues exceed outlays, there is a government budget surplus. For ease of reference we write the definition of the deficit as

$$
\begin{aligned}
\text{deficit} &= \text{outlays} - \text{tax revenues} \\
&= \text{government purchases} + \text{transfers} + \text{net interest} - \text{tax revenues} \\
&= G + TR + INT - T
\end{aligned} \tag{16.1}
$$

A second deficit concept, called the **primary government budget deficit,** excludes net interest from government outlays:

$$
\begin{aligned}
\text{primary deficit} &= \text{outlays} - \text{net interest} - \text{tax revenues} \\
&= \text{government purchases} + \text{transfers} - \text{tax revenues} \\
&= G + TR - T
\end{aligned} \tag{16.2}
$$

The primary deficit is the amount by which government purchases and transfers exceed tax revenues; the primary deficit plus net interest payments equals the deficit. Figure 16.3 illustrates the relationship between the two concepts.

Why have two deficit concepts? The reason is that each answers a different question. The standard or total budget deficit answers the question: how much does the government currently have to borrow to pay for its total outlays? When measured in nominal terms, the deficit during any year is the amount of additional money that the government must borrow during that year.

The primary deficit answers the question: can the government afford its *current* programmes? If the primary deficit is zero, the government is collecting just

**Figure 16.3
The relationship between the total budget deficit and the primary deficit**
The standard measure of the total government budget deficit is the amount by which government outlays exceed tax revenues. The primary deficit is the amount by which government purchases plus transfers exceed tax revenues. The total budget deficit equals the primary deficit plus net interest payments.

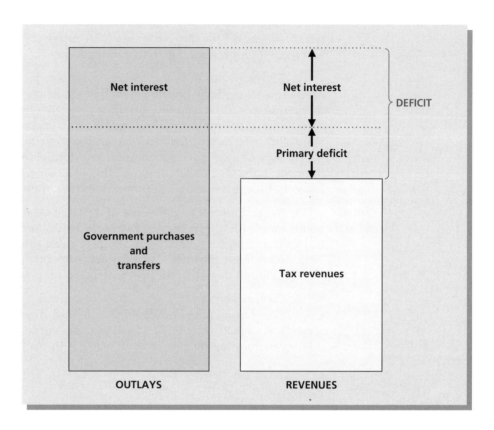

enough tax revenue to pay for its current purchases of goods and services and its current social programmes (as reflected by transfer payments). If the primary deficit is greater than zero, current government purchases and social programmes cost more than current tax revenue can pay for. Net interest payments are ignored in the primary deficit because they represent not current programme costs but costs of past expenditures financed by government borrowing.

Figure 16.4 shows the deficit and primary deficit for both levels of UK government combined as a percentage of GDP since 1930. Again, the World War II period stands out; the government financed only part of the war effort with taxes and thus ran large primary and overall deficits. Large deficits (using both concepts) also occurred in the mid 1970s, although the primary deficit for all levels of government combined was eliminated and turned into a primary surplus in 1980. By the early 1990s, a substantial primary deficit had re-emerged.

16.2   GOVERNMENT SPENDING, TAXES, AND THE MACROECONOMY

How does fiscal policy affect the performance of the macroeconomy? Economists emphasize three main ways by which government spending and taxing decisions influence macroeconomic variables such as output, employment, and prices: (1) aggregate demand, (2) government capital formation, and (3) incentives.

**Figure 16.4
Deficits and primary
deficits in the UK
1930–96**
Shown are the total
government budget
deficit and the primary
deficit, both measured as
a percentage of GDP,
since 1930. The UK
government ran large
deficits during World War
II. Deficits and primary
deficits also occurred
during the mid-1970s and
in the early 1990s. The
widening gap between
the deficit and the primary
deficit during the 1980s
reflected increased
interest payments on the
government's accumulated
debt at that time.

Source: See Figure 16.1

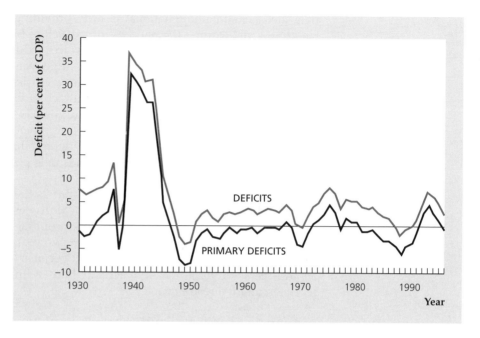

Fiscal Policy and Aggregate Demand

Fiscal policy can affect economic activity by influencing the total amount of
spending in the economy, or aggregate demand. Recall that aggregate demand
is represented by the intersection of the *IS* and *LM* curves. In either the classical or the Keynesian *IS–LM* model, an increase in government purchases
reduces desired national saving and shifts the *IS* curve up and to the right,
thereby raising aggregate demand.

Classical and Keynesian economists have different beliefs about the effect
of tax changes on aggregate demand. Classical economists usually accept the
Ricardian equivalence proposition, which says that lump-sum tax changes do
not affect desired national saving and thus have no impact on the *IS* curve or
aggregate demand.[4] Keynesians generally disagree with this conclusion; in the
Keynesian view, a cut (for example) in taxes is likely to stimulate desired consumption and reduce desired national saving, thereby shifting the *IS* curve up
and to the right and raising aggregate demand.

Classical and Keynesian economists also disagree over the question of
whether fiscal policy should be used to fight the business cycle. Classical economists generally reject attempts to smooth business cycles, by fiscal policy or
by other means. In contrast, Keynesians argue that using fiscal policy to stabilize the economy and maintain full employment – for example, by cutting
taxes and raising spending when the economy is in a recession – is desirable.

However, even Keynesians admit that the use of fiscal policy as a stabilization tool is difficult. A significant problem is *lack of flexibility*. The
government's budget has many purposes besides macroeconomic stabiliza-

---

4. We introduced Ricardian equivalence in Chapter 4. We discuss this idea further in Section 16.3.

tion, such as maintaining national security, providing income support for eligible groups, developing the nation's infrastructure (roads, bridges, and public buildings), and supplying government services (education and public health). Much of government spending is committed years in advance (as in the Eurofighter development programme) or even decades in advance (as for social security benefits). Expanding or contracting total government spending rapidly for macroeconomic stabilization purposes is therefore difficult without either spending wastefully or compromising other fiscal policy goals. Taxes are somewhat easier to change than spending, but the tax laws also have many different goals and may be the result of a fragile political compromise that is not easily altered.

Compounding the problem of inflexibility is the problem of *long time lags* that result from the slow-moving political process by which fiscal policy is made. From the time a spending or tax proposal is made until it goes into effect is rarely less than eighteen months to two years. This lag makes effective countercyclical use of fiscal policy difficult because (for example), by the time an anti-recession fiscal measure actually had an impact on the economy, the recession might already be over.

Automatic Stabilizers and the Full-Employment Deficit. One way to get around the problems of fiscal policy inflexibility and long lags that impede the use of countercyclical fiscal policies is to build automatic stabilizers into the budget. **Automatic stabilizers** are provisions in the budget that cause government spending to rise or taxes to fall automatically – without legislative action – when GDP falls. Similarly, when GDP rises, automatic stabilizers cause spending to fall or taxes to rise without any need for direct legislative action.

A good example of an automatic stabilizer is unemployment benefits. When the economy goes into a recession and unemployment rises, more people receive unemployment benefits, which are paid automatically without further action by Parliament. Thus the unemployment benefit component of transfers rises during recessions, making fiscal policy automatically more expansionary.[5]

Quantitatively, the most important automatic stabilizer is the income tax system. When the economy goes into a recession, people's incomes fall, and they pay less income tax. This 'automatic tax cut' helps cushion the drop in disposable income and (according to Keynesians) prevents aggregate demand from falling as far as it might otherwise. Likewise, when people's incomes rise during a boom, the government collects more income tax revenue, which helps restrain the increase in aggregate demand. Keynesians argue that this automatic fiscal policy is a major reason for the increased stability of the economy since World War II.

A side effect of automatic stabilizers is that government budget deficits tend to increase in recessions because government spending automatically rises and taxes automatically fall when GDP declines. Similarly, the deficit tends to fall in booms. In order to distinguish changes in the deficit caused by recessions or booms from changes caused by other factors, some economists advocate the use of a deficit measure called the full-employment deficit. The

---

5. This statement assumes that the Keynesian view is right, so that an increase in transfers – which is equivalent to a reduction in taxes – raises aggregate demand.

full-employment deficit indicates what the government budget deficit *would be* – given the tax and spending policies currently in force – if the economy were operating at its full-employment level.[6] Because it eliminates the effects of automatic stabilizers, the full-employment deficit measure is affected primarily by changes in fiscal policy reflected in new legislation. In particular, expansionary fiscal changes – such as increases in government spending programmes or (in the Keynesian model) reduced tax rates – raise the full-employment budget deficit, whereas contractionary fiscal changes reduce the full-employment deficit.

Figure 16.5 shows the actual and full-employment budget deficits (as percentages of GDP) for several European countries since 1979. Note that actual budget deficits substantially exceed the full-employment budget deficits during periods of recession, such as 1981–82 in the Netherlands and Germany, 1991–92 in the UK, and 1993 in Germany, France, Italy, and Sweden, when output was below its full-employment level. The difference between the two deficit measures reflects the importance of automatic stabilizers in the budget.

Government Capital Formation

The health of the economy depends not only on *how much* the government spends but also on *how* it spends its resources. For example, as we discussed in Chapter 6, the quantity and quality of public infrastructure – roads, schools, public hospitals, and so on – are potentially important for the rate of economic growth. Thus the formation of **government capital** – long-lived physical assets owned by the government – is one way that fiscal policy affects the macroeconomy. The government budget affects not only physical capital formation but also human capital formation. At least part of government expenditures on health, nutrition, and education are an investment, in the sense that they will lead to a more productive work force in the future.

In Europe, government budget accounting systems distinguish between current expenditures and purchases, such as the salaries of police officers or tuition fees for university students, and expenditures on capital items, such as the construction of a new hospital. When the deficit is measured on a current basis, capital spending is not included as part of government spending. The resulting measure in the UK national accounts is called the *current surplus or deficit.* One component of capital expenditure that is included in this part of the government's accounts is an allowance for capital depreciation, the amount needed to maintain the stock of public capital. This makes sense because depreciation can be thought of as current spending. In the UK, depreciation of the stock of public capital is called *non-trading capital consumption.* When both capital and current government spending are combined the resulting deficit or surplus is referred to as the *financial deficit or surplus* in the UK national account.

---

6. In practice, the calculation of full-employment deficits uses the Keynesian assumption that recessions reflect deviations from full employment rather than the classical assumption that (in the absence of misperceptions) recessions reflect changes in full-employment output.

**Figure 16.5
Full-employment and
actual budget deficits in
selected European
countries 1979–96**
The actual and full-
employment government
budget deficits are shown
for a number of European
countries as a percentage
of GDP. The actual
budget deficit exceeded
the full-employment
deficit, sometimes by
substantial amounts
during the recessions of
the early 1980s and early
1990s reflecting the
importance of automatic
stabilizers.

Source: Deficit from *European
Economy Broad Economic Policy
Guidelines* 1996, Table 76;
Full-employment deficit from
OECD Economic Outlook, June
1997, Annex Table 31.

Incentive Effects of Fiscal Policy

The third way in which fiscal policy affects the macroeconomy is by its effects
on incentives. Tax policies in particular can affect economic behaviour by
changing the financial rewards to various activities. For example, Chapter 4
showed how tax rates influence the incentives of households to save and of
firms to make capital investments.

Average Versus Marginal Tax Rates. To analyse the effects of taxes on
economic incentives, we need to distinguish between average and marginal tax
rates. The **average tax rate** is the total amount of taxes paid by a person (or a
firm), divided by the person's before-tax income. The **marginal tax rate** is the
fraction of an *additional* pound of income that must be paid in taxes. For example, suppose that in a particular country no taxes are levied on the first £10,000

of income, and a 25% tax is levied on all income above £10,000 (see Table 16.3). Under this income tax system a person with an income of £18,000 pays a tax of £2000. Thus her average tax rate is 11.1% (£2000 in taxes divided by £18,000 in before-tax income). However, this taxpayer's marginal tax rate is 25%, because a £1.00 increase in her income will increase her taxes by £0.25. Table 16.3 shows that everyone with an income higher than £10,000 faces the same marginal tax rate of 25% but that the average tax rate increases with income.

We can show why the distinction between average and marginal tax rates is important by considering the individual's decision about how much labour to supply. The effects of a tax increase on the amount of labour supplied depend strongly on whether average or marginal taxes are being increased. Economic theory predicts that an increase in the average tax rate, with the marginal tax rate held constant, will *increase* the amount of labour supplied at any (before-tax) real wage. In contrast, theory predicts that an increase in the marginal tax rate, with the average tax rate held constant will *decrease* the amount of labour supplied at any real wage.

To explain these conclusions, let us first consider the effects of a change in the average tax rate. Returning to our example from Table 16.3, imagine that the marginal tax rate stays at 25% but that now all income over £8000 (rather than all income over £10,000) is subject to a 25% tax. The taxpayer with an income of £18,000 finds that her tax bill has risen from £2000 to £2500, or 0.25(£18,000 − £8000), so her average tax rate has risen from 11.1% to 13.9%, or £2500/£18,000. As a result, the taxpayer is £500 poorer. Because she is effectively less wealthy, she will increase the amount of labour she supplies at any real wage (see Summary table 4, p. 88). Hence an increase in the average tax rate, holding the marginal tax rate fixed, shifts the labour supply curve (in a diagram with the before-tax real wage on the vertical axis) to the right.[7]

Now consider the effects of an increase in the marginal tax rate, with the average tax rate constant. Suppose that the marginal tax rate on income is raised from 25% to 40% and is accompanied by other changes in the tax law that keep the average tax rate – and thus the total amount of taxes paid by the typical taxpayer – the same. To be specific, suppose that the portion of income not subject to tax is increased from £10,000 to £13,000. Then for the taxpayer earning £18,000, total taxes are £2000, or 0.40(£18,000 − £13,000), and the average tax rate of 11.1%, or £2000/£18,000, is the same as it was under the original tax law.

---

7. In terms of the analysis of Chapter 8, the increase in the average tax rate has a pure income effect on labour supply.

Table 16.3 Marginal and Average Tax Rates: An Example (Total Tax = 25% of Income over £10,000)

Income	Income − £10,000	Tax	Average Tax Rate	Marginal Tax Rate
£ 18,000	£ 8,000	£ 2,000	11.1%	25%
50,000	40,000	10,000	20.0%	25%
100,000	90,000	22,500	22.5%	25%

With the average tax rate unchanged, the taxpayer's wealth is unaffected, and so there is no change in labour supply stemming from a change in wealth. However, the increase in the marginal tax rate implies that the taxpayer's after-tax reward for each extra hour worked declines. For example, if her wage is £10 per hour before taxes, at the original marginal tax rate of 25%, her actual take-home pay for each extra hour of work is £7.50 (£10 minus 25% of £10, or £2.50, in taxes). At the new marginal tax rate of 40% the taxpayer's take-home pay for each extra hour of work is only £6 (£10 in before-tax wages minus £4 in taxes). Because extra hours of work no longer carry as much reward in terms of real income earned, at any specific before-tax real wage the taxpayer is likely to work fewer hours and enjoy more leisure instead. Thus, if the average tax rate is held fixed, an increase in the marginal tax rate causes the labour supply curve to shift to the left.[8]

APPLICATION

Labour Supply and Tax Reform in the 1980s

During the 1980s tax reforms were introduced in the UK that dramatically reduced marginal tax rates. At the beginning of the decade the highest marginal tax rate on labour income was 83% and the basic rate of tax was 33%. By the end of the decade the highest marginal rate of tax on personal income had fallen in two stages to 40% whereas the basic rate of tax had dropped to 25%. The average tax rate in the UK is now around 13%, which is higher than that in Germany and France, where it is about 10%, but well below that faced by taxpayers in Sweden where it is over 20%.

These tax reforms were championed by a group of economists, politicians, and journalists who favoured an approach to economic policy called **supply-side economics**. The basic belief of supply-side economics is that all aspects of economic behaviour – such as labour supply, saving, and investment – respond to economic incentives and, in particular, to incentives provided by the tax code. Although most economists agree with this idea in general, 'supply-siders' went further, claiming that the incentive effects of tax policy are much larger than most economists have traditionally believed. In particular, supply-siders argued that the amount of labour supplied would increase substantially as a result of the tax reductions introduced.

What does the theory discussed in this section predict about the likely response of labour supply to these substantial tax reductions? Along with the sharp reduction in marginal tax rates, the average tax rate also fell after 1982 (see the accompanying figure). Between 1982 and 1987 taxes on income fell from 14.7% of GDP to 12.6% of GDP. The theory suggests that the reduction in marginal tax rates should have increased labour supply and that the decline in average tax rates should have reduced labour supply, leading to an ambiguous and probably small effect overall. Actually, the labour force participation rate (the proportion of adults who are working or actively searching for jobs) increased slightly after 1981, so apparently any effect that the tax cuts had on labour supply was indeed small.[9]

---

8. In terms of the discussion in Chapter 8, a change in the marginal tax rate with no change in the average tax rate has a pure substitution effect on labour supply.

9. This slight increase was, in fact, the outcome of two opposite changes: male participation rates were falling slightly but this was offset by a small increase in female activity rates.

Figure 16.6
Tax receipts and the average tax rate in the UK, 1980–96
One curve shows total UK tax receipts in billions of 1990 pounds. The other curve shows the average tax rate expressed as a percentage of GDP. Tax receipts in the UK increased steadily during the 1980s, fell dramatically during the 1990–92 recession, and then rose again. The average tax rate increased in the early 1980s but fell sharply after 1985 before rising again in the late 1980s. During the 1990s the average tax rate has then followed a similar pattern to total tax receipts, falling dramatically in the early 1990s, and then rising again after the end of the recession.

Source: *Economic Trends*, London, HMSO, various issues.

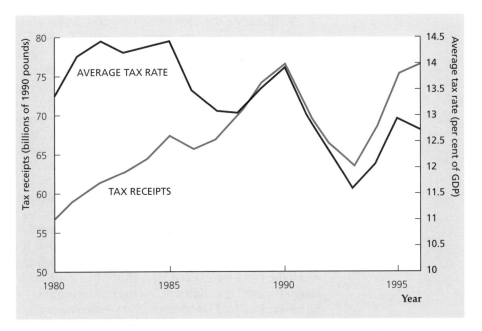

From 1987 onwards the average rate of tax in the UK increased. Because the marginal tax rate is falling and the average tax rate has increased slightly, the overall effect should have been an increase in labour supply. There is some evidence that this increase in labour supply occurred. For example, although the labour force participation rate of women had been increasing since 1950, there was a sharp rise in the labour supply of women in the late 1980s.

Overall, the responses of labour supply to the revisions to the tax law in the 1980s are consistent with our analysis of the effects of average and marginal tax changes. However, contrary to the predictions of supply-siders, the actual changes in labour supply were quite small. In particular, the impact of the tax changes on the labour supply of men and women who work full time has been found to be negligible, although the impact on the hours of work of people working part-time and on non-participants who entered the labour force is more significant. However, the overall impact on labour supply is probably less than 1%.[10]

Tax-Induced Distortions and Tax Rate Smoothing.
Because taxes affect economic incentives, they change the pattern of economic behaviour. If the invisible hand of free markets is working properly, the pattern of economic activity in the absence of taxes is the most efficient, so changes in behaviour caused by taxes reduce economic welfare. Tax-induced deviations from efficient, free-market outcome are called **distortions**.

10. See, for example, Richard Blundell, 'Taxation and labour-supply incentives in the UK', in A. B. Atkinson and G. V. Mogensen, *Welfare and Work Incentives: A North European Perspective*, (Oxford University Press) 1993.

To illustrate the idea of a distortion, let us go back to the example of the worker whose before-tax real wage is £10 per hour. Because profit-maximizing employers demand labour up to the point that the marginal product of labour equals the real wage, the real output produced by an extra hour of the worker's labour (her marginal product) also is £10. Now suppose that the worker is willing to sacrifice leisure to work an extra hour if she receives at least £7 in additional real earnings. Because the value of what the worker can produce in an extra hour of labour exceeds the value that she places on an extra hour of leisure, her working the extra hour is economically efficient.

In an economy without taxes this efficient outcome occurs, because the worker is willing to work the extra hour for the extra £10 in real wages. She would also be willing to work the extra hour if the marginal tax rate on earnings was 25%, because at a marginal tax rate of 25% her after-tax real wage is £7.50 per hour, which exceeds the £7 per hour wage that she is willing to accept. However, if the marginal tax rate rises to 40%, so that the worker's after-tax wage falls to only £6 per hour, she would decide that it is not worth her while to work the extra hour, even though for her to do so would have been economically efficient. The difference between the number of hours the worker would have worked had there been no tax on wages and the number of hours she actually works when there is a tax reflects the distorting effect of the tax. The higher the tax rate is, the greater the distortion is likely to be.

Because doing without taxes entirely is not possible, the problem for fiscal policymakers is how to raise needed government revenues while keeping distortions relatively small. Because high tax rates are particularly costly in terms of economic efficiency, economists argue that keeping tax rates roughly constant at a moderate level is preferable to alternate periods of very low and very high tax rates. For example, if the government's spending plans require it to levy a tax rate that over a number of years averages 20%, most economists would advise the government *not* to set the tax rate at 30% half the time and 10% the other half. The reason is the large distortions that the 30% tax rate would cause in the years that it was effective. A better strategy is to hold the tax rate constant at 20%. A policy of maintaining stable tax rates so as to minimize distortions is called **tax rate smoothing**.

Has the central government had a policy of tax rate smoothing? Statistical studies typically have found that tax rates are affected by political and other factors and hence are not as smooth as is necessary to minimize distortions.[11] Nevertheless, the idea of tax smoothing is still useful. For example, what explains the UK government's huge deficit during World War II (Figure 16.4)? The alternative to deficit financing of the war would have been a large wartime increase in tax rates, coupled with a drop in tax rates when the war was over. But high tax rates during the war would have distorted the economy when productive efficiency was especially important. By financing the war through borrowing, the government effectively spread the needed tax increase over a long period of time (as the debt was repaid) rather than raising current taxes by a large amount. This action is consistent with the idea of tax smoothing.

11. Lynne Evans and Michael Amex 'Seignorage and Tax Smoothing: Testing the Extended Tax-Smoothing Money' *Journal of Macroeconomics*, Winter 1996, pp. 111–25.

THE POLITICAL ENVIRONMENT

THE EUROPEAN UNION'S BUDGET

Although recent debate within the EU has focused on monetary integration and, in particular, the fiscal criteria that need to be satisfied for membership of a single currency, during the 1980s and early 1990s the issue that attracted most disagreement was the European Union's budget. In contrast to other economic unions, the EU has its own fiscal outlays and raises its own revenue over and above the expenditure and tax raising carried out by the governments of member states. Although these expenditures represent only about 1% of the combined GDP of EU member states, total outlays in 1996 still amounted to over 85 billion ECU (over £100 billion). This expenditure is financed in several ways (see below), although the largest receipts involve payments made by member states based on their GDP and on their VAT base.

Enacting the EU's budget is quite a long and complex process, involving both the executive and legislative branches of the European Union. At the start of each year the European Commission prepares a 'statement of estimates' based on the submissions of the various departments, and their spending requirements, anticipated revenue, and something called the multiannual financial perspective. The financial perspective sets out the maximum amount and composition of future expenditure. This preliminary draft will incorporate the spending priorities of the Commission of the Council of Ministers (composed of the Finance Ministers of each of the member states), and of the European

Parliament. It is then submitted by mid June, to the Council of ministers, which, after adding some amendments, will adopt it. The draft budget then goes for its first reading to the European Parliament, which proposes modifications. These are then considered by the Council, which amends the draft budget in the light of the modifications made by the European Parliament, and it is then returned to the Parliament for its second reading in November. Following the second reading, the European Parliament will adopt the budget and it will be implemented.

Although the European Parliament has significant budgetary powers and determines how much will be spent and on what, the budgetary process is a complicated one. There is a lot of 'horse trading' behind the scenes as member states seek to protect or advance the interests of particular groups within their own countries. During the 1980s much of the tension that surfaced between member states was caused by the nature of the budgetary process, which some member states argued lacked budgetary discipline, by the

concentration of expenditure on the system of agricultural support in the EU (the common agricultural policy) which created surpluses (the grain mountains and wine lakes), and by what some countries felt was an unfair system of national contributions to the EU coffers.

The table below shows the breakdown of EU expenditure and highlights the very different composition of spending compared with the pattern of expenditure of member states. In particular, spending on the *common agricultural policy* accounted for half the EU's 1996 budget, whereas spending on social security and on health care are almost completely absent. The objectives of the common agricultural policy are to increase productivity in agriculture, stabilize and set minimum standards for farmers' incomes, and ensure reasonable prices. The policy has, however, been subject to much criticism and has undergone many reforms as a result.

The second largest expenditure is on *structural, social, and regional operations*. These expenditures are used to provide support to the poorer regions of the European

	Million ECU	% of EU Budget
European agricultural guidance, guarantee section, and Guarantee Fund	41,328.0	50.5
Structural, social and regional operations	26,005.6	31.8
Research and Development	3,096.7	3.8
Other internal policies	1,684.4	2.1
External policies and European Development Fund	4,718.2	5.8
Administration	4,128.6	5.0
European Coal and Steel Community	247.0	0.3

Source: The Communitiy Budget: The Facts and Figures, office for offical publications of the EC, 1996.

THE POLITICAL ENVIRONMENT

THE EUROPEAN UNION'S BUDGET CONTINUED

Union and those areas subject to industrial decline. They also include initiatives aimed at combating unemployment. Structural, social and regional operations account for 32% of the EU's budget.

In addition to these two components of expenditure, the EU also has a number of small spending commitments including outlays on research and technological development (4% of the EU budget), on other internal policies such as those in the field of education, training, and youth (3% of the EU budget) and on various aid and other external programmes.

The EU has three sources of revenue that are used to finance its expenditure. First, there are agricultural duties which are levied on imports of agricultural products and customs duties levied on non-agricultural products coming into the EU from a non-member country. These accounted for 18% of total revenue in 1996. Second, there are VAT resources, which are contributions from member states based on their VAT base and which account for just under half of total revenue in 1996. Finally, the EU receives 33% of its revenue from member states, the amount paid by each country being determined by the level of national GDP.

One of the main areas of contention about the EU budget concerns the net contributions each member state must make.

Germany is by far the largest contributor to the budget, accounting for about 30% in 1996, followed by the UK, which contributes roughly 11%. Both these countries are also net contributors, transferring the equivalent of 0.5% of their GDP each year to the EU budget. France is also a net contributor, as is Italy in recent years. The main net beneficiaries have been Greece, Ireland, and Spain, with both Greece and Ireland receiving net payments from the EU budget equivalent to about 6% of their GDP. The net contribution of each country reflect in part the redistributive role of the EU as it seeks to achieve convergence in living standards of member states.

16.3   GOVERNMENT DEFICITS AND DEBT

The single number in any government's budget that is the focus of most public debate is the size of the budget deficit. This is especially the case following the Maastricht treaty which set strict limits on the size of the budget deficit as a pre-condition for membership of the EMU and single currency. During the 1980s and early 1990s a series of unprecedentedly large (for peacetime) deficits led to a barrage of claims and counterclaims about the potential impact of big deficits on the economy. In the rest of this chapter we discuss the government budget deficit, the government debt, and their effects on the economy.

The Growth of the Government Debt

There is an important distinction between the government budget deficit and the government debt (also called the national debt). The government budget *deficit* (a flow variable) is the difference between expenditures and tax revenues in any fiscal year. The **government debt** (a stock variable) is the total value of government bonds outstanding at any particular time. Because the excess of government expenditures over revenues equals the amount of new borrowing that the government must do – that is, the amount of new government debt that it must issue – any year's deficit equals the change in the debt in that year. We can express the relationship between government debt and the budget deficit by

$$\Delta B = \text{nominal government budget deficit} \qquad (16.3)$$

where ΔB is the change in the nominal value of government bonds outstanding.

In a period of persistently large budget deficits, such as that experienced recently by the United Kingdom, the nominal value of the government's debt will grow quickly. For example, between 1990 and 1995, government debt outstanding nearly doubled in nominal terms, from £194.5 billion in 1990 to £348.6 billion in 1995.[12] Measured in terms of 1990 pounds, the (real) value of government debt outstanding in 1995 (£290 billion) was 50% higher than in 1990.

Because countries with a high GDP have relatively more resources available to pay the principal and interest on the government's bonds, a useful measure of government indebtedness is the quantity of government debt outstanding divided by the GDP, or the *debt–GDP ratio*. Figure 16.7 shows the history of the debt–GDP ratio in the United Kingdom.

The most striking feature of Figure 16.7 is the large increase in the debt–GDP ratio that occurred during World War II when the government sold bonds to finance the war effort. By the end of the war the debt–GDP ratio exceeded 2, implying that the value of government debt outstanding was more than double a year's GDP. Since the late 1940s the UK government steadily reduced its indebtedness relative to GDP so that by 1963 the debt–GDP ratio had fallen below 100% and by 1990 it stood at just over one-third. In the early 1990s, larger budget deficits caused the debt–GDP ratio to rise, although it was still less than one-quarter of its size at the end of World War II.

12. *Public Finance Trends 96*, 1996, Table 10.27.

Figure 16.7
Ratio of government debt to GDP in the UK, 1930–96

Total UK government debt is shown as a percentage of GDP. The debt–GDP ratio rose dramatically during World War II, fell steadily for the next forty-five years, and then rose again in the early 1990s

Source: Feinstein, *op cit. Figure 1.4* (1930–65); *European Economy 1996, op cit. Table 1.1(b)*, (1966–96).

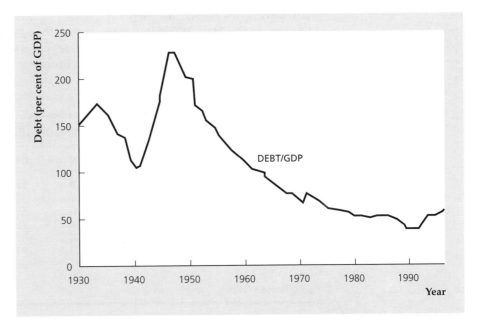

The steady decline in the debt–GDP ratio that has taken place in the UK since the late 1940s is, however, not typical of what has been happening in most other European countries. In Table 16.4 the debt–GDP ratio for a representative sample of countries is shown. Apart from the UK, all the countries shown have seen their indebtedness increase over the past 25 years or so. Indeed, only Luxembourg of all the other EU countries has recorded a fall in the debt–GDP ratio since 1970. Even Germany experienced a three-fold increase in its debt–GDP ratio between 1970 and 1996, although its debt–GDP ratio increased from a very low base of 19% of GDP in 1970 to just over 60% in 1996.

We can describe changes in the debt–GDP ratio over time by the following formula (derived in Appendix 16.A at the end of the chapter):

$$\text{growth rate of debt–GDP ratio} = \frac{\text{primary deficit}}{B} + i - \text{growth rate of nominal GDP} \qquad (16.4)$$

where B is the nominal quantity of government bonds outstanding and i is the nominal interest rate. Recall that the primary deficit is the total budget deficit less interest payments, measured here in nominal terms. Equation (16.4) emphasizes three factors that cause the debt–GDP ratio to rise quickly:

- a high primary deficit;

- a high interest rate, which increases the interest payments the government must make on its outstanding debt and thus increases the total budget deficit; and

- a slow rate of GDP growth.

Equation (16.4) helps account for the pattern of the debt–GDP ratio shown in Figure 16.7. The sharp increase during World War II was the result of large primary deficits. In contrast, for much of the post-World War II period, the government's primary deficit was negative and interest rates were generally lower than GDP growth, so the debt–GDP ratio declined. The debt–GDP ratio increased in the early 1970s and again in the 1990s because the primary deficit was relatively high and because interest rates exceeded GDP growth rates. A factor that may increase debt–GDP ratios in Europe in the not-too-distant future is discussed in Box 16.1.

Table 16.4 Ratio of Government Debt to GDP, 1970–96

	1970	1975	1980	1985	1990	1995
Germany	18.6	24.8	31.8	41.7	43.8	58.2
France	n.a.	20.5*	20.1	31.0	34.4	51.2
Italy	38.0	57.6	57.8	82.3	97.9	124.9
Netherlands	n.a.	42.4	47.6	71.5	78.8	78.1
Sweden	30.5	29.5	41.0	63.8	43.5	85.1
UK	80.3	62.7	54.3	53.8	35.3	51.5

* 1977.

Source: *European Economy 1996 op cit. Table 1.1(b).*

BOX 16.1

The Social Security Surplus and the Budget Deficit

As the generation born in the years after World War II – the 'baby boomers' – ages, the average age in the general population in most European countries will also rise. In 1990, there were about 25 Europeans over the age of 65 for every 100 people of working age (15–64 years). From 2010 to 2040, as the baby boomers retire, this ratio will have more than doubled. In the UK the old-age dependency ratio (the number of people who are of retirement age as a proportion of the working age population) is expected to peak at around 40 people for every 100 people of working age

while in Italy and Germany there will be more than 50 of retirement age for every 100 people of retirement age, and their dependency ratios will still be rising. The prospect of so many retirees raises the question: how will the social security systems of European countries be able to pay promised retirement benefits?

Traditionally, social security systems are *pay as you go*: that is, social security contributions collected from workers approximately equal current benefits paid out to retirees *in each year*. Under a pay-as-you-go system, the prospective bulge in the number of retirees in the twenty-first century will require very high taxes on future workers. Projections of net pension liabilities calculated by Paul Van den Noord and Richard Herd at the OECD[*] show that pension expen-

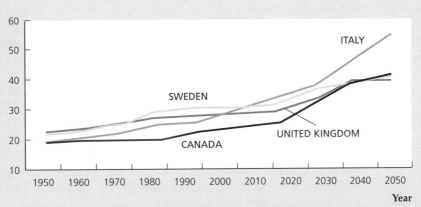

Source: World Economic Outlook, IMF, Washington D.C., May 1996, p. 54, chart 22.

BOX 16.1

diture as a proportion of GDP will rise sharply up to 2040 to over 10% of GDP in Germany and the UK, around 15% in France, and over 20% in Italy. The accompaning figure shows how the dependency ratio will increase sharply in many industrialized countries.

The United States also faces the challenge of financing the retirement of baby boomers. In order to ensure that future generations in the United States do not have to shoulder the burden of paying for the baby boomers' retirement benefits, in 1983 the US Congress changed the method of financing the social security system. Under the system now in effect, funds intended to pay retirement benefits in the twenty-first century are being accumulated in advance. Primarily by raising current Social Security taxes, the social security Amendment of 1983 provided for surpluses in the Social Security Trust Fund (the government account that keeps track of social security taxes and benefits) until several years after the turn of the twenty-first century. The planned surpluses are large: According to the Congressional Budget Office, social security taxes will exceed benefits paid out by $81 billion in fiscal year 1998.[†]

Social Security taxes collected and benefits paid in each year are both counted as part of the current US Federal government budget. Hence the prospective social security surpluses will have a large impact on the overall Federal deficit. Because of the growing social security surpluses, over the next two decades the Federal budget deficit will be significantly lower than it otherwise would have been and (according to some projections) may even become a budget surplus.

Do the large projected social security surpluses solve the problem of high Federal budget deficits? No, not really. A problem with the standard calculation of the deficit (which counts social security taxes and benefits as part of the current budget) is that it ignores the Federal government's obligation to pay social security benefits to the retiring baby boomers in the future. When the baby boomers retire, the social security system will pay benefits to retirees that far exceed the taxes collected from workers at that time. Thus the social security system itself will run large deficits during the middle third of the next century. If the social security surpluses over the next several decades are used simply to offset deficits in the rest of the Federal budget, when the time comes to pay the baby boomers' benefits, no resources will have been accumulated and a new fiscal crisis will occur.

---

[*] 'Estimating Pension Liabilities: A Methodological Framework', OCED, *Economic Outlook*, Winter 1994, pp. 131–66.

[†] *The Economic and Budget Outlook: Fiscal Years 1998–2007*, Congressional Budget Office, January 1997, Table 2–13, p. 46.

The Burden of the Government Debt on Future Generations

People often express concern that the government debt accumulated in many countries in recent years will impose a crushing financial burden on their children and grandchildren, who will someday be taxed to pay off these debts. (Box 16.2, on page 636, discusses the relative tax burdens borne by different generations.) In this view, high rates of government borrowing amount to 'robbing the future' to pay for government spending that is too high or taxes that are too low in the present.

This conventional argument ignores the fact that in most countries government bonds are owned by the countries' citizens. Therefore, although our descendants someday may face heavy taxes to pay the interest and principal of the government debt, these future taxpayers also will inherit the outstanding government bonds and thus will be the *recipients* of most of those interest and principal payments. To a substantial degree, we owe the government debt to ourselves, so the debt is not a burden in the same sense that it would be if it were owed entirely to outsiders.

Although the popular view of the burden of the government debt is faulty, economists have pointed out several ways in which the government debt can become a burden on future generations. First, if tax rates have to be raised substantially in the future to pay off the debt, the resulting distortions could cause the economy to function less efficiently and impose costs on future generations.

Second, most people hold small amounts of government bonds or no government bonds at all (except perhaps indirectly, as through pension funds). In the future people who hold few or no bonds may have to pay higher taxes to pay off the government debt than they receive in interest and principal payments; people holding large quantities of bonds may receive more in interest and principal than they pay in increased taxes. Bondholders are richer on average than non-bondholders, so the need to service the government debt might lead to a transfer of resources from the relatively poor to the relatively rich. However, this transfer could be offset by other tax and transfer policies – for example, by raising taxes on high-income people.

The third argument is probably the most significant. Many economists claim that government deficits reduce national saving: that is, when the government runs a deficit, the economy accumulates less domestic capital and fewer foreign assets than it would have if the deficit had been lower. If this argument is correct, deficits will lower the standard of living for our children and grandchildren, both because they will inherit a smaller capital stock and because they will have to pay more interest to (or receive less interest from) foreigners than they otherwise would have. This reduction in the future standard of living would constitute a true burden of the government debt.

Crucial to this argument, however, is the idea that government budget deficits reduce national saving. As we have mentioned at several points in this book (notably in Chapter 4), the question of whether budget deficits affect national saving is highly controversial. We devote most of the rest of this section to further discussion of this issue.

Budget Deficits and National Saving: Ricardian Equivalence Revisited

Under what circumstances will an increased government budget deficit cause national saving to fall? Virtually all economists agree that an increase in the deficit caused by a rise in government purchases – say, to fight a war – reduces national saving and imposes a real burden on the economy. However, whether a deficit caused by a cut in current taxes or an increase in current transfers reduces national saving is much less clear. Recall that advocates of Ricardian equivalence argue that tax cuts or increases in transfers will not affect national saving, whereas its opponents disagree.

Ricardian Equivalence: An Example. To illustrate Ricardian equivalence let's suppose that, holding its current and planned future purchases constant, the government cuts this year's taxes by £100 per person. (Assuming that the tax cut is a lump sum allows us to ignore incentive effects.) What impact will this reduction in taxes have on national saving? In answering this question, we first recall the definition of national saving (equation 2.8):

$$S = Y - C - G \qquad (16.5)$$

Equation (16.5) states that national saving S equals output Y less consumption C and government purchases G.[13] If we assume that government purchases G are constant and that output Y is fixed at its full-employment level, we know from equation (16.5) that the tax cut will reduce national saving S only if it causes consumption C to rise. Advocates of Ricardian equivalence assert that, if current and planned future government purchases are unchanged, a tax cut will *not* affect consumption and thus will not affect national saving.

Why would a tax cut that raises after-tax incomes not cause people to consume more? The answer is that – if current and planned future government purchases do not change – a tax cut today must be accompanied by an offsetting increase in expected future taxes. To see why, note that if current taxes are reduced by £100 per person without any change in government purchases, the government must borrow an additional £100 per person by selling bonds. Suppose that the bonds are one-year bonds that pay a real interest rate r. In the following year, when the government repays the principal (£100 per person) and interest (£100 × r per person) on the bonds, it will have to collect an additional £100(1 + r) per person in taxes. Thus when the public learns of the current tax cut of £100 per person, they should also expect their taxes to increase by £100(1 + r) per person next year.[14]

Because the current tax cut is balanced by an increase in expected future taxes, it does not make taxpayers any better off in the long run despite raising their current after-tax incomes. Indeed, after the tax cut, *taxpayers' abilities to consume today and in the future are the same as they were originally.*[15] That is, if no one consumes more in response to the tax cut – so that each person saves the entire £100 increase in after-tax income – in the following year the £100 per person of additional saving will grow to £100(1 + r) per person. This additional £100(1 + r) per person is precisely the amount needed to pay the extra taxes that will be levied in the future, leaving people able to consume as much in the future as they had originally planned. Because people are not made better off by the tax cut (which must be coupled with a future tax increase), they have no reason to consume more today. Thus national saving should be unaffected by the tax cut, as supporters of Ricardian equivalence claim.

Ricardian Equivalence Across Generations. The argument for Ricardian equivalence rests on the assumption that current government borrowing will be repaid within the lifetimes of people who are alive today. In other words, any tax cuts received today are offset by the higher taxes that people must pay later. But what if some of the debt the government is accumulating will be repaid not by the people who receive the tax cut but by their children or grandchildren? In that case, would people not react to a tax cut by consuming more?

Harvard economist Robert Barro[16] has shown that, in theory, Ricardian equivalence may still apply even if the current generation receives the tax cut and future generations bear the burden of repaying the government's debt. To

---

13. We assume that net factor payments from abroad, *NFP*, are zero.
14. The government might put the tax increase off for two, three, or more years. Nevertheless, the general conclusion that the current tax cut must be offset by future tax increases would be unchanged.
15. Section 8.2 discusses this point in more detail.
16. 'Are Government Bonds Net Wealth?, *Journal of Political Economy*, November/December 1974, pp. 1095–1117.

state Barro's argument in its simplest form, let us imagine an economy in which every generation has the same number of people and suppose that the current generation receives a tax cut of £100 per person. With government purchases held constant, this tax cut increases the government's borrowing and outstanding debt by £100 per person. However, people currently alive are not taxed to repay this debt; instead, this obligation is deferred until the next generation. To repay the government's increased debt, the next generation's taxes (in real terms) will be raised by £100$(1 + R)$ per person, where $1 + R$ is the real value of a pound borrowed today at the time the debt is repaid.[17]

Seemingly, the current generation of people, who receive the tax cut, should increase their consumption because the reduction in their taxes is not expected to be balanced by an increase in taxes during their lifetimes. However, Barro argued that people in the current generation should not increase their consumption in response to a tax cut if they care about the well-being of the next generation. Of course, people do care about the well-being of their children, as is reflected in part in the economic resources devoted to children, including funds spent on children's health and education, gifts, and inheritances.

How does the concern of this generation for the next affect the response of people to a tax cut? A member of the current generation who receives a tax cut – call him Joe – might be inclined to increase his own consumption, all else being equal. But, Barro argues, Joe should realize that, for each pound of tax cut he receives today, his son Stephen will have to pay $1 + R$ pounds of extra taxes in the future. Can Joe do anything on his own to help out Stephen? The answer is yes. Suppose that, instead of consuming his £100 tax cut, Joe saves the £100 and uses the extra savings to increase Stephen's inheritance. By the time the next generation is required to pay the government debt, Stephen's extra inheritance plus accumulated interest will be £100$(1 + R)$, or just enough to cover the increase in Stephen's taxes. Thus, by saving his tax cut and adding these savings to his planned bequest, Joe can keep both his own consumption and Stephen's consumption the same as they would have been if the tax cut had never occurred.

Furthermore, Barro points out, Joe *should* save all his tax cut for Stephen's benefit. Why? If Joe consumes even part of his tax cut, he will not leave enough extra inheritance to allow Stephen to pay the expected increase in his taxes, and so Stephen will have to consume less than he could have if there had been no tax cut for Joe. But if Joe wanted to increase his own consumption at Stephen's expense, he could have done so without changes in the tax laws – for example, by contributing less to Stephen's education or by planning to leave a smaller inheritance. That Joe did not take these actions shows that he was satisfied with the division of consumption between himself and Stephen that he had planned before the tax cut was enacted; there is no reason that the tax cut should cause this original consumption plan to change. Therefore if Joe and other members of the current generation do not consume more in response to a tax cut, Ricardian equivalence should hold even when debt repayment is deferred to the next generation.

---

17. For example, if the debt is to be repaid in 30 years and r is the one-year real interest rate, then $(1 + R) = (1 + r)^{30}$.

BOX 16.2

Generational Accounts

How are the costs and benefits of a government pro-gramme, such as social security, distributed among the population? We could try to answer this question by noting that in a particular year (say, 1994) social security benefits were received primarily by older people while younger people paid most of the taxes used to fund those benefits. However, to conclude that social security helps old people at the expense of young people fails to recognize that the currently retired paid social security taxes when they were young, and that the people who are paying social security taxes today will someday receive benefits. A better way to measure how the costs and benefits of social security are distributed would be to compare taxes paid and benefits received by various individuals over their *entire lifetimes*. For example, by projecting the lifetime pattern of social security taxes and bene-fits of a worker who is currently 30 years old, we could determine whether, overall, social security is a 'good deal' for that worker, whereas looking at only one year would not allow us to conclude anything about whether the worker should be satisfied to be part of the social security system.

The same lifetime perspective can be applied to all government taxes and transfers combined to see how any group of people – members of a particular genera-tion, for example – fares in terms of benefits and burdens. Alan Auerbach of the University of California at Berkeley, Jagadeesh Gokhale of the Federal Reserve Bank of Cleveland, and Laurence Kotlikoff[*] of Boston University have calculated the taxes paid and transfers received as a fraction of lifetime income for each gener-ation of Americans, starting with people born in 1900 and including projections of taxes and transfers for people who will be born in the future.

Some of their results are summarized in the accom-panying table, which shows lifetime gross tax rates, transfer rates, and net tax rates for various genera-tions. For each generation, the gross tax rate is lifetime taxes paid (Federal, state, and local) as a per-centage of lifetime income, and the transfer rate is lifetime transfers received (such as social security and Medicare) as a percentage of lifetime income. The net tax rate, or the gross tax rate minus the transfer rate, is a measure of the net burden of government borne by each generation. The net tax rate grew with each

generation until the generation born in 1980, implying that, among those alive today, older people have borne a smaller overall burden than younger people have borne or can expect to bear.

The most striking number in the table is the pro-jected 71.1% lifetime net tax rate of US citizens who are yet unborn. This figure is based on numerous pro-jections about the future of the economy and is necessarily speculative. What you should conclude from this calculation is that *without substantial changes in current fiscal policies* future generations will pay significantly higher taxes and receive fewer transfers than generations alive today. However, shifts in fiscal policy could avoid this outcome. For example, Auerbach, Gokhale, and Kotlikoff calculate that if real, per-person expenditures on Medicare, Medicaid, and several other programmes could be held at current levels, the net tax rate faced by future generations would fall to 41.3%.

---

[*] 'Generational Accounts and Lifetime Tax Rates, 1900–1991,' in Fed-eral Reserve Bank of Cleveland, *Economic Review*, First Quarter 1993, pp. 2–13.

Lifetime Tax and Transfer Rates by Generation (%)

Generation's Year of Birth	Gross Tax Rate	Transfer Rate	Net Tax Rate
1900	24.8	3.3	21.5
1910	29.8	5.2	24.7
1920	32.5	6.2	26.3
1930	35.3	7.2	28.1
1940	37.3	8.0	29.3
1950	39.9	9.3	30.6
1960	42.3	10.2	32.1
1970	44.5	11.3	33.2
1980	45.5	11.7	33.8
1990	45.7	12.2	33.6
1991	45.8	12.2	33.5
Future generations	Not available		71.1

Source: Alan Auerbach, Jagadeesh Gokhale, and Laurence Kot-likoff, 'Generational Accounts and Lifetime Tax Rates, 1900–1991,' in Federal Reserve Bank of Cleveland, *Economic Review*, First Quarter 1993, pp. 2–13, Table 5.

This analysis can be extended to allow for multiple generations and in other ways. These extensions do not change the main point, which is that, if taxpayers understand that they are ultimately responsible for the government's debt, they should not change their consumption in response to changes in taxes or transfers that are unaccompanied by changes in planned government purchases. As a result, deficits created by tax cuts should not reduce national saving and therefore should not burden future generations.

Departures from Ricardian Equivalence

The arguments for Ricardian equivalence are logically sound, and this idea has greatly influenced economists' thinking about deficits. Although 25 years ago most economists would have taken for granted that a tax cut would substantially increase consumption, today there is much less agreement about this claim. Although Ricardian equivalence seemed to fail spectacularly in the 1990s in a number of European countries including the United Kingdom and Sweden – when high government budget deficits were accompanied by extremely low rates of national saving – data covering longer periods of time suggest little relation between budget deficits and national saving rates in most European countries.[18] In some other countries, such as Canada and Israel, Ricardian equivalence seems to have worked quite well at times.[19]

Our judgment is that tax cuts that lead to increased government borrowing probably affect consumption and national saving, although the effect may be small. We base this conclusion both on the experience of a number of the European countries cited above and of the USA, and on the fact that there are some theoretical reasons to expect Ricardian equivalence not to hold exactly. The main arguments against Ricardian equivalence are the possible existence of borrowing constraints, consumers' shortsightedness, the failure of some people to leave bequests, and the non-lump-sum nature of most tax changes.

1. *Borrowing constraints.* Many people would be willing to consume more if they could find lenders who would extend them credit. However, consumers often face limits, known as *borrowing constraints*,[20] on the amounts that they can borrow. A person who wants to consume more, but who is unable to borrow to do so, will be eager to take advantage of a tax cut to increase consumption. Thus the existence of borrowing constraints may cause Ricardian equivalence to fail.

2. *Shortsightedness.* In the view of some economists, many people are shortsighted and do not understand that as taxpayers they are ultimately responsible for the government's debt. For example, some people may deter-

---

18. Paul Evans, 'Consumers are not Ricardian: Evidence from Nineteen Countries', *Economic Inquiry*, October 1993, pp. 534–8.

19. For surveys of the evidence by a supporter and an opponent of Ricardian equivalence, respectively, see Robert Barro, 'The Ricardian Approach to Budget Deficits,' *Journal of Economic Perspectives*, Spring 1989, pp. 37–54; and B. Douglas Bernheim, 'Ricardian Equivalence: An Evaluation of Theory and Evidence,' in Stanley Fischer, ed., NBER, *Macroeconomics Annual* (MIT Press, 1987).

20. Section 8.2 discussed the effect of borrowing constraints on consumption and their implications for Ricardian equivalence.

mine their consumption by simple 'rules of thumb,' such as the rule that a family should spend fixed percentages of its current after-tax income on food, clothing, housing, and so on, without regard for how its income is likely to change in the future. If people are shortsighted, they may respond to a tax cut by consuming more, contrary to the prediction of Ricardian equivalence. However, Ricardians could reply that ultra-sophisticated analyses of fiscal policy by consumers are not necessary for Ricardian equivalence to be approximately correct. For example, if people know generally that big government deficits mean future problems for the economy (without knowing exactly why), they may be reluctant to spend from a tax cut that causes the deficit to balloon, consistent with the Ricardian prediction.

3. *Failure to leave bequests.* If people do not leave bequests, perhaps because they do not care or think about the long-run economic welfare of their children, they will increase their consumption if their taxes are cut, and Ricardian equivalence will not hold. Some people may not leave bequests because they expect their children to be richer than they are and thus not need any bequest. If people continue to hold this belief after they receive a tax cut, they will increase their consumption and again Ricardian equivalence will fail.

4. *Non-lump-sum taxes.* In theory, Ricardian equivalence holds only for lump-sum tax changes, with each person's change in taxes being a fixed amount that does not depend on the person's economic decisions, such as how much to work or save. As we discussed in Section 16.2, when taxes are not lump-sum, the level and timing of taxes will affect incentives and thus economic behaviour. Thus non-lump-sum tax cuts will have real effects on the economy, in contrast to the simple Ricardian view.

We emphasize, though, that with non-lump-sum taxes, the incentive effects of a tax cut on consumption and saving behaviour will depend heavily on the tax structure and on which taxes are cut. For example, a temporary cut in sales taxes would probably stimulate consumption, but a reduction in the tax rate on interest earned on savings accounts might increase saving. Thus we cannot always conclude that, just because taxes are not lump-sum, a tax cut will increase consumption. That conclusion has to rest primarily on the other three arguments against Ricardian equivalence that we presented.

Deficits, Debt and the EMU

As we discussed in Chapter 14, the Maastricht Treaty defined various criteria which countries must satisfy if they are to participate in the European Monetary Union and the single currency. One of these criteria involves two conditions that concern the state of the government's budget deficit and the level of government indebtedness. Member states will have to ensure that their deficit–GDP ratio is not more than 3% of GDP and that their debt–GDP ratio does not exceed 60% of GDP. The 'stability pact' agreed by member states in 1997 in Amsterdam went one step further and set out a system of fines for governments which allowed their deficit–GDP ratio to go over the 3% of GDP mark after EMU is established and the Euro is introduced.

The fiscal conditions necessary for participation in the EMU are particularly stringent and have proved a major stumbling block in the progress to complete economic and monetary union. Unlike convergence in terms of the monetary criteria (see page 558 for these), meeting the fiscal conditions for membership has proved to be problematic for most countries. This is especially evident in the difficulties that have developed between France and Germany, for so long the driving force behind EMU, as well as the problems both countries have encountered in meeting the fiscal conditions themselves.

Why then has convergence in terms of the fiscal criteria proved to be so difficult? Figure 16.8 shows the deficit–GDP and debt–GDP ratios for the 15 EU member states for 1996. As the figure shows, only one country, Luxembourg, has been able to satisfy both conditions. Some countries, such as the Netherlands, the UK, Spain, Germany, Finland and France, are reasonably close to satisfying both conditions, whereas Greece and Italy are some way off.

The problem for many European countries is that to satisfy the fiscal criteria involves cutbacks in government spending and/or tax increases at a time when their unemployment rates are already high. The prospect of further fiscal restrictions proved to be unacceptable to the French electorate which, faced with unemployment at about 13%, voted Mr Lionel Jospin's Socialist Party into power in May/June 1997. Mr Jospin is committed to 'softening' the Maastricht criteria for participation in EMU and to pushing for wider responsibilities for the new European Central Bank, requiring it to give greater priority to employment and less to monetary stability than was originally proposed.

Although Mr Jospin has the support of a number of member states, including Sweden and Denmark, the French proposals for modifying the conditions for participation in a single currency have been strongly resisted by Germany's Chancellor, Helmut Kohl. Although Germany had not met the membership criteria at the time of the Amsterdam Treaty (and despite some proposed 'creative accounting' by the German government which brought it into conflict with the Bundesbank), it has remained committed to the original Maastricht conditions, which it believes are essential if monetary integration is

Figure 16.8
Deficit and debt to GDP ratios for EU countries
Government budget deficit–GDP and debt–GDP ratios are shown for EU member states. The horizontal line drawn at 3% and the vertical line drawn at 60% show the EMU membership convergence criteria for the deficit–GDP and debt–GDP ratios respectively. At the time of writing, only Luxembourg had been able to meet both criteria.

Source: *European Economy 1996 Broad Economic Policy Guidelines*, Tables 76 (Net borrowing or net lending of general government) and Table 78 (General government consolidated gross debt) both as percentages of GDP.

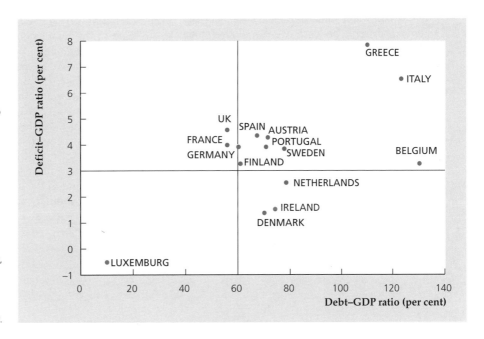

to be a success. Germany, based on its own experience with the mark, is not alone in believing that fiscal prudence is necessary if the Euro is to be a strong and stable currency and that excessive deficits would undermine this. The debate between those countries which want to see the fiscal criteria for participation 'softened' and those which believe that monetary integration can be sustained only with stringent control over government spending has led some observers to doubt that monetary union will actually take place in 1999. They suggest that the German public would be unwilling to accept a currency that is weaker than the German mark. On the other hand, political pressure in the UK, France, Sweden, and Denmark has demonstrated reluctance to join a system that does not place a high priority on combating unemployment.

BOX 16.3

The Politics of Fiscal Adjustment

We have seen that during the past 25 years there has been a significant increase in debt–GDP ratios in most European countries. Moreover, this increase has been associated with a sharp rise in the proportion of government spending accounted for by transfer payments. Much of the analysis carried out by economists tends to ignore the composition of government spending, grouping all expenditure together under one heading. A study by Alberto Alesina of Harvard University and Roberto Perotti of Columbia University[*] has considered whether these two developments are linked. The question that Alesina and Perotti consider is whether changes in the composition of government spending matter. The authors examine three issues: (1) Is there a relationship between whether a government adopts a tight or easy fiscal policy and the composition of government expenditure? (2) Does the composition of a change in fiscal policy affect whether the policy is successful? and (3) Is the composition of government expenditure affected by whether the government is socialist or conservative?

The authors find that tight fiscal policy involves increases in taxation rather than cuts in government purchases, or cuts in transfer payments. Where there are cuts in spending this will typically involve cutbacks in public investment. Easy fiscal policies, on the other hand, tend to be the result of governments increasing expenditure, especially transfer payments and government wages, leaving tax rates unaltered. They suggest that the pattern is one in which increases in government expenditure become permanent and result in subsequent tax increases as governments seek to cut or hold down deficits.

Alesina and Perotti measure the success of a fiscal policy in terms of whether or not it reduces the debt–GDP ratio. They find that the majority of successful fiscal adjustments take place as a result of changes in expenditure, whereas unsuccessful ones are associated with tax increases. Moreover, episodes of successful fiscal policy are ones in which transfers and government wages were cut. Cutbacks in public investment programmes, in contrast, have little impact on the size of the debt–GDP ratio.

Finally, the authors examine whether the composition of fiscal policy changes are affected by the political stance of the government. Recall that in the Application 'Government Elections and Macroeconomic Policy' (p. 492) evidence was reported for the political business cycle in which macroeconomic policy is related to the type of government that is power. Interestingly, Alesina and Perotti find no relationship between the type of fiscal policy and whether the government is socialist or conservative. As one might expect, conservative governments are less likely than socialist ones to adopt easy fiscal policies although, unexpectedly, they are also less likely to adopt tight fiscal policies. Both governments are equally successful in achieving lower debt–GDP ratios. The least successful governments are those coalition governments and those on the centre of the political spectrum. Minority governments, whether socialist or conservative, achieve the most success with fiscal policy in reducing the debt–GDP ratio.

_____

[*] 'Fiscal Expansions and Adjustments in OCED countries' *Economic Policy*, October 1995, pp. 207–48.

16.4 DEFICITS AND INFLATION

In this final section of the chapter we discuss one more concern that has been expressed about government budget deficits: that deficits are inflationary. We show that the principal link between deficits and inflation is that in some circumstances deficits lead to higher rates of growth in the money supply and that high rates of money growth in turn cause inflation.

The Deficit and the Money Supply

Inflation – a rising price level – results when aggregate demand increases more quickly than aggregate supply. In terms of the *AD–AS* framework, suppose that the long-run aggregate supply curve (which reflects the productive capacity of the economy) is fixed. Then for the price level to rise, the aggregate demand curve must rise over time.

Both the classical and Keynesian models of the economy imply that deficits can cause aggregate demand to rise more quickly than aggregate supply, leading to an increase in the price level. In both models a deficit owing to increased government purchases reduces desired national saving, shifting the *IS* curve upwards and causing aggregate demand to rise. This increase in aggregate demand causes the price level to rise.[21] If we assume (as Keynesians usually do) that Ricardian equivalence does not hold, a budget deficit resulting from a cut in taxes or an increase in transfers also reduces desired national saving, increases aggregate demand, and raises the price level. Thus deficits resulting from expansionary fiscal policies (increased spending or reduced taxes) will be associated with inflation.

However, an increase in government purchases or a cut in taxes causes only a one-off increase in aggregate demand. Therefore, although we expect expansionary fiscal policies to lead to a one-off increase in the price level (that is, a temporary burst in inflation), we do not expect an increase in government purchases or a cut in taxes to cause a *sustained* increase in inflation. In general, the only factor that can sustain an increase in aggregate demand, leading to continuing inflation, is sustained growth in the money supply. Indeed, high rates of inflation are almost invariably linked to high rates of national money growth (Chapter 7). The key question therefore is: can government budget deficits lead to ongoing increases in the money supply?

The answer is yes. The link is the printing of money to finance government spending when the government cannot (or does not want to) finance all of its spending by taxes or borrowing from the public. In the extreme case, imagine a government that wants to spend £100 million (say, on submarines) but has no ability to tax or borrow from the public. One option is for this government to print £100 million worth of currency and use this currency to pay for the submarines. The revenue that a government raises by printing money is called **seignorage**. Any government with the authority to issue money can use seignorage; governments that do not have the authority to issue money, such as local governments in most European countries, cannot use seignorage.

---

21. The classical analysis predicts that an increase in government purchases causes aggregate supply to rise too, but we have assumed that the supply effect is smaller than the demand effect.

Actually, governments that want to finance their deficits through seignorage do not simply print new currency but use an indirect procedure. First, the Treasury authorizes government borrowing equal to the amount of the budget deficit (£100 million in our example), and a corresponding quantity of new government bonds are printed and sold. Thus the deficit still equals the change in the outstanding government debt (equation 16.3). However, the new government bonds are not sold to the public. Instead, the Treasury asks (or requires) the central bank to purchase the £100 million in new bonds. The central bank pays for its purchases of new bonds by printing £100 million in new currency,[22] which it gives to the Treasury in exchange for the bonds. This newly issued currency enters general circulation when the government spends it on its various outlays (the submarines). Note that the purchase of bonds by the central bank increases the monetary base by the amount of the purchase (see Chapter 15), as when the central bank purchases government bonds on the open market.

The precise relationship between the size of the deficit and the increase in the monetary base is

$$\text{deficit} = \Delta B = \Delta B^p + \Delta B^{cb} = \Delta B^p + \Delta BASE \tag{16.6}$$

Equation (16.6) states that the (nominal) government budget deficit equals the total increase in (nominal) government debt outstanding, ΔB, which can be broken into additional government debt held by the public, ΔB^p, and by the central bank, ΔB^{cb}. The increase in government debt held by the central bank in turn equals the increase in the monetary base, $\Delta BASE$. The increase in the monetary base equals the amount of seignorage collected by the government.

The final link between the budget deficit and the money supply has to do with the relationship between the money supply and the monetary base. In general, the increase in the money supply M equals the money multiplier times the increase in the monetary base (equation 15.8). In an all-currency economy the money supply and the monetary base are the same and the money multiplier is 1. Nothing significant in this discussion depends on the value of the money multiplier, so for simplicity we focus on an all-currency economy, in which the change in the money supply equals the change in the monetary base. Based on this assumption, equation (16.6) implies that

$$\text{deficit} = \Delta B = \Delta B^p + \Delta B^{cb} = \Delta B^p + \Delta M \tag{16.7}$$

where $\Delta BASE = \Delta M$.

Why would governments use seignorage to finance their deficits, knowing that continued money creation ultimately leads to higher inflation? Under normal conditions developed countries rarely use substantial amounts of seignorage. For example, in recent years the monetary base in the United Kingdom has typically increased about £1 billion per year, which is 4.5% of the government budget deficit and about 0.4% of government outlays. Heavy reliance on seignorage usually occurs in war-torn or developing countries, in which military or social conditions dictate levels of government spending well above what the country can raise in taxes or borrow from the public.

---

22. The new money created by the central bank could also be in the form of deposits at the central bank; the ultimate effect is the same.

Real Seignorage Revenue and Inflation

The amount of real revenue that the government collects from seignorage is closely related to the inflation rate. To examine this link let's consider an all-currency economy in which real output and the real interest rate are fixed and the rates of money growth and inflation are constant. In such an economy the real quantity of money demanded is constant[23] and hence, in equilibrium, the real money supply must also be constant. Because the real money supply M/P does not change, the growth rate of the nominal money supply $\Delta M/M$ must equal the growth rate of the price level, or the rate of inflation π:

$$\pi = \frac{\Delta M}{M} \tag{16.8}$$

Equation (16.8) expresses the close link between an economy's inflation rate and money growth rate.

How much seignorage is the government collecting in this economy? The *nominal* value of seignorage in any period is the increase in the amount of money in circulation ΔM. Multiplying both sides of equation (16.8) by M and rearranging gives an equation for the nominal value of seignorage:

$$\Delta M = \pi M \tag{16.9}$$

Real seignorage revenue, R, is the real value of the newly created money, which equals nominal seignorage revenue ΔM divided by the price level P. Dividing both sides of equation (16.9) by the price level P gives

$$R = \frac{\Delta M}{P} = \pi \frac{M}{P} \tag{16.10}$$

Equation (16.10) states that the government's real seignorage revenue R equals the inflation rate π times the real money supply M/P.

Equation (16.10) illustrates why economists sometimes call seignorage the **inflation tax**. In general, for any type of tax, tax revenue equals the tax rate multiplied by the tax base (whatever is being taxed). In the case of the inflation tax the tax base is the real money supply and the tax rate is the rate of inflation. Multiplying the tax base (the real money supply) by the tax rate (the rate of inflation) gives the total inflation tax revenue.

How does the government collect the inflation tax and who pays this tax? The government collects the inflation tax by printing money (or by having the central bank issue new money) and using the newly created money to purchase goods and services. The inflation tax is paid by any member of the public who holds money, because inflation erodes the purchasing power of money. For example, when the inflation rate is 10% per year, a person who holds currency for a year loses 10% of the purchasing power of that money and thus effectively pays a 10% tax on the real money holdings.

---

23. Real money demand depends on real output and the nominal interest rate (we assume that the interest rate paid on money is fixed). Output is constant, and because the real interest rate and the inflation rate are constant, the nominal interest rate also is constant. Thus the real quantity of money demanded is constant.

Suppose that a government finds that the seignorage being collected does not cover its spending and begins to increase the money supply faster. Will this increase in the money growth rate cause the real seignorage collected by the government to rise? Somewhat surprisingly, it may not. As equation (16.10) shows, the real seignorage collected by the government is the product of two terms – the rate of inflation (the tax rate) and the real money supply (the tax base). By raising the money growth rate, the government can increase the inflation rate. However, at a constant real interest rate, a higher rate of inflation will raise the nominal interest rate, causing people to reduce the real quantity of money held. Thus whether real seignorage revenue increases when the money growth rate increases depends on whether the rise in inflation π outweighs the decline in real money holdings M/P.

This point is illustrated by Figure 16.9, which shows the determination of real seignorage revenue at an assumed constant real interest rate of 3%. The real quantity of money is measured along the horizontal axes, and the nominal interest rate is measured along the vertical axes. The downward-sloping MD curves show the real demand for money; they slope downward because an increase in the nominal interest rate reduces the real quantity of money demanded.

In Figure 16.9(a) the actual and expected rate of inflation is 8%, so that (for a real interest rate of 3%) the nominal interest rate is 11%. When the nominal interest rate is 11%, the real quantity of money that people are willing to hold is £150 million (point H). Using equation (16.10), we find that the real value of seignorage revenue is 0.08 (£150 million), or £12 million. Real seignorage revenue is represented graphically by the area of the shaded rectangle. The rectangle's height equals the inflation rate (8%) and the rectangle's width equals the real quantity of money held by the public (£150 million).

Figure 16.9(b) shows the real amount of seignorage revenue at two different inflation rates. The real interest rate (3%) and the money demand curve in Figure 16.9(b) are identical to those in Figure 16.9(a). When the rate of inflation is 1% per year, the nominal interest rate is 4%, and the real quantity of money that the public holds is £400 billion. Real seignorage revenue is 0.01 (£400 million) = £4 million, or the area of rectangle $ABCD$. Alternatively, when the rate of inflation is 15% per year, the nominal interest rate is 18%, and the real value of the public's money holdings is £50 million. Real seignorage revenue in this case is £7.5 million, or the area of rectangle $AEFG$.

Comparing Figure 16.9(a) and Figure 16.9(b) reveals that real seignorage revenue is higher when inflation is 8% per year than when inflation is either 1% per year or 15% per year. Figure 16.10 shows the relationship between the inflation rate and seignorage revenue. At low inflation rates an increase in the inflation rate increases real seignorage revenue. However, at high inflation rates an increase in inflation reduces real seignorage revenue. In Figure 16.10 the maximum possible real seignorage revenue is £12 million, which is achieved at the intermediate level of inflation of 8% per year.

Figure 16.9
The determination of real seignorage revenue
(a) The downward-sloping curve *MD* is the money demand function for a given level of real income. The real interest rate is assumed to be 3%. When the rate of inflation is 8%, the nominal interest rate is 11%, and the real quantity of money held by the public is £150 million (point *H*). Real seignorage revenue collected by the government, represented by the area of the shaded rectangle, equals the rate of inflation (8%) times the real money stock (£150 million), or £12 million.
(b) The money demand function *MD* is the same as in (a), and the real interest rate remains at 3%. When the inflation rate is 1%, the nominal interest rate is 4%, and the real quantity of money held by the public is £400 million. In this case real seignorage revenue equals the area of the rectangle, *ABCD*, or £4 million. When the rate of inflation is 15%, the nominal interest rate is 18%, and the real money stock held by the public is £50 million. Real seignorage revenue in this case equals the area of the rectangle *AEFG*, or £7.5 million.

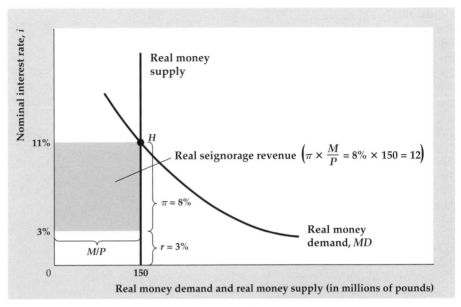

(a) Determination of real seignorage revenue for $\pi = 8\%$

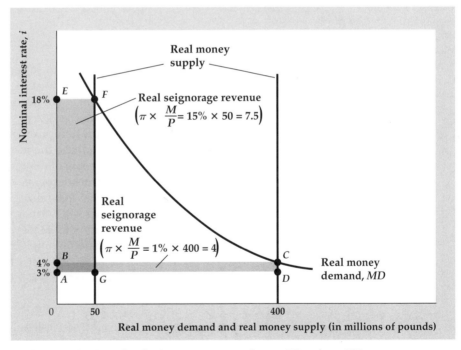

(b) Determination of real seignorage revenue for $\pi = 1\%$ and $\pi = 15\%$

Figure 16.10
The relation of real seignorage revenue to the rate of inflation
Continuing the example of Figure 16.9, this figure shows the relation of real seignorage revenue *R*, measured on the vertical axis, to the rate of inflation π, measured on the horizontal axis. From Figure 16.9(a), when inflation is 8% per year, real seignorage revenue is £12 million. From Figure 16.9(b), real seignorage is £4 million when inflation is 1% and £7.5 million when inflation is 15%. At low rates of inflation, an increase in inflation increases seignorage revenue. At high rates of inflation, increased inflation can cause seignorage revenue to fall. In this example the maximum amount of seignorage revenue the government can obtain is £12 million, which occurs when the inflation rate is 8%.

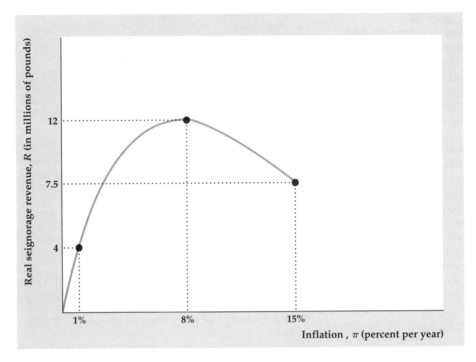

What happens if the government tries to raise more seignorage revenue than the maximum possible amount? If it does so, inflation will rise but the real value of the government's seignorage will fall as real money holdings fall. If the government continues to increase the rate of money creation, the economy will experience a high rate of inflation or even hyperinflation. Inflation will continue until the government reduces the rate of money creation either by balancing its budget or by finding some other way to finance its spending.

In some hyperinflations, governments desperate for revenue raise the rate of money creation well above the level that maximizes real seignorage. For example, in the extreme hyperinflation that hit Germany after World War I, rapid money creation drove the rate of inflation to 322% *per month*. In contrast, in his classic study of the German hyperinflation, Philip Cagan[24] of Columbia University calculated that the constant rate of inflation that would have maximized the German government's real seignorage revenue was 'only' 20% per month.

24. 'Monetary Dynamics of Hyperinflation', in Milton Friedman, ed., *Studies in the Quality Theory of Money* (University of Chicago Press, 1956).

CHAPTER SUMMARY

1. Government outlays are government purchases of goods and services, transfers, and net interest. To pay for them, the government collects revenue by four main types of tax: taxes on income, taxes on expenditure, social security contributions and a number of smaller taxes.

2. The government budget deficit equals government outlays minus tax revenues and indicates how much the government must borrow during the year. The primary government budget deficit is the total deficit less net interest payments. The primary deficit indicates by how much the cost of current programmes (measured by current government purchases and transfers) exceeds tax revenues during the year.

3. Fiscal policy affects the economy through its effects on aggregate demand, government capital formation, and incentives.

4. Increases or decreases in government purchases affect aggregate demand by changing desired national saving and shifting the *IS* curve. If Ricardian equivalence does not hold, as Keynesians usually argue, changes in taxes also affect desired national saving, the *IS* curve, and aggregate demand. Automatic stabilizers in the government's budget allow spending to rise or taxes to fall automatically in a recession, which helps cushion the drop in aggregate demand during a recession. The full-employment deficit is what the deficit would be – given current government spending programmes and tax laws – if the economy were at full employment. Because of automatic stabilizers that increase spending and reduce taxes in recessions, the actual deficit rises above the full-employment deficit in recessions.

5. Government capital formation contributes to the productive capacity of the economy. Government capital formation includes both investment in physical capital (roads, schools) and investment in human capital (education, child nutrition).

6. The average tax rate is the fraction of total income paid in taxes, and the marginal tax rate is the fraction of an additional unit of income that must be paid in taxes. Changes in average tax rates and changes in marginal tax rates have different effects on economic behaviour. For example, an increase in the average tax rate (with no change in the marginal tax rate) increases labour supply, but an increase in the marginal tax rate (with no change in the average tax rate) decreases labour supply.

7. Policymakers must be concerned about the fact that taxes induce distortions, or deviations in economic behaviour from that which would have occurred in the absence of taxes. One strategy for minimizing distortions is to hold tax rates approximately constant over time (tax rate smoothing), rather than alternating between high and low tax rates.

8. The national debt equals the value of government bonds outstanding. The government budget deficit, expressed in nominal terms, equals the change in the government debt. The behaviour of the debt–GDP ratio over time depends on the ratio of the primary deficit to outstanding government debt and on whether the interest rate is greater or less than the GDP growth rate.

9. Deficits are a burden on future generations if they cause national saving to fall because lower national saving means that the country will have less capital and fewer foreign assets than it would have had otherwise. Ricardian equivalence indicates that a deficit caused by a tax cut will not affect consumption and therefore will not affect national saving. In the Ricardian view, a tax cut does not affect consumption because the increase in consumers' current income arising from the tax cut is offset by the prospect of increased taxes in the future, leaving consumers no better off. In theory, Ricardian equivalence still holds if the government debt is not repaid by the current generation, provided that people care about the well-being of their descendants and thus choose not to consume more at their descendants' expense.

10. Ricardian equivalence may not hold – and thus tax cuts may affect national saving – if (1) borrowing constraints prevent some people from

consuming as much as they want; (2) people are short-sighted and do not take expected future changes in taxes into account in their planning; (3) people fail to leave bequests; or (4) tax cuts are not lump-sum. The empirical evidence on Ricardian equivalence is mixed.

11. Deficits are linked to inflation when a government finances its deficits by printing money. The amount of revenue that the government raises by printing money is called seignorage. The real value of seignorage equals the inflation rate times the real money supply. Increasing the inflation rate does not always increase the government's real seignorage because higher inflation causes the public to hold a smaller real quantity of money. Attempts to push the collection of seignorage above its maximum can lead to hyperinflation.

Key Terms

automatic stabilizers, p. 620
average tax rate, p. 622
distortions, p. 625
full-employment deficit, p. 621
government capital, p. 621
government debt, p. 628
inflation tax, p. 643
marginal tax rate, p. 622
primary government budget deficit, p. 617
seignorage, p. 641
supply-side economics, p. 624
tax rate smoothing, p. 626

Key Equations

$$\Delta B = \text{nominal government budget deficit} \quad (16.3)$$

The change in the nominal value of the government debt equals the nominal government deficit.

$$\text{growth rate of debt–GDP ratio} =$$
$$\frac{\text{primary deficit}}{B} + i - \text{growth rate of nominal GDP}$$
$$(16.4)$$

The growth rate of the ratio of government debt outstanding to GDP depends on the ratio of the primary

deficit to outstanding government debt, B, and on the difference between the nominal interest rate, i, and the growth rate of nominal GDP.

$$\text{deficit} = \Delta B = \Delta B^p + \Delta B^{cb} = \Delta B^p + \Delta M \quad (16.7)$$

The government budget deficit equals the increase in the stock of government debt outstanding, B, which in turn equals the sum of additional holdings of government debt by the public, B^p, and by the central bank, B^{cb}. The increase in debt held by the central bank equals the increase in the monetary base, which in an all-currency economy is the same as the increase in the money supply, M.

$$R = \frac{\Delta M}{P} = \pi \frac{M}{P} \quad (16.10)$$

In an all-currency economy, real seignorage revenue, R, equals the increase in the money supply, ΔM, divided by the price level, P. This ratio in turn equals the inflation rate (the tax rate on money) multiplied by the real money supply (the tax base).

Review Questions

1. What are the major components of government outlays? What are the major sources of government revenues? How does the composition of central government's outlays and revenues differ from that of local governments?
2. Explain the difference between the overall government budget deficit and the primary deficit. Why are two deficit concepts needed?
3. How is government debt related to the government deficit? What factors contribute to a high growth rate of the debt–GDP ratio?
4. What are the three main ways that fiscal policy affects the macroeconomy? Explain briefly how each channel of policy works.
5. Define *automatic stabilizer* and give an example. For proponents of anti-recessionary fiscal policies, what advantage do automatic stabilizers have over other types of taxing and spending policy?
6. Give a numerical example that shows the difference between the average tax rate and the marginal tax rate on a person's income. For a constant before-tax real wage, which type of tax rate most directly affects how wealthy a person feels? Which type of tax rate affects the reward for working an extra hour?

7. Why do economists suggest that tax rates be kept roughly constant over time, rather than alternating between high and low levels?

8. In what ways is the government debt a potential burden on future generations? What is the relationship between Ricardian equivalence and the idea that government debt is a burden?

9. Discuss four reasons why the Ricardian equivalence proposition is not likely to hold exactly.

10. Define *inflation tax* (also called *seignorage*). How does the government collect this tax, and who pays it? Can the government always increase its real revenues from the inflation tax by increasing money growth and inflation?

Numerical Problems

1. The following budget data are for a country having both a central government and provincial governments:

Central purchases of goods and services	200
Provincial purchases of goods and services	150
Central transfer payments	100
Provincial transfer payments	50
Grants in aid (central to provincial)	100
Central tax receipts	450
Provincial tax receipts	100
Interest received from private sector by central government	10
Interest received from private sector by provincial governments	10
Total central government debt	1000
Total provincial government debt	0
Central government debt held by provincial governments	200
Nominal interest rate	10%

Calculate the overall and primary deficits for the central government, the provincial governments, and the combined governments.

2. Parliament votes a special one-time £10 million transfer to bail out the gas light industry. Tax collections do not change, and no change is planned for at least several years. By how much will this action increase the overall budget deficit and the primary deficit in the year that the transfer is made? In the next year? In the year after that? Assume that the nominal interest rate is constant at 10%.

3. Because of automatic stabilizers, various components of the government's budget depend on the level of output Y. The following are the main components of that budget:

Tax revenues	$1000 + 0.1Y$
Transfers	$800 - 0.05Y$
Government purchases	1800
Interest payments	100

Full-employment output is 10,000. Find the actual budget deficit and the full-employment budget deficit for

a. $Y = 12,000$. **b.** $Y = 10,000$. **c.** $Y = 8000$.

In general, how does the relationship between the actual deficit and the full-employment deficit depend on the state of the economy?

4. Suppose that the income tax law exempts income under £8000 from the tax, taxes income between £8000 and £20,000 at a 25% rate, and taxes income greater than £20,000 at a 30% rate.

a. Find the average tax rate and the marginal tax rate for someone earning £16,000 and for someone earning £30,000.

b. The tax law is changed so that income of less than £6000 is untaxed, income from £6000 to £20,000 is taxed at 20%, and income of more than £20,000 continues to be taxed at 30%. Repeat part (a).

c. How will the tax law change in part (b) affect the labour supply of the person initially making £16,000? How will it affect the labour supply of the person making £30,000?

5. Suppose that all workers value their leisure at 90 goods per day. The production function relating output per day Y to the number of people working per day N is

$$Y = 250N - 0.5N^2$$

Corresponding to this production function, the marginal product of labour is

$$MPN = 250 - N$$

a. Assume that there are no taxes. What are the equilibrium values of the real wage, employment N, and output Y? (*Hint:* In equilibrium the real wage will equal both the marginal product of labour and the value of a day's leisure to workers.)

b. A 25% tax is levied on wages. What are the equilibrium values of the real wage, employment, and output? In terms of lost output, what is the distortion cost of this tax?

c. Suppose that the tax on wages rises to 50%. What are the equilibrium values of the real wage, employment, and output? In terms of lost output, what is the distortion cost of this higher tax rate? Compare the distortion caused by a 50% tax rate with that caused by a 25% tax rate. Is the distortion caused by a 50% tax rate twice as large, more than twice as large, or less than twice as large as that caused by a 25% tax rate? How does your answer relate to the idea of tax smoothing?

6. Find the largest nominal primary deficit that the government can run without raising the debt–GDP ratio, under each of the following sets of assumptions:

   a. Nominal GDP growth is 10%, the nominal interest rate is 12%, and outstanding nominal debt is 1000.

   b. Nominal interest payments are 800, outstanding nominal debt is 10,000, inflation is 6%, and the economy has zero real growth.

7. In this problem you are asked to analyse the question: By issuing new bonds and using the proceeds to pay the interest on its old bonds, can government avoid ever repaying its debts?

   a. Suppose that nominal GDP is £1 billion and the government has £100 million of bonds outstanding. The bonds are one-year bonds that pay a 7% nominal interest rate. The growth rate of nominal GDP is 5% per year. Beginning now the government runs a zero primary deficit for ever and pays interest on its existing debt by issuing new bonds. What is the current debt–GDP ratio? What will this ratio be after 1, 2, 5, and 10 years? Suppose that, if the debt–GDP ratio exceeds 10, the public refuses to buy additional government bonds. Will the debt–GDP ratio ever reach that level? Will the government someday have to run a primary surplus in order to repay its debts, or can it avoid repayment for ever? Why?

   b. Repeat part (a) for nominal GDP growth of 8% per year and a nominal interest rate on government bonds of 7% per year.

8. Real money demand in an economy is

$$L = 0.2Y - 500i$$

where Y is real income and i is the nominal interest rate. In equilibrium real money demand L equals real money supply M/P. Suppose that Y is 1000 and the real interest rate r is 0.04.

   a. Draw a graph with real seignorage revenue on the vertical axis and inflation on the horizontal axis. Show the values of seignorage for inflation of 0, 0.02, 0.04, 0.06,..., 0.30.

   b. What inflation rate maximizes seignorage?

   c. What is the maximum amount of seignorage revenue?

   d. Repeat parts (a)–(c) for $Y = 1000$ and $r = 0.08$.

9. Consider an economy in which the money supply consists of both currency and deposits. The growth rate of the monetary base, the growth rate of the money supply, inflation, and expected inflation are all constant at 10% per year. Output and the real interest rate are constant. Monetary data for this economy as of 1 January 1994, are as follows.

Currency in circulation	£200
Bank reserves	£50
Monetary base	£250
Deposits	£600
Money supply	£800

   a. What is the nominal value of seignorage over the year? (*Hint:* How much monetary base is created during the year?)

   b. Suppose that deposits and bank reserves pay no interest, and that banks lend deposits not held as reserves at the market rate of interest. Who pays the inflation tax (measured in nominal terms), and how much do they pay? (*Hint:* The inflation tax paid by banks in this example is negative.)

   c. Suppose that deposits pay a market rate of interest. Who pays the inflation tax, and how much do they pay?

Analytical Problems

1. Why is some local spending paid for by grants in aid from the central government, instead of having every locality pay for its own spending by levying taxes on its residents? What are the advantages and disadvantages of a system of grants in aid?

2. Using the *European Economy* compare Finland's government budget in 1979, 1986, and 1992. Express the main components of government spending and receipts in each year as fractions of GDP. Has the increased deficit in 1992 been more the result of increased spending or reductions in revenues?

3. Both transfer programmes and taxes affect incentives. Consider a programme designed to help the poor that promises each aid recipient a minimum income of £7,500. That is, if the recipient earns less than £7,500, the programme supplements his income by enough to bring him up to £7,500.

   Explain why this programme would adversely

affect incentives for low-wage recipients. (*Hint:* Show that this programme is equivalent to giving the recipient £7,500, then taxing his labour income at a high marginal rate.) Describe a transfer programme that contains better incentives. Would that programme have any disadvantages? If so, what would they be?

4. **a**. Show that equation (16.4), which describes how the debt–GDP ratio evolves, still holds if the primary budget deficit, the outstanding stock of government bonds, the interest rate, and the growth rate of GDP are all expressed in real rather than nominal terms. (*Hint:* Use the growth-rate formulas in Appendix A, Section A.7, to show that the growth rate of nominal GDP equals the growth rate of real GDP plus the inflation rate.)

b. Show that, if the primary deficit is zero, the real stock of outstanding government debt grows at a rate equal to the real interest rate. (*Hint:* In this case, the government budget deficit is iB, its nominal interest payments.)

Appendix 16.A   THE DEBT–GDP RATIO

In this appendix we derive equation (16.4), which shows how the debt–GDP ratio evolves. If we let Q represent the ratio of government debt to GDP, by definition

$$Q = \frac{B}{PY} \tag{16.A.1}$$

where B is the nominal value of government bonds outstanding (government debt), P is the price level, and Y is real GDP (so that PY is nominal GDP). A useful rule is that the percentage change in any ratio equals the percentage change in the numerator minus the percentage change in the denominator (Appendix A, Section A.7). Applying this rule to equation (16.A.1) gives

$$\frac{\Delta Q}{Q} = \frac{\Delta B}{B} - \frac{\Delta(PY)}{PY} \tag{16.A.2}$$

The increase in the nominal value of government bonds ΔB equals the nominal value of the government budget deficit (equation 16.3). The budget deficit equals the nominal value of the primary deficit plus interest payments on the government debt so that

$$\Delta B = PD^P + iB \tag{16.A.3}$$

where D^P is the real value of the primary deficit, PD^P is the nominal value of the primary deficit, i is the nominal interest rate, and iB is the nominal value of interest payments on the government debt. Using equation (16.A.3) to substitute for ΔB on the right-hand side of equation (16.A.2), we obtain

$$\frac{\Delta Q}{Q} = \frac{PD^P}{B} + i - \frac{\Delta(PY)}{PY} \tag{16.A.4}$$

As PD^P/B is the ratio of the primary deficit to the government debt and $\Delta(PY)/PY$ is the growth rate of nominal GDP, equation (16.A.4) is equivalent to equation (16.4).

SOME USEFUL ANALYTICAL TOOLS

This appendix reviews some basic algebraic and graphical tools that are used in this book.

A.1 FUNCTIONS AND GRAPHS

A function is a relationship among two or more variables. For an economic illustration of a function, suppose that in a certain firm each worker employed can produce five units of output per day. Let

N = the number of workers employed by the firm;
Y = total daily output of the firm.

In this example, the relationship of output Y to the number of workers N is:

$$Y = 5N \qquad (A.1)$$

Equation (A.1) is an example of a function relating the variable Y to the variable N. Using this function, for any number of workers N we can calculate the total amount of output Y that the firm can produce each day. For example, if $N = 3$, then $Y = 15$.

Functions can be described graphically as well as algebraically. The graph of the function $Y = 5N$, for values of N between 0 and 16, is shown in Figure A.1. Output Y is shown on the vertical axis, and the number of workers N is shown on the horizontal axis. Points on the line $0AB$ satisfy equation (A.1). For example, at point A, $N = 4$ and $Y = 20$, a combination of N and Y that satisfies equation (A.1). Similarly, at point B, $N = 12.5$ and $Y = 62.5$, which also satisfies the relationship $Y = 5N$. Note that (at B, for example) the relationship between Y and N allows the variables to have values that are not whole numbers. Allowing fractional values of N and Y is reasonable because workers can work part time or overtime, and a unit of output may be only partially completed during a day.

Functions such as $Y = 5N$ whose graph is a straight line are called *linear functions*. Functions whose graph is

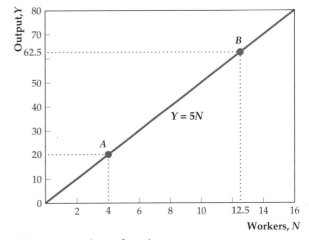

Figure A.1 Linear function
Points on the line $0AB$ satisfy the relationship $Y = 5N$. Because the graph of the function $Y = 5N$ is a straight line, this function is called a linear function.

not a line are called *non-linear*. An example of a nonlinear function is

$$Y = 20\sqrt{N} \qquad (A.2)$$

The graph of the non-linear function $Y = 20\sqrt{N}$ is shown in Figure A.2. All points on the curve satisfy equation (A.2). For example, at point C, $N = 4$ and $Y = 20\sqrt{4} = 40$. At point D, $N = 9$ and $Y = 20\sqrt{9} = 60$.

Both examples of functions given so far are exact numerical relationships. We can also write functions in more general terms, using letters or symbols. For example, we might write:

$$Y = G(N) \qquad (A.3)$$

Equation (A.3) states that there is some general relationship between the number of workers N and the amount of output Y, which is represented by a function G. The numerical functions given in equations (A.1) and (A.2) are specific examples of such a general relationship.

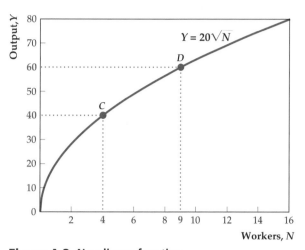

Figure A.2 Non-linear function
The function $Y = 20\sqrt{N}$, whose graph is shown in this figure, is an example of a non-linear function.

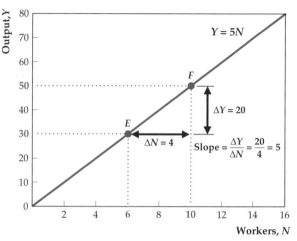

Figure A.3 Slope of a linear function
The slope of a function equals the change in the variable on the vertical axis (Y) divided by the change in the variable on the horizontal axis (N). For example, between points E and F the increase in N, ΔN, equals 4 and the increase in Y, ΔY, equals 20. Therefore the slope of the function between E and F, $\Delta Y/\Delta N$, equals 5. In general, the slope of a linear function is constant, so the slope of this function between any two points is 5.

A.2 SLOPES OF FUNCTIONS

Suppose that two variables N and Y are related by a function $Y = G(N)$. Generally speaking, if we start from some given combination of N and Y that satisfies the function G, the *slope* of the function G at that point indicates by how much Y changes when N changes by one unit.

To define the slope more precisely, we suppose that the current value of N is a specific number N_1 so that the current value of Y equals $G(N_1)$. Now consider what happens if N is increased by an amount ΔN (ΔN is read 'the change in N'). Output Y depends on N; therefore if N changes, Y must also change. The value of N is now $N_1 + \Delta N$, so the value of Y after N increases is $G(N_1 + \Delta N)$. The *change* in Y is

$$\Delta Y = G(N_1 + \Delta N) - G(N_1)$$

The slope of the function G, for an increase in N from N_1 to $N_1 + \Delta N$, is

$$\text{slope} = \frac{\Delta Y}{\Delta N} = \frac{G(N_1 + \Delta N) - G(N_1)}{(N_1 + \Delta N) - N_1}. \quad (A.4)$$

Note that if $\Delta N = 1$, the slope equals ΔY, the change in Y.

Figures A.3 and A.4 show graphically how to determine slopes for the two functions discussed in the preceding section. Figure A.3 shows the graph of the function $Y = 5N$ (as in Figure A.1). Suppose that we start from point E in Figure A.3, where $N = 6$ and $Y = 30$. If N is increased by 4 (for example), we move to point F on the graph, where $N = 10$ and $Y = 50$. Between E and F, $\Delta N = 10 - 6 = 4$ and $\Delta Y = 50 - 30 = 20$, so the slope $\Delta Y/\Delta N = 20/4 = 5$.

In general, the slope of a linear function is the same at all points. You can prove this result for the linear function $Y = 5N$ by showing that for any change ΔN, $\Delta Y = 5 \Delta N$. So for this particular linear function, the slope $\Delta Y/\Delta N$ always equals 5, a constant number.

For a non-linear function, such as $Y = 20\sqrt{N}$, the slope is not constant but depends on both the initial value of N and the size of the change in N. These results are illustrated in Figure A.4, which displays the graph of the function $Y = 20\sqrt{N}$ (as in Figure A.2). Suppose that we are initially at point G, where $N = 1$ and $Y = 20$, and we increase N by 8 units. After the increase in N we are at point D, where $N = 9$ and $Y = 20$ $\sqrt{9} = 60$. Between G and D, $\Delta N = 9 - 1 = 8$ and $\Delta Y = 60 - 20 = 40$. Thus the slope of the function between G and D is $40/8 = 5$. Geometrically, the slope of the function between G and D equals the slope of the straight line between G and D.

Starting once again from point G in Figure A.4, if we instead increase N by 3 units, we come to point C, where $N = 4$ and $Y = 20$ $\sqrt{4} = 40$. In this case $\Delta N = 3$ and $\Delta Y = 40 - 20 = 20$, so the slope between G and C is $20/3 = 6.67$, which is not the same as the slope of 5 that we calculated when earlier we increased N by 8 units. Geometrically, the slope of the line between G and C is greater than the slope of the line between G and D: that is, line GC is steeper than line GD.

Figure A.4
Slope of a non-linear function

Between points G and D the change in N (ΔN) is 8 and the change in Y (ΔY) is 40, so the slope of the function between points G and D is $\Delta Y/\Delta N = 40/8 = 5$. This slope is the same as the slope of the line GD. Similarly, the slope of the function between points G and C is $\Delta Y/\Delta N = 20/3 = 6.67$. The slope of the line tangent to point G, which equals 10, approximates the slope of the function for very small changes in N. Generally, when we refer to the slope of a nonlinear function at a specific point, we mean the slope of the line tangent to the function at that point.

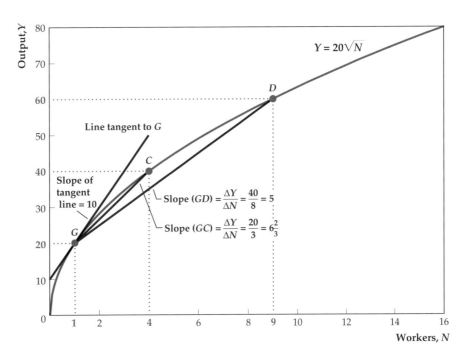

In Figure A.4 we have also drawn a line that touches but does not cross the graph of the function at point G; this line is *tangent* to the graph of the function at point G. If you start from point G and find the slope of the function for different values of ΔN, you will discover that the smaller the value of ΔN is, the closer the slope will be to the slope of the tangent line. For example, if you compare the slope of line GD (for which $\Delta N = 8$) with the slope of line GC (for which $\Delta N = 3$), you will see that of the two the slope of line GC is closer to the slope of the line tangent to point G. For values of ΔN even smaller than 3, the slope would be still closer to the slope of the tangent line.

These observations lead to an important result: *for small values of ΔN the slope of a function at any point is closely approximated by the slope of the line tangent to the function at that point.* Unless specified otherwise, in this book when we refer to the slope of a non-linear function, we mean the slope of the line tangent to the function at the specified point. Thus in Figure A.4, the slope of the function at point G means the slope of the line tangent to the function at point G, which happens to be 10.[1]

The numerical example illustrated in Fig. A.4 shows that the slope of a non-linear function depends on the size of the increase in N being considered. The slope of a non-linear function also depends on the point at which the slope is being measured. In Figure A.4 note that the slope of a line drawn tangent to point D, for example, would be less than the slope of a line drawn tangent to point G. Thus the slope of this particular function (measured with respect to small changes in N) is greater at G than at D.

A.3 ELASTICITIES

Like slopes, elasticities indicate how much one variable responds when a second variable changes. Suppose again that there is a function relating Y to N, so that when N changes, Y changes as well. The *elasticity* of Y with respect to N is defined to be the percentage change in Y, $\Delta Y/Y$, divided by the percentage change in N, $\Delta N/N$. Writing the formula, we have

$$\text{elasticity of } Y \text{ with respect to } N = \frac{\Delta Y/Y}{\Delta N/N}$$

Because the slope of a function is $\Delta Y/\Delta N$, we can also write the elasticity of Y with respect to N as the slope times (N/Y).

If the elasticity of Y with respect to N is large, a 1% change in N causes a large percentage change in Y. Thus a large elasticity of Y with respect to N means that Y is very sensitive to changes in N.

---

1. Showing that the slope of the line tangent to point G equals 10 requires basic calculus. The derivative of the function $Y = 20\sqrt{N}$, which is the same as the slope, is $dY/dN = 10/\sqrt{N}$. Evaluating this derivative at $N = 1$ yields a slope of 10.

A.4 FUNCTIONS OF SEVERAL VARIABLES

A function can relate more than two variables. To continue the example of Section A.1, suppose that the firm's daily output Y depends on both the number of workers N that the firm employs and the number of machines (equivalently, the amount of capital) K that the firm owns. Specifically, the function relating Y to K and N might be

$$Y = 2\sqrt{K}\,\sqrt{N} \qquad (A.5)$$

So, if there are 100 machines and 9 workers, by substituting $K = 100$ and $N = 9$ into equation (A.5), we get the output $Y = 2\sqrt{100}\,\sqrt{9} = 2 \times 10 \times 3 = 60$.

We can also write a function of several variables in general terms using symbols or letters. A general way to write the relationship between output Y and the two inputs, capital K and labour N, is

$$Y = F(K, N)$$

This equation is a slight simplification of a relationship called the production function, which we introduce in Chapter 3.

The graph of a function relating three variables requires three dimensions. As a convenient way to graph such a function on a two-dimensional page, we hold one of the right-hand-side variables constant. To graph the function in equation (A.5), for example, we might hold the number of machines K constant at a value of 100. If we substitute 100 for K, equation (A.5) becomes

$$Y = 2\sqrt{100}\,\sqrt{N} = 20\sqrt{N} \qquad (A.6)$$

With K held constant at 100, equation (A.6) is identical to equation (A.2). Like equation (A.2), equation (A.6) is a relationship between Y and N only and thus can be graphed in two dimensions. The graph of equation (A.6), shown as the solid curve in Figure A.5, is identical to the graph of equation (A.2) in Figure A.2.

A.5 SHIFTS OF A CURVE

Suppose that the relationship of output Y to machines K and workers N is given by equation (A.5) and we hold K constant at 100. As in Section A.4, with K held constant at 100, equation (A.5) reduces to equation (A.6) and the solid curve in Figure A.5 shows the relationship between workers N and output Y. At point C in Figure A.5, for example, $N = 4$ and $Y = 20\sqrt{4} = 40$. At point D, where $N = 9$, $Y = 20\sqrt{9} = 60$.

Now suppose that the firm purchases additional machines, raising the number of machines K from 100 to 225. If we substitute this new value for K, equation (A.5) becomes

$$Y = 2\sqrt{225}\,\sqrt{N} = 30\sqrt{N} \qquad (A.7)$$

Equation (A.7) is shown graphically as the dashed curve in Figure A.5. Note that the increase in K has shifted the curve up. Because of the increase in the number of machines, the amount of daily output Y that can be produced for any given number of workers N has risen. For example, initially when N equalled 9, output Y equalled 60 (point D in Figure A.5). After the increase in K, if $N = 9$, then $Y = 30\sqrt{9} = 90$ (point J in Figure A.5).

Figure A.5
Shifts of a curve
Suppose that output Y depends on capital K and workers N, according to the function in Eq. (A.5). If we hold K fixed at 100, the relationship between Y and N is shown by the solid curve. If K rises to 225, so that more output can be produced with a given number of workers, the curve showing the relationship between Y and N shifts upward, from the solid curve to the dashed curve. In general, a change in any right-hand-side variable that doesn't appear on an axis of the graph causes the curve to shift.

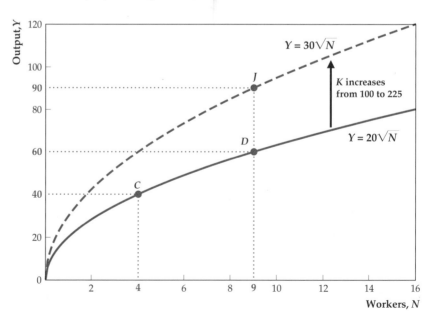

This example illustrates some important general points about the graphs of functions of several variables.

1. To graph a function of several variables in two dimensions, we hold all but one of the right-hand-side variables constant.

2. The one right-hand-side variable that is not held constant (N in this example) appears on the horizontal axis. Changes in this variable do not shift the graph of the function. Instead, changes in the variable on the horizontal axis represent movements *along* the curve that represents the function.

3. The right-hand-side variables held constant for the purpose of drawing the graph (K in this example) do not appear on either axis of the graph. If the value of one of these variables is changed, the entire curve shifts. In this example, for any number of workers N the increase in machines K means that more output Y can be produced. Thus the curve shifts up, from the solid curve to the dashed curve in Figure A.5.

A.6 EXPONENTS

Powers of numbers or variables can be expressed by using superscripts called *exponents*. In the following examples, 2 and 4 are the exponents:

$$5^2 = 5 \times 5 \quad \text{and} \quad Z^4 = Z \times Z \times Z \times Z$$

For any numbers Z, a, and b, exponents obey the following rules:

$$Z^a \times Z^b = Z^{a+b} \quad \text{and} \quad (Z^a)^b = Z^{ab}$$

An illustration of the first rule is $5^2 \times 5^3 = (5 \times 5) \times (5 \times 5 \times 5) = 5^5$. An illustration of the second rule is $(5^3)^2 = (5^3) \times (5^3) = (5 \times 5 \times 5) \times (5 \times 5 \times 5) = 5^6$.

Exponents do not have to be whole numbers. For example, $5^{0.5}$ represents the square root of 5. To understand why, note that by the second of the two rules for exponents, $(5^{0.5})^2 = 5^{(0.5)2} = 5^1 = 5$. That is, the square of $5^{0.5}$ is 5. Similarly, for any number Z and any whole number q, $Z^{1/q}$ is the qth root of Z. Thus $5^{0.25}$ means the fourth root of 5, for example. Using exponents, we can rewrite equation (A.5) as

$$Y = 2K^{0.5}N^{0.5}$$

where $K^{0.5} = \sqrt{K}$ and $N^{0.5} = \sqrt{N}$.

In general, consider any number that can be expressed as a ratio of two whole numbers p and q. Using the rules of exponents, we have

$$Z^{p/q} = (Z^p)^{1/q} = q\text{th root of } Z^p$$

Thus, for example, as 0.7 equals 7/10, $N^{0.7}$ equals the tenth root of N^7. For values of N greater than 1, $N^{0.7}$ is a number larger than the square root of N, $N^{0.5}$, but smaller than N itself.

Exponents also may be zero or negative. In general, the following two relationships hold:

$$Z^0 = 1 \quad \text{and} \quad Z^{-a} = \frac{1}{Z^a}$$

Here is a useful way to relate exponents and elasticities. Suppose that two variables Y and N are related by a function of the form

$$Y = kN^a \qquad (A.8)$$

where a is a number and k can be either a number or a function of variables other than N. Then the elasticity of Y with respect to N (see Section A.3) equals a.

A.7 GROWTH RATE FORMULAS

Let X and Z be any two variables, not necessarily related by a function, that are changing over time. Let $\Delta X / X$ and $\Delta Z / Z$ represent the growth rates (percentage changes) of X and Z, respectively. Then the following rules provide useful approximations (proofs of the various rules are included for reference).

Rule 1. The growth rate of the product of X and Z equals the growth rate of X plus the growth rate of Z.

Proof. Suppose that X increases by ΔX and Z increases by ΔZ. Then the absolute increase in the product of X and Z is $(X + \Delta X)(Z + \Delta Z) - XZ$, and the growth rate of the product of X and Z is

$$\text{growth rate of } (XZ) \qquad (A.9)$$

$$= \frac{(X + \Delta X)(Z + \Delta Z) - XZ}{XZ}$$

$$= \frac{(\Delta X)Z + (\Delta Z)X + \Delta X \Delta Z}{XZ}$$

$$= \frac{\Delta X}{X} + \frac{\Delta Z}{Z} + \frac{\Delta X \Delta Z}{XZ}$$

The last term on the right-hand side of equation (A.9), $(\Delta X \, \Delta Z)/XZ$, equals the growth rate of X, $\Delta X / X$, times the growth rate of Z, $\Delta Z / Z$. This term is generally small: for example, if the growth rates of X and Z are both 5% (0.05), the product of the two growth rates is only 0.25% (0.0025). If we assume that this last term is small enough to ignore, equation (A.9) indicates that the growth rate of the product XZ equals the growth rate of X, $\Delta X / X$, plus the growth rate of Z, $\Delta Z / Z$.

Rule 2. The growth rate of the ratio of X to Z is the growth rate of X minus the growth rate of Z.

Proof. Let W be the ratio of X to Z, so $W = X/Z$. Then $X = ZW$. By Rule 1, as X equals the product of Z and W, the growth rate of X equals the growth rate of Z plus the growth rate of W:

$$\frac{\Delta X}{X} = \frac{\Delta Z}{Z} + \frac{\Delta W}{W}$$

Rearranging this equation to put $\Delta W/W$ on the left-hand side and recalling that $\Delta W/W$ equals the growth rate of (X/Z), we have

$$\text{growth rate of } (X/Z) = \frac{\Delta X}{X} - \frac{\Delta Z}{Z} \quad \text{(A.10)}$$

Rule 3. Suppose that Y is a variable that is a function of two other variables X and Z. Then

$$\frac{\Delta Y}{Y} = \eta_{Y,X} \frac{\Delta X}{X} + \eta_{Y,Z} \frac{\Delta Z}{Z} \quad \text{(A.11)}$$

where $\eta_{Y,X}$ is the elasticity of Y with respect to X and $\eta_{Y,Z}$ is the elasticity of Y with respect to Z.

Proof (informal). Suppose that only X changes so that $\Delta Z/Z = 0$. Then equation (A.11) boils down to the definition of an elasticity, $\eta_{Y,X} = (\Delta Y/Y)/(\Delta X/X)$, as in Section A.3. Similarly, if only Z changes, equation (A.11) becomes $\eta_{Y,Z} = (\Delta Y/Y)/(\Delta Z/Z)$, which is the definition of the elasticity of Y with respect to Z. If both X and Z change, equation (A.11) indicates that the overall effect on Y is approximately equal to the sum of the individual effects on Y of the change in X and the change in Z.

Rule 4. The growth rate of X raised to the power a, or X^a, is a times the growth rate of X,

$$\text{growth rate of } (X^a) = a \frac{\Delta X}{X} \quad \text{(A.12)}$$

Proof. Let $Y = X^a$. Applying the rule from equation (A.8) and setting $k = 1$, we find that the elasticity of Y with respect to X equals a. Therefore, by equation (A.11) the growth rate of Y equals a times the growth rate of X. Because $Y = X^a$, the growth rate of Y is the same as the growth rate of X^a, which proves the relationship in equation (A.12).

Example: The real interest rate. To apply the growth rate formulas, we derive the equation that relates the real interest rate to the nominal interest rate and the inflation rate, equation (2.12).

The real value of any asset, say, a savings account, equals the nominal or money value of the asset divided by the price level:

$$\text{real asset value} = \frac{\text{nominal asset value}}{\text{price level}} \quad \text{(A.13)}$$

The real value of an asset is the ratio of the nominal asset value to the price level, so, according to Rule 2, the *growth rate* of the real asset value is approximately equal to the *growth rate* of the nominal asset value minus the *growth rate* of the price level. The growth rate of the real value of an interest-bearing asset equals the real interest rate earned by that asset; the growth rate of the nominal value of an interest-bearing asset is the nominal interest rate for that asset; and the growth rate of the price level is the inflation rate. Therefore, Rule 2 implies the relationship

Real interest rate = nominal interest rate − inflation rate

which is the relationship given in equation (2.12).

PROBLEMS

1. Graph the function $Y = 3X + 5$ for $0 \leq X \leq 5$. What is the slope of this function?
2. Graph the function $Y = X^2 + 2$ for $0 \leq X \leq 5$. Starting from the point at which $X = 1$, find the slope of the function for $\Delta X = 1$ and $\Delta X = -1$. What is the slope of the line tangent to the function at $X = 1$? (See Problem 3.)
3. For the function $Y = X^2 + 2$, use equation (A.4) to write a general expression for the slope. This expression for the slope will depend on the initial value of X, X_1, and on the change in X, ΔX. For values of ΔX sufficiently small that the term $(\Delta X)^2$ can be ignored, show that the slope depends only on the initial value of X, X_1. What is the slope of the function (which is the same as the slope of the tangent line) when $X_1 = 1$?
4. Suppose that the amount of output Y that a firm can produce depends on its amount of capital K and the number of workers employed N, according to the function

$$Y = K^{0.3} N^{0.7}$$

a. Suppose that $N = 100$. Give the function that relates Y to K and graph this relationship for $0 \leq K \leq 50$. (You need calculate only enough values of Y to get a rough idea of the shape of the function.)
b. What happens to the function relating Y and K and to the graph of the relationship if N rises to 200? If N falls to 50? Give an economic interpretation.
c. For the function relating Y to K and N, find the elasticity of Y with respect to K and the elasticity of Y with respect to N.

5. Use a calculator to find each of the following.

   a. $5^{0.3}$

   b. $5^{0.3}5^{0.2}$

   c. $(5^{0.25})^2$

   d. $(5^{0.5}5^{0.3})^2\,5^{0.4}$

   e. $5^{0.2}/5^{0.5}$

   f. $5^{-0.5}$

6. a. Nominal GDP equals real GDP times the GDP deflator (see Section 2.4). Suppose that nominal GDP growth is 12% and real GDP growth is 4%. What is inflation (the rate of growth of the GDP deflator)?

   b. The 'velocity of money', V, is defined by the equation

$$V = \frac{PY}{M}$$

where P is the price level, Y is real output, and M is the money supply (see equation 7.4). In a particular year velocity is constant, money growth is 10%, and inflation (the rate of growth of the price level) is 7%. What is real output growth?

   c. Output Y is related to capital K and the number of workers N by the function

$$Y = 10K^{0.3}\,N^{0.7}$$

In a particular year the capital stock grows by 2% and the number of workers grows by 1%. By how much does output grow?

GLOSSARY

(The number in parentheses after the glossary term is the chapter in which that term first appears or is most extensively discussed.)

absorption: (5) total spending by domestic residents, firms, and governments, equal to $C + I + G$. (p. 163)

activist: (15) describes a policy strategy that involves active responses by the central bank to changes in economic circumstances. See *discretion*.

acyclical: (9) not displaying a regular pattern of behavior over the business cycle. See *procyclical, countercyclical*. (p. 312)

aggregate demand: (9, 10) the economywide demand for output when the goods market and the asset market are in equilibrium; the level of output corresponding to the intersection of the *IS* and *LM* curves.

aggregate demand (*AD*) curve: (10) in a diagram with output on the horizontal axis and the price level on the vertical axis, the downward-sloping relation between the price level and the economywide demand for output. (p. 365)

aggregate demand for labour: (3) the sum of the labour demands of all employers in an economy. (p. 83)

aggregate demand management: (12) the use of monetary and fiscal policies, which shifts the aggregate demand curve, to try to smooth out the business cycle; also known as macroeconomic stabilization or stabilization policy. (p. 458)

aggregate demand shocks: (12) shocks to the economy that shift the *IS* curve or the *LM* curve and thus affect the aggregate demand for output. (p. 452)

aggregate supply: (10) the amount of output supplied by firms in the economy at any given price level; in the long run, when prices and price expectations have adjusted to their equilibrium levels, aggregate supply equals full-employment output.

aggregate supply (*AS*) curve: (10) in a diagram with output on the horizontal axis and the price level on the vertical axis, the relation between the price level and the total amount of output that firms supply. (p. 369)

aggregate supply of labour: (3) the sum of the labour supplied by everyone in the economy. (p. 83)

aggregation: (1) the process of adding individual economic variables to obtain economywide totals. (p. 15)

appreciation: (14) see *nominal appreciation, real appreciation*.

automatic stabilizers: (16) provisions in the government's budget that automatically cause government spending to rise or taxes to fall when GDP falls. (p. 620)

average labour productivity: (1) the amount of output produced per unit of labour input (per worker or per hour of work). (p. 6)

average tax rate: (16) the total amount of taxes paid divided by the taxpayer's income. (p. 622)

balance of payments: (5) the net increase (domestic less foreign) in a country's official reserve assets; also known as the official settlements balance. (p. 156)

balance of payments accounts: (5) the record of a country's international transactions, consisting of the current account and the capital account. (p. 152)

bank reserves: (15) liquid assets held by banks to meet the demands for withdrawals by depositors or to pay the checks drawn on depositors' accounts. (p. 571)

bank run: (15) a large-scale withdrawal of deposits from a bank, caused by depositors' fear that the bank may go bankrupt and not pay depositors in full. (p. 574)

bequest motive: (8) the desire to leave inheritances. (p. 279)

boom: (9) in a business cycle, the period of time during which aggregate economic activity grows; also known as an expansion. (p. 303)

borrowing constraint: (8) a restriction imposed by lenders on the amount that someone can borrow. If a borrowing constraint causes an individual to borrow less than he or she would choose to borrow in the absence of the constraint, the borrowing constraint is *binding*; otherwise it is *nonbinding*. (p. 276)

budget constraint: (8) a relation that shows how much current and future consumption a consumer can afford given the consumer's initial wealth, current and future income, and the interest rate. (p. 262)

budget deficit: (2) government outlays minus government receipts. See *government outlays, government receipts*. (p. 43)

budget line: (8) the graph of the consumer's budget constraint; the budget line shows graphically the combinations of current and future consumption a consumer can afford given the consumer's initial wealth, current and future income, and the interest rate. (p. 263)

budget surplus: (2) government receipts minus government outlays. See *government outlays, government receipts, government saving*. (p. 43)

business cycle: (9) a decline in aggregate economic activity (a contraction or recession) to a low point (a trough), followed by a recovery of activity (an expansion or boom) to a high point (a peak). A complete business cycle can be measured from peak to peak or from trough to trough. (p. 303)

business cycle chronology: (9) a history of the dates of business cycle peaks and troughs. (p. 302)

capital account: (5) the record of a country's international trade in existing assets, either real or financial. (p. 156)

capital account balance: (5) the value of capital inflows (credit items) minus the value of capital outflows (debit items) in a country's capital account. (p. 156)

capital good: (2) a good that is produced, is used to produce other goods, and—unlike an intermediate good—is not used up in the same period that it is produced. (p. 34)

capital inflow: (5) a credit (plus) item in a country's capital account that arises when a resident of the country sells an asset to someone in another country. (p. 156)

capital–labour ratio: (6) the amount of capital per worker, equal to the capital stock divided by the number of workers. (p. 203)

capital outflow: (5) a debit (minus) item in a country's capital account that arises when a resident of the country buys an asset from abroad. (p. 156)

cash in hand: (15) currency held in the vaults of banks; cash in hand forms a portion of banks' reserves. (p. 581)

central bank: (15) the governmental institution responsible for monetary policy, such as the Bank of England in the UK, the Bundesbank in Germany, and the Federal Reserve System in the US. (p. 569)

chronically unemployed: (3) workers who are unemployed a large fraction of the time. (p. 101)

classical approach: (1) an approach to macroeconomics based on the assumption that wages and prices adjust quickly to equate quantities supplied and demanded in each market. Classical economists generally argue that free markets are a good way to organize the economy and that the scope for government intervention in the economy—for example, to smooth out the business cycle—should be limited.

closed economy: (1) a national economy that does not have trading or financial relationships with the rest of the world. (p. 10)

coincident variable: (9) a variable with peaks and troughs that occur at about the same time as the corresponding business cycle peaks and troughs. See *lagging variable, leading variable*. (p. 312)

cold turkey: (13) a rapid and decisive reduction in the growth rate of the money supply aimed at reducing the rate of inflation; in contrast with *gradualism*. (p. 508)

co-movement: (9) the tendency of many economic variables to move together in a predictable way over the business cycle. (p. 305)

conditional convergence: (6) the tendency of living standards within groups of countries with similar characteristics to become more equal over time. See *unconditional convergence*. (p. 215)

consumer price index: (2) a price index calculated as the current cost of a fixed basket of consumer goods divided by the cost of the basket in the base period. (p. 53)

consumption: (2) spending by domestic households on final goods and services. (p. 36)

consumption-smoothing motive: (8) the preference of most people for a relatively constant or stable pattern of consumption over time, as opposed to having high consumption at some times and low consumption at others. (p. 267)

contraction: (9) in a business cycle, the period of time during which aggregate economic activity is falling; also known as a recession. (p. 302)

contractionary policy: (12) a monetary or fiscal policy that reduces aggregate demand.

convergence: (6) a tendency of living standards in different countries to become equal over time. See *conditional convergence, unconditional convergence*.

corporatism: (13) the extent to which trade unions, management and government cooperate in setting wages in an economy. (p. 498)

countercyclical: (9) tending to move in the opposite direction of aggregate economic activity over the business cycle (up in contractions, down in expansions). See *procyclical, acyclical.* (p. 312)

credibility: (15) the degree to which the public believes the central bank's announcements about future policy. (p. 594)

credit channel: (15) the effects of monetary policy on credit supply and credit demand, which affect the economy in addition to effects operating through interest rates and exchange rates. (p. 588)

currency: (7) paper money and coin issued by the government; cash.

currency–deposit ratio: (15) the ratio of the currency held by the public to the public's deposits in banks. (p. 575)

currency union: (14) a group of countries sharing a common currency, such as members of the European Monetary Union using the euro. (p. 556)

current account: (5) the record of a country's international trade in currently produced goods and services. (p. 153)

current account balance: (2, 5) payments received from abroad in exchange for currently produced goods and services (including factor services), minus the analogous payments made to foreigners by the domestic economy. (pp. 44, 155)

cyclical unemployment: (3) the excess of the actual unemployment rate over the natural rate of unemployment; equivalently, unemployment that occurs when output is below its full-employment level. (p. 102)

debt–GDP ratio: (16) the quantity of government debt outstanding divided by GDP.

deflation: (1) a situation in which the prices of most goods and services are falling over time. (p. 8)

demand for money: (7) the quantity of monetary assets, such as cash and checking accounts, that people choose to hold in their portfolios. (p. 236)

depository institutions: (15) privately owned banks and thrift institutions (such as savings and loans) that accept deposits from and make loans directly to the public. (p. 569)

depreciation: 1. (2) the amount of capital that wears out during a given period of time. (p. 40) 2. (14) a decline in the exchange rate; see *nominal depreciation, real depreciation.*

depression: (9) a particularly severe and prolonged downturn in economic activity. (p. 303)

desired capital stock: (4) the amount of capital that allows a firm to earn the highest possible expected profit. (p. 127)

devaluation: (14) a reduction in the value of a currency by official government action under a fixed exchange rate system. (p. 520)

diminishing marginal productivity: (3) a feature of production functions that implies that, the more a particular factor of production is used, the less extra output can be gained by increasing the use of that factor still further (with the usage of other factors of production held constant). For example, for a given capital stock, adding an extra worker increases output more when employment is initially low than when it is initially high. (p. 73)

discount rate: (15) the interest rate charged by a central bank when it lends reserves to banks. (p. 585)

discouraged workers: (3) people who stop searching for jobs because they have become discouraged by lack of success at finding a job; discouraged workers are not included in the official unemployment rate. (p. 99)

discretion: (15) the freedom of the central bank to conduct monetary policy in any way that it believes will advance the ultimate objectives of low and stable inflation, high economic growth, and low unemployment; in contrast to *rules.* (p. 590)

disinflation: (13) a fall in the rate of inflation. (p. 507)

distortions: (16) tax-induced deviations in economic behavior from the efficient, free-market outcome. (p. 625)

duration: (3) the length of time that an unemployment spell lasts. (p. 100)

economic model: (1) a simplified description of some aspect of the economy, usually expressed in mathematical form. (p. 17)

economic theory: (1) a set of ideas about the economy that have been organized in a logical framework. (p. 17)

effective labor demand curve: (12) in a diagram with output on the horizontal axis and the quantity of labour on the vertical axis, an upward-sloping curve that shows how much labour is needed to produce a given amount of output, with productivity, the capital stock, and effort held constant. (p. 441)

effective tax rate: (4) a single measure of the tax burden on capital that summarizes the many provisions of the tax code that affect investment. (p. 133)

efficiency wage: (12) the real wage that maximizes worker effort or efficiency per unit of real wages received. (p. 432)

efficiency wage model: (12) a model of the labour market in which, because workers exert more effort when they receive a higher real wage, profit-maximizing employers choose to pay a real wage that is higher than the real wage that clears the labour market; the efficiency wage model can be used to help explain real-wage rigidity and the existence of unemployment. (p. 430)

effort curve: (12) the relation between the level of effort put forth by workers and the real wage; its positive slope indicates that a higher real wage induces workers to exert greater effort. (p. 431)

empirical analysis: (1) a comparison of the implications of an economic theory or model with real-world data. (p. 18)

employment ratio: (3) the fraction of the adult population that is employed. (p. 98)

equilibrium: (1) a situation in which the quantities demanded and supplied in a market or set of markets are equal. (p. 21)

European Central Bank: (15) will be the central decision-making body of the European System of Central Banks which will define and implement domestic and external monetary policy for EU member states participating in the European Monetary Union; the organization responsible for issuing bank notes and coins under the single currency. (p. 605)

European System of Central Banks: (15) the organization to be established under European Monetary Union comprising the central banks of member states but controlled by an independent European Central Bank; will have responsibility of monetary policy within the EMU with its main objective of ensuring price stability. (p. 605)

exchange rate: (14) the number of units of foreign currency that can be purchased with one unit of the home currency; also known as the nominal exchange rate. (p. 517)

exchange rate channel: (15) the effects of monetary policy working through changes in the real exchange rate. (p. 588)

exchange rate union: (14) a group of countries that agree to fix exchange rates among themselves while allowing their currencies to fluctuate against those of countries outside the union. (p. 518)

expansion: (9) in a business cycle, the period of time during which aggregate economic activity is rising; also known as a boom. (p. 303)

expansionary policy: (12) a monetary or fiscal policy that increases aggregate demand.

expectations-augmented Phillips curve: (13) an inverse relation between unanticipated inflation and cyclical unemployment. (p. 483)

expected after-tax real interest rate: (4) the nominal after-tax rate of return (equal to the nominal interest rate times 1 minus the tax rate) minus the expected rate of inflation; equals the expected increase in the real value of an asset after payment of taxes on interest income. (p. 121)

expected real interest rate: (2) the nominal interest rate minus the expected rate of inflation; equals the expected increase in the real value of an asset. (p. 58)

expected returns: (7) the rates of return on real or financial assets that financial investors expect to earn. (p. 234)

expenditure approach: (2) a procedure for measuring economic activity by adding the amount spent by all purchasers of final goods and services. (p. 29)

factors of production: (3) inputs to the production process, such as capital goods, labour, raw materials, and energy. (p. 68)

FE line: (10) see *full-employment line*.

final goods and services: (2) goods and services that are the end products of the productive process, in contrast to intermediate goods and services. (p. 34)

fiscal policy: (1) policy concerning the level and composition of government spending and taxation. (p. 13)

fixed-exchange-rate system: (14) a system in which exchange rates are set at officially determined levels and are changed only by direct governmental action. (p. 518)

fixed-weight price index: (2) a price index that measures how much a fixed "basket" of goods costs in each year, relative to its cost in a base period. (p. 53)

flexible-exchange-rate system: (14) a system in which exchange rates are not officially fixed but are determined by conditions of supply and demand in the foreign exchange market; also known as a floating-exchange-rate system. (p. 517)

floating-exchange-rate system: (14) see *flexible-exchange-rate system*. (p. 517)

flow variable: (2) a variable that is measured per unit of time; an example is GDP, which is measured as output per year or quarter. See *stock variable*. (p. 45)

foreign exchange market: (14) the market in which the currencies of different nations are traded. (p. 517)

fractional reserve banking: (15) a banking system in which banks hold reserves equal to a fraction of their deposits so that the reserve–deposit ratio is less than 1. (p. 571)

frictional unemployment: (3) the unemployment that arises as the result of the matching process in which workers search for suitable jobs and firms search for suitable workers. (p. 101)

full-employment deficit: (16) what the government budget deficit *would be*, given the tax and spending policies currently in force, if the economy were operating at its full-employment level. (p. 621)

full-employment (FE) line: (10) a vertical line representing full-employment output in a diagram with output on the horizontal axis and the real interest rate on the vertical axis. (p. 339)

full-employment level of employment: (3) the equilibrium level of employment, achieved after wages and prices fully adjust. (p. 88)

full-employment output: (3) the level of output that firms supply when wages and prices in the economy have fully adjusted to their equilibrium levels. (p. 90)

fundamental identity of national income accounting: (2) the accounting identity that states that total production, total income, and total expenditure during a given period are equal. (p. 31)

fundamental value of the exchange rate: (14) the value of the exchange rate that would be determined by the forces of supply and demand in the foreign exchange market, in the absence of government intervention. (p. 548)

game theory: (15) the study of situations (games) in which individuals (players) use strategy in attempting to achieve their goals, possibly at the expense of the other players. (p. 595)

GDP: (2) see *gross domestic product*.

GDP deflator: (2) a variable-weight measure of the price level, calculated as the ratio of current nominal GDP to current real GDP. (p. 52)

general equilibrium: (10) a situation in which all markets in an economy are simultaneously in equilibrium. (p. 354)

GNP: (2) see *gross national product*.

Golden Rule Capital Stock: (6) the level of the capital stock that maximizes consumption per worker in the steady state. (p. 207)

government capital: (16) long-lived physical assets owned by the government, such as roads and public schools. (p. 621)

government debt: (16) the total value of government bonds outstanding at any given time. (p. 628)

government outlays: (2) the government's purchases of goods and services plus transfers and interest payments; also known as government expenditures. (p. 43)

government purchases: (2) spending by the government on currently produced goods and services. (p. 38)

government receipts: (2) taxes and other revenues collected by the government. (p. 43)

government saving: (2) the government's tax receipts minus its outlays; equal to the government budget surplus. (p. 43)

gradualism: (13) a prescription for disinflation that involves reducing the rate of monetary growth and the rate of inflation gradually over a period of several years; in contrast to *cold turkey*. (p. 508)

gross domestic product (GDP): (2) the market value of final goods and services newly produced within a nation's borders during a fixed period of time. (p. 31)

gross investment: (4) the total purchase or construction of new capital goods. (p. 135)

gross national product (GNP): (2) the market value of final goods and services newly produced by domestically owned factors of production during a fixed period of time. (p. 35)

growth accounting: (6) a method for breaking down total output growth into parts attributable to growth of capital, labour, and productivity. (p. 193)

growth accounting equation: (6) the production function written in growth rate form; it states that the growth rate of output is the sum of (1) the growth rate of productivity, (2) the elasticity of output with respect to capital times the growth rate of capital, and (3) the elasticity of output with respect to labor times the growth rate of labour. (p. 192)

high-powered money: (15) the liabilities of the central bank, consisting of bank reserves and currency in circulation, that are usable as money; also known as the monetary base. (p. 570)

human capital: (6) the productive knowledge, skills, and training of individuals. (p. 217)

hyperinflation: (13) a situation in which the rate of inflation is extremely high for a sustained period of time; one suggested definition is a 50% monthly rate of inflation. (p. 505)

hysteresis: (13) the tendency of the natural rate of unemployment to change in response to the actual unemployment rate, rising if the actual unemployment rate is above the natural rate and falling if the actual unemployment rate is below the natural rate. (p. 499)

income approach: (2) a procedure for measuring economic activity by adding all income received, including taxes and after-tax profits. (p. 29)

income effect: (8) a change in economic behavior (such as the amount a person saves or works) in response to a change in income or wealth; graphically, a change in behavior induced by a parallel shift in the budget line. (p. 272)

income effect (of real interest rate on saving): (8) the tendency of savers to consume more and save less in response to an increase in the real interest rate because they are made wealthier; the tendency of borrowers to consume less and save more in response to an increase in the real interest rate because they are made less wealthy. (p. 283)

income effect (of real wage on labour supply): (8) the tendency of workers to supply less labour in response to an increase in the real wage; arises because an increase in the real wage makes workers wealthier and leads them to want to consume more leisure. (p. 288)

income elasticity of money demand: (7) the percentage change in money demand resulting from a 1% increase in real income. (p. 241)

income-expenditure identity: (2) the accounting identity that states that total income (product) equals the sum of the four types of expenditure: consumption, investment, government purchases, and net exports. (p. 36)

inconvertible currency: (14) a currency that cannot be traded freely for other currencies, usually because of government-imposed restrictions. (p. 548)

index of leading indicators: (9) a weighted average of eleven economic variables that lead the business cycle, used for forecasting future business activity. (p. 312)

indicators: (15) see *intermediate targets*.

indifference curve: (8) shows graphically the combinations of current and future consumption that yield any given level of utility. (p. 266)

industrial policy: (6) a strategy for economic growth by which the government, using taxes, subsidies, or regulation, attempts to influence the nation's pattern of industrial development. (p. 221)

inflation: (1) a situation in which the prices of most goods and services are rising over time. (p. 8)

inflation tax: (16) the resources raised by the government by issuing money and creating inflation; also known as seignorage. (p. 643)

insider–outsider theory: (13) attributes hysteresis of the natural unemployment rate to the supposed tendency of unions to try to obtain the highest real wage consistent with continued employment of employed members (insiders), without taking account of the interests of unemployed workers (outsiders). See *hysteresis*. (p. 501)

instruments: (15) the policy tools that the Central Bank can use to influence the economy; these include reserve requirements, the discount rate, and, especially, open-market operations. (p. 585)

interest elasticity of money demand: (7) the percentage change in money demand resulting from a 1% increase (different from a 1 percentage point increase) in the interest rate. (p. 241)

interest rate: (2) the rate of return promised by a borrower to a lender. (p. 54)

interest rate channel: (15) the effects of monetary policy that work through changes in real interest rates. (p. 588)

intermediate goods and services: (2) goods and services that are used up in the production of other goods and services in the same period that they themselves were produced; an example is wheat used up in making bread. (p. 34)

intermediate targets: (15) macroeconomic variables that the Central Bank cannot control directly but can influence fairly predictably and that, in turn, are related to the ultimate goals the Central Bank is trying to achieve; also known as indicators. Examples of intermediate targets are the growth rates of monetary aggregates and short-term interest rates. (p. 585)

inventories: (2) stocks of unsold finished goods, goods in process, and production materials held by firms. (p. 34)

investment: (2) spending for new capital goods, called fixed investment, and increases in firms' inventory holdings, called inventory investment. See *gross investment, net investment*. (p. 36)

invisible hand: (1) the idea (proposed by Adam Smith) that, if there are free markets and individuals conduct their economic affairs in their own best interests, the economy as a whole will work well. (p. 20)

IS **curve**: (10) in a diagram with output on the horizontal axis and the real interest rate on the vertical axis, a downward-sloping curve that shows the value of the real interest rate that clears the goods market for any given value of output. At any point on the *IS* curve, desired national saving equals desired investment (in a closed economy); equivalently, the aggregate quantity of goods demanded equals the aggregate quantity of goods supplied. (p. 341)

J **curve**: (14) the typical time pattern of the response of net exports to a depreciation of the real exchange rate, in which net exports initially decline but then increase. (p. 524)

Keynesian approach: (1) an approach to macroeconomics based on the assumption that wages and prices may not adjust quickly to equate quantities supplied and demanded in each market. Keynesian economists are more likely than classical economists to argue that government intervention in the economy—for example, to smooth out the business cycle—may be desirable.

Keynesian consumption function: (4) a relationship that states that desired consumption depends on current aggregate output. (p. 116)

labour force: (3) the number of people willing to work, including unemployed people actively searching for work, as well as employed workers. (p. 97)

Labour Force Survey: (3) a quarterly labour market survey undertaken by all EU member states providing information on employment, unemployment and earnings. (p. 97)

labour hoarding: (11, 12) a situation that occurs if, because of the costs of firing and hiring workers, firms continue to employ some workers in a recession that they otherwise would have laid off. (p. 399)

lagging variable: (9) a variable with peaks and troughs that tend to occur later than the corresponding peaks and troughs in the business cycle. See *coincident variable, leading variable*. (p. 312)

large open economy: (5) an economy that trades with other economies and is large enough to affect the world real interest rate. (p. 174)

leading variable: (9) a variable with peaks and troughs that tend to occur earlier than the corresponding peaks and troughs in the business cycle. See *coincident variable, lagging variable*. (p. 312)

leisure: (3) all off-the-job activities, including eating, sleeping, recreation, and working in the yard and on the house. (p. 84)

life-cycle model: (8) a multiperiod version of the basic two-period model of consumer behavior that focuses on the patterns of income, consumption, and saving over the various stages of an individual's life. (p. 276)

liquidity: (7) the ease and quickness with which an asset can be exchanged for goods, services, or other assets. (p. 235)

LM **curve**: (10) in a diagram with output on the horizontal axis and the real interest rate on the vertical axis, an upward-sloping curve that shows the value of the real interest rate that clears the asset market for any given value of output. At any point on the *LM* curve, the quantities of money supplied and demanded are equal. (p. 349)

lombard loans: (15) emergency funding or loans provided by the Bundesbank to credit institutions if they are faced with temporary liquidity problems. (p. 585)

lombard rate: (15) the rate of interest charged by the Bundesbank on lombard loans; traditionally it is the highest interest rate set by the Bundesbank. (p. 585)

long-run aggregate supply (*LRAS***) curve**: (10) in a diagram with output on the horizontal axis and the price level on the vertical axis, a vertical line at full-employment output; indicates that in the long run the supply of output does not depend on the price level. (p. 369)

long-run Phillips curve: (13) in a diagram with unemployment on the horizontal axis and inflation on the vertical axis, a vertical line at the natural rate of unemployment; indicates that in the long run the unemployment rate equals the natural rate, independent of the rate of inflation. (p. 490)

M0: (7) notes and coins in circulation. (p. 232)

M1: (7) the most narrowly defined monetary aggregate, made up of currency and travellers' checks held by the public, demand deposits (non-interest-bearing checking accounts) at commercial banks, and other checkable deposits. (p. 230)

M2: (7) a monetary aggregate that includes everything in M1 and a number of other assets that are somewhat less moneylike, such as savings deposits, small-denomination (under $100,000) time deposits, noninstitutional holdings of money market mutual funds (MMMFs), and money market deposit accounts (MMDAs). (p. 232)

M3: (7) a broad monetary aggregate that includes everything in M2 plus further accounts at banks such as, in Germany, savings deposits at three months' notice held with credit institutions. (p. 232)

M3 extended: (7) a broad monetary aggregate used in Germany which includes everything in M3 plus Euro-deposits, short-term bank debt securities, and certificates of domestic and foreign money market funds. (p. 232)

M4: (7) a broad monetary aggregate which includes notes and coins in circulation plus deposits at banks and other credit institutions (such as building societies in the UK). (p. 232)

macroeconomics: (1) the study of the structure and performance of national economies and of the policies that governments use to try to affect economic performance. (p. 3)

macroeconomic stabilization: (12) the use of monetary and fiscal policies to moderate cyclical fluctuations and maintain low inflation; also known as aggregate demand management or stabilization policy. (p. 458)

marginal cost: (12) the cost of producing an additional unit of output. (p. 440)

marginal product of capital (MPK): (3) the amount of output produced per unit of additional capital. (p. 72)

marginal product of labour (MPN): (3) the amount of output produced per unit of additional labour. (p. 74)

marginal propensity to consume (MPC): (4) the amount by which desired consumption rises when current output rises by one unit. (p. 116)

marginal revenue product of labour (MRPN): (3) the extra revenue obtained by a firm when it employs an additional unit of labour and sells the resulting increase in output; for competitive firms, equal to the price of output times the marginal product of labour. (p. 77)

marginal tax rate: (16) the fraction of an additional pound of income that must be paid in taxes. (p. 622)

markup: (12) the difference between the price charged for a good and its marginal cost of production, expressed as a percentage of marginal cost. (p. 440)

medium of exchange: (7) an asset used in making transactions. (p. 228)

menu cost: (12) the cost of changing prices, for example, the cost of printing a new menu or remarking merchandise. (p. 438)

merchandise trade balance: (5) a country's merchandise exports (exports of goods) minus its merchandise imports. (p. 153)

misperceptions theory: (11) predicts that, because of producers' inability to observe directly the general price level, the aggregate quantity of output supplied rises above the full-employment level when the aggregate price level is higher than expected; hence the short-run aggregate supply curve is upward-sloping. (p. 411)

monetarism: (15) a school of macroeconomic thought that emphasizes the importance of monetary factors in the macroeconomy, but which opposes the active use of monetary policy to stabilize the economy. (p. 591)

monetary aggregates: (7) the official measures of the money supply, such as M1 and M2. See *M1, M2*. (p. 230)

monetary base: (15) the liabilities of the central bank, consisting of bank reserves and currency in circulation, that are usable as money; also known as high-powered money. (p. 570)

monetary neutrality: (10) characterizes an economy in which changes in the nominal money supply change the price level proportionally but have no effect on real variables. The basic classical model predicts neutrality; the classical model with misperceptions and the Keynesian model predict that neutrality holds in the long run but not in the short run. (p. 364)

monetary policy: (1) policies determining the level and rate of growth of the nation's money supply, which are under the control of a government institution known as the central bank. (p. 13)

money: (7) assets that are widely used and accepted as payment. (p. 228)

money demand function: (7) the function that relates the real demand for money to output and the interest rate paid by nonmonetary assets. (p. 239)

money multiplier: (15) the amount of money that can be created from each unit of the monetary base, calculated as the ratio of the money supply to the monetary base. (p. 576)

money supply: (7) the total amount of money available in an economy, consisting of currency in circulation and deposits; also known as the money stock. (p. 233)

monopolistic competition: (12) a market situation in which some competition exists but in which a relatively small number of sellers and imperfect standardization of the product allow individual producers to act as price setters rather than as price takers. (p. 437)

multiple expansion of loans and deposits: (15) in a fractional reserve banking system, the process in which banks lend out some of their deposits, the loaned funds are ultimately redeposited in the banking system, and the new deposits are lent out again; as a result of the multiple-expansion process, the money supply can greatly exceed the monetary base. (p. 573)

multiplier: (12) for any particular type of spending, the short-run change in output resulting from a one-unit change in that type of spending. (p. 448)

national income: (2) the amount of income available to distribute among producers, equal to the sum of employee compensation, proprietors' income, rental income of persons, corporate profits, and net interest. Also measured as gross domestic product plus net factor payments less depreciation and indirect business taxes. (p. 40)

national income accounts: (2) an accounting framework used in measuring current economic activity. (p. 28)

national saving: (2) the saving of the economy as a whole, including both private saving (business and household) and government saving. (p. 43)

national wealth: (2) the total wealth of the residents of a country, consisting of the country's domestic physical assets (such as its stock of capital goods and land) and its net foreign assets. (p. 41)

natural rate of unemployment: (3) the rate of unemployment that exists when the economy's output is at its full-employment level; consists of frictional unemployment and structural unemployment. (p. 102)

net exports: (2) exports of goods and services minus imports of goods and services. (p. 38)

net factor payments from abroad (NFP): (2) income paid to domestic factors of production by the rest of the world, minus income paid to foreign factors of production by the domestic economy. (p. 35)

net foreign assets: (2) a country's foreign assets (for example, foreign stocks, bonds, and factories owned by domestic residents) minus its foreign liabilities (domestic physical and financial assets owned by foreigners). (p. 46)

net investment: (4) the change in the capital stock over the year, equal to gross investment minus depreciation of existing capital. (p. 135)

net national product (NNP): (2) GNP minus depreciation. (p. 40)

new growth theory: (6) research that extends the Solow-Swan growth model to include theoretical explanations of why productivity changes over time. (p. 217)

no-borrowing, no-lending point: (8) on the budget line, the point at which current consumption equals current income plus initial wealth; if the consumer chooses the consumption combination corresponding to this point, he or she neither borrows nor carries over resources into the future. (p. 281)

nominal appreciation: (14) an increase in the nominal exchange rate in a flexible-exchange-rate system. (p. 520)

nominal depreciation: (14) a decrease in the nominal exchange rate in a flexible-exchange-rate system. (p. 520)

nominal exchange rate: (14) the number of units of foreign currency that can be purchased with one unit of the home currency; also known as the exchange rate. (p. 517)

nominal GDP: (2) the value of an economy's final output measured using current market prices. (p. 50)

nominal interest rate: (2) the rate at which the nominal value of an interest-bearing asset increases over time; equivalent to the market interest rate. (p. 56)

nominal shocks: (11) shocks to money supply or money demand, which cause the *LM* curve to shift. (p. 390)

nominal variables: (2) variables measured in terms of current market prices. (p. 49)

normative analysis: (1) an analysis of policy that tries to determine whether a certain policy should be used; involves both analysis of the consequences of the policy and value judgements about the desirability of those consequences. See *positive analysis*. (p. 20)

official reserve assets: (5) assets held by central banks, other than domestic money or securities, that can be used in making international payments; examples are gold, foreign bank deposits, and special assets created by the International Monetary Fund. (p. 156)

official settlements balance: (5) the net increase (domestic less foreign) in a country's official reserve assets; also known as the balance of payments. (p. 156)

Okun's law: (3) a rule of thumb that says that output falls by 2.5% for each percentage point increase in the cyclical unemployment rate. (p. 103)

⸱⸱serve banking: (15) a banking system in which ⸱⸱ld reserves equal to 100% of their ⸱⸱ (p. 571)

open economy: (1) a national economy that has significant trading and financial relationships with other national economies. (p. 10)

open-market operation: (7) an open-market purchase or sale of assets by the central bank, used to affect the money supply. See *open-market purchase, open-market sale*. (p. 233)

open-market purchase: (15) a purchase of assets (such as Treasury securities) from the public by the central bank, used to increase the money supply. (p. 577)

open-market repurchase agreement: (15) an open-market sale (purchase) of an asset by the central bank in which the central bank agrees with the buyer (seller) to repurchase (sell back) the asset at some future date. (p. 578)

open-market sale: (15) a sale of assets (such as Treasury securities) to the public by the central bank, used to reduce the money supply. (p. 578)

overvalued exchange rate: (14) in a fixed-exchange-rate system, an exchange rate that is higher than its fundamental value. See *fundamental value of the exchange rate*. (p. 548)

participation rate: (3) the fraction of adults who are in the labour force. (p. 97)

peak: (9) in a business cycle, the point in time when economic activity stops increasing and begins to decline. (p. 303)

perfect competition: (12) a market situation in which there is a standardized good and many buyers and sellers so that all buyers and sellers are price takers. (p. 437)

permanent income theory: (8) a theory that states that consumption depends on the present value of lifetime resources, with the implication that consumption responds much less to temporary than to permanent changes in income. (p. 272)

persistence: (9) the tendency for declines in economic activity to be followed by further declines and for growth in economic activity to be followed by more growth. (p. 306)

Phillips curve: (13) a downward-sloping relationship between the inflation rate and the unemployment rate; theory suggests that a Phillips curve will be observed in the data only in periods in which expected inflation and the natural rate of unemployment are relatively stable. See *expectations-augmented Phillips curve, long-run Phillips curve*. (p. 476)

portfolio allocation decision: (7) a wealth holder's decision about which assets and how much of each asset to hold. (p. 234)

positive analysis: (1) an analysis of the economic consequences of a policy that does not address the question of whether those consequences are desirable. See *normative analysis*. (p. 20)

present value: (8) the value of a future payment in terms of today's currency; equal to the amount of money that must be invested today at a given interest rate to be worth the specified payment at the specified date in the future. (p. 264)

present value of lifetime consumption (PVLC): (8) the present value of current and future consumption, which equals PVLR according to the budget constraint. (p. 265)

present value of lifetime resources (PVLR): (8) the present value of current and expected future income plus initial wealth; corresponds to the horizontal intercept of the budget line. (p. 265)

price index: (2) a measure of the average level of prices for some specified set of goods and services, relative to the prices of a specified base period. (p. 52)

price setter: (12) a market participant with some power to set prices; see *monopolistic competition*.

price stickiness: (12) in Keynesian theory, the tendency of prices to adjust only slowly to changes in the economy; also known as price rigidity. (p. 436)

price taker: (12) a market participant who takes the market price as given; see *perfect competition*.

primary government budget deficit: (16) a measure of the deficit that excludes government interest payments from total outlays; equal to government purchases of goods and services plus transfers minus tax revenues. (p. 617)

private disposable income: (2) the income of the private sector (households and businesses taken together) after payment of taxes and receipt of transfer payments and interest from the government. (p. 40)

private saving: (2) the saving of the private sector (households and businesses), equal to private disposable income minus consumption. (p. 42)

private sector (2) the household sector and the business sector taken together.

procyclical: (9) tending to move in the same direction as aggregate economic activity over the business cycle (up in expansions, down in contractions). See *acyclical, countercyclical*. (p. 312)

product approach: (2) a procedure for measuring economic activity by adding the market values of goods and services produced, excluding any goods and services used up in intermediate stages of production; equivalently, by summing the values added of all producers. (p. 29)

production function: (3) a function that shows the amount of output that can be produced (by a firm or by an entire economy) by using any given quantities of capital and labour. (p. 69)

productivity: (3) a measure of the overall effectiveness with which the economy uses capital and labour to produce output; also known as total factor productivity. (p. 67)

productivity shock: (11) a change in an economy's production function; equivalently, a change in the amount of output that can be produced using given quantities of capital and labour; also known as a supply shock. (p. 390)

propagation mechanism: (11) an aspect of the economy, such as the behavior of inventories, that allows short-lived shocks to have longer term effects on the economy. (p. 418)

purchase power parity: (14) the idea that similar foreign and domestic goods, or baskets of goods, should have the same price in terms of the same currency. (p. 521)

quantity theory of money: (7) a theory that asserts that nominal money demand is proportional to nominal GDP so that velocity is constant. (p. 244)

rational expectations: (11) expectations about the future values of economic variables that are based on reasoned and intelligent examination of available economic data; although they may make forecast errors, people with rational expectations cannot be *systematically* surprised by changes in macroeconomic policy or in the economy. (p. 417)

real appreciation: (14) an increase in the real exchange rate, which increases the quantity of foreign goods that can be purchased with a given quantity of domestic goods. (p. 520)

real business cycle (RBC) theory: (11) a version of the classical theory that assumes that productivity shocks (supply shocks) are the primary source of cyclical fluctuations. (p. 390)

real depreciation: (14) a fall in the real exchange rate, which decreases the quantity of foreign goods that can be purchased with a given quantity of domestic goods. (p. 521)

real exchange rate: (14) the quantity of foreign goods that can be obtained in exchange for one domestic good; also known as the terms of trade. (p. 519)

real GDP: (2) the market value of an economy's final output measured in terms of the prices that prevailed during some fixed base period. (p. 50)

real interest rate: (2) the rate at which the real value or purchasing power of an interest-bearing asset increases over time; equal to the nominal interest rate minus the rate of inflation. (p. 56)

real shocks: (11) disturbances to the "real side" of the economy, such as shocks that affect the production function, the size of the labour force, the real quantity of government purchases, or the spending and saving decisions of consumers; real shocks affect the *IS* curve or the *FE* line. (p. 390)

real variable: (2) a variable measured in terms of the prices of a fixed base year; a measure intended to represent physical quantities produced or used. (p. 50)

real wage: (3) the real value (measured in terms of goods) of what firms must pay per unit of labour input that they employ; equal to the nominal wage divided by the price level. (p. 79)

real-wage rigidity: (12) from the Keynesian perspective, the apparent tendency of real wages to move too little over the business cycle to keep the quantity of labour supplied equal to the quantity of labour demanded. (p. 430)

recession: (9) in a business cycle, the period of time during which aggregate economic activity is falling; also known as a contraction. (p. 302)

rediscount credit: (15) credit which the Bundesbank provides to domestic banks and other credit institutions. (p. 584)

refinancing: (15) borrowing undertaken by domestic banks and other credit institutions from the Bundesbank either in the form of rediscount credit, lombard loans or open market repurchase transactions. (p. 584)

relative purchasing power parity: (14) the idea that the rate of appreciation of the nominal exchange rate equals the foreign inflation rate minus the domestic inflation rate. (p. 523)

reserve–deposit ratio: (15) the ratio of reserves held by banks to the public's deposits in banks. (p. 571)

reserves: 1. (15) see *bank reserves*. 2. (5) see *official reserve assets*.

revaluation: (14) an increase in the value of a currency by official government action under a fixed-exchange-rate system. (p. 520)

reverse causation: (11) the tendency of expected future changes in output to cause changes in the current money supply in the same direction; used by real business cycle theorists to explain why the money supply leads the cycle. (p. 407)

Ricardian equivalence proposition: (4) the proposition that changes in the government budget deficit caused entirely by changes in (lump-sum) tax collections have no effect on the economy. (p. 125)

risk: (7) the possibility that the actual return received on an asset will be substantially different from the expected return. (p. 235)

rules: (15) a set of simple, prespecified, and publicly announced guidelines for conducting monetary policy; in contrast to discretion. (p. 590)

⸱⸱⸱ ratio: (13) the amount of output lost when the
          ate is reduced by one percentage point

saving: (2) current income minus spending on current needs. (p. 42)

seignorage: (16) government revenue raised by printing money; also known as the inflation tax. (p. 641)

shoe leather costs: (13) the costs incurred in the process of economizing on holdings of cash, for example, in more frequent trips to the bank. (p. 504)

short-run aggregate supply (*SRAS*) curve: (10, 11) in a diagram with output on the horizontal axis and the price level on the vertical axis, the relationship between the price level and the amount of output supplied by firms that applies in the short run. In the extended classical model, the *SRAS* curve slopes upward, as producers are fooled into supplying more output when the price level is higher than expected; the short run in this model is the period of time during which the expected price level remains unchanged. In the Keynesian model the *SRAS* curve is horizontal, as firms meet demand at their initially set prices; the short run corresponds to the period during which prices remain unchanged. (p. 369)

small open economy: (5) an economy that trades with other economies but is too small to affect the world real interest rate. (p. 163)

Solow residual: (11) an empirical measure of total factor productivity. (p. 396)

speculative run: (14) a situation in which financial investors, fearing the imminent devaluation of a currency in a fixed-exchange-rate system, rush to sell assets denominated in that currency. (p. 549)

spell of unemployment: (3) see *unemployment spell*.

statistical discrepancy: (5) the amount that would have to be added to the sum of the current and capital account balances for this sum to reach its theoretical value of zero; arises because of errors of measurement and incomplete reporting. (p. 159)

steady state: (6) a situation in which the economy's output per worker, consumption per worker, and capital stock per worker are constant over time. (p. 204)

stock variable: (2) an economic quantity that is defined at a specific time; examples are wealth or the money supply. See *flow variable*. (p. 45)

store of value: (7) a means of holding wealth over time. (p. 229)

structural unemployment: (3) long-term and chronic unemployment arising from imbalances between the skills and other characteristics of workers in the market and the needs of employers. (p. 101)

substitution effect (of real interest rate on saving): (8) the tendency of consumers to save more, and thereby substitute future consumption for current consumption, in response to a higher reward for saving. (p. 282)

substitution effect (of real wage on labour supply): (8) the tendency of workers to substitute work for leisure in response to a higher real wage. (p. 288)

supply shock: (3) a change in an economy's production function, that is, in the amount of output that can be produced by using given quantities of capital and labour; also known as a productivity shock. (p. 74)

supply-side economics: (16) a school of economic thought based on the premise that all aspects of economic behavior—such as labour supply, saving, and investment—respond strongly to economic incentives, and, in particular, to incentives provided by the tax code. (p. 624)

tax-adjusted user cost of capital: (4) indicates how large the before-tax expected future marginal product of capital must be in order to make a proposed investment profitable; equivalently, the (unadjusted) user cost of capital divided by 1 minus the effective tax rate. (p. 133)

tax rate smoothing: (16) a policy of maintaining stable tax rates over time in order to minimize the distortions created by the tax code. See *distortions*. (p. 626)

terms of trade: (14) the quantity of foreign goods that can be obtained in exchange for one domestic good; also known as the real exchange rate. (p. 523)

trade deficit: (1) a nation's excess of imports over exports. (p. 12).

trade surplus: (1) a nation's excess of exports over imports. (p. 12).

transfers: (2) payments by the government, excluding payments made in exchange for current goods or services; examples of transfers are Social Security benefits, unemployment benefits, and welfare payments. (p. 38)

trough: (9) in a business cycle, the time when economic activity stops falling and begins rising. (p. 303)

turning points: (9) peak or troughs in the business cycle. (p. 303)

turnover costs: (12) the costs associated with hiring and training new workers. (p. 430)

unanticipated inflation: (13) the actual rate of inflation minus the rate of inflation that was expected to occur.

unconditional convergence: (6) a tendency for the living standards of different countries to become more equal over time, independently of the particular characteristics of individual countries. See *conditional convergence*. (p. 215).

underground economy: (2) the portion of the economy that includes both legal activities hidden from government record-keepers and illegal activities. (p. 32)

undervalued exchange rate: (14) in a fixed-exchange-rate system, an exchange rate that is lower than its fundamental value. See *fundamental value of the exchange rate*. (p. 550)

unemployment: (1) the number of people who are available for work and actively seeking work but cannot find jobs. (p. 8)

unemployment rate: (3) the fraction of the labour force that is unemployed. (p. 97)

unemployment spell: (3) the period of time that an individual is continuously unemployed. (p. 100)

unilateral transfers: (5) payments made from one country to another that do not correspond to the purchase of any good, service, or asset; examples are foreign aid and gifts by domestic residents to foreigners. (p. 155)

unit of account: (7) the basic unit for measuring economic value (dollars, for example). (p. 228)

user cost of capital: (4) the expected real cost of using a unit of capital for a specified period of time; equal to the depreciation cost plus the interest cost. (p. 128)

uses-of-saving identity: (2) the accounting identity that states that private saving equals the sum of investment, the government deficit, and the current account balance. (p. 44)

utility: (8) an individual's economic satisfaction or well-being. (p. 266)

value added: (2) for any producer, the value of output minus the value of purchased inputs. (p. 29)

variable-weight price index: (2) a price index that starts with the set of goods and services produced in the current period, then compares the cost of those goods and services today with what they would have cost in the base period. (p. 52)

velocity: (7) the number of times the money stock "turns over" each period; calculated as nominal GDP divided by the nominal money supply. (p. 243)

wealth: (2) the assets minus the liabilities of an individual, firm, or country; also known as net worth. (p. 41)

world real interest rate: (5) the real interest rate that prevails in the international capital market in which individuals, businesses, and governments borrow and lend across national borders. (p. 164)

NAME INDEX

(Note: when page numbers are followed by *n* the reference appears in a footnote.)

Index

(Note: Page numbers in a bold face type indicate where terms are defined; when page numbers are followed by *n* the reference appears in a footnote.)